From the paternal bonding ritual of a
baseball thrown to a small gloved hand
to the shared anxiety and elation of a
football crowd, sport has long been a
central element of cultures throughout
the world. It brings together communities,
nations and people with little else in
common, whether as an activity or a
spectacle, operating as a vital form of
human expression.

Yet despite its importance as a means
of understanding social formations
and interpersonal relations, sport has
often been viewed by social scientists
as a marginal activity. This wide-ranging
collection of essays aims to address this
inconsistency, exploring the ways in which
sport has been marked by the discourses
of race, class, gender, sexuality, and nation
which inform the structure and experience
of wider society.

Both theoretically ambitious and
accessible, *A Companion to Sport* includes
the thoughts of well-known social and
cultural theorists whose work lends
itself to an interrogation of sport. It is an
invaluable extension to the field and is
set to become a default text for anyone
interested in contemporary cultural forms
and their political significance.

WILEY
Blackwell

David L. Andrews is Professor of Physical Cultural Studies in the Department of Kinesiology at the University of Maryland, College Park, USA. He is the author of *Sport-Commerce-Culture: Essays on Sport in Late Capitalist America* (2006) and coauthor of *Sports Coaching Research: Context, Consequences, and Consciousness* (with A. Bush, M. Silk, and H. Lauder, 2013).

Ben Carrington teaches sociology at the University of Texas at Austin, USA and is a Carnegie Research Fellow at Leeds Metropolitan University in England. His most recent book is *Race, Sport and Politics: The Sporting Black Diaspora* (2010).

WILEY
Blackwell

A Companion to Sport

Wiley Blackwell Companions in Cultural Studies

Advisory editor: David Theo Goldberg, University of California, Irvine

This series provides theoretically ambitious but accessible volumes devoted to the major fields and subfields within cultural studies, whether as single disciplines (film studies) inspired and reconfigured by interventionist cultural studies approaches or from broad interdisciplinary and multidisciplinary perspectives (gender studies, race and ethnic studies, postcolonial studies). Each volume sets out to ground and orientate the student through a broad range of specially commissioned articles and also to provide the more experienced scholar and teacher with a convenient and comprehensive overview of the latest trends and critical directions. An overarching *Companion to Cultural Studies* will map the territory as a whole.

A Companion to Sport

Edited by
David L. Andrews and Ben Carrington

WILEY Blackwell

Library of Congress Cataloging-in-Publication Data

A companion to sport / edited by David L. Andrews and Ben Carrington.
        pages, cm – (Blackwell companions in cultural studies ; 15)
    Includes bibliographical references and index.
    ISBN 978-1-4051-9160-9 (cloth : alk. paper)   1. Sports–Anthropological aspects.
2. Sports–Sociological aspects.   3. Sports and society.   I. Andrews, David L., 1962–
II. Carrington, Ben, 1972–
GV706.2.C66 2013
306.483–dc23   2012048373

A catalogue record for this book is available from the British Library.

Cover design: Nicki Averill Design and Illustration
Cover illustration: *Tennis*, c.1933, linocut by Cyril Power © Osborne Samuel Ltd, London / The Bridgeman Art Library

Set in 9.5/11.5 pt Minion by Toppan Best-set Premedia Limited

1   2013

Contents

Notes on Contributors

Edwin Amenta is a professor of sociology, political science, and history at the University of California, Irvine. His most recent books are *Professor Baseball: Searching for Redemption and the Perfect Lineup on the Softball Diamonds of New York* (2007) and *When Movements Matter: The Townsend Plan and the Rise of Social Security* (2008), and he is coeditor (with Kate Nash and Alan Scott) of the *Wiley-Blackwell Companion to Political Sociology* (2012).

Eric Anderson is a professor of sport, masculinities, and sexualities at the University of Winchester, UK. He is recognized as an academician of the British Academy of Social Sciences and a fellow of the International Association of Sex Researchers. His research on sport, masculinities, and sexualities shows an increasingly positive relationship between gay male athletes and sport as well as a growing movement of young heterosexual men's masculinity becoming softer and more inclusive. He also researches matters related to men's monogamy and the positive function of relationship cheating, men's improving recognition of bisexuality, and the increased acceptance of young heterosexual men kissing. He has written 12 books and is regularly featured across the media.

David L. Andrews is Professor of Physical Cultural Studies in the Department of Kinesiology at the University of Maryland at College Park, an affiliate faculty member of the departments of American Studies and Sociology, and a visiting professor in the Faculty of Humanities and Social Sciences at the University of Bath. He is an assistant editor of the *Journal of Sport & Social Issues*, and an editorial board member of the *Sociology of Sport Journal*, the *International Review for the Sociology of Sport*, and *Kinesiological Review*. He is coeditor (with Michael L. Silk) of *Sport and Neoliberalism: Politics, Consumption, and Culture* (2012).

Michael Atkinson is an associate professor in the Faculty of Kinesiology and Physical Education at the University of Toronto, where he teaches physical cultural studies and is director of the Sport Legacies Research Collaborative. His central areas of interest (both teaching and research) pertain to alternative physical cultures, biopedagogical practices in sport, and issues in bioethics within global and local sport cultures. He is author/editor of seven books, including *Battleground Sport* (2008), *Deviance and Social Control in Sport* (with Kevin Young, 2008), and *Deconstructing Men and Masculinities* (2010).

Michael Bérubé is the Edwin Erle Sparks Professor of Literature and Director of the Institute for the Arts and Humanities at Pennsylvania State University. In 2012 he served as the president of the Modern Language Association. His most recent book is *The Left at War* (2009), and he is currently working on a book about cognitive disability and narrative theory.

Amy L. Best is Associate Professor of Sociology in the Department of Sociology and Anthropology at George Mason University. Her research focuses on the study of youth, culture, and social inequalities, with a particular interest in how gender, ethnicity, sexuality, race, and class differently shape the social experiences of contemporary American youth. She is interested in qualitative and feminist approaches to social research. She is author of *Prom Night Youth, Schools and Popular Culture* (2000), selected for the 2002 American Educational Studies Association Critics' Choice Award, and *Fast Cars, Cool Rides: The Accelerating World of Youth and Their Cars* (2006), and editor of *Representing Youth: Methodological Issues in Critical Youth Studies* (2007).

Douglas Booth is Professor of Sport and Leisure Studies and Dean of the School of Physical Education at the University of Otago. His research interests include historiography, extreme sport, and the politics of sport. He is the author of *The Race Game* (1998), *Australian Beach Cultures* (2001), and *The Field* (2005). He serves on the editorial boards of numerous journals, including *Rethinking History*, *Journal of Sport History*, and *Sport History Review*, and is an executive member of the Australian Society for Sport History.

Daniel Burdsey is Principal Lecturer in Sociology at the University of Brighton. He has written and published widely on sport and popular culture within British Asian communities. He is the author of *British Asians and Football: Culture, Identity and Exclusion* (2007) and the editor of *Race, Ethnicity and Football: Persisting Debates and Emergent Issues* (2011). He is also the editor (with Stanley Thangaraj and Rajinder Dudrah) of a special issue of *South Asian Popular Culture* on "Sport and South Asian diasporas" (2013).

Ben Carrington teaches sociology at the University of Texas at Austin and is a Carnegie Research Fellow at Leeds Metropolitan University. He is author of *Race, Sport and Politics: The Sporting Black Diaspora* (2010) and editor (with Ian McDonald) of *Marxism, Cultural Studies and Sport* (2009).

C.L. Cole is a professor of gender and women's studies, sociology, and communications research at the University of Illinois, Urbana-Champaign, where she teaches courses in feminist cultural studies, critical sexuality and race studies, and body studies. She is the author/editor of four books, including the forthcoming *Good Sports? The Boundaries of American Democracy*. She is the editor of the *Journal of Sport & Social Issues*, and serves on the editorial boards of *Cultural Studies ↔ Critical Methodologies*, *Qualitative Research in Sport & Exercise Science*, and the New York University Press book series Biopolitics: Medicine, Technoscience, and Health in the 21st Century.

Scarlett Cornelissen is Professor of Political Science at Stellenbosch University. Her research includes topics on sport and international relations and the politics of sport mega-events. She most recently published Africa and International Relations in the 21st Century (2012, co-edited with Fantu Cheru and Timothy M. Shaw) and Sport Past and Present in South Africa: (Trans) forming the Nation (2012, co-edited with Albert Grundlingh).

João H. Costa Vargas teaches black studies at the University of Texas at Austin. His publications include *Catching Hell in the City Of Angels: Life and Meanings of Blackness in South Central Los Angeles* (2006) and *Never Meant to Survive : Genocide and Utopias in Black Diaspora Communities* (2008).

John Evans is Professor of Sociology of Education and Physical Education in the School of Sport, Exercise, and Health Sciences at Loughborough University; Visiting Adjunct Professor, University of Queensland, Australia, and founding editor of the international journal, *Sport, Education and Society*. He teaches and writes on issues of equity, education policy, pedagogy, identity, and processes of schooling. He has authored and edited many papers, book chapters, and books in the sociology of education and physical education including *Education, Disordered Eating and Obesity Discourse* (2008, coauthored with Emma Rich, Rachel Allwood, and Brian Davies).

Mark Falcous is Senior Lecturer in the Sociology of Sport at the University of Otago. His research focuses on intersections of sport, globalization, national identity, and media. His work has appeared in *Sociology of Sport Journal*, *Continuum: Journal of Media and Cultural Studies*, *International Review for the Sociology of Sport*, *Studies* *in Ethnicity and Nationalism, Journal of Sport & Social Issues, Media and Cultural Politics,* and *Sites.* He coedited (with Joseph Maguire) *Sport and Migration: Borders, Boundaries and Crossings* (2011).

Grant Farred teaches at Cornell University. His works include *What's My Name? Black Vernacular Intellectuals* (2003), *Phantom Calls: Race and the Globalization of the NBA* (2006), *Long Distance Love: A Passion for Football* (2008), and *In Motion, At Rest: The Event of the Athletic Body* (forthcoming) and *Conciliation* (forthcoming).

Gary Alan Fine is John Evans Professor of Sociology at Northwestern University and a former John Simon Guggenheim fellow. Over the course of his career he has published theoretical and ethnographic accounts of several leisure worlds, including little league baseball, fantasy role-play gaming, mushroom collecting, high-school debate, and art collecting. His current research examines the cultures of competitive chess.

Anne Flintoff is Professor of Physical Education and Sport and Head of the Diversity, Equity, and Inclusion Research Center in the Carnegie Faculty of Sport and Education, Leeds Metropolitan University. Her teaching, research, and consultancy center on issues of equity and social inclusion in physical education and sport, with a particular focus on gender. She publishes regularly in both academic and professional journals, and in key readers and textbooks. She is a member of the advisory board of the journal *Physical Education and Sport Pedagogy* (PESP), and is an active member in the British Educational Research Association PESP special interest group.

Michael D. Giardina is a professor of physical cultural studies in the Department of Sport Management at Florida State University. He is the author/editor of 12 books, including *Sport, Spectacle, and NASCAR Nation: Consumption and the Cultural Politics of Neoliberalism* (2011, with Joshua I. Newman) and *Sporting Pedagogies: Performing Culture & Identity in the Global Arena* (2005), which received the 2006 Outstanding Book award from the North American Society for the Sociology of Sport. He is the associate editor of the *Sociology of Sport Journal* and *Cultural Studies ↔ Critical Methodologies,* and the associ-

ate director of the International Congress of Qualitative Inquiry.

Richard Giulianotti is Professor of Sociology at Loughborough University and a visiting professor at Telemark University College, Norway. His current research interests are in the fields of sport, globalization, development and peace, and mega-events. He is author of *Football: A Sociology of the Global Game* (1999) and *Sport: A Critical Sociology* (2005), and he has coauthored *Globalization and Football* (2009, with Roland Robertson) and *Ethics, Money and Sport* (2007, with Adrian Walsh). He has recently acted as guest coeditor of special issues of Global Networks (2007), Urban Studies (2011), and British Journal of Sociology (2012).

Cory Charles Gooding is a doctoral candidate in political science at the University of California, Los Angeles. He is author of the paper "Roots, rhythm and religion: The politics of context, identity and culture among Afro-Caribbeans in New York and Los Angeles" (2011).

John Horne is author of *Sport in Consumer Culture* (2006), co-author (with Garry Whannel) of *Understanding the Olympics* (2011) and (with Alan Tomlinson, Garry Whannel and Kath Woodward) *Understanding Sport* (2013), and coeditor (with Wolfram Manzenreiter) of *Japan, Korea and the 2002 World Cup* (2002), *Football Goes East: Business, Culture and the People's Game in China, Japan and Korea* (2004), and *Sports Mega-Events* (2006).

Davis W. Houck is Professor of Communication in the School of Communication at Florida State University. The author and editor of nine books, Houck is presently at work on a book project on Tiger Woods.

P. David Howe is Senior Lecturer in the Anthropology of Sport in the School of Sport, Exercise, and Health Sciences as well as the Centre for Olympic Studies and Research at Loughborough University. He trained as a medical anthropologist and is author of *Sport, Professionalism and Pain: Ethnographies of Injury and Risk* (2004) and *The Cultural Politics of the Paralympic Movement: Through the Anthropological Lens* (2008).

Douglas Kellner is George Kneller Chair in the Philosophy of Education at the University of

California, Los Angeles and is author of many books on social theory, politics, history, and culture, including *Herbert Marcuse and the Crisis of Marxism* (1984), *Media Spectacle* (2003), and a trilogy of books on postmodern theory (1991–2001, with Steve Best). Kellner is presently editing the collected papers of Herbert Marcuse, four volumes of which have already appeared. His latest books are *Cinema Wars: Hollywood Film and Politics in the Bush/Cheney Era* (2010) and *Media Spectacle and Insurrection, 2011: From the Arab Uprisings to Occupy Everywhere* (2012).

Pirkko Markula is a professor of sociocultural studies of physical activity at the University of Alberta, Canada. Her research interests include social analyses of dance, exercise, and sport in which she has employed several theoretical lenses ranging from critical and cultural studies research to Foucault and Deleuze. While her work is based on qualitative research methods (textual analysis, participant-observation, interviewing, ethnography), she is also interested in methodological experimentation including autoethnography and performance ethnography. Among her many published works are *Foucault, Sport and Exercise: Power, Knowledge and Transforming the Self* (2006, with Richard Pringle), *Qualitative Research for Physical Culture* (2011, with Michael L. Silk), as editor, *Olympic Women and the Media: International Perspectives* (2009), and as coeditor (2011, with Eileen Kennedy), Women and Exercise: The Body, Health and Consumerism.

Ian McDonald teaches sociology, politics and documentary practice at the University of Brighton. He coedited (with Ben Carrington) Marxism, Cultural Studies and Sport (2009) and directed Algorithms (2012), a feature-length documentary about blind chess players in India.

Toby Miller is Distinguished Professor of Media and Cultural Studies at the University of California, Riverside. His latest books are Greening the Media (2012, with Richard Maxwell) and Blow Up the Humanities (2012). You can follow his adventures at www.tobymiller.org.

Brad Millington is a lecturer in the department of education at the University of Bath. His research interests include sport and the environment, fitness technologies, and audience percep-

tions of popular media. His work appears in a range of academic journals such as *New Media & Society*, *Social Identities*, *American Behavioral Scientist*, and *Sociology of Sport Journal*.

Natasha Miric is a graduate student in sociology at the University of California, Irvine. Her interests are in globalization, social movements, and the sociology of sports. She is currently working on a project examining the process of state-making and the role played by linkages to the international community in this process, specifically looking at international soccer.

Jeffrey Montez de Oca is an assistant professor of sociology at the University of Colorado, Colorado Springs with broad research interests in sociological theory, sport, media, identity and inequality, and US imperialism. One of his specialisms is theoretically oriented research on sport during the cultural Cold War. He is author of *Discipline & Indulgence: College Football, Media, and the American Way of Life During the Cold War* (2013) and has been published in *Signs, American Studies, Sociology of Sport Journal, American Behavioral Scientist*, and *Journal of Historical Sociology*.

Abilash Nalapat is based in Mumbai, where he pursues his passion for independent sport research. He has been a full-time sports researcher and sport journalist and is currently employed as a commercial executive in the sport media industry. Publications include a chapter in *Cricketing Cultures in Conflict: World Cup 2003* (ed. Majumdar and Mangan, 2004), and "Sport, celebrity and popular culture" (2005, with Andrew Parker).

Joshua I. Newman is Associate Professor of Sport, Media, and Culture at Florida State University. His research interests focus on the cultural politics of sport, critical body pedagogies, and physical cultural studies. He is the author of *Embodying Dixie* (2010) and *Sport, Spectacle, and NASCAR Nation* (2011, with Michael Giardina). His research has also been published in *Cultural Studies ↔ Critical Methodologies, Review of Education, Pedagogy, and Cultural Studies, American Behavioral Scientist, Journal of Sport & Social Issues*, and *Sociology of Sport Journal*.

Antony Puddephatt is Associate Professor of Sociology at Lakehead University in Canada. His research interests include the sociology of knowledge, science and technology studies, pragmatism and symbolic interactionism, ethnographic research methods, sports and leisure, and the sociology of higher education. His work has appeared in *Symbolic Interaction, Sociological Quarterly, Canadian Sociological Review, Social Epistemology, Sociological Focus, Studies in Symbolic Interaction,* and *American Sociologist.* He is coeditor of *Ethnographies Revisited* (2009).

Emma Rich is a senior lecturer in the Department of Education, University of Bath. Her work draws upon the sociology of education, pedagogy, the body, and physical culture. Her major publications include *The Medicalization of Cyberspace* (2008, with Andy Miah), *Education, Disordered Eating and Obesity Discourse: Fat Fabrications* (2008, with John Evans), *and Debating Obesity: Critical Perspectives* (2011, with L.F. Monaghan and L. Aphramor).

Roland Robertson is Associate Professor of Sociology at the University of Pittsburgh; emeritus professor of sociology and global society at the University of Aberdeen; and honorary professor of cultural studies at Tsinghua University, Beijing. He is the author of many books, articles, and chapters in the fields of globalization and glocalization, religion and culture, sport, and social and cultural theory. His work has been translated into more than 20 languages. He has won a number of prestigious awards, including a Distinguished Career Award from the Global and Transnational Sociology Section of the American Sociological Association.

David Rowe is Professor of Cultural Research in the Institute for Culture and Society, University of Western Sydney. Professor Rowe's principal current research interests are in the sociocultural analysis of mediated sport, popular journalism, cultural policy, and urban leisure. His books include *Sport, Culture and the Media: The Unruly Trinity* (2004), *Global Media Sport: Flows, Forms and Futures* (2011), and *Sport Beyond Television: The Internet, Digital Media and the Rise of Networked Media Sport* (2012, with Brett Hutchins).

Parissa Safai is an associate professor in the School of Kinesiology and Health Science in the Faculty of Health at York University. Her research interests focus on the critical study of sport at the intersection of risk, health, and healthcare. Her most recent book is *The Social Organization of Sports Medicine: Critical Socio-Cultural Perspectives* (2012, with Dominic Malcolm).

Mark Q. Sawyer is a professor of political science, chair of the Afro-American Studies Inter-Departmental Program, and director of the Center for the Study of Race, Ethnicity and Politics at the University of California, Los Angeles. He is author of *Racial Politics in Post-Revolutionary Cuba* (2006).

Sheila Scraton is an emeritus professor at Leeds Metropolitan University. She represented the sociology of sport on the national research assessment panel for RAE2001 and was vice-chair of RAE2008, and pro-vice-chancellor for research at Leeds Metropolitan. She continues advisory board work and supervises postgraduate students. Her interests and commitment remain with women and sport and critical social analysis that challenges inequalities. She has published extensively in the areas of gender and physical education, sport, and leisure.

Michael L. Silk is a reader and director of the Sport, Physical Activity, and Culture Group (@ pcsbath) at the University of Bath. His research and scholarship centers on the relationships between sport and physical activity, the governance of bodies, cultural pedagogies, and identity politics within the context of neoliberalism. He has published extensively on issues concerning the sport media, mega-sporting events, identity, the physically active body, and popular culture.

Barry Smart is Professor of Sociology in the School of Social, Historical, and Literary Studies at the University of Portsmouth. He is the author of many books and articles in the field of social theory. Relevant publications include *The Sport Star: Modern Sport and the Cultural Economy of Sporting Celebrity* (2005) and *Consumer Society: Critical Issues and Environmental Consequences* (2010). He is editor of the four-volume reference work *Post-Industrial Society* (2011) and has coedited the four-volume reference work *Observation Methods* (2013).

Tamir Sorek is an associate professor in the Department of Sociology, Criminology, and Law and the Center for Jewish Studies at the University of Florida. His scholarly interests focus on the processes in which ethnic and national identities are produced, reproduced, and undermined, integrating quantitative and qualitative methods to explore sociohistorical dynamics, power relations, and the juncture of culture and politics. He has published extensively about these subjects in the context of Israel, Palestine, and the Israeli–Palestinian conflict, including *Arab Soccer in a Jewish State: The Integrative Enclave* (2007).

Holly Thorpe is a senior lecturer with the Department of Sport and Leisure Studies, University of Waikato. Her research interests include social theory, gender, physical youth cultures, and action sports. She is coeditor with Douglas Booth of the *Berkshire Encyclopedia of Extreme Sports* (2007) and the Greenwood Guides to Extreme Sports, and recently published her first monograph, *Snowboarding Bodies in Theory and Practice* (2011).

Belinda Wheaton is a senior research fellow with the Centre of Sport Research at the Chelsea School of Sport, University of Brighton. Her research interests include lifestyle sport cultures, the body, identity and difference, sport and transnationalism, sport and environmentalism, and qualitative research methods. She has published widely on lifestyle sport, gender identity, and consumer culture, and is the editor of *Understanding Lifestyle Sports: Consumption, Identity and Difference* (2004).

Brian Wilson is a professor in the School of Kinesiology at the University of British Columbia. He is author of *Fight, Flight or Chill: Subcultures,* *Youth and Rave into the Twenty-First Century* (2006) and *Sport and Peace: A Sociological Perspective* (2012) as well as articles on sport, social inequality, environmental issues, mass media, social movements, and youth culture. His most recent work focuses on environmentalist practices in the Canadian golf industry and on ways that the sport of running is used for peace promotion in Kenya.

Jeff Wiltse is Associate Professor of History at the University of Montana, Missoula. He authored the book *Contested Waters: A Social History of Swimming Pools in America* (2007), named one of the best books of that year by the American Association of University Presses.

Kevin Young is a professor of sociology at the University of Calgary. His research interests bridge criminology and the sociology of sport, and his most recent books include Sport, Violence and Society (2012), Qualitative Research on Sport and Physical Culture (2012, with Michael Atkinson), and Deviance and Social Control in Sport (2008, with Michael Atkinson).

Hui Zhang currently teaches as an assistant professor at the East China Normal University at the Institute of Anthropology. With teaching and research activities mostly based in Shanghai, his recent research projects focus on newly emergent forms of urban culture, on the issues of cinematic representations of body and desire, and on the technology of self and governmentality. His interdisciplinary and multi-methodological research approach tries to bring together ethnography, analysis of media representations, and critique of state cultural policy discourses.

Introduction
Sport as Escape, Struggle, and Art

Ben Carrington and David L. Andrews

Introduction: Anti-sport/Pro-sport

In 2010, the writer Christopher Hitchens published an article in the American weekly political magazine *Newsweek* entitled "Fool's gold." Hitchens, regarded by many as one of the greatest essayists of his generation by the time he died in 2011, sought to debunk a number of popular myths concerning sport. He opens his essay with a list of shameful sports stories that had recently dominated the news media: the attack on the Togolese football (soccer) team during the 2010 African Cup of Nations in Cabinda, Angola, that resulted in the death of the team's assistant coach, its press officer, and the driver of the team bus; the costly overruns of the new stadiums, alleged corruption, and the general disruption caused by that summer's FIFA World Cup finals in South Africa; heightened political tensions between India and Pakistan caused when owners of cricket teams in the Indian Premier League chose not to sign any Pakistani cricketers from the auction list of the world's top players (despite the fact that at the time Pakistan were the world Twenty20 cricket champions); complaints from various nations about the limited opportunities to practice ahead of the Vancouver Winter Olympics, while Canadian Olympians were allegedly given

privileged access to the courses; and the civil unrest and violence that erupted in November 2009 after Algeria had beaten Egypt 1–0 in a football World Cup qualifier, thereby denying Egypt a place in the following year's finals, leading to political and diplomatic tensions between the two countries. Hitchens' view of sport was emphatic and clear:

> Whether it's the exacerbation of national rivalries that you want – as in Africa this year – or the exhibition of the most depressing traits of the human personality (guns in locker rooms, golf clubs wielded in the home, dogs maimed and tortured at stars' homes to make them fight, dope and steroids everywhere), you need only look to the wide world of sports for the most rank and vivid examples. As George Orwell wrote in his 1945 essay "The Sporting Spirit," after yet another outbreak of combined mayhem and chauvinism on the international soccer field, "sport is an unfailing cause of ill-will." (Hitchens, 2010)

Hitchens continues in his *Newsweek* essay to lament the effects of sports metaphors on political discourse, with "lame and vapid and cheery expressions like 'bottom of the ninth', 'goal line', and who knows what other tripe," the absurdity

A Companion to Sport, First Edition. Edited by David L. Andrews and Ben Carrington.
© 2013 Blackwell Publishing Ltd. Published 2013 by Blackwell Publishing Ltd.

of allowing famous athletes (he calls them "thugs and mediocrities") to become role models, as well as the disruption to "serious programming" on television that results from overrunning sports events. Even the print media is not safe from the spread of sports.

> I can't count the number of times that I have picked up the newspaper at a time of crisis and found whole swaths of the front page given over either to the *already known* result of some other dull game or to the moral or criminal depredations of some overpaid steroid swallower. Listen: the paper has a whole separate Part devoted to people who want to degrade the act of reading by staring enthusiastically at the outcomes of sporting events that occurred the previous day. These avid consumers also have tons of dedicated channels and publications that are lovingly contoured to their special needs. All I ask is that they keep out of the grown-up parts of the paper. (Hitchens, 2010)

Hitchens' invective for sport is as much directed at sports *fans* as at the structures and institutions of sports (he notes the connection to the word "fanatic," suggesting as it does an irrational devotion towards an object or belief). Hitchens describes the typical sports bar scene filled with "the pathetic faces of men, and even some women, trying to keep up with the pack by professing devoted loyalty to some other pack on the screen" (Hitchens, 2010). He concludes by suggesting that civilized societies, and a robust political culture, are ultimately threatened by the march of sport across cultural and social boundaries: "the emphasis on sports has a steadily reducing effect on the lowest common denominator, in its own field and in every other one that allows itself to be infected by it" (Hitchens, 2010).

Later that same year, Terry Eagleton, the respected literary theorist and expert on Marxist theory and ideology, wrote an "op-ed" piece for the British newspaper the *Guardian*. In the wake of the 2010 FIFA men's World Cup finals held in South Africa, Eagleton described what he saw as the deleterious effects of sports in general, and football in particular, on working-class consciousness. Although to the political left of Hitchens (Hitchens was regarded as left-wing for much of his career but due to his unequivocal support of the "War on Terror" and the United States-led attack on Iraq in 2003, as well as his public endorsement of George W. Bush, he was seen to have moved to the political right), Eagleton nevertheless comes to similar conclusions regarding the damage sport does to political discourse. Football (soccer), according to Eagleton, pacifies the masses and infantilizes them, allowing the ruling elite to dictate the conditions of everyday existence for ordinary people unopposed. Eagleton (unlike Hitchens) is keen to acknowledge the skill and craft of professional football players, describing their "sublime artistry" and "dazzling individual talent." Eagleton recognizes the power of the sports spectacle to attract millions of devoted fans to its bright lights. Drawing comparisons with the literary form, Eagleton notes that "Football offers its followers beauty, drama, conflict, liturgy, carnival and the odd spot of tragedy." Despite this, and perhaps because of it, football functions as a form of popular entertainment and distraction, a perfect tool for keeping the working class in its lowly place: "If every rightwing thinktank came up with a scheme to distract the populace from political injustice and compensate them for lives of hard labour, the solution in each case would be the same: football" (Eagleton, 2010). True, Eagleton concedes, there are sometimes protests and fan demonstrations, with football in particular often the site for such struggles. But this, Eagleton argues, is really much ado about nothing. Sports politics is not real politics, but merely the flickering of misdirected discontent. Eagleton suggests that the problem for progressive politics is not just that it is held back by football but that progressives must confront the "people's game" directly if any socialist future is to be achieved. Invoking Karl Marx's famous dictum that religion is the opiate of the masses – that is, a social drug that inhibits peoples' ability to understand and change their material conditions with the promise of a better life after death – Eagleton concludes:

> There can be outbreaks of angry populism, as supporters revolt against the corporate fat cats who muscle in on their clubs; but for the most part football these days is the opium of the people, not to speak of their crack cocaine. Its icon is the impeccably Tory, slavishly conformist Beckham. The Reds are no longer the Bolsheviks.

Nobody serious about political change can shirk the fact that the game has to be abolished. (Eagleton, 2010)

These two essays by well-known, if controversial, public intellectuals are worth considering for both the starkness of their arguments and the fact that they encapsulate (albeit in colorful and polemical language) a view of sports that is quite widely held among the general population and particularly amongst academics, intellectuals, and what is sometimes referred to as the "literary class." Both arguments rest on a series of assumptions that position sport as an inherently and intrinsically regressive social force. Sport is regarded as not worthy of serious contemplation (beyond denouncement) as it is a useless activity that at best takes time away from discussing the important political matters of the day (Hitchens), blocks the development of true working-class consciousness (Eagleton), or worse, leads to heightened political tension, increased sectarian feelings with nationalistic if not fascistic undertones, and ultimately violence and death (Hitchens) and the perpetuation of capitalism (Eagleton). Those who follow sports are not fully developed adults (sports are, after all, "just games"), thus sports fans' child-like interests produce immature citizens unable to appreciate more meaningful and challenging forms of culture. Sport, in short, is superficial, irrelevant, infantile *and*, like an infectious disease, destructive to a healthy democratic civil society, whether defined as a liberal public sphere (Hitchens) or a socialist alternative to capitalism (Eagleton).

The essays by Hitchens and Eagleton did not go uncontested at the time. The sports journalist and commentator Dave Zirin charged that Hitchens had merely replaced one exaggerated claim – that sport is always a force for good – with its opposite – that sport is fundamentally bad for society. Hitchens failed to understand, in other words, the fact that sport is what we might call a "contested terrain," a site where politics is at play, where destructive and damaging influences reside, but where we also find moments of political resistance, creativity, and the human emotions of joy, hope, and excitement. Writing in *The Nation* in an article entitled "Christopher Hitchens: Sporting fool," Zirin countered Hitchens'

central thesis that sport is only a domain for regressive politics and immoral behavior:

When racism, sexism, and homophobia have been challenged through struggle in the streets, it has ricocheted with electric results in the world of athletics. This is why we associate Jackie Robinson with the Civil Rights movement or Billie Jean King with the women's liberation struggles of the 1970s. And lest we forget, the most famous draft resister in world history is a boxer, Muhammad Ali. On a far more grass roots level, sports are where many people – particularly young people – find confidence, friendship, and a sense of self. For many it's where the deeply segregated dynamics of our society are broken down. This is not true in every case of course. For every story of sports-as-savior, there are 100 gym class horror stories. Yes, it is absolute truth that sports can bring out the worst in athletes, fans, parents, and coaches. But it can also bring out the best. (Zirin, 2010a)

Zirin was also on hand to denounce Eagleton's article as "elitist hogwash" in *The Guardian* (Zirin, 2010b). Zirin again conceded that the "dark side" of footballing cultures is worthy of critique and admonishment. Yet, Zirin argued, football, and sport in general, is more complex than the caricature painted by Eagleton. Sports are also a space for human creativity and bonding, a physical and competitive art form that shows what the human body – and therefore humanity as a whole – is capable of. It is a space from which a broader humanistic politics might be built that expands rather than diminishes a progressive consciousness.

We don't love sport because we are like babies suckling at the teat of constant distraction. We love it because it's exciting, interesting and at its best, rises to the level of art. . . . By rejecting football, Eagleton also rejects what is both human and remarkable in physical feats of competition. We can stand in awe of the pyramids while understanding the slave labour and misery that comprised its construction. We can stir our soul with gospel music even while we understand that its existence owes itself to pain as much as hope. . . . Sports is as human an act as music, dance, or organising resistance. While sports may in a vacuum have no "significance", the passion we invest transforms it. Sport morphs into something well beyond escape or a vessel for backward ideas and becomes a meaningful part in the fabric of our lives. Just as sports such as football reflect our society, they also reflect struggle. (Zirin, 2010b)

Let us reflect for a moment on some of the issues that arise from these exchanges and the ways in which sport is understood and conceptualized. It is worth noting that it would be unacceptable for a serious public intellectual to denounce any other cultural practice in the way that Hitchens and Eagleton do. Such diatribes would likely not be published in any august journal, newspaper, or magazine on the basis that the writings were simply one-sided and ill-informed. Further, an article that dismissed an entire cultural form, say music for example, would likely be regarded as over-the-top ramblings and the author's own standing and credibility would be brought into question. Neither Hitchens nor Eagleton sought to reference the voluminous social scientific literature on sports that has been developed in a systematic manner since the mid-1960s (Dunning, 1971; Ingham and Donnelly, 1997; Coakley and Dunning, 2000), nor to cite any empirical research to support their arguments. In fact, despite their vast oeuvre, neither writer had written significantly on sports before – Eagleton's commentary on sports reduced to a passing mention or paragraph (e.g., Eagleton, 2000: 70; 2008: 26) and Hitchens even less. As Jason Cowley, the editor of the *New Statesman*, one of Britain's leading political magazines, noted in a remembrance, "Hitchens was an accomplished and prolific writer, but an even better speaker: his perfect sentences cascaded and tumbled, unstoppably. He was one of our greatest contemporary debaters, taking on all-comers on all subjects, except sport, in which he professed to have no interest at all" (Cowley, 2011). A professed and almost celebrated lack of interest in and knowledge about sports, at least among the literary classes, elevates the status of such a learned person as an anti-populist "man of letters" rather than being seen as a sign of ignorance. This fact, in and of itself, is worthy of sociological consideration in terms of what it may tell us, not about the quality and importance of sports studies scholarship, but rather about the place

and intellectual status of sport as an aspect of popular culture within wider society.

Hitchens' argument should be understood as operating from within a long tradition of disdain and moral outrage towards the leisure pursuits of the working classes. With the advent of commercialized forms of leisure in mid- to late nineteenth-century Europe, the middle and upper classes became increasingly concerned about a perceived breakdown of the moral order and the related challenge to the authority of ruling elites (including the church) as cultural and social boundaries were usurped. What become known in Britain as the "rational recreation" movement was an attempt by Victorian moralists to instill better (meaning middle-class) values and mores into the working classes, by the provision of morally improving leisure activities that eschewed the often violent behavior of the sports crowd, the lewdness of the music hall, and the associated "sins" of gambling and drinking (see Bailey, 1978; Walvin, 1978; Clarke and Critcher, 1985; Holt, 1989: 136–148; Waters, 1990).

By the early to mid-twentieth century, these "new" forms of commercialized leisure were seen as birthing a "mass culture" that was disconnected from any organic relationship to traditional forms of folkloric culture, which although looked down upon by the bourgeois elites was still seen to be "authentic" and a natural part of the hierarchical structures of society. Especially in the years following World War II, European cultural elites feared the emerging consumer revolution and what they saw as the "Americanization" of European culture as American films, music, and celebrities saturated Europe. Young people in Europe in particular eagerly embraced the new products (such as jeans and Coca-Cola) and styles of the United States and in so doing disrupted Europe's historically entrenched class-based distinctions. Nothing better illustrated Europe's decreasing authority than the emergence of a global consumer society that was dominated by American (and not European) corporations and commodities, and the related ideals of individualism and "consumer choice" driven by elaborate marketing strategies and the entrepreneurial strength of American companies and finance capital (Judt, 2005; de Grazia, 2006). This new mass culture was viewed by many intellectuals across the political spectrum and on both sides of the Atlantic as amoral and vulgar, appealing to people's base instincts, lacking artistic merit, intellectual depth, or true aesthetic quality, its very popularity a marker of its lowly status and questionable social relevance. As the journalist and cultural critic Dwight Macdonald argued in his essay "A theory of mass culture" (1957), folk art was the culture of the common people, "a spontaneous, autochthonous expression of the people, shaped by themselves, pretty much without the benefit of High Culture, to suit their own needs" (p. 60). But the advent of commercially manufactured mass culture "imposed from above," Macdonald claimed, had destroyed these boundaries and reduced the working classes to "passive consumers" (p. 60) of the "spreading ooze" (p. 73) of a debased and trivial (mass) culture rather than being active producers of their own (folk) culture.

Similarly, Eagleton's position is a modern version of earlier leftist concerns regarding the perceived depoliticizing effects of popular culture on the critical consciousness of the masses and the role of commercial entertainment, or the cultural industries as Theodor Adorno (2001) phrased it, as a form of social control (Lazere, 1987). Whereas conservative "bourgeois idealists" (Holt, 1989: 136) saw the emergence of mass culture and the decline of folk culture as a threat to the social order and class distinctions (and therefore the basis for their own authority and privileged standing), socialist leaders saw the commercial provision of leisure, of which sport was a central part, as a capitalist ploy to deaden the revolutionary spirit by promoting blind allegiance to non-class identities, be they the local factory or town, regional, or even national identifications. For late nineteenth-century socialists, the leisure industries, notes Chris Waters,

> exploited workers who provided entertainment for the masses; it directly threatened the livelihood of those who produced leisure activities in less commercial ways; it encouraged homogeneity; it threatened older, radical ways of organizing leisure; it fostered a dependence on its products, thereby blocking the development of socialist cultural alternatives; and, finally, it began to redefine recreation as a mere purchasable commodity. (Waters, 1990: 29)

Worse, sport's very logic – that celebrated individual success over collective endeavor, competition over solidarity, and violence and aggression over contemplation and reflection – was seen as capitalist ideology made manifest. As Karl Kautsky, one the most influential late nineteenth and early twentieth-century Marxist theorists, argued, the English working class rejected revolutionary struggle as their class emancipation "appears to them as a foolish dream. Consequently, it is foot-ball, boxing, horse racing and opportunities for gambling which move them the deepest and to which their entire leisure time, their individual powers, and their material means are devoted" (1902: 102). Rather than being a realm of freedom, sport, the French intellectual Jean-Marie Brohm (1976) famously claimed, is a *prison of measured time* that leads to alienation of the sporting body, as athletes come to view their own bodies as tools, a place where sports crowds are turned into fascistic cheering machines, and the creative spirit of play transformed into another corporatized and commodified mode of highly rationalized production for capital accumulation and profit maximization (see also Perelman, 2012).

Those familiar with sports studies would also recognize that Dave Zirin's counter-argument to Eagleton and Hitchens is well established within the extant literature. Indeed, the idea of understanding popular culture as a *site of struggle*, as a contested terrain wherein dominant ideologies are found but also resisted, and where ordinary people in their daily lives can still create alternative ways of being and meaning-making that challenge capitalist logics and neoliberal ideologies, is the starting point for cultural studies as an intellectual project (see Miller, 2001); and indeed the rationale for the Blackwell Companions in Cultural Studies book series, of which this present volume is a part. Particularly as associated with the British cultural studies tradition (Carrington, 2001; Hartley, 2003; Turner, 2003), though not exclusive to it, the imperative to read and understand the politics of popular culture in non-reductionist ways; to center but not privilege class analysis and questions of political economy; to theorize power and ideology; and to take seriously the issue of intersectionality – the ways in which various social identities are shaped by each other and "intersect" – has been axiomatic to cultural studies scholars for over half a century. During the 1980s numerous scholars such as Jennifer A. Hargreaves (1982), Richard Gruneau (1983), Garry Whannel (1983), John E. Hargreaves (1986), and Stephen Jones (1988), among others, developed historically grounded and complex theorizations of the ways in which sports are sites for the play of power, ideology, and politics where agency and resistance, constraints and domination, can be found, often simultaneously. As Toby Miller has pointed out (2009: 190), "Sport is a key site of pleasure and domination, via a complex dialectic that does not always produce a clear synthesis from the clash of opposing camps. It involves both the imposition of authority from above and the joy of autonomy from below. It exemplifies the exploitation of the labor process, even as it delivers autotelic pleasures."

It is often the case, as Hitchens notes, that sport (and more often football) is the catalyst for public protests that sometimes result in violence. On February 1, 2012, for example, 74 people died and scores more were seriously injured when fighting broke out between rival fans during a football game between Port Said's Al-Masry and Cairo's Al-Ahly clubs. As a direct result of this tragedy, the entire Egyptian Premier League football season was eventually cancelled. In January 2013, 21 Al-Masry fans (though not any officials) were found guilty and sentenced to death. The sentences provoked jubilation in Cairo among Al-Ahly supporters and further violent clashes in Port Said between Al-Masry fans and the police, prompting Egypt's new President, Mohammed Morsi, to declare a state of emergency in three cities along the Suez Canal. To the uninformed, casual observer it is easy to draw the conclusion that football "caused" the violence. Certainly few other cultural forms and leisure activities seem to invoke the level of passion and commitment that we associate with competitive sports events. There have been few riots or uprisings in recent years associated with the opening of a new musical show on Broadway in New York City or London's Shaftesbury Avenue, or deaths following a disagreement between two authors at one of the many literary and cultural festivals now found across the globe. While it is true that music concerts and nightclub events have occasionally resulted in the tragic deaths of music fans, these tend to be the result of accidents, freak weather storms, collapsing seating, or fires rather than directly caused by the actions of the music-goers themselves. A more complex and complete analysis however would have to look at the specificity of the historical, cultural, economic, and political context of any violent outbreak rather than lazily making a causal argument regarding sport's power to produce violence, as if such events occurred in a social vacuum.

To briefly take the above case as an example, the violence at the Port Said stadium in Egypt was undoubtedly related to the after-effects of the "Arab Spring" that in 2011 led to populist uprisings against many of the authoritarian regimes of the Middle East and North Africa, including that of the subsequently deposed Egyptian president Hosni Mubarak. Some reports suggested that the Egyptian military and authorities had either colluded with some of the fans, or helped to orchestrate the violence (Knell, 2012). In other words, any serious analysis would have to situate the football violence in the wider context of Egypt's ongoing and incremental transition from a military dictatorship that was previously supported by Western countries, towards a nascent independent democratic republic. We would want to consider too the broader question of Egyptian nationalism and the role of political Islam, the place of anticolonial struggles and their aftermath, and national identity in the context of neoliberal globalization that threatens national traditions and customs, as well as the reaction against these destabilizing economic, militaristic, political, and cultural flows that have affected Egypt and the surrounding region (Amar, 2012). This broader sociopolitical context, within which the football game took place, also requires an analysis of the geopolitical and cultural influences resulting from globalization (see CHAPTER 2), US imperialism (CHAPTER 13), and mass media, social networking, and mobile and wireless communication technologies (CHAPTERS 3 AND 14). Further, we would have to consider why other countries and cultures, with similar social dynamics, have not seen sports used as a platform for protest and violence in quite the same way, even when we might expect that this would be the case, as in Israel for example in the context of the Palestinian struggle for statehood. Sociologically informed empirical research actually shows that sport can have a *depoliticizing* effect as regards political violence and protest (see CHAPTER 15), suggesting that there are no universal laws regarding the relationship between sport and political violence. Similarly, we would want to enquire further into the gendered nature of violence, perpetrated as it was in this case overwhelmingly by (and against) men at a men's sports event, and to consider the links between masculinity, sports, status, pride, and violence (see CHAPTERS 5 AND 8). We would have to enquire also why *this particular* match (and *these particular* sets of fans) became the catalyst for the violence by understanding the dynamics of crowd behavior and related questions of identity as well as the group loyalty displayed by the Al-Ahly fans, known as "The Ultras," and those of the other side (see CHAPTER 18) and the important role that football supporters play in Egyptian politics more generally (Zirin, 2013). In the end such a multidimensional reading, moving from the macro-analysis of the structural and historical conditions to a micro-analysis of chance, agency, and intent, would not necessarily provide a definitive answer to the question, asked by many at the time, "why did this happen?" but it would give us a much more nuanced, detailed, and rich appreciation of the complex social, cultural, historical, economic, and indeed *political*, circumstances that made the event possible in the first place. This is what a sociologically informed, non-reductionist but contextually driven cultural studies analysis can produce and what this book as a whole hopes to introduce to students.

In some ways, the arguments put forward by the likes of Hitchens as well as by leftist critics like Eagleton and others (for a discussion of this point see CHAPTER 14) may be seen as an attempt to push back against the often unctuous way in which some boosters talk about sports. Sports fans and players, administrators and governing bodies, and especially sports journalists and commentators, often make overstated and rarely supported claims about the inherently positive effects of sports as an intrinsically moral public good that creates character in young children, produces self-esteem among its participants, and brings families, communities, and even nations together; sport being "the glue" to achieve harmonious social solidarity. Such arguments rest upon a "functionalist perspective" regarding how sport

"functions" to produce a more healthy society; how sport can keep young people busy and therefore reduce crime and delinquent behavior; and how sport functions to maintain balance and equilibrium within society by allowing individuals to harmlessly blow off steam and anger in a controlled and safe environment. Sociological evidence suggests that these commonplace views of sport may in fact be at best exaggerated or worse simply false: under certain conditions, sports may be just as likely to increase bodily harm and decrease physical and mental well-being in the pursuit of sporting excellence (see CHAPTER 6); sports can easily lead to social exclusion and increased racial, ethnic, and national antagonisms (see CHAPTER 9); the evidence that sport actually stops young people from committing crimes or has a meaningful long-term effect in decreasing rates of recidivism tend to be anecdotal at best; and sporting encounters at both the recreational and elite level can as easily produce heightened anxiety, distress, and frustration, sometimes leading to acts of violence, as it can the opposite, according to the supposed theory of sport's "cathartic effect." In other words, what we might term the contrarian "anti-sport" argument (namely, that sport is a negative social force within society) is an attempt to challenge the functionalist "pro-sport" lobby that fervently believe in sport's supposedly irenic effects. (This is perhaps seen most clearly in notions such as the "Olympic truce" whereby wars and national disputes are supposedly "suspended" for the duration of the Olympic Games in order that athletes and others can travel safely to the games to compete in a way that celebrates the values of universal humanism over nationalism and sectarianism). Nearly every major sports institution and governing body (and not just the International Olympic Committee who organize the winter and summer games) subscribe to a version of the pro-sport worldview in which the world would be a safer, more inclusive and healthier place if only more people played (and crucially, given the influence of the media, *watched*) sports.

One of the aims of this book is to encourage students to think beyond the false choice presented here of either being naively "for" sport or condescendingly "against" sport. Instead, students of sport need to develop a more critical approach that strikes a delicate balance between taking sports seriously as an important cultural and social phenomenon in their own right, whilst trying to locate "linkages" and interconnections to the wider social structures and forces that give sport its meaning and significance. The famous historian, novelist, and cricket journalist C.L.R. James once asked, "what do they know of cricket who only cricket know?" What he meant by that question was that it is impossible to fully understand the game of cricket if all that one knows about it are the rules of the game, the scores from previous games, and names of the best players and most successful teams. For James, writing specifically about the English-speaking Caribbean in the middle of the twentieth century, cricket was intimately and unavoidably connected to the politics of the age, namely the Caribbean anticolonial struggle against British racism and domination. In his famous book *Beyond a Boundary* (1963) James argued that to truly make sense of the game of cricket one needs to understand not just a sport's own internal history but also, and simultaneously, the changing *social and political context* within which the game is played: those forces "beyond the boundary" that nonetheless shape and give meaning to the game. In other words, we cannot truly know sports without understanding the society from which they come. Similarly, we would argue that the best way to understand a society or culture or community is to take seriously its pastimes, to examine what its people do in their leisure time, to analyze not just the so-called "high arts" of literature, opera, sculpture, and paintings, but the "popular arts" too. And few cultural activities are as important or popular as sport.

Students need to develop ways of thinking, seeing, and reading sports that avoid the uniformed tirades of the anti-sport lobby and the often naive and idealistic accounts of pro-sports devotees. To think about sport, as C.L.R. James did, as an activity that is simultaneously a space to which we escape for fun, relaxation, and enjoyment, a space charged with social significance and political possibilities for expressing who we are as individuals and the larger communities to which we belong, and as an embodied art form, a physically creative and aesthetic mode of being human, a world replete with all the ugliness and beauty, tragedy and joy, that resides within human societies. The sociological task, then, is to think about sport as an escape from everyday life whilst understanding that no cultural activity is completely autonomous from societal constraints, to examine sport as a form of cultural struggle, resistance, and politics whilst recognizing that it is also compromised by forms of commodification, commercialization, and bureaucratic control, and to consider sport as an embodied art form that is formed in relation to both intrinsic and extrinsic goals and rewards that sometimes over-determine the stated aims of the participants.

What Is Sport? Some Definitional Observations

It is perhaps useful at this point to consider more precisely what we mean when we say "sport" or, as is more common in American parlance, "sports" (for a useful definitional essay see Loy and Coakley, 2007). Sport can be defined as a freely chosen competitive activity requiring physical exertion that centers the body as the main object for expression and creativity and that has some form of quantifiable goal, or external reward, as its main focus. Yet this seemingly simple, obvious, definition perhaps obscures as much as it reveals. Sport, as John Loy (1968) noted many years ago, is surprisingly ambiguous. Exactly how much physicality is required for a sport to qualify as a sport, for example? Tennis and rugby, according to this definition, are "obviously" sports but what about golf or archery, where the level of physical movement is clearly limited. Most, although not all, would include such activities as sports, presumably due to the high skill level required and the competitive element. What then of card games or chess or darts? Here people may raise objections that these are "games" and not "real" sports as the level of physical exertion is minimal, and further that few would pay to see anyone playing chess, for example, or that darts is a game played in a pub or bar for fun and therefore not a proper sport. Such arguments reveal that "our" definition of what constitutes a "proper" sport may be determined not so much by any objective criteria but rather by the specific social expectations and traditions of our own society. For example, darts is recognized as a "real" sport in Britain and much of Europe, with television coverage of the major championships and the leading darts players becoming well known by the general public, a fact that many outside of such nations would find surprising. ESPN and other US television channels now carry coverage of poker games with the leading card-players developing skills such as being able to "read" other players, bluffing and faking, intimidating opponents, and so on, that we would readily associate with "real sports." And an institution none other than the International Olympic Committee (IOC) recognizes the legitimacy of the World Chess Federation and therefore the possibility that chess could one day be an Olympic sport.

Western definitions of sport tend to assume that *competition* is axiomatic but this may be to unduly privilege a particular concept of sport that emerges from a relatively recent moment in European history (Victorian England is usually cited as being the pivotal moment for the codification and institutionalization of "folk games" into modern sports) when, in fact, if we look outside of the West, and to different historical periods, we can find a range of physical cultural practices that could well be understood as "sports," but would not necessarily privilege competition in the way we tend to today. Further, we might want to think more carefully about the extent to which sports are really "freely chosen." For the most part we are introduced to certain sports (and not others) at a young age and encouraged to play (or not) by significant others such as parents and teachers and coaches. But the circumstances from which we get to "choose" are already conditioned by things like money, access, equipment, and knowledge which are themselves linked to broader social structures, particularly those of class, race, and gender, not to mention which region of a country and indeed which country we are born into. As soon as we think more deeply, and sociologically, about the notion that sport is a freely chosen leisure activity we quickly realize that that "choice" is actually limited, partial, and constrained (Bourdieu, 1978; Gruneau, 1983). Further, very few if any of us get to determine the rules and regulations of the sports we play; they are given to us to learn rather than agreed upon, mutually, by the participants themselves. (Try kicking the ball into the ring the next time you play basketball, or suddenly pick up the ball and run with it in soccer, and see how quickly the game falls apart as a social activity with cries of "you can't do that.") In play, unlike in sport, and as anyone who has watched children at play will testify, it *is* possible to make up the rules as you go along, which suggests an important point of ontological distinction between the two.

It could be argued that the traditional "formal-structural" approach to defining sports as largely *secular* activities, premised upon *equality* of opportunity to play, in which each athlete develops *specialized* roles, pursuing *rational* means to achieve goals and success that are *quantifiable* in order to *pursue records*, all overseen by *bureaucratic* institutions (Guttmann, 1978, 2004) may actually reflect a particular and hegemonic account of sport that reinforces the power of sports scholars from the West to define sports for everyone else rather than an accurate and universal definition of the range of activities that might be considered "sports" as they exist in the world (see CHAPTER 1; Carrington, 2010). The definitions of the formal-structural characteristics of sport that try to distinguish between modern and premodern sports, or between "primitive" peoples' games (defined as simplistic and often violent) and those of civilized and modern peoples (defined as complex and emotionally controlled), inadvertently reinforce Eurocentric notions of the civilized West being superior to the developmentally stunted Rest: only those physical cultural practices that fit "our" definitions get to be regarded as "real" sports. An examination of which sports have been recognized by the IOC over the decades would give some credence to this suggestion that "the West" tends to privilege sports played in or codified in Europe or the United States over those from other parts of the world. Indeed some have argued that new lifestyle or action sports, such as skateboarding, BMX riding, surfing, Parkour, snowboarding, and so on, do not fit formal-structural definitions and actually challenge some of the central tenets of traditional, mainstream sports such as the supposed need to pursue records, quantify achievement, and compete for external rewards and honors that are bestowed by an official governing body (see CHAPTERS 20 AND 21).

In other words, the lines between what is merely "play" (often thought of as self-generated, autotelic, child-like fantasy, and therefore not serious), what is "just" a game, and what constitutes a sport, are not as clear-cut as we might at first assume. For example, even our earlier attempt to contrast sport with play needs to be qualified. Whilst it is true that sports require the participants to follow external rules laid down by governing bodies that preexist the participants – whereas the rules of play are self-generated – play is still a *structured activity* that requires the participants to adhere to a set of rules and limits to their play, even if those structures are temporary and subject to change at any moment. Similarly, sports certainly have play-like, or *ludic*, elements that provide meaning and excitement to fans and players alike, but this "freedom" is constrained by the social conditions and environment within which those activities take place. Within this framework, the study and definition of sport suddenly appears to be much more complex than either the pro- or anti-sport advocates acknowledge, suggesting that the sociological approach to studying sport should focus on the dynamics of the struggles to define and control sports and the meanings derived therein (Giulianotti, 2005: xiii) as much as being concerned with trying to find any universal definitions or simple causal explanations of sports' effects "on society," or vice versa. As Richard Gruneau (1983) has argued, in order to truly understand the meaning and significance of sports within society, students and scholars of sport need to situate the "study of play, games, and sports in the context of understanding the historical struggle over the control of rules and resources in social life, and the ways in which this struggle relates to structured limits and possibilities" (1983: 28).

Sports Matter: *A Companion to Sport*

We have suggested in this Introduction that far from "sports" (as a particular form of popular physical culture within the broader leisure field) and "politics" (broadly defined as related to expressions of power, domination, and ideology) occupying separate and discrete domains of social life, the two are deeply interconnected (Street, 1997; Whannel, 2008; Bramham and Wagg, 2011). As the chapters in this *Companion* demonstrate, it is not merely the case that we can

view societal problems reflected in the sports we play and watch – the notion of sport being a "reflection" or "microcosm" of wider society – but rather that individuals, communities, and even societies themselves come to understand who they are *through sports*. One need only look at the importance of football to Brazilian national identity, or of cricket to India's, or the widespread enthusiasm for ice hockey in Finland, or the weight attached to success on the rugby pitch to many New Zealanders, or the pride felt by many British people during the London 2012 Olympic and Paralympic Games, to understand that sport's social significance greatly transcends the small numbers who actually play sports on a regular basis, becoming a part of the "national fabric" of most countries around the world. Beyond the spectacle of international competition, local and regional identities are also often strongly linked to and in part *produced by* affinities to particular sports, whether that be the importance of high school (American) football in small towns across Texas, or the strong attachment to both professional and amateur rugby league teams in parts of West Yorkshire. Thus the line that many try to draw between sport and politics, or between sports and "the rest of society," is misplaced and futile. There is no space "outside" of society where we can find sports, safely removed from the messy problems that confront both communities and individuals. Rather, we should turn such assumptions "upside down" and instead take sport seriously as an object for analytical enquiry so as to help us better understand the complexities of modern societies. Sports, within this framework, can be considered as windows into societies, a way to unveil or "debunk" the superficial, to go beyond surface appearances in order to see the deeper structures of society and the varied histories of local, regional, national, and diasporic cultures. In their different ways, all of the chapters in this book pursue this general premise that *sports matter*.

This attempt to address the social significance of sports in a rigorous, theoretically informed, and critical manner is the basis for the chapters in Part One: Sporting Structures and Historical Formations which collectively lay out "the big picture" as to why and in what ways sports matter, and the relationship of sport to questions of history, globalization, media, class, the body, race, gender, health, and the environment. In CHAPTER 1, CONSTRUCTING KNOWLEDGE: HISTORIES OF MODERN SPORT, Douglas Booth examines the epistemology of sport, or, put more simply, *how* historians of sport (and others) have defined and conceptualized sport as well as the basis upon which claims about the inherent meanings of and facts about sports are made. In CHAPTER 2, SPORT AND GLOBALIZATION, Richard Giulianotti and Roland Robertson look at the effects of globalization on sports and the related issue of how the sports that we play and watch have become more interrelated and connected with the lives and cultures of others, or what is termed "cosmopolitanism." In CHAPTER 3, THE SPORT/MEDIA COMPLEX: FORMATION, FLOWERING, AND FUTURE, David Rowe provides a historical account of the impact of media on sports and the contemporary symbiotic relationship between the two in what he terms the media sports cultural complex. In CHAPTER 4, POLITICAL THEORIES OF SOCIAL CLASS, SPORT, AND THE BODY, Joshua I. Newman and Mark Falcous look at the impact of class on sports and the various theoretical frameworks that have attempted to understand the relationship between capitalism, sport, and the body. CHAPTER 5, GENDER, FEMINIST THEORY, AND SPORT, by Sheila Scraton and Anne Flintoff, provides a summary of the various strands of feminist thought and their contribution to sports studies and the ways in which gender inequality remains a dominant feature of contemporary sports cultures. CHAPTER 6, SPORTS MEDICINE, HEALTH, AND THE POLITICS OF RISK, by Parissa Safai, looks at the emergence of sports medicine and the broader question of health and sports performance. Finally in Part One, CHAPTER 7, SPORT, ECOLOGICAL MODERNIZATION, AND THE ENVIRONMENT, by Brian Wilson and Brad Millington, surveys the often neglected topic of the relationship between sport and the environment as they examine some of the tensions that have existed between forms of economic development based upon a fundamentalist belief in the inherent positive benefits of "free markets" and individual consumer choice (or neoliberalism) and "green" (or environmental) politics.

Sports, of course, are more than just structures and institutions. They are physical activities played by people involving the training, control, and movement of the human body, often in close and sometimes intimate proximity to other bodies. Our bodies are obviously material; we have a physical presence and a biological reality. It is through our bodily senses that we experience the world. But certain bodies and body types are often afforded a privileged status over others. How we read and perceive other bodies, how we shape and think about our own bodies (and therefore our identities), and the ways in which social relations impact the body, are all key issues for sports studies scholars. These questions of "embodiment" are taken up by the authors in Part Two: Bodies and Identities. In CHAPTER 8, PARADOX OF PRIVILEGE: SPORT, MASCULINITIES, AND THE COMMODIFIED BODY, Jeffrey Montez de Oca looks at the importance of sports in shaping masculine identities and how such masculinities have changed in recent years as men's dominant place in society has been challenged, leading some to talk of a "crisis of masculinity." CHAPTER 9, RACISM, BODY POLITICS, AND FOOTBALL, by Mark Q. Sawyer and Cory Charles Gooding, examines the topic of anti-black racism in football, paying particular attention to the ways in which black sporting bodies have become the primary focus for racist attacks in various European countries in recent years. In CHAPTER 10, PHYSICAL CULTURE, PEDAGOGIES OF HEALTH, AND THE GENDERED BODY, Emma Rich and John Evans look at the social expectations on girls and young women to conform to (often contradictory) ideal body types that vacillate between the pressure to be physically active, strong, and fit while remaining "feminine," attractive, and thin. CHAPTER 11, GAY MALE ATHLETES AND SHIFTING MASCULINE IDENTITIES, by Eric Anderson looks at the issue of homophobia within sports cultures and suggests that despite the continuance of anti-gay sentiment, overt forms of homophobia, even within men's competitive team sports, have recently declined leading to more open and egalitarian sporting spaces for men as regards sexual identities and difference. Finally, in CHAPTER 12, SPORT, THE BODY, AND THE TECHNOLOGIES OF DISABILITY, P. David Howe looks at the controversial issue of how bodies are classified (and the complex relationship between technology and performance) within sports for the disabled and the Paralympics in particular.

The chapters in Part Three: Contested Space and Politics explore the politics of sports, paying particular attention to how sport in different locations and spaces becomes a conduit for political beliefs, ideologies, and social change. In CHAPTER 13, US IMPERIALISM, SPORT, AND "THE MOST FAMOUS SOLDIER IN THE WAR," Toby Miller looks at the relationship between sport and US imperialism, engaging, amongst other things, the media coverage and political framing of the former American football player Pat Tillman, who left his NFL career to join the US military and was subsequently killed in Afghanistan in 2004. CHAPTER 14, THE REALITIES OF FANTASY: POLITICS AND SPORTS FANDOM IN THE TWENTY-FIRST CENTURY, by Michael Bérubé explores the politics of sports and virtual spaces by examining the impact of fantasy sports leagues on traditional notions of sports fandom and the wider question of whether sport diminishes or expands the possibilities for progressive politics. In CHAPTER 15, SPORT, PALESTINE, AND ISRAEL, Tamir Sorek looks at the role sport has played in the disputed and highly charged context of the Palestinian–Israeli conflict and tries to answer the question as to why sport has not figured as a site for the overt expression of Arab Palestinian nationalism and anti-Jewish Israeli sentiment that might have been expected given the public platform provided by competitive sports. In CHAPTER 16, CITIES AND THE CULTURAL POLITICS OF STERILE SPORTING SPACE, Michael L. Silk uses the US city of Baltimore to explore the ways cities have used sports as a means to remake urban spaces as sites of consumption based around tourism and entertainment, often at the expense of local concerns and broader notions of the public good. Finally, in CHAPTER 17, SWIMMING POOLS, CIVIC LIFE, AND SOCIAL CAPITAL, Jeff Wiltse provides a historical analysis of the emergence, growth, and subsequent decline of public swimming pools in the United States as a way to think about the politics of race, class, and public space; recent changes within civic life in America related to the privatization of municipal leisure facilities; and the utility of the sociological concept of "social capital."

Both cultural studies and the sociology of culture have long been interested in the development of subcultures wherein alternative, oppositional, and distinctive patterns of dress, speech, behavior, and attitudes could often be found that departed in some significant way from

mainstream society and commercial cultures. Sports *sub*cultures have often emerged from (and sometimes against) traditional sporting cultures whether through the actions of fans and their "deviant," sometimes violent behavior or through the new lifestyle action sports that have challenged orthodox definitions of sports and instead stressed qualities such as beauty and aesthetics, human movement, and an engagement with the environment as their defining characteristics. The chapters in Part Four: Cultures, Subcultures and (Post)Sport seek to interrogate the usefulness and validity of the category of subculture by examining a range of cultural practices and leisure activities that are reshaping how we define and understand sport today. In CHAPTER 18, SPORTS FANDOM, Edwin Amenta and Natasha Miric look at why people become fans of sports, what this means to them, and the development of what they term "player fans" who challenge the binary distinction between participation and spectatorship that has traditionally structured much of the literature on sports fandom. CHAPTER 19, SPORTING VIOLENCE AND DEVIANT BODIES, by Kevin Young and Michael Atkinson, takes up the issue of deviancy in sport, examining the definitional problems scholars continue to face when trying to make sense of activities and actions such as violence and aggression that are rendered not just normal but even desirable, especially within sports that celebrate social behaviors that would otherwise, and outside of certain sports subcultures, be labeled as deviant if not criminal. In CHAPTER 20, DISSECTING ACTION SPORTS STUDIES: PAST, PRESENT, AND BEYOND, Holly Thorpe and Belinda Wheaton focus on the emergence of new alternative lifestyle sports, or what they refer to as "action sports," and how these relatively new sports are challenging traditional and somewhat narrow definitions of sports as a competitive game, driven by scores, that produces a winner, with the rules of the sport sanctioned by an external institution or body. In CHAPTER 21, HEIDEGGER, PARKOUR, POST-SPORT, AND THE ESSENCE OF BEING, Michael Atkinson continues the theme of examining physical cultural practices that either exceed or challenge our idea of what constitutes a "proper" sport through his sociological, historical, and philosophical reading of Parkour. In CHAPTER 22, RACE-ING MEN: CARS, IDENTITY, AND PERFORMATIVITY,

Amy L. Best looks at how the automotive subcultural world of street racing in California becomes a site for the performance and articulation of racialized masculinities. The final CHAPTER 23 in Part Four, CHESS AS ART, SCIENCE, AND SPORT, by Antony Puddephatt and Gary Alan Fine, uses chess as a case study through which to explore traditional notions of sport, how science understands itself, and the broader question of the aesthetic, and in so doing highlights the sometimes mutually constitutive nature of all three categories.

Few, if any, cultural events attract global audiences or levels of corporate sponsorship to anything like the same degree as sports "mega-events." These events, most notably the Olympic summer games organized by the International Olympic Committee and the men's (FIFA) football World Cup finals, and more frequent "multi-site" championships such as Formula One motor racing, are increasingly used by nation states, regions, and cities to influence external perceptions of themselves, to rebrand their identities, and to attract inward investment, making such places desirable tourist destinations and spaces of consumption. As a result, the locations for such events are often "remade," in terms both of the physical structures that are built to host sporting events and of the significant changes to the local environment such as the building and relocation of housing, roads, and public transportation. Who benefits from sporting mega-events (once they have moved on) and who pays for them, especially when large sums of public money – often raised through taxation on local inhabitants – is used to subsidize the events, is clearly a political question. These political questions concern issues related to privatization, the definition of the public good, the role of sport as an agent for social change and redevelopment in the context of corporate profit and local tax revenues, and the nation state's surveillance and security of its citizens and non-citizens alike. The chapters in Part Five: Sport, Mega-events, and Spectacle explore these contentious but important public issues. Scarlett Cornelissen's CHAPTER 24, SPORT MEGA-EVENTS AS POLITICAL MEGA-PROJECTS: A CRITICAL ANALYSIS OF THE 2010 FIFA WORLD CUP, analyzes the 2010 men's FIFA World Cup finals in South Africa as a way to think about

how mega-events serve both external and internal political purposes for the nation states that host them. CHAPTER 25, SPORTING MEGA-EVENTS, URBAN MODERNITY, AND ARCHITECTURE, by John Horne, is an account of the often overlooked role of a global elite of famous architects, or "starchitects," in reshaping the identities of the city spaces following major sports events. In CHAPTER 26, SPORTS, THE BEIJING OLYMPICS, AND GLOBAL MEDIA SPECTACLES, Douglas Kellner and Hui Zhang use the 2008 Olympic summer games in Beijing as a way to think about the nature of the "sporting spectacle" and how this event, and particularly the opening ceremony, was used by the Chinese government to produce narratives of itself as both the protector of China's Communist past and as a forward-looking agent of Chinese modernity. In CHAPTER 27, ALWAYS ALREADY EXCLUDED: THE GENDERED FACTS OF ANTI-BLACKNESS AND BRAZIL'S MALE SELEÇÃO, João H. Costas Vargas provides a critical reading of Brazil's claims to being a racial meritocracy in the context of the lead-up to the 2014 FIFA World Cup finals and the 2016 Olympic summer games in Rio de Janeiro, suggesting that the events are being used to cover and indeed accelerate forms of anti-black racism. CHAPTER 28, TO BE LIKE EVERYONE ELSE, ONLY BETTER: THE US MEN'S FOOTBALL TEAM AND THE WORLD CUP, by Grant Farred, examines the emerging success of the US men's football team via a reflective and personal reading of the 2010 FIFA World Cup finals in South Africa, suggesting that the increased popularity of the game reflects demographic changes and cultural shifts within the United States as a whole. Finally Ian McDonald and Abilash Nalapat's CHAPTER 29, SPORT, SPECTACLE, AND THE POLITICAL ECONOMY OF MEGA-EVENTS: THE CASE OF THE INDIAN PREMIER LEAGUE, critically evaluates the formation and development of the lucrative Indian cricket premier league which, they argue, powerfully illustrates one important aspect of contemporary global sports culture, namely a shift in economic and political power from the West to South Asia, or what some have labeled "post-Westernization."

The chapters in the final Part Six of this *Companion*, Sporting Celebrities/Cultural Icons, trace the myriad ways in which "stars," "celebrities," and "icons" are made by the sports/media complex and further how "reading" sports stars can give us an insight into wider social issues related to class, race, gender, sexuality, and national identity. Barry Smart's CHAPTER 30, GLOBAL SPORTING ICONS: CONSUMING SIGNS OF ECONOMIC AND CULTURAL TRANSFORMATION, provides an authoritative overview of the history of the word "icon," the ways in which icons have been understood over time, and the importance of global sports icons today, linked as they frequently are to global marketing strategies and campaigns. In CHAPTER 31, EMBODYING AMERICAN DEMOCRACY: PERFORMING THE FEMALE SPORTING ICON, C.L. Cole and Michael Giardina look at the ways in which athletes, and particularly female athletes, have come to represent American identity, their bodies becoming a site for wider discussions about race, sexuality, and belonging. CHAPTER 32, MONTY PANESAR AND THE NEW (SPORTING) ASIAN BRITISHNESS, by Daniel Burdsey, examines the career and public reaction to Mudhsuden Singh Panesar, or Monty Panesar as he is popularly known, and how the star cricket player has, somewhat problematically, come to embody a "new" form of British South Asian identity in the context of debates in Britain around the concept of multiculturalism. CHAPTER 33, EARL'S LOINS – OR, INVENTING TIGER WOODS, by Davis W. Houck, analyzes the influence of Earl Woods on his famous son's career, looking in particular at how Earl Woods was a pivotal, contradictory, and somewhat controversial figure in constructing the Tiger Woods "brand" as a transformational icon challenging racism in sports. Part Six ends with Pirkko Markula's CHAPTER 34, DELEUZE AND THE DISABLED SPORTS STAR, which problematizes the very categories of "disability" and the "athletic body" via an exploration of the post-elite sports career of the Finnish Olympic athlete Tuija Helander. In so doing, Markula explores how and in what ways disability in sports and society comes to be constructed as a marginal identity.

Each of the six Parts has its own introduction. Students are encouraged to read these short overviews as a way to better understand the debates that each individual chapter pursues in greater detail. It is also worth pointing out that the construction of each Part and the titles we have given them are somewhat arbitrary, perhaps implying a stronger separation between the themes of each Part than is actually the case. Analytically, we can distinguish questions of embodiment from those of politics, or subcultures from sports celebrities, or mega-events from broader social structures. In reality, of course, these social and cultural phenomenon are deeply interconnected and cannot be neatly separated. Indeed, careful readers will note that some of the chapters could have fitted into a different Part. The arguments contained within them often show how various axes of power, multiple identities, and social forces have to be understood concurrently in order to fully make sense of the particular topic at hand. The six Parts to the *Companion* should be understood as an attempt to highlight or better foreground particular aspects of the case studies or issues under discussion; they are a heuristic structuring device, designed to emphasize certain core conceptual issues that are similar across the other chapters in the same Part, without necessarily implying they are absent in others. As with this Introduction, at the end of each chapter, the authors have provided suggestions for further reading that should help students explore the particular topic of the chapter in greater depth. Note that further reading sections may contain items already listed in the references, whose general suitability for further reading the authors wish to emphasize.

Uninformed polemics against (and sometimes for) sports will likely continue to be written and published in esteemed journals, newspapers, and magazines for some time to come. It is our hope that students of sports will be better informed to make sense of such arguments, and that this *Companion* will be a guide to the best scholarly work on sports that can assist them as they embark on their own interpretive journeys across the sporting landscape.

References

Adorno, T. (2001) *The Culture Industry: Selected Essays on Mass Culture*, London: Routledge.

Amar, P. (2012) "Egypt as a globalist power: Mapping military participation in decolonizing internationalism, repressive entrepreneurialism, and humanitarian globalization between the revolutions of 1952 and 2011." *Globalizations*, 9 (1): 179–194.

Bailey, P. (1978) *Leisure and Class in Victorian England: Rational Recreation and the Contest for Control, 1830–1885*, London: Routledge & Kegan Paul.

Bourdieu, P. (1978) "Sport and social class." *Social Science Information*, 17 (6): 819–840.

Bramham, P. and Wagg, S. (eds.) (2011) *The New Politics of Leisure and Pleasure*, Basingstoke: Palgrave Macmillan.

Brohm, J.-M. (1976) *Sport: A Prison of Measured Time*, London: Ink Links.

Carrington, B. (2001) "Decentering the centre: Cultural studies in Britain and its legacy," in Miller, T. (ed.) *A Companion to Cultural Studies*, Oxford: Blackwell.

Carrington, B. (2010) *Race, Sport and Politics: The Sporting Black Diaspora*, London: Sage.

Clarke, J. and Critcher, C. (1985) *The Devil Makes Work: Leisure in Capitalist Britain*, Basingstoke: Macmillan.

Coakley, J. and Dunning, E. (2000) "General introduction," in Coakley, J. and Dunning, E. (eds.) *Handbook of Sports Studies*, London: Sage.

Cowley, J. (2011) "Christopher Hitchens, the enemy of the totalitarian." *New Statesman*, December 16, http://www.newstatesman.com/blogs/the-staggers/2011/12/hitchens-amis-totalitarian, accessed November 28, 2012.

de Grazia, V. (2006) *Irresistible Empire: America's Advance Through Twentieth-Century Europe*, Cambridge, MA: Harvard University Press.

Dunning, E. (ed.) (1971) *The Sociology of Sport: A Selection of Readings*, London: Frank Cass.

Eagleton, T. (2000) *The Idea of Culture*, Oxford: Blackwell.

Eagleton, T. (2008) *The Meaning of Life: A Very Short History*, Oxford: Oxford University Press.

Eagleton, T. (2010) "Football: A dear friend to capitalism." *Guardian*, June 15, http://www.guardian.co.uk/commentisfree/2010/jun/15/football-socialism-crack-cocaine-people, accessed November 28, 2012.

Giulianotti, R. (2005) *Sport: A Critical Sociology*, Cambridge: Polity.

Gruneau, R. (1983) *Class, Sports and Social Development*, Amherst: University of Massachusetts Press.

Guttmann, A. (1978) *From Ritual to Record: The Nature of Modern Sports*, New York: Columbia University Press.

Guttmann, A. (2004) *Sports: The First Five Millennia*, Amherst: University of Massachusetts Press.

Hargreaves, J.A. (ed.) (1982) *Sport, Culture and Ideology*, London: Routledge & Kegan Paul.

Hargreaves, J.E. (1986) *Sport, Power and Culture*, Cambridge: Polity Press.

Hartley, J. (2003) *A Short History of Cultural Studies*, London: Sage.

Hitchens, C. (2010) "Fool's gold." *Newsweek Magazine*, February 4, http://www.thedailybeast.com/newsweek/2010/02/04/fool-s-gold.html, accessed November 28, 2012.

Holt, R. (1989) *Sport and the British: A Modern History*, Oxford: Clarendon Press.

Ingham, A.G. and Donnelly, P. (1997) "A sociology of North American sociology of sport: Disunity in unity, 1965 to 1996." *Sociology of Sport Journal*, 14 (4): 362–418.

James, C.L.R. (1963) *Beyond a Boundary*, London: Stanley Paul.

Jones, S.G. (1988) *Sport, Politics and the Working Class: Organised Labour and Sport in Inter-war Britain*, Manchester: Manchester University Press.

Judt, T. (2005) *Postwar: A History of Europe Since 1945*, London: Penguin Books.

Kautsky, K. (1902) *The Social Revolution*, Chicago: Charles H. Kerr.

Knell, Y. (2012) "Blame game over Egypt's football clashes." *BBC News*, February 2, http://www.bbc.co.uk/news/world-middle-east-16864901, accessed November 28, 2012.

Lazere, D. (ed.) (1987) *American Media and Mass Culture: Left Perspectives*, Los Angeles: University of California Press.

Loy, J. (1968) "The nature of sport: a definitional effort." *Quest*, 10, May: 1–15.

Loy, J. and Coakley, J. (2007) "Sport," in Ritzer, G. (ed.) *The Blackwell Encyclopedia of Sociology*, Oxford: Blackwell.

Macdonald, D. (1957) "A theory of mass culture," in Rosenberg, B. and White, D.M. (eds.) *Mass Culture: The Popular Arts in America*, New York: Free Press.

Miller, T. (ed.) (2001) *A Companion to Cultural Studies*, Oxford: Blackwell.

Miller, T. (2009) "Foucault and the critique of sport," in Carrington, B. and McDonald, I. (eds.) (2009) *Marxism, Cultural Studies and Sport*, London: Routledge.

Perelman, M. (2012) *Barbaric Sport: A Global Plague*, London: Verso.

Street, J. (1997) *Politics and Popular Culture*, Cambridge: Polity Press.

Turner, G. (2003) *British Cultural Studies: An Introduction* (3rd edn.), London: Routledge.

Walvin, J. (1978) *Leisure and Society 1830–1950*, London: Longman.

Waters, C. (1990) *British Socialists and the Politics of Popular Culture 1884–1914*, Stanford, CA: Stanford University Press.

Whannel, G. (1983) *Blowing the Whistle: The Politics of Sport*, London: Pluto Press.

Whannel, G. (2008) *Culture, Politics and Sport:* Blowing the Whistle, *Revisited*, London: Routledge.

Zirin, D. (2010a) "Christopher Hitchens: Sporting fool." *The Nation*, February 12, http://www.thenation.com/blog/christopher-hitchens-sporting-fool, accessed November 28, 2012.

Zirin, D. (2010b) "Football isn't just about capitalism." *Guardian*, June 21, http://www.guardian.co.uk/commentisfree/cifamerica/2010/jun/21/football-terry-eagleton-sport, accessed November 28, 2012.

Zirin, D. (2013) "Soccer and Egypt's current 'state of emergency.'" *The Nation*, January 29, http://www.thenation.com/blog/172498/soccer-and-egypts-current-state-emergency, accessed January 29, 2013.

Further Reading

The chapters in this volume attempt not only to provide an overview to each topic but also to develop original arguments by pushing previous debates in new directions. Although each chapter should be accessible to most students some technical language is unavoidable and those new to sociology and sports studies may find some of the chapters more difficult to follow than others. With this in mind it is often useful to have a dictionary to hand in order to quickly and easily access key terms and concepts. Although general dictionaries (whether in print form or online) offer a readily available reference point, it is often the case that academics use words in a way that modifies or differs from their commonplace meaning, thus it is vital that students consult *academic* rather than general dictionaries. We recommend the following texts to be read alongside this *Companion* in order to aid your comprehension of the arguments made in this book.

Malcolm, D. (ed.) (2008) *The Sage Dictionary of Sports Studies*, London: Sage.

Tomlinson, A. (ed.) (2010) *Dictionary of Sports Studies*, Oxford: Oxford University Press.

Wagg, S., Carlton, B., Wheaton, B., and Caudwell, J. (eds.) (2009) *Key Concepts in Sports Studies*, London: Sage.

Part One

Sporting Structures and Historical Formations

Introduction

Sport is neither endowed with nor evokes any universal elements, functions, values, or experiences. It possesses no transcendent substance, and is in fact wholly relational. For this reason alone, sport can be considered an important object of sociological inquiry, since its very popularity and ubiquity renders it unavoidably implicated in the myriad relations that structure societal existence. The sheer magnitude of sport's presence within, and influence upon, contemporary societies means it is complexly interconnected to broader social, cultural, spatial, political, economic, and technological forces and formations. As such, this opening section pinpoints some of the key issues pertinent to understanding the sport–society dialectic. These include discussions of: the historical and epistemological foundations of sport; the relationship between sport and globalization; the convergence of media and sport sectors; the social class politics of sport and capitalism; sport, the gendered body, and gender relations; the role of sports medicine and perceptions of health in the context of a risk society; and, finally, the sport industries' collusive engagement with environmentalism. Many of these "big themes" are addressed in more specific detail in subsequent chapters. However, within this opening section, these topics are introduced as key formations of contemporary sporting structures in order to "set the scene" for the rest of the volume.

In CHAPTER 1, Douglas Booth offers a challenging re-examination of the assumptions underpinning how the formations of modern sport have been studied by historians and sociologists of sport. Booth's chapter is doubly useful. First, it provides a broad overview of research pertaining to the origins and causes, diffusion, and reception of modern sport practices and structures. Through recourse to research informed by Marxian, Weberian, Habermasian, and Eliasian theorizing, Booth highlights the objective, if nonetheless partisan, "truths" of modern sport. Second, Booth's empirical survey elucidates the dominant forms of, or approaches to, knowledge adopted by researchers in framing their sporting inquiries. He is critical of the *primary epistemologies* he identifies within much sport research, namely those realist approaches founded on reconstructionist and constructionist ways of knowing, or epistemes. As a remedy to the perceived empirical, methodological, and political inadequacies of reconstructionist and constructionist thought, Booth advances a *deconstructionist-leaning* position. This sporting deconstructionism is based

A Companion to Sport, First Edition. Edited by David L. Andrews and Ben Carrington.
© 2013 Blackwell Publishing Ltd. Published 2013 by Blackwell Publishing Ltd.

on an anti-essentialist and unselfconsciously subjective epistemology. According to this understanding, the generation of knowledge related to modern sport is inveterately contingent, informed as it is by the subjective impulses of both the researcher and the contexts (micro, meso, and macro) within which the research process is enacted. Booth's deconstructionist approach counters the empirical realism, theoretical prefiguration, and associated political insipidity that he identifies as being characteristic elements of extant sport research. As such, Booth's deconstructionist clarion call represents a challenge to the epistemological assumptions (be they reconstructionist or constructionist) framing many chapters in this volume, as it does to the field more generally.

While not concerning themselves overtly with the epistemological underpinnings of their work – something which perhaps belies their constructivist approach toward sociological practice – Richard Giulianotti and Roland Robertson (CHAPTER 2) offer an empirically rich and theoretically nuanced examination of the relationship between sport and globalization. They identify globalization – a multifaceted, complex, yet uneven process of temporal and spatial compression, and social, cultural, political, and economic interconnection – as a defining feature of the contemporary condition (or what is often referred to as "modernity"), and something clearly implicated in the development and contemporaneous expression of modern sport. The discussion utilizes Robertson's six-phase historical periodizing of globalization, as an interpretive schema explaining the development of modern sport from its germinal phase in the fifteenth century, to the millennial phase of the early twenty-first century. Thus follows a considered examination of the sociocultural dimensions and effects of sport's globalization. Through recourse to the constitutive tensions and interpenetrations linking sporting particularism and universalism, heterogenization and homogenization, localization and globalization, Giulianotti and Robertson highlight the varieties of cosmopolitanism (banal, thick, and thin) operating within contemporary sport cultures and social relations. The political-economic aspects of sporting globalization are then discussed, paying particular attention to sport's contribution to the continued political,

economic, and indeed cultural, relevance of the nation state. However, unlike many discussions of sport and globalization, Giulianotti and Robertson scale the discussion down to the subnational level, and illustrate how globally aspirant urban and corporate regimes use sport to advance the interests and particularities of the local. Significantly, they also illustrate the complexities of sport's relationship to the various dimensions of the emergent global civil society.

A significant element of sport's globalization has been its institutional convergence with the various dimensions of the media, beginning with print, and extending into electronic and computer-based media platforms. David Rowe (CHAPTER 3) develops this theme through a focus – inspired and framed by Sut Jhally's groundbreaking critique – on the evolution and operation of the sports/media complex. While acknowledging the political, economic, and technological elements of sport broadcasting, Rowe focuses on the production of *media sport* as an important popular cultural form and practice: the creative appropriation and manipulation of sport as live media content providing the television audience with a simulated experience of the event. According to Rowe, media sport, and especially that involving nationally representative teams and individuals, has played an important role in (re)producing a sense and feeling of national *cultural citizenship* within diverse national politics and sporting economies. The very popularity of live sporting events renders them a prized acquisition as broadcast content for advertising-driven commercial television interests, and is also the root of ongoing tensions regarding the protection of major sporting events for the "free-to-air" television sector, thereby illustrating the enduring commercial/non-commercial, global/local relations operating within media sport. Bringing the discussion of the sport/media complex up to date, Rowe points to the ever more convergent new media technologies and practices (including digital networking, mobile viewing, social media, micro-blogging, and computer gaming) that are radically altering the way sport media content is both produced and consumed, particularly with regards to the ownership and control of the sport media environment.

One of the most domineering formations within modern societies was that related to the hierarchical social class structure through which industrial capitalism was able to enact its productive and accumulative functions. The relationship between sport, shifting modes and relations of industrial production, and social class hierarchies, provides the focus for Joshua I. Newman and Mark Falcous in CHAPTER 4. Focusing on the social class politics of sport, the authors highlight the role played by the sporting body in both challenging and reproducing dominant modes of production and their attendant social class divisions. This is achieved through an exposition of late nineteenth and early twentieth-century literatures examining sport and social class politics. Amongst other things, these works exposed capitalism's consumption-driven class distinctions, and instead offered progressive sport-based programs tied to the principles of the burgeoning Soviet regime. Newman and Falcous then review the place of social class politics within sociology of sport research, highlighting structural functionalist, figurational, neo-Marxist, activist, cultural studies, and Bourdieuian approaches. This is followed by a recognition of the pressing need to revisit the social class politics of sport within an era characterized by global neoliberalism's creative appropriation of productive and consumptive sporting bodies. Nevertheless, and while acknowledging the continued relevance of sport to the reproduction of social class distinctions and divisions, the authors conclude with an acknowledgement of the "intersubjectivity" of the sporting body. Such an understanding requires that theorizations of the sport and social class relation are not abstracted from other subject formations. Rather, the social class analysis of sport has to be simultaneously attuned to pertinent issues of race, ethnicity, generation, (dis)ability, gender, and sexuality.

Sheila Scraton and Anne Flintoff (CHAPTER 5) focus on the relationship between sport and gender. Interestingly, but perhaps not surprisingly given the masculinist orientation of sport more generally, they show how the sociology of sport community in its formative phases was dominated by male academics with little concerted interest in gender and gender relations. Scraton and Flintoff summarize the considerable body of research which addressed the sociology of sport's foundational *malestream*. They illustrate how the field's journey through liberal

feminism, radical feminism, Marxist/socialist feminism, black feminism, poststructuralism, queer theory, and postcolonialism, has heralded a shift from a focus on women and sport to one which engages the complexities and interrelationships of the sport–gender–sexuality nexus more generally. This approach highlights the enactments and operations of power in both the construction and contestation of unequal gender relations, practices, and identities within sport. The authors also identify how recent work focused on sport both denaturalizes assumptions pertaining to male/female, masculine/feminine, heterosexual/homosexual bodies and points to sporting possibilities for resisting and/or redefining these categories. In doing so, they elucidate the dynamic nature of sporting-based gendered power relations, as well as that fluidity of approaches used to interpret them. Like Newman and Falcous, Scraton and Flintoff point to the value of intersectional approaches to understanding sport's role in facilitating the constitutive relations linking gender and other expressions of embodied difference. However, they warn against a pluralist relativism that subsumes gender with other categories of difference and thereby obscures what they consider to be the principal significance, and consequential effects, of gender politics within sport.

Parissa Safai (CHAPTER 6) focuses on sport, health, medicine, and the ways in which the tensions of contemporary risk-society are played out, with sometimes tragic consequences. Hence, and invoking Ulrich Beck's and to a lesser extent Anthony Giddens' conceptualizations, Safai locates sport within the context of risk-society. According to this line of thinking, the rational control associated with the modernization of society is inimitably linked to the emergence of an ethos and culture of risk. An institutionalized structure of risk identification and management (or what Safai refers to as the *safety-industrial complex*) has thus emerged, not least as a response to the dangers and uncertainties posed by modern life itself. This necessarily leads to some internal contradictions within sport spaces. Much of commercial culture glamorizes the risk-taking uncertainties of involvement in sport, almost as an antidote to the banalities of modern everyday existence. Conversely, the very banality of that existence is constituted by the pervasiveness of risk-averse paranoias and initiatives. Thus sport is located at the intersection of the safety/danger, responsibility/irresponsibility, precaution/risk tensions which characterize risk-society. According to Safai, the solution to this seeming sport–risk paradox comes through the production of sporting constituents of the safety-industrial complex. These commodified experiences stimulate the fears and anxieties of their consumer/participants (or sport-risk citizens), while simultaneously addressing their demands for overt risk management strategies and resources. Safai concludes with a dissection of high-performance sport within the context of risk-society. Propelled by the modernist ethos of limitless performance through technological and bureaucratic innovation, risk to the athlete's body (as manifest in severe physical and/or psychological injury, or worse) is understood and experienced as an unavoidable consequence of elite sporting involvement, requiring minimization and management. This is often realized through the collusive actions of sports medicine institutions and intermediaries, who, like the subjugated athletes themselves, contribute to the stability of elite sport's structures and culture of "organized irresponsibility" through their uncritical involvement in the system.

Finally, Brian Wilson and Brad Millington draw attention to another dimension of contemporary existence with which sport is dialectically conjoined, namely, issues of, and approaches toward, environmental degradation and sustainability. Their focus is on the relationship between sport and the values and practices of *ecological modernization*: the steadfast belief in modern assumptions related to the inalienable march of technologically driven progress and innovation ameliorating the negative environmental impacts wrought by earlier phases of industrialization. Wilson and Millington identify the existence of an ecological modernization hegemony that positions it as the unquestioned solution to the potentially negative environmental impacts of the sport industry (broadly construed, and encompassing everything from the production practices of sporting goods manufacturers, to the staging operations of major sport event organizers). Through an overview of the sociology of sport's limited engagement with the environment, an explication of competing positions within environmental sociology, and an illustration of the appropriation and advancement of modernist ecological discourse by sporting corporations and organizations (specifically the London 2012 Olympic and Paralympic summer games and FIA Formula One motor racing), Wilson and Millington elucidate the power dynamics and effects mobilized through the uncritical invocation of the ecological modernization perspective. In doing so, they illustrate how the dominant modernist and neoliberal discourses related to environmental sustainability normalize particular ways of operating – anchored within assumptions about the environmentally responsible and proactive nature of industry in general, and the sport industry more specifically – which obfuscate the very possibility of alternative perspectives or approaches to the environment.

Further Reading

Carrington, B. (2010) *Race, Sport and Politics: The Sporting Black Diaspora*, London: Sage.

Dunning, E. (1999) *Sport Matters: Sociological Studies of Sport, Violence and Civilization*, London: Routledge.

Gruneau, R. (1999) *Class, Sports, and Social Development* (2nd edn.), Champaign, IL: Human Kinetics.

Guttmann, A. (2004) *From Ritual to Record: The Nature of Modern Sports* (2nd edn.), New York: Columbia University Press.

Hargreaves, J.E. (1986) *Sport, Power and Culture*, New York: St Martin's Press.

Hargreaves, J.A. (1994) *Sporting Females: Critical Issues in the History and Sociology of Women's Sports*, London: Routledge.

Maguire, J. (2005) *Power and Global Sport: Zones of Prestige, Emulation and Resistance*, London: Routledge.

Tomlinson, A. (2005) *Sport and Leisure Cultures*, Minneapolis: University of Minnesota Press.

1

Constructing Knowledge
Histories of Modern Sport

Douglas Booth

Introduction

Modern sport is a socially constructed global phenomenon. International sporting federations register players, define the rules of play, stage events, and negotiate with each other, sponsors, broadcasters, and governments. States support ministries and ministers of sport. The media previews, broadcasts, and reviews matches and games 24 hours a day, seven days a week. Sporting teams represent local, regional, and national communities which build sporting infrastructures (and decorate them with sporting insignia, symbols, and flags) and host events to signify their identities. In this chapter I examine the ways historians construct knowledge about modern sport and its form, development, and meanings.

The chapter comprises two substantive parts. I begin with a set of basic questions about the emergence of modern sport, its causes, its motors of diffusion, and its cultural reception. These questions have not only failed to produce a consensus among historians, they have also fueled debates and controversies that raise fundamental questions about the "coherence" of history as a discipline (Thompson, 1995: 51; see also Jenkins, 1991: 15). Thus, in the second part of the chapter, I

I critically examine the primary epistemologies (forms of knowledge) which have framed, and continue to frame, historical enquiries into modern sport. The philosopher of history Alun Munslow (1997) labels these epistemologies *reconstructionism* and *constructionism*. Although these two epistemologies privilege empiricism and proffer primary sources (e.g., official documents) as evidence of the past (which they insist can be recovered), reconstructionists conceptualize history as an objective discipline grounded in the interrogation of sources while constructionists embrace theory to frame their objectivity.[1] The lack of agreement among historians of sport, even among those working within the same epistemological framework, leads me to advocate an alternative deconstructionist-leaning epistemology which contextualizes knowledge about modern sport in the moment of its existence or its narration. Deconstructionist historians are less concerned with reconstructing sport or constructing theoretical interpretations of sport; their goal is to explicate the way historians construct facts, theories, and narratives and the ways they variously "frame," "foreground," "remember," "obscure," and "forget" the past (McDonald and Birrell, 1999: 292). I elaborate on deconstructionist epistemology in the second section with

A Companion to Sport, First Edition. Edited by David L. Andrews and Ben Carrington.
© 2013 Blackwell Publishing Ltd. Published 2013 by Blackwell Publishing Ltd.

reference to the interpretation of modern sporting practices and cultures.

Questions (and Unstable Answers)

Since the late 1960s a set of common questions
has framed scholarly inquiry into modern sport.
When did modern sport begin? What conditions
precipitated and predisposed modern sport? How
did modern sport become a global phenomenon?
How have different cultures received modern
sport? In this section, I summarize the debates
and disagreements ignited by the answers to these
questions under three headings – origins and
causes, diffusion, and reception – and I highlight
the shifting, and unstable, meanings they impose
on modern sport.

Origins and causes

Most reconstructionist historians date the emergence of modern sport as a distinct practice
from the mid-Victorian era. They cite as evidence the formal constitution of a raft of English
governing bodies such as the Football Association (1863), Amateur Swimming Association
(1869), Bicyclists Union (1878), Metropolitan
Rowing Association (1879), Amateur Athletic
Union (1880), and Lawn Tennis Association
(1888). Some reconstructionists, however, point
to the formal constitution of several important
governing bodies at least a century earlier, such
as the Jockey Club, for horse racing, in 1750;
the St Andrews' Society of Golfers, for golf, in
1754; and, for cricket, the Marylebone Cricket
Club in 1787; and then, from the early Victorian
period, the Grand Caledonian Curling Club in
1838 for curling (Tranter, 1998). Of course, dates
marking the formal constitution of sports governing bodies paint only a partial picture and
do not resolve the issue of when modern sport
emerged as a distinct practice, much less its
causes.

Highlighting the "interplay of change and continuity" in the eighteenth and nineteenth centuries, Richard Holt (1989: 12) attributes the idea
of modern sport to mid-Victorian "folklorists"
who, living "in the midst of an unprecedented
upsurge of urban and industrial change," tended
to cast their world as modern and the pre-Victo-

rian era as traditional. Stefan Szymanski (2008: 4)
gives rather more emphasis to continuities across
the eighteenth and nineteenth centuries and
dates modern sport from the early eighteenth
century with the codification of cricket, golf, and
horseracing in rural areas.

Supporters of a mid-Victorian birth point to
quantitative and qualitative differences between
mid-eighteenth- and late nineteenth-century
sport. Although acknowledging eighteenth-
century antecedents, Tranter (1998: 16), for example, insists "the sporting culture of late
nineteenth- and early twentieth-century Britain
was quite unlike anything that preceded it. Sport
in its modern, organised, commercialised and extensive form, was truly an 'invention' of the Victorian and Edwardian age." Steven Riess (2008)
concurs. Referring to the American experience, he
situates modern sport firmly in the nineteenth-
century "process of city building" (p. 37). "Cities,"
Riess argues, "were the primary sites of organized
sports, and the location of players, spectators and
sports clubs" (p. 37). According to Riess, "the
growing city" was the site of countless voluntary
organizations, including elite, middle-class, and
working-class sports organizations and ethnic
sports clubs that engendered a "sense of community and identity" among urbanites (p. 37).

If there is a consensus among reconstructionists that modern sport dates from the mid-Victorian era, Szymanski reminds us that the issue is
unresolved. Deploying the concept of "public
sphere" advanced by the German social theorist
Jurgen Habermas, Szymanski (2008: 1), maintains that the essence of modern sport lies in the
free social associations found in clubs which he
traces to the eighteenth century and the "expansion of private associative activity [in] . . . the
Anglo-Saxon world following the retreat of the
state." Early modern sporting practices, Szymanski elaborates, were largely "dictated by the rules
governing associative activity, and different practices in different countries are a consequence of
these different rules" (p. 3). In Britain and the
United States the state granted individuals more
independence and freedom to "create social networks and organizations outside the family"
(p. 2).

The position adopted by Szymanski (2008)
and the preceding comments by Riess (2008)
reveal that debates over the birth date of modern

sport are difficult to separate from those which engage its causes and the transformation from premodern to modern forms.[2] Reconstructionists mostly attribute this transformation to the by-products of urbanization and industrialization, notably improved standards of living, communications and transport, reduced working hours, and technological innovations (e.g., Lucas and Smith, 1978; Vamplew, 1988). Reconstructionists typically avoid identifying the precise mechanisms of change, which requires engagement with theory and thus a constructionist epistemology. Constructionists largely draw from either modernization or Marxist theories.

Modernization theories of social change once wielded immense influence in the social sciences (Adelman, 1993; Stearns, 1980), but their application to modern sport largely failed to win converts. Allen Guttmann (1978) offers the most sophisticated theory of modernization and modern sport and the transformation of the latter from a form tied to religious customs and interwoven with agrarian rhythms to its contemporary version, which he characterizes as secular, democratic, bureaucratized, specialized, rationalized, quantified, and grounded in an obsession with records. Guttmann locates the basic mechanism of change in human desire and the quest for achievement and status which he proposes underpinned the scientific revolution. According to Guttmann, modern sport is a cultural expression of the scientific world. "The emergence of modern sports," Guttmann says, "represents . . . the slow development of an empirical, experimental, mathematical *Weltanschauung* [worldview]" (1978: 85). This "intellectual revolution . . . symbolized by the names of Isaac Newton and John Locke and institutionalized in the Royal Society," explains how a "relentlessly modern attitude . . . suddenly, even ruthlessly, challenged premodern forms of social organization and ideology" (p. 85).

Guttmann labels his theory of social change after the German sociologist Max Weber. But whereas dialectical interactions between the individual and society, the material and cultural, and the subjective and the objective underpin Weberian theory, Guttmann (1978) locates the origins of the "impulse to quantification" and the "desire to win, to excel, to be the best" in the scientific culture of seventeenth-

century England, about which he offers few details. Nor does he discuss the mechanisms by which this scientific *Weltanschauung* diffused around the globe. Rather, he attributes the mania for records to the *telos* of Western society and modern sport. Criticized for its functionalist assumptions and tenor (Booth, 2005), Guttmann's approach to change also assumes the homogenization of different societies, including their sports, which he implies follow a Western model (Maguire, 1999).

Marxist theories of social change focus on power and political struggles which, in the case of sport, revolve around the capacity to define legitimate sporting practices (Bourdieu, 1978: 826). Historical records reveal intense struggles in the nineteenth century over legitimate sport (John Hargreaves, 1986; Holt, 1989) as the middle classes set out to reform working-class sports. Reforms included restrictions on the times (e.g., Sundays) and places (e.g., public streets) available for sport, and prohibitions on certain forms, especially blood sports (e.g., cockfighting, dogfighting) and those involving gambling. Marxist interpretations identify the emergence of a new form of institutionalized sport in the late nineteenth century, one grounded in the "moral usefulness of games, middle-class respectability, and gentlemanly propriety" (Gruneau, 1988: 21). Critically, "none of this occurred in any evolutionary way, nor did it simply turn on the emergence of new forms of rationality"; the marginalization or incorporation of traditional sports occurred along with the sanctifying of amateur sport which was "part of a broader process of cultural conflict and social change" (Gruneau, 1988: 21).

Proposing motors for these struggles, early Marxist sociologists (e.g., Brohm 1978; Rigauer, 1981) emphasized class conflicts in capitalist social formations. In these theories sport functions as an ideological apparatus of the bourgeois to preserve and perpetuate capitalist structures. In the nineteenth century this meant glorifying skill-based hierarchies and undermining/restricting the development of working-class consciousness. Sport assisted both; in the case of the latter it acted as an "emotional safety valve for the release of aggressive feelings which might otherwise be turned on the real class oppressors" and "a false sense of escape"

(Gruneau, 1982: 23). Reminding us of the one-dimensional nature of these theories, Gruneau comments that they "reduce cultural formations to 'passive reflections' of reality rather than meaningful dramatizations" and "incorrectly assume" that the dominant classes "actually exercise complete control over sport" in ways that enable them to defend their class interests (p. 25).

Notwithstanding these limitations, Marxist theorizing enlightened a generation of scholars. Historian Eric Hobsbawm (1998: 193) described the insights as "charges of intellectual explosive, designed to blow up crucial parts of the fortification of traditional history." According to Hobsbawm, the power of these insights, ironically, lay in their simplicity: "those of us who recall our first encounters with [Marxism] may still bear witness to the immense liberating force of such simple discoveries" (p. 194). Gruneau (1983: 36), too, admits that for all its overstatements, Marxism offers "powerful" and "penetrating" insights, especially into the ways sport helps reproduce the "repressive constraints" of capitalism.

Seeking to escape the reductionism and determinism of Marxism and include expressions of agency while accounting for the ongoing dominance of capitalist structures, left-leaning, constructionist sport historians turned to Antonio Gramsci's concept of hegemony. Gramscian hegemony "refers to the . . . processes through which dominant social groups extend their influences . . . [by] continually refashioning their ways of life and institutionalized modes of practice and belief, in order to win consent for the system and structure of social relations which sustain their dominant position" (Gruneau, 1988: 29). Critically, Gruneau recognizes hegemony as an "ongoing process" as dominant groups confront an endless array of continually emerging practices that seek to redefine and reform social and cultural forms such as sport (p. 29). Thus, through the theoretical lens of hegemony, left-leaning historians, sometimes referred to as *neo*-Marxists, constructed modern sport as a set of practices which emerged "through compromises and struggles" and which were legitimized by the bourgeoisie in capitalist societies who incorporated them into the education system and the media and who reconstituted "the dominant

meanings of sport in a way that separated it from politically dangerous or economically disruptive practices" (Gruneau, 1988: 29–30).

Reconstructionist and constructionist historians concur that modern sport existed as a distinct form in the Anglo-Saxon world during the third quarter of the nineteenth century, although they continue to debate its precise birth date. Empirical evidence supports this position but it alone cannot provide definitive dates, which are inextricably intertwined with specific conceptualizations of modern sport. Nor can empirical evidence resolve ongoing debates over the causes of modern sport which reflect different theoretical conceptualizations of its form. Hegemony may be the most popular explanation among constructionists for the form taken by modern sport in the nineteenth century but it has critics among reconstructionists (e.g., Holt, 1989: 364) and constructionists (e.g., Booth, 2005; see also Donaldson, 1993) for whom the theory is simply too "neat."

Diffusion

Just as they debate the causes of modern sport, so historians dispute the motors which drove, and continue to drive, the diffusion of sport, that is, how individual sports developed and spread, and why some individuals/groups play some sports and not others.[3] Here I analyze the motors of diffusion advanced by four (largely overlapping) theories: modernization, imperialism, dependency, and Americanization.

Modernization   If modernization failed to convince historians about the origins of modern sport, it proved even less persuasive as an explanation for the subsequent diffusion. Reconstructionists typically attribute diffusion to individual agents such as public schoolboys, diplomats, civil servants, military personnel, missionaries, merchants, migrants (e.g., Guttmann, 1993), while constructionists focus more on institutional/structural influences (e.g., bureaucracy, education, economics). In both cases, the process of diffusion often appears as a simple mapping exercise. Commenting on the formation of national soccer federations in Europe in the nineteenth century, Maarten Van Bottenburg (2001: 166) claims they broadly followed the "chronology of modernization and relations between core countries and the periphery," from England, Wales, Scotland, and Ireland to Bulgaria, Greece, Romania, and Albania (see also Clignet and Stark, 1974).

Advocates of modernization also commonly link diffusion to cultural homogenization in which local groups embrace modern organizational principles and transform the formal structural characteristics of traditional sports into modern forms. These scholars emphasize nominal historical continuity, even in traditional sports that have undergone modernization, such as in *buzkashi*,[4] judo, and sumo, where rituals and other characteristics survive from the past (Guttmann, 1991). Few reconstructionists or constructionists consider modernization a satisfactory explanation of diffusion. Whatever commitments to rational organizational principles modern sport expresses, these do not ameliorate economic and political tensions or conflicts and, not surprising, historians generally found imperialism a more persuasive explanation of diffusion.

Imperialism   An imperial system refers to a set of political, economic, and cultural relations between dominant and subordinate nations. In its cultural form, imperialism describes the process by which agents of the dominant power variously attract and or coerce the ruling strata of the subordinate society into creating new social and cultural institutions that correspond to and promote imperialist values and structures (Houlihan, 1994; Guttmann, 1994). Cultural imperialism underpins much of the historical literature dealing with the diffusion of sport in the late nineteenth and early twentieth century as British and American agents introduced cricket, rugby, soccer, track and field, volleyball, and basketball into their respective colonies. These sports supposedly provided colonists with a vehicle to preserve "cultural continuity and social respectability" and a yardstick by which they, and the colonized, measured their imperial identities (Stoddart, 1988: 238). Brian Stoddart's description of cricket in Barbados before World War I captures the received wisdom of imperial sport and its "shared cultural values" (p. 237). The players came from the "elite, respectable section of the community" while the "lower orders,

who . . . had few opportunities to play," cheered their exploits; the two "groups were part of a cultural authority system" based on "British heritage and its attendant ethical idealism through which cricket became as much moral metaphor as physical activity" (p. 237).

Critiques quickly emerged. Guttmann (1994: 174) declared that theories of cultural imperialism rest on the "facile assumption" that sport diffused in one direction only, from Europe and North America to colonies in the East and the South. Citing the diffusion of lacrosse from Canada to the United States, polo from India to Britain, and judo from Japan to Europe and the United States, Guttmann conceptualizes cultural imperialism as a "two-way" process between weaker and stronger states (1994: 173), although he concedes that "receptivity to 'exotic' sports has been limited to . . . more affluent and better educated" groups (p. 174). Guttmann also questions whether cultural imperialism is simply a mechanism of social control; he proposes a raft of "worthier motives" – "the desire to improve health, to encourage the fortitude, to diminish religious animosities" among indigenous populations – which he insists were more than just "colonialist camouflage" (p. 174). In Guttmann's view, the key to understanding nineteenth-century cultural imperialism and the diffusion of sport lies in the concept of muscular Christianity and the "Christianizing" of indigenous populations (1994: 177; see also Gems, 2006).

Elaborating on his theory of cultural imperialism, Guttmann broaches the notion of hegemony which, he says, stresses the complexity of cultural interactions that are usually more than the "totally powerful" subjugating the "entirely powerless" (1994: 178): cultures can be "annihilated" but they can also be "resilient, adaptive, and transformative" (p. 185) and modern sports have helped "crystallize anti-colonial sentiments" (p. 181). Guttmann lists copious examples which support hegemonic conclusions. But ultimately he conflates the concept with ideology and undermines the central tenet of hegemony as a continuous process of political struggle when he insists that "those who adopt a sport are often the eager initiators of a transaction of which the 'donors' are scarcely aware" (p. 179). In the end, Guttmann's version of imperialism disregards theoretical issues of power in favor of functionalist-type assumptions about modern Western society.[5]

Dependency   Power and control, of course, lie at the heart of Marxism, and among left-leaning constructionist historians imperialism captured "the economic and political relationship between advanced capitalist countries and backward countries" in a single world system (Bottomore, 1983: 223; see also Wallerstein, 1974). In the stream of Marxist imperialism known as dependency theory, "industrial metropoles dominate underdeveloped satellites" by expropriating their surpluses and consigning the latter to perpetual states of dependency and under-development (Bottomore, 1983: 498). Aspects of dependency theory appeared in several pieces of sport history in the late 1980s and early 1990s with the authors highlighting exploitative relationships between states (e.g., Arbena, 1988; Jarvie, 1991; Stoddart, 1988). But the two fullest theoretical explications involved American domination of sport in neighboring states: baseball in the Dominican Republic (Klein, 1989) and professional sports in Canada (Kidd, 1982).

American major league baseball teams, says Alan Klein (1989: 95), have had a "deleterious structural effect on the autonomy and quality of baseball in the Dominican Republic" and constricted its development. Among the problems Klein identifies are discrepancies in pay between Dominican and American players, loss of local players, and baseball academies which "cannibalize" amateur leagues in the Republic. Klein likens the academies, which American major league teams introduced to the Republic in the early 1980s, to "colonial outposts" (1989: 103). They "operate more or less in the same capacity as a plantation: locating resources (talent) and refining them (training) for consumption abroad" (p. 103).

Bruce Kidd (1982) blames the subordination of major professional sports in Canada on American interests and the forces of dependency. Referring to hockey, Kidd argues that once city-based teams (e.g., Toronto Maple Leafs) become enmeshed in commercially sponsored competitions they no longer enunciate a sense of community identity. Such competitions, says Kidd, produce commodity markets for players who represent the highest bidder rather than their local communities. By the end of World War II the American-based National Hockey League had, Kidd laments, reduced the Canadian Hockey Association to a "'slave farm of hockey,' controlling rules, revenues, style of play, player development, and even the national team" and it meant that "generations of Canadian boys grew up wearing (and never taking off) sweaters celebrating the cities of another country, while living in ignorance of their own" (Kidd, 1982: 291–292).

In a general critique of dependency theory, Colin Leys (1982) identifies numerous problems including a tendency to see capitalism as "an inexorable process of accumulation" rather than a set of contradictions and constant struggles (p. 307). Implicit in Leys' claim is that assumptions rather than historical evidence drive dependency theory. Elaborating on this point in a response to Klein (1989) which would equally apply to Kidd's (1982) analysis of the dependency in Canadian–American sporting relationships, Stoddart (1989) agrees that Dominican baseball might well be "run for the sole benefit" of American corporations (p. 128). But he maintains that the sociopolitical framework of dependency is considerably more complex and must take into account the place of games within the local economy. "We need to know more," Stoddart argues, about "indirect economic beneficiaries" (p. 128) such as officials, ticket sellers, vendors, souvenir sellers, and the media, and about the economic impact of those who return to the Republic after playing abroad. Moreover, we can never know whether those who left would have been economically successful had they stayed home.

While the concept of dependency has not been overly prominent in sports history, the idea raised interesting questions about capitalism and sport, and about America's imperial influence on sport in the second half of the twentieth century. Sport sociologists, more than historians, took up these questions. At least initially they subordinated questions about capitalism and the increasing commodification of sport to questions about American imperialism and America as the source of professional-entertainment sport. More than simply a form based on paid players, modern professional-entertainment sport is grounded in "management science, with executive directors and specialists in advertising, marketing and public relations," and corporate relationships that include the media and which extend into "player development, equipment, facilities, coaching, dissemination of information, publicity, and administrative costs" (McKay and Miller, 1991: 87). Here I treat Americanization as a fourth motor of diffusion.

Americanization   In the 1990s the American style of marketing and packaging sport attracted the attention of sport sociologists. Describing what they called the Americanization of Australian sport, Jim McKay and Toby Miller (1991: 89), for example, observed popular sports "opting for the showbiz format (e.g., cheerleaders, mascots, live bands, and spectacular displays before, during, and after events)." They also commented on American sport's increasing penetration into the local market: "Australian networks televise the World Series, the Superbowl, the Kentucky Derby, and major events in American golf, tennis, automobile, and motorcycle racing. One of the five national networks televises a 'game of the week' from the [National Football League] and the [National Basketball Association], and professional wrestling matches from the USA are telecast on a regular basis" (p. 87). Such case studies led Peter Donnelly to conclude that American sport is now "the international benchmark for corporate sport" (1996: 246).

Donnelly (1996) believes Americanization has important explanatory power when applied to the diffusion of professional baseball and basketball, the rise and influence of Nike and the International Management Group, and the role of American television in the sport media complex. Notwithstanding their comments about the Americanization of Australian sport, McKay and Miller (1991) deem the concept limited. It tends, they argue, "to flatten out, to homogenize, and to deny the rich heterogeneity and conflict both within and among the supposed donors and legatees" (p. 92). Donnelly agrees. While acknowledging America's influence on modern sport, he believes that any cultural impact must be conceptualized in "hegemonic terms" that affords recipients the power to interpret and resist (1996: 248). Donnelly concurs that Americanization at the corporate level has potential to create a "global sport monoculture" and "doom traditional sports to ... extinction," but he also believes this process can open "cultural space in which new sporting activities may emerge and traditional sports may thrive" (p. 248; see also Andrews, 2009).

Reception

Historians note that when modern sport diffused around the globe it "did not simply take root in virgin soil" (Bale, 1994: 8). For example, ballgames already existed in North Africa (e.g., *om el mahag*), India (e.g., *gulli danda*), Central America (e.g., *tlaxtli*), North America (e.g., *chueco* and *linao*), and Australia (e.g., *marn-grook*). Thus, the diffusion of modern sport raises questions about its reception by cultures that already have conceptualizations of physical movement. In general, theorists of modernization, structural Marxism, imperialism, dependency, and Americanization conceptualize reception in terms of adoption and acculturation and as a process of cultural homogenization in which modern sport emerges as the dominant way of playing, reconfiguring local physical cultures into a single global form. Such reconfiguration takes place either by marginalizing and destroying indigenous movement cultures (e.g., structural Marxism, dependency) or by winning the social acceptance of local elites (e.g., modernization, imperialism, Americanization). By contrast, theories grounded in hegemony refer to reception as a process of struggle leading to cultural heterogeneity.

However, the concept of reception requires clarification. Acceptance of sporting events (e.g., Olympic Games), specific sports (e.g., athletics, soccer), and rational organization (e.g., standardized rules, records, codes of conduct) appear almost universal. In this context, states and groups that claim to use sport as "a tool of cultural, and often explicitly political, resistance" in fact reinforce the idea of a homogeneous global sporting culture (Houlihan, 1994: 363). East Germany, Cuba, and the Soviet Union are classic examples as they claimed their victories in international sport as victories for socialism. But these victories stemmed from imitating the scientific, managerial, and organizational features of modern sport. Thus, claims of cultural difference in sport are often differences grounded in the symbols of identity and in particular national sporting identity rather than different practices (Houlihan, 1994). Here I examine the reception of modern sport and questions of cultural

identity through the debates among constructionist historians and sociologists under two
headings: homogeneity and heterogeneity.

Cultural homogeneity   Recording that 35 codes
have national umbrella organizations in more
than 100 countries, Van Bottenburg (2001: 8)
writes that the level of "cohesion" in sport is such
that one can legitimately speak of "a global sporting system." Numerous scholars advance the view
that this system homogenized physical culture
across the globe and reduced cultural variety. The
champion of modernization, Allen Guttmann
(1991), believes the concept implies that "the
global transformation . . . in the last two centuries
. . . has produced a more secular and a more
rationalized [sporting] world, if not a more
rational one" (p. 188). Jean-Marie Brohm,
working at the other end of the theoretical spectrum, recognizes several universal cultural traits
in global sport including the reproduction of
bourgeois social relations based on "hierarchies,
subservience, obedience," and the transmission of
bourgeois myths around "individualism, social
advancement, success [and] efficiency" (1978:
77). Cultural homogenization shines brightly
among theorists of imperialism. Stoddart (1988:
249) cites a case in 1905 in which "a black spectator kissed the arm of an English bowling star" as
an example of the "outright acceptance of cricket
and its English cultural provenance" in the Caribbean. Scholars of Americanization emphasize the
saturation of global markets by American sporting tastes, even to the extent that tribes in tropical
jungles are now said to use satellite dishes and
generators to watch US sport. Opponents of
homogeneity, however, highlight the "socio-cultural complexity of local–global relations and the
heterogeneity of cultural forms and practices" in
modern sport (Giulianotti, 2005: 202).

Cultural heterogeneity   Sociologists studying
the reception of modern sport employ a range of
concepts to explain cultural heterogeneity in
modern sporting forms and practices. Terms such
as *glocalization, creolization,* and *hybridization*
reflect the dynamic nature of culture and cultural
production, and convey the idea of new cultural
forms emerging from cross-cultural contact.
They "capture," says Richard Giulianotti (2005:
204–205), "the vitality of specific local cultures in

relation to globalization processes." Nowhere is
this vitality better revealed than in the (sociological, historical, and anthropological) literature on
national sporting identities (e.g., Bairner, 2001;
Cronin and Mayall, 1998; MacClancy, 1996;
Mangan, 1996; Mangan, 2001) which reveals "the
values, prejudices, divisions and unifying
symbols" (Guha, 2002: xiv) of individual societies. Here I offer three examples from sport
history.
   Tracing the history of cricket in India, Ram-
achandra Guha (2002: 5) claims expatriate Englishmen had "no intention of teaching the
natives to play cricket"; they viewed the game as
"a source of . . . comfort" and a means to "recreate memories of life in England." Played in
colonial clubs, expatriate cricket was "self-
consciously exclusive" (p. 8) and the Parsees,
Hindus, Muslims, and Sikhs who took up the
game did so on their own initiative as a way to
assert their cultural identity rather than to
express imperial loyalty. Since independence,
cricket has become a symbol of Indian national
identity. In 1971 the national team comprised
Hindus and Muslims, a Parsee, and a Sikh; in
1983 a Christian replaced the Parsee (Guha,
2002: 348). At a time when the World Bank
listed India at 150 in its ranking of nations based
on Gross Domestic Product, Indian cricketers
sustained national pride (p. 351). More recently
Indian "cricket nationalism has become . . .
intense and ferocious" (p. 352), even "ugly and
destructive" (p. 405), and "chauvinism has tri-
umphed over generosity" (p. 352).
   South African rugby, according to Robert
Archer and Antoine Bouillon (1982), highlights
the values held by Afrikaner nationalists who
appropriated the game from British colonists in
the early twentieth century. Rugby carried the
Afrikaner's "convictions, aspirations and dreams"
(p. 73). "Attached to their Voortrekker past, proud
of their civilizing mission in a savage land," Afrikaners "perceive themselves as elected and created
by God to reign on earth"; they are highly "conscious of their vocation as warriors – not soldiers
but freemen under arms – inspired by faith and
an uncompromising moral ethic to defend the
cause of their people and their God" (p. 73).
During the apartheid era, rugby kindled nationalist tensions between Afrikaners and English-
speaking South Africans, and even today, in

post-apartheid South Africa, it remains a source of nationalist hostility between black and white nationalists (Booth, 1998).

Greg Ryan argues that cricket survived an adverse climate, the tyrannies of geography and economics, and provincial rivalries and jealousies to become New Zealand's national game in the nineteenth century because its middle-class patrons subscribed to "a powerful Victorian ethos" that promoted "the game irrespective of cost" (2004: 236); gradually, however, rugby "superseded" cricket (p. 2). Ryan proposes that cricket and rugby reveal fundamental contradictions in New Zealand's national identity. Unlike Indian and Australian nationalists who seized cricket to assert their independence from England (Guha, 2002; Mandle, 1973), New Zealanders appropriated cricket to maintain "ties of affection and loyalty" (Ryan, 2004: 229) and used rugby to break those ties (p. 220).

Logic reinforces the idea that the structure of modern sport nurtures cultural heterogeneity (e.g., Rowe, 2003). The social relationships, dramatic qualities, and affective powers of modern sport may help erode social distinctions within groups (whether they coalesce around region, religion, class, caste, race or gender) but processes of exclusion, demarcation, differentiation, and distinction also disconnect groups from each other. Historians offer supporting evidence. Citing the early twentieth-century financier J.P. Morgan, Guttmann (2004) captures the process of cultural disconnection in sport: advocating the exclusion of merchants from yachting circles at Newport, RI, Morgan told his peers, "you can do business with any one, but you can go sailing only with a gentleman" (p. 155). Such examples lead Guha (2002) to conclude that "those who believe the [batting] crease [is] so narrow as to allow white to become black or Untouchable become Brahmin . . . 'live in a fool's paradise'" (p. 318), and are grist to the mill among supporters of cultural heterogeneity in sport. Yet, for all the evidence in support of, and logic behind, sport as culturally heterogeneous, disagreements rage between those who emphasize cultural autonomy (such as the studies cited above) and those who privilege global forces (e.g., Neubauer, 2008; Roche, 2000). In the case of the latter, David Andrews and George Ritzer (2007: 30), for example, question the autonomy of the local in

the contemporary sporting landscape which they argue has undergone glocalization – "the interpenetration of the global and local, resulting in unique outcomes in different geographic areas" – and which they suggest is modified by the imperialistic ambitions of nations, corporations, and different organizations.

The basic questions framing scholarly inquiry into modern sport since the late 1960s have yielded few definitive answers or stable meanings. Typically, the answers have produced new questions and ignited ongoing debate. For example, sociologist Ben Carrington has argued that traditional models of diffusion reduce the agent of social change to modern rationality. According to Carrington, such reductionism ignores the irrational tendencies – "gratuitous violence, unpredictability, emotional instability" – present in contemporary sport and which he believes require radically different analytical approaches (2010: 45). Notwithstanding the lack of accord, reconstructionist and contructionist historians of sport – and sociologists of sport with historical proclivities (henceforth historical sociologists) – remain committed to objective, factually based, and theoretically informed epistemologies which they (implicitly) believe will deliver the truth about modern sport. Despite their commitments to truth they also, ironically, subscribe to an epistemological skepticism which compels them to continually search for new interpretations, explanations, and meanings. In the following section, I investigate the epistemological assumptions of these scholars who have framed the production of much knowledge pertaining to modern sport. I argue that their epistemologies are limited, limiting, and politically constraining and I propose an alternative deconstructionist-leaning epistemology which questions the relationships between reality and its description and between subjects and objects, as well as the power of concepts, theories, and arguments to produce truth.

Epistemologies (and Floating Truths)

Just as modern sport is socially constructed, so too is our knowledge about it and its forms, development, and meaning. Reconstructionist and contructionist historians of sport and historical sociologists of sport use realist epistemologies to produce much of this knowledge. In this section I identify some fragile and deceptive epistemological assumptions which pertain to facts, theories, concepts, and narratives in these forms of history and sociology. As an alternative, I suggest an anti-essentialist, contextualized epistemology, the first shoots of which are appearing in sports history, notably in the reinterpretation of modern sporting practices and cultures.

Objective knowledge

Reconstructionist and contructionist historians of sport and historical sociologists of sport rarely engage with epistemology and many seem unable, or unwilling, to confront the epistemological brittleness of their endeavors. Indeed, the majority approach their work as a distinct craft, with its own logic, protocols, and methodologies. In so doing they set up epistemological boundaries which create a "'license to ignore'" each other (McDonald and Birrell, 1999: 285) and grounds for intellectual skirmishes (e.g., Collins, 2005; Ingham and Donnelly, 1997; Malcolm, 2008; Rowe, McKay, and Lawrence, 1997; Vamplew, 2007). The latter works expose the epistemological fragility of much historical and sociological knowledge about modern sport and undermine the accompanying claims to objectivity, truthfulness, validity, and relevance.

Reconstructionist historians have long claimed a special relationship with the truth by virtue of their vigilance over the gathering and presentation of historical facts (Collins, 2005; Vamplew, 2007). Notwithstanding the prevalence of constructionist sport history (Hill, 1996; Struna, 2000), reconstructionists remain wary of theory which they believe "infuses predestined meaning" into the study of the past (Elton, 1991: 15). Thus, reconstructionists conceptualize history as a reconstruction of the past, grounded in facts derived from primary sources and represented as narrative. The only problem that reconstructionists acknowledge in this approach is the lack of facts, which they insist can be overcome by digging deeper into the archive or asking new questions. Holt (2009) implies that truths about modern sport will emerge as more historians examine the sixteenth and seventeenth centuries and as they step beyond the national cultures in

which they are currently embedded to examine individual sports at the global level. Caroline Daley (2010), too, urges historians to look beyond the sporting nation and to examine the international circulation of ideas, people, and objects. But the real problem is epistemological not a paucity of evidence.

Historical narratives certainly contain references from the past, but a reference is not a representation: "historians impose narratives on events which they intend to resemble the past" (Phillips and Roper, 2006: 137). The issue, it must be stressed, does not concern the correspondence of simple statements extracted from traces of the past. The dates marking the formal constitution of international sports federations[6] usually survive in archives along with the names of inaugural presidents and committee members and their motives and interests. Assembled in a narrative these dates, names, and interests unquestionably offer factual statements corresponding with the past. However, a narrative representation is quite different from a factual statement: "representation is not reference; [representation] is *about* its subject. That history contains references does not authorise our access to the past's meaning" (Munslow, 2006: 223).

International sports federations exist within multiple contexts (e.g., international relations, national politics, cultural and ideological values), and their founders bear idiosyncratic psychological dispositions. Both contextualizing and psychoanalyzing, which should be integral to histories of international sports federations, incorporate a myriad of assumptions and require judgments on the part of the historian that extend well beyond gathering evidence from primary sources. In practice, reconstructionist historians typically employ at a subconscious level a theory or a concept which directs the questions they ask, guides them to particular sources, organizes their evidence, and shapes their explanations, while constructionists are usually more explicit (Tosh, 2000: 134). Indeed, modernization, imperialism, hegemony, and muscular Christianity are good examples of theories and concepts embraced by historians writing about modern sport.

The origins of these theories and concepts are important because in the main reconstructionist and constructionist historians simply appropriate them from other disciplines, particularly sociology, anthropology, and psychology (Hill, 1996). But the problem for historians dealing in this "second-hand trade," as Alun Munslow (2006: 64) calls it, is the tendency to reify these theories and concepts.[7] Once committed to a theory or concept, few historians will admit that they are engaging a prefigured, constructed, and narrated – i.e., ideological/political – form of knowledge (Munslow, 2003: 176).

Likewise, it is pertinent to ask sociologists how they conceptualize history. The historical orientations of classical social theorists such as Emile Durkheim, Karl Marx, and Max Weber – each of whom viewed the past as the bedrock of the present; in Marx's words, "the tradition of all dead generations weighs like a nightmare on the brain of the living" (1977: 300) – alerted early sociologists of sport to the value of incorporating historical perspectives into their work. Engagements with C. Wright Mills' (1959) notion of the sociological imagination – in which individuals shape and are shaped by society and "its historical push and shove" – reinforced this perspective, at least at the influential Massachusetts school of sports sociology (Ingham and Donnelly, 1997). "The sociological imagination," Mills (1959: 6) espoused, "enables us to grasp history and biography and the relations between the two within society." According to Alan Ingham and Peter Donnelly (1997: 377), Mills' perspective fostered an interest among sport sociologists in a stream of historical sociology informed by critical theory which, in epistemological terms, stood in "sharp contrast" to mainstream North American sport history that subscribed to the canons of empiricism. Indeed, historically inclined sport sociologists – notably Eric Dunning (Dunning and Sheard, 2005), John Hargreaves (1986), Jennifer Hargreaves (1994), and Richard Gruneau (1983) – "borrowed far more from sport historians (mainly, their data) than the other way around" (Ingham and Donnelly, 1997: 377). Of course, there is an irony in the situation where sociologists accept the facts and evidence offered by historians while rejecting their narratives: as noted above, historical explanations are typically framed by implicit theories that guide which facts historians gather and which ones they proffer as evidence.

Just as sport historians appropriate theories and concepts from other disciplines, so sociologists of sport retrieve them from mainstream sociology and classical social theory. How robust are these theories and concepts? Mills (1959) doubted whether the "grand theorizing" in mainstream North American sociology enhanced understanding or helped people to make sense of their experiences. Social historian Arthur Stinchcombe (1978) accused grand theorists of "reckless" theorizing by inventing their concepts at the "level of the large narrative" which he said typically "ignores" the facts in order to generate the concept (p. 16). According to Stinchcombe, the most "fruitful" concepts emerge from examinations of "analogies between historical instances." At the heart of his notion of concept lies the "deep" analogy, a form based on three or more equivalent cases which, of course, demands careful attention to detail.

Lack of detail is a consistent lament among critics examining theories of modern sport. Barry Houlihan (1994) singles out Jean-Marie Brohm's theory that sport reproduces the ideology of bourgeois social relations as one requiring more evidence. Similarly, Houlihan (1994: 360) rejects many of the conclusions relating to the reception of foreign sporting culture as little more than accumulations of eclectic anecdotes. The limited and limiting assumptions underpinning some theories and concepts constitute a second Achilles heel. Richard Gruneau (1988: 17) finds modernization theory bedeviled by assumptions that "direct attention toward certain research questions at the expense of others" and by its use of "hollow liberal clichés about the voluntary and consensual foundations of [Western society and] the extent of social progress." Indeed, structural (i.e., economic, technological) or idealist (i.e., cultural) determinants underpin much of the literature on the origins and diffusion of sport while voluntarism and determinism are hallmarks of the studies into its reception (Gruneau, 1999).

Responding to these issues, Gruneau proposed what he called a "synthetic, multidimensional" approach which binds "history and theory, interpretive cultural analysis, and political economy" (1999: 114) and is sensitive to complexity.[8] Synthetic, multidimensional approaches undoubtedly eliminate much of the reductionism and determinism plaguing early research into modern sport, and better capture the complexity of this phenomenon. Analyzing the reception of soccer in colonial India, James Mills and Paul Dimeo (2003) reveal the simultaneously oppositional and complicit tendencies in, and the complex nature of social relationships around, the game. As well as rejecting the search for cause and effect relationships, they dispose of polar positions that conceptualize soccer as a benign agent of socialization *or* a fully fledged site of resistance to colonial power and authority. Examining the victory of the Mohun Bagan club in the 1911 Indian Football Association Challenge Shield, Mills and Dimeo admit the team's success represented a "moment of nationalist triumph" and a "dramatic and public undoing" of colonial stereotypes about British athletic superiority and Indian effeteness; but the celebrations also endorsed British mores enshrining demonstrations of physical prowess as the true markers of "strength and self-reliance," and the body as the proper "site for judging a people and its destiny" (2003: 119–121). Placing soccer in colonial India in a dynamic cultural system that forged contradictory and paradoxical identities enables Mills and Dimeo to escape the reductionism and determinism befalling much of the work on modern sport.

Jay Scherer, Mark Falcous, and Steven Jackson (2008) display heightened sensitivity to the dynamics of, and shifting power relations in, global capitalism, and especially the media sports cultural complex, a concept that aspires to capture the interrelationships between sporting organizations, the media, and transnational corporations, and to put those interrelationships in a broader cultural context. Scherer and his colleagues transcend many of the problems in the early work on the political economy of sport which, as I showed in the discussion on dependency theory, largely ignored internal relationships and contradictions. While sporting institutions may "financially depend" on transnational corporations, say Scherer and colleagues (2008: 65), this does not mean the media sports cultural complex constitutes a "seamless economic synergy and untrammeled affinity between interest groups" (p. 49). On the contrary, local "conditions, histories, traditions, sporting codes and power relations" ensure that the "processes of commodification and media–sport convergence" are never predetermined (p. 49). They illustrate this point in an empirically rich case study of the media sports cultural complex in New Zealand in which they highlight the fragile and contingent relationships between three key agents: the New Zealand Rugby Union (NZRU), Adidas, and News Corporation. Notwithstanding the shared financial goals of these three agents, Scherer and colleagues maintain that the relationships are "situational, temporary, and dynamic according to the relative market worth of [the] entities at any moment" (p. 65). The market worth of NZRU, for example, is currently threatened by local supporters who resent the Union transforming *their* game into a commodity.

Scherer and colleagues (2008) conclude their analysis with a call for more "empirical studies" to "critically engage" the power brokers and representatives of the media sports cultural complex (p. 66). Such research, they contend, should strive to tease out the ongoing commodification of sport and its increasingly larger place in global capitalism. In many respects their call amounts to testing the concept of the media sports cultural complex. Although widely embraced (e.g., Wenner, 1998; Rowe, 1999; Gruneau, 1999), the media sports cultural complex is not a rigorous formulation in a Stinchcombean sense. David Rowe (1999) embraced the concept as a means to contextualize sport in the broader cultural terrain of late capitalism rather than as an instrument for comparing agents/events/institutions across time/space. In this volume (CHAPTER 3) he notes that the media sports cultural complex continues to "mutate" at a pace which problematizes the integrity of the concept. Similarly, Scherer and colleagues (2008) embrace the media sports cultural complex to locate one set of national power relations in a global context. Yet, notwithstanding the merits of their work as representative of the synthetic, multidimensional approach, which Gruneau (1999) abbreviates to "better histories and more inclusive theories," Scherer and colleagues (2008) and Mills and Dimeo (2003) still express faith in a realist epistemology which they believe captures authentic knowledge about modern sport. But the lack of consensus demonstrates it is an unfounded faith. Not surprisingly then scholars are increasingly challenging realist epistemologies with anti-essentialist, contextualized forms which are more alert to the constructed nature of knowledge.

Contextualized knowledge

Grounded in the ideas of thinkers such as Roland Barthes, Walter Benjamin, Jacques Derrida, Michel Foucault, Clifford Geertz, Maurice Halbwachs, and Hayden White, and commonly labeled postmodernist, anti-essentialist and contextualized epistemologies have established a beachhead in sport history (e.g., Phillips, 2006) and indeed sport sociology (e.g., Rail, 1998). In sport history, for example, Steve Pope (2006) demonstrates the need for such epistemologies when dealing with elusive and indeterminate sources, and Douglas Brown (2003) engages affective sources.[9] John Bale (2004) argues that facts are often "beliefs" and that language is inordinately "complex," "multifaceted," and "slippery," while Jeffrey Hill (2006) examines sport as "negotiated meaning." Incorporating aspects of her personal working life into the broader context of rights for women, Patricia Vertinsky (Vertinsky and McKay, 2004) embraces the idea of reflexive contextualization. I have advocated reconceptualizing archives as sites of power rather than sites of knowledge (Booth, 2005), and Brett Hutchins (2002) deconstructs the function of myths which he links to structures of social power and vested interests. Gary Osmond and Murray Phillips (2004) and Jaime Schultz (2005) approach memory as a process of construction rather than one of retrieving facts and truth. Where reconstructionists ponder the reliability of memory, Osmond and Phillips ask questions about how people relate their memories of the past to the present. Dan Nathan (2003) disposes of reconstructionists and constructionists as disembodied observers in preference for historians as authors, while Synthia Sydnor (1998) has experimented with presenting history in new ways.

None of these historians view knowledge about modern sport as fixed; rather their knowledge is situational and contextualized in the moment of its existence/narration. Importantly, they do not view context as a pure analytical tool. In this regard they follow Frank Ankersmit (2005: 256) who likens contextualization to clouds that obstruct the airline passenger's view of the ground and "prevent us from seeing the past itself or distort our view of it." Instead of searching for the facts pertaining to origins, events, and/or agents, these historians explicate how reconstruc-

tionists and constructionists "frame," "foreground," "remember," "obscure," and "forget" the past (McDonald and Birrell, 1999: 292). Effectively, they "displace the notion of privileged access to 'truth'" and relocate it in the text and in the "complex interrelationship" between the producer and the reader (McDonald and Birrell, 1999: 292).

Michael Oriard (1995) graphically illustrates the fluidity of truth and meaning in sporting "texts" and its highly contextualized nature in his conceptualization of American football as a cultural text grounded in multiple voices and perspectives. For example, Oriard offers a long list of interpretations available to spectators watching a violent collision between a receiver and defender:

> Imagine our receiver as black, the defender white. Or one of them from Notre Dame, the other from Brigham Young; one from the Big Ten, the other from the Southeast Conference; one a candidate for a Rhodes Scholarship, the other a known drug-user or sex-offender; one a street kid from the inner city, the other the son of a wealthy cardiologist; one a well-known volunteer for the Special Olympics, the other an arrogant publicist of his own athletic brilliance. Certain teams have their own distinctive images: think of the Cowboys, the Bears, the Raiders, the 49ers in the National Football League; or, of Penn State, Miami, Oklahoma, Southern California among the colleges. And imagine the fans watching these players and teams not as a "mass" audience but as actual people: European-, African-, Hispanic-, and Asian-American; Catholic, Protestant, Jew, and nonbeliever; WASP and redneck; college graduate and high-school dropout; conservative and liberal; racist and humanitarian; male and female, rich and poor, urban and rural, sick and well; ones just fired from jobs and ones just promoted; ones just fallen in love and ones just separated from a spouse; some pissed off at the world and some blissfully content. (Oriard, 1995: 2–3)

As well as approaching knowledge of modern sport as open to multiple interpretations, contextualized epistemologies also view it as constructed and competing. Murray Phillips (2002) offers an apposite example in a comparative analysis of two narratives about the Australian surf lifesaving movement which, despite drawing from the same archive, are remarkably different. Applying a model developed by Hayden White (1973) to interrogate the construction of narratives, Phillips (2002) unravels the highly technical and complex manner in which the two historian-authors filter their facts through different tropes (e.g., metonymic versus synecdochic), emplotments (e.g., romantic versus tragic), arguments (e.g., formist versus contextualist), and ideologies (e.g., liberal versus radical). In so doing Phillips lends powerful support to White's contention that historians prefigure and construct their narratives rather than discover them in their sources, as well as indicating the fallacies of foundational knowledge upon which scholars can agree and where the truth will emerge (Jenkins, 1999: 28).

An anti-foundationalism lies at the heart of these deconstructionist-leaning approaches. Anti-foundationalism teaches us that "questions of fact, truth, correctness, validity, and clarity can neither be posed nor answered in reference to some contextual, ahistorical, noninstitutional reality, or rule, or law or value" (Jenkins, 1999: 23). In anti-foundationalism, "these matters are intelligible and debatable only within the precincts of the contexts or situations or paradigms or communities that give them their local and changeable shape" (p. 23).

Three questions remain. What are the consequences of constructed knowledge for notions of truth? How should scholars respond to these consequences? How should scholars evaluate anti-essentialist knowledge? Mary McDonald and Susan Birrell (1999) believe constructed knowledge elevates truth to power relations and relocates truth in privileged versions of knowledge or narratives. According to them, privileged narratives are the ones with political import and the ones that constitute useful history. Against this scenario, they encourage scholars to respond by constructing narratives that highlight social conflicts and public debates – many of which abound in modern sport (e.g., racism, sexism, homophobia) – with a view to both adding clarity and shaping the "outcome" (1999: 295). Lastly, McDonald and Birrell recommend that scholars measure the success of contextualized knowledge by its "moral, social and political significance, not simply by [its] empirical or explanatory correctness" (p. 295).

Contextualized epistemologies have exposed scholars to charges of relativism. But rather than "implying licence" as critics charge, relativism introduces "ethical injunctions" (Jenkins, 1999; Jenkins, Morgan, and Munslow, 2007: 6). Ethics are not unique to contextualized knowledge; Scherer and colleagues (2008), for example, examine social access and fairness in their narrative of the sports media and the ways it invites consumers to interpret its functions. However, scholars working with objective epistemologies assume that facts identify and resolve ethical issues. Munslow (2006: 96) counters that facts do neither; nor do they spur political decision-making or action. On the contrary, observing that facts did not prevent genocide in Darfur and that neutrality did not work in Srebrenica,[10] Elizabeth Ermarth (2007: 57) wonders whether there are any examples "where giving us the facts has guided choice." Scholars working with contextualized epistemologies acknowledge that the ethical and moral lessons they build into their narratives reflect their concerns and interests, and their context (i.e., their choices: see Jenkins, 1999: 52). In short, when we recognize that knowledge is a product inextricably intertwined with its social and cultural circumstances, logically and necessarily, attention should shift from questions of truth to questions about authors and their interests, ethics, and intentions.

Conclusion

Modern sport is a global phenomenon whose significance lies not in its origins or development through time but in its meaning in the (never-ending and ever-changing) present. A key task confronting historians is to interrogate the different narratives about modern sport at the time of their production and ask what those narratives reveal about their authors (and the periods in which they write). To this end, the search is not for objective knowledge framed by infallible facts, concepts, and theories which can never capture reality, but for contextualized knowledge that appreciates its temporary and transitory state, and its ethical and political import. While such interrogations – which signal the shift from an epistemological paradigm based on objective knowledge to one based on contextualization – are in their infancy in sport history, their dispersal across the social sciences and humanities, combined with changes in science, technology, and philosophy, suggest a "tectonic change" in assumptions and methodological processes (Ermarth, 2011: xiii). Many sport historians are oblivious to this change, others continue to defend empiricism, and a few even attempt to suppress intellectual experimentation. But while they continue to rely on apparently "natural" objectifying and rational approaches they will continue to deny not only the cultural functions

of their enterprise but also that history is merely a function of the present.

Acknowledgments

Sincere thanks to Mark Falcous and Richard Pringle who generously commented on an early draft of this chapter.

Notes

1 The overwhelming majority of sport historians work at the intersection of reconstructionism and constructionism, appropriating (and not infrequently misappropriating) sociological concepts rather than fully fledged theories to mediate their interpretations of primary sources (Booth, 2005).

2 There are surprisingly few definitions of these two forms of sport. Guttmann (1978) and Dunning and Sheard (2005) offer the most coherent and sophisticated definitions. I refer to Guttmann's (1978) definition in the following paragraph. Loy and Coakley (2006) define sport in a transhistorical sense as a contest-based ludic physical activity which is embodied, structured, goal-oriented, and competitive.

3 According to Van Bottenburg (2001), four of the seven sports with the most participants worldwide come from Britain (soccer, track and field, tennis, and table tennis), two from the United States (volleyball and basketball), and one from Germany (gymnastics). Somewhat surprisingly cricket does not feature in this list.

4 A traditional team sport in Central Asia played on horseback. Players use their arms to grab the carcass of a headless goat or calf, ride clear of their opponents, and then pitch the carcass either across a goal line or into a circle or vat.

5 Nor does Guttmann show any inclination to debate questions of power with his critics.

6 Sixteen international sports federations existed by 1914 (Van Bottenburg, 2001).

7 Scholars approach concepts from a wide variety of angles. Houlihan (1994: 372) draws attention to what he calls the "concept attention cycle" in which a concept is discovered and greeted with "euphoric enthusiasm." This is followed by an awakening to "complexity" and the inevitable

"cooling of enthusiasm" followed by its "quiet transfer . . . to the backburner." Alexander (1995) examines the material conditions under which concepts emerge, while Fiss and Hirsch (2005) discuss the "framing of emerging concepts."

8 Historical sociology also promised to address these concerns (e.g., Abrams, 1982). Figurational sociologists took up the cause of historical sociology with particular vigor in sports studies (e.g., Maguire, 1995) but the five-phased process of "sportization" (Maguire, 1999: 79) which figurationalists advance as an explanation for "the transformation of English pastimes into sports" and their "export" around the globe (p. 80; see also Malcolm, 2006) has won few converts among historians (e.g., Collins, 2005; Vamplew, 2007) or sociologists (e.g., Ingham and Donnelly, 1997; Hargreaves, 1992; Giulianotti, 2005). These sociologists are particularly critical of figurational sociology's failure to adequately theorize power, and charge its adherents with rarely connecting power to "a broader theory and critique of domination in social life, especially in respect to the changing organization of capitalism" (Gruneau, 1999: 121).

9 Sources which are "felt" at the level of the body and which are not easily transcribed into words (see, e.g., Papoulias and Callard, 2010).

10 During the Bosnian war the United Nations declared the town of Srebrenica a "safe area" and assigned its protection to a 400-strong contingent of Dutch peacekeepers. Despite the neutral status of this territory, units from the army of Republika Srpska invaded it and massacred more than 8,000 Bosnian Muslims, mainly men and boys, in July 1995.

References

Abrams, P. (1982) *Historical Sociology*, Somerset: Open Books.

Adelman, M. (1993) "Modernization theory and its critics," in Cayton, M., Gorn, E., and Williams, P.

(eds.) *Encyclopedia of American Social History*, vol. 1, New York: Charles Scribner's Sons, pp. 347–358.

Alexander, J. (1995) "Modern, anti, post and neo." *New Left Review*, 210: 63–101.

Andrews, D. (2009) "Sport, culture and late capitalism," in Carrington, B., and McDonald, I. (eds.) *Marxism, Cultural Studies and Sport*, London: Routledge, pp. 213–231.

Andrews, D. and Ritzer, G. (2007) "The grobal in the sporting glocal," in Giulianotti, R. and Robertson, R. (eds.) *Globalization and Sport*, Oxford: Blackwell Publishing, pp. 28–45.

Ankersmit, F. (2005) *Sublime Historical Experience*, Stanford, CA: Stanford University Press.

Arbena, J. (1988) *Sport and Society in Latin America: Diffusion, Dependency, and the Rise of Mass Culture*, New York: Greenwood Press.

Archer, R. and Bouillon, A. (1982) *The South African Game: Sport and Racism*, London: Zed Books.

Bairner, A. (2001) *Sport, Nationalism, and Globalization: European and North American Perspectives*, Albany: State University of New York Press.

Bale, J. (1994) *Landscapes of Modern Sport*, Leicester: Leicester University Press.

Bale, J. (2004) *Roger Bannister and the Four-minute Mile: Sports Myth and Sports History*, London: Routledge.

Booth, D. (1998) *The Race Game: Sport and Politics in South Africa*, London: Frank Cass.

Booth, D. (2005) *The Field: Truth and Fiction in Sport History*, London: Routledge.

Bottomore, T. (1983) *A Dictionary of Marxist Thought*, Oxford: Basil Blackwell.

Bourdieu, P. (1978) "Sport and social-class." *Social Science Information*, 17 (6): 819–840.

Brohm, J.-M. (1978) *Sport – A Prison of Measured Time*, London: Ink Links.

Brown, D. (2003) "Fleshing-out field notes: Prosaic, poetic and picturesque representations of Canadian mountaineering, 1906–1940." *Journal of Sport History*, 30 (3): 347–371.

Carrington, B. (2010) *Race, Sport and Politics: The Sporting Black Diaspora*, London: Sage.

Clignet, T. and Stark, M. (1974) "Modernization and the game of soccer in Cameroun." *International Review for the Sociology of Sport*, 9 (3): 81–98.

Collins, T. (2005) "History, theory and the 'civilizing process.'" *Sport in History*, 25 (2): 289–306.

Cronin, M. and Mayall, M. (1998) *Sporting Nationalisms: Identity, Ethnicity, Immigration and Assimilation*, London: Frank Cass.

Daley, C. (2010) "'The ref's turned a blind ear': The cultural paradigm and New Zealand's sport history." *Sporting Traditions*, 27 (2): 15–27.

Donaldson, M. (1993) "What is hegemonic masculinity?" *Theory and Society*, 22 (5): 643–657.

Donnelly, P. (1996) "The local and the global: Globalization in the sociology of sport." *Journal of Sport and Social Issues*, 20 (3): 239–257.

Dunning, E. and Sheard, K. (2005) *Barbarians, Gentlemen and Players: A Sociological Study of the Development of Rugby Football*, London: Routledge.

Elton, G. (1991) *Return to Essentials*, Cambridge: Cambridge University Press.

Ermarth, E.D. (2007) "The closed space of choice: A manifesto on the future of history," in Jenkins, K., Morgan, S., and Munslow, A. (eds.) *Manifestos for History*, London: Routledge, pp. 50–66.

Ermarth, E.D. (2011) *History in the Discursive Condition*, London: Routledge.

Fiss, P. and Hirsch, P. (2005) "The discourse of globalization: Framing and sensemaking of an emerging concept." *American Sociological Review*, 70 (1): 29–52.

Gems, G. (2006) *The Athletic Crusade: Sport and American Cultural Imperialism*, Lincoln: University of Nebraska Press.

Giulianotti, R. (2005) *Sport: A Critical Sociology*, Cambridge: Polity Press.

Gruneau, R. (1982) "Sport and the debate on the state," in Cantelon, H. and Gruneau, R. (eds.) *Sport, Culture and the Modern State*, Toronto: University of Toronto Press, pp. 1–38.

Gruneau, R. (1983) *Class, Sports, and Social Development*, Amherst: University of Massachusetts Press.

Gruneau, R. (1988) "Modernization or hegemony: Two views on sport and social development," in Harvey, J. and Cantelon, H. (eds.) *Not Just a Game: Essays in Canadian Sport Sociology*, Canada: University of Ottawa Press, pp. 9–33.

Gruneau, R. (1999) *Class, Sports, and Social Development* (2nd edn.), Champaign, IL: Human Kinetics.

Guha, R. (2002) *A Corner of a Foreign Field: The Indian History of a British Game*, London: Picador.

Guttmann, A. (1978) *From Ritual to Record*, New York: Columbia University Press.

Guttmann, A. (1991) "Sports diffusion: A response to Maguire and the Americanization commentaries." *Sociology of Sport Journal*, 8 (2): 185–190.

Guttmann, A. (1993) "The diffusion of sports and the problem of cultural imperialism," in Dunning, E., Maguire, J., and Pearton, R. (eds.) *The Sports Process: A Comparative and Developmental Approach*, Champaign, IL: Human Kinetics, pp. 125–137.

Guttmann, A. (1994) *Games and Empires: Modern Sports and Cultural Imperialism*, New York: Columbia University Press.

Guttmann, A. (2004) *Sports: The First Five Millennia*, Amherst: University of Massachusetts Press.

Hargreaves, Je. (1992) "Sex, gender and the body in sport and leisure: Has there been a civilizing process?" in Dunning, E. and Rojek, C. (eds.) *Sport and Leisure in the Civilizing Process: Critique and*

Counter Critique, Toronto: University of Toronto Press, pp. 161–182.

Hargreaves, Je. (1994) *Sporting Females: Critical issues in the History and Sociology of Women's Sports*, London: Routledge.

Hargreaves, Jo. (1986) *Sport, Power and Culture*, Cambridge: Polity Press.

Hill, J. (1996) "British sports history: A post-modern future?" *Journal of Sport History*, 23 (1): 1–19.

Hill, J. (2006) "Anecdotal evidence: Sport, the newspaper press, and history," in Phillips, M. (ed.) *Deconstructing Sport History: A Postmodern Analysis*, Albany: State University of New York Press, pp. 117–129.

Hobsbawm, E. (1998) *On History*, London: Abacus.

Holt, R. (1989) *Sport and the British: A Modern History*, Oxford: Oxford University Press.

Holt, R. (2009) "Shift in research topics: The interests of sport historians." Paper presented at the International Symposia of the Research Centre for the History of Sport and Kinesiology, Catholic University, Leuven, Belgium, June 11.

Houlihan, B. (1994) "Homogenization, Americanization, and Creolization of sport: Varieties of globalization." *Sociology of Sport Journal*, 11 (4): 356–375.

Hutchins, B. (2002) *Don Bradman: Challenging the Myth*, Cambridge: Cambridge University Press.

Ingham, A. and Donnelly, P. (1997) "A sociology of North American sociology of sport: Disunity in unity, 1965 to 1996." *Sociology of Sport Journal*, 14 (4): 362–418.

Jarvie, G. (1991) *Highland Games: The Making of the Myth*, Edinburgh: Edinburgh University Press.

Jenkins, K. (1991) *Re-Thinking History*, London: Routledge.

Jenkins, K. (1999) *Why History? Ethics and Postmodernity*, London: Routledge.

Jenkins, K., Morgan, S., and Munslow, A. (2007) *Manifestos for History*, London: Routledge.

Kidd, B. (1982) "Sport, dependency and the Canadian state," in Cantelon, H. and Gruneau, R. (eds.) *Sport, Culture and the Modern State*, Toronto: University of Toronto Press, pp. 282–303.

Klein, A. (1989) "Baseball as underdevelopment: The political-economy of sport in the Dominican Republic." *Sociology of Sport Journal*, 6 (2): 95–112.

Leys, C. (1982) "Sport, the state and dependency theory: Response to Kidd," in Cantelon, H. and Gruneau, R. (eds.) *Sport, Culture and the Modern State*, Toronto: University of Toronto Press, pp. 304–315.

Loy, J. and Coakley, J. (2006) "Sport," in Ritzer, G. (ed.) *Blackwell Encyclopedia of Sociology*, vol. 9, Oxford: Blackwell, pp. 4643–4653.

Lucas, J. and Smith, R. (1978) *Saga of American Sport*, Philadelphia, PA: Lea and Febiger.

MacClancy, J. (1996) *Sport, Identity and Ethnicity*, Oxford: Berg.

Maguire, J. (1995) "Common ground? Links between sports history, sports geography and the sociology of sport." *Sporting Traditions*, 12 (1): 3–25.

Maguire, J. (1999) *Global Sport: Identities, Societies, Civilizations*, Cambridge: Polity Press.

Malcolm, D. (2006) "The diffusion of cricket to America: A figurational sociological examination." *Journal of Historical Sociology*, 19 (2): 151–173.

Malcolm, D. (2008) "A response to Vamplew and some comments on the relationship between sports historians and sociologists of sport." *Sport in History*, 28 (2): 259–279.

Mandle, W.F. (1973) "Cricket and Australian nationalism in the nineteenth century." *Journal of the Royal Australian Historical Society*, 59 (4): 225–246.

Mangan, J.A. (1996) *Tribal Identities: Nationalism, Europe, Sport*, London: Frank Cass.

Mangan, J.A. (2001) *Europe, Sport, World: Shaping Global Societies*, London: Frank Cass.

Marx, K. (1977) "The Eighteenth Brumaire of Louis Bonaparte," in *Karl Marx: Selected Writings*, ed. D. McLellan, Oxford: Oxford University Press, pp. 300–325.

McDonald, M. and Birrell, S. (1999) "Reading sport critically: A methodology for interrogating power." *Sociology of Sport Journal*, 16 (4): 283–300.

McKay, J. and Miller, T. (1991) "From old boys to men and women of the corporation: The Americanization and commodification of Australian sport." *Sociology of Sport Journal*, 8 (1): 86–94.

Mills, C.W. (1959) *The Sociological Imagination*, Oxford: Oxford University Press.

Mills, J. and Dimeo, P. (2003) "'When gold is fired it shines': Sport, the imagination and the body in colonial and postcolonial India," in Bale, J. and Cronin, M. (eds.) *Sport and Postcolonialism*, Oxford: Berg, pp. 107–122.

Munslow, A. (1997) *Deconstructing History*, London: Routledge.

Munslow, A. (2003) *The New History*, Harlow: Pearson.

Munslow, A. (2006) *The Routledge Companion to Historical Studies*, London: Routledge.

Nathan, D. (2003) *Saying It's So: A Cultural History of the Black Sox Scandal*, Urbana: University of Illinois Press.

Neubauer, D. (2008) "Modern sport and the Olympic games: The problematic complexities raised by the dynamics of globalization." *Olympika*, 17: 1–40.

Oriard, M. (1995) *Reading Football: How the Popular Press Created an American Spectacle*, Chapel Hill: University of North Carolina Press.

Osmond, G. and Phillips, M. (2004) "'The Bloke with a Stroke:' Alick Wickham, the 'crawl' and social memory." *Journal of Pacific History*, 39 (3): 309–324.

Papoulias, C. and Callard, F. (2010) "Biology's gift: Interrogating the turn to affect." *Body and Society*, 16 (1): 29–56.

Phillips, M. (2002) "A critical appraisal of narrative in sport history: Reading the surf lifesaving debate." *Journal of Sport History*, 29 (1): 25–40.

Phillips, M. (2006) *Deconstructing Sport History: A Postmodern Analysis*, New York: State University of New York Press.

Phillips, M. and Roper A. (2006) "History of physical education," in Kirk, D., MacDonald, D., and O'Sullivan, M. (eds.) *Handbook of Physical Education*, London: Sage, pp. 123–140.

Pope, S.W. (2006) "Decentering 'race' and (re)presenting 'black' performance in sport history: Basketball and jazz in American culture, 1920–1950," in Phillips, M. (ed.) *Deconstructing Sport History: A Postmodern Analysis*, Albany: State University of New York Press, pp. 147–177.

Rail, G. (1998) *Sport and Postmodern Times*, Albany: State University of New York Press.

Riess, S. (2008) "Associativity and the evolution of modern sport." *Journal of Sport History*, 35 (1): 33–38.

Rigauer, B. (1981) *Sport and Work*, New York: Columbia University Press.

Roche, M. (2000) *Mega-Events and Modernity: Olympics and Expos in the Growth of Global Culture*, London: Routledge.

Rowe, D. (1999) *Sport, Culture and the Media: The Unholy Trinity*, Buckingham, UK: Open University Press.

Rowe, D. (2003) "Sport and the repudiation of the global." *International Review for the Sociology of Sport*, 38 (3): 281–294.

Rowe, D., McKay, J., and Lawrence, G. (1997) "Out of the shadows: The critical sociology of sport in Australia, 1986 to 1996." *Sociology of Sport Journal*, 14 (4): 340–361.

Ryan, G. (2004) *The Making of New Zealand Cricket, 1832–1914*, London: Frank Cass.

Scherer, J., Falcous, M., and Jackson, S. (2008) "The media sports cultural complex: Local–global disjuncture in New Zealand/Aotearoa." *Journal of Sport and Social Issues*, 32 (1): 48–71.

Schultz, J. (2005) "'A wager concerning a diplomatic pig:' A crooked reading of the Floyd of Rosedale narrative." *Journal of Sport History*, 32 (1): 1–21.

Stearns, P. (1980) "Modernization and social history: Some suggestions, and a muted cheer." *Journal of Social History*, 14 (2): 189–209.

Stinchcombe, A. (1978) *Theoretical Methods in Social History*, New York: Academic Press.

Stoddart, B. (1988) "Cricket and colonialism in the English-speaking Caribbean to 1914: Towards a cultural analysis," in Mangan, J.A. (ed.) *Pleasure, Profit, Proselytism: British Culture and Sport at Home and Abroad 1700–1914*, London: Frank Cass, pp. 231–257.

Stoddart, B. (1989) "Sport in the social construct of the lesser developed world: A commentary." *Sociology of Sport Journal*, 6 (2): 125–135.

Struna, N. (2000) "Social history and sport," in Coakley J. and Dunning, E. (eds.) *Handbook of Sports Studies*, London: Sage, pp. 187–203.

Sydnor, S. (1998) "A history of synchronized swimming." *Journal of Sport History*, 25 (2): 252–267.

Szymanski, S. (2008) "A theory of the evolution of modern sport." *Journal of Sport History*, 35 (1): 1–32.

Thompson, E.P. (1995) *The Poverty of Theory: Or an Orrery of Errors*, London: Merlin.

Tosh, J. (2000) *The Pursuit of History: Aims, Methods and New Directions in the Study of Modern History*, Harlow: Pearson.

Tranter, N. (1998) *Sport, Economy and Society in Britain, 1750–1914*, Cambridge: Cambridge University Press.

Vamplew, W. (1988) "Sport and industrialization: An economic interpretation of the changes in popular sport in nineteenth-century England," in Mangan, J.A. (eds.) *Pleasure, Profit, Proselytism: British Culture and Sport at Home and Abroad, 1700–1914*, London: Frank Cass, pp. 7–20.

Vamplew, W. (2007) "Empiricist versus sociological history: Some comments on the 'civilizing process.'" *Sport in History*, 27 (2): 161–171.

Van Bottenburg, M. (2001) *Global Games*, Urbana: University of Illinois Press.

Vertinsky, P. and McKay, S. (2004) *Disciplining Bodies in the Gymnasium: Memory, Monument, Modernism*, London: Routledge.

Wallerstein, I. (1974) *The Modern World System*, New York: Academic Press.

Wenner, L. (1998) *MediaSport*, London: Routledge.

White, H. (1973) *Metahistory: The Historical Imagination in Nineteenth-century Europe*, Baltimore, MD: Johns Hopkins University Press.

Further Reading

Booth, D. (2005) *The Field: Truth and Fiction in Sport History*, London: Routledge.

Ermarth, E.D. (2011) *History in the Discursive Condition*, London: Routledge.

McDonald, M. and Birrell, S. (1999) "Reading sport critically: A methodology for interrogating power." *Sociology of Sport Journal*, 16 (4): 283–300.

2

Sport and Globalization

Richard Giulianotti and Roland Robertson

Introduction

Sport has been one of the most important cultural forces of globalization since the late nineteenth century. Sport mega-events such as the Olympic summer games or the men's football World Cup attract cumulative worldwide television audiences numbered in billions, and thus appear as ideal illustrations of increasing global connectivity.

While the definition of modern sport is relatively straightforward (Giulianotti, 2005: xii–xiii), social scientists have defined globalization in rather more varied ways. Here, we follow Robertson (1992: 8) in understanding globalization as a concept that "refers both to the compression of the world and the intensification of consciousness of the world as a whole." Thus, globalization is characterized by intensified transnational connectivity (e.g., through migration and satellite communication), and greater social reflexivity about the world in general. We stand in some contrast to those analysts who interpret globalization in restricted terms, as being either akin to modernization (cf. Giddens, 1990; Scholte, 2005), or a (late) twentieth-century process (cf. Friedman, 2000), or a shorthand term for the rise of neoliberal capitalism (cf. Bourdieu, 1999;

Wolf, 2004). Alternatively, we posit that globalization is a highly complex, uneven, and multifaceted process, with an extensive history and diverse cultural, social, political, and economic dimensions.

In the following discussion, we explore four key aspects of globalization within the context of sport: first, the *historical* phases; second, *sociocultural* issues; third, *political-economic* questions; and fourth, debates surrounding the emergence of a *global civil society*. Our analysis draws in part upon prior collaborative work, notably on the globalization of football and the development of glocalization theory (Giulianotti and Robertson, 2001, 2004, 2005, 2007a, 2007b, 2009), and also utilizes our separate works on globalization theory (Robertson, 1990, 1992, 1995, 2001, 2004, 2007a; Robertson and White, 2003; Robertson and Scholte, 2007) and the sociology of sport (Giulianotti, 1991, 1999, 2005; Armstrong and Giulianotti, 1997, 2004).

The Historical Aspects of Global Sport: Six Phases

No understanding of the globalization of sport is possible without detailed consideration of the

A Companion to Sport, First Edition. Edited by David L. Andrews and Ben Carrington.
© 2013 Blackwell Publishing Ltd. Published 2013 by Blackwell Publishing Ltd.

historical roots of global processes. Here, we focus on Robertson's (1992, 2007a, 2007b) six-phase historical schema of globalization, which spans the fifteenth to early twenty-first centuries. We should also point out that, in our view, the six phases follow a long proto-phase of globalization which goes back to the beginning of time, as reflected particularly in the ancient civilizations of Egypt, Greece, and Rome. The six-phase schema invites broad application to explain the diffusion of different sports (Giulianotti and Robertson, 2001, 2009; see also Bale and Sang, 1996; Maguire, 1999). Our discussion sets out the main historical and specific sporting characteristics of each of the six phases:

Germinal phase (1400–1750s)

This phase provides the crucial geopolitical and sociocultural foundations for intensive globalization, and for the later diffusion of sports across the world. The germinal phase centers on Europe, and is marked by voyages of discovery, the emergence of national communities, international conflicts between mercantile powers, the international spread of Catholicism and the Gregorian calendar, heliocentric thinking, and the accentuation of ideas regarding the individual and humanity.

In regard to sports, during this period, many "folk" games and pastimes are played across the British Isles and on mainland Europe. These games usually had rudimentary rules, but several were later transformed into modern sports, for example, "folk football" and "patronized" sports like pugilism/boxing, cricket, and horse-racing (Van Bottenburg 2001: 47–52).

Incipient phase (1750s–1870s)

The incipient phase is again centered on European societies, and is marked by the global "moment" of the Lisbon earthquake (1755) and the transcontinental impact of the French Revolution, early colonial expansion and world conflict, the near-global spread of the nation state model, new communication technologies, stronger conceptions of humanity and citizenship, and the staging of early international exhibitions.

In Britain, industrialization, urbanization, new educational systems, and the belated increase in workers' recreational time, provide crucial preconditions for the start and spread of modern national sports like association football, rugby, and athletics (Mangan, 1986). British colonialism facilitates the international diffusion of imperial sports, for example with cricket established in India and Australia in the late eighteenth and early nineteenth centuries; the game's earliest international fixtures were in North America in the 1840s, while England and Australia exchanged touring teams from the early 1860s onwards. Moreover, sport within colonial contexts was a recurring site of social and symbolic struggle, notably for black diasporas in North America and Europe (Carrington, 2010).

In the 1860s and 1870s, association football or soccer is spread by British workers, soldiers, and settlers across mainland Europe, Latin America, and Britain's imperial outposts (Goldblatt, 2006). Early sporting forms of national-cultural differentiation or conflict are evidenced, for example Anglo-Irish settlers in Australia cultivate their own football code (Australian rules football), while post-Civil War Americans prefer, as their national sport, baseball (adapted from the English game of rounders) rather than the more Anglo-centric or elitist game of cricket (Guttmann, 1994: 19–20).

Take-off phase (1870s–1920s)

This phase features the strongest intensification of globalization processes. Moreover, we should emphasize that during this phase, sport becomes increasingly central to globalization processes in general. In this period, personal and national identities, the institutional frameworks of nation states, international relations, and conceptions of global humanity are all given much stronger definition, while major international associations and events are established and staged. Principles of national identification and self-determination are accentuated, notably through the "Wilsonian moment" after World War I, which advances the principle of the equality of all nations and inspires early anticolonial politics, although Woodrow Wilson was not without his racial prejudices (Manela, 2007). National "traditions" are also invented, while "wilful nostalgia" comes to imagine the world in terms of historical decline (cf. Robertson, 1992: 146–163; Stauth and Turner, 1988).

The globalization of sport "takes off," as football, imperial games like cricket and rugby, and many Olympic disciplines (e.g., in track and field, fencing, equestrianism) undergo international diffusion. Highly significant roles are played by local elites and entrepreneurs in promoting sports across local populations (Kaufman and Patterson, 2005). The *Turnverein* (German gymnastic movement) challenges British sporting hegemony in Europe in the late nineteenth century. North American exceptionalism is signified through the popularization of "national" sports like baseball, American football, ice hockey (especially in Canada), and later basketball. Baseball in particular reflects American regional hegemony, as the game is popularized in Central America and parts of the Caribbean, as well as in Japan and its colonies.

The modern Olympic Games, first staged in 1896 and thereafter quadrennially, provide early international exhibitions of sport through *nation-based* competition (Guttmann, 1992). Football's world body FIFA is founded in 1904, along national membership lines. The myopic failure of Britain's football associations to participate fully within FIFA provides an early portent of the old imperialist power's waning global influence.

Different sports are a focus for historical mythology and the "invention of tradition": for example, the modern Olympics are founded to "recreate" ancient Greece's games, while foundation myths are built around the American general Abner Doubleday in baseball and William Webb Ellis in rugby union.[1] International sporting events become rituals of national celebration, while "national" styles of play enable forms of distinctive, masculine national identity to be explored. Sporting successes by non-European nations – for example, by Australians in cricket, New Zealanders in rugby union, and Uruguayans in football – become potent mediums for building strong senses of national solidarity across immigrant-based populations. Finally, on the level of humankind, in many different international settings, sport becomes one important sociocultural space in which those marginalized by class, "race," ethnicity, or gender struggle to overcome this social exclusion, to participate and to compete with more powerful social groups.

Struggle-for-hegemony phase (1920s– late 1960s)

This phase witnesses the outbreak and intensification of global conflicts, alongside attempts to institutionalize world diplomacy and governance. European empires collapse, the "Third World" is created, and nation states are "relativized" by their Cold War positions. The future of humanity is thematized transnationally with reference to atomic weapons and the Holocaust.

Through most of this period, international sporting events and associations experience an exponential growth. In men's football, the first World Cup finals are staged in 1930, and by 1970 feature 16 teams from five continents playing live on color television before tens of millions of international viewers. The Third World has the strongest impact in the growth of global sport movements, with FIFA membership multiplying from 40 in 1925 to 134 in 1969, and competing nations at the Olympics rising from 46 in 1928 to 112 in 1968.

International tensions are deeply embedded within sport, most obviously at Berlin's "Nazi Olympics" in 1936, and Cold War contests between the United States, Western European, and Eastern bloc nations. The infirmity of European hegemony is reflected in football by growing South American influence within FIFA.

Humanity issues are thematized, as obdurate frameworks of exclusion are imposed on sport for much of this period; struggles over racial equality and civil rights are waged in most sports (e.g., North American sports, culminating in the "black power" podium protest by American sprinters at the 1968 Mexico City Olympics), while more equitable status for women is pursued particularly in Olympic sports and tennis (Guttmann, 1991). Attempts to create alternative transnational sport systems, such as through the Workers' Olympics, or the GANEFO sport movement of non-aligned states, are relatively short-lived but help to enhance lower-class, female, and Third World participation within more established sporting events (cf. Kruger and Riordan, 1996).

Uncertainty phase (late 1960s–2000)

This phase features an increasingly complex and multipolar world system of societies, notably after the collapse of Soviet-led state communism and the rise of fundamentalist Islam. Global moments – notably the moon landing – provide fresh ways of imagining the world. International organizations, including intergovernmental organizations (IGOs), non-governmental organizations (NGOs), transnational corporations (TNCs), and new social movements (NSMs), grow exponentially, particularly in the Global North. Cultural and social politics intensify, while conceptions of "global citizenship" and "global civil society" are thematized.

Throughout this period, sport mega-events with worldwide assemblage of participants and television audiences become archetypal world events that produce "global moments" like Olympic world records or World Cup goals (cf. Roche, 2000). Sport's international governing bodies are increasingly reflexive regarding globalization, pursuing global growth strategies.

Political influence within sport becomes increasingly multipolar, through an exponential growth in the variety and volume of politically engaged actors, including athletes, coaches, governing officials, sponsors, television corporations, media reporters, merchandise companies, public sector and governmental sport departments, and sports education institutes. Elites from developing nations and commercial forces gain ground – for example, FIFA is led by a Brazilian (João Havelange, 1974–1998) with strong backing from South American and African nations, while cricket's International Cricket Conference (ICC, renamed in 1989 as the International Cricket Council) is more influenced by Asian and southern African associations. Sport is deeply entrenched within the emerging global economy. Governing bodies engage more fully with commercial backers, competitive inequalities between teams intensify, while some "unprofitable" clubs are merged, closed down, or excluded from new league systems, for example, rugby league teams in Australia and England (Andrews and Ritzer, 2007).

In political terms, sport becomes a major focus for political conflicts and civil rights struggles, notably through the 1972 Olympic terrorist attack, "Title IX" in the United States, US/Soviet-led Olympic boycotts in the 1980s, and the sporting isolation of apartheid-driven South Africa (Guttmann, 1991; Booth, 1998). Sporting successes become potent symbols of ethno-national pride and resistance, notably in West Indian cricket in the 1970s and 1980s (cf. Beckles and Stoddart, 1995). More routinely, sport becomes an increasingly significant domain for the construction of sociocultural identity and particularity.

Millennial phase (from 2001)

This phase features the generalized spread of "millennial moods" and climates of fear, for example regarding terrorism, the environment, and natural resources. Risk and regulation are intensively thematized, for example in governmental monitoring of private spaces and through individual high-risk sports. Cultures of intensive surveillance combine securitization (e.g., "dataveillance"), entertainment (e.g., *Big Brother*), and social networking (e.g., Facebook, Twitter). International relations are marked by the United States' attempts to manage new challenges, notably from China (economically) and from militant Islam (ideologically and militarily).

In sport, the millennial phase is most obviously manifested through the high-cost securitization of mega-events, such as the US$6.5 billion security budget at the Beijing Olympics in 2008 and the official figure of £553 million (US$850 million) for London in 2012. Thus, at the London Olympics, the authorities' fear of a terrorist attack gave rise to a highly detailed security policy which included the mobilization of tens of thousands of police, army, and private security personnel, as well as the use of unmanned aircraft and the siting of surface-to-air missiles at six sites near the main venue. The "security legacies" of sport mega-events become more important, such as new legislation, crowd policing techniques, and high-tech surveillance devices (Giulianotti and Klauser, 2010). The 2009 terrorist attack on the Sri Lankan cricket team in Pakistan, the security-driven relocation of the Indian Premier League cricket tournament to South Africa, and the withdrawal of some athletes from the 2010 Commonwealth games in

Delhi due to concerns over terrorism, all point to the increasing centrality of security issues within global sport.

Sport showcases the dichotomous character of millennial cultures. On one hand, athletes and spectators are assiduously monitored by proactive security agencies and a moralizing mass media, while sport participation is itself subjected to comprehensive risk assessments and insurances; on the other hand, risk-taking sports are embraced, particularly by the new middle classes, while new social network media enable individuals to "blog" their opinions or to "twitter" real-time experiences on sport (Giulianotti, 2009).

In international politics, sport contributes significantly to millennial strategies to assist humankind, as reflected for example in the growing use of sport to promote peace and development, and in the expansion of sporting facilities and competitions for disabled people. However, thus far there has been little analysis of global sport's environmental impact, such as the carbon footprints of urban redevelopment and mass travel surrounding sport mega-events.

Overall, this six-phase model provides the crucial historical context for analysis of the sociocultural, political-economic, and societal aspects of the globalization of sport. The historical model highlights the complexity, unevenness, and openendedness of globalization processes. In broad terms across the *longue durée*, globalization has been marked by trends towards differentiation as well as uniformity. We continue this theme more fully in regard to the sociocultural aspects of global sport.

The Sociocultural Aspects of Global Sport

Discussion of the sociocultural aspects of sport globalization represents the most substantial part of our chapter. In this section, we examine key debates on cultural globalization, and explore their application to sport. We begin by exploring key issues regarding universalism, particularism, and relativization, before moving on to consider the homogenization-heterogenization debate, glocalization, and cosmopolitanism.

Universalism, particularism, and relativization

To begin, we argue that the "universal" and the "particular" are not simply oppositional entities; rather, they are deeply interdependent categories, which possess two types of interrelationship. First, we have the *particularization of universalism*, which is marked by the greater sociopolitical concreteness of the world, for example through the positioning of nations within global time, telephone, or internet systems. Second, there is the *universalization of particularism*, which features the "extensive diffusion of the idea that there is virtually no limit to particularity, to uniqueness, to difference, and to otherness" (Robertson, 1992: 102). In line with the universalization of particularism, the concept of *relativization* helps to explain how forms of differentiation have long been a key feature of globalization. Relativization registers how globalization brings local cultures into sharper comparative focus, thereby giving rise to more complex forms of reflexive, differentiated identity and more diverse types of interrelationship.

Sport has been one potent, popular cultural sphere for the manifestation of these processes. The universalization of particularism is perhaps most evident in the sociocultural *content* of sport. Major sports leagues and tournaments provide symbolic arenas for forms of differentiated identity to be institutionalized and celebrated in ever more potent and elaborate ways. Consider, for example, international fixtures in football, cricket, and rugby, at which spectators are now far more focused on displaying the particularities of their national allegiance (such as through songs, flags, bodily adornments) than was the case in, say, the 1960s or 1970s. Relativization processes underpin this intensification of differentiation; each event brings different national groups into more intensive mutual contact, enabling them to respond to each other in ever more amplified fashions.

The "particularization of universalism" within sport is more evident in regard to *formal*, institutional, and structural aspects. Almost all nation states – including the most "closed" societies – have sought to secure membership within sport's leading global bodies, such as FIFA and the IOC. To gain admission, sport governing bodies within these nations are expected to have established standardized frameworks and procedures. National sports bodies are given further sociopolitical concreteness through their assimilation into the organizational structures of world sport – for example, by being integrated into the sports competitions, administrative frameworks, and communication channels of the global governing bodies.

Homogenization and heterogenization

The homogenization-heterogenization debate is one of the most strongly contested disputes within globalization studies, and has particular relevance for the analysis of global sport. In broad terms, homogenization theories contend that globalization is characterized by intensified forms of cultural convergence and uniformity, while heterogenization theories submit that globalization features heighten cultural divergence and differentiation. We consider both sets of arguments here before exploring how these "polarized" categories may be integrated through the concept of "glocalization."

Homogenization   Most social scientists who advocate the homogenization approach tend to be highly critical of how perceived trends towards cultural convergence are undermining the survival, autonomy, and creativity of local identities and practices. Homogenization theories are, somewhat ironically, associated with a variety of keywords; for reasons of brevity, we consider only a few here.

Many homogenization theories put forward variations of the *cultural imperialism* thesis. In communication studies, this thesis has been particularly influential, notably in arguing that media corporations in the Global North dominate global information flows, so that societies in the North are culturally swamped by the images and products of advanced consumerism (Hamelink, 1995; Schiller, 1976). The specific theory of *Westernization* posits that the West is not simply a geopolitical force but also a techno-economic machine, an "anti-culture," that under the guise of modernization and "development," de-civilizes and destroys non-industrial cultures (Latouche, 1996). Alternatively, Said's (1995) theory of *Orientalism* draws on a Foucauldian standpoint to explore how, over several centuries,

Western power over the East has been established through the construction of discursive knowledge of this other. In turn, "Orientals" come to internalize and to reproduce these discourses as the dominant form of their own self-knowledge. Ritzer's (2004) theory of *grobalization* sets out how, in his view, cultural homogenization is driven by three "grobal" forces: capitalism, notably expansionist major corporations; Americanization, notably through US corporations and culture products; and "McDonaldization," which sees the fast-food chain's highly efficient organizational principles transposed into other social fields.

It is straightforward enough to find some supportive evidence in global sport for these theories. Consider, for example, the Olympic Games or World Cup finals. On cultural imperialism, most "global sports" within these mega-events derive from the Global North; indeed, the relative lack of non-Western sports may also lend support to the Westernization thesis. Global television coverage of these events is saturated in multifarious commercial messages, usually from the Global North's transnational corporations. On Orientalism theory, discourses on sport in both the West *and* East display forms of cultural typologizing along Orientalist lines, for example in media commentaries regarding "natural" African runners or "efficient" German teams. On grobalization theory, many sport mega-events are strongly influenced by American corporations (e.g., in terms of event management, television revenues, or sponsorship); intensively commodified; and highly rationalized in organization. Indeed, ceremonies surrounding sport mega-events seem to have become "grobalized." Leading American event-management TNCs, such as Jack Morton, acquire the contracts to plan and to implement these ceremonies, drawing upon their well-honed, efficient techniques in the emotional and social manipulation of audiences (cf. Clark and Mangham, 2004).

Nevertheless, homogenization theories do have their limitations. Collectively, they fail to account adequately for the critical engagement of social actors – and in particular, those within "peripheral" settings – with "global" cultural forms and processes. Media imperialism theory assumes, wrongly, that those at the end of the communication chain – such as television viewers and newspaper readers – passively absorb media messages. Westernization theory understates how non-Western peoples have seized upon sports, and persistently contested their initial exclusion by Western elites from participation (e.g., football in South America, cricket in south Asia) (Giulianotti, 2005). Orientalism theory exaggerates the degree to which "Orientals" accept their representation within Western culture (cf. Irwin, 2006). Moreover, counter-processes of "Occidentalism" have long been evident, featuring the circulation of anti-Western discourses and values in both East and West (Buruma and Margalit, 2004). Finally, grobalization theory's general flaw is an excessive focus on cultural *commodities*, such as eateries or tourist markets, in contrast to the crucial importance of *values* and *meanings* within cultures, such as styles of play or spectator support in sport.

However, grobalization theory does bring us to consider perhaps the most intriguing variant of all homogenization arguments: Americanization theory. Proponents of Americanization theory contend that the United States and American corporations – led particularly by the usual suspects, such as Coca-Cola, CNN, Disney, McDonald's, Microsoft, and Nike – are the hegemonic cultural imperialists, in remorselessly penetrating other regions, imposing specific and highly profitable beliefs, tastes, practices, and products upon other societies (Crothers, 2007). Americanization processes would appear to have two main levels: "soft Americanization" involves the specific influence of everyday Americanisms within local cultures; and, "hard Americanization" is marked by the domination of American products and practices, usually at the expense of local alternatives.

Despite its initial appeal, significant counter-evidence can be marshaled against the Americanization thesis. First, we may query the continuing legitimacy of the very term *Americanization*, referring as it does not to the continent but to one specific nation, the United States. Moreover, while the term Americanization implies that the United States is a culturally uniform nation, this has never been the case, and indeed is particularly inappropriate now, given the long-term impacts of mass migration and multicultural cosmopolitanism. Indicatively, in sport, while the traditional Big Four men's sports of basketball, American football, ice hockey, and

baseball still dominate, with very strong institutional support from the colleges and television networks, not only does the "non-American" sport of football boast some 18 million players across the United States (especially at college level) but many millions more are enthusiastic supporters of European and Latin American clubs (whose games may be viewed on a myriad of pay-TV systems) and indeed non-American national sides (most obviously Mexico), even in fixtures against the United States (cf. Foer, 2004; Giulianotti and Robertson, 2005, 2007a).

Second, quite obviously, sport provides some compelling illustrations of American exceptionalism rather than forms of American cultural domination (Markovits and Hellerman, 2001). Most North American sports – particularly American football and baseball – have had regional rather than global impact. Their development has been domestically orientated and largely associated with celebrating "the American way of life."

Third, paradoxically, the structures of US major league sports do not fit entirely with the assumption that Americanization is driven by intensified neoliberal commercialism. Major American sports leagues (especially the NFL) promote relatively high levels of revenue-sharing and (through the "draft" system) a relatively equitable distribution of elite players across teams, when compared to the more free-market systems that feature in most European football nations (Szymanski and Zimbalist, 2006). Moreover, American sports teams and stadiums carry far fewer advertisements than their counterparts in football, cricket, and the rugby codes.

Thus, in our view, it is difficult to sustain the "hard Americanization" thesis within sports. Even in locations where US sports seem to be particularly influential – for example, baseball in central America – local populations are still engaged in forms of critical meaning-making and identity-building (cf. Klein, 1991). The "soft Americanization" thesis is more plausible, in accounting for how specific American practices have penetrated some sports – for example, pre-event razzmatazz, or the transfer of US television production techniques into European sports.

As this indicates, we suggest that the homogenization arguments are applied judiciously, with a focus on the cross-cultural sharing of specific sociocultural practices. Homogenization theories are less persuasive when they build from generalized assumptions regarding both the dominant powers of particular nations or regions and the inability of local peoples to work creatively with global cultural forms.

Heterogenization   In contrast, theories of heterogenization highlight the continuation or extension of cultural divergence and differentiation within the context of globalization. For example, the American journalist Jonathan Friedman (1999) uses the concept of *indigenization* in part to explore the proliferation of indigenous cultural-political identities in recent years, such as among "first nation" peoples in North America and Australasia (cf. Niezen, 2003). Ulf Hannerz's (1992) theory of *creolization* explores how individuals and social groups in peripheral societies engage selectively, critically, and creatively with global culture to produce creolized cultural forms. Similarly, Appadurai (1996) employs the concept of *vernacularization* to explain the linguistic adaption of global culture by local populations. The concepts of *hybridity* and *hybridization* have been deployed to bring out the cultural mixing that has long occurred, notably as different societies bring their own interpretations and techniques to bear upon transnational cultural forms, such as music, dance, and sport, particularly in postcolonial contexts (Burke, 2009; Pieterse, 1995, 2007).

In line with these keywords, sport provides some highly potent illustrations of how particular cultural forms are critically and selectively appropriated by local populations. The most radical instances feature fundamental changes to the rules and ethics of particular sports in order to suit local conditions. Trobriand Islanders, for example, transformed cricket, the quintessential English pastime, into an elaborate social ritual in which the home team always wins. More prosaically, North Americans transformed the British game of rounders and variants of folk football or rugby in order to create baseball and American football respectively.

As sports have become more globally diffuse, and as national societies have been more effectively integrated into the international systems within and beyond sport, it has been more common for local populations to "creolize" the content rather than the form of global games, thereby giving rise to technical, aesthetic, and normative variations within the laws of recognized sporting codes. For example, in ice hockey, we find that European players tend to be viewed as more technically proficient than their North American contemporaries; in football, southern European teams and audiences place relatively high value on individual artistry; and, in cricket, the "sledging" or abuse of opponents is relatively prominent among Australian players.

Heterogenization theories help to explain these kinds of processes. Appadurai (1996) has highlighted the way in which Indians have "hijacked" the colonial game of cricket to create their own styles of play and analytical vernaculars. India has become world cricket's most powerful nation, influencing the game's global politics (notably, inside the International Cricket Council), while creating the game's most lucrative and popular tournament (the IPL). These transformations may be symptomatic of more generalized processes of "post-Westernization," as postcolonial societies take stronger control over their cultural practices and destinies (Rumford, 2007).

Indigenism has become a growing force in sport in three particular ways: first, in the foundation of sport movements and organizations by First Nation peoples (e.g., the Inuit Olympics); second, in the long-term appeal or revival of folk sporting "traditions" such as the Highland games or Breton games (Jarvie, 1991; Eichberg, 1994); third, when indigenous movements stage protests around major sporting events in relation to their oppression and denial of human rights (e.g., Australian Aboriginals around the Sydney 2000 Olympics).

The concepts of hybridity and hybridization have been particularly helpful in exploring the cultural self-understandings and practices found within Latin American sports, notably in the interplay between ethnicity, football, and dance. The Brazilian anthropologist Gilberto Freyre claimed that the *mulattos* (people with black and white ancestry) "de-Europeanized football by giving it curves," so that "we dance with the ball" (quoted in Burke 2009: 27–28). A leading Brazilian player from the 1930s, Domingos da Guia, claimed that his short dribbling style was an imitation of the *miudinho* type of samba dance, which also helped him to evade violent challenges

(Bellos 2002: 35). In Argentinian football, Archetti (1998) provides the most concerted and innovative exploration of the links between hybridity and sport. He demonstrates that, through the early twentieth century, football was especially important in enabling Argentina – as an emerging nation with a mix of old and new European migrants – to "hybridize" these diverse influences through a shared symbolic form, and to create a distinctive style of play that reflected an emergent form of male national identity. The equine sport of polo provided a further cultural field for the development of a hybrid, masculine, Argentine identity. Archetti explores also the historical interplay between football and tango, notably in influencing the dribbling techniques of players, and in the football references to be found in tango songs.

Overall, heterogenization theories appear to fit well within sport, notably in registering the creative and critical engagement of different populations with respect to specific sporting forms. However, this is not, of course, to deny that homogenization processes are also at play within sport. Thus, in order to accommodate the dual impulses of homogenization and heterogenization, we advance the concept of *glocalization*.

Glocalization

Since its introduction (Robertson, 1990, 1992, 1995) within the sociocultural realm, the concept of glocalization has been widely debated among globalization theorists (cf. Holton, 2008; Roudometof, 2005; Tomlinson, 1999), and applied to explain particular sport processes and cultures (cf. Andrews and Ritzer, 2007; Giulianotti and Robertson, 2004, 2005, 2007a, 2009). In globalization debates thus far, glocalization theory has tended to emphasize processes of heterogenization, partly to challenge more deterministic arguments regarding cultural convergence. However, more strictly speaking, glocalization refers to the intense *interpenetration* and mutual interdependency of the local and the global (Robertson, 1992: 173–174; 1995, 2001). Glocalization theory thus allows for what might be termed a "duality of glocality," that is, the interplay of convergence/homogenization and divergence/heterogenization impulses in regard to global culture (Giulianotti and Robertson, 2007b).

As our earlier discussions have suggested, the duality of glocality applies to sport, and it is useful here to elaborate upon that initial statement with a couple of illustrations. First, consider how the mass media frame sport mega-events. On the divergence side, as noted, national reporters and audiences will narrate and interpret events in nationally orientated ways. In terms of convergence, some athletes will be global icons who attract intensive levels of support (or, indeed, animosity) from sport followers across the world.

Second, consider the ways in which sports are played across the world. On divergence, as noted, we have strong trends towards differentiation in terms of technical and aesthetic developments. However, homogenizing counter-pulls within modern sport are also apparent, for example in regard to coaching practices that teach "universal" technical skills and tactical knowledge, and in regard to coach instructions which favor "playing the percentages" rather than "risk-taking" innovations.

Overall, glocalization theory helps to explain the interpenetration of homogenization and heterogenization, and also, by extension, the interdependencies of the local and the global. These illustrations also reflect our view that homogenization theories are more persuasive when applied judiciously rather than obliquely, to bring out the complexity of sociocultural processes. These issues acquire intensified vitality through the growing centrality of cosmopolitanism to globalization debates.

Cosmopolitanism

The subject of cosmopolitanism has attracted some of the most substantial and insightful commentary within globalization studies in recent years (cf. Vertovec and Cohen, 2003; Fine, 2007; Robertson and Krossa, 2011). In discussing cosmopolitanism in sociological terms, it is important to recognize that we are not seeking to reify the status claims of self-styled "cosmopolitans" in regard to their presumed superiority to "parochial" locals. Instead, we seek to explore two particular ways in which "the cosmopolitan" may be deployed by sociologists in regard to globalization, and with particular relevance to sport.

First, contemporary cosmopolitanism is a sociocultural fact, in that it registers the heightened levels of connectivity and interrelationship between diverse social groups. For example, most cities are now inhabited by scores of "national" groups, many of which vividly display their distinctive cultural identities through language, dress, cuisine, music, and religiosity. Thus, the term "banal cosmopolitanism" may be employed to describe how encounters with cultural diversity are increasingly mundane features of everyday life (Beck, 2004; Giulianotti and Robertson, 2007b). In sport, banal cosmopolitanism is particularly evident in the international mixture of athletes that are routinely found in professional sport teams, and in the everyday consumption and display of global sporting signifiers (e.g., New York baseball hats, Manchester United football tops, Air Jordan sneakers) (Silk, Andrews, and Cole, 2004).

Second, cosmopolitanism may also be employed to register particular kinds of orientation towards other cultures (Giulianotti and Robertson, 2007b; Robertson and Krossa, 2011). It is therefore useful to differentiate between *thick* and *thin* varieties of cosmopolitanism. *Thick cosmopolitanism* features a full openness towards other cultures, to the extent that individuals and social groups may be willingly and radically transformed through encounters with difference. *Thin cosmopolitanism* features a more pragmatic and utilitarian relationship to other cultures, whereby aspects of the latter are instrumentally utilized in order to sustain or to enhance the host culture.

We should add that the local and the cosmopolitan are not mutually exclusive categories. Indeed, "patriotic" or "rooted" forms of cosmopolitanism are quite commonplace, whereby individuals may engage positively and openly with different cultures, yet still retain strong forms of identification with "home" (Appiah, 1997). As Calhoun (2007: 25) points out, "no one lives outside particularistic solidarities"; cosmopolitans who believe that they do so are following an "illusion."

In sport, thin cosmopolitanism has tended to be most evident, for example as coaches introduce some training and playing methods from other societies in order to improve their own team's performances, and as journalists report only on incidents in foreign sports that might directly affect the interests of local or national teams. Thick cosmopolitanism is reflected in a kind of anthropological openness among sports followers towards, for example, immersing themselves in entirely new sports, or learning and understanding the peculiarities and subtleties of other sporting cultures. Perhaps more commonly, sociocultural relations within sport help to promote forms of "rooted" or "patriotic" cosmopolitanism among participants and spectators. Particularity is facilitated and indeed positively valorized within sport, notably through forms of team allegiance that facilitate intense engagement and enjoyment. On the other hand, even "parochial" players and supporters will be sufficiently cosmopolitan, in terms of knowing and appreciating their sport, to watch and to learn from their opponents. Moreover, most sports followers will still derive great degrees of cosmopolitan pleasure from watching unpredictable, spectacular, and skillful displays by competing athletes or teams to whom the viewers may have little close attachment (cf. Carrington, 2004).

Overall, our reading of the sociocultural aspects of globalization emphasizes the complexity of local–global, particular–universal, and homogeneous–heterogeneous relationships. The interdependencies that underpin these binary oppositions are brought out particularly in the theory of glocalization, and confirmed by the cosmopolitanism of contemporary sociocultural relations. In the next section, we turn to consider some of the major political-economic aspects of globalization in relation to sport.

Political-economic Aspects of Globalization

In this section, we explore two particular debates – on the nation state and the world economic system – in regard to the political-economic aspects of globalization.

Nation state and globalization

According to a variety of analysts, the nation state has been increasingly outmoded by contemporary globalization. For example, for the "hyperglobalist" Ohmae (1994, 1995), the global economy in a "borderless world" is now dominated by transnational investment, industry, information technology, and individual consumerism. For

Beck (2004), the national is one of several old "zombie-categories" that have been transcended by transnational and cosmopolitan processes; furthermore, the "world risk society" features globalizing dangers (such as global warming, pollution, terrorism) that individual nations cannot control (Beck 1999). For Appadurai (1996), the nation state is outmoded by "diasporic public spheres" that are populated in particular by transnational migrant groups, who are themselves served by new global media and communication systems.

However, we would argue that, in line with the subtle arguments of Holton (1998), and in contrast to these somewhat hyperbolic statements, reports of the nation state's demise are premature. Four points underscore our point here, and build in part upon earlier arguments. First, historically, as we have demonstrated, the nation-state system was established hand-in-hand with intensified globalization from the eighteenth century onwards. In the past two decades, following the collapse of East European state socialism, the nation-state model appears to have become *more* relevant to politicians and publics, as reflected in the proliferation of small, transition European states. Second, on the global stage, the Iraq War and China's economic surge have indicated that, for the world's most powerful nations at least, the nation-state model remains a significant player. Indeed, some analysts have identified trends towards "global fascism" or "inverted totalitarianism" in the early twenty-first century, as neoliberal US government policies have undermined domestic democracy while pursuing imperialist foreign policies (Johnson, 2004; Falk, 2005; Wolin, 2008). Third, economically, nation states are increasingly interdependent, yet remain critically important units in establishing particular conditions (neoliberal, or otherwise) for transnational commercial activity. For their part, rather than working to undermine nation states, TNCs are drawn to invest in nations with settled rather than weak state systems. Fourth, the adaptability of nation states is further confirmed in the changes that have occurred in official state ideologies regarding national identity. Many nation states appear to have moved from nationalisms centered on ethnicity to ones that are more civic and inclusive (Nairn, 1995).

In sport, nation states also remain potent entities. First, for many nation states, the participation of national sport teams in international sports events is highly important in political and symbolic terms. International performances are often an important focus in the nation's "global looking-glass," for imagining how the nation is seen across the world. Second, as we argued earlier in relation to the *millennial* phase of globalization, the foreign policies of the United States have had direct ramifications for sport, not least in regard to security issues. Third, since at least the 1970s, national sports organizations have worked closely with the corporate sector in order to secure profitable regimes of accumulation within the elite sport sector. Fourth, new forms of civic and hyphenated nationalism have been displayed in the celebration of national sport successes, particularly in postcolonial contexts (e.g., when France hosted and won the 1998 men's football World Cup).

In our view, the nation state has undergone substantial "glocalization," as a feature of the changing political-economic and sociocultural circumstances of globalization. Analysts in the field of urban studies have advanced similar arguments on this point, notably through their own distinctive development of the concept of "glocalization" (see, in particular, Swyngedouw, 1992; also Brenner, 1998). The urban studies conception of glocalization refers to the "rescaling" of institutional relationships between the subnational, national, and supranational levels. Thus, many of the nation state's old powers are understood as having been shifted upwards to supranational entities (e.g., the European Union, United Nations) and downwards to subnational bodies (e.g., regional assemblies). Nation states themselves have been understood as important agents in directing the rescaling processes.

These glocalization processes have had a direct impact within global sport. At subnational level, since the 1970s local and regional authorities have sought to harness sport as part of their post-industrial and cultural-development strategies – for example, as "world cities" bid to host sport mega-events, or as US cities use "corporate welfare" strategies to attract major league teams. At supranational level, judicial and governmental bodies have had serious impacts upon the governance and regulation of sport. For example, the

European Court of Justice has made crucial rulings (such as the *Bosman* case in 1995, and the *Kolpak* case in 2003) on sport employment rights, thereby greatly increasing the international mobility of athletes within Europe in sports such as football and cricket.

Professional golf demonstrates that glocalization impacts upon both geopolitical boundaries and symbolic solidarities. The European men's tour organizes events in several nations and regions outside Europe, notably Australia, East Asia, and the Middle East. Moreover, the Ryder Cup, a biennial event, has been rescaled since 1979 to feature the United States competing against a European team (previously, it had been a British and Irish team); additionally, we should note that the European side attracts intensive, cosmopolitan support from golf followers and general sport fans across the continent.

Arguably, however, we should be careful to avoid exaggerating the extent to which rescaling has occurred, particularly in sport. Many global governing bodies in sport continue to be comprised of national members. Compared to other social spheres, sport carries few illustrations of governance being devolved downwards to subnational levels. Such rescaling is more evident in symbolic terms, as "submerged nations" have utilized sport to facilitate strong ethno-national differentiation (for example, the 1992 Olympics in Barcelona; see Hargreaves, 2000).

What also needs to be considered here is the powerful interplay of race and ethnicity in relation to the construction of the "nation." As we have seen, the historical diffusion and development of modern sport has been closely tied to different colonial projects and frameworks. In the West, much modern sport reflected the marginalizaton and subjugation of ethnic minorities within national contexts. Yet sport also provided a contested domain in which these communities sought to establish, in real and symbolic terms, their civil status and rights, as well as their distinctive national identities (Back, Crabbe, and Solomos, 2001; Booth, 1998; Carrington, 2010; Edwards, 1969). Thus, in recent times, sport has come to point more towards the everyday possibilities, and routine experiences, of multiculturalism within postcolonial national settings. Thus, media and public debates on athletes drawn from ethnic minorities center less and less on issues of "racial" distinctiveness, while the composition of national teams also signifies the multicultural hybridity of the postcolonial nation. The London 2012 Olympics provide a particularly powerful geocultural illustration of these processes, not least through the location of the Olympic stadium and village in the borough of Newham, one of the most ethnically diverse locales in the entire United Kingdom, with a particularly high Muslim population.

Sport and the global economic system

The nation state is also at the centre of debates on the global economy. World System theories initiated by Wallerstein (1974, 2002) and associated with others such as Frank (1967), Frank and Gills (1993), Arrighi (1994), and Chase-Dunn and Grimes (1995) have examined historically how the modern world economy has been dominated by particular "core" nations (notably the United States, European nations and, latterly, Japan) which control the mode of production and international division of labor, thus ensuring a highly inequitable distribution of resources at the expense of "peripheral" (e.g., African) and "semi-peripheral" (e.g., East European) nations. For Frank (1967), the world economy is characterized by global dependency relationships that systematically "underdevelop" non-core nations in terms of industrialization, market diversification, and education. These structural problems have been exacerbated in recent times by the liberalized world financial system (Wade 2006).

World System theorists identify and examine cyclical crises in the history of the global economy, most recently manifested in the ongoing period of decline since the early 1990s. Wallerstein (2002) has argued that world capitalism is stuck in a deep crisis from which it may not emerge, due in large part to the reduction in cheap labor for rural areas, political pressure for greater welfare rights in developing nations, the rise of "anti-systemic" social movements in the Global North, and the long-term impact of environmental degradation.

Advanced economic globalization draws us into looking beyond nation states to focus particularly on TNCs. TNCs are commercial organizations that, compared to earlier business models, extend far more systematically beyond national borders in investment, labor, and trade. In 2005, TNCs comprised 95 of the 150 largest economic entities in the world; the remaining 55 were nation states (*Forbes Magazine*, July 25, 2005). TNCs have been presented as the catalytic institutions of a "borderless," free-market environment (Ohmae, 1994, 1995). Other analysts have argued that the "global system" is dominated by TNCs, the attendant "Transnational Capitalist Class" (TCC), and their worldwide "culture-ideology of consumerism" (Sklair, 2001).

However, we do need to exercise strong caution in regard to TNCs. It is very rare to find TNCs that are as "truly transnational" as their definition suggests (Doremus *et al.*, 1999; Smith, 1997). Most TNCs retain strong particularistic ties to their home nation, in terms of commercial operations, recruitment of senior management, legal and fiscal regulations, public-sector subsidization, and corporate branding.

It is possible to find some confirming evidence within the realm of sport for these different theories and arguments. It is possible, for example, to differentiate core, peripheral, and semi-peripheral nations in global sport along the lines of World Systems theory. In football, we might say that "core" Western European football systems operate within many of the world's richest markets, while East Europe, Latin America, and Africa are chronically hamstrung by their impoverished wider economies. Many clubs in these latter regions become trapped in cycles of underdevelopment: massive debts press these clubs into selling players into core markets; domestic interest subsequently dwindles, notably as more glamorous fixtures involving European teams are screened live on television. Similar processes of financial crisis and athlete migration may be identified in the world economic systems of athletics and baseball.

However, there are limits to the applicability of the World System model in sport. First, in football, smaller "core" nations within the world economy – such as Scotland, Sweden, and Norway – find themselves in semi-peripheral positions within the Western European football system; arguably, the football systems in Japan and the United States are in a similar position. Second, *pace* arguments regarding the possible demise of world capitalism, structural divisions within

football's economic system appear to be relatively resilient, with few threatening signs from "anti-systemic movements," environmental degradation, or the exhaustion of cheap labor from non-core regions.

The role of TNCs opens up another set of analytical problems within the contemporary global economics of sport. The most obvious and influential TNCs in sport are in merchandise, media, and sponsorship. Merchandise TNCs like Nike, Reebok, and Adidas possess international divisions of labor (notably, production factories in the Global South, and seduction factories in the Global North) and global retail outlet chains. Among media TNCs, the Sky pay TV network has marshaled its premium sport content (e.g., in American football, European football, golf majors, major league baseball, Australian rugby league, rugby union, and Test cricket) in order to "batter" entry into world television markets. Finally, TNCs in electronics, fast food, finance, telecommunications, and transport have become heavily involved in the high-visibility sponsorship of elite sport.

It is intriguing sociologically to explore how the category of TNC maps onto leading sports institutions. Consider, for example, the world's most valuable sport clubs or "franchises." According to *Forbes* (July 12, 2011), 22 sport clubs were valued individually at US$1 billion or more in 2011. The likes of Barcelona, Manchester United, New York Yankees, LA Lakers, Washington Redskins, and Dallas Cowboys are global "brands" or "commodity signs" that are recognized and merchandised across the world marketplace. Their growth as transnational entities is fueled by promotional strategies that include tours in emerging markets (e.g., football summer tours in East Asia and North America, or American football fixtures contested in Europe). However, in line with more cautious definitions of TNCs, these sporting brands do not abandon their "particularities." For example, these teams often sustain a "traditional" playing ethos (e.g., the attacking styles of Barcelona and Manchester United), and feature iconic local or national players (such as Derek Jeter at New York Yankees, or Catalan players at Barcelona). Finally, the civic, regional, and national identities of most clubs remain intact. Nevertheless, the global influence of TNCs looks certain to intensify, with greater competition occurring off-the-field across the world sports markets (cf. Andrews, 2004).

Two final points on the political-economic aspects of sport globalization are worth making. First, the interplay between sport systems and ownership frameworks is becoming increasingly transnational and complex. For example, the majority of clubs in England's Premier League are owned by non-UK citizens, several of whom own or have major stakes in other sports clubs abroad.[2] These arrangements may have important ramifications for international law, as potential clashes between two or more national legal systems may arise – for example, when different national courts provide competing rulings on matters of ownership or regulation.

Second, the corrupt and criminal aspects of sport have become increasingly transnational. In sports like cricket and football, illegal Asian gambling syndicates are alleged to have been behind the fixing of results and specific passages of play in matches played in Europe, Africa, Australia, and South Asia. In one incident, a leading Zimbabwean football official and a Malaysian gambling syndicate allegedly conspired to have a fake Zimbabwe national team lose an official international fixture against Syria during a tour of Malaysia (*Observer*, October 24, 2010). In turn, greater reflexivity regarding world sports corruption has been marked by the work of investigative journalists (e.g., Hill, 2010; Jennings, 2007), and the Danish NGO Play the Game.

Overall, the political-economic aspects of sport globalization point towards the partial applicability of World System or other economic models. However, the more stimulating challenge for sociologists of sport is to explore how these theoretical constructs may be "glocalized" – that is, concertedly applied or, more likely, critically adapted – in order to illuminate and to explain specific aspects of the political economy of sport. TNC sports institutions are illustrative, in terms of showing clear continuities with more qualified analyses of TNCs in general. In terms of the transformation of the existing political-economic structures of power, the "global civil society" has emerged as the most contested field in recent years, and it is to this subject, and its relevance to sport, that we now turn.

The Emerging Global Civil Society and Sport

There has been significant debate in recent years on the subject of the civil sphere in regard to globalization, leading into discussions on the emergence of a global civil society (Alexander, 2006; Habermas, 2001; Kaldor, 2003; Keane, 2003). The *civil society* may be understood as the "third sector" which falls outside of the state and marketplace. As this sphere has extended to become the *global civil society*, so its main identity has centered on the humanitarian possibilities of globalization, notably in facilitating human development, combating poverty, and fostering effective community relations. The future format of the emerging global civil society is contested by a diversity of institutional types, each of which inclines towards a particular political-economic and ideological model. For example, the corporate social responsibility (CSR) sections of TNCs, along with more market-conscious voluntary NGOs, favor a "neoliberal" civil society in which humanitarian organizations are employed to deliver emergency aid or to raise populations from absolute poverty. Alternatively, radical NGOs and new social movements favor an "activist" civil society that more systematically challenges existing relations of domination, notably between the Global North and South. Anti-capitalist movements associated with this radical approach have protested at major international summits, such as the 1999 World Trade Organization meeting at Seattle and the 2001 G8 meeting at Genoa.

In broad terms, the emerging global civil society has been strongly influenced by three interrelated processes. First, there has been a generalized extension of a culture of rights, and the expansion of social justice movements, to include hitherto politically marginalized groups, notably workers in the Global South. Second, international governmental organizations (notably the United Nations, and its various agencies such as UNICEF and UNESCO; also, to a lesser extent, the World Bank) have focused their policies more prominently on achieving specific development goals; for example, the UN Millennium Development Goals aim to achieve specific targets in tackling poverty and other global problems by

2015. Third, NGOs and community-based organizations (CBOs) have grown massively, both numerically and in political significance. However, some critics state that NGO projects in the Global South tend to lack local democratic legitimacy; fail to empower user groups to take ownership of projects; and effectively produce neocolonial relationships between developed and developing nations (Fisher, 1997; Shaw-Bond, 2000).

Many (but far from all) sport organizations fall within the "third sector" definition of the civil society. The most prominent sport/civil society organizations would include governing bodies, and not-for-profit or community-controlled sport clubs. The extent to which elite professional clubs qualify varies in part according to the ownership regulations within nations; in football, for example, most UK clubs are privately owned by individuals or small pools of shareholders, whereas in Germany or Spain leading clubs are often structured entirely as mutual associations.

As the particular sport domain of the global civil society starts to take shape, it is possible to discern the jockeying of different forces with distinctive objectives. For example, from the early 1990s onwards, various NSMs in the Global North have initiated concerted protest campaigns against sport merchandise TNCs (especially Nike) which are responsible for sweatshop conditions within factories in the Global South (cf. Klein, 2000). In response, merchandise TNCs have established their own CSR divisions which, from time to time, produce reports on factory labor conditions.

Elsewhere, national and international sport governing bodies (such as the Norwegian Football Federation, UEFA, FIFA, and the IOC) have introduced CSR departments and "sport for development" programs which seek to promote specific development goals (such as in regard to health, education, and gender inequality) through sport practices. In many instances, these programs are implemented through partnerships with international NGOs, grassroots CBOs, and major IGOs such as UNICEF or UNHCR.

Sport's emergence within the global civil society has been closely associated with the growing centrality of a culture of rights (Giulian-

otti and McArdle, 2006). There are four key aspects to this relationship.

1   The human right to participate in sport has been promoted by various IGOs and NGOs, with the assistance *inter alia* of the UN Universal Declaration of Human Rights (1948) (notably articles 24, 26, and 27) and the UN Declaration of the Rights of the Child (1959) (notably Principle 7) (Donnelly and Kidd, 2000).

2   IGOs and NGOs employ sport to advance the human right to development. The United Nations made 2005 the International Year of Sport and Physical Education, with a strong focus on sport's role in promoting peace and development. However, some critical researchers have argued that sport development programs need to beware reproducing neocolonial relations between the Global North and South, for example by seeking to inculcate "neoliberal" policies at grassroots level, or failing to empower local populations to take ownership of projects (Darnell, 2008; Hognestad and Tollisen, 2004).

3   Human rights abuses *within* sport have been the subject of some scrutiny and investigation – notably, for example, the systematic doping of athletes within East European sport systems up to the early 1990s, or the physical, psychological, and sexual abuse of young athletes by coaches.

4   Critical NGOs have mounted campaigns against the hosts of sport mega-events in relation to human rights abuses. For example, opponents of the Toronto bid for the 2008 Olympic games argued that event-related legislation might infringe civil rights to peaceful assembly or freedom of speech (Lenskyj, 2000). Similarly, Amnesty International and other human rights organizations were highly critical of Beijing's hosting of the 2008 event, with reference to China's human rights record, occupation of Tibet, and involvement in Darfur. Thus, radical NGOs and NSMs level direct criticisms at those sport governing bodies which appear close or supportive towards states with controversial human rights records.

Overall, the issue of human rights provides one of the most contested spaces through which sport engages with the emerging global civil society.

This reflects the centrality of both sport and humankind to globalization processes.

Conclusions: Globalization, Sport, and "Active Glocalism"

We have argued that the globalization of sport is a long-term, complex, and multifaceted process. Sport has played an increasingly prominent role within six historical phases of globalization. In sociocultural terms, sport is a highly vibrant domain within which the "glocal" and increasingly cosmopolitan processes of homogenization and heterogenization are played out. In political-economic terms, World System theory and other all-encompassing analytical frameworks have an uneven utility for explaining contemporary sport. The emerging global civil society provides an ever more significant domain for the interplay of diverse political and ideological agendas within and beyond sport.

Glocalization processes will be increasingly salient within these different aspects of the globalization of sport. These processes actively reflect the interpenetration of the local and the global, the universal and the particular, and processes of homogenization and heterogenization. Glocalization is evidenced in the growing significance of cosmopolitanism within contemporary sport, notably in the ways in which the particular and the universal are integrated through seemingly oxymoronic conditions like "patriotic cosmopolitanism." Moreover, urban studies scholars point us to the importance of glocalization processes within the rescaling of geopolitical frameworks, for example as nation states "glocalize" to accommodate shifting institutional powers at supra- and subnational levels.

A vital ontological precondition within glocalization strategies is the critical, creative, and cosmopolitan empowerment of individuals and social groups. In sport at least, it is important to recognize that these social prerequisites are often identifiable when cultural homogenization or convergence occurs – for example, when local populations seize upon "global" sports, or have sought to emulate the sporting techniques and practices of other cultures.

We would suggest that three contemporary challenges or threats lie before what we might term "active glocalism" within sport. First, the current millennial phase of globalization is marked particularly by the increasing penetration of the civil sphere by juridico-political regulations (from the state) and acute sociocultural prescriptions (from the private sector). In sport, two by-products of these regulative and prescriptive processes are the growing thematization of national security and individual risk assessment. Invariably, these millennial trends challenge the extent to which active glocal strategies and practices may be fully exercised by different social groups.

A second challenge is provided by the political-economic condition of elite global sport. For example, in circumstances in which broad theories of the world economic system apply within sport, we find that non-core nations may be stuck in conditions of underdevelopment, thereby undermining their capacity to initiate active glocal practices or strategies.

A third set of diverse challenges arises in respect of the global civil society. On one hand, the "developmentalist" problem arises over whether "sport for development" institutions, in implementing their projects, facilitate the active glocalism of local user groups. On the other hand, there is the political problem of which institutions and agendas will gain greatest influence within the sport dimension of the global civil society. Will the neoliberal pragmatism of corporate social responsibility have the upper hand over movements that advocate global justice and equality? In turn, there is the human rights problem in relation to sport, which conjoins national governments, sport governing bodies, and diverse NGOs and NSMs.

These three challenges to active glocalism will be increasingly significant within the globalization of sport. Sustaining active glocalism can only be achieved through an effective critical engagement with the historical, sociocultural, political-economic, and civil dimensions of global sport. In each of these domains, the contemporary rise of cosmopolitanism provides one way in which active glocalism may be promoted. Forms of "thick" and "rooted" cosmopolitanism may provide the strongest illustrations of active glocalism. And sport is perhaps *the* social field in which the glocal possibilities of cosmopolitanism may be said to be fully "at play."

Notes

1 In 1907, an investigating commission established by a sports entrepreneur stated that Doubleday had invented baseball in 1839, thus giving the sport, a variation of the English game of rounders, a satisfying foundational myth that was all-American. Historians have long rejected this claim (cf. Guttmann, 1994: 71–72). In 1895, rugby union's own myth of origin centered on Ellis, who is claimed to have invented the game in 1823 by disregarding the rules of football, picking up the ball, and running with it. Again, the historical evidence is highly spurious; the myth itself was more likely to have a political motive, as an attempt by southern rugby clubs to head off the challenge from northern clubs (Holt, 1989: 85–86).

2 For example, Manchester United's Glazer family, with the NFL's Tampa Bay Buccaneers; Liverpool and Boston Red Sox, both owned by New England Sports Ventures; and Randy Lerner, owner of Cleveland Browns and Aston Villa.

References

Alexander, J. (2006) "Global civil society." *Theory, Culture & Society*, 23: 521–524.

Andrews, D.L. (ed.) (2004) *Manchester United*, London: Routledge.

Andrews, D.L. and Ritzer, G. (2007) "The grobal in the sporting glocal." *Global Networks*, 7 (2): 113–153.

Appadurai, A. (1996) *Modernity at Large*, Minneapolis: University of Minnesota Press.

Appiah, K.A. (1997) "Cosmopolitan patriots." *Critical Inquiry*, 23: 617–639.

Archetti, E. (1998) *Masculinities*, Oxford: Berg.

Armstrong, G. and Giulianotti, R. (eds.) (1997) *Entering the Field: New Perspectives on World Football*, Oxford: Berg.

Armstrong, G. and Giulianotti, R. (eds.) (2004) *Football in Africa*, Basingstoke: Palgrave Macmillan.

Arrighi, G. (1994) *The Long Twentieth Century: Money, Power, and the Origins of Our Times*, London: Verso.

Back, L., Crabbe, T., and Solomos, J. (2001) *The Changing Face of Football*, Oxford: Berg.

Bale, J. and Sang, J. (1996) *Kenyan Running*, London: Frank Cass.

Beck, U. (1999) *World Risk Society*, Cambridge: Polity Press.

Beck, U. (2004) "Rooted cosmopolitanism," in Beck, U., Sznaider, N., and Winter, R. (eds.) *Global America?* Liverpool: Liverpool University Press, pp. 15–29.

Beckles, H.McD. and Stoddart, B. (eds.) (1995) *Liberation Cricket*, Manchester: Manchester University Press.

Bellos, A. (2002) *Futebol: The Brazilian Way of Life*, London: Bloomsbury.

Booth, D. (1998) *The Race Game: Sport and Politics in South Africa*, London: Frank Cass.

Bourdieu, P. (1999) *Acts of Resistance*, New York: New Press.

Brenner, N. (1998) "Global cities, glocal states: Global city formation and state territorial restructuring in contemporary Europe." *Review of International Political Economy*, 5 (1): 1–37.

Burke, P. (2009) *Cultural Hybridity*, Cambridge: Polity Press.

Buruma, I. and Margalit, A. (2004) *Occidentalism*, New York: Atlantic.

Calhoun, C. (2007) *Nations Matter: Culture, History and the Cosmopolitan Dream*, London: Routledge.

Carrington, B. (2004) "Cosmopolitan Olympism, humanism and the spectacle of 'race,'" in Bale, J. and Christensen, M. (eds.) *Post-Olympism? Questioning Sport in the Twenty-First Century*, Oxford: Berg, pp. 81–97.

Carrington, B. (2010) *Race, Sport and Politics: The Sporting Black Diaspora*, London: Sage Publications.

Chase-Dunn, C. and Grimes, P. (1995) "World-Systems analysis." *Annual Review of Sociology*, 21: 387–417.

Clark, T. and Mangham, I. (2004) "From dramaturgy to theatre as technology: The case of corporate theatre." *Journal of Management Studies*, 41 (1): 37–59.

Crothers, L. (2007) *Globalization and American Popular Culture*, Lanham, MD: Rowman & Littlefield.

Darnell, S. (2008) "Changing the world through sport and play: A post-colonial analysis of Canadian volunteers within the 'Sport for Development and Peace' movement." Unpublished PhD thesis, University of Toronto.

Donnelly, P. and Kidd, B. (2000) "Human rights in sport." *International Review for the Sociology of Sport*, 35 (2): 131–148.

Doremus, P., Keller, W.W., Pauly, L.W., and Reich, S. (1999) *The Myth of the Global Corporation*, Princeton, NJ: Princeton University Press.

Edwards, H. (1969) *The Revolt of the Black Athlete*, New York: Free Press.

Eichberg, H. (1994) "Traveling, comparing, emigrating: Configurations of sport mobility," in Bale, J. and

Maguire, J. (eds.) *The Global Sports Arena*, London: Frank Cass.

Falk, R. (2005) "Reimagining the governance of globalization," in Appelbaum, R.P. and Robinson, W.I. (eds.) *Critical Globalization Studies*, London: Routledge.

Fine, R. (2007) *Cosmopolitanism*, London: Routledge.

Fisher, W.F. (1997) "Doing good? The politics and antipolitics of NGO practices." *Annual Review of Anthropology*, 26: 439–464.

Foer, F. (2004) *How Soccer Explains the World*, New York: HarperCollins.

Frank, A.G. (1967) *Capitalism and Underdevelopment in Latin America*, New York: Monthly Review Press.

Frank, A.G. and Gills, B. (eds.) (1993) *The World System*, London: Routledge.

Friedman, J. (1999) "Indigenous struggles and the discreet charm of the bourgeoisie." *Journal of World-Systems Research*, 5 (2): 391–411.

Friedman, T. (2000) *The Lexus and the Olive Tree*, New York: Anchor.

Giddens, A. (1990) *The Consequences of Modernity*, Cambridge: Polity Press.

Gimenez, M.E. (2006) "With a little class: A critique of identity politics." *Ethnicities*, 6 (3): 423–439.

Giulianotti, R. (1991) "Scotland"s Tartan Army in Italy: the case for the carnivalesque." *Sociological Review*, 39 (3): 503–530.

Giulianotti, R. (1999) *Football: A Sociology of the Global Game*, Cambridge: Polity Press.

Giulianotti, R. (2005) *Sport: A Critical Sociology*, Cambridge: Polity Press.

Giulianotti, R. (2009) "Risk and sport: An analysis of sociological theories and research agendas." *Sociology of Sport Journal*, 26 (4): 540–556.

Giulianotti, R. and Klauser, F.R. (2010) "Security governance and sport mega-events: Towards an interdisciplinary research agenda." *Journal of Sport & Social Issues*, 34 (1): 49–61.

Giulianotti, R. and McArdle, D. (eds.) (2006) *Sport, Civil Liberties and Human Rights*, London: Taylor & Francis.

Giulianotti, R. and Robertson, R. (2001) "Die Globalisierung des Fussballs: 'Glokalisierung,' transnationale Konzerne und demokratische Regulierung," in Lösche, P., Ruge, U., and Stolz, K. (eds.) *Fussballwelten: Zum Verhältnis von Sport, Politik, Ökonomie und Gesellschaft*, Opladen: Leske and Budrich.

Giulianotti, R. and Robertson, R. (2004) "The globalization of football: A study in the 'glocalization' of the serious life." *British Journal of Sociology*, 55: 545–568.

Giulianotti, R. and Robertson, R. (2005) "Glocalization, globalization and migration: The case of Scottish football supporters in North America." *International Sociology*, 21 (2): 171–198.

Giulianotti, R. and Robertson, R. (2007a) "Forms of glocalization: Globalization and the migration strategies of Scottish football fans in North America." *Sociology*, 41 (1): 133–152.

Giulianotti, R. and Robertson, R. (2007b) "Recovering the social: Globalization, football and transnationalism." *Global Networks*, 7 (2): 144–186.

Giulianotti, R. and Robertson, R. (2009) *Globalization and Football*, London: Sage Publications.

Goldblatt, D. (2006) *The Ball is Round*, London: Penguin Books.

Guttmann, A. (1991) *Women's Sport*, New York: Columbia University Press.

Guttmann, A. (1992) *The Olympics: A History of the Modern Games*, Champaign: University of Illinois Press.

Guttmann, A. (1994) *Games and Empires: Modern Sports and Cultural Imperialism*, New York: Columbia University Press.

Habermas, J. (2001) *The Postnational Constellation*, Cambridge: Polity Press.

Hamelink, C.J. (1995) *World Communication: Disempowerment and Self-Empowerment*, London: Zed Books.

Hannerz, U. (1992) *Cultural Complexity*, New York: Columbia University Press.

Hargreaves, J. (2000) *Freedom for Catalonia? Catalan Nationalism, Spanish Identity and the Barcelona Olympic Games*, Cambridge: Cambridge University Press.

Hill, D. (2010) *The Fix: Soccer and Organized Crime*, Toronto: McClelland & Stewart.

Hognestad, H. and Tollisen, A. (2004) "Playing against deprivation: Football and development in Nairobi, Kenya," in Armstrong, G. and Giulianotti, R. (eds.) *Football in Africa*, Basingstoke: Palgrave Macmillan, pp. 210–228.

Holt, R. (1989) *Sport and the British*, Oxford: Oxford University Press.

Holton, R. (1998) *Globalization and the Nation-State*, Basingstoke: Macmillan.

Holton, R. (2008) *Global Networks*, Basingstoke: Palgrave Macmillan.

Irwin, R. (2006) *For Lust of Knowing: The Orientalists and their Enemies*, London: Allen Lane.

Jarvie, G. (1991) *Highland Games: The Making of the Myth*, Edinburgh: Edinburgh University Press.

Jennings, A. (2007) *Foul! The Secret World of FIFA*, London: Harper Collins.

Johnson, C. (2004) *The Sorrows of Empire*, New York: Metropolitan Books.

Kaldor, M. (2003) *Global Civil Society*, Cambridge: Polity Press.

Kaufman, J. and Patterson, O. (2005) "Cross-national cultural diffusion: The global spread of cricket." *American Sociological Review*, 70 (1): 82–110.

Keane, J. (2003) *Global Civil Society?* Cambridge: Cambridge University Press.

Klein, A. (1991) *Sugarball: The American Game, The Dominican Dream*, New Haven, CT: Yale University Press.

Klein, N. (2000) *No Logo*, Toronto: Knopf.

Kruger, A. and Riordan, J. (eds.) (1996) *The Story of Worker Sport*, Champaign, IL: Human Kinetics.

Latouche, S. (1996) *The Westernization of the World*, Cambridge: Polity Press.

Lenskyj, H. (2000) *Inside the Olympic Industry*, Albany: State University of New York Press.

Maguire, J. (1999) *Global Sport*, Cambridge: Polity Press.

Manela, E. (2007) *The Wilsonian Moment: Self-Determination and the International Origins of Anti-Colonial Nationalism*, Oxford: Oxford University Press.

Mangan, J.A. (1986) *The Games Ethic and Imperialism*, London: Viking.

Markovits, A.S. and Hellerman, S.L. (2001) *Offside: Soccer and American Exceptionalism*, Princeton, NJ: Princeton University Press.

Nairn, T. (1995) "Breakwaters of 2000: From ethnic to civic nationalism." *New Left Review*, 1 (214): 91–103.

Niezen, R. (2003) *The Origins of Indigenism*, Berkeley: University of California Press.

Ohmae, K. (1994) *The Borderless World*, New York: Profile.

Ohmae, K. (1995) *The End of the Nation State*, New York: Free Press.

Pieterse, J.N. (1995) "Globalization as hybridization," in Featherstone, M., Lash, S., and Robertson, R. (eds.) *Global Modernities*, London: Sage Publications, pp. 45–68.

Pieterse, J.N. (2007) *Ethnicities and Global Multiculture*, Lanham, MD: Rowman & Littlefield.

Ritzer, G. (2004) *The Globalization of Nothing*, Thousand Oaks, CA: Pine Forge.

Robertson, R. (1990) "Mapping the global condition: Globalization as the central concept." *Theory, Culture and Society*, 7: 15–30.

Robertson, R. (1992) *Globalization: Social Theory and Global Culture*, London: Sage Publications.

Robertson, R. (1995) "Glocalization: Time-space and homogeneity-heterogeneity," in Featherstone, M., Lash, S., and Robertson, R. (eds.) *Global Modernities*, London: Sage Publications, pp. 25–44.

Robertson, R. (2001) "Globalization theory 2000+: Major problematics," in Ritzer, G. and Smart, B. (eds.) *Handbook of Social Theory*, London: Sage Publications, pp. 458–471.

Robertson, R. (2004) "Rethinking Americanization," in Beck, U., Sznaider, N., and Winter, R. (eds.) *Global America? The Cultural Consequences of Globalization?* Liverpool: Liverpool University Press, p. 257.

Robertson, R. (2007a) "Open societies, closed minds? Exploring the ubiquity of suspicion and voyeurism." *Globalizations*, 4 (3): 399–416.

Robertson, R. (2007b) "Global millennialism: A post-mortem on secularization," in Beyer, P. and Beaman, L. (eds.) *Religion, Globalization and Society*, Leiden: Brill, pp. 9–34.

Robertson, R. and Krossa, S.A. (eds.) (2011) *European Cosmopolitanism: Between Universalism and Particularism*, Basingstoke: Palgrave Macmillan.

Robertson, R. and Scholte, J.A. (eds.) (2007) *Encyclopedia of Globalization*, London: Routledge.

Robertson, R. and White, K.E. (eds.) (2003) *Globalization: Critical Concepts in Sociology* (6 vols), London: Routledge.

Roche, M. (2000) *Mega-Events and Modernity: Olympics, Expos and the Growth of Global Culture*, London: Routledge.

Roudometof, V. (2005) "Transnationalism, cosmopolitanism and glocalization." *Current Sociology*, 53: 113–135.

Rumford, C. (2007) "More than a game: Globalization and the post-Westernization of world cricket." *Global Networks*, 7 (2): 202–214.

Said, E. (1995) *Orientalism*, Harmondsworth: Penguin Books.

Schiller, H.I. (1976) *Communication and Cultural Domination*, Armonk, NY: M.E. Sharpe.

Scholte, J.A. (2005) *Globalization* (2nd edn.), Basingstoke: Palgrave Macmillan.

Shaw-Bond, M. (2000) "The backlash against NGOs." *Prospect*, April: 51–56.

Silk, M., Andrews, D., and Cole, C.L. (eds.) (2004) *Sport and Corporate Nationalisms*, Oxford: Berg.

Sklair, L. (2001) *The Transnational Capitalist Class*, Oxford: Blackwell.

Smith, P. (1997) *Millennial Dreams: Contemporary Culture and Capital in the North*, London: Verso.

Stauth, G. and Turner, B.S. (1988) "Nostalgia, postmodernism and the critique of mass culture." *Theory, Culture and Society*, 5 (2/3): 509–526.

Swyngedouw, E. (1992) "The mammon quest: 'Glocalization,' interspatial competition and the monetary order: The construction of new scales," in Dunford, M. and Kafkalis, G. (eds.) *Cities and Regions in the New Europe*, London: Belhaven Press, pp. 39–67.

Szymanski, S. and Zimbalist, A. (2006) *National Pastime: How Americans Play Baseball and the Rest of the World Plays Soccer*, Washington, DC: Brookings Institution.

Tomlinson, J. (1999) *Globalization and Culture*, Cambridge: Polity Press.

Van Bottenburg, M. (2001) *Global Games*, Urbana: University of Illinois Press.

Vertovec, S. and Cohen, R. (2003) *Conceiving Cosmopolitanism*, Oxford: Oxford University Press.

Wade, R. (2006) "Choking the South." *New Left Review*, 38: 115–127.

Wallerstein, I. (1974) "The rise and future demise of the world capitalist system." *Comparative Studies in Society and History*, 16 (4): 387–415.

Wallerstein, I. (2002) *The Decline of American Power*, New York: New Press.

Wolf, M. (2004) *Why Globalization Works*, New Haven, CT: Yale University Press.

Wolin, S. (2008) *Democracy Incorporated: Managing Democracy and the Specter of Inverted Totalitarianism*, Princeton, NJ: Princeton University Press.

Further Reading

Giulianotti, R. and Robertson, R. (2007) *Globalization and Sport*, Oxford: Wiley-Blackwell.

Giulianotti, R. and Robertson, R. (2009) *Globalization and Football*, London: Sage Publications.

Guttmann, A. (1994) *Games and Empires: Modern Sports and Cultural Imperialism*, New York: Columbia University Press.

Kaufman, J. and Patterson, O. (2005) "Cross-national cultural diffusion: The global spread of cricket." *American Sociological Review*, 70: 82–110.

Lechner, F. (2009) *Globalization: The Making of World Society*, Oxford: Wiley-Blackwell.

Miller, T., Lawrence, G., McKay, J., and Rowe, D. (2001) *Globalization and Sport: Playing the World*, London: Sage Publications.

Robertson, R. (1992) *Globalization: Social Theory and Global Culture*, London: Sage Publications.

Robertson, R. and White, K.E. (eds.) (2003) *Globalization* (6 vols), London: Routledge.

3

The Sport/Media Complex
Formation, Flowering, and Future

David Rowe

Introduction: Three Decades in a Complex Life

In 1984, the year of sundry reflections on the prophetic validity of George Orwell's early Cold War novel *Nineteen Eighty-Four* and on the late Cold War Los Angeles spectacle often referred to as the "Hamburger Olympics," Sut Jhally published an influential article on sport and media in the *Insurgent Sociologist*. The name of the journal itself marks the passage of time and the transformation of sociocultural context – who now, in the post-9/11 world and Iraq-invasion universe, boldly declares the virtues of "insurgency," even if only of an engaged intellectual nature? "The Spectacle of Accumulation: Material and Cultural Factors in the Evolution of the Sports/Media Complex" was one of the few explicitly Marxist works in the English language up to that point to examine the relationship between sport and media in any analytical depth.[1] The critical edge evident in Jhally's work contrasted significantly with other works of the period that either lauded the potential for enhanced capital accumulation through extending and deepening the commercial media's (especially television's) connection to sport, or complained that the modern institution of sport (including its industry, if not its grass-

roots communities) had been taken over by another modern institution – the media.

This chapter returns to Jhally's early intervention in the field of media sport studies to reflect on the history, present, and future of what I prefer to call the "media sports cultural complex" (Rowe, 2004a) but is described variously in this context.[2] It traces the twists and turns in sport's relationship with first print, then electronic, and finally computer-based media, and the continuities and discontinuities in media sport genres, structures, and relations of power. This is not, of course, to imply that a single, towering figure has dominated media sport studies – quite to the contrary, Jhally did not sustain his specific work in this area, and his intervention now constitutes an influential but small footnote to a field of research and scholarship that has grown and prospered in tandem with its object of analysis.[3] Of course, many others have contributed to this intellectual project, and I have dwelt on Jhally's contribution as a convenient point of entry into both the relationship between sport and media, and into the ways in which it might be understood, traced, and deconstructed. Rather than survey the range of significant contributions to this field in the manner of "keeping score," I will draw on them here as they emerge as relevant to the subject in

A Companion to Sport, First Edition. Edited by David L. Andrews and Ben Carrington.
© 2013 Blackwell Publishing Ltd. Published 2013 by Blackwell Publishing Ltd.

question. "The Spectacle of Accumulation" focuses on the key media sport form and technology (television), the significance of its financial dependency at a crucial stage of development in the United States on a source of funds (advertising), the facilitation of highly mediated and widely dispersed sports events and discourses (texts), and reliance on the creation, sustainment, and development of particular types of sociocultural groupings of taste and practice (audiences).

Media sport analysis, therefore, has revolved around production, textuality, and sociality. This tripartite framework (Rowe, 2004b) has developed and changed at different speeds and in various combinations since sports reporting was first industrialized in the print media in the eighteenth century. Sometimes there are periods of relative stability (usually when a particular medium, such as print, radio, or television is dominant), and at others there is considerable volatility (such as the current moment, when the dominance of broadcast television sport is being challenged by online and mobile media). In significant ways, these shifts resemble the "paradigm crises" famously described by Thomas S. Kuhn (1996) in *The Structure of Scientific Revolutions*, as new ways of mediating sport emerge to challenge conventional structures, practices, meanings, and uses. Current and future media sport researchers, it is argued below, must come to terms with a media sport landscape that is in significant flux and, in particular, are required to negotiate, skeptically and critically, the competing claims of both utopian and dystopian diagnosticians of the state and trajectory of this dynamic complex. This chapter concentrates mainly on issues that concern the production of media sport – I will leave the developed discussion of, for example, issues of ideology and representation to other contributions to this *Companion*. Here, the main concern is with the ramifications for cultural citizenship (Miller, 2007) of the emergence and development of the media sports cultural complex.

Complex Prehistory

The histories of media and sport are substantially intertwined, both with each other and, more extensively, with capitalism and modernity (Goldlust, 1987; McChesney, 1989). Sport, as rationalized physical play, developed mainly along two lines. The first was in amateur mode, principally as an expression of institutionalized discipline through schools, clubs, and associations within civil society, and dedicated to the moral, bodily instruction of children and young people, especially males. Sport had many social control utilities in this regard: as a "safety valve" for "unhealthy" impulses (especially sexual and violent); as an ideal model for social relations (incorporating hierarchy, selflessness, compliance, competition, and cooperation), including those expected in factory and office workplaces; training for military combat in the service of the nation state (physical fitness, aggression, and the familiarity with uniforms); gender role instruction (the prescribed demeanor of males and females, the expression of approved dispositions of masculinity through sport in contradistinction to disapproved feminine dispositions), and so on (Hargreaves, 1986; Miller, 2001).

Through physical instruction in which success in sport competition became an alternative source of status beyond scholarly prowess (though ideally combined with it), sport emerged as a cultural form recognizable to the entire populace and celebrated by a sizable (and mainly male) proportion of it. In this way, the "sportization" of physical pastimes could be construed as part of a "civilizing process" (Elias and Dunning, 1986) that helped diffuse violence, promote order, and infuse sport with symbolic values of collective identity, structured competitiveness, and status acquisition. Drawing on and "taming" forms of physical play (such as folk football) that were of a *carnivalesque* and potentially socially disruptive nature (ranging widely across space, taking unspecified amounts of time, and often resulting in substantial physical injury because largely unregulated), sport developed as a form of popular leisure that mirrored the disciplined industrial labor from which it was intended to be distinguished. In "free time," sport was measured in temporal units, practiced in dedicated spaces, and performed through a clear division of labor between producer (athlete) and consumer (spectator) (Brohm, 1978). This structure – largely unrecognizable in relation to the intermittent, unrationalized physical pastimes that preceded it in antiquity (Guttmann, 1978) – enabled the emergence of industrialized sport that could, in turn, offer a new prospect for capital accumulation based on athletic labor and the serviced sports appreciator.

Thus, the second line of sport development was towards the commercial and the professional, in moving from bounded community and local/regional/national state-embodied cultural practice to the sphere of capital exchange, whereby sport became commodified by turning sport contests into controlled events performed by experts for the pleasure of paying spectators. As in all other areas of social, cultural, and economic change, modern sport did not develop evenly across the world but first took root under circumstances where folk-play could be transformed and acted upon most effectively by emergent capitalist values of accumulation and industrial principles of organized production, and within a relatively confined, intensive cultural space favorable to them. It is not surprising, then, that modern sport took shape in Britain (especially England), the first capitalist and industrial nation, and one which, through its associated colonialism and imperialism, was best placed to export sports practices across the world (Guttmann, 1994). As Allen Guttmann puts it:

> It was inevitable, therefore, that England, the homeland of industrial capitalism, was also the birthplace of modern sports. The astonishing readiness of the English to wager money on horse races, foot races, and boxing was commented upon by many observers. In the words of an eighteenth-century French commentator [Jean-Bernard Le Blanc] on English customs, "The probability of life, and the return of ships, are the objects of their arithmetic. The same habit of calculating they extend to games, wagers, and everything in which there is any hazard."
>
> The readiness to wager on horses, cocks, bears, ships, and pugilistic butchers paralleled the increased willingness to risk venture capital in the development of England's expanding industry. From the eagerness to risk and wager came the need to measure time and space. The capitalist's ledgers are close kin to the scorecard. We suddenly enter the world of the bookkeeper and the bookie. (1978: 60)

Although Guttmann's Weberian framework differs from, say, the Marxist analysis of Jhally, the "elective affinity" between sport and capitalism that he proposes resonates with approaches that both emphasize the drive of the bourgeoisie to produce surplus from the exploitation of labor, and the proletariat's propensity for trying (though this was usually a futile quest in strictly financial terms) to break away from exploited labor by "making a killing" through the risky business of betting and wagering. Such working-class "vocabularies of hope" can, from this perspective, at least "transport them from difficulties, frustrations and struggles of day-to-day life, providing a temporary respite" (Lynch, 1990: 200).

This leisure pursuit does not, though, mean that social class precisely demarcates the boundaries of these or any other cultural practices. As John Clarke and Chas Critcher note (1985: 44), "members of all classes may drink, smoke, gamble and watch television but where, when, how, and why they pursue such activities have particular cultural meanings shaped by the social groups to which they belong." They note that the same principle applies to gender (see, e.g., Hargreaves, 1994) and, we might add, other sources of social structure and identity, including "race" (in the sense of constructed racialized identities and groupings, not of genetically constituted groupings) and ethnicity (Carrington and McDonald, 2001; MacClancy, 1996), that can coalesce around sport, be projected onto groups of people, and become implicated in both group formation and resistance to stereotyping.

Some sports contests were, at the outset, little more than opportunities for gambling, drinking, and socializing – most obviously the various types of animal racing, including those involving horses and dogs, that had displaced the now officially disapproved forms of betting-driven animal fighting, such as those using cocks, bears, and (again) dogs. Others, more compellingly, drew on the affective appeal of various forms of social identity, first mainly as touring professionals in sports such as boxing, cricket, and athletics played by local representatives in front of paying crowds supporting their hometown favorites. Later, regular sporting competitions, with common rules and carefully quantified results, enabled expressions of intra/inter-city and regional rivalry, ultimately leading to athletes and teams representing whole nations (Mason, 1989). Commercial gains could be realized, then, through restricting access to significant sport contests to those willing and able to pay for entry, as well as by means of gambling, hospitality, and, of particular interest in the context of this chapter, sponsorship and advertising. Here, the role of the media becomes especially important to the fortunes of the sports industry.

Just as physical play developed under modernity into the cultural form and entrepreneurial practice of sport, similarly unrationalized processes of communication took on a more ordered and sophisticated character through the institution of the media. An analogous pattern of folk practice, state intervention (in this case with institutionalized religion, as with sport, sometimes standing in for the state), and commercial exploitation is evident as human expression through such media as oral storytelling, song, visual illustration, and, later, following widespread instruction in literacy, the printed word, became available for systematic commodification and industrialization. The development of specialist media platforms, deploying print and electronic technologies to communicate across time and space, enabled two especially important functions – the transmission of news and the provision of entertainment. By such means, the world beyond the daily rounds of individuals and groups could be rendered with increasing depth, intensity, and speed, while entertainment genres could be both advertised for sale and provided in mediated form. In Britain, the technical and organizational advancement of capitalism in the late nineteenth and early twentieth centuries had a profound influence on animal sports, which in particular operated as vehicles for gambling. Clarke and Critcher (1985: 74) record that "technology and the market did produce innovations in sport, notably cycle and car racing. Speedway threatened to become a major spectator sport in the late 1920s. But more indicative of the state of organised sport was the introduction of greyhound racing, for this owed its rationale to a continuous and expanding element of popular culture – betting." Gambling had always been an integral part of popular leisure but did not become habitual and widespread until the 1880s, when the telegraph and the popular press made horse-racing results imme-

diately available and improved economic conditions increased discretionary spending power. The result was an increase in the pervasiveness of betting.

Here it can be seen that the intersection of media and sport becomes critical to both institutions and their associated processes and practices. The industrialization of sport required product familiarization and demand stimulation to engender growth that was less reliant on word-of-mouth and rudimentary promotion. The modern media, which increasingly took on a round-the-clock character and so had both copious communicative space to fill and substantial audiences to find, were uniquely well suited to carrying out a range of these tasks (Boyle and Haynes, 2000). Newspapers and magazines, and then radio, newsreels and television, connected potential sport spectators with sports events through mass advertising; sponsors could use the appeal of those events to endorse and advertise their products and enhance their brand image; and sport could become an essential staple of the news media, raising levels of anticipation (and awareness) before events took place, reporting the outcomes, and describing and reflecting on what had occurred (see various contributions to Wenner, 1998). This sport–media relationship became symbiotic, with sport benefiting from the exposure provided by the media (both paid for and free), and the media luring audiences to consult them for information about athletes, teams, clubs, and events, the interest in which they had themselves significantly stimulated.

However useful the functions of advertising, promoting, and reporting of the media were for sport, there remained a considerable distance between them. Two separate entities could still be discerned, with little in the way of integration. As long as sport was predominantly a *subject* for the media, this had to remain the case, but the key change occurred when it became scheduled media *content* in the form of events rendered as audiovisual texts, especially when presented "live" through broadcasting at the same moment as in-stadium spectators were experiencing the temporally and spatially fixed event. Thus, television made possible a sense of "tele-presence" in which viewers at a distance could simulate the experience of "being there."

Television Complex

Before television, those who were absent from a sport contest (necessarily an increasingly vast majority of those interested in it) were mainly reliant on "after the fact" accounts, still photography and radio commentary with, perhaps, some ambient sounds. Newsreels and early films devoted to sports such as boxing also existed, but they were available only periodically and outside the home. Sport television brought moving images of the players and crowds, the atmospheric noises of the unique moment, and explanatory commentary (a rather mixed blessing, it might be observed) directly into the domestic environment. Viewers could be attracted to the screen as *compensation* for their distance from the action, at the same time providing the requisite "eyeballs" for commercial advertisers and, in the case of public, non-commercial television, cultural content that would enhance collective consciousness and so national identity of a citizenry united by the great festivals of televised sport (Roche, 2000; Tomlinson and Young, 2006). This striking simulation of co-presence caused anxiety among several sports, which felt that television's compensation for non-attendance at paying sports events would be so comparatively generous as to constitute an inducement to forgo any intention to attend and pay at all. As television developed (Brookes, 2002), this compensation became ever more lavish, the viewer enjoying the performance of elite sport and savoring its atmosphere without leaving the lounge room, while taking advantage of many media technological innovations unavailable to the co-present spectator. These included the multiple perspectives provided by cameras situated at many vantage points that overcame the limitations of a single viewing position, while action replays, slow motion, and sped-up sequences manipulated singular, unrecorded slivers of time and motion.

Thus, new types of compensation for sport television's "intrusion" were required. For the paying spectator, this might take the form of a seat (even if only an uncomfortable one of molded plastic) rather than a standing space in order to provide at least some of the comforts of home. But, more importantly, television was to add value to the experience of being there, and to reward the spectator for taking the trouble to leave home by bringing the media apparatus of home with them by means of large screens that could show much of the televised action available off site – as well as providing another space for advertising. The second principal form of compensation for accommodating television at sport's most sacred sites was to the sports themselves in the form of paying for broadcasting rights. From modest, tentative beginnings, these were so saleable as to become the most important single component of sport's industrial economy, with sport being one of the few forms of television programming that could assemble large, regular viewerships, and at a fraction of the direct production cost of quality, first-run drama or documentary. The cost of broadcast rights for media companies was offset not only by advertising revenue but later (notably in the 1970s in the pioneering US television market) supplemented through the introduction of the "electronic turnstile," whereby pay television with exclusive rights could outbid free-to-air television in securing substantial subscription and pay per view revenue (Scherer and Whitson, 2009).

Television, although only a part of the far-reaching landscape of media sport that extends across the news and entertainment media, and which takes in everything from feature films to websites, is unquestionably at its heart. It is responsible for sport and media becoming so institutionally and culturally intertwined as to mutate into a phenomenon that, as Jhally (1984) first argued, acquired the ontological status of a *complex*. It is useful to examine this notion, as it signifies a much more intimate and systematic association between sport and media than a more routine organizational and cultural relationship. Jhally sought to theorize the status, in the process of capital accumulation, of the media audience for sport, arguing that the time that its members devote to viewing the advertising material around media texts constitutes a form of labor that produces surplus value to be expropriated by the owners of capital. In a North American context he examines the early phase of the "sports/media complex" between 1890 and 1940, the pre-television era when newspapers first "sold" sports readers to advertisers. This straightforward relationship changed with the advent of radio, as sport was deployed to sell new media technologies to audiences (Jhally, 1984: 43–44). The watershed moment, for Jhally, was the 1939 World Series of baseball, and the concentration resulting from a single network matched with a single sponsor, a manufacturer of men's shaving products:

> [However] it was to be 1939 before the true potential of the sports/media relationship was fully discovered by advertisers. In that year the World Series for the first time went to single-network coverage with Gillette having paid $100,000 for the rights as the sponsor. Although the series finished in the minimum four games, Al Leonard, Gillette's public relations manager recalls, "we couldn't believe our eyes. Sales were up 350% for the Series. It wasn't even a new product and here were these fantastic records coming *in*. We didn't wait, we went running all over the country to buy every major event we could find." (Johnson, 1971: 226, cited in Jhally, 1984: 45)

This was clear recognition in the United States that network sports television could create extraordinary visibility for advertisers by providing a meeting place with massive mediated audiences who were certain, because of the compelling nature of the event, to "turn up." It contrasts with the European experience at the same time (pioneered by the BBC in the United Kingdom, and then found in other places such as Canada, Australia, New Zealand, and, later, much of Asia) of using publicly funded and provided televised sport with considerable success as part of a nation-building rather than an advertising audience-driven project (Whannel, 1992). As Goldlust (1987) has noted, this initial divergence in the underlying ethos of sports television fostered a difference of broadcast styles in which the brashness of audience-seeking, advertisement-punctuated commercial television could be distinguished from the more sober, sedate representation of sport through state-sanctioned broadcasts. As will be discussed below, both the economic underpinning and presentational style of sport television was to change – indeed, converge – in later decades (Rowe, 2004a).

According to Jhally, in the ensuing second phase of the sports/media complex from 1940 onwards, advertising-dependent network television became so important that a fully-fledged, consolidated complex emerged of profound interdependency – or, more accurately perhaps, co-dependency:

> While before 1940 sports and the media had been able to maintain a formal separation, in that neither depended on the other for its continued existence, the coming of television fundamentally disturbed the relationship and ensured that sports could not survive without broadcast revenue. The discovery that Gillette made in 1939 as to the particular value of the sports audience lay at the root of the tremendous changes that the sports/media relationship would go through. (Jhally, 1984: 48)

Television–audience relations, of course, are not of a singular nature, and Jhally notes how, from the mid-1970s onwards, the emergence of subscription television (also including pay per view) and its different model of direct consumer purchase of the right to access media sport texts helped to reconfigure the complex. While he sees this arrangement as essentially hinging on the purchase of new media technologies, more significant, perhaps, is the re-instantiation, as noted above, of the stadium "turnstile," albeit in electronic form, as a new type of payment for entry to sports events was introduced (although one not free of the advertising that produced revenue streams under the regime of network television). Subscription and pay per view (mainly via cable and satellite) televised sport signals a significant shift away from seeing premium broadcast sports texts as public property available to the majority of the population (comfortably exceeding 90 percent by the 1970s) who had purchased what had become a standard item of consumer durable domestic technology. Instead, the trading of access to mediated live sport for exposure to often-intrusive advertising was perceived as not sufficient for the mediators of sport. At the same time, free-to-air television channels, limited in number by spectrum availability, became increasingly incapable of handling the volume of sport that could be televised. Thus, sport on television, especially in cases of uneven popularity, seasonal variations, and unpredictable program length, became a source of considerable uncertainty when placed in the context of the imperatives of television schedules in which viewing habits (for example, of watching the news) and episodic narrative flows (such as of drama series) presented obstacles to programming sport within the established "seasons" of television. Dedicated subscription sports channels, could, therefore, accommodate much more sport without interfering with other types of programming – although, perhaps, not without creating some discord about how much and what television should be watched in individual homes. The subsequent development of free-to-air multi-channeling, especially that precipitated by post-analogue digitization, made it possible to establish dedicated sports television channels on a free-to-air basis (Australian Government, 2009). This change has given new impetus to debates over "free" sport on television, especially that involving national representative teams, as a right of "cultural citizenship" (discussed more fully below).

Jhally's article setting out the creation of the sports/media complex was written in an era before the worldwide web and the internet had emerged as media and information technologies of unprecedented reach and variety, and before digitization had made possible the conversion of media texts of all kinds into so many mutable lines of code that could be made into other texts and placed on multiple platforms. It also, characteristically of both the era and its place of origin, revolved around the nation – or at least the continent – as the fulcrum of analysis. As the next section will demonstrate in greater detail, the ensuing almost three decades have strikingly reshaped the media sports cultural complex.

But it should also be noted that, despite his insistence on the need to understand the material-productive dimension of media sport (following the traditional Marxist precept that the economic basis determines the cultural/ideological superstructure), Jhally was at pains not to ignore the cultural/ideological uses and contexts of media sport. Thus, he argues that, in an industrialized, urbanized nation, the demography of which reflected the diversity that inevitably followed mass migration from across the world, US sports culture became a crucial articulation of what it meant to be *American* (1984: 52). Sport was able to construct, magically, a sense of community that was hard to produce in a nation in transition, and tended to do so by reconstructing a pastoral golden age of stable communities – the *gemeinschaft* of classical sociology – coming

together in communal rituals under circumstances of a *gesellschaft* of urban strangers. As others have proposed (e.g., Brohm, 1978; various contributors to Cantelon and Gruneau, 1982), sport symbolically created a "team ethic" at a point in industrial capitalism where workers were required to coordinate their labor in highly predictable ways, while also being urged to be alive to the possibilities of the individual pursuit of excellence and betterment. Sport, with its simultaneous emphasis on cooperation and collaboration, competition and aggression, could, through extended ideological dissemination via the media, promote capitalist hegemony that simultaneously enjoined the proletariat to be disciplined and realistic but also to aspire to join the bourgeoisie through the assertion of aggressive self interest. In this regard, it is also suggested that the culture of sport offered *tutelage* in the meaning and practice of (in this case American) modern masculinity and crucially, it might be proposed, of racialized inflections of masculinity (Carrington, 1998, 2010). The material/cultural relational issues raised by Jhally have, over the last three decades, remained central to critical analytical work on the subject of sport and media (see, e.g., Andrews, 2006; Whannel, 2009), despite the many changes that have occurred in the period and the new phenomena that urgently demand to be addressed. In the following section, I will address more recent developments in the media sports cultural complex, including those that have "de-centered" to some degree the dominance of the United States and also of television that preoccupied Jhally's first iteration of it.

Complex Today

In the discussion above I have briefly traced the emergence and maturation of the media sports cultural complex, although in looking closely at Jhally's early contribution it gave the context of the discussion a decided "US-centrism." This focus is to some extent justified by the power and influence of US media sport, both in terms of its pioneering of commercial network sport television, the international "weight" of its organizations and market (such as the domination of Olympic broadcasting for several decades by the major US company NBC), and the intercultural influence of US sport genres of visual representation and oral commentary. It was, though, noted above that a counterweight to US television sport hegemony has existed through the influential public broadcast system that was characteristic of Britain, Europe, and other territories (Chandler, 1988; Goldlust, 1987; Whannel, 1992). If this separation of broadcast systems and styles is conceived as a battle, it can be argued that, while there has been no ultimate victory on either side, it is the US television sport "tradition" that has had more influence on its opponent than the reverse, although it would be fallacious to ascribe an American monopoly over the association of capitalism and sport. As was discussed above, professional, commercial sport developed first in Britain and, despite the influence of the ideology and practice of amateurism, capitalism and industrialism have long been a feature of British sport. But while the British sport industry developed rapidly from the late nineteenth century onwards, and the British print media covering sport in considerable depth were unequivocally commercial in nature (except, perhaps, for the regular, detailed coverage of horse-racing for the mainly proletarian readers of the Communist Party daily newspaper the *Daily Worker* – later the *Morning Star*), radio and television were wedded to a strong public service broadcasting tradition that has persisted even after the BBC's monopoly was broken by the arrival of commercial television (ITV) in the 1950s and a range of commercial radio stations such as LBC and Capital Radio in the 1960s (Briggs, 1995; Curran and Seaton, 2003; Goodwin, 1998).

Although the BBC, which receives most of its funding from license fees (and some from merchandising, franchising, and other ancillary sales), has often been comprehensively outbid for principal broadcast rights by first free-to-air and then subscription television (notably, for example, by the Rupert Murdoch-controlled BSkyB for English Premier League football), it has been able to use this comparatively stable funding base to its advantage during times of economic recession. Thus, there is some irony in the aggressive criticism of the BBC by James Murdoch, former chairman and chief executive (Europe and Asia) of News Corporation (and son of the Corporation's chairman and chief executive officer, Rupert Murdoch) in *"The Absence of Trust,"* his 2009

MacTaggart Lecture at the Edinburgh International Television Festival.[4] Although, as befits diversified public and private corporations, the BBC's and Murdoch's concerns go far beyond the domain of broadcast sport, his lecture presents an almost classic exposition of the polar contending positions of a deregulated media sport market (leading potentially to monopoly) and a regulated one that mandates a major role for primarily state-funded (though not state-controlled) media organizations. Murdoch's lecture bears some close analysis as a kind of twenty-first-century media proprietor's "answer" to Jhally's 1980s academic critique. First, he is critical of state control and regulation of the news, sport, information, and entertainment media: "It is hardly a secret that the early years of British broadcasting were dominated by concern about the potential of the new technology for creating social disruption. To deal with that perceived threat, there were two responses: to nationalise broadcasting through the BBC, and to ensure that any other provider was closely controlled and appropriately incentivised" (Murdoch, 2009: Section IV).

State media regulation and national public broadcasting are here condemned by Murdoch, and not only because they are seen to operate as a fetter on industry development and to inhibit the capacity to service customers. They also have more sinister implications relating to political freedom, with George Orwell (ironically, given his socialist beliefs) invoked in a concluding celebration of the profit motive:

As Orwell foretold, to let the state enjoy a near-monopoly of information is to guarantee manipulation and distortion.

We must have a plurality of voices and they must be independent. Yet we have a system in which state-sponsored media – the BBC in particular – grow ever more dominant.

That process has to be reversed.

If we are to have that state sponsorship at all, then it is fundamental to the health of the creative industries, independent production, and professional journalism that it exists on a far, far smaller scale.

Above all we must have genuine independence in news media. Genuine independence is a rare thing. No amount of governance in the form of committees, regulators, trusts or advisory bodies is truly sufficient as a guarantor of independence. In fact, they curb speech.

On the contrary, independence is characterised by the absence of the apparatus of supervision and dependency.

Independence of faction, industrial or political.

Independence of subsidy, gift and patronage.

Independence is sustained by true accountability – the accountability owed to customers. People who buy the newspapers, open the application, decide to take out the television subscription – people who deliberately and willingly choose a service which they value. And people value honest, fearless, and above all independent news coverage that challenges the consensus.

There is an inescapable conclusion that we must reach if we are to have a better society.

The only reliable, durable, and perpetual guarantor of independence is profit. (Murdoch, 2009: Section V)

In this commercial advocacy it can be seen that the independent watchdog role of the news media (Allan, 2005) is connected with, for example, the possibility of sovereign consumers purchasing subscriptions to a range of channels – especially, it might be observed, those dedicated to sport. Notable in this context is Rupert Murdoch's famous declaration to News Corporation shareholders of the need to "use sports as a battering ram and a lead offering in all our pay television operations" (quoted in Millar, 1998: 3), and pronouncement that "sport absolutely overpowers film and everything else in the entertainment genre" (quoted in Eckersley and Benton, 2002: 20). It is safe to say, though, that the reference to "professional journalism" and "honest, fearless, and above all independent news coverage that challenges the consensus" does not refer to the field of sports journalism, and not only because there is disappointingly little critical, investigative sport journalism, in the Anglophone world at least (Boyle, 2006; Boyle, Rowe, and Whannel, 2010; Rowe, 2007). As in other areas involving the economic interests of News Corporation, its own journalism has been far from independent (Neil, 1996; McKnight, 2003; Page 2003). In the specific case of sport and media, examples such as News Corporation's determinedly uncritical coverage of its ultimately failed attempt in 1998 to take over the world-renowned Manchester United

Football Club (Rowe, 2000) has given little confidence that the "only reliable, durable, and perpetual guarantor of independence is profit." Indeed, there is substantial evidence to the contrary regarding News Corporation (Andrews, 2004; Horsman, 1997).

James Murdoch's professed faith in profit as the key to "a better society" was strikingly undermined when, in 2011, News Corporation (through its UK operation, News International) was engulfed in controversy following the exposure of the practices of its now-closed *News of the World* tabloid newspaper of telephone "hacking" (illegally accessing the message banks of citizens), "blagging" (seeking private personal information by deception), and payments to police for inside information. The scandal caused News Corporation to withdraw from its attempted full takeover of BSkyB, the impressive profitability of which (US$1.6 billion pre-tax in 2011) is largely attributable to its subscription sports programming (Guardian, 2011). It also precipitated the ignominious departure of James Murdoch from his senior roles at News International and BSkyB in early 2012.

The unreliability of such reliance on self-interest (a trait, of course, that is by no means exclusive to News Corporation, although it is probably more brazen and outspoken in advancing it than rival organizations such as Disney) is further revealed in the same speech by James Murdoch. Here the rejection of "near-monopoly" by the state is reversed in its embrace of a near (or even absolute) monopoly by a privately controlled corporation, especially in resisting intervention by a suprastate (European Union) regulator:

> To use an example I am familiar with, take the decision of the European Commission to require the broadcasting rights to Premier League football to be divided up so that no one company could buy all the rights. The consequences of that move were predictable enough: customers having to pay more for the same thing because they'd need two subscriptions. However, in defiance of common sense, the Commission apparently believed that prices would instead fall. (Murdoch, 2009: Section III)

Thus, the purchase of all broadcast rights to a major sports competition, and the requirement for all television viewers wishing to watch matches "live" either to pay directly a subscription to BSkyB (News Corporation) or to visit commercial premises such as pubs and clubs which pay the subscription on behalf of their customers (in the expectation of recouping their outlay through the sale of alcohol, food, and related products) is an approved monopoly produced out of economic rather than state-political power. The countering of this monopoly via cheaper foreign decoders has, unsurprisingly, led to court action (unsuccessful so far) by the English Premier League and BSkyB (Rowe, 2011: 53).

As Andrews (2009) has observed, sport is deeply implicated, but by no means unique, in the global extension of such logics of corporate "imperialism" under late capitalism that demand the rolling back of the state and the privileging of privatized consumption. A diversified, vertically integrated media company (involving film, broadcast, cable and satellite television, magazines, newspapers, books, and other media and communication activities) such as News Corporation, which in 2011 had a market value approaching US$50 billion (subsequently reduced on paper by 16 percent after the "phone hacking" scandal discussed earlier) and annual operating income of almost US$5 billion, operates across the globe, finding new markets in which to produce and circulate mediated sports texts (Rowe, 2011). US-based corporations such as News, Disney, and NBC Universal (owned by Comcast and General Electric) are the most global in reach, although Europe-based (e.g., Bertelsmann) and Asia-based (e.g., World Sport Group) corporations have substantial sport television markets. Few public broadcasters can command the capital of the major commercial media sport corporations who, as forcefully argued by James Murdoch in stereotypical terms, promote the figure of the sovereign citizen-consumer with almost limitless choice (providing that they have the means) supplied by efficient, market-led private capital, at the expense of the public citizen whose media services are rationed by a rigid, inefficient, and interfering state.

The lamented "absence of trust" for Murdoch is restored by faith in the profit motive, even under circumstances where it produces a monopoly or quasi-monopoly not only regarding a sports television service but also through the

horizontal and vertical integration that allows a single entity to own and control, say, a leading football club that is a party (irrespective of claimed guarantees of formal separation through organizational processes and structures known as "Chinese Walls") to the selling of its broadcast rights to its owner (Rowe, 2000). The "prices" described above are borne by the viewer, not the broadcaster – awarding of the rights for sport to a free-to-air broadcaster would, of course, not lead to an imposition of a charge. It is for this reason that the state in some countries (including most member states of the European Union) has intervened by means of so-called "anti-siphoning" regulations, which prevent "listed events" from being acquired exclusively by pay television operators. In Australia, for example, the Broadcasting Services Act requires the minister for broadband, communications, and the digital economy to "schedule" sporting events of "national importance and public significance" (such as the Olympic Games, cricket test matches, and finals in the major football codes) to ensure that they are available free to the public (Australian Government, 2009).

Such state intervention in the sport television market, though, raises questions about the extent to which public service broadcasting of commercially saleable content like sport is simply replicating and financially undermining that provided by the private sector. Sport, as argued earlier, has a popular national-cultural role that in some instances has been nurtured and safeguarded by the state (Scherer and Rowe, forthcoming). The proponents of public service broadcasting argue that to restrict its televisual content to "minority" interests – which would mean not showing the most popular sports events – would both marginalize it and attract accusations of elitism, while sport might also be seen to "pull the train into the station," meaning attracting viewers to public channels with other, more diverse and unusual content (Rowe, 2004c, 2004d). James Murdoch (2009: Section IV) argues that pay television first differentiated itself from the BBC and ITV ("When pay-television began in this country, it did so largely by providing programs in genres which public service broadcasting served inadequately: such as 24-hour news, and a broad choice of sport and the latest films") but that it is now more difficult to maintain that differentiation through content, format, and genre exclusivity.

It was, indeed, its successful bid for the new "unlisted" English Premier League competition in the early 1990s, now one of the world's most widely distributed and lucrative media sport properties (Horne, 2006), that is generally credited with the survival and profitability of BSkyB (Horsman, 1997; Dyke, 2004). The insistence of the European Commission over a decade later that the rights should be split into separate packages did have the effect of requiring the most ardent fans of a sport to subscribe to more than one broadcast service. The main beneficiary of this package splitting, the Ireland-based Setanta, could not, though, manage the cost during a recession and against the competitive power of BSkyB (Robinson and Holmwood, 2009; Sweney, 2009). Its Great Britain division (though not its operations in Ireland, North America, and Australia) went into administration in June 2009, and its broadcast rights were relinquished in that territory, in the case of the English Premier League subsequently being purchased by ESPN, the Disney-owned US sports network (BBC, 2009), which, however, sold its rights in early 2013 to BT, the major UK telecoms company.

The Setanta instance and, before it, that involving the Swiss-German consortium ISL and Kirch-Media, which purchased the broadcast rights to the 2002 and 2006 World Cups of association football from FIFA (the sport's world governing body) for €2.3 billion and subsequently collapsed, threatening broadcasts of the world's largest media sport event in several countries (Rowe, 2004c), demonstrates the high stakes and volatility of premium sports television, both subscription and free-to-air. The existence of a sport-media complex, and the interdependencies that it creates between parties including athletes, associations, clubs, fans, media corporations, telecommunications companies, sponsors, advertisers, suprastate bodies, and national governments, does not usher in an inevitable stability but creates the conditions for a series of alignments, alliances, and conflicts around the mutating culture of media sport. The special pleading by one interested party detailed above (News Corporation), whose chairman and chief executive officer, Rupert Murdoch, has frequently been voted "The Most

Powerful Man in Sport" in the annual list produced by *Sporting News*, cannot be easily reconciled with, for example, the mandate claimed by a publicly funded, national public broadcaster like the BBC.[5]

The high levels of public controversy evident when live domestic television access to key sports events moves from free-to-air to subscription television, or off screen altogether, bear directly on questions of the rights pertaining to "cultural citizenship" (Miller, 2007). Conceiving of citizenship in cultural as opposed to the more conventional political or economic terms has particular resonance regarding the media sports cultural complex (Scherer and Rowe, forthcoming). In this domain, there is constant pressure to turn the collective pleasures (non-compulsory, of course) of citizens into modes of consumption that of necessity detach those with lesser material-cultural resources from others. The idea of "sport for all," first proposed as the citizen's right to participate physically, and subsequently extended to that of the right to engage (if desired) freely in its festivals of mediated spectatorship and communal expression, is compromised when high consumerism infringes on the capacity of all citizens to feel suitably involved in significant rituals of popular sociality.

With regard to televised sport, for example, this concept refers to matters of access, equity, inclusion, and exclusion concerning a cultural facility and practice (and in the case of Britain in particular "pioneered" by a public organization) that has become an important part of the fabric of everyday life for a large sector of the population, and which is deeply implicated in notions of national-cultural identity and global cultural inclusion (Rowe, 2004d). Thus the economic, technological, and sometimes spatial barriers that sports pay television presents where the citizenry (or at least a sizable component of it) is accustomed to freely available sports coverage, has led to widespread insistence on such state-interventionist protections as anti-siphoning regimes, which mandate a preference for free-to-air television. An example of the impact of a switch from free-to-air to pay television is the 2009 Ashes cricket series viewership when compared with the earlier 2005 series. Even allowing for such variables as the superior playing standard of 2005 and, perhaps, the emotional atmosphere caused by the

July London tube and bus bombings, there was a very large difference in viewing numbers:

> The climax of England's 2–1 series win over Australia at the Oval in south London was watched by 1.92 million viewers on Sky Sports 1, a 14% share of the multichannel audience, between 5.45 pm and 6 pm.
>
> Nine hours of Ashes coverage on Sky Sports 1 averaged 856,000 viewers, 8% of the multichannel audience, between 10 am and 7 pm.
>
> It was also a good day for [free-to-air] Channel Five, whose highlights show, Cricket on Five, was watched by a record 2 million viewers, 10% of the audience, between 7.15 pm and 8 pm, the channel's highest-rating show of the night . . .
>
> . . . However, Sky's audience was inevitably a fraction of the peak of 7.4 million viewers who saw England's last Ashes triumph in 2005, which was available free-to-air on Channel 4.
>
> On the final afternoon of the 2005 Ashes, an average of 4.7 million viewers were watching Channel 4's live coverage between 1.15 pm and 7 pm. (Plunket, 2009)

Thus, the combined final session viewership of the live pay TV and delayed prime-time highlights free-to-air broadcasts in 2009 was well below that of both the average and, especially, the peak viewership on Channel 4 (an "up-market" free-to-air commercial broadcaster) in 2005. It is for reasons such as these that the New Zealand Labour government reviewed regulations concerning live coverage of sport on broadcast platforms in 2008 (although the succeeding National government decided not to act) and the UK and Australian governments did likewise in 2009 (resulting in some minor listing adjustments).[6]

Australia has the longest list of protected events of any country in the world, partly because of the political power and influence of its free-to-air television sector (especially under the late Kerry Packer) but also because of the centrality of sport to Australian culture (Australian Government, 2009; Cashman, 1995). What has precipitated the pressure for change[7] is not only the desire of pay television broadcasters to gain exclusive access to major sports and, indeed, the demand by sport rights sellers to maximize their returns. Two key developments have made the current regulations problematic: first, the arrival of digital television and the enhanced multi-channeling possibilities

for sport now technically available to free-to-air broadcasters, currently restricted as to which sports they can show on anything but their main channel. Second, the increasing availability of sport in non-traditional broadcast form, such as through the internet and mobile telephony (Hutchins and Rowe, 2009, 2012), and the installation in Australia of a fast national broadband network, means that current broadcast-centric legislation could be bypassed through acquisition of rights by new media platforms and other third parties, including those beyond its national jurisdiction. Here, the issue is not just one of the rights of national-cultural citizenship but also a questioning of the power of the nation itself to set the terms of media sport production, circulation, consumption, and use.

Conclusion: Future Complex

In the last decade, as would be expected in an era when the concept of globalization has moved from fringe academic disciplinary discourse to everyday popular speech, considerable attention has been given to the globalization of both sport and sports media (Bairner, 2001; Bernstein and Blain, 2003; Giulianotti and Robertson, 2007, 2009; Maguire, 1999, 2005; Miller et al., 2001). The global portability and, increasingly, mobility of media sport has been strongly connected to an Americanization process allied with media and cultural imperialism; it is equally implicated in the flow of athletes from the peripheral zones of the media sports cultural complex towards its core, just as media sport texts have moved in the other direction as part of a new international division of cultural labor that creates new, previously unexploited audiences (Miller et al., 2001; Miller, Rowe, and Lawrence, 2011). Although the flows and divisions across the complex are by no means proportionate, they are nonetheless multidirectional. For example, English Premier League football, the US National Basketball Association, and major league baseball are exported to the Asia-Pacific region, often focusing on the athletes from the region who have migrated to play in them and, in the process, frequently overshadowing local sports competitions. At the same time, though, the weight of Indian capital and its multitudinous audience for cricket is in the process of reshaping that sport, drawing it further towards the subcontinent as its economic, political, and administrative centre, and fostering the dominance of the short, spectacular Twenty20 form that derives its aesthetic inspiration from Bollywood rather than Hollywood (Rowe and Gilmour, 2008, 2009).

Yet, the mobility of media sport is not just a matter of transportation of athletes, texts, and techniques of representation and marketing. As the complex has developed, it has breached and redrawn once solid borders, such as those between sport and entertainment, sport and media, and sports workers and fans. As noted earlier, the relative stability of the sports television era of the last six decades is in flux, as internet protocol television (IPTV), internet video, and mobile sport telephony come into view (Hutchins and Rowe, 2012). The movement into the English Premier League rights market of the telecommunications company BT in 2012 is one notable sign of this reconfiguration of the media sport market. Thus, the economics of the media sports cultural complex and the patterns of practice across it are shifting as, for example, the mediated experience of major sports events like the Super Bowl and the FIFA World Cup can, simultaneously, involve broadcast television, mobile viewing, social networking, micro-blogging, and so on. Of particular significance is the BBC's coverage of the 2012 London Olympics, which involved 2,500 hours of live coverage of all games events across 24 digital television and online channels, much in high definition and some in 3D, accessible across multimedia platforms including tablets, mobile (cell) phones, and game consoles, and with a dedicated "app" as well as extensive integration with social media. This "red-button Olympics" pioneered by the world's premier public service media corporation provided a vivid portrait of a sport viewing world that has moved far beyond the mythological couch and the "box in the corner."

How and where media sport is experienced, and who controls it, is now the subject of considerable uncertainty and dispute between sports associations, clubs, athletes, broadcasters, telecommunications companies, sponsors, advertisers, fans, and (supra)national governments. Live broadcasts may be pirated; fans sued for infringing copyright for re-posting club web content; internet and TV news breach conventions on how

much broadcast and still-photographic action to show; athletes defy sports governing bodies' attempts to control blogging and tweeting; additional remuneration for image rights is demanded on multiple platforms, and so on (Hutchins and Rowe, 2009, 2012). Fantasy and video games can operate as collective simulations (often transnational) of the sport experience rather than remain reliant on the unique, "authentic" focus on the professional sports contest (see contributions to Leonard, 2009). There may even be activist-oriented innovations that combine the running of actual sport clubs with the fantasy sport game genre through the construction of web communities using techniques of "crowd sourcing" (Hutchins, Rowe, and Ruddock, 2009).

The key argument is that the media sports cultural complex is constantly subject to disturbance and rebalancing as it is called upon to perform disparate, often competing tasks. It must encourage group cohesion while simultaneously drawing energy from the promotion of division and distinction, and while highly profitable is expected to subjugate market values to those of a non-monetized citizenship. It is meant to privilege the cultural form of sport while engaging in and producing hybrid texts and practices that often make sport as conventionally conceived harder to recognize. Indeed, competitive 'reality' TV shows have taken on a simulated sport-like character. Media sport scholars are required to understand and analyze these rapid, thoroughgoing changes while retaining the sociohistorical sensibility that contextualizes them in terms of how they occurred, who benefited from and resisted them, and their implications beyond the limited preoccupations and well-rehearsed sentiments of interested parties.

It is necessary, therefore, to go way beyond Jhally's seminal formulation of the sports/media complex which, as discussed above, was limited to the US context (including American masculinity), and mainly concerned with network and cable television. Since then, the complex has mutated in ways that Jhally could barely have imagined, and has been used in a variety of ways, and with various conceptual and nominal adjustments, in many works (e.g., Carrington, 2011; Helland, 2007; Maguire, 1999; Phillips, Hutchins, and Stewart, 2005; Skogvang, 2009).

Having become accustomed to analyzing and often critiquing the relationship between sport and media, scholars must now understand the ramifications of the depth and complexity of their interpenetration. This transformation, it is suggested, means that future scholarship applied to the media sports cultural complex must come to terms with a networked digital media sport environment in which the constituent elements can no longer be self-evidently separated. Therefore, even the "forward slash" punctuation that separates "sports/media," as influentially proposed by Jhally, looks increasingly outmoded barely three decades later in the life of the complex.

Acknowledgments

The research on which this chapter is based arises from two Australian Research Council Discovery Projects: "Handling the 'battering ram': Rupert Murdoch, News Corporation and the global contest for dominance in sports television" (DP0556973) and (with Brett Hutchins, Monash University) "Struggling for possession: The control and use of online media sport" (DP0877777).

Notes

1 After two years as a newspaper and 15 as a journal, the *Insurgent Sociologist* was renamed *Critical Sociology* in 1987 in order to "mark its success and adulthood" (Levine, 2004: 1) in the wake of the first, youth-oriented flowering of radical sociology and during the second presidential term of the conservative Ronald Reagan. In relation to this *Companion*, it might be noted that the change also occurred during an intense period of mediated sport development in the United States in which the commercial possibilities of media (especially television), advertising, and sponsorship were fully embraced, as revealed by the statistic that "the three networks together showed 1,500 hours of sports in 1985, double what they programmed in 1960" (Baran, 1997), a level of programming that Baran judges to be excessive and resulting in a negative "effect on the supply-and-demand balance of the commercial spot market." The proliferation of media sport content (but not of academic journals) is discussed in greater detail later in the chapter.

2 Almost a decade later, Joseph Maguire (1993) amended the concept to that of the "media/sport production complex," stressing its industrialized nature. My preference for the adjective "cultural" is that it incorporates more effectively production, consumption, meaning, use, symbolization, ideology, contestation, and so on within a highly relational system that encompasses a range of instrumental and expressive elements.

3 Jhally was to revisit the subject periodically over the years, as is recorded in his collection of essays *The Spectacle of Accumulation: Essays in Culture, Media, and Politics* (2006).

4 James Murdoch's own appointment in 2003 as chief executive of BSkyB at the age of 30 was heavily criticized by some shareholders and commentators as nepotistic (Brand Republic, 2003), while News Corporation's 2004 relocation from Adelaide, Australia, to Delaware, United States, was also condemned on corporate governance grounds given that state's reputation for a looser approach to company regulation (Hobbs, 2007).

5 Highlights and delayed broadcast content is often sold on to other broadcasters. For example, the 2009 Ashes cricket series between England and Australia was shown for the first time exclusively live on Sky Sports in the United Kingdom, with a 45-minute highlights package presented in prime time on the free-to-air Channel Five (Gibson, 2009).

6 The weakening of the political influence of the free-to-air television sector in Australia after the 2005 death of Kerry Packer should be acknowledged, given the progressive withdrawal from the media through private equity sales by his heir, James Packer, whose interests lie mainly in the casino industry (although in 2010 he made a substantial investment in the Ten Network). On a wider basis, this is an exemplification of the *realpolitik* of media policymaking that occurs in all countries with a powerful private media sector (Curran, 2002).

7 This does not mean, of course, that contending parties do not cooperate for strategic reasons. Well-known instances of cooperation, and even of *rapprochement*, include the "truce" between the Murdoch and Packer companies in concluding the "Super League War" over TV rights to rugby league in Australia (Rowe, 2004a); the Premier Media Group joint venture of News Corporation and Consolidated Media Holdings that produces and broadcasts Fox Sports and Fox Sports News in

Australia; and successful joint bids by Setanta and ITV, and BSkyB and the BBC, for British association football rights (UK Competition Commission, 2007).

References

Allan, S. (ed.) (2005) *Journalism: Critical Issues*, Maidenhead, UK: Open University Press.

Andrews, D.L. (2004) "Speaking the 'universal language of entertainment': News Corporation, culture and the global sport media economy," in Rowe, D. (ed.) *Critical Readings: Sport, Culture and the Media*, Maidenhead, UK: Open University Press, pp. 99–128.

Andrews, D.L. (2006) *Sport, Commerce, Culture: Essays on Sport in Late-Capitalist America*, New York: Peter Lang.

Andrews, D.L. (2009) "Sport, culture and late capitalism," in Carrington, B. and McDonald, I. (eds.) *Marxism, Cultural Studies and Sport*, London: Routledge, pp. 213–231.

Australian Government (2009) "Sport on television: A review of the anti-siphoning scheme in the contemporary digital environment." Discussion paper, Department of Broadband, Communications and the Digital Economy, at http://www.archive.dbcde.gov.au/__data/assets/pdf_file/0010/118864/Sport_on_Television_Review_discussion_paper.pdf, accessed February 20, 2013.

Bairner, A. (2001) *Sport, Nationalism, and Globalization: European and North American Perspectives*, Albany: State University of New York Press.

Baran, S.J. (1997) "Sports and television," in Newcomb, H. (ed.) *Encyclopedia of Television* (1st edn.), Chicago: Fitzroy Dearborn, for Museum of Broadcast Communications.

BBC (2009) "Setanta goes into administration." *BBC News*, June 23, http://news.bbc.co.uk/2/hi/business/8115360.stm, accessed December 3, 2012.

Bernstein, A. and Blain, N. (eds.) (2003) *Sport, Media, Culture: Global and Local Dimensions*, London: Frank Cass.

Boyle, R. (2006) *Sports Journalism: Context and Issues*, London: Sage Publications.

Boyle, R. and Haynes, R. (2000) *Power Play: Sport, the Media & Popular Culture*, Harlow, UK: Pearson Education.

Boyle, R., Rowe, D., and Whannel, G. (2010) "'Delight in trivial controversy?' Questions for sports journalism," in Allan, S. (ed.) *Routledge Companion to News and Journalism Studies*, London: Routledge, pp. 245–255.

Brand Republic (2003) "James Murdoch's appointment sparks shareholder anger." *Brand Republic.com*, November 4, http://www.brandrepublic.com/News/194213/James-Murdochs-appointment-sparks-shareholder-anger/, accessed December 3, 2012.

Briggs, A. (1995) *History of Broadcasting in the United Kingdom*, vol. 5, *Competition*, Oxford: Oxford University Press.

Brohm, J.M. (1978) *Sport: A Prison of Measured Time*, London: Pluto Press.

Brookes, R. (2002) *Representing Sport*, London: Edward Arnold.

Cantelon, H. and Gruneau, R. (eds.) (1982) *Sport, Culture and the Modern State*, Toronto: University of Toronto Press.

Carrington, B. (1998) "Sport, masculinity and black cultural resistance." *Journal of Sport & Social Issues*, 22 (3): 275–298.

Carrington, B. (2010) *Race, Sport and Politics: The Sporting Black Diaspora*, London: Sage.

Carrington, B. (2011) "'What I said was racist – but I'm not a racist': Anti-racism and the white sports/media complex," in Long, J. and Spracklen, K. (eds.) *Sport and Challenges to Racism*, Basingstoke: Palgrave Macmillan, pp. 83–99.

Carrington, B. and McDonald, I. (eds.) (2001) "*Race*", *Sport and British Society*, London: Routledge.

Cashman, R. (1995) *Paradise of Sport: The Rise of Organised Sport in Australia*, Oxford: Oxford University Press.

Chandler, J.M. (1988) *Television and National Sport: The United States and Britain*, Urbana: University of Illinois Press.

Clarke, J. and Critcher, C. (1985) *The Devil Makes Work: Leisure in Capitalist Britain*, London: Macmillan.

Curran, J. (2002) *Media and Power*, London: Routledge.

Curran, J. and Seaton, J. (2003) *Power Without Responsibility: The Press and Broadcasting in Britain* (6th edn.), London: Routledge.

Dyke, G. (2004) *Inside Story*, London: HarperCollins.

Eckersley, O. and Benton, N. (2002) "The venue versus the lounge room." *Australasian Leisure Management*, 35: 20–23.

Elias, N. and Dunning, E. (1986) *Quest for Excitement: Sport and Leisure in the Civilising Process*, Oxford: Basil Blackwell.

Gibson, O. (2009) "Ashes series fuels contest for broadcasting rights." *Guardian*, July 6, http://www.

guardian.co.uk/media/2009/jul/06/ashes-test-cricket-broadcast-rights, accessed December 3, 2012.

Giulianotti, R. and Robertson, R. (eds.) (2007) *Globalization and Sport*, Oxford: Blackwell.

Giulianotti, R. and Robertson, R. (2009) *Globalization and Football*, London: Sage Publications.

Goldlust, J. (1987) *Playing for Keeps: Sport, the Media and Society*, Melbourne: Longman Cheshire.

Goodwin, P. (1998) *Television under the Tories: Broadcasting Policy 1979–1997*, London: British Film Institute.

Guardian (2011) *Phone Hacking: How the Guardian Broke the Story*, London: Guardian Books.

Guttmann, A. (1978) *From Ritual to Record: The Nature of Modern Sports*, New York: Columbia University Press.

Guttmann, A. (1994) *Games and Empires: Modern Sports and Cultural Imperialism*, New York: Columbia University Press.

Hargreaves, Jennifer (1994) *Sporting Females: Critical Issues in the History and Sociology of Women's Sports*, London: Routledge.

Hargreaves, John (1986) *Sport, Power and Culture: A Social and Historical Analysis of Popular Sports in Britain*, Cambridge: Polity Press.

Helland, K. (2007) "Changing sports, changing media: Mass appeal, the sports/media complex and TV sports rights." *Nordicom Review*, 28 (Jubilee issue): 105–119.

Hobbs, M. (2007) "'More paper than physical': The reincorporation of News Corporation and its representation in the Australian press." *Journal of Sociology*, 43 (3): 263–283.

Horne, J. (2006) *Sport in Consumer Culture*, Basingstoke: Palgrave Macmillan.

Horsman, M. (1997) *Sky High: The Inside Story of BSkyB*, London: Orion Books.

Hutchins, B. and Rowe, D. (2009) "From broadcast rationing to digital plenitude: The changing dynamics of the media sport content economy." *Television & New Media*, 10 (4): 354–370.

Hutchins, B. and Rowe, D. (2012) *Sport Beyond Television: The Internet, Digital Media and the Rise of Networked Media Sport*, New York: Routledge.

Hutchins, B., Rowe, D., and Ruddock, A. (2009) "'It's fantasy football made real': Networked media sport, the internet, and the hybrid reality of MyFootballClub." *Sociology of Sport Journal*, 26 (1): 89–106.

Jhally, S. (1984) "The spectacle of accumulation: Material and cultural factors in the evolution of the sports/media complex." *Insurgent Sociologist*, 12 (3): 41–57.

Jhally, S. (2006) *The Spectacle of Accumulation: Essays in Culture, Media, and Politics*, New York: Peter Lang.

Johnson, O. (1971) *Super Spectator and the Electric Lilliputians*, Boston: Little, Brown.

Kuhn, T.S. (1996) *The Structure of Scientific Revolutions*, Chicago: University of Chicago Press.

Leonard, D.J. (ed.) (2009) "New media and global sporting cultures." *Sociology of Sport Journal*, 26 (1), special issue.

Levine, R.F. (ed.) (2004) *Enriching the Sociological Imagination: How Radical Sociology Changed the Discipline*, Boston, MA: Brill.

Lynch, R. (1990) "Working class luck and vocabularies of hope among regular poker-machine players," in Rowe, D. and Lawrence, G. (eds.) *Sport and Leisure: Trends in Australian Popular Culture*, Sydney: Harcourt Brace Jovanovich, pp. 189–208.

MacClancy, J. (1996) *Sport, Identity and Ethnicity*, Oxford: Berg.

Maguire, J. (1993) "Globalization, sport development, and the media/sport production complex." *Sport Science Review*, 2 (1): 29–47.

Maguire, J. (1999) *Global Sport: Identities, Societies, Civilizations*, Cambridge: Polity Press.

Maguire, J. (2005) *Power and Global Sport: Zones of Prestige, Emulation and Resistance*, London: Routledge.

Mason, T. (1989) *Sport in Britain: A Social History*, Cambridge: Cambridge University Press.

McChesney, R.W. (1989) "Media made sport: A history of sports coverage in the United States," in Wenner, L.A. (ed.) *Media, Sports & Society*, Newbury Park, CA: Sage Publications, pp. 49–69.

McKnight, D. (2003) "'A world hungry for a new philosophy': Rupert Murdoch and the rise of neo-liberalism." *Journalism Studies*, 4 (3): 347–358.

Millar, S. (1998) "Courtship ends as soccer and TV are united." *MediaGuardian*, September 7: 3.

Miller, T. (2001) *Sportsex*, Philadelphia, PA: Temple University Press.

Miller, T. (2007) *Cultural Citizenship: Cosmopolitanism, Consumerism and Television in a Neoliberal Age*, Philadelphia, PA: Temple University Press.

Miller, T., Lawrence, G., McKay, J., and Rowe, D. (2001) *Globalization and Sport: Playing the World*, London: Sage Publications.

Miller, T., Rowe, D., and Lawrence, G. (2011) "The new international division of cultural labour and sport," in Falcous, M. and Maguire, J. (eds.) *Sport and Migration: Borders, Boundaries and Crossings*, London: Routledge, pp. 217–229.

Murdoch, J. (2009) "*The absence of trust*." MacTaggart lecture, Edinburgh International Television Festival, August 28, http://www.newscorp.com/news/news_426.html, accessed December 3, 2012.

Neil, A. (1996) *Full Disclosure*, London: Macmillan.

Page, B. (2003) *The Murdoch Archipelago*, London: Simon & Schuster.

Phillips, M., Hutchins, B., and Stewart, B. (2005) "The media sport cultural complex: Football and fan resistance in Australia," in Nauright, J. and Schimmel, K.S. (eds.) *Political Economy of Sport*, Basingstoke: Palgrave Macmillan, pp. 85–103.

Plunket, J. (2009) "TV ratings: 2m Sky viewers see England clinch the Ashes." *Guardian*, August 24, http://www.guardian.co.uk/media/2009/aug/24/ ashes-cricket-tv-ratings, accessed December 3, 2012.

Robinson, J. and Holmwood, L. (2009) "Setanta goes off air with loss of more than 200 jobs." *Guardian*, June 23, http://www.guardian.co.uk/media/2009/ jun/23/setanta-goes-into-administration, accessed December 3, 2012.

Roche, M. (2000) *Mega-Events and Modernity: Olympics and Expos in the Growth of Global Culture*, London: Routledge.

Rowe, D. (2000) "No gain, no game? Media and sport," in Curran, J. and Gurevitch, M. (eds.) *Mass Media and Society* (3rd edn.), London: Edward Arnold, pp. 346–361.

Rowe, D. (2004a) *Sport, Culture and the Media: The Unruly Trinity* (2nd edn.), Maidenhead, UK: Open University Press.

Rowe, D. (2004b) "Introduction: Mapping the media sports cultural complex," in Rowe, D. (ed.) *Critical Readings: Sport, Culture and the Media*, Maidenhead, UK: Open University Press, pp. 1–22.

Rowe, D. (2004c) "Watching brief: Cultural citizenship and viewing rights," in McArdle, D. and Giulianotti, R. (eds.) *Sport, Civil Liberties and Human Rights*, London: Routledge, pp. 93–110.

Rowe, D. (2004d) "Fulfilling the cultural mission: Popular genre and public remit." *European Journal of Cultural Studies*, 7 (3): 381–399.

Rowe, D. (2007) "Sports journalism: Still the 'toy department' of the news media?" *Journalism*, 8 (4): 385–405.

Rowe, D. (2011) *Global Media Sport: Flows, Forms and Futures*, London: Bloomsbury Academic.

Rowe, D. and Gilmour, C. (2008) "Contemporary media sport: De- or re-Westernization?" *International Journal of Sport Communication*, 1 (2): 177–194.

Rowe, D. and Gilmour, C. (2009) "Global sport: Where Wembley Way meets Bollywood Boulevard." *Continuum*, 23 (2): 171–182.

Scherer, J. and Rowe, D. (eds) (forthcoming) *Sport, Public Broadcasting, and Cultural Citizenship: Signal Lost?* New York: Routledge.

Scherer, J. and Whitson, D. (2009) "Public broadcasting, sport, and cultural citizenship: The future of sport on the Canadian Broadcasting Corporation?" *International Review for the Sociology of Sport*, 44 (2/3): 213–229.

Skogvang, B.E. (2009) "The sport/media complex in Norwegian football." *Soccer & Society*, 10 (3/4): 438–458.

Sweney, M. (2009) "BSkyB wins Premier League TV rights package back from Setanta." *Guardian*, February 6, http://www.guardian.co.uk/media/2009/ feb/06/sportsrights-bskyb, accessed December 3, 2012.

Tomlinson, A. and Young, C. (eds.) (2006) *National Identity and Global Sports Events: Culture, Politics, and Spectacle in the Olympics and the Football World Cup*, Albany: State University of New York Press.

UK Competition Commission (2007) "Summary of hearing with the FA Premier League on 27 June 2007," http://www.competition-commission.org. uk/inquiries/ref2007/itv/pdf/hearing_summary_ fa_premier_league.pdf, accessed December 3, 2012.

Wenner, L.A. (ed.) (1998) *MediaSport*, London: Routledge.

Whannel, G. (1992) *Fields in Vision: Television Sport and Cultural Transformation*, London: Routledge.

Whannel, G. (2009) "Between culture and economy: Understanding the politics of media sport," in Carrington, B. and McDonald, I. (eds.) *"Race", Sport and British Society*, London: Routledge, pp. 68–87.

Further Reading

Billings, A. (ed.) (2011) *Sports Media: Transformation, Integration, Consumption*, New York: Routledge.

Rowe, D. (2004) *Sport, Culture and the Media: The Unruly Trinity* (2nd edn.), Maidenhead, UK: Open University Press.

Rowe, D. (2011) *Global Media Sport: Flows, Forms and Futures*, London: Bloomsbury Academic.

Wenner, L.A. (ed.) (1998) *MediaSport*, London: Routledge.

Whannel, G. (1992) *Fields in Vision: Television Sport and Cultural Transformation*, London: Routledge.

4

Political Theories of Social Class, Sport, and the Body

Joshua I. Newman and Mark Falcous

Introduction

Sporting activities have long been connected to what social theorists and economists refer to as the "dominant modes of production." In other words, *how we play* has often been influenced by, as well as influential of, a society's industry. From the fields of the agrarian feudal age to the factories that came to define modern capitalism, sporting practices as vastly different as hunting and running or American football and mixed martial arts have emerged from, and often reinforce, the dominant political and economic order. As such, *varieties of play* have often been codified in rhythm with the *systems of work*.

As historians such as Allen Guttmann (1978) have illustrated, in the modern industrial period (*c.*1750–1950) sporting activities were inextricably bound to the logics and systems of factory life. For "modern sport," or those sports cultures developed during the industrial revolution, power relations largely materialized in the form of social class hierarchies established under the sway of industrial capitalism. Specifically, modern industry was characterized by the bourgeois class – those who owned the means of production, the factories, and the machines – expanding their influence and wealth through

the labor of the farming and factory-working masses. Relatedly, many controlling elites of the industrial era shaped and gave patronage to sport not only to further their operational interests and status but also as a means to produce *productive bodies*.

Our focus in this chapter is on the relationship between sport, the dominant modes of production, and how the body, when placed within sporting contexts, (re)produces modern capitalism's social class hierarchies. Looking back, Andrews (2009), drawing up the work of Kellner (2003), notes, "it was only a matter of time before sport (and particularly mass spectator sport) was intensively, and seemingly irreversibly, industrialized, such that it 'emerged as the correlative to a society that is replacing manual labor with automation and machines, and requires consumption and appropriation of spectacles to reproduce consumer society'" (p. 217). In turn, particular sport forms materialized as key features of modern life. These emerging modern sport forms were characterized by: competitive structures, records, and quantification, proliferated market-based values, productive cooperation, an emphasis on training and specialized uses of the productive body, a quest for quantifiable outcomes, rituals of consent, and the principles of

A Companion to Sport, First Edition. Edited by David L. Andrews and Ben Carrington.
© 2013 Blackwell Publishing Ltd. Published 2013 by Blackwell Publishing Ltd.

maximum output (Brohm, 1978; Guttmann, 1978; Loy, 1969).

We learned about modern society through sport; learned how to fit inside its logics and systems of production; learned our place within it. Rob Beamish (1982) reminds us that "sport as a cultural process has two moments to it. The first is directly tied to the concrete labour of the athlete *per se* and the second is the relation of that concrete activity to the context in which it occurs" (p. 172). Put differently, through sport the participating athlete was made into a commercial actor (i.e., a commodity that could be sold or a laborer earning a wage) and at the same time, by *acting within sport* (as consumer, athlete, coach, etc.), the individual was connected to broader commercial forces and capitalistic ideas.

Here we outline how scholars have conceptualized tensions arising from the relations of industrial capitalism, the body, and sport; with a specific focus on power, the sporting body, and social class politics. We look to work that problematizes the mutually influential relationship shared by *the body at play* and *the conditions of social production*. In so doing, we look beyond the vast body of popular thinking on sport that amounts to little more than blithe celebration, whereby sport is "treated as a separate, quasi-sacred realm where values, difficult if not impossible to realise in the normal course of existence, are indeed capable of realisation" (Hargreaves, 1982: 32). Instead, here we emphasize those contributions that have illuminated sport's potential to *reproduce* or *challenge* the dominant modes of production and the associated social class hierarchies. In so doing, we trace the work of critical scholars whose writing has excavated various sports' social class politics. These include, but are not limited to: the assorted codes of football (Andrews, 1999; Andrews *et al.*, 1997; Critcher, 1971, 1974; Giulianotti and Armstrong, 1995; Holt, 1985, 1988; Hughson, 2000; King, 1999; Robson, 2000; Swanson, 2009), rugby (A. Light, 1990; R. Light, 1999, 2001), athletics and Olympic sport (Foote, 2003), basketball (Frey, 1994; Wilson and Sparks, 1996), boxing (Bourdieu and Wacquant, 1999; Sugden, 1987; Wacquant, 1995, 2004), "extreme sports" and emergent sport cultures (Abbas, 2004; Cotter, 2003; Kay and Laberge, 2002; Kusz, 2004), school sports (Armstrong, 1984; Evans, 1986, 1990; Kirk, 1986, 1997; White

and Vagi, 1990; Wright, 1997), cricket (Harriss, 1986, 1990; James, 1963), and auto racing (Howell, 1997; Newman, 2007; Thompson, 2006).

We make the case that when it comes to issues of social class and sport, the material and the conceptual are *always* contested (and contestable), political (and politicized), and incomplete. In this brief review of these developments, we revisit the formalization of a *sociology of sport* discipline and the place of class politics within its analyses. As noted above, there is a sizable body of research devoted to social class politics as mobilized and contested across various sporting contexts which is not easily reducible to a simplistic chronological, ordered sequencing. Mindful of this, we seek to highlight those influential concepts and political movements that have shaped the critical interpretation of culture, sport, and social class.

Sport, Industrial Capitalism, and Revolution

In their formative years, both sport culture and factory life were often symbiotically intertwined; each an increasingly significant feature of the fabric of everyday modern life (Jones, 1982). The intensified intra-national flow of people and culture into industrializing urban centers in the late nineteenth and early to mid-twentieth centuries in particular led to both sport's industrial *necessity* and industrial *cooptation* under the conditions of modernity. In terms of necessity, society's dominant groups found in sport the ability to assert class distinctions (access to sporting grounds, elite clubs, expensive equipment, status, etc.), to congregate bodies for collegial, cathartic social activity, training for optimal physical performance (on the field, in the factory), and to generate consent for the broader capitalist system (competition, performance, etc.). In terms of cooptation, sport was often used to consolidate the foundations of modern industrial life. To play sport often meant to concede the dominant order of things; whereby the individual was disciplined to be socially subordinated, "appropriately" gendered, physically productive, and innately competitive.

In this way, the early foundations of modern sport were often seen by both pragmatists and theorist alike to be *(re)productive* of capitalism's social strata; and the sports field became an important space for expanding the social and material conditions of capitalist production. Indeed, changes in sport culture often supported this thesis. Much as for factory workers, athletes' roles became more specialized; sporting activities became more professionalized (amateur athletes became paid laborers, owners sought to maximize profits by selling their sporting commodities, etc.); styles of play became more standardized; and sporting achievement became more quantified and rationalized. As industrial capitalism grew, new social class divisions materialized, and sport's role in defining and reinforcing capitalism and class increased. Exclusive sport clubs were formed, many sporting spaces (e.g., tennis courts, golf courses, polo grounds, etc.) were restricted to members of the social elite, and sport-based performances on the field or in the park became meaningful expressions of capital-based wealth.

The ideology of amateurism spreading from Victorian England was a powerful mechanism in this regard. Specifically, it provided tightly regulated rules and social expectations designed to maintain sports as exclusive sites for the elite classes, and specifically "gentlemen." Such amateur codes were important in promoting the myth of sport as sacrosanct and untarnished by commercial exchange. Amateur codes also posited sport as distinct from broader social relations.

An early critique of sport's entanglement with the creation and entrenchment of capitalistic class status hierarchies was put forward by Thorstein Veblen (1994) in *The Theory of the Leisure Class*, first published in 1899. Veblen explored the consequences and workings of capitalism in the United States during the late nineteenth century, a period which saw the transformation from a rural, agricultural economy to an urban, industrial one. Veblen was influenced by German sociologist Max Weber's thinking which suggested that status and power could be derived from sources beyond the economy alone. For Weber, wielding economic power *was* significant, but was connected to status that was garnered and displayed in other forms.

Veblen was interested in how social hierarchy was tied to capitalism, but specifically in how ruling elites *actively* used non-working lifestyle choices and physical activities as a means of distinguishing themselves from other groups. In his analysis, Veblen posited that "wealth or power must be put in evidence, for esteem is awarded only on evidence" (1994: 42). That is, status must be actively demonstrated to become tangible. A life of leisure and conspicuous displays of "high" cultural tastes, Veblen argued, were sources of exclusivity and thus generated status which could be demonstrated in valuing particular forms of art, dress/fashion, literature, and physical pastimes (including sports). Leisure activities were then a key means for elite groups to make conspicuous demonstrations that entrenched their privilege and high status. "Addiction to athletic sports, not only in the way of direct participation, but also in the way of sentiment and moral support," Veblen suggested, "is . . . a characteristic of the leisure class" (1994: 271). Thus, Veblen identified a "leisure class" whose promotion and participation in the likes of hunting, angling, and "athletic games" were key means of asserting status.

Ultimately, Veblen's analysis represented a stinging attack on the self-aggrandizing practices of the rich and powerful. He was critical of upper-class sporting devotees, suggesting their "addiction" to sports marked "an arrested development of man's moral nature" (1994: 256). For what he termed the industrial (working) classes, sport, in contrast to the leisure classes "was merely an occasional diversion" (p. 272). Ultimately, Veblen, drawing upon Weber's (and to a lesser extent Karl Marx's) critique of capitalism, theorized that the ruling class used practices and spaces of play to reinforce their status within emerging industrial societies. Veblen's theorizing of leisure, play, and the use of the body as a site of "conspicuous consumption" was an early forerunner to later analyses of the uses of sport in relation to broader industrializing processes.

Veblen's critique of conspicuous consumption and the leisure class came at a time when modern industrial societies were experiencing a previously unforeseen acceleration of commodity production, urbanization, the scientific management of work, and rationalization of everyday life. During that period, sport was simultaneously undergoing international diffusion and codification through, for example, the establishment of governing bodies like the Football Association in

England in 1863 and the United States National Lawn Tennis Association in 1881, James Naismith's invention of basketball in 1891, and the Royal and Ancient's "Rules of Golf" in 1897. The establishment of rules and codes (e.g., amateurism) policed by these governing organizations served two important functions with relation to social class. First, formalized rules standardized sport. Regional idiosyncrasies were eliminated and athletes' participation was regulated and homogenized. Training regimes were put in place which limited what the athletic body was allowed to do on the sports field. Second, these new rules created new forms of spatial regulation, clearly defining who could play, where and when they could play, and who would grant access to the games. In short, sport, like industry, was becoming increasingly rationalized throughout the latter part of the nineteenth century, and this process of bureaucratization and codification encompassed the entrenchment of social class hierarchy and division in the development of modern sport.

In this broader context, Veblen was joined by European scholars who turned their attention toward a better understanding not only of how sport – largely seen by academics as operating outside of the "serious matters" of commerce, industry, and politics – contributed to the rise of industrial capitalism and its social class politics but also of how sport could be used to challenge the dominant order. Basing their ideas and politics within earlier working-class sports movements – and particularly those that can be traced back to the establishment of sports clubs (*Turnvereine*) in 1850s Germany – these public intellectuals sought to organize workers' sporting practices in ways that both symbolically and physically challenged the modern formations of aristocracy, monarchy, and eventually capital-based hierarchy (Rigauer, 2000).

As counter-capitalist revolutionary thinking and action began to spread across much of the developed world, in many nations sport emerged as a site for *confronting* the dominant capitalist order of social and economic life. In this tradition, supporters of sport and critics of capitalism around the world established worker sport movements: in Britain (e.g., the British Sports Workers Federation), in France (e.g., the French workers' sports movements and "play for all" initiatives),

and in the United States (e.g., the "proletarianization" of baseball and the establishment of the player-owned Union Association and Players League) (Wheeler, 1978). In Central Europe, a number of self-described Marxist "sport sociologists" began to outline a new sporting order in line with broader workers' movements. Two German luminaries in particular, Steinitzer through his *Sport and Culture* (1910) and Risse through his *Sociology of Sport* (1921), outlined Marxist-driven analyses on sport as an emancipatory feature of worker's cultural lives. Risse, for instance, situated physical activity and sport as antithetical to the designs of industrial capitalism, writing "Only in the realm of physical culture [i.e., sports] can the mechanized man of today express his will [to be an individual]" (Risse, in Guttmann, 1988: 25).

These texts, as well as several doctrines emanating from progressive hygienists and physical culture scholars in newly formed Communist states in Eastern Europe laid the foundations for the role sport would play in these Eastern bloc nation states. This counter-capitalist sport and physical culture movement was most evidently put into action in the Soviet Union, where sport became part of the workers' revolution in which "forms of artistic, literary and social life would dramatize the workers' state" (Cantelon, 1988: 78). A group of Russian intellectuals, directed by the early revolutionary feminist-hygienist Vera Mikhailovna Bonch-Bruevich and Marxist hygienist Nicholai Bogdanov, formed the Education/ Hygiene Department, which later became the Proletkul'tists movement (Cantelon, 1982). As the Proletkul'tists gained more influence in Vladimir Lenin's Soviet government, they established and codified a state-run workers' initiative that "emphasized personal hygiene, natural movement in the environment, specialized motor skills necessary in industry and some 'approved' sports like track and field, swimming and rowing in which the competitor competed himself and against the clock only" (Cantelon, 1982: 239).

While most critics of Marxism have argued that Marx's theory supposes that the economy determines social and cultural life, and thus social and cultural activities are subordinated to commercial ones, in early Soviet sport the Proletkul'tists popularized programs that corresponded with a newly democratized "Soviet way of life." In the years following the Revolution of 1918, the Proletkul'tists came to hold great influence over the role that sport played in the Soviet Union as well as throughout much of Eastern Europe both in resisting the industrializing processes of modern capitalism and in redefining the body's role on the field as well as in the factory. Similar programs were developed in Romania, Yugoslavia, Czechoslovakia, Hungary, Bulgaria, Poland, and East Germany.

Sport and Social Class: A Critical Sociology

By the time the Cold War had reached its late twentieth-century highpoint, two divergent sporting paradigms had come to define the international sporting landscape. On one side, sport was being used to discipline young athletic bodies along the practices and ethics of capitalism, naturalizing class division in the name of modernization. On the other, sport was being used to challenge – often through spectacularly totalitarian techniques – the seemingly iniquitous hierarchies created by capital.

As twentieth-century industrial societies from East to West and across various political divides morphed and became ever more interconnected, the sport cultures within those societies were variously affirmed, contested, and transformed. In turn, a new academic field of study, a sociology of sport, emerged in response to a growing awareness of the significance of sport as a cultural component. As this new field grew, scholars adopted new paradigms to conceptualize the social influence of sport. As the field evolved, so too did the philosophical foundations upon which such a critical study of sport could be grounded. In what follows, we chart the key, often competing, schools of thought that dominated the analysis of sport and social class during the Cold War Era and beyond.

Structural functionalism

In the United States of America, the political and paradigmatic tenets of structural functionalism – which effectively dominated the social sciences during the 1960s and 1970s – emerged most prominently to address issues of social class in the

sociology of sport's formative years. Loy and Booth (2000), in a review of this early work, note that political conservatism and positivist methodologies were key unifying hallmarks of early approaches to conceptualizing sport and social class. Loy and Kenyon's edited collection *Sport, Culture, and Society* was emblematic of such early work, posited by the editors as a "representative sample of contemporary work" (1969: v). Although there are variations, the approach was largely premised upon exploring the "function" of sport in relation to the maintenance of stability and social order, with elements of symbolic interactionist influences (in theory and method) in studies of particular sporting subcultures. Specifically, sport was viewed as one component of a larger social system and could be evaluated in terms of its role in, for example, effectively socializing youth into particular values, or the extent to which play and games were integrated with other aspects of living such as religion, government, and education. Social class under this approach was largely conceptualized under the term "social stratification," with individuals occupying differing positions and being differentially rewarded according to societal need, and their own "suitability."

As an example, Günther Lüschen's (1969) work, drawing upon quantitative techniques, explored social stratification and social mobility among German youth and, most fundamentally, revealed sports preferences and social class as closely related. Lüschen concluded sports and clubs were "providing important support in [young athletes'] mobility efforts" (p. 276); rendering sport as "primarily characterized by its functioning for the security and advancement of social life" (p. 276). Under this paradigm, sport was envisioned as a site of social (class) mobility and societal equilibrium. That is, as an institution that could effectively distribute rewards and status, and thus help maintain broader societal patterns.

In her oft-cited exemplar of a functionalist approach to sport, Janet Lever's (1983) *Soccer Madness* – a longitudinal case study of Brazilian soccer[1] – was similarly framed in terms of sport's capacity to generate consensus. Lever describes how football was a unique space for the construction of class consciousness, seemingly divorced from other social, political, and economic realms of Brazilian society. Common to this paradigm, sport is conceptualized in Lever's work as an institution distinct from society.[2] Whilst sport is acknowledged as a site that reinforces societal class differences, it is posited as the perfect social domain to overcome such divisions (class-based and otherwise). In this formulation, the "paradox of sport" for Lever is its ability both to symbolize division and also to "integrate through conflict" at the community, metropolitan, national, and world level. Thus, for Lever (1983: 12), "in communities where people are usually divided by . . . relative social power . . . sport can serve to dramatize the strain between these factions, but it can also elicit a temporary truce while all parties are reminded of their commonality." Like most structural functionalist approaches to sport and social class, in Lever's work the capacity of sports to create and reflect social division, then, is subsumed in the analysis to its ultimately unifying function.

Figurationalism

Simultaneous to the conservative theorizations emerging in North America, figurational approaches to sport were being formulated in England. Eric Dunning's work on (con)figurations of interdependence and "processuality" and Norbert Elias' theory of "the civilizing process" emerged as key themes of analysis. Elias' (2000) concept of "figuration" sought to emphasize the interaction between individuals and broader societal structures in contrast to the structure-focused functionalist tradition. The "civilizing process" meanwhile was Elias' metaphor for the long-term historical emergence of constraints on certain types of behavior (particularly sexual norms and violent acts) emanating from the elite classes. Dunning's oft-cited study with Ken Sheard, *Barbarians, Gentlemen and Players* (1979), offered an early exemplar that problematized, in part, the sport–social class connection by exploring the historical emergence of rugby football in Britain. Their study identified that the development of modern rugby football and the subsequent split into two codes was interwoven with the class dynamics of late Victorian England.

Critics subsequently contested the explanatory power of Elias' paradigm and the usefulness of the civilizing process in the context of that early study continues to attract criticism. Scholars such as Collins (2005) have highlighted weaknesses in figurational sociology's understanding of sport's historical development with regard to "civilizing" patterns emerging only from social elites. Ultimately, the figurational school's appeal beyond England (and with some European scholars) remained limited, and was particularly absent in North America, where approaches with clearer political mandates later emerged as central to the study of sport.

Neo-Marxism

Around the same time that structural functionalist and figurationalists were developing their analyses of sport and social class, several European scholars[3] were forging new leftist approaches to the politics of sport and social class. Critiques such as Bero Rigauer's (1969) *Sport and Work* and Jean Marie Brohm's (1978) collection of politically charged essays written between 1964 and 1978, *Sport: A Prison of Measured Time*, captured not only the fervor of the late 1960s/early 1970s countercultural movements (e.g., the student and worker protests in Paris in May, 1968) but also the growing disquiet toward sport as a site of capitalist accumulation and exploitation. Working within a Marxist-inspired frame, these activist-authors resumed the project of their Eastern European counterparts from a generation prior and viewed modern sport as fundamentally productive of the conflicts and dialogues of opposing politico-economic forces and positions to which class division was inherent.[4] For Brohm (1978: 47), "bourgeois sport is a class institution, totally integrated into the framework of capitalist relations and class relations." In this analysis, sport promoted economic exploitation and capitalist expansion; extended imperialist agendas; was repressive and alienating for athletes; and became entangled within oppressive state apparatus.

Sport, Brohm asserted (1978: 50), "conditions people for the oppressive work of the factory." Vinnai (1970) similarly argued that much like the modern factory, the sporting field, with its increasingly regimented and regulated divisions of labor, forced the sports worker to learn and execute structured movements repetitiously rather than freely or without constraint. Historian Allen Guttmann (1988) offered a more succinct appraisal: "in the illusory belief that he is free, the athlete locks the door to his cell" (p. 183). Such scrutiny emphasized the capacity of sport to create and entrench social class division and inequality and vigorously challenged the conservative tenets of functionalism. More importantly, these scholars (particularly Brohm) took their revolutionary ideas into the streets. For example, Brohm organized teachers' unions to call for World Cup boycotts and Olympic protests, wrote in popular media about the oppressive nature of high-performance sport, and lectured on the exploitative potential of unfettered commercialized sport.

Jockraker activism

The rise of these Marxist-inspired critiques from European scholars coincided with several popular (and some quasi-academic) counter-cultural North American interventions such as Harry Edwards' (1969) *The Revolt of the Black Athlete*, Jack Scott's (1971) *The Athletic Revolution*, and Paul Hoch's (1972) *Rip off the Big Game*.[5] This blend of populist writing and neo-Marxist critique of sport came to be known as "jockraking." The centrality of class struggle for these works was clear in Hoch's assertion that "sports partake of all the main contradictions of society, including the most fundamental one – the struggle between those who have power and those who don't, between capital and labor" (1972: 8). He continues, "our quarrel is not with sports, but with the uses some of the most repressive forces in capitalist society would force them to serve" (p. 8).

Interestingly, Jack Scott, writing a brief introduction to Hoch's book, neatly reveals the tensions between the left-wing critical analysis and what was the dominant, institutionalized approach to conceptualizing sport in the United States at that moment. In a revealing attack, and clearly railing against the functionalist tradition, Scott lambasts "sports sociologist-physical educator[s]" on the basis of "nonsensical and spurious" conceptualizations "alleging that sports participation prevents juvenile delinquency or helps social mobility" (in Hoch, 1972: xvi). Janet Lever, noted above, in turn fired a counter-salvo at the Marxist-informed critique in the final few paragraphs of *Soccer Madness*, noting, "it is not

'false consciousness'" that makes people support their teams, "[n]or is soccer an opiate" (1983: 159). Indeed, the intersections of ideology and class consciousness on and in sport became significant points of deviation for sport sociologists of the era.

On the one side, structuralist Marxists such as Roland Barthes (1957, 1979) and Louis Althusser (1969, 1971) wrote impassioned accounts that interpreted sport as an oppressive formation, one which necessarily reproduced the power relations of capital.[6] Conversely, Lever, Lüschen, and their fellow cultural humanists rigidly applied sociological and autobiographical methods to elucidate, and often perpetuate, the longstanding myth of sport as a community-building, integrative feature of modern life. In the context of the overwhelming shift toward critical paradigms that was gaining momentum by this time, however, the latter turned out to be little more than a "last stand" of the conservative, consensus-premised approaches to the sport–social class connection.

The cultural turn

The more enduring conceptual critique of the Marxism(s) of the likes of Rigauer, Edwards, Hoch, and Brohm ultimately came from the academic left, with a turn toward the Italian Marxist Antonio Gramsci's (1971) notion of "hegemony" and the emphasis on social conflict *without* economic determinacy. This "turn" was reflected in Jennifer Hargreaves' appeal that "The most important task . . . is to identify those features specific to sports which may enable them to contribute to the process whereby class rule and class power are translated into 'commonsense' and legitimated" (1982: 121). Incited by a series of contextually specific caricatures of sport – those popular sources which lauded sport as a site of free expression, harmonious teamwork, class-free meritocracy, and civility – a new generation of critical scholars turned toward a more refined critical investigation of sport and social class. Whereas Brohm, Rigauer, and others pointed toward sport as an ideological apparatus (dictating the conditions of social production to the athlete, the fan, or the consumer), this new approach sought to understand how the sporting and working masses were both subjected to macro-forces (economic, political, etc.) and at the same time were architects of their own life experiences – *within* those structural constraints (Andrews and Loy, 1993).

The Gramscian approach, crucially, promised to illuminate the relationships between power, culture, and ideology without denying human agency and resistance. Drawing upon influences that sought to shed light on sport as popular culture, much of this took impetus from the emergence of the field of cultural studies. Born at the University of Birmingham's Centre for Contemporary Cultural Studies (CCCS), the approach had its political roots in the critique of the class politics, literary culture, and circumspection for the free market agenda in Margaret Thatcher's Britain. The centrality of social class is revealed in Stuart Hall's observation that "cultural studies really begins with the debate about the nature of social and cultural change in postwar Britain. An attempt to address the manifest break-up of traditional culture, especially traditional class cultures, it set about registering the impact of the new forms of affluence and consumer society on the very hierarchical and pyramidal structure of British society" (1990: 12). It is thus often interpreted that in his reading of the early Marx of the "Grundrisse" and the idea of the "aggregate of many determinations and relations" (Marx, 1861: 351), Stuart Hall and his cultural studies contemporaries offered a departure from the economic determinism of earlier structural Marxists.

As Lawrence Grossberg (1989) documents, the impetus came from the perceived failure of the left to successfully confront, both theoretically and politically, "the beginnings of late capitalism, the new forms of economic and political colonialism and imperialism, the existence of racism . . . the place of culture and ideology in relations of power and the effects of consumer capitalism" (1989: 117). Consequently, as Grossberg (1997) has gone to great lengths to remind us, cultural studies is foremost a "radically-contextual" enterprise, making culture, particularly "popular" cultural practices such as sport, political by revealing their articulations within broader socioeconomic formations.

For sport, "the socially and historically contingent matrix of social, economic, political, and technological articulations represents the primary method of contextual cultural studies" (Andrews and Giardina, 2008: 406). This *turn toward culture* – toward an emphasis upon relations and articulations of power, identity, and structure – would bring about a significant shift in the interpretation of late modern sport. Sport sociology's *turn toward cultural studies* was significant in that it located sport as a contested cultural practice and signposted new, post-Marxist directions of analysis that ultimately reshaped approaches to theorizing sport (for reviews, see Andrews, 2002; Andrews and Giardina, 2008; Andrews and Loy, 1993; Carrington and McDonald, 2009; Giulianotti, 2005; Hargreaves and McDonald, 2000; Hollands, 1984).

The approach opened the door to differing considerations of social class and also methods of interpreting the class politics of sport at both the levels of abstraction and those of the lived experience. For example, cultural studies scholars used ethnography as a means to explore lived cultures, human agency, and experiences of sport. The early work of E.P. Thompson, and particularly *The Making of the English Working Class* (1963), illustrates how the body at play has been located as oppositional to the body at work in formations of industrial capital (see also Hollands, 1988). Indeed, sport was a site of study in the early work of the CCCS with the likes of Clarke (1973, 1978), Critcher (1971), Willis (1982), Peters (1976), and Hall and colleagues (1978) exploring topics such as football as cultural practice, hooliganism, and sports media. This work, Hargreaves and McDonald later noted, "opened the doors for a specific cultural studies of sport" (2000: 51–52). Through those doors, we find two important works which "are widely believed to have pioneered the use of Gramsci's ideas in the sociology of sport" (Bairner, 2009: 199).

First, Jennifer Hargreaves' edited collection *Sport, Culture and Ideology* (1982) offered a consolidation of this approach to sport in Britain. Drawing heavily on early poststructuralist theories of Michel Foucault, Jacques Derrida, and Jean Baudrillard, these essays explored how bodily appearance, posture, movement, gesture, facial expression, eye contact, adornment, and smell were enacted within sporting contexts to (re) produce relations of power and authority. Hargreaves then called for a turn away from a positivistic sport sociology paradigm largely defined by "quantitative methodology, rigorous

testing, and claims to neutral, context-free procedures" (1982: 2). The weakness of such approaches,
she argued in the book's introduction, were that
they "systematically separated sports 'facts' from
their social and historical context, and, as a result,
sports science methodology [had come to] incorporate taken-for-granted assumptions about the
social function of sport without any attempt to
justify them" (p. 2).

Second, Richard Gruneau's *Class, Sports and
Social Development* (1983) further informed this
new paradigm. Gruneau lambasted the functionalist *and* Marxist directions noted above. He
criticizes Brohm's work, for example, as "left wing
elitism" (p. 17).[7] Thus, Gruneau maps out a key
departure in evaluating sport to broader social
processes. Gruneau's influential text is often credited (see Andrews and Giardina, 2008: 397) as a
break from the deterministic Marxism(s) that
"shackled" the early critical analysis of sport. To
rephrase Critcher (1986: 335), Gruneau introduced a new line of thinking which located sport
as cultural practice neither transcendent of the
social relations of production nor acting as a
simple reflection.

Such directions were also reflected in the subsequent work of British scholars such as Clarke
and Critcher (1985), John Hargreaves (1986), and
Tomlinson (1988). These new approaches broke
the chains of a sport studies influenced by "the
entrenched scientific and positivist bias" that had
been "established in the early days by the strongly
upheld medical and therapeutic justifications for
exercise when the anatomical and physiological
study of the body was the basis from which to
teach physical education" (Jennifer Hargreaves,
1982: 1–2). This "cultural turn" brought with it a
rejection of the "emphasis on quantitative methodology, rigorous testing, and claims to neutral,
context-free procedures" that had largely defined
the social scientific analysis of sport up to that
point (1982: 2).

For example, John Hargreaves' influential
Sport, Power and Culture (1986) mapped sport's
role in the historical production and subsequent
reproduction of British social class hierarchy.
Drawing liberally upon Gramsci, Hargreaves'
analysis details mid-Victorian sport as a key site
of class differentiation, subsequent contestation
by class blocs over the key meanings and forms
sport was to take, consolidation of power through

commercialized sport, and the mediated production of sport within the vision of a national
culture characterized by patriarchal (and racial)
domination. In his work, Hargreaves maps the
complexities of sport's role in British social class
reproduction; along the way exploring how
industrial era mass sport participation became
entangled with "more thrusting capitalistic
elements" (1986: 206). While John Hargreaves
interprets sport as a site of accommodation and
resistance to capitalism (and the even messier
relations between), he nonetheless sees sport as
"fissured" whereby the sporting body is subjected
not only to class stratification and increased
poverty but also to cooptation by commercial
forces, and patriarchal and racial oppression (see
also Giulianotti, 2005; or Hargreaves, 1987, 1992).

The fundamental questions raised within the
cultural turn produced new frames from which
to interrogate the power relations within various
sporting contexts. Such conceptual influences in
the analysis of sport were evidenced in the United
States by the likes of George Sage's *Power and
Ideology in American Sport: A Critical Perspective*
(1990). In his book, Sage explicates sport as a
cultural terrain rife with contemporary class
stratification, namely through limited access to
sport based on economic wealth (or lack thereof);
social barriers to sport participation; and rejuvenated myths asserting social mobility through
sport. Applying a critical theoretical perspective
to examine how "physical activity as a resource
will continue to be withheld from lower class
groups" (Beamish, 1981: 40), such directions
were also evident in Australia (e.g., Rowe, McKay,
and Lawrence, 1997) and Canada (Beamish, 1982,
1985, 1988; Cantelon and Hollands, 1988).

Bourdieu's neo-Weberian approach

In mainland Europe, Pierre Bourdieu (1978,
1988, 1993, 1998) provided perhaps the most
influential critical theorization on the cultural
logics and class politics of sport. Bourdieu revived
Marx's (1861) dialectic materialism, the phenom-
enological theories of Maurice Merleau-Ponty,
and most significantly Max Weber's understanding of the meaning and purpose that individuals
attach to their own actions in his analysis of
sport. His sophisticated approach allowed critical
scholars to interpret the individual's agency or

ability to negotiate structural influences over their everyday sporting experiences (Sugden and Tomlinson, 2000). Bourdieu's work is also significant because, as Jarvie and Maguire (1994) note, the centrality of the analysis of sport, leisure, and the body in his work is a rarity amongst non-sport scholars – and particularly scholars of his stature. In his 1978 article entitled "Sport and Social Class" which preceded the oft-cited, landmark *Distinction* (1984), Bourdieu advocated for analysis of sport to be located within the wider conceptions of social class which are the cornerstone of his work, noting "One would be likely to make serious mistakes if one attempted to study sporting practices . . . without re-placing them in the universe of practices that are bound up with them because their common origin is the system of tastes and preferences that is a class habitus" (1978: 833–834).

For Bourdieu (1990) this notion of *habitus* is central to the analysis of sport, as are the ways in which sport's social class politics is "constituted in practice and is always oriented toward practical functions" (p. 52). In later work, Bourdieu positions habitus as a "normative" arrangement (which would seem to shift away from materiality and toward ideological dimensions), stating "Social class is not defined solely by a position in the relations of production, but by the class habitus which is 'normally' . . . associated with that position" (1984: 372). Thus, for Bourdieu, habitus is not solely the material activity of acting out functions of "installed" economic predilections; rather, an individual's habitus is constituted by predispositions toward social action and the exchange of capital, which both shape the fields of social movement and are shaped by it.

On this basis, Bourdieu viewed the historical emergence of sport and leisure practices within broader bodily habitus codes, strivings for distinction, and wider class power struggles. The key premise of his analysis of sport was that "the field of sporting practice is the site of struggles in which what is at stake, *inter alia*, is the monopolistic capacity to impose the legitimate definition of sporting practice and of the legitimate function of sporting activity" (1978: 826). For Bourdieu, then, the historical emergence and ongoing resonance of particular sports to selective class groupings characterized the contested assertion of particular class-based habitus codes

– reflected in patterns of thought, taste, and preference. That is, sporting practices are entangled in a continual production of capital, in the form of class-based distinction.

The conceptual core of Bourdieu's theory of sporting habitus lies in the embodied form of habitus, the bodily deportment which Bourdieu classifies as *hexis*. Bourdieu (1977) defines bodily *hexis* as "political mythology realized, embodied, turned into a permanent disposition, a durable manner of standing, speaking, and thereby feeling and thinking" (p. 93). In other words, *hexis* is both the shape of idealized bodily formations and the concurrent adoption of the ideology of the dominant way of exhibiting bodily capital. The appeal of various sports, then, is wrapped in their symbolism as bodily demonstrations of the particular tastes and preferences of class groups in the struggle to gain social capital. Upon this basis, Bourdieu (1978) mapped out examples demonstrating how "the constitution of a field of sporting practices" served a distinguishing function to enable "gains in distinction" (p. 828). He noted, for example, the "hidden" entry requirements such as family tradition and early training, markers such as clothing, "bearing," and etiquette that connect particular sports – and provide the distinguishing boundaries – to particular class groups.

Emergent paradigms

The characteristic features shared by Bourdieu, critical theorists, and cultural studies scholars have yielded a new generation of multidisciplinary theory, drawing upon eclectic yet rigorous methods, and engaging diverse sites of empirical analysis.

The "cultural turn" in sport studies, then, has brought with it a breaking down of conceptual barriers and methodological orthodoxy. Many sport scholars today study and conceive the body through a variety of conceptual lenses, articulating physical activity and bodily forms across a range of contexts and in light of a wide range of social issues. Hence, analyses of sport have diversified and been renegotiated to consider varying contexts in relation to unique national, and indeed transnational, contexts (see, e.g., Cole, 1993 and McDonald and Birrell, 1999 for advocacy of analyses along multiple analytical axes).

Scholars studying class politics today articulate the body's potential to reproduce the dominant modes of social production with various other cultural political and economic formations – a departure from the once isolated body of social class analysis. Theorizations of class have been increasingly undertaken alongside intersections with ethnicity, race, gender, sexuality, (dis)ability; and both the critical and cultural turns have brought with them an increased emphasis on the intersubjective politics of the sporting body. Consequently, critical race theories, feminism, postcolonial theory, poststructuralism, postmodernism, and queer theory (see CHAPTER 5, this volume) have converged upon sport in important and elucidating ways, increasingly informing the approach to analyzing sport and its class dimensions.

Conclusion: Social Class, the Sporting Body, and Neoliberalism

Capitalism did not wither away or implode as Marx (1867) predicted it would. In fact, it morphed and expanded across spatial and social domains, expanding the conditions of capital production by way of the lawmaker's pen, the colonialist's gun, the worker's sweat, and the merchant's pitch. New mutations produced new lenses, new paradigms, and new contexts through which capitalism could be imagined, conceived, and critiqued. Such are the forces now exerted upon our sporting lives; times in which capital has more fully integrated itself into our work and play than ever before. Unlike any other point in modern history, corporate capitalism commands the judicial, political, cultural, and technological inner workings of nation states as politically disparate as the United States, the United Kingdom, and the People's Republic of China. Consequentially, the architectures of capital that Marx so vigorously antagonized during his life have become naturalized within the collective consciousness. As such, class, more than ever, *matters*; transmuted into the mechanisms of capital accumulation.

This global proliferation of capital has largely come into being through what critics often refer to as the "neoliberal condition." The term "neoliberalism" refers to a political economic movement which assumes that only through the freeing of markets and market-based relations can the individual achieve freedom. Based largely in the economic theories of Adam Smith and David Ricardo, and the revival of those concepts through the work of Milton Friedman (1962) and Friedrich von Hayek (1944), corporate and political elites around the world now work in tandem, seeking to "open up" all facets of the human condition to uninterrupted forms of market exchange. These initiatives include: abolishing state regulation of economic activity; opening national markets to international trade; loosening or eradicating tax codes (and particularly those that taxed corporations or upper-class earners); promoting the interpenetration of capitalist relations into *every* nuanced social relation; refocusing social activity around individualism and re-emphasizing individual freedom; publicly rejecting the existence of social and economic stratification; and introducing new, rationalized systems of "accountability" within the public sector.

For its part, global sport has been transformed in rhythm with free market capitalism. The result has been wholesale reformulation of the structure, ethics, and organization surrounding many sports. Many local, regional, and national governments have scaled back funding the activities of everything from parks and recreation departments to Olympic committees, insisting that sporting exponents turn to the market and corporate subsidy for operational funding. Today, sport, like most public institutions, has been radically transformed into a site for facilitating heightened commercial activity and extracting new forms of surplus value. Once publicly organized sports clubs have been disbanded or commandeered by globetrotting venture capitalists, public spaces of play (local and national parks) have been turned into revenue-generating apparatuses, and access to education about the benefits of physical activity and exercise has in many places been cut from the public school curriculum. In total, what we have witnessed across the globe is a de-emphasis on "non-market-orientated practices," or as forerunning critic of neoliberalism Karl Polanyi (1944) warned, "the smashing up of social structures" (p. 164) in order to create new forms of consumption and accumulation. Hence, in matters of sport and culture, we have seen the coming of the Proletkul'tists' greatest fear – that the commercial forces of the economic base have increasingly gained sway over the social and cultural dimensions of human activity and play.

Like previous eras, the body under neoliberalism is the primary site for accumulation, exploitation, and distribution of power. Power has been "literally incorporated or invested in the body" (Hargreaves, 1986: 13); and the management of the body, as a site of production, consumption, deviance, neglect (healthism), terror, combat, lifestyle, and "freedom," has become a matter of the utmost importance within the market. Sporting bodies, in this regard, are no different. The living bodies of the global free market are united in and through the economic and cultural formations of neoliberal sport. Today, child workers – stitching sneakers and footballs and bound to the logics of capital found in southeast Asian sweatshops – are connected to multi-millionaire football team owners in Europe or the United States; aspirant ball-dribbling youths in South America practice English media-speak over writing or arithmetic in hopes of joining the traffic on the superhighways of the sport labor trade; and dispossessed peasants in Vietnam, the Philippines, and Cambodia modify their peasant bodies in ways that they hope will seduce the Tiger Woods-fetishizing, golf holidaying sport-sex tourist.

To their credit, many sport sociologists – and particularly those locating their work within the foundations of cultural studies – have maintained an agenda of social justice compared to their colleagues in burgeoning academic fields such as sport management, sport policy, and sport marketing. This is in stark contrast to exponents of *sport as business* paradigms who have effectively cultivated approaches that further subjugate the sporting body (as student, as practicing professional, as athlete, as symbol, etc.) to capitalism – and thereby limit its expressive capacities. Most sociologists have steadfastly sought to envisage and make real a sporting future characterized by democracy and empowerment, not subordination. Sport managers, however, certainly offer a more profitable public pedagogy within the context of neoliberalism. For example, proscribing ways to better *manage*: the bodies and labor(s) of poor women and children in underdeveloped parts of the world; the profitability of sport corporations; the processes and conditions within which sport business is done; and public perceptions of their corporate operations. Both in the academy and on the field, their reward has been a re-formation of sport closely aligned with, if not replicating, those spectacular culture industries that are now thriving within the unbridled market. Against this backdrop, we close by proposing a series of *(re-)turns* that might well position scholars in the field of sport sociology to offer a meaningful intervention into the practices and politics of neoliberalism's social class inequalities.

First, critical sport scholars seeking to recapture the revolutionary impetus of populist movements past, and recast sport as a site of emancipation and *empowerment* rather than subordination and exploitation, must bring social class, power, and exploitation back to the center of analyses. Alan Bairner (2007) recently pointed to a "crisis of the class problem" within sport sociology literature, noting that the cultural turn served the discipline well in rethinking the complex identity politics of sporting experience (bound to intersections of whiteness, postcoloniality, patriarchy, heteronormativity, ableism, etc.). Yet in so doing, he argued that critical sport scholars let the cultural power of residual class politics slip behind the curtain. Bairner picks up an argument made elsewhere in the social sciences, best captured by Slavoj Žižek's notion of the "silent suspension of class analysis" (see Butler, Laclau, and Žižek, 2000). As Andrews (2007) argues, to locate all forms (intellectual, performative, revolutionary, interventionist) of resistance to capitalist oppression under the workers' struggle would wrongly reduce issues of power to the confines of the economic base. That being said, Andrews (2007) follows Bairner in suggesting the importance of social class in shaping contemporary sporting experiences. Class location might well be, indeed it probably is, the single most *overdetermining* "source of common experiences and problems, opening and closing education, social, and economic opportunities" (Gimenez, 2006: 431). Nevertheless, the material experiences of class have to be understood through their relationship with other forms of identity through which the individual subject's is modulated (either positively or negatively) (Andrews, 2007: 42–43).

To engage and contest the ways in which race, gender, sexuality, ability, and nationalism converge on sporting experiences does not necessarily mean we must abandon the field's longstanding commitment to troubling social class inequities. Indeed, in seeking out social and economic justice, these axes of power should be complementary to critiques of social class stratification. As Žižek (2004: 191) explains, class critique was never "the all-encompassing interpretive horizon, but the matrix which enables us to account for (to generate) the multiplicity of narratives and/or interpretations." Hence, contemporary sport sociologists must articulate class suffering and class struggle to broader social axes (gender, sexuality, race, age, ability, etc.), and they must do so in ways that give us constructive and realistic sporting futures.

Brohm's public acts of dissent offer one potential roadmap. Through public pedagogy, political activism, and protest (e.g., against the *junta*-led 1978 Argentina World Cup) Brohm and his comrades sought to "demystify" (Freire, 1970) sport and foster both critical consciousness and revolutionary praxis through sporting encounters. They promised nothing more than this; but unlike a generation of self-proclaimed post-Marxists, *offered nothing less*. Today's critical sport scholars should perhaps take their analyses – and particularly their passions for social justice – to the streets; just as Brohm did.

In the second instance, a theoretical engagement with sport's social class politics alone is not enough to meet the challenge of neoliberalism. In sport sociology, a dangerous dynamic has emerged: one where radical leftist critique is leveraged as critical capital in the education-industrial complex. In other words, Marx and his theoretical successors have become theorists *du jour* for a field dominated by self-contained "critical" analysts. In such a state, sport sociology faces the possibility of rendering itself irrelevant; bound to *a perpetual state of theoretical paralysis*. By turning away from intervention and activism, contemporary sport sociologists run the risk of becoming merchants of an empty argument. I. McDonald (2009) argues that sport sociologists have fallen prey to academic Marxism at the crossroads of the "sports-industrial complex" (Maguire, 2004) and the corporate university. As such, Marxism is reduced to a footnote or carica-

ture that gives both leftist and sociological legitimacy to an otherwise ineffectual class science; and whereby "the study of Marxism became an end in itself rather than a philosophy of practice" (Jarvie and Maguire, 1994: 88).

As McDonald (2009: 41) writes, "the problem is one of politics rather than methodology. Over the past decade or more, as critical theory travelled from neo-Marxism, via Gramsci, to the hegemonic influence of post-Marxism, critical sport sociology has been noticeably detached from an affective class politics." Critical sport scholars would be well advised to rescue this political interventionism; forging not just a critique *of* bodily practice (and its constraints), but a critique *toward* bodily praxis. This will involve renewed emphasis on strategies and actions. For example, becoming forceful public voices, engaging with mainstream media, and engaging directly with political action within the local (sporting) contexts they inhabit. Inevitably, this will involve engaging in the messy *realpolitik* of social change. This will involve compromise, concession, and the necessity of imperfect changes in the service of the goal of better, more just, sporting futures. Sport scholars should at once "thematize sport as an object of struggle, control and resistance, that is as an arena for the play of power relations" and "raise the question of the transformational potential of sport in this regard" (Hargreaves, 1986: 14).

Thus the voice of the critical sociology of sport community is as indispensable as ever (see Zirin, 2008). However, contemporary critical sport scholars are working against the grain on a number of levels: (1) problematizing class politics in an age of increasing mystifications of sport as a site of classless meritocracy; (2) critiquing capital in the age of seemingly indeterminate neoliberal promise; (3) acknowledging class determinacy in that most seemingly egalitarian of cultural fields, sport; and (4) doing work in the contemporary universities, hardly a space of class struggle or proletarian posturing. This is the challenge, and the charge, of contemporary critical sport scholars. In matters of social class, sport sociologists might be well advised to glance backward – to learn lessons of success and failure from the likes of Bogdanov, Brohm, Jennifer Hargreaves and John Hargreaves, Clarke and Critcher, Gruneau, Sage, and Bourdieu – as they move forward with the critical work that is to be done. With urgency, take those lessons into the classroom, take them to policymakers, to business leaders, to sport administrators and athletes, to the masses.

Notes

1 Although published in 1983, the fieldwork for the book was undertaken "during four trips to Brazil, between 1967 and 1973" (Lever, 1983: 22). Thus there was a ten-year lag between the study and its publication.

2 Reflecting this conceptual distinction of sport from society, acknowledging the right-wing militarist leadership in Brazil at the time, she asserts that "we can condemn a regime's cruel tactics of social control and restrictions on civil liberties without condemning soccer" (p. 158).

3 For a detailed review of these Marxist-inspired, but loosely aligned, and indeed conceptually varied "schools" see Beamish (2002).

4 As Beamish (2002) notes, Rigauer's work was influenced far more by the Frankfurt School of "critical theory" than by classical Marxism.

5 Also amongst this genre of "jockraker" literature were: Bernie Parrish's (1971) *They Call It a Game*; Curt Flood's (1971) *The Way It Is*; Dave Meggyesy's (1971) *Out of Their League*; and Gary Shaw's (1972) *Meat on the Hoof*.

6 Althusser wrote that the economic element is still determinant "in the last instance" (1971: 176).

7 It is interesting that Gruneau (1983) charges Brohm's work/writing as "left-wing elitism" (p. 17) yet does not acknowledge Brohm's calls for direct political action. Brohm (1978), for example, closed his book with an "appeal for the boycott of Argentina as organizer of the Football World Cup" (see pp. 183–185). This example, which certainly problematizes the charge of leftist elitism that Gruneau levels at Brohm, is a pivotal one in disconnecting the sociology of sport from popular engagement with political activism and ensconcing it within the academy. In this disconnection, we are left to reflect that maybe something significant was lost in the direction that Gruneau's analysis signaled.

References

Abbas, A. (2004) "The embodiment of class, gender and age through leisure: A realist analysis of long distance running." *Leisure Studies*, 23 (2): 159–176.

Althusser, L. (1969) *For Marx*, New York: Pantheon Books.

Althusser, L. (1971) *Lenin and Philosophy*, trans. B. Brewster, London: New Left Books.

Andrews, D.L. (1999) "Contextualizing suburban soccer: Consumer culture, lifestyle differentiation and suburban America." *Culture, Sport & Society*, 2 (3): 31–53.

Andrews, D.L. (2002) "Coming to terms with cultural studies." *Journal of Sport & Social Issues*, 26 (1): 110–117.

Andrews, D.L. (2007) "Response to Bairner's 'Back to basics: Class, social theory, and sport.'" *Sociology of Sport Journal*, 24 (1): 37–45.

Andrews, D.L. (2009) "Sport, culture, and late capitalism," in Carrington, B. and McDonald, I. (eds.) *Marxism, Cultural Studies and Sport*, London: Routledge, pp. 213–231.

Andrews, D.L. and Giardina, M.D. (2008) "Sport without guarantees: Toward a cultural studies that matters," in *Cultural Studies ↔ Critical Methodologies*, 8 (4): 395–422.

Andrews, D.L. and Loy, J. W. (1993) "British cultural studies and sport: Past encounters and future possibilities." *Quest*, 45 (2): 255–276.

Andrews, D.L., Pitter, R., Zwick, D., and Ambrose, D. (1997) "Soccer's racial frontier: Sport and the segregated suburbanization of contemporary America," in Armstrong, G. and Giulianotti, R. (eds.) *Entering the Field: New Perspectives on World Football*, Oxford: Berg, pp. 261–281.

Armstrong, C.F. (1984) "The lessons of sports: Class socialization in British and American boarding schools." *Sociology of Sport Journal*, 1 (4): 314–331.

Bairner, A. (2007) "Back to basics: Class, social theory, and sport." *Sociology of Sport Journal*, 24 (1): 20–36.

Bairner, A. (2009) "Re-appropriating Gramsci: Marxism, hegemony and sport," in Carrington, B. and McDonald, I. (eds.) *Marxism, Cultural Studies and Sport*, London: Routledge, pp. 195–212.

Barthes, R. (1957) *Mythologies*, trans. Annette Lavers, New York: Hill & Wang, 1972.

Barthes, R. (1979) "The Tour de France as epic," in *The Eiffel Tower and Other Mythologies*, New York: Hill & Wang, pp. 79–90.

Beamish, R. (1981) "Central issues in the materialistic study of sport as cultural practice," in Greendorfer, S.L. and Yiannakis, A. (eds.) *Sociology of Sport: Diverse Perspectives*, West Point, NY: Leisure Press, pp. 34–42.

Beamish, R. (1982) "Sport and the logic of capitalism," in Cantelon, H. and Gruneau, R. (eds.) *Sport, Culture and the Modern State*, Toronto: University of Toronto Press, pp. 141–197.

Beamish, R. (1985) "Understanding labor as a concept for the study of sport." *Sociology of Sport Journal*, 2 (1): 357–364.

Beamish, R. (1988) "The political economy of professional sport," in Harvey, J. and Cantelon, H. (eds.) *Not Just a Game: Essays in Canadian Sport Sociology*, Ottawa: University of Ottawa Press, pp. 141–158.

Beamish, R. (2002) "Karl Marx's enduring legacy for the sociology of sport," in Maguire, J. and Young, K. (eds.) *Theory, Sport and Society*, Oxford: Elsevier Science, pp. 24–40.

Bourdieu, P. (1977) *Outline of a Theory of Practice*, Cambridge: Cambridge University Press.

Bourdieu, P. (1978) "Sport and social class." *Social Science Information*, 17 (6): 819–840.

Bourdieu, P. (1984) *Distinction: A Social Critique of the Judgement of Taste*, Cambridge, MA: Harvard University Press.

Bourdieu, P. (1988) "Program for a sociology of sport." *Sociology of Sport Journal*, 5 (2): 153–161.

Bourdieu, P. (1990) *In Other Words: Essays Towards a Reflexive Sociology*, trans. M. Adamson, Stanford, CA: Stanford University Press.

Bourdieu, P. (1993) "How can one be a sports fan?" in During, S. (ed.) *The Cultural Studies Reader*, London: Routledge, pp. 339–356.

Bourdieu, P. (1998) "The state, economics and sport." *Culture, Sport, Society*, 1 (2): 15–21.

Bourdieu, P. and Wacquant, L. (1999) "The new global Vulgate." *The Baffler*, 12: 69–78.

Brohm, J.M. (1978) *Sport: A Prison of Measured Time*, London: Pluto Press.

Butler, J., Laclau, E., and Žižek, S. (2000) *Contingency, Hegemony, Universality*, London: Verso.

Cantelon, H. (1982) "The rationality and logic of Soviet sport," in Cantelon, H. and Gruneau, R. (eds.) *Sport, Culture and the Modern State*, Toronto: University of Toronto Press, pp. 220–264.

Cantelon, H. (1988) "The Leninist/Proletkul'ist cultural debates: Implications for sport among the Soviet working-classes," in Cantelon, H. and Hollands, R. (eds.) *Leisure, Sport and Working Class Cultures: Theory and History*, Toronto: Garamond Press, pp. 77–98.

Cantelon, H. and Hollands, R. (eds.) (1988) *Leisure, Sport and Working Class Cultures: Theory and History*, Toronto: Garamond Press.

Carrington, B. (2007) "Merely identity: Cultural identity and the politics of sport." *Sociology of Sport Journal*, 24 (1): 49–66.

Carrington, B. and McDonald, I. (2009) "Marxism, cultural studies and sport: Mapping the field," in Carrington, B. and McDonald, I. (eds.) *Marxism, Cultural Studies and Sport*, London: Routledge, pp. 1–12.

Clarke, J. (1973) *Football Hooliganism and the Skinheads*. Birmingham: University of Birmingham Centre for Contemporary Cultural Studies, Stencilled Occasional Paper Series 42.

Clarke, J. (1978) "Football and working-class fans: Tradition and change," in Ingham, R. (ed.) *Football Hooliganism in the Wider Context*, London: Interaction Imprint, pp. 37–60.

Clarke, J. and Critcher, C. (1985) *The Devil Makes Work: Leisure in Capitalist Britain*, London: Macmillan.

Cole, C.L. (1993) "Resisting the canon: Feminist cultural studies, sport, and technologies of the self." *Journal of Sport & Social Issues*, 17 (2): 77–97.

Collins, T. (2005) "History, theory and the 'civilising process.'" *Sport in History*, 25 (2): 289–306.

Cotter, J. (2003) "Eco (ego?) challenge: British Columbia, 1996," in Rinehart, R. and Sydnor, S. (eds.) *To the Extreme: Alternative Sports, Inside and Out*, Albany: State University of New York Press, pp. 207–218.

Critcher, C. (1971) "Football and cultural values." *Working Papers in Cultural Studies*, 1 (Spring): 103–119.

Critcher, C. (1974) *Football since the War: Study in Social Change and Popular Culture*. Birmingham: University of Birmingham Centre for Contemporary Cultural Studies, Stencilled Occasional Papers Series 29.

Critcher, C. (1986) "Radical theorists of sport: The state of play." *Sociology of Sport Journal*, 3 (4): 333–343.

Dunning, E. and Sheard, K. (1979) *Barbarians, Gentlemen and Players: A Sociological Study of the Development of Rugby Football*, Oxford: Martin Robertson.

Edwards, H. (1969) *The Revolt of the Black Athlete*, New York: Free Press.

Elias, N. (2000) *The Civilizing Process: Sociogenetic and Psychogenetic Investigations*, Oxford: Blackwell.

Evans, J. (ed.) (1986) *Physical Education, Sport and Schooling: Studies in the Sociology of Physical Education*, London: Falmer Press.

Evans, J. (1990) "Defining a subject: The rise and rise of the new PE?" *British Journal of Sociology of Education*, 11 (2): 155–169.

Flood, C. (1971) *The Way It Is*, Seattle, WA: Trident.

Foote, S. (2003) "Making sport of Tonya: Class performance and social punishment." *Journal of Sport & Social Issues*, 27 (1): 3–17.

Freire, P. (1970) *Pedagogy of the Oppressed*, New York: Herder & Herder.

Frey, D. (1994) *The Last Shot: City Streets, Basketball Dreams*, Boston: Houghton Mifflin.

Friedman, M. (1962) *Capitalism and Freedom*, Chicago: University of Chicago Press.

Gimenez, M.E. (2006) "With a little class: A critique of identity politics." *Ethnicities*, 6 (3): 423–439.

Giulianotti, R. (2005) *Sport: A Critical Sociology*, Cambridge: Polity.

Giulianotti, R. and Armstrong, G. (1995) "Ungentlemanly conduct: Football hooligans, the media and the construction of notoriety," in Kitt-Hewitt, D. and Osborne, R. (eds.) *Crime and the Media: The Postmodern Spectacle*, London: Pluto.

Gramsci, A. (1971) *Selections from the Prison Notebooks*, London: Lawrence & Wishart.

Grossberg, L. (1989) "The formations of cultural studies: An American in Birmingham." *Strategies*, 2: 114–149.

Grossberg, L. (1997) "Cultural studies, modern logics, and theories of globalization," in McRobbie, A. (ed.) *Back to Reality? Social Experience and Cultural Studies*, Manchester: Manchester University Press, pp. 7–35.

Gruneau, R.S. (1983) *Class, Sports, and Social Development*, Amherst: University of Massachusetts Press.

Guttmann, A. (1978) *From Ritual to Record: The Nature of Modern Sports*, New York: Columbia University Press.

Guttmann, A. (1988) *A Whole New Ball Game*, Chapel Hill: University of North Carolina Press.

Hall, S. (1990) "The emergence of cultural studies and the crisis of the humanities." *October*, 53: 11–23.

Hall, S., Critcher, C., Jefferson, T., *et al.* (1978) *Policing the Crisis: Mugging, the State, and Law and Order*, New York: Holmes & Meier.

Hargreaves, Jennifer (1982) *Sport, Culture and Ideology*, London: Routledge & Kegan Paul.

Hargreaves, Jennifer and McDonald, I. (2000) "Cultural studies and the sociology of sport," in Coakley, J. and Dunning, E. (eds.) *Handbook of Sport Studies*, London: Sage Publications, pp. 106–138.

Hargreaves, John (1986) *Sport, Power and Culture: A Social and Historical Analysis of Popular Sports in Britain*, Cambridge: Polity Press.

Hargreaves, John (1987) "The body, sport and power relations," in Horne, J., Jary, D., and Tomlinson, A. (eds.) *Sport, Leisure and Social Relations*, London: Routledge & Kegan Paul, pp. 139–159.

Hargreaves, John (1992) "Sport and socialism in Britain." *Sociology of Sport Journal*, 9 (2): 131–153.

Harriss, I. (1986) "Cricket and bourgeois ideology," in Rowe, D. and Lawrence, G. (eds.) *Power Play: Essays in the Sociology of Australian Sport*, Sydney: Hale & Iremonger, pp. 179–195.

Harriss, I. (1990) "Packer, cricket and postmodernism," in Rowe, D. and Lawrence, G. (eds.) *Sport and Leisure: Trends in Australian Popular Culture*, Sydney: Harcourt Brace Jovanovich, pp. 109–121.

Hayek, F. von (1944) *The Road to Serfdom*, Chicago: University of Chicago Press.

Hoch, P. (1972) *Rip Off the Big Game: The Exploitation of Sports by the Power Elite*, Garden City, NY: Doubleday.

Hollands, R.G. (1984) "The role of cultural studies and social criticism in the sociological study of sport." *Quest*, 36 (1): 66–79.

Hollands, R.G. (1988) "Leisure, work and working-class cultures: The case of leisure on the shop floor," in Cantelon, H. and Hollands, R. (eds.) *Leisure, Sport and Working Class Cultures: Theory and History*, Toronto: Garamond Press, pp. 17–39.

Holt, R.J. (1985) "Working class football and the city: The problem of continuity." Paper presented at the third annual conference of the British Society of Sports History, Jordanhill College of Education, Glasgow.

Holt, R.J. (1988) "Football and the urban way of life in nineteenth-century Britain," in Mangan, J.A. (ed.) *Pleasure, Profit, Proselytism: British Culture at Home and Abroad, 1700–1914*, London: Frank Cass, pp. 67–85.

Howell, M.D. (1997) *From Moonshine to Madison Avenue: A Cultural History of the NASCAR Winston Cup Series*, Bowling Green, OH: Bowling Green University Press.

Hughson, J. (2000) "The boys are back in town: Soccer support and the social reproduction of masculinity." *Journal of Sport & Social Issues*, 24 (1): 8–23.

James, C.L.R. (1963) *Beyond a Boundary*, London: Stanley Paul.

Jarvie, G. and Maguire, J.A. (1994) "Classical Marxism, political economy and beyond," in Jarvie, G. and Maguire, J.A. (eds.) *Sport and Leisure in Social Thought*, London: Routledge, pp. 86–107.

Jones, G.S. (1982) "Working-class culture and working-class politics in London, 1870–1900: Notes on the remaking of a working class," in Waites, B., Bennett, T., and Martin, G. (eds.) *Popular Culture: Past and Present*, London: Croom Helm, pp. 92–121.

Kay, J. and Laberge, S. (2002) "Mapping the field of 'AR': Adventure racing and Bourdieu's concept of the field." *Sociology of Sport Journal*, 19 (1): 25–46.

Kellner, D. (2003) *Media Spectacle*, London: Routledge.

King, A. (1999) "Football hooliganism and the practical paradigm." *Sociology of Sport Journal*, 16 (3): 269–273.

Kirk, D. (1986) "Health related fitness as an innovation in the physical education curriculum," in Evans, J. (ed.) *Physical Education, Sport and Schooling: Studies in the Sociology of Physical Education*, London: Falmer Press, pp. 167–182.

Kirk, D. (1997) "Schooling bodies in new times: The reform of school physical education in high modernity," in Fernandez-Balboa, J. (ed.) *Critical Postmodernism in Human Movement, Physical Education, and Sport*, Albany: State University of New York Press, pp. 39–64.

Kusz, K. (2004) "Extreme America: The cultural politics of extreme sports in 1990s America," in Wheaton, B. (ed.) *Understanding Lifestyle Sports*, New York: Routledge, pp. 197–214.

Lever, J. (1983) *Soccer Madness*, Chicago: University of Chicago Press.

Light, A. (1990) "'Return to Manderley' – romance fiction, female sexuality and class," in Lovell, T. (ed.) *British Feminist Thought: A Reader*, Oxford: Basil Blackwell, pp. 325–344.

Light, R. (1999) "Learning to be a 'rugger man': High school rugby and media constructions of masculinity in Japan." *Football Studies*, 2 (1): 74–89.

Light, R. (2001) "'Open it up a bit': Competing discourses, physical practice, and the struggle over rugby game style in an Australian high school." *Journal of Sport & Social Issues*, 25 (3): 266–282.

Loy, J.W. (1969) "The nature of sport: A definitional effort," in Loy, J.W. and Kenyon, G.S. (eds.) *Sport, Culture, and Society*, London: Macmillan.

Loy, J.W. and Booth, D. (2000). "Functionalism, sport and society," in Coakley, J. and Dunning, E. (eds.), *Handbook of Sports Studies*, London: Sage Publications, pp. 8–27.

Loy, J.W. and Kenyon, G.S. (eds.) (1969) *Sport, Culture, and Society: A Reader on the Sociology of Sport*, London: Macmillan.

Lüschen, G. (1969) "Social stratification and social mobility among young sportsmen," in Loy, J.W. and Kenyon, G.S. (eds.) *Sport, Culture and Society: A Reader on the Sociology of Sport*, New York: Macmillan, pp. 258–276.

Maguire, J. (2004). "Challenging the sports-industrial complex: Human sciences, advocacy and service." *European Physical Education Review*, 10 (3): 299–322.

Marx, K. (1861) "Grundrisse," in McLellan, D. (ed.) *Karl Marx: Selected Writings*, Oxford: Oxford University Press, 1977, pp. 345–387.

Marx, K. (1867) *Capital*, vol. 1, trans. B. Fowkes, Harmondsworth: Penguin Books, 1976.

McDonald, I. (2009) "One-dimensional sport: Revolutionary Marxism and the critique of sport," in Carrington, B. and McDonald, I. (eds.) *Marxism,* *Cultural Studies and Sport*, London: Routledge, pp. 32–48.

McDonald, M.G. and Birrell, S. (1999) "Reading sport critically: A methodology for interrogating power." *Sociology of Sport Journal*, 16 (4): 283–300.

Meggyesy, D. (1971) *Out of Their League*, New York: Paperback Library.

Newman, J.I. (2007) "A detour through 'NASCAR nation': Ethnographic articulations of a neoliberal sporting spectacle." *International Review for the Sociology of Sport*, 42 (3): 289–308.

Parrish, B. (1971) *They Call It a Game*, New York: Dial.

Peters, R. (1976) *Television Coverage of Sport*. Birmingham: University of Birmingham Centre for Contemporary Cultural Studies.

Polanyi, K. (1944) *The Great Transformation: The Political and Economic Origins of Our Time*, Boston, MA: Beacon Press, 2001.

Rigauer, B. (1969) *Sport and Work*, Guilford, NY: Columbia University Press, 1981.

Rigauer, B. (2000) "Marxist theories," in Coakley, J. and Dunning, E. (eds.) *Handbook of Sport Studies*, London: Sage Publications, pp. 28–47.

Robson, G. (2000) *"Nobody Likes Us, We Don't Care": The Myth and Reality of Millwall Fandom*, Oxford: Berg.

Rowe, D., McKay, J., and Lawrence, G. (1997) "Out of the shadows: The critical sociology of sport in Australia, 1986 to 1996." *Sociology of Sport Journal*, 14 (4): 340–361.

Sage, G.H. (1990) *Power and Ideology in American Sport: A Critical Perspective*, Champaign, IL: Human Kinetics.

Scott, J. (1971) *The Athletic Revolution*, New York: Free Press.

Shaw, G. (1972) *Meat on the Hoof*, New York: St Martin's Press.

Sugden, J. (1987) "The exploitation of disadvantage: The occupational sub-culture of the boxer," in Horne, J., Jary, D., and Tomlinson, A. (eds.) *Sport, Leisure and Social Relations*, London: Routledge & Kegan Paul, pp. 187–207.

Sugden, J. and Tomlinson, A. (2000) "Theorizing sport, social class and status," in Coakley, J. and Dunning, E. (eds.) *Handbook of Sports Studies*, London: Sage Publications, pp. 309–321.

Swanson, L. (2009) "Complicating the 'soccer mom': The cultural politics of forming class-based identity, distinction, and necessity." *Research Quarterly for Exercise and Sport*, 80 (2): 345–354.

Thompson, E.P. (1963) *The Making of the English Working Class*, New York: Vintage Books.

Thompson, N. (2006) *Driving with the Devil: Southern Moonshine, Detroit Wheels, and the Birth of NASCAR*, New York: Three Rivers Press.

Tomlinson, A. (1988) "Good times, bad times and the politics of leisure: Working-class culture in a small northern English working-class community," in Cantelon, H. and Hollands, R. (eds.) *Leisure, Sport and Working Class Cultures: Theory and History*, Toronto: Garamond Press, pp. 41–64.

Veblen, T. (1994) *The Theory of the Leisure Class*, New York: Dover Publications.

Vinnai, G. (1970) *Fußballsport als Ideologie* (Football as Ideology), Frankfurt am Main: Europäische Verlagsanstalt.

Wacquant, L. (1995) "The pugilistic point of view: How boxers think and feel about their trade." *Theory and Society*, 24 (4): 489–535.

Wacquant, L. (2004) *Body & Soul: Notebooks of an Apprentice Boxer*, Oxford: Oxford University Press.

Wheeler, R.F. (1978) "Organized sport and organized labour: The workers' sports movement." *Journal of Contemporary History*, 13 (2): 191–210.

White, P.G. and Vagi, A.B. (1990) "Rugby in the 19th-century British boarding school system: A feminist psychoanalytic perspective," in Messner, M.A. and Sabo, D.F. (eds.) *Sport, Men, and the Gender Order: Critical Feminist Perspectives*, Champaign, IL: Human Kinetics, pp. 67–78.

Willis, P. (1982) "The motor-bike and motor-bike culture," in Waites, B., Bennett, T., and Martin, G. (eds.) *Popular Culture: Past and Present*, London: Croom Helm, pp. 284–293.

Wilson, B. and Sparks, R. (1996) "'It's gotta be the shoes': Youth, race, and sneaker commercials." *Sociology of Sport Journal*, 13 (4): 398–427.

Wright, J. (1997) "The construction of gendered contexts in single sex and co-educational physical education lessons." *Sport, Education and Society*, 2 (1): 55–72.

Zirin, D. (2008) "Calling sports sociology off the bench." *Contexts* (Summer): 28–31.

Žižek, S. (2004) *Revolution at the Gates: Žižek on Lenin, the 1917 Writings*, London: Verso.

Further Reading

Bourdieu, P. (1978) "Sport and social class." *Social Science Information*, 17 (6): 819–840.

Brohm, J.M. (1978) *Sport: A Prison of Measured Time*, London: Pluto Press.

Gruneau, R. (1999) *Class, Sports, and Social Development* (2nd edn.), Champaign, IL: Human Kinetics.

Sage, G.H. (1998) *Power and Ideology in American Sport: A Critical Perspective* (2nd edn.), Champaign, IL: Human Kinetics.

Weber, M. (1958) *The Protestant Ethic and the Spirit of Capitalism*, trans. S. Kalberg, Los Angeles: Roxbury Publishing Company, 2002.

5

Gender, Feminist Theory, and Sport

Sheila Scraton and Anne Flintoff

Introduction

This chapter focuses on the development of critical work on gender and sport and how this has changed over time. In tracing this history new questions emerge as we enter the second decade of the twenty-first century, thus pointing the way to potential future issues and debates. Our journey through the wealth of research on gender and sport involves an engagement with sports feminisms, interrogating how they have contributed to our understanding of sport and the impact (if any) this work has had on policy and practice. How we understand and explain gender and sport is influenced by social, political, and economic change and by developments both within and outside sport. It is impossible to cover all material or issues internationally relating to gender and sport, thus our own heritage as white women in the United Kingdom means that we draw particularly from our own histories and experiences although where possible we also reference research and writing in other societal contexts and cultures.

Early work on gender and sport within the Western academy provided a critique of the "malestream"[1] of sport sociology with the focus very much on women and sport (Hall, 1996; Hargreaves, 1994); not only making women's sport visible but also challenging inequalities seen to be founded on male dominance and male power. Over time the emphasis has shifted from "women and sport" to "gender and sport" with a critical engagement with discourses of masculinities as well as femininities. In the more recent past, the duality of male/female power relations has been further challenged by the developments in poststructuralism with its emphasis on identities, bodies, empowerment, and the significance of difference. This has raised fundamental questions about whether it is any longer appropriate to centralize gender relations or whether we need far more complex engagement with the intersections of difference relating to gender, ethnicity, race, religion, class, sexuality, disability, and/or age.

To explore this development we focus on sports feminisms and how different theoretical explanations have sought to answer very different questions relating to gender and sport. Our starting point is that gender relations are not static but change over time. There are many overlaps between different positions, writers shift their own understandings and "new" feminisms emerge out of existing theoretical positions. As we progress along our journey through sports feminism and gender and sport, we question

A Companion to Sport, First Edition. Edited by David L. Andrews and Ben Carrington.
© 2013 Blackwell Publishing Ltd. Published 2013 by Blackwell Publishing Ltd.

whether some of the "old" questions of early feminism are now outdated and surpassed by new more relevant concerns or whether some questions and issues continue to be pertinent for our sporting lives in the twenty-first century.

Liberal Feminism

Modern liberal feminism bears the legacy of early pioneers such as Mary Wollstonecraft, John Stuart Mill, and Harriet Taylor, who challenged essentialist notions of femininity and the dichotomy that posited rationality as masculine/male and emotionality as feminine/female. Second-wave liberal feminism since the 1960s and 1970s has focused on equality of access and opportunity, different socialization practices, gender stereotyping, and discrimination.

The underlying assumption of all liberal sports feminism is that sport is fundamentally sound and represents a positive experience to which girls and women need access. Differences in female sports participation are seen to be the result of socialization practices carried out by institutions such as the family, the media, and the school (Greendorfer, 1993; Oglesby, 1978). For example, girls are socialized into feminine activities such as netball, gymnastics, or hockey and into a female physicality, and boys are socialized into masculine sports such as football, rugby, or cricket and into a male physicality (Scraton, 1992). Furthermore, discriminatory practices prevent women from having equal access to sporting opportunities including facilities and resources. Despite new legislation, in most private golf clubs in the United Kingdom, in practice, opportunities for "lady" players to play remain unchanged and restricted to one day in the week or tee times later in the day at weekends (Crosset, 1995). Liberal feminist research also focuses on the underrepresentation of women in decision-making positions in sport and in higher coaching and leadership posts (Knoppers, 1994).

Liberal feminism has placed these issues on the agenda of sports organizations, governing bodies, schools, and other institutions involved in delivering, providing, and developing sport. Pressure from activists working on women and sport initiatives such as Women's Sport and Fitness Foundation (WSFF, UK), Women's Sports Foundation (WSF, USA), Canadian Association for Advancement of Women and Sport (CAAWS), Women's Sport International (WSI), and International Association of PE and Sport for Girls and Women (IAPESGW), has resulted in a number of statements targeted at governments as well as national and international organizations. These statements argue for the vital importance of sport and physical education for girls and women (e.g., 1994 Brighton Declaration on Women and Sport; 1998 Windhoek Call for Action; 2008 IAPESGW "Accept and Respect" Declaration). Although there is little doubt that the liberal feminist agenda and the work of activists and pressure groups has opened up opportunities for some women, more radical sports feminists argue that this superficial change has simply hidden more complex gender inequalities that continue to impact on many women and some men.

The early feminist critiques of malestream sport are valuable for their rejection of biological explanations[2] for women's subordination in sport, and for establishing that gender is socially constructed. They are important, also, for documenting the real distributive inequalities between men's and women's sport and for highlighting the significance of women role models, both as participants and decision-makers in sport. Many of the questions raised by early liberal feminists remain pertinent to contemporary sport practice.

The 2012 Olympic and Paralympic Games in London have been heralded as the most "female friendly" games, with every team having women competitors, women now taking part in previously male-only events such as boxing, and female Olympians from the United States outnumbering male Olympians for the first time. Since the Barcelona Games in 1992, the number of women athletes has increased from 25 percent to 45 percent, a significant improvement. However, issues of access and opportunity remain on the agenda. For example, despite these advances, women still do not have as many opportunities to compete, with fewer medals available, and funding is still unequal. Men continue to dominate key decision-making and the percentage of women in governing and administrative bodies in the Olympic movement remains low. As of January 2013, there were only 21 women out of 101 active members of the

International Olympic Committee (IOC, 2013). This reflects sport more widely, where women are still not in decision-making positions, although some small inroads have been made onto committee structures (Talbot, 2001). For example, in 2002 Karren Brady became the first woman to be the managing director of a Premier League association football team in England and in 2012 is the vice-chair of another Premier League football team. Although Sport England (a government agency responsible for building the foundations of sporting success) has three women committee members out of nine, this reflects a minor shift towards gender equity in decision-making with women still very much in the minority.

In addition, the focus on socialization and sex-role differentiation by liberal feminism is problematic as it treats women as a homogeneous group. Although early liberal feminist work has had some impact on policy and practice (as evidenced in the 2012 Olympic and Paralympic Games), many of the early initiatives identified women as a target group, with little regard paid to differences between women (White, 1995). This approach also unquestioningly accepts men's sporting practices and organization, and defines women and their world, not sport itself, as the problem requiring change; the focus is very much on reform, rather than on a fundamental challenge to broader structural power relations.

Radical Feminism

Radical feminism developed out of radical politics in the 1960s and 1970s which saw the development of women's consciousness-raising groups and the beginnings of a women's movement with women campaigning publicly against domestic violence, pornography, and for their rights over reproduction and health matters (Boston Women's Health Collective, 1973). There has always been a strong link between this radical activism and the theories that developed to explain women's oppression. Fundamentally the radical feminist explanation is concerned with underlying structural power relations that are the result of the systematic maintenance of male power through patriarchy, whereby men as a group dominate women as a group. Radical feminists explore the nature of oppression through

the personal experiences of women (the "personal is political") and centralize sexuality as a major site of men's domination over women through the social institutionalization of heterosexuality. This has led to an analysis of compulsory heterosexuality and lesbian feminism. Adrienne Rich (1980) argues that heterosexuality is defined as the norm both for individuals and within institutional settings, thus it becomes the only legitimate form of sexuality. *Compulsory* heterosexuality acts as a form of social and sexual control by normalizing and naturalizing (hetero)sexuality. Through this, radical feminists argue, male power is manifested and maintained. Male violence against women is understood as part of this social control of women and is fundamental to women's oppression (Dworkin, 1981). As men and male power are seen to be the primary cause of women's oppression and inequality, a response has been to celebrate women's values, raise women's consciousness, and develop a separatist philosophy. The degree to which separatism is developed differs from women-only events and spaces to the adoption of a total separatist lifestyle.

Whereas liberal sports feminists argue that women have unequal access to decision-making positions, radical feminists are more interested in the power maintained over women by men within and through sport. Radical feminists working in sport have been interested in the role of sport in the social construction of male sexual dominance and female sexual submission. For example, Lenskyj (1986, 1994) argues that discussions about "femininity" in sport should be better focused on sexuality, such is the strong association between gender and sexuality. Femininity should be viewed as a code name for heterosexuality. Through sport, females are encouraged to develop an acceptable "femininity" central to which is heterosexual attractiveness and availability. Women's involvement in sport is controlled and restricted through their clothing and their need to present a "heterosexy" image (Griffin, 1998; Lenskyj, 1994). For example, the clothing for international women's beach volleyball competitions states that the bikini bottoms must not have a side deeper than six cm. This is less to do with appropriateness of dress for the sport and more about the objectification of women's bodies. Women's objectification in sport is evidenced further in the media portrayal of sportswomen through an emphasis on their appearance, sexuality, and their motherhood/domestic role in the family (Creedon, 1994; Hargreaves, 1993; Pirinen, 1997; Wright and Clarke, 1999). This takes place in our print and broadcast media and is supported by the use of women as display in male sports such as motor racing and boxing.

Radical feminists have contributed to our understandings of lesbianism and homophobia in sport. Research in this area shows how lesbians in sport and physical education are constructed as deviant, silenced, delegitimized, and stigmatized as abnormal. Importantly, they demonstrate, also, the negotiations and resistances developed by lesbians to maintain a presence in homophobic sport contexts (Cahn, 1994; Cunningham, 2012; Griffin, 1998). They do this by the development of various strategies including avoidance, the construction of complex boundaries around themselves, deflection and "playing" the heterosexual (Clarke, 1998). This work has been extended by male pro-feminist writers to an analysis of gay men's position and experiences in sport (Messner, 1992; Pronger, 1990, 1998; Wellard, 2006, 2009).

Radical feminists' work on male violence to women has been applied to sport by demonstrating the continuum of violence from sexually derogative comments to sexual abuse and rape (Brackenridge, 2001; Brackenridge and Kirby, 1997). Within sport, this is a relatively new area of concern dealing with important and sensitive issues; male violence is experienced in sport, both "on and off the field." Examples include domestic violence and male professional sportsmen; the sexual abuse and rape of athletes by male coaches; and sexual assaults by male student athletes on university campuses in the United States (Brackenridge, 2001; Crosset, Benedict, and McDonald, 1995; Fasting, Brackenridge, and Walseth, 2007; Kirby and Greaves, 1996). The conviction in 2012 of a long-serving football coach at Penn State university for child sexual abuse is a recent example, together with the appalling killing in May 2010 of Yeardley Love, a varsity female lacrosse player at the University of Virginia, by her boyfriend, himself a lacrosse player at the university. A radical sports feminist approach emphasizes the importance of consciousness-raising about violence and sexual abuse and supports the development of anti-discriminatory policies challenging homophobia and discrimination against lesbians and gays. In 2006 the Canadian Association for the Advancement of Women and Sport and Physical Activity published a discussion paper entitled "Seeing the Invisible, Speaking the Unspoken" on homophobia and sport. This was part of their strategy for making all sport inclusive and safe. In the past few years the Football Association in England has also included in their equality strategies the need to challenge homophobia. There are now clear statements about their commitment to "ensure every door is open for members of the gay and lesbian communities to participate and progress within football" and to "combat all forms of homophobic language and behaviour – whether by spectators, players or other participants."[3] However, a statement such as this, whilst welcome, is a liberal response to a radical issue and there remains little evidence about how such a statement impacts on actual practices and behaviors.

Radical feminism challenges unequal gender relations in sport particularly by influencing institutional understanding of male violence and homophobia as well as the significance of women-only and gay and lesbian space. This separate provision ranges from local initiatives (e.g., women-only sessions in leisure and sport centers) to large-scale, international sporting events (e.g., women's sports organizations and the Gay Games).[4] Radical sports feminism further encourages the reconstruction of sport into forms that celebrate women's values rather than those more traditionally associated with masculine aggression and competition (Birrell and Richter, 1987; Mitten, 1992).

Radical feminism is criticized for its tendency to essentialism and biological reductionism. Essentialism suggests that there is an essence to being a woman thus emphasizing women's perceived natural or biologically determined qualities. There is a real danger in celebrating the importance of women's values that femininity is reified and becomes fixed and reduced to a biological explanation. In addition, the concentration on patriarchy and the shared oppression of women by men fails to fully explore the divisions between women based on class, race, and ethnicity and homogenizes all men as oppressors.

Marxist/Socialist Feminism

Whereas patriarchy is seen to be the primary structure of oppression in radical feminism, Marxist feminism[5] identifies gender inequalities as deriving from capitalism, class, and economic exploitation. The sexual division of labor is fundamental to this approach and focuses on how capital benefits from women's unpaid domestic labor, maintenance of the future labor force (childcare), and the day-to-day care of male laborers. Because of this narrow focus on capitalism, socialist feminism looks more specifically at the relationships between class and gender and the systems of capitalism and patriarchy. To a large extent socialist feminism has replaced the economic determinist approach of Marxist feminism and remains the feminist approach that seeks to explore the complex dynamics of class and gender relations. Women's oppression cannot simply be explained by class relations and the sexual division of labor (Marxist feminism) or by men's power over women (radical feminism). Socialist feminism attempts to provide a more comprehensive explanation that incorporates both of these areas.

A major problem for socialist feminists is how the relationship between class and gender can be theorized without giving primacy to one over the other – a problem we will return to later when discussing more recent approaches to difference and intersectionality. This has become more complex as socialist feminists have responded to the work of black feminists (which is discussed in the next section) who have argued powerfully against the ethnocentricity of white feminism. Socialist feminism has responded by looking more closely at the interrelationships of gender, race, and class located within capitalism, patriarchy, and neocolonialism. Within sport, socialist feminism highlights the part played by women in servicing both men's and children's sports. For example, women often provide the refreshments at male sporting events; they wash sports clothing for their partner or for men's teams; and they transport their children to sports events and support them in their activities often to the detriment of their own leisure and sporting activities (Thompson, 1999). This sexual division of labor extends into employment in sports organizations and sports clubs, where women are often found in servicing and supporting roles. Women's dual role in the paid labor force and in domestic labor impacts on their time and energies for sport and recreation. Socialist feminism is critical of the disparities between men's and women's opportunities for sponsorship, prize money, and sporting careers (Hall, 1996).

Apart from exploring the complex interrelationships between capitalism and patriarchal power relations, socialist feminism shifts the emphasis from solely concentrating on women's experiences to looking more critically at gender. In order to do this they explore male power through the concept of hegemonic masculinity (Connell, 1987, 1995, 2008). This has developed into a large area of study (men and masculinities) and has created the space for men to engage with feminist theorizing. The early work by Sabo and Runfola (1980) recognized the significance of feminist work for an understanding of men and sport but it is primarily through the work of Sabo (1985), Messner (1992), and Messner and Sabo (1990) that there have developed critical theoretically informed studies of men, masculinity, and sport. This work looks at the historical construction of masculinity and muscularity through sport, male hegemony, and hegemonic masculinity and the relationship between masculinity, male power, and sport. Importantly it explores how men as a group enjoy privileges in sport through the construction of unequal gender relations; how men also pay the cost for their adherence to narrow definitions of masculinity; and the importance of differences and inequalities between men (Messner, 1992, 1997; Wellard, 2006, 2009; Anderson, 2005).

Black Feminism

Black feminists have challenged dominant white feminist theorizing and activism since the early days of second-wave feminism, arguing that black women's experiences have been largely excluded and made invisible (Hill Collins, 1991; hooks, 1981, 1984, 1989). They highlight the fact that the sites of their oppression may be different to those of white women. For example, many white women see the family as a major site of their oppression by both men and the sexual division of labor. Yet for some black women the family is an important site for their resistance and solidarity, where they have control and can wield power (Hill Collins 1991). By focusing only on gendered power relations, white feminist theories have neglected to problematize racial power as central to the production of white feminist knowledge. White women within the feminist movement have not only failed to address the marginalization of black women but have failed to seriously interrogate their own whiteness. Whiteness is the taken-for-granted central position that relegates blackness to "otherness" (Mirza, 1997). The invisibility and marginalization of black women in feminism "speaks of the separate narrative constructions of race, gender and class; it is a racial discourse, where the subject is male; in a gendered discourse, where the subject is white; and a class discourse where race has no place" (Mirza, 1997: 4).

The interrogation of whiteness and sport has begun to be addressed in sport although much of the research remains focused on sportsmen (e.g., Long and Hylton, 2002; King, 2005) with work such as that by McDonald (2009), Fusco (2005), and Azzarito (2009), beginning to shift attention to mapping whiteness in relation to gender, women's sport, and physical education.

Much of the current discourse about women and sport remains ethnocentric and is viewed through a "gendered lens" (Dworkin and Messner, 2001). There is little work that could be defined as offering a black feminist perspective on sport. As Birrell (1990: 193) concludes "we need to increase the awareness of issues in the lives of women of colour as they themselves articulate these issues." Although written over two decades ago, there is little evidence that these omissions have been addressed. Birrell (1990) argues that most of the work that has been done on black women and sport has been categoric (emphasizing differences between categories) or distributive (providing statistics on inequality of opportunity, access, and distribution of resources) (see also Smith, 1992). Often the early work on gender, race, and sport tended to present a simplistic, additive, theoretical model where black women's experiences are simply "added on" to an understanding of gender oppression (Scraton, 2001).

Raval (1989) provides one of the first critiques in the United Kingdom from the position of a South Asian woman in challenging the appropriateness of white academics researching the sporting experiences of black and South Asian women. She argues that their conclusions pathologize South Asian culture, and universalize the notion of South Asian women, failing to recognize differences between these women in relation to ethnicity, religion, and class. Work on the racialization and gendering of sport has been developed by, amongst others, Benn (1996), Benn, Pfister, and Jawad (2010), Kay (2006), and Ratna (2007) on Muslim women and sport and/or physical education; Wray (2001, 2003) in relation to physical activity, exercise, and health of older Muslim Pakistani women; Scraton, Caudwell, and Holland (2005) on race, gender, and women's football, Paraschak (1996, 1997) on native peoples in Canada, and Ifekwunigwe (2009) on sporting celebrity, class, and black feminism. This latter work is located within a theoretical framework of difference that challenges the universalistic approaches of the liberal and radical feminist analyses and will be discussed more fully in the next section.

The more recent development of critical work on gender, race, ethnicity, and women's sport (as discussed above) to some extent redresses the previous androcentric focus by much sports research on black sportsmen. There are also now critical gendered explorations of sportsmen that engage with hegemonic masculinity, recognizing that the image of athletic masculinity is not only about being a man, a dominant powerful image seen in opposition to a subordinate femininity but is also a racialized image that distinguishes between black athleticism and white athleticism (Messner, 1993; Dworkin and Messner, 2001). Sport can be an important site of masculine self-expression for black males that can provide some means of resistance but can also serve to reinforce and lock them into their marginalized positions within a racist society (Majors, 1990; Messner, 1997; Woodward, 2004, 2009). Carrington's (2001) early work on race, racism, and sport is an example of the development of a critical engagement with the complexities of black masculinities and sport. His work suggests that an understanding of sport as a site of black cultural resistance to racism does not always recognize that this is black *male* resistance, often dependent on gendered power relations. Messner, in his discussion of racialized masculinity politics, reiterates Carrington's analysis in suggesting that

> in foregrounding the oppression of men by men, these studies risk portraying aggressive, even misogynist, gender displays primarily as liberating forms of resistance against class and racial oppression. What is obscured or even drops out of sight is the feminist observation that these kinds of masculinity are forms of domination over women. (1997: 77)

Carrington (2007, 2008) has extended his earlier analysis to areas of racialized performativity, bodies, and identities interrogating the complex relationships between racialization and sport.

The policy and practical responses to black feminism have included greater awareness of the needs of different women. In the United Kingdom this has included specific community-based strategies, for example, to encourage South Asian women into physical activity and active lifestyles (Scraton and Stoddart, 2000). However, although some sports organizations may have antiracist policies, these have had little impact on the experiences of many black sportsmen and women (Long *et al.*, 2000; Spracklen, Hylton, and Long, 2006; Hylton, 2009). Indeed, the sporting world has some way to go before the concerns of black feminists become central to sporting practice.

The Impact of Poststructuralism, Queer Theory, and Postcolonialism

Poststructuralist feminists provide conceptual challenges to the macro-analyses of the structural approaches of liberal, radical, and socialist feminism. They argue that it is no longer relevant to seek *the truth* or a single explanation of a particular issue. They reject the view that it is a lack of equal access or opportunity (liberal), patriarchy (radical), capitalism (Marxist) or a combination of patriarchy and capitalism (socialist) that explains women's oppression. Rather they focus on difference and diversity and argue that the very term "women" has little significance in the fragmented and changing world that we live in today. Poststructuralist accounts often draw on the work of Foucault (1980, 1983) who challenges

the structuralist definitions of power (top down, repressive) and considers power as plural and productive in a multiplicity of sites such as the body, discourse, knowledge, subjectivity, and sexuality. Foucault highlights the significance of discourses, such as medical, scientific, and sexual, through which meanings and people are made and, importantly, through which power relations are maintained and changed. His conception of power provides opportunities for women's resistance and struggle, with more of an emphasis on the everyday experiences and agency of individual women. Poststructuralist feminism argues for the deconstruction of the term "woman" and the recognition of a diversity of femininities, masculinities, and sexualities. Judith Butler's (1990) work has been particularly influential to feminist thought, arguing that gender is performative. There is seen to be no inherent identity behind acts that "perform" gender, thus the categories of gender/sex are culturally constructed through the repeated performance of bodily acts.

Research and writing on gender and sport has continued to evolve as it engages with poststructuralist analysis and particularly the work of Foucault and Butler (Rail, 1998; Markula and Pringle, 2006). The focus on the body in poststructuralism is particularly appropriate for analyses of gender and sport. Foucault's work is used in feminist research to explore the notion of the "docile body" and the "disciplined body." Bordo (1993) shows how women engage in self-surveillance of their bodies, disciplining themselves through diet and exercise. Markula's (1995) early work looks at aerobics as a site for disciplining the female body, but it concludes that although they work hard to achieve the ideal body, women also gain pleasure, self-confidence, and self-esteem through their aerobics workout.

The body has also been the focus of critical work exploring and deconstructing femininity. Sport is an ideal arena for the display of gender and sports feminists are engaged with the embodiment of femininity often through analyses of women who take part in sports that have been traditionally defined as "men's sports" such as rugby (Howe, 2001; Wright and Clarke, 1999), ice hockey (Theberge, 2000; Lock, 2006), boxing (Halbert, 1997), body building (Obel, 1996), wrestling (Sisjord and Kristiansen, 2009), and football (soccer) (Caudwell, 1999; Scraton *et al.*,

1999; Mennesson and Clement, 2003). Women who play these sports are negotiating their display of gender particularly in relation to muscles, tough and aggressive gestures, and the clothes they wear. The women in these contexts are doing gender via a body aesthetic but often are still disciplining their bodies in order to adhere to rules of femininity. For example, in body building women's bodies are made to comply with compulsory heterosexual femininity through their swimwear, make-up, breast implants, and styles of walking (Wesely, 2001). However, most importantly this work raises questions about how sport can not only reproduce gender norms in relation to femininity but can also begin to trespass gender frontiers and the potential to recreate and (re)define new femininities. Gender codes or stereotypes are no longer seen as polarized and some commentators argue that female athletes are challenging the boundaries of femininity and masculinity through the development of strong, muscular sporting bodies (Heywood and Dworkin, 2003).

Poststructuralist analyses of sport destabilize traditional notions of the relations between sex, gender, and sexuality (Sykes, 2006) and often provide a more celebratory view of constructions and performances of sexuality. Queer theory has developed from poststructuralist theory with its particular focus on gender and sexuality bringing a deconstructionist approach to sexual identity and heteronormative discourse (Drury, forthcoming). For example, Caudwell's (1999, 2002) work on women who play football deconstructs the dichotomies of sex/gender and masculinity/femininity through an interrogation of the concepts of "butch" and "female masculinity." Whereas radical feminism focuses on compulsory heterosexuality, lesbian/gay sexuality, and homophobia, queer theory is used by sport scholars to move away from "a lesbian and gay politics of identity to a politics of difference, resistance and challenge" (Caudwell, 2006: 2). Caudwell develops this in her examination of an "out" self-defined lesbian football team exploring how femme-ininity/ies disrupt sex-gender-desire imperatives. Broad (2001) also uses queer theory in her research on women's rugby in the United States. In a similar vein to Caudwell, she argues that women's rugby is a sporting context where gender boundaries can be blurred and space

created for the expression of multiple sexualities. Ravel and Rail's research continues to develop poststructuralist and queer readings of sport in their research on young women's discursive constructions of gender and sexuality and their performative acts both in sport and in other contexts. Interestingly their findings suggest that their participants (located in Montreal, Canada), positioned themselves as "*gaie*" not lesbian or queer. "*Gaie*" sexuality is constructed as more "feminine" but, as the authors point out, this construction of alternative sexualities can also still reproduce some "lesbo/butch phobic ideas" (Raval and Rail, 2006: 395).

Pronger (1990, 2000) has been most influential in queering sport analysis particularly in his work on gay sport. Pronger, together with researchers such as Wellard (2006, 2009) and Anderson (2005), argues that we need to go beyond the concept of hegemonic masculinity, as developed most fully by Connell (1995, 2008), to a poststructuralist understanding of masculinities, gender relations, and sport which uses more complex and ambiguous workings of power (Pringle, 2005). Increasingly there are accounts of sportsmen's subjectivities and an attempt to explore the performances of masculinities emphasizing agency, eroticism, desire, bodily pleasures, and subversive acts of gay sports. However, Wellard in particular, whilst using queer theory to analyze his empirical data of gay experiences of sport is mindful of the gap that still exists between academic queer theory and the lived experiences of sports participants. Whilst agency and transformative acts are evidenced in his work he still identifies the continuance of heterosexual hegemonic masculinity and its discriminatory and oppressive impact on his research participants.

Poststructuralism and queer theory have been criticized for their potential for relativism that emphasizes difference and thus loses the notion of women's shared experiences in relation to gender. The issues central to the concerns of poststructuralist analyses are also considered by some, as discussed in relation to Wellard's work above, to be somewhat distanced from the everyday realities of many people's lives (Dworkin and Messner, 2001). Indeed these academic debates around transgressive bodies, female masculinity, and queering of sport are bought into sharp relief when they become a serious challenge to the normative views of the competitive sports world. In 2009, South African athlete Caster Semenya became the women's world champion for the 800 meters in the World Athletic Championships. Her gold medal resulted in the International Association of Athletics Federations (IAAF) instigating gender verification tests (Schultz, 2011). This is an example of the powerful retention, by those in power positions in sport (in this case the IAAF), of notions of gender/sex binaries and gender normativity together with essentialist notions of bodies having a stable sex that can be demonstrated through dress, body shape, muscle, hairstyle, voice, and so on. Anyone transgressing these expectations of normative femininity faces serious and humiliating actions including being asked to "prove" their sex/gender through biological sex testing. The history of gender verification tests goes back to the 1960s when the International Olympic Committee introduced these tests that involved chromosomal testing for the "true woman" with a chromosome XX. This is based on an acceptance of fixed, natural, binary categories of sex: male and female. Whilst academics have developed the work of Butler (1990), who argues for gendered performance and the disruption of any continuity between sex-gender-sexuality, the performance world of sport continues to deny the complexities of gay, lesbian, bisexual, transgender or intersex, and continues to submit athletes to humiliating and inappropriate testing to identify "deviant" athletes whom they see as gaining unfair advantage in women's sports competition.[6]

Theorizing difference and recognizing fluidity and multiple identities is also a key aspect of postcolonialism. The concept of the postcolonial is as contentious as the debates that surround the use of poststructuralism and queer theory. It is also relatively underdeveloped in sport theory generally and specifically in relation to gender.[7] A text by Bale and Cronin (2003) entitled *Sport and Postcolonialism* has few references to women's sport or to gender relations. Postcolonialism destabilizes notions of national identity and engages with diaspora, the transnational, and new identities (Bhabha, 1994; Gilroy, 1993, 2000). As with poststructuralism it disrupts hierarchical understandings of power and focuses on hybridity and resistance (MacDonald *et al.*, 2009).

Postcolonial understandings of gender and sport tend to be textual-based, exploring representations of black sportswomen and sportsmen. There have been a number of interesting accounts of Serena and Venus Williams that seek to deconstruct black womanhood and explore the representations of black sporting bodies (Douglas, 2002; Schultz, 2005; Ifekwunigwe, 2009). This work, particularly the fascinating exploration of Serena and Venus Williams by Ifekwunigwe (2009: 136) engages with multiple subjectivities, agency, and the "nuanced complexities" of sport celebrity, class, and race. One of the few pro-feminist and queer readings of black masculinities is the work of Abdel-Shehid (2005) who again looks at how racism, exclusion, and diaspora shape black masculinities in Canadian sport. Reading representations of black sport stars allows for a better understanding of the contradictions and tensions surrounding national identities, gender, ethnicities, and sexualities.

New Avenues and New Questions for Sport Feminism: Middle Ground Theorizing and Intersectional Analysis

In the final section of this chapter we turn to consider what might be new avenues or questions for feminism, gender, and sport. As noted earlier, feminist theories are fluid and dynamic, with newer theories building on, or challenging, the knowledge and understanding that has gone before, reflecting changes in society and gender relations. However, in this section we also consider whether some of the older theories and questions continue to be relevant to our understandings of contemporary sport practice.

Whilst the contribution of poststructural feminism to our understandings of gender relations and sport has been significant, increasingly it has been criticized for its tendency to overemphasize both difference and diversity at the expense of enduring, material inequalities (Hargreaves, 2001; Walby, 2000). This has led to what could be called *middle ground theorizing* (Archer, 2004), a position that conceives of identities as "situated accomplishments" (Valentine, 2007) *in relation to* material and discursive structures of inequalities.

For example, in the United States, Heywood and Drake (1997) and Heywood and Dworkin (2003) make an interesting contribution to our understanding of gender and sport, arguing for a "third wave" of feminism. This notion of a third-wave agenda grows out of some of the African American feminist writings, particularly the work of bell hooks. The emphasis is on subjectivities, multiplicity, and difference with a view that a politics of hybridity is far more relevant to the twenty-first century. Whilst the third wave emphasizes desire, pleasures, empowerment, and activism, similar to many poststructuralist concerns, it also embraces much of the second-wave legacy particularly its critique of the beauty culture, sexual abuse, and power structures. Whilst moving understandings of gender and sport into new questions of identities, bodies, and empowerment it does this whilst seeing it as a progression from previous feminist theorizing rather than a replacement or rejection of what has gone before. Such middle ground theorizing, drawing on the valuable insights of poststructural analysis, whilst not losing sight of power structures and their impact on sport, is an important avenue for future feminist work. As Hargreaves notes:

> More research is needed to help us understand the realities of injustice and discrimination in sport, the lived social realities of oppressed groups. This is not an argument to throw away all narrative methods but rather to remind ourselves that stories *can* be used as an aid for change, stories *can* persuade others of beliefs and notions of value, they *can* act as arguments, and they *can* influence public opinion. But to nurture such a potential we should link personal, individual, 'different' accounts to wider social circumstances. (2001: 199, original emphasis)

Whilst third-wave feminism begins to engage with this middle ground theorizing, some researchers and theorists are exploring the value of the concept of intersectionality for taking us forward. Davis (2008) has recently suggested that intersectionality has become a "buzzword" for contemporary feminism, precisely because, she argues, of the ambiguities and uncertainties linked to its use . Although, as we have shown, black feminism has always taken an intersectional approach in that it has always theorized across race, ethnicity, class, and gender, Patricia Hill Collins (1998) has also cautioned against the easy invocation of intersectional analysis. However, a number of feminist theorists are exploring the value of an intersectional approach including those working within sport and physical education (Flintoff, Fitzgerald, and Scraton, 2008; Ratna, forthcoming). Flintoff and colleagues (2008) use an intersectional lens to understand contemporary physical education, arguing that this approach moves us beyond the problems of a single category focus on gender *or* race *or* disability. Their work suggests that exploring the material body through an intersectional lens can help us understand the complexities of difference and the relationship of gender to other social categories in sporting contexts. However, whilst intersectional analysis helps move forward our understandings of gender and sport, we also caution against its uncritical theoretical use. There is a danger of slipping into a pluralist approach that potentially loses the significance of gender relations. We would argue that it remains a political and practical imperative, in specific contexts, to retain temporary boundaries if we are to avoid the relativism of difference.

Whilst considering new questions for sports feminism, it is important not to lose sight of some of the "old" questions that still have relevance. As noted earlier, the advances for women at the 2012 London Olympic and Paralympic Games and in other sporting contests, whilst significant, do not mean that equality of opportunity and access have been fully achieved. In understanding gender relations and sport, we seem to have lost the focus on the relationship between gender and class that was so significant in the 1980s work of socialist feminists. As sport has become more commercialized and spectacularized there have been important debates in sport studies around globalization and late capitalism (Silk, Andrews, and Cole, 2005; Andrews, 2009). There are many questions that emerge around the commodification of sport, sport celebrity, and sport media that need to be addressed by sports feminism in the twenty-first century.

Similarly as demographics change and we have an increasingly older population the relationships between gender and aging would seem to be fertile ground for future work. What is the impact of gender for older people previously or currently engaging in sport? Is aging a gendered process in relation to physical activity and sports performance? Similarly disability remains a much marginalized area in sport research generally but in sports feminism in particular. Once again the centrality of the body would suggest that we need to know far more about the disabled body and gender. Smith and Sparkes (2008) through narrative work have begun to explore the disabled male body through sport and this work could be extended, not only through narrative, to learn more about masculinities, femininities, and sexualities for disabled sportsmen and women.

As Birrell highlighted back in 1990, we still know very little about black and minority ethnic women's experiences of sport. Over two decades later we would have to report a similar situation apart from the notable exceptions discussed earlier. We live in a world of complexity and in Great Britain we increasingly have communities with different and mixed heritage. We know little about the relationship of gender and sport in these settings nor the key questions pertinent to sport, physical activity, and active bodies for increasingly diverse, and often marginalized, communities.

Conclusion: Revisiting "Old" Questions in the Twenty-First Century

As we have journeyed through the development of gender and sport it has been increasingly obvious that just as we have new questions that need exploration, the notion of a "post"-feminist era for gender and sport simply does not hold true. Many of the liberal feminist concerns of the 1970s and 1980s may have shifted in detail but remain very much on the agenda. We

do now have significant questions around difference, fragmentation, and identities but this does not mean that "old" questions about inequality do not remain pertinent today. We have a sports media that still provides limited coverage of women's sport (despite the much improved coverage at the 2012 Games) and whilst the sexualization of women on the sports pages may not be so explicit, it remains an issue. In the United Kingdom, approximately 75 percent of all sport coaches are men and approximately 94 percent are white (Sports Coach UK, 2007; Norman, 2010). Similar statistics can be quoted for the United States (Lapchick, 2009). However, it is the continued everyday oppression and inequality experienced by women coaches described by Norman (2010: 100) that is a stark reminder that gender power relations remain at the center of sporting practices: "Women coaches' emotional struggles illustrated that they worked within a male dominated culture. . . . Their oppression was not overt discrimination but more subtle, insidious ideologically based oppressions that contribute to women's continued under-representation."

These examples demonstrate that questions of inequality remain on the agenda for gender and sport. Equally we could highlight sexual abuse of young athletes, the continuing impact of the beauty culture and bodies, eating disorders, and sport amongst other things. What is most important is that sports feminism retains the fundamental principle of linking research to practice and so striving to make a difference in the sporting world. Questions of hybridity and difference are important and can exist alongside questions of inequality and oppression. Research on gender and sport has contributed much to our understandings of the sporting world and will continue to do so in the future.

Notes

1 "Malestream" refers to the mainstream of sport sociology which was seen to be dominated by male academics researching from the point of view of men with no regard for gender relations.

2 Biological explanations emphasize the supposed physical and psychological inferiority of women which, it is argued, make them unsuitable for sport

and accounts for their limited ability and participation.

3 See http://www.thefa.com/football-rules-governance/equality/lgbt-football.

4 The Gay Games takes place every four years and was initiated in 1982. Its founding principles are those of participation, inclusion, and personal best. It is

the world's largest sporting and cultural event organized by and specifically for lesbian, gay, bisexual, and transgender (LGBT) people.

5   Marxist feminism focuses on the economic as the primary source of women's oppression. Socialist feminism tended to develop out of a Marxist approach (although some feminists would still label themselves Marxist) and is usually defined as a

dualist theory that broadens Marxist feminism to consider economic and cultural aspects of women's inequality.

6   Caster Semenya was withdrawn from international competition until July 2010 when the IAAF cleared her to return to competition.

7   See Chapter 1, "Sporting Resistance," in Carrington (2010).

References

Abdel-Shehid, G. (2005) *Who Da Man? Black Masculinities and Sporting Cultures*, Toronto: Canadian Scholars Press.

Anderson, E. (2005) *In the Game: Gay Athletes and the Cult of Masculinity*, Albany: State University of New York Press.

Andrews, D.L. (2009) "Sport, culture and late capitalism," in Carrington, B. and McDonald, I. (eds.) *Marxism, Cultural Studies and Sport*, London: Routledge.

Archer, L. (2004) "Re/theorising difference in feminist research." *Women's Studies International Forum*, 27: 459–473.

Azzarito, L. (2009) "The Panopticon of physical education: Pretty, active and ideally white." *Physical Education and Sport Pedagogy*, 14: 19–40.

Bale, J. and Cronin, M. (2003) *Sport and Postcolonialism*, Oxford: Berg.

Benn, T. (1996) "Muslim women and physical education in initial teacher training." *Sport, Education and Society*, 1 (1): 5–21.

Benn, T., Pfister, G., and Jawad, H. (eds.) (2011) *Muslim Women in Sport*, London: Routledge.

Bhabha, H. (1994) *The Location of Culture*, London: Routledge.

Birrell, S. (1990) "Women of color: Critical autobiography and sport," in Messner, M. and Sabo, D. (eds.) *Sport, Men and the Gender Order*, Champaign, IL: Human Kinetics.

Birrell, S. and Richter, D.M. (1987) "Is a diamond forever? Feminist transformations of sport." *Women's Studies International Forum*, 10 (4): 395–409.

Bordo, S. (1993) *Unbearable Weight: Feminism, Western Culture and the Body*, Berkeley: University of California Press.

Boston Women's Health Collective (1973) *Our Bodies, Ourselves*, New York: Simon & Schuster.

Brackenridge, C. (2001) *Spoilsports: Understanding and Preventing Sexual Exploitation in Sport*, London: Routledge.

Brackenridge, C. and Kirby, S. (1997) "Playing safe? Assessing the risk of sexual abuse to young elite athletes." *International Review for the Sociology of Sport*, 32 (4): 407–418.

Broad, K.L. (2001) "The gendered unapologetic: Queer resistance in women's sport." *Sociology of Sport Journal*, 18 (2): 181–204.

Butler, J. (1990) *Gender Trouble: Feminism and the Subversion of Identity*, London: Routledge.

Cahn, S. (1994) *Coming on Strong: Gender and Sexuality in Twentieth Century Women's Sport*, New York: Free Press.

Carrington, B. (2001) "Sport, masculinity and black cultural resistance," in Scraton, S. and Flintoff, A. (eds.) *A Reader in Gender and Sport*, London: Routledge.

Carrington, B. (2007) "Merely identity: Cultural identity and the politics of sport." *Sociology of Sport Journal*, 24 (1): 49–66.

Carrington, B. (2008) "What's the footballer doing here? Racialised performativity, reflexivity and identity." *Cultural Studies ↔ Critical Methodologies*, 8 (4): 423–452.

Carrington, B. (2010) *Race, Sport and Politics*, London: Sage.

Caudwell, J. (1999) "Women's football in the United Kingdom: Theorizing gender and unpacking the butch lesbian image." *Journal of Sport & Social Issues*, 23 (4): 390–402.

Caudwell, J. (2002) "Women's experiences of sexuality within football contexts: A particular and located footballing epistemology." *Football Studies*, 5 (1): 24–45.

Caudwell, J. (ed.) (2006) *Sport, Sexualities and Queer/ Theory*, London: Routledge.

Clarke, G. (1998) "Queering the pitch and coming out to play: Lesbians in physical education and sport." *Sport, Education and Society*, 3 (2): 145–160.

Connell, R. (1987) *Gender and Power*, Stanford, CA: Stanford University Press.

Connell, R. (1995) *Masculinities*, Sydney: Allen & Unwin.

Connell, R. (2008) "Masculinity construction and sports in boys' education: A framework for thinking about the issue." *Sport Education and Society*, 13 (2): 131–145.

Creedon, P. (ed.) (1994) *Women, Media and Sport: Challenging Gender Values*, London: Sage.

Crosset, T.W. (1995) *Outsiders in the Clubhouse: The World of Women's Professional Golf*, New York: State University of New York Press.

Crosset, T.W., Benedict, J.R., and McDonald, M.A. (1995) "Male student-athletes reported for sexual assault: A survey of campus police departments and judicial affairs offices." *Journal of Sport & Social Issues*, 19 (2): 126–140.

Cunningham, G.B. (ed.) (2012) *Sexual Orientation and Gender Identity in Sport*, College Station: Texas A&M University.

Davis, K. (2008) "Intersectionality as buzzword: A sociology of science perspective on what makes a theory feminist." *Feminist Theory*, 9: 67–85.

Douglas, D. (2002) "To be young, gifted, black and female: A meditation on the cultural politics at play in representations of Venus and Serena Williams." *Sociology of Sport Online*, 5 (2), http://physed.otago.ac.nz/sosol/v5i2/v5i2_3.html, accessed December 5, 2012.

Drury, S. (forthcoming) "Gay sports spaces: Transgressing hetero(/homo) normativity and transforming sport," in Hargreaves, J. and Anderson, E. (eds.) *Routledge Handbook of Sport, Gender and Sexuality*, London: Routledge.

Dworkin, A. (1981) *Pornography: Men Possessing Women*, London: Women's Press.

Dworkin, S. and Messner, M. (2001) "Just do . . . what? Sport, bodies, gender," in Scraton, S. and Flintoff, A. (eds.) *A Reader in Gender and Sport*, London: Routledge.

Fasting, K., Brackenridge, C., and Walseth, K. (2007) "Women athletes' personal responses to sexual harassment in sport." *Journal of Applied Psychology*, 19 (4): 419–433.

Flintoff, A., Fitzgerald, H., and Scraton, S. (2008) "The challenges of intersectionality: Researching difference in physical education." *International Studies in Sociology of Education*, 18 (2): 73–85.

Foucault, M. (1980) *Power/Knowledge: Selected Interviews and Other Writings 1972–77*, ed. Colin Gordon, Brighton: Harvester Press.

Foucault, M. (1983) "The subject and power," in Dreyfus, H. and Rabinow, P. (eds.) *Michel Foucault: Beyond Structuralism and Hermeneutics*, Chicago: Chicago University Press, pp. 208–220.

Fusco, C. (2005) "Cultural landscapes of purification: Sports spaces and discourses of whiteness." *Sociology of Sport Journal*, 22 (3): 283–310.

Gilroy, P. (1993) *The Black Atlantic: Modernity and Double Consciousness*. London: Verso.

Gilroy, P. (2000) "The dialectics of diaspora identification," in Back, L. and Solomos, J. (eds.) *Theories of Race and Racism*, London: Routledge.

Greendorfer, S. (1993) "Gender role stereotypes and early childhood socialisation," in Cohen, G.L. (ed.) *Women in Sport: Issues and Controversies*, Newbury Park, CA: Sage, pp. 3–14.

Griffin, P. (1998) *Strong Women, Deep Closets: Lesbians and Homophobia in Sport*, Champaign, IL: Human Kinetics.

Halbert, C. (1997) "Tough enough and woman enough: Stereotypes, discrimination, and impression management among women professional boxers." *Journal of Sport & Social Issues*, 21 (1): 7–36.

Hall, M.A. (1996) *Feminism and Sporting Bodies*, Champaign, IL: Human Kinetics.

Hargreaves, J. (1993) "Bodies matter! Images of sport and female sexualisation," in Brackenridge, C. (ed.) *Body Matters: Leisure Images and Lifestyles*, Eastbourne, UK: Leisure Studies Association.

Hargreaves, J. (1994) *Sporting Females: Critical Issues in the History and Sociology of Women's Sport*, London: Routledge.

Hargreaves, J. (2001) *Heroines of Sport: Politics of Difference and Identity*, London: Routledge.

Heywood, L. and Drake, J. (1997) *Third Wave Agenda: Being Feminist, Doing Feminism*, Minneapolis: University of Minnesota Press.

Heywood, L. and Dworkin, S.L. (2003) *Built to Win: The Female Athlete as Cultural Icon*, Minneapolis: University of Minnesota Press.

Hill Collins, P. (1991) *Black Feminist Thought: Knowledge, Consciousness and the Politics of Empowerment*, London: Routledge.

Hill Collins, P. (1998) *Fighting Words: Black Women and the Search for Justice*, Minneapolis: University of Minnesota Press.

hooks, b. (1981) *Ain't I a Woman: Black Women and Feminism*, Boston, MA: South End Press.

hooks, b. (1984) *Feminist Theory: From Margin to Center*, Boston, MA: South End Press.

hooks, b. (1989) *Talking Back: Thinking Feminism, Thinking Black*, Boston, MA: South End Press.

Howe, P.D. (2001) "Women's rugby and the nexus between embodiment, professionalism and sexuality: An ethnographic account." *Football Studies*, 4: 77–92.

Hylton, K. (2009) *Race and Sport: Critical Race Theory*, London: Routledge.

Ifekwunigwe, J.O. (2009) "Venus and Serena are 'doing it' for themselves: Theorising sporting celebrity, class and black feminism in the hip-hop generation," in Carrington, B. and McDonald, I. (eds.) *Marxism, Cultural Studies and Sport*, London: Routledge.

IOC (2013) IOC members list, http://www.olympic. org/content/the-ioc/the-ioc-institution/ioc-members-list/, accessed January 17, 2013.

Kay, T.A. (2006) "Daughters of Islam: Family influences on Muslim young women's participation in sport." *International Review for the Sociology of Sport*, 41 (3/4): 339–355.

King, C.R. (2005) "Cautionary notes on whiteness and sport studies." *Sociology of Sport Journal*, 22 (3): 397–408.

Kirby, S. and Greaves, L. (1996) "Foul play: Sexual abuse and harassment in sport." Paper presented to the Pre-Olympic Scientific Congress, Dallas, TX, July 11–14.

Knoppers, A. (1994) "Gender and the coaching profession," in Birrell, S. and Cole, C.L. (eds.) *Women, Sport and Culture*, Champaign, IL: Human Kinetics.

Lapchick, R. (2009) *The 2008 Racial and Gender Report Card: College Sport*, Orlando: The Institute for Diversity and Ethics in Sport (TIDES), University of Central Florida.

Lenskyj, H. (1986) *Out of Bounds: Women, Sport and Sexuality*, Toronto: Women's Press.

Lenskyj, H. (1994) "Sexuality and femininity in sport contexts: Issues and alternatives." *Journal of Sport & Social Issues*, 18 (4): 356–376.

Lock, R. (2006) "Heterosexual femininity: The painful processes of subjectification," in Caudwell, J. (ed.) *Sport, Sexualities and Queer/Theory*, London: Routledge.

Long, J. and Hylton, K. (2002) "Shades of white: An examination of whiteness in sport." *Leisure Studies*, 21: 87–103.

Long, J., Hylton, K., Welch, M., and Dart, J. (2000) *Part of the Game: An Examination of Racism in Grass Roots Football*, London: Kick It Out.

MacDonald, D., Abbott, R., Knez, K., and Nelson, A. (2009) "Taking exercise: Cultural diversity and physically active lifestyles." *Sport, Education and Society*, 14 (1): 1–19.

Majors, R. (1990) "Cool pose: Black masculinity and sports," in Messner, M. and Sabo, D. (eds.) *Sport, Men and the Gender Order*, Champaign, IL: Human Kinetics.

Markula, P. (1995) "Firm but shapely, fit but sexy, strong but thin: The postmodern aerobicising female bodies." *Sociology of Sport Journal*, 12: 424–453.

Markula, P. and Pringle, R. (2006) *Foucault, Sport and Exercise: Power, Knowledge and Transforming the Self*, London: Routledge.

McDonald, M.G. (2009) Dialogues on whiteness, leisure and (anti) racism." *Journal of Leisure Research*, 41 (1): 5–21.

Mennesson, C. and Clement, J.-P. (2003) "Homosociability and homosexuality: The case of soccer played by women." *International Review for the Sociology of Sport*, 38: 311–330.

Messner, M. (1992) *Power at Play: Sports and the Problem of Masculinity*, Boston, MA: Beacon Press.

Messner, M. (1993) "White men misbehaving: Feminism, Afrocentrism and the promise of a critical standpoint." *Journal of Sport & Social Issues*, 16: 136–144.

Messner, M. (1997) *The Politics of Masculinities: Men in Movements*, Thousand Oaks, CA: Sage.

Messner, M. and Sabo, D. (1990) *Sport, Men and the Gender Order: Critical Feminist Perspectives*, Champaign, IL: Human Kinetics.

Mirza, H. (1997) *Black British Feminism: A Reader*, London: Routledge.

Mitten, D. (1992) "Empowering girls and women in the outdoors." *Journal of Physical Education, Recreation and Dance*, 63 (2): 56–60.

Norman, L. (2010) "Feeling second best: Elite women coaches' experiences." *Sociology of Sport Journal*, 27: 89–104.

Obel, C. (1996) "Collapsing gender in competitive bodybuilding: Researching contradictions and ambiguity in sport." *Review for the Sociology of Sport*, 31 (2): 185–202.

Oglesby, C.A. (ed.) (1978) *Women and Sport: From Myth to Reality*, Philadelphia, PA: Lea & Febiger.

Paraschak, V. (1996) "Racialized spaces: Cultural regulation, aboriginal agency and powwows. *Avante*, 2 (1): 7–18.

Paraschak, V. (1997) "Variations in race relations: Sporting events for native peoples in Canada." *Sociology of Sport Journal*, 14 (1): 1–22.

Pirinen, R. (1997) "Catching up with the men? Finnish newspaper coverage of women's entry into traditionally male sports." *International Review for the Sociology of Sport*, 32 (3): 239–249.

Pringle, R. (2005) "Masculinities, sport and power: A critical comparison of Gramscian and Foucauldian inspired theoretical tools." *Journal of Sport & Social Issues*, 29: 256–278.

Pronger, B. (1990) *The Arena of Masculinity: Sports, Homosexuality and the Meaning of Sex*, London: GMP Publishers.

Pronger, B. (1998) "Outta my endzone: Sport and the territorial anus." *Journal of Sport & Social Issues*, 23 (4): 373–389.

Pronger, B. (2000) "Homosexuality and sport – who's winning," in McKay, J., Messner, M., and Sabo, D. (eds.) *Masculinities, Gender Relations and Sport*, London: Sage.

Rail, G. (ed.) (1998) *Sport and Postmodern Times*, Albany: State University of New York Press.

Ratna, A. (2007) "A fair game? British-Asian females' experiences of racism in women's football," in Magee, J., Caudwell, J., Liston, K., and Scraton, S. (eds.) *Women, Football and Europe*, Oxford: Meyer & Meyer.

Ratna, A. (forthcoming) "Playing-up and playing-down intersections of identity: British Asian female footballers and women's football," in Hargreaves, J. and Anderson, E. (eds.) *Routledge Handbook of Sport, Gender and Sexuality*, London: Routledge.

Raval, S. (1989) "Gender, leisure and sport: A case study of young people of South Asian descent – a response." *Leisure Studies*, 8: 237–240.

Raval, B. and Rail, G. (2006) "The lightness of being 'Gaie': Discursive constructions of gender and sexuality in Quebec women's sport." *International Review for the Sociology of Sport*, 41 (3): 395–412.

Rich, A. (1980) "Compulsory heterosexuality and lesbian existence." *Signs*, 5: 631–660.

Sabo, D. (1985) "Sport, patriarchy, and the male identity: New questions about men and sport." *Arena Review*, 9: 1–30.

Sabo, D. and Runfola, R. (eds.) (1980) *Jock: Sports and Male Identity*, Englewood Cliffs, NJ: Prentice Hall.

Schultz, J. (2005) "Serena Williams and the production of blackness at the 2002 US Open." *Journal of Sport & Social Issues*, 29 (3): 338–357.

Schultz, J. (2011) "Caster Semenya and the 'Question of Too': Sex testing in elite women's sport and the issue of advantage." *Quest*, 63 (2): 228–243.

Scraton, S. (1992) *Shaping Up to Womanhood: Gender and Girls' Physical Education*, Buckingham, UK: Open University Press.

Scraton, S. (2001) "Reconceptualising race, gender and sport: The contribution of black feminism," in Carrington, B. and Macdonald, I. (eds.), *Racism and British Sport*, London: Routledge.

Scraton, S. and Stoddart, F. (2000) *An Evaluation of the Zindagi Project*, Leeds: Leeds Metropolitan University.

Scraton, S., Caudwell, J., and Holland, S. (2005) "Bend it like Patel: Centring 'race', ethnicity and gender in feminist analysis of women's football in England." *International Review for Sport Sociology*, 40 (1): 71–88.

Scraton, S., Fastings, K., Pfister, G., and Bunuel, A. (1999) "It's still a man's game? The experience of top-level European women footballers." *International Review for the Sociology of Sport*, 34 (2): 99–111.

Silk, M.L., Andrews, D.L., and Cole, C.L. (eds.) (2005) *Sport and Corporate Capitalism*, New York: Berg.

Sisjord, M.K. and Kristiansen, E. (2009) "Elite women wrestlers' muscles: Physical strength and a social burden." *International Review for the Sociology of Sport*, 44 (2–3): 231–246.

Smith, B. and Sparkes, A.C. (2008) "Changing bodies, changing narratives and the consequences of tellability: A case study of becoming disabled through sport." *Sociology of Health and Illness*, 30 (2): 217–236.

Smith, Y. (1992) "Women of color in society and sport." *Quest*, 44: 228–250.

Sports Coach UK (2007) *Sports Coaching in the UK 11*, Leeds: Sports Coach UK.

Spracklen, K., Hylton, K., and Long, J. (2006) "Managing and monitoring equality and diversity in UK sport: An evaluation of the sporting equals racial equality standard and its impact on organizational change." *Journal of Sport & Social Issues*, 30 (3): 289–305.

Sykes, H. (2006) "Queering theories of sexuality in sport studies," in Caudwell, J. (ed.) *Sport, Sexualities and Queer/Theory*, London: Routledge.

Talbot, M. (2001) "Playing with patriarchy: The gendered dynamics of sports organisations," in Scraton, S. and Flintoff, A. (eds.) *A Reader in Gender and Sport*, London: Routledge.

Theberge, N. (2000) *Higher Goals: Women's Ice Hockey and the Politics of Gender*, Albany: State University of New York Press.

Thompson, S. (1999) *Mother's Taxi: Sport and Women's Labor*, Albany: State University of New York Press.

Valentine, G. (2007) "Theorising and researching intersectionality: A challenge for feminist geography." *Professional Geographer*, 59: 10–21.

Walby, S. (2000) "Beyond the politics of location." *Feminist Theory*, 1: 189–206.

Wellard, I. (2006) "Re-thinking abilities." *Sport, Education and Society*, 11 (3): 311–315.

Wellard, I. (2009) *Sport, Masculinities and the Body*, New York: Routledge.

Wesely, J. (2001) "Negotiating gender: Bodybuilding and the natural/unnatural continuum." *Sociology of Sport Journal*, 18: 162–180.

White, A. (1995) "Towards gender equity in sport: An update on sports council policy development," in Tomlinson, A. (ed.) *Gender, Sport and Leisure: Continuities and Challenges*, Brighton: Chelsea School Research Centre, University of Brighton.

Woodward, K. (2004) "Rumbles in the jungle: Boxing, racialization and the performance of masculinity." *Leisure Studies*, 23 (1): 5–17.

Woodward, K. (2009) *Embodied Sporting Practices. Regulating and Regulatory Bodies*, Basingstoke: Palgrave Macmillan.

Wray, S. (2001) "Connecting ethnicity, gender and physicality: Muslim Pakistani women, physical activity and health," in Scraton, S. and Flintoff, A.

(eds.) *A Reader in Gender and Sport*, London: Routledge.

Wray, S. (2003) "Women growing older: Agency, ethnicity and culture." *Sociology*, 37 (3): 511–527.

Wright, J. and Clarke, G. (1999) "Sport, the media and the construction of compulsory heterosexuality: A case study of women's rugby union." *International Review for the Sociology of Sport*, 34 (3): 227–243.

Further Reading

Benn, T., Pfister, G., and Jawad, H. (eds.) (2011) *Muslim Women and Sport*, London: Routledge.

Dowling, F., Fitzgerald, H., and Flintoff, A. (eds.) (2012) *Equity and Difference in Physical Education, Youth Sport and Health: A Narrative Approach*, London: Routledge.

Hargreaves, J. (2000) *Heroines of Sport: The Politics of Difference and Identity*, New York: Routledge.

Hargreaves, J. and Anderson, E. (forthcoming) *Routledge Handbook of Sport, Gender and Sexuality*, London: Routledge.

Hargreaves, J. and Vertinsky, P. (eds.) (2007) *Physical Culture, Power and the Body*, London: Routledge.

Heywood, L. and Dworkin, S.L. (2003) *Built to Win: The Female Athlete as Cultural Icon*, Minneapolis: University of Minnesota Press.

Markula, P. and Pringle, R. (2006) *Foucault, Sport and Exercise: Power, Knowledge and Transforming the Self*, London: Routledge.

Scraton, S. and Flintoff, A. (2002) *Gender and Sport: A Reader*, London: Routledge.

6

Sports Medicine, Health, and the Politics of Risk

Parissa Safai

Introduction

In early 2012, the Canadian sport community suffered two tragic deaths: in January, freestyle skier Sarah Burke died in hospital from injuries sustained from a fall during a training run at a superpipe event and, only two months later, ski cross athlete Nik Zoricic died one meter from the finish line at a World Cup event in Switzerland as a result of severe neurotrauma from a fall. Both athletes were only 29 years old. A wide range of commentary and criticism about the nature of risk, danger, and safety in contemporary sport followed in the wake of their deaths; Scott Russell (2012) wrote in his blog, "Safety and sport is increasingly becoming the elephant in the room." Yet, the heightened sensitivity to sport-related death among Canadian and global sport enthusiasts may have been blunted – these deaths treated as just freak accidents or normalized as just part-and-parcel of sport – had the tragedy of the 2010 Olympic winter games in Vancouver, British Columbia, not still been fresh in people's memories.

Like other Olympics before it, the 2010 winter Olympics in Vancouver were filled with a dizzying array of spectacle and display, from feats of truly remarkable athletic ability and camaraderie

among Olympic participants, to moments of undisguised pursuit of brand and profit, to the seemingly unexpected and unprecedented display of vigorous Canadian nationalism, to the thoroughly expected production and unfolding of clichéd dramatic narratives in the media coverage of the Games. Sadly, however, the 2010 Games were also marked by pain, injury, and death.

On February 12, 2010, days before the opening ceremonies, Nodar Kumaritashvili, a young Georgian luger, died from fatal injuries suffered during a training run at the Whistler Sliding Centre, the site of all the men's and women's luge, bobsleigh, and skeleton competitions. While his family in Georgia struggled with the news of the loss of the 21-year-old first-time Olympian, officials in Whistler rushed to investigate the circumstances of his death. After a brief investigation, Vancouver Organizing Committee (VANOC) and Fédération Internationale de Luge de Course (FIL) officials declared that Kumaritashvili's death was not the result of an unsafe track but was rather the tragic accident of a young, inexperienced athlete. That said, the track was modified for the official luge competitions during the Games. The walls of the curve on which Kumaritashvili lost his life were raised, exposed metal beams were padded, the ice surface was adjusted

A Companion to Sport, First Edition. Edited by David L. Andrews and Ben Carrington.
© 2013 Blackwell Publishing Ltd. Published 2013 by Blackwell Publishing Ltd.

and, most significantly, the starting points for both the men's and women's competitions were moved down the track in efforts to reduce speed (i.e., the men's starting line was moved down to the women's starting line and the women's starting line was moved down to where junior lugers would start their races). VANOC officials argued that these modifications were necessary not because the track was unsafe but that Kumaritashvili's fellow competitors were emotional and needed such reassurances (Longman, 2010). The well-known saying that "the show must go on" was actualized as the opening ceremonies of the Games were dedicated to Kumaritashvili and the men's and women's luge, bobsleigh, and skeleton competitions were neither canceled nor delayed.

Controversy swirled around the start of the Games as the details of Kumaritashvili's last run – he was travelling in excess of 140 km/hr at moment of impact – and his fear of the course surfaced. According to his father, prior to his death he expressed concern about the dangerous track but had resigned himself to competing and trying to win the event; in a tragic foreshadowing of events, he told his father "I will either win or die" (Dzhindzhikhashvili, 2010). He was not alone in expressing such trepidation about the course. In the months leading up to the Games, athletes (including those in the highest ranks of the sport) and officials from all over the world voiced their concern that the track was too technically demanding and too fast. Some critics acknowledged that the commercial elements of the sport – the need to present itself as an intense, fast-paced, media-friendly winter "extreme" sport – were outweighing the safety requirements of the course. Other criticisms, directed squarely at the Canadian government's Own the Podium (OTP) program, an initiative designed solely to improve Canadian athletes' performances at the 2010 Olympic and Paralympic Games in order to win more medals than any other country – such as the lack of adequate access to the facilities for training by non-Canadian competitors – abounded. Yet the Games did go on and, as each day passed and even while VANOC officials acknowledged that his death would always remain part of the 2010 Games' legacy, there was less and less mention of the young luger's death in mainstream media coverage. There were some critics and journalists, however, who paid more consist-

ent and critical attention to VANOC's and IOC's complicit role in the tragedy. They reframed the tragedy not as the result of the inexperience of a young athlete but as the result of an Olympic machine that bolts together the IOC, corporations, host cities, and countries in the relentless pursuit of (sport, commercial, brand, or otherwise) success at all costs. And what of the athletes who are so centrally wired into – in fact, the very fuel of – the Olympic machinery? What happens to athletes when losing is not an option? Furthermore, what about those individuals who are charged with the care and well-being of athletes willing to risk it all?

In this historical moment, sport occupies a unique place in our "risk society" as one of the few areas of social life to run counter to the prevailing message of risk aversion (cf. Frey, 1991). Although the threshold of risk and risk-taking varies throughout different sport forms and in different sport contexts, sport is still intimately, if not often uncritically, connected with positive and negative risk. Even while Kumaritashvili's death hung over the 2010 Games, televised broadcasts of the Olympics repeatedly employed risk-laden cues and metaphors to depict, valorize and, on many occasions, glamorize athletes who embraced the negative consequences of risk and played through pain in their pursuit of success.[1] Sport remains for many the only place to engage in "edgework" (Lyng, 1990) – to engage in practices that privilege risk-taking and the "uncertainties of the edge" (Lyng, 2005: 4) – at a time when individuals are being inundated, more so than ever, with messages that anything and everything is a potential danger to the health of the individual and collective social body *and* that it is their duty to minimize risk, to exercise caution, and to privilege safety.

Risk remains one of the most widely debated concepts in social and political thought. The scope and focus of existing theories of risk are varied and suggest a wide range of ontologies and epistemologies – from Douglas' cultural/symbolic perspective to Foucauldian notions of governmentality to Giddens' and Beck's critical realist, also referred to as critical structuralist, conceptualizations of the "risk society" (e.g., Beck, 1992a, 1992b; Beck, Giddens, and Lash, 1994; Dean, 1999; Douglas, 1992; Douglas and Wildavsky, 1982; Foucault, 1988; Fox, 1999;

Giddens, 1991).[2] While differences exist between theoretical approaches, some common features include the beliefs that "risk has become an increasingly pervasive concept of human existence in western societies: risk is a central aspect of human subjectivity; risk is seen as something that can be managed through human intervention; and risk is associated with notions of choice, responsibility, and blame" (Lupton, 1999: 25).

These themes all touch upon sport and yet the ways in which risk operates within and through sport remain largely neglected in these theoretical discussions (Lyng, 2005). How do the tensions between taking risk and avoiding risk play out in current sporting practices as they are immersed in the broader "risk society"? This chapter explores this question and others, including: what kinds of risk literacy are being promoted in contemporary sport and what kinds of risk-sport participants are being shaped (cf. Novas and Rose, 2005)? The goal is to demonstrate both the exploitation of the sport-risk tolerance/sport-risk aversion tension for the purposes of selling particular forms of risk management *and* the development and promotion of a particular neurotic type of sport-risk participant who aligns his/her rights and responsibilities with commodified and commercialized forms of risk management. In the last section of the chapter, I examine the relationship between risk and Olympic sport in two ways: first, by exploring sports medicine as a system of risk management in high-performance sport; and second, by exploring the expressions of anxiety and assurance following the death of the young luger.

Locating Sport in the Risk Society

As noted earlier, there are a number of theoretical approaches to the study of risk. One that is particularly useful for our analysis, in spite of its failure to adequately address voluntary risk-taking, is Ulrich Beck's concept of the risk society. This chapter cannot do justice to the full breadth and depth of Beck's work or to the range of critiques leveled at the concept of the risk society, but a limited outline of the central themes is warranted.

Beck (1992a: 21) defines risk as "a systematic way of dealing with the hazards and insecurities

induced and introduced by modernization itself" and suggests that the risk society is a developmental phase of modern society where people confront social, political, and economic dangers on an unparalleled scale, where such threats cannot be spatially, temporally, or socially contained, and where uncertainty has come to consume the thoughts of individuals in social life (Beck, 1994). Health – a phenomenon that takes center-stage within the risk society – is no longer simply undermined by economic hazards but by a host of risks (specifically, for Beck, wide-scale, catastrophic environmental risks) that permeate social, political, and economic systems and which "increasingly escape the institutions for monitoring and protection in industrial society" (Beck, 1994: 5). It is important to note here that other risk theories posit that we choose what risks to attend to (cf. Douglas, 1992). As Ewald (1991: 199; emphasis in original) suggests, "nothing is a risk in itself; there is no risk in reality. But on the other hand, anything *can* be a risk; it all depends on how one analyses the danger, considers the event." This is a key point when considering the "big business" of perceived and imagined risks and risk management referred to in this chapter as the safety-industrial complex (i.e., the burgeoning public and private technologies and industries focused on safety and security, with examples from the provision of personal protection to the detection, monitoring, and management of diseases; cf. Krahmann, 2011). The safety-industrial complex will be discussed in greater depth later in the chapter.

To live in the risk society is to live in a time where "the central problem . . . is not the production and distribution of 'goods' such as wealth and employment in conditions of scarcity . . . but *the prevention or minimization of 'bads'*; that is, risks" (Lupton, 1999: 59; emphasis added). Whereas the twentieth century began with "unprecedented techno-optimism," the twenty-first century has begun with a sobering understanding of the "magnitude of the intended and unintended consequences of . . . massive technologies" (Jaegar *et al.*, 2001: 9). Lupton (1999: 64) adds that "in the early days of industrialization, risks . . . were evident to the senses – they could be smelt, touched, tasted or observed with the naked eye. In contrast, many of the major risks today largely escape perception . . . [and]

exist in scientific knowledge rather than in every-day experience." Beck suggests that risks

> depend on a simultaneously *scientific and social construction*. Science is one of *the causes, the medium of definition and the source of solutions* to risks, and by virtue of that very fact opens new markets of scientization for itself. In the reciprocal interplay between risks it has helped to cause and define, and the public critique of those same risks, techno-scientific development becomes *contradictory*. (1992a: 155; emphasis in original)

Scientific knowledge is contradictory, uncertain, and highly contestable. We need only to listen to a week's worth of news reports to hear "scientific" studies confirm the benefit of a compound, only to find out the next week that other "scientific" studies find the same compound hazardous. Indi-viduals are now "expected to live with a broad variety of different, mutually contradictory, global and personal risks" and to do so in an environment of competing expert discourse and rising uncertainty about what is and what is not a risk (Beck, 1994: 7).

Decision-making has become crucial within the risk society such that, as Elliott (2002: 295) notes, "'risk always depend on decisions – that is, they presuppose decisions. The idea of risk society is thus bound up with the development of instrumental rational control, which the process of modernization promotes in all spheres of life – from individual risk of accidents and illnesses to export risks and risks of war." Elliott continues, "the arrival of advanced modernization is not wholly about risk; it is also about an expansion of choice. For if risks are an attempt to make the incalculable calculable, then risk-monitoring pre-supposes agency, choice, calculation and respon-sibility" (p. 298).

Beck similarly argues that as more and more areas of life are being released from the hold of tradition, individuals are, more than ever, preoc-cupied with and involved in negotiating them-selves in the face of unpredictable surroundings and without clear guidelines that, in earlier stages of modernity, came from such sources as the family or work (cf. Giddens, 1991). Heralded by rapid transformations in gender roles and pat-terns, family structure, mass education, changes

in the labor market, and a general disillusionment with such traditional institutions as religion and science, there is now a plasticity, pliability, *and* anxiety (cf. Wilkinson, 2001) to the construction of identity and lifestyle not seen in other periods of history. As Annandale sums up:

> In the opinion of both Giddens and Beck, the global conditions of late modernity invite us to reconsider the nature of individual experience which, it is argued, is no longer bound by class, gender and race, but exposed to new social parameters of risk and uncertainty which cross-cut traditional social divisions. To be sure, these divisions still have *relevance* for people, but they are no longer, in a straightforward way, the units from which experience derives. (1998: 19, emphasis in original)

It is this set of developments – the subjective backdrop of the risk society – that Beck calls indi-vidualization. Individualization has an increasing effect on the conduct of everyday life for large numbers of people by compelling them to invent new customs and norms for themselves without the certainties of traditional institutions. Indi-viduals are now required to construct their lives "in the absence of fixed, obligatory and tradi-tional norms and certainties," and "individualiza-tion . . . involves a proliferation of new demands upon people at the same time as choices have become more and more complex and difficult" (Lupton, 1999: 69–70).

For Beck, the primacy of agency and the seem-ingly boundless political options for identity in the late (reflexive) modern moment is largely optimistic (Beck and Beck-Gernsheim, 2002). Yet, scholars have pointed to some uneasy fea-tures – a full exploration of which falls beyond the scope of this chapter – about individualiza-tion and the negotiation of self as contextualized within contemporary neoliberal capitalism. Indi-vidualization within the risk society, with its emphasis on lifestyle and choice, demands focus of the self inward to our wants (whether material or otherwise) with a resulting increased focused on consumption as the self we seek is one we buy rather than create (cf. Bauman, 2000). This is framed by, and in turn facilitates, global neolib-eral capitalism and free-market subjectivity: "The rise of capitalist individualism . . . beckons to us as a possible root cause for the modern obsession with isolated interior life. A free-market economy needs the autonomous individual as its fundamental social unit separate from the communal and family identification that could compromise the absolute freedom of movement of entrepreneurs, workers and capital itself" (Mansfield, 2000: 174). In a dangerous cycle of alienation, the self-reflexive turn of individualization within the free market sees consumption become the central feature of social action with decreased attention to communal identity and to people as producers.

Whereas Karl Marx valued individual self-realization – actualized through productive life – as the standard against which social, economic, and political relations should be judged, individualization within the risk society becomes about choice, choice gets taken up as consumption, and the acquisition of material goods and services reproduces alienation: "private property is thus the product, the result, the necessary consequence of alienated labour, the estranged relations of labour to nature and to itself" (Marx and Engels, 1982: 1, 3, 372; see also Beamish, 2009: 94). As Beamish summarizes Marx's work:

> Marx argued that workers producing under conditions of political economy – where the means of production are privately owned and controlled – create not only products and profit; they simultaneously create the very system that confronts them. Workers working under the conditions of bourgeois society live and work under conditions of alienation and estrangement; they are dominated by the end product of their own labour. (2009: 93)

Choice is contextual and socially constructed – under capitalism, individualization demands choice via consumption within a context where not all people have choice equally, where not all people are in a position to purchase the goods and services that supposedly give shape to our identities.

How then are contemporary sporting practices and sport-risk implicated here in this discussion of the risk society? Clearly we recognize that the negative consequences of sport-risk are not nearly as wide or disastrous as global warming or catastrophic nuclear war, but neither should the very real lived experiences arising from the negative consequences of sport-risk (e.g., pain, injury, death) nor the tensions and contradictions involved for individuals as they negotiate sport in the risk society be overlooked or underestimated. Sport does not exist in a social vacuum, so people are called upon to approach sport at a time when anything and everything is a risk and potential danger, when decisions need to be made by individuals (rather than collectives) amidst a growing number of complex choices, and when the prevailing message to individuals is to make those choices and act in ways that minimize risk rather than maximize pleasure or excitement. This is ironic since sport remains for many one of the few remaining areas of social life for people to invent new social traditions and, as noted above, to experience risk and "the uncertainties of the edge" (Lyng, 2005: 4). Individuals are compelled to choose their sporting experiences at a time when sport is contradictory – if safety is privileged in the risk society, sport is potentially unsafe.[3] If people are urged to act responsibly in the risk society, participating in sport is potentially irresponsible. If the "culture of precaution" (Safai, 2003) is what we should be promoting, why the continued production and reproduction of a "culture of risk" (Nixon, 1992) in sport? These sport-risk binaries – safety/danger, responsibility/irresponsibility, precaution/risk – exist and are negotiated by individuals all the time in the risk society and this chapter begins to unpack some of the ways in which these binaries operate and their implications for sport in the risk society by posing two key questions: what kinds of risk literacy are being promoted in contemporary sport and, as a consequence, what kinds of sport-risk participants are being shaped?

Expect the Unexpected: Selling Safety

According to Richard Giulianotti (2009), the study of risk in the sociology of sport has waxed and waned over time. In his essay, both an extensive review of the signature literatures that contribute to the study of risk and sport and an agenda-setting call-to-arms for sport scholars, so to speak, Giulianotti points out that while risk analysis has been employed in the study of sport, as well as "risk-informed analyses of sport and class, gender, childhood and fitness *inter alia*," the theorization of risk – and to an even lesser extent, the theorization of safety – in sport remains relatively underdeveloped, and that "the sociology of sport has yet to witness the emergence of a network of scholars whose defining focus is risk analysis" (2009: 541). While the latter point could be debated given the varied work of scholars on extreme sports (e.g., Wheaton, 2004), social stratification in risk-sport (e.g., Fletcher, 2008; Kay and Laberge, 2002), violence, pain, and injury (e.g., Young, 1993, 2004), social control and governmentality (e.g., Laurendeau and van Brunschot, 2006; McDermott, 2007), and cultural identity (e.g., Atkinson, 2004; Atkinson and Young, 2008), this chapter attempts to contribute to the former call for greater theorization of risk and safety in the sociocultural study of sport via a case study of one particular (and spectacular) sport/medical risk management organization, Immediate Assistants.

Immediate Assistants (IA) is the brainchild of Dr Adrian Cohen, who is perhaps best known for his role as medical director on such Mark Burnett television productions as the (now defunct) Discovery Channel's "Eco-Challenge" and CBS Television's "Survivor." Created by Cohen in 1990, IA is an Australian-based emergency medicine and rescue organization, designed to "ensure that the highest standard of medical care is available to every participant in a wide variety of events."[4] Their clients include a mixture of sport (rugby, triathlon, surfing) and entertainment/media productions (Paramount Pictures, USA Networks, Universal Pictures, Fox Studios, and Baywatch). The Eco-Challenge productions offered a number of fascinating examples of the strategies used by IA to manage and minimize the risks of the race. The mobile medical/rescue team, known as the "Thunderbirds" in homage to the 1960s marionette television show about a futuristic international rescue team, included a specially designed mobile surgical hospital and approximately 12 physicians and rescue workers who were supplemented by local doctors, nurses, and volunteers selected on their clinical expertise and knowledge/familiarity with the surrounding areas.[5] IA personnel trained for months prior to an Eco-Challenge race, reviewing both emergency medical protocols and specialist rescue techniques, so that they could access any and all par-

ticipants regardless of the terrain. If the medical team needed to parachute into a location or climb a mountain or rappel down a vertical cliff face to assist race participants, they did so.

Eco-Challenge is a prime example of commodified contemporary sport practices that sell risk-taking and safety almost simultaneously. Such events continue to be defined by the ideology of excellence as participants still engage in the relentless and calculated pursuit of superior performance; however, one could argue that the nature of risk and risk-taking in these events is, arguably, illusory given the types of safety measures put in place. Such sporting practices do not offer opportunities for the edgework that they market so much as they offer risk minimization and management in the most spectacular ways. In a description of Eco-Challenge's reputation as a safe sporting event, it was acknowledged that

> years of experience, research, training, preparation and planning, combined with comprehensive proactive steps, have established an extremely high safety record for Eco-Challenge. The race itself operates in an uncontrolled wilderness, under extreme conditions. Every discipline in the course has inherent risks and hazards, and while there is no guarantee of personal safety, Eco-Challenge takes months to analyze all potential risks and then takes constant action to mitigate them.[6]

This passage does touch on the risks associated with Eco-Challenge, but the focus is squarely on selling the event's safety (the minimization of its "bads") in light of its dangers via the techno-scientific risk management expertise of the Eco-Challenge organizers. Through "years of experience, research, training, preparation and planning, combined with comprehensive proactive steps," and in spite of "an uncontrolled wilderness," "extreme conditions," and "no guarantee of personal safety," the Eco-Challenge organizers maintain that they can render incalculable risk (arguably, the seductive quality of "edgework") calculable through their practices, techniques, and rationalities (Dean, 1999). The connection to the safety-industrial complex is clear here – the event stimulates the need for techno-scientific risk management and safety experts who then profit from attending to the risk management and safety needs of the participants in the event. Let us remember what Beck suggests about the nature of techno-scientific knowledge in the risk society: "[risks] depend on a simultaneously *scientific and social construction*. Science is one of *the causes, the medium of definition and the source of solutions* to risks, and by virtue of that very fact opens new markets of scientization for itself" (Beck, 1992a: 155; emphasis in original). Eco-Challenge relied on numerous consultants to oversee specific aspects of the competition, to research and plan ahead for potential risks, and to take responsibility for and mitigate those potential risks; this included health risks and involved IA.

Unlike a healthcare team pulled together for an Olympic Games that has a short and temporary lifespan (team members and equipment are brought together before the event and then disbanded afterwards), IA is a professionalized, ongoing, and for-hire medical/paramedical entity that offers specialized services for major high-profile events. We must recognize that there are a host of similarities and differences between what IA do and what sports medicine clinicians in other high-performance sport contexts (e.g., the Olympics) do – this is an area that warrants future research. For the purposes of this chapter, however, it is the language employed by IA in their website that speaks to the exploration of the risk–caution tension. It exemplifies the ways in which sport-risk binaries are used as tools to construct a particular type of sport-risk participant who demands some degree of safety and risk management as part of their sport-risk participation.

IA identify and recognize themselves as medical risk managers and suggest that "Effective Medical Risk Management incorporates anticipating incidents and preparing appropriately for them rather than . . . adopting an 'it didn't happen there so it can't happen here' attitude" (IA website; cf. Kavaler and Alexander, 2012). Similar to the excerpt noted above about Eco-Challenge and its risk management strategies, we see an attempt to persuade readers of the website that IA can render risk calculable and, in doing so, can anticipate, prepare for, and respond to whatever hazards and dangers that may exist. A key question becomes, then: for whom is this website developed? Is this website geared towards

actual sport-risk participants, organizers of the events, or insurers of the events? The short answer is all of the above – while the website covers issues and topics that are of specific interest to each stakeholder, it speaks to all the stakeholders concurrently.

IA claim to "expect the unexpected" and provide "paramedical cover for valuable human assets." One part of the website reads:

> Ask yourself: What is the worst thing that can happen to your people?
> Now ask: What EXACTLY will we do if "the worst" happens?
> Are you happy with the answers??

> 24 hours-a-day, 7 days-a-week, Immediate Assistants personnel and the latest Emergency Medical Equipment can be available to instantly respond to incidents involving your most valuable Human Assets, and those dedicated to their protection.

> Don't leave the safety of your most valuable assets, your Human Assets, to chance . . .

The text of the website can be deconstructed in many ways but this one frame alone highlights the ways in which sport-risk binaries – safety/danger, responsibility/irresponsibility, and trust/distrust – are used to implicitly and explicitly sell this service. In other words, the risk–caution tension associated with these events and marketed through the word play of sport-risk binaries is resolved through the purchase of the services offered by IA (e.g., risks are calculable, dangers are manageable, and you are irresponsible if you do not hire IA).

This section of the website implicates the organizer of the event, but we can extend this example to encompass the sport-risk participant. One potential reading of the way in which the risk–caution tension is resolved for the participant through IA sees the participant recognizing their act of responsibility by choosing to participate in an event that includes this risk management service. For example, risks are calculable, dangers are manageable, and I am responsible if I participate in this event that includes IA. Furthermore, if I do get into trouble while participating, I am acting responsibly (to myself? to my team? to others, e.g., family, friends, colleagues?) by calling on their services. If I participate in an event that does not include such risk management services or if I choose not to call on them in my time of need, than I am acting irresponsibly. The risk–caution tension is resolved to a degree through this line of reasoning, although one cannot avoid questioning whether participants are acting responsibly towards the individuals who are called on to rescue them. Furthermore, from the point of the view of the rescuer, how far are they willing to go in rescuing someone and how responsible/irresponsible are they being?[7]

Anxiety, Assurance, and the Risk–Caution Citizenship Project

The text used in the IA website is underpinned not by techno-scientific data but by a language of anxiety, fear, *and* shame. The use of such language is useful in allowing us to recognize the role of emotions in the risk–caution tension. Wilkinson argues that "the current prominence of the 'language' of risk . . . is generally understood to be related to the fact that people are increasingly disposed to see the world as full of danger" (2001: 6). This is not to suggest that the world is somehow now full of danger and it was not previously. Rather, as noted above, we choose which risks to attend to (and which ones not to attend to) based on a variety of political, social, and cultural factors (cf. Douglas, 1992) and within the risk society, risk has come to dominate our social psyche even though, as Beck (1992a: 55) ambivalently acknowledges "it is not clear whether it is the risks that have intensified, or our view of them."

Sport is much safer and more civilized (cf. Elias and Dunning, 1986) than in previous eras and yet there is a heightened sensitivity, now more so than ever, to the actual and potential risks and dangers of play and sport and this feeds off, in part, the promulgation of anxiety, fear, and shame (see Donnelly, 2004; Furedi, 2012). The IA website feeds anxiety and fear when it states "Ask yourself: What is the worst thing that can happen to your people? Now ask: What EXACTLY will we do if 'the worst' happens? Are you happy with the answers?" It taps into shame when it cautions the

reader not to "leave the safety of your most valuable assets, your Human Assets, to chance." It builds assurance in the services of IA (regardless of whether they can actually "instantly" resolve the crisis put in front of them) when it states "24 hours-a-day, 7 days-a-week, Immediate Assistants personnel and the latest Emergency Medical Equipment can be available to instantly respond to incidents involving your most valuable Human Assets, and those dedicated to their protection."

Readers – whether event organizers or participants – are being asked via a language of anxiety, fear, and shame to risk responsibly and "in order to risk *responsibly* (that is, to show the appropriate level of *caution*) it is necessary to purchase, and *trust* the appropriate equipment (e.g., knee brace, helmet) or service (e.g., lesson from a 'certified' instructor) to participate" (Donnelly, 2004: 53, emphasis in original). The sensational language of anxiety, fear, and shame work normatively in the support of the institutionalization of the safety-industrial complex generally, and the risk management services of IA specifically (cf. Furedi, 2006). With regard to the former point, risk – or to be more specific, the perception or sensation of risk without physical consequence (cf. Holyfield, 1999; Holyfield, Jonas, and Zajicek, 2005; Mohun, 2001) – becomes a commodity to be packaged and sold via the safety-industrial complex. As Krahmann notes:

> the world risk society is not only the outcome of unintended consequences of modernization dangers, but also a creation of private companies which have commodified risks in Europe and North America since the 1970s. Initially, these businesses focused on the provision of security as related to physical dangers such as robbery and burglary. In recent years, however, the search for new sales opportunities has encouraged firms across a widening range of economic sectors, from healthcare and food to consumer goods, to identify a wide variety of risks to the safety and wellbeing of peoples. (2011: 350)

The safety-industrial complex as located within neoliberal capitalism sees the management of risk within industrialized societies through the provision of goods and services for purchase and through, in connection with individualization, individual consumer choices. Ironically, although

Beck argues that industrialization has contributed to the creation of dangers in the risk society through unrestrained global expansion, he also notes that industrial capitalism is reflexive in that "risks are no longer the dark side of opportunities, they are also the market opportunities" (1992a: 46). Krahmann notes in her exploration of the safety-industrial complex (2011: 352), "firms can make profit from managing the risks that they or others have created. Moreover, businesses cannot only manufacture risks in a material sense, but also discursively." She adds, "risk management can take two forms: the first seeks to eliminate the causes of risk in industrial modernization; the second turns the management of the consequences of risk into a new industry sector" (p. 352). The discourse employed in the IA website asks individuals to choose between risk and safety but it promotes choice along certain lines (i.e., the purchase of their services). This is akin to Marx's view that people make history but not under conditions of their choosing; in the sport-risk context, individuals make choices but do so within a broader framework (the safety-industrial complex) that promotes certain choices more so than others.

One could argue that the stimulation of the safety-industrial complex in turn helps in constructing a particular type of citizenship project.[8] Citizenship projects speak to both ways in which people identify themselves and the ways in which they are thought about and acted upon. These sport-risk binaries and the ways in which they tap into and feed off emotions help in constructing a type of sport-risk participant who, as a function of their identification risk as framed by the safety-industrial complex (i.e., something to be managed via the purchasing of specific products or services), recognizes that their affiliation with the risk–caution sport community comes with certain rights and responsibilities. Participants have the right to rescue (which in turn stimulates the safety-industrial complex) and they have a responsibility (as risk-conscious individuals and consumers) to take advantage of all safety and security measures possible; not to do so would be shameful. Risk managers, such as IA, act upon sport-risk citizens by stimulating anxiety and fear and, in turn, their own abilities to mitigate those anxieties and fears. For IA, everything is considered a risk factor of some intensity (cf. Arm-

strong, 1995) and, via their expert discourse and strategy, they promote themselves as the only tacticians able to ensure, calculate, and manage the sport-risk body. This supports Dean's suggestion that "this . . . is not simply about the growing appreciation of risks among certain populations but also how groups of various kinds have come to understand themselves, their futures and their needs, in terms of risks with the assistance of a range of specialists and tutors in the identification and management of risks" (1999: 150).

This discussion of sport-risk citizenship draws on, to a large degree, biological and neurotic citizenship projects. Biological citizenship "encompasses all those citizenship projects that link their conceptions of citizens to beliefs about the biological existence of human beings, as individuals, as families and lineages, as communities, as population and races, and as a species" (Novas and Rose, 2005: 440). Biological citizenship is about identifying oneself in biological terms and using those terms to negotiate along economic, political, and social lines (cf. Petersen, 2012). Petryna's (2002) study of post-Chernobyl Ukraine offers us perhaps the most sophisticated and detailed exploration of the concept of biological citizenship. For Petryna, those who have been, or claim to be, exposed to the radiation effects of the explosion at the Chernobyl nuclear reactor in the Ukraine have come to believe that they have rights to government health services and social supports in the name of their damaged bodies. Thus, individuals who identify themselves as part of this post-Chernobyl biosocial community (cf. Novas and Rose, 2005) demand, as a right of their biological citizenship project, access "to a form of social welfare based on medical, scientific, and legal criteria that both acknowledge biological injury and compensate for it" (Petryna, 2002: 4). This interpretation of biological citizenship and biosociality informs our conceptualization of the sport-risk citizenship project. Where Novas and Rose (2005: 441) state, "biological citizenship can thus embody a demand for particular protections, for the enactment or cessation of particular policies or actions, or, access to special resources," we see a demand for risk management measures and access to special safety/security resources by those who identify themselves as part of a biosocial sport-risk community. In turn, individuals assume responsibility for their approach to risk-taking; as Novas and Rose (2005: 451) note, "part of the obligation of the active biological citizen [is] to live his or her life through acts of calculation and choice." It is important to remember that this demand for risk management measures/resources by, and the assumption of responsibility from, the sport-risk participant is immersed in a broader safety-industrial complex that stimulates and profits from these very demands and assumption.

These acts of calculation and choice are framed by anxiety, fear, and shame which gives rise to a different, but related, citizenship project: neurotic citizenry. As argued by Isin (2004: 223), "the figure that also occupies a central role in our times is the neurotic citizen who governs itself through responses to anxieties and uncertainties." The neurotic citizen is a departure from the rational individual who is "encouraged to conduct themselves in the most beneficial ways to their health, wealth and happiness in ways that are rational, self-interested and calculating" (p. 220). For Isin, the neurotic citizen is "governed through neurosis."

> The subject at the centre of governing practices is less understood as a rational, calculating and competent subject who can evaluate alternatives with relative success to avoid or eliminate risks and more as someone who is anxious, under stress and increasingly insecure and is asked to manage its neurosis. Unlike risk society theories and governmentality studies on risk, the subject at the centre of governing through neurosis is not addressed to mobilize its rational capacities to evaluate truth claims but through affects that manage its anxieties. (2004: 225)

Going back to our examination of the IA website, as argued earlier, the website relies on anxiety and shame – the language of the neurotic citizen – but it also relies upon the rational actor, one who can calculate and act competently (competence as defined by the safety-industrial complex) by choosing IA.

Biological citizenship has important implications for our understanding of contemporary sport as immersed in the risk society and as framed by the safety-industrial complex. To participate in sport is to identify, among many things, with one's embodiment and biology;

simply put, corporeality matters. Within the risk society, and as framed by the safety-industrial complex, the biological sport citizen engages in projects of self, actively shaping his or her life course through acts of biological choice – choosing what sports to participate in, choosing what to eat (whether food or drug), choosing what type of body (e.g., muscular, lithe) to construct, and so on. Biological citizenship in this sense is individualizing (Novas and Rose, 2005). Within the risk society, and as framed by the safety-industrial complex that stimulates and profits from the purchase of risk management measures, these biological choices are made amidst and through the consumption of particular sport-risk experiences (e.g., adventure racing) and particular risk management services (e.g., IA). In this sense, biological sport citizenship is also collectivizing in that athletes have a shared biological identity as sporting bodies and thus become a biosocial group. Yet, in contrast to Petryna's discussion of Chernobyl survivors joining together to advocate for their rights in the name of their damaged bodies as noted above (what Novas and Rose, 2005 refer to as "rights bio-citizenship"), we must question whether contemporary sport-risk participants mobilize together in advocacy for their sporting bodies? With this question in mind, it may be helpful to turn our attention to the study of high-performance sport and health within the risk society.

High Performance Sport and Health within the Risk Society

The very naturalization and institutionalization of sports medicine in high-performance sport represent the entrenchment of the safety-industrial complex and risk management in elite sport. In Canada, as in many other developed nation states competing in the world's high-performance sporting arena, the development and institutionalization of sports medicine in Canada, from the mid-twentieth century onwards, was not simply a function of growing knowledge about human physiology and performance or increased and selfless concern about the health and welfare of athletes. Rather, the institutionalization of sports medicine can also be viewed as a political response to the risks arising from the changes in the production of high-performance sport and one which helped to deflect attention away from the negative health consequences of the emerging intensified and hyper-competitive sport production system (Safai, 2007). In other words, institutionalized sports medicine's developmental momentum came from its role as a risk manager for the professionalized, instrumentally rationalized, and technologically assisted system of sport production that is ideologically centered on excellence at all costs and that has become privileged by many nation states post-World War II (Beamish, 2009; Beamish and Ritchie, 2004; Green and Oakley, 2001; Kidd, 1988; Shogan, 1999).

As a response to a rapidly changing national and international sociocultural, political, and economic climate post-World War II, both within and outside of sport, the ideology of excellence in sport was adopted in the late 1960s and early 1970s in Canada (cf. Macintosh and Whitson, 1990). Success on the world stage of sport was, and still is, culturally, politically, and economically salient for the Canadian state, and the government supported the emerging ideological shift in high performance in the pursuit of sporting success. This shift transformed the nature and culture of high-performance sport in Canada – privileging the professionalized, commercialized, bureaucratized, and instrumentally rationalized production of sport and fostering, as Hoberman (1992: 25) puts it, the "promise of limitless performances." The relentless and calculated pursuit of sporting success (Beamish and Ritchie, 2004) as espoused by this ideology has come to define how high-performance sport is produced and conducted (Kidd, 1988). But, the promise of "limitless performance" has its limits.

Elite athletes, in subscribing to the ideology of excellence and in uncritically accepting and over-conforming to the "sport ethic," regularly train and compete at the borders of physical breakdown (Theberge, 2007; Young and White, 1995; Young, White, and McTeer, 1994). Given this push to perform at the edge in the name of success, we should not be surprised at the widespread use of performance-enhancing drugs in high-performance sport (whether painkillers or anabolic steroids or anything in between). In fact, Beamish and Ritchie (2006: 125) suggest that "risk and danger have become such central aspects of high-performance sport that the care and treatment of injuries is a taken-for-granted aspect of all world-class athletes' training environments." They add:

> While performance-enhancing substances have been singled out for special scrutiny and prohibition under the "harm to the athlete" argument, it is the larger dangers and risks of high-performance sport itself that need to be examined if, indeed, one wants to try to legislate specific protections to ensure the health of high-performance athletes. (2006: 125)

Shilling (2005: 110) notes that while, "success in sport may involve 'subordinating the body completely to the will of the rational mind' . . . attempts to instrumentalize the flesh rarely leave it unmarked." He further adds, "dreams of 'limitless performance' may underpin political and economic investments in sport, but . . . the body remains a mortal, limited phenomenon" (2005: 111).

It is against this sociocultural, political, economic, and ideological backdrop that contemporary sports medicine developed. Although it is important to acknowledge the artificiality of only discussing the therapeutic practice of sports medicine, given that its development is intertwined with the broader growth and development of physical education and sport science, the care, treatment, and rehabilitation of athletes are decidedly phenomena of the twentieth century (Berryman and Park, 1992; Hoberman, 1992; Waddington, 2000). In Canada, discussion of the care, treatment, and rehabilitation of athletes did not gain focused attention until the late 1960s and since that time the therapeutic aspect of sports medicine, including the occupational groups that comprise the field of sports medicine, has enjoyed accelerated, uncritical, and unquestioned development in the high-performance sport system (see Safai, 2007). There was no interrogation of the ways in which "goods" (i.e., sport performance and excellence in performance) are produced or distributed in the high-performance sport system but rather a seemingly obvious need for risk minimization and management, for the need to invest in the control of "bads" (i.e., performance-inhibiting pain and injury).

The state is implicated here, not just in its adoption of a sport production system grounded in the ideology of excellence but also in its active support of the development and institutionalization of sports medicine as risk manager and minimizer; in other words, the capitalist state is an active supporter of the safety-industrial complex.[9] The growth and development of sports medicine was state-supported and subsidized in Canada because doing so was compatible with its agenda of producing success and excellence on the world stage of high performance sport (Safai, 2005). Following the inadequate quality of care provided to athletes at the 1968 Mexico City Olympic Games and the ensuing negative media coverage and public debate, the development and organization of sports medicine for Canadian athletes over the next ten years helped to allay concerns regarding Canadians' ability to compete in international competition and helped to further legitimate state involvement and intervention in high-performance sport (Harvey, 1988). There was and is genuine concern about athletes' health and well-being – it would be inappropriate to suggest that there was not a real desire on the part of sport administrators, officials, and clinicians to help athletes with their pain and injuries. However, a more critical reading of documents in and around this time highlights a different sentiment – concern over the poor performance in relation to and the risk of defeat at the hands of other nation states. If success in high-performance sport was seen as a way in which to bolster Canadian identity and nationalism in the international arena, thus legitimating increased state intervention into sport policy (cf. Harvey, 1988; Kidd, 1988), then state support and subsidy of sports medicine was a way to ensure that success by minimizing the risks to the athletes' "limitless performances." Wrapped in rhetoric of care and concern for the well-being of athletes, sports medicine helped (and helps) in deflecting attention from and softening the dangers of the emerging sport development system.

We can argue, then, that the 2010 Games repeated many of these themes. In the pursuit of winning the most medals, Canada's OTP program created Performance Enhancement Teams (PETs), which included sports medicine clinicians, linked to athletes and teams across the country as they trained for the games (Safai, 2007). As Donnelly (2004: 31) notes, defining risk "is essentially a political act because once a situation has been defined as risky, it becomes necessary for people and governments to attend to it." Thus out of the multitude of risks that arise from the performance-oriented sport system, only certain ones are selected for attention (cf. Douglas, 1992) and those do not include the actual system itself but its by-products – in this case, health problems that interfere with the athlete's performance. The success of sports medicine in deflecting attention is quite surprising, as Donnelly notes:

> the rates of injury in many sports are quite astonishing, but do not seem to have attracted the type of social criticism necessary to bring them to the forefront of public attention. If a similar rate of injury, and even death, existed in other areas of social life (e.g., in schools, factories, or the fast-food industry) it would warrant major legal and policy attention. Imagine a fast-food industry where there are regular accidents such as burns from the hot fat fryer, or falls on grease-covered kitchen floors; where there is a whole sub-specialty of medicine ('fast-food medicine') which included designated clinics, and therapists and specialists in the treatment of such injuries; and where particularly dangerous restaurants have a clinician attached to the workplace. While this may seem absurd with regard to fast-food, it is normal practice in sport. (2004: 33)

We can see this inattention to the sport production system and lack of attribution of systemic health risks to this system as an example of what Beck calls "organized irresponsibility," "in which culpability is passed off on to individuals and thus collectively denied, is maintained through political ideologies of industrial fatalism: faith in progress, dependence on rationality and the rule of expert opinion" (Elliott, 2002: 297–298). The provision of sports medicine as a naturalized and needed support service within the high-performance sport system takes attention away from the sport production process and passes the proverbial buck to the athlete – the injured athlete should not question the way in which the structure of high-performance sport compromises their health because sports medicine, the risk manager/minimizer, is there to help (cf. Fine,

2005). Ironically, as sports medicine deflects attention away from risk in the production of high-performance sport, it also contributes to the increasing medicalization of sport and positions athletes as high-risk patients who require specialized expert advice, surveillance, and regulation (see Safai, 2007).

The role of the sports medicine expert and expert discourse is highlighted within the concept of individualization. In the confrontation with current practices in the risk society, there is an interrogation of the rule of expert opinion and yet that interrogation and critique is routinely short-circuited. This deflection of attention and critique is particularly prevalent with regard to high-performance sport because of the ways in which sports medicine within elite sport is constructed to sell safety and trust. In other words, sports medicine's ability to market and promote itself via the rhetoric of safety and trust helps in deflecting attention from the risks of the ideology of excellence in sport. Beck does not really explore the relationship between risk and trust but for Giddens (1991), whose work on risk parallels Beck's in many ways, trust – "the vesting of confidence in persons . . . made on the basis of a 'leap of faith'" (p. 244) – is a dominant theme. Giddens asserts that within late modern society, there remains a reliance on generalized expert systems and trust is still a necessary part of life; however, that reliance and trust in expert systems is characterized by uncertainty. Thus, people are expected to be more challenging of expert knowledge, requiring of experts that they continually negotiate and win lay people's trust. This is one of the divides between Giddens and Beck. For Beck, reflexivity is a critique of expertise, based not in trust but in distrust of expert systems since "within the context of advanced societies in so-called high modernity, risk is a consequence of the production of wealth, the transformation of society and the institutionalization of scientific knowledge" (Turner, 1995: 220). For Giddens, reflexivity takes place through expert systems and is reliant upon lay people's trust in expertise.

The ideological orientation of sport towards excellence and the performance principle facilitate not just high performance sport's complicity in the production and reproduction of the "culture of risk" but rather its predication on the production and reproduction of the "culture of risk." In

turn, the existence and provision of sports medicine, particularly in the high-performance sport context (e.g., PETs), serves to deflect attention away from the ways in which health is subordinated to the "imperatives of performance" (Shilling, 2005: 111) in the production of high performance sport. Giulianotti (2005: 115) adds, "Beck's 'risk society' illuminates our greater reflexivity regarding sport's body risks. . . . However, the power to act reflexively remains heavily tied to long-standing frameworks of institutional and social domination. . . . [S]ports authorities prioritize doping offences rather than overall athlete health, thereby reflecting greater concern with institutional (not human) profitability." These arguments are not about the reality of the dangers of the production of high-performance sport under the ideology of excellence, but how those dangers are politicized (Carter, 1995; Lupton, 1999). Institutionalized sports medicine, as we know it, is a political response to the risks of the ideology of excellence and performance principle but one that does not disrupt the ethos or practices associated with the ideology of excellence and "performance principle."

Conclusion

It is within the political-economic context of high-performance sport, risk, and the pursuit of limitless performance that we can better understand the tragic death of Nodar Kumaritashvili in the days leading up to the 2010 Vancouver winter Olympic Games. Following his death, Olympic organizers and officials rushed to assure all participants – athletes, coaches, and local/global spectators (including media personnel) – both in rhetoric and action (the modifications of the Whistler Sliding Centre) that the Games were still safe; that the accident was exactly that, an accident. While that strategy worked – the Games did go on – it only worked to a degree as the tragedy fractured the façade of the Games as benign and offered a moment for athletes, coaches, and local/global spectators to challenge and criticize. Some lugers and FIL officials stepped forward to acknowledge that the design of the track met the commercial needs of the sport rather than its safety needs; in other words, the need to keep lugers safe was outweighed by the need to attract audiences with speed and excitement. Others decried the sacrifice of Kumaritashvili's life in pursuit of commercial success, drawing upon communal identity, communal citizenship, the communal biosociality of athletes; as one luger questioned, "to what extent are we just little lemmings that they throw down this track and we're crash-test dummies?" (cited in Zirin, 2010). In the words of Kumaritashvili's father "[Nodar] has passed through all stages of the World Cup and made it to the Olympics. He couldn't have done that if he were an inexperienced athlete. Anyone can make mistake and break a leg or suffer some other injury. But to die!" Some stepped forward to question the pursuit of excellence at all costs – a question repeated again and again over the deaths of Canadian skiers Burke and Zoricic. In a press conference following the death of her son, Nik Zoricic, Silvia Brudar laments, "Every cell in my body hurts – but knowing this could have been avoided, it makes it into agony" (CBC News, 2012).

Sport within contemporary risk society is fraught with tension between risk aversion and risk attraction and this chapter has attempted to explore this tension by posing two questions: what kinds of risk literacy are being promoted in contemporary sport and what kinds of risk-sport participants are being shaped? Through the exploration of the provision of healthcare services by IA, we see the exploitation of the risk tolerance/aversion dialectic for the purposes of selling particular forms of risk management simultaneously with risk (or at least the perception of it) *and* the development and promotion of a particular sport-risk participant who aligns themselves with the capitalistic safety-industrial complex that stimulates and profits from the consumption of risk management services. What also begins to come into focus are the rights and responsibilities of sport-risk participants such that we can explore the potential for biological sport-risk citizenship as both individualizing and collectivizing. Much more research needs to be done in this area, however, and key questions abound. In particular, given the loss of life (Kumaritashvili, Burke, Zorici, and countless others) within the machinations of high-performance sport, we must ask: is there opportunity for resistance to the alienating nature of elite sport (cf. Beamish, 2009), to commodified/commercialized sport and the safety-industrial complex through biological citizenship and, if so, what are the conditions necessary for that?

Notes

1 Slovenia's cross-country skier Petra Majdic was widely praised by journalists and media commentators of the 2010 Games for continuing to compete despite four cracked ribs and a collapsed lung suffered from a fall during a warm-up run. She won her nation's first medal, a bronze, in the women's individual sprint-class cross-country event and was awarded the inaugural Terry Fox Award by VANOC and the Terry Fox Foundation for displaying "courage" and "selflessness."

2 I would be remiss to not acknowledge figurational sociology and the contributions of its proponents to our understanding of risk in social life (e.g., Dunning, 1999; Elias and Dunning, 1986). Although the focus of this article rests on an examination of Beck's "risk society," future analyses of risk and the institutionalization of sports medicine may profit from a figurational sociological approach.

3 However, in another contradiction, sport is infinitely safer than in the past in terms of regulations and equipment while, at the same time, such measures have often encouraged athletes to take further

risks and work the edge of such equipment/regulations.

4 See http://www.immediateassistants.com/about-us/, accessed January 23, 2013.

5 The Eco-Challenge show no longer exists.

6 This description came from the USA Network website (www.usanetwork.com), and is no longer available.

7 In practice, other tensions arise to complicate the responsibility/irresponsibility binary. In early Eco-Challenge races, each team was given a radio transmitter to be used in emergencies. If the team radioed for help, they received assistance as quickly as possible from event organizers (i.e., IA) and were disqualified from further competition. Ironically, given what we already know about overconformity to the sport ethic and the "culture of risk" in sport, it is important to recognize that at some level this encourages unquestioned risk-taking and pain/injury tolerance since participants may push themselves physically and psychologically, either for personal reasons or out of sense of duty to their

teammates, until they find themselves in a situation where they need emergency assistance.

8   As noted earlier in the chapter, Beck conceptualizes individualization as an opportunity for the expansion of an individual's political freedom and yet Bauman, in the foreword to Beck and Beck-Gernsheim's *Individualization*, counters: "the other side of individualization seems to be the corrosion and slow disintegration of citizenship" (2002: xviii).

9   We must remember that the state is not monolithic, neutral or removed from the pushes and pulls of the free market; it is a dynamic institution (comprised of numerous interest groups) that moves back and forth between its, at times incongruous, accumulation and legitimation functions (cf. O'Connor, 2002). This means that the state "must try to maintain or create the conditions in which profitable capital accumulation is possible. However, the state also must try to maintain or create the conditions for social harmony. . . . The legitimization and capital accumulation functions are by no means necessarily mutually contradictory" (Panitch, 1977: 8).

References

Annandale, E. (1998) *The Sociology of Health and Medicine: A Critical Introduction*, Cambridge: Polity Press.

Armstrong, D. (1995) "The rise of surveillance medicine." *Sociology of Health and Illness*, 17 (3): 393–404.

Atkinson, M. (2004) "Tattooing and civilizing processes: Body modification as self-control." *Canadian Review of Sociology and Anthropology*, 41 (2): 125–146.

Atkinson, M. and Young, K. (eds.) (2008) *Tribal Play: Subcultural Journeys Through Sport*, Bingley, UK: JAI Press.

Bauman, Z. (2000) *Liquid Modernity*, Cambridge: Polity Press.

Bauman, Z. (2002) "Foreword," in Beck, U. and Beck-Gernsheim, E. *Individualization: Institutionalized Individualism and its Social and Political Consequences*, London: Sage.

Beamish, R. (2009) "Marxism, alienation and Coubertin's Olympic project," in Carrington, B. and McDonald, I. (eds.) *Marxism, Cultural Studies and Sport*, London: Routledge, pp. 88–105.

Beamish, R. and Ritchie, I. (2004) "From chivalrous 'brothers-in-arms' to the eligible athlete: Changed principles and the IOC's banned substance list." *International Review for the Sociology of Sport*, 39 (4): 355–371.

Beamish, R. and Ritchie, I. (2006) *Fastest, Highest, Strongest: A Critique of High-Performance Sport*, London: Routledge.

Beck, U. (1992a) *Risk Society: Towards a New Modernity*, trans. M. Ritter, London: Sage.

Beck, U. (1992b) "From industrial society to the risk society: Questions of survival, social structure and ecological enlightenment." *Theory, Culture and Society*, 9: 97–123.

Beck, U. (1994) "The reinvention of politics: Towards a theory of reflexive modernization," in Beck, U.,
Giddens, A., and Lash, S. (eds.) *Reflexive Modernization: Politics, Traditions and Aesthetics in the Modern Social Order*, Stanford, CA: Stanford University Press, pp. 1–55.

Beck, U. and Beck-Gernsheim, E. (2002) *Individualization: Institutionalized Individualism and its Social and Political Consequences*, London: Sage Publications.

Beck, U., Giddens, A., and Lash, S. (eds.) (1994) *Reflexive Modernization: Politics, Traditions and Aesthetics in the Modern Social Order*, Stanford, CA: Stanford University Press.

Berryman, J. and Park, R. (1992) *Sport and Exercise Science: Essays in the History of Sports Medicine*, Urbana: University of Illinois Press.

Carter, S. (1995) "Boundaries of danger and uncertainty: An analysis of the technological culture of risk assessment," in Gabe, J. (ed.) *Medicine, Health and Risk: Sociological Approaches*, Oxford: Blackwell, pp. 133–150.

CBC News (2012) "Skier Nik Zoricic's family wants impartial probe into his death," April 25, http://www.cbc.ca/news/canada/toronto/story/2012/04/25/toronto-zoricic-family.html, accessed December 6, 2012.

Dean, M. (1999) "Risk, calculable and incalculable," in Lupton, D. (ed.), *Risk and Sociocultural Theory: New Directions and Perspectives*, Cambridge: Cambridge University Press, pp. 131–159.

Donnelly, P. (2004) "Sport and risk culture," in Young, K. (ed.) *Sporting Bodies, Damaged Selves: Sociological Studies of Sports-related Injury*, Bingley, UK: JAI Press, pp. 29–58.

Douglas, M. (1992) *Risk and Blame: Essays in Cultural Theory*, London: Routledge.

Douglas, M. and Wildavsky, A. (1982) *Risk and Culture: An Essay on the Selection of Technological and Environmental Dangers*, Berkeley: University of California Press.

Dunning, E. (1999) *Sport Matters: Sociological Studies of Sport, Violence and Civilization*, London: Routledge.

Dzhindzhikhashvili, M. (2010) "Georgian luger told dad 'I will either win or die,'" *Huffington Post*, February 15, http://www.huffingtonpost.com/2010/02/15/nodar-kumaritashvili-dead_n_462927.html, accessed January 17, 2013.

Elias, N. and Dunning, E. (1986) *Quest for Excitement: Sport and Leisure in the Civilizing Process*, Oxford: Basil Blackwell.

Elliott, A. (2002) "Beck's sociology of risk: A critical assessment." *Sociology*, 36 (2): 293–315.

Ewald, F. (1991) "Insurance and risk," in Burchell, G., Gordon, C., and Miller, P. (eds.) *The Foucault Effect: Studies in Governmentality*, London: Harvester Wheatsheaf, pp. 197–210.

Fine, M. (2005) "Individualization, risk and the body: Sociology and care." *Journal of Sociology*, 41 (3): 247–266.

Fletcher, R. (2008) "Living on the edge: The appeal of risk sports for the professional middle class." *Sociology of Sport Journal*, 25 (3): 310–330.

Foucault, M. (1988) "Technologies of the self," in Martin, L.H., Gutman, H., and Hutton, P.H. (eds.) *Technologies of the Self*, London: Tavistock, pp. 16–49.

Fox, N. (1999) "Postmodern reflections on 'risk,' 'hazards' and life choices," in Lupton, D. (ed.) *Risk and Sociocultural Theory: New Directions and Perspectives*, Cambridge: Cambridge University Press, pp. 12–33.

Frey, J. (1991) "Social risk and the meaning of sport." *Sociology of Sport Journal*, 8 (2): 136–145.

Furedi, F. (2006) *Culture of Fear Revisited: Risk-taking and the Morality of Low Expectation* (4th edn.), New York: Continuum.

Furedi, F. (2012) "Fearmongers' race to bottom as unseen threats win Olympic status." *The Australian*, July 21, http://www.theaustralian.com.au/national-affairs/opinion/fearmongers-race-to-bottom-as-unseen-threats-win-olympic-status/story-e6frgd0x-1226431226463, accessed December 6, 2012.

Giddens, A. (1991) *Modernity and Self-Identity*, Cambridge: Polity Press.

Giulianotti, R. (2005) *Sport: A Critical Sociology*, Cambridge: Polity Press.

Giulianotti, R. (2009) "Risk and sport: An analysis of sociological theories and research agendas." *Sociology of Sport Journal*, 26 (4): 540–556.

Green, M. and Oakley, B. (2001) "Elite sport development systems and playing to win: Uniformity and diversity in international approaches." *Leisure Studies*, 20: 247–267.

Harvey, J. (1988) "Sport policy and the welfare state: An outline of the Canadian case." *Sociology of Sport Journal*, 5: 315–329.

Hoberman, J. (1992) *Mortal Engines: The Science of Performance and the Dehumanization of Sport*, New York: Free Press.

Holyfield, L. (1999) "Manufacturing adventure: The buying and selling of emotions." *Journal of Contemporary Ethnography*, 28 (1): 3–32.

Holyfield, L., Jonas, L., and Zajicek, A. (2005) "Adventure without risk is like Disneyland," in Lyng, S. (ed.) *Edgework: The Sociology of Risk-taking*, New York: Routledge, pp. 173–186.

Isin, E. (2004) "The neurotic citizen." *Citizenship Studies*, 8 (3): 217–235.

Jaegar, C., Renn, O., Rosa, E., and Webler, T. (2001) *Risk, Uncertainty and Rational Action*, London: Earthscan Publications.

Kavaler, F. and Alexander, R. (2012) *Risk Management in Healthcare Institutions: Limiting Liability and Enhancing Care* (3rd edn.), New York: Jones and Bartlett Learning.

Kay, J. and Laberge, S. (2002) "The 'new' corporate habitus in adventure racing." *International Review for the Sociology of Sport*, 37 (1): 17–36.

Kidd, B. (1988) "The philosophy of excellence: Olympic performances, class power and the Canadian state," in Galasso, P. (ed.) *Philosophy of Sport and Physical Activity*, Toronto: Canadian Scholars' Press, pp. 11–31.

Krahmann, E. (2011) "Beck and beyond: Selling security in the world risk society." *Review of International Studies*, 37 (4): 349–372.

Laurendeau, J. and van Brunschot, E.G. (2006) "Policing the edge: Risk and social control in skydiving." *Deviant Behavior*, 27 (2): 173–201.

Longman, J. (2010) "Quick to blame in luge, and showing no shame." *New York Times*, February 13, http://www.nytimes.com/2010/02/14/sports/olympics/14longman.html?_r=1, accessed December 6, 2012.

Lupton, D. (1999) *Risk*, London: Routledge.

Lyng, S. (1990) "Edgework: A social psychological analysis of voluntary risk-taking." *American Journal of Sociology*, 95: 851–886.

Lyng, S. (2005) (ed.) *Edgework: The Sociology of Risk-taking*, New York: Routledge.

Macintosh, D. and Whitson, D. (1990) *The Game Planners: Transforming Canada's Sport System*, Montreal: McGill-Queen's University Press.

Mansfield, N. (2000) *Subjectivity: Theories of the Self from Freud to Haraway*, New York: New York University Press.

Marx, K. and Engels, F. (1982) *Gesamtausgabe* (Complete Works), Berlin: Dietz Verlag.

McDermott, L. (2007) "A governmental analysis of children 'at risk' in a world of physical inactivity and obesity epidemics." *Sociology of Sport Journal*, 24 (3): 302–324.

Mohun, A.P. (2001) "Designed for thrills and safety: Amusement parks and the commodification of risk, 1880–1929." *Journal of Design History*, 14 (4): 291–306.

Nixon, H. (1992) "A social network analysis of influences on athletes to play with pain and injuries." *Journal of Sport & Social Issues*, 16 (2): 127–135.

Novas, C. and Rose, N. (2005) "Biological citizenship," in Ong, A. and Collier, S. (eds.) *Global Assemblages: Technology, Politics and Ethics as Anthropological Problems*, Oxford: Blackwell, pp. 439–463.

O'Connor, J. (2002) *The Fiscal Crisis of the State*, New York: Palgrave Macmillan.

Panitch, L. (1977) *The Canadian State: Political Economy and Political Power*, Toronto: University of Toronto Press.

Petersen, A. (2012) "Foucault, health and healthcare," in Scambler, G. (ed.) *Contemporary Theorists for Medical Sociology*, London: Routledge, pp. 7–19.

Petryna, A. (2002) *Life Exposed: Biological Citizens after Chernobyl*, Princeton, NJ: Princeton University Press.

Russell, S. (2012) "Risk and sport: The nature of the beast," January 11, http://www.cbc.ca/sports/blogs/scottrussell/2012/01/risk-and-sport-the-nature-of-the-beast.html, accessed December 6, 2012.

Safai, P. (2003) "Healing the body in the 'culture of risk': Examining the negotiation of treatment between sport medicine clinicians and injured athletes in Canadian intercollegiate sport." *Sociology of Sport Journal*, 20 (2): 127–146.

Safai, P. (2005) "The demise of the Sport Medicine and Science Council of Canada." *Sport History Review*, 36 (2): 91–114.

Safai, P. (2007) "A critical analysis of the early development of sports medicine in Canada." *International Review for the Sociology of Sport*, 42 (3): 321–341.

Shilling, C. (2005) *The Body in Culture, Technology and Society*, London: Sage Publications.

Shogan, D. (1999) *The Making of High-Performance Athletes: Discipline, Diversity, and Ethics*, Toronto: University of Toronto Press.

Theberge, N. (2007) "It's not about health: It's about performance," in Hargreaves, J. and Vertinsky, P. (eds.) *Physical Culture, Power and the Body*, New York: Routledge, pp. 176–194.

Turner, B.S. (1995) *Medical Power and Social Knowledge* (2nd edn.), London: Sage Publications.

Waddington, I. (2000) *Sport, Health and Drugs: A Critical Sociological Perspective*, London: E. & F.N. Spon.

Wheaton, B. (ed.) (2004) *Lifestyle Sport: Consumption, Identity and Difference*, London: Routledge.

Wilkinson, I. (2001) *Anxiety in a Risk Society*, London: Routledge.

Young, K. (1993) "Violence, risk and liability in male sports culture." *Sociology of Sport Journal*, 10 (4): 373–396.

Young, K. (ed.) (2004) *Sporting Bodies, Damaged Selves: Sociological Studies of Sports-related Injury*, Bingley, UK: JAI Press.

Young, K. and White, P. (1995) "Sport and physical danger: The experience of female elite athletes." *Journal of Sport & Social Issues*, 19 (1): 45–61.

Young, K., White, P., and McTeer, W. (1994) "Body talk: Male athletes reflect on sport, injury and pain." *Sociology of Sport Journal*, 11: 175–195.

Zirin, D. (2010) "Nodar Kumaritashvili: Never forget," February 22, http://www.edgeofsports.com/2010-02-22-504/index.html, accessed December 6, 2012.

Further Reading

Beck, U. (ed.) (2009) *World at Risk*, Cambridge: Polity Press.

Giulianotti, R. (2009) "Risk and sport: An analysis of sociological theories and research agendas." *Sociology of Sport Journal*, 26 (4): 540–556.

Holyfield, L., Jonas, L., and Zajicek, A. (2005) "Adventure without risk is like Disneyland," in Lyng, S. (ed.) *Edgework: The Sociology of Risk-taking*, New York: Routledge, pp. 173–186.

Le Breton, D. (2000) "Playing symbolically with death in extreme sports." *Body and Society*, 6 (1): 1–11.

Lois, J. (2002) *Heroic Efforts: The Emotional Culture of Search and Rescue Volunteers*, New York: New York University Press.

Magdalinski, T. (2009) *Sport, Technology and the Body: The Nature of Performance*, London: Routledge.

7

Sport, Ecological Modernization, and the Environment

Brian Wilson and Brad Millington

"Looking after the environment is essential if we are to preserve living conditions today and for future generations. Managing environmental issues has also become a critical success factor for business. Environmental awareness drives innovations and resource savings, leading to efficient production and reduced costs."[1] This quotation, taken from the reputable Global Forum for Sports and the Environment (G-ForSE) website (see also Adidas Group, 2009), precedes a review of sustainability practices adopted and modeled by the successful athletic apparel maker Adidas. While the passage is in the first place indicative of the extent to which leading sport corporations now express concern over their environmental impacts, it also offers an initial glimpse into some of the assumptions that often drive environmental "best practices." Indeed, it is not uncommon for businesses to emphasize innovation – especially the development of "clean" technologies – as a means to achieve environmental sustainability, to cater to "green" consumers, and to continue on a path of economic growth. This pertains not only to the production of sports equipment and paraphernalia (as in the case of Adidas) but to the hosting of sporting mega-events like the Olympics as well.

As many scholars have described (e.g., Davidson and MacKendrick, 2004; Gibbs, 2000; Hajer, 1995; Hannigan, 2006; Mol and Sonnenfeld, 2000), this faith in innovation is associated with a particular approach to resolving environmental problems that can be described as the "ecological modernization" approach. In general, ecological modernization is based on the fundamental assumption that existing industrial processes can be altered to become "cleaner" and more efficient while remaining profitable. In this sense, industrialization is imagined as an ongoing process that ideally will reach a "super-industrial" apotheosis whereby technological ingenuity will prevent or undo harmful environmental impacts (Hannigan, 2006: 27). The state is to aid these transitions through a decentralized and flexible style of governance that, while not spurning *dirigisme* altogether, tends to support market-driven approaches to regulation. In this chapter we take the position that while ecological modernization is not *necessarily* problematic, approaches like this become so when they are presented as the *only* reasonable ways of dealing with the potential negative environmental consequences of (for example) developing consumer goods or hosting events. The reason for concern is that inequalities are often reinforced and perpetuated when seemingly commonsensical responses to societal problems go unchallenged. In this case, inequalities

A Companion to Sport, First Edition. Edited by David L. Andrews and Ben Carrington.
© 2013 Blackwell Publishing Ltd. Published 2013 by Blackwell Publishing Ltd.

may arise because a set of ideas (e.g., those under-lying the ecological modernist perspective), and the interests of those promoting these ideas (e.g., athletic apparel companies or Olympic organiz-ing committees) are accepted unconditionally over alternative sets of ideas and interests.

Although concerns about various forms of inequality have been central to writing by critical sociologists of sport, only recently have these topics been discussed for their relevance to the environment. With this shortcoming in mind, one of the authors of this chapter recently wrote an article that critically assessed responses to sport-related environmental problems that are driven by the ecological modernization approach (Wilson, 2012a). The article focused especially on the limitations of the popular "carbon credit" system that allows sport organizations to fund carbon-reducing initiatives as a way of "offset-ting" the environmental impacts of their events. For instance, organizers of a sport mega-event like the Olympics might buy carbon offsets from a wind energy company so as both to promote clean energy production and to counterbalance the greenhouse gas emissions that stem from their own event. While such organizers might be noble in their intentions, it was noted in Wilson's article that carbon offsetting is extremely difficult to implement, and that instituting this practice in "developing" countries (as is often done) brings with it the same concerns that have been raised about other kinds of international development work (e.g., Are practices of local cultures being respected? How is the work being assessed? Is there a well-developed exit plan; cf. Giulianotti, 2004). The article also questioned the tendency to put faith in technological development as a way of lessening the impacts of economic growth. As critics have argued, this often obscures the idea that new technologies are the source of many problems and ignores the possibility that those developing new technologies will be unable to resolve problems fast enough to make a differ-ence, what Thomas Homer-Dixon (2000) has termed the "ingenuity gap." These critiques also call to mind Ulrich Beck's (1992) widely-cited arguments on the "risk society," whereby the pro-duction of risks – including environmental risks that are global in scope – is systematically and inextricably tied to the production of wealth through technological and scientific innovations.

As Beck says, even the technologies now made to combat environmental risks tend to induce new, potentially damaging risks of their own (cf. Giulianotti, 2009). Exacerbating these matters is the fact that collaborations among environmen-tal groups, governments, and corporate partners – collaborations at the core of ecological modern-ization-driven initiatives – are commonly shown to be ineffective, with environmental groups having little influence in these inter-sectoral relationships.

This chapter continues the task of supplement-ing existing research on power relations and inequality in the sociology of sport by addressing various questions left unexamined within the existing literature. These include: If there are so many reasons that ecological modernist responses to environmental problems are contentious, why is it that these responses commonly go unques-tioned? What strategies do sport-related organi-zations use to generate consent for an ecological modernization approach to solving sport-related environmental problems? And, what discourses are commonly mobilized to promote particular ways of understanding sport-related environ-mental issues, and what are the characteristics of texts (e.g., press releases) that broadcast these discourses?

In this chapter we begin to address some of these questions in the following manner. First, we discuss previous research and writing on envi-ronmental issues in the sociology of sport and consider what is already known about these ques-tions and issues. Following this, we identify and describe competing perspectives within environ-mental sociology, with a particular focus on ten-sions between ecological modernists and those who employ the critical, Marxist-influenced "treadmill of production" framework. We then offer two illustrative examples of ways that assumptions underlying the ecological moderni-zation perspective are woven into press releases by sport-related organizations and corporations. Through an analysis of these releases – taken from the aforementioned Global Forum for Sports and the Environment website, which was created to promote the environment-related work of sport organizations and corporations – we comment on how these perspectives are both privileged and taken for granted, outline why these responses are problematic, and offer a set of questions that we think should be asked about these sorts of responses. We ultimately consider how certain power dynamics are sustained by the unchallenged use of ecological modernist discourses.

In pursuing these arguments, we are thus concerned as much with what is omitted – whether strategically or inadvertently – from organizational approaches to environmentalism as we are with what is actually said and done. Michel Foucault's understanding of "discourse" has been widely embraced in the sociology of sport in contexts like these, and we will do the same. While this term takes on multiple meanings in the work of Foucault and those writing in his tradition (see Mills, 2004), it often refers to the ways that broad "conditions of possibility" (e.g., the arrival of neoliberal governance and its faith in unimpeded economic growth) allow for the emergence of specific discursive statements, practices, or policies (e.g., the creation of "clean" business technologies and other practices associated with ecological modernization). Importantly, as Foucault (1990) insists, discourses are also composed of silences – "the things one declines to say, or is forbidden to name" (p. 27).

In developing our arguments, we wish to be clear that the concerns and critiques outlined in this chapter are *not* intended to undermine the proactive environmental work that is being done by various sport-related organizations and the individuals who work within them. Rather, with Foucault's observations in mind, our view is that the space for dialogue around solutions to environmental problems is reduced and compromised when a particular response to environmental concerns appears to be the *only* viable response. For this reason, we are compelled here to consider the processes through which particular perspectives are taken for granted, to identify ways that the (sometimes problematic) assumptions underlying these perspectives might be revealed, and to underscore other questions or perspectives that are silenced under current "conditions of possibility." These questions or perspectives might ultimately be further pursued by others who are interested in responding to environmental concerns, and might help students understand both the importance of environmental issues to the study of sport and the significance of sport to contemporary debates about the environment.

Environmental Issues and the Sociology of Sport: The "Early" Years

Notwithstanding key texts in leisure studies on the implications of leisure pursuits like tourism for urban and rural spaces (e.g., Spink, 1994), research and writing on the relationship between sport and environmental issues has until recently been scarce. David Chernushenko, in his 1994 book *Greening Our Games*, was among the first to focus on these issues and to offer concrete suggestions for sport managers interested in running an environmentally, socially, and economically responsible organization. Although Chernushenko has been critiqued for adopting what Lenskyj (1998) refers to as a "light green" perspective – meaning that he sees economic development and environmental progress to be compatible – his contributions are still relevant for critical sociologists on a variety of levels. At a minimum, he describes some of the main ways that sport impacts the environment. For example, he refers to modifications to lakes and rivers for paddling and canoeing that are known to impact/reduce wetland areas; the soil erosion and destruction of natural vegetation that result from alpine skiing; the implications of golf-course construction for natural habitats, and the impacts of chemicals used on the fairways and greens of these golf courses on wildlife and humans. More generally, he refers to the environmental impacts of hosting sport events, of producing sport apparel and equipment, and of the day-to-day practices associated with running any kind of (sport) organization.

It is also noteworthy that many of the key themes Chernushenko identifies around the politics of space, around consumer culture and environmental destruction, and around sport-related activism and opportunities for social change are at the core of subsequent work in the sociology of sport field. It is especially pertinent for this chapter that Chernushenko recognizes how economic and political interests may undermine pro-environment activities, and that he expresses particular concern about the immense influence that sponsors of professional and amateur sport have over the staging and goals of sport events. In other words, Chernushenko issues an initial warning about the ways that sponsor priorities may negatively impact efforts to develop more sustainable practices.

Although not a focus of his work, Chernushenko's description of the impacts of commercialization is founded on questions about how processes of modernization have affected the development of spaces where sport is played. It is here where the influence of another early writer on issues around sport and the environment – geographer John Bale – has been integral to thinking about environmental issues and sport. Bale, in his foundational 1993 book *Sport, Space and the City* (2001), speaks to the perceived need on the part of sport managers and entrepreneurs not only to upgrade sport facilities on an ongoing basis but also to create playing conditions for athletes that are uniform across contexts. In essence, Bale describes the modernization and rationalization of sport spaces. His work has particular relevance to this chapter because he identifies ways that this tendency leads some "space engineers" to see the environment as a resource to be manipulated, used, and reshaped by humans. In a similar way, Bale (2001: 41) astutely recognizes the link between the "topocidal" tendencies of developers ("topicide" referring to the destruction of affective/emotional ties between people and places that occurs with this sort of destruction) and the increasing focus on attracting "outsiders" or tourists to these sites.

Picking up on these trends, sociologist Brian Stoddart offered a similarly groundbreaking analysis in a 1990 article that described environmental issues associated with the internationalization of golf. Stoddart focuses on how the economic concerns that have driven the expansion of the golf industry – most notably, the construction of luxury golf courses and golf-related holiday resorts – have led to environmentally dangerous practices by developers intent on building and maintaining new courses in (standardized) ways that make them attractive to golf tourists expecting a predictable experience. Stoddart links these transformations with the reshaping and exploitation of environmentally sensitive land, and with the use of hazardous chemicals to keep fairways and greens consistent and "unspoiled." Of course, in the years since Stoddart's article, many sport managers, developers, politicians, and others have come to see themselves as supporters of or members of a "corporate environmentalist" movement. These members/supporters tend to assume that with

the help of new technologies and greener construction and maintenance practices, concerns about these sorts of environmental impacts have been or are on their way to being alleviated. We return to this claim later in the chapter.

Sport, Sociology and the Environment: Contemporary Themes

Additional research on issues around the environment and sport has begun to emerge in the years since Chernushenko, Bale, and Stoddart's foundational works. The intensifying of this research agenda is surely attributable in large part to the fact that "green issues" are a growing concern – if not always a cause for action – for the public, for mainstream and niche media, for governmental and non-governmental organizations, and for industry alike. As Mincyte, Casper, and Cole (2009) write in their introduction to a two-part special issue on sport, leisure, and the environment in the *Journal of Sport & Social Issues*, this creates unprecedented opportunities for scholars to "cross-pollinate environmental sociology's commitment to social and environmental justice with the sociology of sports' focus on embodied experiences of human activity and corresponding issues of labor, power, and inequalities in leisure economies" (p. 105). Recently, authors like Wheaton (2007, 2008), Atkinson (2009), Maguire *et al.* (2002), Lenskyj (2002), Wheeler and Nauright (2006), and Stolle-McAllister (2004) initiated writing about various forms of environmental activism and resistance. Lenskyj (1998) and Beder (2002) described how some sport-related organizations attempt to "brand" themselves as green because it may be appealing to environmentally conscious consumers but do little to actually reduce their impact on the environment (a process referred to as "greenwashing"). Mansfield (2009) reported research focused on ways that various forms of environmentalism have been adopted by fitness cultures in the United Kingdom, describing how interactions between humans and non-humans reflect existing social hierarchies and are connected to processes that underlie the privileging of certain environment-related ideologies over others. Kearins and Pavlovich's (2002) study of the role played by stakeholders in the "greening" of the

Sydney Games explores the potential for undesirable compromises among environmental groups when they are the less powerful member of a collaboration. Tranter and Lowes (2009) examined the environmental, economic, and public health outcomes of mega-events, using motorsport spectacles in Australia as case studies. Cantelon and Letters (2000) addressed the complexities of the International Olympic Committee (IOC)'s decision to integrate environmental concerns into policies that support the Olympic movement, while Pitter (2009) writes about stakeholder relations and political maneuvering around the proposed development of an off-highway vehicle trail system in Nova Scotia. Weiss, Norden, and Hilscher (1998) and M. Stoddart (2012) studied awareness of and perspectives on environmental issues among skiers, and Humberstone (1998) carried out feminist ethnographic research to explore perspectives on and experiences of outdoor wilderness living.

While this is not an exhaustive list of work conducted on sport and the environment, highlighted above are some of the main issues and topics now under pursuit. Despite this progress, there is a long path ahead for sociologists of sport interested in developing a well-rounded and theoretically rich body of research and writing that investigates environment-related issues. We say this because the field of environmental sociology includes a history of work on power relations that inspired the development of various, often conflicting theoretical approaches that are explicitly sensitive to environmental issues. These approaches are seldom referred to by those studying sport.

This argument for more diverse research that is sensitive to links between sport and environmental issues was at the center of Mincyte and colleagues' (2009) aforementioned introduction to a recent two-part journal issue on these topics. They justified their argument by pointing out that while environmental issues are now addressed and acknowledged in mainstream literature on sport – a March 2007 *Sports Illustrated* cover story serves as the featured example of this (Wolff, 2007) – a survey of leading sociology of sport journals as well as environmental sociology and environmental studies journals reveals an incredible lack of attention to the topic. The authors indicate that in the three decades leading up to

the special issue, only 14 articles focused on sport and the environment appeared in the two major peer-reviewed sociology of sport journals – the *Sociology of Sport Journal* and the *International Review for the Sociology of Sport* (IRSS) – with six of these appearing in a special issue of IRSS on environmental issues in 1998. They also note that in environmental studies and environmental sociology journals there has been just a "handful" of articles that refer to sport, perhaps due to "the misconception that sports are disconnected from labor, inequalities, social movements, development politics, as well as to a disciplinary gaze that sees 'true' environmental issues in terms of eco-disasters, social movements, national parks and wilderness preserves, resource management issues, and economic relations" (Mincyte et al., 2009: 105).

The authors go on to emphasize how concerns with inequality and social justice are inseparable from thinking about environmental issues – thus supporting the view that a broader, multidisciplinary perspective is needed. To demonstrate this point, the authors describe how the impacts of ecological degradation, hazards created by unsafe industrial practices, and natural disasters have particular implications for marginalized and vulnerable groups (as Hurricane Katrina starkly demonstrated). Others, like Maguire et al. (2002: 84–85), have elaborated on this idea, identifying concepts like "intergenerational equity" (the need to consider how environment-related activities by current generations may impact future generations), "transfrontier equity" (the need to consider how the environment-related activities in local contexts may impact those living in other places), and intra-generational equity (referring to the need to account for existing social inequalities when devising sustainability projects) as guiding concepts for those concerned with power relations and the environment.

Many of those who have studied sport and the environment express concern about developments in sporting worlds that are driven by the "modernizing project" referred to above – especially the modernist assumption that there is a fundamental separation between humans and nature, and the related belief that human "progress" can be equated with "mastering nature." Mincyte and colleagues (2009) allude to these points in their discussion of how "nature" is a term commonly used to refer to "pristine, sacred space[s]," that are "external to human endeavors" (p. 105). Mansfield (2009) and Barnes (2009) address this as well in their writing about ways that wilderness/outdoor fitness programming and exercise experiences are commonly advertised as being "free" from the constraints associated with more "unnatural," overly structured spaces. Mansfield (2009), Barnes (2009), and Mincyte *et al.* (2009) challenge these depictions of nature by pointing out that "human activities, including movement of sporting bodies through space and time, can and do deeply affect the environment" (Mincyte *et al.*, 2009: 105). Underpinning this critique is the argument that the "modern separation between nature and society is imaginary (though consequential) and that natures and bodies do not exist prior to their cultural representations but are produced through discursive practices and relationships of power" (Barnes, 2009: 233, drawing on Berlant, 1997, Cronon, 1983, Haraway, 1989, and Stern, 2005).

Sport, the Environment, and Neoliberalism

Several of the authors referred to above make the argument that the perspectives commonly privileged in contemporary approaches to the environment (i.e., about how to respond to environmental problems, and about relationships between humans and non-humans) tend to reflect and support the views and interests of more powerful groups. For example, Barnes (2009), Mansfield (2009), Schaffner (2009), Tranter and Lowes (2009), and Pitter (2009) describe how responses to environmental issues and/or relationships with "nature" and "wilderness" are commonly framed in ways that privilege economic interests over concerns about the environment in subtle and sophisticated ways. In this sense, strategies of environmental management are increasingly under the directive of neoliberalism – a system of governing that privileges economic growth by optimizing the conditions for market-based exchange and by downloading responsibility for social concerns onto businesses and individual (consumer-)citizens (Harvey,

2005; Rose and Miller, 2008). Barnes (2009) in particular argues that wilderness competitions like "adventure sports" are valued by participants because they are thought to be free from the interventions and regulations associated with other sporting activities. For this reason these activities are "perfectly suited to the production of the kinds of subjects imagined through neoliberal political formations, that is, subjects who are free, autonomous, flexible, and constantly seeking their potential" (p. 233, following the work of Foucault, 2007, Ong, 2005, and Rose, 1999). In a related way, Mansfield (2009) suggests that health and fitness industries that market their products and activities as "natural," "green," and/or environmentally friendly are actively encouraging forms of "moral" or "ethical" consumption. In her view, outdoor exercise, holiday park environments, and beauty spas "reflect a type of fitness and health-oriented symbolism in 'spectacular consumption environments'" that promote "consumer freedom in a realm of elite consumption practices" (p. 358, following Silk and Andrews, 2006).

Taken together, these works are instructive in their recognition of how individuals' relationships with "nature" are increasingly structured around a taken-for-granted form of citizenship that is articulated through "consumer choice" and "personal responsibility." From this (neoliberal) perspective, it is assumed that individuals negatively or positively impact the societies they live in primarily through the decisions they (inevitably) make about *purchasable* goods and services. The problem with this emphasis on conspicuous consumption of morally and ethically superior fitness-related items and activities (e.g., "green" spas) is that, while framed in terms of lifestyle choices, it ultimately is structured in ways that exclude those without the economic or cultural resources required for participation. That is to say, there is no choice for environmental action for some people, and for other people (with adequate resources), the only choices are *consumer* choices.

Equally disconcertingly, some scholars suggest that certain kinds of participation in and consumption of wilderness activities are also based around deceptive associations with environmentalism. Returning to Barnes' analysis of adventure sports, she explains how some environmentalists were taken by surprise at the damage outdoor tourism, especially mountain bikes, could inflict on the land. . . . Though mountain biking initially seemed preferable to cattle ranching, uranium mining, and gas/oil exploration [activities historically associated with the wilderness areas in Utah that Barnes was writing about], it quickly came to be viewed as a primary threat to the very existence of the landscape. . . . The detrimental effects of mountain biking on the land eventually came to be embodied in the need to protect delicate, living soil structures known as cryptobiotic or cryptogamic soils. . . . According to educational campaigns designed by the NPS [National Park Service] and environmental organizations, once damaged by footprint or bike tread, soil structure regeneration can take up to 250 years. (2009: 245–246)

In a similar way, Tranter and Lowes (2009), argue that developments of urban spaces in the name of "public good" are done in ways that serve "the interests of hegemonic groups in society" (p. 155). As an example, the authors point out that the development of sport facilities in the "most expensive and 'spectacular' spaces of a city" – a common practice in the Australian cities studied by the authors – ultimately undermines "the values of environmental and public health through the promotion of [potentially environmentally unfriendly forms of] conspicuous consumption" (p. 155).

In the next part of this chapter we build on the work of the above-mentioned sociologists of sport who have brought attention to the ways that neoliberal discourses and to a certain extent "modernist" discourses are privileged in rhetoric produced by many sport-related organizations and corporations. We do this in two ways. First, we consider how the "ecological modernization" concept – a concept developed in the 1980s and revised and rethought by environmental sociologists in the years since – could be helpful for thinking about some key concerns raised by sociologists of sport. Second, we offer examples of ways that assumptions underlying an ecological modernist response to environmental issues are woven into promotions of "green" initiatives by sport-related organizations.

Ecological Modernization and Environmental Sociology

Authors like Davidson and MacKendrick (2004) describe how assumptions underlying an ecological modernization discourse have begun to act as a "reformative management directive" for policymakers and businesses looking to focus on economic concerns while remaining (or at least appearing) sensitive to pressures to adopt "greener" organizational practices. Although Davidson and MacKendrick's research was focused on Alberta, Canada – specifically on the province's adoption of ecological modernization to reframe the relationship between natural resource development and environmental protection in a context rife with debate about the impact of the resource industry – the practice is widespread and, as we will show, has particular relevance for those interested in sport-related responses to environmental concerns.

So what is "ecological modernization," and why is it a preferred guide for environmental responses within industries? Although there is ongoing controversy about the meaning and implications of the concept, advocates of the term and associated approaches generally assume that existing industrialization processes can be altered so they become more efficient. That is to say, it is believed that industries can "switch" from practices that are more harmful to the environment to ones that are "sustainable" (i.e., those that do not do further harm to the planet – see Spaargaren and Mol, 1992; Hannigan, 2006). An early advocate of this perspective was Huber (1982, 1985), who argued that processes of industrialization in modern societies progress/develop from: (1) an initial industrial breakthrough; to (2) the construction of an industrial society; to (3) the development of a super-industrial society, where technology is developed that can "deal with" environmental impacts (Hannigan, 2006: 27). Of course, underlying this perspective is the belief that economic development and environmental progress are compatible, and that innovation and the design/implementation of new technologies are crucial if these progressions are to take place.

While most ecological modernist thinkers and advocates share these general principles, there are different "strands" of the approach. "Strong" versions of the theory are more sensitive to the need for public consultation, for critical self-reflection about how technology is used, and for open consideration of the role that government and regulation can play in supporting pro-environment goals. Advocates of "weaker" versions have more faith in the power of market-driven mechanisms to inspire environmental change as a response to consumer demand (not government regulation) – and are more clearly aligned with a neoliberal perspective on environmental problems.

It is not difficult to see why this perspective – especially weaker versions – would be favored by for-profit industries expected to adopt more environmentally friendly practices. Indeed, "ecological modernization" is increasingly favored ahead of terms such as "sustainable development" to characterize business practices that engender economic and environmental benefits. This latter term is ambiguously defined – it has been described as "the form that economic activity would take if we were to be able to meet the material needs of human society without further harming the planet" (Chernushenko and van der Kamp, 2001: 10) – and thus is seen by some as missing ecological modernization's "concrete agenda" for change (Davidson and MacKendrick, 2004: 48–49).

There are many critiques of both strong and weak versions of ecological modernization. Although some of these are outlined in the introduction to this chapter (and in related work by Wilson, 2012a, 2012b), there are other important critiques offered in well-developed theoretical statements by scholars like Harvey (1996) and Schnaiberg and Gould (2000). Most notably, ecological modernist approaches do not account for ways that unequal power relationships impact the functioning of collaborations between corporations and other environmental stakeholders. This is an especially serious problem for "strong" ecological modernists who support public consultation. Furthermore, these approaches do not acknowledge the emergence of "greenwashing" techniques by some businesses intent on *appearing* green – which, in a market-driven model (i.e., a weak ecological modernist model), could be seen as a logical response to consumer demand for more environmentally friendly products and services. Critics of neoliberalism have also been

clear in their view of the weaker version of ecological modernization as little more than "a lifeline for capitalist economies threatened by ecological crisis" (Gibbs, 2000: 12, following Hajer, 1995).

Schnaiberg and Gould (2000) offer perhaps the most developed critique of ecological modernist-guided responses to environmental problems through the introduction of the "treadmill of production metaphor" – a metaphor they use to describe how government policies that are generally designed and redesigned to promote economic growth are inevitably more focused on promoting (rather than reducing) consumption. Hannigan builds on this idea by suggesting that problems arise when governments that are mandated to promote economic growth *and at the same time* regulate activities that impact the environment look for a middle ground:

> governments often engage in a process of "environmental managerialism" in which they attempt to legislate a limited degree of protection sufficient to deflect criticism [about environmental concerns] but not significant enough to derail the engine of economic growth. By enacting environmental policies that are complex, ambiguous and open to exploitation by the forces of production and accumulations the state reaffirms its commitments to strategies for promoting economic development. (2006: 21)

Hannigan's point is interesting because it speaks to ways that governments, wanting to garner public support, must promote their actions on the environment in ways that would be satisfactory both to businesses that are reliant on economic growth and to consumers who are increasingly interested in the implementation of environmentally sensitive measures. With this in mind it would make political sense to promote the idea that environmental sensitivity and economic growth are not only compatible but inseparable – and that the only strategies for addressing environmental problems must be linked with a concern for economic growth. In other words, it would make sense for governments, as for many organizations and corporations, to promote a response to environmental problems that is guided by ecological modernist principles.

Environmental Discourses and Promotional Culture: Examples from the Global Forum for Sports and the Environment

To demonstrate some of the ways that ecological modernist principles are embedded in promotional texts produced by or about sport-related organizations and corporations, we looked to the self-identified "largest database on environmental action in sports," the Global Forum for Sports and the Environment (G-ForSE). The G-ForSE website functions as a publicity site for "sports federations, sporting goods manufactures [sic], event producers and sports enthusiasts" interested in finding out more about work that is currently taking place to address sport-related environmental concerns. In doing so, it also acts as a database that "highlights a broad spectrum of environmental action in sports from around the world in order to educate and promote these activities." Although the platform includes "featured" articles, conferences, and videos related to sport and the environment, in our view the website is most notable for the database it hosts. The database is divided into three sections: (1) sports facilities and the environment; (2) sports events and the environment; and (3) sports goods and the environment. Under each heading/link is a long list of press releases or media articles featuring information about various ways that sport-related businesses/organizations are responding to environmental issues. Taken together, there are hundreds of releases/articles that can be viewed under these headings. The site is supported and hosted by the United Nations Environment Program (UNEP) and the Global Sport Alliance (GSA) – a non-profit organization mandated to "promote environmental awareness and action across all sport." The GSA has a "memorandum of understanding" with UNEP and is a partner with the IOC's Sports and Environment Commission.

With this background, we have identified an example of a press release and an example of a news article (both from G-ForSE) that, together, help us demonstrate how ecological modernist themes can be embedded in and taken for granted in the reporting of "green" responses to environmental problems by sport-related organizations.

Example 1 – Olympic Park and London 2012

The following press release from the London Organizing Committee of the Olympic and Paralympic Games (LOCOG) was featured on the G-ForSE website in September of 2009:

> The clean-up of the Olympic Park is almost complete and the Olympic Delivery Authority (ODA) is on track to beat its target of recycling and reusing 90 per cent of demolition materials. Recycling has also significantly reduced the number of lorry journeys in the local area, as only a minimal amount of contaminated material was taken off site. There have been nearly 3,000 site investigations carried out into contamination on site since October 2006 with nothing unexpected uncovered. Industrial contamination that was found on site included oil, petrol, tar, cyanide, arsenic and lead, as well as some very low-level radioactive material. The contaminated soil has been cleaned and reused on site using innovative techniques including soil washing and bioremediation – a technique that uses bacteria, fungi and other microbes to clean the soil. The clean-up process began three years ago and enabled construction to start on or ahead of schedule on all of the permanent Park venues. The "big build" is now well underway with venues coming out of the ground. Work also continues on the 21 bridges, roads, a new energy centre and utilities network, and transport infrastructure. This will not only benefit the Games but also the communities that will live and work in the area after 2012.[2]

For supporters of an ecological modernist response to environmental problems, there is much to be optimistic about here. For example, by reporting the use of "innovative techniques" such as soil washing and bioremediation, it would appear that contamination problems around the site for the Olympic Park were being dealt with. More than this though, environmental damage created by "less efficient" industries of years past – industries that are the reason for the recent state of oil, petrol, tar, cyanide, arsenic, lead, and radioactive contamination – were being reversed because of new clean-up technologies. In these ways, environment-related problems were being dealt with through innovation and the development of new technologies. These are fundamental strategies to ecological modernists. The "meta-narrative" that is implicit in this press release – that contemporary industries have adopted practices that allowed them to "move beyond" the polluting, contaminating industries of the past – aligns well with Huber's (1982) vision of an inevitable progression from an industrial society to a "greener, cleaner" super-industrial society.

It is also notable that these changes were taking place as part of an event based around a partnership of NGOs (LOCOG and the IOC), the British government that supported the bid to bring the Olympic Games to London in 2012, and corporate sponsors. That is to say, the clean-up efforts can be attributed to the collective work of private, public, and non-profit organizations. Again, the strategy is based around an ecological modernist assumption: that stakeholders from various sectors can effectively collaborate, and that solutions to environmental problems can be achieved through largely market-driven mechanisms (e.g., by hiring industry partners who will creatively respond to pressures to be environmentally friendly). In the end, this is presented as a vision of responsible capitalism.

Consider also LOCOG's uninhibited enthusiasm about the fact that the "big build is underway with venues coming out of the ground." By including references to these kinds of big-money projects/contracts in the context of an article about progressive responses to contamination, economic growth and environmental progress are implicitly linked. As noted earlier, this is characteristic of an ecological modernist approach to resolving environmental problems, or for preventing more perilous ones from arising in the first place.

Since the release of this article on the G-ForSE website in 2009, LOCOG has continued to boast of its environmental stewardship. For example, in 2011 they unveiled their first sustainability report: a meticulously crafted document that updated LOCOG's progress *vis-à-vis* their sustainability goals and underscored the organization's responsible approach to creating new infrastructure. Among many other initiatives, this approach was said to include delivering 45 new hectares of space for wildlife habitat, reclaiming demolished materials from the Olympic Park construction for reuse or recycling, and building new venues according to a BREEAM (an environmental

assessment method and rating system) rating of "excellent." Notably, however, the goal of generating 20 percent of energy costs from local, renewable sources proved "unviable." According to the report, the original commitment was written at a time (in 2004) when "it was expected that the London renewable energy market would grow significantly, but this has not happened" (London 2012 Sustainability Report, 2011: 45). If this admission shows, on the one hand, the noble intentions of the organizing committee, on the other hand it demonstrates the limitations of relying on market-based, technologically dependent approaches to "sustainable" development that critics of ecological modernization have been wary of for some time.

Example 2: Formula One and climate change

Consider also the following excerpt from a newswire article from Reuters (dated July 2007) that appeared on the G-ForSE website.

The world's top motor sport competition is for many the epitome of gas-guzzling wastefulness with powerful engines burning nearly a liter of fossil fuel per kilometer while a vast entourage of people and machines jets to races round the world. But green winds of change are blowing through one of the world's most popular sports, and a growing number of team bosses say they want to make Formula One a high-tech pioneer and leader in fighting climate change rather than a whipping post. Proposed changes include smaller engines [and] using bio-fuel. . . . "Unless Formula One can become a contributor to the technology that might help the environment, it's likely it will become a dinosaur," Nick Fry, team principal of Honda racing, told Reuters in an interview at Sunday's European Grand Prix. "It's almost come true with the floods in England last week. If there are environmental disasters happening around the world in the future before races, people will say it's inappropriate to then put on a glitz show, burning lots of fossil fuel." Fry, a catalyst in the push to cut carbon emissions and waste in a sport known for its conspicuous consumption, put a huge picture of the earth on his team's two race cars this year, uncorrupted by the usual commercial logos. "Formula One is one of the best marketing tools in the world," said Fry, pointing to the 600 million television viewers. F1 technology breakthroughs trickle down to road cars, he said. "If we get behind it, the potential is unsurpassed." . . . "We are discussing rule changes to make Formula One a real pioneer," BMW team boss Mario Theissen told Reuters. "Formula One does not have to be on the defensive. It's on our agenda to take developments in Formula One and use them for road cars."[3]

This article, while obviously less self-congratulatory than the press release described above, also includes several themes that support the idea that an ecological modernist approach is the only reasonable approach to resolving (sport-related) environmental problems. For example, a key message in the article is that "consumer demand" (e.g., for sport events that are more environmentally friendly) is an excellent catalyst for behavior change among sport-related businesses. More than this though, quotations from Formula One representatives selected for the article sustain the idea that this sport-related industry is responding independently to environmental problems. Therefore, it would seem, there is no reason to feel "under attack" (e.g., by regulators). The quotation "Formula One does not have to be on the defensive . . . it's on our agenda to take developments in Formula One and use them for road cars" from BMW's Mario Theissen articulates this view that industry is an excellent self-regulator when inspired by market-driven mechanisms.

These messages are aligned with a weaker version ecological modernization, and are fully compatible with neoliberalism's belief in unfettered market-exchange. When these messages are considered alongside excerpts that portray Formula One as "one of the best marketing tools in the world" and describe how "F1 technology breakthroughs [could] trickle down to road cars," then Formula One's positioning as an industry that can continue to be a profitable global sport enterprise while driving economic growth more generally (through the production of green technologies) is reinforced. In this sense, the ecological modernization approach is taken-for-granted in Formula One's "green strategy." As authors like McCarthy and Prudham (2004) observe, this particular version of ecological modernization "is

suspiciously coterminous with the self-regulation and neo-corporatism characteristic of neoliberalism more broadly" (p. 280).

Like LOCOG, Formula One has not ceased in championing its environmental "best practices" since the release of this article on the G-ForSE website. The sport's governing body, the Fédération Internationale de l'Automobile (FIA), continues to make their perspectives on sustainability available to the public. This includes, for example, a document entitled "Make Cars Green," which outlines FIA's position on motoring and air quality, climate change, and fuel economy (see FIA, 2012). FIA has announced that smaller, "greener" engines would be mandated across racing so as to reduce fuel expenditure by 35 per cent. Tony Fernandes, the owner of a prominent racing team, once again articulated the presumed trickle-down effect of these changes in high-level sport: "35 per cent less fuel is amazing. Imagine what that would do to the world if the technology being used in Formula One can be brought to all cars and reduce fuel consumption by 35 per cent" (Climate Action, 2011). This strategy of relativizing consumption (rather than, for example, stressing expected overall emission levels even after the new engine mandate) goes far in depicting industry as responsible and proactive.

Conclusion

Among Foucault's many influential contributions, sports scholars have been inspired by his view that power has a productive capacity. In one of his more revered texts, Foucault (1990) describes how the will to speak about sexuality in the Victorian age lead not only to the authorization of certain statements, policies, and practices (e.g., about "deviant" bodies and personas) but also to the production of silence – to the production of that which was *unauthorized*. "There is not one but many silences," says Foucault, "and they are an integral part of the strategies that underlie and permeate discourses" (1990: 27). Examining these excerpts from the G-ForSE website offers some insight into ways that a particular discourse – in this case the ecological modernization discourse – is authorized in subtle but important ways. There are many questions and concerns that are not raised on a website that is fundamentally driven by the work of those who benefit from a response to environmental problems inextricably linked with economic growth. For example, and as noted earlier in this chapter, critics commonly raise concerns about organizations that *promote* their work on environmental issues without following through on their publicized commitments ("greenwashing"). Others raise important questions about the leap of faith that is frequently made by those who are blindly optimistic about the potential of new technologies (and those who develop them) to solve environment-related problems – problems that, in many cases, have not been anticipated or recognized yet. Furthermore, questions about the need for and potentially negative impacts of hosting major sport events would likely not appear on G-ForSE's webpages because of the site/network's affiliation with the IOC. Questions about why environmental advancements cannot take place without the immense resource commitments required by events like the London 2012 Olympics would also not appear in a context like G-ForSE.

Ultimately, and although the analysis and commentary offered above was intended to be illustrative of *how* ecologist modernization themes are woven into these messages, we argue that the presence of these themes in the promotion of major sporting events (such as the Olympic Games) suggests that ecological modernization discourses are *the* central discourses in the promotion of environmental action by sport-related businesses and organizations. Preparations for the 2016 Olympics in Rio de Janeiro, for instance, have included talks of solar paneling in the favelas in the city's Baixada region (Rio2016, 2010). Given that sustainability initiatives of this kind show no signs of abating, further research is needed on their material impacts and on their discursive promotion.

Indeed, in pointing out how organizations like LOCOG and Formula One promote a particular approach to environmental issues – an approach that unproblematically links economic growth with environmental progress – our work will hopefully inspire further studies about how particular ways of thinking come to be privileged in subtle but powerful ways. In doing so, our intention is to make room for those interested in challenging the environmental-related (promotional) images and messages they encounter in everyday contexts, and to support a more open dialogue and debate about best strategies for addressing one of the key concerns of our time.

Notes

1　Global Forum for Sports and the Environment, http://en.g-forse.com, accessed December 7, 2012. Quotation from "Adidas environmental report," G-ForSE website archive, italics added.

2　Press release at the G-ForSE website, accessed January 25, 2010.

3　G-ForSE website archive, "Climate change fears reach even Formula One Racing."

References

Adidas Group (2009) "Sustainability," at http://www.adidasgroup.com/en/sustainability/welcome.aspx, accessed December 7, 2012.

Atkinson, M. (2009) "Parkour, anarcho-environmentalism, and poiesis." *Journal of Sport & Social Issues*, 33 (2): 169–194.

Bale, J. (2001) *Sport, Space, and the City*, West Caldwell, NJ: Blackburn (first published 1993).

Barnes, B.A. (2009) "'Everybody wants to pioneer something out here': Landscape, adventure, and biopolitics in the American Southwest." *Journal of Sport & Social Issues*, 33 (3): 230–256.

Beck, U. (1992) *Risk Society*, Beverly Hills, CA: Sage Publications.

Beder, S. (2002) *Global Spin: The Corporate Assault on Environmentalism*, White River Junction, VT: Chelsea Green Publishing Company.

Berlant, L.G. (1997) *The Queen of America Goes to Washington City: Essays on Sex and Citizenship*, Durham, NC: Duke University Press.

Cantelon, H. and Letters, M. (2000) "The making of the IOC policy as the third dimension of the Olympic movement." *International Review for the Sociology of Sport*, 35 (3): 249–308.

Chernushenko, D. (1994) *Greening our Games: Running Sports Events and Facilities that Won't Cost the Earth*, Ottawa: Centurion.

Chernushenko, D. and van der Kamp, A. (2001) *Sustainable Sport Management: Running an Environmentally, Socially and Economically Responsible Organization*, New York: United Nations Environment Programme.

Climate Action (2011) "Formula One changes to a green future," http://www.climateactionprogramme.org/news/formula_one_changes_to_a_green_future, accessed December 7, 2012.

Cronon, W. (1983) *Changes in the Land: Indians, Colonists, and the Ecology of New England*, New York: Hill and Wang.

Davidson, D. and MacKendrick, N. (2004) "All dressed up with nowhere to go: The discourse of ecological modernization in Alberta, Canada." *Canadian Review of Sociology and Anthropology*, 41 (1): 49–65.

FIA (2012) "Mobility Policy," http://www.fia.com/mobility/mobility-policy, accessed January 16, 2013.

Foucault, M. (1990) *The History of Sexuality*, vol. 1: *An Introduction*, London: Penguin Books (first published 1978).

Foucault, M. (2007) *Security, Territory, Population: Lectures at the Collège de France, 1977–1978*, trans. G. Burchell, New York: Palgrave Macmillan.

Gibbs, D. (2000) "Ecological modernisation, regional economic development and regional development agencies." *Geoforum*, 31 (1): 9–19.

Giulianotti, R. (2004) "Human rights, globalization and sentimental education: The case of sport." *Sport in Society*, 7 (3): 355–369.

Giulianotti, R. (2009) "Risk and sport: An analysis of sociological theories and research agendas." *Sociology of Sport Journal*, 26 (4): 540–556.

Hajer, M. (1995) *The Politics of Environmental Discourse*, Oxford: Clarendon Press.

Hannigan, J. (2006) *Environmental Sociology* (2nd edn.), New York: Routledge.

Haraway, D.J. (1989) *Primate Visions: Gender, Race, and Nature in the World of Modern Science*, New York: Routledge.

Harvey, D. (1996) *Justice, Nature and the Ecology of Difference*, Oxford: Blackwell.

Harvey, D. (2005) *A Brief History of Neoliberalism*, Oxford: Oxford University Press.

Homer-Dixon, T. (2000) *The Ingenuity Gap: Can We Solve the Problems of the Future?* New York: Knopf.

Huber, J. (1982) *Die verlorene Unschuld der Ökologie. Neue Technologien und superindustrielle Entwicklung* (The Lost Innocence of Ecology: New Technologies and Superindustrialized Development), Frankfurt am Main: Fischer Verlag.

Huber, J. (1985) *Die Regenbogengesellschaft: Ökologie und Sozialpolitik* (The Rainbow Society: Ecology and Social Policy), Frankfurt am Main: Fischer Verlag.

Humberstone, B. (1998) "Re-creation and connections in and with nature: Synthesizing ecological and feminist discourse and praxis?" *International Review for the Sociology of Sport*, 33 (4): 381–392.

Kearins, K. and Pavlovich, K. (2002) "The role of stakeholders in Sydney's Green Games." *Corporate Social Responsibility and Environmental Management*, 9 (3): 157–169.

Lenskyj, H. (1998) "Sport and corporate environmentalism: The case of the Sydney 2000 Olympics." *International Review for the Sociology of Sport*, 33 (4): 341–354.

Lenskyj, H. (2002) *The Best Olympics Ever: Social Impacts of Sydney 2000*, Albany, NY: State University of New York Press.

London 2012 Sustainability Report (2011) "A blueprint for change," http://www.mma.gov.br/estruturas/255/_arquivos/london_2012_sustainability_report_a_blueprint_for_change_relat_255.pdf, accessed January 23, 2013.

Maguire, J., Jarvie, G., Mansfield, L., and Bradley, J. (2002) *Sport Worlds: A Sociological Perspective*, Champaign, IL: Human Kinetics.

Mansfield, L. (2009) "Fitness cultures and environmental (in)justice?" *International Review for the Sociology of Sport*, 44 (4): 345–362.

McCarthy, J. and Prudham, S. (2004) "Neoliberal nature and the nature of neoliberalism." *Geoforum*, 35 (3): 275–283.

Mills, S. (2004) *Discourse*, New York: Routledge.

Mincyte, D., Casper, M. J., and Cole, C.L. (2009) "Sports, environmentalism, land use, and urban development." *Journal of Sport & Social Issues*, 33 (2): 103–110.

Mol, A.P.J. and Sonnenfeld, D.A. (2000) "Ecological modernization around the world: An introduction," in Mol, A.P.J. and Sonnenfeld, D.A. (eds.) *Ecological Modernisation Around the World: Perspectives and Critical Debates*, London: Frank Cass, pp. 3–14.

Ong, A. (2005) "(Re)articulations of citizenship." *PS: Political Science & Politics*, 38 (4): 697–699.

Pitter, R. (2009) "Finding the Kieran way: Recreational sport, health, and environmental policy in Nova Scotia." *Journal of Sport & Social Issues*, 33 (3): 331–351.

Rio2016 (2010) "Cabral reveals major urban investment program for Rio 2016," http://www.rio2016.org/en/rio-2016-now/cabral-reveals-major-urban-investment-program-for-rio-2016, accessed December 7, 2012.

Rose, N. (1999) *Powers of Freedom: Reframing Political Thought*, Cambridge: Cambridge University Press.

Rose, N. and Miller, P. (2008) *Governing the Present: Administering Economic, Social, and Personal Life*, Cambridge: Polity Press.

Schaffner, S. (2009) "Environmental sporting: Birding at superfund sites, landfills, and sewage ponds." *Journal of Sport & Social Issues*, 33 (3): 206–229.

Schnaiberg, A. and Gould, K. (2000) *Environment and Society: The Enduring Conflict*, West Caldwell, NJ: Blackburn Press.

Silk, A. and Andrews, D. (2006) "The fittest city in America." *Journal of Sport & Social Issues*, 30 (3): 315–327.

Spaargaren, G. and Mol, A.P.G. (1992) "Sociology, environment, and modernity: Ecological modernization as a theory of social change." *Society and Natural Resources*, 5 (4): 323–344.

Spink, J. (1994) *Leisure and the Environment*, Oxford: Butterworth-Heinemann.

Stern, A. (2005) *Eugenic Nation: Faults and Frontiers of Better Breeding in Modern America*, Berkeley: University of California Press.

Stoddart, B. (1990) "Wide world of golf: A research note on the interdependence of sport, culture, and economy." *Sociology of Sport Journal*, 7 (4): 378–388.

Stoddart, M. (2012) *Making Meaning Out of Mountains: The Political Ecology of Skiing*, Vancouver: UBC Press.

Stolle-McAllister, J. (2004) "Contingent hybridity: The cultural politics of Tepoztlán's anti-golf movement."

Identities: Global Studies in Culture and Power, 11 (2): 195–213.

Tranter, P.J. and Lowes, M. (2009) "Life in the fast lane: Environmental, economic, and public health outcomes of motorsport spectacles in Australia." *Journal of Sport & Social Issues*, 33 (2): 150–168.

Weiss, O., Norden, G., and Hilscher, P. (1998) "Ski tourism and environmental problems: Ecological awareness among different groups." *International Review for the Sociology of Sport*, 33 (4): 367–379.

Wheaton, B. (2007) "Identity, politics, and the beach: Environmental activism in surfers against sewage." *Leisure Studies*, 26 (3): 279–302.

Wheaton, B. (2008) "From the pavement to the beach: Politics and identity in 'Surfers against Sewage,'" in Atkinson, M. and Young, K. (eds.) *Tribal Play: Subcultural Journeys through Sport*, Bingley, UK: Emerald Group Publishing, pp. 113–134.

Wheeler, K. and Nauright, J. (2006) "A global perspective on the environmental impact of golf." *Sport in Society*, 9 (3): 427–443.

Wilson, B. (2012a) "Growth and nature: Reflections on sport, carbon neutrality, and ecological modernization," in Andrews, D. and Silk, M. (eds.) *Sport and Neo-Liberalism*, Philadelphia, PA: Temple University Press, pp. 90–108.

Wilson, B. (2012b) *Sport & Peace: A Sociological Perspective*, Don Mills, ON: Oxford University Press.

Wolff, A. (2007) "Going, going green." *Sports Illustrated*, March 6, http://sportsillustrated.cnn.com/2007/more/03/06/eco0312/, accessed December 7, 2012.

Further Reading

Chernushenko, D., van der Kamp, A., and Stubbs, D. (2001) "Sustainable sport management: Running an environmentally, socially and economically responsible organization," Nairobi, Kenya: United Nations Environment Programme.

Dryzek, J. (2005) *The Politics of the Earth: Environmental Discourse*, Cambridge: Cambridge University Press.

Foster, J., Clark, B., and York, R. (2010) *The Ecological Rift: Capitalism's War on the Earth*. New York: Monthly Review Press.

Giddens, A. (2011) *The Politics of Climate Change*, Cambridge: Polity Press.

Hannigan, J. (2006) *Environmental Sociology*, New York: Routledge.

Urry, J. (2011) *Climate Change and Society*, Cambridge: Polity Press.

Part Two

Bodies and Identities

Introduction

Although the body, and issues pertaining to the politics of sporting embodiment, have become a core dimension of the sociology of sport, it should not be overlooked that this is a relatively recent occurrence. Up until the late 1980s (which, after all, is not that long ago, even in academic terms), sociology of sport research largely circumvented any recognition of the embodied nature of sport culture. With the benefit of the contemporaneous preoccupations with bodies and embodiment, this oversight may seem surprising at the very least. However, the previous absence of the body within the sociology of sport can be attributed to the influence of prevailing structural theories (both functionalist and critical in orientation), within which the body was a derivative phenomenon of macro-analyses, as opposed to being a key point of empirical engagement. From the late 1980s onwards, sociology of sport research has been at the forefront of trends within the sociology of the body/embodied sociology that reawakened interest in the body as an important social and cultural construct. This is largely due to the body's status as the material subject of sporting practice, in addition to being the definitive object of sporting representation. Hence, "the sporting body" is unavoidably implicated in the formations of power hierarchies and relations, through which individual identities and experiences are (sometimes actively, sometimes passively) constructed. The chapters within this section examine various dimensions and iterations of the sport–body–identity relation, oftentimes keying in on the operation of power within and through the sporting body.

Focusing on the masculine body as the symbolic and political center of sport culture, Jeffrey Montez de Oca (CHAPTER 8) explicates the extensive sociology of sport literature focused on sport and masculinities, while also drawing attention to sport's importance as a fruitful area of inquiry within critical masculinities studies, and gender studies more generally. Through recourse to research drawn from various theoretical influences – including Elias, Gramsci, Foucault, and Bourdieu – Montez de Oca fashions a fluid and contextual understanding of sporting masculinities. This is illustrated within a number of empirical settings. First, he summarizes research examining the construction and normalization of masculine subjectivities within the sport media, which focuses on depictions of both the form and function of idealized masculine sporting bodies, and their associated off-the-field consumption

A Companion to Sport, First Edition. Edited by David L. Andrews and Ben Carrington.
© 2013 Blackwell Publishing Ltd. Published 2013 by Blackwell Publishing Ltd.

practices. Second, Montez de Oca speaks to the role of masculine sporting subjectivities as pointedly raced symbols of nationhood. While in many Western societies the sporting nation has traditionally been embodied by white male subjects, this process has been subverted by the emergence of prominent non-white athletes as metonyms for the multicultural nation, not all of whom are readily accepted as such. Third, he speaks to new forms of masculinity, performed and represented through various aspects of sport culture, that have arisen in response to contemporaneous crises of traditional masculinity. Through this overview, Montez de Oca elucidates the contradictions and paradoxes at the heart of the performance and production of the masculine condition. For while (white) men, (white) male bodies, and expressions of traditional (white) masculinity, are institutionally and symbolically privileged within sport culture, this position of privilege is increasingly questioned by the actions and aspirations of women and other groupings empowered by broader sociopolitical shifts, and now in a position to challenge the heterosexual, masculinist, and racially exclusionist orientation of traditional sports cultures.

Mark Q. Sawyer and Cory Charles Gooding (CHAPTER 9) examine the embodied racial politics of international football (soccer) culture. Unlike many political scientists, the authors recognize the significance of sport as a discursively constituted semiotic practice, produced by the institutional and ideological arrangements which surround it. For this reason, Sawyer and Gooding approach sport, and football in particular, as events with profound political significance. Developing themes discussed in the preceding chapter, they focus on the relationship between football and national identity, and the symbolic function played by (almost exclusively male) players and teams in representing the body politic of broader constituencies, be they cities, regions, or nations. Although acknowledging the representative possibilities of professional team sports, Sawyer and Gooding identify national teams as the most infectious and emotive embodiments of nation, and the forms of racialized citizenship with which the nation is most readily associated. Through recourse to the periodic manifestations of anti-black racism within football in Europe, they highlight the existence of an *inclusionary discrimination* wherein athletes from non-white

racial groupings are afforded formal rights of citizenship (as manifest in their selection for the nation's representative side). However, and under the symbolic weight of populist and racially exclusionary understandings of nationality, these non-white athletes are effectively prohibited from inhabiting any authentic sense of national belonging: something customarily and unquestioningly afforded members of Europe's majority white populations. The bodies of black athletes are thus discursively positioned as primarily representatives of an amorphous and transnational *black mass*, and secondarily, if indeed at all, as embodiments of locality, team, or nation. Hence, through recourse to incidents in various European countries including Spain, Italy, Germany, the United Kingdom, France, Serbia, and Russia, Sawyer and Gooding identify a global inventory of anti-black racist acts and sentiments within football, which oftentimes transcend the racial histories of the local, confirming the status of the black body as the ultimate pan-global "other."

Emma Rich and John Evans (CHAPTER 10) explore the social, cultural, political, and economic contexts framing the representation, perception, and experience of girls and young women's (in)active bodies in the United Kingdom. Their discussion is based upon qualitative data drawn from a study of girls' attitudes and experiences from eight schools, encompassing a range of social, cultural, and policy contexts, yet all framed by the seemingly omnipresent moral panics related to the existence of a youth obesity epidemic or crisis. The authors examine the discursive constitution of valorized *fit* bodies, and demonized *fat* bodies, and how the associated subjectivities are negotiated by girls in their day-to-day lives. In specific terms, they focus on the broader domain of physical culture (encompassing various aspects of active embodiment, including fitness, exercise, wellness, movement, and dance, in addition to sport practices), and illustrate how (in)active young female bodies are rendered visible, and subsequently viewed, disciplined, and governed, by the influence of pervasive "healthiest" and neoliberal discourses. Indeed, Rich and Evans demonstrate how the bodies of girls and young women are the vanguard of a particular neoliberal subjectivity pertaining to issues of self-determination, personal responsibility, and moral self-worth, as manifest within the expected realization of the active, fit, and thin body. They illustrate how various social institutions – schools, health policy, the mass media, and consumer culture – act as pedagogical agents, normalizing specific practices of health and physical activity, and idealizing particular gendered forms of embodiment. Crucially, Rich and Evans also underscore the depoliticizing nature of this "active body" pedagogy. The abstracted individualism embedded within this neoliberal "healthism" obfuscates the enduring social inequalities and exclusions (i.e., those related to race, ethnic, social class, generation, gender, sexuality, and disability differences) which preclude many from being able, quite literally, to embody the social and moral responsibility of the productive citizen.

Whereas Rich and Evans highlight the practice of disciplining female sporting bodies to particular gendering norms, Eric Anderson (CHAPTER 11) points to the contested state of sporting bodies, with his analysis of the changing nature of the relationship between (hetero)sexual norms and masculine sport identities. Based upon more than a decade of qualitative inquiry, carried out within both the United States and the United Kingdom, Anderson points to a progressive social change that has swept through organized sport. This is expressed within significant shifts in the prevalence and expression of homophobia, and the concomitant experience and reception of gay male athletes, within sporting culture. Such a dramatic transformation is attributed to a number of interrelated factors linked to the familiarizing of homosexual bodies and practices to the wider population. These factors include: the increased presence of sexual minorities in the popular media; a raft of legal initiatives advancing the rights of homosexuals; and the prevalence of individuals "coming out" to their various social constituencies. According to Anderson, Western society's new found familiarity – and apparent comfort – with homosexuality has, when transposed to the sporting context, led to a radical revision of entrenched linkages between sport, bodies, and sexuality. As a result, the rate and intensity of active and passive hostility toward those identified as being homosexual within sport has been radically reduced. Numerous Western male sport settings are now eschewing the overt homophobia that previously defined them as sexually discriminatory and exclusionary institutions. This is manifest in the performance

of *inclusive masculinities*, as expressed within: a problematizing of essentialized associations between sport, the athletic body, and heteronormative masculinity; a greater acceptance of, and empathy for, homosexuals within mainstream sport culture; and an increased prevalence of heterosexual athletes engaging in behaviors and emotive expressions previously coded as "homosexual."

P. David Howe's focus on sport for the disabled and specifically Paralympic high-performance sport (CHAPTER 12), provides a graphic illustration of the complexity of sporting body politics more generally. However, he also elucidates some of the specificities of the power relations operating within sport for the disabled, particularly concerning those related to the contested nature of disabled athletic bodies, and the prevalent cultural politics of representation which privilege some disabled athletic bodies over others. At the heart of Howe's argument is the recognition that the classification of disabled bodies for the purposes of sporting competition is a politically contentious and contextually contingent issue. Thus, it can be seen that the present system of athlete classification, which positions the wheelchair athlete at its "originary core," are far from objective formulations. Rather, these classificatory systems are a product of the institutional history and evolution of the Paralympic movement. Furthermore, as Howe notes, the performance and aesthetically driven body hierarchies evident within able-bodied sport, and which distinguish between acceptable and unacceptable sporting bodies, are also evident within Paralympic sport. Howe maps the role of technology in the reproduction of these hierarchies. For instance, the use of sophisticated technology by elite wheelchair athletes helps them, particularly over longer distances, realize performances which far surpass those of able-bodied athletes. Due to their superlative physical performances, wheelchair athletes are thus more likely to become the embodiment of Paralympic athleticism. Conversely, those athletes with cerebral palsy or an intellectual impairment – whose impairment is visibly manifest in their physical performance, in that it is oftentimes mechanically different and considerably slower than an able-bodied counterpart – are relegated to the institutional and cultural margins. Such are the body politics of Paralympic sport.

Further Reading

Hoberman, J. (1992) *Mortal Engines: The Science of Performance and the Dehumanization of Sport*, New York: Free Press.

Miller, T. (2001) *Sportsex*, Philadelphia: Temple University Press.

Shogan, D. (1999) *The Making of High-performance Athletes: Discipline, Diversity, and Ethics*, Toronto: University of Toronto Press.

Wacquant, L. (2004) *Body and Soul: Notebooks of an Apprentice Boxer*, Oxford: Oxford University Press.

Woodward, K. (2009) *Embodied Sporting Practices: Regulating and Regulatory Bodies*, New York: Palgrave Macmillan.

8

Paradox of Privilege
Sport, Masculinities, and
the Commodified Body

Jeffrey Montez de Oca

Introduction

Modern sport provides a spectacular cultural arena for the performance and production of masculinities. As a result, the study of sport has been and remains an important site of research in the area of critical masculinities studies (CMS) (Connell and Messerschmidt, 2005: 833). Leading masculinities theorists such as R.W. Connell (1990) and Michael Kimmel (1990) have written on sport. More importantly, the research of profeminist sport sociologists Michael Messner and Don Sabo amongst others have helped develop the field of critical masculinities studies. The current literature on sport and masculinities is informed by Gramscian, Foucaultian, Bourdieuian, and figurational theory, and as such has much to offer cultural studies research. Some key areas of research include men's violence, media and ideology, nationalism and imperialism/militarism, bodily commodification, and intersectionality.

The sport and masculinities literature has consistently focused on relations of power, patriarchy, and exclusion. At its heart, the literature is concerned with the problems and paradoxes of masculine identities that arise in competitive and hierarchically ordered institutions. Transformations in the organization of society over time, in

social relations, and in inter-group positioning make masculinity an unstable and crisis-prone identity category at the same time that it remains socially dominant (Connell and Messerschmidt, 2005). In other words, men as a group are powerful, but individual men often feel powerless and insecure (Capraro, 2000: 184; also Kaufman, 1999: 59; Hearn, 2004; Kimmel, 1994; Pleck, 1983). Moreover, a crucial force in the construction of masculinity is not only men's inter-group domination of women but also the intra-group domination of men over men (Brod, 1990; Connell, 2000; Connell and Messerschmidt, 2005; Curry, 2000; Grindstaff and West, 2006; Kimmel, 1994; Loy, 1995; Messner, 2002, 2007a; Pleck, 1983; Remy, 1990; Sabo and Jansen, 1998; Schacht, 1996; Smith, 2007; Trujillo, 1991; Whannel, 1993). The paradox and pain of masculinity is captured well in the title of Alan Klein's (1990) excellent essay "Little Big Man" that finds male body-builders tend to build hypermasculine bodies as a means to hide an inner sense of masculine insecurity. The desire to explain the problematic and paradoxical nature of masculinity without equating it to the experience of women became a central concern of CMS in the 1980s and has continued into the present (Messner, 2004: 75).

A Companion to Sport, First Edition. Edited by David L. Andrews and Ben Carrington.
© 2013 Blackwell Publishing Ltd. Published 2013 by Blackwell Publishing Ltd.

A result of the paradoxical nature of masculinity is that masculinity is crisis-prone. Michael Messner in his groundbreaking book *Power at Play* (1992) argues that industrialization removed many of men's opportunities to prove their manhood through physical labor. Without a clear ability to differentiate themselves from women and thus justify masculine privilege, industrialization created a crisis in masculinity where the meaning of manhood became unclear and thus difficult to perform (Dunning, 1986b). Messner goes on to argue that sport emerged in the late nineteenth century as a masculinizing institution used by men to prove their manhood and legitimate a dominant position in society. The sports that emerged in this time period privileged men's physicality (Bale, 1994). At the same time, women were either excluded from sports or forced to wear cumbersome clothes that made them appear less athletic than men (Hargreaves, 2002). Modern sport thus emerged out of the nineteenth century as a major pillar of patriarchy by excluding women and emphasizing the masculinity of men.

Crises of masculinity have proven endemic to Western modernity. In addition to industrialization, social movements throughout the twentieth and early twenty-first centuries have destabilized the once unquestioned dominance of white men. The different waves of the feminist movement opened (white) women's access to social power in what had been male preserves, such as politics, education, labor, and sport. Similarly, the civil rights movement and the gay rights movement opened similar access for racial and sexual minorities. Ben Carrington shows that in addition to class, race structures relations of inequality between men, and that sport has been a site of both racial domination and racial contestation (Carrington, 1998a, 2010). The ability of historically subordinated groups to make claims upon white male privilege and white men often triggers angry reactions from men who experience any movements in society towards more egalitarian relations as a net loss of privilege (Messner, 2004). Indeed, many men will subordinate class, race, or institutional interest in order to protect patriarchal interest (Messner, 2004; Messner and Solomon, 2007).

Capitalist development also creates new social and cultural conditions that affect the configurations of masculinity. The ascendance of neoliberal capitalism has made higher education and white-collar labor the avenue to a middle-class lifestyle; it expands men's obligation to engage in self-conscious consumerism as style, appearance, and manners become increasingly important; and with more women in the workforce, cultural norms increasingly valorize sensitive men who participate in domestic labor. These transformations present men with a paradoxical image of manhood. While traditional aspects of masculinity, such as strength and the ability to control others, remain culturally valued, new characteristics, such as sensitivity and gender egalitarianism, are also revered. The result is that many men experience their identities as unstable and under siege (Messner, 2004), especially young white men, who are unsure about how to achieve manhood (Kimmel, 2008; Messner and Montez de Oca, 2005; Tragos, 2009). Nostalgia for a mythical time when men enjoyed unquestioned privilege has a triggered a reaction in popular culture sometimes called "new laddism" that can be seen in the representation of sport stars, sport bars, fraternities, and male popular culture (Whannel, 1999; Nylund, 2004; Kusz, 2001).

This chapter is organized to explore some of the contradictions and paradoxes that the sport and masculinities literature reveals. The chapter begins by reviewing the dominant theoretical perspectives in the sport and masculinities literature. This review is intended to provide the reader with a sense of the theoretical stakes and tensions in the sport and masculinities literature. The next section looks at how sport media represents male and female bodies since the sport-media complex is a preeminent masculinizing institution. Sporting bodies in the media are complicated by the fact that they represent more than themselves. Bodies in sport media operate as commodities that symbolize idealized ways of being a man in society and desirable styles of life, and as symbols of the nation itself. In this sense, individual male bodies become masculine texts that the manhood, lifestyle, and nation is written upon (Dworkin and Wachs, 2009). The following section looks directly at how contemporary social-cultural conditions led to the rise of a New Man and a New Lad reaction. The tension between the New Man and the New Lad reflects the crisis-prone nature of highly commodified versions of masculinity. The clearest example of this is in the configuration of metrosexuality that blurs traditional demarcations of manhood in a spectacle of style and consumption. The chapter concludes by returning to the paradoxical and crisis-prone nature of masculinity to argue that although men are universally privileged by gender, that privilege is not simple or unitary. Manhood as gender category is filled with cleavages and contradictions that men negotiate differently given their idiosyncratic tendencies and structural position in society. I hope that this chapter will, ultimately, demonstrate that the subject of sport and masculinities has a lot to offer any scholar interested in gender and cultural studies.

Theoretical Perspectives on Sport and Masculinity

The sport and masculinities literature offers scholars a range of different theoretical traditions to use, including figuration theory, Gramscian, Foucaultian, and Bourdieuian. A good place to begin is with Eric Dunning's (1986b) "Sport as a Male Preserve" because, as a relatively early article in the figuration tradition, it indicates areas more fully developed in later literature. Dunning theorizes gender relations as a power struggle between men and women that is responsive to broader transformations in society and that is worked out in cultural formations, such as sport. As a figurational theorist, Dunning argues that the civilizing process that Western society underwent in the modern era suppresses relations of direct expressive violence in favor of symbolic relations of power (see Dunning, 1972, 1975, 1986a, 2004; Dunning and Mennell, 1998; Goudsblom and Mennell, 1998). The rise of symbolic relations of power through the nineteenth and twentieth centuries, Dunning contends, provided middle-class women with an increased opportunity to claim authority in society (e.g., suffrage) and to exert a civilizing force on men and boys in the home (Dunning, 1986b: 81–83). Middle-class men reacted to women's increased social power by retreating into the gender-segregated space of sport to construct a masculine identity in contradistinction to femininity.

A sporting manhood emerged in the nineteenth century that was courageous, aggressive, and violent in opposition to a timid, nurturing,

and compassionate non-sporting womanhood (Dunning, 1986b: 82–84; see also Nelson, 1994). The narrow construction of masculinity in opposition to femininity within a homosocial environment made the alterity of women and homosexual men a threat to heterosexual men's self-construction as *naturally* powerful and dominant (see also Brown, 2006). Misogynistic and homophobic traditions developed in the middle-class sport of rugby to purify femininity from its homosocial space and keep it from sliding into the homoerotic (Dunning, 1986b; also Sedgwick, 1992). Drawing upon the work of R.W. Connell (1987), Steven Schacht (1996) confirms the continuation of homophobic and misogynistic traditions amongst collegiate men's rugby players in the United States, and goes beyond Dunning to argue that the rugby pitch provides a mental and physical training ground for heterosexual male domination characteristic of an expansionistic Western culture (Schacht, 1996: 562; see also Stoddart, 1988). Later theorists, such as Schacht, added to Dunning's early work by offering greater empirical specificity and more robust theories of gendered power. Probably the most significant in this regard is Connell's notion of hegemonic masculinity.

R.W. Connell developed the concept *hegemonic masculinity* in the 1980s to correct the static, ahistorical, and depoliticized concept of sex role theory that grew out of structural functionalism (Carrigan, Connell, and Lee, 1987). Connell drew loosely upon Antonio Gramsci's notion of hegemony to describe how idealized versions of masculinity become ascendant at different social and historical moments. The concept of hegemonic masculinity assumes that an idealized masculinity dominates or attains leadership over subordinated masculinities and femininity through the organization and deployment of both material and discursive force. The attainment of hegemony makes the social ideal appear as *the* natural, normal, and desirable way of being a man in the world while viable alternatives appear undesirable or deficient. As a corollary, men and women participate in, or at least give tacit consent to, their own domination but also have the potential to resist and subvert gender domination through the development of "aspirational" hegemonies (Howson, 2009). Therefore, what is hegemonic at any given moment is neither universal nor static since the idealized form of masculinity emerges out of dynamic, historically specific patterns of gender relations, or "gender regimes," that form in institutions such as workplaces, families, schools, sports, and religions. Every institution contains its own gender regime, for instance the gender relations on most college football teams in the United States are far more rigid and exclusionary than in most US college classrooms. Since college football teams and classrooms do not exist in isolation, institutions come together to form tense fields of power that Connell calls the "gender order" where the gender regime of different institutions are situated together within a tense "state of play" (see Connell, 1987, 1995; Connell and Messerschmidt, 2005; Messner and Sabo, 1990; McKay, Messner, and Sabo, 2000; Messner, 1992, 2002; Davis, 1997; Trujillo, 1991).

The idealized version of manhood is in fact an impossible *ideal* for most men and a temporary status for the minority that approach the ideal. Michael Oriard (2007) relates the poignant story of Mike Webster, who was the epitome of hegemonic masculinity as a center for the Pittsburgh Steelers from 1974 to 1990. He was a powerful, dominating man; he was superbly skilled at his profession; and he endured superhuman levels of pain. Ironically, when inducted into the NFL Hall of Fame in 1997, Webster no longer embodied the masculine ideal. He had lost his home, his money, his wife, and his physical health had disintegrated to the point that (amongst other ailments) varicose veins in his legs regularly popped open and squirted blood. Mike Webster died at the age of 50, just five years after his induction into the NFL Hall of Fame (Oriard, 2007: 206–209). Webster was not the statistical norm in society but as a football star he presented a normative image for non-hegemonic men to strive towards and to measure themselves by (Connell and Messerschmidt, 2005: 832). Mike Webster's life suggests that hegemonic masculinity signifies an ongoing quest that many men engage in to express social power, though not exclusively in the physical realm (Trujillo, 1991; Messner, 2007b; Connell and Messerschmidt, 2005; Howson, 2009). However, that quest comes at enormous physical and emotional costs (Sabo, 2001; Sabo and Jansen, 1998; Connell, 1990; Miller *et al.*, 2006).

Hegemonic masculinity continues to hold conceptual value for the study of masculinity and sport. However, the concept has also been criticized for a top-down, binary model of power split that operates along the axes of super- and subordination; for being too general and categorical to explain individual athletes; for leading to an overemphasis on elite athletes; and for being unable to explain ambiguities in male subjectivities (Markula and Pringle, 2006; Miller, 1998a; Pringle, 2005; Pringle and Markula, 2005). The preponderance of hegemonic masculinity research led Pringle (2005) to worry "that if researchers continue to examine sport and masculinities through a lens filtered by neo-Gramscian understandings of power they risk conceptualizing and representing linkages between sport and masculinities in one particular manner" (p. 257). Moreover, Alan Bairner argues that gender theorists misuse Gramsci's conception of hegemony (Bairner, 2009) though others would contest this claim (Howson, 2009). Given its conceptual limits, more recent theorizations are expanding the study of sporting masculinities.

Foucaultian research on sporting masculinities complicates the dynamics of power in which bodies become the bearers of discourse, and emphasizes underlying systems of thought, or discursive formations, that open some ways of being human while closing down others. Toby Miller (1998a) charges that Connell's theory constructs a universal, patriarchal desire of men to dominate women but it does not capture men's feeling of powerlessness or performances of masculinity separate from domination.[1] Pringle and Markula (2005) found in a study of non-elite (mostly) former rugby players that rugby did not produce a single hegemonic masculinity but instead men negotiate the discursive field of masculinity and produce different forms of manliness. I found Foucault's notion of governmentality useful in understanding how Cold War discourse became inscribed onto the bodies of young men as they produced themselves as cultural citizens in physical education regimes (Montez de Oca, 2005, 2006). While some Foucaultian research takes an overly individualistic ("local") approach that obscures material and group relations of power, Foucaultian approaches push the literature in new directions and challenge some of the core assumptions in CMS.

The work of Pierre Bourdieu also adds a powerful institutional dimension to the research on sport and masculinities (Washington and Karen, 2001). David Brown (2006) argues that Bourdieu's (2001) perspective on masculine domination forces sport scholars to look at the micro-practices and politics of everyday life. A problematic that masculinities scholars must grapple with, Brown suggests, is that the cultural reference point for our critiques of gender domination are structured by the very relations of domination that we wish to critique. Bourdieuian tools help scholars reflect upon and analyze the institutional processes that weaves domination into the habitus (Brown, 2006: 167). Loïc Wacquant's writings on boxing theorizes how social practices of the everyday lead to the embodiment of a masculine habitus in fighters (Wacquant, 1992, 1995, 2004). Bourdieu's notion of capital, understood as the currency or fluid forms of power that circulates within *fields* (institutional settings) and regulates the distribution of resources in those fields, animates many sport studies (Bourdieu, 1986, 1991; Bourdieu and Wacquant, 1992). Lee, Macdonald, and Wright (2009) deploy an analysis of economic and cultural capital to reveal how a complex notion of class becomes embodied in the habitus of different young male athletes as their everyday practices participate in the reproduction of social inequality. Stempel (2006) develops a concept of "masculinist moral capital" to explain why viewers of the National Football League, National Basketball Association, and boxing were *less likely* to support the 2003 US invasion of Iraq than were viewers of NASCAR, major league baseball, tennis, and golf. Stempel (2006) finds that it is not the violence of the sport that leads viewers to support military interventions, as hegemonic masculinity would predict but the whiteness of the sport that appeals to viewers who associate moral capital with authority and hold a worldview that interprets war as a reasonable solution to fearful situations (pp. 97, 99). Although hegemonic masculinity has been the most broadly adopted perspective on sporting masculinities, as new scholars enter the field other theoretical perspectives become enriched and increasingly sophisticated.

Media, Nation, and Race

The media is a key site for constructing the norms and ideals of masculinity. Studies find that the corporate sport media fosters a conservative, competitive, unreflexive, and patriotic worldview consistent with the hegemony of a dominative masculinity and imperialistic national agenda (Burstyn, 1999; Frey and Eitzen, 1991; Hilliard, 1994; Jhally, 1984; Messner *et al.*, 2000; Nylund, 2004; Real, 1979; Sabo and Jansen, 1998; Sabo, Gray, and Moore, 2000; Silk and Falcous, 2005; Stempel, 2006; Trujillo, 1991). Women's and girls' sports are marginalized, trivialized, and sexualized in most sport media (Billings, Halone, and Denham, 2002; Buysse and Embser-Herbert, 2004; Duncan, Messner, and Cooky, 2000; Fink and Kensicki, 2002; Lee, 1992; Messner, Duncan, and Cooky, 2003; Messner, Duncan, and Wachs, 1996; Parker and Fink, 2008) which serves to construct male sport not only as "real" sport that people "want" to watch but also men as "naturally" athletic and powerful (Messner and Solomon, 2007). The greater success of US women athletes at the 2012 London Olympics presents a very clear and visible challenge to the narrative of male superiority. Given the shifting gendered *mediascape*, Sabo and Jansen (1998) call upon researchers to interrogate sport media that construct the male body as naturally powerful and valorizes the "pain principle" – a process of self-construction based on enduring physical and mental suffering (Sabo, 2001). Televised sport celebrates players "playing through the pain" and the athlete who heroically emerges from physical and mental trauma is a repeating metaphor or trope of masculinity in sport films (Burstyn, 1999; Cook, 1982; Grindon, 1996, 1998; Messner, 2002; Messner, Dunbar, and Hunt, 2000; Sabo and Jansen, 1998). Images that represent the male body ritually tortured as a rite of passage in sport media create powerful nationalistic rhetoric and discourse (Mrozek, 1995; Montez de Oca, 2005; Dworkin and Wachs, 2009).

Constructions of masculinity in sport media are closely tied to the commodification of the athletic male body (Tomlinson, 2006: 272). Lifestyle marketing constructs desirable images of masculinity for insecure, non-hegemonic men based on consumption (Messner and Montez de

Oca, 2005). Messner *et al.* (2000) describe a pedagogical metanarrative in sport media that valorizes an aggressive, risk-taking masculinity realizable by the average male only through consumption, which they call "the televised sport manhood formula" (TSMF). The TSMF constructs a "traditional" (albeit commodified) masculinity that appears stable, coherent, and powerful. As a pedagogy on manhood, the TSMF appeals to young men whose sense of privilege has been eroded by economic restructuring on the one hand and a broad array of social movements on the other (Messner *et al.*, 2000; Messner, 2004; Messner and Montez de Oca, 2005). Smith and Beal (2007) found that the TV show *MTV Cribs* provides two powerful, racialized images of masculinity, one a "*white*" *James Bond* image based on extensive knowledge of upper-class taste and one a "*black*" *Cool Pose* image that defines itself outside of the norms of the upper class. "Importantly, both [of] these fantasy models are physically strong, actively heterosexual, and independent from women and children" (p. 110). In other words, athletic masculinity on *MTV Cribs* represents two sides of a consumeristic, racialized manhood. The neoliberal emphasis on lifestyle marketing and cross-promotion has created a contemporary sport-media context where star athletes become highly commodified celebrities most clearly embodied by stars such as Michael Jordan, Tiger Woods, and David Beckham (Andrews, 2001; Carrington, 2010; Cashmore and Parker, 2003; Cole and Hribar, 1995; Harris, 2006; Harris and Clayton, 2007; Moor, 2007; Whannel, 1999, 2001; Whitson, 1998).

Sport media not only constructs commodified subject formations, it also constructs national formations. The articulation of sport as national allegory transforms teams and athletes into national hero(es) that serve as symbols of the nation (Rowe, McKay, and Miller, 1998; Montez de Oca, 2005, 2008). For instance, professional male hockey players come to represent Canadian masculinity (Allain, 2008). For a brief moment in 1980 the US Olympic hockey team represented the indefatigable masculinity of American men during a time of economic restructuring (McDonald, 2007). Sport media in New Zealand smoothed class, race, and national contradictions to construct Sir Peter Blake, two-time Americas

Cup winner, as a national hero symbolic of a white New Zealand masculinity in a multicultural society (Cosgrove and Bruce, 2005). Similarly, Sammy Sosa successfully negotiated the global mediascape to signify Venezuelan masculinity while playing major league baseball in the United States (Juffer, 2002). On the other hand, the multivocality of Lennox Lewis' transatlantic blackness made it difficult for sport media to place him in a particular national and ideational category so that he could symbolize more than his own complicated identity (McNeil, 2009). In sum, athletes and teams come to symbolize the nation not based on performance but on how those performances are interpreted in specific sociohistorical situations.

The coeval development of the modern nation, imperialism, and sport makes the articulation of white supremacy central to the construction of masculinity in sport and sport media. White supremacy's discursive and material structuring of Western societies produces a key contradiction between sport as the proving ground of manhood and the fact that many of the most successful and high-profile athletes are not white. This generates a tension between the desire for successful athletes and anxiety over powerful, athletic black bodies that resist and subvert white authority (Andrews, 2001; Bloom, 2000; Carrington, 1998a; Cole, 2001; Cole and King, 2003; Cunningham, 2009; Ferber, 2007; Hartmann, 2003, 2007; King, 2007; King, Leonard, and Kusz, 2007; Streible, 1996). This tension in part explains the heavy coverage of the very successful white swimmer Michael Phelps by US media during the 2012 Olympics. The meaning of athletic black bodies become even more complicated as those bodies are increasingly commodified in the global flows of sport media that reach heterogeneous audiences across the globe (Carrington, 2001; Juffer, 2002; Kellner, 2001; McNeil, 2009). Sport as national allegory makes athletic performance symbolize white masculinity at the same time that the dominance of non-white athletes places white masculinity in a constant state of insecurity and crisis (Carrington, 2010; Cosgrove and Bruce, 2005; Cunningham, 2009; Ferber, 2007; King, 2007; King et al., 2007; Kusz, 2001; Walton and Butryn, 2006).

Israel presents an interesting example since its diminutive size creates a powerful "David and

Goliath" national allegory played out in international sport competition (see CHAPTER 15). As national allegory, sport creates an arena for Israeli men to perform a heroic and physically powerful New Jewish masculinity tied to the modern state of Israel. Ironically, the diminutive size of Israel forces Israeli teams to rely on Israeli Arab and foreign black players in international competition. The centrality of non-Jewish athletes makes Jewish athletes appear physically inferior and dependent on the non-Jewish athletes. However, the articulation of white supremacy in the Ashkenazi-dominated state positions physically powerful Arab and black men as childlike and thus not manly in a modern civil society. The result is a complex and contradictory social space that breeds insecurity in all men (Shor, 2008). Studies of sporting masculinities continue to reveal the deeply paradoxical and crisis-prone nature of masculinities, a nature that is only exaggerated in the highly commodified new economy.

Commodity Relations of the New Man and the New Lad

The significance of commoditization becomes clearest in the literature on "new masculinities." Since the 1990s, a "New Man" has emerged. The New Man, often termed a *metrosexual*, is more comfortable with his feelings, more compassionate, more tolerant, and more concerned with how other people view him. The rise of young heterosexual men's growing comfort with expressing affection and closeness for other men has led to the emergence of a category of relationships called *bromances*.[2] The metrosexual is symbolized most clearly in the television show *Queer Eye for the Straight Guy* and celebrity athletes such as David Beckham (see Gotting, 2003; Berila and Choudhuri, 2005; Burton, 2006; Cashmore and Parker, 2003; Miller, 2005; Williams, 2005). While there is some debate about *Queer Eye* (see O'Barr et al., 2004), most research has found that it produces a pedagogy on masculinity that teaches urban, middle-class, white gayness to suburban heterosexual white men and depoliticizes the critical potential of a queer subject position (Berila and Choudhuri, 2005; Miller, 2005).

The emergence of metrosexuality highlights the intersection of identity and political economy

in masculinities research. Barber (2008) situates the current emphasis on male grooming and appearance within a symbolic economy of bodily self-presentation that marks status relations between middle- and working-class men as well as between professional men and professional women (Barber, 2008: 473). The present "dress for success" ethos grew out of the mid-twentieth-century rise of the corporation and consumerism that forced middle-class, salaried men to become increasingly aware of other people's opinions of them (see Riesman, Glazer, and Denney, 1950; Whyte, 1956; Mills, 1951; Marcuse, 1964). In fact, sociologists struggled for a language to express how men negotiated a crisis of masculinity in the 1950s that was tied to the changing gender relations associated with the rise of corporations, expansion of suburbanization, and shifts in postwar labor relations (Gilbert, 2005; Cuordileone, 2000; Spigel, 1992). The current shift away from an industrial manufacturing economy to a service and informational economy in addition to the broad extension of lifestyle marketing throughout social life places even greater pressure on middle-class men – the so-called New Men – to conform to corporate taste arbiters most clearly signified in *Queer Eye* (Barber, 2008).

The term New Masculinities suggests a turning away from or moving beyond "traditional," "old," or hegemonic masculinity that is widely celebrated in sport media. This seems appropriate if one understands hegemonic masculinity as essential, fixed, and monolithic rather than unstable, dynamic, and contextual (Connell, 2000). Straight men showing emotion and affection for each other in public space, hugging their gay makeover artists at the end of *Queer Eye*, and some pro-homosexual Facebook pages[3] provide evidence of a decreasing trend in homophobia as well as a greater range of acceptable masculine performances. Eric Anderson calls this "inclusive masculinity" because it is less homophobic and "femphobic" and more sexually ambiguous than "orthodox" masculinity (Anderson, 2005, 2008a, 2008b). Similarly Bridel and Rail (2007) find that marathon running allows some gay, white Canadian men to engage in "exercises of freedom" and self-creation resistant to self-images that dominate even in the gay community (p. 140). While recognizing the positive developments across the cultural landscape, researchers must also be careful not to separate styles of masculine performance from the structure of inter- and intra-group dynamics (see Hondagneu-Sotelo and Messner, 1994) and remain careful of unwittingly facilitating a form of liberation at the expense of reproducing other forms of domination (King, 2008). For instance, Price and Parker (2003) studied an amateur rugby union club for gay and bisexual men in Britain that through a liberal discourse of inclusion achieved access to and recognition from a traditionally homophobic sphere of society. But the inclusion came at the cost of depoliticizing the potentially radical politics of a queer rugby team and ultimately legitimated the rugby mainstream.

When contemplating the New Man, it is important to recall that *men* remain dominant across political and economic institutions (Connell, 2000: 1). Further, parallel to the 1990s emergence of the New Man was the emergence of a New Laddism, a consciously immature and anti-intellectual trend that emphasizes leisure in homosocial settings (Knowles, 2004), such as sports bars, on AM radio, and in magazines (Messner and Montez de Oca, 2005; Whannel, 1999; Nylund, 2004). In their socially exclusive settings, young and often underemployed white men bond by engaging in racist, misogynistic, and homophobic banter. Ben Carrington shows how New Lad culture, sport, and popular music converged around Euro 96 (the 1996 European football championships) to construct a nostalgic and racially pure image of Britain that was implicitly white and masculine (Carrington, 1998b). While ironic and humorous, New Lad discourse still reproduces traditional modes of domination along the axes of race, gender, and nation (Carrington, 1998b; Messner, 2004; Messner and Solomon, 2007; O'Barr *et al.*, 2004).

A case in point is a group of South Australian soccer fans known as the "Grog Squad" who were studied by Catherine Palmer and Kirrilly Thompson (2007). The Groggies are a group of heavy-drinking young men who perform a misogynistic, homophobic, and xenophobic masculinity. Palmer and Thompson argue that the Grog Squad's New Lad behavior does not mean they are a purely anti-social, dominative group since the Groggies' public expression of self also

emphasizes social, emotional, and economic support (2007: 199). In other words, Groggies may be sexist, racist, and homophobic louts in the stadium, which the researchers found abhorrent (p. 201), but on their social networking website they express "bonding capital" that allows for social and emotional support and "bridging capital" that creates institutional access to social resources (pp. 189, 199).[4] However, CMS research finds that the operation of bridging and bonding capital across socially homogenous, all-male institutions by their very exclusive nature actively supports the domination of men and women outside of their fraternal orders (see Boswell and Spade, 1996; Booth, 2001; Brod, 1990; Curry, 1991, 2000; Kimmel, 2007; Loy, 1995; Mechling, 2008; Messner, 2002; Messner and Stevens, 2002; Nelson, 1998; Remy, 1990).

The New Man and the New Lad can be seen as two sides of the same contemporary male subject attempting to negotiate a highly commodified and objectifying social world. Whereas the New Man is positioned to compete in the new economy, the New Lad rebels and, to a certain degree, opts out by performing a blasé, juvenile attitude (Messner and Montez de Oca, 2005). More than anything else, the new masculinities indicate a marketing-driven crisis of masculinity where masculine identities fluctuate with transformations in society and capital formations. Boundaries around gender, class, race, and sexuality may grow more flexible but do not disappear any more than society's hierarchical order (Harris and Clayton, 2007: 160). Shows like *MTV Cribs* and *Queer Eye* teach a lifestyle that expresses class position through the purchase and display of symbolic power in public settings, which is what Veblen (1899) truly meant by the term "conspicuous consumption." In effect, older systems of exclusion are dressed up in new forms, styles, and aesthetics.

Conclusion

My review of the sport and masculinities literature indicates that masculinity is contextual, performative, and reacts to political challenges by women and other minorities. The literature situates individual identity within broader transformations in society that occurred with the advent of modernity. The images, the meanings, and the performances of gender are thus in flux along with society, which had profound consequences for the production of gendered identities. Further, the study of sports such as rugby and sport media provide empirical windows into gendered power dynamics at the individual and social levels as well as the complex ways that men perform masculinity. Challenges to men's privilege and authority create crises of masculinity or anxiety over what it means to be a man and the privileges assumed to flow from a masculine identity. Crisis invoking challenges upon masculinity result from social-historical transformations that create opportunities for minorities to make group-based demands upon dominant groups and is driven by men's perceived loss of privilege and authority (see also Messner, 2004; Messner and Solomon, 2007; Messner and Montez de Oca, 2005). The professionalization of sport, even at the amateur level, and the expanse of the sport-media complex will only increase the commodification of athletes and athletics (Burstyn, 1999; Jhally, 1984; Smith, 1988; Zimbalist, 1999). The objectification of identity that stems from its commodification will continue to make masculinity a crisis-prone and paradoxical subject position.

Notes

1   Miller's more recent work on metrosexuality has led him to modify his position on positive transformations in gender relations driven by commercial industries. See Burton, 2006; Miller, 1998b, 2001.

2   Bromance refers to intense, non-sexual friendships between, typically, two heterosexual men but can occur between a heterosexual and a homosexual male. The very naming of the relationship, however, normalizes a relationship that clearly invokes a certain degree of discomfort.

3   An example is *Typical, average straight guys in favor of gay rights* that describe its members as "typical, average straight guys. We like sports, beer, and yeah, women. But you know what? We've got absolutely no problem with people who don't prefer the opposite sex. Live and let live. If you agree, join us." See www.facebook.com.

4   Palmer and Thompson employ Robert Putnam's (1995) notion of social capital (see also CHAPTER 17).

References

Allain, K.A. (2008) "'Real fast and tough': The construction of Canadian hockey masculinity." *Sociology of Sport Journal*, 25 (4): 462–481.

Anderson, E. (2005) "Orthodox and inclusive masculinity: Competing masculinities among heterosexual men in a feminized terrain." *Sociological Perspectives*, 48 (3): 337–355.

Anderson, E. (2008a) "'Being masculine is not about who you sleep with . . .': Heterosexual athletes contesting masculinity and the one-time rule of homosexuality." *Sex Roles*, 58: 104–115.

Anderson, E. (2008b) "Inclusive masculinity in a fraternal setting." *Men and Masculinities*, 10 (5): 604–620.

Andrews, D.L. (2001) "The fact(s) of Michael Jordan's blackness: Excavating a floating racial signifier," in Andrews, D.L. (ed.) *Michael Jordan, Inc.: Corporate Sport, Media Culture, and Late Modern America*, Albany: State University of New York Press, pp. 107–152.

Bairner, A. (2009) "Re-appropriating Gramsci: Marxism, hegemony and sport," in Carrington, B. and McDdonald, I. (eds.) *Marxism, Cultural Studies and Sport*, New York: Routledge, pp. 195–212.

Bale, J. (1994) *Landscapes of Modern Sport*, Leicester: Leicester University Press.

Barber, K. (2008) "The well-coiffed man: Class, race, and heterosexual masculinity in the hair salon." *Gender and Society*, 22 (4): 455–476.

Berila, B. and Choudhuri, D.D. (2005) "Metrosexuality the middle class way: Exploring race, class, and gender in *Queer Eye for the Straight Guy*." *Genders Online Journal*, http://www.genders.org/g42/g42_berila_choudhuri.html, accessed January 17, 2013.

Billings, A.C., Halone, K.K., and Denham, B.E. (2002) "'Man, that was a pretty shot': An analysis of gendered broadcast commentary surrounding the 2000 men's and women's NCAA Final Four Basketball Championships." *Mass Communication and Society*, 5 (3): 295–315.

Bloom, J. (2000) *To Show What an Indian Can Do: Sports at Native American Boarding Schools*, Minneapolis: University of Minnesota Press.

Booth, D. (2001) *Australian Beach Cultures: The History of Sun, Sand, and Surf*, New York: Taylor & Francis.

Boswell, A.A. and Spade, J.Z. (1996) "Fraternities and collegiate rape culture: Why are some fraternities more dangerous places for women?" *Gender & Society*, 10 (2): 133–147.

Bourdieu, P. (1986) *Distinctions: A Social Critique of the Judgement of Taste*, Cambridge, MA: Harvard University Press.

Bourdieu, P. (1991) *Language & Symbolic Power*, Cambridge, MA: Harvard University Press.

Bourdieu, P. (2001) *Masculine Domination*, Palo Alto, CA: Stanford University Press.

Bourdieu, P. and Wacquant, L.J.D. (1992) *An Invitation to Reflexive Sociology*, Chicago: University of Chicago Press.

Bridel, W. and Rail, G. (2007) "Sport, sexuality, and the production of (resistant) bodies: De-/Re-Constructing the meanings of gay male marathon corporeality." *Sociology of Sport Journal*, 24 (2): 127–144.

Brod, H. (1990) "Pornography and the alienation of male sexuality," in Hearn, J. and Morgan, D. (eds.) *Men, Masculinities and Social Theory*, London: Unwin Hyman, pp. 124–139.

Brown, D. (2006) "Pierre Bourdieu's 'masculine domination' thesis and the gendered body in sport and physical culture." *Sociology of Sport Journal*, 23 (2): 162–188.

Burstyn, V. (1999) *The Rites of Men: Manhood, Politics and the Culture of Sport*, Toronto: University of Toronto Press.

Burton, J. (2006) "Metrosexuality: What's happening to masculinity? Interview with Toby Miller," *M/C Dialogue*, http://www.tobymiller.org/images/press/print/metrosexint.pdf, accessed January 17, 2013.

Buysse, J.A.M. and Embser-Herbert, M.S. (2004) "Constructions of gender in sport: An analysis of intercollegiate media guide cover photographs." *Gender & Society*, 18 (1): 66–81.

Capraro, R. L. (2000) "Why college men drink: Alcohol, adventure, and the paradox of masculinity," in Kimmel, M.S. and Messner, M.A. (eds.) *Men's Lives* (7th edn.), New York: Pearson, pp. 182–195.

Carrigan, T., Connell, B., and Lee, J. (1987) "Toward a new sociology of masculinity," in Brod, H. (ed.) *The Making of Masculinities: The New Men's Studies*, Boston: Allen & Unwin, pp. 61–100.

Carrington, B. (1998a) "Sport, masculinity, and black cultural resistance." *Journal of Sport & Social Issues*, 22 (3): 275–298.

Carrington, B. (1998b) "Football's coming home, but whose home? And do we want it? Nation, football and the politics of exclusion," in Brown, A. (ed.) *Fanatics! Power, Identity and Fandom in Football*, London: Routledge, pp. 101–123.

Carrington, B. (2001) "Fear of a black athlete: Masculinity, politics and the body." *New Formations*, 45: 91–110.

Carrington, B. (2010) *Race, Sport and Politics: The Sporting Black Diaspora*, Thousand Oaks, CA: Sage.

Cashmore, E. and Parker, A. (2003) "One David Beckham? Celebrity, masculinity, and the soccerati." *Sociology of Sport Journal*, 20 (3): 214–231.

Cole, C.L. (2001) "Nike's America/America's Michael Jordan," in Andrews, D.L. (ed.) *Michael Jordan, Inc.: Corporate Sport, Media Culture, and Late Modern America*, Albany: State University of New York Press, pp. 65–103.

Cole, C.L. and Hribar, A. (1995) "Celebrity feminism: Nike style, post-Fordism, transcendence, and consumer power." *Sociology of Sport Journal*, 12, 347–369.

Cole, C.L. and King, S. (2003) "New politics of urban consumption: Hoop dreams, clockers, and 'America,'" in Wilcox, R.C. (ed.) *Sporting Dystopias: The Making and Meaning of Urban Sport Cultures*, Albany: State University of New York Press, pp. 17–34.

Connell, R.W. (1987) *Gender and Power: Society, the Person and Sexual Politics*, Palo Alto, CA: Stanford University Press.

Connell, R.W. (1990) "An iron man: The body and some contradictions of hegemonic masculinity," in Messner, M.A. and Sabo, D. (eds.) *Sport, Men and the Gender Order: Critical Feminist Perspectives*, Champaign, IL: Human Kinetics, pp. 452–478.

Connell, R.W. (1995) *Masculinities*, Berkeley: University of California Press.

Connell, R.W. (2000) "Understanding men: Gender sociology and the new international research on masculinities." Clark lecture, Lawrence: University of Kansas.

Connell, R.W. and Messerschmidt, J.W. (2005) "Hegemonic masculinity: Rethinking the concept." *Gender & Society*, 19 (6): 829–859.

Cook, P. (1982) "Masculinity in crisis? Tragedy and identification in *Raging Bull*." *Screen*, 23 (3/4): 39–46.

Cosgrove, A. and Bruce, T. (2005) "'The way New Zealanders would like to see themselves': Reading white masculinity via media coverage of the death of Sir Peter Blake." *Sociology of Sport Journal*, 22 (3): 336–355.

Cunningham, P.L. (2009) "'Please don't fine me again!!!!!': Black athletic defiance in the NBA and

NFL." *Journal of Sport & Social Issues*, 33 (1): 39–58.

Cuordileone, K.A. (2000) "Politics in an age of anxiety: Cold War political culture and the crisis of American masculinity." *Journal of American History*, 87 (2): 515–545.

Curry, T.J. (1991) "Fraternal bonding in the locker room: A profeminist analysis of talk about competition and women." *Sociology of Sport Journal*, 8 (2): 119–135.

Curry, T.J. (2000) "Booze and bar fights: A journey into the dark side of college athletics," in McKay, J., Messner, M.A., and Sabo, D. (eds.) *Masculinities, Gender Relations, and Sport: Research on Men and Masculinities*, Thousand Oaks, CA: Sage Publications, pp. 162–175.

Davis, L.R. (1997) *The Swimsuit Issue and Sport: Hegemonic Masculinity in* Sports Illustrated, Albany: State University of New York Press.

Duncan, M.C., Messner, M.A., and Cooky, C. (2000) "Gender in televised sports: 1989, 1993, and 1999." Report for the Amateur Athletic Foundation of Los Angeles.

Dunning, E. (1972) "The development of modern football," in Dunning, E. (ed.) *Sport: Readings from a Sociological Perspective*, Toronto: University of Toronto Press, pp. 133–151.

Dunning, E. (1975) "Industrialization and the incipient modernization of football: A study in historical sociology." *Stadion: Journal of the History of Sport and Physical Education*, 1 (1): 101–139.

Dunning, E. (1986a) "Introduction," in Elias, N. and Dunning, E. (eds.) *Quest for Excitement: Sport and Leisure in the Civilizing Process*, Oxford: Basil Blackwell.

Dunning, E. (1986b) "Sport as a male preserve: Notes on the social sources of masculine identity and its transformations." *Theory, Culture and Society*, 3: 79–90.

Dunning, E. (2004) "'Figuring' modern sport: Autobiographical and historical reflections on sport, violence and civilization." Occasional paper, Chester Centre for Research into Sport and Society: University College Chester.

Dunning, E. and Mennell, S. (1998) "Elias on Germany, Nazism and the Holocaust: On balance between 'civilizing' and 'decivilizing' trends in the social development of Western Europe." *British Journal of Sociology*, 49 (3): 339–357.

Dworkin, S. and Wachs, F. (2009) *Body Panic: Gender, Health, and the Selling of Fitness*, New York: New York University Press.

Ferber, A.L. (2007) "The construction of black masculinity: White supremacy now and then." *Journal of Sport & Social Issues*, 31 (1): 11–24.

Fink, J.S. and Kensicki, L.J. (2002) "An Imperceptible difference: Visual and textual constructions of femininity in *Sports Illustrated* and *Sports Illustrated for Women*." *Mass Communication and Society*, 5 (3): 317–339.

Frey, J.H. and Eitzen, D.S. (1991) "Sport and society." *Annual Review of Sociology*, 17: 503–522.

Gilbert, J.B. (2005) *Men in the Middle: Searching for Masculinity in the 1950s*, Chicago: University of Chicago Press.

Gotting, P. (2003) "Rise of the metrosexual." *The Age*, http://www.theage.com.au/articles/2003/03/10/1047144914842.html, accessed January 17, 2013.

Goudsblom, J. and Mennell, S. (1998) *The Norbert Elias Reader: A Biographical Selection*, Oxford: Blackwell.

Grindon, L. (1996) "Body and soul: The structure of meaning in the boxing film genre." *Cinema Journal*, 35 (4): 54–69.

Grindon, L. (1998) "Getting into shape: Classic conventions make their move into the boxing film, 1937–1940." *Journal of Sport & Social Issues*, 22 (4): 360–372.

Grindstaff, L. and West, E. (2006) "Cheerleading and the gendered politics of sport." *Social Problems*, 53 (4): 500–518.

Hargreaves, J. (2002) "The Victorian cult of the family and the early years of female sport," in Scraton, S. and Flintoff, A. (eds.) *Gender and Sport: A Reader*, London: Routledge, pp. 53–65.

Harris, J. (2006) "(Re)Presenting Wales: National identity and celebrity in the postmodern rugby world." *North American Journal of Welsh Studies*, 6 (2): 1–13.

Harris, J. and Clayton, B. (2007) "The first metrosexual rugby star: Rugby union, masculinity, and celebrity in contemporary Wales." *Sociology of Sport Journal*, 24: 145–164.

Hartmann, D. (2003) *Race, Culture, and the Revolt of the Black Athlete: The 1968 Olympic Protests and Their Aftermath*, Chicago: University of Chicago Press.

Hartmann, D. (2007) "Rush Limbaugh, Donovan McNabb, and 'a little social concern.'" *Journal of Sport & Social Issues*, 31 (1): 45–60.

Hearn, J. (2004) "From hegemonic masculinity to the hegemony of men." *Feminist Theory*, 5 (1): 49–72.

Hilliard, D.C. (1994) "Televised sport and the (anti) sociological imagination." *Journal of Sport & Social Issues*, 18 (1): 88–99.

Hondagneu-Sotelo, P. and Messner, M.A. (1994) "'Gender displays and men's power': The 'New Man' and the Mexican Immigrant man," in Brod, H. and Kaufman, M. (eds.) *Theorizing Masculinity*, Thousand Oaks, CA: Sage, pp. 200–218.

Howson, R. (2009) "Deconstructing hegemonic masculinity: Contradiction, hegemony and dislocation." *Nordic Journal for Masculinity Studies*, 4 (1): 7–21.

Jhally, S. (1984) "The spectacle of accumulation: Material and cultural factors in the evolution of the sports/media complex." *Insurgent Sociologist*, 12: 41–57.

Juffer, J. (2002) "Who's the man? Sammy Sosa, Latinos, and televisual redefinitions of the "American" pastime." *Journal of Sport & Social Issues*, 26 (4): 337–359.

Kaufman, M. (1999) "Men, feminism, and men's contradictory experiences of power," in Kuypers, J.A. (ed.) *Men and Power*, Halifax: Fernwood Books, pp. 59–83.

Kellner, D. (2001) "The sports spectacle, Michael Jordan, and Nike: Unholy alliance?" in Andrews, D.L. (ed.) *Michael Jordan, Inc.: Corporate Sport, Media Culture, and Late Modern America*, Albany: State University of New York Press, pp. 37–63.

Kimmel, M.S. (1990) "Baseball and the reconstitution of American masculinity, 1880–1920," in Messner, M.A. and Sabo, D.F. (eds.) *Sport, Men, and the Gender Order: Critical Feminist Perspectives*, Champaign, IL: Human Kinetics, pp. 55–66.

Kimmel, M.S. (1994) "Masculinity as homophobia: Fear, shame, and silence in the construction of gender identity," in Brod, H. and Kaufman, M. (eds.) *Theorizing Masculinity*, Thousand Oaks, CA: Sage, pp. 119–141.

Kimmel, M.S. (2007) "Ritualized homosexuality in a Nacirema subculture," in Kimmel, M.S. and Messner, M.A. (eds.) *Men's Lives* (7th edn.), Boston, MA: Allyn & Bacon, pp. 174–181.

Kimmel, M.S. (2008) *"Guyland": The Perilous World Where Boys Become Men*, New York: HarperCollins.

King, C. (2007) "Staging the winter Olympics." *Journal of Sport & Social Issues*, 31 (1): 89–94.

King, C., Leonard, D., and Kusz, K. (2007) "White Power and Sport." *Journal of Sport & Social Issues*, 31 (1): 3–10.

King, S.J. (2008) "What's queer about (queer) sport sociology now?" *Sociology of Sport Journal*, 25 (4): 419–442.

Klein, A.M. (1990) "Little Big Man: Hustling, gender, narcissism, and body building subculture," in Messner, M.A. and Sabo, D.F. (eds.) *Sport, Men and the Gender Order: Critical Feminist Perspectives*, Champaign, IL: Human Kinetics, pp. 127–140.

Knowles, J. (2004) "'New Lad' fiction," in Kimmel, M.S. and Aronson, A. (eds.) *Men and Masculinities*, Santa Barbara, CA: ABC-CLIO, pp. 569–570.

Kusz, K.W. (2001) "'I want to be the minority': The politics of youthful white masculinities in sport and popular culture in 1990s America." *Journal of Sport & Social Issues*, 25 (4): 390–416.

Lee, J. (1992) "Media portrayals of male and female Olympic athletes: Analyses of newspaper accounts of the 1984 and the 1988 summer games." *International Review for the Sociology of Sport*, 27 (3): 197–219.

Lee, J., Macdonald, D., and Wright, J. (2009) "Young men's physical activity choices: The impact of capital, masculinities, and location." *Journal of Sport & Social Issues*, 33 (1): 59–77.

Loy, J. (1995) "The dark side of agon: Fratriarchies, performative masculinities, sport involvement and the phenomenon of gang rape," in Bette, K.H. and Rutten, A. (eds.) *International Sociology of Sport Contemporary Issues: Festschrift in Honor of Günther Luschen*, Stuttgart: Verlag Stephanie Naglschmid, pp. 69–81.

Marcuse, H. (1964) *One-Dimensional Man: Studies in the Ideology of Advanced Industrial Society*, Boston, MA: Beacon Press.

Markula, P. and Pringle, R. (2006) *Foucault, Sport and Exercise: Power, Knowledge and Transforming the Self*, London: Routledge.

McDonald, M.G. (2007) "'Miraculous' masculinity meets militarization: Narrating the 1980 USSR–US men's Olympic ice hockey match and Cold War politics," in Wagg, S. and Andrews, D. (eds.) *East Plays West: Sport and the Cold War*, London: Routledge, pp. 222–234.

McKay, J., Messner, M.A., and Sabo, D. (2000) *Masculinities, Gender Relations, and Sport*, Thousand Oaks, CA: Sage Publications.

McNeil, D. (2009) "Lennox Lewis and black Atlantic politics: The hard sell." *Journal of Sport & Social Issues*, 33 (1): 25–38.

Mechling, J. (2008) "Paddling and the repression of the feminine in male hazing." *Thymos*, 2 (1): 60–75.

Messner, M.A. (1992) *Power at Play: Sports and the Problem of Masculinity*, Boston, MA: Beacon Press.

Messner, M.A. (2002) *Taking the Field: Women, Men, and Sports*, Minneapolis: University of Minnesota Press.

Messner, M.A. (2004) "On patriarchs and losers: Rethinking men's interests." *Berkeley Journal of Sociology*, 48: 76–88.

Messner, M.A. (2007a) "Becoming 100 percent straight," in Kimmel, M.S. and Messner, M.A. (eds.) *Men's Lives* (7th edn.), Boston, MA: Allyn & Bacon, pp. 361–366.

Messner, M.A. (2007b) "The masculinity of the governator: Muscle and compassion in American politics." *Gender & Society*, 21 (4): 461–480.

Messner, M.A., Duncan, M.C., and Cooky, C. (2003) "Silence, sports bras, and wrestling porn: The treatment of women in televised sports news and highlights." *Journal of Sport & Social Issues*, 27 (1): 38–51.

Messner, M.A., Dunbar, M., and Hunt, D. (2000) "The televised sports manhood formula." *Journal of Sport & Social Issues*, 24 (4): 380–394.

Messner, M.A., Duncan, M.C., and Wachs, F.L. (1996) "The gender of audience-building: Televised coverage of men's and women's NCAA basketball." *Sociological Inquiry*, 66 (4): 422–439.

Messner, M.A. and Montez de Oca, J. (2005) "The male consumer as loser: Beer and liquor ads in mega sports media events." *Signs: Journal of Women in Culture and Society*, 30 (3): 1879–1910.

Messner, M.A. and Sabo, D.F. (1990) *Sport, Men and the Gender Order: Critical Feminist Perspectives*, Champaign, IL: Human Kinetics.

Messner, M.A. and Solomon, N.M. (2007) "Social justice and men's interests: The case of title IX." *Journal of Sport & Social Issues*, 31 (2): 162–178.

Messner, M.A. and Stevens, M.A. (2002) "Scoring without consent: Confronting male athletes violence against women," in Gatz, M., Messner, M.A., and Ball-Rokeach, S.J. (eds.) *Paradoxes of Youth and Sport*, Albany: State University of New York Press, pp. 225–239.

Miller, K.E., Melnick, M.J., Farrell, M.P., *et al.* (2006) "Jocks, gender, binge drinking, and adolescent violence." *Journal of Interpersonal Violence*, 21 (1): 105–120.

Miller, T. (1998a) "Commodifying the male body, problematizing 'hegemonic masculinity.'" *Journal of Sport & Social Issues*, 22 (4): 431–446.

Miller, T. (1998b) *Technologies of Truth: Cultural Citizenship and the Popular Media*, Minneapolis: University of Minnesota Press.

Miller, T. (2001) *Sportsex*, Philadelphia, PA: Temple University Press.

Miller, T. (2005) "A metrosexual eye on *Queer Guy*." *GLQ: A Journal of Lesbian and Gay Studies*, 11 (1): 112–117.

Mills, C.W. (1951) *White Collar: The American Middle Classes*, Oxford: Oxford University Press.

Montez de Oca, J. (2005) "'As our muscles get softer, our missile race becomes harder': Cultural citizenship and the 'muscle gap.'" *Journal of Historical Sociology*, 18 (3): 145–171.

Montez de Oca, J. (2006) *All-American Sport for All Americans: Collegiate Gridiron as Citizenship Practice during the Early Cold War*. Los Angeles: University of Southern California.

Montez de Oca, J. (2008) "Football as national allegory: A meeting of hegemony and govermentality." Unpublished conference paper, North American Society for the Sociology of Sport, Denver, CO.

Moor, L. (2007) "Sport and commodification." *Journal of Sport & Social Issues*, 31 (2): 128–142.

Mrozek, D.J. (1995) "The cult and ritual of toughness in Cold War America," in Wiggins, D.K. (ed.) *Sport in America: From Wicked Amusement to National Obsession*, Champaign, IL: Human Kinetics, pp. 257–267.

Nelson, D.D. (1998) *National Manhood: Capitalist Citizenship and the Imagined Fraternity of White Men*, Durham, NC: Duke University Press.

Nelson, M.B. (1994) *The Stronger Women Get, the More Men Love Football*, New York: Harcourt, Brace & Co.

Nylund, D. (2004) "When in Rome: Heterosexism, homophobia, and sports talk radio." *Journal of Sport & Social Issues*, 28 (2): 136–168.

O'Barr, W.M., Cameron, D., Paxton, M., *et al.* (2004) "Roundtable on advertising and the new masculinities." *Advertising & Society Review*, 5 (4).

Oriard, M. (2007) *Brand NFL: Making and Selling America's Favorite Sport*, Chapel Hill: University of North Carolina Press.

Palmer, C. and Thompson, K. (2007) "The paradoxes of football spectatorship: On-field and online expressions of social capital among the 'Grog Squad.'" *Sociology of Sport Journal*, 24 (2): 187–205.

Parker, H.M. and Fink, J.S. (2008) "The effect of sport commentator framing on viewer attitudes." *Sex Roles*, 58 (1–2): 116–126.

Pleck, J.H. (1983) "Men's power with women, other men, and society: A men's movement analysis," in Richardson, L. and Taylor, V. (eds.) *Feminist Frontiers: Rethinking Sex, Gender, and Society*, Reading, MA: Addison-Wesley, pp. 371–377.

Price, M. and Parker, A. (2003) "Sport, sexuality, and the gender order: Amateur rugby union, gay men, and social exclusion." *Sociology of Sport Journal*, 20 (2): 108–126.

Pringle, R. (2005) "Masculinities, sport, and power: A critical comparison of Gramscian and Foucauldian inspired theoretical tools." *Journal of Sport & Social Issues*, 29 (3): 256–278.

Pringle, R. and Markula, P. (2005) "No pain is sane after all: A Foucauldian analysis of masculinities and men's experiences in rugby." *Sociology of Sport Journal*, 22 (4): 472–497.

Putnam, R.D. (1995) "Bowling alone: America's declining social capital." *Journal of Democracy*, 6 (1): 65–78.

Real, M.R. (1979) "The Super Bowl: Mythic spectacle," in Newcomb, H. (ed.) *Television: The Critical View* (2nd edn.), Oxford: Oxford University Press, pp. 170–203.

Remy, J. (1990) "Patriarchy and fratriarchy as forms of androcracy," in Hearn, J. and Morgan, D. (eds.) *Men, Masculinities and Social Theory*, London: Unwin Hyman, pp. 43–54.

Riesman, D., Glazer, N., and Denney, R. (1950) *The Lonely Crowd: A Study of the Changing American Character*, Garden City, NY: Doubleday Anchor Books.

Rowe, D., Mckay, J., and Miller, T. (1998) "Come together: Sport, nationalism, and the media image," in Wenner, L.A. (ed.) *MediaSport*, London: Routledge, pp. 119–133.

Sabo, D.F. (2001) "Pigskin, patriarchy and pain," in Rothenberg, P.S. (ed.) *Race, Class, and Gender in the United States: An Integrated Study* (5th edn.), New York: W.H. Freeman, pp. 373–376.

Sabo, D.F., Gray, P.M., and Moore, L.A. (2000) "Domestic violence and televised athletic events: 'It's a man thing,'" in Mckay, J., Messner, M.A., and Sabo, D. (eds.) *Masculinities, Gender Relations, and Sport*, Thousand Oaks, CA: Sage Publications, pp. 127–146.

Sabo, D.F. and Jansen, S.C. (1998) "Prometheus unbound: Constructions of masculinity in sports media," in Wenner, L.A. (ed.) *MediaSport: Cultural Sensibilities and Sport in the Media Age*, New York: Routledge, pp. 202–217.

Schacht, S.P. (1996) "Misogyny on and off the "pitch": The gendered world of male rugby players." *Gender and Society*, 10 (5): 550–565.

Sedgwick, E.K. (1992) *Epistemology of the Closet*, Berkeley: University of California Press.

Shor, E. (2008) "Contested masculinities: The New Jew and the construction of black and Palestinian athletes in Israeli media." *Journal of Sport & Social Issues*, 32 (3): 255–277.

Silk, M. and Falcous, M. (2005) "One day in September/A week in February: Mobilizing American (sporting) nationalisms." *Sociology of Sport Journal*, 22 (4): 447–471.

Smith, J. (2007) "'Ye've got to 'ave balls to play this game sir!' Boys, peers and fears: the negative influence of school-based 'cultural accomplices' in constructing hegemonic masculinities." *Gender and Education*, 19 (2): 179–198.

Smith, M.M. and Beal, B. (2007) "'So you can see how the other half lives': MTV 'Cribs' use of 'the other' in framing successful athletic masculinities." *Journal of Sport & Social Issues*, 31 (2): 103–127.

Smith, R.A. (1988) *Sports and Freedom: The Rise of Big-Time College Athletics*, Oxford: Oxford University Press.

Spigel, L. (1992) *Make Room For TV: Television and the Family Ideal in Postwar America*, Chicago: University of Chicago Press.

Stempel, C. (2006) "Televised sports, masculinist moral capital, and support for the US invasion of Iraq." *Journal of Sport & Social Issues*, 30 (1): 79–106.

Stoddart, B. (1988) "Sport, cultural imperialism, and colonial response in the British Empire." *Comparative Studies in Society and History*, 30 (4): 649–673.

Streible, D. (1996) "Race and the reception of Jack Johnson fight films," in Bernardi, D. (ed.) *The Birth of Whiteness: Race and the Emergence of US Cinema*, New Brunswick, NJ: Rutgers University Press, pp. 170–200.

Tomlinson, A. (2006) "Leisure studies: Progress, phases and possibilities – an interview with Alan Tomlinson." *Leisure Studies*, 25 (3): 257–273.

Tragos, P. (2009) "Monster masculinity: Honey, I'll be in the garage reasserting my manhood." *Journal of Popular Culture*, 42 (3): 541–553.

Trujillo, N. (1991) "Hegemonic masculinity on the mound: Media representations of Nolan Ryan and American sports culture." *Critical Studies in Mass Communication*, 91 (8): 290–309.

Veblen, T. (1899) *The Theory of the Leisure Class: An Economic Study in the Evolution of Institutions*, New York: Macmillan.

Wacquant, L.J.D. (1992) "The social logic of boxing in black Chicago: Towards a sociology of pugilism." *Sociology of Sport Journal*, 9: 221–154.

Wacquant, L.J.D. (1995) "Through the fighter's eyes: Boxing as a moral and sensual world," in Cantu, R.C. (ed.) *Boxing and Medicine*, Champaign, IL: Human Kinetics, pp. 129–153.

Wacquant, L.J.D. (2004) *Body and Soul: Notebooks of an Apprentice Boxer*, Oxford: Oxford University Press.

Walton, T.A. and Butryn, T.M. (2006) "Policing the race: US men's distance running and the crisis of whiteness." *Sociology of Sport Journal*, 23 (1): 1–28.

Washington, R.E. and Karen, D. (2001) "Sport and society." *Annual Review of Sociology*, 27: 187–212.

Whannel, G. (1993) "No room for uncertainty: Gridiron masculinity in *North Dallas Forty*," in Kirkham, P. and Thumim, J. (eds.) *You Tarzan: Masculinity, Movies, and Men*, London: Lawrence & Wishart, pp. 200–211.

Whannel, G. (1999) "Sport stars, narrativization and masculinities." *Leisure Studies*, 18 (3): 249–265.

Whannel, G. (2001) *Media Sport Stars: Masculinities and Moralities*, London: Routledge.

Whitson, D. (1998) "Circuits of promotion: Media, marketing and the globalization of sport," in Wenner, L.A. (ed.) *MediaSport*, London: Routledge, pp. 57–72.

Whyte, W.H. (1956) *The Organization Man*, Garden City, NY: Doubleday Anchor Books.

Williams, A. (2005) "60 second interview: Mark Simpson," *MetroCafe*, http://www.metro.co.uk/

metro/interviews/interview.html?in_page_
id=8&in_interview_id=1169, accessed January 17,
2013.

Zimbalist, A. (1999) *Unpaid Professionals: Commercialism and Conflict in Big-Time College Sports*, Princeton, NJ: Princeton University Press.

Further Reading

Burstyn, V. (1999) *The Rites of Men: Manhood, Politics and the Culture of Sport*, Toronto: University of Toronto Press.

Carrington, B. (2010) *Race, Sport and Politics: The Sporting Black Diaspora*, Thousand Oaks, CA: Sage Publications.

Connell, R.W. (2005) *Masculinities*, Berkeley: University of California Press.

Messner, M.A. (1992) *Power at Play: Sports and the Problem of Masculinity*, Boston, MA: Beacon Press.

Stempel, C. (2006) "Televised sports, masculinist moral capital, and support for the US invasion of Iraq." *Journal of Sport & Social Issues*, 30 (1): 79–106.

9

Racism, Body Politics, and Football

Mark Q. Sawyer and Cory Charles Gooding

Introduction

In his classic work, *Beyond a Boundary*, C.L.R. James (1963) chronicles how cricket became a form of anticolonial resistance for members of his Trinidadian town and the Caribbean region. The contests between former Caribbean colonies and Great Britain, who invented the game, took on added symbolic meaning that challenged multiple hierarchies: colonial, racial, and class. James, a scholar of the Communist International as well as of the Haitian Revolution and one of the premier intellectuals of the Caribbean, aptly captured the symbolic importance of such a seemingly trivial game. Conceptions of nation, identity, worth, and belonging were at stake in the matches and West Indians took pride in defeating those who had first been their slave masters and later colonial masters. For James, cricket became a central part of the development of West Indian political identity and aesthetics and it shaped relationships between black West Indians and their former owners and colonial power Great Britain.

The lessons learned through James' exploration of cricket have been applied to the world's most popular sport, football, or soccer as it is known in the United States. Sociopolitical historian Eduardo Galeano (2003) and journalist

Simon Kuper (1994) have sought to understand the relationship between football and political development in Latin America, Europe, and Africa. Others have also explored from a sociological perspective the politics of sports in general and football in particular as they relate to class, race, religion, immigration, and politics more broadly. They find that football and its interpretations by masses and elites form a critical part of political culture. There is, from sociology, a growing literature developed to understand the sociopolitical effects of sport on society as well as the way sports symbolize key ideas and conflicts (Giulianotti, 1999). As political scientists and scholars of race, we have been disappointed by the lack of attention our discipline has paid to sports as part of a broader neglect of symbolic and cultural politics outside of the realm of things like political campaign advertising. In many cases, political culture is a "black box," which is on one hand essential and unique across polities but which is also ultimately unintelligible to political scientists other than to suggest that race, religion, or perhaps geography produce essential differences in populations that cause them to have different norms and values (Huntington, 2004). Thus, there is little broader discussion of culture and symbol and its role in

A Companion to Sport, First Edition. Edited by David L. Andrews and Ben Carrington.
© 2013 Blackwell Publishing Ltd. Published 2013 by Blackwell Publishing Ltd.

understanding how they reflect political culture and help shape political and social events.

We use "political culture" in a very specific sense to mean what Lisa Wedeen (2002) refers to as "semiotic practices." For Wedeen,

> semiotic practices refers to what language and symbols *do* – how they are inscribed in concrete actions and how they produce observable political effects. At the same time, insofar as semiotic practices are also the effects of institutional arrangements of structures of domination, and of strategic interests, activities of meaning-making can be studied as effects or dependent variables. (2002: 714)

Borrowing from Wedeen, we argue that studying football as a semiotic practice allows us to understand how it affects politics and is also a product of the sets of institutions and arrangements that surround it. While Wedeen opens a space for these considerations within political science, sociologists have long recognized the symbolic importance of sports (Carrington, 2010; Dubois, 2010). This is most obviously the case if we examine anti-black racism in Europe in the current moment. The racist practices around football matches are an outcome of broader dynamics that allow us to understand the contested meanings of nation and citizenship in Europe (MacClancy, 1996; Back, Crabbe, and Solomos, 2001; Kassimeris, 2009, 2011; Dubois, 2010; Carrington, 2010; Adair, 2011). They outline something that is quite unique, a ritualized practice of anti-black racism that transcends local histories of colonization or relationships with the transatlantic trade in human beings. Further, we argue that the unique symbolic nature of sports makes it a perfect mode of the kind of analysis described by Wedeen where we move beyond static invocations of political culture; "in an empirically grounded, practice-oriented approach to cultures, meanings are understood to exist inside historical processes, which themselves are always enmeshed in changing relations of power" (Wedeen, 2002: 714).

As we stated above, political science has not paid much attention to the world of sports. The tendency to see political culture as a static unchanging entity in many modes of analysis renders things like sport a sideshow that neither confirms nor affects what the "true" political culture really is. However, if we think in terms of semiotic practices and political culture as ever changing, or at least contested, we can recognize how activities in popular culture confirm, challenge, and transform societal norms, opinions, activities, and maybe in some cases policies (Carrington, 2011). If we map this on to one of the most fluid and unsettled issues in modern politics, that of identity, we see that sport can play a profound role in providing meaning and interpretations for such an ever-changing and unsettled phenomena. Thus, sports are a part of popular culture and sporting events frequently have profound political significance. Football is an important venue for understanding themes of nationalism (Bairner, 2001; Hargreaves, 2002). This chapter will examine the relationship between race, immigration, and citizenship as it relates to sports. We argue that football games are not just sporting events but have political significance because of the symbols they embody and the ways in which they challenge and affirm group identity and membership (Valeriano, 2006; MacClancy, 1996; Adair, 2011). Many of these symbols are racial and are why football has become a site of contestation over norms of racial equality versus expressions of national pride and purity (Carrington, 1998). Thus, our understandings of politics in general and racial politics in particular need to focus on the uses and aims of political symbols and how we interpret those symbols.

Sports have long been seen as important societal symbols. While we have many examples of it, as political scientists we do not often recognize the power and salience of symbols around sports. Symbolically, the dramatic victories of African American sprinter Jessie Owens at the Berlin Olympics were so powerful that German leader Hitler could not stand to face such visible repudiation of Aryan superiority and in consequence a fundamental part of the Nazi ideological project (Large, 2007). From the defeat of German boxer Max Schmelling by Joe Louis, to the 1968 medal stand protest by Juan Carlos and Tommie Smith, sports have had huge political significance. The use of flags, military metaphors, and the long history of participating in sports as members of nation states and not just individuals continually move sports beyond simple contests between individuals and teams to contests between broad groups. The Olympic movement, one of the world's most prominent international sports organizations, still has athletes compete for their "nations." While the movement encourages non-discrimination and universalism, it has yet been the hallmark of medal counts as expressions of political activity. To be clear, while there are politics *in* sports, meaning the allocations of goods, services, and resources through legislative bodies and governing organizations, this chapter will look at the impact that sports have *on* politics and political discourse. In that sense, discourse surrounding sports is both a product of and a way to measure existing political discourse. Moreover, discourse around sport also operates as a realm of contestation that helps shape political discourse. This dual role is especially important and salient in the realm of team sports. This chapter first establishes a theoretical connection between football and national identity. We then discuss the issue of anti-black racism and its symbolic function. We finally examine a series of racist incidents in order to advance the argument of the similarity of anti-black racist symbols and tropes across cultures, suggesting a global lexicon of anti-black racism.

The Body Politic and Race

Many observers of modern politics speak to the role of population dynamics and the way in which political ideals and discourse are embodied by individuals and groups. Nations themselves are constructions of disparate groups that must be harnessed to produce what appear to be homogenous identities for the ultimate purpose of forming and maintaining nation states (Anderson, 1991). These constructions of nations and their exclusions are always embodied through citizens and through the perceptions of who is in or outside of the nation. That is, in many cases we embody "things" as symbols of nations or countries. We often allow the bodies of individual human beings to represent ideals, nations, and lands that transcend the limits of individual corporeal existence. Ernst Kantorowicz in his now famous work, *The King's Two Bodies* (1957) points out how the king's body was understood in one way as his normal human form, like all other

bodies, and also as a representation of the sovereign. We argue that athletes, and in particular sports teams, represent the "body politic" and in many cases nations or cities. The athlete or team, in this way, can represent the ideologies and values of a nation or locality and come to stand as a symbol of the power, intelligence, and will of the people through their triumphs on the field of play (Carrington, 1999). In the way that armies, firefighters, and police forces represent nations and localities through their discipline and triumphs on battlefields and success in defeating crime, fires, and enemies, the physical achievements of individual athletes and teams represent the power, will, cunning, intelligence, and perseverance of the nation or locality (James, 1963; Dubois, 2010). It is worth noting that these forms of national representation are profoundly gendered and in this case gendered male. The team in its triumph or defeat symbolizes more than just the players but the values, hopes, and aspirations that the teams represents. While we argue this is the case for local professional sports teams, it is even more pronounced in the realm of national teams who represent the nation more explicitly.

It is here where race becomes of central importance. Athletes who are of different races face profound questions about their worthiness to represent the entire body. Moreover, fans sometimes either lament the lack of representativeness of their athletes or laud how their team racially reflects the body politic and their notion of how a citizen of their country or locality is supposed to look (Dubois, 2010). In this sense, the bodies of black athletes are particularly controversial in spaces like Europe where somatic norms define "whiteness" as a part of social belonging (Hine, Keaton, and Small, 2009). Further, these ideas offer opportunities to understand quotidian practices of citizenship through sport that are often reproduced on the street (Hine *et al.*, 2009). In this case, black athletes and race are both separate from and yet help define everyday meanings of citizenship. Further, we see a common set of practices or attacks against black athletes that define a series of rituals of anti-black racism that are international and transcend particular histories of colonial or other kinds of relationships with the African diaspora. It is here that we can better understand the practice and boundaries of citizenship than through either juridical or cultural lenses.

Citizenship and Race

Scholars of citizenship have begun to grapple with the problem of race. However, there remains a significant gap between understandings of racial phenomena that are seen as existing in places like the United States and South Africa and the prevalence of questions of ethnicity (Fredrickson, 1981; Hanchard, 1994; Laitin, 1998; Marx, 1998; Sidanius, Peña, and Sawyer, 2001; Winant, 2001; Goldberg, 2009). When viewed through the lens of citizenship there are more opportunities for comparison. Race or birth, while not determinative of citizenship status – outside of either apartheid regimes or societies with overtly ethnic, as opposed to civic, forms of citizenship – frequently determines the qualitative experience of citizenship (Brubaker, 1998). This pattern of work by political scientist Mark Sawyer has been referred to as "inclusionary discrimination" (Sidanius et al., 2001; Sawyer, Peña, and Sidanius, 2004; Sawyer, 2006). Sawyer describes this as the unequal inclusion of racialized individuals into the national polity. Frequently, racialized individuals have formal citizenship rights but in quotidian interactions as well as common understandings of culture, national belonging, and the operation of institutions, they are treated unequally and perceived to be permanently unlike other citizens. This perspective departs dramatically from the perspective of Rogers Brubaker who argues, "The citizenry of every modern state is internally inclusive. Defined to coincide roughly with the permanent resident population of the state, the modern citizenry excludes only foreigners, that is, persons who belong to other states" (Brubaker, 1998: 21). While this may be true in the juridical sense it is far from the case in popular practice and discourse. Thus, citizenship while formally undifferentiated is frequently differentiated and hierarchical in practice.

Literature on immigration, assimilation, and/or the concepts of immigrant incorporation have largely ignored the ways that for groups like African Americans, Chicanos, Puerto Ricans, Roma, Black Britons, or Black French, citizenship is not enough. In each case, second- or third-generation native citizens are still faced with questions of belonging and societal membership. In many cases, while not formally treated as legally different, their life chances, day-to-day interactions, and semiotic practices demonstrate that while citizens, there are components of societal membership that are not captured by the twin notions of legal citizenship and cultural assimilation. What does it mean when a politician, academic, or pundit characterizes a third-generation Frenchman as Algerian or a second-generation American as Mexican? Or discusses such people in the context of immigration?

For example, Samuel Huntington focuses his concerns about Mexican migration to the United States not on the questions raised by first-generation migrants but on the identity and cultural choices of second- and third-generation Mexican Americans who consider themselves to be American, speak English, and in every way imaginable are part of the American cultural and social landscape (Huntington, 2004). Thus, the use of assimilation to define immigrant incorporation never poses the question of assimilation into what? And, on what terms are groups assimilated or not allowed to assimilate or blend into the dominant culture (Alba and Nee, 2003)? Further, writers analyzing immigrant "incorporation" who study immigrant reception in legalistic terms and through the openness or ease of naturalization miss the ongoing aspects of societal membership that are conditioned by race (Bloemraad, 2006). In the case of assimilation and racial conceptions of national belonging, writers often miss that some groups by virtue of race are considered generally inassimilable regardless of which language they speak, whose wars they fight, how they take their tea, or what nationality they claim. Further, the literature on citizenship or immigrant incorporation fails to capture the differential terms of incorporation and experiences of both immigrants and native-born citizens based upon racial hierarchy that cuts across legal status, citizenship, or nativity (Hanchard and Chung, 2004). We argue that race, and in particular blackness, undercuts both cultural and juridical notions of citizenship and renders status and nativity problematic in many everyday contexts. This is not to say that culture and legal regimes of citizenship are meaningless but rather that they only get us part of the way toward understanding the politics of immigration, race, and national belonging.

Globalized Anti-Black Racism

Anti-black racism is one of the social forces that challenge undifferentiated notions of citizenship. That is, in almost every society, blacks regardless of citizenship status find themselves in a position of alterity (Grosfoguel, 2003) and are marginalized by racist discourses. Jemima Pierre discusses this when she writes:

> Very few of us doubt (or so I would presume) that African and other racialized black peoples are linked to a global discourse and exploits. Yet many, including scholars, continue to treat the U.S., with its large and politicized "minority" populations, and South Africa, with a legacy of a savage racial minority rule, as the only sites with potent expressions of race and practices of racialization. This move, I argue is often based on the assumption that race need only be studied in terms of overt and state-sanctioned conflict. (2003: 38)

Societies like Cuba, France, and Brazil where blacks have enjoyed formal citizenship under Marxist, liberal, or republican ideals are thought to be inherently different or non-racist. Other European countries are thought to have experiences with "ethnicity" and ethnic difference but not race. As a result, Rogers Brubaker points to "cultural difference" based on ethnicity and not race. Thus, for Brubaker it is culture that generates the negative discourse about immigrants and ethnic others, or in the context of France, Spain, Italy, and the United Kingdom, black Europeans (Brubaker, 1998).

However, when looking at sport, the myth of a raceless Brazil or the idea that problems in Western Europe are a result of ethnicity and culture and not race fall apart (see CHAPTER 27). There are few activities that culturally bond people together as strongly as the practice of sport. Footballers playing for national teams or national leagues are part of an enterprise that is culturally marked as acceptable. While it is international, football is a mark of modernity and belonging and in many cases a symbol of cultural

"assimilation." However, the growing anti-black racism around both national teams and local leagues demonstrates (1) the ways that race undercuts citizenship and national membership and (2) the globalized nature of anti-black racism. Racist incidents in international football are semiotic practices that demonstrate both of these points. Further, both issues have attracted the attention of different political forces due to their potential to undermine other state and multinational projects. This exemplifies the importance of sports as a central symbolic terrain in political discourse. The following section of this chapter will focus exclusively on the experience of blacks and anti-black racism. However, we are fully aware of the dynamics and similar issues of anti-Semitism or intersections with Islamophobia surrounding European soccer. We do not believe anti-black racism is more important, prevalent, or serious than these other forms of racism; they are simply outside the limited scope of this chapter. Here we are concerned more exclusively with anti-black racism and its international manifestations around "black" athletes.

Black Athletes and Racial Politics

In this case, we focus on black athletes and their trials and travails. In an increasingly globalized world, the black athlete currently and historically has come to represent the aspirations and perceptions of the larger black mass. Here we use "black mass" to mean that the actual national location of the black athlete, while sometimes material, is not a superordinate location and comes to represent some group of blacks that transcend time, space, nativity, nationality, and citizenship status. This black mass is profoundly undifferentiated by conceptions of class, nationality, and other important markers that we suggest might determine one's place in society. In some cases, even individual racial identities do not matter. Players who in their local context do not consider themselves "black" are targeted. Here again, citizenship or perception of belonging is conditioned by perceptions of race (Farred, 2004). However, it is at this (political) juncture that the black athlete plays an important semiotic practice.

In a gripping moment in his autobiography, Malcolm X, then Malcolm Little, is working as a sleeping-car porter, being referred to as "George" (a moniker that was preferable to "Boy") and serving white patrons (Haley, 1991). He writes of his joy at the moment when in their rematch Joe Louis defeated Max Schmelling. Athletes like Muhammad Ali (USA), Pélé (Brazil), Joe Louis (USA), Jack Johnson (USA), Cathy Freeman (Australia), Ben Johnson (Canada), Linford Christie (UK), and others from a multiplicity of national contexts came to represent the hopes and aspirations beyond the playing field of "black" people both in their countries of origin and beyond (Carrington, 2010). In this moment, we see what Hanchard describes:

> The social and cultural capital accrued in one sphere of society, even the body capital of the professional athlete, was invariably brought into question, interrogation and use in other spheres of society. The public – and sometimes private – lives of Jack Johnson, Althea Gibson and Joe Louis, among others, exemplify the manner in which . . . rationalization for the persona/charisma distinction for the US African-American professional athlete is problematic. (2003: 25)

Hanchard is suggesting that athletes offer a form of charismatic leadership – figures who argue for full citizenship rights within nations – that in many cases is read by individuals beyond a given national context. For this reason, we can see why the activities and exploits of black athletes have been so heavily policed or manipulated. White crowds did not attack Jackie Robinson because they could not bear to see him hit a baseball or run the bases but because his activities challenged the very ideology of white supremacy that justified the maintenance of Jim Crow and other forms of second-class citizenship for blacks (Thomas, 2002). In the case of the Cold War, the US State Department sought to use black athletes to counter Soviet Third World propaganda that used racism in the United States to undermine US foreign policy objectives (Thomas, 2002). The success of black athletes for the United States represented the possibilities of capitalism and the justice of the US system. Similarly, Cuba has used the achievements of Afro-Cuban athletes to demonstrate the successes of socialism in eliminating racism and building a strong and capable Cuban nation (Sawyer, 2006).

Thus, the warrants for understanding sports as a semiotic practice are never clearer than in the realm of race and in the case of the black athlete.

Black athletes in nations with ideologies of white supremacy challenge these notions and also challenge notions of who national or local teams represent. Black athletes represent the black mass primarily and only secondarily the nation, team, or locality. It is this contingent status that produces racist acts against black athletes on the playing field. It is their transgression of boundaries of citizenship, ideologies of white supremacy, and notions of homogenous communities that create the friction around sporting contests. That transcendence is exemplary of processes of European and global integration that are helping to push patterns of immigration but it is also symbolized by the increasing internationalization of European football leagues. These incidents have been quite prevalent in recent years in international football.

Despite the diversity of the clubs and nations involved in anti-black racist incidents, many of the cases are characterized by allusions to black players being related to monkeys and apes (monkey chants, thrown bananas). The relative consistency in the type of attacks highlights the fact that these acts take place on a global scale, as opposed to evolving out of specific cultural contexts. While local politics, news, and events may heighten the likelihood of such occurrences, the attacks manifest themselves in a manner that is relatively global/universal. Whether in Western or Eastern Europe, the Americas or Australia, the use of monkey and ape references, stereotypes of blacks as lazy, and even use of the term "nigger" remain consistent. These references are long-held stereotypes bolstered by late nineteenth- and early twentieth-century race "science" that cast African Americans as less than human relative to the superior races of Europe. The work of scholars and others during this period associated people of African descent with being inferior, primitive, and closer to apes in morphology, behavior, and intelligence (Gould, 1981; Shohat and Stam, 1994; Goff et al., 2008).

Incidents in Western Europe

Spain

One of the most highly publicized incidents of anti-black racism in international football occurred in 2004 during a training session of the

Spanish national team. Spanish TV cameras captured coach Luis Aragonés telling player José Antonio Reyes to "Give him the ball, and then show that black little shit that you are better than him." The "black little shit" that Aragonés was referring to was Thierry Henry, Frenchman and striker for the English football club Arsenal. When English fans learned of the incident there was uproar. However, while the initial incident reflected the racist views of an individual, the tension between Spanish and English football fans escalated later that year when Spanish supporters in Santiago Bernabeu stadium in Spain persistently imitated monkey noises whenever black English players touched the ball during a friendly match (Kelso and Tremlett, 2004). As a result of those actions, Spanish fans were punished when their local team, Real Madrid, was not allowed to have fans in the stadium for its following match. Unfortunately, despite the punishment this type of behavior was not unique to this match.

In February 2005, Cameroonian FC Barcelona striker Samuel Eto'o received similar treatment during a match against Real Zaragoza. Zaragoza supporters hurled peanuts onto the field and showered Eto'o with monkey chants whenever he had possession of the ball (Zirin and Cox, 2006). As the match proceeded Eto'o scored a goal and responded to the crowd's actions by dancing like a monkey in celebration. After the match, when asked about his actions Eto'o told reporters, "I danced like a monkey because they treated me like a monkey." Despite the events of the tumultuous match, referee Fernando Carmona Méndez only commented that the behavior of the crowd was "normal" in his report. Consequently, the Spanish football federation was unable to take official action against Real Zaragoza and their supporters (BBC Sport, 2005a).

The incident surrounding Samuel Eto'o highlights the impact that these incidents have on individual players. In a February 2011 interview, Brazilian full-back Dani Alves described the racism in Spanish football as "uncontrollable." He stated that "I live with racism in every game, but I'm not offended. Fans insult me and call me 'monkey'... My family is sad about it. They complain, but I try to distance myself from it. I believe these people are uneducated" (*Daily Mail*, 2011). Such behavior has become so pervasive in the

game that players such as Barcelona midfielder Sergio Busquets have been accused of participating in the taunting as well. TV cameras covering a May 2011 match between Barcelona and Real Madrid captured Busquets attempting to cover his mouth while allegedly calling Madrid defender Marcelo Vieira a monkey.

Incidents where black players are singled out while being subjected to racist taunts from opponents, fans, and even coaches highlights assumptions about their perceived membership in some specific "black mass." Members of this mass are understood to possesses similar "qualities" (laziness, dirtiness, etc.) and have primary allegiance to an entity that is neither the team nor the nation. Unfortunately, such chants and behavior are not exclusive to Spain.

Italy

Ivorian defensive player Marco André Kpolo Zoro brought attention to the presence and persistence of anti-black racism in Italian soccer during a match between his club Messina and Inter Milan in November 2005. After enduring monkey chants from Inter Milan supporters throughout the match, Zoro's frustrations came to a head in the 67th minute when he picked up the ball and began walking off the field in tears. It took several minutes and the intervention of black Brazilian Adriano and Nigerian forward Obafemi Martins to quiet the crowd and convince Zoro to finish the match (BBC Sport, 2005b). The monkey chants also turned into expressions of derision toward the black players of Inter Milan who were perceived to be choosing their racial interests over those of Messina when supporting Zoro.

Similarly, black Inter Milan striker, Mario Balotelli has also endured racist taunts. Balotelli is an Italian born in Palermo but of Ghanaian descent. In April of 2009, Balotelli was subjected to racist taunts after scoring two goals in the second half of a match with Roma. Roma was subsequently fined US$10,000 by the Italian league. A month later, Balotelli was once again the victim of racial abuse in a game against Juventus. After scoring, Balotelli was subjected to chants of "a black Italian does not exist" and songs that contained racist sentiments from sections of the Juventus crowd in Turin. In response to these events, the league required Juventus to play their next home Serie A game behind closed doors. The explicit statement of what an Italian is not relies on a commonly understood conception of what an Italian *is* in overtly racial terms. During these incidents, Italian fans are expressing a specifically racial conception of national identity while disqualifying nativity from granting membership in the nation to blacks.

Like the Spanish cases, the Italian cases are interesting in that nationalism and racism have been synonymous with overtly Fascist parties who have taken to making Nazi salutes and other racist expressions at football matches. The forms of hooliganism that once were the hallmark of Italian fans and focused generally at other "European" fans and athletes have now turned against black athletes, some of whom were born in Italy. Such racist and fascist expressions publicly define citizenship and national membership in racial terms and unfortunately are reproduced even in the context of strict anti-Fascist laws in Germany.

Germany

Frustration similar to that experienced by Zoro and Balotelli spurred Nigerian midfielder, Adebowale Ogungbure to retaliate against fans during a March 2006 match. After the match, as Ogungbure was walking off the field spectators approached him, spat at him, and called him "Dirty Nigger," "Shit Nigger," and "Ape." As he walked past them he heard fans in the main stand making monkey noises at him. Upon hearing this Ogungbure put two fingers above his mouth to symbolize a Hitler moustache and performed a Nazi salute to the crowd. In an ironic turn of events Adebowale Ogungbure was investigated for making the illegal Hitler salute; however the charges were dropped within 24 hours (Lodde, Glindmeier, and Todt, 2006).

These incidents raise questions about the participants and the origins of these beliefs. The question remains, are these the actions and beliefs of racist nationalist fans or growing right-wing extremism? Rolf Heller, president of German football club Sachsen Leipzig, played down the Ogungbure incident and said it was an isolated case. "This has nothing whatsoever to do with right wing extremism, it is just misguided fervor on the part of the fans," he said (Lodde *et al.*,

2006). However, the prevalence of these incidents throughout Germany and the rest of Europe seems to invalidate Heller's statements.

In an August 2007 match between Borussia Dortmund (BVB) and Schalke, Ghanaian striker Gerald Asamoah and German goalkeeper Roman Weidenfeller collided in the 51st minute of the match. During the collision Weidenfeller reportedly called Asamoah a "black pig." The BVB keeper apologized to Asamoah after the game but denied using those words. Following an investigation by the German football federation, Weidenfeller was banned for three games and fined €10,000 for making "disparaging and insulting" remarks.

United Kingdom

Patterns of racism in English football have been well documented. Back, Crabbe, and Solomos (1998) point out the contingent nature of racist expressions and chanting and that the totality of late twentieth-century racism in English football should not be reduced to the phenomenon of "hooliganism" alone. Around the English game racism was and continues to be intermittent, contingent, and largely banal (Back *et al.*, 1998). While racism has declined in the English game there are still moments around the game where it is expressed. For example, Ron Atkinson, former Manchester United coach and pundit for television channel ITV, highlighted the presence of racist sentiments among the media when he made a racist comment on the air while speaking with commentator Clive Tyldesley. At the end of the broadcast of a 3–1 Chelsea loss in April of 2004, Atkinson referred to Chelsea's Marcel Desailly as a "fucking lazy nigger." Atkinson apparently thought his microphone had been turned off but his comments were broadcast live to channels in the Middle East who continued the live feed after the final whistle. Atkinson, an award-winning pundit and well-known figure in British football, subsequently quit his job at ITV and his position as a columnist for the *Guardian* newspaper.

Unfortunately, sentiments like those held by Atkinson have not been restricted to English announcers. Players, supporters, and even political figures have used racist language and taunts to address and deride black players. While there has been a change in the English game and a tentative embrace of multiculturalism along with international marketing of the Premier League that has encouraged clubs and the English Football Association to work with groups like FARE and "Kick It Out" to eliminate racism from the game (Back *et al.*, 1998, 2001; Garland and Rowe, 2001; Carrington, 2011), incidents of anti-black racism still persist.

The 2011–2012 English premiership season was marred by two incidents of racial abuse on the pitch. In a matter of just a few weeks Luis Suárez, the Uruguayan striker for Liverpool, and John Terry, captain of the England and Chelsea football teams, were both accused of using racial references to abuse black players during matches. Luis Suárez was found guilty by the English Football Association of using the term "negro" in a derogatory manner at least seven times in referring to Manchester United and French international defender Patrice Evra. Suárez was given an eight-match ban and a £40,000 fine, although he received backing from Liverpool with fellow players wearing T-shirts in support. The Terry case was much more complicated and protracted.

John Terry was accused of using the word "black" in a stream of abuse hurled at Queens Park Rangers defender Anton Ferdinand. The English Football Association delayed the case initially as it was addressed as a criminal matter. However, when Terry was acquitted in the criminal trial, the Football Association convicted him and gave a four-match ban and a £220,000 fine. Chelsea, who had supported Terry until the conviction by the Football Association, then announced they would take undisclosed disciplinary action as well. Terry was allowed to play for England at the 2012 UEFA European football championship (Euro 2012) while the criminal and Football Association proceedings were pending. Further, it was revealed that while Chelsea has in the past banned fans for life involved in racist chanting, Terry would keep his club captaincy following his four-match ban. Following the ban, Anton Ferdinand's brother Rio, a player for England and Manchester United, as well as Jason Roberts, a striker for Reading FC and a radio pundit, challenged the "Kick it Out" campaign, accusing the antiracism pressure group of not demanding more severe punishment and being too beholden to the Premier League and the English Football Association.

The two incidents taken together raised serious questions for many in the United Kingdom about the commitment to eradicating racism when it involves high-profile players and in particular when it involved a high-profile English player. In 2012, the England football authorities struggled with the meaning of "zero tolerance" and the different standards applied to fans versus high-profile players. That is aside from a number of incidents involving criminal charges against fans who racially abused black players and pundits via Twitter.

France

The relationship between nationalism and international soccer was most clearly stated by president of the French Languedoc-Roussillon region, Georges Frêche. In January 2007, Frêche remarked that the French national team was "too black." He expressed embarrassment over the racial composition of the team because nine of the eleven members of the team were black. Furthermore, he expressed concern about the possibility of an entirely black French national team. Frêche's comments resulted in his expulsion from the French Socialist Party of which he was a leading and founding member (Associated Press, 2007). Despite his position as a leading politician in French regional government, Frêche's comments strongly conflict with the tradition of French republicanism and dispel the myth that France is a raceless or color-blind society.

Frêche was not the only political leader who expressed these concerns. Leader and founder of the hyper-nationalist National Front party, Jean Marie Le Pen, attacked the French coach for including too many black players on the national team. In particular, the ambivalent feelings towards stars like Zinedine Zidane (Zizou) of Algerian descent and Thierry Henry of Caribbean descent dramatized the limitations of French racial thinking in ways that were also reflected in the fall 2005 riots on the outskirts of Paris by French youth who grew weary of discrimination and poverty (Janmohamed, 2006). French officials attacked the rioters as "immigrants" when most were second- and third-generation French citizens. Thus, despite the attempt by French politicians and pundits to cast the youths as "immigrants" they were French in every way imaginable except for the color of their skin.

Erik Bleich and Laurent Dubois point to a lack of policy engagement on racial difference in France that is driven by a lack of recognition of racial difference and underwritten by French republican notions of citizenship and universalism (Bleich, 2003; Dubois, 2010). Laurent Dubois situates French football success and controversy in the basic field of the fall of French empire and post-imperial politics since the 1930s (Dubois, 2010). Thus, despite the myth of the French republican tradition and even a moniker created by the French football federation, "not black or white just Blue," in reference to the French jersey color, race in these contexts still trumps citizenship status. Ironically, this became especially clear during a January 2005 antiracism initiative in the French league where Paris Saint-Germain players wore all white jerseys and RC Lens players wore all black. The white jerseys moved the crowd to sing "Come on whites" while making monkey chants when Lens players touched the ball. Zizou and Henry are always "immigrants," despite the fact that they were both born in France, both speak the French language, and neither claims any nationality than French. However, France in response to Le Pen, the riots, and racism around football lacks a real language or specific policy response to address racism other than to encourage French natives to "assimilate."

The extent to which racism persists from the fans to the federation level became clear when senior official Mohammed Belkacemi secretly recorded a meeting of high-ranking members of the federation. Transcripts of the meeting indicate that officials discussed plans of how to limit the number of black and African players eligible for the national team. The recordings indicate that officials believed that there were too many black players on the national team and developed plans to establish ethnic quotas of 30 percent on non-white players as early as age 12 or 13 (Chrisafis, 2011). Such high-level proposals seek to "reestablish," express, and affirm racialized conceptions of who is French and therefore eligible to represent the nation in international competition. The actions of French officials reflect a concern that is not exclusive to the federation, players, or fans. The multiracial make-up of the French national team is the subject of taunts and derision in other nations as well.

In a European Championship qualifier match between Lithuania and France in March 2007, Lithuania fans displayed a banner showing a map of Africa, painted with the colors of the French flag (blue, white, and red) and a slogan saying "Welcome to Europe." Like the statements of fans, players, and politicians, the banner was a commentary about the many black players on the French team (FARE, 2007).

Incidents in Eastern Europe

Serbia

As in Western Europe, the cases where slogans, banners, and commentary graduate to instances of violent interaction and abuse are of special concern. Such cases have presented themselves in Serbia. In October of 2006, 37 Borac Cacak fans were arrested after racially abusing the club's Zimbabwean player Mike Temwanjira during a first division match. Temwanjira subsequently left the club.

In 2007, UEFA fined the Serbian Football Association for racial insults by fans aimed at England's black players during the under-21 European Championship match. Tension in the stadium mounted on the field when a dispute over the legitimacy of England's second goal led to a confrontation between the players. English players reported that Serbian players repeated the racist rants shouted by the fans.

One year later in March of 2008, Serbian fans again attacked a member of their own team, Ghanaian player Solomon Opoku. Opoku, a striker for Borac Cacak, was returning to his hotel with friends after a match when he was struck in the back of the head. His attackers proceeded to beat and kick him while declaring their hatred for blacks (BBC Sport, 2008). Such incidents where players are berated and abused by fans of their own team bring further attention to the view that race trumps national and team affiliation in the eyes of football supporters.

Further, in October of 2012 Serbian fans assailed the England under-21 squad with monkey chants during a home match. England player Danny Rose, frustrated by the abuse, kicked a ball into the stands. He was sent off by the referee and left the field making monkey gestures in response to the constant abuse. Following the incident UEFA threatened to fine Serbia but also seemed to consider punishing the England players for expressing anger and frustration at racist abuse.

Russia

The hostile conditions that black players are forced to endure in Eastern European football became an issue of significant concern when Russia was announced as the host nation for the 2018 World Cup. While Russian officials worked to develop a culture of tolerance using various campaigns in schools and colleges, racist incidents persisted in Russian football.

During a June 2011 match between Krylia Sovetov Samara and Anzhi Makhachkala, Brazilian and Makhachkala player Roberto Carlos had a banana thrown at his feet during the final minutes of the game. The incident prompted Carlos to remove the banana from the field and leave the game. This was the second time that Carlos had been confronted by such taunts. During a March 2011 match, a fan of Zenit St Petersburg was photographed taunting Carlos with a banana. This incident highlighted the prevalence of racism in football at large but it also shone a light on the history, practices, and culture of Zenit St Petersburg football.

Investigations into Zenit St Petersburg revealed that the team remains the only major Russian team never to have signed a player of African heritage. While past manager Vlastimil Petrela stated that there were players of African heritage of interest to him, he was consistently told that the club was not interested. Such resolve by the club to maintain racial restrictions on club membership serves to reaffirm the behavior of Zenit supporters who frequently greet opponents of African ancestry with monkey chants and other forms of racial derision (Coomarasamy and Goldberg, 2011).

Regardless of who drives the racist atmosphere present in Zenit St Petersburg, Krylia Sovetov Samara or Russian football at large, it is clear that although Russian and Eastern European teams have no real colonial history in Africa and no history of slavery, the symbols and terms used in cases of racism in Eastern Europe demonstrate the global nature of anti-black racism and the ubiquity of the stereotypes and representations. The incidents continue relatively unabated in countries where governmental and sport-governing bodies have not taken decisive action in combating racism. Some European societies struggle with the distinction between the freedom of fans to express themselves and a strong stance against racism. For some countries, ultras (organized groups of fans) are part of the basic structure of football clubs. Although some ultras are implicated in racial incidents, sanctioning those fans can have negative financial and cultural implications for clubs and leagues in the short term. In some cases, racist fans are not a vocal minority but a core part of the support for major European clubs. UEFA and FIFA while symbolically decrying racism have only levied small fines against clubs, and have awarded the 2018 World Cup to Russia, a country where serious incidents of anti-black racism have occurred on and off the field.

The persistence of such incidents and the need to combat them were highlighted at Euro 2012. During the 16-team tournament hosted by Poland and Ukraine, Germany, Croatia, Russia, and Spain were all fined for racist incidents involving their supporters. While the penalties communicated a stand made by UEFA against racism, it was coupled with their stance before the tournament that players who responded to racist taunts or left the field would also be penalized. Given the robust history of referees ignoring racist taunts, this stance fueled player concerns about whether they would be adequately supported, protected, and defended by the governing body.

Over the years, groups of players have sought to challenge these practices through organizations such as FARE and Kick it Out. However, while writing this chapter we requested a systematic report and/or statistics on incidents and the organization was unable to provide them. Further, players' unions in major leagues like Italy and Spain have not taken strong steps to fight racism, in part due to government and club inaction. But this dynamic is also driven by the strength of supporters within the club structure. In Spain, supporters are the "owner" of many clubs with a voice in selecting the chairman democratically.

In sum, these incidents demonstrate the universality of tropes of anti-black racism. It has been elevated to a ritual practice in many European football grounds. That practice, while including polities with direct involvement in colonialism and the transatlantic slave trade, is actually more prevalent in places that have less of a direct history and certainly fewer immigrants of African descent. This suggests that the circulation of anti-black stereotypes is near-universal, but that antiracism is more likely to occur where substantial contact with populations of African descent have created movements to challenge it. European anti-black racism crosses boundaries, historical contexts, and demographic contexts; however, the signs and rituals remain eerily similar and the football ground is one of the prime places where they appear.

Conclusion

Unfortunately, condemnation of racism in soccer may only be treating the symptom without appropriately dealing with the deeper issue that is at least partly responsible for the epidemic. The growing anxieties around immigration and economic integration combine with long-held racial hostilities that in the case of Europe stem back to colonialism and in the case of the Americas to the slave trade and conquest of indigenous peoples (Hine et al., 2009). What is remarkable however is that anti-black racism transcends nations with a palpable history of colonialism or participation in the transatlantic slave trade. Anti-black racism has become a global phenomenon with the figure of the black becoming the ultimate "other," regardless of nationality, citizenship, or legal status.

Race and in particular anti-black racism cuts across categories of citizenship, status, class, and culture (Higginbotham, 1992). In the post-9/11 world only one other group enjoys such universal attacks, Muslims. At the same time, the discourse around Muslims, while including discourses about race, focuses more explicitly on "culture" rather than race. Still, in some cases race and religion are used as a proxy to connect Muslims to a range of unassimilable cultural practices. However, it is only in the case of blacks that acculturation in some other aspects

of life does not overcome perceptions of otherness.

While we have witnessed the rise of right-wing/fascist parties and anti-black racism in the context of Europe and around the world, we have also seen an equally global set of actors and organizations that have risen to combat it (Long and Spracklen, 2011; Burdsey, 2011). The organs of the United Nations through the Durban World Conference on Racism, the football federation FIFA, and a host of other non-governmental and quasi-social movement organizations have emerged to challenge racial attacks on blacks in a myriad of societies. What is noticeable is how these efforts mirror the concerns by blacks in all corners of the globe about segregation in the United States, colonialism, and later South African apartheid. While the American mass public and blacks are largely not watching this particular aspect of the drama, there are increasing interconnected interchanges between groups, individuals, and organizations interested in combating racism. Some of these connections are facilitated by foundations and organizations like the World Bank but others are grassroot. They use mass media, the internet, and other forms of communication to facilitate challenges to racist practices. Blacks in France self-consciously cited challenges to racism and social unrest in disparate cases like the Rodney King riots and in Soweto, South Africa. In fact, one of the authors observed a black French commentator on Brazilian television drawing similarities between universal notions of citizenship in France and Brazil and the denial of obvious racism in both countries. As students of politics, our notions of antiracist movements can no longer be contained within national boundaries. We must focus on international groups and organizations as well as on the interchange between "national" groups and organizations.

Finally, as students of politics we cannot ignore, in particular, how symbols and events within popular culture such as football simultaneously measure and help to form racial attitudes. The discourse and activities around international football serve as a corrective to the discussion of race, immigration, and citizenship that suggest that legal status or citizenship policies, in particular *jure soli vs. jure sanguinis*, determine racial or ethnic politics (Brubaker, 1998). While not diminishing the importance of legal notions of citizenship, this distinction only gets us part of the way towards understanding attitudes and formation of ideals and the political effects of migration on given polities. We also cannot have unique national explanations to forms of anti-black racism. Its existence in places with unique histories, differing notions of citizenship, different policies, welfare states, and so on, suggests that our studies of "immigrant incorporation" need to incorporate both global and local formations of worthiness and citizenship. While football is not the only terrain for this exploration, nor does it exhaust all the research questions, it suggests that serious students of racial politics cannot avoid discussions of symbols and discourse in shaping racial and political landscapes. This challenges both the methodological tendencies and theoretical orientations of the studies of race and calls us to push beyond the legal and to consider events and discourses as important variables in constructing racial politics.

References

Adair, D. (2011) *Sport, Race, and Ethnicity: Narratives of Difference and Diversity*, Morgantown, WV: Fitness Information Technology.

Alba, R. and Nee, V. (2003) *Remaking the American Mainstream: Assimilation and Contemporary Immigration*, Cambridge, MA: Harvard University Press.

Anderson, B.R.O.G. (1991) *Imagined Communities: Reflections on the Origin and Spread of Nationalism*, London: Verso.

Associated Press (2007) "French politician pays for racial soccer remark: Socialist party expels Freche for saying national team had too many blacks." *NBC Sports*, http://nbcsports.msnbc.com/id/16842366/, accessed December 11, 2012.

Back, L., Crabbe, T., and Solomos, J. (1998) "Racism in football: Patterns of continuity and change," in Brown, A. (ed.) *Fanatics! Power, Identity and Fandom in Football*, London: Routledge.

Back, L., Crabbe, T., and Solomos, J. (2001) *The Changing Face of Football: Racism, Identity and Multiculture in the English Game*, Oxford: Berg.

Bairner, A. (2001) *Sport, Nationalism, and Globalization*, New York: State University of New York Press.

Bleich, E. (2003) *Race Politics in Britain and France: Ideas and Policymaking since the 1960s*, New York: Cambridge University Press.

Bloemraad, I. (2006) *Becoming A Citizen: Incorporating Immigrants and Refugees in the United States and Canada*, Berkeley: University of California Press.

Back, L., Crabbe, T., and Solomos, J. (1998) "Racism in football: Patterns of continuity and change," in Brown, A. (ed.) *Fanatics! Power, Identity and Fandom in Football*, London: Routledge.

BBC Sport (2005a) "Eto'o responds to racist abuse." *BBC Sport*, http://news.bbc.co.uk/sport2/hi/football/africa/4261881.stm, accessed January 17, 2013.

BBC Sport (2005b) "Zoro suffers more racist abuse." *BBC Sport*, http://news.bbc.co.uk/sport2/hi/football/africa/4476412.stm, accessed January 17, 2013.

BBC Sport (2008) "Serb fans jailed for Opoku attack." *BBC Sport*, http://news.bbc.co.uk/sport2/hi/football/africa/7686213.stm, accessed January 17, 2013.

Brubaker, R. (1998) *Citizenship and Nationhood in France and Germany*, Cambridge, MA: Harvard University Press.

Burdsey, D. (2011) *Race, Ethnicity and Football: Persisting Debates and Emergent Issues*, London: Routledge.

Carrington, B. (1998) "Sport, masculinity and black cultural resistance." *Journal of Sport & Social Issues*, 22 (3): 275–298.

Carrington, B. (1999) "Cricket, culture and identity: An ethnographic analysis of the significance of sport within black communities," in Roseneil, S. and Seymour, J. (eds.) *Practising Identities: Power and Resistance*, New York: St Martin's Press.

Carrington, B. (2010) *Race, Sport and Politics: The Sporting Black Diaspora*, London: Sage Publications.

Carrington, B. (2011) "'What I said was racist – but I'm not a racist': Anti-racism and the white sports/media complex," in Long, J. and Spracklen, K. (eds.) *Sport and Challenges to Racism*, Basingstoke: Palgrave Macmillan.

Chrisafis, A. (2011) "French football official admits blowing whistle in race row." *Guardian*, http://www.guardian.co.uk/world/2011/may/04/french-football-official-race-row, accessed December 11, 2012.

Coomarasamy, J. and Goldberg, A. (2011) "Racism in Russian football: Zenit fans let side down." *BBC News*, http://www.bbc.co.uk/news/world-europe-12848838, accessed December 11, 2012.

Daily Mail (2011) "'Uncontrollable' racism in Spanish football will never go away, insists Barcelona's Alves." *Daily Mail*, http://www.dailymail.co.uk/sport/football/article-1354944/Dani-Alves-Racism-

Spanish-football-away.html, accessed January 23, 2013.

Dubois, L. (2010) *Soccer Empire: The World Cup and the Future of France*, Berkeley: University of California Press.

FARE (2007) "Racist banner exhibited at Lithuania-France Euro 2008 qualifier." FARE, http://www.farenet.org/default.asp?intPageID=7&intArticleID=1290, accessed January 17, 2013.

Farred, G. (2004) "Fiaca and Veron-ismo: Race and silence in Argentine football." *Leisure Studies*, 23 (1): 47–61.

Fredrickson, G.M. (1981) *White Supremacy*, Oxford: Oxford University Press.

Galeano, E.H. (2003) *Soccer in Sun and Shadow*. London: Verso.

Garland, J. and Rowe, M. (2001) *Racism and Antiracism in Football*, Basingstoke: Palgrave.

Giulianotti, R. (1999) *Football: A Sociology of the Global Game*, Cambridge: Polity Press.

Goff, P.A., Eberhardt, J.L., Williams, M.J., and Jackson, M.C. (2008) "Not yet human: Implicit knowledge, historical dehumanization, and contemporary consequences." *Journal of Personality and Social Psychology*, 94 (2): 292.

Goldberg, D.T. (2009) *The Threat of Race*, Oxford: Blackwell.

Gould, S.J. (1981) *The Mismeasure of Man*. New York: Norton.

Grosfoguel, R. (2003) *Colonial Subjects: Puerto Ricans in a Global Perspective*, Berkeley: University of California Press.

Haley, A. (1991) *The Autobiography of Malcolm X*, New York: Ballantine Books.

Hanchard, M.G. (1994) *Orpheus and Power: The Movimento Negro of Rio de Janeiro and São Paulo Brazil, 1945–1988*, Princeton, NJ: Princeton University Press.

Hanchard, M.G. (2003) "Acts of misrecognition: Transnational black politics, anti-imperialism and the ethnocentrisms of Pierre Bourdieu and Loïc Wacquant." *Theory, Culture, and Society*, 20 (4): 5–29.

Hanchard, M.G. and Chung, E.A. (2004) "From race relations to comparative racial politics: A survey of cross-national scholarship on race in the social sciences." *Du Bois Review: Social Science Research on Race*, 1: 319–343.

Hargreaves, J. (2002) "Globalisation theory, global sport, and nations and nationalism," in Sugden, J.P. and Tomlinson, A. (eds.) *Power Games: A Critical Sociology of Sport*, London: Routledge.

Higginbotham, E.B. (1992) "African American women's history and the metalanguage of race." *Signs*, 17 (2): 251–274.

Hine, D.C., Keaton, T.D., and Small, S. (2009) *Black Europe and the African Diaspora*, Urbana: University of Illinois Press.

Huntington, S.P. (2004) *Who Are We? The Challenges to American's National Identity*, New York: Simon & Schuster.

James, C.L.R. (1963) *Beyond a Boundary*, London: Hutchinson.

Janmohamed, Z. (2006) "A much needed head-butt." *Altmuslim Comment*, http://www.patheos.com/blogs/altmuslim/2006/07/a_much_needed_head_butt/, accessed January 17, 2013.

Kantorowicz, E.H. (1957) *The King's Two Bodies*, Princeton, NJ: Princeton University Press.

Kassimeris, C. (ed.) (2009) *Anti-Racism in European Football: Fair Play for All*, Plymouth, UK: Lexington Books.

Kassimeris, C. (2011) "Black, blanc and beur: French football's 'foreign legion.'" *Journal of Intercultural Studies*, 32 (1): 15–29.

Kelso, P. and Tremlett, G. (2004) "Spanish apologise for soccer racism." *Guardian*, http://www.guardian.co.uk/spain/article/0,2763,1354973,00.html, accessed January 23, 2013.

Kuper, S. (1994) *Football Against the Enemy*, London: Orion.

Laitin, D. (1998) *Identity in Formation: The Russian Speaking Populations in the Near Abroad*, Ithaca, NY: Cornell University Press.

Large, D.C. (2007) *The Nazi Games: The Olympics of 1936*, New York: Norton.

Lodde, E., Glindmeier, M., and Todt, J. (2006) "Player silences German racists with Hitler salute." *Spiegel Online*, http://www.spiegel.de/international/0,1518,409517,00.html, accessed January 15, 2013.

Long, J. and Spracklen, K. (eds.) (2011) *Sport and Challenges to Racism*, Basingstoke: Palgrave Macmillan.

MacClancy, J. (1996) *Sport, Identity, and Ethnicity*. Oxford: Berg.

Marx, A.W. (1998) *Making Race and Nation: A Comparison of the United States, South Africa and Brazil*, New York: Cambridge University Press.

Pierre, J. (2003) "Race, migration, and the re-imagining of contemporary African diasporas." *Wadabagei: A Journal of the Caribbean and its Diaspora*, 6 (3): 37–77.

Sawyer, M.Q. (2006) *Racial Politics in Post Revolutionary Cuba*, New York: Cambridge University Press.

Sawyer, M.Q., Peña, Y., and Sidanius, J. (2004) "Cuban exceptionalism: Group-based hierarchy and the dynamics of patriotism in Puerto Rico, the Dominican Republic, and Cuba." *Du Bois Review*, 1 (1): 93–113.

Shohat, E. and Stam, R. (1994) *Unthinking Eurocentrism: Multiculturalism and the Media*, London: Routledge.

Sidanius, J., Peña, Y., and Sawyer, M.Q. (2001) "Inclusionary discrimination: Pigmentocracy and patriotism in the Dominican Republic." *Political Psychology*, 21 (4): 827–851.

Thomas, D.L. (2002) "'The good Negroes': African-American athletes and the cultural Cold War, 1945–1968." PhD dissertation, University of California, Los Angeles.

Valeriano, B. (2006) "Latino cultural assimilation: Divided loyalties and the World Cup." Unpublished manuscript, Department of Political Science, University of Illinois at Chicago.

Wedeen, L. (2002) "Conceptualizing culture: Possibilities for political science." *American Political Science Review*, 96 (4): 713–728.

Winant, H. (2001) *The World is a Ghetto: Race and Democracy Since World War II*, New York: Basic Books.

Zirin, D. and Cox, J. (2006) "Who's to blame for racism in soccer." *Socialist Worker*, http://www.socialist worker.org/2006-2/593/593_13_WorldCup.shtml, accessed December 11, 2012.

Further Reading

Anderson, B.R.O.G. (1991) *Imagined Communities: Reflections on the Origin and Spread of Nationalism*, London: Verso.

Burdsey, D. (ed.) (2011) *Race, Ethnicity and Football: Persisting Debates and Emergent issues*, New York: Routledge.

Goldberg, D.T. (2002) *The Racial State*, Oxford: Blackwell.

Hanchard, M.G. (2006) *Party/Politics: Horizons in Black Political Thought*, Oxford: Oxford University Press.

Kassimeris, C. (ed.) (2009) *Anti-racism in European Football*, Plymouth, UK: Lexington Books.

Wedeen, L. (1999) *Ambiguities of Domination: Politics, Rhetoric, and Symbols in Contemporary Syria*. Chicago: University of Chicago Press.

10

Physical Culture, Pedagogies of Health, and the Gendered Body

Emma Rich and John Evans

Introduction

In 2010, Michelle Obama launched "Let's Move!", a healthy eating and exercise campaign against obesity. At that time, she said of her own children, Sasha and Malia, "In my eyes I thought my children were perfect . . . I didn't see the changes" and that "the doctor was concerned that something was getting off balance" (*Daily Mail*, 2010). Earlier, in 2008, Barack Obama also commented in an interview with *Parents Magazine*, "A couple of years ago – you'd never know it by looking at her now – Malia was getting a little chubby" (Henderson, 2010). More recently, Olympic gold medalist Jessica Ennis was subject of controversy when her coach claimed that a high-ranking person in UK athletics had said "that she's fat and she's got too much weight" (see Smith, 2012). In the lead-up to and during the London 2012 Olympics a number of other female participants also experienced comments about their physiques in the media. It seems the size, shape, and weights of even female Olympians are not immune from critical public scrutiny.

These comments reflect the way in which the "obesity crisis," as it is now commonly known, is a powerful element in the way in which physical activity and health is storied into existence in the public domain. Specifically, sport and physical activity is commonly constituted as a panacea, and charged with combating all manner of social problems from obesity to youth disaffection. In this chapter, we explore how these contemporary visions of health and physical activity within social-cultural and political contexts shape how we come to understand the "sporting female," focusing specifically on the UK context. Following Pirkko Markula's observation (2008: 384) that physical cultural studies (PCS) "has embraced the challenge of studying the body," we draw upon this approach to aid our exploration. David Andrews defines physical cultural studies as the

> synthesis of empirical, theoretical and methodological influences (drawn from, among other sources, the sociology and history of sport and physical activity, the sociology of the body, and cultural studies) that are focused on the critical analysis of active bodies and specifically the manner in which they become organized and represented, and experienced in relation to the operations of social power. (Andrews, 2008: 45)

Scholars elsewhere, many of whom have drawn upon Foucaultian concepts, have already alluded to the continued disciplining, governance, and

A Companion to Sport, First Edition. Edited by David L. Andrews and Ben Carrington.
© 2013 Blackwell Publishing Ltd. Published 2013 by Blackwell Publishing Ltd.

surveillance of sporting and (un)fit bodies (Markula and Pringle, 2006; Shogan, 1999; Smith-Maguire, 2002; Woodward, 2009). In building on this work, we endeavor to explore how discourses of femininity, physicality, health, and neoliberalism come to shape current configurations of the sporting (female) subject within contemporary physical culture (see also Woodward, 2009) within the United Kingdom. It has been argued that the shift of attention from "sport" to physical culture within PCS informs our understanding of physicality in more nuanced and contextually sensitive ways (Andrews, 2008; Silk and Andrews, 2011). This shift is significant because in understanding the physically active body, "sport" is no longer the sole focus but is considered instead to be "one, of many constituted elements within the broader domain of physical culture" (Andrews, 2008: 50). In understanding the various aspects of the physical, "the range of sociology of sport research has expanded to incorporate the empirical domains of fitness, dance, exercise, movement, wellness, and health" (Andrews, 2008: 51). PCS thus locates and analyzes these domains within broader social, political, economic, cultural, and technological contexts. In this way we are therefore able to connect how seemingly disparate issues (such as the comments above made by leading political figures) come to bear upon how we understand "physically active" or "inactive" bodies.

That this chapter's focus is on girls and young women is not to suggest that boys' and young men's bodies are not subject to inequitable practices and cultural politics in the representation of physically active and "fit" bodies. Rather, the analytical and conceptual focus is on girls and young women because of the integral positioning they have come to hold within current sociocultural and socioeconomic discourses about the "future" of neoliberal society. Much has been written separately about these two issues. For example, physical culture and the active body have long caught the attention of sociologists of sport and PCS scholars (Hargreaves and Vertinksy, 2007; Ingham, 1997; Pronger, 1998). Equally, cultural studies and childhood studies have been interested in contemporary visions of girlhood and the positioning of girls and young women as the vanguard of particular neoliberal subjectivity (Harris, 2004). In recent times, via "celebratory discourses"

(Lucey and Reay, 2002: 322), young women (middle-class in particular) have been celebrated for the ostensible progress they have made in various social contexts such as education and employment, as if somehow reflecting the progression around gender equality. In this chapter, we highlight how these discourses coalesce via the utilization of the "fit" body (Cole, 1998; King, 2003), and now the "obese" body as culturally symbolic of sedentariness, as part of the neoliberal constitution of personal responsibility.

Much of the chapter focuses specifically on how contemporary discourses of health, configured through governing technologies of neoliberalism, come to bear upon physical culture and in particular sport, in ways which constitute female physicality. Whilst we recognize that these representations of gender might not necessarily be new (Cole, 1993; Fisette, 2011; King, 2003; Markula, 2001), we argue that they are made more visible and prevalent via emerging body pedagogies which focus on the particular health crisis of a putative obesity epidemic. Individuals in neoliberal societies are increasingly being incited to maintain responsibility for their weight as part of a broader culture of healthism and moral panics about obesity and sedentariness. These pedagogies thus reveal how current imaginings of the "future can-do girl" (Harris, 2004) converge with new health imperatives as part of "the ways in which subjective gender is constituted and mobilised" (Zannettino, 2008: 66).

Moreover, drawing upon research with school-aged girls and young women, the chapter reveals how exercise and physical activity practices associated with new health imperatives tend to homogenize young people's diverse interests, needs, and opportunities across ethnicity, class, age, culture, and ability. Within obesity discourse the possibilities for health are often announced through "one size fits all" policies advocating practices that are deemed appropriate for everyone and fail to give due attention to the socioeconomic contexts which may mediate opportunities and prohibit choice, and thus reifies a form of political individualism. Throughout, we examine the complex interplay between discourses of health, sport, young women's physicality, and the active negotiations around their subjectivity. Following Michel Foucault (1979) the body is taken as a site on which various discourses are contested and negotiated; the convergence of sport and health brings into play a particular gendered body politic (Fusco, 2006). This is not to suggest that young women's bodies are acted upon by these discourses in ways which reductively determine their subjectivity. Indeed, understanding contemporary visions of girlhood demands complex explanatory frameworks which avoid monolithic categories and recognize not only the pervasive impact of health discourse but also the *active role* that girls may play in constituting their subjectivities in relation to this. Elsewhere a growing body of work has begun to reveal the active role that girls may play in constituting their subjectivities (Davies, 1989; Francis and Archer, 2005; Skelton and Francis, 2009; Susinos, Calvo, and Rojas, 2009; Youdell, 2005).

Obesity, Health, and Girlhood

Complex sociocultural, socioeconomic, and sociopolitical dynamics demand a nuanced approach to understand the relationships between physical culture and female physicality. Whilst contemporary neoliberal health messages may be announced through "universal" (essentially white, middle-class, Westernized) *ideals*, their meanings may not be experienced uniformly but are recontextualized, resisted, made meaningful in the lives of girls as they intersect with other categories of experience such as age, family location, social class, sexuality, gender, and ethnicity. In understanding the constitution of gendered bodies through physical culture and in particular sport, we must remain cognisant of the ways in which girls may variously invest in, resist, and negotiate discourses. Thus, rather than simply reading girls and young women's bodies as being acted upon by global neoliberal discourses, such approaches allow us to explore how different girls and young women invest in, negotiate, and/or resist discourses of health via particular practices of the body (see Atencio and Wright, 2009; Skeggs, 1997; Youdell, 2005, 2006; Hauge, 2009; Zannettino, 2008).

In the United Kingdom, as in many other Western and Westernized societies, something of a crisis has been constructed around the relationships between childhood inactivity, young people's diets, and rising obesity levels, and promoted through various sites of physical culture. This discourse cultivates the idea that reduced activity and poor diets are leading to increased rates of obesity, resulting in imminent decline in health and increased mortality rates. Fueled by a moral panic,[1] these concerns have recast attention towards the weight, size, shape, and lifestyles of young people, intensifying the pressures on them to regulate their bodies and lifestyles, for example to alter their eating habits, take more exercise, and lose weight. This interest in obesity reflects a biopolitical shift toward organizing, shaping, and regulating bodies in particular ways, through a simplistic focus on "weight" (see Evans *et al.*, 2008: Wright and Harwood, 2009) rather than health. Moreover, such fears about the declining future health of current generations of young people are used as justification for intervening in people's lives at an increasingly younger age and on an ever greater scale. Rarely have so many people been made to feel so bad about their bodies or their routine maintenance through eating, moving, exercising, and so forth, with so little concern or sensitivity as to the potentially damaging effects of this especially on the lives of girls and young women (see Halse, Honey, and Boughtwood, 2008; Evans *et al.*, 2008).

Anti-obesity discourse has resulted in a barrage of policies and initiatives in schools to get children more physically active, slimmer, and eating less, fueled by concerns about the increase in sedentary behavior (see Evans *et al.*, 2008). In England and Wales for example, central government has sought joint action from its agencies, the Department of Health and the Department for Children, Schools and Families (formerly Department for Education and Skills), to address health matters through policy affecting the whole environment of schools. In the United Kingdom, a government white paper (Department of Health, 2010) identified children in early-years settings as a key target group, highlighting the importance of early intervention and prevention as crucial for their future health and well-being. In the same context, physical activity guidelines for children under 5 years of age have been recently released for the first time (Department of Health, 2011).

While concerns about children's health, weight, and physical activity might not be new, following the broader concerns associated with a putative "obesity epidemic" the scrutiny of young people's bodies has not only become relentless but also converges with broader discourses of neoliberalism.

As Jan Wright (2009) observes, the "obesity epidemic" offers one of the most powerful and pervasive discourses influencing ways of thinking about health and the body. In keeping with liberal individualism, this has led to a renewed interest in the need for populations to monitor their own and others' weight and health against perceived risks associated with deteriorating lifestyles. These concerns are driving what might be described as "new health imperatives" prescribing the choices people should make around lifestyle, in particular relating to physical activity and food. Work elsewhere has begun to explicate the connections between these health imperatives and neoliberal politics (Halse, 2009; Halse, Honey, and Boughtwood, 2007: Rich and Evans, 2005) and demonstrate how they are infused with moral ethics of citizenship, advocating how individuals ought to "appear" and behave (Evans, 2006). These new health imperatives constitute subjectivity, in that they deeply influence the visceral experience (and ongoing assessment) of one's own body size; such that the thin or slender body is taken to represent not only a state of "good health" but also an indication of personal control, virtue, and goodness, of making the "right choices" (Rich, Holroyd, and Evans, 2004) and adopting the "right lifestyle." Some argue that body pedagogies which instruct populations on "good health" are underpinned by a new-right political ideology asserting particular versions of citizenship. Such body pedagogics (Shilling, 2005, 2007) not only provide instructional charges oriented towards weight, diet, and lifestyle but also produce embodied subjectivities which act as corporeal orientations to one's own and others' bodies. Body pedagogies in this sense define whose and what bodies have status and value, constituting acts of inclusion and exclusion imbued with moral imperatives and an ethic of particular forms of citizenship. In obesity discourse, for example, individuals' character, value, and sense of self are to be judged essentially in terms of "weight," size, or shape. The responsibility placed on populations to protect themselves from the assumed risks associated with obesity reflects a broader shift towards "surveillance

medicine" (Armstrong, 1995). Indeed, this recognizes that the control of populations through medicalization is not an enforced action but one which normalizes particular health practices within everyday contexts. Practices of this kind are now recognized as part of the biopolitical landscape of contemporary Western and Westernized cultures oriented towards healthism and more specifically escalating concerns associated with obesity. Drawing on Foucault's (1979) concept of biopower, Wright and Harwood (2009) have developed the notion of biopedagogies as a theoretical concept through which to examine the relationships between biopower, obesity discourse, and pedagogical practices. We take up some of their ideas in the analyses below which offer clear indication of how obesity discourse forges consciousness and impacts the lives of young people, sometimes negatively, especially if mediated insensitively through the body pedagogies of schools.

The data are drawn from an ESRC-funded research project (RES-000-22-2003) exploring young people's experiences of new health imperatives associated with weight loss, examining their manifestation across particular cultural sites and practices. The study has investigated how health imperatives and associated curriculum initiatives are operationalized within and across a range of schools located in Middle England with parallel studies pursued in Australia and New Zealand. The methodology was designed to explore the relationships between demographic "resources" (sociocultural capital) born of age, gender, class, ethnicity, and (forms of) schooling, sites and sources of influence on "body knowledge," and individuals' relationships to their embodied selves. Data sets were collected across eight schools in England selected to reflect a range of social, cultural, and policy contexts enabling the in-depth analysis required to capture the interplay between cultural forces, social institutions, and their impact on young people's embodied identities. This chapter draws specifically on a combination of quantitative and qualitative data derived from some 1,176 questionnaires administered to pupils aged from 9 to 16 years of age, in eight schools in central England (see Table 10.1), and qualitative data drawn from interviews with 90 pupils and 19 staff (see De-Pian, Evans, and Rich, 2008). All interview quotes are reported

Table 10.1 School contexts.

School	Type/Description	Age groups included in research sample
B	Large, independent, secondary school for boys (10–18 years old)	12–13 and 15–16 (Years 8 and 11)
F	Large, independent, coeducational, preparatory school (4–11 years old)	9–11 (Years 5 and 6)
G	Secondary school for girls (11–18 years old)	12–13 and 15–16 (Years 8 and 11)
H	Large, coeducational, rural state middle school (11–14 years old)	11–14 (Years 7–9)
L	Large, coeducational, multiethnic, state middle school (11–14 years old)	12–13 (Year 8)
R	Large, coeducational, multiethnic, inner-city, state primary school (4–11 years old)	9–11 (Years 5 and 6)
W	Very small, coeducational, middle-class, rural/village, state primary school (4–11 years old)	9–11 (Years 5 and 6)
X	Large, coeducational, deprived, multiethnic, inner-city college (11–16 years old)	13–15 (Years 9 and 10)

using pseudonyms, school year where appropriate, and the school type represented by a letter (e.g., school X).

Healthy Girls, Healthy Futures

In a time of dramatic social, cultural and political transition, young women are being constructed as a vanguard of new subjectivity. They are supposed to offer clues about the best way to cope with these changes. Power, opportunities, and success are all modelled by the "future girl", a kind of young woman celebrated for her "desire, determination and confidence" to take care of her life, seize chances, and achieve her goals. (Harris, 2004: 1)

Recent theorizations of contemporary girlhood have endeavored to make sense of the integral role that young women play in relation to the future of society (Harris, 2004). Many of the seemingly "progressive" steps made towards gender equity have been attributed to the work of previous feminist movements and changing social conditions which have provided increased opportunities for education, career pathways, and the like (Walby, 1997) underpinned by the pressing "socioeconomic need for young women to take up places in the new economy" (Harris, 2004: 7). However, many of these opportunities

have been available only to an elite "few" rather than the many, and social conditions for other young women across different social class, race, and cultural status remain limited but obfuscated within these discourses of individualism. In other words, rather ironically, this overly individualistic discourse of "success" serves only to celebrate and privilege the "worth of the individual at the expense of the collectivity" (Budgeon, 2001: 18).

This individualist approach is clear to see within contemporary visions of health, as manifested within current policies and practices associated with tackling the "obesity epidemic." Increasingly, both individuals and populations are being ascribed responsibility for their health and its reductive constituent "weight," and are relentlessly monitored in their capacity so to do. The imperative to dutifully take care of one's body emerges from a neoliberal hegemony that has come to shape contemporary Western life (Giroux, 2004; Nettleton, 1997: 213). Obesity discourse, constituted through a focus on risk (or rather "risk avoidance" – of falling foul of obesity and related illnesses: Gard and Wright, 2005) has become a defining characteristic of both contemporary Western society and individualized health discourses.

Within obesity discourse young women are assumed to be both in control of their own destiny and able to shape their future lives and health if only they undertake the regulative practices which it prescribes (e.g., pursuing "good" diets, exercising, and losing weight). Such thinking reflects the image of "future girls" outlined by Harris (2004), that is, girls who are able to demonstrate control over their own lives and futures. The focus is on personal responsibility and an ethic of self-care (Jette, 2006; Cole, 1998; King, 2003). Body pedagogies and physical culture have thus been mobilized to embody and encourage the neoliberal individual who "enters into the process of self-examination, self-care and self-improvement" (Petersen, 1996: 48–49), to monitor and regulate their bodies against the future risks of ill health through increased physical activity, weight loss, and better diets. These broader sociopolitical relations of power shape the ways in which ideas around health, physical activity, and food are being produced.

The girls in our research, refracting such expectations, reported that they sought to demonstrate personal responsibility of health specifically through an engagement with exercise. Many reported taking up exercise as a practice on the body to constitute themselves in particular ways:

> Just so that I can like if I do it once a week I won't get such a big change because I'm really small but once a month I can see a big change. We used to have these old scales that were really awful but now we've got these new ones and it can either do it in kilograms or stones and I do it in kilograms and I'm pretty happy with my weight.
>
> I make sure that I'm always going for a gain, a goal or a target in cross country so three laps of the field, try and beat someone in a relay and it makes me feel a lot better. (Kirsty, Year 5, W)

The gendered nature of particular practices of exercise and physical activity is evident in the focus on individual parts of the body, such as thighs or tummies: "I enjoy swimming and I really enjoy bike riding 'cause it works all of your muscles and so does swimming. I'm trying to work on my thighs at the minute" (Marie, Year 6, F). Whilst many may constitute the benefits of exercise through the focus on working on one's muscles, Marie's reference to working on her thighs alludes specifically to the focus of body practices towards the breakdown/reshaping of specific body parts in an effort to constitute a specific subjectivity: "Yeah, I try *to work* on it.

When I'm sitting down I try and lift my legs up and down so I'm working them . . . I go on my mum's foot pedals as well and she's got a sit-up machine and I've got a Davina exercise DVD that I do with my mum" (Marie, our emphasis).

The emphasis on the health benefits of exercise in this way also produces practices through which young women come to work on particular body parts (e.g., reshaping thighs) as means through which to enact not only the dutiful healthy citizen but also the particular body ideals associated with femininity (Bordo, 1990; Hesse-Biber, 2006; Markula, 1998; Garrett, 2004).

In this sense, a thin body complies with gendered norms, through becoming the hetero-feminine subject, and also with official discourse of obesity. The convergence of health with certain physical cultural practices thus also works to legitimate readings of the body connected to the hetero-feminine subject, reflecting the body's role in "the inseparability of sex–gender–sexuality" (Youdell, 2005: 268). Through such physical cultures, exercise is a practice by which young women like Marie come to shape their bodies to meet the ideals around what a healthy girl should look like. Drawing on particular physical cultural artefacts such as fitness DVDs, Marie is also able to demonstrate an active responsible subjectivity, where she is seen to be working on her body. She is thus constituted through a middle-class, neoliberal discourse in which the individual is deemed responsible for solving their own health problems (Armstrong, 1995; Crawford, 1980) and working on oneself as the dutiful citizen. A neoliberal ethic of selfhood plays a significant role in the formation of gendered subjectivities. Girls and young women in particular, as the subjects of governmentality (Harris, 2004) are thus positioned as responsible for advancing particular projects of the state. Health and weight feature as aspects of contemporary girlhood, through a body politic that blends gendered norms with individualized notions of health and citizenship.

Sculpted Lean Femininity

Although girls and young women like those in the research project may present themselves in ways which elicit self-control, responsibility, and determination, it is equally clear that achieving an "appropriate physicality" presents many dilemmas and contradictory discourses. Bodies of young girls are subject to an array of physical cultural demands, which far from offering freedom towards endless possibilities of who they might be, suggest that the "can do" girl (Harris, 2004) is reserved for the few and constituted through an individualized, personal project. Although a thin body was admired, many young women were conscious of walking a very delicate tightrope between constructing an ideal body and a body that was too thin. Being a "healthy girl" was intimately related to their embodied gendered subjectivities and mediated by their engagement with and complex reading of wider popular and consumer culture, for example, teenage magazines (see McRobbie, 2000; Oliver and Lalik, 2000), through which they also learnt about acceptable bodies. In extolling the image of the self-directed, can-do, neoliberal girl, many of the young women made reference to not simply a "thin" body but also to the "sculpted lean muscled femininity" (Heywood, 2007: 113) which circulates in consumer culture (representing a particular expression of fitness) and which was considered to reflect both self-control and a body which has been manifestly worked upon and altered in positive ways. As Kala (School R) put it, "I'd like to be like her 'cause she's like a bit sporty and stuff." In this sense, whilst many girls and young women offered a critical reading of thinness, this was complicated by an accompanying critique of the can-do sporty future girl. Particular celebrity figures such as Victoria Beckham (former pop star and wife of David Beckham, often criticized in popular magazines for being "too thin") were frequently positioned as "overstepping the boundary" and "too thin":

INTERVIEWER: What about Victoria Beckham, do you like the way she looks?
MARIE: I think she's really pretty and she's got a really good figure but she's just too skinny for me ... hmm the right weight ... well I wouldn't like to be Paula Radcliffe [an international runner].
ABI: Personally I wouldn't like to be that skinny.
MARIE: Because she's so skinny. I'd more like to be her really [points to picture of Anna Kournikova, a tennis player]. (Year 6, F)

As Huckaby (2010: 76) argues, public life is saturated with images of the mediated body that are "exaggerated, less attainable and often unrealistic ideals of real bodies" which "draw our energies into maintaining and reifying the illusion, which we live through our embodied beings." While slenderness has long been the ideal, a more nuanced reading of thinness and gender is necessary reflecting the increasingly narrow normative femininity purveyed through obesity discourse and neoliberal ideals. This narrow femininity was incontrovertibly (hetero)sexualized, racialized, and able-bodied. Some girls and young women for example, made reference to exercise as a way to constitute a different, "fit, strong and toned" body . Only 16.9 percent said that being healthy is important to them for physical reasons such as being able to participate in sport (36.5 percent). Over half of those girls (51.6 percent) were located in the girls' independent secondary school and located in the higher social classes (1–3) where reputation and recognition of sports performance was vital, and part of the broader neoliberal incentive towards marketization of the school. In such cases, socioeconomic and sociocultural influences intersect to bear upon the relationships between gender, citizenship, and physical activity in young women's reading of the sporting female:

ELIZABETH: Yeah, like I agree with Hannah, toned is good because it makes you look healthy.
HANNAH: For example in this picture you can see that without doing anything you see she's got like muscles not like a body builder or anything, you just see they're there and she's obviously played sport whereas if you went and had a look at these guys (Posh Spice) you can see their muscles because they've got no fat there. They just have no fat on them at all, it's like "oh my God, it's like skin and bones" – and the only reason you can see the muscles because they've got no fat there.
ELIZABETH: Yeah, that's just a bit minging – that just scares me. (Year 11, G)

For girls like Hannah from the independent (fee-paying) school, athletic toned bodies define the "fit" and "sporty" body which accords with the emphasis placed on the progressive, achievement-oriented construction of "future girl" (Harris, 2004) who is flexible enough to negotiate being "toned but she's [Anna Kournikova] not too thin" (Hannah, School G). Hannah's aspirations towards having a body like Anna Kournikova's reflects this knowledge to display the correct "sculpted lean muscled femininity" (Heywood, 2007: 113); "she's not like a stick thin person, she's just really toned and looks really good." In trying to cultivate such a femininity, young women interviewed drew on imagery of girlhood which reflected the can-do girls (Harris, 2004) who are educated, flexible, healthy, self-determined, employable, (hetero) sexual, middle-class, white (see also Heywood, 2007):

> Because I do a lot of sport I would say I'm quite a healthy person: I eat healthily and I would say that I have quite a good body but then there's always an issue, because I cut down on sport so like I have my rest period then I put on weight and then I lose weight so I prefer how I am when I'm being sporty, when I'm doing loads of sport rather than in the summer when I'm doing it perhaps once or twice a week rather than once a day, so that's my preference. (Hannah, Year 11, G)

As Walkerdine (2003: 240) suggests, the neoliberal self is expected to be "autonomous and flexible to negotiate, choose, succeed in the array of education and retraining forms." Some of the young women via middle-class narratives of choice and mobility experience themselves within a discourse which positions them as humanist subjects, "to have the chance to consider their options, choose and think critically" (Jones, 1997: 263). This particular feminine subject has been recognized by other scholars as having historical roots in a middle-class femininity which is disciplined, slender, and normalized through whiteness (see Azzarito, 2010; Seid, 1989). To this end, the neoliberal constitution of the toned, sporting female who is actively responsible in adopting a "healthy" lifestyle and reflects this through the sculpting of a particular physique, glosses over the many ways in which the opportunities to enact particular "health" practices are mediated by social class, gender, ethnicity, and culture. The constitution of a successful healthy girl in the

independent schools carried very clear expectations which coalesced with broader physical cultures and thus required a flexible individual who could negotiate the display of particular corporeal identities across a variety of social-cultural contexts (see Ali, 2003).

The Healthification of Sport and Physical Activity

It is important to explore how physical physical culture has been utilized in political processes and through institutions, inciting girls and young women to participate in particular strategies of what Fusco (2007: 45) refers to as "healthification" involving "the political processes through which institutions and individuals invite and incite youth to participate in the new public health's strategies." Many of the girls/young women described exercise as vigorous activities involving sweating and getting out of breath in order to "work off weight." Various physical cultural sites played a significant role in shaping and constraining their "body management practices" (Riley et al., 2008), such that various forms of physical activity were undertaken in instrumental ways:

> Eat good food and exercise everyday 'cause it will burn off your carbs and make you fitter . . . I feel really happy with myself because I've gone on a bit of a diet. This morning I didn't have any breakfast . . . I have, I've got one on my bike, it tells me how many meters I've done in a day and when I clip it onto my belt it will tell me how many steps I've done in a day . . . I just want to know if I need to do more. I try to improve it, so say if I've done fifty in a day I'd do like seventy, and it also tells me how many carbs you've burnt off and how many stones you've lost. (Marie, Year 6, F)

In doing so, young women like Marie undertake exercise as a practice of the body (Hauge, 2009) in ways which constitute the morally good citizen. Through processes of healthification exercise became less about the pleasure of movement, or experiencing different physicalities, and focused more on the means through which bodies can be shaped and trained towards achieving often "unachievable ideals" (Markula, 1998): "But if you ate a whole pizza you would have to run a whole marathon to burn it off so I'm not having pizza" (Lauren, Year 5, W). Particular practices of the body thus afford positions through which young women are able to recognize themselves or others as particular subjects. These meanings of physical activity converge with broader neoliberal discourses and physical cultural practices through which these young women understood exercise, sport and physical activity:

> Go outside even if it's just walking, it could still burn a calorie or two instead of staying inside and watching the TV. (Elise, Year 7, H)

> I'm not always conscious about it but just like . . . I feel better in myself that I'm doing something, I'm not like lounging around. And dancing is proper hard work, isn't it, proper sweat. (Jordan, Year 10, X)

> I would prefer to be not too fat but then not too skinny because if you're too skinny then people say you're too skinny and then you start getting depressed and you start eating a lot and then you're saying "Ooh, I'm eating too much I should stop" and you keep on going back and fore but when you're too fat you worry yourself about being too fat and then sometimes you have to pay all this money to get operations done but even though you're fat you can keep warm but you don't get a lot of exercise. So it's better to feel good about yourself and do as much exercise as you can. (Bryony, Year 6, F)

Such comments reflect the moral imperative and duty to be healthy and the body as an indicator of one's health (e.g., Crawford, 1980; Shilling, 1993; Markula, 1997). Many young women in this study supposed that one's weight was a result of whether one exercised and ate well (as prescribed in obesity discourse). The neoliberal discourses running through these comments emphasizes the need to work on oneself, act responsibly and productively as part of an appropriate feminine subjectivity (Fusco, 2006). In this way, various political, economic, sociocultural norms about future girlhood are intertwined through practices of and on the body.

Understandings of exercise and health such as those described above draw upon "meritocratic principles that explain any failure to 'achieve' and to 'have' as personal failure" (Lucey, Melody, and Walkerdine, 2003: 285). Within the neoliberal life project, one is expected to handle uncertainty, such as health risks, but in this sense it produces an almost "inevitable failure that will be lived as personal failing" (Walkerdine, 2003: 241). The focus on "effort," "proper exercise," acts in a depoliticizing way that obfuscates inequitable social structures which may impact on the opportunities in the lives of these young women. Certain opportunities to enact health (Burrows, 2010) and subjectivities may only be available to some girls depending on the particular contexts of their lives. Moreover, the illusion of individual autonomy contributes to the production of particular forms of pedagogy, wherein young people are "required to collectively invent the neoliberal systems they are part of, making sure each time that they come closer and closer to the correct discourse" (Davies, 2005: 10). Such pedagogies incentivize individuals such as Marie to monitor and regulate their bodies against standards constructed by others, such as schools, media, health policy, consumer culture. Many girls and young women, like those above, dutifully undertake regulation, policing, and monitoring of the self (Fusco, 2006) via physical practices.

Body pedagogies constructed in line with obesity discourse and its associated practices of the body may thus provide certain "subject positions" (Davies and Harré, 1990) which cultivate ways of being and naming oneself or others. Moreover, the incitement of girls to invest, manage, and work on their bodies in extensive, and often limitless ways, in an effort to be a particular subject and constitute a particular subjectivity, can lead to excessive and sometimes harmful body practices. Indeed, a majority of the girls in our survey (60.9 percent) reported that they "NEVER feel good about their bodies," and 54.3 percent were "NEVER happy about their current weight and size." Research elsewhere reports similar findings where improved "appearance" consistently emerges as the reason for young women to exercise (Strelan, Mehaffey, and Tiggemann, 2003). When asked "Have you tried to lose weight?" 45 percent of boys responded "yes" compared to 64.5 percent of girls. Thus, girls expressed a particularly strong desire to get thinner compared to boys. Of those that had tried to lose weight, 44 percent said that they had tried to lose weight *through exercise*. Whilst the survey data revealed that girls were clearly able to see the value in exercise as means to lose weight, very few alluded to potential dangers associated with over-exercising. While 50.4 percent of participants listed patterns of exercise as one of, if not the main thing that stops people being healthy, 72 percent of those participants claimed "no exercise or sport" was unhealthy whereas only 1.2 percent referred to over-exercising as unhealthy.

Affect, Body Pedagogies, and Gender Differentiation

> So like me now I'm always worried about what I look like and I always have to be perfect . . . I've done it since I've been 9–10 really, I've been wanting to make my hair look nice. I'd like make myself look perfect if there was a boy I liked and I wanted to impress him. I just want to make myself look perfect and I want to make myself look skinny and I want my hair to be right. (Marie, Year 6, F)

Comments such as those above implore us to think about how "discursive processes work in and through desires, feelings, anxieties and defenses" (Zannettino, 2008: 477). Schools, media, and other physical cultural sites play an instrumental role in the classification of dividing practices associated with fatness, thinness, and physical activity. For example, many of the young people in the research alluded to the powerful pedagogic moments that occurred through emerging technologies which had become part of their everyday lives. The role cyberspace has played in the construction of health discourses (Miah and Rich, 2008) ,particularly those associated with the corporeal governance promulgated through obesity discourse, is now well recognized. Girls and young women demonstrated a discerning reading of various forms of pedagogical address such that certain cultural artefacts held more meaning over others:

> I read lots of magazines that say that you have to have a balanced diet . . . Yeah. There was this article about which foods count as five a day and I learnt a lot from that so which I could eat and

would help me keep healthy, and there's lots of adverts on television and they say keep healthy and all that. (Philippa, Year 6, F)

In learning about health and the body these young people often referred to the significance of reality media on weight and health which had a "surveillant" focus (see Andrejevic, 2002), for example through the direct observation of participants' weight, health, or lifestyle. These include media that fall within the genres of "reality science" (Cohen, 2005) and "reality television," involving "first person programming" (Wood and Skeggs, 2008) and non-actors. These reality media seek not only to entertain audiences but to "instruct" on how to undertake surveillance of their own and other's bodies (Rich, 2011). Such media provided them with the "knowledge" of what sort of problem obesity is, and a vision of what life would be like as a "fat" or "obese" person:

> I was watching GMTV[2] with my Mum this morning. There's that Inch Loss Island . . . I think it's kind of inspiring showing people how you can lose weight if you want to but they're not like portraying images of like really skinny models and things like that so they don't really pressure you into being like that but they're just saying how you could change your lifestyle to be more healthy. (Laura, Year 8, H)

The pedagogies cultivated through these media promote orientations to the body specifying its maintenance, development, enrichment, and repair. The instructional format of weight/health-related media utilizes the television "lifestyle expert" (Biressi and Nunn, 2008; Lewis, 2007; Wood and Skeggs, 2004; Rich, 2011) but also announce to these young women who is deemed to be an "appropriate provider and evaluator" (Bernstein, 2000: 78):

> Well it depends what it is, because sometimes like on the internet there could be things about healthy eating but you don't know if it's true so it's hard to believe but I think that if you've seen it on a TV program like if there's someone who's saying they've been unhealthy and now they're healthy it must be true. (Elise, Year 7, H)

With the advent of a range of digital platforms that merge entertainment with the regulation of the body, such as internet-based nutrition games – along with the use of games consoles such as Nintendo Wii Fit and exergaming in schools (Vander Schee and Boyles, 2010) – cyberspace becomes more recognizable to young people as contexts for learning of the constitution of gender subjectivities (Francombe, 2010).

However, such "pedagogies, public and institutionalized, in and of themselves are neither good nor bad, but as an apparatus of power they do hold the potential to harm or benefit" (Huckaby, 2010: 74). What is clear is that whilst this may affect girls and young women in different ways, many reported a "fear" of fatness in terms of both social stigma and also potential health risks. For example: "and there's always that thing will I have a heart attack earlier because of my weight and there's consequences" (Abi, Year 6, F); "child obesity has doubled in 10 years, because it's children. It's scary" (Rhiannon, Year 8, L).

The construction of all bodies as potentially at risk underpins the need to constantly work on oneself to be protected from the risks of obesity. However, the fat body is not a preexisting entity that is stable, bounded, unified, but it becomes multiple things as it connects with other bodies (e.g., thin bodies), knowledges, and images. In this sense, "we need to take into account the body in movement, involved in a complex set of relations to the spaces around it. Not just operating as an object of which we have a clear image" (Featherstone, 2010: 208). In this vein, the affective responses young women have in relation to weight are not only attached to the "health risks" of weight but also the various images circulating in physical culture. Such images were drawn upon in processes of differentiation around the gendered body and physical activity. Girls across all school settings reported that when they did display alternative bodies, they were often called names like "fatty": "You get called more names if you're overweight" (Leonne, Year 9, H). Such naming reveals the often affective and emotional consequences of trying to develop alternative ways of being: "When I was younger I was quite fat [laugh] at primary school, about year 4 or 5 and some people used to call me names and I think children will grow up and other people will start taking the mick out of them and they'll feel shy and they might want to change, they might starve themselves" (Emma, Year 8, H); "Yeah my

teacher told me to stay healthy because if you are overweight people won't be your friend and they'll like be mean to you" (Salina, Year 5, R).

Many were aware that girls and young women's bodies were being read by others not only as an indicator of one's health but also of one's moral worth (Crawford, 1980; Markula, 1997). Fatness was constructed as a visible sign of lack of self-control and a failure to gain rational control over one's body (Evans *et al.*, 2008; Sobal, 1995; Throsby, 2007). Prevailing discourses of health and obesity thus provided powerful ways of framing exercise as a meaningful practice *upon* the body, as reflected in official discourse on obesity. "'Cause if you're too fat you could not be really fit and walk around as much as you normally do and it would be more unhealthy to be more fat than thin I think it would be hard to exercise and I think I wouldn't really like it 'cause I would just like to be normal like everyone else" (Phillipa, Year 6, F).

This way of thinking (as evident in new health imperatives) appeared to grant young people moral license to comment, often negatively, on the body size, shape, and weights of their peers: "And they get pushed around and no-one wants to be friends with them and no-one wants to meet them" (Ingrid, Year 5, F). In such physical cultures the body acts as a form of currency through which to distinguish between their neoliberal can-do girlhood and other forms of femininity. The responsible, thin, controlled neoliberal citizens who are considered to have made the correct choices to care for their bodies are differentiated from those deemed to be "fat" whose subjectivity is instead depicted as lacking in confidence, immobile, lacking in empathy, socially isolated, and thus displaying an inappropriate femininity. This could be most clearly seen in the use of the term "O-Beast" as a derogatory term (and play on words) for someone who was Obese, implying a negative aesthetic: "A lot of people just can't be bothered to do the exercise if they have obesity or whatever" (Kirsty, Year 6, W); "That it [obesity] has risen in the country and that lots more people are obesed" (Sarah, Year 8, G).

However, constituting the "obesed" subjectivity provided no discursive space for the complexities of weight (i.e., that one might be overweight and healthy, or physically active). In the construction of "truth" in this body politic (Fusco, 2006) these discourses (re)produce particular understandings about the healthy girl. Broader macro-structures of neoliberalism are thus enacted through these girls and young women's bodies.

From Postergirls to Looters: Physical Culture and Consumption Practices

Processes of "healthification" not only construct particular kinds of gendered civic citizenship but also "consumerist subjectivities" (Fusco, 2007). In this final section we explore how physical culture and the positioning of girls is integral to free market logics through which they are incited to enact particular neoliberal subjectivity as self-determined, flexible consumers. In this way, the marketing of health and physical activity and associated consumption practices are also intimately connected to the contemporary constitution of the gendered body through sport.

Girls and young women are positioned not only as valuable to the future employment/labor force but also as target of consumption practices and a "commodity" (Harris, 2004). In this sense, body pedagogies are to be understood in terms of the "interests of pre- or proscribed ideals (for example, around employment or health)" (Evans et al., 2008: 80). As Huckaby (2010: 74) argues, these pedagogies translate into "everyday politics and enacted pedagogies made real on our bodies and sustained through practices of our bodies." Harris (2004: 47) argues that particular girls become the "postergirls" of the have-it-all femininity – becoming implicated in particular narratives about what all girls/women might become, despite the social inequalities which mean only few may achieve such status. However, for some of the girls and young women in our research, "the image of successful, individualized girlhood itself is one of the most profitable products being sold to them and others" (Harris 2004: 20): "Like in the papers or in TV if you look at the clothes section, they're always for slim people" (Rhiannon, Year 8, L); "I don't wanna look like her because she doesn't wear suitable clothes and I don't like how she looks. She kind of looks like a boy" (Salina, Year 5, R).

The marketization of sports clothing/products is central to this postergirl imagery as the consumptive practices of young women are intimately bound up in the constitution of neoliberal subjectivity and the body. As Nadia (School, L) suggested, when you are thin "You get to wear nice clothes."

> They wear like really tight clothing to make them look really skinny and they have bum jobs and everything. (Marie, Year 6, F)

> I don't feel that, I just don't like clothes that make me look bigger than I am. I just like clothes that make me look my size, not skinnier, not fatter, just what I am instead of making me look really slim and long or something that makes me look short and fat. (Abi, Year 6, F)

> I think if I had a body like theirs I would have the confidence to wear that kind of outfit. If you don't look very good you tend to wear stuff that covers up everything (Kirstin, Year 8, G)

This was also something that was observed by some of the teachers interviewed in our research study, as reflected in the following quote:

> I don't know. Well I think a lot from television and adverts, I would think. Us, parents. I mean there's a whole world out there of influence. When we were little, my mother told me what I did and I did it. I mean now you've got the television, the internet, they're all big tools, marketing tools. That's why I'm really pleased we have a school uniform and they don't all have to come in in their own clothes because it would be like in America . . . Guns and daggers because I want your Nike shoes. Where do they get their messages from? (Jane, Head of PE, School F)

Far from being a "freedom," the pressures placed on young women to make correct consumption choices are another means through which they learn the practices and embodiment of particular subjectivities. The model citizen (as neoliberal subject) is constituted as someone who not only works hard but is also able to demonstrate the correct consumption practices. This is in line with developments in broader physical culture in which the body as a symbolic form of distinction has become intimately connected with health and well being (see Shilling, 2010; also CHAPTER 6).

Equally, whilst offered up as a paradigm of opportunity within which all young women/girls have the opportunity to reshape themselves, Gill (2007: 149) notes the "stark and continuing inequalities and exclusions that relate to 'race' and ethnicity, class, age, sexuality and disability as well as gender." The opportunities to freely undertake consumption practices was thrown into the public spotlight in the summer of 2011 when England witnessed a hitherto unprecedented level of rioting which also involved the looting of high street stores, in particular sports shops and mobile phone shops. Those without the purchasing power to seize the opportunity to craft a particular subjectivity had gone to excessive measures of looting stores to take sports clothing, trainers, and other products. Connections between the riots, social class, and consumerism occupied much of the media coverage of the riots. As Naomi Klein (2011) reports, "This is the global *saqueo*, a time of great taking. Fuelled by a pathological sense of entitlement, this looting has all been done with the lights on, as if there was nothing at all to hide."

Elsewhere, sociologist Zygmunt Bauman (2011) commented: "These are not hunger or bread riots. These are riots of defective and disqualified consumers." In a social context and time when the "over achievement" of girls is a dominant storyline in the media landscape, the presence of girls on media footage seen engaging in the riots and looting caught the attention of the public. "Two girls who took part in Monday night's riots in Croydon have boasted that they were showing police and 'the rich' that 'we can do what we want'" (BBC, 2011).

At this juncture one can only speculate about the relationship between the neoliberal market targeting girls/young women and the events that took place in England in August 2011. However, the classed discourses running through the media reporting of these events revealed the presence of commodification and consumption as a contemporary gendered body politic (Fusco, 2006) which is incontrovertibly classed, racialized, able-bodied, and gendered. Whilst not embodying the middle-class neoliberal dutiful citizen heralded in the "alpha girl" status and "can-do" femininity, the responses of the girls above allude to the appropriation of a complex and diversified, popularized and classed feminism in which young

women can "do what they want" as some form of post-feminist sensibility (Gill, 2009). Similar responses were reported in other UK media:

> The 17-year-olds were drinking stolen rosé wine at 9.30 a.m. yesterday as they laughed about the previous night's disturbances in south London and made vague complaints about "rich people."
>
> One told the BBC: "Everyone was just on a riot, going mad, chucking things, chucking bottles – it was good, though."
>
> Her friend added: "Breaking into shops – it was madness, it was good fun."
>
> One of the girls bragged about "getting a couple of free things," before insisting: "It's the government's fault. I don't know. Conservatives, whoever it is. It's the rich people who've got businesses and that's why all this happened." (*Metro*, 2011)

In a culture where young women's worth is judged not only by their bodies but by their consumption practice, the opportunities to consume, to make the "right choices," are increasingly rendered more difficult. As Bauman (2011) suggests:

> We are all consumers now, consumers first and foremost, consumers by right and by duty. The day after the 11/9 outrage George W. Bush, when calling Americans to get over the trauma and go back to normal, found no better words than "go back shopping." It is the level of our shopping activity and the ease with which we dispose of one object of consumption in order to replace it with a "new and improved" one which serves us as the prime measure of our social standing and the score in the life-success competition. To all problems we encounter on the road away from trouble and towards satisfaction we seek solutions in shops.

The responses of those girls above speak to broader political and socioeconomic conditions (in which expectations are high but opportunities minimal); as Deb Orr (2011) suggested, "that opportunistic looters exist, in such numbers, is ghastly evidence of a host of societal flaws and ruptures – not least among them educational and parental failures." The classed nature of this symbolic and actual violence, excessive as it is, alludes amongst many other things to the complexities of the distillation of post-feminist logics along class, cultural, and ethnic lines. If nothing else, one might observe that these events alarmingly reveal how "young women in contemporary society may be negotiating discourses of gender, the self and discourses of equality in often multiple and contradictory ways" (Rich, 2005: 496) but not always consciously so.

Conclusion

This chapter has highlighted the pressures placed on girls and young women to display appropriate physically active, fit, and "thin" subjectivities in contemporary societies where consumption practices, body ideals, and obesity discourse converge on and through their bodies. Drawing on UK research, the chapter highlights how, in cultures where the "future girl" is being held up as integral to the future of society, girls as young as 10 are being pressed towards demonstrating the neoliberal subject whose body reflects control and self-determination, and balances precarious and narrow definitions of female physicality. Whilst obesity discourse emphasizes weight-loss practices and thinness, mediated physical culture also emphasizes a toned femininity (Heywood, 2007). In this sense, various economic, political, and social struggles converge on and through young women's physical cultural practices and reiterate the centrality of the body and physical culture in contemporary visions of girlhood. What this chapter demonstrates is the importance of broader physical culture in terms of how we "learn" through body pedagogies about the value, importance, and meaning of particular physically (in)active bodies. Whilst the focus for this particular discussion has been on "gender" and the implications for how these broader physical cultures come to define the sporting female subject, so too are these processes are mediated by class, gender, ability, race, and other categories.

Notes

1 Stanley Cohen (1972) refers to a moral panic as "a condition, episode, person or group of persons which emerge to become defined as a threat to societal values and interests" (p. 9). Cohen makes specific reference to the role of the media in intensifying and shaping these moral panics.

2 GMTV refers to the UK Channel 3 (ITV) breakfast television national broadcasting.

References

Ali, S. (2003) "To be a girl: Culture and class in schools." *Gender and Education*, 15 (3): 269–283.

Andrejevic, M. (2002) "The kinder, gentler gaze of Big Brother." *New Media & Society*, 4 (2): 251–270.

Andrews, D.L. (2008) "Kinesiology's 'Inconvenient Truth': The physical cultural studies imperative." *Quest*, 60 (1): 46–63.

Armstrong, D. (1995) "The rise of surveillance medicine." *Sociology of Health and Illness*, 17 (3): 393–404.

Atencio, M. and Wright, J. (2009) "'Ballet it's too whitey': Discursive hierarchies of high school dance spaces and the constitution of embodied feminine subjectivities." *Gender and Education*, 21 (1): 31–46.

Azzarito, L. (2010) "Future girls, transcendent femininities and new pedagogies: Toward girls' hybrid bodies?" *Sport, Education and Society*, 15 (3): 261–275.

Bauman, Z. (2011) "The London riots: On consumerism coming home to roost." *Social Europe Journal*, August 9, http://www.social-europe.eu/2011/08/the-london-riots-on-consumerism-coming-home-to-roost/, accessed December 12, 2012.

Bernstein B. (2000) *Pedagogy, Symbolic Control and Identity*, Lanham, MD: Rowman & Littlefield.

Biressi, A. and Nunn, H. (2008) "Bad citizens: The class politics of lifestyle television," in Palmer, G. (ed.) *Exposing Lifestyle Television: The Big Reveal*, Aldershot: Ashgate, pp. 15–24.

Bordo, S.R. (1990) "The body and reproduction of femininity: A feminist appropriation of Foucault," in Jagger, A. and Bordo, S. (eds.) *Gender/body/knowledge*, New Brunswick, NJ: Rutgers University Press, pp. 13–33.

BBC (2011) "London rioters: 'Showing the rich we do what we want.'" *BBC News*, August 10, http://www.bbc.co.uk/news/uk-14458424, accessed December 12, 2012.

Budgeon, S. (2001) "Emerging feminist(?) identities: Young women and the practice of micropolitics."

European Journal of Women's Studies, 8 (1): 7–28.

Burrows, L. (2010) "Kiwi kids are weet-bix kids – body matters in childhood." *Sport, Education and Society*, 15 (2): 235–253.

Cohen, D. (2005) "The rise of reality science." *British Medical Journal*, 330 (7501): 1216.

Cohen, S. (1972) *Folk Devils and Moral Panics*, London: MacGibbon & Kee.

Cole, C.L. (1993) "Resisting the canon: Feminist cultural studies, sport, and technologies of the self." *Journal of Sport & Social Issues*, 17 (2): 77–97.

Cole, C.L. (1998) "Addition, exercise, and cyborgs: Technologies of deviant bodies," in Rail, G. (ed.) *Sport in Postmodern Times*, Albany: State University of New York Press, pp. 261–276.

Crawford, R. (1980) Healthism and the medicalisation of everyday life. *International Journal of Health Services*, 10: 365–388.

Daily Mail (2010) "Reform begins at home: Michelle Obama puts daughters on a diet as she launches anti-obesity campaign," *Daily Mail*, http://www.dailymail.co.uk/news/article-1247254/Michelle-Obama-puts-daughters-diet-launching-obesity-campaign-U-S.html, accessed December 12, 2012.

Davies, B. (1989) *Frogs and Snails and Feminist Tails: Preschool Children and Gender*, Sydney: Allen & Unwin.

Davies, B. (2005) "The (im)possibility of intellectual work in neoliberal regimes." *Discourse: Studies in the Cultural Politics of Education*, 26 (1): 1–14.

Davies, B. and Harré, R. (1990) "Positioning: The discursive production of selves." *Journal for the Theory of Social Behaviour*, 20 (1): 44–63.

Department of Health (2010) *Healthy Lives, Healthy People: Our Strategy for Public Health in England*, London: Department of Health.

Department of Health (2011) *UK Physical Activity Guidelines*, http://www.dh.gov.uk/en/Publicationsandstatistics/Publications/PublicationsPolicyAndGuidance/DH_127931, accessed January 24, 2013.

De-Pian, L., Evans, J., and Rich, E. (2008) "Mediating health? A preliminary analysis of how social class and culture refracted through different forms of schooling are reflected in young people's actions toward their bodies and their health." Paper presented at Australian Association for Research in Education Conference, Brisbane, December 3.

Evans, B. (2006) "Gluttony or sloth: Critical geographies of bodies and morality in (anti)obesity policy." *Area*, 38 (3): 259–267.

Evans, J., Rich, E., Davies, B., and Allwood, R. (2008) *Education, Disordered Eating and Obesity Discourse: Fat Fabrications*, New York: Routledge.

Featherstone, M. (2010) "Body, image and affect in consumer culture." *Body and Society*, 16 (1): 193–221.

Fisette, J. (2011) "Exploring how girls navigate their embodied identities in physical education." *Physical Education and Sport Pedagogy*, 16 (2): 179–196.

Foucault, M. (1979) *Discipline and Punish*, London: Peregrine.

Francis, B. and Archer, L. (2005) "Negotiating the dichotomy of boffin and triad: British Chinese pupils' constructions of laddism." *Sociological Review*, 53 (3): 495–520.

Francombe, J. (2010) "'I cheer, you cheer, we cheer': Physical technologies and the normalized body." *Television & New Media*, 11 (5): 350–366.

Fusco, C. (2006) "Inscribing healthification: Governance, risk, surveillance and the subjects and spaces of fitness and health." *Health & Place*, 12 (1): 65–78.

Fusco, C. (2007) "Healthification and the promises of urban space: A textual analysis of play, activity, youth (PLAY-ing) in the city." *International Review for the Sociology of Sport*, 42: 43–63.

Gard, M. and Wright, J. (2005) *The Obesity Epidemic: Science, Morality and Ideology*, London: Routledge.

Garrett, R. (2004) "Negotiating a physical identity: Girls, bodies and physical education." *Sport, Education and Society*, 9 (2): 223–237.

Gill, R. (2007) "Postfeminist media culture: Elements of a sensibility." *European Journal of Cultural Studies*, 10 (2): 147–166.

Gill, R. (2009) "Beyond the 'sexualisation of culture' thesis: An intersectional analysis of 'sixpacks,' 'midriffs,' and 'hot lesbians' in advertising." *Sexualities*, 12 (2): 137–160.

Giroux, H. (2004) "Cultural studies, public pedagogy, and the responsibility of intellectuals." *Communication and Critical/Cultural Studies*, 1 (1): 59–79.

Halse, C. (2009) "Bio-citizenship: Virtue discourses and the birth of the bio-citizen," in Wright, J. and Harwood, V. (eds.) *Biopolitics and the "Obesity Epidemic": Governing Bodies*, New York: Routledge, pp. 45–49.

Halse, C., Honey, A., and Boughtwood, D. (2007) "The paradox of virtue: (Re)thinking deviance, anorexia and schooling." *Gender and Education*, 19 (2): 219–235.

Halse, C., Honey, A., and Boughtwood, D. (2008) *Inside Anorexia: The Experiences of Girls and Their Families*, London: Jessica Kingsley.

Hargreaves, J. and Vertinsky, P. (eds.) (2007) *Physical Culture, Power and the Body*, London: Routledge.

Harris, A. (2004) *Future Girl. Young Women in the Twenty-First Century*, London: Routledge.

Hauge, M.-I. (2009) "Bodily practices and discourses of hetero-femininity: Girls' constitution of subjectivities in their social transition between childhood and adolescence." *Gender and Education*, 21 (3): 293–307.

Henderson, N.-M. (2010) "Obama's new book raising questions about when his kids are off-limits to the public." *Washington Post*, September 15, http://www.washingtonpost.com/wp-dyn/content/article/2010/09/15/AR2010091506587.html, accessed December 12, 2012.

Hesse-Biber, S. (2006) *Am I Thin Enough Yet? The Cult of Thinness and the Commercialization of Identity*, Oxford: Oxford University Press.

Heywood, L. (2007) "Producing girls: Empire, sport, and the neoliberal body," in Hargreaves, J. and Vertinsky, P. (eds.) *Physical Culture, Power, and the Body*, London: Routledge, pp. 101–120.

Huckaby, F.M. (2010) "Public pedagogies: Everyday politics *on* and *of* the body," in Sandlin, J.A., Schultz, B.D., and Burdick, J. (eds.) *Public Pedagogy: Education and Learning Beyond Schooling*, New York: Routledge, pp. 71–81.

Ingham, A.G. (1997) "Toward a department of physical cultural studies and an end to tribal walfare," in Fernandez-Balboa, J. (ed.) *Critical Postmodernism in Human Movement, Physical Education and Sport*, Albany: State University of New York Press, pp. 157–182.

Jette, S. (2006) "Fit for two? A critical discourse analysis of *Oxygen Fitness Magazine*." *Sociology of Sport Journal*, 23: 331–351.

Jones, A. (1997) "Teaching poststructuralist feminist theory in education: Student resistances." *Gender and Education*, 9 (3): 261–269.

King, S.J. (2003) "Doing good by running well," in Bratich, J.Z., Packer, J., and McCarthy, C. (eds.), *Foucault, Cultural Studies and Governmentality*, Albany: State University of New York Press, pp. 295–316.

Klein, N. (2011) "Looting with the lights on." *Guardian Online*, August 17, http://www.guardian.co.uk/commentisfree/2011/aug/17/looing-with-lights-off, accessed December 12, 2012.

Lewis, T. (2007) "'He needs to face his fears with these five queers!': *Queer Eye for the Straight Guy*, makeover TV and the lifestyle expert." *Television and New Media*, 8 (4): 285–311.

Lucey, H., Melody, J., and Walkerdine, V. (2003) "Uneasy hybrids: Psychosocial aspects of becoming educationally successful for working class young women." *Gender and Education*, 15 (3): 285–301.

Lucey, H. and Reay, D. (2002) Carrying the beacon of excellence: Social class differentiation and anxiety at a time of transition. *Journal of Education Policy*, 17 (3): 321–323.

Markula, P. (1997) "Are fit people healthy? Health, exercise, active living and the body in fitness discourse." *Waikato Journal of Education*, 3: 21–39.

Markula, P. (1998) "Women's health, physical fitness and ideal body: A problematic relationship." *Journal of Physical Education New Zealand*, 31 (1): 9–13.

Markula, P. (2001) "Beyond the perfect body: Women's body image distortion in fitness magazine discourse." *Journal of Sport & Social Issues*, 25: 134–155.

Markula, P. (2008) "Affect[ing] bodies: Performative pedagogy of Pilates." *International Review of Qualitative Research*, 1: 381–408.

Markula, P. and Pringle, R. (2006) *Foucault, Sport and Exercise: Power, Knowledge and Transforming the Self*, London: Routledge.

McRobbie, A, (2000) *Feminism and Youth Culture*, New York: Routledge.

Metro (2011) "Croydon riot girls boast that looting was 'good fun,'" *Metro*, August 9, http://www.metro.co.uk/news/871891-croydon-riot-girls-boast-that-looting-was-good-fun, accessed December 12, 2012.

Miah, A. and Rich, E. (2008) *The Medicalization of Cyberspace*, London: Routledge.

Nettleton, S. (1997) "Governing the risky self: How to become healthy, wealthy and wise," in Petersen, A. and Bunton, R. (eds.) *Foucault, Health and Medicine*, London: Routledge, pp. 207–222.

Oliver, K. and Lalik, R. (2000) *Bodily Knowledge: Learning about Equity and Justice with Adolescent Girls*, New York: Peter Lang.

Orr, D. (2011) "UK riots: Society must change fundamentally if we are to move on." *Guardian Online*, August 10, http://www.guardian.co.uk/commentisfree/2011/aug/10/uk-riots-society, accessed December 12, 2012.

Petersen, A. (1996) "Risk and the regulated self: The discourse of health promotion as politics of uncertainty." *Australian and New Zealand Journal of Sociology*, 32: 44–57.

Pronger, B. (1998) "Post-sport: Transgressing boundaries in physical culture," in Rail, G. (ed.) *Sport and Postmodern Times*, Albany: State University of New York Press, pp. 277–300.

Rich, E. (2005) "Young women, life choices and feminist identities and neo-liberalism." *Women's Studies International Forum*, 28 (6): 495–508.

Rich, E. (2011) "'I see her being obesed!': Public pedagogy, reality media and the obesity crisis." *"Health": An Interdisciplinary Journal for the Social Study of Health, Illness and Medicine*, 15 (1): 3–121.

Rich, E. and Evans, J. (2005) "'Fat ethics' – the obesity discourse and body politics." *Social Theory & Health*, 3 (4): 341–358.

Rich, E., Holroyd, R., and Evans, J. (2004) "'Hungry to be noticed': Young women, anorexia and schooling," in Evans, J., Davies, B., and Wright, J. (eds.) *Body Knowledge and Control*, London: Routledge: 173–190.

Riley, S.C.E., Burns, M., Frith, H., and Markula, P. (eds.) (2008) *Critical Bodies: Representations, Practices and*

Identities of Weight and Body Management, Basingstoke: Palgrave Macmillan.

Seid, P.R. (1989) *Never Too Thin. Why Women Are at War with Their Bodies*, London: Prentice Hall.

Shilling, C. (1993) *The Body and Social Theory*, London: Sage.

Shilling, C. (2005) "Body pedagogics: A programme and paradigm for research." Paper presented to the School of Sport and Exercise Sciences, Loughborough University, UK.

Shilling, C. (2007) *Embodying Sociology: Retrospect, Progress and Prospects*, Oxford: Blackwell.

Shilling, C. (2010) "Exploring the society–body–school nexus: Theoretical and methodology issues in the study of body pedagogics." *Sport Education and Society*, 15 (2), special edition on *Body Pedagogies, Health and Education*: 151–167.

Shogan, D. (1999) *The Making of High Performance Athletes: Discipline, Diversity, and Ethics*, Toronto: University of Toronto Press.

Silk, M.L. and Andrews, D.L. (2011) "Toward a physical cultural studies." *Sociology of Sport Journal*, 28 (1): 4–35.

Skeggs, B. (1997) *Formations of Class and Gender*, London: Sage.

Skelton, C. and Francis, B. (2009) *Feminism and the Schooling Scandal*, London: Routledge.

Smith, E. (2012) "Jessica Ennis coach hits out at UK athletics for labeling her 'fat.'" *Guardian*, May 24, http://www.guardian.co.uk/sport/2012/may/24/jessica-ennis-fat-olympics, accessed December 12, 2012.

Smith-Maguire, J. (2002) "Michel Foucault: Sport, power, technologies and governmentality," in Maguire, J. and Young, K. (eds.) *Theory, Sport and Society*, Oxford: Elsevier Science, pp. 293–314.

Sobal, J. (1995) "The medicalization and demedicalization of obesity," in Maurer, D. and Sobal, J. (eds.) *Eating Agendas: Food and Nutrition as Social Problems*, New York: Aldine De Gruyter, pp. 67–90.

Strelan, P., Mehaffey, S.J., and Tiggemann, M. (2003) "Self-objectification and esteem in young women: The mediating role of reasons for exercise." *Sex Roles*, 48: 89–95.

Susinos, T., Calvo, A., and Rojas, S. (2009) "Becoming a woman: The construction of female subjectivities and its relationship with school." *Gender and Education*, 21 (1): 97–110.

Throsby, K. (2007) "Happy re-Birthday: Weight loss surgery and the 'new me.'" *Body & Society*, 14 (1): 117–133.

Vander Schee, C. and Boyles, D. (2010) "'Exergaming,' corporate interests and the crisis discourse of childhood obesity." *Sport Education and Society*, 15 (2), special edition on *Body Pedagogies, Health and Education*: 169–185.

Walby, S. (1997) *Gender Transformations*, London: Routledge.

Walkerdine, V. (2003) "Reclassifying upward mobility: Femininity and the neo-liberal subject." *Gender and Education*, 15 (3): 237–248.

Wood, H. and Skeggs, B. (2004) "Notes on ethical scenarios of self on British 'reality' TV." *Feminist Media Studies*, 4 (2): 205–208.

Wood, H. and Skeggs, B. (2008) "Spectacular morality: Reality television, individualisation and the re-making of the working class," in Hesmondhalgh, D. and Toynbee, J. (eds.) *The Media and Social Theory*, London: Routledge, pp. 177–193.

Woodward, K. (2009) *Embodied Sporting Practices: Regulating and Regulatory Bodies*, Basingstoke: Palgrave Macmillan.

Wright, J. (2009) "Biopower, biopedagogies and the obesity epidemic," in Wright, J. and Harwood, V. (eds.) *Biopolitics and the "Obesity Epidemic": Governing Bodies*, London: Routledge, pp. 1–14.

Wright, J. and Harwood,V. (2009) *Biopolitics and the "Obesity Epidemic": Governing Bodies*, New York: Routledge.

Youdell, D. (2005) "Sex – gender – sexuality: How sex, gender and sexuality constellations are constituted in secondary schools." *Gender and Education*, 17: 249–270.

Youdell, D. (2006) "Subjectivation and performative politics – Butler thinking Althusser and Foucault: Intelligibility, agency and the raced-nationed-religioned subjects of education." *Gender and Education*, 27: 511–528.

Zannettino, L. (2008) "Imagining womanhood: Psychodynamic processes in the 'textual' and discursive formation of girls' subjectivities and desires for the future." *Gender and Education*, 20 (5): 465–749.

Further Reading

Evans, J., Rich, E., Davies, B., and Allwood, R. (2008) *Education, Disordered Eating and Obesity Discourse: Fat Fabrications*, London: Routledge.

Rich, E. (2011) "Exploring the relationship between pedagogy and physical cultural studies: The case of new health imperatives in schools." *Sociology of Sport Journal*, 28: 64–84.

Wright, J. and Harwood, V. (2009) *Biopolitics and the "Obesity Epidemic": Governing Bodies*, London: Routledge.

11

Gay Male Athletes and Shifting Masculine Identities

Eric Anderson

Introduction

This chapter concerns a dramatic shift in masculine sporting culture: a shift away from a disposition of extreme homophobia toward one of inclusivity. In this chapter I discuss not only how this shift has come to be but also the positive impact that it has had on the lives of gay and straight male athletes alike. However, because there are important differences between the way men construct their masculinity, compared to the way women construct their femininity; and because the experiences of gay men in sport are likely different than those of lesbians in women's sport, the arguments I make can only be valid for men's sport.

While I explicate the increasingly positive experiences of young gay males in Western sporting cultures today, it is important to realize that the shift toward a gay-friendly culture is relatively new. Decreasing cultural homophobia is an uneven social process, and the experience of these athletes does not necessarily reflect the experience that every, or even any, particular gay male athlete would have coming out of the closet to his teammates: Anderson (2005a) provides a more accurate assessment of individual circumstances. Still, the results of my decade of using ethno-graphic methods suggest that the relationship between sport, masculinity and homophobia is rapidly changing (Anderson, 2011b). Matters were not always so hopeful.

Researchers who have examined issues related to gay men in sport during the 1980s and 1990s largely agreed that organized sports in Western cultures were a highly homophobic institution. For example, Michael Messner (1992: 34) wrote, "The extent of homophobia in the sports world is staggering. Boys (in sports) learn early that to be gay, to be suspected of being gay, or even to be unable to prove one's heterosexual status is not acceptable." Gert Hekma (1998: 2) wrote, "Gay men who are seen as queer and effeminate are granted no space whatsoever in what is generally considered to be a masculine preserve and a macho enterprise." And Brian Pronger (1990: 26) suggested, "Many of the (gay) men I interviewed said they were uncomfortable with team sports ... orthodox masculinity is usually an important subtext if not *the* leitmotif" in team sports.

However, there exist a number of cultural trends related to sexuality and gender that may influence how university-aged men reconstruct their sexual and gendered identities. The most salient trend concerns the rapid reduction of cultural homophobia. This has increased the social

A Companion to Sport, First Edition. Edited by David L. Andrews and Ben Carrington.
© 2013 Blackwell Publishing Ltd. Published 2013 by Blackwell Publishing Ltd.

legitimacy of alternative categories of sexuality, and expands upon the social and political landscapes for gay males (Anderson, 2009).

Team sport athletes have not been immune from this progressive social change. There is a growing body of literature regarding heterosexual men and their increasingly inclusive attitudes toward homosexuality in sport (cf. Bush, Anderson, and Carr, forthcoming, or Southall *et al.*, 2011). In multiple studies (Anderson, 2002, 2005a, 2008a, 2008b, 2008c, 2009, 2011b) I find heterosexual men displaying positive attitudes toward homosexuality. This is theorized to occur through a combination of media, political, and culturally driven influences; however, it also comes through contact with gay men, who are coming out in increasingly rapid numbers, even in team sports (Anderson, 2002, 2005a, 2011a). And, as athletes continue to come out, they challenge sport's hegemonic perspectives in creating an orthodox form of masculinity.

This chapter begins by explaining the difficulty of counting gay men (or any sexual minority) in society, and thus the impossibility of accounting for what percentage of athletes maintain a sexual orientation of something other than heterosexual. It then moves toward a discussion of the dominant theory used to account for the way in which boys and men have traditionally created inter-masculine hierarchies (reflected in hegemonic masculinity theory), explicating that it was overt homophobia and homohysteria that maintained the stratification of men. However, the chapter then details how and why Western cultures are rapidly losing their homophobia. As this occurs not only are gay male athletes shown to have a better experience in sport, but heterosexual male athletes are given more gendered freedom. I discuss this as "inclusive masculinities" and I use data from three pieces of my research to explicate these findings.

The first research project I draw from concerns the first-ever research published on the experiences of openly gay male athletes throughout American high school and universities (Anderson 2002). Updated research concerning the experience of gay men in sport is now available (Anderson 2011a), together with a special volume of the *Journal of Homosexuality* dedicated to the experiences of gay men in sport and physical cultures (Anderson 2011b). Here, a host of research

highlights that matters continue to improve for gay men, both those who play and those who work within the institution of sport.

The second research project that I draw upon for this article concerns ethnographic work conducted on a British rugby team. This is just one example of many studies conducted on British teams (Anderson, 2009), but this particularly research saw my assistant embed himself (as a player) into a highly competitive rugby team (one of the best in the country) with a homophobic coach. This gave him unprecedented insider access.

Finally, the third piece of research I draw from comes from an ethnography of an American university soccer team (Anderson, 2011c). Here my research assistant and I spent ten days training and playing with the team, as well as conducting in-depth interviews. What is unique about this team, however, is that they represent men not only from a small, Catholic college but also one located in a rural area, in the Midwest – demographics that suggest elevated homophobia. It should be noted, however, that the overall findings I relate in this chapter, the pattern of decreasing homophobia and increasing gendered expression for straight men, is formulated from a decade of research. Particularly since 2008, my research assistants and I have investigated hundreds of gay and straight male athletes.

My research teams exhibit diversity of identities and attributes in conducting this research. I am white, openly gay, and a running coach and one of my colleagues who helps me with this research is a gay male non-athlete in his early twenties, but my assistants (who are the same age as the athletes we study) are straight soccerplayers. It is impossible to know how one's sexual identity impacts one's research findings. Hopefully having various researchers, with differing sexual identities, collecting data in different locations (yet all reporting similar findings) helps add validity to the findings I report here.

The Presence of Gay Men in Sport

Although we understand that the reason there are few openly gay athletes in sport is because of cultural homophobia (and not because gay men lack athletic talent), we still do not know whether gay men are overly, underly, or evenly represented in sport, as compared to the population at large. The only way to know the answer is to discover the percentage of gay men in the population, and then compare this to what the percentage is in sport. This is a tricky proposition because the presence of cultural homophobia nullifies the possibility of knowing what percentage of the general population is gay. And this excludes the complications of also counting bisexuals.

It is impossible to survey people about their same-sex desires if they are compelled to lie about these desires. Accordingly, the only accurate way to answer this question of what percent of the population is gay is to ask it once the last vestiges of homophobia have long been erased from our culture. Until then, we can only theorize, and in this theorizing, we can be relatively certain that whatever rates of sexual minorities sociologists come up with, they will remain vastly underestimated. As long as homophobia exists, heterosexuality will always be overly estimated from empirical data.

Making matters more complex, it is also difficult to understand just what it means to be "homosexual" or "heterosexual." Sexuality proves to be an extremely complicated affair that can be described by at least three separate dimensions: sexual behavior (what one does), sexual orientation (what one desires), and sexual identity (how one views one's sexual self). Sexuality scholars rightfully and easily complicate matters to the point that definition is near impossible. Therefore, the question of whether gay athletes are overrepresented or underrepresented in team sports can only be theoretical. The question is too vague, and definitions of sexuality are too fluid. If we cannot agree on what it is to be gay or straight, we certainly cannot ascertain what percentage of the population is gay or straight.

These complications aside, we can be readily assured that at the lowest level of sport (youth sports), the percentage of whatever it means to be gay is in statistical equality to whatever the percentage of gay males are in the culture at large. This is because sporting participation has been made a cultural (and sometimes institutional) requisite for boyhood in the Western world (Anderson, 2005a). Therefore, the question of importance is: As athletes advance in the sporting world, does the proportion of gay athletes change?

In other words, we know that gays are being assimilated into the culture of athletics at the same age as heterosexuals, but as one matures, how might their sexuality influence whether they drop out of or remain within the institution of sport?

The weight of empirical evidence *suggests* that gay male adult athletes are exceedingly underrepresented in sport. Hekma (1998) found that once closeted gay men come out in team sports (in the Netherlands), they no longer needed the heterosexualizing façade of sport. He also reported that many gay youths believed that excelling in sport and being gay were incompatible (my research shows this no longer to be the case). Pronger (1990) suggested that the mandates of orthodox masculinity found in sport create a sense of "not being" for many gay athletes: that they continually feel like an outsider, even if they are on the inside. Pronger suggested that this alienation engenders indifference and/or aversion to sport for young gays. But clearly at least some gay men exist in sport (Anderson, 2002, 2005a, 2011a).

Although these are good theories, Pronger (1990) and I alternatively suggest it to be possible that some gay men may be drawn to team sport precisely *because* of its homophobic and masculinist culture. Gay athletes who are motivated to conceal their sexual identity may actually be attracted to team sports (or motivated to remain within them). This is because, as team-sport athletes, they are largely protected from gay suspicion. The presence of muscles and violence in sport is normally considered incompatible with homosexuality. The more muscle-bound athletes are, the less likely they are suspected of being gay (due to increased masculine capital). This buys them "insurance" against homosexual suspicion. Since football and basketball players are generally more muscular than cross-country runners, these athletes are less likely to have their heterosexuality questioned than those in "lower" sports or social arenas. Therefore, if a deeply closeted gay man is attracted to muscle and also seeks a veneer from homosexual suspicion, team sports are a particularly attractive social arena.

Still other gay males might erroneously think that participation in a hyper-masculine enterprise will actually change their sexual desires (it does not). Many of the gay men in my (Anderson,

2005a) study suggested that their fathers forced them into sport because they feared that their sons were gay. Others, who played individual as opposed to team sports, found one parent blaming another for not forcing him to play team sports (i.e., more macho sports). Finally, adolescent males who are not consciously aware of their sexuality might find themselves drawn to team sports because of their homoeroticism: men playing sport together is erotic to men with sexual desire in men, and there is nothing wrong with enjoying that eroticism (Anderson, 2005a). It is one of the many benefits of being fortunate enough to be born gay or bisexual.

But team sports provide more than just a feast for the gay gaze, they also exist as an opportune space for athletes (gay or straight) to bond with other boys and men, to engage with them on an emotional and a physical level. Thus, it is for the erotic desire of men with low body fat and visible muscle, alongside the fraternal bonding that those muscles permit, that leads Pronger and myself to suggest that the most deeply closeted gay men are the ones drawn to the competitive team-sport arena. Conversely, lesser-closeted gay men might join individual sports, or sports requiring more aesthetics. As the years pass, this dichotomy fades. Some young gay men joining team sports are already out of the closet today (Anderson, 2011a).

Theoretical Underpinnings into Masculinity and Homophobia

Sociologists recognize that there are various forms of masculinities found among differing cultures, and that there is no singular way of being masculine within any given culture. We recognize that, in response to social forces, the definitions of what it means to be masculine shift within the same culture – and that not all masculinities are treated equally in any culture. In her influential book *Masculinities* (1995), Robert (then) Raewyn (now) Connell gives an excellent discussion of the various and often competing forms of masculinities in Western cultures, especially in regard to understanding the operation of hegemony as it relates to masculinity.

Hegemony, a concept created by Antonio Gramsci (1971), refers to a particular form of dominance in which a ruling class legitimates its position and secures the acceptance – if not outright support – of the classes or archetypes below. While a feature to Gramsci's hegemony theory is that there is often the threat of force structuring a belief, the key element is that force cannot be the causative factor that elicits complicity. This is what separates hegemony from overt rule. In order to compel people to empathize with the ruling class or identity, those who do not fit within the dominant ideal must believe that their subordinated place is both *right* and *natural*. Of relevance to this research, the concept of hegemony has been applied to a more nuanced understanding of how men and their masculinity and sexuality are stratified in society (Connell, 1995). Much of the study of masculinities examines how men construct hierarchies that yield decreasing benefits the further removed one is from the flagship version, hegemonic masculinity.

It is important to clarify that hegemonic masculinity, however, is not an archetype. "It is, rather, the masculinity that occupies the hegemonic position in a given pattern of gender relations, a position always contestable" (Connell, 1995: 76). And while Connell does describe the contemporary form of hegemonic masculinity as including the tenets of homophobia and antifemininity, she does not assign a categorical label to this group. This makes it easy to conflate the process of hegemonic masculinity with an archetype of masculinity, and this explains why there is such usage confusion among scholars. Accordingly, as a theoretical concept hegemonic masculinity is unclear, carries multiple contradictions, and fails to demonstrate the independence of the gender system. Because of this I discuss the behavioral and attitudinal aspects of hegemonic masculinity as "orthodox masculinity" (Anderson, 2005b).

Orthodox masculine behaviors

There are a few central tenets that all scholars (of all epistemological orientations) use in their work to describe orthodox/hegemonic masculinities. Some of these behavior components include emotional stoicism, a willingness to fight, the ability to drink copious amounts of alcohol, a disinterest in style, and (of course) participation in invasion team sports. However, most scholars highlight that the first rule of "acting like a man" is that of antifemininity (Kimmel, 1994). Here, the primary element toward being a man has been not to *be*, *act*, or *behave* in ways attributed to women. Robert Brannon (1976: 12) summarizes this nicely, saying that the first rule toward being a man is "no sissy stuff." However, the reason for this underlying discontent of femininity is because effeminacy among men is correlated with homosexuality (Anderson, 2008b).

This rigid contention carries with it a measurable cost for heterosexual men. Under this system homophobia becomes the primary policing weapon of boys' and men's gendered behaviors. If a man steps outside the range of acceptable behaviors, or expresses an attitude out of step with other men's thinking, he is pushed back by homophobic discourse: he is made out to be homosexual (homosexualized) by his peers, regardless of whether he is or is not bi/gay.

This policing begins as early as primary school. For example, psychologist William Pollack (1999) maintains that fear of homosexual stigmatization prevents young boys from engaging with anything that is designated feminine. Sociologist Michael Messner (1992) suggests that grown men, too, avoid compassion, weakness, fear, or the appearance of vulnerability because these are traits also associated with women. Both Pollack and Messner agree that if a boy or man violates these rules, he risks being labeled a sissy or a fag, and when this happens, he must either deflect attention by calling someone else a fag, or stand and fight for his "heteromasculinity" (Kimmel, 1994). This obsession with policing men's gendered and sexual behaviors is a social condition that I describe as *homohysteria*.

Homohysteria

Homophobia, directed at men, has been central to the production of orthodox masculinity, and this helps maintain orthodox masculinity as a hegemonic version of masculinity. Homophobia serves as an ordering principle of valued or subjugated individuals in Western cultures (Anderson, 2008a, 2008b), making hypermasculinity compulsory for boys. When one combines a culture of men's homophobia (a dislike of gay or bisexual men), femphobia (a dislike of men, gay or straight, acting in ways that are associated with

femininity), and compulsory heterosexuality (the belief and promotion that we should all be heterosexual and that being gay is second-best), one has the make-up of what I call homohysteria (Anderson, 2009). In a culture of homohysteria, boys and men are so afraid of being thought gay that they severely police their behaviors. Boys and men watch what they say, and monitor what they do, or else they might be thought a "fag."

But what happens to the traditional, conservative, orthodox version of masculinity when our culture of homohysteria decreases (Anderson, 2005b)? What implications might this have for men who were once forced into a narrow ascription of masculinity? In my multiple research ethnographies of heterosexual team sport athletes, in both the United Kingdom and the United States, I argue that the existence of inclusive masculinities (Anderson, 2009) means that there is awareness that heterosexual men can act in ways once associated with homosexuality, with less threat to their public identity as heterosexual. This, I show, has positive effects for straight men as well (Anderson, 2005b, 2008b, 2008c, 2009).

The reduction in cultural homohysteria in the Western world is a result of a myriad of legal rulings. The steady advancement of gay marriage is just one example. In Western cultures, the plight of sexual minorities has sparked public debates regarding the status of gays and lesbians in nearly every sector of Western culture, including cherished American institutions like the boy scouts (who have come under increasing fire for their discriminatory practices), and most synagogues and churches (which frequently fracture over issues pertaining to homosexuality).

These legal gains are, however, merely a reflection of shifting attitudes. Decreasing cultural homophobia is fueled by increased numbers of people coming out (almost all high schools have a gay–straight alliance these days); the visibility of sexual minorities on the internet (Facebook asks for one's sexual interest, and MySpace asks for one's sexual orientation); as well as the increased visibility of sexual minorities on television (where having a gay character is almost a compulsory part of today's Hollywood formula). The ubiquity of pornography on the internet also means that many of today's young males grow up accessing volumes of free porn, where they see a panoply of sexualized behaviors, including homosexuality (Anderson, 2012).

It seems that in the new millennium, Anglo-Americans are increasingly accepting of, perhaps even desensitized to, homosexuality. This is particularly true of younger Americans. For example, whereas most major polls show that around 50% of the United States population supports gay marriage, this number is considerably higher among 18–29 year olds (Gallup, 2012). This decrease in cultural homophobia is also true of the youth who play sport (Bush et al., forthcoming).

Coming Out in Sport

The threat that gay men pose to hegemonic masculinity comes from the fact that gay men comply with the principal gendered script of orthodox masculinity (through their sporting prowess), while also violating the principal rule of masculinity (through their same-sex desires). For this reason, in my *Gender and Society* article (2002) I suggested that gay male athletes may threaten sport's ability to reproduce orthodox masculinity. I argued that gay men expose the falsity of the notion that femininity is weak. It is because of this threat that homophobia has traditionally presented itself as resistance toward the intrusion of a gay subculture within sports.

Research on male athletes who are publicly out to their ostensibly heterosexual teammates was nonexistent until my article on the experiences of openly gay male athletes (Anderson 2002). My later book *In the Game: Gay Athletes and the Cult of Masculinity* (Anderson 2005a) expanded this sample to 68. Prior to this, our best understanding of the relationship between the gay male athlete and sport came through interviews with closeted gay male athletes (Hekma, 1998; Pronger, 1990), from athletes on all-gay teams (Price and Parker 2003), or from attitudinal research of heterosexual male athletes toward the possibility of openly gay athletes being on their teams (Wolf-Wendel, Toma, and Morphew, 2001). Indeed, studying openly gay athletes was not possible in what might be called the first wave of discrimination against gay athletes. This is because the social sanction for coming out of the closet was too high. The transformative potential of gay athletes

in sport was neutralized through overt homophobia and covert mechanisms, like the normalization of homophobic language and the silencing of gay discourse, identity, and behaviors.

While matters are quickly improving, openly gay males are still vastly underrepresented at all levels of sport (Anderson, 2002, 2005a, 2011a, 2011b). For example, there have only been two openly gay male athletes at my university (a bisexual rugby player and a lacrosse player) in the last four years. Matters are even worse at the professional level. When examining the ranks of professional team sports (where tens of thousands of men have matriculated through the various sporting systems), there has *never* been an openly gay professional athlete to emerge from the closet while playing in the United States (in the top four sports), and only four have come out in the three most popular British team sports. Furthermore, there have only been a handful of players who have emerged from the closet after retiring from professional sports. This omission raises the question: is this the product of there being so few gay men in professional team sports or a result of the near-seamless heterosexual hegemony that prevents them from coming out once in sport?

The segmented identities of openly gay male athletes

Given the homophobia theorized to still exist within sporting culture, one would hardly expect gay athletes to report positive experiences after coming out to their teams. But my research into openly gay high school and university athletes shows just the opposite. For example, Ryan typifies some of the positive experiences of my interviewed athletes. Ryan, a 19-year-old first-year student at a private university in Southern California came out to his crew team in a rather public manner. "The whole school knows about me, so from the first day of practice the team also knew about me," he said (Anderson, 2002: 867). Ryan, like the other athletes in my study, said that he had no difficulty with teammates. There was no homophobic taunting.

When I probed for situations that might make homophobia more salient, Ryan said, "I thought the real test would be when we were out on the road, when we had to share a bed. That was when it would come down to it." When the bedding configuration placed three athletes in a room with two beds, the rowers did not want Ryan to have one of the beds alone. They feared that not sharing a bed with him would send a message that they were homophobic. "We talked about it for a while, and we just pushed the two beds together and made one big one. That way nobody felt bad" (Anderson, 2002: 867).

Perhaps not all of the athletes I interviewed felt as supported as Ryan, but most were unexpectedly pleased with their coming-out experience, even those who played American football. I asked all of the informants, "If you could do it all over again, what, if anything, would you do differently?" to which almost all responded that they would have come out earlier. One athlete said, "It was so much easier than I thought. Now I look back and wonder why the hell I didn't do it sooner" (Anderson, 2002: 867). Another said, "I forgot what I was supposed to be so worried about after I came out" (Anderson, 2002: 867).

But some of these informants over-generalized how well things were for them. For many, their stories highlight the persistence of heterosexism. For example, Gabriel initially spoke of his coming out in glowing terms. He and two of his fellow distance runners came out all on the same day, and Gabriel praised his coach for creating a supportive environment for them. However, because Gabriel attended a private Christian school, the team decided to keep their identities concealed from the rest of the school. This was justified because the school had kicked one of its students out the previous year, simply for saying that he was gay. Highlighting how homophobia of the institution still controlled his life, Gabriel talked about his state finals 1600-meter relay race, and how he and his teammates enacted their agency to contest their subordination:

My friend (also openly gay) and I were approached by our other two (heterosexual) teammates, right before the final race. They reached into their bag and pulled out two pairs of gay pride socks and said that they wanted us to wear them. We were really touched. And then they pulled out two more pairs and said that they were going to wear them in support of us. (Anderson, 2002: 867)

Gabriel's experience was perceived as being positive to him. Together, he and his teammates symbolically stood against the school's homophobic policies.

The glory of this story is unquestionable. However, as enjoyable as those tingles were when I first heard them, there was a problem that they concealed: the athletes had to keep their identities secret in the first place. Gabriel's story, in fact, typifies how gay athletes normally relay their experiences to me. Gay athletes generally first begin by speaking of their experience as a general positive, praising their teammates, and talking about how accepted they felt by them. However, when I inquire about their richer experiences, a different story often (though not always) emerges. While these are not the stories of outright violence that many would predict, they remain stories of (often) extreme heterosexism, silencing, and sometimes the use of homophobic discourse. Nonetheless, athletes remain in high spirits about their coming out; they are unbothered or even unaware as to the high degree of heterosexism and homophobic discourse around them.

Whereas sociologists usually discuss people who compare themselves to those who have it better, these athletes seem to compare themselves to those who had it worse – something I call *reverse-relative deprivation*. They do not actually have examples of those who fared worse after coming out; instead they compare their experience to their worst-imagined fears.

Fear, of course, is the hallmark of the closet. Gay athletes and gay men in general fear all types of things: losing friends, respect, and even the emotional (and sometimes financial) support of their families should they come out. Yet, to this day, I have never known an athlete who regretted coming out – and this is so after interviewing another 26 openly gay athletes for a follow-up to this research (Anderson, 2011a). This suggests a wider pattern of fear-based control that keeps men closeted.

Thus, one way that orthodox masculinity can adapt to include gay men, without compromising much of the institutional values, is to permit gay men to play, but deny their existence and mute their voices. As an openly gay tennis player, Tim exemplifies how one is able to challenge orthodox masculinity while simultaneously reproducing it. I asked him if he was treated any different after coming out. "No," he replied. "They didn't really treat me as gay, if that's what you mean. In fact, they didn't even mention it really. They just treated me like one of the guys" (Anderson, 2002: 870). I then asked Tim if his teammates continued to include him in locker-room talk about women. "Yeah, they ask me like who I think is hot and stuff." When I questioned if his teammates ever asked what guys he thought attractive, he replied, "Hell no. They'd never do that. They don't want to hear that kind of stuff" (Anderson, 2002: 870). It is for this reason that I suggest that a culture of inclusive masculinities does not necessarily imply one of decreased heterosexism. Heterosexism is an independent variable to homohysteria.

I suggest that Tim lives with a *segmented identity*: overtly his teammates know that he is gay, but they continue to treat him as if he were not. This means that he is caught between two identities, gay and straight. Perhaps his teammates think they are doing what is best for Tim; and perhaps Tim thinks it is what is best too. Without interviewing his teammates I cannot be sure what the motivations are. But the situation is one of *don't ask, don't tell*. Silencing gay men's identities and politically avoiding discussions of their teammates' sexuality is, in some ways, a compromise between tenets of orthodox masculinity. The silencing of gay identities and the promotion of heterosexuality serves to venerate heterosexuality and marginalize homosexuality. Tim is allowed to *be* gay but he is not permitted to *act* gay. Ken, an NCAA champion track runner, illustrated this policy when he said, "Even to this day, people know, but people just won't say it . . . It's like they just can't talk about it" (Anderson, 2002: 870).

Gay athletes often fail to recognize that their identities are partially denied within their sporting spaces. Highlighting the hegemony of orthodox masculinity, they frequently take part in their own oppression by self-silencing and by partaking in heterosexual dialogue. Of course, the athletes do not see it this way. This is the operation of hegemony in heterosexism. Victimized by hegemony, many (though not all) athletes avoid discourse about homosexuality. Frank's stated opinion was that "sport is not the appropriate place for such discussions" (Anderson, 2002: 871) and another openly gay athlete said simply, "The gay thing was never talked about" (p. 871).

Shifting narratives of gay male athletes

Because I have been interviewing openly gay athletes (formally and informally) since 1998, I have seen a shift in the way athletes tell their stories. Collectively, what can be said from their experiences is that even though sport is still a macho enterprise, openly gay athletes *increasingly* exist within sporting spaces (even among football and basketball teams). Many of these athletes conform to all other mandates of orthodox masculinity, but many do not. Increasingly, they suggest that their heterosexual teammates also do not (Anderson, 2011a). More recent stories of athletes to emerge from the closet, I argue, threaten the ability of sports to seamlessly reproduce orthodox masculinity. In doing so, they may help open the doors to increased acceptance of once-subjugated masculinities and perhaps even the acceptance of female athleticism. While the culture of sport may not yet permit the creation of a formidable gay subculture, gay athletes alongside straight athletes are beginning to contest sport as a site of orthodox masculine reproduction (Anderson, 2005b). This highlights that hegemony in the athletic arena is not seamless – gay men are increasingly accepted within the belly of masculine sports.

Supporting this statement, when I first published on gay men (Anderson, 2002), I found that virtually every openly gay athlete I could locate was not only good but he was truly outstanding. Of my sample of just 36 openly gay men, I had four national champions (representing various sports). But by the time I published my updated research on gay athletes in 2005, I was able to locate dozens of lesser-quality athletes. Although these are small numbers, they are also significant. In my later research (Anderson 2011a), I found gay men no better than their heterosexual teammates.

The coming out of lesser athletes cannot be attributed to others blazing the path for them; these represent individuals who made individual decisions to come out to their teams without having other openly gay athletes to lay the groundwork. If 32 of 36 were extraordinary prior to 2000, but only 8 out of 22 were extraordinary after 2003, it highlights that individuals felt more confident in coming out due to a wider spread of phenomena. Similarly, whereas I had a difficult time locating gay men to interview in the early parts of 2000, today they are much more accessible.

If I am right, and decreased homohysteria is the hallmark of inclusive masculinities, we should see a similar tolerance and acceptance of diversity occurring throughout multiple sectors of sport and society. Supporting this, a *Sports Illustrated* magazine poll on February 27, 2006 of 1,401 professional American team sport athletes also found that the majority (and 80 percent of those in the National Hockey League) would welcome a gay teammate today. This combined with the finding of nearly 100 percent support for gay male teammates among 252 incoming undergraduate athletes in a major British university (Bush *et al.*, forthcoming) suggests that (certainly in England) matters have improved rapidly. Explicating how reduced homophobia not only improves the lives of gay athletes but of straight ones as well, I now turn to examine men who play rugby in an inclusive environment.

Heterosexual Team Sport Athletes

Within British and many other Western cultures, university rugby players are known for promoting and valorizing masculinist acts of hooliganism, alcohol abuse, and hazing, as well as perpetuating masculinist bravado and risk-taking (cf. Donnelly and Young, 1988). Grundlingh (1994: 197) describes rugby as the "ultimate manmaker," inculcating characteristics of courage, self-control, and stamina, alongside a deeply ingrained culture of homophobia.

As with other team-sport athletes, rugby players are also thought to project their masculine attributes at the expense of marginalized and subordinated men (Price and Parker, 2003). Coaches, administrators, and fans are thought to lend institutional and cultural support to the promotion of rugby men to their exalted peer status so that the playing pitch serves as a figurative "proving ground" (Muir and Seitz, 2004) or "training field" (Schacht, 1996: 562) for a socially conservative hegemonic embodiment of masculine behaviors and attitudes. Yet matters are changing.

I was prompted to conduct research on a rugby team because I was told they did not meet the definition of orthodox masculinity I expected of them. Dubious of this claim, I took the opportunity to investigate the team with one of my graduate students the following year. Results indicate a coordination of data between our notes, interviews, and experiences with members of the team. Collectively, they all show that these rugby players are actually very accepting of homosexuality. Interestingly, interviews with students at the university who were not rugby players indicate that they too thought rugby players would exhibit orthodox masculinity.

I asked Graham why he thought non-rugby players perceived his teammates as homophobes. He laughed, "We probably used to be" (referring to the traditional culture of rugby), "but sexuality shouldn't really matter to anyone," he said. "There are still people stuck in the past, I guess. But that isn't the way I see it. I have absolutely no problems with gay men" (Anderson and McGuire, 2010: 255). When asked if he would mind having an openly gay player on the team he said, "Maybe my coach would, but I wouldn't." His answer reflects the myriad of gay affirmative responses to questions designed to probe for homophobia among the players interviewed on this rugby team. "I wouldn't give a shit," one responded. "Not in the slightest." Another said, "Seriously what kind of people do you think we are?" (Anderson and McGuire, 2010: 255).

My observations of members of this team concur with the interviews. Often, on Wednesday nights, I used to go clubbing at the university's dance club. Here, I socialized with a number of the men from this team. I was frequently bought drinks, players came to talk with me, and occasionally we danced together. These are not the actions of homophobic men. An equally strong measure of their inclusivity came at a home game. Here, all of the men on the sidelines sat on the bench in front of the student-filled arena waiting to be called into the game. During the middle of the game, I walked onto the field into the "player only" arena, so that I might say hello to a few of the athletes. Here, in full view of thousands of men, and without the use of alcohol, I was greeted with hugs. When I then said goodbye to one player before the match was over, he smiled and squeezed my backside.

What is interesting about these men, however, is how they came to their inclusive perspective.

There were no openly gay men on their team at the time I conducted this research (although the following year an openly bisexual player joined the team and was later elected captain), and they were not molded by organizational or institutional culture, either (as I will next show). Instead, these men suggest that they grew up in a peer group that found homophobia unacceptable. This is interesting considering that their rugby coaches still value orthodox notions of masculinity. Accordingly, the heuristic utility of inclusive and orthodox masculinity is made salient when comparing these men's attitudes and behaviors to that of their coaches. Here, a distinctive variance exists in the two groups' masculinity making process. My student's observations show that the team's coaches use homophobic and misogynistic discourse with regular frequency.

"Don't be a fucking poof," a coach screamed after a player failed to properly complete a play. And when another player told his coach that he did not think he should practice because of an ankle injury, the coach said, "For God's sake, what are you, gay?" Graham said, "He calls players 'poofs' when they are injured and he frequently says, 'You're fucking gay,' just to put a player down" (Anderson and McGuire, 2010: 256). Interviews with other athletes confirm that they perceive their coaches' homophobic and misogynistic comments as intended to hurt, degrade, and objectify, all in a failed attempt to motivate the players to pursue and value physical risk and pain. "I can see why he does it," Graham said, referring to the homophobic and misogynistic banter. "That's his generation. But it doesn't work for us. It doesn't make us jump up and perform better. It doesn't make me think, 'Oh, no. I'm not a real man, I need to play harder.'" Graham added, "It just makes me think he's a fucking idiot" (Anderson and McGuire, 2010: 256).

Collectively, the athletes despise their coaches' approach, and they are fairly adamant that they are opposed to their coaches' behaviors and beliefs. Still, it is interesting to note that they do not actively contest their coaches. "No. You don't say anything," Graham said. "That would be a sure way to sit on the bench" (Anderson and McGuire, 2010: 256). When asked why that should matter, he said, "You have to remember that most of us are trying to make the next level.

Or earn more money. You don't prove yourself on the bench" (Anderson and McGuire, 2010: 256).

However, athletes do support and encourage each other to "shake off" the abuse. Ollie said, "Yeah, he says those things all the time. And no, I don't like it or appreciate it, but it doesn't, you know, get to me." He continued, "First, I can't be bothered to care too much about what a jerk like him thinks. So you just ignore him, really." Mark added, "But the other guys are there for you when the coach screams this shit at you. They give you a hug and say, 'don't listen to him, he's a jerk'" (Anderson and McGuire, 2010: 256).

In addition to using homophobic and misogynistic language against the players, the coaches occasionally tried to relate to their players through a failed attempt at bantering with them. Graham explained, "Occasionally he uses it [homophobic discourse] in what he thinks is good humor, to try to be one of the boys. To banter with us about being gay the way we do. But it is just bad most of the time" (Anderson and McGuire, 2010: 256). Alex said, "No. They don't banter like we do. They don't relate to us like they might think they do . . . He [the head coach] talks about gay people in ugly and disparaging ways" (Anderson and McGuire, 2010: 256). Mark agreed: "Yeah, like I'll say to a mate, you're gay, and that will bring us closer, but he does it differently. He said, 'That guy's gay,' and it's a totally different thing" (Anderson and McGuire, 2010: 256). Once, when discussing the fact that Mark had a gay roommate, the coach went off about how "fucking gross" it must be to see the roommate bring a guy home. And once, when some of the players were discussing me (I'm well known on campus), the head coach (who has never met me) said, "That guy is just fucking gay. Gay. Gay. Gay."

This ethnography not only shows that the form of masculinity these men desire and construct is fundamentally inclusive, it also shows that these players are constructing this inclusive perspective despite the masculinity they have modeled to them by their coaches. I suggest that the coaches' reliance upon orthodox tactics of homophobic intimidation and masculine subordination reflects their socialization into an orthodox sporting ethos, one that holds increasingly less weight with these younger men. Athletes and coaches on this team therefore share a discursive field in which variations in language and belief systems are (mostly covertly) contested. Instead of direct confrontation, however, these athletes utilized their agency through protested silence and changing the meaning associated with discourse. They do not speak the language of their coaches, maintain the same attitudes, or even perform on the pitch as their coaches desire. Instead, they bond in *opposition* to the gendered understandings that their coaches maintain, offering each other emotional comfort and shoring up their version of inclusive masculinity against their coaches' gendered perspectives.

Accepting Gay Athletes in the Heart of America

The exuberant embrace of homosexuality I found in England is matched by multiple ethnographic studies I have recently conducted on soccer players in the United States. For example, while researching a soccer team at a very small, conservative, Catholic college in the rural Midwest, one of their players, Jake, told me and my co-researcher, Adrian Adams, that he wanted to come out (Adams and Anderson, 2012).

On the second day of our research (before Jake came out) Jeff, one of his team-mates, asked Jake about his recent trip to Amsterdam. "Did you pay for pussy?" he asked, referencing the legal trade of heterosexual prostitution in Amsterdam. Jake simply answered, "No." He later told us that this is how he normally managed his sexuality, to which Jake offers short, direct answers that do not give away his sexuality. This is a common strategy among closeted gay athletes (Anderson, 2005a), and it permitted Jake to be heterosexualized by the heteronormative standards of his team-mates. By all accounts, Jake's strategy worked: Other than the three friends he has already told, the remainder of the players did not know he was gay. His best friend, Tyler, said, "They have no clue that he's gay. None at all" (Adams and Anderson, 2012).

Before outing Jake, we first asked six team-mates (in formal interviews) whether or not they thought they had any closeted gay team-mates on their squad. While two of the six athletes referred to the myth that one in ten men is gay, and therefore deduced that it was theoretically possible that a player or two were gay, none suspected any

athletes in particular. However, none of these six athletes maintained that they would be concerned if one of their team-mates were to come out, either. And while three of the men suggested that a gay athlete might not be accepted by *all* members of the team, none could name any athletes that they thought might have difficulty with it. These athletes also did not feel that an openly gay player would negatively impact the team's cohesion. Although a few said it might make showering situations awkward, they maintained that it would generally make no difference to them. Tom said, "It might be strange in the locker room, but I think you'd get used to that pretty quick" (Adams and Anderson, 2012).

Once Jake determined that he was ready for us to begin outing him to his team-mates, we strategically selected informal interviews in hopes of recording a genuine emotional reaction. While talking about homosexuality over a meal with Ben, we asked, "How do you feel about the fact that Jake is gay?" Ben responded, "Jake is gay? You serious?" After confirming, he said, "That's cool. I just had no idea, that's all." And when sitting in Tom's room after dinner, we said, "Yeah, we are glad Jake decided to come out." Tom responded, "What? Jake is gay?" We confirmed, "Yeah, of course. You didn't know?" Tom answered, "No. That's cool though" (Adams and Anderson, 2012).

These responses reflect the lack of socio-negative views that we found among the next nine players we told using this particular outing method. In the moment of realization, none of the athletes spoke negatively about Jake's homosexuality. Although a few expressed that they wished Jake had told them earlier, none felt that his outing was inappropriate. Interestingly, while none thought that this would improve team morale, none felt that it would lower it either.

We next strategized about how to gauge players' reactions that avoided some of the research effect (athletes might have upgraded their response to our questions because they desired to please the researchers). Thus we recruited one of Jake's team-mates, Tyler, to collect data on his team-mates' reactions for us. Tyler told players, both in groups and individually, that Jake was gay, recording notes of the conversation immediately after. Results of these outings suggest that there was no discernible researcher effect, as there was no discernible reaction difference between the two methods. For example, Tyler told us that he talked with Jeff about the Amsterdam conversation, saying, "I thought it was funny that you asked a gay guy if he paid for 'pussy.'" "Wait, you're saying Jake is gay?" Jeff asked. "Yeah, of course," Tyler answered. "Oh. I didn't know that. Well, shit, I feel bad now." Jeff clarified, "It's no big deal. I just didn't know" (Adams and Anderson, 2012). And while other players learned of Jake's sexuality in other ways, the finding of importance is that of the 21 heterosexual men on this team, none provided a homophobic reaction. There were no negative emotional reactions toward his sexuality; there were no intellectual statements critical of his homosexuality.

Although I have found highly inclusive attitudes among team-sport athletes in other research locations (cf. Anderson, 2009), this is a particularly important finding, because these men represent a demographic of Midwestern rural youth who have been socialized into a Catholic ethos. We theorize that part of the positive reactions toward Jake's homosexuality is attributable to players' previous contact with gay men. Interviews with informants show that all but three of the 22 players knew a gay male other than Jake or myself. Most maintained informal relationships with gay men. John, for example, said, "One of my girlfriend's friends is gay . . . He's a cool guy," and Justin said, "One guy came out at high school, and I didn't want to talk to him at first. But I grew up, you know. I figured that he's gonna do what he's going to do and you can't change it, so I was cool with him" (Adams and Anderson, 2012). Thus, the common narrative among players was that most had a friend or family member who is gay, and they used this association to express that they learned a degree of social inclusion through this contact.

Thus, perhaps the most *salient* research finding from this particular study is that men traditionally described as belonging to two categories of conservative sexuality beliefs (Catholics and team-sport athletes) appear to have come to a place of relative social inclusivity for gay men long before this research took place. This has mostly been accomplished through contact with extended gay friends or family members.

The most *significant* finding, however, is that the ability to openly discuss the particulars of

homosexual sex seems to further upgrade emotional feelings about homosexuality. For example, Kyle said, "I wasn't homophobic before I knew Jake was gay. But knowing him has made me pretty positive about gay stuff . . . Today, we're like brothers, I could talk to him about anything." When Kyle is asked how, specifically, knowing Jake has facilitated this, he answered, "We've spent so many nights just lying on the couches talking about sex . . . I've grown to understand things from his [gay] perspective. . . . Hell, I can even tell you what kind of guys he's attracted to." He continued, "We will be walking down the street and I'll just know Jake is checking out a guy, and I'll just say, 'Yep, I saw him, too.'"

When Tyler was asked about how his friendship with Jake has shaped his understandings of homosexuality, he said, "Yeah, Jake is great. I mean, you can talk to him about anything, and I learned a lot about homosexuality from him. I think his coming out has really bonded us. We're great friends." When Tyler was asked about his comfort level with homosexuality before meeting Jake, he said, "The thought of two guys getting it on just sort of grossed me out. But now I'm over that" (Adams and Anderson, 2012). Mike added, "We've both been here for four years, and I've always considered him a good friend. Things are the same as they were before I found out he was gay, but now he can be more honest. I think that's real cool." When I asked if talking about homosexuality has made him feel more endeared to Jake, he said, "Absolutely, it's like he's told us this, and he didn't have to. I just love him even more now" (Adams and Anderson, 2012).

Conclusion

Largely because of a decline in homophobic religiosity, increased gay and lesbian presence on the internet, and (particularly) the visibility that the internet has provided sexual minorities, large-scale quantitative studies like the General Social Survey show that since 1993 attitudes toward homosexuality have grown increasingly progressive in Western cultures (Anderson, 2012; Loftus, 2001). While sport (and by extension athletes), once used to represent extremely elevated rates of homophobia, it is no longer sociologically sound to say that sport *is* homophobic, or that contact-sport athletes are, either. There has been a rapid reduction in cultural homophobia within the institution.

I have spent over a decade studying the relationship between men, sport, and homosexuality, conducting dozens of studies in multiple states and two countries concerning the issue. Collectively, my research shows, without exception, that matters continue to improve for gay men in Western cultures. This is particularly true of young men, whose attitudes toward homosexuality are markedly better than older men (Anderson, 2012; McCormack, 2012).

The decrease in cultural homophobia has also lead to an equally impressive reduction in homohysteria. Thus, sports are not only more accepting of gay men but they are also more inclusive of heterosexual men acting in ways that were once coded as gay. As cultural homohysteria continues to decrease it permits heterosexual men

to be more emotional with each other (even developing bromances), to be more physically tactile with each other (McCormack and Anderson, 2010), and even to kiss one another. Highlighting this, research of university men in the United Kingdom shows that 90 percent of heterosexual male students have kissed one (or more) of their male friends on the lips (Anderson, Adams, and Rivers, forthcoming). These kisses, stripped of their sexual significance, exist as a testament to the type of emotional and physical intimacy that can occur when heterosexual men cease to care if they are thought gay or not. Today's heterosexual male athletes are more permitted to emote, dress with style, and maintain strong emotional friendships with their gay team-mates (Anderson, 2009). This is the advantage of a generation who have dared to challenge orthodox notions of masculinity. We increasingly live in a progressive culture, and the benefits are astounding.

References

Adams, A. and Anderson, E. (2012) "Homosexuality and sport: Exploring the influence of coming out to the teammates of a small, Midwestern Catholic college soccer team." *Sport, Education and Society*, 17 (3): 347–363.

Anderson, E. (2002) "Gays in sport: Contesting hegemonic masculinity in a homophobic environment." *Gender and Society*, 16 (6): 860–877.

Anderson, E. (2005a) *In the Game: Gay Athletes and the Cult of Masculinity*, Albany: State University of New York Press.

Anderson, E. (2005b) "Orthodox and inclusive masculinity: Competing masculinities among heterosexual men in a feminized terrain." *Sociological Perspectives*, 48 (3): 337–355.

Anderson, E. (2008a) "Inclusive masculinity in a fraternal setting." *Men and Masculinities*, 10 (5): 604–620.

Anderson, E. (2008b) "'I used to think women were weak': Orthodox masculinity, gender-segregation and sport." *Sociological Forum*, 23 (2): 257–280.

Anderson, E. (2008c) "'Being masculine is not about who you sleep with . . .': Heterosexual athletes contesting masculinity and the one-time rule of homosexuality." *Sex Roles: A Journal of Research*, 58 (1–2): 104–115.

Anderson, E. (2009) *Inclusive Masculinity: The Changing Nature of Masculinities*, New York: Routledge.

Anderson, E. (2011a) "Updating the outcome: Gay athletes, straight teams, and coming out at the end of the decade. *Gender and Society*, 25 (2): 250–268.

Anderson, E. (2011b) "Masculinities and sexualities in sport and physical cultures: Three decades of evolving research." Special edition, *Journal of Homosexuality*, 58 (5): 1–14.

Anderson, E. (2011c) "Inclusive masculinities of university soccer players in the American Midwest." *Gender and Education*, 23 (6): 729–744.

Anderson, E. (2012) *The Monogamy Gap: Men, Love and the Reality of Cheating*. Oxford: Oxford University Press.

Anderson, E. and McGuire, R. (2010) "Inclusive masculinity and the gendered politics of men's rugby." *Journal of Gender Studies*, 19 (3): 249–261.

Anderson, E., Adams, A., and Rivers, I. (forthcoming) "You wouldn't believe what straight men are doing with each other: Kissing, cuddling and loving." *Archives of Sexual Behavior*.

Brannon, R. (1976) "The male sex role and what it's done for us lately," in Brannon, R. and David, D. (eds.) *The Forty-Nine Percent Majority*, Reading, MA: Addison-Wesley.

Bush, A., Anderson, E., and Carr, S. (forthcoming) "The declining existence of men's homophobia in British sport." *Journal for the Study of Sports and Athletes in Education.*

Connell, R. (1995) *Masculinities,* Berkeley: University of California Press.

Donnelly, P. and Young, K. (1988) "The construction and confirmation of identity in sport subcultures." *Sociology of Sport Journal,* 5: 223–240.

Gallup (2012) "Half of Americans support legal gay marriage." *Gallup.com,* http://www.gallup.com/poll/154529/Half-Americans-Support-Legal-Gay-Marriage.aspx, accessed January 17, 2013.

Gramsci, A. (1971) *Selections from the Prison Notebooks,* London: New Left Books.

Grundlingh, A. (1994) "Playing for power? Rugby, Afrikaner nationalism and masculinity in South Africa, c.1900–70." *International Journal of the History of Sport,* 11: 408–430.

Hekma, G. (1998) "As long as they don't make an issue of it . . .": Gay men and lesbians in organized sports in the Netherlands." *Journal of Homosexuality,* 35 (1): 1–23.

Kimmel, M. (1994) "Masculinity as homophobia: Fear, shame and silence in the construction of gender identity," in Brod, H. and Kaufman, M. (eds.) *Theorizing Masculinities,* Thousand Oaks, CA: Sage.

Loftus, J. (2001) "America's liberalization in attitudes toward homosexuality, 1973 to 1998." *American Sociological Review,* 66 (5): 762–782.

McCormack, M. (2012) *The Declining Significance of Homophobia: How Teenage Boys are Redefining Masculinity and Heterosexuality,* Oxford: Oxford University Press.

McCormack, M. and Anderson, E. (2010) "'It's just not acceptable any more': The erosion of homophobia and the softening of masculinity at an English sixth form." *Sociology,* 44 (5): 843–859.

Messner, M. (1992) *Power at Play: Sports and the Problem of Masculinity,* Boston, MA: Beacon Press.

Muir, K. and Seitz, T. (2004) "Machismo, misogyny, and homophobia in a male athletic subculture: A participant observation study of deviant rituals in collegiate rugby." *Deviant Behaviors,* 25: 303–327.

Pollack, W. (1999) *Real Boys: Rescuing OUR SONS from the Myth of Boyhood,* New York: Henry Holt and Company.

Price, M. and Parker, A. (2003) "Sport, sexuality and the gender order: Amateur rugby union, gay men, and social exclusion." *Sociology of Sport Journal,* 20 (2): 108–126.

Pronger, B. (1990) *The Arena of Masculinity: Sports, Homosexuality, and the Meaning of Sex,* New York: St Martin's Press.

Schacht, S. (1996) "Misogyny on and off the 'pitch': The gendered world of male rugby players." *Gender & Society,* 10: 550–565.

Southall, R., Anderson, E., Southall, C., *et al.* (2011) "An investigation of ethnicity as a variable related to US male college athletes' sexual-orientation behaviors and attitudes." *Ethnic and Racial Studies,* 34 (2): 293–313.

Wolf-Wendel, L., Toma, J.D., and Morphew, C. (2001) "How much difference is too much difference? Perceptions of gay men and lesbians in intercollegiate athletics." *Journal of College Student Development,* 42 (5): 465–479.

Further Reading

Anderson, E. (2005) *In the Game: Gay Athletes and the Cult of Masculinity,* Albany: State University of New York Press.

Anderson, E. (2009) *Inclusive Masculinity: The Changing Nature of Masculinities,* New York: Routledge.

Anderson, E. (2011) "Updating the outcome: Gay athletes, straight teams, and coming out at the end of the decade." *Gender and Society,* 25 (2): 250–268.

McCormack, M. (2012) *The Declining Significance of Homophobia: How Teenage Boys are Redefining Masculinity and Heterosexuality,* Oxford: Oxford University Press.

12

Sport, the Body, and the Technologies of Disability

P. David Howe

Introduction

Over the last 50 years there has been an increasing interest in provision for sports programs designed for populations with disabilities. Adapted physical activity (APA), as the academic and practical field is widely known, includes not only the high-performance end of the sporting spectrum, most notably the Paralympic Games, but also grassroots events in schools and clubs where participation in physical activity is the objective. In writing a chapter concerning technologies of disability such as this one it is perhaps best to focus on Paralympic high-performance sport as this is more high profile than the participation end of the APA spectrum. However, readers should remember that to a greater or lesser extent the issues highlighted within this chapter can have an impact right across the APA spectrum.

It is in Paralympic sport that we most often see aerodynamic and feather-light racing wheelchairs as well as biomechanically and ergonomically responsive prostheses which have helped create a legion of cyborg bodies that is manifest in the image of the sporting *supercrip* (Berger, 2004, 2008; Silva and Howe, 2012). These technological developments have made it difficult for political advocates for the rights of people with disabilities

to expunge the dichotomous relationship represented in the image of heroic versus tragic impaired figure. In other words, referring to high-performance athletes with disabilities as high achievers in spite of their impairment further marginalizes the ordinary disabled population. Hence, these mobility enhancements, such as wheelchairs and prosthetic limbs, have also created a divide between different impairment groups because there are whole classes of athletes that cannot benefit from the use of such hi-tech mobility devices.

This chapter will begin by focusing upon some of the salient points highlighted in social scientific literature that is at the nexus between sport, the body, and disability. Following this there will be a discussion of how the field of APA with its key management tool, classification, has become a disability industry that has until recently marginalized sport people with disabilities from important decision-making roles both at the participation and elite ends of the sporting spectrum. The chapter will then explore technology and how the process of its continual advancement and development of wheelchairs and prosthetic limbs, used in track and field athletics, have led to the Paralympic Games becoming increasingly commercial and relatively high

A Companion to Sport, First Edition. Edited by David L. Andrews and Ben Carrington.
© 2013 Blackwell Publishing Ltd. Published 2013 by Blackwell Publishing Ltd.

profile. As a result of the influence of technology certain impaired bodies of athletes may be seen as a product of cyborgification that ultimately leads to the successful competitors being seen as supercrips. By highlighting the ubiquitous case of bilateral below-the-knee amputee athlete Oscar Pistorius, who through his sporting endeavors in mainstream and Paralympic sport has become the international symbol of disability sport, this chapter will then develop these issues in relation to how the disabled body is viewed more generally in Western society. In doing so the chapter will highlight the development of a technocentric ideology within the Paralympic sport that makes the classification of impaired bodies a politically contentious issue. Ultimately this chapter will ask whether the advances in technology are actually empowering disabled athletes, and the disabled community more generally.

Marginal Bodies

Work in the field of disability studies has suggested that individuals with impairment are pushed to the margins of society (Oliver, 1996; Thomas, 1999). The radicalization of the disability movement (see Oliver, 1990) has not until recently been very influential in the social exploration of disability sport. It has been widely accepted within disability studies circles that a person-first approach should be adopted when addressing athletes with a disability, and in this chapter I have stuck to this convention except when referring to sport as an institution. Here I use the term "sport for the disabled" instead of disability sport because through my research it is clear that sporting provision for the disabled is part of what might be labeled a "disability industry" (see Albrecht, 1992; Campbell and Oliver, 1996). The disability industry is characterized by increased provision for the disabled community that is staffed, organized, and managed by the "able" majority. However, being politically explicit about the agenda of sport for the disabled is a stance that is contrary to the agenda of the International Paralympic Committee (IPC) to make high-performance disability sport more visible.

Since the late 1980s there has been a considered effort on the part of the IPC to force the issue of sport for the disabled into mainstream consciousness (Steadward, 1996). The problem is that it is a particular type of impaired body that is celebrated over others. The hierarchy inside and outside Paralympic sport places those bodies that use mobility technologies to facilitate the participation above those who do not (Sherrill and Williams, 1996; Howe, 2008). In other words some disabled bodies are even marginalized within the confines of sport for the disabled and as such there is a need to re-evaluate what is an acceptable sporting body. In an environment where the body is essential, such as sport, imperfection becomes evident. Karen DePauw (1997) examines how sport marginalizes the impaired and argues that we need to re-examine the relationship between sport and the body as it relates to disability. "Ability is at the centre of sport and physical activity. Ability, as currently socially constructed, means 'able' and implies a finely tuned 'able' body. . . . To be able to 'see' individuals with disabilities as athletes (regardless of the impairment) requires us to redefine athleticism and our view of the body, especially the sporting body (1997: 423).

Hahn (1984) suggests that, because sport for the disabled is based on physical tasks, those in this community who are not as physically able as others become further marginalized. The problem is that sporting performance including the Paralympics glorifies physical ability. As a result more severely impaired competitors are being marginalized within the Paralympic program because their bodies do not fit the image that is associated with the ideal able body. These elite participants are being given sporting opportunities in events like boccia, a game of skill similar in many respects to lawn bowling played by severely impaired athletes with cerebral palsy who use wheelchairs. The game of boccia removes the athletes from the environs of the athletics stadium and swimming pool that are the focus of most media attention during the games. This makes the more severely impaired participants liminal to the Paralympic Games. The involvement in competitive sport of impaired performers is in effect accepting the social definitions of the importance of physical prowess – in essence disabling them (Hahn, 1984).

The bodies of impaired athletes have continually been judged in relation to an able-bodied[1] "norm" and the standards of play and performance are compared with those of main-stream competitions. This can have an adverse effect on participation rates within sport for the impaired because "it is through the study of the body in the context of, and in relation to, sport that we can understand sport as one of the sites for the reproduction of social inequality in its promotion of the traditional view of athletic performance, masculinity, and physicality, including gendered images of the ideal physique and body beautiful" (DePauw, 1997: 420). Sport is an embodied practice and as such many people who possess less than normal bodies may shy away from the masculine physicality associated with sport. Classification as a tool for managing bodies with different levels of ability facilitates organized and high-performance sport such as the Paralympic Games. Yet in many respects it is not only the complex classification system that separates APA activities from the mainstream but also the adoption of performance-specific technologies that are used by these groups to distinguish disability sport from that of the able-bodied sports world.

Managing Classified Bodies

Classification is simply a structure for competition similar to the systems used in the sports of judo and boxing where competitors perform in distinctive weight categories (Jones and Howe, 2005; Howe and Jones, 2006). Within sport for the disabled, competitors are classified by their body's degree of function within their chosen sport. Classification takes the form of a series of functional tests that determine the appropriate category in which to place the athlete in order to provide equitable sporting contests. This process is conducted by a group of qualified classifiers who have between them an expertise in physical impairments and the sporting practice in which they are classifying athletes. It is therefore important that the classification that is the result of the process of examination of the impaired bodies[2] of athletes is robust and achieves equity across the Paralympic sporting practice and enables athletes to compete on a "level playing field" (Sherrill, 1999).

The IPC currently organizes and administers both the Paralympic Games and the quadrennial World Championships for individual Paralympic

sports such as athletics, using athletes who have been through a process of classification. Using the resources of the International Organizations of Sport for the Disabled (IOSDs) (including athletes, volunteer administrators, and classification systems) the IPC made the Paralympic Games into the most recognizable and influential vehicle for the promotion of sport for the disabled. The IOSDs are: Cerebral Palsy International Sports and Recreation Association (CPISRA), International Blind Sports Association (IBSA), International Sports Federation for Persons with Intellectual Disability (INAS-FID), and the International Wheelchair and Amputee Sports Association (IWAS). The latter, launched in 2004 at the Athens Paralympic Games, is the result of a merger of two federations, the International Stoke Mandeville Wheelchair Sports Federation (ISMWSF) and the International Sport Organization for the Disabled (ISOD), that have been part of the Paralympic movement since its inception after World War II.

The classification system within Paralympic sport has continued to be very complex simply because of the nature of various impairments that the IOSDs service. This complexity and the number of classes that were produced made it initially difficult for the IPC to attract the desired media attention simply because there were so many events that it was hard for them to know where to focus. For example there are two 100-meter races at the Olympics, one for men and one for women. At the Paralympics Games in London in 2012 on the other hand there were 15 for men and 14 for women. Since the establishment of the IPC in 1989, there has been constant pressure to remove the IOSDs from decisions regarding classification systems in order to streamline Paralympic programs. However, many of the first officials of the IPC had previously held posts within these founding federations. Consequently, there was initially *carte blanche* acceptance of the IOSDs' classification systems in the early days of the Paralympic movement. According to Bob Steadward, the IPC's first president (1996: 36), "the potential benefit of decreasing classes by using a functional integrated classification system is that it may simplify the integration into the rest of the sports world." Such a functional integrated classification system was developed in some sports such as swimming and downhill skiing. In this system athletes are classified according to what they can and cannot achieve physically within the sport rather than by the severity of their disability, as is the case with the disability-specific classification system. The use of the functional integrated classification system reduces the number of classes for a group of athletes by focusing upon functional ability rather than disability and ultimately leads to an increase in the number of viable events at major championships (Vanlandewijck and Chappel, 1996).

The IPC has implemented rules that state that there must be six athletes from four nations in order for an event to be considered eligible to be run in the Games. Because of the complexity of the classification system some events in sports such as athletics do not attract enough athletes to run since this sport requires ten athletes to be on the worldwide ranking list in order to be eligible for the final Paralympic program. As a result many events are canceled for the more severely impaired athletes who are generally lower in numbers and therefore have less opportunity to compete at the Paralympic Games (Howe and Jones, 2006). In effect this move was to force the sport of athletics into adopting the integrated functional classification system used in swimming. However there is still resistance to this system within athletics since it is believed that this system is akin to performance-banding where athletes are grouped together based on results they have achieved rather than by the results they could achieve, since this system is based on a performance curve (Sherrill, 1999; Steadward, 1996; Vanlandewijck and Chappel, 1996).

Processes of classification for the disability-specific system used by the IOSDs makes a distinction between the physical potential of athletes and attempts to achieve an equitable environment whereby after competition the successful athletes in each class will have an equal chance of accumulating physical capital (Jones and Howe, 2005). In reality however a number of factors impact upon the accumulation of capital (both physical and cultural) in various classifications, the most salient of which for the purpose of this chapter is whether or not the athlete uses mobility technologies instrumentally while they perform. The second factor is the number of athletes within a particular event. Another important factor in terms of whether winners ultimately gain capital from their involvement in sport is the nature and degree of their impairment. The more minimally impaired a wheelchair athlete is for example the more likely that they will become the embodiment of what it is to be a Paralympic athlete. Certainly there is evidence to suggest elite sport for the disabled illuminates a hierarchy of "acceptable" impairment within the community of athletes as well as mainstream society (Sherrill and Williams, 1996; Schell and Rodriguez, 2001).

Classification of course can be seen as a fundamental component of Paralympic culture (Howe, 2008) but it is the insistence that the system is somehow socially neutral that is problematic (Dupré, 2006). The original classification system was developed by the ISMWSF, an organization that has subsequently become known as the International Wheelchair and Amputee Sports Association (IWAS). This system classified athletes with spinal-cord injuries according to where the lesion was in their spine because back function is of great importance in sport. It was believed that athletes with a greater level of function in their spine should be in a different class from those athletes who have less. Athletes who were leg amputees could easily be fitted into this system in the most able class that had full use of the spine. As more and more athletes with different impairments wished to get involved in sport for the disabled, ISMWSF established a broad class known as *les autres*, a French phrase used within disability sport circles meaning "the others." Originally the term referred to athletes with a disability who did not directly fit into the classification system established by ISMWSF. Today *les autres* is used to highlight any athlete who is not specifically referred to in the classification systems of the IOSDs and who is able to be slotted into an existing classification system. I use the term here specifically to refer to athletes with a disability who do not use either a wheelchair or prosthesis while competing in athletics. Some athletes who use wheelchairs and were *les autres*, including people with spina bifida and polio, were able to be slotted into the ISMWSF system, but it was and never has been an exact science. However, many *les autres* were ineligible because they did not need to use a wheelchair, which eventually led to the development of the remaining IOSDs and ultimately the development of the

IPC. As a result the classification system that led to the development of sport for the disabled was not political or culturally neutral.

The original classification system began with athletes who used wheelchairs, and this legacy has continued to the present day where athletes who use performance technologies such as racing wheelchairs and space-age prosthetic limbs are more celebrated within the Paralympic movement than *les autres*. One simple explanation for this may be the fact that these athletes more than any others expose the "ability" in disability sport. Elite wheelchair racers over distances longer than 800 meters are considerably faster than able-bodied ambulant runners and those athletes who wear hi-tech prostheses to perform have a greater "wow" factor associated with their performances that an ambulant athlete with cerebral palsy certainly will not. It is important to remember that it is not possible to create a politically neutral classification system in spite of inclinations to the contrary.

> It is often supposed that one of the goods delivered by successful science is the right way of classifying the things in the world. Surely there is something right about this: any body of scientific knowledge will include ways of classifying, and will not serve its intended aims unless the classifications it embodies reflect real differences and similarities in the world. (Dupré, 2006: 30)

Following Dupré, a philosopher of science, we can see that a classification system can be developed to make sense of the world, in this case that of Paralympic sporting practice, but importantly he adds a caveat to the statement above suggesting "there is a highly questionable implication of there being some unique best classification . . . Classifications are good and bad for particular purposes, and different purposes will motivate different classifications" (2006: 30). In other words the systems of classification developed and adopted within the cultural context of Paralympic sport are the product of the history of this practice. Since the history of the Paralympic movement places athletes in wheelchairs[3] at its center in part because athletes with spinal-cord injuries and amputations were the first to compete in disability sport (Howe, 2008), it is likely that the classification system currently in place favors

these athletes who are reliant on constantly improving mobility technologies to enhance their performances. It is to the issue of technology that this chapter now turns.

Technology

A discussion of the technological improvements in wheelchairs and prosthetic limbs will be used to shed light on how these developments have been and continue to be used not only to improve performances of elite disabled athletes, but to continually focus the Paralympic spotlight on athletes who are members of IWAS. The importance placed on the development of improved technologies to enhance mobility of both amputee and wheelchair athletes has influenced the cultural politics of the Paralympics movement. It is important however to remember that these technologies have to be purchased and therefore the Paralympic movement represents a developing market for the sale of technologically advanced mobility aids. As such many of the most up-to-date mobility technologies highlighted in this chapter are inaccessible to athletes from much of the "developing" world. In this sense Paralympic athletics may be seen as technologically advanced on the one hand, but isolationist and exclusionary on the other. There are many eligible athletes who are unable to gain access to these technologies for financial reasons. In other words the importance of technology in the context of sport for the disabled can best be expressed in the phrase "technocentric ideology" (Charles, 1998: 379).

The move to hi-tech mobility devices specifically designed for sport is a response to the desires of the athletes to perform with greater proficiency. Today many of the top athletes work with leading wheelchair and prosthesis suppliers to ensure their future success is based on the technologies they use as much as it is on the training regimes they follow. In other words technology is literally pushing the Paralympic movement. As Charles suggests:

> Technology and kinesiology are symbiotically linked. They have a mutually beneficial relationship. As technology advances, so does the quality of scientific research and information accessible

in the field. As kinesiology progresses and gains academic acceptance and credibility, technology assumes a more central role in our field. The more scientific the subdiscipline, the more we can see technology at play. (1998: 379)

Following this statement it is clear that the field of high-performance sport (of which Paralympic sport is a subset) has benefited from an increase in technologies that have been developed to harness the power of the human body (Davis and Cooper, 1999). This is most obvious in the Paralympic movement in developments in technologies associated with mobility, namely the wheelchair and prosthetic legs. Able-bodied high-performance athletes rely on technology in their day-to-day training (Hoberman, 1992; Shogan, 1999) yet when these athletes perform in sports like athletics the technology that has got them to the sporting arena may be completely absent from view. Able-bodied athletes do take technology with them to the start of an Olympic final, as their clothing and footwear are products of advanced technology. However, specialist clothing and shoes appear less like advanced technology in comparison to racing wheelchairs and space-age prosthetic limbs as they are not explicitly aids for mobility. "When persons with disabilities use technologies to adjust the participation in 'normal' physical activity, the use of these technologies constructs this person as unnatural in contrast to a natural, nondisabled participant, even though both nondisabled participants and those with disabilities utilize technologies to participate" (Shogan, 1998: 272).

Technology such as racing wheelchairs and flex-feet (artificial legs biomechanically designed for running) have enhanced the performances of athletes whose impairments benefit from their use and are central to the identity of the Paralympic movement. Bodies that are able to successfully adapt to technology that wherever possible normalizes their movements within society generally and on the athletics track specifically are seen as successful. According to Seymour (1998: 119), "a winning wheelchair athlete is seen as the epitome of rehabilitative success. The vision of the strong male bodies competing for honours on the sports field is an image that has currency in the able-bodied world. Bravery in overcoming the catastrophe of a damaged body is a quality

everyone can admire." This image extends to amputee athletes who have also suffered traumatic injuries and who use prosthetic limbs that can be used to enhance performance. The use of mobility technologies provides an opportunity for the user of re-embodiment (Seymour, 1998). That is, users of both wheelchairs and prosthetic limbs who have acquired their impairment, or are born with an inability to walk unaided, are able to establish a distinctive identity with their new bodies. Moves to transform the technology used for movement in the sport of track-and-field athletics, the racing [wheel]chair, static platforms like those used in throwing events, and the prosthetic limbs can be seen as an attempt to use technologies to enhance the impaired body's performance and reinforce this newly acquired identity not as something to hide, but rather as something of which to be proud. It is after all the bodies that are the hallmark of IWAS and central to the public understanding of the Paralympic movement.

Wheelchairs in track and field athletics

In the mid-1980s racing wheelchairs were four-wheeled and cumbersome by the standards of today's "space age" technology, but they were a great improvement on the technologies of the rehabilitative sport era of the Paralympic movement (Howe, 2008). Specially designed racing wheelchairs may be seen as the first major step toward a high-performance Paralympic Games. Indeed performances at the Paralympic Games have been improving with the turning of every Paralympiad, as a close examination of the athletics results from the IPC website will attest. The desire of athletes to move better and faster and also to assist in the production of technology by offering expert advice has allowed them to achieve these aims. However, developing improved technology is only half the battle. First of all, technologies develop at different rates. Some nations might make advances in performance simply because of their access to superior technology. Medal tables at the Paralympic Games have been traditionally dominated by Western nations in part because they are at the forefront of the technological revolution. Like the Cold War arms race the Paralympic movement quite literally, in the race to produce the most efficient and advanced mobility aids, has a "leg race" on its hands.

Today's high-performance racing wheelchair has three wheels, is aerodynamically built of lightweight carbon fiber so that developing more speed takes considerably less effort than it did on the heavier models of two decades ago. The frame is "T" shape which provides stability, through the long front, and a degree of rigidity, both of which are required when the chairs travel at high speeds (Yilla, 2000). For events over 800 meters both men and women T54 are faster than their able counterparts. This is in part due to the fact that drafting is allowed in the IPC athletics rules. As a result elite races on the track are similar (at least in terms of tactics) to road cycling where drafting is an advantageous way to save energy. Racing machines with very thin highly pressurized tires and a carbon fiber frame that year on year weigh less and less also benefit from a steering mechanism called a compensator. This is a technology that has been developed to allow wheelchair racers to "forget" about turning their chairs through a corner. The compensator can be set to direct the chair around the bend once it has been activated by the athlete. Compensators are fixed to the axial front wheel so that the athlete hits it upon entering and exiting a turn. This is all they have to concern themselves with (that is apart from the art of racing) while on the bend. This technological advance has allowed racers to improve their performances markedly. Not only are their chairs lighter and more aerodynamic than ever, but they are also easier to handle.

Within track-and-field athletics throwing events (discus, javelin, shot put, and club)[4] wheelchairs have, since the early 1990s, been replaced by throwing frames which do not have wheels. These frames are more robust than a wheelchair and as a result are easier to tie down to a solid position. The frame is tied to a series of points on the ground either in a shot put or discus circle or behind the line on the javelin "run-up." Each frame is specifically designed for the athlete and therefore enables them to get the most out of their throwing technique. Because of the complex nature of the technique associated with throwing implements such as the shot, discus, and javelin the rules regarding seated throws have come under close scrutiny in recent years (Frossard, O'Riordan, and Goodman, 2006). Some classes of

athletes are not allowed to let their gluteus leave the seat of the throwing frame. Breaking of this rule has been increasingly been monitored by officials at top-level events including the Paralympic Games and IPC World Championships. Those throwers who are able to use their legs as well as their upper body ultimately face the prospect of being reclassified into a more able class since the use of one's legs can be an obvious advantage in a sport where the longest distance thrown in six attempts establishes the winner.

There has also been concern about the use of materials in the frames that allow for a "spring like response" to the throwing action. Athletes hold onto a pole that is part of their frame, recoil the body, and then release the implement. Excess energy generated by this action cannot force the body outside the throwing area. In other words if the force from the pole is so great it allows the body to break the plane of the throwing arena the resulting effort will be considered a foul. What is important with regards to discussions about technology is that there is a strong correlation between "the interaction between the design of the athletes' throwing frame and their throwing technique" (Frossard et al., 2006: 1). There is a direct link therefore, between the impaired body and technology to the extent that the technology becomes an extension of the body.

For the top racers and throwers, their wheelchairs and throwing frames are now an extension of their bodies. As a result, the most successful wheelchair athletes can be seen as cyborgs, that is "a coupling between organism and machine" (Haraway, 1991: 150; see also CHAPTER 21). These athletes are all individuals who are accustomed to using a wheelchair for mobility, to the degree that moving in a wheelchair becomes habitual, and allows them to develop a hybrid body (Haraway, 1991: 178). While this is the case with wheelchairs it is perhaps more obvious with users of prosthetic limbs.

From wooden leg to carbon-fiber blade

Perhaps the most popular imagery of the past associated with prosthetic limbs is that associated with the haggard old "sea dog" who hobbles around on a wooden peg-leg. These wooden prostheses have a long history and are more than adequate mobility aids (Webling and Fahrer,

1986; Chaloner, Flora, and Ham, 2001). The term *prosthesis* is Greek for an addition and is designed to remove physical stigma. "Prosthetic medicine is dedicated to physical normalisation and is devoted to the artificial alteration of both function and appearance, but it enters the realm of biopolitics because it uses the "normal" body as its tribunal and blueprint for action, and treats the impaired body as a spoilt entity that must be hidden and corrected" (Hughes, 2000: 561). There is therefore a desire to "create" the normal and at the same time allow individuals to be more mobile and therefore independent. In the context of sports participation as well as day-to-day mobility one of the problems associated with traditional technology is the development of pressure ulcers and painful stumps that develop where the prosthesis joins the body (DesGrosseilliers *et al.*, 1978). Such dermatologic ailments are at their most painful during the process of rehabilitation where part of gaining an ability to use a prosthetic limb is that the skin at the point of contact needs to "toughened up" (Rossi 1974). This is particularly acute for leg amputees as the act of bearing weight on a prosthesis can create a good deal of pressure on the "stub" that is the result of the amputation.[5] Regardless of technological advances the pull of gravity means that this pressure will always have to be dealt with.

Since 1988 there has been a marked improvement in the technology associated with leg prosthetics. The materials from which prostheses are made has changed markedly from wood to fiberglass to all manners of carbon fiber and lightweight metals used in advanced scientific design. These mobility aids have been a product of state-of-the-art "space age" technologies and as a result the athletes who are in the vanguard of this new technology are producing performances that would have been considered impossible 20 years ago. Technology has advanced with three aims in mind: to produce better performances; to increase the comfort for an individual, athlete or otherwise; and to enable an improvement in efficiency of movement. Advancement is most evident on the track, but also in field events where athletes with amputations have the option of competing as standing athletes or as athletes who use throwing frames. Traditionally a large percentage of track-and-field athletes with full or partial leg amputations have for reasons of comfort competed from a wheelchair. The treatment of the nexus between the prosthesis and the body has developed at pace with the actual replacement limb. Today the top of the range "flex foot" legs are built around the individual's stump and are secured in place by a vacuum seal device which often includes gel padding which greatly reduces the risk of injury from swollen stumps (Howe, 2006, 2008).

The use of flex-foot technology – that is, the carbon-fiber blades that are used instead of the old-fashioned prosthesis where flexion of the ankle was either mechanical or non-existent – is universal at the highest level of Paralympic sport. As a result there is little advantage to having this technology once you are at the Paralympic Games, but it is required to get there. Countries who are at the developmental stages of sport for the disabled programs may find it unrealistic to train runners and throwers in leg amputee classes as the cost of up-to-date technology can be prohibitive (Walker, 2012). This is a problem with the "leg race" for technology. Such technology is available only to those who have the economic capital as a state-of-the-art leg can be extremely expensive. "A pair of prosthetic racing legs of the sort used by Paralympic poster-boy Oscar Pistorius come in at around £15,000" (Walker, 2012). While the technology is getting more affordable there will likely always be nations and athletes left behind in the "leg race." Therefore eligibility can be limited by economic factors as well as physical ones. However, performance standards have improved dramatically across the board within the classification of leg amputees, in a large part due to the increased accessibility, in the West at least, to state-of-the-art technology, since more athletes with leg amputation opted to stand rather than sit as athletes as more affordable hi-tech prostheses become available.

Supercrips, Cyborgs, and *Les Autres*

The bodies that have been absent from this chapter thus far are those that do benefit from advances in sport science support, such as biomechanical and physiological analysis, but do not require a mobility aid such as the use of a wheelchair or prosthesis. Visually impaired, ambulant cerebral palsy, and those with intellectual impairments are able to compete in sport without the use of special technologies of mobility. The relative normality in which they compete compared to the able-bodied can be seen as detrimental to how these groups may be treated both inside and outside the Paralympic movement. Athletes with visual impairment are relatively easily understood by the public. A high percentage of the world's population use either spectacles or contact lenses which are designed to help us better appreciate the world around us. As our eyesight deteriorates through the passage of time and old age we can understand poor sight. As a result athletes with visual impairment are not treated as marginal in Western society to the same extent as those who have cerebral palsy or an intellectual impairment (Sherrill and Williams, 1996).

For those whose impairment is more difficult to understand, such as the uncontrollable spasticity of an individual with cerebral palsy or for those where the physical manifestation of their condition is only evident in social environments, such as an athlete with an intellectual impairment, technological intervention will not manage their body in a manner that is acceptable to the normality assumed of sporting practices. As such it is often rather difficult for the general public to see ability in some of the performances of individuals with impairments. In referring to athletes with cerebral palsy a former president of CPISRA, Colin Rains stated, "It's tough to say but I believe people think that athletes with cerebral palsy are not totally media friendly, visually. They can be slightly uncoordinated both in their running and their visual expressions. It is possible people find this off-putting" (Mott, 2000). The result of this can be stigmatization of a young person with an impairment that cannot benefit from mobility technologies and therefore is unable to actively engage with explicit cyborgification. Butryn (2002, 2003) has highlighted that high-performance (able-bodied) track-and-field athletics is surrounded by technologies that enable athletes to become cyborgs. Training for track-and-field athletics does have a technological element that scholars have argued dehumanizes it (Hoberman, 1992), but when I refer to cyborg athletes here I am explicitly referring to those who adopt mechanical devices which allow movement that otherwise would not be possible for them.

Following Shogan (1999) I would argue that the mobility technology used in sport for the disabled is unnatural in the context of high-performance sport, but in light of the "superhuman" results achieved through the use of either state-of-the-art wheelchairs or prosthetic limbs it has become an accepted currency over the last decade. Mobility technology allows for exceptional sporting performances in the sport of athletics that to some extent are celebrated by the able-bodied public, but such performances are unlikely to be achieved by athletes who compete without these mobility aids. The use of what Butryn (2003) coined as "implement technology" has made the Paralympic Games into a significant sporting spectacle. In other words in the media attention surrounding certain role models that use the technology of wheelchairs or prosthetic limbs have become synonymous with Paralympic sport.

The use of these technologies has led to a litany of supercrip stories. According to Berger:

> "Supercrips" are those individuals whose inspirational stories of courage and dedication, and hard work prove that it can be done, that one can defy the odds and accomplish the impossible. The concern is that these stories of success will foster unrealistic expectations about what people with disabilities can achieve, what they *should* be able to achieve if only they tried hard enough. Society does not need to change. It is the myth of the self-made man. (2004: 798)

By and large these narratives follow closely athletes who benefit from technological aids as it is "easier" to see ability in a fast sprinter on *blades* like Oscar Pistorius or a wheelchair racer who can "run" a mile faster than the current able-bodied world record. However, many Paralympians who are highly trained and motivated athletes but do not require these technologies, therefore can never live up to these ideals which appear imperative in the commercialized world of the twenty-first-century Paralympic Games.

More recent work by Berger highlights the role-model capacity of the supercrip that clearly indicates that celebrated athletes are more than a media construction and can act as "real" mentors (Berger, 2004). While this is a useful point, Berger's research (2004, 2008) is conducted within the context of wheelchair basketball, a sport where high-performance technology is also self-evident. His conclusions would likely have been different if he had used the ambulant athletes described above who receive very little media coverage and whose role-model capacity is hence diminished. The same tension Berger (2008) mentions between athletes and non-athletes in his study could be made between athletes who are accepted (technology users) as supercrips and those who are not. The conundrum is clear – elite sport is concerned with enhanced bodily performance, yet how do you show this with a continuum of impaired bodies?

In an increasingly commercial world, however, the technocratic ideology (Charles, 1998) that surrounds the sport of track-and-field athletics at the Paralympics will be hard to transform. The athletes who use wheelchairs and prostheses are at the center of the Paralympic movement and will be better consumers simply because they have specialist materials to purchase if they wish to compete at the highest level. The body policing (Cole, 1993, 1998) that goes on in mainstream high-performance sport, between what is accept-ably human and what is not, in the Paralympic world has been, in an odd way, reversed.

Issues concerning eligibility for elite sporting contests may have never been more debated than when South African 400-meter runner Oscar Pis-torius decided that he was searching for a new challenge. Pistorius is a bilateral below-the-knee amputee who came to the attention of those interested in Paralympic sport following success in the Athens 2004 Paralympic Games and to the general public at the London 2012 Games, where he ran in both the Olympics and Paralympics, and became the ubiquitous symbol of disability. It is clear that the case of Pistorius is eye-catching not only for his physical achievements, but also because an absence of lower limbs required the adoption of two prosthetic limbs that have cata-pulted him beyond the horizon of the Paralympic movement. The cyborg body that Pistorius pos-sesses has led him to be referred to as the *Blade Runner* (Howe, 2011). When Pistorius first attempted to compete in mainstream sport his cyborg body was seen as not human enough (Howe, 2011; Swartz and Watermeyer, 2008) yet in the Paralympic world this body is the most

highly celebrated. Pistorius was cleared by the IAAF to run in its events in 2007 but was unable to achieve qualifying times until 2011. In August of that year Pistorius ran in the IAAF World Championships in Daegu, South Korea where he was a semi-finalist and a silver medalist in the 4×400 meters relay. A year later he competed in both the Olympic and Paralympic Games in London. Because Pistorius had been successful at both Games his status as a Paralympian was called into question (Howe, 2012) yet for most people the exposure that both Pistorius and his fellow cyborgs received at the Paralympics was celebrated.

It appears that in Paralympic track-and-field athletics the closer a body is to a cyborg the more capital it holds, which is the opposite to the world articulated by Haraway (1991) in relation to the boundaries between humans and non-humans. Explicitly wheelchair users and amputees who use prostheses are tied to sport technologies and therefore blur the lines between "natural" and "ar-tificial" and are perhaps the best example of the cyborg in contemporary society. Butryn (2003) sees the nexus between the natural and legal and the artificial and illegal as hegemonic humanness. However, Paralympic sport celebrates "trans-gressing the taboo boundary between blood, sweat, and tears, and blood, sweat and gears" (p. 28) because the cyborg (manual) wheelchair-user and the prosthetic limb-wearer are the role mod-els and supercrips the movement celebrates, in a way that Olympic and other mainstream sport has failed to achieve.

Where does this leave *les autres*? They certainly have a part to play in the Paralympic movement, but the more marginal the physicality of the body, the further away from the potential of cyborgifi-cation, the more likely a tragic rather than a heroic allegory will follow them. This analysis tells us a great deal about the politics of disable-ment. While it is considered an infringement for the able to become too cyborg, for the disabled it is highly advantageous because technology can normalize their "inferior" bodies to the point where in the case of elite wheelchair racers they can produce superhuman results. Of course there is a tension here. MacIntyre (1999) tells us that vulnerability and affliction and the related facts of dependence are central to the human condi-tion. That is, the susceptibility to injury and misery, distress and pain are likely to befall us all at some point in our existence. We all will be reliant on others from time to time. It begs the question why impaired bodies are so harshly disabled by society and, at least in the context of Paralympic sport, only those that are cyborgs are celebrated at length.

Conclusion

The classification system at the center of the Paralympic movement was established by the now defunct ISMWSF but lives on in IWAS. This system classifies bodies that use wheelchairs to compete in the sport of athletics and creates *les autres* who are unable to use this mobility technology. While the development of mobility technology that enhances sport performance is beneficial for the impairment groups concerned, it marginalizes further those athletes who do not use technologies directly in their competitive performance. Because the high-end wheelchair athlete is able to perform at the same level as or better than an able-bodied athlete, to the public the abilities of these athletes is obvious. On the other hand it might be difficult to see the ability of an athlete who has cerebral palsy which affects both legs and runs 100 meters much slower than his/her able-bodied counterpart.

The possibility of a re-embodiment for certain athletes with disabilities is provided through acquiring expensive sporting technologies. This economic exclusion makes much of the world's population of potential Paralympians ineligible. In elite sport for the disabled, there are increasing numbers of athletes with mechanical, artificially designed bodies, creating new sporting potential. These athletes are the most celebrated in part because the sport for the disabled movement developed around them. The technology they use has the capacity to "normalize" their bodies, and in so doing produces "sporting cyborgs." Unlike in mainstream sport these athletes are celebrated within the Paralympic movement and outside it as long as they know their place. In other words cyborgs are treated like royalty in the Paralympic movement, but are *persona non grata* within mainstream sport. Technocentric ideology has great influence within Paralympic sport as long as it stays within that field. Those who have the most sophisticated aids are traditionally from the West, and they are the athletes who have the greatest chance of winning medals and breaking records. As a result, the Paralympics risk becoming a show of radical technology, rather than a show of athleticism, leaving behind those from the developing world without performance-enhancing technology at their disposal, a process that certainly creates a less than level playing field.

Notes

1   I use the term "able-bodied" here because it is the term used by athletes within the cultural context of the Paralympic Games. As a former Paralympic athlete and ethnographer I think it is important to use this term rather than the commonly used "non-disabled."

2   In the case of athletes with mental impairments the classification focuses on determining mental ability. Athletes from the International Sports Federation for Persons with Intellectual Disability (INAS-FID) were banned from competition in IPC events from autumn 2000 due to a perceived lack of robustness in their classification process. The process of classification has been changed and these athletes did compete once again at the 2012 Paralympic Games.

3   In the early days of Paralympic sport athletes with amputations would have more often than not competed from a wheelchair and as such the group of athletes I consider to be at the center of the Paralympic movement are those with spinal-cord injuries and amputations.

4   Club is an event for class F32/F51 athletes who either have very involved and severe cerebral palsy (F32) or a very high lesion on their spinal cord (F51) and as a result throwing a javelin is impractical and dangerous.

5   The connection between the prosthesis and the upper body obviously does have gravity to deal with, but the lack of "weight bearing" means that pressure ulcers and the like are less troublesome. Also arm prostheses are much less prevalent in the sport of track-and-field athletics.

References

Albrecht, G.L. (1992) *The Disability Business: Rehabilitation in America*, London: Sage Publications.

Berger, R.J. (2004) "Pushing forward: Disability, basketball, and me." *Qualitative Inquiry*, 10: 794–810.

Berger, R.J. (2008) "Disability and the dedicated wheelchair athlete: Beyond the 'supercrip' critique." *Journal of Contemporary Ethnography*, 37 (6): 647–678.

Butryn, T.M. (2002) "Cyborg horizons: Sport and the ethics of self-technologization," in Miah, A. and Easson, S. (eds.) *Sport, Technology: History, Philosophy, and Policy*, Bingley, UK: JAI Press, pp. 111–134.

Butryn, T.M. (2003) "Posthuman podiums: Cyborg narratives of elite track and field athletes." *Sociology of Sport Journal*, 20: 17–39.

Campbell, J. and Oliver, M. (1996) *Disability Politics: Understanding Our Past, Changing Our Future*, London: Routledge.

Chaloner, E.J., Flora, H.S., and Ham, R.J. (2001) "Amputations at the London Hospital 1852–1857." *Journal of the Royal Society of Medicine*, 94: 409–412.

Charles, J.M. (1998) "Technology and the body of knowledge." *Quest*, 50: 379–388.

Cole, C.L. (1993) "Resisting the canon: Feminist cultural studies, sport, and technologies of the body." *Journal of Sport & Social Issues*, 17: 77–97.

Cole, C.L. (1998) "Addiction, exercise, and cyborgs: Technologies and deviant bodies," in Rail, G. (ed.) *Sport and Postmodern Times*, Albany: State University of New York Press, pp. 261–275.

Davis, R. and Cooper, R. (1999) "Technology for disabilities." *British Medical Journal*, 319: 1–4.

DePauw, K. (1997) "The (in)visibility of disability: Cultural contexts and "sporting bodies." *Quest*, 49: 416–430.

DesGroseilliers, J.-P., Desjardins, J.-P., Germain, J.-P., and Krol, A.L. (1978) "Dermatologic problems in amputees." *Canadian Medical Association Journal*, 118: 535–537.

Dupré, J. (2006) "Scientific classification." *Theory, Culture and Society*, 23 (2/3): 30–32.

Frossard, L., O'Riordan, A., and Goodman, S. (2006) "Applied biomechanics for evidence based training of Australian elite seated throwers." International Council of Sport Science and Physical Education research paper.

Hahn, H. (1984) "Sports and the political movement of disabled persons: Examining nondisabled values." *Arena Review*, 8: 1–15.

Haraway, D.J. (1991) *Simians, Cyborgs, and Women: The Reinvention of Nature*, London: Routledge.

Hoberman, J. (1992) *Mortal Engines: The Science of Human Performance and the Dehumanization of Sport*, New York: Free Press.

Howe, P.D. (2006) "The role of injury in the organization of Paralympic sport," in Loland, S., Skirstad, B., and Waddington, I. (eds.) *Pain and Injury in Sport: Social and Ethical Analysis*, London: Routledge, pp. 211–225.

Howe, P.D. (2008) *The Cultural Politics of the Paralympic Movement: Through the Anthropological Lens*, London: Routledge.

Howe, P.D. (2011) "Cyborg and supercrip: the Paralympics technology and the (dis)empowerment of disabled athletes." *Sociology*, 45 (5): 868–882.

Howe, P.D. (2012) "Pistorius shouldn't be allowed to compete at the Paralympics." *The Conversation*, http://theconversation.edu.au/pistorius-shouldnt-be-allowed-to-compete-at-the-paralympics-9278, accessed December 14, 2012.

Howe, P.D. and Jones, C. (2006) "Classification of disabled athletes: (Dis)empowering the Paralympic practice community." *Sociology of Sport Journal*, 23: 29–46.

Hughes, B. (2000) "Medicine and the aesthetic invalidation of disabled people." *Disability and Society*, 15 (4): 555–568.

Jones, C. and Howe P.D. (2005) "Conceptual boundaries of sport for the disabled: Classification and athletic performance." *Journal of Philosophy of Sport*, 32: 133–146.

MacIntyre, A. (1999) *Dependent Rational Animals: Why Human Beings Need the Virtues*, Chicago: Open Court.

Mott, S. (2000) "Impaired logic keeps heroes off the stage." *Daily Telegraph*, December 11.

Oliver, M. (1990) *The Politics of Disablement*, London: Macmillan.

Oliver, M. (1996) *Understanding Disability: From Theory to Practice*, London: Macmillan.

Rossi, L.F.A. (1974) "Rehabilitation following below-knee amputation." *Proceeds of the Royal Society of Medicine*, 67: 37–38.

Schell, L.A. and Rodriguez, S. (2001) "Subverting bodies/ ambivalent representations: Media analysis of Paralympian, Hope Lewellen." *Sociology of Sport Journal*, 18: 127–135.

Seymour, W. (1998) *Remaking the Body: Rehabilitation and Change*. London: Routledge.

Sherrill, C. (1999) "Disability sport and classification theory: A new era." *Adapted Physical Activity Quarterly*, 16: 206–215.

Sherrill, C. and Williams, T. (1996) "Disability and sport: Psychosocial perspectives on inclusion, integration and participation." *Sport Science Review,* 5 (1): 42–64.

Shogan, D. (1998) "The social construction of disability: The impact of statistics and technology." *Adapted Physical Activity Quarterly,* 15: 269–277.

Shogan, D. (1999) *The Making of High Performance Athletes: Discipline, Diversity and Ethics,* Toronto: University of Toronto Press.

Silva, C.F. and Howe, P.D. (2012) "The [in]validity of *supercrip* representation of Paralympic athletes." *Journal for Sport & Social Issues,* 36: 174–194.

Steadward, R. (1996) "Integration and sport in the Paralympic movement." *Sport Science Review,* 5: 26–41.

Swartz, L. and Watermayer, B. (2008) "Cyborg anxiety: Oscar Pistorius and the boundaries of what it means to be human." *Disability and Society,* 23 (2): 187–190.

Thomas, C. (1999) *Female Forms: Experiencing and Understanding Disability,* Buckingham, UK: Open University Press.

Vanlandewijck, Y.C. and Chappel, R.J. (1996) "Integration and classification issues in competitive sports for athletes with disabilities." *Sport Science Review,* 5: 65–88.

Walker, P. (2012) "Paralympics tries to shake off image as games for rich countries." *Guardian,* http://www.guardian.co.uk/sport/2012/aug/30/paralympics-games-for-rich-countries, accessed December 14, 2012.

Webling, D.D. and Fahrer, M. (1986) "Early bent knee prostheses: Ancestors of K9." *British Medical Journal,* 293: 1636–1637.

Yilla, A. B. (2000) "Enhancing wheelchair sport performance," in Winnock, J. (ed.) *Adapted Physical Education and Sport* (3rd edn.), Leeds: Human Kinetics, pp. 419–431.

Further Reading

Berger, R.J. (2008) "Disability and the dedicated wheelchair athlete: Beyond the 'supercrip' critique." *Journal of Contemporary Ethnography,* 37 (6): 647–678.

Dupré, J. (2006) "Scientific classification." *Theory, Culture and Society,* 23 (2–3): 30–32.

Howe, P.D. (2008) *The Cultural Politics of the Paralympic Movement: Through the Anthropological Lens,* London: Routledge.

Hughes, B. (2000) "Medicine and the aesthetic invalidation of disabled people." *Disability and Society,* 15 (4): 555–568.

Part Three

Contested Space and Politics

Introduction

Researchers have long recognized the temporal dimensions of sport culture, specifically in terms of the importance of historical context in shaping sport institutions, practices, identities, and experiences. Nonetheless, in recent years, there has been a growing recognition of the *spatial relations* within which sport is implicated. As numerous commentators have identified, space represents a social construct dialectically linked to the social practices and relations enacted within and through it. This can be attributed to the fact that space cannot be divorced from the expressions and relations of power extant within that social formation. Space is a contingent and contested entity. This understanding has particular relevance for the analysis of sport, which can be considered an embodied and embodying social practice that is delimited by time and space. However, the scale of sport's spatial dimensions are variable. As the chapters in this section illustrate, sport can occupy, and help to constitute, global, national, city, and even virtual spaces, and work in the service of differing spatially-based power arrangements (be they based upon national, ethnic, gender, and/or social class divisions), thus highlighting the politically charged and contested nature of sporting spaces.

In his broad-ranging and provocative discussion, Toby Miller (CHAPTER 13) disinters the routinely submerged relationship between sport and contemporary US imperialism. In doing so, he identifies the (internally and externally) spatially contested nature and paradoxes of US sport. Although continuing to masquerade, however spuriously, behind the façade of American sporting *exceptionalism*, Miller identifies how sport, in a concomitant fashion to the less bellicose strands of US foreign policy, has engaged in an often indirect and mediated form of imperialism. Reconceptualizing elements of economic dependency theory, Miller advances a theory of the New International Division of Cultural Labor (NICL), as the interpretive framework for understanding the spatial expansion of US professional sport. According to the theory of the NICL, labor market's global expansion, coupled with developments in global communications systems and transportation networks, proved instrumental in promulgating a more expansionist sensibility that rescued a floundering US economy from its own parochial excesses. In sporting terms, this imperialism developed in response to the capitalist crisis caused by the systemic problem of overproduction. The maturation (read stagnation) of the US professional sport marketplace prompted

A Companion to Sport, First Edition. Edited by David L. Andrews and Ben Carrington.
© 2013 Blackwell Publishing Ltd. Published 2013 by Blackwell Publishing Ltd.

sport organizations to turn overseas to secure cheaper forms of labor, and to develop expanding overseas audiences. Thus, the American sporting empire adopts what Miller refers to as a "classic imperialist economic move": although it may be construed as being more neo-imperialist in execution, committed as it is to the symbiotic exploitation of overseas constituencies as both producers and consumers of US sport. Miller juxtaposes the critical dissection of the sporting NICL with that of Pat Tillman, the ex-NFL soldier whose "friendly-fire" death was cynically rearticulated as a means of bolstering popular support for the United States' ongoing global military incursions. He offers a re-reading of Tillman as a critic of American empire, which demonstrates the possibilities of contesting imperialist practice, whether within the sporting arena or beyond.

Michael Bérubé (CHAPTER 14) interrogates the same professional sport space, albeit offering a different – and at times seemingly oppositional – interpretation to that offered by Miller. Plainly critical of what he perhaps considers to be the default and superficial reading of sport offered by leftist intellectuals such as Noam Chomsky and Terry Eagleton, Bérubé suggests there is considerably more to the contemporary sport formation than simply being a late-capitalist corporate-entertainment conspiracy, that is to say a meaningless and pacifying diversion for the disempowered masses. Furthermore, he counters Chomsky and Eagleton's failure to recognize the active and self-reflexive practices of sport fandom, wherein fans plainly recognize the inadequacies and contradictions exhibited within their sporting obsessions, and frequently ruminate upon them (utilizing social media platforms for example) in critical and informed ways which would doubtless surprise the leftist sport cynic. Indeed, Bérubé identifies these new technologies of sport fandom (internet-based sports fantasy leagues and message board discussions), and the virtual communities and conversations they elicit, as being significant factors in the development of sport culture. Far from nurturing the "irrational jingoism" that Chomsky associated with sport fandom, these technologies – when harnessed by the informed user – allow individuals to transcend the strange mix of residual parochialism and accelerating transience that characterizes sport within the age of hypermobil-

ity. Through involvement in fantasy sports leagues, in Bérubé's terms, fans are rendered more "rhizomatic" in their ability to manufacture a virtual team able to circumvent physical, organizational, and indeed mythological boundaries that separate them from players in the "real" world. While his analysis suggests that developments within the sport-entertainment industrial complex both confirm and contest the sport-as-distraction/pacification thesis, he clearly privileges the potentialities of the latter. As he concludes – and despite the incontrovertibly masculinist orientation of virtual sports fandom communities and spaces – the fun-inducing and playful mental labor associated with practices of active involvement in fantasy sport represents a strategy for nurturing the type of informed and committed popular involvement presently absent within the democratic sphere.

Focusing on the relationship between sport and the contestation for space within contemporary Israel, Tamir Sorek (CHAPTER 15) unearths a sporting-political paradox within a society fraught with tensions between Zionist and Palestinian nationalist movements. Given the decades of conflict and violence between these populations, the author acknowledges that one would have expected sporting contests between representative individuals and teams from the Jewish and Palestinian communities to be the venues for acts of protest and resistance against the Israeli state by the subjugated Palestinian population. The fact that this is not the case represents the paradox of organized sport within contemporary Israel, and speaks to its multidimensional complexity. While Jewish Israeli and Arab Palestinian representatives are not regular combatants on the sporting field, their meetings are sufficiently frequent to have sparked some forms of intercommunity conflict, were it not for the somewhat surprisingly complementary machinations of the Israeli state and the aspirations of the Palestinian populace. These factors have combined to depoliticize Arab–Jewish sporting encounters, by effectively isolating them from the discursive and material tensions of the Israeli–Palestinian conflict. Sorek identifies how the Israeli state attempted to enact this concerted depoliticization of sport through the active – though ultimately unsuccessful – discouraging of Palestinian participation in sports involving overt aggression towards an opponent (i.e., soccer, wrestling, and boxing). This was due to the fear that such sporting contests would provide a forum for the expression and development of Palestinian national consciousness, especially when the opponent was from the Jewish Israeli community. Ironically, as Sorek notes, it was precisely in these combative and emotive sports that Palestinians have excelled. While the Israeli state found it impossible to suppress Palestinian involvement in them, it has been able to govern them in a manner which has rendered them largely impotent as sites for the expression of ethno-national protest. Since the early 1960s, this has been achieved by encouraging Arab sport teams as long as they played within the structures of the Zionist sport organization. Despite providing what are effectively sporting opportunities for the expression of a combative masculinity targeted against Jewish Israeli opponents, Sorek asserts that sport's perceived status as an expression of modernity rendered Arab Palestinian involvement in state-sanctioned sporting institutions a tangible source of ethno-nationalist pride and positive self-image. Hence the hegemony of the Israeli state has worked sufficiently to ensure that Arab–Jewish sporting encounters are consciously depoliticized by athletes, organizers, and spectators alike, so as not to compromise sport's perceived function as an integrative agent for the subjugated Palestinian minority.

Having discussed the global and national dimensions of the sport–space–politics nexus, Michael L. Silk (CHAPTER 16) reduces the scale of analysis down to that of the "cityspace." Using Baltimore – the emblematic deindustrialized city – as his empirical focus, Silk theorizes the emergence of the contemporary American city (although many of the processes and practices of neoliberal urbanism are manifest in cities around the world) fundamentally divided by structural inequalities, yet which nonetheless hides behind a sophisticated façade of commercially driven urban "glamor zones," predicated on experiences and practices of consumption. He depicts the multifarious neoliberal forces and processes that are shaping contemporary deindustrializing cityscapes (deregulation, privatization, public fiscal austerity, and spectacularized commercial redevelopment), which have resulted in the emergence of cityspaces and populations bifurcated by

the competing (and oftentimes incongruent) interests of public interest and private capital. Silk thus maps the shift from regimes of city governance based on the public-service obligations of an overarching welfare managerialism, to those founded on the economic rationalities of urban entrepreneurialism. Within the latter context sport-related consumption experiences play an important role in the material and symbolic reconstitution of cityscapes: in the reformation of cities as spectacular consumptive spaces, or what Silk refers to as the instantiation of *sterile* cityspaces. With regard to Baltimore, he cites Orioles Park at Camden Yards baseball stadium, the Baltimore Ravens' Stadium, and the hosting of various high-profile events (including a leg of the round-the-world yacht race, and an Indy car race), as exemplars of how sport has helped to mobilize public monies to reinvigorate the city's tourist bubble as a playful, vital, and healthy environment. However, Silk also points to the detrimental effects of this market-driven urban repackaging, which marginalize and exclude those of insufficient financial wherewithal to partake of Baltimore's spectacular consumption spaces. This population is also doubly disadvantaged, through the compromised public services that result from the diversion of public monies into the motors of privatized urban growth. In this way, sport – while oftentimes purporting its function as an agent of communal cohesion – plays a significant role in the spatial and social segregation of contemporary urban spaces and populations.

Jeff Wiltse (CHAPTER 17) scrutinizes one spatial component of twentieth-century cityscapes: the swimming pool. Through a detailed exposition of the evolution of public and private, municipal and residential swimming pools, he indexes the changing role played by these important social resources in fostering socially interactive spaces which contribute to the integration of a wider community. Critically engaging Robert Putnam's widely cited conceptualizing of social capital, Wiltse corroborates that – as evidenced by changing patterns of swimming pool development and usage – the twentieth century marked a significant decline in civic engagement amongst the American populace. However, he offers some important correctives to Putnam's social capital schema, not least of which being Wiltse's recognition of race-based discrimination's role in the diminution of civic engagement and integration. Wiltse identifies three distinct periods in the changing relationship between swimming pools and social capital. First, during the early twentieth century, municipal pools were developed for the social class in which the facility was located. Oftentimes this allowed for the simultaneous use by the different racial groupings that comprised the local population, but a strict separation of men and women was enforced. Second, the 1920s and 1930s saw an expansion in funding to public recreation, leading to the development of greater numbers of municipal swimming pools. Rather than being socially exclusive as in earlier times, these new facilities were intended to act as agents of community sociability; integrating social class groupings from across the social spectrum, largely resultant from the middle class's newfound toleration for the working class. However, this increased social class integration at the municipal swimming pool developed at the expense of racial minorities (particularly African Americans). The residual social stigma against them as being a dual threat to social and public health resulted in the effective racial segregation of municipal swimming pools. Third, in the postwar period, the legally mandated desegregation of publicly funded swimming facilities mobilized the enduring racial anxieties of the white population with regards to the possibility of increased interaction with black bodies at the swimming pool. Hence, as Wiltse demonstrates, beginning in the 1950s, white Americans abandoned public swimming pools in their droves, preferring instead the racial exclusiveness offered by either private swim clubs or residential pools, both of which rapidly expanded over subsequent decades as the usage of, and funding for, municipal pools declined. As Wiltse concludes, the very space of the swimming pool has, and continues to be, an illuminating window into the nature of American civic life, and the broader social and political forces and processes shaping it.

Further Reading

Andrews, D.L. (2006) *Sport–Commerce–Culture: Essays on Sport in Late Capitalist America*, New York: Peter Lang.

Bale, J. (1994) *Landscapes of Modern Sport*, Leicester: Leicester University Press.

King, S.J. (2006) *Pink Ribbons, Inc.: Breast Cancer and the Politics of Philanthropy*, Minneapolis: University of Minnesota Press.

Silk, M. (2012) *The Cultural Politics of Post-9/11 American Sport: Power, Pedagogy and the Popular*, New York: Routledge.

Sugden, J. and Bairner, A. (1993) *Sport, Sectarianism and Society in a Divided Ireland*, Leicester: Leicester University Press.

13

US Imperialism, Sport, and "the Most Famous Soldier in the War"

Toby Miller

United States imperialism poses many complexities for opponents, analysts, and fellow-travelers alike. It has involved invasion and seizure, in the case of the Philippines and Cuba; temporary occupation and permanent militarization (Japan); naked ideological imperialism (the Monroe doctrine[1] and Theodore Roosevelt); and a cloak of anti-imperialism (Franklin Delano Roosevelt and Barack Obama). "Yanqui"[2] imperialism is quite different from the classic nineteenth-century model. It's much harder to gain independence from the United States than it ever was from European colonists, because US imperialism is often indirect and mediated. It produces few dramatic moments of resistive nation building, unlike the painful but well-defined struggles towards sovereignty that threw off conventional colonial yokes across the twentieth century.

This is because Yanqui imperialism began at a well-developed stage of industrial capitalism and developed – in fact led into – the post-industrial age, seeking to break down colonialism in order to gain access to labor and consumption on a global scale. Its mature form coincided with the Cold War, which favored imperial proxies over possessions, owing to both prevailing ideology and the desire to avoid direct nuclear conflict with an equal. And once that conflict was over, the free markets that had been undermined by classic imperialism were firmly re-established in the 1990s as rhetorical tropes in ways that confirmed the drive towards a loose model of domination, with economic power underwritten by militarism rather than colonialism, via the exploitation of a global division of labor.

That mobile model was itself tied to technological and socioeconomic developments. Jacques Attali (2008: 31) explains that a new "mercantile order forms wherever a creative class masters a key innovation from navigation to accounting or, in our own time, where services are most efficiently mass produced, thus generating enormous wealth." He recognizes that new eras in knowledge and communication index homologies and exchanges between militarism, colonialism, and class control. The First World recognizes that its economic future lies in finance capital and ideology rather than agriculture and manufacturing – seeking revenue from innovation and intellectual property, not minerals or masses. Hence the advice given by the consulting firm of former US secretary of state and master of the dark art of international relations Henry Kissinger that the United States must "win the battle of the world's information flows, dominating the

A Companion to Sport, First Edition. Edited by David L. Andrews and Ben Carrington.
© 2013 Blackwell Publishing Ltd. Published 2013 by Blackwell Publishing Ltd.

airwaves as Great Britain once ruled the seas" (Rothkopf, 1997: 38, 47). Today's imperialism is as much a discursive formation as a military struggle, of governmentality as much as government. Culture is crucial, and sport a core aspect of it.

Alongside Japan and Western Europe, the United States forms a power triad of the technical and ideological world. China and India are finally becoming the economic powers that their population numbers should ensure. But while they provide many leading software engineers in addition to a huge army of labor, they have lacked the domestic venture capitalists, the military underpinnings to computing innovation, and the historic cross-cultural textual power that characterize Sony, the BBC, Hollywood, or the Pacific Northwest. It comes as no surprise, for example, that the triad still accounts for 80 percent of the globe's TV programming market.

None of this means that the US variety of imperialism lacks the drive or the horror of Old World imperialism – just the overt policies and colonial *rites de passage*. The country that advertises itself as the world's greatest promise of modernity has been dedicated to translating its own national legacy, a nineteenth-century regime of clearance, genocide, and enslavement as much as democracy – a modernity built, as every successful one has been, on brutality – into a foreign and economic policy with similar effects and, at times, methods. Consider the astonishing acts of brutality funded, supported, and undertaken by the United States government across Latin America throughout the 1970s and 1980s and in Honduras in 2009. Yanqui governments and corporations take as a self-ascribed divine right that they may intervene in the political economy of the region in any way and at any time that the United States deems fit. The outcome for Chile after the CIA-engineered *golpe* of 1973 was thousands murdered and tortured, and a so-called economic miracle that was nothing of the kind. Under the democratically elected socialist Salvador Allende, unemployment had run at 4.3 percent. Under the military dictator Augusto Pinochet, it reached 22 percent. Real wages decreased by 40 percent and poverty doubled thanks to intellectual allies and corporate chiefs affiliated with US foreign and economic policy. Many were freshly minted from University of

Chicago graduate seminars in neoliberalism, under the signage of Milton Friedman, who even attended the court of Pinochet (during the same period, he was wheeled around Australia and other US client states to preach his warlockcraft) (Miller, 2007a).

The United States relies on ideology more than colonization, albeit underwritten by self-interested military and commercial power. Europeans wanted to occupy and exemplify conduct to conquered peoples up close; Gringos prefer to invade then instruct from a distance. They learnt a great deal from the old European powers via Spain's religious *conquista de América*, Portugal's *missão civilizadora*, and France's *mission civilisatrice*. Just after World War I, British prime minister David Lloyd George told the Imperial Conference that the empire was "the most hopeful experiment in human organisation which the world has yet seen," because its *modus operandi* was ethical rather than coercive, "based not on force but on goodwill and a common understanding. Liberty is its binding principle" (quoted in Mansergh, 1969: 158). These logics of cultural policy have been central to Yanqui imperialism.

This history seems largely unknown to the US population. When surveys address popular knowledge of US foreign policy, again and again we find the incorrect assumption that the state's primary overseas role has been helping others or securing the nation (Miller, 2007b). How could this happen in the case of a country with a million warriors across four continents, 702 military facilities in 132 sovereign states, battleships in each key ocean, a much-vaunted desire to mount wars on at least two international fronts at the same time as ensuring domestic security, and a "defense" budget greater than those of the next 12 biggest countries put together? How many destabilized governments and rigged elections will it take, from Lebanon, Indonesia, Iran, and Việt Nam in the 1950s, through Japan, Laos, Brazil, the Dominican Republic, Guatemala, Bolivia, and Chile in the 1960s, Portugal, Australia, and Jamaica in the 1970s, and Central America in the 1980s, before *gringos* realize that US imperialism is bellicose, anti-democratic, and dedicated to economic self-interest (Miller, 2007a)?

We can only understand such ignorance in the light of the ideology and hegemony of nationalism. There is a long mythic history of delusional popular thought in the United States that dates from the simultaneously anti-British and anti-imperial rhetoric and imperialistic conduct of early white invaders (Pope, 2007). Today, the laughable quality of US journalism, specifically news coverage of military conflicts, is a vital component of the mix (Miller, 2005, 2006, 2010a). And sport?

It has long been a core component of this ideological mystification, not least for its capacity to recruit and train servants of empire. Sport helps to fuel nationalism and militaristic adventurism through its invocation of struggles for territory and identity as grandiose and collective violence as purifying. Historically, processes of internal Americanization equated sport with nationalism. For instance, the push towards Americanizing Native Americans and new immigrants in the late nineteenth and early twentieth centuries was embodied in the formation of compulsory sporting schools and voluntary sporting associations respectively, while black slaves provided crucial labor in the emergence of southern horse-racing. In the two decades from 1881, the US birthed national bodies to regulate and represent tennis, golf, and college sports. The American Legion sponsored baseball to counter working-class radicalism and encourage social integration. Baseball, hockey, and (American) football professionalized and associated themselves with patriotic rhetoric. This soon became part of a new image overseas. In 1888, an international baseball tour was staged to promote sporting goods and display the new nation's missionary zeal, and World War I saw a major articulation of sporting values with militarism and citizenship (Miller et al., 2001; Pope, 2007; Shapiro, 1989).

Sport also became an arm of US foreign policy. The US Peace Corps argued in Sports Illustrated in 1963 that sport was more productive terrain for its mission than teaching because it was less "vulnerable to charges of 'neo-colonialism' and 'cultural imperialism.'" John F. Kennedy established a President's Council on Youth Fitness to counter a "growing softness, our increasing lack of physical fitness," because it constituted "a threat to our security" (Lasch, 1979: 183; Kang, 1988: 431; Montez de Oca, 2005). In the run-up to normalizing relations with China, table tennis became a proxy via "ping-pong diplomacy." And consider executive hectoring of the US Olympic Federation to boycott the 1980 Moscow Games, Congressional censure of Beijing's 2000 Olympic bid, the Treasury denying ABC a license to telecast the 1991 Pan-American games because they were held in Havana, or the government opposing major league (MLB) baseball's attempts to open up Cuban links until 1999 (Miller et al., 2001).

In keeping with the complexities of US imperialism, this chapter looks at both political-economic and symbolic elements in Yanqui sport. It applies the New International Division of Cultural Labor (NICL) to US professional sports and the bourgeois media utilizing a global labor pool and audience to modulate an oversupplied local market where players are too wealthy and crowds too poor to permit the restless drive to growth that both fuels and frustrates capitalism. The chapter then shifts to ideological analysis, via a case study of how sport signifies within the United States in the context of nationalism and imperial warfare, looking at the circumstances surrounding the life, death, and legacy of college and National Football League (NFL) player and military recruit Pat Tillman.

The two halves of the chapter are rather distinct. They do not obey the norms of US academic life, where integration of an argument is crucial and a clear narrative path is prized. That neatness is satisfying but unreal. It militates against political-economic and symbolic analyses being forced together, for methodological reasons as much as anything else. But we see those forces in creative tension across the work of a Marx, an Adorno, or a Foucault, without the need to tie them together or keep them apart via an interpretive violence that guarantees a neat story. Without claiming to mimic those maîtres à penser, their capacity to allow for threads to spool chaotically at the same time as drawing on grand narratives is exemplary. US imperialism and sport are both animated by the division of labor and ideology, and each is in need of address with due recognition of their relative interdependence with and autonomy from each other.

Professional Sports and the NICL

The theory of the NICL is a reconceptualization of economic dependency theory. By the 1970s, developing markets for labor and products, and the shift from the spatial sensitivities of electrics to the spatial *in*sensitivities of electronics, pushed businesses in the Global North beyond treating countries in the South as suppliers of raw materials into viewing them instead as shadow-setters of the price of work. That process broke up the prior division of the world into a small number of industrialized nations and a majority of under-developed ones, as production was split across continents. Folker Fröbel, Jürgen Heinrichs, and Otto Kreye (1980) christened this phenomenon the New International Division of Labor. They sought to comprehend what Andrew Herod calls "the economic geography of capitalism through the eyes of labor" (2001: 18).

The idea behind the NICL is that just as manu-facturing fled the First World, cultural produc-tion has also relocated: popular and high-cultural texts, computer-aided design and manufacture, sales, marketing, and information may now be created and exchanged globally, based on the division of labor. The NICL has been most dramatically applied to film and television pro-duction (Miller *et al.*, 2005; for sport, see Miller *et al.*, 2001, 2003; Andrews, 2006b). In order to understand it, we must give equivalent attention to the global, where capitalism is ordered; the national, where ideology is determined; and the local, where reception is experienced.

Labor-market expansion and developments in global transportation and communications tech-nology have diminished the need for co-location of sporting management, labor, and consump-tion. At the top of certain sports, rates of pay for workers who compete internationally have com-bined with a deregulated world TV market to create labor cosmopolitans across football, ice hockey, swimming, basketball, track, cycling, baseball, golf, tennis, and cricket. In keeping with other new professional diasporas, they migrate on both a seasonal and a permanent basis (Cohen 1997: 155–176).

In the United States, this trend really began in the so-called amateur sphere. In 1960, colleges recruited 8 percent of their athletes from Africa. Then came the "latter-day scramble for Africa" that resembled nineteenth-century imperial powers seeking new territory: an unseemly search by US colleges to attract athletes who could heighten their national standing. By 1980, African

track-and-field athletes provided 33 percent of the campus total, as numerous Olympic successes by middle-distance runners from African nations spurred Yanqui schools to recruit them. When these student athletes came to the United States, they were frequently overworked to service boos-terism, leaving town with devastated bodies that allowed no room for further success on behalf of themselves and their countries (Bale, 1991: 79, 74). The acme of this story is Henry Rono, a Kenyan brought to the United States who set four world records in three months in 1978 as a college runner but never won Olympic gold medals. Of course, Africa is not the only source of cannon fodder – tens of thousands of student athletes from abroad compete in the United States each year from dozens of nations, with the numbers rising steadily over time (Popp, Hums, and Greenwell, 2009; NCAA, 1996).

The NICL has since moved into the heart of the professional leagues. Because of the classic capitalist problem of overproduction, US profes-sional sports are being forced to transcend the provincialism of domestic arenas and media outlets. Foreign recruiting is also designed to cir-cumvent the historic gains made by local athletes to secure income redistribution. For instance, between 1974 and 1991, the proportion of revenue spent on MLB players' salaries increased from 17.6 percent to 42.9 percent, because base-ballers achieved free agency in 1975, following court and union action. From that time on, wealthy clubs could hire the most desirable players, leaving poorer teams struggling. These circumstances stimulated the desire to develop players outside the US college system in order to cut beginners' compensation. In 1970, fewer than 10 percent of MLB players were born outside the United States; by 2003, the proportion was almost 20 percent (Marcano Guevara and Fidler, 1999: 517–518; Brown, 2005: 1117). The 2009 season featured 229 players from 15 nations and territo-ries, amounting to 28 percent of the total roster.[3] It's all about minimizing development costs.

Officially bi-national leagues, where teams themselves come from outside the United States, must comply with multiple legal systems. For example, North American baseball, basketball, and hockey are all subject to Canadian as well as US labor legislation (see Jarvis and Coleman, 1999: 347). This has not been a problem for baseball in its dealings with Latin America, however. Academy members fall outside the US amateur draft's protection of wages and conditions – sporting corporations are uninterested in applying the labor laws and conditions that protect their own executives! That's not surprising: the Monroe Doctrine licenses dismissive attitudes towards legal frameworks of the region.

Most infamously in terms of these secondary labor markets, MLB teams set up baseball academies across Latin America in the 1980s. They search for young men (defined as 11 years of age and older) who will sign up for much less than equivalently gifted players domiciled in the United States. Some US-based *hispano hablantes* even drop out of high school to join the Dominican amateur leagues, in the hope of being noticed by MLB representatives (Brown, 2002). Teams discourage young boys from attending school, and require them to avoid agents (whose bargaining skills have been so important in the domestic arena). The biggest source of talent is the Dominican Republic, with Puerto Rico, Venezuela, and Mexico of increasing importance. In the 2002 season, 89 Dominicans had major-league contracts, and 1561 were playing in the minor leagues, accounting for almost 25 percent of all pro-ballplayers in the United States. MLB teams have 30 baseball academies in the Republic, and the sport ranks among the top five national industries. Life in the academies is brutish and short, and there are many tragic stories of players destined for the equivalent of a wrecking yard if injuries or skill levels militate against their success. Rejected in their early twenties, they lack marketable skills (Marcano Guevara and Fidler, 2002; Gmelch, 2006; Klein, 2006).

When US-based players have sought to play off-season back home in Latin America, MLB has often blocked them, lest there develop an alternative baseball system. So there was great irony and symbolic violence in baseball's nomination of March 2000 and 2001 as "The Month of the Americas," a putative recognition of Latin@ contributions to the sport.[4] As if in mocking preparation for this moment, *Sports Illustrated* offered a photo-essay of young boys in the Dominican Republic using makeshift equipment in the dirt, overlooked by satellite dishes bringing coverage of US games (Chass, 1998a, 1998b; Winegardner, 1999; Marcano Guevara and Fidler,

1999: 512, 518).[5] It is especially significant that these programs are aimed at states in the Global South. The North has an entirely different type of aid, based on developing spectator interest in baseball rather than schooling stars (Japan, not the Dominican Republic, was the first place outside North America to host an official MLB series, in 2000) (*Sports Illustrated*, 2000).

Secondary labor markets overseas also provide a place to test home-grown players – for example, in 1998, more than 130 NFL "footballers" had played in league-sponsored competitions outside the United States. There are few foreign-born NFL players – under 2 percent in 1970, rising to no more than 3 percent over the next three decades (Millman, 2009). Canada has always been the largest supplier. In the 1999–2000 season, the league featured 50 overseas players from 23 states (some born of US parents living abroad as part of the work of empire, such as soldiers quartered overseas, while others were the children of economic migrants, and few were direct recruits to the NFL) (Brown, 2005: 1121). The sport has never been of great international interest, for three reasons: its choreography features centralized control, lack of initiative, and suppression of individual expression and finesse, as per US labor practices; its development and attempted export occurred later than baseball and basketball; and it competes seasonally and semiotically with "real" football.

Having saturated the domestic supply of good, cheap, obedient athletes and affluent consumers, the National Basketball Association (NBA) went overseas in search of cheap talent and likely customers during the 1990s, opening offices in Switzerland, Spain, Australia, Hong Kong, and Mexico. Whereas three international players were drafted into the NBA for the 1993–1994 season, opening rosters for 1999–2000 contained 37 athletes from 25 countries, while in 2002–2003, 69 players from 33 countries featured. They comprised almost 14 percent of all NBA professionals. The numbers tripled in the past two decades. The 2008–2009 season included 77 players from 33 nations, and 2009–2010 a record 83 from 36 countries, with slightly more on opening-night roster the next year (Jackson and Andrews, 1999: 34; Brown, 2005: 1119).[6]

Of course, the corollary of this development is the disintegration of essentialist Yanqui shibboleths, notably that "white men can't jump" (a position that was always implausible, given the history of the high jump, pole vault, and triple jump). US discourses of racialization, which held that black people could play high-quality basketball and leap high while others could not, were shown to be intensely local. With the growing presence of Latin, Asian, and European players across the NBA, such assertions looked increasingly anachronistic. They finally tumbled to the floor in 2002, when the US national team was easily defeated on successive nights in the World Basketball Championship by Argentina and Yugoslavia – on a US court. By that point, most lists of the 20 leading players in the NBA included a Yugoslavian (Pja Stojakovic), a Virgin Islander (Tim Duncan), a German (Dirk Nowitzki), and a Canadian (Steve Nash), while the best of the young included representatives from France (Tony Parker), Spain (Pau Gasol), and Turkey (Hedo Turkoglu) (Wilbon, 2002). Gasol was NBA rookie of the year and was joined in the All-Rookie team by Parker and Russia's Andrei Kirilenko. The following season, the number one basketball draft pick was Yao Ming from China, and 29 percent of NBA draftees came from outside the United States. In 2007, the NBA championship was won by a team with backgrounds in four countries, against a team with backgrounds in one (the United States). That year, like the two previous ones, the MVP Award went to a foreigner, and Nowitzki won the finals MVP in 2011 (Coffey, 2002; Price, 2002b; Steele, 2002; Wells, 2008).

For its part, the Women's National Basketball Association (WNBA) *began* with use of the NICL, rather than turning to it once the domestic market in players and fans had become supersaturated in cost/quality and wealth/quantity respectively. The NICL was a means of immediately moving to a high standard of player ability and global spectator appeal. Twenty-three nations were represented by 46 players in the 2002 season, with 25 percent of WNBA professionals born outside the United States. The most powerful countries were Brazil and Australia. Five All-Stars were foreign nationals, from Australia (Lauren Jackson and Penny Taylor), Portugal (Ticha Penicheiro), Canada (Stacey Dales-Schuman), and Congo (Mwadi Mabika) (Orton, 2002). In 2005, 29 players came from 19 countries and in 2010,

22 from 13. The WNBA was also sending its players overseas in the off-season to supplement their meager incomes.[7]

But the NICL is not simply an unfolding narrative of US domination. It references fiscal crises for the national sports system at the levels of both demand and supply, necessitating an outreach that also undermines the hermetically-sealed domestic world. The NICL runs counter to a potent brand of amateur intellectualism and reactionary academia that celebrates a putative "American exceptionalism," which supposedly makes US sport an export rather than an import culture.

The concept of exceptionalism began as an attempt to explain why socialism had not taken greater hold in the United States. It has since turned into an excessive rhapsody to Yanqui world leadership, difference, and sanctimony. So we encounter claims made – in all seriousness – that "foreignness" can make a sport unpopular in the United States and the media will not accept practices coded as "other" (Brown, 2005). Consider the *Village Voice*'s denunciation of football: "Every four years the World Cup comes around, and with it a swarm of soccer nerds and bullies reminding us how backward and provincial we are for not appreciating soccer enough" (Barra, 2002). During the 2010 World Cup, this anti-leftist xenophobia became focused domestically. Glenn Beck, one of the right's pitchmen in the bourgeois media, referred to Obama's policies as "the World Cup" of "political thought," advising us that "the rest of the world likes Barack Obama's policies, we do not" and "we don't want the World Cup, we don't like the World Cup, we don't like soccer." Gordon Liddy, the convicted Watergate conspirator, decried the game on his talk show because it "originated with the South American Indians" and asked "[w]hatever happened to American exceptionalism?" His guests from the coin-operated Media Research Center said it was "a poor man or poor woman's sport" that "the left is pushing . . . in schools across the country" (Willis, 2010).

Perhaps the most appalling instance of "American exceptionalism" was provided by the Reaganite Republican Jack Kemp, who derided football before Congress as a "European socialist" sport by contrast with its "democratic" US rival (quoted in *Economist*, 2006). Similarly ethnocentric denunciations – predicated, of course, on letting Latin@s and migrants know they're not "American" – largely flow from the intemperate keystrokes and irate penmanship of angry white men. Frustrated at the prominence and popularity of the sport, they are desperate to attack its "European . . . death and despair" (Webb, 2009). As at December 2009, Google offered 31,000 hits for "soccer is un-American," many of which, unsurprisingly, dwelt on the sexuality of its players and followers. But these are death-throes against the tide of history. Wiser critics, such as Habte Selassie (2002), connect such protectionist expressions to Cold War scapegoating of immigrants, with the rejection of football in the 1940s and 1950s a rejection of difference. By 2005, the United States had English- and Spanish-language TV networks dedicated to the sport, covering leagues in Britain, Germany, Japan, Africa, France, Spain, the Netherlands, Australia, Mexico – and the United States (men's and women's by 2009). In Los Angeles, 93,000 people turned up to watch a football match in 2009. The clouds had grown heavy and thick around elderly, inadequate ways of understanding the US sporting market, via "American exceptionalism."

Time magazine's European business correspondent (Ledbetter, 2002) offers a better model for explaining the world-historical extent of cultural protectionism in the United States, which applies across the entertainment spectrum (Miller *et al.*, 2005). One might regard the level of protection in US sport as akin to socialism – a draft for *faux* students who have been trained for free in directly and indirectly state-subsidized universities; limits on salaries; revenue sharing; stadiums paid for through taxation; exemptions from antitrust legislation; and limits on cable competition (Ford, 2002). This is a planned, command economy by any other name – one that works with the recognition that, in sport, firms need opponents in order to survive. Unlike its role in other forms of capitalism, competition in sport is more an end than a means. And it is in cahoots with imperialism's means of dealing with economic crises.

There is considerable debate about whether the sporting media are immune to recessions. Premium sports claim that their brand will protect them from reductions in television rights and sponsorship revenue, while media companies confront balance sheets with reduced advertising and subscriptions. In barely a decade, overbidding for TV rights, fueled by Rupert Murdoch's dual ambition of creating a global sporting television service while achieving hegemony in its foundational market, has turned broadcast sport from a prized commodity to a valued loss leader, and finally into a contractual liability. As one commentator put it, during the largest slump in spending on advertising since World War II, but before the debt-driven crisis of five years later, "the US media market is glutted with more sports and entertainment properties than there is ad money to go round" (McCarthy, 2002: 27).

The early twenty-first century clearly shows that the protectionism of the US sports market has produced a domestic oversupply. Television networks, cable and satellite companies, universities, and municipal governments have begun to question the vast public subsidies given to the four major professional men's sports of "football," ice hockey, basketball, and baseball, and the nature and extent of their externalities. Expansion teams are under close scrutiny – Disney immediately looked to sell the 2002 "World" Series winners, the Anaheim Angels, which it had only bought as a means of "relandscaping and reinvigorating" the location that housed Disneyland (Goldsmith, 2002). Morgan Stanley suggests that the major TV networks lost US$1.3 billion on sports between 2002 and 2006. The NFL's fortunes went into a steep decline, with a decrease in ratings of 13 percent in the five seasons to 2002. Disney dispatched *Monday Night Football* from ABC to ESPN in 2006 due to falling audience numbers, where it was a success at that much lower ratings threshold. In 2009, NBC was unable to sell all its advertising slots for the Super Bowl (Hiestand, 2002; J. Solomon, 2002; Nunn and Rosentraub, 2003; *Economist*, 2009a).

This oversupply led to write-downs of US$3 billion in the value of rights to sport paid by US media companies. Such hard-fought deals as NBC's contract for future Olympic games are financial albatrosses around corporate necks (Chenoweth and O'Riordan, 2002). Murdoch's News Corporation lost US$5.4 billion in 2008–2009, partly because of declining advertising revenue for regional cable sports networks and increased marketing and sports-rights costs, such as the National Association for Stock Car Racing (NASCAR). When rights come up for renegotiation, television's losses are passed onto sports. Competition for shrinking resources between owners, administrators, coaches, elite players, and other fractions of the sporting industries were not pretty in the early years of this century, and uglier still in the post-2007 global financial crisis. By 2009–2010, the NBA needed a US$200 million line of credit to subsidize bankrupt teams. Under these circumstances, smaller sports (including many Olympic and US college codes and the WNBA) and media companies vulnerable to the credit squeeze are in jeopardy (Arango, 2009; News Corporation, 2009; Sherlock, 2008; Zirin, 2009).

Along the way, the working-class pretensions of professional sports – especially powerful in asinine claims made against football – have been eroded. In the five years from 1997, the proportion of NFL fans earning below US$30,000 decreased by over 7 percent, while the proportion earning over US$100,000 increased by 30 percent. In keeping with this gentrification, banks moved to the center of US sports sponsorship, even as they were dealing with the public opprobrium resulting from their role in the Great Recession and subsequent reward of corporate welfare. The 2009–2010 NFL season saw ticket prices soar and attendance numbers crash as average prices for the hour or less of actual action per match went to around $100 (Goetzl, 2008; Economist, 2009a, 2009b; Zirin, 2009).

The response to this overproduction has been a classic move of imperialism: stimulating overseas demand. The NFL's increasing reliance on a global marketplace has even produced "collaborations" with rival codes: in 2002, FC Barcelona, the leading Catalan football club, signed a cross-promotional deal with the league. American "football," a minor sport globally, gained from this association with a truly competitive sport, while Barcelona obtained a certain entrée to the United States. The Barcelona deal followed one struck by Manchester United with the Yankees, the only US sporting club with any real meaning across the globe since the demise of Michael Jordan (Martin and Reeves, 2001; G. Solomon, 2002; Miller, 2004). The NFL invested forlornly in overseas teams via NFL Europe/Europa until it

gave up in 2007, and continues to subsidize thousands of hours of television across the globe and offer feckless exhibition games and a few league fixtures attracting expats and followers of the odd and the banal (Times-Picayune, 2002; Carrington, 2009: 23).

The NBA commissioner euphemized the drastic impact of domestic over-expansion as a sign that "the American sports market is mature," as he unveiled plans to draw 50 percent of the league's revenue from overseas (Hiestand, 2002). This movement from provincial protectionism to an NICL that addresses the crisis of domestic overproduction is the key to the future of US basketball, with white European stars an added "advantage" both internationally and at home via racialized marketing. As the famous anti-racist black coach John Thompson said, "it's only economically smart" (quoted in Coffey, 2002). Basketball's use of Yao Ming and other leading players to attract audiences in their countries of origin and diasporic contexts is a conspicuous example of global marketing (Rowe and Gilmour, 2008). When he retired, the reaction was as much about his sales impact in China as his career.[8] The NBA also legalized zone defense in order to diminish the boredom of US players backing opponents into the low post, favoring instead the skilled European jump shooter through the application of international rules in a hitherto protected environment (Price, 2002a). Meanwhile, the stubbornly parochial, race-baiting world of NASCAR has struggled, with logos dropping from vehicles like flies, and teams amalgamating to counter desperate financial straits (Economist, 2009a).

TV's response to the crisis is to look for new markets overseas. ESPN, a series of Yanqui sports television cable channels owned by Disney that modestly styles itself the "worldwide leader in sports," has 31 networks outside the United States, in addition to related interests in promotions and other media. Its texts are on sale in 194 countries and territories, across 15 language groups: a Latin American network started in 1989 and operates alongside three subregional networks, plus there are five networks in Canada, several EU channels, and programming throughout the Arab world, in addition to 13 stations across Asia. ESPN customizes programs established in the United States, notably the highlights show *SportsCenter*, and emphasizes local interests in materials devised for particular audiences, especially football. At issue here are the expropriation of profit and the consolidation of already dominant sports (Miller, 2010b). When the Irish-based Setanta television company went bankrupt in 2009, ESPN bought up its rights to screen the English Premier League in the United Kingdom. In 2008, ESPN Star Sports, a joint Disney–News Corporation venture (Mickey-meets-Rupert) invested US$1 billion over a decade in the new Twenty20 cricket world championships (Gibson, 2009; Hutton, 2009; Rowe and Gilmour, 2009). NBA TV began in 1999, and is now available worldwide.[9]

To summarize these findings, we can say that the sporting cartels of the United States are endeavoring to use the NICL to minimize the price of their overproduction. Protectionism has consequently eased somewhat in terms of player origins and rules of the game, but major barriers remain to truly international exchange. Massive resources are dedicated to importing and exporting players and exporting tastes, but few to importing the latter. The empire wants to expropriate and buy human capital, and develop audiences, from elsewhere. This is a classic imperialist economic move.

Ideological Ramifications – Tillman Time

In returning to my earlier query about how it is possible for vast swathes of the US population to be so gullible about imperialism, "the sporting star" can be seen as embodying the brutality of the nation blended with its beauty (also see PART FOUR). The sports star is simultaneously a product of popular culture, a marketing system, a social sign, a national emblem, an outcome of capitalism and individualism, and an object of personal and public consumption. Joseph Maguire (1993) typifies this sporting body as a model of discipline, a mirror, a site of domination, and a form of communication. The disciplined body is remodeled through diet and training. The mirroring body functions as a machine of desire, encouraging mimetic conduct via the purchase of commodities. The dominating body exercises power through physical force,

both on the field and – potentially – off it. Finally, the communicative body is an expressive totality, balletic and beautiful. These taxonomies bleed into one another, and can be internally conflictual or straightforwardly functional. They are carried by human, commercial, and governmental practices that stretch and maintain boundaries between athletes, sporting performance, and aspiration. A man becomes a sports star when his off-track lifestyle and personality merge with his sporting achievements as amalgams of training, playing, and the self. Whilst bodies may be caked in mud or clad in uniforms, their names, numbers, sponsors, case histories, and smiles can all be retrieved and replayed by the electronic brush of history under the sign of nationalistic fervor, and their dedication metaphorized to humanize and endorse imperialism. The internal ideological work of nationalism and the external violent work of imperialism meet neatly under the sign of the NFL with its efforts to generate a global hyper-masculinist *demesne* that symbolizes brutality and produces revenue. These attempts may not have succeeded internationally, but domestically, their hold over the national imaginary remains regrettably powerful.

It comes as no surprise that studies of US television sports fans indicate high correlations with support for imperialist warmongering, principally among white men (Stempel, 2006). Sporting allegory has traditionally reinforced masculinism and patriotism, especially at times of great conflict or formal celebration. To cite some prominent US instances: Andrew Johnson hosted the New York Mutuals baseball club at the White House in 1867; Theodore Roosevelt indexed his manliness by riding horses; opening day MLB pitches have regularly been thrown by presidents since 1910; the first network TV broadcast in the United States was a 1945 "football" game with Harry S. Truman in the stadium, binding sport, politics, and corporate power together in a symbolic whirl; Dwight D. Eisenhower favored golf; and Ronald Reagan was carefully if comically depicted as a cowboy. Sport has also provided linguistic tropes of empire and masculinity: Richard M. Nixon's secretary of defense Melvin Laird euphemized the mining of Haiphong Harbor and increased bombing of North Việt Nam as "an expansion ball club"; the Nixon

White House staff called itself "operation line-backer"; and Tricky Dicky's own nickname was "quarterback." The oleaginous Reagan regularly cited the role he played as student "football" player George Gipp in the 1940 biopic of a Notre Dame football coach, *Knute Rockne, All American*. Reagan repeatedly quoted Gipp's dying words that had inspired his side to new heights – "win one for the Gipper" – in a 1981 Commencement address at the university commemorated in the film, when opening the 1984 Los Angeles Olympics, as a rallying cry during the Nevada senate race in 1986, and at George H.W. Bush's nomination two years later. Reagan also trivialized his 1984 presidential opponent Walter Mondale as "Coach Tax Hike." In 2000, Bill Bradley's campaign for the Democratic nomination played on his Olympic gold medal in basketball and subsequent title-winning career with the New York Nicks. George W. Bush solidified his public image in the 1990s as owner of the Texas Rangers baseball franchise, and spent much of his presidency riding bikes and running trails when he wasn't sleeping or invading, while John Kerry fruitlessly countered with "I've been a hunter all my life" in 2004. During the 2008 presidential campaign, Barack Obama played basketball with soldiers in Iraq, John McCain appeared at NASCAR events, and Sarah Palin announced that she enjoyed shooting caribou from planes (Miller, 2001, 2010b; Zirin, 2008a).

Beyond presidential politics, militarists deploy this type of symbolism all the time: officers see themselves as all-rounders, as pentathletes (Keenan, 2006). "Football" has specialized in nationalistic fervor through coordination with the military since the American War in Việt Nam, and there is now even an Armed Forces Bowl, in which college "football" is sponsored by Bell Helicopter-Textron, one of the vast array of "private-enterprise" companies whose livelihoods rely on public-sector welfare via the development and purchase of murderous technology. In this instance, promotional activities are not about selling products to fans, as per most sports underwriting. Instead, they are dedicated to creating goodwill towards corporate militaristic welfare through homologies between sport, nation, and *matériel*, via a contest that is televised – and owned – by ESPN, featuring ghoulish recruiters looking to prey on young

spectators plus the presentation of a "Great American Patriot Award." For its part, baseball offers "Welcome Back Veterans" and "Military Appreciation" events (Butterworth and Moskal, 2009).

At both encoding and decoding levels, it seems as though sporting metaphors associate romantic male sacrifice with national glory through classic second-order meaning. The Gipp exemplar takes the mythic last words of an historical character as replayed in a film. Four decades later, the actor playing him redisposes the words for political purposes, cleaving to himself the *persona* of the original speaker. Enunciation loses historical specificity, banality benefits, and thought disorder reigns. And that is where the story of Pat Tillman begins.

Tillman was a successful Arizona State University (ASU) "football" player who became a successful NFL player with the Arizona Cardinals, then turned down the opportunity to further his career through a US$3.6 million contract, due to his ideological affinities with US imperialism: Tillman had interpreted the horrors of September 11, 2001 as justifications for military retribution. His decision became a crucial aspect of US imperial propaganda, because of his status as a "football hero" (a bizarre Yanqui neologism). His prominence made him individually symbolic, rather than *lumpen*-fodder, and he was sent a very public note of congratulation by the soon-to-be-disgraced secretary of defense, Donald Rumsfeld (*Democracy Now!*, 2008). Why? Because Tillman's recruitment delivered a "testosterone cocktail" that "was impossible to resist" (Zirin, 2005): "Journalists simply could not write about Tillman without evoking his role as a protagonist of mythic proportions" (Chidester, 2009: 366). When he died in Afghanistan in April 2004, Tillman was immediately hailed for his sacrifice by the state, academia, the NFL, and the bourgeois media, and was posthumously awarded a distinguished medal, the Silver Star, for "gallantry in action against an armed enemy" which he had supposedly pursued and "forced to withdraw" (Couric, 2008).

McCain (2004) gave a eulogy at Tillman's nationally televised (ESPN) funeral that quickly turned the occasion into a hymn to "our blessed and mostly peaceful society," supported of course by military service, where "the purpose of all good courage is love." McCain said that soldiers' "blood debts" and "goodness" would endure, and reassured Tillman's family as it waited "to see him again, when a loving god reunites us all." This courage and these debts had driven Tillman from football to fighting, according to this ideologue – who had never met him, and whose "thoughts" were immediately published by the far-right *National Review* magazine. Hack conservative intellectual Ann Coulter called Tillman "an American original – virtuous, pure and masculine like only an American male can be" (quoted in Collier, 2005). And the libertarian simpletons over at the Cato Institute took his volunteerism as a sign that a military draft was not necessary, so pure was the population's desire to serve the nation while sidestepping the state (Healy, 2004).

The White House hailed Tillman as "an inspiration on and off the football field . . . who made the ultimate sacrifice in the war on terror" (quoted in Zirin, 2005). The Governor of Arizona ordered that flags at ASU be flown at half-mast, and the university began to market match tickets under his name. The Cardinals divined that he "represented all that was good in sports" and placed his uniform in a glass case alongside bouquets and teddy bears. The league said Tillman "personified all the best values of his country and the NFL." Much was made of his non-stop energy and desire to hurt opponents in tackles (quoted in *Sports Illustrated*, 2004).

Meanwhile, the league's appalling record of metabolic syndrome and cardiovascular mortality amongst its "athletes" – much higher than ordinary people, let alone by comparison with authentic sporting stars – was matched by dreadful health reports in terms of their lack of fitness and overall likelihood of early death, and new research that indicated an alarming, in fact astonishing, correlation with neurodegeneration (Selden *et al.*, 2009; Wojtys, 2009). Tillman may have died on the field of adventurism but his former colleagues were set for less glamorous deaths as empire's symbolic stars whose bodies were ultimately worth nothing.

But Tillman's story became more complex and contradictory as time passed. He was an atheist, as his youngest brother Richard explained to McCain and ESPN at the funeral: "Pat isn't with God. He's fucking dead. He wasn't religious. So thank you for your thoughts, but he's fucking dead" (quoted in Tillman with Zacchino, 2008). And during his time abroad, Tillman had become anti-war and a fan of Noam Chomsky's – he was going to meet the veteran analyst of imperialism had he returned from theater (Zirin, 2005). Then it turned out that Tillman had been the victim of manslaughter by his colleagues, not murder by his enemies. In short, he failed the tasks laid down for him by history – he was not what he looked like, not what he had been built up to be, and not what the war machine had manufactured. He was a critic of US imperialism at the very moment that he was celebrated as its epigone and epitome. His movement into the NICL had gone from sporting recruit to nationalistic recruit to ideological recruit to fallen recruit to dead activist.

General Stanley McChrystal is notorious for several things, foremost among them having been Obama's chief warmonger of Afghanistan, a key long-term operative in the empire's mistreatment of detainees, and a very amateurish *Rolling Stone* interviewee.[10] He was also a central player in the scandalous, mendacious propaganda use of Tillman's name, service, and death. When McChrystal was appointed to run the empire in Afghanistan, Tillman's father accused him of having conducted "a falsified homicide investigation." Tillman's brother Kevin referred to him as a "fraud," because McChrystal had approved the award of a Silver Star to Pat despite the Ranger's death at the hands of compatriots (which McChrystal admitted under oath that he had known, even though the citation referred to "devastating enemy fire"). In 2007, the Pentagon's acting inspector general held McChrystal "accountable for the inaccurate and misleading assertions" in the citation, but he was overruled by the army (Fox News, 2009; *Democracy Now!*, 2008; Laidlaw and Mendoza, 2007; Krakauer, 2009; Tillman with Zacchino, 2008). The military later determined that the Silver Star citation was "based on what he [Tillman] intended to do" (White, 2005). Got it.

Tillman's family spent years trying to penetrate the Pentagon's obfuscation and propaganda simply to establish what had been known from the moment of his death – that he'd been killed by Yanquis, heroized by Yanquis, and used by Yanquis in a way that was first and foremost dedicated to lying to his family members as part of a massive cover-up of the kind that color Republican and Democrat administrations alike (Collier, 2005; Camacho and Hauser, 2007; Andrews, 2006a). As second-order meaning, this bought into a long and disgraceful association of whiteness with sporting and military valor versus an association of blackness with flashiness and selfishness (Kusz, 2007). As a white man, Tillman was fodder for this binary.

Tillman's brother and fellow-recruit Kevin testified before Congress that the impending disclosures about Abu Ghraib had driven the Pentagon to clutch at Pat and claim him for nationalism: "Revealing that Pat's death was a fratricide would have been a political disaster during a month already swollen with political disasters and a brutal truth that the American public would undoubtedly find unacceptable, so the facts needed to be suppressed. An alternative narrative had to be constructed" (*Democracy Now!*, 2008). Kevin went on to explain how repulsed the family was to learn that "our elected leaders were subverting international law and humanity" through the seizure and torture of people, because "suspension of Habeas Corpus is supposed to keep this country safe" and "reason is being discarded for faith, dogma, and nonsense" (Tillman, 2006).

Any attempt to rearticulate Tillman's death and its *faux* heroization led to immediate and maddened calumny from the right. When ASU art professor John Leaños generated a poster of Tillman entitled "Friendly Fire" that questioned these militaristic distortions "and the quasi-religious and dogmatic adherence to Tillman's mythological heroic image by mainly conservative male Americans," he was immediately subjected to scrutiny by CBS, CNN, and ABC. That produced angry outbursts by viewers, hundreds of violent, splenetic emails and threats, and an inquiry into Leaños by ASU and denunciations of him by the school's bureaucrats (Leaños, 2005). When the *San Francisco Chronicle* disclosed that Tillman had regarded the invasion of Iraq as "fucking illegal" (Collier, 2005), Coulter thundered that "I don't believe it" (quoted in Zirin, 2005). There was even an embarrassingly performative, sentimental academic lament for him that fretted over the loss of US servicemen as if

they were the central sufferers of imperial overreach (Lockford, 2008).

As Kevin Tillman noted to Congress, querying the official rendition of his brother's death was equated with "casting doubt on Pat's bravery and sacrifice." It was nothing of the sort. Rather, once the nature of the scandal was exposed, "Pat was no longer of use as a sales asset." Needless to say, Rumsfeld did not contact the family once this "asset" had been compromised – but did find the time to deny there had been a cover-up. His typically torturous prose announced that the story had been "handled in a way that was unsatisfactory." This was an oblique reference to the fact that Tillman's mother learnt her son was the victim of fratricide from the *Arizona Republic*, not an Arizona Republican. For questioning the Pentagon, she and her surviving sons were routinely derided by the right. One of the Army's principal investigators, and a recommender of the Silver Star award, Tillman's commander Ralph Kauzlarich, suggested to the network that the Tillman family had been unable to accept that this was "an unfortunate accident" because it was not religious (i.e., superstitious) and hence saw Pat's fate as to become "worm dirt." (This "reasoning" was also evident in an internal military memo; Breslau, 2008.) At least Tillman's worm-afterlife had a name – the Afghan soldier killed alongside him was left unidentified for years (Fish, 2006; Goff, 2006; *Democracy Now!*, 2008; Couric, 2008; Breslau, 2008; Greenwald, 2007).

But even true believers came to question the administration's propaganda. The TV drama series *Bones* offered a thinly veiled fictionalization of the cover-up (Takacs, 2009). Once the Republicans lost their Congressional majority in 2006, the House of Representatives committee system mounted inquiries, albeit ineffectual ones (Greenwald, 2007; Tillman with Zacchino, 2008). ESPN had already done a very thorough job of investigative journalism, extremely rare in the fawning fandom that characterizes the US sporting press. It essentially showed that everyone in the chain of command understood this was a fratricide within hours of the event (Fish, 2006). The depth and breadth of ESPN's research may be taken as one of those fissures that occur when the empire is viewed as a compromised bureaucratic thicket rather than a pure national *esprit de corps* – when the state overdetermines the nation, and reflexive Yanqui dislike of government overtakes the association of military command with, to quote McCain, "love."

Conclusion

The NICL governs the material relationship between US sport and empire. The national sporting economy has been compromised by overreach, such that it relies on talent from overseas to play and money from overseas to watch. Ironically, the NFL, a global failure, recently produced a significant ideological debate about the violence of Yanqui imperialism.

We need to understand the fissures between capital and the sovereign state, between the rhetoric and reality of US imperialism. Like Pat Tillman, the US public is not monolithic or entirely gullible, US academia is not entirely nationalistic, and the US press is not completely imperialistic. There are long and profound histories of Yanqui anti-imperialism in unions, political parties, churches, critical intellectual circles, and international feminism. Sport has generated its own stellar literature of dissent (summarized and exemplified in Zirin, 2008b). A progressive, pacific internationalism has deep strains in US thinking, and ultimately determined the Tillman story in both life and death. Tillman himself was clearly a complex figure, a bizarre amalgam of *machismo* and subtlety, of militarism and criticism, of nationalism and cosmopolitanism. He was all the contradictory subjects suggested by Maguire's typology of the peak athlete, because he embodied the violence at the heart of contemporary empire with its relatively autonomous discursive side – a Yanqui who saw the constitution as a political, not a religious document, and was able to reconsider his ideological commitments in accordance with international law and material experience. His death, as tragic as all others in war, rearticulates an entire history of US sport's imbrication with imperial endeavor. It reminds us that the world of work and the fragility of bodies are central to sport in both its economic and political signification. This chapter may not have followed the dictates of essay writing in terms of a neatly reasoned, unitary argument, but I hope that it has offered a realistic account of a polyvalent phenomenon and offered some valuable tools for engaging and dismantling imperial practice.

Acknowledgments

My thanks to Dave Andrews for rescuing me from several infelicities and errors.

Notes

1   The Monroe Doctrine, adopted as US foreign policy in the 1820s under President Monroe in opposition to European intervention in the Western Hemisphere, holds that any and all activities taking place in the Americas can basically be taken as the business of the US whenever it sees fit.

2   Yanqui is the term used by the countries to whom the adjective "American" applies but which are not part of the USA.

3   See http://mlb.com/news/press_releases/press_release.jsp?ymd=20090406&content_id=4139614&vkey=pr_mlb&fext=.jsp&c_id=mlb, accessed December 17, 2012.

4   "Latin@" is the non-sexist form favored across the Americas of "Latino/a."

5   See also "MLB honors Latin impact in 2000 with 'Month of the Americas.'" MLB press release, November 10, 1999.

6   See http://www.voanews.com/english/news/usa/people/International-Players-Impact-on-NBA-Grows-in-Past-Two-Decades-116426514.html; http://www.reuters.com/article/2010/10/26/us-nba-internationals-idUSTRE69P3T020101026, accessed December 17, 2012.

7   See http://wnba.com/players/international_roster.html; http://www.wnba.com/news/rosters_100514.html, accessed December 17, 2012.

8 See http://shanghaiist.com/2011/07/20/yao_ming_retirement_press_conferenc.php, accessed December 17, 2012.

9 See http://nba.com/global; http://nba.com/Fan-Night, accessed December 17, 2012.

10 See http://www.rollingstone.com/politics/news/the-runaway-general-20100622, accessed December 17, 2012.

References

Andrews, D.L. (2006a) "Introduction: Playing with the pleasure principle." *South Atlantic Quarterly*, 105 (2): 269–276.

Andrews, D.L. (2006b) *Sport–Commerce–Culture: Essays on Sport in Late Capitalist America*, New York: Peter Lang.

Arango, T. (2009) "News Corporation posts a loss on MySpace charge." *New York Times*, August 5.

Attali, J. (2008) "This is not America's final crisis." *New Perspectives Quarterly*, Spring: 31–33.

Bale, J. (1991) *The Brawn Drain: Foreign Student-Athletes in American Universities*, Urbana: University of Illinois Press.

Barra, A. (2002) "Nil and void." *Village Voice*, July 9.

Breslau, K. (2008) "'They were lying.'" *Newsweek*, May 5.

Brown, J. (2002) "Diamonds in the rough." *Christian Science Monitor*, March 25.

Brown, S.F. (2005) "Exceptionalist America: American sports fans' reaction to internationalization." *International Journal of the History of Sport*, 22 (6): 1106–1135.

Butterworth, M. and Moskal, S.D. (2009) "American football, flags, and "fun": The Bell Helicopter Armed Forces Bowl and the rhetorical production of militarism." *Communication, Culture & Critique*, 2 (4): 411–433.

Camacho, P.R. and Hauser, W.L. (2007) "Civil-military relations – who are the real principals? A response to 'Courage in the service of virtue: The case of General Shinseki's testimony before the Iraq War.'" *Armed Forces & Society*, 34 (1): 122–137.

Carrington, B. (2009) "Sport without final guarantees: Cultural studies/Marxism/sport," in Carrington, B. and McDonald, I. (eds.) *Marxism, Cultural Studies and Sport*, London: Routledge, pp. 15–31.

Chass, M. (1998a) "A new baseball strategy: Latin-American bargains." *New York Times*, March 22.

Chass, M. (1998b) "Baseball's game of deception in the search for Latin talent." *New York Times*, March 23.

Chenoweth, N. and O'Riordan, B. (2002) "The sick business of sport." *Australian Financial Review*, June 4.

Chidester, P.J. (2009) "'The Toy Story of life': Myth, sport and the mediated reconstruction of the American hero in the shadow of the September 11th terrorist attacks." *Southern Communication Journal*, 74 (4): 352–372.

Coffey, W. (2002) "Global warming changes the NBA landscape." *New York Daily News*, July 18.

Cohen, R. (1997) *Global Diasporas: An Introduction*, Seattle: University of Washington Press.

Collier, R. (2005) "Family demands the truth." *San Francisco Chronicle*, September 25.

Couric, K. (2008) "What really happened to Pat Tillman?" *CBS News*, May 4, http://www.cbsnews.com/8301-18560_162-4061656.html, accessed January 18, 2013.

Democracy Now! (2008) "Mary Tillman, mother of slain Army Ranger and former NFL star Pat Tillman, on her four-year quest to expose the military cover-up of her son's death by members of his own unit." *Democracy Now!*, May 22.

Economist (2006) "The odd man out," *Economist*, June 10: 32 (Lexington column).

Economist (2009a) "Is it recession-proof?" *Economist*, February 14: 69.

Economist (2009b) "Play on." *Economist*, May 30: 79.

Fish, M. (2006) "E-ticket: An un-American tragedy." *ESPN.com*, http://sports.espn.go.com/espn/eticket/story?page=tillmanpart1, accessed January 18, 2013.

Ford, P. (2002) "In business of sport, US one of less-free markets." *Christian Science Monitor*, June 19.

Fox News (2009) "Parents of slain army ranger Tillman: McChrystal shouldn't get top Afghanistan post." *Foxnews.com*, May 13, http://www.foxnews.com/story/0,2933,520071,00.html, accessed December 17, 2012.

Fröbel, F., Heinrichs, J., and Kreye, O. (1980) *The New International Division of Labor: Structural Unemployment in Industrialised Countries and Industrialisation in Developing Countries*, trans. Burgess, P., Cambridge: Cambridge University Press.

Gibson, O. (2009) "Where will the big bucks go when the bubble bursts?" *Guardian*, January 22.

Gmelch, G. (ed.) (2006) *Baseball Without Borders: The International Pastime*, Lincoln: University of Nebraska Press.

Goetzl, D. (2008) "ESPN: Monday night football top '08 cable series." *Media Daily News*, December 30, http://www.mediapost.com/publications/article/97357/espn-monday-night-football-top-08-cable-series.html, accessed February 24, 2013.

Goff, S. (2006) "Playing the atheism card against Pat Tillman's family." *Truthdig*, July 28, http://www.truthdig.com/report/item/20060728_worm_dirt/, accessed January 18, 2013.

Goldsmith, J. (2002) "Mouse house chief flies with angels." *Variety*, November 13–14.

Greenwald, G. (2007) "The Pat Tillman and Jessica Lynch frauds." *Salon*, April 25, http://www.salon.com/2007/04/25/tillman_lynch/, accessed January 18, 2013.

Healy, G. (2004) "You gotta serve somebody." *Cato Institute*, May 7, http://www.cato.org/publications/commentary/you-gotta-serve-somebody, accessed January 18, 2013.

Herod, A. (2001) *Labor Geographies: Workers and the Landscapes of Capitalism*, New York: Guilford Press.

Hiestand, M. (2002) "Spanning the globe." *USA Today*, April 30.

Hutton, P. (2009) "2009 Promises to be more about consolidation in challenging economic times." *Indiantelevision.com*, January 13, http://www.indiantelevision.com/special/y2k9/Peter-Hutton-yearender.php, accessed January 23, 2013.

Jackson, S.J. and Andrews, D.L. (1999) "Between and beyond the global and the local: American popular sporting culture in New Zealand."*International Review for the Sociology of Sport*, 34 (1): 31–42.

Jarvis, R.M. and Coleman, P. (1999) *Sports Law: Cases and Materials*, St Paul, MN: West Group.

Kang, J.-M. (1988) "Sports, media and cultural dependency." *Journal of Contemporary Asia*, 18 (4): 430–443.

Keenan, J. (2006) *Developing the Pentathlete: The Army Congressional Fellowship Experience*, Carlisle Barracks, PA: United States Army War College.

Klein, A.M. (2006) *Growing the Game: The Globalization of Major League Baseball*, New Haven, CT: Yale University Press.

Krakauer, J. (2009) *When Men Win Glory: The Odyssey of Pat Tillman*, New York: Doubleday.

Kusz, K.W. (2007) "From NASCAR nation to Pat Tillman: Notes on sport and the politics of white cultural nationalism in post-9/11 America." *Journal of Sport & Social Issues*, 31 (1): 77–88.

Laidlaw, S. and Mendoza, M. (2007) "General suspected cause of Tillman death." *Washington Post*, August 4.

Lasch, C. (1979) *The Culture of Narcissism: American Life in an Age of Diminishing Expectations*, New York: Warner.

Leaños, J. (2005) "Intellectual freedom and Pat Tillman." *Bad Subjects*, http://bad.eserver.org/reviews/2005/leanosstatement.html, accessed January 18, 2013.

Ledbetter, J. (2002) "The culture blockade." *The Nation*, November 4.

Lockford, L. (2008) "Investing in the political beyond." *Qualitative Inquiry*, 14 (1): 3–12.

Maguire, J. (1993) "Bodies, sportscultures and societies: A critical review of some theories in the sociology of the body." *International Review for the Sociology of Sport*, 28 (1): 33–52.

Mansergh, N. (1969) *The Commonwealth Experience*, London: Weidenfeld & Nicolson.

Marcano Guevara, A.J. and Fidler, D.P. (1999) "The globalization of baseball: Major league baseball and the mistreatment of Latin American baseball talent." *Indiana Journal of Global Legal Studies*, 6: 511–577.

Marcano Guevara, A.J. and Fidler, D.P. (2002) *Stealing Lives: The Globalization of Baseball and the Tragic Story of Alexis Quiroz*, Bloomington: Indiana University Press.

Martin, C.R. and Reeves, J.L. (2001) "The whole world isn't watching (but we thought they were): The Super Bowl and United States solipsism." *Culture, Sport, Society*, 4 (2): 213–236.

McCain, J. (2004) "Courage and honor: Remembering Pat Tillman." *National Review*, May 4.

McCarthy, M. (2002) "Bowl, Olympics compete for gold." *USA Today*, January 31.

Miller, T. (2001) *SportSex*, Philadelphia, PA: Temple University Press.

Miller, T. (2004) "Manchester, USA?" in Andrews, D.L. (ed.) *Manchester United: A Thematic Study*, London: Routledge, pp. 241–248.

Miller, T. (2005) "Financialization, emotionalization, and other ugly concepts," in Nohrstedt, S.A. and Ottosen, R. (eds.) *Global Wars – Local Views: Media Images of the Iraq War*, Göteborg: Nordicom, pp. 263–276.

Miller, T. (2006) "US journalism: Servant of the nation, scourge of the truth?" in Cole, B. (ed.) *Conflict, Terrorism and the Media in Asia*, London: Routledge, pp. 5–22.

Miller, T. (2007a) *Cultural Citizenship: Cosmopolitanism, Consumerism, and Television in a Neoliberal Age*, Philadelphia, PA: Temple University Press.

Miller, T. (2007b) "The American people cannot be trusted," in Denzin, N.K. and Giardina, M.D. (eds.) *Contesting Empire, Globalizing Dissent: Cultural Studies After 9/11*, Boulder, CO: Paradigm, pp. 121–135.

Miller, T. (2010a) "Journalism and the question of citizenship," in Allan, S. (ed.) *The Routledge Companion to News and Journalism*, London: Routledge, pp. 397–406.

Miller, T. (2010b) *Television Studies: The Basics*, London: Routledge.

Miller, T., Govil, N., McMurria, J., et al. (2005) *Global Hollywood 2*, London: British Film Institute/Berkeley: University of California Press.

Miller, T., Lawrence, G., McKay, J., and Rowe, D. (2001) *Globalization and Sport: Playing the World*, London: Sage Publications.

Miller, T., Lawrence, G., McKay, J., and Rowe, D. (2003) "The over-production of US sports and the New International Division of Cultural Labor." *International Review for the Sociology of Sport*, 38 (4): 427–440.

Millman, J. (2009) "These days, everybody's All-American just may be a Haitian: Football-mad Florida fills US gridirons with Kreyol-speaking stars." *NFL International*, December 4, http://online.wsj.com/article/SB125987130978175269.html?mod=slideshow_overlay_mod, accessed January 18, 2013.

Montez de Oca, J. (2005) "'As our muscles get softer, our missile race becomes harder': Cultural citizenship and the 'muscle gap.'" *Journal of Historical Sociology*, 18 (3): 145–172.

NCAA (1996) *NCAA Study of International Student-Athletes: A Comparison of Data Regarding International Student-Athletes from 1991–92 and 1995–96*. National Collegiate Athletic Association, http://fs.ncaa.org/Docs/library/research/international_s-a/1996_international_s-a.pdf, accessed January 18, 2013.

News Corporation (2009) "Earnings release for the year and quarter ended June 30, 2009," August 5, http://www.newscorp.com/investor/download/NWS_Q4_2009.pdf, accessed January 18, 2013.

Nunn, S. and Rosentraub, M.S. (2003) "Sports wars: Suburbs and center cities in a zero-sum game," in Lewis, T. and Miller, T. (eds.) *Critical Cultural Policy Studies: A Reader*, Oxford: Blackwell, pp. 211–224.

Orton, K. (2002) "A modern League of Nations." *Washington Post*, July 14.

Pope, S.W. (2007) "Rethinking sport, empire, and American exceptionalism." *Sport History Review*, 38: 92–120.

Popp, N., Hums, M.A., and Greenwell, T.C. (2009) "Do international student-athletes view the purpose of sport differently than United States student-athletes at NCAA division I universities?" *Journal of Issues in Intercollegiate Athletics*, 2: 93–110.

Price, D. (2002a) "Mavs, Kings globetrotting." *Star-Telegram*, May 3.

Price, D. (2002b) "NBA goes global." *Star-Telegram*, June 27.

Rothkopf, D. (1997) "In praise of cultural imperialism." *Foreign Policy*, 107: 38–53.

Rowe, D. and Gilmour, C. (2008) "Contemporary media sport: De- or re-westernization?" *International Journal of Sport Communication*, 1 (2): 177–194.

Rowe, D. and Gilmour, C. (2009) "Global sport: Where Wembley Way meets Bollywood Boulevard." *Continuum*, 23 (2): 171–182.

Selassie, H. (2002) "Warming up to soccer." *Village Voice*, June 4.

Selden, M.A., Helzberg, J.H., Waeckerle, J.F., et al. (2009) "Cardiometabolic abnormalities in current National Football League players." *American Journal of Cardiology*, 103 (7): 969–971.

Shapiro, M.J. (1989) "Representing world politics: The sport/war intertext," in Der Derian, J. and Shapiro, M.J. (eds.) *International/Intertextual Relations: Postmodern Readings of World Politics*, Lexington, MA: Lexington Books, pp. 69–96.

Sherlock, M. (2008) "Downturn could offer sporting opportunity." *Sport Business*, November 19.

Solomon, G. (2002) "Barcelona, NFL agree to a 3-year partnership." *Washington Post*, January 31.

Solomon, J. (2002) "The sports market is looking soggy." *New York Times*, April 21.

Sports Illustrated (2000) "Leading off." *Sports Illustrated*, February 14, http://sportsillustrated.cnn.com/vault/article/magazine/MAG1018244/index.htm, accessed January 18, 2013.

Sports Illustrated (2004) "Tillman killed in Afghanistan." *Sports Illustrated*, April 23.

Steele, D. (2002) "It's finally a global game." *San Francisco Chronicle*, May 3.

Stempel, C. (2006) "Televised sports, masculinist moral capital, and support for the US invasion of Iraq." *Journal of Sport & Social Issues*, 30 (1): 79–106.

Takacs, S. (2009) "The body of war and the management of imperial anxiety on US television." *International Journal of Contemporary Iraqi Studies*, 3 (1): 85–105.

Tillman, K. (2006) "After Pat's birthday." *Truthdig.com*, October 19.

Tillman, M. with Zacchino, N. (2008) *Boots on the Ground at Dusk: My Tribute to Pat Tillman*, New York: Modern Times.

Times-Picayune (2002) "The world's fare?" *Times-Picayune*, January 29.

Webb. S.H. (2009) "Soccer is ruining America." *Wall Street Journal*, March 12.

Wells, S. (2008) "Johnny foreigner has taught US basketball a painful lesson." *Guardian*, April 7.

White, J. (2005) "Army withheld details about Tillman's death," *Washington Post*, May 4, A3.

Wilbon, M. (2002) "Basketball's new world order." *Washington Post*, September 6.

Willis, O. (2010) "As the World Cup starts, conservative media declare war on soccer." *MediaMatters for America*, June 11, http://mediamatters.org/research/2010/06/11/as-the-world-cup-starts-conservative-media-decl/166099, accessed December 17, 2012.

Winegardner, M. (1999) "Los naturales." *New York Times Magazine*, October 3.

Wojtys, E.M. (2009) "Big hits." *Sports Health: A Multidisciplinary Approach*, 1 (6): 459.

Zirin, D. (2005) "Pat Tillman, our hero." *The Nation*, October 6.

Zirin, D. (2008a) "Sarah Palin's extreme sports." *The Nation*, October 7.

Zirin, D. (2008b) *A People's History of Sports in the United States: 250 Years of Politics, Protest, People, and Play*, New York: New Press.

Zirin, D. (2009) "Big League blues." *The Nation*, November 16.

Further Reading

Andrews, D.L. (2006) *Sport–Commerce–Culture: Essays on Sport in Late Capitalist America*, New York: Peter Lang.

Maguire, J. (1993) "Bodies, sportscultures and societies: A critical review of some theories in the sociology of the body." *International Review for the Sociology of Sport*, 28 (1): 33–52.

Shapiro, M. J. (1989) "Representing world politics: The sport/war intertext," in Der Derian, J. and Shapiro, M.J. (eds.) *International/Intertextual Relations: Postmodern Readings of World Politics*, Lexington, MA: Lexington Books, pp. 69–96.

Zirin, D. (2008) *A People's History of Sports in the United States: 250 Years of Politics, Protest, People, and Play*, New York: New Press.

14

The Realities of Fantasy
Politics and Sports Fandom in the Twenty-first Century

Michael Bérubé

Introduction

Sunday, November 15, 2009 will be remembered as an epochal moment in the history of sports – or at least in the history of North American fantasy sports leagues. That day, the National Football League (NFL) match-up between the Jacksonville Jaguars and the New York Jets produced a dramatic and bizarre finish, a duel of coaching wits that ended when Maurice Jones-Drew, the Jaguars' running back, deliberately downed himself on the Jets' one-yard line rather than score a touchdown. The situation was this: with just over five minutes remaining, the Jaguars took possession of the ball on their own 17-yard line, trailing the Jets 22–21. Converting two third downs, they made their way to midfield before busting open a 33-yard pass that put them at the Jets' 14-yard line. At that point, of course, the Jaguars were well within field-goal range and poised to regain the lead. After the two-minute warning, Jones-Drew ran for four yards, whereupon the Jets used their last timeout to stop the clock at 1:48. And then the game took a strange turn. During the timeout, the Jets evidently determined that their only chance to win the game, now that the Jaguars were looking at a

short field goal and could run the clock down far enough to prevent the Jets from retaking possession, was to refuse to tackle the ball-carrier on the next play. That way, the Jaguars would score, going up 28–22 but allowing the Jets one more possession with roughly 90 seconds remaining. Meanwhile, on their sideline, the Jaguars evidently decided that if the Jets were to refuse to tackle their ball-carrier, he would run for a first down but take a knee short of the end zone, so as to allow the Jaguars to retain possession of the ball before kicking a very short field goal as time expired. For that is precisely what happened when play resumed: the Jaguars handed the ball to Jones-Drew, the Jets refused to play defense, and Jones-Drew sprinted toward the goal line, stopping at the 1 and touching a knee to the turf. The Jaguars proceeded to run down the clock, and kicked the winning field goal with three seconds remaining.

The game's conclusion was notable for its relatively high level of strategic thinking: most head coaches in the NFL are notoriously conservative playcallers, and few would have gone the route chosen by Jets coach Rex Ryan – allowing an opponent to score in order to get the ball back with time enough for a final drive. (The fact that

A Companion to Sport, First Edition. Edited by David L. Andrews and Ben Carrington.
© 2013 Blackwell Publishing Ltd. Published 2013 by Blackwell Publishing Ltd.

it was, indeed, the most likely winning scenario would not have mattered to most coaches, who would opt instead to try to stop the offense and try to block the field goal – futile though that might be.) Likewise, the Jaguars deserve credit for anticipating the Jets' desperation strategy and instructing their running-back not to score. "Smartest play of the game," Jets quarterback Matt Sanchez said afterwards. "That's an MVP play right there" (Waszak, 2009).

Indeed it was an exceptionally smart play, but that's not why I'm describing it here, or nominating November 15, 2009 as an epochal moment in sports. Rather, it was Jones-Drew's postgame comment that seemed to me to mark a new era in sports fandom: "Sorry to my fantasy owners," he said of his final-yard kneeldown. "I apologize. I had myself today. It was a tough call, but whatever it takes to get the victory, that's what counts" (Waszak, 2009). He was speaking tongue in cheek, of course. But that's why the event was notable: a professional athlete jokingly apologized to his "fantasy owners" for making a play that enhanced his team's chances to win but did not show up in his personal statistics. The day that happens is the day we realize we inhabit a world in which the outcomes of games in fantasy leagues are more important to many fans than the outcomes of games in real leagues. Moreover, the fact that Jones-Drew not only apologizes to his fans/owners but claims to have "had himself" in his own fantasy league makes the remark all the more piquant, since it suggests that Jones-Drew's play was doubly unselfish: it affected not only his individual performance stats but also his fantasy team's place in its league's standings. And not least, the idea of owning oneself in a fantasy league opens up a conceptual hall of mirrors (as we shall see in a moment) while playing complexly on the notion of "self-possession"– namely, the kind of restraint and awareness required to take a knee at the 1-yard line even when your team is down by a point.

In other words, the line between the "real team" and the fantasy league, though "real," is not as clear as it might seem. For weirdly enough, during the week prior to the game, *Yahoo! Sports'* "The Gentlemen's League" (2009) did an interview with Jones-Drew *about* fantasy football, in which the interviewer and Jones-Drew refer-

enced another similar play, Brian Westbrook's decision to down himself at the 1 in a game against the Dallas Cowboys on December 17, 2007. That situation was a bit different, insofar as the Eagles were leading 10–6 with two minutes left, not trailing and planning a last-second field goal, and Westbrook downed himself not because of any crafty planning on the sidelines but because the Eagles' right tackle, Jon Runyan, followed Westbrook down the field yelling at him to take a knee so that the Cowboys would not be able to come back from 17–6 in a freak finish. "In a crazy game like this, you never know," Runyan said, "you are a long kickoff return or a crazy play and an onside kick away from possibly losing the game" (NBC Sports, 2007). The repercussions of Westbrook's play, for fantasy owners, can be gauged by the degree of outrage it generated on the internet: "Brian Westbrook screws over fantasy owners, stops at 1-yard line," read the headline of one fan's report (*Fan IQ*, 2007); the article went on to say, "You know Runyan's fantasy opponent this week had Westbrook on his team. That's the only plausible explanation." Lest this plausible explanation appear to be deliberately silly, take a look at the transcript of the *Yahoo!* interview (Chase, 2009) about fantasy football with Jones-Drew (and note that at the time, Jones-Drew was the number one running-back in most of *Yahoo!*'s fantasy leagues):

> JONES-DREW: When running these long runs, in the back of my mind, I'm like, I have to score, this is fantasy, these are fantasy points.
>
> YAHOO: I'm so happy to hear you say that, because finally, I feel like I have peace of mind now.
>
> JONES-DREW: You have to, 'cause, I mean, football is football, but pride comes into it, you know, pride comes into it. So you have to – when you get, you know, you get there and you hit a wall, and it's two yards to the end zone you gotta drive, fantasy is what gives you that extra drive.
>
> YAHOO: I remember Brian Westbrook –
>
> JONES-DREW: – took a knee! (Shakes head.)

In one sense Jones-Drew's remarks about the power of fantasy are grounded firmly in the

real world, insofar as the outcome of every player's contract negotiations depends on his or her
individual statistics. Yet for sports fans who follow
"real" teams rather than fantasy teams (for the
record, I have never participated in a fantasy
league), all this talk of the importance of fantasy
stats – no matter how facetious it may be – sounds
ridiculous. For people who aren't sports fans, it
probably sounds insane. But there is no question
that fantasy leagues represent an important
development in sports fandom. Not only do they
expand the reach of the real leagues, as well as the
sports/entertainment media apparatus, by inducing fans to follow players' movements from the
moment they are drafted; they also render
fandom more rhizomatic, by breaking up local
and regional allegiances and requiring "owners"
to follow recaps and box scores from teams in
remote cities. In this respect, fantasy leagues have
abetted – and, in turn, have been abetted by –
those aspects of the expanded sports/entertain-
ment media apparatus that allow fans to follow
individual players on remote teams, from the
internet to cable packages (such as NHL Center
Ice and NFL Sunday Ticket) that offer fans a
chance to see nearly every game on the league
schedule.

Furthermore, as every fan knows, the days are
long gone when a star player would spend his
entire career with one team; professional players
are now so mobile that even a reasonably successful team experiences enormous personnel turnover. When the Florida Marlins won the baseball
World Series in 2003, their roster included only
one player – Luis Castillo – who had played for
the Marlins in their previous World Series victory
only six years earlier. In the major professional
North American sports, then, the greatest continuity most fans experience with any individual
franchise is their relationship with other fans – a
feature that professional-sports fandom now
shares with sports like college football and basketball, where of course rosters are in constant
flux. Fantasy leagues would seem to disperse the
affections of fandom still further, allowing fans to
maintain rooting interests in their local franchises while hoping, watching out of the corners
of their eyes, that "their" players on other teams
do well – so that, say, a San Diego Chargers fan
watching his team beat Philadelphia can nevertheless care whether or not Maurice Jones-Drew

takes a knee in a stadium in the swamps of New
Jersey.

As Steven G. Hill and Chang Wan Woo (2011:
86) noted, "despite widespread participation by
Americans and potential for even more dramatic
growth worldwide, the fantasy-sports phenomenon has received scant attention from communication scholars or other academic researchers."
Hill and Woo, however, focus their research on 13
(all male) leaders in the fantasy sports industry,
concluding that "on the whole, interviewees felt
that research conducted on behalf of two trade
associations in particular – the Fantasy Sports
Trade Association and the Fantasy Sports Association – had produced a valuable set of demographic and consumer-spending information for
the industry" (p. 97). By contrast, in their 2007
essay, "Types of fantasy sports users and their
motivations," Lee K. Farquhar and Robert Meeds
conducted a fan-centered, uses-and-gratifications
study that interviewed 42 students, 38 male and
four female "which," they note, "is similar to the
male–female participation rates reported by
the Fantasy Sports Trade Association" (2007:
1212), from a large Midwestern university in the
United States.

Farquhar and Meeds employed Q-methodology
to classify their interviewees as "casual," "skilled,"
"isolationist thrill-seekers," "trash-talkers," and
"formatives" (neophytes), and they concluded
that their subjects "were either highly involved
and enjoyed the statistics, knowing that they out-
smarted those who did not win, or they were less
involved and sought the thrill of victory and subsequent bragging rights" (2007: 1224). Farquhar
and Meeds open fascinating avenues for understanding fantasy sports from the perspective
of the fantasy players themselves. But I am less
interested in individual fans' motivations for
participating in fantasy sports than I am in two
other questions: (1) how does fantasy fandom
reshape sports fandom more generally? (2) What
about the possibility that fantasy sports are
simply a massive waste of time?

False Sports Consciousness

ESPN television now includes, as part of its
sports-media empire, statistics and "crawls" tai-
lored specifically to fantasy leagues; likewise, for

the major North American team sports, the individual player webpages on *CBSSports.com* offer (in this order) "player updates," "injury reports," and "fantasy analysis." On *NBCSports.com*, "fantasy" appears in the dropdown boxes for the NFL, NBA, NHL, and MLB just ahead of "scores" and "standings." But I want to resist the temptation to suggest that fantasy leagues are driven by corporate media conglomerates. They may be *enabled* by corporate media conglomerates, fueled by the internet, and warmly embraced by sports entrepreneurs, but fantasy leagues were created, as were many other aspects of contemporary sports fandom, by fans themselves. This seems a simple enough proposition, but I offer it as a companion and a challenge to the common leftish dismissal of sports, in which sports are the quintessential bread-and-circuses nonsense that keep the general populace content and compliant. In Noam Chomsky's discussion of the subject in the film *Manufacturing Consent*, to take a deservedly famous example, sports are a convenient way to keep the masses distracted and disempowered:

> Take, say, sports – that's another crucial example of the indoctrination system, in my view. For one thing because it – you know, it offers people something to pay attention to that's of no importance. [*audience laughs*] That keeps them from worrying about [*applause*] keeps them from worrying about things that matter to their lives that they might have some idea of doing something about. And in fact it's striking to see the intelligence that's used by ordinary people in [discussions of] sports [as opposed to political and social issues]. I mean, you listen to radio stations where people call in – they have the most exotic information [*more laughter*] and understanding about all kind of arcane issues. And the press undoubtedly does a lot with this.
>
> You know, I remember in high school, already I was pretty old. I suddenly asked myself at one point, why do I care if my high school team wins the football game? [*laughter*] I mean, I don't know anybody on the team, you know? [*audience roars*] I mean, they have nothing to do with me, I mean, why I am cheering for my team? It doesn't mean any – it doesn't make sense. But the point is, it does make sense: it's a way of building up irrational attitudes of submission to authority, and group cohesion behind leadership

> elements – in fact, it's training in irrational jingoism. That's also a feature of competitive sports. I think if you look closely at these things, I think, typically, they do have functions, and that's why energy is devoted to supporting them and creating a basis for them and advertisers are willing to pay for them and so on. (Chomsky, 2010)[1]

Chomsky's delivery is deadpan, almost Woody Allen, and the laughter and applause he elicits suggests that he knows his audience well. But notably, he does not attempt to account for why it is that ordinary people seem so intelligent when discussing sports. Nor is it clear, more broadly, why they would seem to participate so eagerly in their indoctrination – though one might suggest that indoctrination works especially well when people participate eagerly in it; that argument can never be refuted, because every demurral from it must surely be a confirmation of it. All one needs to know is that (1) people are induced to care about something of no importance, and (2) the real object of the game is training in irrational jingoism and irrational attitudes of submission to authority. That doubtless explains why nothing of consequence to the history of race in the United States ever took place in a sporting venue, and it accounts for the inability of C.L.R. James to say anything of social significance about cricket.

Chomsky is not an outlier in this respect; on the contrary, he is one of the more eloquent spokesmen for this strain of thought on the left. Especially among intellectuals (who are, I suppose, demographically less likely to have been friends with the guys on their high-school football teams), this attitude of mystified bemusement about sports is often twinned with outright disgust and disdain. Thus Terry Eagleton's rant about the evils of soccer, published in the *Guardian* just in time for the 2010 men's World Cup finals:

> If every rightwing thinktank came up with a scheme to distract the populace from political injustice and compensate them for lives of hard labour, the solution in each case would be the same: football. No finer way of resolving the problems of capitalism has been dreamed up, bar socialism. And in the tussle between them, football is several light years ahead. . . .
>
> The sport is a matter of spectacle but, unlike trooping the colour, one that also invites the intense participation of its onlookers. Men and

women whose jobs make no intellectual demands can display astonishing erudition when recalling the game's history or dissecting individual skills. Learned disputes worthy of the ancient Greek forum fill the stands and pubs. Like Bertolt Brecht's theatre, the game turns ordinary people into experts. (Eagleton, 2010)

The Chomskian note of scorn and amazement is sounded right on cue, produced by the spectacle of ordinary people becoming experts in such trivial matters. The idea that sports might have a Brechtian function is promising – but, alas, for Eagleton soccer is very unlike Bertolt Brecht's theater in the end, because really, the game turns ordinary people into dope fiends: "football these days is the opium of the people, not to speak of their crack cocaine."

Perhaps many readers have come to expect this kind of thing from figures such as Chomsky and Eagleton. I know I have. But as a matter of fact, the text that led me to write this section of the essay came from a much less distinguished source. It was just a random pseudonymous comment on the internet, in response to an innocuous *New York Times* column by the journalist Bob Herbert. On January 1, 2010, Herbert wrote a column in which he expressed the wish that the New York Jets would meet with success during the playoffs after 40 years of ineptitude and a couple of near-misses, and expressed the certainty that they would not: "I've been fortunate enough to avoid drug addiction and alcoholism, and I gave up smoking cigarettes a very long time ago. But I am a Jets fan. And being a New York Jets football fan is an illness. So keep that in mind, and please be kind as you read this" (Herbert, 2010). For various reasons, most readers decided not to be kind. Because Herbert was the *Times'* most liberal columnist, the op-ed writer most likely to call attention to economic and social injustice, readers weighed in to chastise him for caring about sports. Many of the 186 comments that followed his column pointed out that the Jets' sorry history pales before that of the Chicago Cubs, who have not won the World Series since 1908 (if I recall correctly): "When you've enjoyed a full century of futility, you'll be in the same league as Cubs fans."[2] Those comments were, in turn, "recommended" by a handful of like-minded readers. But the most popular comment, by far (recom-

mended by 97 other readers, where the second most recommended comment drew a mere 40 approvals), was this stern dressing-down:

> Don't you get it Bob? Pro-sports teams are for profit corporations. They exist for one purpose only: to grind every penny possible out of the community they operate in. Here in Seattle, the taxpayers have spent a billion dollars on stadiums for the Mariners and The Seahawks. Ten years ago, after the voters said no to financing a new stadium for the Seattle Mariners, the state legislature passed emergency legislation to fund the stadium with tax dollars anyway. In the ten years since no other emergency legislation has been passed. Not to house the homeless, feed the hungry, or provide medical care to the children. Versions of that event play out in every community in America that "hosts" a pro-sports team. You get it on so many other issues Mr. Herbert. I am amazed that you don't see pro-sports for what they really are: a means of exploiting the community while distracting us from the exploitation we experience by corporations of every stripe.[3]

It is true that from Cleveland to Arlington to Minneapolis to New York, taxpayers get stuck with the bills for billion-dollar stadiums whose revenues remain, mysteriously, wholly private. But unfortunately, this commenter got some of the details wrong about Seattle's Safeco Field. The vote to raise public funds for the stadium occurred in 1995, the year after the Mariners had had to play a bunch of "home" games on the road after their old stadium, the Kingdome, was rendered unusable when acoustic tiles fell from its roof. Voters rejected a 0.1 percent rise in the sales tax, whereupon the state legislature passed taxes on car rentals and restaurant and tavern meals. The final cost of the stadium was US$520 million, and the Mariners picked up the US$130 million cost overrun, though not without trying to pass it off to the public first. (One might add, if one knew something about Seattle sports, that the Mariners franchise was more recently run into the ground, insult-upon-injury style, when Bill Bavasi's tenure as general manager, 2003–2008, transformed one of baseball's more successful teams into one of baseball's least successful teams, thanks entirely to Bavasi's devastatingly poor baseball judgment.) Meanwhile, Seattle's NBA franchise, the

SuperSonics, made good on their threat to leave the city, delighting the sports fans of Oklahoma when they set up shop as the Oklahoma City Thunder in 2008 and proceeded to become one of the most exciting young teams in the league. But why any of this should prevent Bob Herbert from following the New York Jets since the late 1960s is not clear.

I might as well acknowledge the obvious: athletes can be arrogant, swaggering assholes. Owners can be still worse. And to give Chomsky his due, there certainly is something arbitrary about fandom, whether it's a matter of cheering for State High against Central High on the grounds that you go to school at State, or cheering for Cleveland rather than Cincinnati because you're from Toledo rather than Dayton. But amazingly enough, *none of this is news to sports fans*, some of whom manage to enjoy watching games of high and difficult technique played spectacularly well regardless of whether we know the players personally, or whether said players are nice people, or whether the public was bilked out of a billion bucks by unscrupulous owners and corrupt public representatives. Indeed, fans are at least as likely to know the details of those deals as are non-fans. It is inconceivable that there can be a fan of the Washington Redskins who does not despise mercurial, swaggering, nickel-and-dime-chiseling owner Dan Snyder,[4] and I doubt whether there are many fans of the New York Knicks or New York Rangers who do not root for those teams *against* the incompetent management of Madison Square Garden executive chairman James Dolan. And if it is hard to understand why any liberal or leftist would enjoy a sporting event underwritten by for-profit corporations, perhaps it is hard to understand why any earnest, right-thinking person could take pleasure in art, music, or literature that was underwritten by the patronage system.

Owning the Fantasy

Fantasy baseball leagues began when a group of men (including future *New York Times* public editor Daniel Okrent and statistician Glen Waggoner, who "is commonly cited as the originator of the first fantasy sports league"; see Farquhar and Meeds, 2007: 1209) met at La Rotisserie Française restaurant in New York in 1980: the term "rotisserie baseball" persisted for many years thereafter. A predecessor fantasy form, Strat-O-Matic baseball, a tabletop game with stat cards for each player in the major leagues, began in 1963. The appeal was obvious: a game like Strat-O-Matic allows you to be your own manager. Since the statistics on the cards are based on players' actual performances each year, Strat-O-Matic players can simulate individual games in great detail, basing their decisions to pinch-hit, to bunt, to hit-and-run, and to go to the bullpen (pitchers in Strat-O-Matic tire in the late innings, just like their flesh-and-blood counterparts) on the idiosyncrasies of each individual player. Every Red Sox fan who groaned at Grady Little's infamous decision to leave Pedro Martinez on the mound in game 6 of the 2003 ALCS against the Yankees can replay the game the *right* way, by managing the team him- or herself, which certainly beats screaming helplessly at the television or gloating with *schadenfreude* at Little's subsequent firing.

It may seem to be something of a coincidence that ESPN began life in the same year those baseball fans met at La Rotisserie Française. But coincidence it was. And over the next twenty years, ESPN grew into a behemoth sports-media conglomerate; rotisserie baseball grew into fantasy leagues in every major team sport; and the internet, as the saying goes, changed everything. Together, they produced a world in which even the annual NFL combine and draft somehow became popular *televised* events, as opposed to arcana about which one reads in the remote back pages of the local paper's sports section. Finally, as I noted earlier, innovative (and lucrative) deals were devised that made "season ticket" sports packages – from the NFL and MLB to the English Premier League and international cricket – available to anyone with cable or satellite TV. Together, these developments have transformed the landscape of sports fandom, in ways that both contest and confirm the complaint that sports amount to a corporate-sponsored distraction from inequality and social injustice. Obviously, fantasy fandom is more intense, more time-consuming, and more distracting than simply watching the mid-1970s Mets on the back stoop of your house in Bayside, Queens with a six-pack of Rheingold. Fantasy leagues thus intensify Eagleton's complaint that sport "invites the intense participation of its onlookers," and depend precisely on the fact that "men and women whose jobs make no intellectual demands can display astonishing erudition when recalling the game's history or dissecting individual skills."

But then again, *every* mass-cultural production invites the intense participation of its onlookers. That is why people watch *American Idol*, and why Susan Boyle's appearance on *Britain's Got Talent* was an international phenomenon; it is why people write fanfic about Harry Potter, *Twilight*, *Star Trek*, and all the countless progeny of *Lord of the Rings*; it is why viewers will actually stay on message boards and blog comment sections while watching *Mad Men* or *The Sopranos*, to record their reactions to each episode in real time along with a virtual community of fellow-travelers. Everywhere you look, it seems, people are paying close attention to all the wrong things. They have, as Chomsky (2010) put it, "the most exotic information and understanding about all kind of arcane issues." Surely, one is asked to imagine, we would be better off if they brought all that exotic information and astonishing erudition to bear on social policy.

There are two things to be said about that (implied) desire. The first is that it may be illusory: in the United States, the rise of the political blogosphere has given a platform to any number of ordinary citizens who follow politics closely, and on the left-liberal side, I have discovered many whose insights about social policy are more acute than most of the superannuated op-ed writers for major daily newspapers; but I have also found that there is no simple correlation between enthusiasm and erudition. Many of the most widely read conservative blogs, such as Michelle Malkin's "Hot Air" and Jim Hoft's "Gateway Pundit," are mind-numbingly awful, ever ready and willing to run with any story no matter how ludicrous.[5] The second is that although every mass-cultural production invites the intense participation of its onlookers, not all those invitations are answered; many mass-cultural productions are flops, failing to draw even tepid-to-moderate participation from their onlookers. There is no way, in other words, of saying that people *would* be deeply invested in combating political injustice if only they were not distracted by sports; and among all the entertainments and distractions available to people in developed nations, it remains to be determined why people would become so invested in fantasy sports leagues rather than anything else.

As I noted above, it is not uncommon for sports fans to rail about incompetent general managers, foolish franchises, and stupid, overbearing owners. It's part of the game. Fantasy leagues give fans a rich outlet for that frustration, just as Strat-O-Matic baseball gave them the chance to manage a simulated baseball game: in the fantasy league, you are your own *general* manager, and you are your own scouting system. Is this fantasy experience of general-managerdom an illusory form of control? Of course it is. Even if you are so lucky or so skilled as to win some cash in your fantasy league, you're not pulling down a general manager's salary, and you're not really signing real players to a real team. For that matter, even though Maurice Jones-Drew also "had himself" on his fantasy team in his 2009 game against the Jets, he probably doesn't *really* rely on the power of fantasy for that "extra drive" to break through the defensive line's goal-line stand and reach the end zone. And yet, just as Jones-Drew's fantasy points represent real achievements and have consequences for contract negotiations, participants in fantasy leagues actively select and manage their fantasy teams, performing mental labor that is in turn based on those players' real achievements.

Conclusion

It is – or should be – undeniable that fantasy leagues have done a great deal to erode what Chomsky (2010) calls the "irrational jingoism" of sports. In the fantasy world, you aren't simply rooting for whatever team happens to be geographically closest to your home or affectively closest to your heart; you are pulling for a team that you yourself have selected on the basis of your astonishing erudition and command of exotic information (and on the basis of the availability of players unselected by your astonishingly erudite peers). And more generally, it is – or should be – undeniable that fantasy plays an enormous role in every aspect of human life. It may not be the secret motivation behind the feats of NFL running-backs, but it is certainly part of the reason why anybody does anything, whether they harbor utopian fantasies of establishing a single-payer healthcare system in the United States or whether they have delusional rock-n-roll fantasies of taking the world by storm on *American Idol*.

In *Dream: Re-imagining Progressive Politics in an Age of Fantasy*, Stephen Duncombe (2007) makes this point at some length, arguing that a left politics that is anchored solely in the "reality-based community" will be roughly as attractive as a diet consisting solely of oatmeal and leafy greens. Championing a wide range of alternative forms of politics, from street theater to *BUST* magazine, Duncombe audaciously makes a case even for the infamous video game *Grand Theft Auto: San Andreas*, in part because the game's interior landscape is so rich that even the most hardened gangbanger can, if s/he so desires, take a wrong turn, ignore the assigned mission, abandon the city altogether, and ride a dirt bike through a forest or take a swim in a river. Duncombe (2007: 72) draws from this the conclusion:

> if a game offers power, excitement, and the room to explore, people will play evening after evening after evening, almost regardless of the results. Perhaps the problem is not that people don't want to get involved in politics, but rather that they don't want to take part in a professionalized politics so interested in efficiency that there is no space for them, or they don't want to spend time in a political world so cramped that there's no freedom to explore and discover, to know or master. People don't get involved in politics because the process, figuratively and literally, does not involve them.

Though I remain unpersuaded that the *Grand Theft Auto* family of games offers a useful model for what game designers Katie Salen and Eric Zimmerman call "transformative play" (Duncombe, 2007: 73), I do agree that most people don't get involved in politics because politics makes no place for them. And I think it's worth entertaining the thought that inasmuch as we do live in a world of fantasy, we should take seriously the kind of play of mental labor that is also fun, of active fandom that is neither arbitrary nor jingoistic, afforded by fantasy sports leagues. They have not made fans' fantasies into reality, elevating the casual softball player to the position of third

baseman for the Los Angeles Dodgers or offering the weekend warrior a spot on the San Antonio Spurs. Fantasy sports leagues have accomplished something else entirely: by allowing and encouraging fans to create a game based entirely on the achievements of athletes, unencumbered by the bloviations of owners and the blunders of incompetent general managers, they have turned the realities of sports into the realities of a form of fantasy that can be realized by any fan.

The problem with this argument, unfortunately, is related to the problem with Duncombe's (2007) argument about *Grand Theft Auto*: if one is looking for forms of "transformative play" that elicit player interest and build grassroots (virtual) communities, one needs to acknowledge that the communities built by fantasy sports leagues are overwhelmingly – indeed, almost exclusively – made up of men. According to Hill and Woo (2011: 85), "27 million Americans now play fantasy sports – an Internet-fueled upswing from an estimated 2 million in 2000." That's an explosion of interest by any measure, but if the Fantasy Sports Trade Association's figures, as cited by Farquhar and Meeds (2007), are correct, then it's an explosion that involves roughly nine men for every woman. If fantasy leagues involve a form of fantasy that can be realized by any fan, it bears noting that most sports fans are men to begin with, and that fantasy leagues seem to intensify the male-bonding aspects of sports fandom to the point at which they might seem to serve as He-Man Women Haters Clubs.

Such is the argument of Nickolas W. Davis and Margaret Carlisle-Duncan, whose study of three fantasy sports participants concluded that "participants did indeed use fantasy sport participation as a means of affirming their masculinity" and that "fantasy sport is another way in which men symbolically bolster their superiority over women in the sport domain" (2006: 251). Certainly, 9:1 gender ratios cannot be explained away as naturally occurring phenomena, even in a domain so male-dominated as that of sport. What's especially interesting about the domination of white men in fantasy sport is that it occurs at a time when "women are challenging the sport domain" (Davis and Carlisle-Duncan, 2006: 261). The functionalist conclusion thus seems irresistible: perhaps fantasy sports leagues are a way for men to escape from a more gender-equitable sports world in which commentators and commercial advertisers seem to care about women's World Cup soccer, women's tennis, women's basketball and volleyball, and to retreat into a boys-only domain of trash talk and nut-flexing. As Davis and Carlisle-Duncan write (2006: 261):

> In many respects, fantasy sport leagues act as an "Old Boy's Club" that allows men to communally meet, bond, and redefine what it is to be masculine. Within this space, men can act like men without fear of feminization. Although on a less extreme basis, fantasy sport leagues may be compared to such movements as the Promise Keepers and the mythopoetic men's movement, insofar as they allow men the opportunity to reconstruct hegemonic masculinity in a safe environment, free from feminine influence.

These conclusions also suggest one possible answer to the question of why the number of women participants in fantasy sports leagues is so low. Although women may have as much access to computers as men as well as the requisite computer skills, the construction of the young, White, middle-class, heterosexual male domain of fantasy sport leagues creates a climate that is actively hostile to women.

I submit that it involves some interpretive strain to liken fantasy sports leagues to an explicitly patriarchal initiative launched under the aegis of Christian fundamentalism (the Promise Keepers) on the basis of a study of three male fantasy sports participants. And although it involves less interpretive strain, I am not convinced by Davis and Carlisle-Duncan's conflation of correlation with causation: "it is no surprise to the authors that fantasy sport participation has increased dramatically since the late 1990s, which Kusz (2001) suggests spawned the beginning of 'White male backlash politics'" (2006: 391). But then, one reason I am not convinced by this argument is that I see white men as having engaged in backlash long before the late 1990s, all the way back to the days when Bobby Riggs took it upon himself to try to delegitimate women's tennis.

That said, Davis and Carlisle-Duncan are undoubtedly right to claim that the combination of fantasy sport and internet culture makes for an especially hostile environment for female fans, who generally do not place as much importance on detailed knowledge of sports minutiae and who generally do not imagine themselves as players, managers, general managers, or owners:

> When women are recruited to participate in fantasy sports leagues, it is because there are not enough men to fill out the ranks; thus, they are seen as placeholders for men, who are judged to be far more knowledgeable. In addition, sports in which women have an advantage over men (i.e., sports stressing agility and long-term endurance) are absent from fantasy leagues. It's even possible that some women also find the prospect of owning and managing a professional sports team so unimaginable (given the low number of female owners and managers in actuality) that they cannot engage with it. (2006: 261)

Davis and Carlisle-Duncan interviewed no women for their study, so I decided to test their argument with an even smaller sample – my oldest son, Nicholas, and his girlfriend Rachel, both 27. Nick is an enthusiastic participant in fantasy sports, and does not mind that his father's curiosity about them is purely intellectual (in the sense that I have no interest in joining a fantasy league); he readily (if a bit sheepishly) agreed with the argument that few women participate in fantasy sports, and are usually recruited as placeholders or as girlfriends of league members – very clearly as second-class citizens in the masculine world of sports knowledge and its strategic deployment. But he insisted – and Rachel confirmed – that women of their cohort (white, twenty-something, college-educated, professional) regard fantasy sports with disdain, as a form of sports fandom that drains sport of its intrinsic interest (in the playing of real games with real objects and real bodies) and turns it into another kind of pointless video game like *Grand Theft Auto* or *Call of Duty*.

If that is true – and I hope it is at least two-thirds as true as the findings of Davis and Carlisle-Duncan – then it poses problems both for their argument and for mine. On the one hand, it confirms their sense that fantasy sports are a domain in which men can perform rituals of masculinity that are effectively hostile to women and to women's sports; but on the other hand, if men are using fantasy sports (deliberately or not) as a means of establishing hegemony over sports fandom, it would seem to be a kind of hegemony most women are not interested in contesting. To put that another way: in the United States, most women with an interest in sports know the value of Title IX of the Education Amendments of 1972, which barred discrimination in "any education program or activity receiving Federal financial assistance" and transformed women's high-school and collegiate sports. For American women, Title IX seems like a serious (and, to date, largely successful) challenge to male domination of scholastic sports: it matters *on the field*, so to speak, in the sense that it changed the rules for who could play the game(s). By contrast, male hegemony over fantasy sports seems more like the idea of "sport" held by Chomsky and Eagleton – just not worth the time and trouble. This in turn poses problems for my suggestion that it's worth exam-

ining the kind of "fun" mental labor involved in fantasy sports, for it raises the possibility that if we want to understand why people engage in play and feel that politics makes no place for them, we also have to account for why women sense that *this* form of play makes no place for *them*. Davis and Carlisle-Duncan are very likely correct to surmise that "some women also find the prospect of owning and managing a professional sports team so unimaginable (given the low number of female owners and managers in actuality) that they cannot engage with it"; the question remains whether, in the foreseeable future, this is a form of fantasy female sports fans will find realistic enough to be meaningful, and whether the boy-culture of fantasy sports will be challenged or transformed as a result.

Notes

1 *Manufacturing Consent: Noam Chomsky and the Media*, dir. Mark Achbar and Peter Wintonick, perf. Noam Chomsky, Edward S. Herman (Humanist Broadcasting Foundation, 1992). The relevant excerpt from the film is available online at YouTube: http://www.youtube.com/watch?v=Vz1nIHv6P6Q, accessed January 15, 2013.
2 "Dan S.," comment on Herbert, January 2, 2010.
3 "Proxxy," comment on Herbert, January 2, 2010.
4 Famous for, among other things, selling fans year-old packages of peanuts and charging US$3,000 for "Dream Seats" located at field level behind the players on the sidelines, where the view of the field

consists of players' backs (McKenna, 2010), as the Oklahoma City Thunder started in 2008 and proceeded to become one of the most exciting young teams in the league, reaching the NBA finals in 2012.
5 Malkin is famous for insisting that Rachael Ray's scarf, in an advertisement for Dunkin Donuts, is really a keffiyeh that signals support for Islamism (MSBNC, 2008); Hoft, similarly, claimed that the logo of the 2010 Nuclear Safety Summit, which was based on the Rutherford–Bohr model of the atom, was really an Islamic crescent (Dimiero, 2010).

References

Chase, C. (2009) "Maurice Jones-Drew takes a knee, apologizes to fantasy owners." *Yahoo! Sports Shutdown Corner*, November 15, http://sports.yahoo.com/nfl/blog/shutdown_corner/post/Maurice-Jones-Drew-takes-a-knee-apologizes-to-f?urn=nfl-202651, accessed January 18, 2013.

Chomsky, N. (2010) "Excerpts from *Manufacturing Consent*: Noam Chomsky interviewed by various interviewers." *Chomsky.info*, http://www.chomsky.info/interviews/1992----02.htm, accessed January 18, 2013.

Davis, N.W. and Carlisle-Duncan, M. (2006) "Sports knowledge is power: Reinforcing masculine privilege through fantasy sport league participation." *Journal of Sport & Social Issues*, 30 (3): 244–264.

Dimiero, B. (2010) "Jim Hoft: Dumbest man on the internet?" *Media Matters for America* September 21, http://mediamatters.org/blog/201009210034, accessed December 17, 2010.

Duncombe, S. (2007) *Dream: Re-imagining Progressive Politics in an Age of Fantasy*. New York: New Press.

Eagleton, T. (2010) "Football: A dear friend to capitalism." *Guardian*, June 15, http://www.guardian.co.uk/commentisfree/2010/jun/15/football-socialism-crack-cocaine-people, accessed December 17, 2012.

Fan IQ (2007) "Brian Westbrook screws over fantasy owners, stops at 1-yard line." *Fan IQ*, December 16, at http://www.faniq.com/blog/Video-Brian-Westbrook-Screws-Over-Over-Fantasy-Owners-Stops-

At-1yard-Line-Blog-5398, accessed December 17, 2012.

Farquhar, L.K. and Meeds, R. (2007) "Types of fantasy sports users and their motivations." *Journal of Computer-Mediated Communication*, 12 (4): 1208–1228.

The Gentlemen's League (2009) Episode: Max vs. Jerry, November 13, http://sports.yahoo.com/video/player/fnfl/16637286#fnfl/16637286, accessed January 18, 2013.

Herbert, B. (2010) "The miracle that never happens." *New York Times*, January 1, http://www.nytimes.com/2010/01/02/opinion/02herbert.html, accessed January 15, 2013.

Hill, S.G. and Woo, C.W. (2011) "New media, new audiences, and new questions: Exploring a communication research agenda for fantasy sports." *Journal of Sports Media*, 6 (1): 85–114.

Kusz, K.W. (2001). "'I want to be the minority': The politics of youthful white masculinities in sport and popular culture in 1990s America." *Journal of Sport & Social Issues*, 25 (4): 390–416.

McKenna, D. (2010) "The cranky Redskins fan's guide to Dan Snyder." *Washington City Paper*, November 19, http://www.washingtoncitypaper.com/articles/40063/the-cranky-redskins-fans-guide-to-dan-snyder/, accessed December 17, 2012.

MSNBC (2008) "Rachael Ray ad pulled as pundit sees terror link." *MSNBC.com*, May 29, http://www.msnbc.msn.com/id/24860437/ns/business-retail/t/rachael-ray-ad-pulled-pundit-sees-terror-link/, accessed December 17, 2012.

NBC Sports (2007) "Who knew? Westbrook lauded for not scoring." *NBC Sports.com*, December 17, http://nbcsports.msnbc.com/id/22301082, accessed December 17, 2012.

Waszak, D., Jr. (2009) "Jets lose to Jags 24–22; Playoff hopes fade: Scobee's FG as time expires lifts Jags over Jets." *NBC Sports*, November 16, http://www.nbcnewyork.com/news/sports/Jets-Get-Pawed-By-Jags-24-22-70149437.html, accessed January 18, 2013.

Further Reading

Davis, N.W. and Carlisle-Duncan, M. (2006) "Sports knowledge is power: Reinforcing masculine privilege through fantasy sport league participation." *Journal of Sport & Social Issues*, 30 (3): 244–264.

Farquhar, L.K. and Meeds, R. (2007) "Types of fantasy sports users and their motivations." *Journal of Computer-Mediated Communication*, 12 (4): 1208–1228.

Hill, S.G. and Woo, C.W. (2011) "New media, new audiences, and new questions: Exploring a communication research agenda for fantasy sports." *Journal of Sports Media*, 6 (1): 85–114.

Zirin, D. (2012) *Bad Sports: How Owners Are Ruining the Games We Love*, New York: Scribner.

15

Sport, Palestine, and Israel

Tamir Sorek

Introduction

The sport dynamics in Palestine/Israel are characterized by an interesting paradox. Among both the Zionist and Palestinian national movements, institutional sport has historically emerged as a nationalist project aimed to bridge intra-national cultural/communal differences and to rehabilitate a collective self-image which suffered from humiliation and subjugation. However, the sport sphere in Israel/Palestine has rarely become an explicit ethno-national battleground. It has not provided unforgettable moments of national conflict, of the kind provided by India–Pakistan cricket, by the United States–Soviet Union hockey games during the Cold War, or by soccer games in the Basque and the Catalan regions in Spain.

There are two reasons for that; one is self-evident, and the other needs much more elaboration and is the focus of this chapter. The obvious reason is that because the level of hostility and mutual denial between Israelis and Palestinians is so strong, sport encounters between formal representatives of the two sides have been uncommon. The Israeli–Palestinian conflict is popularly seen by both sides as a total and a zero-sum conflict, and for many years the mere recognition of

the legitimacy of the other's collective identity has been out of question. So far, the only time when official representatives of the State of Israel and the Palestinian national movement have met in the sport sphere was in the 1972 summer Olympic Games in Munich, when members of the Israeli Olympic team were taken hostage and eventually executed by Black September, an organization affiliated with the Palestine Liberation Organization (PLO).

In one context Jews and Arabs do meet each other on a regular basis. Jewish and Arab Palestinian citizens of Israel (the latter number about 1.3 million people, 17 percent of Israeli citizens) do share the same sport sphere. In this context, however, another dimension to the paradox is added. The more "warlike" and masculinist the sport is, the more Arabs in Israel are represented and also successful in it. One would expect that overrepresentation and success of a discriminated minority in combative sports would lead to the emergence of figures like the boxer Muhammad Ali, an opinionated and vocal athlete who used his status to promote political protest (Saeed, 2002). But this is not the case. A unique combination of social, political, and economic forces has "depoliticized" Arab–Jewish athletic

A Companion to Sport, First Edition. Edited by David L. Andrews and Ben Carrington.
© 2013 Blackwell Publishing Ltd. Published 2013 by Blackwell Publishing Ltd.

encounters within Israel and partly isolated them from the Israeli–Palestinian conflict. The nationalist connotations are blurred, and rarely do these encounters become an explicit Israeli–Palestinian battleground. In this chapter I follow the historical development which has led to this depoliticization and suggest a solution to the double-layered paradox.

The Gramsci-inspired literature in the sociology of sport has highlighted the dialectic of sport as a political sphere. Sport is seen as a contested terrain, which can be potentially used by both the state and by subjugated groups to promote their interests (Hargreaves, 1986; Hartmann, 2000; McKay, 1991; Sugden and Bairner, 1993). This dialectic can also be found in the case of sport among the Palestinian citizens of Israel. As a general tendency, however, the potential for sport to be a stage of protest and resistance has rarely materialized.

In order to understand the political role of sport in Israel/Palestine, one should first conceptualize the conflict itself, a task which usually exposes the political sympathy or affiliation of the scholar. In this chapter, I refer to this conflict as a struggle of a native population against a settler-immigrant movement and at the same time a struggle between two national movements. From this point of view, Zionism is both a national movement (an aspect that is evident from its discourse and practices aimed to mobilize national identification among Jews) and a colonial movement (an aspect which is evident from its political practices toward the native population of Palestine). Sport, as an institution that has been used both to mobilize national identification (Ehn, 1989; Houlihan, 1997; Lever, 1983) as well as to stabilize and legitimize colonial control (Jacob, 2005; Mahlmann, 1988; Mandle, 1979; Mangan, 2001; Nauright, 1997; Sugden and Bairner, 1993) is a sphere in the conflict that is usually underestimated.

Before dealing with the above-mentioned paradox we need first to briefly describe the essence of the conflict with a focus on the development of sport until 1948. Since 1948 the Palestinians have been dispersed in different countries and lived under different political conditions and therefore the pre-1948 outline is followed by a separate discussion for each of these contexts. The political role of sport is most evident in the context where Jewish Israelis and Arab Palestinian citizens of Israel do encounter each other regularly in the sport field, and therefore a more detailed analysis is dedicated to the ways sport has shaped and reflected the relations between Jewish and Arab citizens of Israel. Finally, I evaluate the possible contribution of sport for Israeli–Palestinian reconciliation.

Sport in Zionism and the Palestinian National Movement

"The conflict" is an historical clash between the Zionist movement and the Palestinian people. Respectively, both Zionism and the Palestinian national movement have been shaped to a large extent as a reaction to collective existential threats and collective humiliations. For Jews as a discriminated and persecuted minority in Europe and the Arab Palestinians as a colonized population, sport has been a way to rehabilitate their collective self image and especially to redeem threatened manhood through nationalism.[1]

The Zionist movement was a European Jewish reaction to the emergence of ethnic national movements in Europe in the nineteenth century. The discourse of ethnic nationalism emphasizes cultural homogeneity and the Jews found themselves frequently as the "ultimate other" of these movements and suffered persecutions. Having been rejected by the European nations, some Jews were looking for alternatives such as emigrating to the New World or adopting universalist ideologies like Marxism. At the end of the nineteenth century a minority was attracted by the idea that Jewish people should establish themselves as a separate nation and, following the emerging European model, to set up a national state of their own – a solution that became known as Zionism.

At least in Western Europe, this new development was accompanied by a growing interest in sport, as a tool for developing national consciousness. As several scholars of Zionism and sexuality have shown, the way in which early Zionist leaders saw the body of the European Jewish man reflected a remarkable internalization of contemporary anti-semitic stereotypes and pseudo-scientific literature, which depicted the Jewish male body as inferior and drew similarities between the physiology of Jewish men and female bodies (Biale, 1992; Boyarin, 2000). Therefore, Zionism strove to redeem the Jewish man from his "femininity" by "converting" him into "an Aryan man." The "sportization" of the Jew was seen as a cure to his non-masculine character. In his extensively quoted speech from 1898, the Zionist leader, Dr Max Nordau, called for the establishment of a "Muscular Jewry" and emphasized the link between national redemption and masculine rehabilitation: "We shall develop a wide chest, strong limbs, a courageous look – we will become a people of valor. Sport is educationally significant to us, the Jews, for not only do we have to recover physically, but also spiritually" (Israel and Forman, 1994). The names given to Zionist sports clubs, for example, reflected the yearning for mythological muscular warriors found in the Jewish ancient past: for example Maccabi, Shimshon (Samson), Bar-Kokhba, and so on (Kaufman and Bar-Eli, 2005: 180).

Although Zionist thinkers considered several territorial options for gathering Jews to establish their own state, traditional and religious motives drew the Zionist movement to Palestine (the "Land of Israel" in Jewish tradition). At the turn of the twentieth century, Palestine had a population of around 700,000, the great majority of which was Muslim Arab. Christian Arabs numbered around 72,000 and Jews around 60,000 (Campos, 2010: 12–13).

The Arab national movement appeared almost at the same time as the Zionist movement, initially confronting the Ottoman empire and later the colonial regimes founded in the region at the end of World War I. In 1917 the British empire promised to support the Zionist movement's efforts to establish a national home for the Jewish people in Palestine. The British conquered the country shortly after this, and initially enabled Jewish immigration to Palestine. The Zionist immigrants and their declared plan to establish a Jewish homeland in Palestine alarmed the native Arab population and gradually led to a direct resistance. As a reaction to the Zionist immigration and land purchase, a separate Arab Palestinian national movement emerged (Khalidi, 1997; Kimmerling and Migdal, 1993; Muslih, 1988; Porath, 1974).

The British authorities noticed the Arab frustration, and their initial sport policy was shaped by it. Sports were considered by the Mandatory government as a mechanism that might promote inter-ethnic cooperation between Jews and Arabs (Ben Porat, 2001) and invited both Arabs and Jews to join sports competitions they organized. Arab and Jewish athletes did play in the same associations during the 1920s but separated in the early 1930s, a separation which served the nationalist agenda of both sides. For both Zionists and Arab Palestinians, sports organization at this point served as an organizational as well as symbolic platform, which was especially important for a stateless national movement.

The Arab Palestinian sport movement in the 1930s and 1940s was an integral part of the nationalist movement (Sorek, 2007). The constitution of the Arab Palestinian Sport Association established in 1944, for example, explicitly prohibited the participation of Jewish players. The Zionist football association (officially named Palestine Football Association) kept inviting Arab clubs to join its ranks, in order to keep its recognition by FIFA as the official representative association of the country. Like the Zionist sport movement, the nationalist-masculinist character of the Palestinian sport movement was exemplified through youth sports teams that were named after historically renowned Muslim and Arab military commanders, such as Khaled Ibn al-Walid and Sallah al-Din al-Ayubi. The rhetoric of the newly born Arabic-language sports media frequently emphasized the militaristic functions and meanings of sports.

Furthermore, the sport–militarism connection on both sides went beyond simple rhetoric. The physical education of the Arab and Jewish youth was intended to train the young generation for combat. Among the Jews, in 1939, following the Arab Great Revolt,[2] the National Committee established the Department for Physical Training, with the explicit aim of training Jewish youth to protect settlements. This department had significant personal and organizational overlap with the existing Jewish sport infrastructure in Palestine.[3] Among the Arabs, some sport clubs in the mid-1940s were used to prepare Arab youth for a military conflict with the Zionists (Levenberg, 1993: 126–154).

As the conflict intensified in the region, and with the resounding impact of the Holocaust of European Jewry, the United Nations decided in 1947 to divide the country into two states, Jewish and Arab. Most of the Zionist movement accepted the partition resolution, convinced that the crucial issue was to establish a firm foundation for Jewish sovereignty. The Arabs, on their part, could not understand why they should pay the price for crimes committed against the Jews by Europeans, and violently objected to the plan. In the subsequent 1948 war, Palestinians lost their modern urban centers on the coast, hundreds of villages were destroyed, and around 750,000 Palestinians were uprooted, became refugees, and were not allowed to return to their home (Morris, 1987). This series of events is remembered by the Palestinians as the *Nakbah* (catastrophe) and it is the central pillar of contemporary Palestinian national narrative. The State of Israel was established in May 1948 and during the war expanded its territory to 78 percent of Mandatory Palestine.

The 1948 war created a new sociopolitical reality with far-reaching implications on sports institutions. The effect of the war on Palestinian sport (as on Palestinian society generally) was devastating. In 1947 dozens of Arab Palestinian sports clubs were active, most of them in cities. The large-scale destruction of the war and the forced exile of urban elites brought an end to almost all the sports clubs that flourished in the territory that became Israel. Following the war, the Palestinians were divided and lived under different sovereignties: Jordanian, Egyptian, Israeli, Lebanese, and Syrian. Their sporting activities in the first two decades after 1948 reflected the interests and strategies of the different governments who controlled their lives. The level and form of inclusion/exclusion of Palestinians in the sport organizations in every country has been a very good indicator for their status of (or lack of) citizenship.

Palestinian refugees, Jordan granted citizenship to most of them and implemented a "Jordanization policy." As a result, the Jordanian policy toward sports also derived from aspirations to promote cultural unity after the drastic demographic transformation following the 1948 war (Khalifeh, 1986). Palestinian refugees were prevented from reorganizing sports clubs with a potent Palestinian character (Sayigh, 1997: 52) but were encouraged to integrate into the Jordanian sports organization. These efforts intensified after "Black September," the Jordanian–Palestinian civil war in 1970, as Jordanian–Palestinian soccer encounters became highly tensioned and sometimes violent (Brand, 1991: 183; Massad, 2001: 256–257). It is unclear to what extent this policy was successful in the field of sport, but the existing evidence suggests that Palestinians in Jordan tend to express collective national pride in the soccer sphere, through their flagship team, al-Wihdat (Tuastad, 1997).

Only about a quarter of the 100,000 Palestinian refugees who arrived in Lebanon received citizenship. On the one hand, the Palestinians in the refugee camps were not allowed to join the Lebanese sports organization. On the other hand, with severe restrictions on their employment, housing, and movement, and a prohibition on establishing independent organizations in the camps, they were very limited in developing their own sports infrastructure. It was not until 1969 that Palestinians were allowed to establish institutions and organizations to serve refugees, following the Cairo agreement.[4] As a result of this agreement, the PLO embarked on a campaign to establish a number of such institutions and organizations, including sports clubs (PRRN, 2007). However, most of the 23 sports clubs that existed in 2001 did not have any playgrounds or proper coaches.

Palestinian Sports under Jordanian and Lebanese Rule

Following the 1948 war, about 380,000 Palestinian refugees settled in the West Bank and about 70,000 arrived on the eastern bank of the Jordan river, both of which areas were then under Jordanian control (Jordan officially annexed the West Bank in 1950 and lost it to Israel during the 1967 war). Unlike other countries that absorbed the

Sports and Arab–Jewish Relations in Israel

After the 1948 war, approximately 160,000 Palestinians remained under Israeli rule and today they number about one-sixth of Israeli citizens. This is the only context where Jews and Arabs have shared the same sport sphere since 1948. This context, therefore, is the most interesting for a sociological examination of sport in the conflict, since it provides an important field for investigating the political role of sports.

As Palestinians by their ethno-national identification and Israelis by citizenship, the Palestinians in Israel face persistent predicaments regarding their sociopolitical location and self-presentation for several interrelated reasons. First, historically, Israel as a Jewish state was established in 1948 on the ruins of the local Palestinian society – and this historical association is the major anchor of Palestinians' collective memory and national identity. This zero-sum-game narrative makes the holding of both self-identifications, Palestinian and Israeli, extremely challenging; therefore, diverse strategies have been developed to solve the dissonance (Bishara, 1999). Second, Palestinians in Israel face contradictory expectations on the part of Israeli Jews and by Palestinians outside Israel. While their Arab Palestinian identity places them in the position of "an enemy within" for the Jewish majority, they are simultaneously considered suspicious – "Israelified Arabs" – by Palestinians outside Israel. Third, but no less important, as Arab citizens in a state that defines itself as Jewish, they suffer from prolonged forms of discriminatory policies in diverse spheres (Haider, Awad, and Mahmoud, 2010). They are systematically excluded from the major political, economic, and social centers of power in the state, their culture and language hold an inferior status in Israeli public life, and they are alienated from the exclusivist Jewish Zionist symbols of the state. At the same time, they do not see any realistic political alternative to the current situation. A viable Palestinian state does not exist, and a return of the Palestinian refugees which will transform the demographic balance in their favor is unlikely to occur. In addition, with all the above-mentioned deficiencies they still enjoy more political freedom and economic opportunities than any other Palestinian group in the Middle East (i.e., refugees in several countries and Palestinians in the West Bank and the Gaza Strip) and even than most Arab citizens in neighboring countries. These contradictions further complicate questions of belonging and identification. This multidimensional complexity must be taken into consideration when we analyze Arab sports in Israel.

A cursory examination of the involvement of the Arab Palestinian citizens of Israel in the sport sphere might create the impression that sport is a site of ethno-national protest. This is because the branches of sports in which Arabs have achieved significant presence and success are those sports that legitimize a higher level of aggression toward the opponent. Furthermore, these are the exact same sports that the Israeli authorities initially intended to discourage Arabs from playing, out of concern that they would serve as a platform for the development of national consciousness (Sorek, 2007).

Modern sport is based on maintaining a delicate balance between the pleasurable "de-controlling" of human feelings of excitement on the one hand and the maintenance of a set of checks and balances to keep those emotions under control (Elias and Scotson, 1994). Sports allow and legitimize the expression of aggression (de-controlling), and at the same time sports regulate that aggression by a set of previously agreed rules. In ethno-national conflicts, and especially when these conflicts involve severe forms of discrimination or are embedded in colonial and postcolonial contexts, this dialectic of modern sports is translated into a tension between the potential of sports to serve as a platform for anticolonial, ethnic, or national pride and the pacifying potential of the ethnically blind discourse, which makes sports a potential sphere of integration and suspension of protest. Different sports are located differently on this controlling/de-controlling continuum. As a rule of thumb, in the State of Israel the closer a sport is to the de-controlling edge of the continuum, the higher the presence of and success of Arab citizens in it.

The two most popular sports in Israel, basketball and soccer, illustrate well this phenomenon. Basketball was among the games the Israeli military government (in effect between 1948 and 1966) intended initially to encourage (together with volleyball, track and field, and table tennis), while soccer was "not recommended" (together with wrestling, boxing, weightlifting). From the governmental point of view, the "dangerous sports" included combative and warlike sports – exactly those sports which were the most desired for oppressed men who needed them to compensate for their political subordination (women as rebels were probably less of a concern).

This policy, if it was ever seriously implemented, completely failed. In the long term, it is exactly in the "dangerous sports" where Arab men became extremely overrepresented, or even gained complete dominance. Arab men in Israel are underrepresented and unsuccessful in basketball. An Arab team has never played in the first division, the Israeli national team has never included an Arab player, and the total number of Arab men teams officially registered in the Israeli basketball union is only 24 (out of 228 teams, around 11 percent).[5]

Soccer, however, represents the opposite pole. More than one-third of the men's soccer teams playing in the Israeli Football Association represent Arab towns, villages, or neighborhoods. Furthermore, over the last decade Arab teams have gained a stable presence in the first division and in 2004 an Arab team, Ittihad Abna Sakhnin, won the Israel State Cup and represented Israel in Europe in the following season. Interestingly, this tendency is reversed among women. Arab women are overrepresented in basketball (21 out of 110 teams, or 19 percent),[6] and underrepresented in soccer (one team out of 17, or 6 percent).[7] These invert tendencies might represent the masculine image of soccer in Israel as opposed to the more gender neutral image of basketball and the differential implications of these images on those who hold the political power as opposed to the subjugated and colonized minority.

Arab men are overrepresented as well in other sports, which were "not recommended" for Arabs by the Israeli government in the early 1960s. As early as 1959, an Arab weightlifter 'Ali Khudruj from Acre, was the first Arab athlete to win an Israeli national championship. In subsequent years, 'Ali and his brothers 'Adnan and Muhsin, dominated Israeli weightlifting. The Arab domination in weightlifting diminished later with the influx of immigration from the Soviet Union, but it still exists in other "masculinist" sports. For example, among the 57 Israelis who held a black belt in traditional karate in 2009, 23 (40 percent) were Arabs.[8]

But the most striking example is boxing, a sport located on the edge of the controlling/decontrolling of violence spectrum since it literally legitimizes punching the opponent in the face. Starting in the 1980s, Arabs gained complete domination in boxing in terms of participation, achievements, and representation in administrative positions. In the 2005 championships, for example among the 460 participants more than half (234) came from clubs representing Arab towns, in addition to 75 (16 percent) which came from clubs representing mixed towns and cities.[9] Furthermore, between the years 2001 and 2004, 40 out of 52 (77 percent) championship titles for male seniors were won by Arab boxers.[10] The Israeli Boxing Association is the only sport association whose offices are located in an Arab town, which usually organizes its major competitions in Arab towns, and which has Arabs as chair and general director.

The intriguing aspect of this overrepresentation in physically violent sports is that it is rarely translated into explicit expressions of political protest or ethno-national confrontations. Palestinian flags are an extremely rare vision in the Israeli boxing sphere. Active Arab boxers avoid any Palestinian nationalist statement and the Arab administration of the Israeli Boxing Association maintains an Israeli patriotic tone in the media (Sorek, 2009). The question is, if Arab citizens are attracted to these physically intense sports, why are articulations of ethno-national protest absent from the sports sphere?

Modernity and Sport: Muting the Protest

With the establishment of the State of Israel sport activities were seen by the state authorities as a tool for forging an Israeli national identity, enhancing the ties between Israel and the Jewish diaspora, and promoting Israel's image in the world (Harif, 2011). Sport had the potential to overcome a fundamental paradox in the Zionist ideology: the founding fathers of this movement and the leading political parties have been secular, and at a certain point even anti-religious with the explicit aim of secularizing Judaism (Avineri, 1981), but the most stable common ground for Jews from different continents and cultures was religion. This tension intensified during the first decade of the state's existence while the Jewish demographic in the country drastically changed with the absorption of mass Jewish immigration from Muslim countries, an immigration which ended the almost exclusive European character of the Jewish population in the country until that time. Promoting national pride through sport was one strategy of the secular elite to bridge the cultural differences between Jews while bypassing the religious–secular question.

The Arab Palestinians who remained under Israeli rule after the 1948 war and received a nominal Israeli citizenship were not the target audience of the efforts to shape an Israeli national identity. In fact, during the first decade of the State of Israel it is difficult to identify a coherent policy toward this population (Bauml, 2001; Robinson, 2005), except a suspicion and fear that was expressed in the imposition of a strict military rule which severely curtailed their freedom of movement, speech, and livelihood (Jiryis, 1969; Lustick, 1980). The humiliation of Arab men who were defeated in the war was multiplied by the loss of significant tracts of their land, which before 1948 had been an important element in the masculine self-image of peasant men (Katz, 1996).

A major principle in the policy of state authorities in the 1950s and 1960s was to prevent the emergence of a nationalist consciousness among the Arab Palestinian minority, and to attempt to develop a non-Palestinian local Arab identity for the new, unwanted Israeli citizens. The development of state-dependent sports clubs was one expression of these efforts. Hence, after 1948, sport in Israel was not only assigned the role of rehabilitating the image of Jewish men and consolidating a modern Hebrew national identity but also was used as a mechanism to facilitate the control and surveillance of the Arab Palestinian minority.

The Arab Palestinian population who remained under Israeli rule was mainly rural, with significant parts of it previously somewhat detached from the Palestinian sporting movement. Israel became the sponsor of sports, which grew to be an element in a set of strategies through which the state presented itself as a facilitator of modernity. The state functionaries, or more precisely, the functionaries of the Histadrut (General Federation of Labor Unions), who were assigned by the government to encourage the establishment of sports clubs in Arab villages, took advantage of the opposition of the elder rural leadership to the game in order to emphasize their image as the bearer of modernity. This Arab Palestinian leadership did not welcome the idea of youth playing games like soccer. At best, they considered the

sight of barely dressed young men purposelessly running around after a ball a waste of time, and at worst as a licentious, "unmasculine" activity.

"Modernity" is a key concept for understanding the lure of the game and the power relation between the state and the Palestinian citizens. Modernity is a powerful discourse which plays a specific role in colonial contexts (Mitchell, 2000), and sports is an important element in the production of this discourse. The representation of sports as "modern" and their association with certain political agents enabled the accumulation of significant political assets.

The adoption of sports has been a strategy of delineating the border between the modern and the traditional. This association between sports and modernity was used by the Palestinian elite in the pre-1948 period to promote a secular Palestinian national identity. The institutional development of modern Palestinian sports was tightly connected to the "discourse produced by modernity about itself" (Delanty and O'Mahony, 2002: 6). Namely, sports, in the eyes of certain parts of the Palestinian elite under British rule, were a significant component in a "cultural model of modernity, the basic normative, symbolic and aesthetic structures underlying societies that consciously aspire to become 'modern'" (Delanty and O'Mahony 2002: 6).

After 1948, sport as a badge of "modernity" was used by the agencies of state in order to present themselves as modernizing agents. For men of the younger generation, masculine sports provided an outstanding opportunity to rehabilitate their collective self-image. Sport has a wide and flexible range of interpretations, and while for the elders the game was "play" (and therefore associated with childhood and immaturity), for the younger generation it provided an opportunity to test their masculinity in competition, shortly after their people suffered a catastrophic and humiliating defeat in the war. This nexus of masculinist-nationalist pride was embedded in a prevalent discourse about body and modernity which has emerged in the region since the late nineteenth century (Jacob, 2005; Schayegh, 2002). Following colonial penetration, this rhetoric incorporated explicit consideration of the relationship between national success and physical culture (Jacob, 2005: 126–156), to some extent as a reaction to images of masculinity produced by the colonizers, in which the native's male body was described as weak and undisciplined (p. 122). Therefore, before 1948 sport's assumed power to cultivate modernity in Palestine made it a necessary tool of both nation-building and anticolonial struggle.

This meaning of sport enabled an ad hoc alliance between the Israeli political establishment and the young men in the Israeli-ruled Palestinian towns and villages. Both were interested in developing Arab sport but for different reasons: the latter to support self-image, and the former for control. Particularly since the early 1960s, Arab sport clubs in Israel were spreading. Although initially it was considered a dangerous game from the point of view of the authorities, soccer's popularity was too strong to defeat and therefore the game was encouraged, as long as it was under the complete control and supervision of the state. Israeli authorities considered the new clubs a useful antidote to nationalist consciousness and deliberately encouraged and supported them if they played under the official umbrella of the Zionist sports organization. Independent Arab sports organizations were banned and quickly dismantled if they appeared. Under these circumstances, soccer and boxing became a safe ground for Arab men to display a combative, quasi-nationalist masculinity (Sorek, 2009), which did not involve the risk of confrontation with state authorities.

Paradoxically, by muting their expression of nationalist aspirations, or by relegating them to other spheres, Arab male athletes were able to simulate a war against Jewish men. For Arab sport fans in the late 1960s, identification with successful Arab soccer players or boxers, even if they played for Jewish teams, could reinforce masculinity and national self-respect. These identifications did not risk the potential sanctions involved in identifying with other heroes, such as the Fatah movement[11] which was beginning to gain momentum at exactly the same time.

The military government was officially removed in 1966 (and paradoxically was exported immediately to the territories occupied in 1967) and Israel in its pre-1967 borders experienced a period of relative liberalization in many spheres of life, especially from the 1980s. The disciplinary power of the state, however, was soon replaced by market forces. The accelerated commercialization of some sports, mainly soccer, since the early 1980s (Ben Porat, 1998) has significantly contributed to the pacifying role of sports. The liberalization of the public sphere meant that an Arab athlete who wished to protest would no longer risk legal sanctions or harassment by the security forces. This protest, however, had the potential to prevent him from gaining a place in the roster of a leading Jewish club or in the Israeli national team. This, in turn, might lead not only to direct loss of income but also to less exposure to European agents and hinder his or her chance of a lucrative European athletic career.

It was only in the 1990s, with the proliferation of an independent Arab press, the relative liberalization of the Israeli public sphere, and the growing confidence of the Palestinian elite inside Israel, that an explicit combative nationalist discourse was attached to Arab sport in Israel. Since the mid-1990s it has become more common to find in the Arabic press warlike metaphors to describe Arab–Jewish encounters in the sports sphere, sometimes with concrete reference to events from the Arab–Israeli wars. Still, it seems that there is a gap between sport journalists, who are more educated than the average fan, and the set of symbols that are actually visible in the stadiums. Palestinian national symbols are mostly excluded from the sports site (even though they have not been illegal since 1993). In addition, violent outbreaks in Arab–Jewish encounters are not more common than with other competitions (Arab–Arab or Jewish–Jewish), statistics which testify that "sport as a substitute for war" is too a simplistic as a theme for describing sport dynamics in Israel.

While Jewish working-class soccer fans sometimes aspire to intensify the national conflict in soccer stadiums, Arab soccer fans are in a more ambiguous position. Soccer is indeed an opportunity to "beat the Jewish men" in a physical competition. But it is also a unique opportunity for Arab citizens to obtain integration and acceptance by the Jewish majority. It is a sphere that glorifies a meritocratic ethos and therefore offers players some protection from the discriminatory practices they face in many other spheres of Israeli society. Therefore, Arab fans manage their confrontation with Jewish fans with great care.

This does not mean that Arab–Jewish tension is absent from the soccer stadium but that Arab fans and players tend to under-articulate it. Toward the end of the 2011–2012 soccer season, for example, Israeli soccer fans could watch on their TV an Arab team from Nazareth letting another Arab team from Lyda win 6–0 in order to help the latter to climb to the Premier League.[12] This case of Arab solidarity against Jewish teams reminds us of the undercurrent of tension that does exist below the surface of the integrative rhetoric on the bleachers. At the same time, we have evidence that the integrative and conservative orientation of the sport sphere in Israel exists beyond the rhetorical level. It is illustrated in the results of a survey I conducted in 2000 with a representative sample of young Arab men in Israel (Sorek, 2007). It was found that Arab men who attend the soccer stadium are more likely to vote for Zionist parties in the election and less likely to feel proud of their Palestinian identity. These results imply that any planned attempt of the authorities to manipulate the collective consciousness of citizens by sports has gained some success.

During the first decade of the twenty-first century Arab–Jewish relations in Israel deteriorated drastically (Smooha, 2010). Toward the end of the decade even the soccer field witnessed a slight increase in the frequency of appearance of Palestinian national symbols. Still, a Palestinian flag is an exception that attracts the Hebrew sports media and is covered with a magnifying glass. Only time will tell if we are witnessing the beginning of a change in the political role of sport in Israel.

Palestinian Athletes in the West Bank and the Gaza Strip

The meaning of sport as a mechanism for "limited inclusion" became even clearer after the 1967 war. In this war Israel occupied more territories and imposed its control over the Palestinians in these territories, including the Gaza Strip (which was held until 2005) and the West Bank.[13] The Palestinians in the West Bank and the Gaza Strip have never been considered as potential Israeli citizens, and therefore have never been invited to join the Israeli sport associations under any conditions. The only place where Israeli authorities were involved in organizing sports competition was in East Jerusalem, a territory that was officially annexed to Israel without international recognition. The Israeli municipality of Jerusalem has been involved in developing some sport projects for youth, and a small number of athletes have participated in Israeli competitions.

In the other parts of the 1967 occupied territories, the Palestinians have competed only in their separate athletic frameworks. Under Israeli occupation a separate soccer league for the West Bank was established in 1977 and later on a separate boxing federation. The Palestinian Olympic Committee was recognized as a member of the International Olympic Committee in 1995 and Palestine has been represented in the Olympic summer games since 1996. In 1998 the Palestine Football Federation was recognized by FIFA and the Palestinian national team has been playing in official international games since then. The important aspect for our discussion is that these frameworks have included almost only Palestinians from the West Bank and the Gaza Strip and has rarely included Arab Palestinian citizens of Israel.

Although the Palestine Football Association hired for the national team a Palestinian coach who was a citizen of Israel and a former player in a Jewish Israeli team (the late Azmi Nassar) it was clear to everyone involved that Arab soccer players from inside Israel would not be invited to the team. According to FIFA rules (which reverberate a classic discourse of modern nationalism) throughout his or her career a soccer player can play for only one national team. For this reason Arab players who already played in the Israeli national team could not be invited. Even for those who have not played in the Israeli national team there is a strong incentive to refuse an invitation to the Palestinian team, since playing for Israel would increase their exposure to European player agents. Whatever would be the reason for it, the separation between Palestinian athletes from inside pre-1967 Israel and those from the West Bank and the Gaza Strip is clear, and it becomes even clearer among the top athletes. This separation adds another dimension to the "Israeli" orientation of Arab athletes inside Israel.

At the same time, there is evidence that Israeli soccer has, or at least had in the past, followers among Palestinians in the West Bank and the

Gaza Strip, although it is hard to estimate the extent of this phenomenon. This interest goes back to the time period between 1967 and 1992, when the significant part of the Palestinian male labor force was employed inside pre-1967 Israel (in its peak, over 40 percent), was exposed to Israeli daily life, and learned Hebrew. A striking illustration for the construction of sport as an ex-territorial sphere, where conflict is not allowed to penetrate, can be found in Dan Setton's documentary movie *Shaheed: The Making of a Suicide Bomber*. Based on an interview with Palestinian prisoners who were sent on suicide bombing missions in Israel, this film examines the justifications they give for their readiness to sacrifice their lives. One of the interviewees, Rashid Saker, a would-be suicide bomber in an Israeli jail, was talking about his interest in Israeli soccer.

> QUESTION: Had you were [sic] requested to commit your mission in a soccer stadium, in the Teddy stadium in Israel, for example – what would you have done?
> ANSWER: In the soccer stadium I couldn't have done that.
> QUESTION: Even though these are Jews, Zionists, and infidels?
> ANSWER: I couldn't have done it.

The documentary does not go further, to explore the reasons for Saker's reluctance to kill Israeli fans and himself in a soccer stadium, but it is clear that soccer has a special symbolic value for him. As a Palestinian who was employed in Israel, Saker might have been exposed to the same forces that shaped the attitude of Palestinian citizens of Israel toward the game. Namely, soccer might have symbolized a hope for normality, an island of egalitarian relationship between Jews and Arabs. While Saker imagined the fans in the stadium they might have looked too similar to him to be enemies who deserve to die.

Sport and Reconciliation?

Sport has not become a field of explicit nationalist confrontation between Jewish Israelis and Arab Palestinians, even though in a specific context they do share the same sport sphere. The case of sport among the Arab Palestinian citizens of Israel is a good illustration of the way sport might contribute to the maintenance of hegemonic structures and ideas, through its ability to generate ethnically blind discursive elements. Even though there is ample evidence that national frustration and humiliation play an important role in the attraction of the Palestinian citizens of Israel to the sport sphere as fans and athletes, their frustration remains frequently muted and is heard mainly outside the sport sphere.

Consequently, over the past decade several initiatives to promote peace between Jewish Israelis and Arab Palestinians have been launched. The most extensive and best-known program, Football for Peace, is run by the Chelsea School of Sport at the University of Brighton, the German Sport University Cologne, the British Council, and the Israeli Ministry of Culture and Sport (Sugden and Wallis, 2007). The program brings together Jewish and Arab children to practice and play football, and its declared aims are to "provide opportunities for social contact across community boundaries; promote mutual understanding; engender in participants a desire for and commitment to peaceful coexistence; and enhance sports skills and technical knowledge about sport" (Sugden, 2010).

Since Jewish and Arab children have so few opportunities to interact, one should not underestimate the potential positive contributions of this program. At the same time, we should evaluate the possible political implications of it based on what is known about the history and the contemporary role of sport as a site of depoliticization of Arab–Jewish relations. Providing opportunities for social contact would lead to lasting coexistence in an ideal world where divisions are only horizontal and social conflict is the result of a "cultural gap"; assuming a natural flow from the former to the later does not take into account the initial hierarchy and power relations between the two communities. Stated plainly, when Jewish and Arab children leave their football practice, the Arab players return home to denser streets and a substantially lower quality of education, health, welfare, and public services. These gaps, which are on the rise (Haider *et al.*, 2010), are not only the consequences of the capitalist market but also embody the cumulative effect of an active semi-colonial political reality in which the unequal distribution of resources is compatible with the state's ethnocratic ideology. The exclusion of any discussion of this reality is a precondition for a smooth Arab–Jewish encounter on the sport field.

John Sugden, the leading academic figure in the project, believes that "if imbued with socially progressive values and organized and managed correctly, [sport] can play a role in promoting peace and reconciliation in even the most fractured and deeply divided societies" (Sugden, 2010: 263). This statement might be valid as long as there is recognition by both sides that something is wrong with the existing political system and that sportive reconciliation does not come instead of political change. Otherwise, by depoliticizing the Arab–Jewish encounter, sport joins other uncommon isolated enclaves in Israel, such as pharmacies or the operating room, in which the Jewish political advantage is suspended and

replaced only temporarily by an egalitarian interaction based on commercial, professional, or sportive criteria. Regardless of the specific input of Football for Peace, as a general tendency sport in Israel/Palestine has not contributed so far to reconciliation, even though it clearly has the potential to do so. Unfortunately, the relatively liberal discourse which has been produced in the sport sphere has played a role in justifying and legitimizing the existing ethnic hierarchy in other spheres by providing an illusionary egalitarian model that cannot realistically be exported to other contexts.

Sport might not have the power to transform Israeli politics, but its proven sociopolitical power could significantly support such a transformation if and when it happens simultaneously in other spheres. We should not rule out, therefore, that under different future circumstances sport would support large-scale structural societal change in the country.

Notes

1 For a discussion of nationalism and masculinity in the history of the Israeli–Palestinian conflict, see Katz (1996) and Boyarin (2000).

2 The 1936–1939 Arab revolt in Palestine was an uprising against the British Mandatory authorities in Palestine in protest against accelerated Jewish immigration and Zionist land purchase in the mid-1930s.

3 In 1949 Israel's first prime minister, David Ben Gurion, hesitated whether the department should be annexed to the Ministry of Defense or the Ministry of Education and Culture, and decided in the end for the latter.

4 The Cairo agreement between the PLO and the Lebanese army established principles under which the activities of Palestinian guerrillas based in Lebanon would be tolerated and regulated by the Lebanese authorities. Subsequently, the PLO effectively created "a state within a state" in Lebanon.

5 See the Israeli Basketball Association website, http://www.ibba.one.co.il/, accessed December 17, 2012.

6 See http://www.ibba.one.co.il/, accessed December 17, 2012.

7 Calculation based on information available on the Israel Football Association website, http://football.org.il/Leagues/Pages/LeagueDetails.aspx, accessed December 17, 2012.

8 Calculation based on the Israeli Institute for Martial Arts website, http://www.israel-martialarts.org, accessed January 15, 2013.

9 Calculation is based on information available on the Israeli Boxing Association website: http://www.boxingisrael.com/index.php, accessed December 17, 2012.

10 Calculation is based on information available on the Israeli Boxing Association website, http://www.boxingisrael.com/index.php?option=com_content&task=view&id=33&Itemid=56, accessed January 15, 2013.

11 A major Palestinian party established in 1959 which advocated independent Palestinian action, autonomous from the interests of Arab states. The Fatah adopted armed struggle as a strategy and started implementing it from 1965.

12 The Jewish coach of Nazareth, Shimon Hadari decided to leave the team after this game. Some players were arrested by the police but were released later.

13 With the implantation of the Oslo accords in the mid-1990s in some territories the Palestinian Authority gained partial control over incongruent territories which accumulate to approximately 30 percent of the West Bank. The tangible control of the land, however, remains practically in Israeli hands.

References

Avineri, S. (1981) *The Making of Modern Zionism: The Intellectual Origins of the Jewish State*, New York: Basic Books.

Bauml, Y. (2001) "The attitude of the Israeli establishment toward the Arabs in Israel: Policy, principles, and activities: the second decade, 1958–1968." PhD thesis (in Hebrew), University of Haifa, Haifa.

Ben Porat, A. (1998) "The commodification of football in Israel." *International Review for the Sociology of Sport*, 3 (33): 269–276.

Ben Porat, A. (2001) "'Linesmen, referees and arbitrators': Politics, modernization and soccer in Palestine," in Mangan, J.A. (ed.) *Europe, Sport, World: Shaping Global Societies*, London: Frank Cass, pp. 131–154.

Biale, D. (1992) *Eros and the Jews: From Biblical Israel to Contemporary America*, New York: Basic Books.

Bishara, A. (1999) "The Arabs in Israel: Reading a fragmented political discourse," in Bishara, A. (ed.) *Between the "Me" and the "Us" (in Hebrew), Jerusalem: Van Leer Institute, Ha-kibbutz Ha-meuchad*, pp. 169–191.

Boyarin, D. (2000) "Outing Freud's Zionism, or, the bitextuality of the diaspora Jew," in Patton, C. and Sánchez-Eppler, B. (eds.) *Queer Diasporas*, Durham, NC: Duke University Press, pp. 71–104.

Brand, L. (1991) *Palestinians in the Arab World: Institution Building and the Search for State*, New York: Columbia University Press.

Campos, M. (2010) *Ottoman Brothers: Muslims, Christians, and Jews in Early Twentieth-century Palestine*, Stanford, CA: Stanford University Press.

Delanty, G. and O'Mahony, P. (2002) *Nationalism and Social Theory: Modernity and the Recalcitance of Nation*, London: Sage Publications.

Ehn, B. (1989) "National feeling in sport: The case of Sweden." *Ethnologia Europaea*, 19 (1): 56–66.

Elias, N. and Scotson, J.L. (1994) *The Established and the Outsiders: A Sociological Enquiry into Community Problems*, London: Sage Publications.

Haider, A., Awad, Y., and Mahmoud, M. (2010) *The Equality Index of Jewish and Arab Citizens in Israel (2009)*, Jerusalem: Sikkuy.

Hargreaves, J. (1986) *Sport, Power and Culture*, Cambridge: Polity.

Harif, H. (2011) *Muscular Zionism: The Political Roles of the Representative Sport in the Yishuv and the Formative Years of the State of Israel, 1898–1960* (in Hebrew), Jerusalem: Yad Ben Zvi.

Hartmann, D. (2000) "Rethinking the relations between sports and race American culture: Golden ghettos and contested terrain." *Sociology of Sport Journal*, 17 (3): 229–253.

Houlihan, B. (1997) "Sport, national identity and public policy." *Nations and Nationalism*, 3 (1): 113–137.

Israel, S. and Forman, S. (1994) *Great Jewish Speeches Throughout History*, Northvale, NJ: Jason Aronson.

Jacob, W.C. (2005) "Working out Egypt: Masculinity and subject formation between colonial modernity and nationalism, 1870–1940." PhD dissertation, Department of History and Middle Eastern and Islamic Studies, New York University.

Jiryis, S. (1969) *The Arabs in Israel*, Beirut: Institute for Palestine Studies.

Katz, S.H. (1996) "Adam and Adama, 'Ird and Ard: Engendering political conflict and identity in early Jewish and Palestinian nationalisms," in Kandiyoti, D. (ed.) *Gendering the Middle East: Emerging Perspectives*, Syracuse, NY: Syracuse University Press, pp. 85–101.

Kaufman, H. and Bar-Eli, M. (2005) "Processes that shaped sports in Israel during the 20th century." *Sport History Review*, 36 (2): 179.

Khalidi, R. (1997) "The formation of Palestinian identity: The critical years, 1917–1923," in Gershoni, I. and Jankowski, J. (eds.) *Rethinking Nationalism in the Arab Middle East*, New York: Columbia University Press, pp. 171–190.

Khalifeh, S.M. (1986) *The History of Organized Sports in Jordan*, Coral Gables, FL: University of Miami Press.

Kimmerling, B. and Migdal, J. (1993) *Palestinians: The Making of a People*, New York: Free Press.

Levenberg, H. (1993) *Military Preparations of the Arab Community in Palestine 1945–1948*, London: Frank Cass.

Lever, J. (1983) *Soccer Madness*, Chicago: University of Chicago Press.

Lustick, I. (1980) *Arabs in the Jewish State*, Austin: University of Texas Press.

Mahlmann, P. (1988) "Sport as a weapon of colonialism in Kenya: A review of the literature." *Transafrican Journal of History*, 17: 152–171.

Mandle, W.F. (1979) "Sport as politics: The Gaelic Athletic Association 1884–1916," in Cashman, R. and McKernan, M. (eds.) *Sport in History*, St Lucia: University of Queensland Press, pp. 99–123.

Mangan, J.A. (2001) "Soccer as moral training: Missionary intentions and imperial legacies." *Soccer and Society*, 2 (2): 41–56.

Massad, J. (2001) *Colonial Effects: The Making of National Identity in Jordan*, New York: Columbia University Press.

McKay, J. (1991) *No Pain, No Gain? Sports and Australian Culture*, Brunswick, Victoria: Prentice Hall.

Mitchell, T. (2000) "The stage of modernity," in Mitchell, T. (ed.) *Questions of Modernity*, Minneapolis: University of Minnesota Press, pp. 1–34.

Morris, B. (1987) *The Birth of the Palestinian Refugee Problem: 1947–1949*, Cambridge: Cambridge University Press.

Muslih, M.Y. (1988) *The Origins of Palestinian Nationalism*, New York: Columbia University Press.

Nauright, J. (1997) *Sport, Cultures and Identities in South Africa*, Leicester: Leicester University Press.

PRRN (2007) Palestinian Refugees ResearchNet, http://prrn.mcgill.ca, accessed January 18, 2013.

Porath, Y. (1974) *The Emergence of the Palestinian-Arab National Movement, 1918–1929*, London: Frank Cass.

Robinson, S.N. (2005) "Occupied citizens in a liberal state: Palestinians under military rule and the colonial formation of Israeli society, 1948–1966." PhD thesis, Stanford University, Stanford.

Saeed, A. (2002) "What's in a name? Muhammad Ali and the politics of cultural identity." *Sport in Society*, 5 (3): 52–72.

Sayigh, Y. (1997) "Armed struggle and state formation." *Journal of Palestine Studies*, 26 (4): 17–32.

Schayegh, C. (2002) "Sport, health, and the Iranian middle class in the 1920s and 1930s." *Iranian Studies*, 35 (4): 341–369.

Smooha, S. (2010) *Index of Arab–Jewish Relations in Israel, 2003–2009*, Haifa: Jewish–Arab Center, University of Haifa.

Sorek, T. (2007) *Arab Soccer in a Jewish State: The Integrative Enclave*, New York: Cambridge University Press.

Sorek, T. (2009) "'The only place where an Arab can hit a Jew and get a medal for it': Boxing and masculine pride among Arab citizens of Israel," in Galily, Y. and Ben-Porat, A. (eds.) *Sport, Culture, and Ideology in the State of Israel. Sport in Society: Cultures*, 12 (8), special issue, *Commerce, Media, Politics*.

Sugden, J. (2010) "Critical left-realism and sport interventions in divided societies." *International Review for the Sociology of Sport*, 45 (3): 258–272.

Sugden, J. and A. Bairner (1993) *Sport, Sectarianism and Society in a Divided Ireland*, Leicester: Leicester University Press.

Sugden, J. and Wallis, J. (2007) *Football for Peace?: The Challenges of Using Sport for Co-existence in Israel*, Oxford: Meyer & Meyer.

Tuastad, D. (1997) "The political role of football for Palestinians in Jordan," in Armstrong, G. and Giulianotti, R. (eds.) *Entering the Field: New Perspective on World Football*, Oxford: Berg, pp. 123–140.

Further Reading

Ben-Porat, A. and Galily, Y. (eds.) (2012) *Sport, Culture and Ideology in the State of Israel*, London: Routledge.

Gelvin, J.L. (2007) *The Israel–Palestine Conflict: One Hundred Years of War*, New York: Cambridge University Press.

Kimmerling, B. (2001) *The Invention and Decline of Israeliness: Society, Cultures, and Military in the Israeli State*, Berkeley: University of California Press.

Sorek, T. (2007) *Arab Soccer in a Jewish State: The Integrative Enclave*, New York: Cambridge University Press.

16

Cities and the Cultural Politics of Sterile Sporting Space

Michael L. Silk

Introduction

According to Frederic Jameson (1991: xx), the United States of America acted as the "hothouse" for the reformation of capitalism during the second half of the twentieth century. If this was indeed the case, then the American city – both in its mythologized and materialized iterations – can be considered the generative core and geographical locus of the emergent late capitalist order. Shorn of its mass industrialist (pre)occupations (whose very operationalizing, let alone ultimate demise, became redolent of modernity's disingenuous relationship with public culture) the late capitalist American city speaks of a new social, political, and economic urban order in which the American urbanscape (or, more accurately, select parcels thereof) now represents the built instantiation and celebration of the highly commercialized, privatized, and deregulated marketplace that defines the late capitalist American condition in general (cf. Giroux, 2003, 2005; Grossberg, 2005; Harvey, 2003). Differently put, the exalted (as opposed to the demonized) spaces of urban America are those commercially reconstituted, multifaceted, and spectacularized urban environments designed and justified for the express purpose of stimulating tourist-generated capital accumulation (e.g., Bianchini and Schwengel, 1991; Friedman, Andrews, and Silk, 2004; Lowes, 2002; Zukin, 1991).

Building upon recent work (see, e.g., Bockmeyer, 2000; Brenner and Theodore, 2002a, 2002b; Friedman et al., 2004; Harvey, 2001; Judd and Simpson, 2003; Peck and Tickell, 2002; Sheller and Urry, 2003; Silk, 2004, 2010; Soja, 1989; Turner and Rosentraub, 2002; Walks, 2001) which has addressed the careful orchestration of city space as an arena for market-oriented growth and elite consumption practices – place marketing, tourism, enterprise and empowerment zones, local tax abatements, urban development corporations, public–private partnerships, property redevelopment schemes – this chapter is concerned with ongoing processes involved in the constitution of sporting experiences as they relate to the symbolic reconstitution of cityscapes. As a telling exemplar, I point towards a city that David Harvey (2001) termed emblematic of the conditions that have molded cities under late capitalism: Baltimore.

Cities have shed their industrial exo- and endoskeleton and capitalized upon the cultural landscape of the city. This "visually seductive"

A Companion to Sport, First Edition. Edited by David L. Andrews and Ben Carrington.
© 2013 Blackwell Publishing Ltd. Published 2013 by Blackwell Publishing Ltd.

celebration of the commercial monumentalities of late capitalism – which elevates tourism and tourist discourse to new heights – interrupts the perception of the inner city as an unsafe area of unchecked blight, racial strife, criminality, and deviance (Friedman *et al.*, 2004; Judd and Simpson, 2003). Thus, the presentation of a commercially reconstituted and spectacularized downtown – what de Certeau (1984) terms a "concept city" – may well work to negate the unpredictability of preconceived urban experiences, yet this is merely a sophisticated façade (Harvey, 2001) that belies the structural inequalities in the contemporary cityscape, routinely manifest in polarized labor markets, extreme economic disparities, and racially differentiated housing, population distribution, schooling, and welfare provision. Therefore, and perhaps as the nefarious counter to neoliberal urban policy regimes (deregulation, privatization, liberalization, enhanced fiscal austerity, symbolically oriented tourist economies), it is important to think of cityspace as polarized or segregated, creating a divided city: a container of multiple narratives within the context of transformation in the predominant mode of social regulation (Walks, 2001). For, as with many expressions of neoliberalism, the new urban glamour zones – upon which many cities have based their economic revival – conceal a brutalizing demarcation between winners and losers, included and excluded, lionized and demonized populations (MacLeod, 2002); crude binary distinctions between those included in social, political, and cultural practices and those excluded, in which the poor or degenerate are rigidly disciplined through a range of discursive, legal, and architectural methods (Davidson and Wyly, 2012; Graham, 2012; MacLeod, Raco, and Ward, 2003; Raco, 2012; Smith, 1998). The careful orchestration of cityspace, then, is suggestive of a "regulatory capitalism" in which hybrid relationships emerge between states and powerful corporations, to the point that distinctions between providers and policymakers become increasingly blurred (Raco, 2012); a condition that provides the context for the manipulation of place identity by public/private agencies pursuing strategies promoting the advantages of their cities, in light of the domineering processes and rhetoric of interregional, national, and, global competition

(Rowe and McGuirk, 1999). In this respect, key questions emerge within the practices of destination repositioning with respect to *whose* aesthetics really count, *who* benefits, *whose* collective memory is being performed, and *whose* interests are being furthered (Harvey, 2001; Graham, 2002; Silk and Amis, 2005).

The focus, then, is on addressing the "lean and mean" urban geographies in which cities engage in aggressive place management and marketing initiatives (Smith, 1998), often predicated on sporting experiences and consumption. These processes, I argue, bifurcate urban spaces and populations, creating stark distinctions between bodies that do and do not matter (Butler, 1993; Zylinska, 2004): between the generative affluent and the degenerate poor; between the private (tourist) consumer and the public recipient; between the civic stimulant and the civic detriment; and, between the socially valorized and the socially pathologized (Silk and Andrews, 2006, 2008). To explicate this argument, the chapter begins by addressing the shift towards the material and discursive constitution of cityspace. I then turn to Baltimore, as emblematic exemplar of the neoliberal forces that act to shape and are contested within the city. Conclusions center on the lessons that we might learn from Baltimore, in which I offer tentative suggestions for, and scholarly directions in, addressing sterile cityspaces.

Sporting the Late Capitalist Tourist Bubble

Without wishing to circumvent the acknowledged complexities of nineteenth-century urbanization and industrialization, and the subsequent twentieth-century corollaries of deindustrialization, population decline, and suburbanization (see, e.g., Dyerson, 1999; Gottdiener, 1994, 2000; Riess, 1995), for the purposes of brevity, my focus is the new urban morphology (more closely aligned with the symbolic regimes of production and consumption underpinning the late capitalist economy; Jameson, 1991) adopted by many Western cities from the 1970s onwards. The breaking down of the national bargain, the rolling back of the Keynesian welfare state, the emergence of post-Fordist patterns of production and consumption (e.g., MacLeod *et al.*, 2003; Walks, 2001), compounded by the problems of deindustrialization, a falling tax base due to suburban flight, and the associated concentration of impoverished residents in inner areas (Brenner and Theodore, 2002b; Goodwin, 1993), has meant – faithfully evoking the political hegemony of neoliberal ideologies and policies – that urban governments have sought to (re)capitalize upon the cultural landscapes of their cities (Brenner and Theodore, 2002b; MacLeod, 2002). Engaging in a competitive process of cultural economic restructuring to reposition and represent themselves as the service centers for the financial services, for information and communication services central to the network society, and as spaces of consumption (Gottdiener, 2000; MacLeod *et al.*, 2003; Sassen, 2001; Whitson and Macintosh, 1996), by the early 1990s numerous formerly industrial cities had begun to revive their fortunes on the basis of corporate-oriented downtown strategies and new economies based on tourism, leisure, entertainment, and culture (Cohen, 1999; Gottdiener, 2000; Judd and Simpson, 2003). While they may belie the mid-twentieth-century processes of suburbanization and the perception of the inner city as problematic spaces of social deviance and spatial decay (Friedman *et al.*, 2004; Hannigan, 1998; Judd, 1999), these "spectacular spaces of consumption" (Bélanger, 2000) – what I term sterile cityspaces – are predicated on capital, leisure, and tourism: shopping malls, themed restaurants, bars, theme parks, mega-complexes for professional sport franchises, gentrified housing, conference complexes, and waterfront pleasure domes (Gottdiener, 2000; Macleod *et al.*, 2003; Waitt, 1999; Wilcox and Andrews, 2003).

As part of the efforts to attract middle-class, suburban consumers back into downtown areas (see Florida, 2002) and promote (no matter how false) an image of the city as a central cog – a necessary destination, if you will – within the "global circuits of (tourist) promotion" (Whitson and Macintosh, 1996), these sterile spaces of consumption are often specially designed, scrubbed, and reinvented entertainment districts concentrated in small areas, physically bounded "tourist bubbles" (Judd, 1999: 53) that cordon off and cosset the desired visitor as they simultaneously ward off the threatening "native" (Fainstein and Gladstone, 1999; Harvey, 2001; Jamieson, 2004; Lash and Urry, 1994; Silk, 2004).

To attract tourists, it is important for these local boosters to be able to project an identity that can transform ordinary places and times into extraordinary tourist worlds – something not easily accomplished for formerly mercantile and industrial cities (Judd, 1999; MacLeod and Ward, 2002). According to Lowes (2002) organizing and imaging a city through such consumption-biased spaces (Zukin, 1991, 1995), often fueled by private investment, has become a dominant means of attracting (desired) capital and people in such periods of intensified inter-urban competition and entrepreneurialism, attracting residents, businesses, and tourists to downtown areas, and creating a positive impact on the downtown economy. These "tourist bubbles" are often predicated on convention facilities and sporting investment (Judd and Simpson, 2003), which are argued to have the potential to generate significant economic activity, promote the brand image of a city, function as a locus of community affect and identity, and reproduce the concept of a spatially constructed (imagined) unity (Rowe and McGuirk, 1999). Indeed, international sport, major events, franchises, new stadia, and other sporting experiences have thus become one of the most powerful and effective vehicles for the showcasing of place and for the creation of a "destination image" (Whitson and Macintosh, 1996; see also Hinch and Higham, 2004; Gibbons and Wolff, 2012; Gibson, 2005; Silk, 2002, 2007, 2011; Silk and Amis, 2005). Investment in sports appears crucial for a city to legitimately claim a position on the world stage. In addition to playing a significant role in transnational (financial and communication) business, a city must become a significant "place" in the global sports marketplace (Wilcox and Andrews, 2003), and with sporting events having arguably eclipsed other forms of mega-event, they have assumed increased significance in global city promotion and urban renewal strategies (Chalkey and Essex, 1999; Silk, 2002). In sum, the construction of new facilities devoted to tourism and entertainment has transformed the built environment of many cities (Judd and Simpson, 2003); the social institution of sport and local sporting character are part of the fabric of place identity and the fortunes of sporting performance are frequently invoked in various dimensions of place representation (Rowe and McGuirk, 1999).

The Model of Urban Renaissance?

Clearly the articulations between sport and urban space processes are felt, albeit with different emphasis and with differing (localized) inflections, in a multiplicity of metropolitan spaces across the world (see, e.g., Bélanger, 2000, 2009; Friedman, 2009; Fusco, 2007; Lowes, 2002; Misener and Mason, 2008; Sam and Scherer, 2006; Schimmel, 2006; Silk, 2004; Silk and Andrews, 2008; Wilcox and Andrews, 2003). The American city of Baltimore, however, has not only been credited with having undergone a "model" urban renaissance – the London *Sunday Times* proclaiming in 1987 that "the decay of old Baltimore slowed, halted, then turned back" (Harvey, 2001; Hula, 1990; Wagner, 1996) – it has also provided the isomorphic blueprint for many cities keen to capitalize on their own cultural economy.[1] Initial redevelopment of the central business district (CBD) started in the 1950s with the US$180 million Charles Center office and retail complex, which was targeted towards white-collar professional corporations in the legal, finance, insurance, and real estate industries (Harvey, 2001; Hula, 1990; Wagner, 1996). Business leaders then turned their focus toward the Inner Harbor, which had been a "cradle" of the city's development and had long been a center for Baltimore's industrial, warehousing, and wholesaling activities, but had fallen into disuse and decay by 1960 and was characterized as an area of urban blight (Wagner, 1996). Following the election of Mayor Schaefer in 1971, whose campaign and administration focused on the redevelopment of the urban core (Hula, 1990), the Inner Harbor was gradually transformed into a space predicated on consumption. The berthing of the USS *Constellation*, a mid-nineteenth-century US Navy sloop-of-war, in 1963; the relocation of the Baltimore City Fair, attended by two million people, to the Inner Harbor in 1973; the completion of the Maryland Science Center (1974); and the 27-story World Trade Center (1977) offered early momentum (Friedman *et al.*, 2004; Hula, 1990; Silk and Amis, 2005; Wagner, 1996).

Overcoming opposition from citizens who wanted to preserve the waterfront for public use, subsequent developments formed the Inner Harbor's flagship projects: the Harborplace festival mall, the redevelopment of the former Baltimore city power plant that now houses the ESPN zone, the Hard Rock Café, Golds Gym, Barnes and Noble, the National Aquarium, the Hyatt Regency Hotel, and the Baltimore Convention Center (Harvey, 2001; Wagner, 1996). With the backbone of the Harbor's new infrastructure in place, the Baltimore Strategic Management Committee announced a 20-year renaissance strategy for downtown as "a place for people," a place of "opportunity," "uncommonly liveable," "easy to get to," and "especially attractive" for residents and tourists to consume a diverse array of leisure options offered around Baltimore's Inner Harbor (quoted in Friedman *et al.*, 2004). Encouraged by public–private partnerships and federal initiatives (e.g., Empowerment Zone and Renewal Community designation), Baltimore's resuscitation has been grounded in a turn to the cultural economy – leisure, tourism, entertainment, and culture (Allon, 2004; Cohen, 1999; Judd and Simpson, 2003) – that has attracted the "creative class" (Florida, 2002), tourists, and international media attention to the city's once moribund CBD. This reputation was bolstered in 2005 by Frommer's, which touted Baltimore as one of the top 10 up-and-coming tourist destinations in the world. Despite the ongoing and global economic downturn and recession that began in late 2007, Baltimore continues its upward trajectory as a tourist destination. In the first quarter of 2011, hotel occupancy was at the highest level since 2008, the Thurgood Marshall Baltimore–Washington International Airport reported international and domestic arrivals 6.1 percent and 3.1 percent respectively higher than the previous year, and the convention center reported a 45 percent increase in use on a year-to-date basis (Baltimore Tourism Barometer, 2011). These figures are in the context of a new US$500,000 tourist slogan released in 2010, "Bmore Happy," a slogan derived from research that suggests that, in a time of economic downturn, people are embracing simpler things that make them laugh and smile (Donnell, 2010; Gunts, 2010).

Cities such as Baltimore are clearly adapting their physical urban environment and the imagined representations of cityspace to attract and accommodate the types of economic activities – financial and specialized service industries, sites of hi-tech innovation and production, spaces of consumption – they desire (Castells, 1994; Pagano and Bowman, 1997; Sassen, 2001; Savitch and Kantor, 2003). Given these processes, a greater importance becomes attached to promoting the positive, unique – often through the management and manufacture of heritage – and differential amenity and service attributes of a city in as much as the entire urban core is looked upon as a recreational environment and as a tourism resource (Jansen-Verbeke, 1989). This "symbolic commodification of place" (Whitson and Macintosh, 1996) is based around the manufacturing and promotion of a positive brand identity for a city that is designed to appeal to and attract tourists who want to visit this must-see destination. This of course gives an enhanced role to those in the culture industries who produce the range of symbolic goods and imaged experiences of "culture" within, and for, the contemporary city: branded consumption spaces for (suburban) tourists.

Yet Ritzer (1999: xi) claimed consumers "grow bored easily" with consumption environments; as such Baltimore turned to "increasingly spectacular displays and a continual escalation of efforts to lure consumers." In an effort to differentiate itself from other cities and ensure the freshness of the consumption environment, in the late 1980s Baltimore unveiled plans for the construction of a baseball stadium in Camden Yards (Friedman et al., 2004; Silk and Amis, 2005). Located on the western fringe of the Inner Harbor, Camden station and warehouse were closed and abandoned in the early 1970s as industrial production in the city waned – an image that was inconsistent with the newly developed tourist-oriented Inner Harbor space of consumption. Bound with concern over the potential relocation of the Orioles baseball team (following the 1984 departure of the National Football League's Colts to Indianapolis) and the decrepit Memorial Stadium, the city was desperate to find a new home for its remaining major league franchise. By architecturally incorporating the Camden Yards warehouse within the retro-design of the ground, the stadium provided Baltimore with a landmark that caught the attention

of baseball fans and players, professional sports owners, the general public, and architectural critics. Under the dictates of the late capitalist consumption economy, such an approach speaks to the intensified commodification of "pastness" – a repository of history (Bale, 1994) – that often, although it is certainly not preordained to, emphasizes style over substance; an interpretation of the past *manipulated in the interests of capital* (Apostolakis, 2003; Ashworth and Larkham, 1994; McIntosh and Prentice, 1999; Markwell, Stevenson, and Rowe, 2004; Waitt, 2000). In this sense, the incorporation of the warehouse in the design of the stadium and the construction of a "new-old" stadium creates a baseball environment replete with a *faux* historical authenticity (Andrews, 2000) built on "nostalgia as an antidote to modernity" (Bale, 1994: 170).

Camden Yards, then, offers a telling exemplar of the distortion, disappearance, or staging, of the "authentic" in the name of *capital* (Chhabra, Healey, and Sills, 2003; Jamal and Kim, 2005). That is, under the dictates of a consumer economy, the past is revised, recast instead as an innocent place of play that bears little resemblance to the city's deep industrial and working-class histories (see, e.g., Ashworth, 1990; Ashworth and Tunbridge, 1990; Edson, 2004; Kearns and Philo, 1993; Markwell et al., 2004; Waitt, 2000). Indeed, the (re)production of these images and memories symbolizes who belongs in specific places. Camden Yards is thus imbued with social relations, it is a space that is "accompanied by a complex and often conflicting array of identifications and potential conflicts, not least when heritage places and objects are involved in issues of legitimation of power structures" (Graham, 2002: 1006).

The construction of a publicly financed US$210 million stadium for the Baltimore Orioles baseball (Camden Yards) team not only provided a solution to the potential perceived loss of the city's major league status (see Friedman et al., 2004) but also provided an opportunity to extend the tourist bubble (Judd, 1999) westwards. This has been manifest in the creation of the Baltimore "Westside," an area of the downtown anchored by the Camden Yards ballpark, the M&T Bank Stadium (home of the NFL franchise, the Baltimore Ravens), the Hippodrome Theater, the new

Centerpoint and Zenith retail complexes, a city-run hotel, and a number of newly renovated upscale apartment buildings and hotel complexes. The Westside includes the ballpark and extends north incorporating the two hotels indicated and Eutaw Street. Connecting to the Inner Harbor along the Pratt Street tourist corridor, flanked by the Baltimore Convention Center, these developments extend the Inner Harbor retail and commercial zone approximately one mile west to the University of Maryland Medical School and Hospital (Silk and Amis, 2005). Baltimore's Westside, containing the medical, consumer, sporting, and tourist-oriented facilities so desired by civic leadership, is hawked under a revitalization campaign: "The West has Zest." Yet, this zest leaves a bitter taste in the mouth for those businesses rendered incongruent by the latest efforts to revitalize the Westside. The Upper Deck bar and carry-out and the Goddess Gentlemen's Club sit dwarfed by monopoly rent apartments (Harvey, 2001) in renovated warehouses, brand-new towering apartments and condos, and the two new retail complexes. However, it is not so much their presence but those attracted to these businesses that is causing concern for those who operate the high-end apartment communities. In a letter encouraging residents to be wary of these two businesses, management of the Redwood apartment community encouraged residents to report any "adverse experiences" outside the Upper Deck or the Goddess as part of the "necessary steps to ensure our community and immediate surroundings will continue to be a great place to live" (letter to residents, March 2, 2005; see also Silk, 2010).

The reputation of Baltimore's tourist bubble as a space of play was furthered through hosting a leg of the 2006 Volvo Ocean Round the World yacht race. Re-energizing the Inner Harbor as a place for ships – there had previously been calls to remove certain ships from the harbor area given that their "disturbing" physical presence obstructs the view of the monumentalities of consumption upon which the Harbor's new economy is based (see Gunts, 2006) – the race, as with the yearly Preakness Stakes (one-third of horse-racing's triple crown) at the world-famous Pimlico racetrack, offers opportunities for the city to enter into the tourist circuit of promotion. However, the Pimlico racetrack is located some

five miles north of the city's tourist bubble. Thus, in an effort to centralize Baltimore's "sporting bubble" and place the Preakness Stakes alongside the Ravens' and Orioles' stadiums, plans were mooted for an 189-acre racecourse, the Baltimore Gateway International, that would host the Preakness Stakes and be built within the historic Pigtown neighborhood. Adjacent to the tourist bubble, Pigtown is a neighborhood described in *American Demographics* magazine as a ragged symbol of everything that was wrong with American cities, and is still very much on the periphery of the city's capital extension.[2] The redevelopment of Pigtown would extend the tourist bubble beyond its material and symbolic border, Martin Luther King Expressway, and thereby encompass the B&O Railroad museum, and potentially the Baltimore International Gateway. The project was contested and subsequently shelved, with opposition centering on how the development would wipe out seven core blocks of the neighborhood – seven blocks that have traditionally been inhabited by African Americans. Indeed, the original residents were descendants of slaves or freed slaves who worked at the nearby Carroll Mansion and bought their homes after freedom; many descendants from these families, as well as those black people employed at the B&O railroad, still populate the area (Royster-Hemby, 2005). According to Shawn McIntosh, executive director of the Washington Village/Pigtown Neighborhood Planning Council, 160 homes would be displaced: "What this racetrack is proposing to do is to take out the heart of the African-American community here" (quoted in Royster-Hemby, 2005).

An altogether different form of racing, however, provides a physical albeit ephemeral boundary between the tourist bubble and Pigtown. The inaugural Baltimore Grand Prix (part of the IndyCar Series) took place in September 2011. The circuit quite literally can be seen to locate dromological desires and the desires of the roads (based on Paul Virilio's notion that that which moves with speed will dominate that which is slower) with the material and symbolic regeneration of Baltimore City. The eastern fringes of the circuit in particular provide a physical buffer between the tourist bubble and the "less desirable" (Pigtown) communities that it borders. Drawing on Gwee's (2008: 38–39) reading of

Singapore's Formula One Grand Prix event, the circuit links the "awe and applause for practically everything criminal in the pure rush of high speed: the flouting of normal traffic rules and road direction, the anticipation of some spectacular crashes, and utter disregard for air and noise pollution" with the backdrop of landmarks that stand for legal and economic prowess. Indeed, the event offered spectacular and highly visible images of the material landscape, with skyscrapers as the epitome of symbolic corporate power and global cultural capital – tangible evidence, monuments if you like, to the global city moniker. Likening the event to the Greek orgiastic festivals held in honor of Dionysus which heralded both Greek tragedy and comedy, Gwee (2008) suggested that such race circuits are a curious and sublime reverse celebration of life in a conundrum which combines the relative speed of urbanization – relative because it relies on, and is always competing with, the speeds of other economic centers – with the absolute limits for such volatility to take place. In this sense, in Baltimore as in Singapore, and in light of the fact that physical change cannot catch up adequately or uniformly with the rate of economic change, there becomes no ontological difference between the city and the road: it is the road – as much as the skyscraper or the economy – that becomes the quintessential image of urban processes; a pathological reliance on cosmetics when one has lost one's coordinates for natural processes (Gwee, 2008).

While it is unlikely that many of Pigtown's residents, or indeed the residents of those communities on the periphery of Baltimore's tourist bubble (see Silk, 2010), were invoked, the city was bestowed with another honor that furthers Baltimore's playful "vitality" and "healthy" labeling, despite the noise and air pollution associated with the IndyCar Series. Fully complicit with the physical monumentalities to sport, a contrived allusion to the "health" of Baltimore came in the January 2006 issue of Men's Fitness, in which the magazine named Baltimore as the "Fittest City in America." Derived from admittedly non-scientific criteria, the survey was based on: ratios of parks to population; use of fitness facilities (such as gyms); diet patterns; reactions to public health "emergencies" such as obesity; and, most importantly for Men's Fitness, the role of civic

legislation and leadership in creating fitness- and health-education directives, including requiring developers to create open spaces and trails and enacting fitness-promotion initiatives (Lucia, 2006; Silk and Andrews, 2006). Baltimore achieved this place of honor for apparently having "one of the healthiest diets around" with "half the average number of junk-food places per capita of all the cities in our survey," for a "citizenry who has taken to exercise," for "excellent air quality," for "top-notch health-care," and for the efforts of Mayor Martin O'Malley to make "his populace more active" (Lucia, 2006). In cahoots, then, with the material and symbolic transformations of this select parcel of Baltimore, rhetoric such as the "Fittest City in America" offers a symbolic augmentation to the sanguine, if not delusional, representation of the city as a healthy, safe, and sanitized tourist space (Silk and Andrews, 2006).

Pre-dating the Bmore Happy tagline, in May 2006 the Baltimore City Planning Commission (2006) unveiled its seven-year comprehensive master plan. The report, titled Live. Earn. Learn. Play: A Business Plan for a World Class City, 2007–2012, had been eight years in the making and was adopted by Baltimore City Council in September 2006. The master plan is, in many respects, a blueprint for the material imposition of market logics onto the city given its focus on, to offer just a few examples, the safety of neighborhoods, the attraction of desired residents to the city, the encouragement of entrepreneurship, the concentration of earning in health, biosciences, hi-tech industries, hospitality, and tourism, and, most importantly for our present purposes, the cultural economy of the city. Perhaps not surprisingly, the Play section of the report centers on tying together tourism, heritage, nightlife, and sport as the fabric of a healthy "24-hour world-class city" (2006: 8). Keen to build upon the 15.7 million visitors and business travelers the city attracted in 2004 and their US$2.9 billion spend, the plan emphasizes capitalizing upon Baltimore's uniqueness, visual arts, music, histories, theater, nightlife districts, entertainment, and sports through major promotional campaigns in target tourist markets. Thus, as a component of the comprehensive master plan, the latest layer of urban imagineering was conceived. The plan gives elevated responsibility and funding to the Baltimore Area Convention and Visitors Association (BACVA), suggesting the return, increased tourist dollars, would outweigh the costs. Thus, in late 2005 the city paid US$500,000 to Landor Associates – famed for building brands for Madrid, the state of Florida, Hong Kong, Gatorade, Altoids, Fed Ex, and Kentucky Fried Chicken – to create a slogan for the city (Donovan, 2005). The brand image, "destination re-positioning" as it is labeled by Landor, sets out to draw on the "critical points of difference," the uniqueness and peculiarities of the city (2005 Landor Associates Report to Baltimore City Council, quoted in Donovan, 2005). These particularities of place not surprisingly include the waterfront as well as the "genuine" character of Baltimoreans – a character centered on the "quirky," "funky," "off-kilter," "hilarious," "bizarre," "off-center attitude" – labeled in the report as the "Hon factor." The "Hon factor," rooted in Baltimore's working-class white communities – whiteness, once again, rendered as "genuine" and "authentic" – is best captured in the works of city resident John Waters (Silk and Andrews, 2006). Perhaps best known for the 1988 movie, *Hairspray*, now a major Broadway success, Waters' own off-beat and eccentric version of Baltimore constructs a particular, and admittedly stylized, symbolic rendering of the city: a rendering annually "performed" each year at the Baltimore Hon festival, and commemorated daily in the locally famous Café Hon diner.[3]

In May 2006, coinciding with the launch of the city's master plan, BACVA unveiled the new slogan "Get in on it." The brand platform is centered on Baltimore's "central gathering spot," the Inner Harbor, the space (or "stage" in the promotional vernacular) from which visitors can explore Baltimore's arts, culture, food, history, neighborhoods, and, of course, sports. Based on a nine-month research exercise incorporating mail-out surveys, one-on-one management interviews with key stakeholders and community partners, focus groups in feeder markets (Washington, DC, Philadelphia, and northern New Jersey), and research and visitor profiling conducted by tourism research consultancy Longwoods International, Landor built upon the "uniqueness" of Baltimore as a quirky, laid-back city that is "very rich in that which it has to offer." "Get in on it" is a "rallying cry" that is said to communicate that there is "something special going on here and it's

exciting" (Landor, 2006). The connotative value of the brand is built upon a

> colorful visual identity [that] communicates a city on water and uses icons to represent the fun, carefree and spontaneous nature of the city. The cap suggests baseball at Camden Yards; the guitar represents the nightlife and entertainment at Fells Point; the crab honors the well-known city mascot, while the dinosaur and the shark speak of the Science Center and Aquarium respectively. (Landor, 2006)

Aimed at both tourist, convention, and meeting planners, the new brand is being communicated via a series of promotions including print, radio, and web campaigns, public relations, downtown promotions, and most markedly a television commercial (to be shown in external markets) featuring local residents enjoying the arts, sports, food, and culture of the Inner Harbor. Other neighborhoods that speak to the particularities of the city's cultures and histories are also represented (although the focus is very much centered on the Inner Harbor) in the strategizing (such as Hampden, location of the Café Hon diner), yet, interestingly, the city's own comprehensive master plan suggests that inadequate transportation and signage along with concerns about safety outside the cosseted tourist bubble make it difficult to draw tourists away from the Inner Harbor to other neighborhoods.

In cahoots with the material transformations of this select parcel of Baltimore, these monikers offer a series of symbolic accoutrements to the sanguine, if not delusional, representation of the city as a healthy, safe, and sterile urban space. As an appetizing appurtenant to the market-oriented dictate of the ascendant neoliberal order, those auteurs responsible for contouring the city – that loose conglomeration of private/public coalitions and the symbolic mavens of late capitalist consumer culture that are increasingly difficult to tell apart – are interpellating with this image a desired new urban populace: an amalgam of the gentrified, creative, or tourist classes. That is, as part of an ongoing circuit of cultural production (du Gay *et al.*, 1997), this symbolic armory produces or assembles certain subjects that become aligned to spatial expressions of capital. Such symbolic machinations are part of an array of practices that shape identities and forms of life – advertising, marketing, the proliferation of goods, the multiple stylizations of the act of purchasing, cinemas, videos, pop music, lifestyle magazines, television soap operas, advice programs, and talk shows – and which contribute toward a "civilizing project very different from the 19th-century attempts to form moral, sober, responsible, and obedient individuals, and from 20th century projects for the shaping of civility, social solidarity, and social responsibility" (Rose, 1999: 1399).

These practices and technologies constitute the assemblage, and display, of the bodily habitus of the normalized and regulated subject – the stylized display of (fitness) clothing obtained through acts of consumption, working out in the "right" gym in Federal Hill, being seen jogging along the Inner Harbor, drinking Propel Fitness water (not the *passé* Evian), cheering the performative and brutalizing displays of the overrepresented and "othered" male bodies playing for the Ravens or the Orioles, consuming sushi at Nichiban under the gaze of local artists or authentic regional Mexican cuisine amid the maize and coral cantina hues of the Blue Agave Restaurante and Tequileria, drinking US$5 "Bud-Lites" at ESPN Zone viewing one of the ubiquitous flat screens, passing the same beer in the urinals without missing a pitch as you listen to the radio (ESPN Radio, of course) while the kids engage in the sensory overload of the Game Zone, creating hybrid fleshy-digital displays/bodies as they meander on a stationary bike/horse/car around a racetrack in an exotic location, shopping for collectibles or antiques at Vanessa's Vintage Treasures, or drinking coffee post-work in Metropolitan Café's coveted *al fresco* seating – serving not only to further constitute consumerism but to *exercise* power over the "body that matters." This is a sporting symbolism that offers a powerful "civilizing project," a discourse of social regulation that infuses the desired subjects with the consumer "freedoms" afforded to them as privileged groups in consumer capitalist society; the ability to experience, consume, and play in sterile spaces. However, in championing an idealized, consumerized, sporting existence through succumbing to Baltimore's visually seductive, privatized public culture, there is little more than a superficial engagement with a neoliberal "concept," an urban core that presents an appealing *unified impression* (de Certeau, 1984) yet masks and simplifies the contingencies and multiplicities of urban lived experiences (Jamieson, 2004).

Multiple, pejorative, and starkly divergent (Walks, 2001) city narratives provide a far more accurate, if messier and more complex, account of city life. A tiny peek behind the hallucinatory neon, fitness discourse, and the monumentalities of sporting consumption, exposes the stark lived realities that appear when one tears off the mask and peers behind the façade of the Inner Harbor (see Harvey, 2001). While there have been long histories that detail the decline of manufacturing in Baltimore, the segregated school system, and the increased poverty among African Americans in the city, three times higher than the state average (see Quirk and Binder, 2006), it is the publication of the 2010 Baltimore City health disparities report card that most markedly points towards the actualization of structural inequalities in distinct Baltimore neighborhoods.[4] The report details the health inequities – the result of systematic social, political, economic, and environmental policies and practices – driven by differences in residents' access to opportunities that promote and enhance health and points to a variety of social determinants of health (e.g., access to healthy food, healthy housing, healthcare, safe neighborhoods, education and employment opportunities, and transportation). Utilizing a number of disparity ratios (such as age, gender, education, income, and location) the report offers a gruesome testament to deeply engrained and socially and economically divisive operations of racial containment within the city. African American men, for example, are more than twice as likely than white men to suffer from prostate cancer; African Americans are eight times more likely to contract HIV/AIDs than is the white population in the city; over three times more likely to live in a "dangerous" neighborhood; twice as likely to be obese or to suffer from high blood pressure or diabetes, to have no healthcare, and to report food insecurity (concern about having enough food); five times more likely to have childhood asthma; and three-and-a-half times more likely to have unmet mental healthcare needs; and African American men are 11.5 times more likely to be the victims of homicide than white males.

The "rot beneath the glitter" (Harvey, 2001) that one discovers in Baltimore has itself been symbolically constituted with far less friendly labels – the Heroin Capital, the Murder Capital – that focus on the perception of the city as "hopeless, depressed, unemployed and crack addicted" (2005 Landor Associates report to Baltimore City Council, quoted in Donovan, 2005). These perceptions and labels are based on popular, commercial representations of the city such as the television serials *Homicide: Life on the Street*, *The Wire*, and *The Corner*; rap renditions by Jay Z about taking cocaine to Baltimore for sale and by 50 Cent, whose album *The Massacre* contained a drug serenade titled "A Baltimore Love Thing"; the computer game *The Suffering: The Ties That Bind* centered on the "horror along the industrial waterfront and in neighborhoods like Druid Hill Park"; in "underground primers on the contemporary drug scene in Baltimore," such as Stop Snitchin'; in Nike's latest "B'More" campaign, featuring NBA star Carmelo Anthony and centering on the urban depravity whence he came (Ollison and Kiehl, 2005; Tucker, 2005); and in the lived realities of Baltimore. These lived realities reveal that 24 percent of the city's residents live in poverty (compared with 14 percent nationally) as Baltimore's per capita income level fell to 57 percent of Maryland's average (Johns Hopkins, 2000), life expectancies are 14 years below national averages, teen pregnancy was the highest among the nation's 50 largest cities in 1999, and 34 percent of children under 18 in the city live below the poverty level (nationally, this figure is 10 percent) (Harvey, 2001; Johns Hopkins, 2000; Siegel and Smith, 2001; Silk and Andrews, 2006; US Census, 2004). Homicide rates in the city averaged around 300 per year (around seven times higher than the national rate, six times higher than New York City, and three times higher than Los Angeles) in the last decade, the majority homicides endemic to drug- and gang-related violence (Dao, 2005). Furthermore, large parcels of the city are characterized by block after block of vacant row houses; the city has led the nation in violent crime, in juvenile homicide, and in heroin, cocaine, and syphilis rates; and a higher percentage of the city's population tested positive for heroin than any other US city, with some 59,000 addicts in a city of 675,000 (Cannon, 1999). Indeed, and in direct contradistinction to official destination positioning, readers of *Travel and Leisure* in June 2011 voted Baltimore the sixth dirtiest city in the United States (based on litter, air pollution, and the taste of drinking water). Put simply, and although there have been recent fluctuations in murder rates and violent crime, Baltimore is, like many cities whose civic administrations operate less in the interests of citizens and more in the interests of bolstering the "logics" of the marketplace (see, e.g., Sheller and Urry, 2003), the "home of the comfortable and the prison of the choiceless" (Johns Hopkins, 2000: 48).

Conclusion: Learning from Baltimore

The juggernaut of cultural capitalism, then, may well have enveloped particular entities, places, and peoples. It may well have elevated tourism, sport, and entertainment to new heights in the repackaging of corporatized, sterile pockets of cityspace. More accurately, it positions a particular form of sport, that is resigned to, if not embedded in, the seeming inevitability of regulatory capitalism (Raco, 2012), one which is constituted by, and serves to constitute, the ubiquity of a haunting, nebulous neoliberalism. Yet it concurrently marginalizes and excludes from such sanctioned spaces the abject other, and further marks this abject other from the "healthy body politic." For, within capital-produced space (Harvey, 2001), the *sterile* sporting sphere (and its associated populace) is rendered visible through the preservation, management, and sustenance of the boundary between the *bodies proper* that fulfill the "obligations" of participatory democratic citizenship (in this sense through appropriate rates and acts of sporting consumption) and those constitutive of socially, morally, and economically pathologized *outsiders*. Expelled to spaces outside the circuits of security and inclusion, spaces which are increasingly avoided and feared by those who used to walk, shop, and visit there, the poor, the street people, the homeless, the workless, the abject, are cast out and excluded as degenerates or public pollutants (Rose, 2000). These outsiders become positioned as an invisible source of life that protects the constitution of the healthy consuming polis by rendering it visible and thereby distinguishing it from those who do not *properly belong* to it (Butler, 1993; Zylinska, 2004) and are increasingly subject to "legitimate" technologies of regulation, increased social surveillance, and strategies of control (policing, surveillance, and "carceralization"): the technologies of social and moral regulation that will secure the extension, maintenance, reproduction, and management of the consequences of market rule (Peck, 2003; see also Devas, 2001; MacLeod *et al.*, 2003). That is, following Ahmed (2000), the abject are rendered strange, or, in her terms, dangerous strangers. Strangers, for Ahmed, are those already recognized as not belonging, as *being out of place*. Recognition of strangers – those who look out of place in sterile cityspace, becomes, then, the means by which inhabitable (no matter how temporarily) or bounded spaces become produced (Ahmed, 2000). This linguistic and bodily integrity of the stranger embodies – and provides justification for – that which must be expelled from the purified space of the community and the purified life of the *good* citizen (Ahmed, 2000). In this sense, the discursive constitution of the healthy sporting body politic, and even the built environment that helps sustain it, operates as a form of ocular self-subjectifying and self-persecuting governance that renders even more visible – and thus subject to control and regulation – those bodies that are deemed or perceived to threaten normalized, consumerized, healthy bodies and social practices. Thus, and fully complicit with civic regimes centered less on the public good and more on bolstering and extending the logics of the market, pernicious consumer capitalist sporting discourse – acting as a form of neoliberal racism (see Goldberg, 2008) – names, shames, and makes discernible the degenerate, and thereby through discursively-based subjectification facilitates the disappearance of the social, economic, and political conditions responsible for the proliferation of degeneracy, ultimately providing the justification for the systematic evisceration of those bodies that do not matter. Such discourses offer but "a utopian geography that is so powerful and all-encompassing that it ensures the very real processes of exploitation and social exclusion which sustain the vision remain out of sight" (Whittaker, 2011: 126).

Sadly, it appears that we have not come that far since Venturi, Scott-Brown, and Izenour's (1972) call to learn from Las Vegas. Written before Vegas became a monument to the phantasmagorical (Benjamin, 2002) and prior to instantiation of a new neoliberal urban politics, Venturi and colleagues' perceptive and insightful text calls for receptivity to the tastes and values of "common" people. Yet the "common people" are increasingly subject to "justified" authoritarian modes of control sustained through fear, suspicion, Draconian forms of policing and scrutiny, the suspension of their rights, and the promotion of an atmosphere of perpetual emergence and panic (Back, Sinha, and Bryan, 2012). Writing about the impact on London of the 2012 Olympic regeneration, S. Graham (2012) suggests the legacy is one which better resembles lockdown London as opposed to landmark London: a reshaped urban environment in which a range of new punitive measures and potentially invasive laws legitimize the use of force, in which new surveillance technologies, methods of dealing with protest, and precedents of joint army, municipal, and private security action become "normalised" (Gibbons and Wolff, 2012: 441). This is likely to be especially the case the further one ventures from the phantasmagorical locus of Olympic consumption, with "omniscient surveillance" (Graham, 2012: 446) further deepening the city's existing inequalities and the social and spatial fragmentation of London's poor, and exacerbating the multiple industrial, ethnic, educational, and religious planes of division within the city's socioeconomic groups (Davidson and Wyly, 2012). Poor and minority multiethnic bodies who border the Olympic Park are likely be subject to increased regulation, surveillance, and policing techniques (Gibbons and Wolff, 2012), raising important questions about the longer-term "liberty-cost" (Raco, 2012), which bodies matter – and which do not, i.e., the pathologized abject – to the vast technical rule-making, legal doctrine, and complex bureaucracies of the sporting spectacle (Raco, 2012).

Somewhat rearticulating Venturi and colleagues, and taking into account the seemingly ubiquitous, kaleidoscopic, and global tsunami of urban regeneration under a regime of regulatory capitalism – most recently expressed at London 2012 – we should learn from Baltimore. Following Ahmed (2000), as academics we need to expose and avoid "stranger fetishism": that is, the process of welcoming or expelling the stranger as a figure with linguistic and bodily integrity. To do so requires "examining the social relationships that are concealed by this very fetishism. That is, we need to consider how the stranger is an effect of processes of inclusion and exclusion, or incorporation and expulsion, that constitute the boundaries of bodies and communities, including communities of living (dwelling and travel), as well as epistemic communities" (p. 6). We need to be receptive to, and provide the conditions for the mobilization of the excluded, the marginalized, the abject; and we need to connect these stories to structural and discursive relations of power. Further, as Anouk Bélanger (2009) suggests, we need to understand how resistance to sterile cityspaces is an integrated component of the processes of spectacularization. We need to ensure that we see such spaces are not merely imprints of capital or produced by it. Rather, we need to recognize how such spaces are used by different people in various contexts, and that these spaces can be put to use in divergent, even subversive ways (Bélanger, 2009). We need to explicate how spectacularized sterile sporting spaces are negotiated, enacted, performed, lived in and lived through, contested, and (un)representative (MacLeod, 2002). This is likely to involve telling stories, from diverse and different voices, about the contestations of space and the multiple narratives of the city, challenging and (actively) disrupting the cartographic revision of the spaces of late capital, and stepping outside our comfortable zones of depersonalized and detached research into a messier world that de-centers questions of power dynamics, authority, the ability to represent, and what "counts" as meaningful, ethical, and, moral research (Morgan and Pritchard, 2005; see also Denzin, 2002). We need to contextualize the "embodied practices of the tourist/resident 'subject'" (Jamal and Kim, 2005: 74) and those bodies constituted as antithetical to the workings of the market – witness the homeless populations, the panhandlers, and the abject moved on from Eutaw Street around noon prior to every Orioles home game – whose sporting and leisure practices we know so little about. We need to understand and expose these stories, their (sporting) worlds that differ so much from those

aligned with capital, stories of survival from the borders of the tourist bubble: the street vendor serving fast food, plastic paraphernalia, and unofficial sporting merchandise; the performative display of racialized sporting clothing; the active embodiments of sporting (and militarized) style and performance; the cries of joy from pick-up games in the street; the distinctly non-corporatized sporting organizations (churches/youth clubs) offering a space for structures sporting involvement; the tireless and timeless commitment of the volunteer acting as teacher, taxi, carer, sibling, parent, disciplinarian, mentor, counselor, pastor, social worker, role model, and coach.

These are stories from, and pathways through, Baltimore's archipelago (Soja, 2000) of normalized enclosures – interdictory spaces (Flusty, 2001) – that rub closely against each other, proffering physical and institutional barriers that cosset private worlds that share little in common with adjacent neighborhoods, and, both voluntarily and involuntarily, "barricade individuals and communities in visible and not-so-visible urban islands, overseen by restructured forms of public power and private authority" (Soja, 2000: 299). To counter the repressive cultural politics of sterile neoliberal cityspace, and indeed to avoid representing sporting spaces purely as the apex of neoliberalism (MacLeod and Ward, 2002), we need multiple, pejorative, stories and actions (see, e.g., Denzin, 2002; Lincoln and Denzin, 2005; Silk, 2010): we need to begin to sketch a political project (McLaren, 2008) in which researchers and teachers addressing the articulations between sport and urban space are able to speak the "truth of power and facilitate the speech of the powerless" (Tribe, 2006: 377). This would be a critical project, one that takes sides, one that is not resigned to the seeming inevitability of capital (McLaren, 2005). Following Darder and Miron (2006), Giroux (2005), Giroux and Giroux (2006), McLaren (2008, 2009), and MacLeod (2002) our academic contributions to understanding and intervening into sterile sporting cityscapes should contribute towards an urban insurgency; a strategy that can resist, transgress, and oppose, can unshackle the padlocks of purified sporting spaces, and thereby challenge the official, growth-machine dominated representations of urban spaces.

282   MICHAEL L. SILK

Notes

1   For a full length article detailing competing repre-
    sentations of urban space in Baltimore see Silk and
    Andrews (2011). In this article, we address the ways
    in which the competing narratives of Baltimore
    (evident in programs like *The Wire*) rub against
    "official" destination narratives.
2   City officials had renamed the area Washington
    Village, yet in an effort to symbolically reconstitute
    the neighborhood, residents campaigned to restore
    the name "Pigtown" and thereby recognize the
    unique history of the community. The community,
    which stretches from the birthplace of American
    railroading – the head of the B&O railroad – to the
    home of the Baltimore Ravens (the M&T Bank
    stadium), was named Pigtown because pigs were

run through the streets from the rail terminal to
slaughter houses (the current site of the M&T Bank
stadium).
3   The city does have full and rich African American
    histories. With the exception, however, of the
    recently opened Reginald F. Lewis Museum of
    Maryland African American History and Culture,
    these histories do not tend to feature heavily in
    the city's promotional campaigns – although the
    recent comprehensive master plan does recognize
    the supposed $90 billion potential in "minority
    tourism."
4   Available at http://www.baltimorehealth.org/info/
    2010_05_25_HDR-FINAL.pdf, accessed December
    17, 2012.

References

Ahmed, S. (2000) *Strange Encounters: Embodied Others in Post-coloniality*, London: Routledge.
Allon, F. (2004) "Backpacker heaven: The consumption and construction of tourist spaces and landscapes in Sydney." *Space and Culture*, 7 (1): 49–63.
Andrews, D.L. (2000) "Dead and alive? Sport history in the late capitalist moment sporting traditions." *Journal of the Australian Society for Sport History*, 16 (1): 73–85.
Apostolakis, A. (2003) "The convergence process in heritage tourism." *Annals of Tourism Research*, 30 (4): 795–812.
Ashworth, G. (1990) "The historic cities of Groningen: Which is sold to whom?" in Ashworth, G. and Goodall, B. (eds.), *Marketing Tourism Places*, London: Routledge, pp. 138–155.
Ashworth, G. and Larkham, P. (eds.) (1994) *Building a New Europe: Tourism, Culture and Identity*, London: Routledge.
Ashworth, G. and Tunbridge, J. (1990) *The Tourist-Historic City*, London: Belhaven.
Back, L., Sinha, S., and Bryan, C. (2012) "New hierarchies of belonging." *European Journal of Cultural Studies*, 15 (2): 139–154.
Bale, J. (1994) *Landscapes of Modern Sport*, London: Leicester.
Baltimore City Planning Commission (2006) *Live. Earn. Learn. Play: A Business Plan for a World Class City, 2007–2012*, http://msa.maryland.gov/megafile/msa/speccol/sc5300/sc5339/000113/002000/002899/unrestricted/20066308-0001e.pdf, accessed January 21, 2013.
Baltimore Tourism Barometer (2011) *1st Quarter 2011 in Review*, Baltimore: Sage Policy Group.

Bélanger, A. (2000) "Sport venues and the spectacularization of urban spaces in North America: The case of the Molson Centre in Montreal." *International Review for the Sociology of Sport*, 35 (3): 378–397.
Bélanger, A. (2009) "The urban sport spectacle: Towards a political economy of sports," in Carrington, B. and McDonald, I. (eds.) *Marxism, Cultural Studies and Sport*, New York: Routledge, pp. 51–67.
Benjamin, W. (2002) *The Arcades Project*, trans. Eiland, H. and McLaughlin, K., Cambridge, MA: Belknap Press.
Bianchini, F. and Schwengel, H. (1991) "Re-imaging the city," in Corner, J. and Harvey, S. (eds.) *Enterprise and Heritage: Crosscurrents of National Culture*, London: Routledge, pp. 212–234.
Bockmeyer, J. (2000) "A culture of distrust: The impact of local political culture on participation in the Detroit EZ." *Urban Studies*, 37 (13): 2417–2440.
Brenner, N. and Theodore, N. (2002a) "Preface: From the new localism to the spaces of neoliberalism." *Antipode*, 34 (3): 341–347.
Brenner, N. and Theodore, N. (2002b) "Cities and the geographies of 'actually existing neoliberalism.'" *Antipode*, 34 (3): 349–379.
Butler, J. (1993) *Gender Trouble: Feminism and the Subversion of Identity*, New York: Routledge.
Cannon, A. (1999) "The charm city blues." *US News and World Report*, 126 (1): 24–26.
Castells, M. (1994) "European cities, the informational society and the global economy." *New Left Review*, 204: 18–32.
Chalkey, B. and Essex, S. (1999) "Urban development through hosting international events: A history of

the Olympic games." *Planning Perspectives*, 14: 369–394.

Chhabra, D., Healey, R., and Sills, E. (2003) "Staged authenticity and heritage tourism." *Annals of Tourism Research*, 30 (3): 702–719.

Cohen, P. (1999) "In visible cities: Urban regeneration and place-building in the era of multicultural capitalism." *Communal/Plural*, 7 (1): 9–28.

Dao, J. (2005) "Baltimore street meaner, but message is mixed." *New York Times*, February 9: A1.

Darder, A. and Miron, L. (2006) "Critical pedagogy in a time of uncertainty." *Cultural Studies ↔ Critical Methodologies*, 6 (1): 5–20.

Davidson, M. and Wyly, E. (2012) "Class-ifying London." *City: Analysis of Urban Trends, Culture, Theory, Policy, Action*, 16 (4): 395–421.

de Certeau, M. (1984) *The Practice of Everyday Life*, Berkeley: University of California Press.

Denzin, N. (2002) "Confronting ethnography's crisis of representation." *Journal of Contemporary Ethnography*, 31 (4): 482–489.

Devas, N. (2001) "Does city governance matter for the urban poor?" *International Planning Studies*, 6 (4): 393–408.

Donnell, S. (2010) "Don't worry, Bmore Happy: Baltimore sells city with a smile." *NBC Washington*, http://www.nbcwashington.com/the-scene/events/Dont-Worry-Bmore-Happy-93418229.html, accessed January 18, 2013.

Donovan, D. (2005) "Baltimore: The city in search of a slogan." *Baltimore Sun*, November 8: A1.

du Gay, P., Hall, S., Janes, L., *et al.* (eds.) (1997) *Doing Cultural Studies: The Story of the Sony Walkman*, London: Sage Publications.

Dyerson, M. (1999) "Nature by design: Modern American ideas about sport, energy, evolution, and republics, 1865–1920." *Journal of Sport History*, 26 (3): 447–469.

Edson, G. (2004) "Heritage: Pride or passion, product or service?" *International Journal of Heritage Studies*, 10 (4): 333–348.

Fainstein, S. and Gladstone, D. (1999) "Evaluating urban tourism," in Fainstein, S. and Judd, D. (eds.) *The Tourist City*, New Haven, CT: Yale University Press, pp. 212–234.

Florida, R. (2002) *The Rise of the Creative Class*, New York: Basic Books.

Flusty, S. (2001) "The banality of interdiction: Surveillance, control and the displacement of diversity." *International Journal of Urban and Regional Research*, 25 (3): 658–664.

Friedman, M.T. (2009) "The transparency of democracy: A Lefebvrean analysis of Washington's National Park." Unpublished doctoral dissertation, Department of Kinesiology, University of Maryland, College Park.

Friedman, M., Andrews, D., and Silk, M. (2004) "Sport and the façade of redevelopment in the post-industrial city." *Sociology of Sport Journal*, 21: 119–139.

Fusco, C. (2007) "Healthification and the promises of urban space: Textual analysis of place, activity, youth (PLAY-ing) in the city." *International Review for the Sociology of Sport*, 42 (1): 43–63.

Gibbons, A. and Wolff, N. (2012) "Introduction: Re-writing London and the Olympic city: Critical implications of 'faster, higher, stronger.'" *City: Analysis of Urban Trends, Theory, Policy, Action*, 16 (4): 439–445.

Gibson, H. (2005) "Sport tourism: Concepts and theories." *Sport in Society*, 8 (2): 133–141.

Giroux, H. (2003) *The Abandoned Generation*, New York: Palgrave Macmillan.

Giroux, H. (2005) *The Terror of Neoliberalism*, New York: Palgrave Macmillan.

Giroux, H. and Giroux, S. (2006) "Challenging neoliberalism's new world order: The promise of critical pedagogy." *Cultural Studies ↔ Critical Methodologies*, 6 (1): 21–32.

Goldberg, D. (2008) *The Threat of Race: Reflections on Racial Neoliberalism*, Oxford: Wiley-Blackwell.

Goodwin, M. (1993) "The city as commodity: The contested spaces of urban development," in Kearns, G. and Philo, C. (eds.) *Selling Places: The City as Cultural Capital, Past and Present*, Oxford: Pergamon, pp. 145–162.

Gottdiener, M. (1994) *The Social Production of Urban Space*, Austin: University of Texas Press.

Gottdiener, M. (2000) "Lefebvre and the bias of academic urbanism: What can we learn from the new urban analysis?" *City*, 4: 93–100.

Graham, B. (2002) "Heritage as knowledge: Capital or culture?" *Urban Studies*, 39 (5–6): 1003–1017.

Graham, S. (2012) "Olympics 2012 security." *City: Analysis of Urban Trends, Theory, Policy, Action*, 16 (4): 446–451.

Grossberg, G. (2005) Caught in the Crossfire: Kids, Politics, and America's Future, Boulder, CO: Paradigm.

Gunts, E. (2006) "Are ships cramping aquarium's style?" *Baltimore Sun*, February 12: B1.

Gunts, E. (2010) "Find your happy place in Baltimore: Smile-themed marketing campaign to be launched." *Baltimore Sun*, May 10, http://articles.baltimoresun.com/2010-05-10/business/bs-bz-smile-campaign-20100509_1_visit-baltimore-happy-place-oriole-bird, accessed January 18, 2013.

Gwee, L. (2008) "The road people: Poetry and urban (im)mobility in Singapore." *Asiatic*, 2 (2): 38–51.

Hannigan, J. (1998) *Fantasy City: Pleasure and Profit in the Postmodern Metropolis*, London: Routledge.

Harvey, D. (2001) *Spaces of Capital: Towards a Critical Geography*, London: Routledge.

Harvey, D. (2003) *The New Imperialism*, Oxford: Oxford University Press.

Hinch, T. and Higham, J. (2004) *Sport Tourism Development, Clevedon*, UK: Channel View Publications.

Hula, R. (1990) "The two Baltimores," in Judd, D. and Parkinson, M. (eds.) *Leadership and Urban Regeneration: Cities in North America and Europe*, Newbury Park, CA: Sage, pp. 191–215.

Jamal, T. and Kim, H. (2005) "Bridging the interdisciplinary divide: Towards an integrated framework for heritage tourism research." *Tourist Studies*, 5 (1): 55–83.

Jameson, F. (1991)*Postmodernism, or, the Cultural Logic of Late Capitalism. Post-Contemporary Interventions*, Durham, NC: Duke University Press.

Jamieson, K. (2004) "Edinburgh: The festival gaze and its boundaries." *Space & Culture*, 7 (1): 64–75.

Jansen-Verbeke, M. (1989) "Inner cities and urban tourism in the Netherlands: New challenges for local authorities," in Bramham, P., Henrey, I., Mommas, H., and van der Poel, H. (eds.) *Leisure and Urban Processes: Critical Studies of Leisure Policy in Western European Cities*, London: Routledge.

Johns Hopkins (2000) "Baltimore in transition: How do we move from decline to revival?" Proceedings of the 30th Annual Conference, International Urban Fellows Program, Johns Hopkins Institute for Policy Studies, http://ips.jhu.edu/elements/uploads/fck-files/file/2000conf.pdf, accessed January 18, 2013.

Judd, D. (1999) "Constructing the tourist bubble," in Fainstein, S. and Judd, D. (eds.) *The Tourist City*, New Haven, CT: Yale University Press, pp. 35–53.

Judd, D. and Simpson, D. (2003) "Reconstructing the local state: The role of external constituencies in building urban tourism." *American Behavioral Scientist*, 46 (8): 1056–1069.

Kearns, G. and Philo, C. (eds.) (1993) *Selling Places: The City as Cultural Capital, Past and Present*, Oxford: Pergamon.

Landor (2006) "Baltimore: Get in on it!" Landor Associates case study, http://landor.com/#!/work/case-studies/baltimore/, accessed January 21, 2013.

Lash, S. and Urry, J. (1994) *Economies of Signs and Space*, London: Sage Publications.

Lincoln, Y. and Denzin, N. (2005) "Epilogue: The eighth and ninth moments: Qualitative research in/and the fractured future," in Denzin, N. and Lincoln, Y. (eds.) *The Sage Handbook of Qualitative Research* (3rd edn.), Thousand Oaks, CA: Sage Publications.

Lowes, M. (2002) *Indy dreams and Urban Nightmares: Speed Merchants, Spectacle, and the Struggle over Public Space in the World-Class City*, Toronto: University of Toronto Press.

Lucia, J. (2006) "How fit is America?" *Men's Fitness*, February, http://www.obesitydiscussion.com/forums/information-on-obesity/how-fit-is-america-764.html, accessed January 15, 2013.

MacLeod, G. (2002) "From urban entrepreneurialism to a 'revanchist city'? On the spatial injustices of Glasgow's renaissance." *Antipode*, 34 (3): 602–624.

MacLeod, G. and Ward, K. (2002) "Spaces of utopia and dystopia: Landscaping the contemporary city." *Geografiska Annaler*, 84, B (3–4): 153–170.

MacLeod, G., Raco, M., and Ward, K. (2003) "Negotiating the contemporary city." *Urban Studies*, 40 (9): 1655–1671.

Markwell, K., Stevenson, D., and Rowe, D. (2004) "Footsteps and memories: Interpreting an Australian urban landscape through thematic walking tours." *International Journal of Heritage Studies*, 10 (5): 457–473.

McIntosh, A. and Prentice, R. (1999) "Affirming authenticity: Consuming cultural heritage." *Annals of Tourism Research*, 26 (3): 589–612.

McLaren, P. (2005) "Critical pedagogy and class struggle in the age of neoliberal globalization: Notes from history's underside." *International Journal of Inclusive Democracy*, 2 (1): 1–62.

McLaren, P. (2008) "This fist called my heart: Pedagogy in the belly of the beast." *Antipode*, 40 (3): 472–481.

McLaren, P. (2009) "Critical pedagogy for a post-capitalist future." Keynote paper presented at the 3rd Critical Tourism Studies Conference: Connecting Academies of Hope, Zadar, Croatia, June 21–24.

Misener, L. and Mason, D. (2008) "Urban regimes and the sporting events agenda: A cross-national comparison of civic development strategies." *Journal of Sport Management*, 22 (5): 603–627.

Morgan, N. and Pritchard, A. (2005) "On souvenirs and metonymy: Narratives of memory, metaphor and materiality." *Tourist Studies*, 5 (1): 29–53.

Ollison, R. and Kiehl, S. (2005) "City gets a bad rap in song by 50 Cent: Baltimore is in title of a cut about heroin." *Baltimore Sun*, March 5: D1.

Pagano, M. and Bowman, A. (1997) *Cityscapes and Capital: The Politics of Urban Development*, Baltimore, MD: Johns Hopkins University Press.

Peck, J. (2003) "Geography and public policy: Mapping the penal state." *Progress in Human Geography*, 27 (2): 222–232.

Peck, J. and Tickell, A. (2002) "Neoliberalizing space." *Antipode*, 34 (3): 380–403.

Quirk, P. and Binder, S. (2006) *The Legislative Branch*, Oxford: Oxford University Press.

Raco, M. (2012) "The privatization of urban development and the London 2012 Olympics." *City: Analysis of Urban Trends, Theory, Policy, Action*, 16 (4): 452–460.

Riess, S. (1995) *Sport and Industrial America*, Wheeling, IL: Harlan Davidson.

Ritzer, G. (1999) *Enchanting a Disenchanted World: Revolutionizing the Means of Consumption*, Thousand Oaks, CA: Pine Forge Press.

Rose, N. (1999) "Community, citizenship, and the third way." *American Behavioral Scientist*, 43 (9): 1395–1411.

Rose, N. (2000) "Government and control." *British Journal of Criminology*, 40: 321–339.

Rowe, D. and McGuirk, P. (1999) "Drunk for three weeks: Sporting success and the city image." *International Review for the Sociology of Sport*, 34 (1): 125–142.

Royster-Hemby, C. (2005) "Bettor off? Residents of Pigtown tell Annapolis they don't want a racetrack in their backyards." *City Paper*, http://www.citypaper.com/news/story.asp?id=8657, accessed December 17, 2012.

Sam, M. and Scherer, J. (2006) "The steering group as policy advice instrument: A case of 'consultocracy' in stadium subsidy deliberations." *Policy Sciences*, 39 (2): 169–181.

Sassen, S. (2001) *The Global City: New York, London, Tokyo* (2nd edn.), Princeton, NJ: Princeton University Press.

Savitch, H. and Kantor, P. (2003) "Urban strategies for a global era: A cross-national comparison." *American Behavioral Scientist*, 46 (8): 1002–1033.

Schimmel, K. (2006) "Deep play: Major sports and urban social conditions in the USA." *Sociological Review*, 54 (s2): 160–174.

Sheller, M. and Urry, J. (2003) "Mobile transformations of public and private life." *Theory, Culture and Society*, 20 (3): 107–125.

Siegel, E. and Smith, V. (2001) "Can Mayor O'Malley save ailing Baltimore?" *City Journal*, 11 (1): 64–75.

Silk, M. (2002) "'Bangsa Malaysia': Global sport, the city and the mediated refurbishment of local identities." *Media, Culture and Society*, 24: 775–794.

Silk, M. (2004) "A tale of two cities: Spaces of consumption and the façade of cultural development." *Journal of Sport and Social Issues*, 28 (4): 349–378.

Silk, M. (2007) "Come downtown and play." *Leisure Studies*, 26 (3): 253–277.

Silk, M. (2010) "Postcards from Pigtown." *Cultural Studies ↔ Critical Methodologies*, 10 (2): 143–156.

Silk, M. (2011) "Towards a sociological understanding of London 2012." *Sociology*, 45 (5): 733–748.

Silk, M. and Amis, J. (2005) "Sport tourism, cityscapes and cultural politics." *Sport in Society*, 8 (2): 280–301.

Silk, M. and Andrews, D. (2006) "The fittest city in America." *Journal of Sport & Social Issues*, 30 (3): 1–13.

Silk, M. and Andrews, D. (2008) "Managing Memphis: Governance and spaces of inequality." *Social Identities*, 14 (3): 395–414.

Silk, M.L. and Andrews, D.L. (2011) "(Re)presenting Baltimore: Place, policy, politics, and cultural pedagogy." *Review of Education, Pedagogy, and Cultural Studies*, 33(5): 433–464.

Smith, N. (1998) "Giuliani time: The revanchist 1990s." *Social Text*, 57: 1–20.

Soja, E. (1989) *Postmodern Geographies*, New York: Verso.

Soja, E. (2000) *Postmetropolis: Critical Studies of Cities and Regions*, Oxford: Blackwell.

Tribe, J. (2006) "The truth about tourism." *Annals of Tourism Research*, 33 (2): 360–381.

Tucker, A. (2005) "Harm city: Three men familiar with the city's crime and grime take on a virtual Baltimore via a new video game." *Baltimore Sun*, October 11: 1E.

Turner, R. and Rosentraub, M. (2002) "Tourism, sports and the centrality of cities." *Journal of Urban Affairs*, 24 (5): 487–492.

US Census (2004) "Population and housing narrative profile." US Census Bureau, http://www.census.gov/prod/www/abs/h170.html, accessed January 18, 2013.

Venturi, R., Scott-Brown, D., and Izenour, S. (1977) *Learning from Las Vegas (revised edn.)*, Cambridge, MA: MIT Press.

Wagner, P. (1996) "The construction of urban tourism space: Baltimore's Inner Harbor, 1964–1990." Unpublished Master's thesis, University of Maryland, College Park.

Waitt, G. (1999) "Playing games with Sydney: Marketing Sydney for the 2000 Olympics." *Urban Studies*, 36 (7): 1062–1073.

Waitt, G. (2000) "Consuming heritage: Perceived historical authenticity." *Annals of Tourism Research*, 27 (4): 835–862.

Walks, R. (2001) "The social ecology of the post-Fordist/global city? Economic restructuring and socio-spatial polarisation in the Toronto urban regional." *Urban Studies*, 38 (3): 407–447.

Whitson, D. and Macintosh, D. (1996) "The global circus: International sport, tourism and the marketing of cities." Journal of Sport & Social Issues, 20: 239–257.

Whittaker, T. (2011) "Between the dirty and the pretty: Bodies in utopia in Dirty Pretty Things." *International Journal of Cultural Studies*, 14 (2): 121–132.

Wilcox, R. and Andrews, D. (2003) "Sport in the city: Cultural, economic and political portraits," in Wilcox, R., Andrews, D., Pitter, R. and Irwin, R. (eds.) *Sporting Dystopias: The Making and Meanings of Urban Sport Cultures*, Albany: State University of New York Press, pp. 1–16.

Zukin, S. (1991) *Landscapes of Power: From Detroit to Disney*, Berkeley: University of California Press.

Zukin, S. (1995) *The Culture of Cities*, Oxford: Blackwell.

Zylinska, J. (2004) "The universal acts: Judith Butler and the biopolitics of immigration." *Cultural Studies*, 18 (4): 523–537.

Further Reading

Brenner, N. and Theodore, N. (2002b) "Cities and the geographies of 'actually existing neoliberalism.'" *Antipode*, 34 (3): 349–379.

Harvey, D. (2001) *Spaces of Capital: Towards a Critical Geography*, London: Routledge.

Sassen, S. (2001) *The Global City: New York, London, Tokyo* (2nd edn.), Princeton, NJ: Princeton University Press.

Turner, R. and Rosentraub, M. (2002) "Tourism, sports and the centrality of cities." *Journal of Urban Affairs*, 24 (5): 487–492.

Whitson, D. and Macintosh, D. (1996) "The global circus: International sport, tourism and the marketing of cities." *Journal of Sport & Social Issues*, 20: 239–257.

17

Swimming Pools, Civic Life, and Social Capital

Jeff Wiltse

Introduction

In 1990, a long simmering dispute over the fate of McCarren Pool in Brooklyn, New York, escalated into a public controversy. The pool dated back to 1936, when New York City Parks Commissioner Robert Moses opened 11 giant pool complexes funded by the federal government through the Works Progress Administration. McCarren Pool measured 165 × 330 feet (50 × 100 meters) and could accommodate 6,800 swimmers. Throughout much of its history, the enormous pool had served as "the hub of the working-class neighborhood's summertime social life," according to the *New York Times* (Brozan, 1990). Local citizens who could not afford the time or expense of seaside vacations gathered together at this urban oasis and forged social bonds. As a study commissioned by the city's Parks Department concluded, the pool "provided a special sense of community identity."[1]

During the 1970s and early 1980s, however, the pool deteriorated due to neglect and turned into a social battleground. New York City suffered a series of budget crises that forced it to cut maintenance funding for its swimming pools. McCar-

ren Pool became so dilapidated that one city official deemed it a public hazard (*New York Times*, 1985). At the same time, an increasing number of Puerto Ricans and African Americans from nearby Williamsburg began using the facility, which angered the neighborhood's longtime Polish, Italian, and Irish American residents. "There were riots," recalled Junior Nieves. "The Puerto Ricans were on one side, the Polish were on the other, and all hell was breaking loose" (Stelloh, 2006). Many locals abandoned the pool because it no longer seemed to be a safe, neighborhood space. By the early 1980s, the pool had become "overrun" by rowdy teenagers, according to some residents, and a "haven for drug dealers and prostitutes." The city closed McCarren Pool in 1983 (Brozan, 1990).

The public controversy in 1990 centered on what should be done with the pool's crumbling remains. Some in the community, especially black and Latino residents, wanted McCarren Pool restored to its former splendor. For them, a large public space where thousands of people could gather together represented the promise of a rejuvenated and vibrant community life. "McCarren is a deep-rooted part of the area's social history," a leading advocate of restoration explained. "It is

A Companion to Sport, First Edition. Edited by David L. Andrews and Ben Carrington.
© 2013 Blackwell Publishing Ltd. Published 2013 by Blackwell Publishing Ltd.

as big as a lake, and it is this community's waters" (Yampolsky, 1990). Other area residents, mostly whites, wanted the pool closed permanently or rebuilt on a much smaller scale. They feared that such a large public pool would become a locus for urban crime and social disorder. "Put 6,000 people in one pool and you can imagine the chaos that will follow," explained one critic (Brozan, 1990).

The McCarren Pool controversy and the history of swimming pools more generally reveal much about civic life in America.[2] For one, they reveal the vital role public space can play in fostering a vibrant and sociable community. For several generations, McCarren Pool provided a common ground where neighbors gathered together to recreate, socialize, and participate in the public life of their community. Because pools are intimate and sociable spaces, they enable people to interact with one another in meaningful ways and thereby form personal and social bonds. Swimmers spend hours, sometimes the entire day, at pools – lying out in the sun, navigating through crowded water, flirting, and engaging in conversation. Socially interactive public spaces such as these counteract the atomizing and sometimes alienating effects that the widespread trend toward privatization has had on civic life. In general, swimming pools and other public recreation facilities provide an accurate barometer of a community's commitment to civic life. The construction of many new public pools and increasing attendance are strong indicators of a flourishing civic life. The closing of existing pools, the construction of few new pools, and declining attendance are strong indicators of deteriorating civic life.

And yet, precisely because swimming pools are such intimate and sociable spaces, they have been intensely contested and reveal the limits many Americans have placed on their participation in the public life of their communities. Social anxieties about gender, class, and racial differences are easily piqued at pools. As a consequence, Americans have mostly used swimming pools in ways that divided communities along class and racial lines and thereby reinforced these social distinctions. Even though New York City pools were not racially segregated, McCarren Pool primarily served the working-class whites who lived in the surrounding Greenpoint neighborhood. When blacks and Latinos began to use the pool during the 1970s, many locals rejected their presence and abandoned the facility. Eventually they sought to eliminate this public space from their community. Rather than nurturing social bonds, McCarren Pool sparked racial conflict, generated a public controversy that hardened perceptions of social difference, and caused many in the community to retreat from public life. In the present as in the past, social anxieties hinder Americans from creating a civic life that transcends the boundaries of race and class.

The history of swimming pools also informs the burgeoning scholarly literature on social capital. Although theorists have defined the concept slightly differently, social capital generally refers to the benefits that accrue to individuals, communities, and societies from networks of personal relationships.[3] These benefits can include improved access to jobs, lower crime rates, dynamic civic activism, improved physical and mental health, better schools – the list goes on.[4] Scholars have examined social capital in many different contexts – including workplaces, extended families, schools, service organizations, churches, neighborhood associations, and marketplaces (Field, 2008; Halpern, 2005; Putnam, 2000). Recently, social capital scholars have also turned their attention to sports, studying the extent to which participatory sports, sports clubs, and professional sports teams contribute to the generation of social capital (Nicholson and Hoye, 2008; Harvey, 2007). Scholars have also examined how ideas about social capital have influenced public policies related to sports and leisure (Blackshaw and Long, 2005). Thus far, however, social capital scholars have ignored community recreation venues and the informal interaction that occurs at these public spaces. Public recreation spaces – swimming pools in particular – warrant attention by social capital scholars because historically many Americans integrated themselves into communities and socialized with their neighbors at swimming pools. The relationships formed at pools were not as formalized as at workplaces, churches, and Elks clubs, but they nonetheless enabled people to participate actively in the public life of their communities, interact with neighbors, and develop shared values. Swimming pools also served as a common interest and concern for people within a community. Neighbors frequently banded together to oppose pool closings, demand new regulations, or protest admission policies. In each case, people used the personal linkages created by the pool to resolve a civic concern.

Much of the recent attention devoted to social capital has focused on Robert Putnam's bestselling book *Bowling Alone* (2000). In it, Putnam celebrates the civic virtues of social capital, claiming that networks of interpersonal relationships – what he terms social and community "connectedness" – benefit not only individuals but communities and societies more generally. They increase levels of civic trust and tolerance, lead to the establishment of shared values, create "norms of reciprocity," and encourage more active civic involvement (2000: 287–349). Much of Putnam's book measures the varying levels of social capital in American society during the twentieth century. He claims that social capital was abundant during the Progressive Era and after World War II but has been declining since the 1960s (pp. 31–180). He attributes the recent decline to several factors: the passing away of the civic-minded generation that came of age during the Great Depression and World War II; the expanding appeal of electronic entertainment; mass suburbanization; and increased pressures on time and money resulting from longer commutes, two-career families, and financial insecurity (pp. 183–284). Putnam's analysis resonated with many Americans, probably because it affirmed popular reverence for the "greatest generation," lent scholarly authority to widespread anxiety about the current state of community life in America, and yet held out the possibility of future redemption.

Scholars have been more critical of Putnam's assumptions and conclusions. Many have challenged what they see as his overemphasis on the positive benefits of social capital and underemphasis on the "dark side" of social capital, namely the ways social capital has been used to reinforce inequality and support antisocial behavior (Field, 2008: 79–100; Arneil, 2006). They have also questioned whether social capital has actually declined over the past several decades or whether the nature of social relations has changed and the sites where social connections are formed have shifted to areas where Putnam did not look (Field, 2008: 101–131). Scholars also dispute Putnam's claims about what caused the supposed

decline in civic engagement, especially his claims that generational turnover and increasing numbers of women in the workforce are responsible (Blackshaw and Long, 2005; Arneil, 2006). The amount of criticism that has been generated by Putnam's work on social capital testifies to its public and scholarly significance.

The history of swimming pools in America corroborates Putnam's general point that civic engagement has been declining during recent times, but it also complicates some of his more specific assertions. Putnam claims that the decline in civic engagement began in the 1970s and that racial prejudice did not contribute to Americans' retreat from public life. The history of swimming pools tells a different story. White Americans abandoned public pools *en masse* beginning in the 1950s in direct response to racial desegregation. The use of public pools is certainly not the only measure of civic engagement, but it is a significant one because of the numbers involved. Attendance at municipal pools nationwide plummeted by many millions when black and Latino Americans began to swim at pools that had previously been used only by whites. This was a profound retreat from public life motivated primarily by racial prejudice. Furthermore, the history of swimming pools highlights the "dark side" of social capital. In many instances, the relationships formed at pools were utilized – sometimes in violent ways – to intimidate groups of people from accessing these public facilities. In particular, white swimmers frequently acted in concert with one another to intimidate African Americans and Latino Americans from using swimming pools earmarked for whites only. As a result, blacks and Latinos were denied access to public facilities, and the public life of many communities further fractured along racial lines.

The history of swimming pools also informs several more specific questions that interest social capital scholars. Recent scholarship has become increasingly concerned with the role, if any, that government and public policy can play in increasing stocks of social capital and in ensuring that social capital is not used to reinforce inequality. The history of swimming pools suggests that one way government can encourage the development of social capital is by providing public spaces – the common ground – where citizens can gather together and develop relationships. Government's role is particularly vital to create opportunities for networks of relationships to develop between people with different social identities. Formal institutions – such as universities and businesses – tend to create social linkages between people of similar class standing. And private spaces tend to fragment communities along class and racial lines. Private swim clubs, for example, have served white, middle-class Americans almost exclusively. These clubs have generated social capital among their socially homogenous members but have also reinforced class and racial divisions. Public spaces by contrast have the potential to bring together people from different social groups. During the 1920s and 1930s, public officials throughout the United States purposely and successfully integrated municipal swimming pools – and the public life of their communities more generally – along class, gender, and generational lines by constructing enormous resort-like pools that appealed to a broad cross-section of citizens.

And yet, government provision of public space has not been without problems. Historically, public officials have denied particular social groups access to public facilities or forced them to use separate, inferior facilities. Even well-intentioned public policy has led to discrimination and inequality because public officials are limited in their control over how people use public space. When northern cities first permitted mixed-gender use of municipal pools in the 1920s, most whites suddenly objected to swimming with blacks and some whites quite literally beat black swimmers out of the water (Wiltse, 2007: 125–139). Many public officials surely supported the imposition of *de facto* segregation, but that was not the intention of the gender-integration policy. It was, however, the consequence.

Social capital scholars have also focused much attention on social trust,[5] and debated to what extent it is a prerequisite for the development of social capital and to what extent it is an outcome of the development of social capital. Swimming pools provide a useful setting for examining the relationship between social trust and social capital because of the visual and physical intimacy involved in their use. Stripping mostly naked and sharing an enclosed body of water through which dirt and disease can be passed

from one person to another necessitates substantial trust that others at the pool do not pose a physical, sexual, or health threat. The history of swimming pools in the United States suggests that social trust is a prerequisite for the type of meaningful interaction – especially between people from different social groups – that could lead to the development of social capital. The mere presence of swimming pools did not bring people of different class and racial backgrounds together, where they could then develop trust between them. Rather, a certain level of trust had to be preexisting for them to be willing to gather together at municipal pools. Historically, this trust was produced by broad social, ideological, and economic developments that generally diminished the perceived significance of social differences. Middle-class northerners, for example, first became willing to use the same pools as the working class during the 1920s, only after improved material conditions, the end of large-scale European immigration, and the increasing presence of black Americans all combined to make working-class whites seem less foreign, poor, and dirty than they had previously.

This chapter examines the history of swimming pools in the United States during the twentieth century, focusing on what the changing patterns of social interaction at pools reveal about civic life in America. The first section briefly looks at the early twentieth century, when blacks and whites swam together but men and women and rich and poor did not. The second section examines the social transformation that occurred in pool use during the 1920s and 1930s, when pools became integrated along class and gender lines but segregated along racial lines. The final section interprets the splintering of pool use that occurred after World War II, when millions of Americans abandoned municipal pools and chose to swim instead at private clubs or in their own backyards.

Swimming Pools and Civic Life in Industrial America

Historically, municipal swimming pools both restricted and enlarged the social boundaries of civic life in American communities. During the late nineteenth and early twentieth centuries, pool use in the northern United States divided public life along gender and class lines. Public officials forbid males and females from using pools together in order to protect the modesty of female swimmers and restrict interaction between unacquainted men and women. Cities provided separate pools or set aside separate hours for males and females (Wiltse, 2007: 22, 32–33). Public officials also encouraged class-segregated use by locating municipal pools within working-class slums or in isolated sections of cities. In 1910, for example, the proposal to build a large municipal pool in New York's Central Park generated intense opposition from the city's middle and upper classes precisely because it would have attracted more working-class children into their oasis of genteel recreation. "I have never been in favor of putting a swimming pool in Central Park," declared New York City parks commissioner Charles Stover. "I should consider it disastrous if the only swimming pool belonging to the city was put there. It would attract all sorts of undesirable people" (*New York Times*, 1910a). Instead, Stover and the *New York Times* recommended that municipal pools be located underneath the Manhattan and Queensboro bridges in order to seclude working-class swimmers and protect the city's class-segregated social geography (*New York Times*, 1910a, 1910b).

While early municipal pools reinforced class and gender divisions in American cities, they brought Americans from different racial and ethnic groups into close public contact. In an article titled "All races and creeds flock to public bath," the *St. Louis Post-Dispatch* described the scene in 1907 at the city's bathhouse: "Greek, Italian, negro, Irish, German, French, American – they were all there, sweating, grinning, and scolding at one another in strange tongues" (August 11: 6). The crowds at municipal pools in Chicago were similarly diverse. At Union Park Pool, roughly half of the swimmers were black and half white (CCRR, 1922: 279). At another Chicago pool, a group of reformers claimed that the close mingling of boys from different ethnic groups had reduced conflict in the neighborhood:

On any Saturday afternoon, a few years ago, the streets of the West Side of Chicago were a battle ground for rough and tumble fights between Italian and Slav boys. National characteristics and international misunderstandings were fertile causes for combat. . . . Now on any Saturday afternoon long lines of Italians and Slavs, as well as Hungarians, Scandinavians, Irish and Germans, may be seen at the door of the swimming pool, awaiting their turn – with the peace preserved.[6]

Despite the close intermingling, municipal pools did not necessarily foster friendships across racial and ethnic lines. At Chicago's Union Park Pool, blacks and whites used the same pool, but, according to the pool manager, "they stayed in separate groups" (CCRR, 1922: 279). In some cases, shared pool use led to violence. A pool located on New York's Upper West Side turned into a racial battleground in 1907, when black and Irish swimmers fought for control over this desirable public space. One commentator concluded that it was a fallacy for the city to think it could "wash out the race problem in a swimming pool" (Todd, 1907: 901). At another Chicago pool, a gang of white boys reportedly held a young black swimmer under water until he was close to drowning (CCRR, 1922: 279). In these instances, shared use of the pool did not lead to increased trust and understanding but, rather, enabled young swimmers to act out social antagonisms.

Swimming Pools and the Social Transformation of Civic Life between the World Wars

During the 1920s and 1930s, public officials and swimmers redrew the social boundaries of public life at municipal pools. Cities throughout the country constructed enormous swimming pools – many of them larger than football fields – and surrounded them with sand beaches and concrete sun decks. The construction occurred in two phases. Throughout the 1920s, cities and towns built swimming pools to meet Americans' increasing demand for outdoor recreation and leisure activities. The approximately 1,000 municipal pools constructed during this period helped popularize swimming as a recreational activity. Whereas swimming had previously been a fringe activity that appealed mostly to boys and young men, it became the most popular form of outdoor recreation in America during the 1920s, appealing to young and old, males and females, and rich and poor (Wiltse, 2007: 90–93, 95–97). The 1920s pool-building spree came to a sudden end in late 1929, after the stock market crashed and the nation began to descend into the Great Depression. Beginning in 1934, however, the federal government initiated a second wave of pool building, funding nearly 750 swimming pools throughout the country (Wiltse, 2007: 93–95). These pools testified to the nation's commitment to funding public recreation, even during the depths of the Great Depression.

The social divisions that characterized the use of earlier pools evaporated during the interwar years. Across the northern United States, swimming pools became social melting pots into which males and females and working class and middle class all plunged together. Public officials initiated this widespread social transformation. They permitted males and females to swim and sunbathe together, because they intended the new resort pools to promote family and community sociability. A parks department official in Wilmington explained that the city opened an enormous pool in Price's Run Park so that "young folks can swim together and dads can bring their families" (*Wilmington Star*, 1930). Public officials also encouraged the class integration of municipal pools. Whereas earlier pools intended only for the working classes had been austere facilities located in residential slums, cities typically located the new resort pools in open and accessible parks so they would appeal to middle-class residents as well. After Bethlehem, PA, opened a large municipal pool in Saucon Park, Mayor Archibald Johnston proudly claimed that it had brought about a "thorough intermingling of our citizens" and "a fuller understanding of, and the better co-operation of, all classes" (Bethlehem, 1920: 7). In short, public officials intended swimming pools to bring families together and foster a community life that transcended the social lines of gender and class. "Let's build bigger, better and finer pools," exhorted Nathan Kaufmann, Recreation Director for Allegheny County, Pennsylvania, "that's real democracy. Take away the sham and hypocrisy of clothes, don a swim suit, and

we're all the same" (*Beach & Pool*, "Splashes," November 1939: 13).

The class integration of municipal pools reflected a significant shift in social values – namely a widespread weakening of class prejudice. During the Progressive Era, middle-class Americans avoided swimming in the same pools as the working classes largely because they viewed them as poor, dirty, and foreign (Wiltse, 2007: 22–46). Beginning in the late 1910s, however, several factors mitigated these prejudices. First, the decline in European immigration to the United States made the urban working class seem less foreign than it had previously (Roediger, 2005). At the same time, the material conditions for working-class northerners improved, which made them seem less poor. Some moved out of urban slums and into working-class suburbs, and most participated in the consumer economy (Biggott, 2001; Crawford, 1995; Cross, 2000: 59). Public health campaigns and widely publicized studies showing declining rates of disease among working-class whites also made them appear less unhealthy in the 1920s than they had previously (Tomes, 1998: 204, 219, 242–243; Hoy, 1995: 121, 123–149). Finally, the Great Black Migration – in which approximately 1.5 million African Americans migrated from the South to northern cities between 1915 and 1930 – heightened perceptions of racial difference in the North, which helped whites of all social classes forge a common identity out of their shared whiteness (Nasaw, 1993: 60). Because of these large-scale historical developments, middle-class whites generally became willing to swim in the same pools as working-class whites.

Millions of Americans embraced the new social landscape at municipal pools and transformed them into vibrant civic spaces. *Fortune* magazine estimated in 1934 that upwards of 30 million Americans swam in pools a total of 350 million times each year (*Fortune*, 1934: 81, 85). Municipal pools became the centers of summertime community life. When Ellsworth, KA, opened an outdoor pool in 1924, it quickly became the town's principal gathering spot. "The new swimming pool is the most popular place in town," noted city clerk Elden Shaw. Locals gathered at the pool not only to swim but also to "eat their supper." Shaw further noted that "people who do not swim go there to look on and visit"

(Shaw, 1924: 668–669). People actually chatted with one another at the pool. The same was true in Palmerton, a mining and smelter town in eastern Pennsylvania. According to longtime resident Joseph Plechavy, the municipal pool, which opened in 1929, attracted just about everyone in town. "It didn't matter who you were, you swam at the pool." Plechavy spent countless afternoons and weekends at the pool "yakking with whoever was there." The Palmerton pool also hosted summertime community events, including the American Legion "community picnic," the Fourth of July celebration, and the annual Palmerton picnic. These events brought the whole town together at the pool, where neighbors swam, chatted, devoured ice cream, and celebrated their shared identity as Americans and Palmertons (Wiltse, 2007: 107–108). Municipal pools likewise fostered a vibrant community life in larger cities. In 1925, Wilmington, DE, opened a giant pool in Price's Run Park that measured 480 feet (146 meters) long and between 120 and 180 feet (36–54 meters) wide. A local reporter visited the pool and celebrated its effect on the city's civic life. The pool had generated "a wonderful neighborhood and fraternal spirit. . . . Everyone seemed imbued with the community spirit and bent on having a good time." Because of the intimate and sociable environment at the pool, swimmers actually became "acquainted with each other." People otherwise separated by urban geography and social differences recreated together and "cement[ed] bonds of community friendship" (*Wilmington Evening Journal*, 1925: 13). All of these pools were shared social spaces and community meeting grounds. In using them, residents developed attachments to their communities and to one another.

The municipal pools of the interwar years also served as social and cultural laboratories, where community standards were contested and new shared values were developed. Hundreds and often thousands of people gathered together at municipal pools during this period. They changed clothes next to one another, showered together, negotiated crowded spaces, and lay out side by side on sandy beaches. This novel environment necessitated social and cultural adjustments at the same time that it enabled interaction and dialogue. The conversations and contact that occurred at swimming pools were not fleeting as at most public spaces. People spent hours, sometimes the entire day, at municipal pools – swimming, chatting, sunbathing, and picnicking. Furthermore, the visual and physical intimacy at pools gave rise to thorny issues that often necessitated community dialogue to resolve. What swimsuit styles were appropriate? What should be the boundaries of male–female interaction? Should any social group be prohibited from using the pool? In short, a meaningful public discourse occurred at and about municipal pools that caused Americans to establish new standards of public decency and new patterns of public social interaction (Wiltse, 2007: 82–85, 108–109).

The opening of Price's Run Pool in Wilmington exemplifies the cultural adjustments that occurred at swimming pools during this period. Thousands of males and females crowded together in the enormous pool, and thousands of "spectators" came to watch. In an effort to dampen the sexual charge sparked by mixed-gender swimming and sunbathing and uphold existing standards of public decency, the local park board banned tight-fitting one-piece bathing suits for women and insisted that men wear loose-fitting jersey tops outside their trunks. And yet, according to the *Wilmington Evening Journal* (1925), many of the thousands that congregated at the pool ignored these rules. Men tucked in their jerseys to make them more form-fitting, and women wore tight-fitting, one-piece suits "with impunity." In response to the public's disregard of its policies, Wilmington's park board called a special meeting to reconsider the bathing-suit restrictions. Several citizens complained about swimmers' immodesty, but even their remarks indicate that a new standard of public decency was quickly developing at the pool. Speakers did not object to attractive young men and women displaying their svelte bodies at the pool but rather to people with unattractive bodies wearing skimpy suits. "Many unsightly conditions prevail [at the pool]," C.A. Chader told the board, "and if I dare say, the most is the appearance of stout women in one-piece bathing suits" (*Wilmington Every Evening*, 1925). Public decency was being redefined at the new swimming pool to mean exhibiting an attractive appearance rather than protecting one's modesty.

Americans also redrew the social boundaries of community life at municipal pools by excluding certain social groups. At the same time that municipal pools in the northern United States became gender and class integrated, they became racially segregated. In some cities, especially in the southern tier of Northern states, public officials mandated racial segregation at public pools. Mayors, city councils, and park boards determined that blacks and whites should no longer swim together and instructed pool managers and police officers to forbid identifiably black people from entering pools earmarked for whites (Wiltse, 2007: 141–152). Even the federal government mandated racial segregation at public pools during this period. The federal government administered the District of Columbia, so Congress was responsible for funding its recreation facilities. In 1925, the Senate considered a bill authorizing the construction of two giant outdoor pools for the capital. Senator Lee Overman of North Carolina objected to the bill because it did not specify that the pools would be racially segregated. The bill's sponsor, Royal Copeland of New York, assured him that district officials intended to operate the pools on a segregated basis, but Overman required more conclusive assurance. "I know the Senator from New York is all right; I have every confidence in him; but he will not have the authority to construct these pools and arrange for the bathing. . . . There ought to be some language in the bill requiring that the pools be separate." Senator Copeland consented to make explicit what had been understood. He amended the bill by adding the line, "one for the white race and the other for the colored race."[7] The amended bill passed both houses of Congress and was signed by President Calvin Coolidge on May 5, 1926 (*Washington Tribune*, 1926). Just as public officials helped engineer the class and gender integration of municipal pools during the interwar years, they also engineered the separation of blacks from whites.

In more northern cities, white swimmers themselves imposed racial segregation through coordinated violence and intimidation. At Pittsburgh's Highland Park Pool, which was supposedly open to all, white swimmers regularly punched and kicked black swimmers in the changing room and dunked them under the water in the pool. On one occasion, several hundred white swimmers simultaneously climbed out of the pool when two young black men plunged into it. As the two youths swam alone in the gigantic pool, hundreds of menacing white faces stared at them. When they climbed out, an estimated 100 whites "brutally pummeled and slugged [them] with clubs." Police officers stationed at the pool frequently encouraged these attacks and then typically arrested the black victims, charging them with "inciting to riot" (*Pittsburgh Press*, 1932). The imposition of racial segregation at the municipal pool in Elizabeth, NJ, was likewise a coordinated effort. The city opened Dowd Pool in 1930. At first, pool officials explicitly barred blacks from entering. After protests from the local chapter of the National Association for the Advancement of Colored People (NAACP), the city's recreation commission promised no further discrimination would occur. Days later, Morgan Dickinson and Walter Gordon entered the facility, but never made it into the water. As they exited the changing room, dozens of "menacing swimmers" stood shoulder to shoulder blocking their path to the pool. A police officer then "advised the two youths not to make use of the pool." Undeterred, Dickinson and Gordon tried to enter the pool but were "somewhat roughly handled by the crowd." The two young men finally managed to escape from the assault after 14 more police officers arrived to restore order ("Race riot near at Dowd Pool," *Elizabeth Daily Journal*, August 11: 1). This concerted violence effectively intimidated local blacks from using Dowd Pool. Eight years later, when the black community again attempted to integrate Dowd Pool, white swimmers and pool officials orchestrated a more sustained effort to maintain segregation. Groups of whites pelted blacks with rocks and tomatoes as they approached the pool. White swimmers dunked and punched blacks who entered the pool. Lifeguards offered no assistance to endangered black swimmers. Citizens sent scores of abusive letters to public officials threatening widespread racial violence if the city did not officially bar blacks from using the pool ("Trouble flares at Natatorium," *Elizabeth Daily Journal*, August 16: 13). The sustained violence eventually caused black residents to abandon their integration efforts. A swim in Dowd Pool was not worth the threat to their safety (Wiltse, 2007: 139). In these ways, whites utilized the social linkages that had been established at the pools to exclude blacks and thereby redraw the social boundaries of community life.

Several factors contributed to Northern whites' sudden refusal to swim in pools with blacks, but the most direct causes were gender integration and race-based health concerns. As soon as city officials permitted males and females to swim together, whites suddenly objected to the presence of blacks. Although the rationale remained mostly unspoken, Northern whites in general objected to black men having the opportunity to interact with white women at such intimate and erotic spaces. As Matthew Guterl argues in *The Color of Race in America* (2001: 6), pernicious racial prejudice increasingly infected the minds of Northern whites during this period. This led them to fear that black men would act upon their supposedly untamed sexual desire for white women by touching them in the water and assaulting them with romantic advances (Wiltse, 2007: 132–133). White Northerners also became increasingly concerned about the health and cleanliness of black Americans at this time. Most of the Southern blacks that migrated to Northern cities during the Great Black Migration settled in trash-laden, run-down slums, and many worked at dirty, low-level industrial jobs (Grossman, 1989: 153). As a result, blacks became the most conspicuous poor in Northern cities. At the same time, widely publicized health studies reported relatively high rates of communicable diseases such as tuberculosis, smallpox, and syphilis among Northern blacks (McBride, 1991: 16–30, 34–40; Hoy, 1995: 117–121). The combined effect was to stigmatize them as threats to public health. Whites now objected to swimming in the same pool with blacks, in part, because they feared contracting a communicable disease and becoming contaminated by their supposed dirtiness.

The simultaneous occurrence of class integration and racial segregation at municipal pools in the North during this period offers some insight into the relationship between social trust and social capital. Middle-class Americans became willing to swim in the same pools with working-class whites during the 1920s because the end of large-scale European immigration, improving material conditions among the working classes, and the emergence of race as the predominant social division in the North made working-class whites seem less different than they had previ-

ously. This increased general trust across class lines, which was a prerequisite for them sharing the same swimming pools. Conversely, working-class whites and blacks had commonly swum together at municipal pools during the late nineteenth and early twentieth centuries. And yet, this shared use had not generated enough social trust between blacks and whites to counteract the intensifying racial prejudice that resulted from the Great Black Migration, increasingly conspicuous poverty among Northern blacks, and media reports that emphasized racial difference. In both cases, levels of social trust were determined by larger social, economic, and ideological circumstances more than by direct interaction.

Even though interaction at municipal pools between blacks and whites did not necessarily generate social trust, the absence of interaction could harden perceptions of racial difference and intensify distrust. An incident at a municipal pool in Pittsburgh reveals this most clearly. Even as Pittsburgh's Highland Park Pool became a racial battleground when it opened in 1931, blacks and whites continued to swim in relative harmony at the city's other municipal pools, which, not coincidently, remained gender segregated. Four years later, however, racial violence spread to the city's gender-segregated pools as well. On July 7, 1935, a group of white youths "beat and kicked" 9-year-old Frank Reynolds at the Paulson Playground pool. Frank's mother reported the assault to Inspector Kellie of police station no. 6. Rather than investigating the alleged crime, Kellie admonished her, "Why can't you people use the Washington Boulevard pool, I don't approve of colored and white people swimming together" (*Pittsburgh Courier*, 1935). For two generations prior to 1935, it had been socially normal for blacks and whites of the same sex to swim together in Pittsburgh. At first, the assumption that blacks and whites should not swim together was narrowly applied to gender-integrated pools. As whites experienced swimming only with other whites at Highland Park Pool, however, this narrow social assumption expanded into a more general social value that blacks and whites should not swim together regardless of the gender mix. As a result, white swimmers began to beat black Americans out of gender-segregated pools as well. What began at Highland Park Pool had developed into a more general assumption that racial separation was natural and normal, even though it was a very recent development.

Although black Americans resented and resisted pool segregation in many Northern cities, Jim Crow pools nonetheless provided African Americans with a public space that strengthened their social attachments to one another during this period of social flux caused by the Great Black Migration. Washington, DC, for example, opened a large, modern pool for black residents in 1928, and it quickly became a center of community life. Newspaper reports indicate that it attracted a large number of children and adults and was frequented by all levels of black society (*Washington Tribune*, 1928). An early manager of the pool claimed that it served as a summer resort for blacks throughout the area. They flocked to the pool not just to swim and enjoy the sun but also to socialize and people-watch. In 1932, "spectators" accounted for nearly 10 percent of all admissions (Tyson, 1939: 3). The pool also hosted numerous special events, including frequent swim meets and an annual Fourth of July celebration (*Washington Post*, 1936). Shared concern about the pool also motivated Washington's black residents to organize community protests. When district officials planned to hire a white man to manage Francis Pool, swimmers mobilized to protest the decision. According to a local paper, they were "united in their determination to organize a boycott" and conducted extensive "picketing operations" (*Washington Post*, 1928). Francis Pool brought black Washingtonians together and their shared use of the pool enabled cooperative efforts to protect their common interest.

Swimming Pools and the Segmenting of American Society after 1945

The use of swimming pools in the United States splintered after World War II. Middle-class whites largely vacated public pools, choosing instead to swim at private clubs and backyard residential pools. Club pools largely re-segregated swimming along class lines, whereas residential pools fenced families into their own backyards. At municipal pools, desegregation opened many more pools to blacks and Latinos, but it rarely led to meaningful racial integration. When blacks and Latinos began using a pool, whites generally abandoned it. Because most working-class whites could not afford to access private pools, they resisted pool desegregation most stridently. The legacies of these post-World War II developments persist. In contemporary times, the use of swimming pools still clearly reveals the social fault lines in American communities.

Racial desegregation was, paradoxically, a key cause of the splintering. In the decade following World War II, municipal pools throughout the northern United States were desegregated through the efforts of local citizen groups and NAACP chapters. Initially, they challenged segregation by repeatedly seeking admission to whites-only pools, thereby forcing cities to actively enforce segregation. They also lobbied local public officials, encouraging them to open all pools to blacks and whites alike (Wiltse, 2007: 154–160, 166–168). If these social and political protests failed, the groups typically filed suit seeking a court order to desegregate their local pools. The first pool desegregation decision was handed down in 1948 by federal district judge Ben Moore, who ordered Montgomery, WV, to either open its one municipal pool to black residents or construct an "equal swimming facility" for their use. Since the city could not afford to construct a second pool, the ruling amounted to a desegregation order.[8] Two years later, federal district judge Rubey Hulen ordered St Louis to open its outdoor pools to black residents. When the city's attorney pointed out to the judge that his ruling upset the "status quo" and would anger white citizens, Hulen responded, "Does the viewpoint of the community set aside the Constitution? Is the Constitution to be shelved for an hour, or set aside, because one part of the community has antipathy towards it? . . . I have no intention of putting my ear to the ground, to see what the people are thinking. I think any judge that would do that would be a dishonor to the bench."[9] When Thurgood Marshall read a transcript of this exchange several weeks later, he forwarded it to two other NAACP attorneys with a note attached exclaiming, "This is really good."[10] The US Supreme Court finally ruled, if only indirectly, on racial segregation at public pools in 1955. The US Court of Appeals for the Fourth Circuit had ordered Baltimore to desegregate its public pools. Unwilling to accept the judgment of the appeals court, the city appealed to the Supreme Court, but the nine justices effectively upheld the ruling by declining to review the case (*Washington Star*, 1956). And so by 1956, public pools throughout the northern United States had been racially desegregated.

Desegregation held the promise of integrating African Americans and other racial minorities into the communities whites had created at municipal pools. The same "bonds of community friendship" forged between males and females, young and old, and rich and poor at the resort pools of the interwar years could now potentially be cemented between blacks and whites. At least some Americans at the time hoped this would indeed occur. The day after Baltimore desegregated its municipal pools in 1956, the *Sun* (June 24, 1956: 38) printed a highly suggestive photo of two boys, one white and one black, clasping hands as they plunged into the water from a diving board. The image symbolized the hope that racially integrated municipal swimming pools could help bridge the social divide which separated blacks from whites.

This hope went largely unfulfilled. Desegregation rarely led to meaningful interaction across racial lines because Northern whites generally abandoned municipal pools rather than swim with blacks. In the summer of 1948, prior to the desegregation of St Louis' Fairgrounds Pool, the city recorded 313,000 swims, all by whites. In the years after desegregation, the number of swims per year averaged only 15,000 and almost all the swimmers were now black. "It appears likely," the city's parks and recreation division explained with considerable understatement, "that the failure of the large outdoor pools to draw the huge number of swimmers that were attracted in the past may be a reflection of passive resistance to inter-racial swimming" (St Louis Parks and Recreation, *Annual Report*, 1954: 18). Warren, OH, was forced by a pending court order to desegregate its municipal pool in 1948. The local Warren newspaper covered the first day of interracial swimming by printing a front-page photo showing a dozen children waiting to enter. The last two children in line were clearly black and the caption read, "Last one in the water is a monkey" (*Warren Tribune Chronicle*, June 16, 1948: 1). The racial antipathy expressed in the newspaper was shared by many local whites.

When they realized that black residents intended to use the pool, they mostly abandoned it. Although it did not provide exact numbers, the local paper reported that "records indicate that nowhere near as many persons are using the pool this year as last" (*Warren Tribune Chronicle*, "Court rules on pool case," July 3, 1948: 4).

At the same time that public pools were being desegregated throughout the North, private swim clubs began to flourish. Americans organized thousands of club pools during the 1950s, mostly in the nation's burgeoning suburbs. Approximately 150 swim clubs appeared just in the suburbs surrounding Washington, DC, between 1953 and 1960. The *Philadelphia Evening Bulletin* (1958) reported that "swim-club pools have sprung up in every direction." The same was true in cities across the country. If the 1920s and 1930s was the age of municipal pools, the 1950s was the age of private swim clubs (Wiltse, 2007: 193–194).

Club pools fulfilled a vital social function in America's burgeoning postwar suburbs. These new communities lacked the social bonds that knit older communities together. Neighbors did not know one another, nor did they necessarily share the same ethnic or religious heritage. Furthermore, single-family homes in sprawling suburbs best navigated by car tended to isolate families from their neighbors. Swimming pools, however, brought suburban families together. They were one of the few civic spaces where suburbanites could socialize and integrate themselves into the community. The *Philadelphia Evening Bulletin* (1958) commented that joining a swim club served as "a means of becoming acquainted with neighbors, forming friendships among children and uniting a community in a common purpose. The community swim pool is an investment in . . . neighborhood co-operation, enjoyment and friendliness." In short, club pools were vital social centers in America's postwar suburbs.

Suburban communities could have chosen to fund public pools – which would have served the same social function as club pools – but most did not. In July 1954 Donald Hunt, chairman of the Montgomery County Council in Maryland, noted there was "no interest" in public pools, even though a dozen local groups were organizing private swim clubs at the time (*Washington Star*,

1954). Montgomery County did not open its first public pool until 1968 (*Washington Star*, 1968a). As late as 1974, Montgomery County and neighboring Prince George's County operated a total of two public pools. By contrast, there were well over 100 club pools scattered throughout the two counties (*Washington Post*, 1974). The same was true in suburban Philadelphia. The *Philadelphia Inquirer* (1964) reported that "private swim clubs are flourishing in all areas of suburban Philadelphia," but counted only one public pool in the city's suburbs.

Suburbanites organized private club pools rather than fund public pools during the 1950s and 1960s because club pools enabled them to control the social composition of swimmers, whereas public pools did not. As one critic commented in 1955, club pools were built "not for all persons regardless of race or creed, but for a group of affluent [white] citizens" (*Washington Star* 1955a). Class exclusion was achieved through residency requirements and membership fees. Many pool associations mandated that most or all members had to live within a certain distance of the club or within a particular subdivision. This limited the social makeup of the membership to the social makeup of the community. The typical US$200 membership fee and US$30 annual dues reinforced the residency requirement by restricting membership to families earning a middle-class income (Wiltse, 2007: 194–196). As a result of this social exclusivity, club pools re-divided swimmers along class lines. Americans from different social classes once again swam and socialized at different pools.

The primary appeal of club pools for white suburbanites, however, was the assurance of not having to swim with black Americans. Civil rights laws applied only to "public accommodations," so private clubs could legally exclude blacks from becoming members even after courts had forced cities to desegregate public pools. Many club pools, especially those located in suburbs accessible to black Americans, explicitly barred them from joining (Wiltse, 2007: 195). Other swim clubs relied on the racial exclusivity of their surrounding neighborhood to ensure a whites-only membership. One club in suburban Washington, DC, passed a residency requirement in 1958 mandating that members live within three-quarters of a mile (1.2 km) of the club. So few blacks lived in

the area that the club did not receive a membership application from a black family until 1968. When the first black family applied, the club rejected its application and then quickly established an official policy limiting membership to whites.[11] Since the club could no longer rely on residential segregation to protect the racial composition of its membership, it now needed an explicit policy. Noting the pervasive discrimination against black Americans at club pools, a Washington, DC judge lamented, "I suppose like many people I really didn't believe that when the issue had to be faced that intelligent, well-educated, financially secure suburban middle-class people would effectively exclude a neighbor from a community [swimming pool] solely on the basis of race" (*Washington Star*, 1968b). In this case, he clearly misunderstood the suburban middle class.

It is also clear that racial desegregation deterred suburban communities from building public pools during the 1950s and 1960s. Montgomery County, MD offers a particularly clear example. In May 1955 the county council authorized construction of two public swimming pools. Its stated rationale was that moderate-income residents could not necessarily afford membership at a private club (*Washington Star*, 1955b). The council suddenly scrapped the two public pools a couple of months later, however, just days after a federal court ordered the desegregation of public recreation facilities throughout Maryland (*Washington Star*, 1955c). A year earlier, a local citizen had asked rhetorically, "Is [approving club pools] to be the easy way for the County Council, other municipal bodies and civic associations to avoid the issue of public pools?" (*Washington Star*, 1954). In many suburban communities, the answer was yes.

Backyard residential pools were the second wave of private pool construction during the postwar period. In 1950, there were only 2,500 residential pools in the United States. At the time, Americans rightly associated them with Hollywood stars and Long Island estates. Thereafter, however, the number of residential pools in the United States increased rapidly. The building spree began in 1952, when Americans built 7,000 residential pools, but really took off during the 1960s, when an average of 50,000 new residential pools was built each year. By 1970, Americans owned a total of 800,000 residential pools. New construction continued to accelerate thereafter. By the end of the 1990s, Americans were building 170,000 residential pools annually and the total number in the United States topped 4 million (Wiltse, 2007: 199, 201, 203).

Several factors enabled this rapid growth. Mass suburbanization and expanding economic prosperity created the material conditions necessary for millions of American families to install backyard pools. These material developments, however, do not explain why having a pool in one's backyard appealed to so many Americans. Residential pools were so popular during the second half of the twentieth century because they satisfied several desires common among the suburban middle class. For one, they advertised material success and upward mobility. Installing a backyard pool was a conspicuous way for "status-seeking" Americans to show they were getting ahead. "Of all the symbols of wealth you can imagine," the *Washington Star* recognized in 1957, "having a private swimming pool for your own family would probably rank among the highest" (Porter, 1957). Residential pools also enhanced domestic family life by keeping mom, dad, and children at home to recreate. At a time when many parents feared that cars, movies, and youth culture were eroding domestic relationships, residential swimming pools promised to strengthen family bonds by providing an appealing at-home gathering space. Finally, backyard pools enabled Americans to retreat from public life and thereby avoid interacting with people they did not already know at club pools or public pools. Residential pools provided the privacy, security, and social exclusivity that so many suburbanites desired during the tumultuous postwar decades (Wiltse, 2007: 200–201).

The history of swimming pools clearly corroborates Robert Putnam's central claim in *Bowling Alone* that the quality of community life in America has declined over the last several decades due to a widespread retreat from public life. The choices of millions and millions of Americans to abandon public pools and either join a swim club or install a backyard pool exemplify what Putnam terms "civic disengagement." And yet, the timing and causes of pool privatization complicate Putnam's interpretation. He claims (2000: 31–180) that community life flour-

ished during the 1950s and 1960s and then began to decline in the 1970s. He explains the flourishing and then the decline primarily by generational turnover. Americans who came of age during the Great Depression and World War II, he claims, were exceptionally active in the civic life of their communities. By the 1970s, this generation was beginning to pass away. Subsequent generations, according to Putnam, have been less civically active (2000: 247–276). Furthermore, Putnam explicitly downplays racial prejudice and racial desegregation as causes of Americans' retreat from public life. "[My] evidence is not conclusive," Putnam concludes, "but it does shift the burden of proof onto those who believe that racism is a primary explanation for growing civic disengagement" (2000: 280, 283–284).

The history of swimming pools locates the beginning of civic disengagement in the 1950s and 1960s – the period when Putnam claims community life flourished – and links it quite clearly with racial prejudice and racial desegregation. Between 1950 and 1970, millions of Americans chose to stop swimming at municipal pools. This represented a mass abandonment of public space and was caused most directly by racial prejudice. When municipal pools were desegregated, white swimmers generally fled because they were unwilling to use these public spaces with blacks and Latinos. Those who could afford the expense organized or joined private club pools. The primary appeal of club pools was that white, middle-class members could avoid interacting with people who were socially different from themselves, especially African Americans. Club pools contributed to a vibrant community life, but access was narrowly restricted along class and racial lines. The frequent and sustained interactions that had occurred between middle-class and working-class Americans at municipal pools during the interwar years diminished. Although difficult to prove empirically, the absence of meaningful interaction between socially diverse people and the lack of an immediate common interest – such as a shared swimming pool – surely hardened social divisions, limited understanding across social lines, and segmented civic life. At the very least, pools no longer served as spaces where social capital could be generated among Americans from different social classes.

The proliferation of residential pools repre-sented a much more profound civic disengage-ment. Between 1950 and 1970, nearly 800,000 American families spent considerable sums of money in order to recreate at home rather than in public. They installed backyard pools precisely because they wanted to turn inward and privilege family over community. As Alexis de Tocqueville observed back in the nineteenth century:

> each person, withdrawn into himself, behaves as though he is a stranger to the destiny of all the others. His children and his good friends consti-tute for him the whole of the human species. . . . And if on these terms there remains in his mind a sense of family, there no longer remains a sense of society. (Quoted in Sennett, 1974: vii)

This retreat from public life accelerated after 1970, when 3 million more American families installed at-home pools. But it originated during the postwar period among the generation that came of age during the Great Depression and World War II.

The privatization of swimming pools has degraded civic life in more tangible ways as well. For one, it contributed to the decline of munici-pal pools. When middle-class Americans largely abandoned public pools in favor of private pools, cities downgraded the importance of public pools. As a result, relatively few municipal pools were built during the postwar period. Washing-ton, DC and New York, for example, opened no new pools between 1945 and 1960. Kansas City likewise built no new pools during this period, even though it operated only three at the time (Wiltse, 2007: 184–185). In addition to not build-ing new pools, many cities underfunded mainte-nance on existing pools and eventually closed many of them – especially those serving minority swimmers – when they became dilapidated. In Washington, DC, for example, federal officials let McKinley Pool fall into disrepair after it was racially desegregated in 1950 and its use changed from exclusively white to predominantly black. By 1960, the "pipes were corroded," the drainage system backed up, and the filtration system did not work properly. According to city engineers, the pool had become "a health hazard" (Washing-ton Star, 1962). Local residents organized a series of rallies encouraging the federal government to

repair McKinley Pool, but it decided to close the pool instead (Washington Star, 1963). Public offi-cials in Kansas City closed one of its pools in 1957 for similar reasons. After Grove Pool was deseg-regated in 1954, attendance plummeted and city officials began to view it as a financial burden not a civic asset. Rather than pay the yearly operating deficit of US$6,000, the city closed the facility even though it operated only two other swim-ming pools (Kansas City Times, 1957). In 1966, Philadelphia closed its municipal pool located at Memphis and Albert streets and replaced it with a parking lot (Philadelphia Evening Bulletin, 1966). Swimming pools were clearly no longer the high civic priority that they had been previously.

A second wave of pool closures occurred during the 1980s and 1990s in response to declin-ing attendance and budget shortfalls. As late as 1984, Youngstown, OH operated eight municipal pools, but attendance at the pools was 80 percent lower than it had been in previous decades. Over the next seven years, the city permanently closed six of its pools, leaving residents with only two public pools in which to swim (Wiltse, 2007: 190–192). The destruction of municipal pools in Pittsburgh came later than in Youngstown but was equally severe. Between 1996 and 2004, the city permanently closed 20 of its 32 pools in an effort to reduce its ballooning budget deficit. Some members of the city council complained – but to no avail – that public pools should be the last city services suspended because they pro-vided one of the few forms of active recreation for poor residents during the summer. As a result of the closings, Pittsburgh offered residents fewer municipal pools in 2005 than it had in 1925 (Wiltse, 2007: 192–193).

In 1991 a New Yorker article commented on a rash of pool closings in New York City. The author claimed that closing municipal pools sig-nificantly degraded the quality of community life in the city. The neighborhood pools, he observed, brought people together and provided a public space – amid the high-rise apartments, passing cars, and hurrying pedestrians – where neighbors actually communicated with one another. Closing the pools, he implied, would make local residents more anonymous to one another and erode the local sense of community that they fostered. The author also related the pool closings to what he saw as the increasing privatization of life in the city. New Yorkers, he noted, spent untold billions on Hampton summer homes, artwork and furnishings, and entertainment. And yet, amidst such plenty, the city could not afford to operate its municipal pools.

> We are not poor as a people, yet somehow we have become bankrupt as a society. We are – to use an old fashioned word – *ruined*. . . . We seem to have accepted two separate economies: one of abundance, ruling the way that many of us eat and sleep and entertain ourselves, and one of absolute hand-to-mouth impoverishment, ruling our civic life. ("Talk of the Town," *New Yorker*, August 5, 1991: 22–23)

While readers of the *New Yorker* may have shared the author's concern about impoverished civic life, the closing of municipal pools affected poor and working-class Americans most directly and severely. They could least afford to join a private swim club or install a backyard pool, which meant they relied on public recreation facilities. Fewer public pools meant reduced opportunities for recreation. When Youngstown, OH was considering closing one more of its pools in 1989, city councilwoman Darlene Rogers pointed out the obvious: "If we close the pool, there won't be any place for those kids to swim. And we don't have many other recreational activities for them" (*Youngstown Vindicator*, 1989). The same was true elsewhere. As a result of pool closings, many poor and working-class neighborhoods in American cities lack appealing public spaces where residents can gather to socialize, exercise, play, and forge community bonds.

Conclusion

On June 29, 2009, 65 campers from the Creative Steps day camp in North Philadelphia arrived at the Valley Swim Club in suburban Montgomery County to swim and play for an hour and a half. The camp director, Althea Wright, had paid the private club US$1,950 to use the facility Monday afternoons throughout the summer. The camp had to rely on the private club for a place to swim, in part, because budget shortfalls had forced Philadelphia to close many of its public pools that summer. As the campers entered the water, some club members reportedly pulled their children out of the pool and wondered aloud what all these black and Latino kids were doing there. A few days later, the Valley Swim Club returned the US$1,950 to Wright and informed her that the club had decided to cancel the use agreement (Tillman and Stendahl, 2009). When later pressed to explain why the club would not permit the campers back at the pool, club president John Duesler stated "there was concern that a lot of kids would change the complexion . . . and the atmosphere of the club" (Gerhart, 2009). This incident quickly erupted into a national news story. Journalists, bloggers, USA Swimming, and even then-senator Arlen Specter expressed shock that such apparently blatant racial discrimination could occur in contemporary times. "This is the sort of thing you'd hear about in 1966 during the height of the Civil Rights Movement," commented Chuck Wielgus, executive director of USA Swimming, "not in 2009 and not in [Philadelphia]" (Gerhart, 2009).

The Valley Club incident highlights how the history of swimming pools shapes the ongoing relationship between civic life and social capital in contemporary America. The Valley Club was founded in 1956, when private swim clubs were being developed in response to the racial desegregation of public pools. Suburbanites chose to organize private swim clubs rather than fund public pools in large part because they could still legally exclude non-whites from private clubs. The racial prejudice at the time caused middle-class whites to create restricted environments that ensured they would not have to interact with people socially different from themselves.[12] Since the 1950s, racial prejudice has surely diminished, but the relatively homogeneous social environments created at that time still remain. The Valley Club, for example, had no African American members when the camper controversy occurred in 2009 (*Philadelphia Inquirer*, 2009). As a result of these homogeneous environments, civic life remains socially fragmented. Many Americans do not publicly interact in a meaningful way with people from different class and racial backgrounds. Ideologically they may embrace social and cultural pluralism, but they do not have the social experiences that would enable them to feel comfortable around people who are socially different from themselves. This was why, it seems to me, some members of the Valley Club reacted as they did to the Creative Steps campers. They were not racists – they were suburbanites accustomed to recreating only with people just like themselves.

If Americans want to avoid future Valley Club incidents and increase the type of interaction across class and racial lines that generates social capital, they need to consciously break from the long trend towards privatization – which has contributed to the creation of homogeneous social environments – and recommit themselves to funding public spaces where diverse Americans can comfortably gather together. The resort-like municipal swimming pools of the interwar years served this function for whites of all social classes. Blacks were excluded because of the pervasive racial prejudice that existed at the time and the absence of social trust across racial lines. Today, the historical circumstances are much different. Black Americans are integrated into the political and cultural mainstream. Many occupy a secure place within the middle class and even upper class. Racial prejudice has become publicly untenable. In other words, the social, economic, and ideological circumstances of today suggest that sufficient social trust exists for Americans from different racial backgrounds to gather together at public spaces. What communities need now are appealing and sociable public spaces where this can occur.

Notes

1   New York City Parks Department, "Restoration of the WPA Era Pools in New York City," (undated) "Sports-Swimming" vertical file, Irma and Paul Milstein Division, New York Public Research Library.

2   My research has focused exclusively on the United States and, thus, I limit to my conclusions to it. Even though anxieties about racial and ethnic difference, which are rooted in historical circumstances particular to the United States, have profoundly shaped the history of swimming pools in the country, my conclusions may, nonetheless, be relevant to other societies. On February 23, 2008, the Economist published an article "The search for social glue" about segregation at public swimming pools in Great Britain that drew direct parallels to the social conflict that has characterized the use of swimming pools in the United States.

3   Theorists have identified three basic variants of social capital. Pierre Bourdieu conceives of social capital as a resource that is accessible to individuals through networks of relationships within formal institutions, such as universities and corporations (Bourdieu and Wacquant, 1992: 119). James Coleman likewise focuses on the individual benefits of social relationships, but he studies the benefits derived through social relationships that develop within less formal and less exclusive institutions, such as families and community organizations. Coleman also theorizes that social capital contributes to the overall good of the social group by promoting cooperation among individual members (Coleman, 1994). Robert Putnam extends Coleman's consideration of the larger, group benefits of social capital to include entire communities and even whole societies. He is especially attentive to the trust and shared norms that he claims develop in communities and societies with strong and abundant networks of interpersonal relationships (Putnam, 2000). Too many words have been written dissecting the differences between these variants of social capital and privileging one over the others (Crabbe, 2008; Blackshaw and Long, 2005). Different forms of social capital can accrue from relationships in different social contexts, and scholars can usefully draw from the insights of different thinkers without accepting any of them whole. In the case of public recreation sites, such as swimming pools, the social capital generated is mostly of the types identified by Coleman and Putnam. The relationships are informal, and the interaction clearly affects the larger community. And yet, Bourdieu's recognition that social capital can be used in ways that reinforce privilege is also germane to understanding how the social capital generated at swimming pools has been used.

4   For good introductions to the concept of social capital and the scholarship that has been written about it, see Field (2008) and Halpern (2005).

5   By social trust, I mean the general assumption on the part of people within a community that others will not harm, exploit, or defraud them.

6   Playground Association of America, "Citizen as Playmaker." Annual Report (1909), Philadelphia.

7   Congressional Record, 69th Cong., 1st Session, Washington, DC (1926): 3629, 7949–7950, 8232, 8747.

8   Lawrence v. Hancock (1948), 76 F. Supp. 1004, 1007–1008.

9   "Judge refuses to delay opening pools to negroes," St. Louis Post-Dispatch, July 18, 1950: 3.

10 Note attached to "Transcript of Proceedings," Draper v. City of St. Louis (1950), "Discrimination – Swimming Pools – St. Louis" folder, box B-66,

Part II: 1940–1955, NAACP Papers, Manuscript Division, Library of Congress, Washington, DC.

11 Tillman v. Wheaton-Haven Recreation Association (1973), 410 US 431, 432–433.

12 Postwar suburbs were likewise products of racial prejudice. Developers restricted ownership to whites, and many suburbanites moved out of cities in order to escape the breakdown of residential segregation in urban neighborhoods (Jackson, 1985: 241–243; Sugrue, 1996: 181–230).

References

Arneil, B. (2006) *Diverse Communities: The Problem with Social Capital*, New York: Cambridge University Press.

Bethlehem (1920) *Third Annual Message of Mayor Archibald Johnston to the Members of Council and Citizens of Bethlehem, Pa., and Reports of the Superintendents of the Various City Departments*, Bethlehem, PA.

Biggott, J. (2001) *From Cottage to Bungalow: Houses and the Working Class in Metropolitan Chicago, 1869–1929*, Chicago: University of Chicago Press.

Blackshaw, T. and Long, J. (2005) "What's the big idea? A critical exploration of the concept of social capital and its incorporation into leisure policy discourse." *Leisure Studies*, 24 (3): 239–258.

Bourdieu, P. and Wacquant, L. (1992) *An Invitation to Reflexive Sociology*, Chicago: University of Chicago Press.

Brozan, N. (1990) "A crumbling pool divides a neighborhood." *New York Times*, July 30: B1.

CCRR (Chicago Commission on Race Relations) (1922) *The Negro in Chicago: A Study of Race Relations and a Race Riot*, New York: Arno Press, reprint.

Coleman, J.S. (1994) *Foundations of Social Theory*, Cambridge, MA: Belknap Press.

Crabbe, T. (2008) "Avoiding the numbers game: Social theory, policy and sport's role in the art of relationship building," in Nicholson, M. and Hoye, R. (eds.), *Sports and Social Capital: An Introduction*, Burlington, MA: Butterworth-Heinemann.

Crawford, M. (1995) *Building the Workingman's Paradise: The Design of American Company Towns*, New York: Verso.

Cross, G. (2000) *An All-Consuming Century: Why Commercialism Won in Modern America*, New York: Columbia University Press.

Field, J. (2008) *Social Capital* (2nd edn.), New York: Routledge.

Fortune (1934) "Swimming . . . the new great American sport." *Fortune*, June: 81.

Gerhart, A. (2009) "Alleged prejudice starts probe at club." *Washington Post*, July 11: A2.

Grossman, J. (1989) *Land of Hope: Chicago, Black Southerners, and the Great Migration*, Chicago: University of Chicago Press.

Guterl, M. (2001) *The Color of Race in America, 1900–1940*, Cambridge, MA: Harvard University Press.

Halpern, D. (2005) *Social Capital*, Cambridge: Polity Press.

Harvey, J. (2007) "Sport and social capital," in Ritzer, R. (ed.) *The Blackwell Encyclopedia of Sociology*, vol. 9, Oxford: Wiley-Blackwell: 4693–4694.

Hoy, S. (1995) *Chasing Dirt: The American Pursuit of Cleanliness*, Oxford: Oxford University Press.

Jackson, K. (1985) *Crabgrass Frontier: The Suburbanization of the United States*, Oxford: Oxford University Press.

Kansas City Times (1957) "Grove Pool is closed." *Kansas City Times*, October 21.

McBride, D. (1991) *From TB to AIDS: Epidemics among Urban Blacks since 1900*, Albany: State University of New York Press.

Nasaw, D. (1993) *Going Out: The Rise and Fall of Public Amusements*, New York: Basic Books.

New York Times (1910a) "Stover wants no park wading pools." *New York Times*, July 4: 3.

New York Times (1910b) "The Central Park plans." *New York Times*, July 4: 3.

New York Times (1985) "Goldin cites hazards at swimming pools." *New York Times*, April 1: B4.

Nicholson, M. and Hoye, R. (2008) *Sport and Social Capital*, Burlington, MA: Butterworth-Heinemann.

Philadelphia Evening Bulletin (1958) "Communities are pooling their interests for everyone's benefit." *Philadelphia Evening Bulletin*, April 6.

Philadelphia Evening Bulletin (1966) "3 Councilmen want more swim pools." *Philadelphia Evening Bulletin*, July 19.

Philadelphia Inquirer (1964) "Booming public pools lag behind rise in swimmer population." *Philadelphia Inquirer*, July 30.

Philadelphia Inquirer (2009) "Stagnant pool." *Philadelphia Inquirer*, November 18.

Pittsburgh Courier (1935) "Police look on as whites beat youth at pool." *Pittsburgh Courier*, July 13: 1.

Pittsburgh Press (1932) "2 negro swimmers attacked by mob." *Pittsburgh Press*, July 9: 16.

Porter, S. (1957) "Boom in swimming pools." *Washington Star*, May 22: B22.

Putnam, R. (2000) *Bowling Alone: The Collapse and Revival of American Democracy*, New York: Simon & Schuster.

Roediger, D. (2005) *Working Toward Whiteness: The Strange Journey from Ellis Island to the Suburbs*, New York: Basic Books.

Sennett, R. (1974) *The Fall of Public Man*, New York: Norton.

Shaw, E. (1924) "Ellsworth – 2,100 population – builds a municipal swimming pool." *American City*, June: 668–669.

Stelloh, T. (2006) "Seeking to recapture the glory of the past. Or maybe not." *New York Times*, April 9: CY7.

Sugrue, T. (1996) *The Origins of the Urban Crisis: Race and Inequality in Postwar Detroit*, Princeton, NJ: Princeton University Press.

Tillman, Z. and Stendahl, M. (2009) "Montco club accused of racial discrimination." *Philadelphia Inquirer*, July 9: A1.

Todd, R. (1907) "The municipal baths of Manhattan." *Charities and the Commons*, 19: 896–903.

Tomes, N. (1998) *The Gospel of Germs: Men, Women, and the Microbe in American Life*, Cambridge, MA: Harvard University Press.

Tyson, J. (1939) "The Francis Swimming Pools of the Welfare and Recreational Association of Public Buildings and Grounds," James G. Tyson Papers, Moorland-Spingarn Research Center, Howard University, Washington, DC.

Washington Post (1928) "Colored citizens fight on head of pool." *Washington Post*, June 28: 20.

Washington Post (1936) "DC awaits greatest '4th' in its history." *Washington Post*, July 1: X17.

Washington Post (1974) "It's hard for most to get in the swim." *Washington Post*, May 26: B1.

Washington Star (1954) "Montgomery heated on community swimming pools." *Washington Star*, July 11: A13.

Washington Star (1955a) "County rejects plea in Donaldson Run for swimming pool." *Washington Star*, April 3: A8.

Washington Star (1955b) "Civic federation asks two $150,000 Montgomery pools." *Washington Star*, March 15: A10.

Washington Star (1955c) "Pool program to share budget hearing interest." *Washington Star*, June 14: A16.

Washington Star (1956) "Integration delays swim pool opening in city of Baltimore." *Washington Star*, May 20: A15.

Washington Star (1962) "McKinley Pool, in bad condition, to be shut down." *Washington Star*, March 30: A3.

Washington Star (1963) "Pickets ask reopening of closed pool." *Washington Star*, July 6: A16.

Washington Star (1968a) "Montgomery readies first county pool." *Washington Star*, July 14: B5.

Washington Star (1968b) "Club in New Carollton excludes negro family." *Washington Star*, July 14: B4.

Washington Tribune (1926) "Beach bill passed with color line." *Washington Tribune*, April 30: 1.

Washington Tribune (1928) "Society views splash events at swim meet: Many prominent in Baltimore and Washington social circles at Francis Pool." *Washington Tribune*, September 14: 3.

Wilmington Evening Journal (1925) "1900 bathe in Price Run Pool." *Evening Journal*, July 7: 13.

Wilmington Every Evening (1925) "Price's Run Pool not to be open during Sundays." *Wilmington Every Evening*, July 15: 10.

Wilmington Star (1930) "Resulting from annual drives city now has splendid pools." *Wilmington Star*, June 15: 9.

Wiltse, J. (2007) *Contested Waters: A Social History of Swimming Pools in America*, Chapel Hill: University of North Carolina Press.

Yampolsky, P. (1990) "In Brooklyn, people say, 'I grew up at McCarren Park Pool.'" *New York Times*, August 18: 24.

Youngstown Vindicator (1989) "Youngstown may close 2nd city pool." *Youngstown Vindicator*, April 21: 1.

Further Reading

Arneil, B. (2006) *Diverse Communities: The Problem with Social Capital*, New York: Cambridge University Press.

Field, J. (2008) *Social Capital* (2nd edn.), New York: Routledge.

Putnam, R. (2000) *Bowling Alone: The Collapse and Revival of American Community*, New York: Simon & Schuster.

Wiltse, J. (2007) *Contested Waters: A Social History of Swimming Pools in America*, Chapel Hill: University of North Carolina Press.

Part Four

Cultures, Subcultures, and (Post)Sport

Introduction

As evidenced within the first section of this book, modern sport is an inveterately global institution. Nonetheless, the embodied nature of sport performance renders it an intimately local experience too. Differently put, the contingencies of social, cultural, spatial, economic, political, and/or technological settings mean that sport is an unavoidably localized practice which can incorporate the peculiarities of the local within its ritualized performance. The chapters in this Part acknowledge the global–local tensions imbued within the performance of sport. Each of them points to broader global structures and sensibilities responsible (even in opposition) for the existence and operation of the sport practice, while simultaneously pointing to the localized subcultural dimensions, through which the activity becomes a vehicle for the advancement and/or contestation of class, race, gender, sexuality, generational, or nation-based cultures and power relations. Thinking about these subcultural dimensions – and how they challenge, extend, or confirm traditional definitions of what constitutes "sport" – is a central theme of the section, which is taken up in various ways by the different authors.

Developing upon numerous themes introduced within earlier sections of the book, Edwin Amenta and Natasha Miric (CHAPTER 18) contextualize and complicate the performative and ritualistic phenomenon of sport fandom. Acknowledging its varied iterations, they conceptualize the traditional sports fan as an individual who regularly follows, and displays a meaningful level of appreciation for and an emotional attachment to, sport teams and/or individual sport athletes. Amenta and Miric also theorize the career trajectories of the sport fan, and the proliferating possibilities for developing new sport fan allegiances and practices, resulting from technologically driven changes in the production and delivery of sport. Focusing on the United States, they disentangle the complexities of sport fandom, beginning with an explanation for the dominant team-sport culture that generates the majority of fan interest and involvement. By identifying the macro-social considerations underpinning the rise to ascendancy of football, basketball, baseball, and to a lesser extent, ice hockey, Amenta and Miric illustrate the processes whereby certain sports become institutionalized, and thereby socially, culturally, and economically dominant, to the extent that they preclude the establishment of sporting rivals to their hegemonic position. The authors also discuss the role played by social class differences in determining

A Companion to Sport, First Edition. Edited by David L. Andrews and Ben Carrington.
© 2013 Blackwell Publishing Ltd. Published 2013 by Blackwell Publishing Ltd.

a potential fan's choice of sport. With reference to Pierre Bourdieu's theorizing, and as a result of variable access to economic and cultural capital, Amenta and Miric point to the socially distinguishing function of sport fandom, most often realized by the sport choices of the middle and upper classes. These groupings are able to (re) produce their social status either through involvement in the elitist sporting practices from which the lower classes are effectively prohibited, or through more socially intensive involvements in those sport cultures with a mass appeal. Finally, through recourse to an ethnographic study of New York City softball players, Amenta and Miric chart the rise of the "player fan," that is, those individuals who root their identities, and indeed their fandom, within the teams for whom they actually play.

Identifying an important dimension of sport performance, Kevin Young and Michael Atkinson (CHAPTER 19) point to the dearth of research focused on the practice of social deviance by theorists within the sociology of sport community. This is particularly ironic due to the continued prevalence of deviant sporting acts, such that within many settings the performance of deviance – of various types – has become a quasi-sanctioned, and largely anticipated aspect of sport culture. As such, Young and Atkinson's chapter can be considered a corrective to this glaring absence, through a concerted effort to bring the issue of *sporting deviance* to the fore. This is achieved through a conceptually derived discussion of the complex phenomenon of sport deviance; an overview of the major theoretical approaches used to interpret embodied deviance in sport cultures (including violence and aggression theories, subculture theories, identity politics theories, and victimology theories); and an empirically-based and multifocused rationale explaining the endurance, and perhaps even the necessity, of sports deviance. Focusing primarily on elite or corporate sport, the final section of the chapter points to the varied reasons, and indeed tacit encouragement, for the persistence of specific forms of *tolerable* embodied sport deviance, many of which are attributable to the contextual forces shaping contemporary sport and society. These include: a general perception of the low place of sport deviance on the wider social problems hierarchy; the perceived ability for sport

organizations to effectively police and govern their own miscreants; the mimetic social function played by violent sporting acts in eliciting excitement amongst spectators; the positioning of athletes as a specially protected population, whose indiscretions are willingly often overlooked by many; the pathologizing of individual deviant athletes, as opposed to social and sporting formations which helped nurture their deviance; the perceived futility of legal cases against athletes; and, finally, the general sensationalization and over-amplification of deviance within popular culture, rendering people less outraged by its occurrence.

Holly Thorpe and Belinda Wheaton (CHAPTER 20) dissect the performative and ritualistic dimensions of action sports (i.e., skateboarding, surfing, snowboarding, kite-surfing, BMX) that have emerged as an alternative to the highly rationalized and competitive structures of traditional achievement sport. Based on a thorough analysis of the voluminous action sports studies literature (including reference to a number of their own important studies), Thorpe and Wheaton focus on the evolution of the action sports sector, through an examination of the different theoretical approaches used to inform the understanding of the power, politics, and agency shaping these highly individualized and seemingly expressive sporting activities. The discussion originates with an exposition of the profound influence of the Centre for Contemporary Cultural Studies' subcultural theory within the sociology of action sports cultures. Acknowledging the importance of this work, Thorpe and Wheaton nonetheless are candid with regards to its flaws. Uppermost amongst these, they cite action sports studies that reinscribe the understanding of action sports subcultures as fixed and immutable (as opposed to dynamic and contingent) sociocultural formations and the illusory nature of subcultural opposition, wherein performative expressions of subcultural membership are oftentimes erroneously conflated with meaningful political resistance. The authors then turn to the influence of *post-subcultural studies* within action sports studies. This body of work offers a more complex understanding of action sport cultures, which avoids the pitfalls of dichotomous understandings privileging either subcultural resistance or subcultural incorporation. Many action sports scholars working within the post-subcultural studies framework have illustrated the agentic possibilities of subcultural involvement, through recourse to studies of how some participants operate in active and creative ways within the contingencies imposed by their sport's comprehensive commercialization. Thorpe and Wheaton subsequently discuss the myriad power relations explicated by action sports studies researchers (including those associated with identity politics, spatial politics, representational politics, and bodily and aesthetic politics of action sports formations). Finally, they suggest the importance of enhancing action sports studies, through the adoption of an approach founded on methodological reflexivity, theoretical versatility, and transformational possibility.

From the broad overview of action sports studies provided by the preceding chapter, Michael Atkinson (CHAPTER 21) delves into the specificities of the reemergence of an alternative action sport: Parkour or free running. This physical cultural practice involves the incorporation of elements of the built urban environment into creative and exhilarating gymnastic journeys between two established points. Drawing upon Martin Heidegger's existential phenomenology, and to a lesser extent Guy Debord's neo-Marxism, Atkinson positions Parkour as an expressive embodied performance revealing important essences of the human condition, through which participants (or *traceurs*) explore the existential dimensions of athleticism. Many aspects of action sports have been irrevocably incorporated into the modernist, techno-capitalist strictures of performance or achievement sport. Such "transhumanist" approaches to sport advocate the utilization of technological interventions on the athlete's body as a means of enhancing performance through scientific innovation, leading to a *de facto* blurring of the boundaries between nature, humanity, and technology. Informed by ethnographic data derived from engagement with Parkour communities in two Canadian cities, Atkinson advances Parkour as an antidote to the dehumanizing tendencies of transhuman sport. It is a resistant *post-sport* response to, and a form of moral, reflexive, community-oriented, anarchic athleticism and active rejection of, the disciplining and framing constraints of modern sport's

preoccupation with the scientific mastery of the human condition. Atkinson identifies Parkour as a technique of late modern *poiesis*: the expression of subjective human realities and possibilities, or what Heidegger referred to as the coming to presence as Beings. For many traceurs, Parkour provides a bringing forth of poiesis, as evidenced in their ambivalence toward the measuring and accountability of the Parkour performance, in favor of a recognition of its role in accenting knowledge about the human condition. Thus, the performance of Parkour becomes a site of existential experience.

Focusing on the role of sport performance in the process of identity construction, Amy L. Best (CHAPTER 22) examines the world of illegal street-racers within San Jose, California. Utilizing a range of qualitative methods, yet resting largely on in-depth and focus group interviews with young men and women, she explores the practices and symbolism of this grouping. Best argues that the culture of street-racing provides a venue for the materialization, and indeed intersection, of negotiated understandings of gender, class, ethnicity, and nation. Her study focuses largely on the "Import Car Scene" favored by many first- and second-generation immigrant populations (particularly those from various parts of Southeast Asia), as juxtaposed against the "American muscle" cars preferred by white racers. Interestingly, Best notes the important social and symbolic function played by car ownership within each of these antagonistic working-class groups, particularly with regard to expressions of masculine status and identity. She acknowledges the breakdown of traditional sources of working-class masculinity that resulted from the collapse of the modern industrial manufacturing complex, precipitated by the economic restructuring of the 1970s and 1980s. Within this context, cars – historically a defining feature of American masculinity – have taken on added significance within the gender-identity projects of these young men. Despite the fact that these two antagonistic groups rarely race against each other, much of Best's argument focuses on the material and symbolic differences between import and domestic racing car cultures, through which ethnic differences and conflicts are (re)inscribed. Thus, the very structure and design of the cars become metonyms for the broader ethnic grouping, and, quite literally, the vehicles for inter-group conflict. For instance, the lightweight, low-cost quickness of the import cars are as celebrated by their Asian American advocates, as they are derided by their white American detractors, who favor the heavier and larger-engined domestic frame. As Best concludes, the culture of street-racing provides young men with a highly visible forum for the assertion and contestation of their racially and ethnically inflected masculinities.

Lastly in this Part, Antony Puddephatt and Gary Alan Fine (CHAPTER 23) utilize a symbolic interactionist perspective in examining the social world of chess. Based upon independent ethnographic explorations of chess players and chess culture, Puddephatt and Fine combine to provide a nuanced and empirically rich understanding which evidences the fluid and complex nature of the chess subculture, or *community in action*. As with other chapters in this Part, the authors also elucidate the role played by chess in shaping participants' identities and lifestyles, especially to those for whom the game becomes an all-consuming activity. Following a discussion of the broad range of research unpacking the diverse elements of chess as a field of action, Puddephatt and Fine offer a typology of chess as art, science, and sport, which points to both the discrete and the interrelated aspects of each category. In terms of *chess as art*, they suggest that aesthetic elements play an important role in the popularity of the game, particularly in its ability to immerse the participant subjects in the game to a sufficient degree that it becomes a temporary refuge from life's problems and anxieties. Through reference to Thomas Kuhn's epistemology of the scientific paradigms, Puddephatt and Fine highlight the notion of *chess as science*. Specifically, they illustrate how the evolution of chess paradigms has been punctuated by periods of *normal science* (in which incremental advances characterize the development of the game), followed by intense bouts of chess revolution, that ultimately lead to phases of normal cumulative development. Finally, the authors detail the rationalized, bureaucratic, and intensely competitive structure of the chess community in action, thereby pointing to the characterization of *chess as sport*. Indeed, although it may be viewed as a tangential sporting activity by many, the authors demonstrate how the competitive, symbolic, and institutionalized dimensions of chess draw suggestive parallels to more routinely acknowledged sport formations and in so doing expand our understanding as to what sport is and can be.

Further Reading

Crawford, G. (2004) *Consuming Sport: Fans, Sport and Culture*, London: Routledge.

Klein, A.M. (1993) *Little Big Men: Bodybuilding Subculture and Gender Construction*, Albany: State University of New York Press.

Messner, M. (2007) *Out of Play: Critical Essays on Gender and Sport*, Albany: State University of New York Press.

Thorpe, H. (2011) *Snowboarding Bodies in Theory and Practice*, New York: Palgrave Macmillan.

Wheaton, B. (2013) *The Cultural Politics of Lifestyle Sports*, London: Routledge.

18

Sports Fandom

Edwin Amenta and Natasha Miric

Introduction

With the expansion of leisure since the middle of
the twentieth century, sports fandom has become
an increasingly widespread and important phenomenon. There are many additional opportunities for people across class, race, and gender lines
to play and to follow sports. The process of being
a fan has changed in qualitative ways, too, with
the emergence of new technologies, such as the
internet and cable and satellite television, and
with new uses of old technologies, such as sports
talk radio. In this chapter we review some sociological and related literatures on sports fans to
highlight some under-studied questions about
fans and suggest new lines of research. We structure our review around the insights of Pierre
Bourdieu (1978, 1984, 1988; see also Guttmann,
1978; Tomlinson, Markovits, and Young, 2003)
regarding sport as a social field with its own
integrity, not easily reduced to the wider culture,
society, or states surrounding it, and meeting
both a supply and demand for sports activities
(see also Gruneau, 1999). Also important in our
discussion are Bourdieu's (1984) concepts of
class, status, and distinction.

A series of important questions about fans
reside at a macro-level of analysis, involving
sports as an arena and place of production,
processes, and institutions connected to what
Bourdieu (1978) refers to as the supply of
activities in the sports field. The possibilities
of individuals becoming fans are related to the
configuration of the wider sports cultures of
localities, countries, and the world and lead to the
following questions: Why do some societies have
the dominant sports cultures they do? Why is the
dominant US sports culture, with its many sports
not including football/soccer, so unusual? What
aspects of dominant sports cultures tend to close
off possibilities for further entrants? Under which
conditions is it possible for sports to enter or
exit sports cultures? Under which conditions
do sports cultures gain political resonance and
inflections? Have sports cultures changed in ways
similar to other leisure cultures dominated by
viewing and spectatorship, such as for television,
films, and music, in which audiences have become
increasingly fragmented across competing venues
for attention?

Scholars have also identified many important
questions about individuals and their connection
to following sports, mainly an issue surrounding
what Bourdieu (1978) calls the "demand" side of
sports. Among the questions we find most pressing are the following: Why does someone become

A Companion to Sport, First Edition. Edited by David L. Andrews and Ben Carrington.
© 2013 Blackwell Publishing Ltd. Published 2013 by Blackwell Publishing Ltd.

a sports fan? Why do people follow certain sports over others and choose between the different sports that are possible? Are there standard fan career trajectories, similar to employment careers or to sports entering the sports culture, with path dependencies at key decision points? How are fans' allegiances to teams similar to individuals' commitments to social movements? How does being a sports fan differ from being a fan connected to other leisure activities, such as following a television show or a movie star? What does being a sports fan mean and what ways of acting, thinking, and feeling are associated with being a sports fan? Under which conditions do fans become violent? Are there standard types of fans and are some becoming more prevalent than others? In which ways have new technologies and social conditions opened the possibilities for new fan allegiances and activities?

In the first part of the chapter, we consider the research on these questions. We find that much is known about why some sports rather than others became parts of national sports cultures, the meaning of being a fan, the different types of fan affiliations and various fan activities, and the ways that participating as a fan have changed over time. But more work is needed in understanding changes in sports cultures and what specifically constitutes barriers to entry given new changes in the technological delivery of sports events and news. Also, we need to know more about why fans become fans of sports and fans of the particular sports they follow, and about the career trajectories of fans. From there we discuss some possibilities for expanding the definition of a sports fan, given the rise of newly popular sports and games, the expansion of the industry of leisure, and the surge in various new technological possibilities to follow sports.

Next we discuss a new concept and phenomenon – the "player fan" (Amenta, 2007) – that has become more important as leisure activity and the ability to pursue sports in adulthood has extended beyond the upper classes. The player fan breaks down the distinction between participation and spectatorship. Player fans are adult amateur sports players who are typically fans of professional teams of the sport they play. Yet they are also act in fan-like ways with regard to the teams for which they play, identifying with and rooting for the team. The situation is one, however, in which the player fans have considerable control over and say in the operations of the team. The player fan is connected to other possibilities and new ways of following sports that increase opportunities for participation and break down the distinction between being a spectator and being a participant.

Our review is in no way meant to be a comprehensive treatment of the extensive academic literature on fans and instead highlights the work of exemplars addressing the questions outlined above and theoretical approaches that have been or may prove fruitful in addressing them, especially those approaches in areas of sociology that seem analogous and related to sports affiliations. In addition, we focus on the US case in comparative and historical perspective, largely within a Western context. We do this in part because of the many sports that exist in its sports culture (Markovits and Hellerman, 2001), in part because the processes of the commodification of fan experience, such as replacing playing fields with museum-like ones, and the advancement in new technologies in sports have carried furthest there. We also focus on relatively under-studied questions and ones suggested by these recent technological and other developments. After reviewing this literature, we suggest hypotheses and lines of research that may help to answer some of the important and under-studied questions. In doing so, we hope to suggest some valuable new ways of thinking about fans and sports cultures, some of which are related to sociological literatures on social movements and careers.

What Is a Sports Fan?

The term "sports fan" has been claimed to be derived from both "fancy" (Dickson, 1999) and "fanatic" (see Crawford, 2004), the latter derived from a Latin term meaning "of a temple" and implying zealous enthusiasm of a quasi-religious sort. The enthusiastic follower of sport has also been referred to historically by terms such as "bug" or "crank," and in British usage as "supporters." Such people are sometimes called "aficionados," which provides a more positive valence suggesting a more rarefied appreciation. Here we define a sports fan as someone who regularly follows sports and has developed a significant emotional attachment to and appreciation for teams or individuals who play sports (see also Crawford, 2004; see Giulianotti, 2002, on different types of fans). A fan is typically interested in specific teams or players, though in some instances may also be attached simply to the sport itself. Although fans often have face-to-face contact with other fans and attend in person athletic contests, their key characteristic is participating in an imagined community (Anderson, 1991) of the like-minded. One can be a fan despite never having played the sport in question, having witnessed a team play in person, or having convened with other fans (Wann *et al.*, 2001).

We see sport as involving an athletic competition, in which teams and individuals seek to prevail against opponents in contests that importantly involve physical activity and skill. At the borders of sport are many competitive activities that are only marginally athletic, such as bowling, chess, and poker, which may induce similar followings and activity. Sports fans have a deep connection to this sort of competition, with its focus on winning and losing and uncertain outcomes, conditions that distinguish sports fans from fans of film stars, rock bands, and television shows, and a more purposive approach to their viewing (see Rowe, 1995; Schimmel, Harrington, and Bielby, 2007). Most sports fans are attached to the major mass team sports, notably football/soccer, which has fans worldwide, the big three US sports, baseball, basketball, and American football, as well as the Canadian import ice hockey, which have only partial resonance outside North America and Scandinavia, and British Commonwealth sports, such as cricket (Markovits and Hellerman, 2001). However, extensive numbers of fans also follow major individual sports including professional tennis, golf, boxing, horseracing, and auto-racing and a series of mainly "Olympic" sports, such as track and field, swimming, figure-skating, and gymnastics. The vast majority of fans are male, as are most participants in the sports with a significance presence in the wider "sports culture" (Crawford, 2004; Markovits and Hellerman, 2001, 2003).

Sports fan action and behavior resides largely in the realm of consumption (Crawford, 2004) and, like the participation in sport, is associated with lifestyles and status maintenance (Bourdieu, 1978). Sports fans are also participants, and frequently vigorous ones, in fan cultures (Giulianotti, 2002; Crawford, 2004). Despite the status differential of adults playing in sports versus being fans of them and sports fans' attachment to what Bourdieu (1978) refers to as "vulgar" sports, many sorts of fan activity may not signify a loss of cultural capital or distinction (Bourdieu, 1984; Peterson, 1992). Indeed, some fans achieve such great expertise that they can make living from it (Crawford, 2003). Other fans blur the distinction between playing and being fans (Amenta, 2007). In addition, in some instances fans are politically mobilized as fans to alter the policies of their team's ownership or to replace owners with objectionable policies or records (Nash, 2000; Zirin, 2010). However, there is no getting around the facts that typically fans are deeply engaged in sports that they are not playing, that following sports is not as health-producing as playing them, that fans rarely exert significant control over the organizations and people in charge of their sports teams and favored athletes, and that acting and performing as a sports fan, or any type of fan, tends to crowd out possibilities of engaging in political behavior focused on states and governments and other forms of civic engagement (Bourdieu, 1978; Putnam, 2000). Most sports fans follow sports by way of television, which dwarfs attending sports activities in time-use surveys, in both amount of time and percent of people engaged (see, e.g., US Bureau of Labor Statistics, 2011). Most sports fans, like television fans of all sorts with regard to their objects of interest, have only a tenuous connection to sport (Wann *et al.*, 2001; Crawford, 2004: Chapter 7). All the same, we are not evaluating sports fans' behaviors, denigrating some as "passive" and elevating others as "resistant," and instead seek to make sense of variations across place and time of fan activity and sports cultures.

On the Supply of Sports Available for Fans: The Historical Trajectories of Sports Cultures

One key set of questions about sports fans has to do with what Bourdieu (1978) refers to as the "supply side" of the sports field, the area of production of sports products. Although individuals may choose to become fans of some sports rather than others, for most people this choice is severely circumscribed by macro-social considerations, notably which sports are available to be followed by fans. To paraphrase Marx, men (and men constitute the vast majority of sports fans) make their own decisions about following sports, but they do not make them as they please. They occur under circumstances given and transmitted from the past, notably in the context of what Markovits and Hellerman (2001: 9) call "hegemonic" or dominant "sports cultures," which they define as concerning "what people follow as opposed to what people do." The main questions about sports cultures include the following: Why do some sports rather than others become part of the dominant sports culture? Why do national sports cultures vary in the different sports that appear in their dominant sports cultures? Markovits and Hellerman address specifically why the world's game, football/soccer, has not taken hold in the United States, whereas four sports have done so. Other key questions are these: Under which conditions is it possible for sports to emerge in a sports culture that already has a hegemonic sport or sports? Under which conditions do sports exit the dominant sports culture, after securing positions there? Do new technologies and types of sports make it easier or more difficult to produce shifts in the sports culture?

To explain why dominant sports cultures take root, Markovits and Hellerman (2001, 2003) provide a compelling path-dependent argument rooted in historical institutionalist accounts of macro-social change. These accounts point to critical junctures and self-reinforcing processes (Pierson, 2000) and rely on "historicist causation" (Stinchcombe, 1968). A series of conditions, some "accidental," happen at a crucial moment to select one plausible result over another. Afterward, self-reinforcing processes or positive feedback loops protect the initial choice, and the conditions that brought it about in the first place no longer are causally influential. These processes typically result in the creation of strong organizations and institutions that resist competition. To put it into sporting terms, once a nation has chosen football or baseball as its dominant sport, a series of institutions, activities, and relationships develop and progress to a point where other sports are hindered from entering the sports space. Business organizations profiting from fans'

patronage and lucrative television contracts, television networks and newspapers that assign space and reporters to cover the sport, a large base that passes down its allegiances to the sport across generations – all of these protect the hegemonic sports and provide barriers to entry for challengers. Although the sports space is culturally rather than physically constructed (Tomlinson et al., 2003), the US space is deemed to be filled about to capacity with American football, baseball, basketball, and ice hockey.

For Markovits and Hellerman (2001, 2003), the key period for the construction of hegemonic sports cultures for most countries was between 1870 and 1930 and was connected to processes of industrialization and democratization (see also Hargreaves, 1986). For them, sport as mass culture exists only in countries with an extensive working class and a modern middle class, and for most of the industrialized world, sports spaces were "frozen" by the 1930s, much in the manner of political party systems (Lipset, 1967).

Players of the incipient hegemonic sports tend to originate in working classes, and nationalism also influences sports cultures. This argument explains differences across countries in sports cultures, the main one being that in most of Europe football/soccer is the hegemonic sport, whereas in the United States the sports culture is dominated by the "big three and a half." This result is somewhat puzzling in terms of the disjuncture between playing a sport and following it. About 20 million US youths play football/soccer, but relatively few Americans follow it, in comparison with the others, whereas relatively few play American football (Markovits and Hellerman, 2003), which has the most fans. Surveys consistently show that some form of American football is the favorite sport of US fans by a large margin (with 43 percent preferring professional or collegiate football, 17 percent preferring baseball, 10 percent preferring professional or collegiate basketball, with soccer increasing in popularity, but remaining somewhat below auto-racing and ice-hockey at 4 percent (Harris, 2010). A series of historical, cultural, and organization reasons favored the big three and disfavored football/soccer in the years leading up to the crucial period. Because of anti-English feeling and Americans' quest for uniqueness (Sugden, 1994), football was deemed un-American, unlike baseball and American football, both Americanized versions of English sports, and the native sport basketball; organizational leadership in soccer was also lacking during the crucial period (Markovitz and Hellerman, 2001; see also Bairner, 2001). Football/soccer was crowded out from below by baseball, the sport favored by the working classes, and from above by American football, an altered form of rugby that became popular on collegiate campuses. These sports in turn pressed their institutional advantages and further secured their places once television arrived in the 1950s. This provides a plausible explanation for why the US sports space is filled with its peculiar set of team sports and why soccer has been unable to join it.

Another reason for differences in sports spaces, and the difficulties faced by football/soccer in the United States and by American football elsewhere, is the likelihood that with sports "families," some sports serve as substitutes for others. The dominance of one sport in a family in a culture may impede another from the same family in gaining a footing later. The sports of football/soccer, rugby, Australian-rules football, and American football have similar origins, are typically played in similar seasons, and are nearly functional substitutes, an additional reason for the inability of American football to gain a foothold in the soccer-centered European sports space (Van Bottenburg, 2003). A similar substitutability seems true for baseball and cricket; in no countries are both sports part of dominant sports cultures, with cricket drawing many adherents among former colonies in the British empire and baseball in the US sphere of influence. The dominant sport in a family is typically associated historically with working-class support; others in the family are relegated to secondary status, maintaining or developing an association with middle and upper classes, as with soccer in the United States and rugby in Britain.

Yet even these tradeoffs within sports families leaves open the question of why the sports spaces of other countries are so different and in most instances not nearly so full as the American one. One key difference is in terms of which sports family dominates. In most countries, football/soccer dominates the sports space, and the functional equivalents American football and Australian-rules football dominate theirs. In many countries, the ball and bat games dominate, such as Cuba, Japan, and the Dominican Republic with baseball, and others, such as India and Pakistan, with cricket. A second difference involves the number of sports. Whereas the US calendar is filled with major events by different sports, in many countries one sport dominates the sports space. This group notably includes the baseball countries of Japan and the Dominican Republic, and Brazil, where football/soccer is central to national identity (Pardue, 2002; see CHAPTER 27). Why a sport from some other family has not joined these spaces is perhaps due to the fact that in some of these countries the sports culture dominates the popular culture, with sports stars and teams gaining far more attention than their counterparts in film, television, or music, impeding the entry of additional sports. From the sports-family point of view, basketball has a comparative advantage in not being derived from or even closely connected to other team sports (save perhaps the minor Olympic sport of team handball and the Commonwealth women's sport of netball). Although basketball has become an increasingly important part of the sports cultures of many European countries, especially Mediterranean ones, and China, it has been mainly thwarted elsewhere, despite its attempts at a global appeal and the lack of other competing members in its sports family.

In many aspects of cultural life globalization is synonymous with Americanization, especially in popular music, movies, and celebrity culture, but not so in sports (Markovits and Hellerman, 2001; Van Bottenburg, 2003), which took root in an earlier period for most places. Yet there were diffusion processes, notably from hegemonic powers Britain and the United States to countries within their spheres of influence, and from other turn-of-the-century European powers, and these influences account in large part for differences in sports cultures across countries (see also Maguire, 1999; Miller et al., 2001). This is further due to the search for "native" sports in the nineteenth century among Americans (Sugden, 1994), who ended up nonetheless mainly adapting British sports. The US sports dominant after World War II, however, have been differently diffused. Basketball has been successfully transplanted in many new countries, whereas baseball has made some inroads in Europe in places like the

Netherlands and Italy, with American football largely quarantined to its homeland (Van Bottenburg, 2003).

The standing of individualistic sports in sports cultures, which get short shrift in Markovits and Hellerman's (2001, 2003) accounts given their prominence, may answer some parts of the above riddles. Although individual sports lack the continuity provided by teams rooted to specific locations, they are typically run by organizations that are sometimes international in scope, have rooting interests often colored by nationalism, and feature regularly scheduled competitions, often in sacred sports venues, such as the Tour de France, the Masters, and Wimbledon. The organizational ensconcing of some of these individual sports, such as cycling in France, likely crowds out potential team entrants.

Paying more attention to non-team sports also makes it possible to address two other key but neglected questions: why some sports have exited the dominant sports culture, despite having strong presences during the crucial period, and why some others may gain a foothold, despite having little profile during the crucial period. For instance, among the most followed US sports through the first half of the twentieth century were professional boxing and horse-racing. Yet both have been shunted to the margins of the sports culture, each now the preferred sport of about 1 percent of US fans in Harris polling. The decline of these sports happened while individual sports, notably professional tennis and golf, rose to greater prominence, and with NASCAR emerging as the fourth "half" sport in the US sports culture. The precipitous drop of interest in boxing suggests that organizational integrity among the organizations or individuals in charge of scheduling and the crowning of champions is a prerequisite for a sustained presence in the sports culture.

Although team sports that gain a foothold during the crucial period have not disappeared from the sports culture, they can decline or otherwise significantly change places in attention, in part at least for similar reasons. Extended problems in labor relations, such as those throughout the history of major league baseball, and suffered recently by the National Hockey League, can lower the profile of a dominant sport in the sports culture, by igniting fans' anger at the disruption of the orderly progression of championship contests. Similarly, well-run sports leagues, like the NFL, or the Australian AFL, can significantly boost the fortunes of a sport in the sports culture. There may be some "advantages of backwardness," as these sports had made an impression on the sports culture during the crucial era, but were able to form their main organizations during the era of television and in response to crises surrounding gambling in other sports. The decline of professional baseball in the United States relative to professional football was dramatic over the last half-century, with professional football eclipsing baseball in the early 1980s as the most popular sport in surveys and increasing its advantage since then.

More generally, modeling the sports field as being akin to a social movement sector (McCarthy and Zald, 1977) may fill gaps in our understanding of the production of fans. The resource mobilization model of social movements poses questions on what accounts for commitments of time, energy, and money to voluntary organizations seeking social and political change. Key theoretical claims refer to the resources, forms, and resourcefulness of organizations in social movement "industries," which compete for the discretionary income and time of socially conscious "conscience constituents." Other arguments focus on the appeals made by these organizations, and the political and cultural contexts in which these organizations maneuver for support (Andrews and Edwards, 2004). In some ways, the standard movement sector and industries model is more fitting for sports organizations than for voluntary political ones or for most corporations (Hirschman, 1970). Sports organizations seek to mobilize mass allegiance, enthusiastic support, and time commitments from consumers to achieve their pecuniary goals. By contrast, most profit-seeking corporations simply seek purchases, and movement organizations need to interact intensively with political institutions (Amenta et al., 2010). Organizations are at the center of the production of sports products both as spectacle and as activity; their make-up and relative power helps to determine where sports will end up situated in sports cultures. There are also struggles, mainly one-sided, about the meaning of sport between the organizations that produce sport as spectacle and those that promote participation in sports (on sports as a spectacle and resistance to it, see Jhally, 2006; Tomlinson, 2002; Bélanger, 2009; CHAPTER 26).

Why Does Someone Become a Sports Fan?

Our discussion of why someone becomes a sports fan and why they choose to be fans of certain sports and teams and not others begins with Bourdieu's (1978) questions: What are the "social conditions" that affect whether or not people follow a sport? In this we address the changing class bases of sport. Why do people follow certain sports over others? How do people choose among different sports that are offered to them as possible? We go on to discuss the "careers" of sports fans and their connections to employment careers and to participating in social movements. We also discuss the connections between sports fans and violence.

Why someone becomes a sports fan is a question with a variety of dimensions. There are broad "risk factors" in becoming a sports fan, such as being male, adult, having played organized sports and enjoyed the experience, and having parents or friends who are sports fans (reviews in Crawford, 2004; Wann et al., 2001). For Bourdieu (1978, 1984), becoming a fan of the dominant entrants of the team-sports culture also had an irreducible class element, with working classes highly represented in the following of team sports and middle and upper classes tending to avoid fandom and to play country-club, individual sports into adulthood. Across countries, as we have seen, the place of a sport in the culture is a key factor in a fan's choice of sport, with the central sports in the sports culture historically associated with working-class fans and less central ones with middle-class fans (Markovits and Hellerman, 2001). Also, changes in the commodification of sports (Giulianotti, 2002), technological possibilities to follow sports, and general changes in cultural consumption patterns (see review in Lizardo and Skiles, 2008) have altered the class composition of followers of sport.

Recent sociological scholarship has adopted a natural history approach. In this view why someone becomes a sports fan is a matter of indicating the sequences by which someone becomes a sports fan, in the manner that Crane Brinton (1965) explained revolutions and Howard Becker (1963) traced the progression of marijuana users. Relying on Glaser and Strauss (1971), Crawford (2003) posits a stage model of "moral careers" of sports fans though status passages. The concept of career allows us to understand the development of fans over the life course, and Crawford maps the stages from "general public," adults who care little about sports through the progressive stages of "interested," "engaged," "enthusiastic," and "devoted," categories which include most sports fans. For instance, for enthusiastic fans, their sporting interest is comparatively important in their lives and watching and attending games and matches absorbs a significant amount of free time. At the levels above these are "professional" fans, who seek to distance themselves from others by their expertise, and "apparatus," whose vocation it is to run sports teams (Crawford, 2004: 42). This research is among fans attending games of ice hockey, a hopeful entrant to the English sports culture. This situation may not capture typical sports fans, who become attached to dominant team sports in youth; many devoted and even professional fans may not attend games of the dominant sports culture regularly.

Markovits and Hellerman (2001) add to this stage model by beginning it sooner in a fan's career and applying path dependencies to it. For them, becoming a fan is more like an employment career, in which there are choice points after which it is difficult to turn back. Once someone becomes a fan of one sport and a specific team in that sport it is more difficult to shift fan allegiances to another team and to other sports because of sunk emotional and knowledge costs. In addition, there is the sticky influence of surrounding oneself in a community of the like-minded, who will reinforce allegiances. They also argue that team sports are better than individual sports for attracting lifelong fans because they are "continuous institutions with clear identities" (Markovits and Hellerman, 2001: 17) and focus on the initial adoption of allegiances, not ones later in life. In short, in their view once a fan, almost always a fan of that sport and team.

This perspective has value because choosing a sports team has surface similarities with choosing a career, in its sunk costs and path dependencies, and fan allegiances may find critical periods and choice points for a specific team much earlier in life than in making a career choice. Similarly, the supply of available jobs, like the availability of sports teams in one's locality, and one's class background will greatly influence the possibilities in choosing. As with paid employment, most people will not have careers in the sense of gaining the advancement opportunities to become professional, and will be stranded at medium high levels of enthusiasm and knowledge. But unlike with job choice, a sports fan often does not have all or even most of his or her eggs in one basket. One can be a fan of different sports, adding on new "specialties," without as much conflict, and the transition from following one sport to another can be fluid in sports cultures with many successful entrants, as in the United States. There fans can accumulate allegiances with teams in different sports over a lifetime, paying closest attention to the local team whose sport is in season or which achieves the greatest successes. More important, fans can completely opt out of following sports in ways that are not possible for adults and their jobs or careers.

Giulianotti (2002) takes into account changes in the larger economic situation facing fans, notably the increased commodification of sports, in a model of fan allegiances based on hot, cool, traditional, and consumer qualities of fandom. Hot and cool forms of loyalty represent the degree to which the club is central to the individual's project of self-formation. Traditional and consumer relationships address the basis of the individual's investment in a specific club. He designates the traditional/hot spectators as "supporters," traditional/cool spectators as "followers," consumer/hot spectators as "fans," and cool/consumers are *flâneurs*. With the increased commodification of sports, fans increasingly exit the "supporter" category, in which sports teams are central to the identity and investments are deep, in favor of types of sports fandom more lightly held and with fan investments that are more diversified. The image of the fan as being local with local outlooks, loyalties, and concerns was once the standard for fans, largely those of the working classes, but this model is less sustainable with the development of mass capitalistic sports. There are also pressures in the cool and consumer

directions from new technologies for following sports, and new ways of being fans.

The increased commodification in sports as well as new technologies and opportunities to be fans can be connected to new distinctions conferred in following the sports at the center of sports cultures, which, in Bourdieu's (1978) terms, makes such following far from "vulgar," as it once was. For Bourdieu, sport is a field with its own autonomy, contested by those seeking to define sport as participatory or spectacle; sport also performs a distinguishing function across and within classes, with the participation in sport, notably sports requiring considerable money or cultural capital, upholding status distinctions for upper-class groups of adults and the following of popular sports typically reserved for working and lower middle classes. Bourdieu sees being a fan of popular sports as perpetuating the domination of lower and working classes, and turning them into consumers dominated by experts. However, the transformation of events at the center of sports cultures into expensive tickets, the changes in sports stadiums and the experiences promoted by them, and the increased possibilities of following sports in an expert fashion, such as through websites, blogging, and "fantasy" sports (see CHAPTER 14) each of these have opened the way for more extensive middle-class and upper-class participation in sports fandom.

That middle-class fans are dominating spectatorship in the sports of the dominant sports cultures is due largely to the increasing costs of admission and the more museum-like nature of new modern sports stadiums (Inglis, 2001). With sports franchises needing ever more revenue to meet expanding payrolls, working-class spectators mainly follow them remotely, typically on television. All new sports stadiums are equipped with luxury or "sky" boxes and "club" seating catering to big-ticket corporate customers, and older venues have introduced more high-priced seats. In baseball, the vast majority of major league teams have built new stadiums since 1990. Bleacher tickets at Chicago's Wrigley Field, in the late 1960s the base of fans whose blue-collar identity was signified by their claim to be "hardhats," have increased in price from US$1 in 1970 to US$6 in 1991 to a median price of US$42 in 2011, and US$72 for high-profile "marquee" games, pricing out many potential attenders (Sullivan, 2010). Only a tiny fraction of its poorer fan base has any chance of witnessing in person a favorite team playing in the Super Bowl, given the increased prices over already expensive season prices and a lack of availability. Working-class and lower-middle-class fans can more readily become regular spectators at sports at the margins of the sports culture, such as major league soccer or the Women's National Basketball Association. All this suggests that understanding sports fans requires a greater focus on those who fill the state-of-the-art stadia in the manner of a holiday or pilgrimage.

More than that, there are larger social trends in which distinction is no longer lost, but may be increased by upper-class members who augment their culture consumption with more popular or low cultural offerings; the cultural "omnivore" can now signify the highest status (Peterson, 1992; Ollivier, 2006). For instance, omnivores in musical taste can like the popular forms of hip hop, or rock, so long as they are combined with classical music and jazz, or if rock or other popular forms are enjoyed in an informed way (Trondman, 1990). Devotion to some cultural forms likely confers a kind of negative distinction, such as country music or death metal (Bryson, 1996), and among recent US sports, for instance, following NASCAR or extreme fighting likely confers negative distinction. But most of the main sports in the mass sports cultures, notably baseball with its rich historical and literary tradition, and football/soccer can be part of a high-distinction cultural consumption menu. The high-distinction followers of mass culture typically follow sports in ways that Crawford (2004) would deem "expert." Bourdieu (1978) notes that within sports culture there are expert fans whose appreciation of sport approaches that of music in music-lovers (see also Giulianotti, 2002), and these experts stand in opposition to the great mass of supporters.

Even among expert fans, however, new class distinctions have formed, notably between those who have played the game and know the "inside game," beyond simply mastering standard plays and strategies, and those who focus on analyzing the records of players and can manipulate new metrics with which to judge them – the "outside" game (Lewis, 2004). How one follows sport is key.

The first sort of fan is epitomized by radio and TV color commentators, who typically enter their career from the ranks of professional players. The more prevalent non-remunerated sort of "inside" fan may become experts on such matters of the history of their chosen team simply by intensive following through the mass media, ascending to the highest level of fan in the stage model of Crawford (2003, 2004). Similarly, with sports talk radio and the rise of the internet, sports discourse has been democratized and become coarsened and personalized, with expert fans calling in to make suggestions and register complaints. Unbridled criticism of and expressions of anger at the members of a fan's favorite team who fail to meet expectations in on-field performance or off-field behavior are now standard. Players, coaches, and front offices are found deficient in personal qualities, ranging from talent and smarts to diligence and courage, which are publicly and bluntly called into question daily. This sort of passionate discourse may not be the most prevalent in the mass sports culture (Wann et al., 2001), but it has the highest profile.

The middle-class expert fan tends to be more highly educated and analytical in approach, as with other forms of cultural consumption, with high cultural capital returns from education (Lizardo and Skiles, 2008). Through this different mode of following, middle-class expert fans fill the burgeoning ranks of fantasy sports leagues (notably in baseball and American football, whose fantasy history began in the 1960s and took off in the last decade with the rise of the internet and the easy transmission of sporting data). There is greatly increased participation in such leagues, which are hosted en masse by sites such as ESPN and CBS Sports. To take baseball as an example, these expert fans also provide the mass market for books by writers like Bill James and the output of other commercial "sabermetric" enterprises, such as the website of Baseball Prospectus and many others like it. For this group of active fans their following is more analogous to running a team and leads to a professionalized if non-remunerated mode of fandom. Serious fantasy or rotisserie players often lose interest in the fates of a favorite team and its players, as they track the statistical progress of their own roster draftees, which typically range across teams. Their fandom, while involving considerable investments of time and emotion, is instrumental and more akin to the activity of general managers or, perhaps more closely, gamblers. Unlike fans of teams, fantasy followers do not make great emotional investment in the players on their rosters. A star player on the fantasy roster who falls to injury does not dash dreams and diminish hopes the way Chicago Cubs fans mourned the loss to injury of the highly promising young pitchers Kerry Wood and Mark Prior in the mid-2000s. For the fantasy fan, injuries to players are merely annoying holes to be filled. The battle in baseball management outlined by Michael Lewis (2004) between the old-school scouts, usually former ballplayers, and the new-school statistical analysts, often with postgraduate degrees including statistical training, has class dimensions and also plays out among fans.

Because of these battles, it seems unlikely that the career trajectories of sports fans proceed smoothly across the highest stages. Only in rare instances is it possible to make the leap from expert fan to a career in the management of sports franchises or media sports commentary, without additional higher education and certification in business or media. A far easier career path is to move from professional athlete to a paid position in sports franchises or communications media, as least in the US context where many players' careers pass through university settings. The exceptions are mainly among the educated middle class of expert fans. In baseball it has been possible for analysts to be paid for their work on subscription websites and move to positions in baseball front offices. The pioneering "sabermetrician" Bill James began his career as an expert fan, published baseball books drawing a mass audience, and was named a special assistant to the general manager of the Boston Red Sox in 2002 (Lewis, 2004); less prominent baseball analyst/fans have found positions in other baseball franchises. Most likely this is as rare as members of tribute bands being tapped to replace retired or deceased members of original ones. A much likelier path from fan to career in sports is from personal blog to paid positions on websites supported by advertising revenue and subscriptions.

Negative distinction is typically conferred on those whose mode of following sports involves a specific sort of participation: violence. Literature on sports violence has focused mainly on football

fans and hooligans. John Williams, Eric Dunning, and Patrick Murphy, often referred to as the "Leicester school," have attributed the violence to class differences. They argue that before World War I "a larger proportion of the British working class were relatively unincorporated into dominant and hegemonic values" (1994: 151) so they were more likely to violate dominant norms by behaving violently at football matches. Also, downwardly mobile middle-class fans see violent working-class fans as a reference group and participate in fan violence, whereas upwardly mobile working-class fans will participate in fan violence to keep in touch with their working-class roots. Stott and Reicher (1998: 361), however, argue that this model does not explain "how and why in the context of football, violence becomes a crowd behavior." Their "elaborated social identity model of crowd behaviour" emphasizes intergroup dynamics and holds that if the in-group perceives the actions of the out-group as illegitimate, they redefine their identities, and violence, which had been seen as inappropriate, then becomes legitimate. Also, applying Stott's model to policing at sporting events has shown that high-profile police presence "sustained and validated conflictual forms of England fan identity" (Stott, Hutchison, and Drury, 2001: 94). Crawford (2004: 100) argues, however, that the social control of violent fans has shifted from reactive strategies to preventive strategies, such as crowd surveillance and the creation of family-friendly environments. Also, football hooliganism is mainly seen as a phenomenon of England, where it originated, though it has spread to other countries, notably Italy, Germany, and Croatia.

In the North American setting, sports fans' violence tends to take the form of the celebratory riot and is typically theorized through the lens of collective behavior. Jerry Lewis (2007: 8–19) adapts Smelser's theory of collective behavior and McPhail's model of categories of behavior, theorizing that riots are more likely to involve fans of the winning team and that the fans involved in the riots will be young, white males. Riots are also more likely to occur after championship games, the deeper the series goes into a championship, if the final game is close, and if the team has not won in over five years. Riots are also facilitated by access to an urban gathering area (Lewis, 2007: 95–100). McCarthy, Martin, and McPhail (2007: 292) found that on college campuses, when many such riots occur, police are more likely to use the "aggressive tactics of making arrests or employing tear gas or pepper spray and riot batons" during convivial gatherings than at protest events. They also argue that the lack of formal organization in these types of gatherings, which include disorderly sporting events, makes it more difficult for police to negotiate with participants than at protest events, where police are accustomed to negotiating a solution with protest participants. The episodic nature of such disruptive activity rarely confers the sort of distinction attached to football hooliganism.

The Rise of Player Fans

Next we address a condition that combines aspects of spectatorship and participation in the sports themselves: player fandom. This is an approach to leisure and life for adults who play team sports that combines the joys and trials of playing for a team with those of also being a follower or fan of it, blurring the distinction between sports as activity and as spectacle and providing a new site for class status struggles. Bourdieu (1978) argues that less well-off youths play to win team sports at all costs, and in adulthood as family and economic obligations increase and as free time, disposable income, and physical health decline they no longer play sports, but root to win. The "vulgar" sports that form the main parts of mass sports cultures serve as potential means of economic betterment for some of the working classes, but in adulthood most working-class and lower-middle-class adults live partly vicariously through the exploits of their working-class heroes. By contrast, their privileged class counterparts tend to play team sports as youths in order to learn lessons in leadership and sportsmanship and to form class ties. Those who remain sports-minded as they age discard the team sports of youth in favor of individualized country-club sports such as tennis or golf, or opt for skiing, sailing, polo, or mountaineering, or focus on athletic activity inducing bodily health, as through jogging or yoga.

Yet different classes have mixed in recent decades as adults continuing to play team sports, and these adults are the source of player fans. There are pressures producing this outcome from different class directions. As incomes rose in the third quarter of the twentieth century and jobs became more flexible, leisure increased in importance. These changes provided lower-middle-class and working-class adults in the postwar West with greater time and means to pursue sports as adults, while retaining a class-based preference for team sports (Amenta, 2007), though these opportunities have not increased in recent decades, as inflation-adjusted median incomes have been stagnant and have dipped during the Great Recession beginning in 2008 (Carrington, 2008). Middle-class adults also pursue team sports, in part because of increased venues available to do so, and involvement in team sports is no longer *déclassé*. For Bourdieu, middle classes following team sports would confer a loss of distinction, but as noted above the high price and museum-like nature of major sporting venues along with trends toward cultural omnivores has altered the situation. The phenomenon may be particularly evident in the United States, which has historically combined extreme economic inequality with less severe social inequalities; players with varying economic class trajectories and statuses are likely to combine on the playing field or court. Most of the organizations involved in mobilizing these activities are at the town or community level, and are highly decentralized, in comparison to the organizations mobilizing sports as spectacle for the mass sports culture.

The fact that player fans are adults means that they have already been fully formed as fans, unlike, say, youth players of sports. Some adult fans can live vicariously by way of their favorite professional teams. Other adults root their identities more in highly participatory avocations. Adult players of sports can do both, identifying with their sports avocation and following the exploits of teams on which they play. Though falling far short of having professional talent and with little potential for improvement in skills, like most adult fans of commercial sports, a player fan's identity is bound up with being a skilled athlete, and thus is engaged in a form of serious leisure (Stebbins, 2007). Yet like a spectator he or she develops an emotional attachment to the teams he or she plays for.

In what follows, we address player fandom among competitive softball players. In an ethnographic, observant participation (see Wacquant, 2004) study of New York City softball players,

Amenta (2007) compared different types of teams, playing for five teams and organizing a weekly pickup game, which was expected to be less serious and more about sociability than the league games were. Although American adults rarely play baseball for fun, many play softball, which has replaced baseball as a mass participation ball-and-bat sport, or as a "pastime." For the most part, male competitive recreational softball players rarely know or identify with the top ranks of softball players, who include college women or unsung virtuosos of a kind of offbeat, inferior minor league baseball, and instead follow professional baseball. US basketball has a similar combination of players and fans, and player fans appear in US soccer leagues as well, though not typically as fans of major league soccer (MLS). The author's experiences covered teams that won and teams that lost, teams that were constituted mainly of players with working-class and lower-middle-class backgrounds, teams constituted largely of professional and upper white-collar workers, and teams that mixed classes. The author's status also varied considerably, ranging from being a star player to being a marginal one. As manager of one team, the author elicited conflict through the application of sabermetric or baseball analytic principles on a team largely consisting of player fans who saw themselves as experts, but from the experiential knowledge base of their previous play. His approach contrasted with the application of practice-based expert authority exhibited by a rival manager.

Although adult amateur competitive players are neither the best players nor the ones who care most about their team, they constitute the purest form of player fan. Paid athletes simply have too professional an attitude and approach, and their activity falls outside the usual definitions of leisure. No major league player continues to support the team of his childhood unless he is acquired by it. At the one extreme there is the hyper-professional approach of former major leaguer Jim Bouton (1970), who found baseball games interesting only when he was pitching in them. The stakes have increased for professional baseball players since the massive salary increases after the revolution of free agency and arbitration in the 1970s. Unlike through most of the twentieth century, when teammates would orally replay games in the clubhouse, professional players now often see the clubhouse as a place of surveillance, where they can run into public trouble by releasing a poorly chosen comment, and tend to scatter. Although schools probably produce the player fans that care most about their teams, many players hope to advance to a higher level and are thus partly professionalized. The authority structure is vastly different from organized adult competitive sports. Unlike competitive recreational adult players, the players of high-school and collegiate teams are led by formal coaches with extensive authority and often great power, such as whether a player will remain on the team and when and where players will play. In adult sports, the teams are usually led by peers. Finally, adults playing team sports typically have already been socialized as fans of the team sport of the dominant sports culture.

Like other sports fans, the player fan lives and dies a little each week during his or her team's game – though like most fans, player fans are predominantly but not exclusively male – but more personally than the analogous fan of a big league team. The player fan glories in the exploits of his favorite player – himself – and can be obsessed with that same player's failures. He also is likely to idolize and demonize other players. Unlike the objects of typical fan attention, however, these players, his team-mates, are much more socially proximate; often they are friends, not the distant celebrities of today. Being a player on an amateur team does not so much extinguish rooting and following so much as add a new target and object. The players root for their own team and probably their home major league team as well, but in new and often lopsided proportions.

Although one of the main reasons to engage in recreational sports is to have fun and to enjoy sociability (Fine, 1987), playing competitive softball and similar team sports available to grown-up amateurs is a more serious pursuit (Stebbins, 2007) fraught with conflict and trouble for player fans. That is due to several related circumstances. Like other serious amateurs, adults playing competitive sports are more concerned with upholding and validating their identities as good players than with sociability, as compared with those in less competitive leagues. Yet unlike with individual sports, where, for instance, runners or swimmers can improve or maintain their times, a team player's identity is more bound up with collective results. There is a kind of caste nature to teams in which the players' individual statuses can move upward in a stratification hierarchy only as members of a group. Teams that lose will tend to have that status applied to each member of the team, regardless of the individual contributions of any member of the team. The numbers are grim, and most teams and their players become some species of loser. Most teams ultimately lose and thus players are often forced to question their value as players. Frequently their value is questioned directly by their own team-mates, who are searching for reasons for why the team is losing. Fans of losing teams suffer, but almost never feel personally responsible nor are held accountable for the losing.

Class-based battles that sometimes play out among fans also play out among player fans. Often there are also conflicts within and across teams on the relative importance of winning, harking back to the class conflicts addressed by Bourdieu (1978). Class conflicts within and across teams are accentuated because most players also see themselves as expert fans, their expertise being experiential, based on playing and viewing the sport. Yet there is also class conflict among expert fans, reflecting rifts among experts in professional baseball front offices regarding the relative value of statistics and eyewitness observations. Adult player fans may not root as hard for their own teams as high-school or college players and may not have as much of their identity invested in being a player, but for adults the situation is more difficult and conflict is more in the foreground because the authority structures on adult teams is tenuous. The person in charge of the team is typically a player colleague, usually with no special authority to be in charge, and is always subject to being replaced by a team-mate.

Conclusion

In this chapter we have addressed a number of issues in the study of sports fandom, notably the development of sports cultures, why someone becomes a fan, and the changing class nature of being a fan. As we have seen, much is known about sports cultures and sports. Indeed this review touches on only a few areas of research and study. But much more research is needed even in the areas we have addressed. Here we suggest some lines of activity to advance understanding of the historical development of sports cultures and the careers and sports allegiances of individual fans. To advance our knowledge we suggest the application of comparative historical, career, social movement, and production of culture approaches to sport.

As for sports cultures, some basic comparative research would be welcome to situate comparisons across sports cultures. One way to track historically the sports space of different countries, to pinpoint more precisely when sports entered the sports culture, is through analyses of newspapers and records regarding attendance at events. Establishing the different sports space trajectories will make it possible to engage in more extensive comparative research. One important comparison will be between countries that had their modernization and democratization periods at times similar to those of the United States and Europe and those that did not. We probably need to move beyond the question of why the United States is so different in its sports culture, analogous to the way that scholars have moved beyond asking why the United States welfare state is different from those of Europe. It is worth addressing more refined questions, analogous to those regarding conservative, Christian Democratic welfare states in Central Europe, such as how it was possible for basketball to make the inroads that it did in Mediterranean countries. It is also well worth comparing across similar countries with differently filled sports spaces, such as in Latin America, where in some countries football/soccer dominates and others baseball. In such comparisons it might be possible to isolate geopolitical influences, given the varied histories of European powers with these countries. Is it simply a matter of adopting the most invasive imperial power's top sport? Or are there countervailing influences?

Although the rise of the dominant sports in the United States has been well researched, some questions remain. It is worth addressing all recent entrants to sports cultures, such as NASCAR in the United States, to see what paths are available to sports attempting to breaking into more or less filled systems.

Similarly, it is worth isolating those sports that had a seemingly secure place in the dominant sports culture, but then faded, as did boxing in the United States and elsewhere. Note that in the United States even among the dominant sports there were major shifts in prominence, such as the rise of professional NFL football and NBA basketball over their better-followed collegiate counterparts, and the complete demise of rooting for almost anything aside from major league baseball. It seems possible that organizational models like those of the resource mobilization model will be able to help sort out why some sports sector "industries" gain, while others decline.

Applying career models to the historical development of individual fans has already revealed its promise, but it is worth studying further the origins of the initial allegiances of fans, and the conditions under which playing a sport as a child leads to sustained following as an adult. Research should also focus on gender issues. Although it is well known that men are more involved as sports fans than women, less well understood is whether the processes of becoming a sports fan differ between men and women, especially given the sea change in female participation in sport in the United States over the last four decades in the wake of Title IX. More also needs to be known about the conditions under which fans decide to switch allegiances, or add new allegiances onto old ones, or end their fan careers. Similarly, we need a better understanding of everyday fan behavior, about fans who spend much time and emotional energy following sports and favorite teams and players, but rarely attend sporting contests. Most serious fans have an intense and often quite time- and emotion-consuming attachment to sports, but only the better-off can afford to attend the most popular sports in the sports culture more than occasionally, unlike the more extreme fans who have been more closely studied. New technological developments have altered individual fan sporting habits, which provides many more opportunities to follow intensively at a distance.

Another way to a better understanding of these issues is to examine the struggles among organizations regarding the meaning of sports. Much of the relative change in sports spaces is likely due to the jockeying among or dysfunctions within the organizations promoting or regulating sports spectacles. The decline of boxing in the sports culture is certainly related to deficiencies and dysfunctions in the organizations promoting it, just as the rise of the National Football League to its current heights in the US sports culture, leaping both beyond collegiate football and baseball, is similarly due in large part to organizational factors, including its far-sighted collectivist strategy and the organizational constraints on universities' ability to compete with fully commercialized organizations. Given the ability of adults across classes to continue to pursue the sports of childhood as well as others, it would be worth addressing the relative ability of organizations to further this goal. It is at the adult level that the conflicts between sport as participation and as spectacle may be strongest. These organizations serve as the link between the development of sports cultures writ large and the possibilities for the careers of individual sports fans. Attention to the meso-level of organizational struggle would complement the main theoretical accounts of sports cultures and sports fans, which usually reside, respectively, at the macro-social and individual levels of analysis.

These investigations may be aided by a return to Bourdieu's approach, especially by employing ideas from sociologists studying the production of culture. Sports are a cultural consumption like other cultural goods and processes and need to be seen for their similarities as well as their differences. It seems helpful to see how far general theories of the production of culture help to explain fan sports' cultural outcomes and processes. It is also worth further applying some of Bourdieu's ideas about status struggles and cultural capital to the brave new world where adults of all classes continue to pursue sports, fans have the kind of technological access to sporting events never before dreamed of, the well-off have the best access to the most prominent sporting events, and cultural omnivores dominate across the land.

References

Amenta, E. (2007) *Professor Baseball: Searching for Redemption and the Perfect Lineup on the Softball Diamonds of Central Park*, Chicago: University of Chicago Press.

Amenta, E., Caren, N., Chiarello, E.S., and Su, Y. (2010) "The political consequences of social movements." *Annual Review of Sociology*, 36: 287–307.

Anderson, B. (1991) *Imagined Communities: Reflections on the Origin and Spread of Nationalism*, New York: Verso.

Andrews, K.T. and Edwards, B. (2004) "Advocacy organizations in the US political process." *Annual Review of Sociology*, 30: 479–506.

Bairner, A. (2001) *Sport, Nationalism, and Globalization: European and North American Perspectives*, Albany: State University of New York Press.

Becker, H.S. (1963) *Outsiders: Studies in the Sociology of Deviance*, New York: Free Press.

Bélanger, A. (2009) "The urban sport spectacle: Towards a critical political economy of sports," in Carrington, B. and McDonald, I. (eds.), *Marxism, Cultural Studies and Sport*, New York: Routledge, pp. 51–67.

Bourdieu, P. (1978) "Sport and social class." *Social Science Information*, 17: 819–840.

Bourdieu, P. (1984) *Distinction: A Social Critique of the Judgment of Taste*, trans. R. Nice, Cambridge, MA: Harvard University Press.

Bourdieu, P. (1988) "Program for a sociology of sport." *Sociology of Sport Journal*, 5 (2): 153–161.

Bouton, J. (1970) *Ball Four: My Life and Hard Times Throwing the Knuckleball in the Big Leagues*, New York: World Publishing Co.

Brinton, C. (1965) *The Anatomy of Revolution*, New York: Vintage Books.

Bryson, B. (1996) "Anything but heavy metal: Symbolic exclusion and musical dislikes." *American Sociological Review*, 61: 884–900.

Carrington, B. (2008) "Introduction: Rethinking labour and leisure." *Leisure Studies*, 27 (4): 368–374.

Crawford, G. (2003) "The career of the sport supporter: The case of the Manchester storm." *Sociology*, 37: 219–237.

Crawford, G. (2004) *Consuming Sport: Fans, Sport and Culture*, New York: Routledge.

Dickson, P. (1999) *The New Dickson Baseball Dictionary*, New York: Harcourt Brace & Co.

Fine, G.A. (1987) *With the Boys: Little League Baseball and Preadolescent Culture*, Chicago: University of Chicago Press.

Giulianotti, R. (2002) "Supporters, followers, fans, and flaneurs: A taxonomy of spectator identities in football." *Journal of Sport & Social Issues*, 26 (1): 25–46.

Glaser, B.G. and Strauss, A.L. (1971) *Status Passage*, Chicago: Aldine Transaction.

Gruneau, R.S. (1999) *Class, Sports, and Social Development*, Champaign, IL: Human Kinetics.

Guttmann, A. (1978) *From Ritual to Record: The Nature of Modern Sports*, New York: Columbia University Press.

Hargreaves, J. (1986) *Sport, Power, and Culture: A Social and Historical Analysis of Popular Sports in Britain*, Cambridge: Polity Press.

Harris (2010) "Football expands lead over baseball as America's favorite sport." Harris Poll, at http://www.harrisinteractive.com/vault/Harris-Interactive-Poll-Research-Sports-Popularity-2010-02.pdf, accessed January 21, 2013.

Hirschman, A.O. (1970) *Exit, Voice, and Loyalty: Responses to Decline in Firms, Organizations and States*, Cambridge, MA: Harvard University Press.

Inglis, S. (2001) *Sightlines: A Stadium Odyssey*, London: Yellow Jersey Press.

Jhally, S. (2006) *The Spectacle of Accumulation: Essays in Culture, Media, Politics*, New York: Peter Lang.

Lewis, J. (2007) *Sports Fan Violence in North America*, Lanham, MD: Rowman & Littlefield.

Lewis, M. (2004) *Moneyball*, New York: Norton.

Lipset, S.M. (1967) "Cleavages, party, and democracy," in Lispet, S.M. and Rokkan, S. (eds.) *Party Systems and Voter Alignments*, New York: Free Press, pp. 2–8.

Lizardo, O. and Skiles, S. (2008) "Cultural consumption in the fine and popular arts realms." *Sociology Compass*, 2 (2): 485–502.

Maguire, J.A. (1999) *Global Sport: Identities, Societies, Civilizations*, Cambridge: Polity Press.

Markovits, A.S. and Hellerman, S.L. (2001) *Offside: Soccer and American Exceptionalism*, Princeton, NJ: Princeton University Press.

Markovits, A.S. and Hellerman, S.L. (2003) "Olympianization of soccer in the US." *American Behavioral Scientist*, 46 (11): 1533–1549.

McCarthy, J.D., Martin, A., and McPhail, C. (2007) "Policing disorderly campus protests and convivial gatherings: The interaction of threat, social organization, and First Amendment guarantees." *Social Problems*, 54: 274–296.

Miller, T., Lawrence, G., Mckay, J., and Rowe, D. (2001) *Globalization and Sport: Playing the World*, London: Sage Publications.

McCarthy, J.D. and Zald, M.N. (1977) "Resource mobilization and social movements: A partial theory." *American Journal of Sociology*, 82: 1212–1241.

Nash, R. (2000) "Contestation in modern English professional football: The Independent Supporters Association Movement." *International Review for the Sociology of Sport*, 35 (4): 465–486.

Ollivier, M. (2006) "Snobs and quétaines: Prestige and boundaries in popular music in Quebec." *Popular Music*, 25: 97–116.

Pardue, D. (2002) "*Jogada lingüística*: Discursive play and the hegemonic force of soccer in Brazil." *Sport and Social Issues*, 26 (2): 360–380.

Peterson, R.A. (1992) "Understanding audience segmentation: From elite and popular to omnivore and univore." *Poetics*, 21 (4): 243–258.

Pierson, P. (2000) "Increasing returns, path dependence, and the study of politics." *American Political Science Review*, 94 (2): 251–267.

Putnam, R.D. (2000) *Bowling Alone: The Collapse and Revival of American Community*, New York: Simon & Schuster.

Rowe, D. (1995) *Popular Cultures: Rock Music, Sport, and the Politics of Pleasure*, London: Sage Publications.

Schimmel, K., Harrington, C.L., and Bielby, D. (2007) "Keep your fans to yourself: The disjuncture between sport studies' and pop culture studies' perspectives on fandom." *Sport in Society*, 10 (4): 580–600.

Stebbins, R.A. (2007) *Serious Leisure*, New Brunswick, NJ: Transaction Publishers.

Stinchcombe, A.L. (1968) *Constructing Social Theories*, New York: Harcourt, Brace, & World.

Stott, C. and Reicher, S. (1998) "How conflict escalates: The inter-group dynamics of collective football crowd 'violence.'" *Sociology*, 32: 353–377.

Stott, C., Hutchison, P., and Drury, J. (2001) "'Hooligans' abroad? Inter-group dynamics, social identity and participation in collective 'disorder' at the 1998 World Cup Finals." *British Journal of Social Psychology*, 40: 359–384.

Sugden, J. (1994) "USA and the World Cup: American nativism and the rejection of the people's game," in Sugden, J. and Tomlinson, A. (eds.) *Hosts and Champions: Soccer Cultures, National Identities and the USA World Cup*. Aldershot, UK: Ashgate, pp. 219–252.

Sullivan, P. (2010) "Deciphering the Cubs ticket pricing system." *Chicago Tribune*, October 15, http://www.yardbarker.com/mlb/articles/deciphering_the_cubs_ticket_pricing_system/3422323, accessed January 21, 2013.

Tomlinson, A. (2002) "Theorizing spectacle, beyond Debord," in Sugden, J. and Tomlinson, A. (eds.) *Power Games, a Critical Sociology of Sport*, London: Routledge, pp. 44–60.

Tomlinson, A., Markovits, A.S., and Young, C. (2003) "Mapping sports space." *American Behavioral Scientist*, 46 (11): 1463–1475.

Trondman, M. (1990) "Rock taste – on rock as symbolic capital," in Carlsson, U. and Roe, K. (eds.) *Popular Music Research*, Gothenburg: Nordicom, pp. 71–85.

US Bureau of Labor Statistics (2011) "American time use survey: Leisure and sports." US Bureau of Labor Statistics, http://www.bls.gov/tus/current/leisure.htm, accessed December 20, 2012.

Van Bottenburg, M. (2003) "Thrown for a loss? (American) football and the European sport space." *American Behavioral Scientist*, 46 (11): 1550–1562.

Wacquant, L. (2004) *Body and Soul: Notebooks of an Apprentice Boxer*, Oxford: Oxford University Press.

Wann, D.L., Melnick, M.J., Russell, G.W., and Pease, D.G. (2001) *Sport Fans: The Psychology and Social Impact of Spectators*, New York: Routledge.

Williams, J., Dunning, E., and Murphy, D. (1984) *Hooligans Abroad: The Behaviour and Control of English Fans in Continental Europe*, London: Routledge.

Zirin, D. (2010) *Bad Sports: How Owners are Ruining the Games We Love*, New York: Scribners.

Further Reading

Amenta, E. (2007) *Professor Baseball: Searching for Redemption and the Perfect Lineup on the Softball Diamonds of Central Park*, Chicago: University of Chicago Press.

Bourdieu, P. (1978) "Sport and social class." *Social Science Information*, 17: 819–840.

Crawford, G. (2004) *Consuming Sport: Fans, Sport and Culture*, New York: Routledge.

Giulianotti, R. (2002) "Supporters, followers, fans, and flaneurs: A taxonomy of spectator identities in football." *Journal of Sport & Social Issues*, 26 (1): 25–46.

Markovits, A.S. and Hellerman, S.L. (2001) *Offside: Soccer and American Exceptionalism*, Princeton, NJ: Princeton University Press.

19

Sporting Violence and Deviant Bodies

Kevin Young and Michael Atkinson

Introduction: Is "Deviance" Still Relevant?

Deviancy theory has never really found a home in the sociology of sport (Coakley and Donnelly, 2005). Perhaps this is a historical artifact of how and when the sociology of sport (and now physical culture) blossomed in the last quarter of the twentieth century (much later than the heyday of deviancy theory in the United States) or reflective of how sociologists of sport tend to see the concept of deviance as overly functionalist, conservative, and reaffirming of some imaginary status quo. In an often left-leaning subdiscipline, it is understandable why an academically "old school" concept like deviance would be unappealing. Many in the sociology of sport now dismiss the concept as irrelevant on these grounds alone. Further still, perhaps many within the subdiscipline reject the notion of deviance because for so long people within sport cultures have shown considerable resistance to stereotypes within sport that categorize particular gendered, sexed, disabled, raced, ethnic, or other bodies as abnormal and unworthy of inclusion. We understand why, in the continual battle to secure equal rights for inclusion and acceptance for all in sport, the concept of deviance may be unpopular or controversial.

But we are reminded of Paul Willis' idea in Profane Culture (1978) that research on "moving cultures" can save us much philosophy. Our research ventures into the world of sport and exercise continually illustrate how there are both formal and informal "rules of order" in these worlds that are policed, tested, sanctioned, and altered. In many ways, how is culture possible without these processes? People breaking such rules face private and public sanctions from time to time, and these sanctions carry concrete consequences for those labeled as "offenders." To borrow from Norbert Elias (1991), there is more than a twinge of "reality congruence" in this observation. Whether or not sociologists of sport acknowledge or "like" the social processes by which cultural definitions of right and wrong are inserted into the practice of sport is another matter entirely. For people on the front lines of sport and physical activity, the processes, conditions, and impacts of being labeled and treated as deviant are very real and, for scholars, they are worthy of study, explanation, and reflection.

What is especially interesting to us is how sports institutions and cultures themselves

A Companion to Sport, First Edition. Edited by David L. Andrews and Ben Carrington.
© 2013 Blackwell Publishing Ltd. Published 2013 by Blackwell Publishing Ltd.

actively promote and then punish rule violations, player misconduct, and general "bad behavior" in a full range of ways. Simply put, sport and exercise cultures are rife with the performance of "wanted deviance." Wanted deviance is a behavior, perspective, or symbol that violates an accepted social or cultural standard. It tends not to be defined as proper or just and is generally understood, even by perpetrators, to be controversial. It is an amalgam of Robert Hughes and Jay Coakley's (1991) categories of positive and negative deviance. When wanted rule violations are relatively controlled, they are not seen as being symptomatic of pathological circumstances – yet neither are they viewed as fully socially acceptable. Considerable evidence suggests that the embodied rule violation in sport is indeed wanted by players, coaches, leagues, audiences, and other stakeholders. Watching physical manifestations of deviance, such as a fistfight in ice hockey, can be physiologically pleasurable and thus emotionally meaningful for audiences. Learning that an athlete "doped" to win is interesting, and discovering that a player cheated with illegal equipment brings an added element of excitement to the sport spectacle itself. The violation may thrill, intrigue, or reinforce meaningful social allegiances between participants and audiences. However, rule violators are not always excused of their wrongdoing or granted an unchecked license to thrill with their particular behavior – witness the increasing intervention of the authorities into "headshots" or "high" hits in ice hockey and, increasingly, American football regarding concussions and other head injuries.

The lines demarcating wanted and unwanted deviance in any sport are not always clear, nor are they negotiated by athletes, coaches, officials, or league administrators with reckless abandon. Additionally, what sports insiders and their audiences define as acceptable and unacceptable behavior is, at best, inconsistent and contested. As such, theorizing (wanted and unwanted) sport deviance, misconduct, inappropriate behavior or whatever term we might like to apply, is challenging. In contact sports such as rugby, ice hockey, soccer, and football, there is considerable tension regarding the tactical use of wanted deviance by coaches and athletes in the throes of competition and its mass mediation by sport promoters (Coakley and Donnelly, 2005). Marketers of

North American ice hockey might find permissible on-ice violence hard to sell if both wanted (e.g., body checks or fistfighting) and unwanted (e.g., stick swinging leading to injury) forms of physical violence in the game did not create excitement and tension for audiences. To make sense of such accommodations and contradictions, figurational sociologists suggest that the emotional tension balances of safety and risk underpinning competitive sports are a defining feature of their appeal (e.g., Elias and Dunning, 1986: 21).

Marxist and neo-Marxist sociologists of sport (e.g., Gruneau and Whitson, 1994) caution figurationalists and others to acknowledge the groups who are hurt by the mass marketing of wanted and unwanted sports deviance. Both types of deviance are lucrative for the established hegemony in sport – a hegemony in which business policy monitors standards of play and influences cultures of violence embedded in sports like ice hockey. Profit-driven entrepreneurs know that deviance sells seats and encourages the public consumption of sport media, which in turn fuels advertising and promotional revenues (Blackshaw and Crabbe, 2004). Ironically, those paying the heftiest price for deviant behavior may be the athletes themselves. Professional cyclists are banned for taking drugs despite institutional networks that place enormous pressures on racers to push past the barriers of human ability and establish new records.[1] Basketball stars are fined thousands of dollars for brawling on court despite their corporate branding and consumption as "thugs" (Wilson, 2006). In ice hockey, enforcers are punished, sometimes by the criminal courts, for their coach- and peer-approved brutality, which is routinely lauded on "Hits of the Day" segments on television news and sport programs (Young, 2012). While owners, sponsors, and officials prosper from on-field deviance, athletes are fined, suspended, or shamed when their behavior is perceived to cross the ambiguous line from *wanted* to *unwanted*. Although the contradictions and hypocrisy are obvious, the theoretical roadmaps for understanding sports deviancy in its wanted and unwanted forms are not.

In the remainder of this chapter, we examine the tensions, contradictions, and overall problems in defining and then "policing" what constitutes embodied deviance in sports cultures. We review major theoretical ways of "seeing" embodied deviance in sport and physical activity, and examine the main arguments offered as to why sports deviance is difficult to either define or contain across cultural settings.

The Social Control of Deviant Bodies in Sport

Although the literature goes much further back, any discussion of sport deviancy theory must surely start with Hughes and Coakley's (1991) seminal essay. Hughes and Coakley explain how athletes in competitive amateur and professional sports learn what Erving Goffman (1974) calls "interpretive frames" regarding what is appropriate conduct, and use these frames to gauge commitment to the group and sport. The authors describe how athletes are taught to strive for distinction, make sacrifices for their sport, and play through pain and injury as part of an overarching *sport ethic*. While not all athletes are socialized quite so completely or assess all social interactions and athletic performances in relation to this ethic, this maxim is so pervasive that most athletes encounter it and must reconcile themselves to it at some point over the course of their careers.

Hughes and Coakley suggest that the bulk of athlete behavior observed during competition and training, or even in social settings outside of sport, jibes with the requisites of the sport ethic. They illustrate athlete behavior on a statistical normal curve, and locate everyday athlete behavior at the heart of the curve. Athlete behavior that deviates from the sport ethic is located at either tail of the normal curve. "Sport deviance," as they see it, is considered statistically rare. On the one tail, they place a category of behaviors they refer to as *positive deviance*. These are athlete behaviors that pursue the principles of the sport ethic to an unhealthy extent such as dangerous weight loss (e.g., through dehydration strategies) in order to make a weight category in boxing or wrestling or in order to please judges in an "appearance sport" such as gymnastics or figure-skating. What is important is that, by and large, positive deviance goes unpunished by sport insiders or outsiders. On the other tail, Hughes and Coakley describe *negative deviance*. This includes athlete behaviors that reject the importance of the sport ethic, such

as disobeying a coach's instruction to attend every practice session or to work hard in training.

While Hughes and Coakley's (1991) model of (embodied) deviance in sport continues to have empirical merit, the schematic tends to ignore the ways in which wanted deviance is promoted in sport, or the ways in which people become conscientious, political dissidents in the sport process in order to challenge dominant social structures and codes through embodied acts. Consider, for instance, some of the following substantive areas in which news stories of corruption, abuse, cheating, and violations of rules or laws take place on an almost daily basis: the rise and proliferation of so-called alternative sport cultures designed to contest social normalcy in mainstream sports (snowboarding, skate and street boarding, Parkour, X Games, extreme fighting cultures, mixed martial arts, animal blood sports); health, drug, and doping cultures in sport (steroid use and abuse, gene manipulation, corruption in drug-testing policies, obesity, anorexia and body pathologies, the use of supplements and so-called fitness products); and participant misconduct (cheating, abusing opponents and officials, player–fan conflicts, initiation traditions, cultures of sexual aggressiveness and rape, overtraining, injury, self-abuse, gambling). This list is far from exhaustive, but we are struck by how little empirical research exists on most of the behaviors mentioned, and how mainstream sociologists of sport, bodies, and deviance have ignored the situational, cultural, and political-institutional aspects of these behaviors. Each of these empirical categories of sport deviance *could* spawn hundreds of research ventures across the globe to better understand the behaviors of those involved, and ultimately, to better understand sport.

With all of the above said, the concept of deviance continues to "creep" through existing strands of sociological research on sport bodies and their performances in a range of ways. For the sake of comparison, we bracket these into four strands: *violence and aggression theories, subculture theories, identity politics theories*, and *victimology theories*.

Violence and Aggression Theories

"Deviance" in sport is often understood to be synonymous with violence and aggression in sport. Whether showcased as eye-catching behavior during a "Highlight of the Night" feature on sport TV or critiqued in the popular press as reprehensible, on- and off-field violence involving athletes, fans, and officials is the subject of widespread public attention and debate. Numerous sociologists of sport have theorized the causes of violence and aggression and related sociocultural experiences in a variety of games.

There is no definitive work on either aggression or violence in the sociology of sport or physical cultural studies. However, a review of that literature reveals that the term *aggression* is typically conceived of as behavior that intentionally threatens or inflicts physical injury on another person or thing. The definition of aggression may include assertive behaviors (such as a verbal attack), discriminatory behaviors, or economic exploitations that need not produce physically injurious outcomes. By comparison, Dan Olweus (1993) suggests that the term *violence* is confined to the use of physical force. He defines violent behavior as behavior in which a perpetrator uses his or her own body as an object to inflict injury upon another person. Using such a definition there is an obvious overlap between violence and, say, bullying in sport, where bullying is carried out via physical aggression. Sebastien Guilbert (2004) expands on traditional definitions by identifying certain forms of sport intimidation as violence. He classifies *hard* violence as actions designed to impose pain and injury on opposing players and *soft* violence as verbal, symbolic, and psychological actions.

Many attempts to understand violence and aggression in sport focus on how situations of emotionally intense competition trigger aggressive cues within individuals. These are essentially "bio-psychological theories"; or simply, theories that root human behavior and expression deep within genes and/or minds. One of the earliest examples can be found in John Dollard and colleagues (1939) who explain all forms of aggression and violence as a product of situationally experienced frustration arising from blocked goals. From this perspective, a wide range of violent acts on the playing field, from "beanballs" in baseball to fistfights in ice hockey to reckless tackles in soccer, can be explained as reactionary and relatively unreflexive emotional responses to conditions of frustration occurring between contestants. Violent outbursts between athletes are explained as natural, genetically expressive, and predictable phenomena that occur in social spaces defined by intense competition for an object or a prize. Frustration may also manifest itself in response to officiating that is perceived to be inept or biased, or as a result of taunting by other players, or fans.

Central among theoretical accounts that emphasize the bio-psychological dimensions of sport violence is the Freudian-inspired "instinct theory." Popularized by the ethological ideas of Konrad Lorenz (1963), instinct theory explains violence and aggression in terms of Darwinian struggles for social superiority. Lorenz also posits that violence and aggression occur naturally in any competitive context, and attributes the manifestation of aggression in competition to its role in clarifying the ranking of the members of a group (such as a sports team). Lorenz and other instinct theorists suggest that frustration is a motivator to participate in close, hand-to-hand struggles as a form of instinctual release.

A second subcategory of violence and aggression theories commonly employed in the sociology of sport literature is social psychological in orientation, and includes Ted Gurr's (1970) "relative deprivation" theory that has been used to explain grievance, social hostility, and aggression. Gurr defines relative deprivation as "actors' perception of discrepancy between their value expectations and their value capabilities" (p. 24). In other words, relative deprivation is the gap between that "to which people believe they are rightfully entitled" and that which "they think they are capable of getting and keeping" (p. 24). Deprivation leads to frustration and aggression and is not based on wants or needs alone but on wants and needs that people feel they deserve. Therefore, an athlete who feels that his or her performance warrants victory also feels a sense of entitlement to accolade. When an entire group such as a sports team holds a similar skill–outcome mindset, a collective sense of entitlement toward winning, recognition, and success develops. If an individual or team feels deprived by the outcome, violence toward the source of the perceived deprivation may result.

John Kerr's (2004) "reversal theory" attempts to explain why athletes or spectators may conform to rules in one context but revert to violence and aggression in others. He outlines a number of what he calls *bipolar meta-motivational states*. These states determine passive or aggressive behavior in any sport setting and may be altered due to factors such as frustration and satiation. He identifies four meta-motivational states (*telic-paratelic, conformity-negativism, mastery-sympathy*, and *autic-alloic*) and explains violence in sport by arguing that aggressors spend more time in a particular combination of meta-motivational states than in any other combination – namely, they spend more time in paratelic (risk-taking), negativism (norm-violating), mastery (dominance), and autic (self-concerned) states. The crucial point for Kerr is how such states are cognitively and physiologically experienced when combined with arousal and what he calls the *hedonic tone*. To be relaxed is to be in the telic state with low arousal and high hedonic tone. For Kerr, whose substantive focus is soccer hooliganism, the combination of meta-motivational states and the feelings they create explains the motivation behind aggressive or violent acts of sport deviance.

Finally, figurational or process-sociologists (Elias, 1994, 1996; Elias and Dunning, 1986; Dunning, 1999) have examined the role of violence and aggression in arousing emotion and creating exciting significance for spectators. A central principle in figurational research on long-term civilizing processes is that Western societies have become relatively unexciting social environments. With the general pacification of cultures that occurs over time, a collective need to devise and institutionalize cultural activities that strike a balance between personal pleasure and restraint arises. As outward displays of emotion are pushed behind the scenes of social life (Elias, 1994), people pursue activities that elicit exciting significance in highly controlled contexts. Sports involving a moderate degree of physical violence (including rule-violating violence) thus become tolerable, allowing individuals to participate either as competitors or as spectators in behaviors that are taboo in other social spheres.

Subculture Theories

Influenced by social anthropology scholars of the early twentieth century, sociologists have studied groups of sports and athletes as distinct collectivities replete with their own subterranean value systems. For some authors, such as Gary Fine (1987), a sport subculture might be a Little League team that shares perspectives on its characteristics and goals. Chicago School symbolic interactionism (Blumer, 1969) focuses on how people in everyday life define their social realities as meaningful and act according to learned and shared ways of viewing the self and the surrounding social world. Children in Little League sports such as baseball or ice hockey, for instance, are approached as special populations, distinct in their shared statuses, identities, and collective rituals. Symbolic interactionism highlights the uniqueness of sport subcultures by explaining what it means to be a member of such a group.

Others have explored theoretical offshoots of symbolic interactionism, such as dramaturgy (Goffman, 1959, 1963), in order to learn how definitions of normativity and deviance are negotiated within sport subcultures. Elizabeth Pike (2005) offers a grounded investigation of the ways in which traditional and alternative medical ideologies clash and are negotiated between injured rowers and their chosen physicians. She shows how female rowers occasionally define their available health care as restrictive (or as medically deviant) and pursue unorthodox healthcare strategies as a subcultural solution. Michael Atkinson (2000) blends symbolic interactionism with ethnomethodology to study the deviant street subculture of ticket scalpers in Canada. His Toronto-based study focuses on how scalpers define the activity as tolerable deviance and devise subculturally appropriate means of conducting illegal trade.

One of the rare clear links between the sociology of deviance and the sociology of sport emerged in the 1980s and later as sport researchers tapped subcultural research initiated at the University of Birmingham's Centre for Contemporary Cultural Studies (CCCS). Members of the CCCS used a blend of Gramscian Marxism, semiotics, and labeling theory to conceptualize subcultures as reaction-formation groups that evolve in response to collectively experienced social problems. Sociologists of sport began adopting the CCCS interest in the politics of subcultural style and group disaffection in the 1980s to explain how specific youths utilize sport as a site of opposition and often highly stylized "resistance." The CCCS-inspired perspective views do-it-yourself (DIY) youth sports with avant-garde styles as such symbolic gestures of opposition toward sport orthodoxy. For instance, Becky Beal (1995) understands skateboarding as a strategy of resistance against mainstream competitive sports that stress middle-class, white, and male norms, Brian Wilson (1997) deconstructs the use of particular athletic footwear and uniforms by urban black basketball participants as a symbol of racial resistance to white hegemony in the sport, and Andrew Thornton (2004) views the development of ultimate Frisbee subcultures as part of the early eco-sport movement (see also CHAPTER 20).

A turn to risk theory (Beck, 1991) in the parent discipline has encouraged a recent generation of sport researchers to view thrill-seeking via dangerous forms of athleticism as an example of deviance. During the 1990s, the term *risk* became associated with a sizable corpus of research in the sociology of sport, and risk ascended to become one of the most popular research areas within the subdiscipline. Of particular interest are accounts of risk mentalities in sport, lifestyles of athletic risk taking, and the rise of extreme sports. Robert Rinehart and Synthia Sydnor (2003) and David le Breton (2000) deconstruct sports insiders' ideologies of risking the body through surfing, hang gliding, skydiving, and backcountry snowboarding as a type of symbolic death and power game. The term *deviance* rarely appears in such analyses of risk, extreme, or death sports, but the empirical research in this theoretical vein nevertheless typically classifies willful risk-taking as contranormative, alternative, or marginal activity.

Identity Politics Theories

Robert Dunn (1998: 20) defines identity politics as the process of aligning oneself with others who share feelings of marginality and oppression. Eschewing conventionally ascribed characteristics revered by dominant social hierarchies such as white or heterosexual, individuals engage in identity struggle to redefine personal (and collective) identity in the process of "winning space" (Cohen, 1972). In this process, violating dominant norms, values, and beliefs that provide the ideological support for cultural practices is criti-

cal. Research on identity politics in the sociology of sport is so common that it has been tackled using a wide range of approaches, including postmodern and poststructural theories, cultural studies, feminist and queer theories, discourse theories, and existential theories (Atkinson, 2007).

A consistent thread in this research is the reproduction and contestation of dominant gender codes/bodies. Gender-power objectivists examine how opportunities for participation and leadership in sport (i.e., access to sport for men and women, coaching and administration opportunities, economic power positions in sport, and so on) are structured rigidly by traditional ideologies that place masculinity (i.e., strong, powerful, aggressive, authoritarian) as the gender norm and femininity (i.e., weak, docile, dominated, domestic) as the deviant gender. For instance, Michael Messner's (2002) work on gender paints a sobering portrait of the structural barriers that endure for female athletes and the ways in which women are systematically marginalized in sports organizations. Rita Simon's (2004) historical review of American legislation designed to remedy gender inequality in sport, including Title IX, suggests that even formal attempts to correct gender discrimination in sport receive limited public support.

Gender-power subjectivists, by contrast, examine how dominant gender logics are negotiated or resisted in sport contexts. Nancy Theberge's (2002) research on femininity in Canadian ice hockey and Jean Williams' (2003) analysis of women's football in Britain show how contact sports provide contexts for consciously subverting cultural constructions of the "passive woman." Theberge and Williams underscore how women come to associate athleticism, as well as the ability to exert power over others in athletic competition, with the performance of gender identity in sport.

Genevieve Rail's (1990) work on the experience of "masculine-like" physicality in women's basketball also explores how participants receive physical, psychological, and emotional satisfaction by culturally standing out as powerful figures. Kevin Young and Philip White's (2007) Canadian volume on the identity politics of gendered sport and resistance in sport examines how deviant gender performance is deliberately choreographed by athletes, and David Kestenbaum's (2003) research on a traditionally "docile" and feminine sport – figure-skating – also reveals how young female athletes assert individuality in their sport to an unprecedented, and heretofore deviant, degree. Racial and ethnic discrimination is also an important dimension of gender politics in sport. For more than 50 years, racialized athletes have been portrayed as deviant and as biologically gifted (Entine, 1999; Hoberman, 1997; Wiggins and Miller, 2005) or as part of a criminal or bestial athlete underclass characterized by hubris and aggression (Miller, 2003). Similar research has been conducted on the systematic exclusion of Latinos (Mangan and DaCosta, 2001) and Native Canadians (Paraschak, 2007) from mainstream white, middle-class sport cultures in North America and elsewhere.

Contemporary research on definitions of ethnicity and the politics of "doing race" through sport underlines ways in which minority identities are asserted publicly as non-deviant through sports practices. Embedded cultural antagonisms toward Asian, Indo-Asian, African, and other minority ethnicities in the West have been exposed and challenged through sport research (Coakley and Donnelly, 2005). Caroline Pluss' (2005) study of cricket in China and Greg Gillespie's (2000) analysis of cricket in Canada draw attention to how sporting excellence is produced on playing fields without mainstream cultural recognition. Ellis Cashmore (2002) argues that the systematic public under-appreciation of non-white sports is a measure of a broader cultural exclusion of minorities and that their continuance indicates minority resolve. At the same time, minority groups have publicly confronted racist and ethnically insensitive representations in mainstream white sport, such as those found in the previously discussed team mascot images. The efforts of groups promoting Native Americans, such as the Society for the Study of the Indigenous Languages of the Americas, to eliminate the racist use of Native American names, images, and iconography in sport show how some people envision sport as a key venue for negotiating minority rights (King, 2004).

Finally, identity politics continues to be the dominant focus of research on the exercise of heteronormativity of sport (Eng, 2007). Heteronormativity is an ideology and a set of disciplinary practices that enforce heterosexual relations and related gender roles. Pat Griffin (1998) describes sport as a heteronormative *deep closet* for the ways in which gay and lesbian athletes have been culturally and structurally ostracized. By interrogating how gay, lesbian, and transgender identities and symbols have been historically denigrated in sports worlds, authors such as Eric Anderson (2005; also CHAPTER 5), Jayne Cauldwell (2006), and Brian Pronger (1990) reveal how Western sport cultures remain some of the last bastions of overt and socially tolerated homophobia. Queer identities and sexual preferences were, until relatively recently, blatantly denied, excluded, and even aggressively marginalized in the masculine and heteronormative world of sport (Eng, 2007). Even today, gay and lesbian identities are among the least publicly acknowledged and celebrated within, for instance, the sports media.

Victimology Theories

A radical departure from existing thinking about deviance in sport, victimological perspectives encourage us to focus on people who are affected first-hand by rule violation (Young, 1991; Young and Reasons, 1989). Victimology is rooted in the idea that people who participate in sport hold inherent rights to freedom, safety, and personal welfare. Moreover, athletes who are paid to participate in sport and are members of complex economic organizations – that is to say, workplaces – should be viewed as workers who deserve institutional and legal protections. Early victimological research in the sociology of sport displayed Marxist and cultural studies leanings, addressing the myriad ways in which athletes or other sports insiders may be systematically victimized (physically, socially, economically, or psychologically) by exploitative and corporate sport hegemonies (Young, 1991).

Victimologists shift attention from the expression of deviance to the pressures placed on individuals in certain settings to behave in certain ways. For example, studies of sport violence like those of Young (1991) and Young and Reasons (1989) challenge labor officials and courts to view the exploitation of athletes as a type of white-collar crime. Practices such as requiring that athletes gain or lose an unnatural amount of weight in the off-season, urging or even forcing athletes to play while injured, or implicitly threatening their job security if they do not play while in pain may be considered as a violation of their civil rights (Young, 1993).

To date, however, few sociologists of sport have pursued a victimological perspective; far more emphasize the subcultural kudos athletes receive for competing while under physical, emotional, or psychological duress (Howe, 2004; Young, White, and McTeer, 1994). Psychologists and sociologists of sport do, however, study sexually abused athletes from quasi-victimological perspectives (Brackenridge, 2001). Pastiche analyses of the sexual exploitation of young players by coaches have been achieved through psychoanalytic and feminist readings. Paulo David (2005: 12) identifies the sexual and physical abuse of children in sport (including child trafficking through sport) as a theoretical "black hole." He argues that the abuse of children in local or global sport cultures is relatively ignored and that sports insiders in highly competitive athletic circles rarely question whether intensive training, ideological indoctrination into winning at all costs, isolation from non-athletes, emotional manipulation, dietary control, sexualization, and corporeal punishment for performance failure are appropriate for children and youth.

The expanding globalization literature attends to how the mass commercialization and market development of Western sport creates "victim communities" in economically developing nations (Sage, 1999). The labor practices of corporations such as Nike, the spread of professional sports cultures into new regions, and even Olympic movements are linked to the economic exploitation of indigenous labor (through product development, facility construction, and gentrification) in countries like Mexico, Argentina, Brazil, South Africa, Indonesia, China, and Pakistan (Liao, 2006; Maguire, 1999). Other work addresses the non-human victims of global sport through its investigations of the environmental effects of organized sports like golf. Hyun Duck Kim's (1995) account of the golf industry's contribution to deforestation, water pollution, energy consumption, and the destruction of wildlife exemplifies how sport victimizes a range of sentient life forms and in

return faces minimal social, legal, or cultural accountability. In brief, victimological research is "cutting edge" in the parent discipline of sociology and certainly in the field of criminology, but it remains seriously underutilized in the sociology of sport.

Why is Sports Deviance *Wanted*?

In this respect, many forms of *wanted* sport deviance are quintessential examples of what Robert Stebbins (1996) calls *noncriminal tolerable deviance*. A culturally tolerable deviance violates a normative code but is not interpreted by audiences as a legitimate threat to the collective (or moral) good. Tolerable deviance, Stebbins (1996) argues, may be undertaken for personal pleasure or private experimentation. It encompasses moderately proscribed deviant behaviors in Western cultures, such as certain sexual activities, gambling, and the use of illegal drugs. A wide range of sport behaviors may also be viewed as tolerable deviance. Stebbins acknowledges sport as a site of tolerable deviance, noting how athletes in risky sports such as snowboarding or mountain-climbing pursue extreme challenges. These behaviors may oppose common sensibilities for self-protection, responsibility, and personal care but are tolerable because they pose little risk to broader populations outside of the individual participant.

Stebbins' emphasis on tolerable rule violation most likely resonates for anyone who has participated in, or studied, sport cultures. Tolerable deviance is connected conceptually with our descriptions of wanted forms of rule violation in sport because it adds excitement in the sporting context – it adds what Jack Katz (1988) calls *sneaky thrills*, or what John Hagan (1991) terms *disreputable pleasures*. In this way, sport deviance may provide an emotional "double whammy" for audiences since the tone and content of the rule violation poses little public threat and the act (e.g., a particularly brutal and rule-violating hit in American football) may be culturally and emotionally fascinating for those drawn to the aggressive dimensions of the game.

We believe that sport deviance (in most forms) is viewed as tolerable by audiences for seven key reasons.

1 Hierarchy of social problems argument

The criminological literature on police work shows that any urban police force creates a hierarchy of crimes to monitor. Serious ("index") crimes such as murder, drug trafficking, and armed robbery regularly appear at the top of these lists. The ranking of each crime on such lists is, of course, influenced by the perspectives of powerful social lobbyists and moral entrepreneurs, including collective interest groups, economic stakeholders in the community, corporations, and private citizens. From a social problems perspective, when communities face pressing social and physical challenges such as health and disease crises, unemployment, environmental degradation, and discrimination, issues that may be perceived as only mildly criminal or culturally allowable tend to receive minimal public or official attention. Social problems involving statistically few members of a population also tend to be placed at the bottom of the agenda for social control.

Underscoring how a hierarchy of social problems argument might resonate for sport is the fact that scholars have uncovered troubling cultures of body distortion and self-starvation among female athletes in sports such as gymnastics, figure-skating, and track athletics. By investigating girls' eating pathologies (such as bulimia and anorexia) as types of body dysmorphic disorder, Mark Reinking and Laura Alexander (2005) show how certain athlete personalities are more predisposed to eating problems than others are. The precise extent of eating disorders in young female sport, or in sport more generally, is not known, but it seems unlikely that anorexia in female sport is any more pressing than obesity in adolescent populations in North America and elsewhere. From this perspective, it might be argued that time and money are better directed toward addressing more common eating, body, and weight problems in the broader population than in the relatively smaller athlete population.

2 Internal policing argument

In 2003 Dr Wade Exum, the former director of the drug control administration for the United States Olympic Committee (USOC), spoke to a global television audience about the extent of drug cheating in American track and field. As a longtime insider to American track and field, he controversially released private files indicating that 19 American medalists were allowed to compete at various Olympic games from 1988 to 2000 despite having failed drug tests leading up to the respective competitions (Knapp, 2003). Exum alleged that more than 100 American athletes in several different sports tested positive for banned substances between 1988 and 2000. The athletes were cleared by internal appeals processes within respective sport federations such as the USOC, IOC, International Association of Athletics Federations (IAAF), and the World Anti-Doping Agency (WADA). Acclaimed American sprinter Carl Lewis was one of three Olympic gold medalists who tested positive for banned stimulants (pseudoephedrine, ephedrine, and phenylpropanolamine) in the months preceding the 1988 Games. In Seoul, Lewis originally finished second but was eventually awarded the gold medal by default when Ben Johnson of Canada was discovered to have failed a drug test. Exum's files, summarized in an April 12, 2003 Orange County Register exposé, sent shock waves through the Olympic community (Knapp, 2003). Critics of the US dominance in track and field demanded intervention in order to eliminate drug cheating in the sport. Over half a decade later, no such external intervention has been initiated in amateur sports in the United States. The long-standing argument, promulgated by the USOC and IAAF following Exum's claims, is that only sport federations themselves understand how to police their own forms of deviance. At the minimum, Exum's files should have encouraged critics to ask how the extensive network of drug consumption and distribution within sports like track and field has avoided legal scrutiny (Knapp, 2003). Given that steroid possession and distribution violates criminal law in the United States and other countries, why do sport federations continue to receive discretionary power to enforce, or ignore, anti-drug rules?

The answer to this question in part lies in the way that sport federations such as the IAAF and IOC scapegoat particular athletes (e.g., stripping Canadian sprinter Ben Johnson of his Seoul gold medal and awarding it to Carl Lewis) and cite their punishment as a measure of institutional efficacy. For example, Irish swimmer Michelle

Smith won four medals (three gold and one bronze) at the 1996 Olympic Games in Atlanta. During her two previous Olympic Games, Smith's best result was a modest 17th place in the women's 200-meter backstroke. In the time leading to the Atlanta Games, Smith won three European swimming titles and trimmed more than 17 seconds from two of her personal bests in the pool. Following these unheralded performances, the Fédération Internationale de Natation (FINA), the governing body of amateur swimming, suspected Smith of doping. FINA expressed concern to the IOC that Smith refused out-of-season drug testing in 1995. FINA testers surprised Smith at her home in 1998 and requested a urine sample. The tests found a bizarre alcohol concentration in her urine sample, and testers concluded that Smith doctored the sample by adding whiskey as a masking agent. FINA immediately suspended her from international competition for four years. The sleuthing of Smith's doping practices was lauded by the IOC and WADA as an example of how internal control in amateur sport functions effectively. The sports world is filled with teams, leagues, and administrative structures that justify their internal policing by pointing to individual cases when many more cases involving precisely the same behaviors escape such close scrutiny.

3 Mimesis argument

Elias and Dunning (1986) and Dunning and Rojek (1992) argue that a primary role of sport within complex societies is to make social life less routine. Sport is seen a social theater in which spectators are deliberately aroused by the tension balances created through athletic contests. Figurational sociologists describe sport as *mimetic* because it deliberately resembles warlike competition. It is socially and emotionally significant to individuals because it elicits excitement through controlled violence in a battle that is not as perilous to the participants as an actual war. Spectators are excited by the often rough and rule-violating competitive exchange between the participants yet feel neither guilt nor repugnance in watching the action since the struggles are not real acts of war.

The figurational construction of mimesis is pivotal for grasping why sport deviance is tolerated or promoted as wanted. For example, using the car as a battering ram in American NASCAR racing is a mimetic form of interpersonal violence in the sport. During a race, drivers illegally push, nudge, or crash into each others' vehicles as a maneuvering and jockeying strategy. High-speed crashes, rollovers, and multiple-car pileups occasionally result from the bumping. In a 2003 NASCAR race in Miami, Juan Pablo Montoya collided cars with Ryan Newman. Newman bumped Montoya at high speed and sent his car head on into the track's inner wall. Montoya, a former Formula One driver, received only minor injuries from the incident, even though flames engulfed his car shortly after the crash. Newman received no reprimand from NASCAR officials for the accident.

4 Athletes as a special population argument

Another sport perspective views athletes as a special population with a license to participate in rule-violating behavior. Athletes, especially young males participating in power and performance sports, are socialized into believing that they are privileged people whose social transgressions in and around the playing field will be excused by parents, coaches, teachers, and even police (Benedict, 1997). Athletes who participate in highly visible and culturally revered sports, even at young ages and amateur levels, may become celebrities in their communities. The public fall and punishment of an athlete celebrity because of rule-violating behavior not only challenges cultural constructions of the athlete's moral character but also challenges cultural ideals about sport itself as a virtue-producing social institution. Coakley and Donnelly (2005) describe how hubris germinates within athletes who feel as if their actions are beyond reproach. Studies by Harry Bissinger (2000, on American high-school football), Laura Robinson (1998, on amateur ice hockey), and others underline the degree to which communities remain willing to overlook the deviance and crimes of athletes who are protected as special populations.

5 Isolated offender argument

The indiscretions of athletes, however common and statistically typical, tend to be perceived as unusual and unrepresentative of sport culture by sport apologists. Pete Rose's (baseball) or Michael Jordan's (basketball) gambling is defined as atypical, Michael Irvin's (American football) or Theoren Fleury's (ice hockey) use of recreational drugs is interpreted as individually problematic but not widely victimizing, and the spousal abuse perpetrated by star athletes such as O.J. Simpson (football), Sugar Ray Leonard (boxing), and Stan Collymore (soccer) is interpreted using "rotten apple" rather than "spoiled barrel" logic. By pathologizing individuals and not the cultures that help produce their psychologies, characteristics, and patterns of action, sport advocates deflect attention away from sport as a system of values that allows certain behaviors and personalities to emerge, endure, and remain relatively immune from sanction.

6 Impossibility of legal intervention argument

Michael Smith's (1983) and John Barnes' (1988) respective work on sport violence led them to conclude that criminal deviance in sport is difficult to establish. Sport is likely one of the few remaining social institutions that consistently escapes the modern reflex toward settling order and controlling problems litigiously. Among the most cited reasons as to why the police and criminal prosecutors avoid cases of violence and aggression in sport is the perceived lack of criminal intent in a player's actions, the inherent risks and dangers in competitive sport, and the apparent consent players give to being hurt during play (Barnes, 1988). A considerable amount of sport violence is summarily dismissed by agents of social control due to a belief in the impossibility of convincing athletes, the public, and the courts that sport deviance actually constitutes criminal behavior. More than a century's worth of case examples of failed police intervention into North American athletics supports this claim.

Consider the example of the "beanball" in American baseball. Pitchers deliberately throw fastballs at opposing batters' heads as a tactic of competition or revenge. Legendary pitchers Bob Gibson, Nolan Ryan, Roger Clemens, and Randy Johnson are among the most recognized pitchers throwing beanballs in the sport's history. The beanball is an especially dangerous rule violation,

as a batter's reaction time at the plate – and ability to dodge such a pitch – is a matter of microseconds. The Major League Baseball Players Association instituted a mandatory helmet rule for players. Rather than crack down on rule violators and ban the practice altogether, improving equipment that allowed the practice to continue – in this case encasing players' heads in tough plastic – was the chosen route. One of the most notorious examples of the beanball in the modern era occurred during the 1981 World Series. Pitcher Goose Gossage of the New York Yankees intentionally hit Ron Cey of the Los Angeles Dodgers in the head with a fastball, knocking Cey off his feet and concussing him. Given that athletes like Cey disavow their own victimization and consider such rule violations as just part of the game, legally intervening into sport violence cases becomes complicated, and the successful prosecution of offending players becomes extremely unlikely (Young and Wamsley, 1996; Young, 2012).

7 Overamplification of sport problems argument

Stanley Cohen's (1972) account of how community "folk devils" are constructed through amplified media reports emphasizes the role of moral entrepreneurship in the deviancy process. It also highlights the way in which the public may grow desensitized toward social deviance because of its spectacular representation in the press. Deviants are initially villainized in the media through sensational accounts of their activities, and their disreputable images galvanize over time as they become recognized folk devils. According to criminologist Vince Sacco (2005), the media often hyperbolize cases of rule violation and crime, thus distorting public understanding of social problems in the community. Sacco notes that with such media overexposure, grand claims about the sheer presence of deviance, and sensationalization of deviance, people become accustomed to seeing deviance in everyday life and thus are less shocked by its occurrence.

The Nike corporation experienced intense media scrutiny in the mid-1990s after the publication of troubling reports detailing worker victimization in several of the company's manufacturing facilities located in developing countries. Accounts of corporal punishment, sexual abuse, slave wages, dangerous and unhealthy working conditions, and forced labor surfaced out of countries such as Thailand, Pakistan, China, and Vietnam. A subsequent global "Anti-Nike," "Boycott Nike," and "Just Don't Do It" social movement and a massive media blitz into Nike's corporate practices demanded that the company and certain nations, including the United States, initiate immediate industry reform. Nike acknowledged problematic behavior in a few regions but maintained that several alleged and isolated cases of (especially female) worker abuse were exaggerated by the global media. Apparently, consumers of Nike products agreed, as the company set profit records during the second half of the 1990s (Frisch, 2004), a trend that continues.

has been and continues to be comfortably rationalized by audiences using special arguments that render it tolerable, even preferred. When sociologists have taken its manifestations seriously, there is also no doubt that behavior considered as sport deviance almost always falls under one of the explanatory umbrellas we have reviewed here – violence and aggression, subcultural identity, political and ideological identity, and the realm of abuse and victimization. But this is just the "state of play" so far, and it seems extremely likely that as students of crime and deviance continue to take sport deviance seriously, the applicability of the concept of wanted deviance will become ever more obvious. It is our contention that as this happens our understanding of problematic sport behavior, and what to do to about it, will also widen and deepen.

Conclusion

There is no doubt that theorizing sport deviance is difficult, at least in part because so much of it

Note

1   For example, in 2013 the American cyclist Lance Armstrong finally admitted that he had taken performance enhancing drugs and banned substances throughout most of his career. In a revealing interview with the television host and entertainer

Oprah Winfrey, Armstrong was asked, "In your opinion was it humanly possible to win the Tour de France, without doping, seven times in a row?" Armstrong replied, "Not in my opinion" (Armstrong, 2013).

References

Anderson, E. (2005) In *the Game: Gay Athletes and the Cult of Masculinity*, Albany: State University of New York Press.

Armstrong, L. (2013) "Lance Armstrong confession: Cyclist admits doping during Oprah interview." *Huffington Post*, January 17, http://www.huffingtonpost.com/2013/01/17/lance-armstrong-confession-doping_n_2500857.html, accessed January 17, 2013.

Atkinson, M. (2000) "Brother can you spare a seat: Developing recipes of knowledge in the ticket scalping subculture." *Sociology of Sport Journal*, 17: 151–170.

Atkinson, M. (2007) "Sport, gender and research method," in Young, K. and White, P. (eds.) *Sport and Gender in Canada*, Don Mills, ON: Oxford University Press, pp. 29–54.

Barnes, J. (1988) *Sport and the Law in Canada*, Toronto: Butterworths.

Beal, B. (1995) "Disqualifying the official: An exploration of social resistance through the subculture of skateboarding." *Sociology of Sport Journal*, 12: 252–267.

Beck, U. (1991) *Risk Society: Towards a New Modernity*, London: Sage Publications.

Benedict, J. (1997) *Athletes and Acquaintance Rape*, Thousand Oaks, CA: Sage Publications.

Bissinger, H. (2000) *Friday Night Lights: A Town, a Team, and a Dream*, Cambridge, MA: Da Capo Press.

Blackshaw, T. and Crabbe, T. (2004) *New Perspectives on Sport and Deviance*, London: Routledge.

Blumer, H. (1969) *Symbolic Interactionism: Perspective and Method*, Englewood Cliffs, NJ: Prentice Hall.

Brackenridge, C. (2001) *Spoilsports: Understanding and Preventing Sexual Exploitation in Sport*, London: Routledge.

Cashmore, E. (2002) *Sports Culture: An A–Z guide*, London: Routledge.

Cauldwell, J. (2006) *Sport, Sexualities and Queer Theory*, London: Routledge.

Coakley, J. and Donnelly, P. (2005) *Sport in Society: Issues and Controversies*, Toronto: McGraw-Hill.

Cohen, S. (1972) *Subcultural Conflict and Working Class Communities*, Birmingham: Centre for Contemporary Cultural Studies.

David, P. (2005) *Human Rights in Youth Sport*, London: Routledge.

Dollard, J., Doob, L., Miller, N., *et al.* (1939) *Frustration and Aggression*, New Haven, CT: Yale University Press.

Dunn, R. (1998) *Identity Crises: A Social Critique of Postmodernity*, Minneapolis: University of Minnesota Press.

Dunning, E. (1999) *Sport Matters: Sociological Studies of Sport, Violence, and Civilization*, London: Routledge.

Dunning, E. and Rojek, C. (1992) *Sport and Leisure in the Civilizing Process*, London: Macmillan.

Elias, N. (1991) *The Society of Individuals*, Oxford: Blackwell.

Elias, N. (1994) *The Civilizing Process*, Oxford: Blackwell.

Elias, N. (1996) *The Germans: Studies of Power Struggles and the Development of Habitus in the Nineteenth and Twentieth Centuries*, Oxford: Polity Press.

Elias, N. and Dunning, E. (1986) *Quest for Excitement: Sport and Leisure in the Civilizing Process*, Oxford: Blackwell.

Eng, H. (2007) "Queer athletes and queering in sport," in Cauldwell, J. (ed.) *Sport, Sexualities and Queer Theory*, London: Routledge, pp. 49–61.

Entine, J. (1999) *Taboo: Why Black Athletes Dominate in Sports and Why We are Afraid to Talk About It*, New York: Public Affairs.

Fine, G. (1987) *With the Boys: Little League Baseball and Preadolescent Culture*, Chicago: University of Chicago Press.

Frisch, A. (2004) *The Story of Nike*, San Francisco: Smart Apple Media.

Gillespie, G. (2000) "Wickets in the West: Cricket, culture and constructed images of 19th century Canada." *Journal of Sport History*, 27: 51–66.

Goffman, E. (1959) *The Presentation of Self in Everyday Life*, Garden City, NY: Doubleday-Anchor.

Goffman, E. (1963) *Stigma*, Garden City, NY: Doubleday-Anchor.

Goffman, E. (1974) *Frame Analysis*, Cambridge, MA: Harvard University Press.

Griffin, P. (1998) *Strong Women, Deep Closets: Lesbians and Homophobia in sport*, Champaign, IL: Human Kinetics.

Gruneau, R. and Whitson, D. (1994) *Hockey Night in Canada: Sport, Identities, and Cultural Practices*, Toronto: Garamond.

Guilbert, S. (2004) "Violence in sports and among sportsmen." *Aggressive Behavior*, 32: 231–240.

Gurr, T. (1970) *Why Men Rebel*, Princeton, NJ: Princeton University Press.

Hagan, J. (1991) *The Disreputable Pleasures: Crime and Deviance in Canada*, Toronto: McGraw-Hill Ryerson.

Hoberman, J. (1997) *Darwin's Athletes: How Sport has Damaged Black America and Preserved the Myth of Race*, Wilmington, MA: Houghton Mifflin.

Howe, D. (2004) *Sport, Professionalism and Pain: Ethnographies of Injury and Risk*, London: Routledge.

Hughes, R. and Coakley, J. (1991) "Positive deviance among athletes: The implications of overconformity to the sport ethic." *Sociology of Sport Journal*, 8: 307–325.

Hyun, D.-K. (1995) "Environmental movements against golf course development in Korea since the late 1980s." *Korea Journal of Population and Development*, 24: 57–70.

Katz, J. (1988) *Seductions of Crime*, New York: Basic Books.

Kerr, J. (2004) *Rethinking Violence and Aggression in Sport*, London: Routledge.

Kestenbaum, E. (2003) *Culture on Ice: Figure Skating and Cultural Meaning*, Middletown, CT: Wesleyan University Press.

King, R. (2004) "This is not an Indian: Situating claims about Indianness in sporting worlds." *Journal of Sport & Social Issues*, 28: 3–10.

Knapp, G. (2003) "USA covered up positive tests." *San Francisco Chronicle*, April 18: C1.

le Breton, D. (2000) "Playing symbolically with death in extreme sports." *Body and Society*, 6: 1–11.

Liao, H. (2006) "A brief review of Olympic urbanization." *International Journal of the History of Sport*, 23: 1232–1252.

Lorenz, K. (1963) *On Aggression*, San Diego, CA: Harcourt Brace.

Maguire, J. (1999) *Global Sport: Identities, Societies, Civilization*, Cambridge: Polity Press.

Mangan, J. and DaCosta, L. (2001) *Sport in Latin American Society*, London: Frank Cass.

Messner, M. (2002) *Taking the Field: Women, Men and Sports*, Minneapolis: University of Minnesota Press.

Miller, P. (2003) *Race and the Sport Color Line*, London: Routledge.

Olweus, D. (1993) *Bullying at School: What We Know and What We Can Do*, Oxford: Blackwell.

Paraschak, V. (2007) "Doing race, doing gender: First nations, sport, and gender relations," in Young, K. and White, P. (eds.) *Sport and Gender in Canada*, Don Mills, ON: Oxford University Press, pp. 137–154.

Pike, L. (2005) "Doctors say 'just rest and take ibuprofen.'" *International Review for the Sociology of Sport*, 40: 201–219.

Pluss, C. (2005) "Constructing globalized ethnicity: Migrants from India and Hong Kong." *International Sociology*, 20: 201–205.

Pronger, B. (1990) *The Arena of Masculinity: Sports, Homosexuality, and the Meaning of Sex*, New York: St Martin's Press.

Rail, G. (1990) "Physical contact in women's basketball: A first interpretation." *International Review for the Sociology of Sport*, 25: 269–285.

Reinking, M. and Alexander, L. (2005) "Prevalence of disordered eating behaviors in undergraduate female collegiate athletes and nonathletes." *Journal of Athletic Training*, 40: 47–51.

Rinehart, R. and Sydnor, S. (2003) *To the Extreme: Alternative Sports, Inside and Out*, Albany: State University of New York Press.

Robinson, L. (1998) *Crossing the Line: Violence and Sexual Assault in Canada's National Sport*, Toronto: McClelland & Stewart.

Sacco, V. (2005) *When Crime Waves*, Thousand Oaks, CA: Sage.

Sage, G. (1999) "Justice do it! The Nike transnational advocacy network." *Sociology of Sport Journal*, 16: 206–235.

Simon, R. (2004) *Fair Play: The Ethics of Sport* (2nd edn.), Boulder, CO: Westview Press.

Smith, M. (1983) *Violence and Sport*, Toronto: Butterworths.

Stebbins, R. (1996) *Tolerable Differences: Living with Deviance*, Whitby, ON: McGraw-Hill.

Theberge, N. (2002) *Higher Goals: Women's Ice Hockey and the Politics of Gender*, Albany: State University of New York Press.

Thornton, A. (2004) "Anyone can play this game," in Wheaton, B. (ed.) *Understanding Lifestyle Sports: Consumption, Identity and Difference*, London: Routledge, pp. 175–196.

Wiggins, P. and Miller, D. (2005) *Sport and the Color Line*, London: Routledge.

Williams, J. (2003) *A Game for Rough Girls*, London: Taylor & Francis.

Willis, P. (1978) *Profane Culture*, London: Routledge & Kegan Paul.

Wilson, B. (1997) "Good blacks and bad blacks: Media constructions of African American athletes in Canadian basketball." *International Review for the Sociology of Sport*, 32: 177–189.

Wilson, B. (2006) *Fight, Flight, or Chill: Subcultures, Youth, and Rave into the 21st Century*, Montreal: McGill-Queen's University Press.

Young, K. (1991) "Violence in the workplace of professional sport from victimological and cultural studies perspectives." *International Review for the Sociology of Sport*, 26: 3–14.

Young, K. (1993) "Violence, risk, and liability in male sports culture." *Sociology of Sport Journal*, 10: 373–396.

Young, K. (2012) *Sport, Violence and Society*, Abingdon, UK: Routledge.

Young, K. and Reasons, C. (1989) "Victimology and organizational crime: Workplace violence and the professional athlete." *Sociological Viewpoints*, 5: 24–34.

Young, K. and Wamsley, K. (1996) "State complicity in sports assault and the gender order in 20th century Canada: Preliminary observations." *Avante*, 2: 51–69.

Young, K. and White, P. (2007) *Sport and Gender in Canada*, Don Mills, ON: Oxford University Press.

Young, K., White, P., and McTeer, W. (1994) "Body talk: Male athletes reflect on sport, injury and pain." *Sociology of Sport Journal*, 11: 175–194.

Further Reading

Atkinson, M. and Young, K. (2008) *Deviance and Social Control in Sport*, Champaign, IL: Human Kinetics.

Hughes, R. and Coakley, J. (1991) "Positive deviance among athletes: The implications of overconformity to the sport ethic." *Sociology of Sport Journal*, 8: 307–325.

Kerr, J. (2004) *Rethinking Violence and Aggression in Sport*, London: Routledge.

Smith, M. (1983) *Violence and Sport*, Toronto: Butterworths.

Young, K. (2012) *Sport, Violence and Society*, Oxford: Routledge.

20

Dissecting Action Sports Studies
Past, Present, and Beyond

Holly Thorpe and Belinda Wheaton

Introduction

The term "action sports" broadly refers to a wide range of mostly individualized activities such as BMX, kite-surfing, skateboarding, surfing, and snowboarding that differed – at least in their early phases of development – from traditional rule-bound, competitive, regulated Western "achievement" sport cultures (Booth and Thorpe, 2007; Kusz, 2007a; Wheaton 2004, 2010). Various categorizations have been used to describe these activities, including extreme, lifestyle, and alternative sports. In this chapter, however, the term *action sports* is used as it is currently the preferred term among committed participants and industry members in North America and Australasia (many of whom reject the overly commercialized "extreme" moniker imposed upon them by transnational media and mainstream sponsors during the mid- and late 1990s).

Many action sports gained popularity during the new leisure trends of the 1960s and 1970s and increasingly attracted alternative youth, who appropriated these activities and infused them with a set of hedonistic and carefree philosophies and subcultural styles (Booth and Thorpe, 2007; Thorpe and Wheaton, 2011a; Wheaton, 2010).

While each action sport has its own unique history, identity, and development patterns (Wheaton, 2004), early participants *allegedly* sought risks and thrills, touted anti-establishment and do-it-yourself philosophies, and subscribed to an "outsider identity relative to the organized sports establishment" (Kusz, 2007a: 359; Beal, 1995). Developing during a "historically unique conjuncture" of transnational mass communications and corporate sponsors, and entertainment industries, and amongst a growing affluent and young population, many action sport cultures have "diffused around the world at a phenomenal rate" (Booth and Thorpe, 2007: 187). Over the past five decades, action sports have become a highly visible feature of popular culture. Action sports athletes appear on the covers of *Rolling Stone*, *Sports Illustrated*, and *FHM* and feature in advertisements for corporate sponsors such as Nike, Mountain Dew, and American Express. Recent estimates suggest there are more than 22 million Americans currently participating annually in the four most popular action sports – skateboarding, snowboarding, BMX riding, and surfing – with many participating on a regular basis and engaging in an array of other action sports (AMG, 2007). Reliable

A Companion to Sport, First Edition. Edited by David L. Andrews and Ben Carrington.
© 2013 Blackwell Publishing Ltd. Published 2013 by Blackwell Publishing Ltd.

international statistics are scarce, yet similar trends have been observed in many Western, and some Eastern (e.g., China, Japan, South Korea), countries (see Booth and Thorpe, 2007; Thorpe, 2008; Wheaton, 2004, 2010). As these sports continue to gain popularity, many become highly fragmented, with enthusiasts engaging in various styles of participation, demonstrating philosophical differences and various levels of skill and commitment.

Since the mid-1990s, scholars from many disciplinary backgrounds, including anthropology, cultural geography, history, philosophy, psychology, sociology, and youth studies, have employed an array of methodological and theoretical approaches in order to understand and explain the experiences of action sports cultures within local, national, global, and virtual contexts in historical and contemporary conditions. In this chapter we focus on the qualitative efforts of critical sports scholars to understand the various forms of power operating on and through action sport bodies. In so doing, we explain how trends in theoretical and conceptual approaches have revealed various forms of politics including symbolic resistance, cultural politics, identity politics, spatial politics, representational politics, and bodily and aesthetic politics, as well as action sport related social movements. This chapter consists of two parts. First, we provide an overview of some of the past and present trends in action sports research, illustrating how different theoretical approaches have informed (and limited) our understanding of power, politics, and agency during various historical junctures. Second, we offer some suggestions for constructing more nuanced social explanations of action sports cultural politics into the twenty-first century.

Understanding the Politics of Action Sports Cultures: From Symbolic Resistance to Social Movements

Since the 1970s, the stylistic practices of youth have been an important theme in sociological works emerging from Birmingham University's Centre for Contemporary Cultural Studies (CCCS) tradition. Early subcultural theorists associated with the CCCS focused on youth style as symbolic resistance to mainstream or "hegemonic" society. They examined symbolic cultural aspects of youth subcultures, such as music, language, and especially dress. Dick Hebdige (1979), for example, argued that subcultural youths engage in "semiotic guerrilla warfare" through their construction of style (p. 105). Early subcultural theorists described subcultures emerging in resistance to dominant culture, and reacting against a sense of blocked economic opportunities, lack of social mobility, alienation, adult authority, and the "banality of suburban life" (Wooden and Blazak, 2001: 20). A variety of spectacular postwar subcultures such as Teddy boys, Mods, punks and skinheads, provided CCCS theorists with evidence of youth styles challenging the dominant order. These theorists turned to Antonio Gramsci's (1971) notion of hegemony to give their evidence theoretical expression, proposing that subordinate classes operate by "winning space" through their modes of presentation and apparently antisocial behaviors.

Some of the pioneering work on action sports cultures drew inspiration from the theoretical approaches developed by the CCCS tradition, as well as methodological approaches employed by the more ethnographically oriented Chicago School (see Wheaton, 2007a). For example, in her early ethnographic work on a local skateboarding culture in Colorado, Becky Beal (1995, 1996) describes a group of young male skateboarders practicing and performing an alternative form of masculinity. According to Beal (1995), this group of skateboarders distinguished their subculture from traditional sport and hegemonic masculinity via an array of symbolic (e.g., dress, language) and physical (e.g., embracing styles of participation that deemphasized competition and embraced individual expression) practices. But she also observed contradictions within the local skateboarding culture under investigation; she explained that, while the young male skateboarders overtly resisted the hypermasculine "jock" identities of male athletes in more traditional sports (e.g., football) and embraced skateboarding as an alternative to the dominant sports culture, they simultaneously reproduced patriarchal relations via the exclusion and marginalization of female participants (Beal, 1996).

The influence of the Birmingham School approach to subculture and style on the sociology of action sports cultures has been profound, yet the hegemonic understandings of power and resistance inherent in this approach, like all concepts and theories, were a product of its time. To paraphrase Lawrence Grossberg (1997), concepts are measured, and their truth and validity judged, by their ability to give a better understanding of the context (p. 262). The early subcultural research on alternative sports developed at a time when neo-Marxist, and particularly hegemonic, understandings of power were dominant in both youth cultural studies and sport sociology. Since then, however, there have been major changes in the development of action sports, and "generational shifts" in research on youth cultural formations and understandings of power, politics and social change in sport, which call into question much of this earlier work (see Donnelly, 2008; Thorpe, 2006; Wheaton, 2007a).

Operating within a specific conjuncture (the 1970s and 1980s), the theoretical concepts developed by the CCCS (and later appropriated by some action sports scholars) were limited by the material conditions of their times. In recent years hegemony theory, as advocated by the CCCS subcultural studies theorists, has drawn substantial criticism for ignoring participants' subjectivity, failing to study subcultural groups empirically, focusing too much on Marxist/class-based explanations and grand theories, reifying the concept of subculture, overemphasizing style, and over-politicizing youthful leisure (e.g., Haenfler, 2004; Muggleton, 2000). As Hebdige (1988) acknowledged, he may have conflated subordinance with the resistant among certain youth groups who were not overly political. Indeed, while the CCCS emphasized that subcultural style was a form of resistance to domination, ultimately the actions of subcultural members reinforced class relations because they focused on (superficial) stylistic resistance rather than political organization, employment or education (see Willis, 1978). In this sense, resistance was illusory; subcultural participation gave members a feeling of resistance while leaving existing social and political relations firmly in place.

Many accounts of postwar youth subcultures also "overlooked the dynamic quality of style" and discussed subcultures as though they are "immutably fixed phenomena, frozen statically at a particular point" (Osgerby, 1998: 76). In reality youth cultures exist in a constant state of change and flux. The dialectical relationship between dominant culture and resistance – which is implicit in the idea of subculture – is a fluid process; "resistance is contextual and many layered rather than static and uniform" (Haenfler, 2004: 409). Yet, scholars tended to overlook this relationship and portrayed subculture "as a homogenous and static system" (Fine and Kleinman, 1979: 5). In fact, work associated with the CCCS tradition ignored the *development* of subcultures, considering them "only when they were fully mediated and ripe for critical interpretation" (Thornton, 1996: 152). Members of the Centre admitted this shortcoming in their methodology: "Homological analysis of a cultural relation is synchronic. It is not equipped to account for changes over time, or to account for the creation or disintegration, of homologies: it records the complex qualitative state of a cultural relation as it is observed in *one quantum of time*" (Willis, 1978: 191, emphasis added).

Thus there is an "uncomfortable absence" in the early literature of how subcultures are "sustained, transformed, appropriated, disfigured or destroyed" and what the consequences of those processes might be (Clarke, 1982: 8). In short, CCCS subcultural analysis omitted the "whole dimension of change" (Muggleton, 2000: 22). As we have explained elsewhere, there has been a similar tendency in some ethnographic studies of action sports cultures which focus on the micro-politics within particular locations, often to the exclusion of the broader social and historical context (Thorpe, 2006; Wheaton, 2007a). Moreover, by focusing on single groups, such as skateboarders or snowboarders, in "one quantum of time" (Willis, 1978: 191), such accounts ignore dimensions of cultural change and development. Arguably, more social historical approaches are necessary for understanding contemporary action sports cultures, and explaining how cultural signs, practices, and politics change along with the cultural and social context.

The politics of incorporation: from subcultural studies to post-CCCS

Cultural incorporation was an important theme emerging from the CCCS tradition of subcultural research. Much of this research focused on the power of commercial agents to define and co-opt youth cultures. "Authentic" youth cultures were characterized as distinct from mass-produced, commercial, or mainstream culture, that is, until the commercial sphere appropriated the alternative images of the subculture as a means of making money. For many CCCS scholars, opposition to mainstream politics and philosophies evaporated in the processes of incorporation and the appropriation of these groups who subsequently forfeited their subcultural status (Barker, 2000).

While alternative or lifestyle sporting subcultures have received less attention in the mainstream sociological literature (see Wheaton, 2007a), similar debates about their commercial or mainstream inclusion, particularly the lamented shift from "alternative" to "mainstream" sports, have been prevalent in the sport sociology literature (e.g., Beal and Weidman, 2003; Beal and Wilson, 2004; Donnelly, 1993; Humphreys, 2003; Rinehart, 2005; Thorpe, 2006; Wheaton, 2007a). In one of the first in-depth investigations of the commercialization of action sports in the post-Fordist culture and economy, Duncan Humphreys (1996, 1997) examined the processes by which "alternative sports" such as skateboarding and snowboarding increasingly became controlled and defined by transnational corporations seeking to tap into the highly lucrative youth market. In his examination of youth cultural participants' symbolic and political responses to the forces and constraints of the commercialization process, Humphreys (1997) presented the much-publicized case of Norwegian snowboarder Terje Haakonsen's critique of the International Olympic Committee (IOC). Undoubtedly the world's best half-pipe rider at the time, Haakonsen refused to participate in the 1998 winter Olympics because he believed that the IOC comprised a group of Mafia-like officials and that taking part in the event was tantamount to joining the army. Haakonsen publically criticized the IOC's lack of understanding of snowboarding culture, and protested against snowboarders being turned into a "uniform-wearing, flag-bearing, walking logo[s]" (Mellgren, 1998: para. 8). Other snowboarders expressed similar sentiments. Yet Humphreys (2003) concludes by lamenting that such senti-

ments seemed to do nothing to stem the process of incorporation.

The X Games – the self-defined "worldwide leader" in action sports (Rinehart, 2008: 175) – was the brainchild of the cable television network ESPN (Entertainment and Sports Programming Network), and gained financial support from a range of transnational corporate sponsors. The inaugural summer Extreme Games (later renamed the X Games) held in 1995 in Rhode Island (USA) featured 27 action sport-related events in nine categories: bungee jumping, eco-challenge, in-line skating, skateboarding, sky-surfing, sport climbing, street luge, cycling, and water sports. Following the success of the summer games, ESPN staged the first winter X Games in 1997 in California, featuring events such as snowboarding and snowmobiling. With its "spectacular footage, distinctive sporting and cultural personalities, innovate representation styles and ubiquitous reach" (Thorpe and Wheaton, 2011a: 183), the X Games have played a significant role in the global diffusion and expansion of the action sports industry and culture (Rinehart, 2000). Indeed, the X Games have been integral to the institutionalization of action sports, especially cultural attitudes to formalized competitions, professionalization, and outsider regulation and control, such that it is not surprising that they attracted considerable academic interest (Beal, 1995; Beal and Wilson, 2004; Booth and Thorpe, 2007; Messner, 2002; Rinehart, 1998, 2000, 2008; Thorpe and Wheaton, 2011a, 2011b).

As action sports became popular and incorporated into the mainstream via mega-events such as the X Games and the Olympics, they appeared to assume many of the trappings of other modern sports including corporate sponsorship, large prize monies, "rationalized systems of rules," hierarchical and individualistic star systems, win-at-all costs values, and the creation of heroes, heroines and "rebel" athletes who look like "walking corporate billboards" (Messner, 2002: 82). As Wheaton (2004: 14) and others have revealed, "selling out" debates relate not just to commodification but also to the appropriation of action sports ethos and ideologies, such as attitude to risk, responsibility, freedom and regulation, repacking and selling their values and lifestyles for mass consumption (Humphreys, 1996, 1997; Rinehart, 2000, 2003, 2008). Reflecting CCCS-inspired research on youth cultures, however, much of the early work on action sports overlooked the potential for participants to practice agency or resistance *within* the processes of commercialization, incorporation, and institutionalization. For Humphreys (1996, 1997, 2003), for example, the radical potential of snowboarding largely evaporated once the sport became incorporated into the Olympic juggernaut.

Since the late 1990s, a new generation of sociologists and cultural studies scholars has emerged that is seeking to re-evaluate the idea of subculture, including previous explanations of the processes of commercial incorporation in youth, music, and style cultures (e.g., Bennett, 2011; Bennett and Kahn-Harris, 2004; Muggleton and Weinzierl, 2003). A key argument put forward by proponents of "post-subcultural studies" is that scholars typically paid little systematic attention to the role of media and commerce in youths' cultural formations, and rarely provided an explanation of what occurs "after the subculture has surfaced and become publicized" (Hebdige, 1979: 122). Drawing on, and reflecting theorizations of youth subcultures influenced by the CCCS, much of the early research on the institutionalization and commercialization of action sports tended to focus on the negative effects of these processes, seeing incorporation as a process that undermined the "authentic" oppositional or resistant character of the alternative sports, and typically conceptualizing commercialization as "a top-down process of corporate exploitation and commodification" (Edwards and Corte, 2010: 1137). As Richard Giulianotti (2005) suggests, the CCCS approach is insufficient for "explaining 'resistant' subcultures that actively *embrace* commodification, to function as niche businesses within the sport industry" (p. 56).

Recognizing the complex politics involved in the commercialization and incorporation of action sports in the early twenty-first century, a number of action sports scholars are working within this post-subcultural studies framework. Wheaton and Beal (2003) explain that, while participants in contemporary action sports cultures may not resist market incorporation, many contest the discourses about commercialism, regulation, and control, and importantly, raise the question, who defines and shapes sport? Revisiting Beal's earlier research on skateboarding culture, Beal and Wilson (2004: 32) explain that "internal contradictions are more common than a clear-cut sense of social resistance" in contemporary skateboarding culture. They describe the commercialization process in skateboarding culture as a set of contingent negotiations between "youths cultural expression, the cultural industry and mass media representations" (p. 33). Similarly, Wheaton (2004) observes that contemporary action sports participants are not simply victims of commercialization but active agents who continue to "shape and 'reshape' the images and meanings circulated in and by global consumer culture" (p. 14). In his analysis of the continuing and multiple forms of contestation around the X Games, Rinehart (2008) argues that there is "no simplistic dichotomy for resistance and co-optation in the alternative sport world" and thus we need to "move beyond constraining binaries – e.g., resistance vs. co-optation, mainstream vs. emergent, traditional vs. new" (p. 192; also see Booth, 2002; Edwards and Corte, 2010; Thorpe, 2006; Wheaton, 2004).

More recently, Thorpe and Wheaton (2011a, 2011b) employed a post-subcultural theoretical approach to examine the cultural politics surrounding the incorporation of action sports into the Olympic program via case studies of windsurfing, snowboarding, and bicycle motocross (BMX). Ultimately, our analysis reveals that "the incorporation processes, and forms of (sub)cultural contestation, are in each case unique, based on a complex and shifting set of intra- and inter-politics between key agents, namely the IOC and associated sporting bodies, media conglomerates, and the action sports cultures and industries" (Thorpe and Wheaton, 2011b: 830). Drawing upon post-CCCS arguments, recent research reveals contemporary action sport cultures as highly fragmented and in a constant state of flux, such that myriad types of cultural production, consumption and contestation are occurring, often simultaneously. As Wheaton (2010) explains, in this context, "resistance is not a struggle with dominant hegemonic culture but is located at the levels of the everyday and in the body" (p. 1063).

Everyday politics in action sports cultures:
identity, representation, experience,
and reflexivity

Questions of identity and inequality feature strongly in contemporary research on action sports cultures. Despite recent concerns over the "usefulness of identity as a basis for scholarly analysis and political action" after the "poststructuralist turn" (King and McDonald, 2007: 1), many action sports scholars continue to work within an identity politics framework, employing an array of methodological and theoretical approaches to "discern injustices" done within and through the realm of action sports to particular social groups on the basis of their cultural identities (King and McDonald, 2007: 1). While class-based identity politics were central to subcultural studies associated with the CCCS, class and privilege often go under-analyzed in action sports scholarship. In contrast, researchers have dedicated considerable attention to gender politics in action sports cultures.

Researchers have examined the young hypermasculinity celebrated within climbing (Robinson, 2008), snowboarding (Anderson, 1999; Thorpe, 2010), surfing (Evers, 2004; Waitt and Warren, 2008), and windsurfing (Wheaton, 2000) cultures, and the hierarchical power relations between groups of "other" men and women within them. Some have also investigated the multiple (and often contradictory) ways women negotiate space within male-dominated action sports cultures such as adventure racing (Kay and Laberge, 2002), skateboarding (Pomerantz, Currie, and Kelley, 2004; Young and Dallaire, 2008), sky-diving and snowboarding (Laurendeau and Sharara, 2008), snowboarding (Thorpe, 2006, 2008), surfing (Booth, 2002; Comer, 2010; Heywood, 2007; Knijnik, Horton, and Cruz, 2010; Spowart, Hughson, and Shaw, 2010), and windsurfing (Wheaton and Tomlinson, 1998). To facilitate their analyses of the complex gender practices, performances, and politics operating within action sports cultures, researchers have engaged an array of theoretical perspectives, including hegemonic masculinity, various strands of feminism (liberal, radical, and third-wave feminism), and, more recently, some poststructural feminist engagements with the work of Bourdieu (see Thorpe, 2009), Deleuze and Guattari (see

Knijnik *et al.*, 2010), and Foucault (Crocket, 2012a; Spowart *et al.*, 2010; Thorpe, 2008). With distinct understandings of power, structure, agency, and resistance, the various theoretical perspectives have facilitated different insights into the place of action sports bodies in the "reproduction of social and sexual structures" (Shilling, 2005: 198), as, too, the various forms of agency available to some male and/or female action sports participants within existing social, economic, and cultural structures.

Despite a growing number of theoretically sophisticated and empirically nuanced studies of the gender power relations and politics within local, national, and global contexts, there is a paucity of intersectional research that engages the various forms of identity-based politics operating within and across action sports cultures. Some notable exceptions include Brayton (2005), Kusz (2003, 2004, 2007b), and Yochim's (2010) partial intersectional analyses of the youthful, privileged, white masculinity celebrated in extreme sports – and particularly skateboarding for Brayton (2005) and Yochim (2010) – in North America. Despite some efforts toward more intersectional analyses, scholarship that reveals the complexities between multiple identifiers (e.g., gender, sexuality, race, class and privilege, nationality, physical, age) in action sports cultures has yet to emerge (see Wheaton, 2009). Arguably, many of our current theoretical approaches struggle under the weight of such a task. As well as engaging with broader debates about "identity and inequality, subjectivity and agency, and materiality and discourse" (King and McDonald, 2007: 1), in order to better capture the intersecting axes of social difference and identity-based inequalities in action sports cultures, we may also need to revise fundamental assumptions underpinning dominant theoretical, methodological, and/or representational approaches.

The cultural politics between groups within action sports cultures based on cultural commitment, physical prowess, and/or styles of participation, and between "outsider" groups, have gained considerable academic attention. Pierre Bourdieu's concepts of field, capital, practice, and to a lesser extent habitus, have been particularly popular among those seeking to explain how distinctions among individuals and groups expressed as differences in embodied tastes and styles, and uses of cultural products and commodities, are practiced, performed, and regulated, in various locations (e.g., skate-parks, waves, mountains) (see Atencio, Beal, and Wilson, 2009; Ford and Brown, 2006; Thorpe, 2011). Some scholars have explained embodied dress and language practices, as well as displays of cultural commitment, physical prowess, and risk taking, as contributing to the social construction and classification of group identities within action sports fields (e.g., Beal and Wilson, 2004; Robinson, 2008; Thorpe, 2004; Wheaton, 2003b). Others have examined the cultural politics involved in negotiating space and access to physical, social, and economic resources within hierarchically organized sporting, cultural, or industry contexts; the struggles among surfers seeking to navigate space in the "line up," and thus access to a limited number of waves, have been particularly well documented (see Ford and Brown, 2006; Olivier, 2010; Scheibel, 1995; Waitt, 2008). A few have examined the gender politics and hypermasculinity in high-risk natural environments, such as the backcountry for skiers (Stoddart, 2010) and snowboarders (Thorpe, 2011), and big waves for surfers (Booth, 2011; Stranger, 2011). Some scholars have also drawn upon highly interdisciplinary approaches (e.g., cultural geography, architecture, urban studies) to describe the spatial politics practiced by action sports participants, especially skateboarders and Parkour practitioners, in their attempts to challenge dominant meanings ascribed to public spaces in urban environments (e.g., Atkinson, 2009; Borden, 2001; Jones and Graves, 2000; Stratford, 2002).

Some critical sport scholars have also examined the politics involved in representing bodies in various forms of mass, niche, and micro action sports media. Wheaton and Beal (2003) examined the production and consumption of discourses of cultural "authenticity" in niche skateboarding and windsurfing magazines; Kusz (2006), Wheaton (2003a), and Frohlick (2005) described the young, white, hyper-masculinity celebrated in the skateboarding film *Dogtown and Z-Boys* (Peralta), niche windsurfing magazines, and big mountain films, respectively; and Henderson (2001), Rinehart (2005), and Thorpe (2005) examined the representation of female bodies in the surfing, skateboarding, and snowboarding media, respectively. Drawing upon

Gramscian understandings of power (particularly hegemonic masculinity), Henderson (2001) and Rinehart (2005) focused on the ways female action sports participants and non-participants (e.g., models) are sexualized and trivialized in the niche media. In contrast, Thorpe (2008) engaged Foucault's concepts of power/knowledge, discourse, and technologies of self, to show that representations of female snowboarding bodies are not inherently oppressive; some men and women are adopting critical and reflexive interpretations of various discursive constructions of snowboarding bodies in the mass, niche, and micro media.

Adopting a particularly innovative approach toward the politics involved in the production and consumption of mediated surfing bodies, Booth (2008) reveals the various photographic, editorial, and design techniques employed, and decisions made, by *Tracks* surfing magazine as designed primarily to evoke the affect of "stoke" among the predominantly young male readers.

Given the richness and cultural significance of the images, narratives, representations, and meanings so powerfully associated with action sports as a cultural form, it is sometimes "easy to forget that these are all epiphenomena" (Ford and Brown, 2006: 149). Participants frequently reiterate that the embodied and immediate experience is the key to the cultural practice and words cannot articulate the experience. In critical research on action sports cultures, however, the lived experience is often reduced to language or discourse or representation, or neglected in favor of politics. But affect and sensation, and power and politics, are not mutually exclusive. According to Howes (2003), "sensation is not just a matter of physiological response and personal experience. . . . Every domain of sensory experience is also an arena for structuring social roles and interactions. We learn social divisions, distinctions of gender, class and race, through our senses" (p. xi). Drawing inspiration from the recent affective and sensual turn in the social sciences and humanities, some action sports researchers are moving away from theory and toward more embodied forms of research (e.g., sensuous ethnography) in their attempts to better understand and explain experience (Evers, 2004, 2006, 2010; Ford and Brown, 2006; Laviolette, 2010; Saville, 2008; Thorpe, 2011). Some scholars write critical auto-ethnographies and ethnographic fiction to shed light on their own and others' lived and embodied action sports experiences, and draw attention to the various forms of power operating within the culture (Evers, 2006; Thorpe, 2011).

According to Atkinson and Wilson (2002), the bodily experiences or everyday performances of action sports participants can resist constraints imposed by mainstream culture. Emphasizing the "micro level, the performative, and the everyday" (Wheaton, 2007a: 299), they contend that a creative skateboard trick or riding a wave may be thought of as a form of "free expression," a "temporary escape or sense of empowerment through movement" (Atkinson and Wilson, 2002: 386; also see Stranger, 2011). Similarly, scholars adopting more psychological approaches suggest that participation in so-called "extreme sports" can prompt transcendental experiences (Celsi, 1992) and/or "positive transformations in courage and humility" (Brymer and Oades, 2009). Elsewhere, however, Wilson (2002) warns that, while such embodied pleasures may be empowering – enabling the individual to escape the norms of discipline and conformity and thus offer a potentially subversive challenge to mainstream society – they are ultimately resistance "that makes no difference" (p. 401, cited in Wheaton, 2007a: 299).

Developing these ideas further, some scholars are examining the potential for action sports participants to develop critical reflexivity and agency within existing power relations. Thorpe (2009, 2010) has drawn upon recent feminist extensions of Pierre Bourdieu's work, particularly the concepts of field-crossing and "regulated liberties," to explain how some female and male snowboarders come to reflect critically upon their past and present cultural participation and problematic aspects of the snowboarding culture (e.g., sexism, homophobia, celebration of risk and injury) and engage in an array of embodied practices to subtly challenge dominant cultural norms and values within existing power relations. A few scholars are drawing upon Michel Foucault's later work on the technologies of self to explain how some action sports participants make meaning of various discourses and engage in ethical and/or aesthetic practices to minimize the effect of power relations on themselves and others (Crocket, 2012b; Spowart et al., 2010; Thorpe, 2008). Despite many differences in their work, however, Bourdieu and Foucault both acknowledge that an individual's conscious awareness does not by itself lead to fundamental social change. Certainly, as suggested in much of the action sports literature, while some individual participants are critically aware of the problematic power relations and inequalities, and engage in various forms of everyday micro-level politics, their efforts have tended to be isolated to various dimensions of the action sports culture, sport, or industry.

Since the mid-1990s, however, some action sports participants have established non-profit organizations and movements relating to an array of social issues including health (e.g., Boarding for Breast Cancer; Surf Aid International, see Thorpe and Rinehart, 2012), education (e.g., Chill – providing underprivileged youth with opportunities to learn to snowboard, skate and surf; Skateistan – co-educational skateboarding schooling in Afghanistan, see Thorpe and Rinehart, 2012), environment (e.g., Protect Our Winters – POW; Surfers Environmental Alliance – SEA; Surfers Against Sewage – SAS; see Heywood and Montgomery, 2008; Laviolette, 2006; Wheaton, 2007b, 2008), and anti-violence (e.g., Surfers for Peace – an informal organization aimed at bridging cultural and political barriers between surfers in the Middle East). In her analysis of the complex relationships between action sports, identity, consumption, politics, and new forms of media, Wheaton (2007b) describes action sports participants as "individualistic and part of a collectivity: they are hedonistic and reflexive consumers, often politically disengaged yet environmentally aware and/or active" (p. 298, original emphasis). Building upon Wheaton's earlier thesis, we argue that, while many contemporary young physical cultural participants are politically engaged, their politics often take different shapes, and occur in different spaces and places, than in previous decades. Relying on traditional conceptions and "conventional indicators" of what constitutes politics, however, we risk being "blind" to some of the highly nuanced and variegated forms of political agency being expressed by youth in the early twenty-first century (Norris, 2002: 222).

Seeking to further examine the innovative political practices employed by (some) contemporary action sports participants, Thorpe and

Rinehart (2010) drew upon Nigel Thrift's (2008) non-representational theory and particularly his work on the "politics of affect" and "politics of hope." In so doing, they reveal action sports-related social movements drawing heavily upon new technologies to produce new forms of passionate politics within local, regional, national, global, virtual, and imagined communities. For example, POW, a non-profit organization dedicated to educating and activating snowsport participants on issues relating to global warming (see Thorpe, 2011) and Surf Aid International (SAI) – a non-profit humanitarian organization dedicated to "improving the health and well-being of people living in isolated regions connected to us through surfing"[1] – readily employ an array of new social media to educate and activate action sports enthusiasts around the world (e.g., websites, YouTube videos, blogs, Twitter, Facebook). Discursive analyses of these various media reveal POW and SAI staff and supporters (e.g., journalists, professional athletes) taking "affect and entrancement" (Thrift, 2008) into their workings in an attempt to not only inform, but also evoke a political response from those in the snow (Thorpe, 2011) and surf (Thorpe and Rinehart, 2010) industries and cultures, respectively. A key point in these works was that the affective practices and political strategies of action sports-related social movements and organizations, such as POW and SAI, deserve further critical exploration. Arguably, a Thriftian approach can facilitate such projects by encouraging us to pay closer attention to some of the "diverse ways in which the use and abuse of various affective practices is gradually changing what we regard as the sphere of 'the political'" (Thrift, 2008: 173) in contemporary action sports cultures.

In sum, action sports research has drawn widely from trends in critical sport studies and the social sciences more broadly (e.g., anthropology, cultural studies, cultural geography, philosophy, and youth studies), to expand understandings of the various forms of symbolic, bodily, aesthetic, and cultural politics being practiced and performed by participants in various geographies. Apart from a few studies that are examining the recent trend toward action sports-related social justice movements, much of this research has focused on the micro-politics operating within particular action sports in local spaces,

with little consideration given to trends across action sports cultures (for exceptions, see Booth and Thorpe, 2007; Wheaton, 2004, 2007a, 2010), or the broader political and economic context (also see Donnelly, 2008; Thorpe, 2006; Wheaton, 2007b, 2008). Arguably, the meaning of these cultural, symbolic, or embodied practices can only be understood by the way they articulate into a particular set of complex historical, economic, and political relationships (Thorpe, 2006). Acknowledging the highly complex and nuanced power relations involved in contemporary action sports, Wheaton (2007a) advocates that future studies of subcultural formations attend to both the micro-political and the macro-political contexts. The emphasis on aesthetics and micro-level cultural power relations, however, may tell us more about the politics of academic research on action sports (i.e., the theoretical and methodological choices we are making, and research questions being asked) than it does about the sporting cultures themselves. In the final part of this chapter we suggest that, to make meaning of the complexities and nuances of action sports in the twenty-first century, we may need to rethink our use of theory, method and representational styles.

A "Politics of Hope" for Action Sports Studies: Notes from the Field

Contemporary action sports cultures are complex, multidimensional, and in a constant state of change and flux. While such features are often part of the appeal for participants and researchers alike, making meaning of such dynamic and multilayered social phenomena can prove challenging for both new and experienced scholars alike. Arguably, future investigations seeking to construct nuanced social explanations of action sports cultures would do well to adopt a position of theoretical and conceptual reflexivity, and analytical dynamism and openness. In so doing, our research has the potential to become more personally and socially meaningful for the researcher(s), readers, and action sports participants. Here we draw primarily upon the first author's research on global snowboarding culture (Thorpe, 2011) to illustrate our key arguments.[3]

Methodological flexibility and researcher reflexivity

It is not our intention here to advocate a particular methodological approach for studying action sports cultures. Rather, methods should be selected based on the research questions being posed, theoretical approach(es) employed, and the resources available to the researcher. Based on our own research experiences, however, we recognize the value in adopting flexible and multi-methodological approaches (Thorpe, 2011; Wheaton, 2002). In her book *Snowboarding Bodies in Theory and Practice*, Thorpe (2011) explains that her understanding of the complexities of snowboarding bodies derived from multiple modes of data generation, a type of methodology used extensively by Bourdieu and which he describes as "discursive montage" of "*all sources*" (Bourdieu and Wacquant, 1992: 66, emphasis added). Bourdieu (1992) adds that this is "the only possible attitude toward theoretical tradition" (p. 252). Similarly, Grossberg recommends using "any and every kind of empirical method, whatever seems useful to the particular project" in order to "gather more and better information, descriptions, resources," and improve one's interpretations (Wright, 2001: 145). Throughout her project she seized "all types of data, evidence, sources, and artefacts to enlighten [her] inquiry into snowboarding bodies" (Thorpe, 2011: 6). According to C.W. Mills (1959), sociologists do not study projects, rather they become tuned, or sensitive, to themes that "they see and hear everywhere in [their] experience" (p. 211). Indeed, as Thorpe became increasingly sensitive to the themes of the snowboarding body, she gathered evidence from personal observations and experiences, magazines, websites, newspapers, interviews and personal communications, videos, internet chat rooms, promotional material, television programs, press releases, public documents, reports from snowboarding's administrative bodies, and promotional material from sporting organizations and from associated industries. "Even the humblest material artefact is," as Eliot (1948) explains, "an emissary of the culture out of which it comes" (cited in Vamplew, 1998: 268). As Thorpe (2011) explains, using cultural sources in conjunction with multi-sited fieldwork and interviews,

"helped deepen my understanding of snowboarding's cultural complexities and the multidimensional snowboarding body" (p. 12).

It is important to keep in mind, however, that research is a process that occurs through the medium of a person – "the researcher is always inevitably present in the research" (Stanley and Wise, 1993, cited in Wheaton, 2002: 246). This is certainly true in critical studies of action sports cultures. To date, many (though not all) action sports scholars have approached their subject with an embodied understanding of cultural norms and values developed via past or present active participation. The strengths and limitations of studying these sporting cultures from an "insider" perspective have been the subject of much debate within the field (Evers, 2006; Donnelly, 2006; Wheaton, 2002, 2004). The challenges of negotiating multiple roles (i.e., critical researcher, active participant, feminist) in the field of ethnographic inquiry also garner increasing critical reflection (Olive and Thorpe, 2011; Thorpe, 2011; Wheaton, 2004). For example, approaching her ethnographic study of windsurfing culture as a highly proficient female athlete, journalist, and partner of a male windsurfer, Wheaton (2002) notes that while this "insider knowledge" helped her develop rapport with participants and identify relevant sources and themes, it also carried potential pitfalls. She explained that one of the hardest tasks during the early phases of her research was negotiating the path that allowed her to understand and acknowledge the participants' worldviews and their subjectivities, while also gaining the "critical distance" necessary to contextualize those views and actions (Wheaton, 2002: 262; see also Carrington, 2008; Olive and Thorpe, 2011).

Upon embarking on her project on snowboarding culture, Thorpe could also have been considered a cultural insider. Prior to commencing this study, she had already held many roles in the snowboarding culture (i.e., novice, weekend-warrior, lifestyle sport migrant) and industry (i.e., semi-professional athlete, snowboard instructor, terrain-park employee, and journalist). While her physical abilities and knowledge about snowboarding initially gave her access to the culture and a head start in discerning relevant sources, her position in the culture changed over time and varied depending on location (see Thorpe, 2011; Thorpe, Barbour, and Bruce, 2011; Olive and Thorpe, 2011). The length of her project and the dynamic nature of the snowboarding culture also meant that, as her research progressed, she became further removed in terms of age and generation (i.e., clothing styles, language) from the majority of core participants (mostly in their late teens and early twenties), which prompted her to further reflect on issues relating to cultural access and participant rapport while conducting research in the field, as well as individual participants' embodied experiences of movement into, within, and out of, the snowboarding culture. Thus, the key issue here is not whether one approaches their study as a past or present (non)active participant, or conducts interviews, focus groups, observations, or discourse analysis, but rather the reflexivity of the researcher in terms of how his or her dynamic position in the action sports culture *and* the academy, and movement between these fields, influences research questions, methodological choices, and theoretical approaches and representational styles, at various stages during the project (Olive and Thorpe, 2011; Wheaton, 2002).

Theoretical adventures in action sports studies

Sociology hosts a wide variety of theories and theoretical perspectives, each drawing on different sets of assumptions about social reality and how it should be explained. The tendency in action sports scholarship (and indeed many fields of critical sociological inquiry) has been to pick one primary theorist and regard the rest as secondary:

> There is often a sense that we should align ourselves with one theoretical school, or even one theorist. In the process of drawing from this work, the scholar defines him or herself as a particular type of researcher. Thus, using a theoretical work is not just a question of being interested in particular ideas but also how one represents him or herself to others. (Thorpe, 2011: 268)

However, we argue that action sport scholars should be cautious about confining themselves to one theory or one theoretical tradition. As Andrews (2002) reminds us, there is a very real

danger of being lulled into a "false sense of conceptual security" (p. 116), in which individuals see only what fits into their preexisting schema and ignore conflicting evidence. Indeed, Barrett (1995) argues that theoretical disciplines offer a "license to ignore," since disciplinary boundaries create "an informal division of labor in which certain questions are assigned to one subject and can thus legitimately be ignored" by others (cited in McDonald and Birrell, 1999: 285). Despite each theory claiming to best interpret the facts it identifies as significant, no single theory is adequate to deal with the various forms of power operating on and through the bodies of action sports participants (Thorpe, 2011). In each of the studies discussed above, particular forms of power are foregrounded while others fade into the background; no theory has proved adequate to attend to "both the micro-political and macro-political contexts" in action sports cultures (Wheaton, 2010). Furthermore, because all "theories are created by individuals in their search for meaning" in response to concrete material conditions (Alexander, 1995: 79–80), some theories prove more suitable for explaining some aspects of the power and politics within action sports in the current historical moment than others.

All theories have strengths and shortcomings and, because they are a matter of perspective, are always open to debate. If we approach our research with the knowledge that the search for the exact theoretical fit is futile, perhaps we can begin to use social theory differently, that is, with the aim to "think differently than one thinks" and "perceive differently than one sees" (Foucault, 1985, cited in Mills, 2003: 6). Arguably, rather than employing one theoretical perspective to frame our research (as has been the dominant approach in action sports scholarship), there is much to be gained by experimenting with a range of theoretical perspectives from commensurate paradigms. In *Surfing and Social Theory*, for example, Ford and Brown (2006) employ an array of theoretical perspectives to offer an insightful multidimensional analysis of global surfing culture and the embodied, lived experience of surfing. Importantly, we are not advocating employing multiple theoretical approaches to understand the different forms of power and politics operating within action sports cultures. Rather, we are proposing that action sport scholars need to reflexively consider how and why we are using particular theoretical approaches in our projects, and not be afraid to explore the potential of other theoretical perspectives (Thorpe, 2011). According to Fredric Jameson, we should "learn theories like languages, and explore as every good translator does the expressive gaps between them – what can be said in one theory and not another" (cited in Leane and Buchanan, 2002: 254). Indeed, sometimes those "theoretical languages" that require the most "struggling," or as Hall (1992) terms it "wrestling with the angels" (p. 280), can be the most fulfilling because they challenge us to think differently about our data, action sports cultures, and the social world around us.

Balancing theory and empirical research – or "wrestling with the angels" – is a prime goal of sociology, yet its practice is "all too rare" (Waters, 2000: 4). Concerned that many intellectual products have lost their analytical dynamism and openness, and remain bent on "illustrating the applicability of *their* framework" (Baert, 2004: 362, emphasis added), philosopher Richard Rorty (1980) pleads for a critical approach that challenges "accepted taxonomies and lenses rather than merely reiterating them" (cited in Ford and Brown, 2006: 146). With Rorty, Baert (2004) is concerned by the contemporary trend that measures theory-inspired research by the "extent to which a theory . . . neatly . . . fits the data . . . and to which the various components of the theory . . . weave easily into the myriad of empirical experiences" (p. 367). Rather than employing one theoretical perspective (often late in the analysis) to frame our empirical investigations, scholars should seek to make theoretical ideas "live" through "empirical discussions" (Alexander, 2003: 7–8) with the action sports culture under investigation. In other words, we should aim to "move back and forth between theorizing and researching, between interpretations and explanations, between cultural logics and pragmatics" (Alexander, 2003: 6) throughout our projects. In her book, Thorpe (2011) argues that action sports scholars should be more willing to "play" with theoretical concepts; "pushing, pulling and stretching theories and concepts in relation to our empirical evidence can help us identify their strengths and limitations for explaining particu-

lar aspects of contemporary society" (p. 269) and action sports cultures.

Making a difference: Towards a political action sports studies

Theory is the heart and soul of sociology and central to the discipline's contribution to "the development of self-knowledge *and* the guidance of human society" (Waters, 2000: 1, emphasis added). While scholars of action sports cultures have employed various theoretical approaches with the goal of developing new ways of knowing and identifying the multiple forms of power, politics, and inequality operating within and across local and global contexts, it is also important to consider the social responsibility and/or ethics of our scholarship. Here we might recall Karl Marx's observation that "philosophers have interpreted the world in various ways; the point, however, is to *change* it" (McLellan, 1977: 158). Yet few action sports scholars appear to be invested in transforming the inequitable power relations they identify, thus raising the long-debated question: What constitutes socially responsible sociology? Perhaps the answer lies not in how much change scholars can personally initiate, but rather our ability to explain and present our critical analyses in an accessible manner so that readers can use them to make sense of their own (and others') embodied and bodily experiences and inform their involvement in related practical and political issues.

In our efforts to "strategically disseminate" potentially empowering forms of knowledge to wider audiences (Andrews, 2008), we might draw some salient lessons from action sports participants themselves in terms of their creative and savvy use of new social media (e.g., niche magazines, websites, and blogs) for sharing information, engaging in local, national and transnational conversations, and inspiring individual and collective political action. Some action sports scholars are using or creating niche and/or micro-media to share their work and raise critical issues among their peers and participants (e.g., blogs, see Olive, 2013). A particularly good example is *Kurangabaa*, a highly creative and thought-provoking not-for-profit "journal of literature, history and ideas from the sea" co-produced by an international board of critical scholars and educated surfers.[2] In *Notes for a Young Surfer* (2010), Clifton Evers – an Australian cultural studies scholar and key member of the *Kurangabaa* board – offers an accessible and engaging commentary on the various forms of power operating within surfing culture. Written primarily for young male surfers, Evers raises critical issues, such as homophobia, sexism, and misogyny, via beautifully crafted, thought-provoking, and deeply affective narratives based on his own experiences and observations from a lifetime immersed in the practice and culture of surfing. Interestingly (and perhaps somewhat surprisingly), despite exposing and challenging some of the fratriarchal practices at the core of the surfing culture, *Notes for a Young Surfer* has received some positive reviews from within the surfing culture; his position as a highly committed and proficient surfer, and his willingness to position himself in his narratives, seem to help him find space to raise these critical issues among his surfing peers. It is worth noting here that, at various stages in our sporting and academic careers, we have also both worked to address gender politics in the snowboarding and windsurfing cultures, respectively, through engaging with, and working in, action sport media (particularly niche magazines) – see, for example, Thorpe (2012). As these examples suggest, alternative styles of representation may further enhance the accessibility of our theoretically informed research and help us raise critical social issues about various dimensions of action sports cultures (e.g., reflexivity, power, ethics, identity, pleasure, pain, risk, performance, and gender) among wider audiences (see Laurendeau, 2011, 2012).

Conclusion

Since the foundational work of a select group of critical sociohistorical scholars of sport during the mid- and late 1990s (e.g., Becky Beal, Douglas Booth, Peter Donnelly, Duncan Humphreys, Nancy Midol, Robert Rinehart, and Belinda Wheaton), the sub-field of action sports studies has continued to flourish. Today, researchers – particularly graduate students and emerging scholars – from various disciplinary backgrounds are examining a plethora of action sports-related topics in an array of local, national, global, and virtual contexts, and publishing across the social science and humanities. But, for scholarship to continue developing in new and important ways, we need to reflect critically upon some of the methodological and theoretical assumptions underpinning our work. Rather than asking familiar questions in different contexts, or drawing upon common theoretical and methodological approaches to reveal somewhat predictable findings, we should seek to approach our work with a new "sociological imagination" (C.W. Mills, 1959) with the aim to (re)imagine more meaningful action sports research in the early twenty-first century. In sum, action sports scholarship that embraces more transdisciplinary, multi-methodological and theoretical, contextual, and political approaches could go a long way toward helping us "identify and analyze how dominant power structures become expressed in, and through, [the] socially and historically contingent embodied experiences, meanings, and subjectivities" (Andrews, 2008: 53) of action sports participants in local, national, and global contexts.

Notes

1 *Annual Report: Surf Aid International 2006/2007*, www.surfaidinternational.org/LiteratureRetrieve.aspx?ID=86872, accessed January 21, 2013. See also Thorpe and Rinehart (2010, 2012).

2 See http://kurungabaa.net/, accessed December 20, 2012.

3 The authors are grateful for permission from Palgrave Macmillan to reprint parts of Thorpe's (2011) chapter "Body politics, social change and the future of physical cultural studies" here.

References

AMG (2007) "Action sports: The action sports market." Active Marketing Group, http://activemarketing-group.com/Assets/AMG+2009/Action+Sports.pdf, accessed January 21, 2013.

Alexander, J. (1995) "Modern, anti, post and neo." *New Left Review*, 210: 63–101.

Alexander, J. (2003) *The Meaning of Social Life: A Cultural Sociology*, Oxford: Oxford University Press.

Anderson, K. (1999) "Snowboarding: The construction of gender in an emerging sport." *Journal of Sport & Social Issues*, 23 (1): 55–79.

Andrews, D. (2002) "Coming to terms with cultural studies." *Journal of Sport & Social Issues*, 26 (1): 110–117.

Andrews, D. (2008) "Kinesiology's *Inconvenient Truth* and the physical cultural studies imperative." *Quest*, 60: 45–62.

Atencio, M., Beal, B., and Wilson, C. (2009) "The distinction of risk: Urban skateboarding, street habitus and the construction of hierarchical gender relations." *Qualitative Research in Sport and Exercise*, 1 (1): 3–20.

Atkinson, M. (2009) "Parkour, anarcho-environmentalism, and poiesis." *Journal of Sport & Social Issues*, 33 (2): 169–194.

Atkinson, M. and Wilson, B. (2002) "Bodies, subcultures and sport," in Maguire, J. and Young, K. (eds.) *Theory, Sport & Society*, Oxford: Elsevier Science, pp. 375–395.

Baert, P. (2004) "Pragmatism as philosophy of the social sciences." *European Journal of Social Theory*, 7 (3): 355–369.

Barker, C. (2000) *Cultural Studies: Theory and Practice*, London: Sage Publications.

Barrett, M. (1995) "Words and things: Materialism and method in contemporary feminist analysis," in Barrett, M. and Phillips, A. (eds.) *Destabilizing Theory: Contemporary Feminist Debates*, Stanford, CA: Stanford University Press, pp. 201–219.

Beal, B. (1995) "Disqualifying the official: An exploration of social resistance through the subculture of skateboarding." *Sociology of Sport Journal*, 12: 252–267.

Beal, B. (1996) "Alternative masculinity and its effects on gender relations in the subculture of skateboarding." *Journal of Sport Behavior*, 19: 204–221.

Beal, B. and Weidman, L. (2003) "Authenticity in the skateboarding world," in Rinehart, R. and Sydnor, S. (eds.) *To the Extreme: Alternative Sports, Inside and Out*, Albany: State University of New York Press, pp. 337–352.

Beal, B. and Wilson, C. (2004) "Chicks dig scars: Commercialisation and the transformations of skateboarders identities," in Wheaton, B. (ed.) *Understanding Lifestyle Sports: Consumption, Identity and Difference*, London: Routledge, pp. 31–54.

Bennett, A. (2011) "The post-subcultural turn: Some reflections 10 years on." *Journal of Youth Studies*, 14 (5): 493–506.

Bennett, A. and Kahn-Harris, K. (eds.) (2004) *After Subculture: Critical Studies in Contemporary Youth Culture*, Basingstoke, UK: Palgrave Macmillan.

Booth, D. (2002) "From bikinis to boardshorts: Wahines and the paradoxes of the surfing culture." *Journal of Sport History*, 28 (1): 3–22.

Booth, D. (2008) "(Re)reading the surfers' bible: The affects of *Tracks*." *Continuum: Journal of Media and Cultural Studies*, 22 (1): 17–35.

Booth, D. (2011) *Surfing: The Ultimate Guide*, Santa Barbara, CA: Greenwood Publishing.

Booth, D. and Thorpe, H. (2007) "The meaning of extreme," in Booth, D. and Thorpe, H. (eds.) *Berkshire Encyclopedia of Extreme Sports*, Great Barrington, MA: Berkshire, pp. 181–197.

Borden, I. (2001) *Skateboarding, Space and the City: Architecture and the Body*, Oxford: Berg.

Bourdieu, P. (1992) *The Logic of Practice*, trans. R. Nice, Cambridge: Polity Press.

Bourdieu, P. and Wacquant, L.J.D. (1992) "The purpose of reflexive sociology," in Bourdieu, P. and Wacquant, L.J.D. (eds.) *An Invitation to Reflexive Sociology*, Cambridge: Polity Press, pp. 61–215.

Brayton, S. (2005) "'Back-lash': Revisiting the 'white negro' through skateboarding." *Sociology of Sport Journal*, 22: 356–372.

Brymer, E. and Oades, L. (2009) "Extreme sports: A positive transformation in courage and humility." *Journal of Humanistic Psychology*, 49 (1): 114–126.

Carrington, B. (2008) "'What's the footballer doing here?' Racialized performativity, reflexivity and identity." *Cultural Studies ↔ Critical Methodologies*, 8 (4): 493–506.

Celsi, R. (1992) "Transcendent benefits of high-risk sports." *Advances in Consumer Research*, 19: 636–641.

Clarke, G. (1982) *Defending Ski-Jumpers: A Critique of Theories of Youth Subcultures*, Birmingham: Centre for Contemporary Cultural Studies.

Comer, K. (2010) *Surfer Girls in the New World Order*, Durham, NC: Duke University Press.

Crocket, H. (2012a) "This is *men's* ultimate: (Re)creating multiple masculinities in elite open Ultimate Frisbee." *International Review for the Sociology of Sport*, online before print.

Crocket, H. (2012b) "Playing with ethics? A Foucauldian examination of the construction of ethical subjectivities in Ultimate Frisbee." Unpublished PhD dissertation, University of Waikato.

Donnelly, M. (2006) "Studying extreme sport: Beyond the core participants." *Journal of Sport & Social Issues*, 30: 219–224.

Donnelly, M. (2008) "Alternative *and* mainstream: Revisiting the sociological analysis of skateboarding," in Atkinson, M. and Young, K. (eds.) *Tribal*

Play: Subcultural Journeys through Sport, Bingley, UK: JAI Press, pp. 197–214.

Donnelly, P. (1993) "Subcultures in sport: Resilience and transformation," in Ingham, A. and Loy, J. (eds.) *Sport in Social Development: Traditions, Transitions and Transformations*, Champaign, IL: Human Kinetics, pp. 119–145.

Edwards, B. and Corte, U. (2010) "Commercialisation and lifestyle sport: Lessons from twenty years of freestyle BMX in 'ProTown' USA." *Sport in Society*, 13 (7/8): 1135–1151.

Eliot, T.S. (1948) *Notes Towards the Definition of Culture*, London: Faber & Faber.

Evers, C. (2004) "Men-who-surf." *Cultural Studies Review*, 10: 27–41.

Evers, C. (2006) "How to surf." *Journal of Sport & Social Issues*, 30 (3): 229–243.

Evers, C. (2010) *Notes for a Young Surfer*, Melbourne: Melbourne University Press.

Fine, G. and Kleinman, S. (1979) "Rethinking resistance: An interactionist perspective." *American Journal of Sociology*, 85: 1–20.

Ford, N. and Brown, D. (2006) *Surfing and Social Theory*, London: Routledge.

Foucault, M. (1985) *The Use of Pleasure: The History of Sexuality*, vol. 2, London: Penguin Books.

Frohlick, S. (2005) "'That playfulness of white masculinity': Mediating masculinities and adventure at mountain film festivals." *Tourist Studies*, 5: 175–193.

Giulianotti, R. (2005) *Sport: A Critical Sociology*, Cambridge: Polity Press.

Gramsci, A. (1971) *Selections from the Prison Notebooks*, ed. Q. Hoare and G. Nowell Smith, London: Lawrence & Wishart.

Grossberg, L. (1997) *Bringing It All Back Home: Essays on Cultural Studies*, Durham, NC: Duke University Press.

Haenfler, R. (2004) "Rethinking subcultural resistance: Core values of the straight edge movement." *Journal of Contemporary Ethnography*, 33 (4): 406–436.

Hall, S. (1992) "Cultural studies and its theoretical legacies," in Grossberg, L., Nelson, C., and Treichler, P. (eds.) *Cultural Studies*, London: Routledge, pp. 277–294.

Hebdige, D. (1979) *Subculture: Meaning of Style*, London: Methuen.

Hebdige, D. (1988) *Hiding in the Light*, London: Routledge.

Henderson, M. (2001) "A shifting line up: Men, women, and *Tracks* surfing magazine." *Continuum: Journal of Media and Cultural Studies*, 15 (3): 319–332.

Heywood, L. (2007) "Third wave feminism, the global economy, and women's surfing: Sport as stealth feminism in girls' surf culture," in Harris, A. (ed.) *Next Wave Cultures: Feminism, Subcultures, Activism*, London: Routledge, pp. 63–82.

Heywood, L. and Montgomery, M. (2008) "Ambassadors of the last wilderness: Surfers, environmental ethics, and activism in America," in Young, K. and Atkinson, M. (eds.) *Tribal Play: Sub-Cultural Journeys through Sport*, Bingley, UK: JAI Press, pp. 153–172.

Howes, D. (2003) *Sensual Relations: Engaging the Senses in Culture and Social Theory*, Ann Arbor: University of Michigan Press.

Humphreys, D. (1996) "Snowboarders: Bodies out of control and in conflict." *Sporting Traditions*, 13 (1): 3–23.

Humphreys, D. (1997) "Shredheads go mainstream? Snowboarding and alternative youth." *International Review for the Sociology of Sport*, 32 (2): 147–160.

Humphreys, D. (2003) "Selling out snowboarding," in Rinehart, R. and Sydnor, S. (eds.) *To the Extreme: Alternative Sports, Inside and Out*, Albany: State University of New York Press, pp. 407–428.

Jones, S. and Graves, A. (2000) "Power plays in public space: Skateboard parks as battlegrounds, gifts, and expression of self." *Landscape*, 1–2: 136–148.

Kay, J. and Laberge, S. (2002) "The 'new' corporate habitus in adventure racing." *International Review of the Sociology of Sport*, 37 (1): 17–36.

King, S. and McDonald, M. (2007) "(Post)identity and sporting cultures: An introduction and overview." *Sociology of Sport Journal*, 24: 1–19.

Knijnik, J., Horton, P., and Cruz, L. (2010) "Rhizomatic bodies, gendered waves: Transitional femininities in Brazilian surf." *Sport in Society*, 13 (7/8): 1170–1185.

Kusz, K.W. (2003) "BMX, extreme sports, and the white male backlash," in Rinehart, R. and Sydnor, S. (eds.) *To the Extreme: Alternative Sports, Inside and Out*, Albany: State University of New York Press, pp. 153–175.

Kusz, K.W. (2004) "'Extreme America': The cultural politics of extreme sports in 1990s America," in Wheaton, B. (ed.) *Understanding Lifestyle Sports: Consumption, Identity and Difference*, London: Routledge.

Kusz, K.W. (2006) "Interrogating the politics of white particularity in Dogtown and Z-Boys," in King, C.R. and Leonards, D. (eds.) *Visual Economies of/in Motion: Sport and Film*, New York: Peter Lang, pp. 135–163.

Kusz, K.W. (2007a) "Whiteness and extreme sports," in Booth, D. and Thorpe, H. (eds.) *Berkshire Encyclopedia of Extreme Sport*, Great Barrington, MA: Berkshire Publishing, pp. 357–361.

Kusz, K.W. (2007b) *Revolt of the White Athlete: Race, Media and the Emergence of Extreme Athletes in America*, New York: Peter Lang.

Laurendeau, J. (2011) "'If you're reading this, it's because I died': Masculinity and relational risk in BASE jumping." *Sociology of Sport Journal*, 28 (4): 404–420.

Laurendeau, J. (2012) *BASE Jumping: The Ultimate Guide*, Santa Barbara: ABC Clio.

Laurendeau, J. and Sharara, N. (2008) "'Women could be every bit as good as guys': Reproductive and resistant agency between two 'action' sports." *Journal of Sport & Social Issues*, 32 (1): 24–47.

Laviolette, P. (2006) "Green and extreme: Free-flowing through seascape and sewer." *Worldviews*, 10 (2): 178–204.

Laviolette, P. (2010) "Fearless trembling: A leap of faith into the devil's frying pan." *Senses and Society*, 4 (3): 303–322.

Leane, E. and Buchanan, I. (2002) "What's left of theory?" *Continuum: Journal of Media and Cultural Studies*, 16 (3): 253–258.

McDonald, M.G. and Birrell, S. (1999) "Reading sport critically: A methodology for interrogating power." *Sociology of Sport Journal*, 16: 283–300.

McLellan, D. (ed.) (1977) *Karl Marx: Selected Writings*, Oxford: Oxford University Press.

Mellgren, D. (1998) "AP reports Terje boycotting Nagano?" *Transworld Snowboarding*, January 7, http://snowboarding.transworld.net/1000025710/news/ap-reports-terje-boycotting-nagano/, accessed January 21, 2013.

Messner, M. (2002) *Taking the Field*, Minneapolis: University of Minnesota Press.

Mills, C.W. (1959) *The Sociological Imagination*, Oxford: Oxford University Press.

Mills, S. (2003) *Michel Foucault*, London: Routledge.

Muggleton, D. (2000) *Inside Subculture: The Postmodern Meaning of Style*, Oxford: Berg.

Muggleton, D. and Weinzierl, R. (eds.) (2003) *The Post-subcultures Reader*, Oxford: Berg.

Norris, P. (2002) *Democratic Phoenix: Reinventing Political Activism*, Cambridge: Cambridge University Press.

Olive, R. (2013) "'Making friends with the neighbours': Blogging as a research method." *International Journal of Cultural Studies*, 16 (1): 71–84.

Olive, R. and Thorpe, H. (2011) "Negotiating the F-word in the field: Doing feminist ethnography in action sport cultures." *Sociology of Sport Journal*, 28 (4): 421–440.

Olivier, S. (2010) "'Your wave, bro!': Virtue ethics and surfing." *Sport in Society*, 13 (7/8): 1223–1233.

Osgerby, B. (1998) *Youth in Britain since 1945*, Oxford: Blackwell.

Pomerantz, S., Currie, D., and Kelly, D. (2004) "Sk8er girls: Skateboarders, girlhood and feminism in motion." *Women's Studies International Forum*, 27: 547–557.

Rinehart, R. (1998) "Inside of the outside: Pecking orders within alternative sport at ESPN's 1995 'The EXtreme Games.'" *Journal of Sport & Social Issues*, 22 (4): 398–414.

Rinehart, R. (2000) "Emerging/arriving sport: Alternatives to formal sports," in Coakley, J. and Dunning, E. (eds.) *Handbook of Sports Studies*, London: Sage Publications, pp. 504–519.

Rinehart, R. (2003) "Dropping into sight: Commodification and co-optation in in-line skating," in Giardina, M.D. and Donnelly, M.K. (eds.) *Youth Cultures and Sport: Identity, Power and Politics*, New York: Routledge, pp. 71–89.

Rinehart, R. (2005) "'Babes' and boards." *Journal of Sport & Social Issues*, 29 (3): 232–255.

Rinehart, R. (2008) "ESPN's X Games, contests of opposition, resistance, co-option, and negotiation," in Atkinson, M. and Young, K. (eds.) *Tribal Play: Subcultural Journeys through Sport*, vol. 4: *Research in the Sociology of Sport*, Bingley, UK: JAI Press, pp. 175–196.

Robinson, V. (2008) *Everyday Masculinities and Extreme Sport: Male Identity and Rock Climbing*, New York: Berg.

Rorty, R. (1980) *Philosophy and the Mirror of Nature*, Oxford: Blackwell.

Saville, S. (2008) "Playing with fear: Parkour and the mobility of emotion." *Social and Cultural Geography*, 9 (8): 891–914.

Scheibel, D. (1995) "'Making waves' with Burke: Surf Nazi culture and the rhetoric of localism." *Western Journal of Communication*, 59: 253–269.

Shilling, C. (2005) *The Body in Culture, Technology and Society*, London: Sage Publications.

Spowart, L., Hughson, J., and Shaw, S. (2008) "Snowboarding moms carve out fresh tracks: Resisting traditional motherhood discourse?" *Annals of Leisure Research*, 11 (1–2): 187–204.

Stanley, L. and Wise, S. (1983) *Breaking Out: Feminist Consciousness and Feminist Research*, London: Routledge.

Stoddart, M. (2010) "Constructing masculinized sportscapes: Skiing, gender and nature in British Columbia, Canada." *International Review for the Sociology of Sport*, 46 (1): 108–124.

Stranger, M. (2011) *Surfing Life: Surface, Substructure and the Commodification of the Sublime*, Aldershot, UK: Ashgate.

Stratford, E. (2002) "On the edge: A tale of skaters and urban governance." *Social and Cultural Geography*, 3 (2): 193–206.

Thornton, S. (1996) *Club Cultures: Music, Media and Subcultural Capital*, Middletown, CT: Wesleyan University Press.

Thorpe, H. (2004) "Embodied boarders: Snowboarding, status and style." *Waikato Journal of Education*, 10: 181–201.

Thorpe, H. (2005) "Jibbing the gender order: Females in the snowboarding culture." *Sport in Society*, 8 (1): 76–100.

Thorpe, H. (2006) "Beyond 'decorative sociology': Contextualizing female surf, skate and snowboarding." *Sociology of Sport Journal*, 23 (3): 205–228.

Thorpe, H. (2008) "Foucault, technologies of self, and the media: Discourses of femininity in snowboarding culture." *Journal of Sport & Social Issues*, 32 (2): 199–229.

Thorpe, H. (2009) "Bourdieu, feminism and female physical culture: Gender reflexivity and the habitus-field complex." *Sociology of Sport Journal*, 26: 491–516.

Thorpe, H. (2010) "Bourdieu, gender reflexivity and physical culture: A case of masculinities in the snowboarding field." *Journal of Sport & Social Issues*, 34 (2): 176–214.

Thorpe, H. (2011) *Snowboarding Bodies in Theory and Practice*, Basingstoke, UK: Palgrave Macmillan.

Thorpe, H. (2012) "Over exposed: Using sex to sell (the soul) of snowboarding: a hot debate." *Curl Magazine*, August: 60–69, http://hollythorpe.com/wp-content/uploads/Holly-1.pdf, accessed December 21, 2012.

Thorpe, H. and Rinehart, R. (2010) "Alternative sport and affect: Non-representational theory examined." *Consumption and Representation of Lifestyle Sport*, 13 (7/8), special issue, *Sport in Society*: 1268–1291.

Thorpe, H. and Rinehart, R. (2012) "Action sport NGOs in a neoliberal context: The cases of Skateistan and Surf Aid International." *Journal of Sport & Social Issues*, online before print.

Thorpe, H. and Wheaton, B. (2011a) "The Olympic movement, action sports, and the search for generation Y," in Sugden, J. and Tomlinson, A. (eds.) *Watching the Olympics: Politics, Power and Representation*, London: Routledge, pp. 182–200.

Thorpe, H. and Wheaton, B. (2011b) "'Generation X Games,' action sports and the Olympic movement: Understanding the cultural politics of incorporation." *Sociology*, 45 (5): 830–847.

Thorpe, H., Barbour, K., and Bruce, T. (2011) "Feminist journeys: Playing with theory and representation in physical cultural fields." *Sociology of Sport Journal*, 28, special issue: *Physical Cultural Studies*: 106–134.

Thrift, N. (2008) *Non-Representational Theory: Space, Politics, Affect*, London: Routledge.

Vamplew, W. (1998) "Facts and artefacts: Sports historians and sports museums." *Journal of Sport History*, 25 (2): 268–282.

Waitt, G. (2008) "'Killing waves': Surfing, space and gender." *Social and Cultural Geography*, 9 (1): 75–94.

Waitt, G. and Warren, A. (2008) "'Talking shit over a brew after a good session with your mates': Surfing, space and masculinity." *Australian Geographer*, 39 (3): 353–365.

Waters, M. (2000) *Modern Sociological Theory*, London: Sage.

Wheaton, B. (2000) "'New lads?'Masculinities and the 'new sport' participant." *Men and Masculinities*, 2: 434–456.

Wheaton, B. (2002) "Babes on the beach, women in the surf: Researching gender, power and difference in the windsurfing culture." Sugden, J. and Tomlinson, A. (eds.) *Power Games: A Critical Sociology of Sport*, London: Routledge.

Wheaton, B. (2003a) "Lifestyle sport magazines and the discourses of sporting masculinity," in Benwell, B. (ed.) *Masculinity and Men's Lifestyle Magazines*, Oxford: Blackwell, pp. 193–221.

Wheaton, B. (2003b) "Windsurfing: A subculture of commitment," in Rinehart, R. and Sydnor, S. (eds.) *To the Extreme: Alternative Sports, Inside and Out*, New York: State University of New York, pp. 75–101.

Wheaton, B. (2004) "Selling out? The globalization and commercialization of lifestyle sports," in Allison, L. (ed.) *The Global Politics of Sport: The Role of Global Institutions in Sport*, London: Routledge.

Wheaton, B. (2007a) "After sport culture: Rethinking sport and post-subcultural theory." *Journal of Sport and Social Issues*, 31: 283–307.

Wheaton, B. (2007b) "Identity, politics, and the beach: Environmental activism in 'Surfers Against Sewage.'" *Leisure Studies*, 26 (3): 279–302.

Wheaton, B. (2008) "From the pavement to the beach: Politics and identity in Surfing Against Sewage." Atkinson, M. and Young, K. (eds.) *Tribal Play: Subcultural Journeys through Sport*, Bingley, UK: JAI Press, pp. 113–134.

Wheaton, B. (2009) "The cultural politics of lifestyle sport (re)visited: Beyond white male lifestyles," in Ormond, J. and Wheaton, B. (eds.), *On the Edge: Leisure, Consumption and the Representation of Adventure Sport*, Eastbourne, UK: Leisure Studies Association.

Wheaton, B. (2010) "Introducing the consumption and representation of lifestyle sports." *Sport in Society*, 13 (7/8): 1057–1081.

Wheaton, B. and Beal, B. (2003) "'Keeping it real': Subcultural media and discourses of authenticity in alternative sport." *International Review for the Sociology of Sport*, 38: 155–176.

Wheaton, B. and Tomlinson, A. (1998) "The changing gender order in sport? The case of windsurfing subcultures." *Journal of Sport & Social Issues*, 22: 251–272.

Willis, P. (1978) *Profane Culture*, London: Routledge & Kegan Paul.

Wilson, B. (2002) "The Canadian race scene and five theses on youth resistance." *Canadian Journal of Sociology*, 27 (3): 373–412.

Wooden, W. and Blazak, R. (2001) *Renegade Kids: Suburban Outlaws: From Youth Culture to Delinquency* (2nd edn.), Belmont, CA: Wadsworth.

Wright, K.H. (2001) "'What's going on?' Larry Grossberg on the status quo of cultural studies: An interview." *Cultural Values*, 5 (2): 133–162.

Yochim, E. C. (2010) *Skate Life: Re-imagining White Masculinity*, Ann Arbor: University of Michigan Press.

Young, A. and Dallaire, C. (2008) "Beware *#! Sk8 at your own risk: The discourses of young female skateboarders," in Atkinson, M. and Young, K. (eds.) *Tribal Play: Subcultural Journeys through Sport*, Bingley, UK: JAI Press, pp. 235–254.

Further Reading

Booth, D. and Thorpe, H. (eds.) (2007) *The Berkshire Encyclopedia of Extreme Sports*, Great Barrington, MA: Berkshire Publishing.

Rinehart, R. and Sydnor, S. (eds.) (2003) *To the Extreme: Alternative Sports, Inside and Out*, Albany: State University of New York Press.

Thorpe, H. (2011) *Snowboarding Bodies in Theory and Practice*, Basingstoke, UK: Palgrave Macmillan.

Wheaton, B. (ed.) (2004) *Understanding Lifestyle Sports: Consumption, Identity and Difference*, London: Routledge.

21

Heidegger, Parkour, Post-sport, and the Essence of Being

Michael Atkinson

Introduction

Two weeks prior to the opening ceremonies of the 2008 Beijing Olympic Games, Nike launched its "Courage" promotional campaign. A marquee television commercial spearheaded the pre-Olympic advertising blitzkrieg, partially commemorating the twentieth anniversary of Nike's "Just do it" slogan. The high-energy commercial, brought to life by The Killers' song, "All These Things That I've Done," began with the slogan "Everything You Need is Already Inside" blazoned across the screen. It featured no less than 31 Nike-branded athletes from over a dozen different countries, including the United States, Russia, Portugal, Switzerland, Afghanistan, and South Africa.[1] The commercial ends with a long, panoramic focus on controversial double-amputee Oscar Pistorius running in his "cheetah" prosthetics.

Amidst the dizzying array of athletic prowess and achievement displayed by athletes in the commercial are images of animals jumping and running, neon-colored brain synapses firing and other microscopic bodily wonders, flowers blossoming, planets and celestial bodies glowing, babies in the womb, rockets launching, astro-nauts floating, tribal peoples adorned in ceremonial regalia, tapestries and other global *objets d'art*, hurricanes and tornadoes, fashion shows, and pristine mountain vistas. The frenetic visual pastiche is both engrossing and mentally destabilizing. Beyond the crass and overtly commercial connections between athlete bodies, Nike gear, nations, and sporting excellence are more subtle and nuanced significations of capitalism, progress, technology, and scientific discovery; or more simply, the fulfillment of the Enlightenment dream of mastery over the human condition (in this case, displayed in the context of sport). The commercial taps into (embracing without critique) one of the many battleground issues in contemporary elite sport; the blurring of nature/humanity/technology through/in athletics. Gazelles leaping with great ability, zebras running frantically across a savanna, and birds effortless in flight are juxtaposed against three-dimensional representations of microbiological processes, and athletes performing incredible feats. The signification in the assemblage is clear, as is the framing of contemporary sport as a zone where human performance is now more of a matter of science and the destabilization of boundaries between animals and machines than athletes' hard work or poetic chance alone. Athletics has become the field of all scientific discovery and cutting-edge knowledge; to be a Nike athlete is to be at the forefront of scientific enhancement in a brave new world of *transhumanist* sport.

Transhumanist philosophy and associated ethical debates remains relatively novel in the sociology of sport (Butryn, 2002, 2003, 2007; Miah, 2004, 2007, 2008a). A transhuman, or transitory human, is one who is on the path to becoming more intensively merged with biotechnology. Predominantly the terrain of sports ethicists and philosophers, transhumanist philosophy is a body of thought that deals with biological enhancement technologies for humans, and the associated bioethical dilemmas accompanying the penetration of the human body by science. In brief, transhumanists favor the radical technological "enhancement" of human cognitive and physical capacities toward a "post-human" state: one in which the individual is entirely liberated from the trappings and limitations of the natural body via a complete interface with technology – where the person is actually "uploaded" completely into/through biotechnology. The history of transhumanism as a social philosophy and practice appears to be as old as human consciousness itself, and indeed, proponents argue that the very moment humans started to produce the means of our own subsistence as primitive beings we became transhumanists. But the word "transhumanism" and the seeds of it as a new social movement first appear in Julian Huxley's *Religion Without Revelation*:

> The human species can, if it wishes, transcend itself – not just sporadically, an individual here in one way, an individual there in another way – but in its entirety, as humanity. We need a name for this new belief. Perhaps *transhumanism* will serve: man remaining man, but transcending himself, by realizing new possibilities of and for his human nature. (1927: 19)

For transhumanism advocates[2] including Nick Bostrom and David Pearce, with the advent of late twentieth-century medical and scientific technology the human species is receiving a self-made evolutionary, transhuman "turbo-boost." Instead of unplanned biological evolution – a slow process of survival, reproduction, and adap-

tation over geological time – human futures are powered via deliberately employed technologies that will increasingly work their way inwards, radically transforming our bodies and minds. Transhumanism, though not a homogenous movement, generally advocates the use of invasive technology and human physical, genetic, mental manipulation to correct "quality of life problems" and human limitations such as disease, vulnerability to aging, maximum lifespan, and biological constraints on physical and cognitive abilities. Transhumanists like Bostrom (2005, 2008) contend that by unlocking the genetic secrets of human development, we can veritably "upgrade" humanity like an outmoded computer into something more efficient, streamlined, liberated, and perfect.

Transhumanists support the emergence and convergence of radical bio-interventions on the body such as nanotechnology, biotechnology, information technology, and cognitive science, and hypothetical future technologies such as simulated reality, artificial intelligence, super-intelligence, mind-uploading, and cryonics. They believe that humans can and should use these technologies to become "more than human," or pursue a state of being *beyond contemporary sociocultural understandings of corporeal wellness*. They therefore support, in a radical libertarian fashion, the recognition and/or protection of cognitive liberty, morphological freedom, and procreative liberty as basic civil liberties to guarantee individuals the choice of using human enhancement technologies on themselves and their children (Bostrom, 2008). A model transhuman would transcend basic modes of human existence and reality, becoming a postmodern Gilgamesh or Nietzsche's *Overman*; two-thirds engineered god, and one-third human. Groups including the World Transhumanist Association (WTA, now called Humanity+), Cryonics Institute, Transhumanist Arts, Alcor Life Extension Foundation, the Future of Humanity Institute, the Extropy Institute, and the Foresight Institute have for the better part of the last 40 years promulgated transhuman visions and futures. Key transhuman texts in this growing new social movement include Ettinger's (1972) *Man into Superman*, Esfandiary's (1989) *Are You a Transhuman?*, Regis' (1990) *Great Mambo Chicken and the Transhuman Condition*, Drexler's (1992)

Nanosystems, Newman's (2004) *Promethean Ambitions: Alchemy and the Quest to Perfect Nature*, and the WTA's (2002) *Transhumanist Declaration*.

Transhumanist projects, for example, seek to strengthen or transcend basic human characteristics such as youth, creativity, and intelligence by using medical technology to develop, correct, repair, activate, or eliminate certain defective, weak, or limiting genes; or, the use of other scientific innovations such as robotics to enhance movement. Posthumans, as the transhuman credo promotes (WTA, 2002), will be capable of achievements of which present generations write about only in science fiction. Transhumanists point to many potential human futures through corporeal manipulation such as the development of super-intelligence via cerebral interface with computers, lifelong emotional well-being via the recalibration of the brain's pleasure centers, the use of personality pills and complementary gene therapy to correct "pathological conditions" like shyness, the development of biological nanotechnology to increase the lifespan, the uploading of thoughts and consciousness into virtual reality via neuroprostheses, and cryogenic freezing and then reanimation of "dying" bodies or body parts. In the future, humans will reap the benefits of altered DNA, selective reproduction, prosthetic limbs, nanorobotics, synthetic organs, sensory magnification, anti-aging regimens, portable telecommunication devices, and drug therapy (Miah, 2008a, 2008b). Model posthumans are, then, engineered X-Men, who might receive injections of anti-aging serum that replenishes cells, are embodied with telecommunication systems transmitting text, voice, video, and large knowledge/data files to other machines, whose eyes are rigged with an artificial oculus that measures color, depth, heat, and distance, whose DNA has been genetically altered so they are virtually immune to disease, and whose emotions are regulated by receptors implanted deep in their brains to render them free from stress, fear, doubt, paranoia, or depression. Skeptics including Max Dublin (1992) and Francis Fukuyama (2002) argue that transhumanism is more or less a misnomer for *posthumanism*.

Elite sport culture is a zone pregnant with transhuman significance and possibility because of its diffuse emphasis on performance, perfection, science, and physical manipulation. Indeed, so much of the transhumanist development in sport has arrived without significant critique. As Lovnik argues:

> There is no radical critique of the new technologies. The few luddites refuse to develop a systematic understanding and can only act as kamikaze fighters. The dream of a nomadic counter-movement, constantly in fear of being appropriated, prevents any serious form of organization or the accumulation of enough knowledge, power, and even capital to make it a serious threat. So transhumanism does not even have to present itself as an ideology – it can immediately enter the room of the ruler. And so it happens, willingly supported by artists, visionaries, followed by marketing researchers. The rest is history. (2002: 119)

At the academic forefront of transhumanist philosophy in sport is Andy Miah (2004, 2007, 2008a, 2008b). Miah's corpus of work does not only present transhumanism as an inevitable state of development in sport but advocates it as desirable, exciting, and pleasurable for athletes. Miah's (2004) deontological meta-narrative maintains that through the use of sports equipment, nutrition, techniques training, and other scientific interventions on the human body in sport, athletes are already transhuman players. Instead of shackling sport/athlete development with excessively conservative and reactionary ideologies against the increased biological intervention into/onto the athletic body, Miah (2004, 2007) suggests that athletes should be allowed, as a matter of ethical and autonomous choice, to freely request and use genetic therapy and manipulation (that would stimulate muscle growth, expand blood and oxygen carrying capacities in athletes, reduce tissue damage through training, and speed recovery time), drugs, and nanotechnology to explore their own performance abilities; that is, to simultaneously transcend their own physical abilities and articulate the power of science to transport human potential and essence into a zone of awe-inspiring mega-performance.

In the remainder of this chapter, I discuss the implications of transhumanism on sport culture, and the resistance to transhumanist tendencies in sport through the case study of Parkour. In largely drawing upon the existentialist and phenomeno-logically informed work of Martin Heidegger and neo-Marxist thinking of Guy Debord (1967), I present an alternative to the largely hegemonic condition of technological dominance in sport.

Transhumanism and the Sociology of Sport

Sociologists of sport like Ted Butryn (2003, 2007) often reveal a complacent, classically critical, but academically/morally detached position on the nature of athlete–technology coupling. Through his collective work on the cyborgification of sport, Butryn (2002, 2003) presents an analysis of how bodies are progressively aligned and inter-faced with machines in late modern performance cultures. Other sociologists and psychologists of health, illness, and sport point to the emancipa-tory potential of increased medication interven-tion into sport, as new technologies, drugs, scientific procedures, and technological gear are made available to athletes suffering from disa-bility, injury, or disease. If biotech sciences can be employed as a means to grant access to physical activity to those with impaired abilities, the standard narrative implies, intervention is morally sound. However, sport and leisure policy researchers continue to raise important questions regarding the consequences of transhuman ide-ologies in sport, by reminding audiences of the spread of performance-enhancing drug use accompanying the insurgence of sport science logics and training practices in elite sport worlds (Culbertson, 2007; McNamee, 2007). What remain absent from these discussions (save for the literature on disability sports) are analyses of transhumanist tendencies in sport starting with athlete-informed desires, wishes, beliefs, atti-tudes, or accounts. Sociologically intriguing are the broad and overarching claims about athlete agency, choice, and freedom to compete as enhanced beings, when we consider how few analyses of transhumanism are buttressed by the thoughts, experiences, or existential beliefs of athletes themselves. Not only do transhumanists advocate the transcendence of human potential in sport, then, they also appear to transcend the notion of athletes as the existential subjects informing sport development processes.

As a result of the above, central to any discus-sion of transhumanism, science, and sport is the bioethical question of *enhancement for whom, and for whose good*? In a majority of the sport and transhumanism literature, morality is either ignored or explained away. Sociologists, notes Thiele (2005), are stereotypically reticent of engaging debates about morality (i.e., under claims of detachment, scientific inquiry, value freedom, or objectivity), and philosophers of transhuman sport like Miah (2007, 2008a, 2008b) tactically sidestep such issues by discounting the very idea of *humanness* to which moral debates are linked. While overt instances or the cultural residues of homophobia, sexism, racism, xeno-phobia, jingoism, classism, or other forms of prejudice in mainstream sports cultures are regu-larly exposed by sociologists of sport, rarely do researchers seek to engage moral commentary on those forms of discrimination (Atkinson and Young, 2008: Long and McNamee, 2004). Too few follow Pronger's (2002) lead by either promoting alternative (i.e., anti-biotech) sports moralities and practices, or offering visions of how sport might look if stripped of systematic forms of dominance, inequality, and exploitation. There-fore, tabling interventionist questions regarding who sports enhancement via human transcend-ence is for, what social and cultural ends it serves, issues of power and agency accompanying enhancement, the human risks associated with it, the cultural messages it conveys, and the ability for enhancement to improve the human condi-tion in lasting and meaningful ways is, however, universally critical.

Physical cultural studies theorists question whether transhumanist discourses advocate an unequivocally secular, pro-choice ethos of unhinged democracy, and are wrapped in contemporary liberal logics of free choice, self-determination, personal fulfillment, and self-reflexive identity exploration. The thin veneer of libertarianism slathered across transhumanist discourses only slightly blurs a neo-conservative, pro-institutional sentiment clearly indicating how contemporary body enhancement processes in sport are coupled with late modernist techno-capitalist agendas. As Andrews (2006, 2008) notes, sport is a primary site of unbridled neolib-eral/neo-conservative logics and practices, and more recently there has been a groundswell of sociological attention directed toward the social, physical, and cultural implications of neoliberalism in/on sport. Few have acknowledged the rise of transhumanism in sport cultures as an offshoot of neoliberalism, or the genesis of human transcendence ideologies and practices in this milieu. As a beginning, Henry Giroux's (2005) warning about the cultural and social trappings of neo-liberalism in broader society is salient:

> As neo-liberal policies dominate politics and social life, the breathless rhetoric of the global victory of free-market rationality is invoked to cut public expenditures and undermine those non-commodified public spheres that serve as the repository for critical education, public dialogue, and collective intervention. Public services such as health care, childcare, public assistance, education, and transportation are now subject to the rules of the market. Social relations between parents and children, doctors and patients, teachers and students are reduced to that of supplier and customer just as the laws of market replace those non-commodified values capable of defending vital public goods and spheres. . . . Under neo-liberalism, the state now makes a grim alignment with corporate capital and transnational corporations, legitimating the dangerous presuppositions that corporations should be planning our future and that progress should be defined almost exclusively in economic and technological terms rather than in social and ethical terms. Corporations, in turn, are not designed to be responsible citizens.

Stanley Aronowitz (2003: 102), like Giroux, argues that the deregulation of Western business at all levels of enterprises and trade, limitations on labor's right to organize and bargain collectively, social policies favoring commercial and industrial development at the expense of humanism, reduced governmental aid to public education and health, and limitations on the right of aggrieved individuals to sue employees and corporations who provide services are consequences of Western neoliberalism. Sport has not, of course, been impervious to such social and cultural shifts, but rather it neoliberally produces and reproduces ideologies of neoliberalism. Elite athletes, Young (1993) reminds us, are incredibly vulnerable groups subject to the pressures of coaches, sponsors, and sport scientists (who are

themselves increasingly agents of private corporations via grants, endowments, and financial "gifts") who wield considerable power over athlete's bodies. Constructions of the athlete's ability to choose transhumanist possibilities and interventions totally freely in a neoliberal world seems both naïve and empirically unwarranted.

Quite simply, the rapid movement toward transhuman sport enhancement is a quintessential neoliberal "spectacle" in Guy Debord's sense. As a major intellectual influence in the French neo-Marxist Situationist movement of the 1950s and 1960s, Debord wrote scathing critiques of capitalist, bourgeois, middle-class hegemony in France. His landmark book, *Society of the Spectacle* (1967), is a rejectionist and rebellious tome that eviscerates normative modernist cultural ideologies of economic production, technology, media, and social order. At the heart of Debord's analysis, so much akin to Jacques Ellul's (1967), is that all of everyday experience is geared toward the worship and reification of the capitalist social modality of living; from the production of commodities, to their consumption and display, to their lauding as evidence of Western progress. On a grand scale, this is the Spectacle, and everyday acts become spectacles reaffirming the larger. Debord (1967) contends that humans become willing but yet unwitting drones to capitalist production and commodity fetishism. The Spectacle of life is capitalist order, reason, and social organization (e.g., the form and content of our social structures and our cultural ideologies), while small-scale spectacles (such as the use of sport biotech for the purposes of "enhancement") become the fabric of everyday life. For Debord or Ellul we might add that hegemonic capitalist order is historically achieved through overt and covert instances of scientific discovery (*qua* reason and rationality) and the extension of scientific logic to market capitalism (production, innovation, distribution, marketing, etc.). Most theorists of late modern, neoliberal consumer society and those who study the sport-industrial complex like Maguire (2005) instruct similarly; such are foundational aspects of the Spectacle and spectacles. Science is an essential component of the modern Spectacle, and micro-spectacles of human enhancement (such as the process of making an athlete run faster, jump higher, or swim farther) veil how deeply related science, medicine, and technology are within market capitalism. The agenda of transhumanism has Spectacular roots and deeply impacts how athletes' "choices" congeal in sport contexts; a thought or recognition carefully glossed over or ignored by its advocates.

If unfettered self-reflexivity and Me-making through consumption are self-delusionary norms in deceptively Spectacular societies, then beliefs that the scientific engineering of athletes levels the playing field in sport by providing athletes with more agency, autonomy, self-determination, and *biocapital* (Miah, 2008b) – the production and representation of the physical body (its contents and abilities) as a form of social capital – is equally deceiving. Transhumanists like Miah (2008a, 2008b) find little problem with scientific engineering in sport, and discount criticisms that once legalized, institutionalized, and normalized, genetic manipulation *will become a must*, not an open choice, for athletes. Lining up in the proverbial starting blocks alongside a genetically "perfected" athlete holds no allure for those still humanly raw. Rather than liberation or transcendence within sport, then, genetic modification poses a coercive human future. Miah (2004: 158) discounts messy issues like coercion by stating that "elite sport is already the kind of activity where individuals participate under pressure. Sport is already a coercive environment and this is constitutive of what makes it valuable." If there can be no human essence, universal moral values underpinning sport, or need for protecting athletes against coercion, then certainly transhumanist practice appears ethical.

Indeed, the record-setting, goal-achieving, personal-best logics of most mainstream sports cultures closely parallel transhumanist discourses advocating human perfection, genetic tampering, and possibility exploration. Here, what counts as *human nature, human essence,* or *human desire* becomes quantitatively assessed through a continuum of empirical performance metrics and ideas. Any athletic deficiency (i.e., a problem of the raw, unfixed human essence) is probed, mapped, evidenced, re-sourced, and conquered much like a new market problem. Through scientific regulation and control of athletic bodies, coupled with their moral deregulation in sports cultures, the essential athlete

body can be solved, extended, and reborn in transhuman fashion (McNamee, 2007). Neo-traditionalist cultural concerns regarding human essence, nature, and the perversion of fair play in sport, the ethos of hard work and chance, are merely outdated social regulations impairing progress – a progress achieved only when (free market) scientists are granted unbridled intervention into sports performance circles. If the scientific Pandora's Box of biotech is fully opened, the human essence of competitive athletics – the unscientifically produced human doubt, drive, joy, effort, pain, uncertainty, bonding, effort, suffering, chance, spirituality, and divinity testified to by athletes and participants, what Elias and Dunning (1986) called sports-based "tension balances" – is forever stripped from its culture in a Fordist, assembly-line athlete production world. Here is precisely where "post-sport" advocates like *traceurs* (Parkour practitioners) enter into the late modern, transhumanist sport movement with a resistant physical culture response.

Parkour, Heidegger, and Post-Sport Physical Culture

In recent years I have become fascinated by physical cultural practices underpinned by a "post-sport" ethos that seeks to reject the trappings of neoliberalism and transhumanism in athletics (Atkinson, 2009). A post-sport, anti-transhumanist physical culture is one which subverts modernist sports ideologies and practices outright, and in which corporeal boundaries demarcating the sacred and profane, the raw and the cooked, the civilized and the primordial body are challenged through subaltern and autonomous forms of athletic movement. Whereas traditional sports practice contain, discipline, and enframe physical bodies as resources to be deployed toward the attainment of external goals (i.e., competitive and performative sport outcomes) and fulfillment of cultural-institutional discourses, post-sport athletic practices eschew the modernist body-as-resource (Heidegger, 1954) schematic. Post-sport athletics are at once moral, reflexive, community-oriented, green, spiritual, anarchic, and potentially Eros-filled physical cultural practices. They often adorn the guise of mainstream sports forms and techniques of play (e.g., swimming, running, cycling) – what Wheaton (2004) describes as the "residual" elements of modernist sport – but their individual or collective engagement and experience bears little similarity. Post-sport is, then, sinewy and connected athletic practices that are decisively anti-commercial, cooperative over competitive, rejectionist of advanced material technology, socially inclusionary rather than hierarchical, process-oriented, holistic, and internally differentiated in their orientation and engagement. A post-sport physical culture values human spiritual, physical, and emotional development (or rather, realization) through athleticism, beyond medical-technical or power and performance terms.

The philosophical roots of Parkour (or "free running") as a post-sport physical cultural practice date back over 100 years. The late modern manifestation of Parkour is a particular offshoot of a style of training called *hébertisme*. Hébertism emerged in the early twentieth century through the athletic philosophies and practices of French naval officer George Hébert. A lifelong advocate of exploring intense physical training as a means of developing human virtue, Hébert came to believe that the pursuit of physical perfection and communion with one's local environmental surroundings is a technique for developing one's sense of (moral and spiritual) place in the physical and social environment; and as a vehicle for bringing forth the underlying essence of one's humanity (Delaplace, 2005). Hébert tutored at the College of Reims in 1903 where he innovated a pathbreaking physical cultural lifestyle. He designed a series of apparatuses and exercises to teach what he dubbed the "Natural Method" of training. Hébert believed that individuals should train in the open environment as an unfettered animal species traversing a variety of landscapes and obstacles. Hébert's physical cultural method eschewed remedial gymnastics and the Swedish methods of athletic training popular in France at the time. For Hébert, these methods seemed unable to develop the human body harmoniously with nature, or to prepare students for the moral requirements of everyday life (i.e., courage, confidence, truth, calmness, and oneness). Hébert believed that by concentrating on competition

and performance within contrived environmental spaces (such as a gymnasium), mainstream sports cultures rather negatively impacted moral development in youth.

Hébert's Natural Method typically placed practitioners in a wooded setting, wherein they would be instructed run a course of 5–10 km (3–6 miles). Practitioners were simply told to run through the woods, over bushes, and through streams, climb up and down trees, and traverse fields as a method of stimulating their instincts, intuitions, and natural abilities to move. Students were also instructed, at particular time or distance points, to lift fallen logs, carry and throw heavy stones or even hang from trees as a means of developing their musculature. Hébert believed that by challenging his students to practice basic human muscular-skeletal movements in wilderness settings, they would develop qualities of strength and speed toward being able to walk, run, jump, climb, balance, throw, lift, and swim in practically any geographic landscape. Hébert felt that Natural Method practitioners would progressively learn to encounter and control any emotions or social situations they encountered in life. The Natural Method demanded that one possessed sufficient energy, willpower, courage, coolness, and *fermeté* (hardness) to manage any physical or mental obstacle; that is, to transcend limitations placed on people's abilities to think, react, sense, and use intuition via learned cultural norms, values, and ideologies. In a moral sense, by experiencing a variety of mental and emotional states (e.g., fear, doubt, anxiety, aggression, resolve, courage, and exhaustion) during training, one cultivated a self-assurance that would lead to inner peace and personal connection with one's environment – a state Hébert felt that was the ultimate essence of Being. The Natural Method could not be construed, then, as a transhuman venture, but rather as a sacred method of energetic communion.

Hébert thus became the earliest proponent of the French physical cultural practice of *le parcours* (obstacle course). The contemporary subcultural moniker Parkour clearly derives from the Hébert's use of the term *parcours*, and the French military term *parcours du combattant*. Indeed, Hébert's Natural Method of training had a special impact on French military training in the 1960s. Among the French soldiers exposed to the Natural Method was Raymond Belle. After his tour of duty in Vietnam, Belle taught his son David the principles of the Natural Method. David Belle had participated in martial arts and gymnastics as a young teen, and immediately took to the method. After moving to the Parisian suburb Lisses, David Belle further explored the rigors and benefits of the Natural Method with his friend Sébastien Foucan. By the age of 15, Belle and Focuan had developed their own suburban style of the Natural Method which they termed "Parkour." Belle and Foucan gathered recruits across Europe through the 1990s. By the end of the decade, the media in France, the United Kingdom, and the Netherlands had documented the Parkour physical culture. Media reports predictably framed the practice as a vacuous and style-oriented urban youth counter-culture. Belle later referred to Parkour's insertion into the media as part of a generational "prostitution of the art."[3] As a result of media attention, widespread youth interest, the commercialization of Parkour images and identities, and movement away from the spiritual to the spectacular aspects of the practice, Foucan and Belle disagreed vehemently over its vision and purpose. Belle continued, at least for a time, to adhere to the original principles of Parkour and the essence of the Natural Method. Belle pioneered a more dare-devilish, sport-like, and aesthetically oriented lifestyle that increasingly adherents referred to as *urban freeflow, free running,* or *Parkour.*

In the summer of 2005, I met and first started collecting data on two traditional *traceur* (Parkour exponent) groups in Toronto and Hamilton, Canada. I launched the project by hanging around with a core group of four traceurs in an eastern borough of Toronto, and eight in a west-end suburb of Hamilton. I first encountered a traceur while teaching an undergraduate course in Hamilton, Ontario, who invited me to watch a training session (what they often call "jams") involving 13 traceurs in Toronto. By July of 2005, I found myself fully immersed in the local Hamilton crew, investigating the meaning of Parkour for the young men in the crew on a first-hand, participatory basis. A free runner in the crew invited me to travel with him to a training jam in Toronto, where I met six of his friends. Within the next

month, I traveled to Toronto on a weekly basis to train in the city with them. In these jam sessions, I learned about conducting the physical practice of Parkour: how a typical session involves running, jumping, and hurling oneself over urban landscapes as a gymnastic exercise. One leaps up walls, over railings, across statues; jumps out of windows; rolls across park spaces; and moves as quickly as one can from a jam's starting point to its predetermined finishing point. The goal in these sessions is to move with rather than around urban obstacles in the spirit of the Natural Method.

Although difficult to quantify precisely, the number of traceurs in Canada appears to be growing. Through my participant observation with traceurs over a 12-month period, I met nearly 300 local practitioners in the metropolitan areas, and formally interviewed 17 as part of the research process. Through participant observation and interviewing, I came to note several important sociodemographic commonalities among the traceurs. Nearly 90 percent of the traceurs I encountered were male, 86 percent lived in either the greater Hamilton or Toronto urban core, 72 percent were middle class, and 64 percent were white. The mean age of the group was 21, and nearly all had experience as a player in a traditional sport during their adolescence.

The general ethos among those observed and interviewed reflected stereotypical resistance subculture attitudes toward mainstream sport; in other terms, they are emerging *post-sport enthusiasts.* Traceurs expressed disdain for highly organized, scripted, contained, authoritarian, competitive, and consumer-based sports experiences. They preferred free and creative forms of athletic movement devoid of techno-sport *accoutrements.* Among those with whom I interacted, Parkour is a method of personal exploration through movement, a do-it-yourself form of running and urban gymnastics, rejecting modernist ways of seeing and training a body in scientific-rational terms (Atkinson, 2009). In terms of their "playing field," the traceurs described a need to reappropriate local space for their own leisure and self-exploration purposes, and to use their natural environment to meet their own needs. Most described Parkour as a way of life and an ideology permeating all of their thoughts and actions, and as a vehicle for "finding themselves" outside of the highly controlling and claustrophobic sociocultural zones (e.g., families, schools, and workplaces).

Traceurs engage existential questions about the self in late modern social life through their post-sport, Parkour lifestyles. Principally, they ask whether core truths about the nature of existence and one's essence are to be learned through ascetically grounded forms of athleticism. They venture into Parkour and explore what multiple truths lay beneath the culturally-institutionally discursive framed self; as such, they describe a collective desire to tap knowledge of the existing body which precedes, and cannot be wholly assembled through, or by, extant late modern (sport) discourses. Parkour is, then, a bio-pedagogical project designed to bring what traceurs believe to be an *essential* life force, spirit, and desire underpinning all human existence to presence. Zen Buddhist scholars, as with other Chinese Buddhists, refer to such a force as the *qi* of life. In the *Upanishads*, Hindu philosophers refer similarly to the *prana*; the vital, life-sustaining force of living beings and energy in the universe. Pronger (2002) describes a similar life force as the *puissance* of the free, desiring body and spirit.

Transcendence and the Pursuit of *Dasein*

To understand the essence of Parkour practices and traceurs' interests in transcendence, sociologists of physical activity might first commence by excavating (sport) philosophy. Early on in my ethnographic research on Parkour I turned to existential theories, most notably Heidegger (1954, 1962), in an attempt to grasp the logic of the Natural Method and its emphasis on the discovery of human essence through movement. Heidegger (1947, 1954) searches deeply into the question of human essence (*Wesen*). For Heidegger, personally understanding human essence is the matter of *coming to presence*; of being present and reflexively mindful in the here and now of life. In "The Question Concerning Technology" (1954) and *Being and Time* (1962), Heidegger launches an

extended analysis of the ontology of Being through such a framework.[4]

Traceurs practice and preach very similarly to Heidegger regarding the nature of human condition in (late) modernity and the benefits of "coming to presence." Parkour traditionalists will firstly argue that the majority of Western sports experiences are dominated by external power (*pouvoir*); or more simply, that one's desire to participate in athletics, the relationships and positions forged through sport, experiences therein, and identities as athletes are pre-shaped by cultural goals and values (i.e., late capitalist logics of dominance, winning, external reward, social distinction through vanquishing others, the cultivation of cultural ideal-type bodies, and the maintenance of political-economic social hierarchies) which are not one's "own"; thus, questions are posed regarding what consciousness is bred in mainstream competitive sport. Derrick (aged 21) told me one day:

> I played hockey and football as a kid and hated it, not because I was a wimp or small or had the other guys pushing me around. But because I hated the atmosphere of everyone yelling, and coaches talking about how important winning is and that shit. Like we'd sit there and listen to a coach blab on, like, about all of the plays we had to memorize and techniques, or like moves we had to get down perfect. I loved throwing the ball around in a field with my friends or playing street hockey on Sundays, but that was where you actually did what you wanted. Right, if you ask me, sport is not for kids, it's for parents who want their kids to be like little robots or worker bees.[5]

For traceurs like Derrick, bodily energies and desires to move, to express and find joy in athletics are literally *re-sourced* (Heidegger, 1954) and channeled into competition for external reward – be it against a clock, against an opponent, or against the natural elements. For them, the desire to move and to engage athletics *should* come from an inner, mindful, present desire to explore the parameters of Being removed from such tightly controlled and alienating contexts. Fred (aged 26) said, "my dad used to tell me that I would learn how to be a better person in sport [baseball]. I only ever learned to be like everyone else. It never felt like I could express myself in baseball or be an individual. Just one of the team."

Heidegger (1954) describes the Western idea of technology (including capitalist modes of production and design), as loosely dialogical with the ancient Greek idea of *techne* (an act or process of applied discovery). In a traditional scientific sense, *techne* is the process of applying knowledge and apparatuses to discover "truths" about the physical (and social) world; and, of course, to employ such truth discoveries to produce the means of human subsistence and development. Such is the ethos of transhumanism in sport. It is a means of realizing modernist progress, discovery, and truth via athletics and not the existential enhancement of sport for athletes principally. Athletic movement techniques, one might argue, reveal and reaffirm truths about scientifically determined human essence/potential. Applying biotech to sport is a vehicle for the coming to presence of scientific theory and knowledge. Heidegger notes that technology for Western (sports enthusiasts) is thus conceived as the "bringing-forth" of capitalist truths and values (Heidegger, 1954), and testing theories regarding the metaphysics underpinning all life. Late modern sport spectacles are technological wonders in these respects, as physical, social, and interpretive spaces embedded with rule-bound logics of scientific production and control. Contrast this with Levi's (aged 22) construction of Parkour:

> I don't need gizmos, gadgets, or high-tech gear to go on a run. I have a beaten up, old pair of shoes, shorts and T-shirts for running. I'm not paranoid about how I look, or what electronics I need to guide me. The only thing I need is out there and here [*points to chest*]; I use what's in my neighborhood, like walls and fences and stairs ... I never go into sports stores and buy all kinds of stuff for running, or anything like that, because it would be stupid. Like, Parkour is about freedom, yeah, so you should need less to be free, not more.

For Levi, late modern sport is completely *enframed* (Heidegger, 1954) by techno-scientific and commercial ontologies. In Heidegger's (1954) theoretical schematic, typical athletes are merely standing reserve armies within and against which production technology is deployed, extended, tested, and improved. Many traceurs in Toronto and Hamilton tend to agree with Heidegger, expressing how the human potential for effort, the desire and energy to move and even the physical environments in which humans live are systematically *re-sourced* to serve technological needs and purposes (i.e., production efficiency, tool refinement, market expansion, and consumption). Like Heidegger, some traceurs contend that sports technology uses humans more than humans use technology. Clint (age 19) noted, "my mom does marathons, and it's funny. Watch everyone at the start line, starting their watches or setting their GPS systems, with fuel belts on, and special hats and really expensive glow in the dark shoes. I fucking laugh at those guys because without the cool shit, they'd be lost!"

Heidegger (1954) notes, and Pronger (2002) echoes, that Westerners have generally understudied the ancient Greek's holistic notion of *techne* in physical cultures. Heidegger (1954) stresses that not all ontological questions or human needs (like that of moving or being athletic) may be addressed by quantitatively demarcating the boundaries of lived experience or the possibilities of transhuman potential through applied mechanical and scientific means. He exposes the other side of *techne*: the bringing forth or revealing of aesthetic and poetic human realities through subjective emotional expression and reflection – what the ancient Greeks called *poiesis*. In many ways, such is Heidegger's (1954) description of the process of coming to presence by transcending modernist ideological baggage where people carry their mindsets and dispositions. Poiesis is an artistic, aesthetic, emotional, and public method of revealing "different" human truths and values. These truths are, according to Heidegger (1954), humanistic, moral, ethical, spiritual, and green realities. Poiesis arises from an act, a symbol, a thought, feeling or expression that brings forth knowledge of the human condition falling outside of rationally technological ways of understanding human essence(s). Many traceurs in Toronto and Hamilton are less concerned, for example, with measuring and accounting for performance in their daily free-running exploits, than the possibility of coming to presence and learning about what defines them as Beings. Stan (age 30) told me:

> I've been doing this for about ten years and each year it teaches me something new about me as a person. Free runs have no script, so you become the script. I use my mind to navigate a terrain and slip through the city, and I have to make choices and reflect on why I made the choices I did, and moved in turn. If you study that process after the run, you learn who you are at your core . . . the choices we make on a run are telling since it lets you know your own fears, hopes and sense of person. If I can deal with that, focus on the positive of my Being and my strength, and manage my self-doubts, I find a kind of inner peace.

Heidegger (1947, 1954) suggests that social and personal explorations of poiesis provide moments of catharsis for people like Stan, or moments of *ecstasis* wherein the conscious and calculating mind is "let go" and the body and mind move as one. But what, precisely can poiesis bring forth or reveal for traceurs that stands in opposition to transhuman leanings in sport cultures? To Heidegger (1962), reflexive engagement with a practice like Parkour can allow for the important explorations and experiences of *Dasein*.

There can be no doubt or misinterpretation regarding Heidegger's central interest in *Dasein*, and the processes involved in a present-minded sense making (also termed *Being-there-in-the-world*). *Dasein* often proves a thorny, if not at times completely untenable, concept for sociologists of physical culture (Atkinson, 2009). At its core, the concept relates to experiential authenticity versus inauthenticity. *Dasein* is roughly a human "first-nature" or a pre-Descartesian mode of "Being-in-the-world" (Heidegger, 1962). Through the socialization process, culturally instilled languages, logical systems, and modes of rational thinking, honed emotional states, social psychologies, and ideologies obscure the experience of *Dasein*. Heidegger (1954, 1962) refers to the sociocultural layers cloaking *Dasein* as "moods." Simply put, one acquires a social-psychologically reflexive self and this becomes, as

Mauss (1973), Elias (1978), and Bourdieu (1984) outline, the basis of a personal *habitus* – or one's socially instilled second nature, tastes, dispositions. and preferences. Beings are *Dasein* even when they are ontologically encased in systems of habit and consciousness that obscures what Heidegger calls "authentic" – one's choice to live within and transmit this tradition. To Heidegger (1962), *Dasein* is therefore thrown or projected onto the possibilities for thought and action presented before it in the social world, and a Being interprets and understands the world in terms of such learned possibilities.

Over the course of interaction with traceurs, they regularly spoke to me about the importance of unplugging from stereotypical ways of conceiving and practicing sport (i.e., learned *moods*) in order to experience human movement in polyvalent, existential ways as *Dasein*. The reproduction of dominant ideologies through sport and its framing along typical class, gender, nationalistic, and race lines of identification, occurs via the uncritical acceptance of what sport must be, how it should be practiced, and what personal desires have to be stimulated, mobilized, and experienced through athletic movement. Because Parkour runs are generally unscripted, not bound by rigidly taught codes of movement, nor judged by officials, one is able to move how one feels and how one senses. Stated differently, one is encouraged to be present with one's body and to use running, jumping, climbing, and other athletic techniques to bring forth, or reveal, *Dasein*. Eoghan (aged 27) said:

> Being on the edge made me learn who I am at my core. When I look into myself, and confront my humanity, I realize what makes me function. It's when my body and mind are punished [through Parkour] that I learn about me. In the middle of a run, when nothing else in the world matters and I'm tired, I realize how controlled and forced the rest of my life is . . . so a monkey vault or cat leap is not agony or pain to me. It's the rest of my life and what's in my head every day that makes me hurt. That's the truth about me which I learn from Parkour.

The rigor and poiesis of Parkour, as advocated by Natural Method pioneers, is partially located in its stance on sporting anti-Method. One listens to the body, movement is based on intuition, and learns to tap one's own understanding or existential meaning of what athleticism fosters. Alan (aged 28) said:

> Some kids think that if you have a run or two with us every month, some magic enlightenment will happen. No chance of that. If you want to benefit from the practice, you have to practice the mindset of freedom with every breath, every move you make, and do this all the time. That really means giving up and letting go of the mental and cultural clutter that people carry around and just feel free to move and to be. It means sacrifice to practicing and reflecting on what makes you tick, the relationships you make, and the impact you have on the earth ... Parkour is only a gateway; it's a series of movements intended to change your life, and it has to start from within.

To Alan, people do not experience "existential enlightenment" in modernist sporting contexts, but instead one only reveals the *Dasein* one has always been without knowing through post-sport contexts. Steve (age 26) said to me, "Parkour helped me become a free-thinker and self-aware. A thing I always could be, but never was."

Heidegger (1947, 1962) still argues that *Dasein* is immersed in the physical, literal, tangible day-to-day world. For Heidegger, authentic existence and the experience of *Dasein* comes to presence when individuals arrive at the realization of who they are as thrown Beings, and grasp the fact that each human being is a distinct entity projected in the world. In thinking about his own projection, and the learned needs contouring his existence, Patrick (age 25) said:

> Doing it [Parkour] day in and day out, and shifting my mind to Parkour didn't allow drugs or sex, or video games or online shit, or whatever, to rule my head. It also teaches me to not be concerned with how much someone else has or what they are doing, and only worry about what you can control. ... Oh yeah, and to take the time to stop and enjoy the beauty around you. How can I say this, it's like the body can be the most beautiful thing on earth because of how it can move – not because my body beat another body in a sport, but because it moves explosively for

itself. That kind of nature is beautiful, not things you buy in a store or put on display for other people to envy.

For Patrick and others, once people examine the moods shaping their existence, then concern with the world will no longer be to emulate the masses but rather to explore one's own existence as a minded, present Being.

What, then, is the existential experience of Parkour? Of course this is not a straightforward question to answer. Individuals assess, use, or deconstruct Parkour in any number of ways, and for a full range of purposes. Still, one cannot overlook the striking consistency of traceurs' constructions of "free running" as a technique of late modern poiesis. Heidegger (1954) proclaims that people may utilize particular activities (he discusses art, music, and literature, for example) as poiesis in the process of revealing one's nature of Being-in-the-world and Being-with (others). Through poetic activities, people may eventually expose and scrutinize the pervasive *Das Man* (The One) mentality underwriting our choices as agents in the world. *Das Man* (Heidegger, 1947, 1954) is a state of consciousness and acting derivative of the impersonal singular pronoun *man* such as the "one." Heidegger refers to this concept of *The One* in explaining inauthentic modes of existence, in which one moves, thinks, or feels in a particular way (from a particular state of thrownness, social mood, or mode of "Being-in-the-world") because "that is what One does." Cam (aged 21) said:

> Mike, you know why I didn't like organized sport? It's like to be an athlete you had to be a position, not a player with a mind, and act in a specific way. I played hockey because my dad pushed me, and like all my friends did or whatever. And like if you get to a certain level, or play in the right league, only then are you a true hockey player. I hated that because if I am going to play something, I want to do it because I love it and no one should be able to tell me if I am doing it right, or like have been recognized as good. ... Parkour is not a sport you are good at, it's more like a mindset than a status you have. The traceurs you know in the group, Mike, well those guys are not traceurs because I say they are, or you say they are, but because they believe they are and move that way.

A *Das Man* athlete constitutes a state of Being-in-the-world of sport as determined by dominant norms, conventions, values, and moods as Cameron illustrates. Heidegger (1947: 113) states that, "The 'They' prescribes one's state-of-mind, and determines what and how one sees (experiences) *Dasein*. This is a feature of 'the They' as it functions in society, an authority that has no particular source, group boundary, reference point or conscious justification." Heidegger (1947) contrasts the authentic self (my *owned self, Dasein*) with the "They self" (my *un-owned self*), to argue how one's general state of presence may be wholly determined by the cultural and social forces into which the individual is born and exposed, and internalizes as normative.

In bringing his complex existentialism full circle, Heidegger (1954, 1962) differentiates between a person who is *present-at-hand* and one who is *ready-at-hand*. People ready-at-hand are involved in the world in an ordinary and relatively unreflexive manner. They are, in the terms of technology, science, and capitalist agendas, Beings who are ready to deploy their bodily energies and desires toward the fulfillment of dominant structures of power; to affirm the modernist Spectacle (Debord, 1967). Athletes ready-at-hand abound in recreational, amateur, and elite sport figurations (Atkinson, 2009). Traceurs take significant issue with such a one-dimensional emphasis on athletic Being, and triumph the benefits of using exhausting and personally challenging forms of athletic movement as a means of distancing oneself from non-essential personal concerns or moods. Glenn (aged 27) told me:

The more I push myself with a jump or a really hard leap on a jam [a free run], well, it takes me away from most of the nonsense I worry about in life. There's like a spring coil of stress I used to feel compressing at the back of my neck throughout the day. Sometimes when I was sitting at my desk or stuck in traffic, it was like it was going to pop out of my brain. Jams have allowed me to forget about most of those petty little stressors and self-crippling pet peeves. The frenzy and the openness and the self-direction of the jams helps you center and focus only on what counts in life. I changed my career, life focus and

basically everything about me after doing Parkour for three years.

A traceur like Glenn approaches a "jam" as a meditative process, where intense internal introspection about what "makes you tick" is stimulated on the *parcours*.

Those present-at-hand come to terms with, relish, and advocate chosen behavior as a means of living dialogically with one's everyday existence as a subject in and of itself. A fundamental basis of our Being-in-the-world as people present-at-hand is for Heidegger (1947, 1962), not the cultivation of pure spirit but acknowledgement of central *cares* (*Sorge*). All ways of Being-in-the-world have concern or care. But to Heidegger, one must excavate and understand the nature of one's concerns, moods, and cares as the basis for all personally relevant action, or *Dasein*. Just as the sport scientist investigates, presumably neutral in the process of "bettering" the human condition through transhumanist activities, we see that beneath this there is the *care* to reveal the "truth" of theory of movement and possibility. For traceurs, if athletics are employed in a poetic manner (i.e., as part of resisting mainstream sport-techno-capitalist concerns), it signals a care to promulgate athletic modes of Being and alternative logics of sports presence as part of the transcendence of modernist sport. The thrust of the post-sport, anti-transhumanist challenge to mainstream sports cultures and their modalities of Being is precisely this; traceurs deliberately question why particular states of Being are privileged over others in athletics, and what athletics might look like if new sensibilities and existential experiences are nurtured within physical cultures.

Conclusion

The particular cluster of urban traceurs I studied in Toronto and Hamilton are highly critical of hyper-competitive and transhumanist currents in both amateur and elite athletics. Many, but clearly not all, decry athletics' domination by transhuman agendas, and the deleterious social-cultural impact of capitalist *pouvoir* on mainstream sports cultures. To this end, they seek to disrupt social constructions of sport by reifying capitalist *pouvoir* and its deployment through subaltern Parkour movements. Parkour is their *techne* for laying bare the central social, cultural, and spiritual ethics in transhumanist sport cultures, and its impact on human will/desire/suffering. Parkour, on a far more individual level, is an ascetic and aesthetic form of self-exploration. By focusing on the aesthetics of gymnastic movements, the spiritual experience of physical rigor, and communion with one's (urban) environment, they pursue something about bodily experience which ventures beyond utterly rational knowledge. Parkour can be an innovative late modern form of community formation and self-exploration through intensely reflexive athleticism. As Saville (2008), Marshall (2010), and Gilchrist and Wheaton (2011) illustrate in their respective studies of Parkour, post-sports are clearly appealing to youth generations who are dissatisfied with and alienated from mainstream sports cultures.

Upon even further reflection, a critical component of Parkour appears to lie in its configuration as a practice geared toward using athletics as technique for touching *Dasein*. Given their interests in connecting athletics with moral development and personal truth seeking (i.e., experiencing *Dasein* and being present-at-hand), urban traceurs are not simply sporting *flâneurs* without purpose. Their street athletics are predicated on heavily flamboyant and spectacular moves because they are designed to bring forth spectacular presences and existential experiences among practitioners. As an offshoot, Parkour is a physical cultural disruption of the taken-for-grantedness of corporatized and denaturalized (i.e., transhuman) sports practices. Traceurs' desire to practice Parkour in heavily ascetic styles symbolizes how they feel, in Heidegger's (1954) terms, that in order to reframe athletics in an alternative manner, one has to spectacularly destabilize the enframing nature of its transhuman state. Like the nature of their selves, it has to be stripped bare before it can be reassembled as present "whole." The sheer growth of the traceur movement in Toronto and other urban zones is a loose indicator that their message is being received; and that more young people in these environments embrace the idea of the downtown core (and indeed their own selves) as a site of existential experience.

Notes

1 The athletes in question are: LeBron James, Vasily Alekseyev, John McEnroe, Cristiano Ronaldo, Paul Gasol, Ralph Boston, Lasji Doucourè, Wayne Rooney, Maria Sharapova, Henry Marsh, David Lega, Mary Lou Retton, Zhu Jianhua, Liu Xiang, Carlos Lopes, Daiane dos Santos, Steve Prefontaine, Paula Radcliffe, Joan Benoit-Samuelson, Wallace Spearmon Jr., Julie Moss, Omar Salazar, Miho Shinoda, Lance Armstrong, Kenny Bartram, Garrett Reynolds, Hasely Crowford, Carl Lewis, Kobe Bryant, Bernard Lagat, Mary Decker Slaney, Kerry O'Brien, Pete Sampras, Manfred Naumann, Derek Redmond, Arthur Ashe, Roger Federer, Sherone Simpson, Jon Lester, Michael Johnson, Michael Jordan, and Romualdo Kubiak.

2 See http://humanityplus.org/about, accessed January 21, 2013.

3 In the Channel 4 TV program *Jump London*, directed by Michael Christie, first aired September 9, 2003.

4 *Dasein* may be roughly translated as "being" or (human) "existence."

5 The observations made by the young traceurs are taken from Atkinson (2009).

References

Andrews, D.L. (2006) *Sport–Commerce–Culture*, New York: Peter Lang.

Andrews, D.L. (2008) "Kinesiology's 'Inconvenient Truth': The physical cultural studies imperative." *Quest*, 60 (1): 46–63.

Aronowitz, S. (2003) *How Class Works*, New Haven, CT: Yale University Press.

Atkinson, M. (2009) "Parkour, environmentalism and poiesis." *Journal of Sport & Social Issues*, 33: 164–194.

Atkinson, M. and Young, K. (2008) *Deviance and Social Control in Sport*, Champaign, IL: Human Kinetics.

Bostrom, N. (2005) "In defence of posthuman dignity." *Bioethics*, 9: 202–214.

Bostrom, N. (2008) "Why I want to be posthuman when I grow up," in Gordijn, B. and Chadwick, R. (eds.) *Medical Enhancement and Posthumanity*, New York: Springer, pp. 107–137.

Bourdieu, P. (1984) *Distinction: A Social Critique of the Judgement of Taste*, Cambridge, MA: Harvard University Press.

Butryn, T. (2002) "Cyborg horizons: Sport and the ethics of self-technologization," in Miah, A. and Eassom, S. (eds.) *Sport Technology: History, Philosophy, and Policy*, Oxford: Elsevier Science, pp. 111–134.

Butryn, T. (2003) "Posthuman podiums: Cyborg narratives of elite track and field athletes." *Sociology of Sport Journal*, 20: 17–39.

Butryn, T. (2007) "Technology, sport and the body," in Klavora, P. (ed.) *Foundations of Exercise Science: Studying Human Movement and Health*, Toronto: Sport Books.

Culbertson, L. (2007) "Human-ness, dehumanisation and performance enhancement." *Sport, Ethics and Philosophy*, 1: 195–214.

Debord, G. (1967) *The Society of the Spectacle*, trans. F. Perlman and J. Supak, Detroit, MI: Black & Red, 1970, 1977.

Delaplace, J.-M. (2005) *George Hébert: Sculpter du Corps*, Paris: Vuibert.

Drexler, K. (1992) *Nanosystems: Molecular Machinery, Manufacturing, and Computation*, New York: John Wiley & Sons Inc.

Dublin, M. (1992) *Futurehype: The Tyranny of Prophecy*, New York: Penguin Books.

Elias, N. (1978) *The Civilizing Process*, Oxford: Basil Blackwell.

Elias, N. and Dunning, E. (1986) *The Quest for Excitement: Sport and Leisure in the Civilizing Process*, Oxford: Basil Blackwell.

Ellul, J. (1967) *The Technological Society*, London: Vintage.

Esfandiary, F. (*FM-2030*) (1989) *Are You a Transhuman?*, New York: Warner Books.

Ettinger, R. (1972) *Man into Superman: The Startling Potential of Human Evolution*, New York: St Martin's Press.

Fukuyama, F. (2002) *Our Posthuman Future*, New York: Farrar Straus & Giroux.

Gilchrist, P. and Wheaton, B. (2011) "Lifestyle sport, public policy and youth engagement: Examining the emergence of Parkour." *International Journal of Sport Policy*, 3: 109–131.

Giroux, H. (2005) "Cultural studies in dark times: Public pedagogy and the challenge of neoliberal-ism." *Fast Capitalism* 1.2, www.fastcapitalism.com, accessed December 22, 2012.

Heidegger, M. (1947) "Letter on humanism," in Krell, D. (trans. and ed.) *Martin Heidegger: Basic Writings*, New York: Harper & Row, 1977, pp. 213–265.

Heidegger, M. (1954) "The question concerning technology," in Krell, D. (trans. and ed.) *Martin Heidegger: Basic Writings*, New York: Harper & Row, 1977, pp. 99–124.

Heidegger, M. (1962) *Being and Time*, London: SCM Press.

Huxley, J. (1927) *Religion Without Revelation*, London: E. Benn.

Long, J. and McNamee, M. (2004) "On the moral economy of racism and racist rationalizations in sport." *International Review for the Sociology of Sport*, 39: 405–420.

Lovnik, G. (2002) *Dark Fiber: Tracking Critical Internet Culture*, Cambridge, MA: MIT Press.

Maguire, J. (2005) *Power and Global Sport: Zones of Prestige, Emulation and Resistance*, London: Routledge.

Marshall, B. (2010) "Running across the rooves of empire: Parkour and the postcolonial city." *Modern and Contemporary France*, 18: 157–173.

Mauss, M. (1973) "Techniques of the body." *Economy and Society*, 2: 70–88.

McNamee, M. (2007) "Whose Prometheus? Transhumanism, biotechnology and the moral topography of sports medicine." *Sport, Ethics and Philosophy*, 1: 181–194.

Miah, A. (2004) *Genetically Modified Athletes: Biomedical Ethics, Gene Doping, and Sport*, London: Routledge.

Miah, A. (2007) "Genetics, bioethics and sport." *Sport, Ethics and Philosophy*, 1: 146–158.

Miah, A. (2008a) *Human Futures: Art in an Age of Uncertainty*, Liverpool: FACT & Liverpool University Press.

Miah, A. (2008b) "Justifying human enhancement: The accumulation of biocultural capital," in Wint, S.M.E. (ed.) *Our Ethical Future: Boundaries to Human Enhancement*, London: Royal Society for the Encouragement of the Arts.

Newman, W. (2004) *Promethean Ambitions: Alchemy and the Quest to Perfect Nature*, Chicago: University of Chicago Press.

Pronger, B. (2002) *Body Fascism: Salvation in the Technology of Physical Fitness*, Toronto: University of Toronto Press.

Regis, E. (1990) *Great Mambo Chicken and the Transhuman Condition: Science Slightly Over the Edge*, Reading, MA: Addison-Wesley.

Saville, S.J. (2008) "Playing with fear: Parkour and the mobility of emotion." *Social & Cultural Geography*, 9: 891–914.

Thiele, D. (2005) "The problem with sociology: Morality, anti-biology and perspectivism." *Quadrant*, 10: 210–224.

Wheaton, B. (2004) *Understanding Lifestyle Sport: Consumption, Identity and Difference*, London: Routledge.

WTA (2002) *The Transhumanist Declaration*. World Transhumanist Association, http://transhumanism.org/index.php/WTA/declaration/, accessed December 22, 2012.

Young, K. (1993) "Violence, risk and liability in male sports culture." *Sociology of Sport*, 10 (4): 373–396.

Further Reading

Debord, G. (1967) *The Society of the Spectacle*, trans. F. Perlman and J. Supak, Detroit, MI: Black & Red, 1970, 1977.

Ellul, J. (1967) *The Technological Society*, London: Vintage.

Fukuyama, F. (2002) *Our Posthuman Future*, New York: Farrar Straus & Giroux.

Heidegger, M. (1954) "The question concerning technology," in Krell, D. (trans. and ed.) *Martin Heidegger: Basic Writings*, New York: Harper & Row, 1977, pp. 99–124.

Pronger, B. (2004) *Body Fascism: Salvation in the Technology of Physical Fitness*, Toronto: University of Toronto Press.

22

Race-ing Men
Cars, Identity, and Performativity

Amy L. Best

Introduction

This chapter explores the collective life of illegal street-racers of San Jose, California, focusing on the dynamics of race, risk, and masculinity. I examine the ways cars are encoded racially and ethnically as young men struggle to find their place as men in a changing social world as they transition to adulthood. Late-night street-racing has long been a popular activity among young men, serving as a space where race, class, and gender identities materialize as young men negotiate the symbolic boundaries of place. A handful of media images of street-racing tell of the prominent place cars have had in post-World War II American youth culture for young men. The image of James Dean engaged in a perilous game of chicken (drag-racing) in *Rebel Without a Cause* is perhaps the most enduring. More recently, popular franchise films such as, *Gone in 60 Seconds* and *Fast and Furious* depict a cultural scene populated largely by young men with deep investment in the car. Absent from these films, however, is an accounting of the economic transformations and the changing global and racial landscape that shape the identity investments young men make in cars and the underground

street-racing scene today. At the dawn of a new century, young people confront a world of economic, political, and social uncertainty (Beck, 1998; Giddens, 1991), wrought by dramatic economic and social changes often associated with the global economy (Cieslik and Pollock, 2002; Newman and Giardina, 2011; Sassen, 1998). Economic restructuring in the 1970s and 1980s leading to the collapse of the modern industrial complex eroded the opportunity structures once available for a large percentage of young American men (Giroux, 1995; Fine and Weis, 1998; Kellner, 1997; Newman and Giardina, 2011). Yet, as young men encounter an adult world of emptying opportunity, they are also drawn into a culture of hyper-consumption, whereby objects provided in the consumer market, such as cars, serve as significant identity resources.

Cars have what French theorist Jean Baudrillard called "identity value" in that they act as markers of social and cultural difference, and thus communicate ideas about who we are in relation to whom others are. Through this system of signs, cars serve as symbols of masculinity (Baudrillard, 2000). Car culture is often seen as a space where men can be men, and in many instances provides one of the few opportunities for men to forge

A Companion to Sport, First Edition. Edited by David L. Andrews and Ben Carrington.
© 2013 Blackwell Publishing Ltd. Published 2013 by Blackwell Publishing Ltd.

emotional ties with other men, often across generations. "Traditional notions of separate spheres and the control of technology ensured that the car came to be identified with masculinity," argues cultural historian Sean O'Connell (1998: 44). The car has long been an object for young working-class men to claim respect and dignity as men, to deflect the repeated assaults on their manhood staked elsewhere. But as much as the car and the culture that develops around it can bring men together, the car also creates and deepens divisions among men (Gilroy, 2010). These divisions have grown increasingly antagonistic in a global context where struggles over moral, political, and economic resources intensify. In an increasingly global economy marked by a steady stream of bodies crossing ever-changing borders, masculinity is increasingly bound up with race and national identity struggles, such that claims to masculine capital are sorted through a racial system of domination (Collins, 1990; Connell, 1995; Connolly, 1998; Mac An Ghaill, 1994; Messner, 1992). In what follows, we will see how masculine struggles, as they come into being through the underground street-racing scenes, are racially and nationally coded.

In this formulation, identities can be treated as "projects," emergent features of ongoing social interaction, set within a set of structural relations, formed out of the discursive repertoires youth use to make sense of, interpret, and narrate their worlds. Identities materialize as young people occupy different interactional and discursive fields, realized in the practices they take up, the activities that occupy their time, the objects they use, and a complex of relations organizing their everyday worlds, even if they do not originate in those worlds (Best, 2000). As educational scholar and cultural critic Henry Giroux (1995) has argued, youth "identities merge and shift rather than becoming more uniform and static. No longer associated with any one place or location, youth increasingly inhabit shifting cultural and social spheres marked by a plurality of languages, ideologies and cultures" (p. 32).

Methods

To capture how cars figure in the everyday lives of young people, and also understand how a complex of social and economic forces mediates this relationship, requires the use of different research strategies, including participant observation, in-depth interviewing, focus-group interviewing, and examination of archival and contemporary documents such as films, print media, advertisements, bulletin boards, and personal websites maintained by car enthusiasts (Best, 2006). As with most projects of this kind, my focus is not on drawing broad generalizations about all young men and their relationship to cars. Instead, this research is guided by an interest in excavating layers of social meanings and understanding the connection between the process of meaning-making and youths' identity projects (Best, 2007).

At the center of this project is in-depth and focus-group interviews with young men and women, representing different economic locations, all between the ages of 15 and 23. All reside in San Jose, California and its surrounding suburbs – often called Silicon Valley, which was the center of the technological boom of the last decade. San Jose bears visible markers of its increasing involvement in a post-industrial, global economy that has transformed the everyday life of the community (Benner, 2002). One such change has been the emergence of San Jose as a major immigrant-receiving city with Santa Clara County now constituting a "majority minority" county (Castellanos, 2001). An estimated 60 percent of the county's residents are direct descendants of immigrants. Asian American and Latino/as represent over 55 percent of the Silicon Valley population.[1] San Jose is comprised of a number of ethnic enclaves across class groups. This ethnic segmentation is meaningful for the city's car culture, because it has given rise to ethnically segmented car scenes.

The youth who participated in this study represent the ethnic and racial diversity that characterizes the multicultural America we have become as we move into the twenty-first century. A significant number of participants are first- or second-generation American. The voices of Filipino American, Indo-American, Southeast Asian, Chicana, Latino/a, Black American, and European American youth fill these pages. In total, 44 semi-structured and open-ended face-to-face interviews were conducted with young men and women (age 15–23) who represent widely different income and racial/ethnic groups. Through focus groups, I interviewed 52 additional young women and men. I conducted five focus groups in total, each having between 7 and 15 participants.

To contextualize the accounts collected through in-depth and focus-group interviews, I draw upon a series of observations conducted at a number of different car sites over a period of several years between 2000 and 2004. I attended car shows, visited car dealerships, and patronized various car washes around the San Jose community. I spent a number of afternoons walking around high-school parking lots after school talking with kids and observing as they made their way out of school to their cars. I also spent time observing auto-shop class at Freedom High School, a low-income school in Santa Clara County, primarily comprised of Latino/as and Vietnamese students. I spent a portion of the 2004 spring semester observing four sections of auto-shop class. These classes were dominated by young men of color.

The Boys at Freedom High

On a Tuesday morning in the late spring of 2004, I am at Freedom High School hanging around auto shop. I spend much of my morning moving between the groups of boys who are scattered throughout the room charged with different tasks: measuring tire pressure, checking fluids, testing battery levels, before making my way over to a huddle of boys attempting to recharge the battery of a Honda CRX, a beat-up old car that is official property of auto shop. Moments before two of the boys, Justin and David, had pushed the CRX over beside a much newer Honda Civic parked in the lot a few feet from the car bays. The Civic is painted a purplish-blue and is outfitted with a sleek body kit and shiny chrome rims, its frame resting much lower to the ground than any stock Honda but just enough above the shiny rims to still be "street legal." I ask the group whose car it is and a tall South Asian boy who I come to know as Shrini offers up, "Mine." Don, who is sitting in the driver's seat of the CRX, with both hands firmly placed on the steering wheel, leans his head out of the car's window to ask if I like it, which is met with snickering laughs. "You can buy

it if you want," Shrini tells me with a more serious tone. I ask him why he's selling it. He explains, he wants to get a Subaru STi, a much faster car. Shrini's car is an automatic, a fact he reluctantly offers only after I ask. Though his car has undergone some changes to its exterior, there have been no performance upgrades. Right now, the car isn't fast enough and as an automatic it never will be. A slow car, especially if its exterior has been customized to look fast, confers little respect in the world of underground street-racing. Such a look will eventually discredit a racer. Speed, driver skill, and a willingness to take calculated risks behind the wheel are what matter most in the world of street- and organized racing. A slow car, no matter its appearance, provides little chance to demonstrate any of these virtues.[2]

This band of boys race imports: Honda Civics and Accords, Nissans and Acura Integras. They are part of what has been called "the import car scene" which emerged in southern California in the early 1990s but has extended north to San Jose and San Francisco and east beyond California in the last decade. The import scene in southern California and in San Jose at the time of this study (2000–2004) was dominated by Asian and Asian American young men in their teens and early twenties with auto imports principally from Japan, not continental Europe (Namkung, 2004). These young men are all Asian, 1.5- and second-generation Chinese, Indian, and Vietnamese, with exceptions like Daniel, who is Mexican.[3] And they are students at Freedom High School, a low-income school in San Jose, California with a large population of immigrants and students of color and few academic resources and opportunities for upward mobility. They comprise a loosely organized network that extends beyond their school, made up of small crews who know each other primarily by the cars they drive.

Most in this group at Freedom High School own used cars. For most in this loosely formed network of boys, these low-priced cars serve as templates for a series of modifications that in the end can more than double the initial cost of the car. Body kits, lowered suspensions, engine upgrades, multimedia systems, and altered exhaust systems comprise a multi-billion dollar industry of after-market car parts, an industry that has exploded in recent years in large part because of these young men and others like them who on weekend nights gather in the early hours of the morning on darkened streets and empty business parking lots to see whose car will out-drive whose.

How do they afford these expensive car modifications? For a small number of young men tied to the import car scene, parents finance these excesses but not in the case of these boys. Hours are spent doing low-wage work to provide just enough money for them to gain entry to this world of pulleys and H-pipes (aftermarket exhaust pipes), adjustable struts, sway bars, inter-cooler kits, and injectors defined in large measure by the practice of "moding" or alternately "tuning." Few in the group drive new cars because they can't afford them but others in the import car scene do. The middle and upper-middle-class Asian American young men from Orange County, California in Victoria Namkung's (2004) study "Reinventing the Wheel," focused on the import car scene and its role in Asian American youth culture, largely drove new cars, spending upwards of US$25,000 when figuring the upgrades and the initial cost of the car, according to Namkung's estimates. Those in Namkung's study came from more affluent families than the boys at Freedom High School, most were enrolled in college and had considerable disposable income of their own. Within the larger import scene in San Jose, this is also the case.

For this group of high-school boys, their time is consumed by their cars and racing, often at the expense of other activities. Few participate in organized team sports inside or outside school or other extracurricular activities; school itself is secondary in importance to racing for many. Like diehard footballers, snowboarders, and mountain climbers, these boys eat, sleep, and breath racing and cars (Wheaton, 2004, 2010). Their economic situation restricts directing the same amount of money into their cars that upper income and older kids do but it doesn't stop them from dedicating whatever money they do have into "tuning" their cars.

Thuy Vo, who owns a custom Honda Civic hatchback, works at Great America, a theme park where local youth toil for modest wages. All his income, he admits, is devoted to modifying his car's engine and exterior. To date he has installed a sway bar, allowing him to better handle turns at high speeds, he tells me, and a new exhaust. His door handles have been "shaved," leaving a smooth surface on driver and passenger side door, and he has removed the windshield wipers. In their place he has sprayed a commercial sealant on the windshield designed to repel the rain. The car has been lowered several inches, the "H" that normally resides on the car's hood, identifying it as a Honda, has been removed, and the back lights have been replaced. These exterior changes enable Thuy Vo to achieve what he considers "a clean look." In many ways a clean appearance achieves an aesthetic of speed. With sleek stream-lining, its center of gravity hugging the road, the car visually appears faster and not "frumpy" and "rumpled" like a standard stock Civic or worse a lumbering American giant like a Dodge or Chevy. In addition to these changes his car has been painted "egg shell white," a custom color, and he has installed red car seats, new "racing" seatbelts, a new steering wheel, a red racing stripe and red-and-gold rims, which he painted himself to resemble from a distance a very expensive set of rims he confides he cannot afford. Thuy Vo, like a number of these boys, uses his time in auto shop to work on his car (usually at the expense of completing the official class projects). On the weekends Thuy Vo along with the others in his crew convene at secret meeting spots to race against other imports. During the week, his time when not in school or at work is spent cruising the lots of shopping malls and local streets in the hope his car will be recognized, especially after all the work he has put into its transformation. Thuy Vo's car, which was always parked just beyond the auto shop's car bays, was the focus of much discussion among the students, racers and non-racers alike, in the four classes I observed. On one occasion I overheard one of the boys from a class remark to another, "Daammmn, I see that car everywhere." Thuy Vo has gained what he had hoped, a much sought-after visibility for his unique styling through his car.

Imports versus American Muscle

Thuy Vo, Don, Shrini, Vicrum, and Justin, along with other boys who participate in the import car scene, distinguish themselves from another groups of racers, boys whose allegiance is given unapologetically to American Muscle – Ford and

Chevy drivers who at Freedom High School number less than a dozen at best. Since the 1950s American Muscle has held sway over the "illegal" street and "legal" organized car-racing and hot-rodding scenes. Yet, in the last decade this booming import scene has threatened to denude hot-rodders of their claim to a number one slot. Writing on the wider social relevance of the import car scene in southern California, Victoria Namkung asserts that "the growing import racing scene has unquestionably changed the automotive industry and altered the dynamics of the vibrant car culture. . . . Import racing has propelled a historically invisible ethnic group onto center stage of the previously Anglo-dominated consumer market and culture" (2004: 160). Many would agree that the ascendance of import racing and import racers in the commercial world and the world of car enthusiasts has subverted the longstanding rivalry between Chevy and Ford, replacing it with a new one – a rivalry between domestics and imports. Two different logics organize the domestic and import scenes. Within the world of American Muscle, having a car that is either "fast," "loud," or "big," a car with "serious metal" – that is, engine power – translates into what the late French scholar Pierre Bourdieu (1997), writing on the social practices that produce social distinction and symbolic boundaries between dominant and dominated, called "symbolic capital." Symbolic capital, as Bourdieu argued, converts into "profits of distinction," serving thus as the foundation for the exercise of symbolic forms of violence, as the analysis that follows will demonstrate.

A car's "muscle" is not celebrated among participants in the import scene where far less emphasis is placed on horsepower or having a large engine. Instead quick, light-weight cars are coveted. Acuras and Hondas are regarded as superior to Mustangs – the reigning modern American Muscle car – because they are low cost and lightweight. A more powerful Honda engine (like the Prelude) can be easily "dropped" into a Civic. The more powerful engine in a lightweight car can make the car tremendously quick, particularly if it also has a nitrous oxide boost. The boys from Freedom High School insist that such a Honda could easily outrace a 4.6 or 5.0-liter Mustang. This claim, of course, is met with protest from those whose loyalty remains with American

Muscle, like Kenny and Tom who both drive brand-new, modified Mustangs and are part of the same crew. When I ask if they ever race against the imports, they are quick to tell me theirs is the superior car, assuring me it would hardly be considered a "fair" match. "It's not worth it," Tom says with a firm and confident nod of his head. "If you call it racing," Kenny adds with both sarcasm and exasperation. "Their car's really slow, my car's really fast."

Imports and American Muscle serve as axes around which the illegal street-racing scene, fluid in its form, membership, rituals, and rules coalesces. These two distinct sets of racers routinely convene in the same meeting places but import racers and domestics rarely race against each other. The groups are largely ethnically split, "You got your Asian Rice Rockets. Honda Civics that are supped up, got their Na's, their flo master's," JP, a white kid and self-described racer who drives a restored Chevy, explains. Melissa, who as a young woman sits on the sideline of these overlapping scenes, echoes JP's remarks, "Trust me, if you go out there and look, you'll see a complete difference between a Vietnamese car and a white person's car. Asian cars they'll always do a body kit. And that's why they call them *Rice Rockets*. Because their cars sound a lot different. . . . They do something different with their mufflers and their intakes." The antagonism between the two groups has intensified over the last several years as the ranks of the import racers swell and loyalists to American Muscle have attempted (with only some success) to reassert their claim to dominance over the world of car-racing.

Formally and informally, the racing scene operates as a space of competition and antagonism, where challenges by other racers are a routine and constitutive practice. Respect and recognition is bestowed to those who can "step up" and "hold their own" against those who already are recognized as the most skilled drivers with the fastest cars. Street-racing and car customizing are activities dominated by men – a set of performative practices, rituals, relations, and interactions through which young men work to craft coherent narratives of self and position themselves against other men (see Connell, 1995; Messner, 1992). These ritual encounters and displays can confer respect or disqualify and discredit work to solidify a ranking among men. It is this sense of intense competition that permits the link between cars and masculinity to endure (Gilroy, 2010). Perhaps this explains why high-level risk-taking assumes such prominence in this scene; the level of risk one is willing to take becomes the means to set oneself apart and lay claim to masculine authority and authenticity; in short, it is the measure of a man.

Risky Business: Boys Who Race

AB: Um, what's the fastest you've ever driven?

KENNY: 142 miles an hour.

AB: Really, on a highway?

KENNY: Uh-huh, on the freeway.

AB: Were you scared?

KENNY: Yeah.

AB: Well describe what it's like, I mean, I've never driven that fast.

KENNY: It's a rush, it's like crazy, like.

AB: Well, how do you feel?

KENNY: Calm, I feel really calm when I do it, like I don't know it just feels like you're flying or something. Yeah, it feels like you're floating across the road.

Daring, danger, and peril reside at the center of this competitive world of racing, constituting this as a world of risk. These boys race in search of a profound "experience" enabling them to transcend the shackles of time and place, to step outside the self as they step into the flow to engage risk and defeat it (Csikszentmihaly, 2008). They race to *feel* the intense sensation, difficult to describe on paper, that provides the means to anchor themselves within a physical world where one's existence is known because it is felt, and that provides a semblance of self-coherence against self-fragmentation made all the more meaningful at this moment in time. Kevin McDonald (1999) sees the search for intensity and visibility as central to the project of self-creation at this historical moment, a period of late modernity. Zygmunt Bauman (2000) defines late modernity, emerging in the last quarter of the twentieth century principally by flow, movement, fragmentation, and incoherence over stability and stasis. Bauman has called this moment "liquid modernity," which stands in contrast with "solid modernity," the period preceding it, and is marked by

disorganization, uncertainty, and a weakening of modern institutions of socialization such as family and school. Others have also recognized this as a period marked by rapid transformations in social organization and social experience, with profound effect on the identity projects of young adults and their transition into adulthood (Arnett, 2000; Furlong and Cartmel, 2007; Cieslik and Pollock, 2002).

These boys talk endlessly about the "rush" from racing, the "high" they get from being at the edge. The source of the rush? To test themselves against themselves and against others as they push the limits of danger and daring and, in doing so, gain highly coveted respect and recognition by other young men who race. Perhaps that is why when not racing they spend hours with others in their crew exchanging stories of near peril, what adolescent psychologist Cynthia Lightfoot (1997) regards as "risk narratives." These narratives comprise these boys "storyworlds" through which they forge a sense of self as worthy and build symbolic capital (see also Mirón and Inda, 2000). The auto shop is a particularly appropriate space in this regard since it provides opportunity to talk about cars, risk, and peril of all sorts. The boys spend hours hashing and rehashing details of past races, revising and revisiting wins and losses. "I used to race people on the freeway 'cause this car it always attracts people that want to race me so I always end up racing," Olie explains, "I'm really good at maneuvering through traffic and I make really crazy moves and stuff." On another morning boys trickle into auto-shop class settling into their seats as they chatter about the last weekend. John, a racer, begins to tell Mr O'Malley, the teacher, about his racing at Sacramento raceway over the weekend, describing how the rear axle and drive-shaft broke on his friend's Camaro SS, as a now large number of students listen. In this moment I am reminded of Daniel telling me the week before how he had blown up the engine of his Civic in an intense race where victory would have been his had he not pushed his engine beyond capacity. I hear countless stories of driving on bald tires, stripped struts, and ever-thinning break pads, all told with the apparent aim to affirm and be recognized for their participation in a world of risk.

I also hear several stories of tickets. Speeding tickets, especially tickets issued for "exhibition speed" and "reckless driving," which carry serious financial penalty, provide evidence of a willingness to take risk. Because tickets serve a symbolic role, carrying their own cachet, they are always announced to the group. Consider David's remarks: "I have a Civic at home," he offers, but he is prohibited to drive it since having his license suspended, he tells me and his now growing audience as he chuckles to himself. When I ask why, he clarifies, "reckless driving." He and another guy were "just fooling around" in a parking lot. He says in earnest, "we weren't even racing" but the cops detained them and inspected their car "because they think we do drugs." This resulted in a US$1,500 ticket and a suspended license which won't be returned for 10 months. Surprisingly, he is hardly upset. Perhaps he has resigned himself to the fact, or just as likely, it is because this has become a good story to tell, a story that earns him his rightful spot as a man among men.

The Need for Speed: Masculinity and Performance Vehicles

Cars have long served as objects for men to position themselves in terms of masculinity, providing occasion to perform and enact contemporary notions of the masculine. But the relationship these young men forge between cars and being masculine is far from straightforward, to the contrary it is beset by contradiction and struggle. To understand the nature of this struggle demands an understanding of the rapidly changing world in which boys are becoming men, which I alluded to earlier, and the place of gender in its organization. Michael Kimmel (1997) among other scholars has argued that modern masculinity is in crisis, its foundation rapidly eroding as the traditional anchors of manhood recede in importance or become all but impossible to obtain. Financial independence, for example, is increasingly unattainable since most young men will be unable to earn what labor union advocates once called "the family wage," especially if they intend to reside in communities like San Jose where cost of living is considerable (Benner, 2002). Outside the realm of sports, physical competence, a traditional marker of masculinity, carries little occupational prestige in a world organized around the exchange of information not displays of muscle. In an increas-

ingly post-traditional world, where "social roles" (e.g., the breadwinner) are less likely to serve as guides for action and identity formation, as Anthony Giddens (1991) and Zygmunt Bauman (2000) have separately argued, young men inevitably will face what Giddens himself has called "ontological insecurity and existential anxiety." Their participation in the world of cars and car-racing provides a space to manage the existential dilemmas of masculinity, where these young men work to construct and sometimes rework a set of boundaries to shore up masculine power and their legitimate claim to it through the expression of symbolic forms of violence.

These boys make significant investments of the self in fast cars and this "fast scene" as they traverse a changing world in search of recognition, visibility, and respect, in part because the traditional ways to gain respect as men are out of reach. They also confront other problems because their struggle to become men occurs in a context where masculinity is increasingly transparent as a social construct. Against a masculinity that reveals itself to others as an elaborate performance, these boys struggle to be authentic men. "I think, um, there's always some internalized pressures to drive a certain way in terms of my gender. There seems to be some expectation to drive fast and live and do everything fast," Richard, one particularly insightful 20-year-old, remarked. These young men must be convincing as men to others and also to themselves. As Giddens (1991) has argued, identity formation today occurs in a context where "the self is seen as a reflexive project for which the individual is responsible," demanding a heightened sense of self-awareness (p. 75). Men are increasingly expected to be reflective about their manhood in order to be seen as authentic and to avoid being pigeonholed as either hypermasculine or feminine. This sense of struggle to achieve an authentic masculine self by debasing and discrediting other men is well illustrated in the following example drawn from one of the countless electronic bulletin boards organized around street racing. The following posts represent an ongoing conversation occurring over several days about the meaning of a "real" racer.[4]

MALACHI #1: I've been in the game since 94. Not that duration is important, but for the last 9 years I've eaten, slept, dreamed and worked for going faster. My driving is always being examined, and my mechanical skills are always improving. The name racer always sounded stupid to me, but it's what I am. Who here is a real racer? Post up and tell me why. *Do not post if your just gonna list the parts you bought, and why your euro style tailights were a performance upgrade.*

Green Goblin #2 is the first to respond, offering the following:

> A racer is a one who races. I drive a Ford Explorer, but I've raced other SUVs. I know it isn't the fastest vehicle on the road, and I don't act like it is, but it IS at least faster than a lot of other SUVs. I don't go around places saying "I am a racer" but I have raced others in the past and I still do, so therefore, I am a racer.

This is followed by a series of messages. Their conversation rapidly becomes hostile, with repeated attempts by these men to debase other young men as they talk about their own relationship to cars. They position themselves against a particular group of racer who are recognized as "all show and no go," the aforementioned, "RICERS."

> ABCD123 #3: I see what you're getting at. I have a few friends like that. Some keep at it for more power, some keep at it, but for more speed. I don't consider myself a real racer. Maybe back in the day, I would drag anything that moved. Cars weren't as powerful, and the police was not an issue. There was more emphasis on being able to cut through traffic than actual horsepower, since mods were unheard off.
>
> SL PORN SERIES #4: I've been racing since 94 also back in high school. I guess I caught the bug from when pops was a kid. He raced anything from lola's old chevy station wagon, his triple deuce, GTO, Sting ray, Vet, his Suburban.
>
> We always BS about comparing apples vs oranges as no replacement to displacement. etc. . . He's a strong vette follower and a supervisor mechanic for PG&E. He's a real racer from drag to autoX, to go carts, to road courses. He's pretty impressed with imports and he also likes driving my turbo hatch. I do it for fun and not to be trendy. I've dragged charged buicks, Pop's C5, and a lot of Hondas. I respect anybody that

races and works on their cars. I do it for sport. *Unlike most ricers these days who drive to be trendy and be "noticed". Peace!*

> SLEEPER #5: Street . . . well that's just full of posers . . . it would be so easy for me to claim something that my car obviously does do . . . but it happens at the scene all the time (we usually call them ricers or idiots). I do push my car to the limits on the way back roads . . . if I have to drive 2 hours to find a remote spot, I will . . . with minimal risk to me, my car and more importantly others who wish not to be involved. I also, usually don't take anyone with me . . . the main reason is that most of the people in my town are all talk and I don't trust the abilities of other drivers. I do accept the risks and have no problem taking tickets if I'm doing something wrong . . . cops usually respect that too. I accept responsibility for my mistakes.
>
> LT. WHAT? #6: Fake racer. I pretend to drive my cars. They really drive themselves, they're the real racer.
>
> *Another thing, you ignorant prick, if you're going to talk shit in your sig, you might want to spell check. I'm sure you'll respond saying I don't know anything about the english language, much the same as engines, and 'your are' is proper english.*
>
> Lastly, did you really need to include a setup for your little rib at Nick? I'm sure only one with your intellect could put together that the comment in YOUR sig was FROM you. Thank you for labeling it for us mere mortals. *Eat a dick, bitch.*
>
> RUNNER #8: Let's not get into what is racing and what is not. I really don't like to drag now. I road race exclusively. I will drag once in a while though, I haven't for few years though.
>
> I wrench, I don't really like to. But when it's my ass on the line, I gotta know my car will be there for me. I don't trust anyone. I've been screwed. No one will care like I do. I've only bought one aftermarket body panel in my life, a Spoon CF lip for my old EG. I drive a WRX now. It's ugly and fast as fock. Not done yet, it's being built as a well rounded car. Suspension/Brakes/Power-Driving skill. That's all that matters to me. No euro tails, no Z3 gills, no supra headlights, no lighted washer nozels and no 15 year old on my hood! But the WRX will have some nicer panels in the end.
>
> *I remember when the scene was pure. When all we wanted to do was go faster. I sold my civic*

because I was tired of being associated with scum. Too harsh? Stop doing ghetto shit to the car, get rid of the euro tail lights.

These writers/racers define the boundaries clearly: "real" racers modify the performance of their cars and "imposters" make modifications for aesthetic appeal. In this sense, gender tropes are in play as examples of display are linked to feminine activity. In their struggle to be recognized as real racers, these young men distance themselves from feminine practices of paying too much attention to the body (car body in this case). Spending too much time "primping" renders the racer un-masculine. This can be seen primarily in the recurring challenge to gratuitous display that emerges, beginning in the first instance with Malachi: *"Do not post if your just gonna list the parts you bought, and why your euro style tailights were a performance upgrade."* At several points driving skill is privileged over aesthetic changes as they draw firm lines between those who are of the scene and those who are not.

I also witnessed attempts to draw distinctions between real racers and posers in the auto-shop class. On one occasion a group of import racers, Ping, Brad, and Vicrum, are at work on Ping's Civic hatchback. They are planning to attach a black lip to the bottom of the body of the car to give the appearance of the car being closer to the ground. Other kids hover around watching them as they work to figure how precisely they are to attach this lip. As I look on, I ask why they want to attach the lip to the car and one of the guys, the only non-import racer in the group responds with noted sarcasm: "To make it *look* lower," as he chuckles to himself before walking off. A few moments later another non-import racer approaches asking the group at work sarcastically, "Does it make it faster?"

American Muscle and Talking Trash

The comments posted on the bulletin boards that defined as "ricers" racers who focus on exterior changes rather than performance upgrades are revealing, as was the observation from auto-shop class. As SL Porn #4 remarked in his post, "most ricers these days who drive to be trendy and be noticed." Runner #8 comments, "I remember

when the scene was pure. When all we wanted to do was go faster. I sold my Civic because I was tired of being associated with scum. Too harsh? Stop doing ghetto shit to the car, get rid of the euro tail lights. " Sleeper #5 writes, "Street . . . well that's just full of posers . . . it would be so easy for me to claim something that my car obviously does do . . . but it happens at the scene all the time (we usually call them ricers or idiots)." Within the world of car-racing the term "ricer" or "rice rocket" is used interchangeably with the term "import." Ricers and rice rockets are Hondas, Nissan, and Acuras. Fords and Chevys are never called rice rockets.

The condemnation of "ricers" was widespread on these message boards. "All show and no go, that's rice," one post declares. "Ricer burners want to look performance but can't perform. I would rather have performance than looks," another wrote. The distinction between an authentic racer, somebody who is focused on power, speed, and skill, and a "poser" is presented through racialized metaphors that align cars and aesthetics with particular ethnic/race groups. This rivalry might be explained because these car scenes are ethnically organized. American Muscle continues to be dominated by whites, while the import scene is predominantly Asian. Recall my earlier remarks that American Muscle's reign in the racing world has been challenged more recently by Imports. American Muscle racers have managed this threat through attempts to discredit imports and import racers and by physically and discursively distancing themselves from this group. I repeatedly listened to young white, Mexican, and African American men aligned with domestics denounce any association with the import car scene, the cars, rice rockets, and its participants known as "ricers." "Yeah, I'm not into the car scene where they all like rice rockets," 17-year-old Cesar explains. Jorge echoes Cesar:

Rice rockets the small, you know, Hondas I don't like em. Honda Civics souped up, stereotypically Asian . . . I have no respect for imports . . . they give them too much credit . . . for what they've done and if it wasn't for I guess the American cars you've got bigger muscle cars . . . they wouldn't be around. And they still have to give respect to those cars cause you know who you're messing with and who you're not messing with [*laughing*].

Even within the group of import racers at Freedom High School the distinction between a ricer and racer was made. Brad tells me, "to hot rodders and cruisers we're all ricers in the [import] racer community." But to Brad and his friends there is a difference between an import racer and a ricer. In the words of sociologist Erving Goffman (1963), they "stratify their own" as they must manage a stigmatized identity (p. 107). Brad and his friends distance themselves from "excessive" exterior changes (pointing out some of the cars in the lot that are "ricers" or "border on ricers") as they struggle to maintain legitimacy within this world of risk and competition.

This disparaging talk directed at import racers and its reliance on a racial schema of "us and them" also emerges in a conversation during one of the focus-group interviews I conducted at another high school. While this was a racially mixed group of kids, significantly, there were no Asian kids. As was the case in other focus groups, the young men dominated the conversation. In this particular focus group, one of the boys, JP, a white kid and the oldest in the group, carried much of the discussion.

JP: I don't like imports.

AB: You don't like imports, how come?

JP: I just don't.

AB: So what do you like then, like what's kind of?

JP: Oh no, I have, I respect them, I don't say anything about them at all, I just –

AB: It's just not your style?

JP: Like them, they don't like muscle cars, and then they actually do go and talk crap about muscle cars.

AB: Who's they?

ADAM: I know.

JP: Imports.

ADAM: Asian people.

JP: If you think about it, you go buy a $20,000 car okay, it might have some advantages like air conditioning, CD Player and all that, but then you get a car for half the price, an American one, and it ends up out running all those cars, for half that price, and you put, you work that other half of the money into your car, and then you have a machine . . . it's crazy.

ADAM: What you call them is you call them imports and domestics, me and him both drive domestics, so that's Chevy, Ford all those, those are domestics.

JP: And then you got your imports which is like Honda, your Integra –

ADAM: Your Acuras.

TOM: Integra.

JP: All that crap is imports and that's the ones you hear nnneeeennneeeee goin' down the street, and stuff like . . . See I just like domestic cars a lot better.

JP starts out talking about cars but shifts his talk to the drivers. Ricers are no longer cars but people, Asians, as he condemns imports and import racers. Asians are constructed as the outsiders – the others against whom he and other hot-rodders craft their identities as men. This is further illustrated by additional comments he made in the course of the focus group. He draws specifically on the emergent stereotype of Asians as "bad drivers" as he again attempts to discredit not simply the import scene but an entire racial group.

JP: I think Chinese shouldnt really drive because they don't even really know how to drive.

CYNTHIA: Oh my God!

AB: Who?

ADAM: Asian people.

JP: No actually a lot of Asians.

AB: So why do you think that?

JP: [*imitating a Chinese accent*] Ohhhh, oh, you son of bitch, you wreck my car [*laughter from the group*].

AB: Well, what about American born Asians?

JP: Then they get out and they start yelling at you for parking your car.

AB: What do other folks think? So, is this like all Asian folks, like Asian born folks or –

JP: They can't see [*laughter again from the group*].

AB: [*referring to a comment by AS*] Well, okay, well he just said that your comment was racist.

TOM: No, actually Asian people are very good at racing, like I know lots of guys –

AB: [*referring to DH*] You just said it's because they are rich?

DH: Cause they always have nice cars.

AB: So are there any Asian kids that go to this school?

TH: A lot.

AB: So, well what do you think about that? So what if there was an Asian person sitting here right now would you be saying the same thing, or –

CJ: Maybe.

AM: I don't think so.

AB: You don't think so.

CC: I don't think so.

CJ: But, I mean they can't drive, seriously, they can't drive, they drive piece of shit cars, sounds like a god damn mouse running through your house. It's like come on now, get a real car. I don't like the ones that make so damn, so much noise, like the, the ones they call "rice rockets."

The idea that Asians can't drive also emerged in auto-shop class. On one occasion a group of us are gathered around Brad's red Civic hatchback as he balances his tires. The group of young Asian men around the car are talking about another car on the lot whose fender has a large scratch and Sean, one of the Asian boys, remarks as he explains the scrape, "He can't drive, he's Asian." Incredulous, Daniel, the only Mexican boy who hangs around with the import racers, responds, "Daaaammmnnn, and you're Asian." To this Sean retorts, "Yeah I can't drive I can admit it," as the groups collapses in laughter.

Interpreted one way, this comment reflects the psychosocial dynamics of racial dominance. After all, this statement is articulated by a young Asian man and is met with laughter by other young Asian men and in this sense reflects what Goffman (1963) called "identity ambivalence" in his analysis of stigma and stigma management. Yet, this comment about Asian drivers in the context of this largely Asian, all-male group also could be interpreted as a way to manage the enduring stereotypes, what Patricia Hill Collins (1990) refers to as "controlling images," used to discredit Asian men as less than men and thus justify their subordination. These boys know that JP is not alone in his censure of the import car scene or of Asians. By preemptively making the charge they

can control the joke themselves as they attempt to preserve a sense of being men in a context of an intense competition over the symbolic resources that define what is masculine and who may legitimately claim it.

This point is also illustrated in another instance. One early evening in 2001 I am driving across town to a restaurant for dinner and I pull up behind a Honda Civic at a stop light; it is an older model of the very car I have, but unlike mine its suspension has been lowered and while my muffler is barely audible, its exhaust buzzes each time the driver, a young Asian guy with short black hair shaped into small spikes, taps his foot on the accelerator. As I sit waiting for the light to turn green, I inspect this car, curious about its driver, who he is and where he's going. I notice that just above the car's back bumper is written in white script "*Got Rice?*" Within moments the light turns green and the small vehicle idling in front of me is gone, its rear lights fading as the distance between us grows. I am left in its wake. I imagine a scenario where this car is racing against another on a highway or empty street, it pulls ahead, leaving its rival behind, with a derisive, *Got Rice? Got Rice?*, all the more powerful as the last word is loaded with intention and mocking, a means to invert and convert the pejorative meaning of ricer and to call into question American Muscle's preeminence. Paul Connolly (1998) argues that young men will express deep racial animus in situations of tense competition, though they might not in other situations. Certainly car-racing is a space of hyper-competition. Because many import drivers are Asian, this struggle over dominance appears to be largely directed toward Asian young men and reflects the historical legacy of anti-Asian, nativist rhetoric.

Race constructs are routinely used to work out deep anxieties about masculinity, to define what is masculine and what is not. R.W. Connell (1987, 1995) has argued that normative masculinity depends on the hypermasculinization of black men on the one hand and the hyperfeminization of Asian men on the other. Certainly these struggles over definitional boundaries of masculinity are in play and thus useful for making sense of these exchanges among young men who participate in the car racing scene (see also Gilroy, 2010). The import car culture emerged as a distinctly

Asian American male youth culture within a broader context of hyperfeminization of Asian men. Cars became central to constructing masculine identity for young Asian men who had otherwise been excluded from the muscle car culture of the 1970s and 1980s since cars are coded as masculine. Yet many of these Asian young men as they forged alternative masculinities through the import car racing scene came to reject a "brutish" mode of masculinity epitomized in the muscle car of the 1970 and 1980s, distancing themselves from a masculinity rooted in white working class culture, a form traditionally defined by one's physical strength and skill in working with one's hands (e.g., mechanics).

Asian import racers, as a group who have historically been feminized, get discredited in this car world as others actively (re)feminize them. Yen Le Espiritu (1997) has argued, "Asian American men have been excluded from white-based cultural notions of the masculine," noting Asian American men are regularly depicted in a variety of media sites as "impotent eunuchs" and emasculated "model minorities" (p. 90). Feminizing Asian men is achieved in two specific ways. First, by arguing Asians can't drive, Asian men are positioned outside of a masculine world of skill, risk, and competence. Similar arguments made about women drivers also once served as justification to keep women off the road (Scharff, 1991). Second, Asian import drivers are feminized with "rice rockets" represented as cars with gratuitous display "all show, no go." Consider comments made by one writer, "jdanger": "I hope you guys see where I am coming from. These little jap cars are nothing but the nastiest, dumbest girl in school with plastic surgery."

One might also consider the possibility that attempts to discredit import racers as ricers through a critique of gratuitous display are also part of a backlash against Asians and Asian immigrants in a post-1965 American context. Changes in immigrant policy in the mid-1960s led to an influx of immigrant groups in the 1980s and 1990s, a time of eroding economic opportunity as manufacturing sectors have crumbled in the United States. A number of scholars and activists have noted a heightened anti-Asian, anti-immigrant sentiment in California and across the United States in the context of economic uncertainty. The charge of gratuitous display against

"ricers" may express hostility toward Asians for claiming too large of a piece of the proverbial pie thereby, displacing other groups from employment and housing opportunities (Espiritu, 1997; Rubin, 2004; Wu 2002). A deep racial animus against upwardly mobile Asians is present in JP's focus group where all Asians are defined as "being rich." Indeed, this has served as the very basis of the model minority myth that continues to target Asians as interlopers.

A larger narrative appears to be at work here reflecting deepening inequalities and conflict in an increasingly global world marked by ever-growing economic and social polarization. The rise of distinct ethnically based car scenes and the emerging rivalry between domestics and (Asian) imports arise out of a changing, competitive global world order where the perception that "America" must continually demonstrate their supremacy in the face of unwarranted attacks by outsiders. Consider these comments posted on another message board by "jdanger":

> You guys that LOVE imports can say all you want about how they're cool and stuff, but they still will be little jap cars. You say NOS this and turbo that, but nothing is gonna beat American Muscle. I know maybe some American companies are manufacturing in other countries but they still make better cars than Honda, acura and all the other jap brands. I do want to ask you one question. . .why fix up little crappy 4 bangers, when you can fix up a muscle car and get at least twice the power?

Comments posted of this kind often become the source of disagreement but seem to reflect long-standing anti-Asian ideas, ideas that catalyzed a chain of reactionary policies, panics, and sentiments against Asians and Asian countries over a century. From the Immigration Exclusion Acts of the 1800s and 1900s directed at Chinese immigrants and others, to the Japanese internment camps during World War II, to the "Buy American" movements that emerged in the 1970s and 1980s as US multinationals shifted production to outside the United States and US laborers (many of whom were white union men) lost their jobs (Newman and Giardina, 2011). Lillian Rubin (2004) has argued that anti-immigrant sentiments are often articulated by white working-class men because they are the ones who have lost the most (and are increasingly vulnerable) in a post-industrial America (see also Fine and Weis, 1998). This certainly is evident here.

Conclusion: Masculine Distinctions in a Changing World

At the center of the competitive and antagonist world of street-car racing, where what you know serves to define where you are and where the level of risk you're willing to take is the measure of a man, is a heated rivalry between domestics and imports: Hondas against Mustangs, "Ricers" against "American Muscle." I have argued that this struggle, because it is organized to position whites and Asian at odds, is racialized. Terms like "rice rockets," "ricers," and "riced out" operate as code words to talk about race, to participate in racial discourses, to express a veiled racism important to the exercise of symbolic violence by one group of young men against another. What stands behind these racial repertoires are young men's struggle for masculinity in a context where the traditional measures of being a man are increasingly out of their reach. For young men of color perhaps this has always been so. But young white men who align themselves with American Muscle, many of whom are working-class and have experienced a loss of status as they confront eroding job opportunities for the future and as those jobs that remain open to them in the service economy are defined as women's work, struggle to reassert their dominance in other ways. In this instance it is through the symbolic work of distinction. As Sarah Thornton (1997: 201) observes "distinctions are never just assertions of equal distance; they usually entail some claim to authority and presume the inferiority of others."

A study of cars provides an opportunity to map the messy cultural terrains where racialized masculine identities are formed, anchored, enacted, and transformed as young men are drawn into a complex of ideological, economic, social, and political processes through the uses of cultural objects. As Paul Gilroy (2001) has argued, an investigation of cars and the cultural fields they cross must "encompass the alienated but nonetheless popular pleasures of auto-freedom – mobility, power and speed – while appreciating their conspicuous civic, environmental and polit-

ical costs" (p. 89). Particular attention is given in this chapter then, to how these practices occur within a transforming social landscape, a post-traditional order where the traditional moorings for identity have been changed by globalization and the acceleration of production and consumption in late capitalism. Ours is a post-industrial world, where new forms of selfhood and social experiences have arisen, tied less to traditional organizations and institutions and increasingly to cultural objects available in a commodity culture (McDonald, 1999). Sociologist Don Slater (1997: 30) explains, "In a post-traditional society, social identity must be constructed by individuals because it is no longer given or ascribed, but in the most bewildering of circumstance: not only is one's position in the status order no longer fixed but the order itself is unstable and changing and is represented through ever changing goods and images." The consumer culture assumes critical importance as young people are called upon to craft their own identities.

The car-racing scene is also a significant site where young men construct accounts of who "we" and "they" are, and in this sense serves as a space through which racial ideas are formed and circulated in ways that have consequences for masculine identity formation as young men transition to adulthood in a changing racial and economic landscape wrought by global capitalism. As these young men construct their own identities they rely heavily on notions of the hypermasculine "other" and the feminized "other," both constructs recognized by the group as masculine imposters. The repeated use of racial repertoires in which other young men are discredited is one means by which claims to masculine authority, legitimacy, and authenticity are made. A legacy of race becomes meaningful to the boundaries invoked by these young men as they attempt to draw both symbolic and moral distinctions between real racers and imposters, between authentically masculine men and mere posers. Thus, young men, as they struggle to gain recognition and visibility as authentic men, reinscribe a racial order of masculinity through their participation in the world of cars and street-racing. They do so in a context where opportunity structures are increasingly insecure and anchors for the self elusive. Class, race, and nation mediate the struggles that unfold as young men vie for masculine capital in a global landscape marked by profound economic and social change. What the future holds in store for them as they move toward middle adulthood remains unclear. Uncertain economic futures suggest dramatic change in the identity projects undertaken and the objects used to anchor the self as men work to find a place in a world of men. Future investigations would be well served by attention to changes in the landscape of cultural life and its consequences for the life course and life transitions for this group of young men and others.

Notes

1   See   http://www.sanjoseca.gov/index.aspx?nid= 2046, accessed January 21, 2013.
2   The low-rider scene, as Best (2006) and Chappell (2010) have demonstrated, is organized by a different cultural logic.
3   1.5-generation migrants are immigrants who came to the host country when they were children or young teenagers, usually with migrant parents.
4   These passages appear as they were posted on the bulletin boards. I did not change typographical or grammatical errors. I have placed in italics those portions of the text that I identify as particularly important to this masculine struggle.

References

Arnett, J. (2000) "High hopes in a grim world: Emerging adults' views of their futures and Generation X." *Youth and Society*, 31 (3): 267–286.

Baudrillard, J. (2000) "The ideological genesis of needs," in Schor, J.B. and Holt, D.B. (eds.) *The Consumer Society Reader*, New York: New Press.

Bauman, Z. (2000) *Liquid Modernity*, Cambridge: Polity Press.

Beck, U. (1998) "Politics of risk society," in Franklin, J. (ed.) *The Politics of Risk Society*, Cambridge: Polity Press.

Benner, C. (2002) *Work in The New Economy: Flexible Labor Markets in Silicon Valley*, Oxford: Blackwell.

Best, A. (2000) *Prom Night: Youth, Schools and Popular Culture*, New York: Routledge.

Best, A. (2006) *Fast Cars, Cool Rides: The Accelerating World of Youth and Their Cars*, New York: New York University Press.

Best, A. (ed.) (2007) *Representing Youth: Methodological Issues in Critical Youth Studies*, New York: New York University Press.

Bourdieu, P. (1997) *Outline of a Theory of Practice*, Cambridge: Cambridge University Press.

Castellanos, T. (ed.) (2001) *KIN: Knowledge of Immigrant Nationalities in Santa Clara County*, San Jose, CA: Office of Human Relations of Santa Clara County and West Valley-Mission Community College District.

Chappell, B. (2010) "Custom contestations: Lowriders and urban space." *City and Society*, 22 (1): 25–47.

Cieslik, M. and Pollock, G. (eds.) (2002) *Young People in Risk Society: The Restructuring of Youth Identities in Late Modernity*, London: Routledge.

Collins, P.H. (1990) *Black Feminist Thought: Knowledge, Consciousness and The Politics of Empowerment*, New York: Routledge.

Connell, R.W. (1987) *Gender and Power: Society, The Person and Sexual Politics*, Stanford, CA: Stanford University Press.

Connell, R.W. (1995) *Masculinities*, Berkeley: University of California Press.

Connolly, P. (1998) *Racism, Gender Identities and Young Children: Social Relations in a Multi-Ethnic, Inner-City Primary School*, London: Routledge.

Csikszentmihaly, M. (2008) *Flow: The Psychology of Optimal Experience*, New York: Harper Perennial Modern Classics.

Espiritu, Y.L. (1997) *Asian American Women and Men: Labor, Laws and Love*, Thousand Oaks, CA: Sage Publications.

Fine, M. and Weis, L. (1998) *The Unknown City: The Lives of Poor and Working Class Young Adults*, Boston, MA: Beacon Press.

Furlong, A. and Cartmel, F. (1999) *Young People and Social Change: Individualization and Risk in Late Modernity*, Buckingham, UK: Open University Press.

Furlong, A. and Cartmel, F. (2007) *Young People and Social Change: New Perspectives*, Buckingham, UK: Open University Press.

Giddens, A. (1991) *Modernity and Self Identity: Self and Society in the Late Modern Age*, Stanford, CA: Stanford University Press.

Gilroy, P. (2001) "Driving while black," in Miller, D. (ed.) *Car Culture: Materializing Culture*, Oxford: Berg.

Gilroy, P. (2010) *Darker Than Blue: On the Moral Economies of Black Atlantic Culture*, Cambridge, MA: Harvard University Press.

Giroux, H. (1995) *Fugitive Cultures: Race, Violence and Youth*, New York: Routledge.

Goffman, E. (1963) *Stigma: Notes on the Management of Spoiled Identity*, New York: Simon & Schuster.

Kellner, D. (1997) "Beavis and butthead: No future for postmodern youth," in Steinberg, S.R. and Kincheloe, J.L. (eds.) *Kinder Culture: The Corporate Construction of Childhood*, Boulder, CO: Westview Press.

Kimmel, M. (1997) "The contemporary 'crisis' of masculinity in historical perspective," in Brod, H. (ed.) *The Making of Masculinties: The New Men's Studies*, Boston, MA: Allen & Unwin.

Lightfoot, C. (1997) *The Culture of Adolescent Risk-Taking*, New York: Guilford Press.

Mac An Ghaill, M. (1994) *The Making of Men: Masculinities, Sexualities and Schooling*, Buckingham, UK: Open University Press.

McDonald, K. (1999) *Struggle for Subjectivity: Identity, Action and Youth Experience*, Cambridge: Cambridge University Press.

Messner, M. (1992) *Power At Play: Sports and The Problem of Masculinity*, Boston, MA: Beacon Press.

Mirón, L. and Inda, J. (2000) "Race as a kind of speech act." *Cultural Studies: A Research Annual*, 5: 85–107.

Namkung, V. (2004) "Reinventing the wheel: Import car racing in Southern California," in Lee, J. and Zhou, M. (eds.) *Asian American Youth: Culture, Identity, and Ethnicity*, New York: Routledge.

Newman J. and Giardina, M. (2011) *Sport, Spectacle and Nascar Nation: Consumption and the Cultural Politics of Neo-Liberalism*, New York: Palgrave Macmillan.

O'Connell, S. (1998) *The Car in British Society: Class, Gender and Motoring, 1896–1939*, Manchester: Manchester University Press.

Rubin, L. (2004) *Families on the Fault Line: America's Working Class Speaks about the Family, the Economy and Race and Ethnicity*, New York: Harper Collins.

Sassen, S. (1998) *Globalization and its Discontents*, New York: New Press.

Scharff, V. (1991) *Taking the Wheel: Women and the Coming of the Motor Age*, Albuquerque: University of New Mexico Press.

Slater, D. (1997) *Consumer Culture and Modernity*, Cambridge: Polity Press.

Thornton, S. (1997) "The social logic of subcultural capital," in Gelder, K. and Thornton, S. (eds.) *The Subcultures Reader*, London: Routledge.

Wheaton, B. (ed.) (2004) *Understanding Lifestyle Sports*, New York: Routledge.

Wheaton, B. (2010) "Introducing the consumption and representation of lifestyle sports." *Sport in Society*, 13 (7/8): 1057–1081.

Wu, F. (2002) *Yellow: Race in America Beyond Black and White*, New York: Basic Books.

Further Reading

Bauman, Z. (2000) *Liquid Modernity*, Cambridge: Polity Press.

Best, A. (2006) *Fast Cars, Cool Rides: The Accelerating World of Youth and Their Cars*, New York: New York University Press.

Bourdieu, P. (1984) *Distinction: A Social Critique of the Judgement of Taste*, Cambridge, MA: Harvard University Press.

Chappell, B. (2012) *Lowrider Space: Aesthetics and Politics of Mexican American Custom Cars*, Austin: University of Texas Press.

Cieslik, M. and Pollock, G. (eds.) (2002) *Young People in Risk Society: The Restructuring of Youth Identities in Late Modernity*, London: Routledge.

Furlong, A. and Cartmel, F. (1999) *Young People and Social Change: Individualization and Risk in Late Modernity*, Buckingham, UK: Open University Press.

Giddens, A. (1991) *Modernity and Self Identity: Self and Society in the Late Modern Age*. Stanford, CA: Stanford University Press.

23

Chess as Art, Science, and Sport

Antony Puddephatt and Gary Alan Fine

Introduction

Former world chess champion Anatoly Karpov was once quoted as saying "chess is everything: art, science, and sport." Is chess all of these things? Why and how do these images resonate with chess players? In this chapter, we argue that chess can plausibly be linked to claims of art, science, and sport, yet the boundaries of these three realms are by no means neatly divided. How, for example, does chess complement but also expand traditional assumptions of sport, and how does "sport" link to both "art" and "science"? Beyond using chess to think about the relationship between sport, art, and science, we argue that chess informs a number of generic features of human association, including focus and attention, affiliation, beauty, status, collective memory, consumption, and competition. This chapter emerges from each of our separate research projects on chess as a social world. Both authors have conducted their own independent ethnographies of chess players, exploring the sociological implications of chess as a set of competitive, symbolic, and institutionalized social activities. Drawing on these ethnographic studies, we compare chess to other studies across the sociol-

ogy of art, science, and sport, in order to explore how chess fits into each of these categories, and how the essence of these categories are mutually dependent, fluid, and relational.

Both Fine and Puddephatt treat the social world of chess as a "subculture," though this term is not without controversy, particularly in the field of cultural studies. Put another way, chess is a community of action. As Andy Bennett (1999) and David Muggleton (2005) have argued in the context of youth subcultures, the term has gone through a number of changes since its origin in the Birmingham Centre for Contemporary Cultural Studies. Traditional conceptions of subculture as deterministic, rigidly conceptualized, and class-based designations of youth collectives were rejected by newer postmodern theorists, who would eschew all static categories of subculture, since the identities, activities, and beliefs of most groups are too heterogeneous, shifting, and fluid to pin down. Muggleton's solution in his (2000) study of punk subculture was to acknowledge that both traditional modernist Weberian notions of more stable "authenticity" exist in subcultural group definitions as much as fluidity, fragmentation, and hyper-individualism in members' ability to generate creative assemblages of cultural

A Companion to Sport, First Edition. Edited by David L. Andrews and Ben Carrington.
© 2013 Blackwell Publishing Ltd. Published 2013 by Blackwell Publishing Ltd.

images to furnish their identity. If chess is not a social category of participants, a shared commitment to action provides the game with a cultural vitality that characterizes chess as a subculture.

We argue that this image of subculture, as having both relatively fixed but also shifting and contested definitions, is consistent with a symbolic interactionist perspective (Fine and Kleinman, 1979; Prus, 1997). Interactionists (e.g., Blumer, 1969; Strauss, 1993) have always problematized static or structural definitions of what are better considered shifting subcultural arrangements. They also used the term subculture more broadly, to characterize myriad groups within the wider culture, not just those that are deviant or alienated. It is true that interactionist scholars have put less emphasis on the cultural "bricolage" of postmodern hyper-individualism than scholars working in cultural studies. Nevertheless, the symbolic interactionist conception of subcultural analysis is well suited to "cover the large complexes of interlaced activities [and the] . . . large variety of relations between the participants" (Blumer, 1969: 35), as well as the "local, embedded, and translocational" (Prus, 1997: 43) character of shifting subcultural involvements, activities, and identities.

While we are working largely from this symbolic interactionist framework, we also take inspiration from Belinda Wheaton's (2004) more recent argument for the concept of "lifestyle sports." The chapters in her book emphasize extreme sports, but the idea of a sport or leisure activity that shapes one's identity and lifestyle is right and proper. While many sport cultures are technically organized around specific forms of activity (e.g., surfing), the members' identities and secondary activities often go far beyond just these alone. Rather than people simply "playing at" surfing or chess, the activity becomes an all-consuming lifestyle and identity, bringing with it a host of relationships, philosophies, politics, and worldviews that people carry around whether they are engaged in the particular leisure activity or not. In the same way, any observation of the world of chess will demonstrate the relevance of the concept of "lifestyle sport" for many of the players, particularly as it becomes an all-consuming activity. With its share of misfits, cynics, and eccentrics, those "in" the social world of chess resonate with a certain common worldview and

set of sympathies that are carried far beyond the confines of tournaments and friendly games at the club. Those who might be outsiders elsewhere are often accepted within the chess community where eccentricity is put at a premium (Puddephatt, 2008; Desjarlais, 2011).

Over the years, chess has been a frequent topic for social scientists, perhaps because so many have been chess players themselves. Freudians believed that the unconscious appeal of chess was a result of the oedipal dynamics revealed in the game (Jones, 1931; Coriat, 1941). Psychoanalysts ask why many strong chess players displayed psychiatric disorders (Fine, 1956); the suggestion is that chess is often learned at puberty and pre-puberty by boys, and that the pieces represent various symbols that are key to ego-development (e.g., the king is a phallic symbol representing castration anxiety, the queen represents the mother, etc). Chess plays out oedipal dynamics of aggression and sex via the symbolic representations of the game. Those drawn to chess are thought to have problems balancing aggressive and sexual impulses due to a weakly developed super-ego, and hence are good candidates for neurotic traits later in life, echoing grandmaster Victor Korchnoi's observation that "no Chess Grandmaster is normal; they only differ in the extent of their madness."[1] While researching his recent ethnography of chess, Fine was told half in jest that each tournament should hire a psychiatrist. Others analyzed the supposed unconscious aspects of the game that pointed to aggressive and sexual tendencies (Cockburn, 1974; Melamed and Berman, 1981). Chess players enjoy describing the dysfunctions of their colleagues, both in matches and outside of the game, even while these colleagues are accepted as members of the community. Many of these psychoanalytic claims have been challenged since. For one thing, focusing on atypical cases such as Paul Morphy's paranoia or the drunken rages of some contemporary players is inadequate for generalizing to all chess players (Binet, 1966). Further, much of the analysis is based entirely on speculative Freudian assumptions that have little empirical support (Huaco, 1976), coupled with the irony that many psychoanalysts are also serious chess players.

Other psychologists have used chess to understand spatial memory, pattern recognition, and decision-processing. Testing strong players provides insight into perception, mental capacity, planning, and problem-solving abilities that extend beyond the game itself (Chase and Simon, 1973; Degroot, 1978; Grabner, Stern, and Neubauer, 2007). Others use chess to understand learning in relation to practice (Campitelli and Gobet, 2008), as well as the effects of gender (Chabris and Glickman, 2006), age (Fair, 2007), and personality (Bilalic, McLeod, and Gobet, 2007). The belief that chess has educational benefits is widespread, and has led to the growth of scholastic chess programs in the United States and elsewhere. Csikszentmihalyi (1975, 1997) used chess to develop the concept of "flow," the ability to achieve a level of focus where one loses self-consciousness, such that creative concentration is maximized. Other psychologists consider the more practical, "sports psychology" aspects of managing emotion, maintaining focus, building confidence, and avoiding time trouble in competition (Benko and Hochberg, 1991; Avni, 2001).

Sociologist Michael Carroll (1981) built on the French structuralist tradition of Lévi-Strauss to study the history of chess rules in regard to the legal movement of the pieces. He found that the logic of the moves through history, without exception, is built upon a patterned foundation of oppositions, mimicking Lévi-Strauss's argument about the necessity of opposition as the basis of cultural constructions. Galitis (2002) considered an Australian school chess club as a site of gendered stratification, where gender inequality is reinforced in nuanced ways through play and social organization. Building on ethnographic analysis, anthropologists Wendling (2002) and Desjarlais (2011) both focus on the creation of status systems and community within the world of chess, examining France and the United States respectively. Kunnen (2002), a Dutch scholar, suggested that the development of chess style reflects a process of "sportification," suggesting the linkage of performance with competition. Puddephatt (2003) considered the sociological aspects that contribute to the experience of focus, or the "flow" experience, as players strive to eliminate self-conscious thoughts and outside distractions in order to implement "strategic activity." He also considered the career mobility experienced by amateur players as they try to improve their skills and climb the hierarchies of local clubs (Puddephatt, 2005). More recently, he analyzed the concept of "devotion" by exploring the intersection of ritual and social organization in chess, treating the chess world as a "greedy institution" (Puddephatt, 2008).

This range of research suggests the richness of chess as a field of action. In considering the social psychological aspects of chess, Benko and Hochberg (1991), both strong players themselves, argue that the game takes many forms, depending on the style and approach of the player. They consider chess as a "fight," an "art," a "sport," a "life," and a "war." Fine found these metaphors in his ethnography of adult players – including those at the grandmaster level as well as at local clubs – many of which could coexist in the same experience. Players approach the game itself from different philosophical perspectives, but they also feel drawn to chess clubs or casual games for different reasons (Puddephatt, 2003). Players define the benefits of social membership as belonging, competition, personal enrichment, excitement, challenge, and status rewards. Some treat chess aesthetically, as an art form and a rewarding psychological experience. Others see it as the ultimate form of competition, and find motivation in the experience of closely contested battles, and climbing the ladder of local or national rankings. Still others treat chess as a science, a set of puzzles waiting to be solved. To capture these diverse meanings, we use a typology of chess as art, science, and sport, examining the game in light of these alternative yet related realms of social and institutional meaning.

Chess as Art

"The Chess pieces are the block alphabet which shapes thoughts; and these thoughts, although making a visual design on the chessboard, express their beauty abstractly, like a poem" (Marcel Duchamp). No two games in chess are identical and, as a result, the seemingly unending avenues of mystery have enticed many players, adding to the cultural status of the game. Purdy once quipped "chess is as much a mystery as a woman." Fine has heard players liken chess to improvisational jazz in the way that combinations of pieces emerge over the course of a game. The mystery, art, and beauty of chess is a theme that appeals to many, and to compliment a particularly inspired combination, players use the term "brilliancy." Of course, on the other hand, many chess games, even at the elite level of play, can be drawn out, mundane, and boring. Players may win out of a brilliant and elegant sacrifice, or may simply grind out a fairly predictable or even ugly win, based on slowly leveraging a dominant position. We are not arguing that chess is any more inherently beautiful than other games in any real sense, just that the aesthetic moments of chess do capture a significant romantic appeal, according to the players. This artistic appeal can also be seen in the intricate designs of boards and pieces, the use of chess analogies in poetry and stories, and as a motif for designs in marketing and advertising.

The artistic aspect of chess play is certainly a major appeal of the game, and this appreciation is not lost on amateur players. The talk of symmetry and beauty is not seen just in poems and romantic slogans from grandmasters, but is described by amateur players as well. Consider the following quotation from an amateur (male, 21):

It's kind of hard to see, but there's beauty in it. The symmetry of the pieces and the idea of threatening, sometimes it all just comes together and it gets distracting at points, but sometimes I really just sit back and go "Wow, look at this game." It's like a perfect balance, an absolutely perfect piece of art . . . for instance the idea of a checkmate that's six moves away is just beautiful. (Puddephatt, 2003: 275)

Much of this beauty is perceived as the elegance of solving a complex problem that has only one possible solution, requiring an exacting plan that envisions all potential contingencies. William James (1909) posited that truth is best located not in a correspondence of knowledge with the real world but in the deeply gratifying psychological experience of realizing an action that was previously frustrated or blocked. Grandmaster Siegbert Tarrasch is often quoted as saying "Chess is a form of intellectual productiveness; therein lies its peculiar charm . . . in chess everyone can, everyone must, be intellectually productive, and so can share in this select delight." This is true in mathematics as well, since style is observed through the most elegant solutions or proofs and as Fine was told, "Chess is all about style." Undoubtedly these are the most heralded moments in chess, from the awe experienced from an exacting answer to a daunting and complex problem.

Creative moves, counter-intuitive plays, and unexpected sacrifices or combinations add a romantic element to the game. Furthermore, if they are decisive in forcing a winning position, they represent elegant solutions to seemingly impenetrable defenses. The mid-century grandmaster and chess scholar Reuben Fine (1956) famously stated:

Combinations have always been the most intriguing aspect of Chess. The masters look for them, the public applauds them, the critics praise them. It is because combinations are possible that Chess is more than a lifeless mathematical exercise. They are the poetry of the game; they are to Chess what melody is to music. They represent the triumph of mind over matter.

If combinations are the climax of chess games, it implies that each game has a narrative from which a climax could emerge. In support of this idea, Gary Alan Fine spent time with players as they reviewed their games after they concluded, creating an account of what went right and what went wrong, and showing alternative lines of play. Since players exchange moves and respond to each other's play in a cumulative manner, they reveal how the tension of the game builds. To an outsider, the board is comprised of a random formation of pawns, knights, rooks, and other pieces. But to the players involved, these configurations are anything but random, having their own history, meanings, logic, emotional content, and aesthetic appeal. Positions are shared by the players and onlookers, and are constituted by a localized and symbolically meaningful sense of collective memory. Chess games are aesthetically intense because each player had a constructive hand in how the configuration on the board was developed to that point. The players may imagine potential outcomes taking root from controlling squares, critical turning points, and different tactics and strategies based on the texture of the game.

Linked to this aesthetic experience is the degree to which participants can become involved in the game subjectively, and block out external distractions. Csikszentmihalyi (1975, 1997) developed the concept of "flow" to capture the capacity of people to focus on an activity to such a powerful extent that they lose awareness of time, external surroundings, and self-consciousness. Such experiences become "autotelic," since the boundaries between the self and the activity fade. For Csikszentmihalyi, this is when we are most creative, productive, and happy in our work, leisure, and personal lives. It is no surprise to us that Csikszentmihalyi (1975) selected chess as a prime example through which individuals generate flow through focused activity. The players he talked with reported performing best when the flow experience is maximized and they could "dig in" to the game (p. 66). Sara Ahmed (2010) recently critiqued Csikszentmihalyi since he misses the fact that one's place within social, economic, and cultural locations greatly determines whether individuals will have the privilege to experience flow. She argues that flow has been treated as an overly psychological concept, which fails to ask who in society is lucky enough to "let go" in their everyday lives and engage in meaningful, creative activity that leads to such enriching experiences. This is an important sociological corrective. While many of the players in our samples were from underprivileged socioeconomic positions, and often marginal to mainstream society, they were nevertheless able to become deeply engrossed in chess, and experienced considerable enjoyment from these flow experiences. Indeed, this is a major draw for those who might otherwise be unhappy since it provides a place to go that is far away from life's problems and worries. Both Fine and Puddephatt found this idea emerge in discussions with players: "It's a kind of stress, but it's a kind of positive stress. And it brings you even more into the game, so . . . you forget about all of the things around you. . . . It was all about the game, nothing else" (Puddephatt, 2003: 274).

Such a model of flow is mirrored in sociological theorizing. Durkheim (1912) posited that religion is important not because belief systems address a higher spiritual reality but because religious assemblies enable intense ritual activity. By participating in shared rituals, group members strengthen their bonds, invest intense emotional energy in each other, and, from this state of "collective effervescence," generate, reshape, and or reinforce shared beliefs and symbols, which both echo and direct the moral order of society.

Goffman (1967) built on Durkheim's work on the analysis of ritual, demonstrating how this process applied to different spheres of modern society. Considering games, Goffman (1961) argued that the ritual experience of play would be maximized, and most engrossing, when the sides were relatively even, such that the outcome is not predictable from the beginning. He wrote "Not only are games selected and discarded on the basis of their ensuring euphoric interaction, but, to ensure engrossment, they are sometimes also modified in a manner provided within their rules" (Goffman, 1997: 129; see Fine, 1983: 182). This sociological concept of engrossment parallels the psychological concept of flow in that activities are more all-encompassing when the frame of the game, in contrast to the frame of mundane reality, is emphasized. Randall Collins (2004) extended Durkheim's ritual theory to explain when such engrossing ritual encounters are likely. He argues that four factors characterize successful (engrossing) versus failed (unfocused) rituals: (1) bodily co-presence; (2) barriers to outsiders; (3) mutual focus of attention; and (4) shared mood. Csikszentmihalyi (1975, 1997) adds that in addition, "flow" experiences are maximized when people (5) receive constant and relatively immediate feedback; and (6) feel control over the activity. Since chess scores highly in each of these categories, there is little wonder that players report being engrossed in closely contested games. In tournament play, directors enforce quiet to reduce distractions and set time limits to keep the game active while increasing tension. Given that winning and losing affects players' ratings, games have significance for the identity of participants. As such, tournament chess tends to increase engrossment in contrast to casual games.

If chess can be seen as art, then its culture and social organization might be considered an art world, raising questions of how reputation and status develop from its inner workings. Examining art in light of structural inequality, Pierre Bourdieu (1993) considered how positions are organized relationally to one another within an art field, as actors struggle for upward mobility by incorporating the evaluative rules of their artistic peers. However, high-status positions are scarce, and require competitive advantage in both art (Becker, 1982; Bourdieu, 1993; Fine, 2004) and science (Bourdieu, 1975; Collins, 1998). In the field of chess, gaining "rating points" (a numeric and widely utilized indicator of chess skill) is always relative to the performance of others, so the ranking one enjoys in a local city club, or the world stage, is only meaningful in terms of one's competitors.[2]

Status is not only internal to fields but, as Bourdieu (1993) argued, is also related to positions in the wider society. Puddephatt (2008) found that many players who are devoted to the game in local clubs hail from meager socioeconomic positions. Some of the stronger players enjoy an almost priest-like status, and garner much positive attention and praise from the other players even though they may be seen as "misfits" in the outside world. The idea of the chess player as weird or deviant was a common trope in both authors' research. Many of the top local club players are often socially awkward, and at times so devoted to the game that they did not hold regular jobs. A classic adage from chess lore is that "the ability to play chess is the sign of a gentleman; the ability to play chess well is the sign of a wasted life." We take an agnostic position on this, but marvel at the commitment demonstrated by players as they devote themselves so fully to the game.

Chess as Science

Many players view chess as a science, and often chess players have jobs in technical or scientific vocations (many high-school chess coaches teach science). The metaphor of chess as science relies on the traditional image of science as a value-free, objective, and rigorous process to uncover the truth. In the case of chess, this suggests the struggle to find the one best move. For these players, worrying about "chess psychology" is a wasted effort; preying on opponents' perceived weaknesses is not necessary if the best possible move in a position can be found through rational deliberation. As a result, players often have postmortems after their games to attempt to discover what move they should have made at certain critical points. In this vein Bobby Fischer once announced, "I don't believe in psychology. I believe in good

moves." The idea is that long-term strategies and short-term tactics can be developed through close study of the basic principles of chess and a rigorous understanding of the logic of moves. Aron Nimzovich's (1936) *Chess Praxis: The Praxis of My System* was intended to emphasize such fundamental principles as "centralization" and "over-protection," basic principles (or laws) of the game, using a scientific rhetoric to argue for the superiority of his system.

This view of chess as rational and objective is challenged when one realizes that like science itself (Merton, 1938), the development of chess has had a contingent historical development. Theories of chess have evolved over history with fits and starts, and much of what stands as "objective theory" cannot be easily detached from stylistic preferences. Innovation in chess is necessary for grandmasters to dethrone their predecessors and earn their stature; the tactical and strategic answers that worked in relation to previous models are translated into an approach that is alleged to be objectively superior. As games are won and lost, the "correct" approaches to the game change, and become newly affirmed and reframed, which suggests a further metaphorical likeness to science.

Of course, scholars in the social sciences have long challenged traditional assumptions about science as a value-free enterprise to discover truth. Kuhn's (1962) analysis of scientific paradigms as well as contemporary studies of scientific practice (Pinch, 2007) have shown that the rational and objective basis of science cannot be easily detached from cultural and institutional contexts, practical contingencies, and career trajectories. Objectivity and truth claims are judged relative to reputations and scientific politics, which are often contested and fought over (see Bourdieu, 1975; Collins, 2009). In chess, as in science, players may claim allegiance to one paradigmatic approach over another, for example preferring the strategic approach of Botvinnik over the tactical attacking style of Tal.

Kuhn (1962) famously rejects the model of scientific knowledge as a steady and linear accumulation of neutral facts. Instead, he argues that knowledge progresses, much like other social and political institutions, in dramatic shifts. Kuhn argues that scientists do not study the natural world from scratch but are oriented by culturally acquired scientific paradigms that provide the basic assumptions, theories, and methods appropriate to investigate a given set of phenomena. As paradigms begin to fail due to the steady build-up of anomalous evidence, new paradigms arise in response, which fundamentally split off from the beliefs of the prior period. To appreciate how this model of scientific progress relates to chess, we briefly detail the centuries old history of the game (Krogius, 1976; König, 1977; Kopec and Pritchett, 1980; Euwe and Nunn, 1997). What is most apparent in the development of chess theory is that, as with Newton or Einstein in the natural sciences, the role of "exemplars" is key to establishing the "paradigm," or the accepted style or approach valorized in a given period of chess theory. Euwe and Nunn (1997: 8) note that "succeeding generations of experts have contributed to the development of chess play, but it was the style of some outstanding individual which moulded the thinking and style of play of his time." The reputation of these chess exemplars furnished the paradigm-like understandings of the game that would develop at various historical moments, which eventually trickled down to everyday players (König, 1977: xiv).

Much like Kuhn's description of pre-paradigm science, the development of theory in chess represented a slow development in the early years. In the first recorded chess games that used modern rules, there did not seem to be much coherent theory in place. Of course, modern players can find "flashes of genius" in the games, but a systematic account of chess principles to orient play seemed to be absent for many centuries. Discussing games documented from the 1600s, Euwe and Nunn (1997: 9) explain that:

> the primitive chess player lived, so to speak, from hand to mouth. He made his move and hoped for the best. It was a matter of excursions with the pieces, punctuated by pleasant little episodes such as winning a piece or giving check – especially giving check, which had a rare fascination for the early players. However systematic play was virtually non-existent; what happened on the board was largely a matter of chance.

In the early days of chess, there was no unifying theory, systematic principles, or strategies around which players could converge. It is true that the success of the seventeenth-century player Greco served as an "exemplar" of sorts (his style influential for at least 100 years afterward), but his approach was never systematized.

This lack of systematic theory in chess changed with the advent of Philidor (1726–1795), the first famous chess master to write an approach to the game that outlined basic principles or fundamental laws of chess. Philidor famously argued that "pawns are the soul of chess." Rather than treating pawns as unimportant, and emphasizing the rapid development of the other pieces, Philidor believed that a strong pawn structure framed one's attack and defense. As such, he recommended a slow, methodical approach, delaying major operations until a dominant pawn structure was secured (Euwe and Nunn, 1997: 14–15).[3] Today Philidor's belief in the power of pawns is emphasized less, but the importance of pawn structure remains central. Nevertheless, he presented a clear set of principles with which players could view and approach the game. As such, Philidor's legacy of play represents the first key exemplary contribution to a coherent paradigm for modern chess.

In time, Philidor's preference for a slow positional approach to careful pawn development was challenged as opponents found alternative strategies that proved successful. Suffering defeats using Philidor's system can be considered as theoretical anomalies to the model of chess strategy that he championed. A new paradigm set to solve the shortcomings of the perceived passive approach of Philidor was required. Thus, a new focus on combinations of pieces, gambits, and strong attempts to checkmate without regard for material considerations became the organizing principle of the game.

> Everything turned on attack and counterattack. Passive play, defence, refusal of sacrifices . . . the setting up of a pawn phalanx – these and all such ideas were right outside the mentality of the chess player of the first half of the 19th Century. He was spellbound by the beauty of combination, and in this realm many an elegant production resulted. (Euwe and Nunn, 1997: 19)

The major protagonist of this approach was Adolf Anderssen. Anderssen had little interest in the "sober truth" of searching for an objective set of basic principles, but he emphasized the sacrificing of pieces in order to achieve exciting tactical forays and attacks that might lead to checkmate. This unrelenting style became popular in the chess world. As Anderssen was the dominant chess player in the mid-nineteenth century, his success publicized his model of play. Following the success of Anderssen and subsequently Paul Morphy (1837–1884), the preferred style of chess for most of the nineteenth century tended to be full of tactical assaults without much explicit consideration of pieces or position. Following Kuhn's logic, this is because it solved the weaknesses of Philidor's approach, coupled with the powerful charismatic and sponsoring effect of endorsement by emerging chess players of the subsequent generation.

This approach would undergo another radical shift as Wilhelm Steinitz (1836–1900) first presented a scientific rendering of chess by explicitly analyzing the game through fundamental principles of positional play. Steinitz developed his thought on the long-term, strategic elements of positional advantage. As the most prolific writer in chess of his time, publishing the *International Chess Magazine*, Steinitz had an institutional forum to disseminate and popularize his beliefs. Eventually his theories of chess began to coalesce into a body of systematic knowledge that is still routinely taught to amateur players. Steinitz believed that all chess positions could be objectively evaluated as each side would have advantages as well as weaknesses (Euwe and Nunn, 1997: 44–45). Today players will often refer to particular squares as "strong" or "weak" and pieces as "good" or "bad." Equilibrium was the point at which the advantages and weaknesses of each side, based on the positions of their pieces, cancel each other out and could be measured numerically – today, a feature of computer chess programs.

After Steinitz, many players added refinements to the existing stock of knowledge about chess, and "virtuoso players" (e.g., Lasker, Capablanca) developed hybrid versions of both positional and tactical/combinative skills; in Kuhn's terms, they were engaging in "normal science." Siegbert Tarrasch (1862–1934) was a key writer of chess theory in this period as he developed simple practical rules (still followed by amateur players) based on these principles. In time, new approaches

developed that challenged the stagnancy developing from this previous era, giving rise to yet another paradigm. This is often referred to as the "hyper-modern" approach of players such as Alexander Alekhine, a world champion in the 1930s. One of the ideas that came about with this movement was to develop control of the center squares using pieces placed near the edges of the board (Euwe and Nunn, 1997: 114–117). Hyper-modern openings looked different from and contrary to traditional openings. Opening principles that were previously thought to be eternally valid were being overturned in favor of new, creative possibilities.

Chess knowledge continues to evolve into the contemporary period. Today we are perhaps in another phase of "normal science," seen through the incremental advances and styles of such players as Bobby Fischer, Anatoly Karpov, Garry Kasparov, Vladimir Kramnik, and Viswanathan Anand. The development of sophisticated computer programs and large databases of previous games allows players to test their theories, but as yet no revolutionary approach has developed, and most players attempt to incorporate different models that have withstood the test of time. Technique, skill, calculation, and knowledge of the positional principles of the game have become overshadowed by detailed research and preparation and the memorization of deep opening repertoires where innovative moves can be tested. Chess, mired in a sophisticated normal science, awaits a new paradigm.

For chess knowledge to be influential it must be effectively disseminated and sponsored, a process with parallels to academic knowledge. First, a dizzying literature is available to the players, as more writings exist on chess than all other games combined. Books are available for beginners that introduce all aspects of the game, which are analogous to introductory textbooks for physics, psychology, or sociology. As players become more experienced, they advance to discussions of particular topical issues. They might purchase a book on opening principles, or tactics and combinations, akin to more advanced academic treatises. As players progress, there is no end to the specificity and specialization of topics. They may read material, for example, on the finer points of one variation of a specific opening line, paralleling "reference books" aimed at professional academics with sufficient training to understand them.

In the world of chess, players cannot simply develop their skills by reading theory books in isolation; the development of expertise is a social activity. Advancement relies on a dialectical process of reading chess literature, learning from others, and applying this knowledge in practice. Through becoming embedded in networks of knowledge producers and consumers, as well as rituals of competitive activity, players begin to develop a chess *habitus*. They develop stocks of taken-for-granted habits, preferences, and dispositions, which shape how they approach all aspects of the game. The same can be said for scientists, whose knowledge and expertise does not develop purely through the acquisition of diagrams and book-learning but also through tacit skill development that can only be accrued through a long immersion in scientific networks (Collins, 2009). As such, much knowledge in chess is not internalized entirely at the conscious level. Krogius (1976: 13) quotes grandmaster Richard Reti's statement that "players ask me how many moves ahead do I normally calculate in my combinations and are very surprised when I reply (truthfully) that generally it is not even one." Why? Because the knowledge players develop toward the game is, like in science, largely the development of trusted habits of thought and intuitive practice. He trusts the move is correct even though he does not justify this to himself explicitly in the moment of action.

Chess as Sport

How does chess fit into a sociological conception of modern sport? Building off of the modernization theory of Durkheim, Weber, and Parsons, Allen Guttmann (1978) put forth seven criteria for modern, as opposed to premodern, forms of sport. These included secularism, universalism, specialization of roles, rationalization, bureaucracy, quantification, and the quest for records (p. 16). Giulianotti (2005: 22–24) has criticized Guttmann's model, arguing for the counterpoints to each of these ideas. For example, modern sport is not entirely secular, as we still have need for pregame ritual ceremonies and superstition. While counter-examples can undoubtedly be found for

each category, Guttmann (2004) argues that it is all a matter of degree: modern sports are much more characterized by these properties than premodern sports even if counter-examples abound for each category. While some aspects (e.g., universalism) are not realized in full (many people will never get the opportunity to access certain sports let alone thrive in them), the more sports modernize, the more universal they become.

So where does chess fit in Guttmann's criteria for modern sport, and how might it challenge some of these categories? Certainly chess seems to be a secular game, and is often used as a cultural symbol that is emblematic of rationalization. The game is largely universal since those from broad social spheres participate, and it is found throughout the globe. Still, women are strikingly underrepresented in chess, and Russians and Eastern Europeans still dominate as chess elites. The roles of players are not specialized, though the various segments of the game certainly are. Certainly the bureaucracy of chess has a wide institutional canopy and extensive formal rules, linking tournaments to the same rating system and player rankings the world over. Statistics and records are important in chess, evidenced by the obsessive move-by-move documenting, annotation, analysis, and dissemination of grandmaster games. History is maintained in terms of the heroic lore of chess players such as Bobby Fischer successfully dethroning the Soviet champion Boris Spassky. There is a heavy rhetorical emphasis in chess on keeping equal conditions of competition, with strict rules and an exacting time system used to ensure no side has an advantage. This modern norm is evident in players' complaints about the fairness of tournament conditions, such as Kasparov's belief that the computer match against "Deep Blue" was rigged because humans were illegally "coaching" the computer behind the scenes.

Ensuring equality of conditions is important because chess games can be highly competitive. This thrills and motivates players, and shapes local hierarchies and status structures. It is difficult to imagine an activity that is more competitive, and the organizational basis of chess provides for intense competition during the match and the distribution of status rewards afterwards. Many players describe their love for chess as a result of the "cut-throat" competitive aspects of play. In this sense, chess resembles a fight or a war: a desire to kill and avoid being killed. Benko and Hochberg (1991: 108) describe this aptly: "If you have ever had the experience of suddenly realizing that you were about to lose a game you thought you were winning, you know your body reacted exactly as though your life were being threatened: your heart pounded, your pulse raced, your stomach did flip-flops, your skin broke out in a sweat." Puddephatt (2008: 168) quotes a master-level player who describes the hyper-competitive approach of some of the top players of a local big city club: "The masters at the top . . . very competitive, and big egos . . . their whole attitude . . . that I am going to crush you. And I will be extremely rude. And I will do whatever is necessary to crush you." Another player responded to Fine, "Chess is like hand-to-hand combat. It's so visceral. How can I hurt you?" Such metaphors are so common as to be unremarkable.

Why is chess so competitive? Much of the answer is found in how chess is organized, and in the institutional framework embedding local club play. Of course, chess need not only be played at competitive tournaments, and often is a simple pastime for fathers and sons, siblings, and friends on a lazy weekend afternoon – a more complex version of "Candyland." This is markedly different from competitive, club-level, tournament play, where chess as sport is evident. Local clubs are organized under the rules governed by national chess organizations. In the United States, this is the US Chess Federation (USCF), while in Canada it is the Canadian Chess Federation (CFC); the world chess federation is FIDE (Fédération Internationale des Échecs). Many clubs pay dues to national organizations so that their tournaments are officially tracked, so players in the club can gain or lose "rating points" that measure their skill in comparison to others. Ratings range from the hundreds for a rank novice to over 2800 for a top grandmaster. As of 2004, the average rating for a member of the USCF was 1068.

The players' ratings often serve as a form of identification to the chess community and for the chess players themselves. Thus, calling someone a 1900 or 2300 player has meaning within the subculture and resonates with the player's sense of self. Ratings determine what tournaments players

can access, and what divisions (or "classes") within the tournament they can play. Players receive adjustments to their ratings based on a mathematical computation of the game's outcome in light of the ratings of their opponents. Rating points are treated as accurate, reliable, and universal indicators of chess skill, even though these can be misleading at times. For example, a player can never lose more than 200 ratings points from his/her highest level (this is known as one's rating floor), and so may be far weaker than what their ratings suggest. Others – particularly younger players on the way up – may rapidly improve before their ratings are updated, and are often far stronger than their ratings suggest. Still others might intentionally lose games to be placed in a lower, less competitive, category in a tournament for a better chance to win the prize fund, known as "sandbagging." Nevertheless, ratings are generally viewed as accurate designations of skill, and therefore translate into social status, prestige, and respect, as the following interview excerpt explains:

They are judged by their current rating. If they are clean, dirty, doesn't matter. We are aware there are people there who are nuts, or they don't dress well, they might be poor, they might be rich. I guess we are aware of these things, but as far as who we want to talk to? The cliques that form and so on? It's chess skill and rating. (Puddephatt, 2008: 165)

The flip side is that players who often lose have low ratings and thus low status. Since ratings are public, this creates a "visible weakness" (Goffman, 1963) in the identity of low-rated players, sometimes pushing such players away from clubs where they feel unappreciated. This is evident in the self-deprecating humor, insults, and deferential behavior often exhibited to others by the weaker players. These players are often not given much respect by the stronger players, and Fine discovered that some players choose to cultivate a role for themselves as pushovers, easy to beat, thus being pleasant partners whose games are usually satisfying for their opponents. One's chess skill and rating trump traditional sociological indicators of social status within the club, bolstering the relevance of micro-sociological inquiries into the performance and presentation of status

(Sauder, 2005) and situational stratification (Collins, 2004).

If people join a chess club it is expected that they are eager for sanctioned, competitive play, and hence their skill will be assessed to place them in a hierarchy. Clubs are routinely organized around competitive match play, or most often, local tournaments. Most clubs hold an annual club championship, with several other tournaments that run throughout the year. As mentioned, the outcomes of all of these games are recorded with the results available to others. As such, strong players often wish to avoid weaker players who are on their way up so as not to sacrifice rating points should they lose. In open tournaments, however, strong players often have to face those of a lesser rating, and risk the potential of what Orrin Klapp (1964) referred to as "fool-making encounters." Accounts of tirades and flare-ups are not uncommon; losing a game unexpectedly, especially with the threat of lost rating points, can be a devastating emotional experience for a devoted and ambitious player.

Since players' ratings are in jeopardy, so is their status, and to some extent, their sense of identity. As one player explains, "chess is such an ego sport . . . it is supposed to be wrapped up in your intellect, and is much closer to what we think of as our identity. And so I think it is harder to lose" (Puddephatt, 2008: 167). Players who are striving to attain a higher level of status at their local club are invested in maintaining their ratings, which requires studying chess theory, working through chess problems, recruiting stronger players to coach them, and above all, practicing. Players who wish to compete successfully and maintain a strong record may spend large blocks of time on chess. This underlines the importance of chess as science, since for players to improve in any tangible way, they must adhere to studying the game and breaking it down systematically. Like many sports, chess relies on scientific preparation to succeed.

Of course, not all players invest extensive time to improve. As Welser (2002) points out in his study of rock-climbers, commitments in competitive hierarchies follow from the logic of social comparisons and judgments of the success or failure in relation to what they have invested (see also Williams and Donnelly, 1985; Stebbins, 2005, 2009). Players near the bottom of the club hierarchy may study just enough so they can participate in the tournaments without "getting blown away." Such players are satisfied by taking stronger players into the later stages of the game, experiencing the intrinsic fun of competition, and having their opponent's status rub off on them. They may not have many victories, but they do have stories to tell. In contrast, mid-level players who have achieved prior success may be motivated to commit, since moderate amounts of work may yield tangible benefits. These status rewards, coupled with increased respect at the club, may motivate further study. Once players plateau and realize their increased investments no longer generate the same rewards, their study may be curtailed.

How investment strategies and symbolic rewards are distributed among participants follows from the nature of the chess rating system as well as the "activity logic" that determines the implicit "rules of the game" within this competitive field of practice (Bourdieu, 1993). As noted, the rating system is visible and public, but more importantly, it is treated as an accurate marker of skill. Chess, unlike poker, is highly predictable in the outcomes of competition (stronger players reliably defeat weaker players). The complexity of the game does not allow for many upsets, since the degree of chance in chess is low. In network terms, "system noise" is low; the hierarchies are stable, reproducible, and easy to track. In poker, world champions, many of whom have won millions of dollars over their careers, may nevertheless lose early in large tournament formats if their cards are not favorable (Siler, 2009). Poker depends on a level of chance that chess lacks, so that the marginal advantages in skill and decision-making abilities in poker can only reap benefits over the long term.

Ironically, this noise leads many amateurs to invest more than they probably should in online and casino gambling. Since they experience lucky breaks and stumble upon excellent choices from time to time, they may develop higher opinions of their skills than are warranted. Since there is no objective, comparative indicator of skill, they form their opinions based on anecdotal moments of success or failure. It is the high level of noise in poker's widely dispersed and highly fluctuating outcomes, coupled with the lack of any visible reified marker of skill, that brings people to the tables in droves, encouraging repeated investments. This may be why poker is profiled centrally on ESPN programming in North America, while chess is largely absent. Because of the wide fluctuations of outcomes in poker, viewers often "choose correctly" while playing along, and hence, gain reinforcement that their beliefs about the game are correct. This media exposure would probably then lead players to participate in more casual, online, and casino play because of this consistent reinforcement for some good plays, even if this would lose money over the long run.

In chess, the role of luck is less relevant, so the chance of an amateur upsetting former world champion Garry Kasparov in a competitive match is remote. This stability, and the power of a chess rating to predict the outcomes of games, provides the rating system with an obdurate reality that is trusted. Having a visible and reliable means to evaluate their status, investment strategies are made within a more constrained field of performance appraisals and social comparisons. Lower-ranked players in chess are less likely than players in poker to invest as they have a clearer, more certain view of their chances of mobility. Even though rankings and even ratings occur in some other sports, the precision and durability of the chess rating system is unique in shaping player identities, organizing status rankings, and encouraging or dissuading investment by the players. Comparing chess to other organized sports helps decipher the effects of different status reward systems. For example, baseball players are judged by a number of statistics (batting average, home runs, runs batted in, fielding percentage, or stolen bases) that are taken together to describe their competence. These varied statistics reduce competition between players on the same team since they defer to each other's strengths and find esteem in their specific skills. In Guttmann's (2004) terms, baseball has a high level of role specialization. Even though chess players may have strengths and weaknesses at different aspects of the game, chess does not craft separate measures for these, and players are assigned a single, all-encompassing rating. This is similar to the golf handicap, which describes a general level of play but says nothing of how well one putts in comparison to driving the ball off the tee. These are excellent examples of "commensuration," or "the transformation of different

entities into a common metric" (Espeland and Stevens, 1998: 314), carrying direct behavioral consequences in terms of personal investment, social comparison, and status competition.

Conclusion

The presence of a chapter on chess in a scholarly companion to sport might seem eccentric. Chess is famously an activity of the mind with only the briefest movement of light, carved pieces. It is true that long games may involve some measure of bodily stress, but chess players have not been known for their physical fitness, even if prior to long matches some players do include exercise in their preparation. Although Chess Olympiads are held, chess is not yet part of the quadrennial international summer Olympic Games. One should keep in mind that while North Americans may not rank chess as a sport, the game is definitely considered as such in Russia and other countries with stronger chess traditions. Indeed, chess players once routinely received the "Soviet Hero of Sport" award and the matches that played out gained wide media coverage. The game takes on multiple meanings cross-culturally, pointing to the fact that sport itself is often a matter of contested definitions in relation to other cultural realms.

In this chapter we characterized chess as "art, science, and sport." The patterns of chess style that have evolved through its history suggest an aesthetic appeal that links chess to the world of art. If it is neither quite a material art nor a performance art, the beauty of a well-played chess match has been commented upon by many. Likewise, there are ways in which we can link chess to science. As we described, over the centuries chess has developed a body of systematic knowledge that is known as "chess theory." Like scientific paradigms, there are periods of revolution, periods of active incorporation, periods of satisfaction, and other moments of normal cumulative development. To the extent that it is believed that there are proper styles of play, chess is linked to the creation of truth regimes. Finally, and most directly relevant for this *Companion*, chess involves an intense and focused competition. Whether we call chess a sport, it depends on the creation of a status system built on past victories and defeats. Further, while we may be predisposed to speak of chess as a leisure pursuit, it also creates solidarity and identification: a desire to demonstrate one's commitment to the local world and its status markers. With the uncertain outcomes often characteristic of sport, chess has some of the same features of the other zones of activity discussed elsewhere in this volume.

The fact that chess spans the worlds of art, science, and sport has lessons for the sociological analysis of sport in other substantive contexts. It is not just that chess is art, science and sport but that each category is somewhat arbitrary, hinting that it feeds off and is partially constituted by the others. How does one succeed in competitive chess without treating it as a science, and holding a belief in the surety of a rationalized method toward improvement? Where do the heralded stories of competition and romantic heroism come from if not from the more artistic and elegant aspects of the game? Certainly the mutual interdependence of these categories of thought are consequential for a host of other sports. Increasingly athletes – runners, rowers, and wrestlers – are collaborating with physicians and physiologists to get the greatest advantages in systematic diets and exercise regimes in the belief that "science" will provide a competitive advantage. Simultaneously, audiences look for artistic flair that reveal genius whether these be flying lay-ups on basketball courts or graceful serves on tennis courts. Chess does not stand apart from other sports because it also fits into the hallmarks of art and science. Quite the opposite: all sports should be analyzed for their reliance on aesthetic appeal and scientific exactitude if they are to grow in popularity and thrive in their appeal for participants.

Notes

1   We will be using famous chess quotes throughout the essay. Unfortunately, the chess community does not subscribe to the meticulous citation practices of academics, and most famous quotations in chess do not have an official reference source, so citing the work is difficult if not impossible. Nevertheless, we wanted to include these quotations throughout the essay since they help the reader gain a sense of the mystique and lore of the game.

2   Gaining rating points in a city like New York with a robust chess community is more difficult than earning the same number of points in an isolated community with players less devoted to the game.

3   Philidor placed so much importance on the pawns that he would recommend bishops playing a supporting role behind pawns; today this is considered a bad positional decision since bishops are best when they are allowed free movement across open lines. This is another example of how new paradigms do not simply add new things to the existing stock of knowledge but often fundamentally disagree with the ideas of previous generations.

References

Ahmed, S. (2010) *The Promise of Happiness*, Durham, NC: Duke University Press.

Avni, A. (2001) *Practical Chess Psychology: Understanding the Human Factor*, London: B.T. Batsford.

Becker, H. (1982) *Art Worlds*, Berkeley: University of California Press.

Benko, P. and Hochberg, B. (1991) *Winning with Chess Psychology*, New York: David McKay Co.

Bennett, A. (1999) "Subcultures or neo-tribes? Rethinking the relationship between youth, style, and musical taste." *Sociology*, 33 (3): 599–617.

Bilalic, M., McLeod, P., and Gobet, F. (2007) "Personality profiles of young chess players." *Personality and Individual Differences*, 42 (6): 901–910.

Binet, A. (1966) *Mnemonic Virtuosity: A Study of Chess Players*, Provincetown, MA: Journal Press, pp. 127–162.

Blumer, H. (1969) *Symbolic Interactionism: Perspective and Method*, Berkeley: University of California Press.

Bourdieu, P. (1975) "The specificity of the scientific field and the social conditions of the progress of reason," repr. in Biagioli, M. (ed.) *The Science Studies Reader*, New York: Routledge, 1998, pp. 31–50.

Bourdieu, P. (1993) *Field of Cultural Production: Essays on Art and Literature*, New York: Columbia University Press.

Campitelli, G. and Gobet, F. (2008) "The role of practice in chess: A longitudinal study." *Learning and Individual Differences*, 18 (4): 446–458.

Carroll, M. (1981) "A structuralist looks at chess." *Semiotica*, 31 (3/4): 273–287.

Chabris, C.F. and Glickman, M.E. (2006) "Sex differences in intellectual performance: Analysis of a large cohort of competitive chess players." *Psychological Science*, 17 (12): 1040–1046.

Chase, W.G. and Simon, H.A. (1973) "Perception in chess." *Cognitive Psychology*, 4 (1): 55–81.

Cockburn, A. (1974) *Idle Passion: Chess and the Dance of Death*, New York: Simon & Schuster.

Collins, H. (2009) "Walking the talk: Doing gravity's shadow," in Puddephatt, A., Shaffir, W., and Kleinknecht, S. (eds.), *Ethnographies Revisited: Constructing Theory in the Field*, London: Routledge, pp. 289–304.

Collins, R. (1998) *The Sociology of Philosophies*, Princeton, NJ: Princeton University Press.

Collins, R. (2004) *Interaction Ritual Chains*, Princeton, NJ: Princeton University Press.

Coriat, I.H. (1941) "The unconscious motives of interest in chess." *Psychoanalytic Review*, 28: 30–36.

Csikszentmihalyi, M. (1975) *Beyond Boredom and Anxiety: The Experience of Play and Games*, San Francisco: Jossey-Bass.

Csikszentmihalyi, M. (1997) "Happiness and creativity: Going with the flow." *Futurist*, 31 (5): A8–A12.

Degroot, A.D. (1978) *Thought and Choice in Chess*, New York: Mouton.

Desjarlais, R. (2011) *Counterplay: An Anthropologist at the Chessboard*, Berkeley: University of California Press.

Durkheim, E. (1912) *The Elementary Forms of the Religious Life*, trans. K.E. Fields, New York: Free Press, 1995.

Espeland, W. and Stevens, M. (1998) "Commensuration as a social process." *Annual Review of Sociology*, 24: 313–343.

Euwe, M. and Nunn, J. (1997) *The Development of Chess Style: An Instructive and Entertaining Trip through the Heritage of Chess*, London: B.T. Batsford.

Fair, R.C. (2007) "Estimated age effects in athletic events and chess." *Experimental Aging Research*, 33 (1): 37–57.

Fine, G.A. (1983) *Shared Fantasy: Role Playing Games as Social Worlds*, Chicago: University of Chicago Press.

Fine, G.A. (2004) *Everyday Genius: Self Taught Art and the Culture of Authenticity*, Chicago: University of Chicago Press.

Fine, G.A. and Kleinman, S. (1979) "Rethinking subculture: An interactionist analysis." *American Journal of Sociology*, 85 (1): 1–20.

Fine, R. (1956) *The Psychology of the Chess Player*, New York: Dover.

Galitis, I. (2002) "Stalemate: Girls and a mixed gender chess club." *Gender and Education*, 14 (1): 71–83.

Giulianotti, R. (2005) *Sport: A Critical Sociology*, Cambridge: Polity Press.

Goffman, E. (1961) *Encounters: Two Studies in the Sociology of Interaction*, Indianapolis, IN: Bobbs-Merrill.

Goffman, E. (1963) *Stigma: Notes on the Management of Spoiled Identity*, Englewood Cliffs, NJ: Prentice Hall.

Goffman, E. (1967) *Interaction Ritual: Essays on Face to Face Behavior*, New York: Doubleday.

Goffman, E. (1997) "Social life as a game," in Lemert, C. and Branaman, A. (eds.) *The Goffman Reader*, Oxford: Blackwell, pp. 129–146.

Grabner, R.H., Stern, E., and Neubauer, A.C. (2007) "Individual differences in chess expertise: A psychometric investigation." *Acta Psychologica*, 124 (3): 398–420.

Guttmann, A. (1978/2004) *From Ritual to Record: The Nature of Modern Sports*, New York: Columbia University Press, revised 2004.

Huaco, G.A. (1976) "Review feature: Symposium review of *Idle Passion: Chess and the Dance of Death*." *Sociological Quarterly*, 17: 130–133.

James, W. (1909) *The Meaning of Truth*, Cambridge, MA: Harvard University Press.

Jones, E. (1931) "The problem of Paul Morphy: A contribution to the psycho-analysis of chess." *International Journal of Psycho-Analysis*, 12: 1–23.

Klapp, O. (1964) *Symbolic Leaders: Public Dramas and Public Men*, Chicago: Aldine.

König, I. (1977) *Chess from Morphy to Botvinnik: A Century of Chess Evolution*, New York: Dover.

Kopec, D. and Pritchett, C. (1980) *Chess World Title Contenders and Their Styles*, New York: Dover.

Krogius, N. (1976) *Psychology in Chess*, New York: R.H.M. Press.

Kuhn, T.S. (1962) *The Structure of Scientific Revolutions*, Chicago: University of Chicago Press.

Kunnen, R. (2002) *Schaken in Stijl: De ontwikkeling van schaakstijlen als een proces van sportificatie*, Zoetermeer: Swob De Kade.

Melamed, D. and Berman, E. (1981) "Oedipal motives in adolescent chess players." *Journal of Adolescence*, 4 (2): 173–176.

Merton, R. (1938) "The Puritan spur to science," repr. in Merton, R. *The Sociology of Science: Theoretical and Empirical Investigations*, Chicago: University of Chicago Press, 1973, pp. 228–253.

Muggleton, D. (2000) *Inside Subculture: The Postmodern Meaning of Style*, Oxford: Berg.

Muggleton, D. (2005) "From classlessness to clubcul-
ture: A genealogy of post-war British youth cultural
analysis." *Young: Nordic Journal of Youth Research*,
13 (2): 205–219.

Nimzovich, A. (1936) *Chess Praxis: The Praxis of My
System*, New York: Dover Publications.

Pinch, T. (2007) "The sociology of science and technol-
ogy," in Bryant, C. and Peck, D. (eds.) *21st Century
Sociology: A Reference Handbook*, vol. 2, Thousand
Oaks, CA: Sage Publications, pp. 266–275.

Prus, R. (1997) *Subcultural Mosaics and Intersubjective
Realities*, New York: State University of New York
Press.

Puddephatt, A. (2003) "Chess playing as strategic activity." *Symbolic Interaction*, 26 (2): 263–284.

Puddephatt, A. (2005) "Advancing in the amateur chess
world," in Pawluch, D., Shaffir, W., and Miall, C.
(eds.) *Doing Ethnography: Studying Everyday Life*,
Toronto: Canadian Scholars' Press, pp. 300–311.

Puddephatt, A. (2008) "Incorporating ritual into greedy
institution theory: The case of devotion in organized chess." *Sociological Quarterly*, 49 (1): 155–180.

Sauder, M. (2005) "Symbols and contexts: An interactionist approach to the study of social status." *Sociological Quarterly*, 46: 279–298.

Siler, K. (2009) "Preference adaptation and the challenge of poker." Unpublished manuscript.

Stebbins, R. (2005) *Challenging Mountain Nature: Risk,
Motive, and Lifestyle in Three Hobbyist Sports*,
Calgary, AB: Detselig.

Stebbins, R. (2009) "The development of leisure
theory," in Puddephatt, A., Shaffir, W., and
Kleinknecht, S. (eds.) *Ethnographies Revisited: Constructing Theory in the Field*, London: Routledge, pp.
169–179.

Strauss, A. (1993) *Continual Permutations of Action*,
New York: Aldine.

Welser, T. (2002) "For love of glory: Performance, self-
evaluation and competition among rock climbers."
Paper presented at Annual Sociological Association
meeting, Chicago, August 18.

Wendling, T. (2002) *Ethnologie des joueurs d'échecs*,
Paris: Presses Universitaires de France.

Wheaton, B. (2004) *Understanding Lifestyle Sports:
Consumption, Identity and Difference*, London:
Routledge.

Williams, T. and Donnelly, P. (1985) "Subcultural production, reproduction, and transformation in
climbing." *International Review of Sociology of Sport*,
20 (1/2): 3–17.

Further Reading

Ahmed, S. (2010) *The Promise of Happiness*, Durham,
NC: Duke University Press.

Csikszentmihalyi, M. (1975) *Beyond Boredom and
Anxiety: The Experience of Play and Games*, San
Francisco: Jossey-Bass.

Desjarlais, R. (2011) *Counterplay: An Anthropologist at
the Chessboard*, Berkeley: University of California
Press.

Guttmann, A. (2004) *From Ritual to Record: The Nature
of Modern Sports*, New York: Columbia University
Press.

Muggleton, D. (2000) *Inside Subculture: The Postmodern Meaning of Style*, Oxford: Berg.

Part Five

Sport, Mega-events, and Spectacle

Introduction

A voluminous literature exists related to the recognition and analysis of sporting mega-events as key components of the global sport landscape. These studies have identified a hierarchy of sporting mega-events (at the pinnacle being the FIFA men's World Cup finals and the summer Olympic Games, with events such as the Commonwealth games and the IAAF athletics world championships being further down the ranking in terms of magnitude and influence) as important manifestations of both the globalization and the commercialization of sport culture, and the attendant increased importance placed upon sporting mega-events by various scales of governance (city, region, and nation) attuned to the place-based competitiveness inherent within the global age. Simultaneously, an equally fecund literature exists focused on the economy of global sport spectacles that have proved to be crucial elements in constituting the political and cultural economy of contemporary sport, and oftentimes those of the national constituencies from which the spectacle is framed. The chapters in this section disrupt what is a false dichotomy between the sporting mega-event and spectacle, through examinations which point to their mutual interdependency, and the political mobilizations (be they urban, national, regional, or global in focus) which arise from their confluence.

Scarlett Cornelissen (CHAPTER 24) examines the politics of the sport mega-event, through a detailed examination of the 2010 FIFA World Cup finals in South Africa. Her analysis provides a general overview of the sport mega-event phenomenon but concentrates on highlighting the differences in the motivations, planning, and staging of such events in the Global North and the Global South. In terms of the former, Cornelissen identifies how the hosting of sport mega-events has become a means by which urban governments have attempted to stimulate economic development through the regeneration of city spaces and infrastructure, and the reimaging of the city as a desirable destination for tourists and corporate interests alike. Although strategies of urban regeneration have underpinned some sport mega-event initiatives within the Global South, more typically they are centered around broader national, and sometimes regional, objectives, often targeted at projecting the image and reputation of the host nation to the rest of the globe. As such, the sport mega-event is used as a form of *soft power* by developing nations – in recognition of their dearth of *hard power* – in

A Companion to Sport, First Edition. Edited by David L. Andrews and Ben Carrington.
© 2013 Blackwell Publishing Ltd. Published 2013 by Blackwell Publishing Ltd.

their attempts to secure a greater presence and influence on the world stage. Cornelissen cites various examples of how sport mega-event hosting become *totalizing endeavors*: initiatives incorporating all levels of statecraft, including political and economic policies, and their development within domestic and foreign theaters. Turning to South Africa's 2012 FIFA World Cup, she identifies how the event was mobilized by South African leaders as part of broader strategies of reincorporating South Africa into the world economy, while simultaneously looking to build a cohesive sense of national community within the post-apartheid nation, all of which were tied to the significant infrastructural and facility investments needed to successfully host the tournament. Importantly, Cornelissen also points to the strategic use of the World Cup by South African politicians with more expansive agendas, looking to position Africa and its peoples in a more positive light as a modern and progressive continent.

Having discussed the political economy of sport mega-events, John Horne (CHAPTER 25) delves into a related yet much neglected area of inquiry, the built environments, and specifically the iconic architectural structures built as part of the mega-event staging. Horne engages this issue through a cultural and political economic-oriented examination of the agents and institutions responsible for the design and building of stadia and facilities, as the material infrastructure of sporting mega-events. However, his examination of sports architects and architecture is preempted by an exposition of the political economy of urban modernity, as manifest in transformations within the built environment of contemporary cities. He identifies architects as being important members of the transnational capitalist class that has propelled the forces and products of capitalist globalization, and created a global economy of inter-city competition. Architects have thus played a central role in the reimagining and reconstruction of cities as spectacularized spaces designed as new hubs, and attractors, of corporate, finance, and tourist capital. At one time, sport stadia and facilities may have been a minuscule aspect of architectural practice. However, the post-industrial reconfiguring of city spaces and functions, combined with the rise in the cultural, political, and economic significance of sporting

mega-events as highly coveted motors of urban transformation, has resulted in a significant growth in sports architecture. Horne captures this development through an overview of the leading firms working within the area of sports architecture. Many of these have produced iconic buildings, linked to specific sports mega-events, that have played an important part in the construction of transnationally attractive, cosmopolitan, and progressive consumption spaces that benefit cities by announcing and promoting their place in the world. Horne poses a number of important questions related to the form and function of contemporary sports architecture, specifically with regard to the global–local tensions they elicit, and their demonstrably positive and negative legacies. He concludes with a motivating call for further research within the sociology of sport architecture.

Whereas Cornelissen and Horne make inferences toward the sporting mega-event as a global sport spectacle, Douglas Kellner and Hui Zhang (CHAPTER 26) bring this into more direct focus. They provide a nuanced conceptual overview of the sport spectacle as a key component of the contemporary sporting mega-event. Their discussion looks to address this deficiency through a critical explication of the sports spectacle, followed by an in-depth analysis of the 2008 Beijing Olympic Games as an example of the phenomenon. According to Kellner and Zhang, the sports spectacle is formed by an *unholy alliance* conjoining the commercialization of sport, sport celebrity, and media spectacle. They illustrate how, within post-industrial consumption-oriented societies, the implosion of sport performance and media entertainment has realized the emergence of post-industrial sport, with the sports spectacle at its symbolic and economic core. Despite locating the paradigmatic illustrations of the sports spectacle within the North American context – with the excitement-laden telegenicism of professional basketball identified as being the exemplary manifestation of sports/entertainment society – Kellner and Zhang point to the transformation of the FIFA World Cup and the Olympic Games into global sports spectacles necessarily implicated in local political agenda. They focus on the 2008 Beijing Olympic games as a complex and contested amalgam of localism, nationalism, and globalism, in which the calculated choreographing of the Olympic spectacle sought to marry potentially contradictory themes: universalist sentiments designed for a global audience sensitive to the issues associated with the totalitarian Chinese regime staging an Olympic games, and a triumphant localism celebrating China's history and confirming its rise as a global superpower. The global–localism of the Beijing Olympic spectacle was most vividly and pointedly expressed within the performative politics of the opening ceremony. From a revisionist historicizing of China's ancient civilization juxtaposed against allusions to China's contemporary emergent status as a modern nation, to the strategic positioning of celebrated Chinese athletes, and through to the mobilization of children as representations of universal innocence and hope, the spectacle of the opening ceremony historicized, mythologized, and aestheticized communicative bodies as emotive servants of the Chinese state's dualistic nationalist/transnationalist agenda.

Furthering the examination of the political and cultural economy of sporting mega-events, João H. Costa Vargas (CHAPTER 27) uses the FIFA World Cup as a site for understanding the ongoing tensions related to the black influence upon Brazilian sport and society. He examines the racialized narratives emanating from various World Cup experiences of the Brazilian men's football team (both triumphal and tragic, victorious and vanquished, glorious and inglorious), tracing back to the national catastrophe of the defeat in the final of the 1950 tournament through to a prophetic vision of racial politics likely to envelop the 2014 tournament. Vargas shows how a sporting mega-event, and the performance of the Brazilian team (or *seleção*) within it, provides a forum for the discursive management of racial difference according to the hegemonic interests and hierarchy of the Brazilian racial formation. He identifies a residual racial logic operating within Brazilian society (and as expressed in various ways through Brazilian football culture), which positions the white population at the political and symbolic core of the Brazilian nation. Hence, those black (Afro-descended) or mixed-race Brazilians are *always already* excluded from occupying an unquestioned place within the national body, and, within times of national decline or struggle, are positioned as embodied detriments to the realization of Brazil as a flourishing modern nation. This marginalizing of "non-white" Brazilians is clearly apparent within the narrativizing of the instances where the *seleção* failed to live up to national expectations. Within such moments, the playing performances and styles, personalities, and intellects of non-white players were routinely pilloried through the mobilization of crude racial stereotypes that rendered such individuals (and the wider populations they symbolically represented) suspect as athletes and citizens. Even in times of triumph and celebration, Vargas notes how the incorporation of non-white players into the national dialogue is done on a temporary and contingent basis. At such moments, positive representations of black players are positioned as racial anomalies, thereby reinforcing the default anti-black ideology that continues to leave its imprint on Brazilian culture and society.

Grant Farred (CHAPTER 28) brings the experience of global sporting mega-events to a more individual level, through his anecdotal recounting of reactions to the US men's teams exploits in the 2010 FIFA World Cup finals in South Africa. Farred begins with a nuanced contemplation on the reasons for the United States' seemingly perpetually neophyte status on the world football (soccer) stage. At least in part, he attributes this to the minor status of the sport within the nation (if not in terms of participation, then perhaps with regards spectatorship and cultural embeddedness). Indeed, Farred invokes right-wing admonitions of football as a putatively anti-American pastime. And yet, as he identifies through his own observations and experiences, there does appear to be a growing sense of popular interest in the game, perhaps stimulated by its new-found accessibility by means of digital and internet technologies. Within this moment, it is as if "American exceptionalism" (it being a nation in which the game is not widely engaged or celebrated), within the specific context of the global football landscape, is being eroded in front of Farred's very eyes, through what he considers to be the surprising – in his terms, astonishing – expressions of support for US football. However, what arguably catches Farred most off-guard is the possibility of developing an affinity with, and unconcealed support for, a US football team that is thoughtful, culturally nuanced, politically savvy, and, crucially, does not exhibit the forms of nationalist jingoism that are all-too-readily associated with football culture. He is clearly surprised, and to some degree enthused, by the progressive political possibilities made visible to him through "Uncle Sam's Army."

In the final chapter in Part Five, Ian McDonald and Abilash Nalapat (CHAPTER 29) dissect the recent emergence of another sporting mega-event as sport spectacle, again within a non-Western setting. They focus on the Indian Premier League (IPL). As the authors demonstrate, the IPL is a franchise-structured Twenty20 cricket league originated and administered by the Board of Control for Cricket in India (BCCI). It began in 2008, is presently based in 10 Indian cities, and offers a condensed, accelerated, and intensified version of cricket. The IPL is a highly corporatized, commodified, and spectacularized professional sport league, incorporating many elements (specifically with regard to marketing and promotional expertise, branding strategy, merchandizing, and spectacularizing media presentation) of a largely North American/Western model of sports entertainment. Not least of these is the conscious and concerted packaging and promotion of the IPL as a media spectacle designed to attract a mass audience in cricket-loving India

and, specifically through the utilization of new media technologies, to engage members of the vast Indian diaspora. However, as McDonald and Nalapat note, as well as being a localized iteration of what is a Western, corporate model of sport structuring and delivery, the IPL simultaneously speaks to elements of the *post-Westernization of global sport*. As Cornelissen (South Africa, 2010), Kellner and Zhang (Beijing, 2008), and Vargas (Brazil, 2014; Rio de Janeiro, 2016) illustrate, the once Western-dominated economy of sporting mega-events has recently been challenged by the emergence of previously subordinate (in global economic, political, and indeed sporting terms) non-Western nations. The IPL can be understood as the cricketing expression of Indian sport administrators' growing global aspirations (also illustrated in the hosting of the 2010 Commonwealth games in New Delhi, and the inaugural Indian Formula One grand prix in 2011). As such, and as McDonald and Nalapat distinguish, the IPL's *cricketainment* represents a portent of sport's global–local future, wherein highly spectacularized, non-Western located sporting mega-event structures have an increased presence within, and influence upon, the global sport landscape.

Further Reading

Dubois, L. (2010) *Soccer Empire: The World Cup and the Future of France*, Berkeley: University of California Press.

Lenskyj, H.J. (2000) *Inside the Olympic Industry: Power, Politics, and Activism*, Albany: State University of New York Press.

Newman, J. and Giardina, M. (2011) *Sport, Spectacle, and NASCAR Nation: Consumption and the Cul-tural Politics of Neoliberalism*, New York: Palgrave Macmillan.

Perelman, M. (2012) *Barbaric Sport: A Global Plague*, London: Verso.

Roche, M. (2000) *Mega-events and Modernity: Olympics, Expos and the Growth of Global Culture*, London: Routledge.

24

Sport Mega-events as Political Mega-projects
A Critical Analysis of the 2010 FIFA World Cup

Scarlett Cornelissen

Introduction

South Africa's hosting of the finals of the Fédération Internationale de Football Association (FIFA) World Cup in 2010 carried much symbolic significance that extended beyond the fact that it was the first sport tournament of its kind and magnitude to be staged on the African continent. The event's importance should be seen, first, in the larger context of the politics of mega-events in the Global South, where event hosting is often underpinned by political motivations and ambitions of a particular kind. These include the use of events to strategically position the country in the world system, as a conduit of soft power[1] or to help fortify the state (Black and van der Westhuizen, 2004). South Africa's football World Cup was one among a range of other mega-events used as strategic tools by the bigger and rising states of the Global South (Cornelissen, 2010a). Second, the organizational achievements of the finals negated the widespread skepticism that flavored discourse about the country's capabilities in the international arena. In this regard South Africa's World Cup and its seeming organizational successes are likely to have ramifications for other future hosts from the developing world,

encouraging different measurements of state capacities.

The third significance of the event lies in the internal function it was meant to play. The World Cup should be seen as part of an ongoing process of state and societal reconstitution in the post-apartheid era. It was constructed as a central component of a three-pronged process of transition that has been underway in the country since 1994 (consisting of democratic consolidation, socioeconomic change, and national and racial unification). Linked to a grand narrative of African modernity, potential, and revival, the World Cup was intended to help advance this transformation agenda. Given this, it is, fourthly, significant that the event's apparent success appeared to validate pre-tournament boosterist projections of growth and change.

In many ways, therefore, South Africa's World Cup is exemplary of the dynamics that typify mega-event hosting in the Global South: often held in circumstances where state–society relationships are tenuous, and frequently aimed at meeting larger foreign-policy objectives, the staging of mega-events takes on a dual function. This is to highlight to the international community the state's capacities (and to underscore its

A Companion to Sport, First Edition. Edited by David L. Andrews and Ben Carrington.
© 2013 Blackwell Publishing Ltd. Published 2013 by Blackwell Publishing Ltd.

sovereignty and prowess), and to reinforce the idea of the state to its own domestic audiences. Political ambitions therefore constitute the over-riding impetuses. Under these conditions, *mega-event hosting constitutes a political mega-project*, characterized by the comprehensive mobilization and deployment of national resources and ration-alized as a vehicle for big national goals (mod-ernization, development, transformation, unity; also see Flyvbjerg, Bruzelius, and Rothengatter, 2003). They are therefore an aspect of statecraft. Further, staging a mega-event is for these states an all-encompassing or totalizing endeavor, incorporating various elements of the state bureaucratic machinery.

The treatment of sport mega-events as signifi-cant sociocultural affairs with attendant symbolic dimensions and outcomes is well established in the scholarship on mega-events. What is less explored is the way in which mega-events consti-tute political commodities in the contemporary era and how they are used in instrumental and strategic ways for large-scale objectives by politi-cal forces. Seeing events as mega-projects focuses attention on how event processes reflect some-thing about the society and the state they are hosted by, and how societal processes shape event outcomes. It also enables understanding of the role of mega-events in the plotting of new trajec-tories for the polity and society.

This chapter examines these dimensions in relation to the 2010 FIFA World Cup. It follows two lines of analysis, one which explores *sport mega-events as political mega-projects* and the processes around that in the Global South; and a second, which views such events as *adversarial sites*, reflecting the ambivalent internal dynamics between the state and its society and the func-tions and impacts that mega-events have in those circumstances. The first part of the chapter provides an overview of the politics of sport mega-events in the Global South and the princi-pal contrasts there are in relation to the patterns and dynamics of mega-event aims, planning, and staging in the Global North. In the second part the role of sport and sport mega-events in the South African political economy is discussed. This constitutes a backdrop to a more detailed discussion of the motivations and main features of planning for the 2010 finals. A concluding section reflects on some of the emergent out-comes of South Africa's World Cup and their implications for scholars of sport. Hall's (1992) definition of mega-events as major sporting com-petitions of limited duration and regular occur-rence, held on a rotating basis across the world, is adopted here, as is his differentiation of such events whether they are of a first-order magni-tude (such as the Olympic Games and the FIFA World Cup) or of lower rank (such as the Com-monwealth games or continental competitions) in terms of the spectatorship, participation, and commercial turnover they command.

The Politics of Sport Mega-events in the Global South

The past decade or so has been marked by a strong and discernible shift in the international geography of sport mega-event hosting away from the Global North, where historically most mega-events have been held, to their staging by states located in the Global South. Beijing's 2008 Olympic Games, the 2010 Commonwealth games hosted in India, South Africa's 2010 FIFA World Cup, Brazil's prospective staging of the 2014 FIFA World Cup and the 2016 Olympic Games, and Qatar's 2022 FIFA World Cup, are all part of a trend in recent years for some of the most promi-nent and commercially significant events on the world sport calendar to be held in the developing world. Countries from the former Communist bloc, the so-called transition states, have also been party to this, as seen in Russia's hosting of the Winter Olympics in 2014 (in the Black Sea resort of Sochi) and the 2018 FIFA finals, and Ukraine and Poland's co-hosting of the 2012 Euro football finals. Notably, interesting bid dynamics have tended to precede the awarding of hosting rights to these states, which are as telling of the nature of sport politics in the contempo-rary era as they are of the high premium that is being attached to sport mega-events today. It is important to recognize that the more intense competition to stage a mega-event among states from the Global South occurs within a particular world context, is a feature of the international relations of a certain type of developing state, and as a result, is conditioned by unique sets of objectives.

In a general sense, the increased significance of sport mega-events – which relates to both the growth in their scale and appeal and the growing enthusiasm to host them – is most usefully understood in terms of the economic and socio-cultural changes associated with globalization (Roche, 2000), and more specifically neoliberal globalization. The various dimensions of globalization have been widely documented (e.g., Appadurai, 1996; Ohmae, 1990; see also CHAPTER 2). Four particular aspects of globalization can be highlighted to help explain the new economic role of sport and major sport events. These are: (1) the increased mobility and transferability of capital from one sector to another and across national boundaries; (2) the new ways in which capital is valorized and/or created; (3) the related commodification of "non-traditional" (i.e., non-manufactured) products and services and the resultant higher value that is given to consumption goods; and (4) from a policy perspective, the attempts by governments to "capture" mobile international capital or at least align national development processes with perceived international tendencies (see Harvey, 1990; Zukin, 1995).

Sport and leisure are two consumption goods that have gained greater significance in the international economy (Slack, 2004), and sport mega-events have become platforms for the further commodification of these goods (Horne and Manzenreiter, 2002). Encouraged in large measure by corporate stakeholders such as sport, media, and other firms, as well as sport federations, large-scale international sport competitions have become highly commoditized and commercialized affairs. They are mediatized or framed in certain ways to heighten not only their popular but also their commercial allure.

As such, new semiotic and economic functions have arisen for these types of events in recent years, which have had ramifications for national and subnational planning and development processes across the world. From the vantage point of policymakers, but also of the private sector in bidding countries, sport mega-events are regarded as useful creators and conduits of capital in a competitive international environment. This is arguably based on a perception that as an activity that generates economic output, sport has lower entry costs, and given its widespread appeal, that it offers the potential for higher yields.

Thus, bid campaigns are commonly justified by an economic narrative that stresses the catalytic potentials of an event. This usually relies on claims about an event's ability to attract foreign investments; to stimulate domestic investments in under-resourced areas or vulnerable sectors; to consolidate urban or national brands; and to expand revenue and tax bases or create new employment (Horne and Manzenreiter, 2006).

For many national or urban governments, therefore, hosting a sport event of the magnitude of the FIFA World Cup finals (a multi-city or national event) or the Olympic Games (hosted by one city), is part of their strategic politics and policies formed within the context of the prevailing neoliberal, globalized order. Bid campaigns by prospective hosts from the developed and developing worlds generally share the language of economic revitalization and competitiveness. However, there are significant nuances in their overall aims and ambitions that point to an important dimension of the geopolitics of sport mega-event hosting in the Global South. Further, the divergences in the primary motives for staging an event are reflected in how differently hosts from the Global South and those from the Global North generally view and employ such events.

For instance, in the case of the Global North, many urban governments have turned towards hosting mega-events to stimulate new forms of economic development (particularly in culture industries, leisure or sport tourism), to regenerate dilapidated urban regions, to spur on tourism growth and/or to help re-image the city. Urban regeneration is a common objective for the majority of host cities in the developed world. For many planners in the Global South, mega-events can often also be a tool to rejuvenate urban economies. Cape Town's bid for the 2004 Olympic Games, for instance, intended to use the city's staging of the event as a platform to promote development across the city, to help foster physical integration by means of new transportation and other infrastructure linkages, and to boost foreign and domestic tourism (see Swart and Bob, 2004). Kuala Lumpur, host to the 1998 Commonwealth games, sought to use its staging of the event *inter alia* to advance the diffusion of technology in the city (Dobson and Sinnamon, 2001).

However, it is typical that for hosts in the Global South there are also other motives for putting up a mega-event that override urban development goals. While they might seek to stimulate local economic development, this is mostly coupled with larger national objectives. Accelerating widespread development, rather than encouraging the targeted regeneration of specific local areas (such as London's aim to regenerate its impoverished East End with the staging of the 2012 Olympics), is one significant difference. Another is the way in which hosting a mega-event is often intended to achieve greater exposure for the nation state, or to demonstrate national achievements. Poynter's (2006) analysis of the motives underlying the 2008 Beijing and 1988 Seoul Olympics is illustrative in this regard. For these two countries, their hosting of the Games was as much aimed at displaying the host city's features to the outside world as they were intended to demonstrate national prowess. In the case of the Beijing Games, for example, the event was designed to represent "the shop window for a Chinese economy that is experiencing record growth rates and one that seeks international recognition for its relatively recent re-entry into the world economic system" (Poynter, 2006: 6). While an important concern for the Chinese authorities, boosting Beijing's local economy was not the chief motivation for their hosting of the Games. (Although it should be noted that the city did benefit in terms of new and upgraded infrastructure, with some of the most prominent being the newly built Olympic stadium and the rapid rail connection to the neighboring city of Tianjin.) Instead, the Games were meant to showcase China's economic accomplishments (Close, 2010). The scale at which the Games were staged, moreover, and the volume of resources that were invested (at an estimated US$42 billion the Games were the most expensive in the history of the modern Olympic movement) suggest that the Chinese authorities had another intention: to project a particular idea of the country in the international arena, one which proclaimed its greatness and the success of China's variant of modernity (also see Cornelissen, 2010a; CHAPTER 26).

Using variously participation in, or the staging or even boycotting of, a major sport event to display prowess is a tactic well established in world politics (see for instance Levermore, 2004; Rosner and Low, 2009; Wenn and Wenn, 1993),

with many historical examples to be drawn, particularly from the Olympic movement. Yet the contemporary dynamics of sport mega-event hosting in the Global South appear to have different foundations. In these settings putting up an event is often linked to national ideologies of modernization. Such ideologies are used to legitimate the wholesale (and generally unaccounted for) mobilization and deployment of national resources. Staging a mega-event becomes in this way a *totalizing endeavor*, a state-driven project that incorporates various machinations of statecraft, and which is a central component of the country's foreign as well as domestic policies.

When Thabo Mbeki, then South African president, made a submission to the FIFA executive during the last stages of his country's bid to host the 2010 World Cup, for instance, he stated:

> This is an African journey of hope – hope that in time we will arrive at a future when our continent will be free of wars, refugees and displaced people, free of tyranny, of racial, ethnic and religious divisions of conflict, of hunger and the accumulated weight of centuries of our denial of human dignity. . . . Nothing could ever serve to energise our people to work for their and Africa's upliftment more than to integrate among the tasks of our Second Decade of Democracy and the African Renaissance our successful hosting of the 2010 Soccer World Cup. (Mbeki, 2004)

As discussed in greater detail below, for South Africa hosting the FIFA World Cup was part of an extended strategy of domestic transformation and the creation of a new future for the entire African continent. Similar political framing is evidenced by the Brazilian government's responses to being awarded the rights to host the 2016 Olympic Games (see CHAPTER 27). President Lula was reported to have named it "the end of the street dog complex" for the country, and a validation by the International Olympic Committee (IOC) of Brazil's importance in the world. In the view of a foreign ministry official, the IOC's decision reflected the organization's recognition of Brazil's greater success in weathering the effects of the global financial crisis relative to the other countries it was competing against at the time ("09Brasilia1439"). Moreover, the chance to stage the Olympics – a first for a South American country – was taken as an opportunity for Brazil to raise its stature on the continent and to consolidate its influence over other South American states.

The statements by these leaders demonstrate the strategic utility that playing host to a mega-event can hold for countries from the Global South, particularly for those of a certain level of advance with aspirations of greater world prominence. It is not only sport events but other kinds of large-scale events that can be politically instrumentalized in different ways too. China's staging of the Shanghai Expo shortly after the Beijing Games, for example, was even more costly than the 2008 summer Olympics, and was intended to reinforce the messaging of national prowess which characterized the Games. The Shanghai event was an example of the long-established practice by states to use hallmark events such as World Fairs to showcase domestic achievements (e.g., Hall, 1992). South Africa's hosting of global diplomacy summits in the early 2000s (such as the United Nations' World Summit on Sustainable Development in 2002 and the World Conference against Racism, Racial Discrimination, Xenophobia, and Related Intolerance in 2001) was part of a cumulative strategy of staging both sporting and political events in the post-apartheid era (Cornelissen, 2004). Typically, therefore, for many states in the Global South sport mega-event hosting is part of a wider range of tactics to position themselves more favorably in the international arena, or as a means to buttress broader foreign policy aims.

The reasons for using mega-events in this way reflect the nature of power in the contemporary world system and the novel forms of international relations that substantive shifts in this system are provoking. The states of the Global South that successfully canvass to host mega-events share a number of features: although not fully industrialized they display rapid levels of growth and related social change. Their status as middle-income countries means that they have an expansive and growing middle class, although they are often highly stratified societies with the pace of their advance frequently associated with greater income inequalities. Many of these states are home to large deposits of valued primary resources such as minerals, precious metals, and oil that enable commodity-driven export

growth. This, coupled with swift economic change, gives them substantial and growing influence over trajectories in the world economy. However, their economic influence is often in disjuncture with their political influence. Although many may be powerful actors in their immediate regional sphere (Brazil in South America, South Africa in Africa, India in South Asia, and so on), and may be viewed as leaders in the developing world, they often do not have the same political leverage that the major states of the Global North (in particular the United States) have – at least not in the domains of international politics associated with *hard power*. As a form of statecraft, sport mega-event hosting is therefore one of the strategies of soft power used by many of these developing countries, in part to mitigate their lack of hard power but also as an element of a process to gain greater influence and prominence in the world system (also see Nye, 1990; Black and van der Westhuizen, 2004). This is often based on a distinctive national role conception – a self-view of the nature and place of the state and its role in the immediate region and in the wider international domain (which, variably, can be self-conceptions of these countries as regional leaders, as middle powers, or as aspiring hegemons) – which shapes foreign policies.

Mega-event bidding and hosting processes are molded by these broader foreign-policy aims. It is noteworthy, for example, that several developing countries frame their hosting of a particular event with their regional neighbors as explicit points of reference. As discussed in greater detail below, South Africa defined its World Cup as "an African World Cup," a political language that was related to the country's established policy towards the continent and its regional leadership ambitions (also see Habib, 2009). Similarly, Brazil's 2014 FIFA World Cup campaign highlighted its powers *vis-à-vis* those of its regional neighbors. It is also significant how hosts from the Global South center their bidding and planning campaigns on constructed discourses which draw heavily on historical analogies and idioms that evoke recollections of past glories and one-time international preeminence. India's bid to stage the Commonwealth games strongly featured the symbolic remnants of former civilizations, drawing connections between the country's role in earlier historical epochs and its current emergence (Black, 2007). Similarly, China's 2008 Games projected elements of both former and contemporary Chinese civilization (Close, 2010).

These kinds of processes have important material and symbolic dimensions which are further aimed at cementing the idea of the state (see CHAPTER 25). Not only do they entail extensive volumes of public investments, they also usually rely on the development of large-scale signature architectures, whether in the form of a new national stadium, a national convention center or other infrastructures. Beijing's Bird's Nest and the large international airport refurbished for the Olympic Games, for instance, are memorable leftovers from the event, but they are also symbols of China's recent and continuing global ascent.

There are also domestic elements which constitute important subsidiary motives for embarking on event strategies and shape the politics of hosting in the Global South. More often than not, the societal make-up of these countries is highly heterogeneous as far as their ethnic, racial, and class composition is concerned, which can be sources for societal tensions and outright conflict. The nature of the relationship between the state (or governing authority) and the society is often also distinctively fragile, and the legitimacy of the state or dominant political classes is often questioned or challenged. Delhi's hosting of the 2010 Commonwealth games, for example, occurred in a context of vulnerability of the Indian state towards domestic insurgencies. A significant part of the Brazilian authorities' preparations for the 2014 FIFA World Cup and the 2016 Olympic Games, furthermore, centers on neutralizing domestic challenges to the government's sovereignty emanating from organized and "disorganized" crime, the latter mostly located in the country's infamous favelas.

Further, political and social diversity is often accompanied by varied and divergent recollections of histories that shape societal engagement and counteract national processes of unification. Often, as is the case in the transition societies of the former Communist bloc, strong minority identities exist that fragment new national identities. Major social cleavages can fuel societal processes that become the basis for counter-narratives to grand narratives of national unity. The frail underpinnings of the political compacts between the elite and the masses imply uncertain trajectories and futures. Mega-events are often supposed to offer identitarian pillars for national endeavors towards social harmony, and government actors may use a variety of narratives linked to the event to try to engender this. Often this rests on a discourse of successfully delivering the event in order to galvanize the society, which becomes the focal point for unity.

In these settings the processes of event planning and implementation are heavily colored by the wider aims of state-building. This leads to the distinctively top-down structuring of event organization. Event delivery becomes defined as a political and national task with a much stronger implementation role for the public sector and often much closer involvement of the central organs of state. This is also accompanied by the garnering of national resources and the linking of mega-event planning to broader, large-scale infrastructural programs. Whilst planning for the 2010 Commonwealth games, for example, India's government fast-tracked a very comprehensive upgrade program, constituting one of the largest public–private initiatives in the developing world, that aimed to develop 20,000 kilometers of new roads and other infrastructure linking the country's populous cities (BBC, 2010). Brazil's political authorities have the ambition to use the sport events it will host to help upgrade the country's dated infrastructure.

Because so much is at stake as far as their reputations are concerned, host authorities from the Global South often adopt a cost-is-no-obstacle attitude, and they would spend comparatively much more than Northern countries on the development of event sites, other signature architecture, and event-related "propaganda." The exorbitant costs of the Beijing Games have been cited. Qatar's ambitions to create "artificial clouds" for the 2022 FIFA World Cup, in an attempt to try to lower temperatures and to ensure there is no disruption to FIFA's standard summer World Cup schedule (*Guardian*, 2011), is another example of the lengths to which states from the Global South will go and the investments they are willing to make in order to bolster their international standing. Given the character of these polities, there are fewer checks and balances for public expenses made in the name of a mega-event, and fewer recourses for societal admonishment. This contrasts with the situation for most hosts in the Global North where institutionalized feedback loops between public office-holders, planners, and civil society act as democratic controls on spending – although as noted by Lenskyj (2008) and others, in the latter settings political regulations and checks and balances are often sidestepped and regular infringements of civil liberties also occur.

South Africa's 2010 FIFA World Cup

The dynamics of sport mega-events in post-apartheid South Africa

South Africa's bid for and hosting of the 2010 FIFA World Cup finals reflected much of the intentions and dynamics that have characterized processes around mega-events in other parts of the Global South. There were also important particularities which stemmed from the country's very singular past of lengthy institutionalized racial separation, its colonial and twentieth-century trajectories of political and economic development, and the country's unique international position in relation to other countries on the African continent. Rapid evolution in socioeconomic and sociopolitical circumstances after the end of apartheid made for a highly changeable environment which, through policymaking, South Africa's post-apartheid authorities attempted to shape towards a nationally unified, democratized, and internationally competitive society.

South Africa was awarded the rights to host the FIFA World Cup in May 2004, after a lengthy bid campaign that was initiated in 1998. At the time, leaders in South Africa's national football organization bid to host the 2006 World Cup. When this failed – Germany was conferred the rights to host the 2006 finals – South Africa renewed its bid for 2010. A new continental rotation system introduced by FIFA at that point amid some controversy over the possible political reasons for the 2006 bid outcome meant that South Africa competed only against other African contenders (Egypt, Morocco, and, during the initial stages of the bid process, Tunisia, Libya, and Nigeria; Cornelissen, 2004). The rotation system was subsequently applied once more when South American

countries could bid to host the 2014 World Cup, but it has since been abandoned by FIFA.

South Africa's World Cup campaigns should be understood within the emergent international political economy of sport mega-events and the way in which mega-events are seen as instruments towards economic and political objectives, as described above, as well as in terms of the relationship between sport and politics in the country in the post-apartheid era. First, the process of dismantling apartheid from the late 1980s onward coincided with fundamental ideological and politico-economic shifts in the international arena. The latter dramatically shaped developments in South Africa. Facing an increasingly globalized, competitive, and interdependent international environment, South Africa's new leaders had to consider how to most effectively reincorporate the country into the world economy. At the same time the national policy-making process after the first democratic elections in 1994 had to respond to pressing internal conditions. These included the need to transcend the racial and socioeconomic legacies of apartheid, and in particular the inequities this system established. It also entailed bigger goals to create a sustainable path of transformation and to establish a new social order.

As many analysts of post-apartheid South Africa have noted, it has not been an easy task to marry aims defined in relation to processes of globalization with national transformation (e.g., Southall, Daniel, and Pillay, 2010). Indeed, multiple, overlapping, and sometimes conflicting national narratives have characterized South Africa's political developments since 1994, which have been mirrored in the tone and content of policymaking processes and in overarching political programs. These narratives have ranged from the emphasis on redress and redistribution (reflected, for instance, in the early post-apartheid macroeconomic policy of Reconstruction and Development), to national unity based on transitional justice (which has been a consistent theme throughout and has influenced major political processes such as the establishment of the Truth and Reconciliation Commission in the late 1990s), to international competitiveness, which prioritized policies with strong neoliberal objectives. The country's diplomatic orientation has tended to be underpinned by a narrative of moral leadership – strongly normative in tone, laying emphasis on the lessons that the country could teach the rest of world due to its peaceful, negotiated transition and the role it could play in bargaining for a more stable world order. The country also placed African revival at the center of its foreign policy. Thus, framed implicitly on an understanding that South Africa's future was intimately connected with that of the wider continent, the country's leadership robustly pursued Africa-focused foreign policies. The African Renaissance initiative of Thabo Mbeki of the late 1990s, which later branched into the establishment of the New Economic Partnership for Africa's Development (NEPAD) and the restructuring of the continent's main diplomatic organ into the African Union, are two particularly important examples in this regard.

The staging of mega-events has been an element of these internationalist and domestic orientations by South Africa's leadership, valued as a tool to raise the country's global prominence, to increase competitiveness, and to solidify nascent processes of nation building. Indeed, even if not framed as explicit policy, it is noteworthy how active the country has been bidding for and staging large-scale sport and political events. In 1992, for instance, the city of Cape Town bid to host the 2004 Olympic Games. The city failed in its Olympic bid, but there has been speculation that another South African city, Durban, may bid for the 2024 Games. In 1995 South Africa hosted the Rugby World Cup, something the country's rugby fraternity sought to repeat with a failed bid to stage the rugby finals in 2011. In 1996 the country provided the venue for the biennial continental football championship, the Africa Cup of Nations. In 1999 South Africa hosted the All Africa Games and then two further world championships in 2003 – the International Cricket Council's World Cup, and the women's World Cup of golf. The country also sought prominence in the diplomatic sphere, by hosting two major United Nations meetings, as noted. However, securing the rights to host the 2010 FIFA World Cup was a particular victory to South Africa's bid campaigners, since this presented a unique opportunity to showcase the country on the world stage.

But the pursuit to host sport events has also been underpinned by a second rationale on the part of South Africa's leaders, which relates to the powerful connection which has historically existed between sport and politics in the country. It has long been recognized by historians and sociologists that sport has played an important role in the formation of societal identities and the maintenance of racial separation (Archer and Bouillon, 1982; Grundlingh, Odendaal, and Spies, 1995; Nauright, 1997). During the time of apartheid the sport of rugby was, for instance, associated with values of masculinity, cultural pride, and supremacy by some people in the Afrikaner community and was viewed by them as a key symbolic attribute of Afrikanerdom (Black and Nauright, 1998). In contrast, football developed as a sport generally supported by the country's black population, for whom the game's association with the working classes held major appeal. From the 1950s onward, moreover, as the popularity of football grew and the game expanded in the cities, it became symbolically connected with the social protest movement against the minority white government (Couzens, 1983; Merrett, 2009). Sport has been a sphere in which many of South Africa's racial politics played out domestically.

In the international arena the policy of apartheid also had dramatic ramifications in the sport domain. South Africa was barred from participating in the 1964 and 1968 Olympic Games, for instance, held respectively in Tokyo and Mexico. Following threats of further boycotts, the IOC expelled the country as member in 1970. This amounted to a bold indictment of the government of South Africa of the day, but the IOC's actions came many years after similar steps were taken by other sport organizations and international federations. For instance, FIFA expelled the whites-only national federation in 1955 and the Commonwealth excluded South Africa from the 1962 games (South Africa having previously chosen to leave the Commonwealth in 1961). International federations representing sports such as weightlifting, judo, and boxing had also expelled South Africa during the 1960s. From that point on, South Africa entered a lengthy period of international sport isolation which paralleled the growing diplomatic and later economic isolation to which the country was subjected. Since sport was such an important part of the sociocultural imaginary, the international

sport boycotts arguably held very tangible ramifications for the society at large (Booth, 1998;
Black, 1999).

In the post-apartheid era sport has gained new
significance as a means to help overcome racial
differences and to build a common national identity. A former minister of sport for instance
stated:

> sport is a very important part of society. . . . Our
> country too has a responsibility to use sport to
> assist the country and our people to move in a
> particular direction; the direction of a deracial-
> ised South Africa. . . . So indeed we must use
> sport for nation building. We must use it to build
> self-esteem and national pride. We cannot con-
> tinue with paradigms that perpetuate apartheid
> stereotypes of some who are destined for great-
> ness while others are destined for mediocrity and
> inferiority. (Stofile, 2007)

The linkage between sport and nation building
in the context of major events was established
soon after South Africa's first democratic elections, during the 1995 Rugby World Cup. The
tournament victory by the mostly white South
African rugby team was celebrated after the final
match by then President Nelson Mandela, who
appeared at the stadium wearing the Springbok
jersey – the colors of national rugby, which during
the time of the liberation struggle were regarded
as a symbol of apartheid's racism. Nelson Mandela's apparent embrace of this symbol signaled
a new era of reconciliation in which all population groups should participate in the construction of a unified and prosperous South Africa
poised to assume its place in the international
community (Grundlingh, 1998; Black and Nauright, 1998). The same symbolism was evident
during the Africa Cup of Nations hosted by South
Africa in 1996, the first time the country had
participated in the Africa-wide football championship, and a tournament intended to signify
the country's integration with the rest of the
continent.

Intentions, processes, and challenges around the World Cup

These aspects have continued to inform South
Africa's endeavors to host major sport events in

subsequent years. Indeed, it is noteworthy that
two elements characterized South Africa's bid for
the 2010 World Cup, the first an effort to use the
event as a means to reinforce a common national
identity, and the second an emphasis on how the
event could help the country play an important
role within Africa and beyond. Fostering African
unity was a further goal. Shortly before the start
of the tournament, for instance, then South
African president Jacob Zuma stated:

> We need to find resonance between the ability of
> sport to unite a people and to establish the roots
> for peace and development. This international
> event, to which all of us can rightly claim owner-
> ship, should be used to deepen our understand-
> ing of our shared cultures and ensure that
> dialogue and cooperation among Africans is pro-
> moted. (Zuma, 2010a)

South Africa's authorities sought to use the event,
which was named "the African World Cup" to
represent the continent in a more favorable light.
This was mostly aimed at countering the effects
of Afro-pessimism on investments and tourist
arrivals to the continent. The 2010 Local Organizing Committee (LOC) had defined their aim,
"to strengthen the African and South African
image, promote new partnerships with the world
as we stage a unique and memorable event . . .
[and] be significant global players in all fields of
human endeavour" (South African Football Association, 2007). Tied to this was a projection of
African modernity, a conception of the continent
which sought to emphasize its existing achievements and the potentials towards innovation and
progress that lay in its population – a view very
different from the usual imagery of conflict and
the continent internationally. Notably, therefore,
by the time the tournament took place, its official
slogan was "*Ke Nako,*" which translates as "Celebrate Africa's humanity." The official "Africa
Legacy Programme" had several objectives,
namely to "support the realisation of African renaissance"; to ensure that all African countries
participated in the event; to further the development of African football; and to improve the
international image of the continent (South
Africa Government, 2010a). The aim to create a
continent-wide legacy and to extend potential
benefits beyond the host country set the 2010

World Cup apart from previous World Cups and centralized a key political feature.

At the same time, staging the event was rationalized for the boost it could give to national development processes, and was promoted to the domestic population as an important vehicle to change the circumstances of the country's mass unemployed and poor (Cornelissen and Swart, 2006; Pillay, Tomlinson, and Bass, 2009). From an official perspective, the World Cup was regarded as an opportunity "to speed up development and growth in the country so that it leaves behind a proud legacy that will benefit generations of South Africans to come" (South Africa Government, 2010b). Thus, an economic argument about the potential impacts of the World Cup was an important part of political leaders' efforts to gain domestic support for the World Cup bid.

Therefore, much was anticipated from the tournament as far as its symbolic, political, and economic legacies were concerned. There were a number of significant challenges which the country's authorities and planners faced during the planning and preparation phases, however, which cast into doubt whether the myriad expectations would be met. The first concerned the very critical question of whether South Africa had the capacity in physical and human resources to host the event to an appropriate standard. Over the years there was much skepticism in the international arena over South Africa's chances of successfully hosting the tournament and completing all preparations on time; on the potential effects of crime; and the possibility that political instability may jeopardize the event (see Korth and Rolfes, 2010, for a comprehensive review). For a significant period before the tournament there was speculation that the event would be moved to another location.

Such skepticism was not totally unwarranted. In preparation for the World Cup much emphasis was placed on the timely development or preparation of three types of infrastructure: the competition venues/stadia, transportation, and tourist accommodation. Of the ten stadiums that were used for matches, six were newly built or refurbished, while four existing stadiums – used in the past mostly for rugby – were upgraded. All of the stadiums were completed on time, but this was often accompanied by excessive cost escalation and persistent allegations of corruption

around tendering processes (see *Business Day*, 2008; Schulz Herzenberg, 2010). The development of road and other transport infrastructure that was undertaken as part of the tournament (many host cities use the World Cup as an opportunity to develop new urban commuter networks) also often saw delays and increases in costs.

Further, early planning assessments by South Africa's tourism authorities showed that the country had a significant accommodation deficit, with the shortfall quite acute in some of the largest host cities (SA Tourism, 2005). In the years leading to the tournament host cities endeavored to ensure that there was sufficient accommodation for visitors and spectators, but it is noteworthy that less than a year before the start of the World Cup, some high-ranking FIFA officials voiced concern that that might not be achieved. Jerome Valcke, FIFA's secretary-general, for instance stated in an interview in late 2009, "I am not worried about ticket sales but instead about accommodation for the fans. It is our concern that every fan in the world who has bought a ticket also gets a flight and a room. . . . We need enough accommodation for the guests and a high and secure transport capacity" (South African Press Association/Deutsche Presse Agentur, 2009).[2]

Finally, the implementation of an appropriate World Cup security plan presented another challenge to South African authorities. This was because in addition to the standard security measures which needed to be undertaken for a tournament of this kind – directed against hooliganism and the prevention of potential terror attacks – authorities also needed to take measures against crime. South Africa has gained international notoriety for the extent of crime and social violence in the country; indeed, this reputation was widely regarded as a potential deterrent to foreign visitors to the World Cup. In addition, during the country's hosting of the Confederations Cup in 2009, an event which is linked to the FIFA tournament and is meant to be a dry run for the big finals, the LOC failed to secure a security company on time. Although the event progressed without any incident, it was clear that security planning had to be improved for the World Cup. These experiences fueled many cynics' questioning of South Africa's organizational capacities, and there was highly negative media reporting right up to the start of the tournament which framed international discourse about the country's state of preparedness.

A second cluster of challenges for South Africa's authorities was that they were faced with the threat of social unrest during the tournament. The rise to power of the president, Jacob Zuma, in 2009, although initially underlain by populism, was soon accompanied by social protest, municipal strikes, and demands for improved service delivery which progressively expanded in scale and violence. While not directly related to the upcoming World Cup, it was noteworthy that there was a growing tide of civic action that questioned what the real social benefits of the event would be. An illustrative case is a violent demonstration in late October 2009 in the township bordering the Soccer City stadium, the main tournament venue in Johannesburg, during which residents vowed that "there will be no 2010 [World Cup] because they had no houses and no jobs," and stating that the government is "pouring money into [the] 2010 [World Cup] . . . why are they not pouring money into housing?" (*Times*, 2009).

Thus, there was the possibility that the World Cup could constitute a platform for civic protests. More worrying for the country's political leadership was the possibility that generalized social unrest – both organized and spontaneous in origin – could arise during the World Cup which, although voicing a broader range of socioeconomic grievances beyond the World Cup itself, could derail the tournament. The authorities had to consider both the potential impacts on the country's image if this were to occur and the long-term political fallouts that could come from a failed tournament. In the end, while a number of civic protests took place during the tournament, they were tightly controlled by the national police.

Given the above, the question of whether the World Cup could spark national pride and become the basis for social cohesion became all the more important. The attempts to foster unity through the tournament rested on three pillars. First, there was the popularization of the World Cup in the months before the tournament. This consisted of national promotion and loyalty campaigns led by the public sector

(urban authorities and the national government) which declared, *inter alia*, certain days of the week to be national football days (e.g., "Football Fridays"). On these days the public were encouraged to wear the colors of the national football team, Bafana Bafana, and to brandish World Cup paraphernalia. Programs were also held at schools to raise awareness of the event among youths. This was accompanied, second, by private marketing campaigns by prominent South African corporations which had the World Cup as central theme. Two of the largest telecommunications firms for instance ran publicity campaigns championing the World Cup. These efforts were linked to a third, which was an attempt by political and private-sector actors to galvanize public support for Bafana Bafana, who along with sport heroes from the domain of rugby were put forward as a symbol of national prowess.

This aspect of the unity promotion endeavors was the most revealing of the societal context within which the World Cup was being held and the unpredictability of the real nation-building potential of the event. As indicated, in the post-apartheid era successful sport performance has become one of the main ingredients of the country's nascent nation-building process. Yet the experience in hosting and competing in sport mega-events has been a speckled one, with performances by national teams generally falling well below expectations, concomitantly affecting not only domestic support for teams but in many instances, popular regard for sport events too. For example, the national cricket team underperformed during the 2003 cricket World Cup hosted in South Africa, and the team's early exit from the tournament dampened the population's enthusiasm and support for the event as a whole. There have been lackluster performances in the Olympics by Team South Africa over the years, and Bafana Bafana had a very poor record in international competitions. It was particularly unclear how Bafana would perform in the World Cup tournament and whether an early exit would undermine national unity. Thus, while the country's elites still considered sport events as important nation-building instruments, they were facing a critical and cynical public. The fact that rugby heroes such as the captain, John Smith, and players Brian Habana and Schalk Burger were used to promote the football World Cup was another irony.

Some outcomes and ramifications

All of these dimensions are pertinent for understanding the outcomes of the World Cup and the event's importance for future societal trajectories. In spite of some initial organizational hitches, South Africa's tournament was prevailingly successful and safe; most security concerns were addressed; and although numerous civic protests were staged, they were small in scale.

In the aftermath of the tournament a few dynamics can be highlighted for their longer term implications. One concerns the politics around the event's economic legacies. Projections toward and expectations of the tournament's economic legacies have been highly variable. Pre-tournament estimations of the event's likely macroeconomic impacts ranged from R30 billion in 2003 to R93 billion (approximately US$13.2 billion) in 2010. In 2010 it was projected that the event would generate around US$2.7 billion in tax revenue for the government, and that up to 415,000 new jobs would be created (Grant Thornton, 2010). The number of foreign visitors to the tournament was expected to be around 373,000, and it was projected that the event could generate US$1.2 billion in tourism income for the country.

The national authorities spent about R21 billion (approximately US$3 billion) on the construction of stadiums and event-related infrastructure. A further US$1.7 billion was spent on aspects such as policing, marketing, the procurement of new technologies, and the tournament's opening and closing ceremonies (South Africa Government, 2010c). However, for several years before the tournament, the government had been engaged in a large-scale infrastructure development program, which though linked to the World Cup was meant to spearhead broader development. In total around US$85 billion was spent on the upgrade of ports of entry, roads, railway lines, and energy provision (South Africa Government, 2010c).

The positive aspect of this is that as part of World Cup preparations, public investment was made on needed infrastructure programs. A significant part of the spending, for instance, was dedicated to the upgrade of South Africa's dated road network, and the improvement of public transport. In relative terms, these investments are significantly more than what was spent by the Chinese authorities on the Beijing Games and its aftermath, and make up a significantly larger portion of South Africa's annual GDP of around US$500 billion.

While South Africa's authorities intended to use the World Cup to stimulate new large-scale developments in the country, it arguably came at a very high cost. As such, it is significant that early indicators of the World Cup's economic impacts are mixed, and it is uncertain whether most of the projected impacts will materialize. The estimated number of tournament visitors was 309,000 (SA Tourism, 2010), about one-third less than the predicted number of arrivals. Tourism receipts were significantly less than those projected pre-event. Evidence from other economic sectors also suggests that little new, permanent employment has been created. For instance, the construction sector experienced an increase in employment at first but then a drop of around 25 percent in the months leading to the tournament.

It is perhaps not surprising that competing narratives have arisen around the issue of the event's long-term benefits and costs. One narrative advanced by the national government persistently emphasizes the World Cup's significance for the country's agenda of socioeconomic transformation, and another, looser narrative arising from the ranks of civil society questions the distributional benefits and possible debt implications (see, e.g., Ndlovu-Gatsheni, 2011). This partly reflects the major political schisms of the day and the continued demands faced by the government from its constituency for improved basic service delivery (including the delivery of housing). These are issues which have been shaping electoral processes and broader political processes. But, importantly, the World Cup did become part of South Africa's larger politics of class contestation as the developmental messaging constructed in official circles around the event created expectations. The fact that the tournament is the most profitable in the history of the World Cup, with FIFA's earnings estimated at US$3.6 billion (Soccerex, 2011) suggests that despite the event's pro-poor casting, it benefited a fairly small and elite number of players in South

Africa and beyond (also see Cornelissen, 2010b). It remains to be seen whether this becomes a factor in future political dynamics in the country. Further, the ultimate long-term impacts – positive or negative – on the macro-economy will only be known after a substantial number of years.

The juxtaposition between an official narrative of progress and unity on the one hand and a societal narrative of polarization on the other is also of significance for another matter, which is the World Cup's longer-term consequences for social identity processes. It is noteworthy that during the tournament there was widespread domestic support and scenes of euphoria and unity reminiscent of the celebrations for the 1995 rugby World Cup. The *vuvuzela* – much reviled in the international arena but very popular among South Africans from all racial and class backgrounds – became a symbol of an ascendant and harmonious South Africa, an accessory to the metaphoric "rainbow nation." From the perspective of the national government, the World Cup successfully achieved the historical mission towards racial harmony. President Zuma heralded the event as one of post-apartheid South Africa's greatest achievements, and noted that "the wearing of Bafana Bafana jerseys and the display of the rainbow flag everywhere in our country by patriotic South Africans will forever be part of our heritage . . . these national colours unite us and strengthen solidarity" (Zuma, 2010b).

It is unclear, however, what the longevity or even authenticity of these expressions of unity are or what they mean in a country where racial divisions persist. A critical view advanced by some of the country's prominent civil-society leaders and intellectuals admonishes South Africa's short-lived moment of "fake nationhood" (Ndlovu-Gatsheni, 2011). In addition, several months after the tournament, a public spat between two top politicians, one black and one coloured, over South Africans' racial traits and differences (Manuel, 2011), demonstrated the continued centrality of race in everyday public and private life in the country, as well as how it continues to shape political dynamics.

The issue of race also figured in a more unexpected fashion, when soon after the end of the World Cup there was speculation that a xenopho-bic campaign might be waged against persons from other parts of the African continent. Anti-African xenophobia has increased in South Africa over the past number of years. In 2008 xenopho-bic sentiments led to widespread attacks against "outsiders" from the rest of Africa. Over the period of a month, more than 60 persons were killed. Fortunately, there was no resurgence in xenophobia after the World Cup, and indeed during the tournament it was noteworthy how South Africans supported all competing African teams. But this aspect did undermine the official pan-African narrative in which South Africa's World Cup campaign had been framed. The messaging of continental renaissance and unity was contrasted by societal narratives of hatred and disunity/polarity.

A more cynical reading of the disjuncture between the official and societal narratives around the "African World Cup" is that pan-Afri-canism and Afro-pride were rhetorical devices employed by the country's football elite, first to gain African support for the South African bid campaign, and second to engender empathy for the continent in the international arena that could be transformed into support for the World Cup (also see Desai and Vahed, 2010; Ndlovu-Gatsheni, 2011). Promises by South Africa that the tournament's economic benefits will be shared with other African countries through the joint hosting of matches or accommodation of teams and visitors did not materialize, largely because other states were prevented by FIFA from being involved in the tournament's staging due to security concerns. It is also unclear how inclusive other aspects of the tournament were. In the view of some, representations of Africa consisted of collaged clichés with little depth (e.g., Mbembe, 2010). The curiously ahistorical narrative of "African modernity" upon which the World Cup was built may ultimately change little about the continent's position in the wider international arena.

Conclusion

For many states in the Global South hosting a sport mega-event has become part of their modernization strategies. The scale at which many of these states plan and stage such an event, and the way in which this dovetails with their broader foreign-policy ambitions and domestic transformation agendas makes sport events a significant new form of political mega-project in the Global South. These mega-projects involve the development of infrastructures that are intended both to catalyze modernization and to symbolize the transcendence of the country from its former "underdeveloped" (or colonial) status and its advance towards enhanced sovereignty and leadership in the international arena.

The FIFA World Cup was South Africa's mega-project that was meant to give momentum to processes of social and political change underway in the country over the past two decades. The most pertinent questions of the event's ramifications – economic, material, symbolic, and political – should center on how it might have reshaped the foundations of the polity and have influenced outlooks for the future.

In the years before the tournament many expectations had been raised by the country's leaders of the event's potential employment and growth impacts. While, as a result, there was much societal anticipation about the tournament's possible legacies, public opinion about the event was also varied and ambivalent. On a symbolic level, the World Cup saw a number of achievements, particularly as far as temporarily inverting negative images of Africa in the international domain. In addition, the smooth delivery of the event is sure to enhance the country's international image in the short to medium term. The country also has much to contribute to future World Cup hosts as far as its experiences in best and worst practice and institutional lessons are concerned.

Finally, the tournament did momentarily help unify a nation that still carries the legacies of racial division. Without demonstrable and widely distributed material benefits however, these positive symbolic spin-offs may hold little tread over the longer term in a society marked by the levels of inequality and class and racial divisions as exist in South Africa.

Notes

1   As used by Joseph Nye in his study of international relations (1990), *soft power* refers to the influence or prominence a country has in the international arena, which stems from aspects related to its society, culture, or economy (e.g., a national dish, national dress, or film industry), rather than *hard power* built on military might.

2   "Fußball-WM 2010: Herausforderungen und Hoffnungen." South African Press Association/Deutsche Presse Agentur, June 8, 2010, http://www.bpb.de/gesellschaft/sport/fussball-wm-2010/64142/herausforderungen-und-hoffnungen?p=all, accessed January 21, 2013.

References

"09Brasilia1439," http://wikileaks.tetalab.org/mobile/cables/09BRASILIA1439.html, accessed December 24, 2009.

Appadurai, A. (1996) *Modernity At Large: Cultural Dimensions of Globalization*, Minneapolis: University of Minnesota Press.

Archer, R. and Bouillon, A. (1982) *The South African Game: Sport and Racism*, London: Zed Press.

BBC (2010) "Will India's highways project be path to growth?" *BBC News*, April 21.

Black, D. (1999) "'Not cricket': The effects and effectiveness of the sport boycott," in Crawford, N. and Klotz, A. (eds.) *How Sanctions Work: Lessons from South Africa*, London: Palgrave Macmillan, pp. 213–231.

Black, D. (2007) "The symbolic politics of sport mega-events: 2010 in comparative perspective." *Politikon*, 34 (3): 261–276.

Black, D. and Nauright, J. (1998) *Rugby and the South African Nation: Sport, Cultures, Politics and Power in the Old and New South Africas*, Manchester: Manchester University Press.

Black, D. and van der Westhuizen, J. (2004) "Going global: The promises and pitfalls of hosting global games." *Third World Quarterly*, 25 (7): 1215–1232.

Booth, D. (1998) *The Race Game: Sport and Politics in South Africa*, London: Frank Cass.

Business Day (2008) "2010 stadiums R3.2 bn over budget." *Business Day*, December 2.

Close, P. (2010) "Olympiads as mega-events and the pace of globalization: Beijing 2008 in context." *International Journal of the History of Sport*, 27 (16/18): 2976–3007.

Cornelissen, S. (2004) "'It's Africa's turn!' The narratives and legitimations of the Moroccan and South African bids for the 2006 and 2010 FIFA finals." *Third World Quarterly*, 25 (7): 1293–1309.

Cornelissen, S. (2010a) "The geopolitics of global aspiration: Sport mega-events and emerging powers." *International Journal of the History of Sport*, 27 (16/18): 3008–3025.

Cornelissen, S. (2010b) "The economic impact of South Africa's 2010 World Cup: Ex ante ambitions and possible ex post realities," in Southall, R., Daniel, J., and Pillay, D. (eds.) *The New South African Review*, Johannesburg: Wits University Press.

Cornelissen, S. and Swart, K. (2006) "The 2010 FIFA World Cup as a political construct: The challenge of making good on an African promise." *Sociological Review*, 54 (2): 108–123.

Couzens, T. (1983) "An introduction to the history of football in South Africa," in B. Bozzoli (ed.) *Town and Countryside in the Transvaal*, Johannesburg: Ravan Press, pp. 198–214.

Desai, A. and Vahed, G. (2010) "World Cup 2010: Africa's turn or the turn on Africa?" *Soccer & Society*, 11 (1/2): 154–167.

Dobson, N. and Sinnamon, R. (2001) "A critical analysis of the organisation of major sports events," in Gratton, C. and Henry, I. (eds.) *Sport in the City: The Role of Sport in Economic and Social Regeneration*, London: Routledge, pp. 63–77.

Flyvbjerg, B., Bruzelius, N., and Rothengatter, W. (2003) *Megaprojects and Risk: An Anatomy of Ambition*, Cambridge: Cambridge University Press.

Grant Thornton (2010) "Updated economic impact of the 2010 FIFA World Cup." Media release, April 21.

Grundlingh, A. (1998) "From redemption to recividism? Rugby and change in South Africa during the 1995 Rugby World Cup and its aftermath." *Sporting Traditions*, 14: 67–86.

Grundlingh, A., Odendaal, A., and Spies, B. (1995) *Beyond the Tryline: Rugby and South African Society*, Johannesburg: Ravan Press.

Guardian (2011) "Qatar hopes 'artificial clouds' at World Cup can ease heat concerns." *Guardian*, March 24, http://www.guardian.co.uk/football/2011/mar/24/qatar-world-cup-clouds, accessed January 21, 2013.

Habib, A. (2009) "South Africa's foreign policy: Hegemonic aspirations, neoliberal orientations and global transformation." *South African Journal of International Affairs*, 16 (2): 143–159.

Hall, C.M. (1992) *Hallmark Tourist Events*, London: Belhaven Press.

Harvey, D. (1990) *The Condition of Postmodernity: An Enquiry into the Origins of Cultural Change*, Oxford: Blackwell.

Horne, J. and Manzenreiter, W. (2002) *Japan, Korea and the 2002 World Cup*, London: Routledge.

Horne, J. and Manzenreiter, W. (2006) "An introduction to the sociology of sports mega-events," in Horne, J. and Manzenreiter, W. (eds.) *Sports Mega-Events: Social Scientific Analyses of a Global Phenomenon*, Oxford: Blackwell, pp. 1–24.

Korth, M. and Rolfes, M. (2010) "Unsicheres Südafrika – Unsicheres WM 2010? Überlegungen und Erkenntnisse zur medialen Berichterstattung im Vorfeld der Fußball-Weltmeisterschaft," in Haferburgh, C. and Steinbrink, M. (eds.) *Mega-Event und Stadtentwicklung im globalen Süden – Die Fußballweltmeisterschaft 2010 und ihre Impulse für Südafrika*, Frankfurt: Brandes & Apsel.

Lenskyj, H. (2008) *Olympic Industry Resistance: Challenging Olympic Power and Propaganda*, Albany: State University of New York Press.

Levermore, R. (2004) "Sport's role in constructing the 'inter-state' worldview," in Levermore, R. and Budd, A. (eds.) *Sport and International Relations: An Emerging Relationship*, London: Routledge.

Manuel, T. (2011) "An open letter to Jimmy Manyani." *City Press*, March 2.

Mbeki, T. (2004) "Presentation to the FIFA Executive Committee on South Africa's bid for the 2010 Soccer World Cup," May 14, http://www.info.gov.za/speeches/2004/04051708151001.htm, accessed January 21, 2013.

Mbembe, A. (2010) "2010 World Cup: Where is the moral argument?" http://www.africultures.com/php/index.php?nav=article&no=5757, accessed January 21, 2013.

Merrett, C. (2009) *Sport, Space and Segregation: Politics and Society in Pietermaritzburg*, Scottsville: University of KwaZulu Natal Press.

Nauright, J. (1997) *Sport, Cultures and Identities in South Africa*, London: Leicester University Press.

Ndlovu-Gatsheni, S. (2011) "The World Cup, vuvuzelas, flag-waving patriots and the burden of building South Africa." *Third World Quarterly*, 32 (2): 279–293.

Nye, J. (1990) "Soft power." *Foreign Policy*, 80: 153–171.

Ohmae, K. (1990) *The Borderless World: Power and Strategy in the Inter-linked Economy*, London: Collins.

Pillay, U., Tomlinson, R., and Bass, O. (eds.) (2009) *Development and Dreams: Urban Development Implications of the 2010 Soccer World Cup*, Cape Town: HSRC Press.

Poynter, G. (2006) *From Beijing to Bow Creek*. London: London East Research Institute.

Roche, M. (2000) *Mega-events and Modernity: Olympics and Expos in the Growth of Global Culture*, London: Routledge.

Rosner, S. and Low, D. (2009) "The efficacy of Olympic bans and boycotts on effectuating international political and economic change." *Texas Review of Entertainment and Sports Law*, 11 (1): 27–79.

SA Tourism (2005) *Tourism Supply-Side Diagnostic of Potential Host Cities for the 2010 Soccer World Cup*, Pretoria: Department of Environmental Affairs and Tourism.

SA Tourism (2010) *Impact of 2010 FIFA World Cup*, Johannesburg: South Africa Tourism.

Schulz Herzenberg, C. (ed.) (2010) *Player and Referee: Conflicting Interests and the 2010 FIFA World Cup™*, Pretoria: Institute for Security Studies.

Slack, T. (ed.) (2004) *The Commercialisation of Sport*, London: Routledge.

Soccerex (2011) "FIFA unveils profit, World Cup allocations and event hosts." *Soccerex Business Daily*, March 4.

South Africa Government (2010a) "2010: Celebrate Africa's Humanity," http://www.southafrica.info/2010/slogan.htm, accessed January 21, 2013.

South Africa Government (2010b) "South Africa is ready for the World Cup," http://www.info.gov.za/issues/world_cup/index.htm, accessed January 24, 2013.

South Africa Government (2010c) "Government assessment of 2010 Fifa World Cup," July 14, www.sa2010.gov.za.

South African Football Association (2007) "The LOC vision," http://www.safa.net/index.php?page=organisation_matters, accessed 28 December, 2012.

South African Press Association/Deutsche Presse Agentur (2009) "World Cup accommodation a 'challenge,'" http://www.ioltravel.co.za/article/view/5164469, accessed October 22, 2009.

Southall, R., Daniel, J., and Pillay, D. (eds.) (2010) *The New South African Review*, Johannesburg: Wits University Press.

Stofile, M. (2007) "Budget vote speech, National Assembly." Cape Town, May 22. Cape Town: Government Communication and Information System.

Swart, K. and Bob, U. (2004) "The seductive discourse of development: The Cape Town 2004 Olympic bid." *Third World Quarterly*, 25 (7): 1311–1324.

Times (2009) "Riverlea residents demand 2010 employment." *The Times*, October 22.

Wenn, S.R. and Wenn, J.P. (1993) "Muhammed Ali and the convergence of Olympic sport and US diplomacy in 1980: A reassessment from behind the scenes at the US State Department." *Olympika: The International Journal of Olympic Studies*, II: 45–66.

Zukin S. (1995) *The Cultures of Cities*, Oxford: Blackwell.

Zuma, J. (2010a) "Africa: Address by President Jacob Zuma on the occasion of the Africa Day gala dinner," May 29, http://www.thepresidency.gov.za/pebble.asp?relid=300, accessed January 21, 2013.

Zuma, J. (2010b) "Address by the President of the Republic of South Africa, Mr J.G. Zuma on the occasion of National Heritage Day Celebrations in Moses Mabhida Stadium, Durban," September 24, http://www.thepresidency.gov.za/pebble.asp?relid=2120&t=79, accessed January 21, 2013.

Further Reading

Cornelissen, S. and Grundlingh, A. (eds.) (2012) *(Trans)forming the Nation: Sport Past and Present in South Africa*, London: Routledge.

Nauright, J. (2010) *Long Run to Freedom: Sport, Cultures and Identities in South Africa*, Morgantown, WV: Fitness Information Technology.

Pillay, U., Tomlinson, R., and Bass, O. (eds.) *Development and Dreams: Urban Development Implications of the 2010 Soccer World Cup*, Cape Town: HSRC Press.

25

Sporting Mega-events, Urban Modernity, and Architecture

John Horne

Introduction: Cities and Sporting Spectacles

Cities are spatial manifestations of broader social forces and struggles. The built environment and architecture play their part as both metric and motor of change. In the West for the past 250 years the urban environment has been created by industrial capitalist modernity, or perhaps, as the famous poem "Questions from a Worker Who Reads" by Bertholt Brecht (1976) reminds us, we should say by workers operating under the conditions of industrial capitalist modernity. In the past 30 years most of the developed and developing world, including emerging economies such as Brazil, China, and India (with the inclusion of Russia sometimes called "BRIC economies") have joined in the competitive marketing of places as social and economic opportunities seeking capital investment. Places have become commodities and "converted into products to be sold in competitive markets" (Philo and Kearns, 1993: 19).

It is not surprising then that several members of what Deyan Sudjic (2005: 117) called the "flying circus of the perpetually jet-lagged" were invited on to the 13-strong jury that judged the architectural competition to design the Olympic (Beijing National) stadium for the 2008 summer Olympic Games. The jury comprised seven Chinese and six foreign "starchitects," including Jean Nouvel, Rem Koolhaas, and Dominique Perrault. The winners, Jacques Herzog and Pierre de Meuron, also designed the Allianz Arena football stadium in Munich before the 2006 FIFA football World Cup, the Tate Modern in London, and the Forum Building in Barcelona. Architectural critic Sudjic (2005: 117) considered their proposed "bird's nest" stadium would be the most distinctive Olympic stadium since "Munich's Teflon-coated tents" in 1972. In addition to the Olympic stadium, nearby was the National Aquatics Center (or "Water Cube"), designed by Australian architectural firm PTW, and Digital Beijing, the information control and data center for the games. The building of Terminal 3 of Beijing Airport (designed by Lord (Norman) Foster, who also helped design the new Wembley Stadium in London), the National Theater, and the headquarters of China Central Television (CCTV) designed by Rem Koolhaas, completes a list of some of the most iconic architectural structures that have been built in Beijing since the awarding of the Olympic Games in 2001.

A Companion to Sport, First Edition. Edited by David L. Andrews and Ben Carrington.
© 2013 Blackwell Publishing Ltd. Published 2013 by Blackwell Publishing Ltd.

For the 2012 summer Olympic and Paralympic Games held in Stratford, east London, six permanent venues were constructed including the Olympic stadium designed by architectural firm Populous, a velodrome by Hopkins Architects (the firm of Sir Michael Hopkins), and an aquatics center designed by the architect Zaha Hadid. While there were severe criticisms of the cost of the latter (£269 million for a swimming pool) and the additional "water wings" attached to boost seating accommodation during the staging of the Olympics and Paralympics, the designs for all three received widespread acclaim within the field of architecture and amongst the crowds of sports fans who attended events in the Olympic park. The stadium was shortlisted for the largest annual prize in British architecture (the Royal Institute of British Architects' (RIBA) Stirling Prize). In this and many other ways it is clear that sports and other mega-events have long provided opportunities for nations to signal emergence or re-emergence on the international stage.

Whilst there are and can only be a few "global cities" (Sassen, 1991), attempts to promote locations is a commonplace of the past 30 years. Whether as new hubs for business and finance or as tourist destinations, cities increasingly build and utilize iconic architecture and urban spaces to flag their presence in the world. Sports mega-events play their part in this competition for global promotion and branding. But this is only one of their contributions. As Eisinger (2000) notes, the "politics of bread and circuses" is about building cities for the wealthy "visitor class"; iconic stadium construction is about flagging transnational places and creating symbolic capital to attract middle- and upper-middle-class visitors.

Some sociologists of sport have identified these developments and begun to explore them critically (see, e.g., Horne, 2011; Horne and Whannel, 2012; Friedman, Andrews, and Silk, 2004; Silk and Amis, 2005; Zhang and Silk, 2006). Reviews of the impact of sports mega-events on the urban environment have noted at least three vested interests involved in their production: sport, corporate, and urban. With a focus on impacts, legacy, or as Hiller (2003) prefers, "outcomes," studies have considered the different phases (Essex and Chalkley, 2003) and patterns (Liao and Pitts, 2006) of urban development that have resulted from the Olympic Games. I agree with Hiller (2003) that it is important to consider the controversial nature of urban developments related to sports mega-events. Legacies cannot be considered to be simply positive ones. As Jonathan Glancey remarked in his review of architecture for 2008 in the *Guardian* newspaper, the Beijing National Stadium was "the architectural star of the Olympics," even if, he added, "it was strangely quiet and empty during the games" (2008b: 23). Looking back a year later he included the Bird's Nest in his top ten list of buildings of the "noughties" decade, yet also noted that since the Olympics, "this charismatic structure has been largely redundant" (Glancey, 2009: 19).

Rather than rehearse various "knowns" about sports mega-events (Horne, 2007), such as the likely production of "white elephants" and the overestimation of benefits and underestimation of costs, this chapter sets out some notes and critical observations on a less often researched aspect of sport spectacles and mega-events: who the agents and institutions are that assemble, build, and especially design the material infrastructure, including the stadia and facilities.

Ren (2008: 176) suggests "social scientists have just begun to explore the linkage between architectural mega-projects and nation-building practices in global or globalizing cities." Whilst Garry Stevens (1998: 137) estimated that less than 1 percent of the buildings designed by architects listed in the *Macmillan Encyclopedia of Architects* were for sports, these figures relate to the late 1970s. Preuss, in his (2004) study of the economics of the Olympics, suggests that architectural design "applies less to sports venues and Olympic villages than to the smaller ticket-selling information stands" (pp. 235–236). I propose that both authors underestimate the symbolic power and economy of the sports mega-events infrastructure. Adopting a "production of consumption" approach to the study of sport in consumer culture, related to, but not completely informed by, the critical political economy of sport (found, e.g., in the work of Bélanger, 2009; Horne and Whannel, 2012; Whannel, 2008; Whitson and Macintosh, 1993), this chapter seeks to dig below the surface of the reified world of the material infrastructure of global cities to discuss the creators of the emblematic buildings and the leisure and sport spaces constructed to assist in the pursuit or maintenance of "world-class" status.

The chapter has the following structure. In the next section I consider the production of the material infrastructure of urban modernity and particularly debates about the political economy of the built environment, architecture, and architects. Included here is an outline of the growth of what Sklair (2001) calls the "transnational capitalist class" (TCC) and the place of architects in this class. Next an historical overview of architecture and architects in relation to urban sport spectacles in both the United Kingdom and North America is presented. The leading firms and architects that build sport stadia, and especially stadia for sports mega-events, are then discussed and their key characteristics identified. My conclusion summarizes the discussion and identifies future research questions for a critical sociology of sports architecture.

Architecture and the Production of the Material Infrastructure of Cities

Architecture and the social role of architects in particular have not been a significant topic for sociological analysis. Partly this has been supported by the view that architecture is an artistic practice, the creation of individual genius, and therefore cannot be adequately comprehended by sociological theories. Three books however demonstrate that it is possible to produce a sound understanding of the social world of architecture, architects and architectural education, utilizing contemporary social theories.

Garry Stevens (1998) found great value in Pierre Bourdieu's work for understanding the way the architectural "field" produces cultivated individuals with distinctive styles and tastes, and thus the way in which individual architectural creativity is derived from a social process. Like other artistic practices contemporary architecture can be examined in Marxist and sociological terms by looking at the social relations of production within which it emerges and operates. These approaches pay attention to the institutions through which architects are educated, how building designs are produced, and hence how architecture is socially constructed (see, for another example, Imrie, 2007). Architects may

operate today within conditions that are determined by market forces for design and iconicity, but also, as Donald McNeill (2009) suggests, architecture is a *heteronomous* practice – it is reliant on other agents and practices in order to take place. As the managing principal at the world's largest architectural practice in 2008, Chris Johnson of Gensler told *Building Design* magazine, "we don't really do projects, we do relationships" (*Building Design*, 2007: 6). Taking this notion of architectural dependency further is the study *Architecture Depends* by Jeremy Till (2009), which demonstrates the *contingency* of architecture and architects via a discussion of the sociological ideas of Zygmunt Bauman, Henri Lefebvre, and Bruno Latour amongst others. In addition to those mentioned in the main body of the text recent sociological accounts include Fowler and Wilson (2004) on women in the architectural profession, and Jones (2006) and Delanty and Jones (2002) on the relationship between architecture and identity in post-national contexts.

How buildings are made to look like one another, with particular messages about place and identity being transmitted, and why some buildings are seen to be more culturally important than others (Ballantyne, 2002) are important questions but I do not look at them in detail here. As McNeill (2009) suggests, architecture also needs to be understood from the perspectives of the firm, fame, and form. In this chapter the focus is on identifying the firms involved in the building of sport facilities and stadia, and charting the changing relationship between architects and sport. Whilst Ewen (1988) alludes to the changing celebrity status of architects and architecture during the twentieth century, Till (2009: 42) comments that "the values and currency of the famous" dominate architectural culture, and the production and marketing of architectural icon buildings and signature architects (Larson, 1994: 470) or "starchitects," has certainly grown since the 1980s. Whilst architecture may have a cultural and aesthetic existence independent of those paying for it, it is unquestionably the case that "architecture is about power" (Sudjic, 2005: 6). As Garry Stevens notes (1998: 86), "The field of architecture is responsible for producing those parts of the built environment that the dominant classes use to justify their domination of the social order. Buildings of power, buildings of state, buildings of worship, buildings to awe and impress."

Politically architecture tells a story about those who determine that something is built. Whether democratic or totalitarian, a regime utilizes architecture as a tool of "statecraft" (Sudjic, 2005: 8; see also Marvin, 2008 for the role of architecture in Chinese statecraft). One very important economic feature is the growth of the marketplace for building design. The market provides the basic economic structure that encloses and also creates the experiences of architects. The structure makes some aspirations possible, and others inconceivable. A brief consideration of the political economy of architecture would reveal that whilst architects design buildings they do not do so under circumstances of their own choosing. As Till (2009: 123) states, "qualities of hard space that dominate architectural production allow that space to be easily appropriated by the market." This is exacerbated by the architects' code of conduct, whereby they provide a service for clients (not users) whose own demands are most often driven by market and "short-term opportunism" (p. 123). If "architects can never fully control the actions of users" (p. 41) they most certainly cannot easily dictate to those for whom they provide a service. This is one of the ways that the position and role of architects is contingent.

Architects are involved in the construction of 30–50 percent of the contract value of buildings in the developed world (Stevens, 1998: 228, n. 64). Traditionally it has been considered that there are three types of architectural firm: "strong-delivery," "strong service," and "strong ideas" firms (Gutman, 1988). The first types are highly commercial and rarely win awards but build a lot. The second includes architectural practices such as Skidmore, Owings, and Merrill which designed Canary Wharf in London and is currently designing the Freedom Tower at "Ground Zero" in Manhattan, New York City. The third types of firm contain well-known "starchitects" such as Frank Gehry, Norman Foster, and Robert Venturi, all famous for producing iconic buildings. Gehry's design for the Guggenheim Museum in Bilbao, for example, became the world's most famous new building in the 1990s and led to calls to replicate the "Bilbao effect." The building, a titanium-covered museum juxtaposed against central Bilbao's river valley and built on the site of a former steelworks, "brought together deeply politicized place marketing, the architectural branding of an aspirational art institution, and the worldwide projection of Frank Gehry as a celebrity architect" (McNeill, 2009: 81–82). Gehry even featured in an episode of *The Simpsons*. Gehry is not impressed with being described as a "starchitect," however, as an interview with him published in the *Independent* newspaper showed (Day, 2009).

Despite the symbolic value of such iconic architecture designed by celebrity architects, Sklair (2005: 487) noted that entry level to the *Fortune* Global 500 – the annual list of the world's largest transnational corporations (TNCs) identified by *Fortune* magazine – was US$10 billion in 2003. No leading architectural firm reached anywhere near this figure then and the same applied to the US$19 billion entry-level figure recorded in the 2011 list (Forbes, 2011). Even strong delivery firms that produce a lot of buildings but few icons, operate in consortia chasing mega-projects (here defined as construction projects estimated to involve expenditures over US$1 billion). The two main locations for most mega-projects in the past decade have been the United States and China.

In 2006 the United States had an estimated 150 projects that provided the bulk of opportunities for engineering, architectural, and construction firms there (RKMA, 2006: 46). The restructuring of the financial sector globally has had an impact on these projects, and as one observer noted by the end of 2009, "the money, the work and the power have irrevocably headed East" (Puckett, 2009). Economic growth in Pacific Asia (especially stimulated by China's building boom since the 1990s, see Olds, 1997, 2001) and the Middle East (until recently) has in turn encouraged more celebrity architects to operate globally. These architects have taken on an increased role in planning and building in cities in the Asia-Pacific region. The so-called Global Intelligence Corps including architectural celebrities have been used to brand local developments by indigenous developers, politicians, and bureaucrats, who thus in turn gain symbolic capital by association (Olds, 1997; Larson, 1994; Rimmer, 1991). As Broudehoux (2004: 21) notes, since the death of Mao Zedong Beijing has been "turning itself into a scenographic venue for the hosting of world class media events and the staging of grand urban spectacles." This works in sport as much as any other form of spectacle, as Trumpbour (2007) points out in his discussion of the stadium construction boom that has beset the United States since the late 1990s. As cities in the United States have competed to retain or gain "major league" or "world class" status, association with a professional sports franchise is seen as a valuable source of symbolic capital.

In the contemporary globalizing world Leslie Sklair (2005) argues that the emergence of "iconic architecture" (IA) is a result of transformations in the production, marketing, and reception of architecture, which is itself a consequence of capitalist globalization. Producing iconic buildings has increasingly become useful to what Sklair (2005; see also 2001, 2002, 2006) refers to as the transnational capitalist class. IA refers to two things, buildings and spaces that are famous because of the architects who design them and also those with special symbolic/aesthetic significance attached to them. Architects can be iconic in this sense, hence the media label "starchitect." Before the 1950s, which in Sklair's formulation is the pre-globalization era, the interests of the state and/or religion drove IA. In the globalization era he argues that the dominant force driving iconic architecture is the TCC (Sklair, 2005: 485).

Architecture has been internationalized as its source of patronage and sponsorship has altered (King, 2004). Modes of production and associated ideologies increasingly shape architectural design rather than the nation state (although see Brownell, 1995, on stadium building in Beijing). Globalized production aided by new technologies of communication and design in addition to an already internationalized profession (formalized by the formation of the International Union of Architects in 1948) led to the growth of architecture as a global cultural form. The 1950s and 1960s saw the building of American-style hotels throughout the world, prompting debates about homogenization and plurality that became familiar in subsequent decades with respect to the notion of sociocultural globalization.

According to Sklair the TCC comprises people with globalizing as well as localizing agendas, who have a home in more than one place, and who have a cosmopolitan outlook. The TCC seeks to secure the conditions under which its interests and largely capitalist interests are furthered in global and local contexts. The TCC has four fractions: corporate, state, technical, and consumerist. The corporate fraction own and control major transnational corporations and their local affiliates. In architecture these are the major architectural, architecture-engineering, and architecture-developer-real estate firms listed in such magazines as the (now defunct) *World Architecture* and *Building Design's* World Architecture 100.[1]

As I have suggested, the revenues of these companies are relatively small compared to firms in the *Fortune* 500, and the number of starchitects with the biggest firms is also small, but they have great significance for the built environment and their cultural importance for cities outweighs their financial muscle. This is one reason why Preuss (2004: 235–236) is mistaken to ignore the symbolic role and value of architectural design in sports mega-events such as the Olympic Games. Nor is it enough, without further investigation, to say that the impacts of sports mega-events on urban, spatial, architectural, and built form of cities (including negative ones such as mass evictions; on this see COHRE, 2007) are "obvious" (King, 2004: 35). The state fraction of the TCC includes politicians and bureaucrats who decide what gets built where and how changes to the built environment are regulated (at central, regional, and municipal levels of government). The technical TCC are professionals involved in the design of structural features and services of new buildings, as well as the education of students and the public in architectural discourse. The consumerist TCC are the merchants and media responsible for the marketing and the consumption of architecture (Sklair, 2005: 485–486).

In the next section I sketch some examples of how stadium architects (another type of "starchitect") contribute to the construction of not only sport stadia and spectacles but also urban built environments, and thus help to produce symbolic capital for localities seeking a global profile.

Stadium Architecture and Urban Sport Spectacles

The allure of hosting sports mega-events has increased greatly in the past 30 years. When Los Angeles hosted the summer Olympics in 1984 there were no competing cities. Nagoya was the only rival to Seoul to host the summer Games in 1988. Clearly the significant alteration in the global geopolitical landscape at the end of the 1980s – the collapse of the Soviet Union, the highly symbolic but also material demolition of the Berlin wall, and the associated break-up of the East European bloc of nations – has helped the Olympic "mega" develop into the position it now holds in the global imagination and the global economy of appearances. As noted earlier, journalist and architectural critic Deyan Sudjic (2005: 326) suggests that architecture "is constantly about . . . power, glory, spectacle, memory, identity" whilst it always changes in form. That this is as true for the buildings and facilities underpinning sport and sports mega-events as it is for other construction projects can be seen through a brief examination of selected buildings designed for summer Olympic Games (see Table 25.1).

As I have suggested the role of architects in the creation of memorable Olympic infrastructures has not been analyzed much until relatively recently. This may partly be to do with the fact that whilst stadia built prior to 1984 included the well-received Tokyo and Munich projects, it also included Montreal, which stands out as one of the most negative examples of contemporary architectural ambition. The complex design and ambitious *grand projet* left the city with an enormous debt only paid off completely 30 years later in November 2006 (CBC News, 2006; also see Morin, 1998; Whitson and Horne, 2006). As a result the stadium, popularly called "The Big O," gained the additional nickname of "The Big Owe" and even in late 2008 the website of the architectural practice concerned, Paris-based Roger Taillibert,[2] contained a note from "the Stadium's Friends" on the history of the stadium, defending his role. It argued that

- The Olympic park has become the largest industrial wasteland of the Olympic sports.
- Jean Drapeau [former Mayor of Montreal] who put all his energy to offer it to the youth of Quebec and of eastern Montreal has been betrayed.
- Baseball disappeared. – Cycling committed suicide. – Indoor sports have never been realized. – Swimming has been neglected, if we consider the importance of the equipment. – The outside surroundings have been neglected too and the fountains became jardinières. – The work of the great Canadian artist Riopelle, considered at that time as a permanent fixture, was removed from the site. – Projects related to offices to be incorporated into the mast were evoked, whereas this is a quite unrealizable idea, surprising and destructive. – Suppression of a walking surface originally designed for the quality of the complex and of its annexes.
- The great mistake was to have considered Jean Drapeau as a spendthrift politician, whereas he will remain forever a visionary for his city and his country. As for the Olympic funding, we can say that the amount of the tobacco tax and its income would have made it possible to build 6 Olympic stadiums. (French original)

It is clear that the Olympic Games and other sports mega-events have long provided opportu-

Table 25.1   Selected Olympic Games and architects.

Olympic Games	Architect
Tokyo 1964	Tange Kenzo (Yoyogi National Gymnasium, Tokyo)
Munich 1972	Gunter Behnisch and Frei Otto (Olympiastadion, Munich)
Montreal 1976	Roger Taillibert (Montreal Stadium)
Sydney 2000	Bligh Lobb Sports Architecture (Stadium Australia, Sydney)
Athens 2004	Santiago Calatrava Valls (Olympic Sports Complex, Athens)
Beijing 2008	Jacques Herzog/Pierre de Meuron (Beijing National Stadium)
London 2012	HOK Sport/ Populous™ with McAlpine (Olympic Stadium); Zaha Hadid (Aquatics Centre)

nities for nations to signal emergence or re-emergence on the international stage. Whilst there are and can only be a few "global cities," attempts to promote locations has become a commonplace of the past 20 years. Whether as new hubs for business and finance or as tourist destinations, cities increasingly build and utilize iconic architecture and urban spaces to flag their presence in the world. Sports mega-events play their part in this competition for global promotion and branding.

Researchers have noted that the attraction of hosting sports mega-events has grown since the 1980s because it enables multiple sets of agendas to be addressed. The main ones are place promotion, internal (social, cultural, and economic) development, and global status. The hosting of a major event enables symbolic as well as material nation building to take place. Short (2004: 68ff.) identifies four modalities of global cities: transportation hubs and networks; global cultures and cosmopolitanism; global imaginings and place marketing; and global spectacles, signature architects, and cosmopolitan urban semiotics. The summer Olympic Games is "the mega-event with the ability to create, reinforce and consolidate global city status" (Short, 2004: 108) as it condenses these modalities. The summer Olympics are "global spectacles, national campaigns and city enterprises" at one and the same time (Short, 2004: 86).

Globally the International Olympic Committee (IOC), prompted by concerns about its environmental impact, wavering public opinion in the light of corruption revelations, and interest in the amorphous concepts of "legacy" and "sustainability" that developed in the 1990s, has helped shape the environment in which the change in the role of architecture and stadium architects in sport has taken place (see also CHAPTER 7). Concerns about legacy have been the focus of one IOC conference and transfer of knowledge has become a vital part of the organization of Olympic events. The related concern with "sustainability" has existed since 1994 when the IOC adopted the environment as the third pillar of the Olympic movement (Hayes and Horne, 2011). Former IOC president Samaranch and current president Rogge have written highly positive forewords to books on stadium design (see John and Sheard, 2000; John, Sheard, and Vickery, 2006).

The growth in ambition and significance of sports architects and architecture can be illustrated in the titles of three books published over the past 20 years: *Handbook of Sports and Recreational Building Design*, vol. 1, *Outdoor Sports* (John and Campbell, 1993); *Stadia: A Design and Development Guide* (John and Sheard, 2000);[3] and *The Stadium: Architecture for the New Global Culture* (Sheard, 2005). There has been a shift from the technical/descriptive, to the nostalgic (including works like the widely popular and pictorial study of football grounds, Inglis, 1987) and the sociocultural, such as the Played in Britain series of books edited by Simon Inglis (see, e.g., Inglis, 2005).

Sklair argues that "starchitects" assist the TCC through the construction of transnationally attractive consumption spaces and the production of IA forms. Since the 1980s starchitects have been invited to build iconic buildings and consumption spaces and the ideological role of these reflects other processes going on in cities. This includes the reimagining/imagineering of cities as consumption centers, rather than centers of production; the building of urban entertainment destinations and other themed environments; and the construction of spaces for the consumption of experiential commodities, such as sports and recreational events, concerts, and other commercial gatherings, which include stadia or "tradiums" often increasingly named after a sponsor rather than their location in the city (Rutheiser, 1996; Hannigan, 1998). Examples of these would include QualComm Park, Gillette Stadium, FedEx Field, and Coors Field, in the United States, the Rodgers Center in Canada, and the JJB Stadium, Reebok Stadium, and Emirates Stadium in the United Kingdom. Saunders (2005: viii) suggests "*Spectacle* is the primary manifestation of the commodification or commercialization of design." This has also involved a "simulated de-McDonaldization" according to George Ritzer and Todd Stillman (2001). What they mean by this is that in some sporting venues the rebuilding of ballparks as theme parks, for example, has involved a deliberate attempt to re-enchant the place whilst also retaining a rationalized and efficient location in which to maximize consumption. As they write "the magical allure of the ballpark is simulated to increase the consumer appeal of a rationalized setting" (Ritzer and Stillman, 2001: 99). In addition this process has seen architects become brands in their own right (Frampton, 2005) creating "architainment" for some.

As already noted, some sociologists have already responded to these developments critically. In North America journalist Dave Zirin has identified the building of iconic sports and leisure spaces as a poor "substitute for anything resembling an urban policy in this country" (2009: 262). He describes the way that the Louisiana Superdome became a shelter for 30,000 of New Orleans' poorest residents left homeless by Hurricane Katrina in August 2005. Built from public funds 30 years earlier, it would normally have been beyond their means to enter the arena. The homeless people were then moved on from there to the Houston Astrodome in Texas, not to government housing, public shelters, or somewhere nearer to their devastated homes. Zirin (2009: 262) argues, "stadiums are sporting shrines to the dogma of trickle-down economics." A total of US$16 billion of US public money had been spent on stadium construction and upkeep in the previous decade. Despite evidence to the contrary that they function as financial cash cows "the domes keep coming" (Zirin, 2009: 262), however. The opening of two new baseball arenas in 2009 in New York, CitiField (New York Mets) and the new Yankee Stadium (New York Yankees) – the latter the most expensive sport stadium in the world, ahead of the new Wembley stadium in London – testifies to the continuing allure of sports facilities (Cornwell, 2009).

Trumpbour (2007: 57) noted that if the pace of stadium building in the United States continued at the same rate as it commenced the twenty-first century, then it would surpass the value for the entire twentieth century by 2015. The situation in the United Kingdom is not much different, although the rebuilding began in the 1990s. Inglis (2000, 2005) identifies two moments when sport stadium architecture underwent fundamental change in the United Kingdom, at the end of the nineteenth century and at the end of the twentieth. The local stimulus to the most recent shift in Britain has been the sustained investment in the infrastructure of football stadia in England, Wales, and to a lesser extent Scotland, since the publication of the Taylor Report (1990) into the Hillsborough Stadium disaster in 1989 that rec-

ommended, amongst other things, the move toward all-seat football stadia.

One of the first fruits of this tragic stimulus was the Alfred McAlpine (now Galpharm) Stadium in Huddersfield, designed by Rod Sheard, which became the first sports venue to win a RIBA Building of the Year award in 1995. Following the merger of Sheard's Lobb Partnership and HOK in 1999, Sheard and HOK Sport (now known as Populous™) have become even more prominent in promoting sports architecture, including, for example, through sponsoring Inglis' (2005) book.

The 2012 Olympic Games had a massive influence on architecture in the United Kingdom in the lead up to the Games and the links connecting leading politicians, architectural practices, the construction industry, academics, and the London 2012 Olympics became evident. Sport-related projects, not only in the mega-event form, may become more important for architects as they look to diversify in the sectors in which they operate. In doing so architects will be drawn even more into urban, spatial politics (Glancey, 2011).

Bélanger (2009) identifies several contradictory and contested features of the urban sport spectacle in which architects can become enmeshed as they produce (trans)national sport spaces. First, the paradox of distinctiveness is that if everywhere has iconic architecture then there is a global sameness to the pursuit of distinction. This can lead to the creation of unspectacular spectacles, or the predictable monotony of the spectacular in commodified space, as geographer David Harvey once argued (1989) was the case with respect to postmodernist architecture (see Merrifield, 2002, especially pp. 144–155). Second, there are various urban narratives, imaginaries, and themes that can create a division between, in architectural as well as other terms, the spectacular global and the vernacular local. This in turn can lead to spectacular local resistance to and/or negotiation with the global spectacle through novel uses and vernacular appropriation of the built environment (Stevens, 2007). Third, the production of consumption spaces, such as the new-made-to-look-old nostalgic baseball parks in the United States (e.g., Camden Yards in Baltimore or PNC Park in Pittsburgh), uses collective memory to reformulate a new consumerized public sphere.

Yet as spaces sports stadia are both public and private, both popular and disciplining, intimate as well as commercial. They are shaped by public meanings and form the basis of popular memories, including, at times of disaster, becoming the forum for cultures of commemoration (Russell, 2006). Hence Bélanger (2009) alerts us to the ever-present gap between capital's intentions and the use values of spectacular urban sport spaces.

To summarize the argument so far: the involvement of the various fractions of the TCC in the shaping of the built environment relates to sports facilities and stadia as much as to any other public building. In the next section I illustrate this with some case studies that illustrate which firms build these sports facilities as monuments. I then ask how they make their buildings mean something. In short, what is the spatial and political impact of architecture?

The Leading Firms in Sports Architecture

Building Design magazine's World Architecture 100 ranks architectural practices by size (number of architects and other "creative" staff employed), regional prominence by fee income, and market-sector share. Interpreting the annual league tables requires some caution – results are produced from questionnaire returns from the firms, fee income revealed is an approximation, and of course the tables provide only a snapshot of the situation from one year to the next which may reflect specific market conditions in sectors, regions, or the global economy. Despite these qualifications the data is of interest in identifying the leading firms in building sport stadia.

The top ten in the "sports stadium" sector is outlined in Table 25.2. Of the leading companies in the sector four had their headquarters in the United States, two in Europe, two in Japan, and one each in Australia and the People's Republic of China (PRC). The leading company in the design of sports facilities was HOK International or Hellmuth, Obata, and Kassabaum. In the World Architecture 100 for 2008, overall HOK was the second largest architectural practice with total fee income in excess of US$250 million and 2,493 employees. Founded in 1955 by George Hellmuth, Gyo Obata, and George

Kassabaum, HOK had 26 regional offices on four continents – North America, Europe, Asia, and Australia.[4] A specialist company division – HOK Sport + Venue + Event (HOKSVE) – dealt with sport, venues, and event management following a merger with the Lobb Partnership in 1999 and Anderson Consulting in 2002. As the division's website noted in 2007, "Our global client list is diverse and comprehensive, and it includes 24 Major League Baseball franchises, 30 NFL franchises, 80 professional and civic arena clients, 40 soccer and rugby teams and 120 colleges and universities. Our reach is worldwide. Our passion is undeniable and we approach the architecture of sport unlike anyone else."

HOKSVE employed over 70 principal and senior principal architects – although only three of them were women. In this respect it has a significantly smaller percentage of women than in the male-dominated architectural profession as a whole: "the practice of creating large scale buildings is still virtually monopolized by men," as Fowler and Wilson (2004: 101) noted. The firm has engaged in projects covering most sports – aquatic, track and field, Australian football league, major league and minor league baseball, basketball (including collegiate), cricket, equine, field and ice hockey, American football, soccer, motor-racing, speed-skating, and tennis – over a 25-year period. In 2008 HOK's apparent ascendancy as the number one sports stadium architectural firm was reflected in terms of its regional status. HOK appeared in the top ten practices in Australasia, the Middle East, Central Asia, and North and South Central America in the 2008 World Architecture 100.

In the second half of 2008 HOKSVE was subject to a management buy-out led by senior principal architect Rod Sheard. It was relaunched with the new corporate name and brand Populous™ in March 2009. The website of the new practice stated that "Populous is a global design practice specializing in creating environments that draw people and communities together for unforgettable experiences."[5]

According to the Populous website the following numbers applied to the firm in December 2009: US$20 billion total construction value of Populous projects; 1,000 Populous-completed projects around the world; 520 million people have attended a Populous facility in the past 10

Table 25.2 The top ten sports stadium architectural practices in 2008 ranked by fee income.

Practice	HQ	Fee income from sport US$m	Total fee income US$m	No. of architects	No. of employees	World position	Exemplary project(s)
HOK(SVE)	St Louis, USA	85.4	>250	1,205	2,493	2nd	Wembley Stadium; London 2012 Stadium
HKS	Dallas, USA	17.0	190–199	651	1,426	9th	Liverpool FC (proposed new stadium)
JSK Architects	Frankfurt, Germany	12.0	70–79	201	n/a	48th	Warsaw National Stadium
Cox Architects/Planners	Sydney, Australia	10.0	70–79	350	450	23rd	Melbourne Cricket Ground; Aquatic Center, Thailand
ACXT-IDOM	Bilbao, Spain	5.8	50–59	145	n/a	72nd	New San Mamés Stadium, Bilbao
Leigh & Orange	Hong Kong, PRC	5.5	30–39	220	670	42nd	Happy Valley Racecourse; Al Shaqab Equestrian Academy, Doha, Qatar
Leo A Daly	Omaha, USA	5.0	180–189	327	1,074	24th	Reliant Stadium, Houston
Kume Sekkei	Tokyo, Japan	4.7	80–89	311	527	27th	Nagano Olympic Games Memorial Arena (M-Wave)
Nikken Sekkei	Tokyo, Japan	4.6	>250	1,174	2,008	3rd	"Big Swan" Stadium, Niigata
NBBJ	Seattle, USA	3.1	150–159	442	759	17th	Staples Center, Los Angeles; Samsan World Gymnasium, Incheon

Source: BD 2008 World Architecture 100, http://emag.digitalpc.co.uk/cmpi/worldarch08.asp, accessed 29 December, 2012.

years alone; 510 million square feet of buildings Populous has designed; 18 million seats in Populous-designed stadia; 351,000 club seats Populous has designed; 15,500 suites Populous has designed; 30,000 times Populous has been mentioned in the media; 34 countries where Populous has done work; 24 major league baseball franchise clients; 30 NFL franchise clients; 80 professional and civic-arena clients; 40 soccer and rugby team clients; 120 college and university clients; 40 convention center clients; 30 sports-related events Populous has coordinated; 500 employees around the world; and 150 design awards the firm has received (Populous, 2009a). Notably however a number Populous did not list was that in December 2009 only one woman featured in the renamed "Populous" practice.

Populous continues to achieve considerable success in attracting commissions – including both the main stadium for the winter Olympic and Paralympic Games to be held in Sochi, Russia in 2014 and London's 2012 Olympic stadium (Populous, 2009b).[6] None of the other companies in the sports stadium sector has such a global presence as HOK/ Populous™, although NBBJ – tenth in the sports stadium sector but seventeenth largest architectural firm in the world in 2008 – featured in both the North America and Central and Eastern Europe regional top ten.

In addition to the Liverpool FC commission, Dallas-based HKS were selected to design a multi-sport stadium scheduled to be built on the site of the former Maze/Long Kesh prison in Belfast, Northern Ireland. Owing to the political situation the Belfast project was eventually canceled in May 2008, while in late 2012 Liverpool confirmed that they would work with the city council to redevelop their home ground Anfield instead into a 60,000 seater stadium, at an estimated cost of £150 million. Most of the other sports stadium-sector leaders have a more regional, rather than global, presence. Cox was ranked second overall in the Australasia region, ACXT-IDOM and JSK were ninth and tenth in Western Europe, Leo Daly and HKS are third and fourth biggest in North America, whilst Nikkon Seikei, Kume Seikei, and Leigh & Orange were first, fourth, and ninth respectively in the Pacific Rim region (*Building Design*, 2007: 35, 37). Nikkon Seikei, the largest firm in Japan, whose major projects range from golf course and

country club design to bridge and road building, has nearly all its projects in Asia.

The website of Leo Daly, a large Omaha-based practice, responsible for several sports arenas and public venues, outlined the complexity of the sector's needs in 2008:

> Whether they serve as anchor for a civic complex that revitalizes a downtown area or become a symbol of school pride, public assembly and sports venues must be exceptional and generate excitement. . . . Their multipurpose nature requires flexibility to accommodate and rotate activities. . . . Our designers work closely with owners, municipalities, operators, food service providers, sports teams and performers because they understand these facilities must meet the goals of multiple stakeholders.[7]

To summarize this section, five features are immediately noticeable about sport-sector architectural firms, practices, and projects. First, in common with most other architectural work, as McNeill (2009) and Till (2009) both demonstrate well, is the necessity of working in partnership with other architectural practices and construction and design services such as service and structural engineers, project managers, and building contractors. Both JSK and Cox have worked in collaboration with HOK on projects in Germany (World Arena, Berlin) and Australia (MCG, Melbourne) respectively. Dependence also applies with respect to the necessity of conformity to local building regulations and safety guidelines (e.g., DCMS, 2008) that are as much a feature of the sports facilities and stadia sector as other areas of architectural practice. Second, as the long quotation above from Leo Daly affirms, the stakeholders', or clients', needs come before those of potential users or citizens of the locations where stadia or arenas are built. Third, the leading firms tend to be those with a more global presence. Those that seek a global presence will use any successes in design competitions to enhance their reputation and thus sustain their presence in the market sector. Fourth, despite apparent globalization, there has been a tendency for most sports-related work in North America, Europe, and the Pacific Rim region (including East Asian countries) to be designed by local companies, although the Beijing Olympic stadium and the associated

"Water Cube" aquatic center were exceptions to this. Fifth and finally, high-profile "starchitects" and well-respected companies, such as Foster and Partners and Herzog and de Meuron, are not part of the sport stadium top ten even though they have been and will be involved in some highly significant developments in the sector.

The Spatial and Political Impact of Architects

Individuals, companies, practices, and consortia are required to produce sports mega-events and its material infrastructure. Yet in building and designing for sport firms such as Populous™ have come to dominate international stadium design by arguably "turning out an interchangeable series of huge spectator machines that can process crowds quickly and efficiently yet entirely lack personality or charisma" according to Sudjic (2005: 117). The potential implications of this for urban space – regenerated but homogenized and ahistorical with sports stadia and buildings lacking personality – is taken up the British writer Iain Sinclair (2011).

As some "starchitects" have taken on an increased role in planning and building in cities in the Asia-Pacific, as well as the rest of the developed world, their global influence in stadium architecture can be seen as much as in any other form of IA. That the design of the built environment has been increasingly "engulfed in and made subservient to the goals of the capitalist economy" in the past 30 years is almost a truism (Saunders, 2005: vii).

Nonetheless, while architects are caught in the dilemmas of involvement in the market, some seek to imbue their designs with greater public access (Bauman Lyons Architects, 2008; McNeill, 2009). According to architect Irena Bauman, "Architects need to become sociologists as well as researchers" (quoted in Wainwright, 2008: 2). Jones (2006: 550) suggests that architecture may have become an increasingly significant expression of diverse collective identities in recent years. While landmark buildings were once a central way of "expressing and developing the national code," Jones notes that they are now increasingly sites of symbolic conflict and competition over identities. In what he considers could be a post-

national context, architecture can provide a cultural space for new identities to be expressed and contested. The role of architects as cultural intermediaries in all of this is to make their buildings meaningful to non-architects. The "architect's role in translating and disseminating meanings is key" (Jones, 2006: 556). They do this by reflexively situating their buildings in terms of identity projects.

We all might ask: but how can architects align their buildings with various identity discourses? There are three ways that architects can engage with their designs' meanings – interpreting the buildings they design, conveying the meaning of the buildings, and linking the buildings to identities both collective and personal. First, architects have become more active in disseminating their interpretations of their buildings (Jones, 2006: 551–553). They appear more on television, give more lectures, write more books and letters to newspapers, and generally have a higher media profile. Rod Sheard's recent output is one good example of this. In his books, contributions to collections, and in articles discussing his work, he has even developed a theory of the development of stadia, "the five generations of stadia" theory (Sheard, 2001a, 2001b, 2005: 100ff.; Culf, 2005; Inglis, 2000). This firmly places the contemporary stadium at the center of urban regeneration projects with the potential for inspiring urban change through the building of iconic sports architecture.

A second way architects communicate the meaning of their work is to create symbolic narrative associations between their work and positive or warm political concepts such as "democracy," "transparency," and "openness" (this was especially evident in the relationship between architects EMBT headed by Enric Miralles and the design of the new Scottish Parliament building). With respect to stadium architecture, as a member of the World Stadium Team (WST) consortium of HOK and Foster and Partners that developed the new Wembley Stadium, the guided tour of the building given by Lord (Norman) Foster that was broadcast during the FA Cup Final preview on May 19, 2007 on BBC TV was another example of this. Throughout Foster referred to the stadium as "intimate," praised the "closeness" of the "fantastic views" (even from the "cheap seats") and how much more the new stadium resembled "a spa," "a luxury hotel," or "a cultural building like an opera house or a hotel" than a football stadium. The arch, on the other hand was "one of those inspirational things."

The third way architects make their buildings mean something is to avoid privileging one collective identity over another, focusing instead upon concepts such as "multiculturalism," "diversity," and "accessibility." In this way the architects create links between buildings and collective identities, even though some are very exclusive and privileged identities. Meanings can change and values linked to buildings can be detached. Architecture reflects tensions in global and local identity. So how buildings are coupled to collective identities is best understood as a process over time, involving a "complex web of highly charged discourses about identities" (Jones, 2006: 562). Since meanings are not self-evident they have to be identified, translated, interpreted, and communicated.

Some architects can also be producers of alternative, protest, hybrid, and more locally relevant, meanings and identities. Ai Wei Wei, consultant designer on the Beijing Bird's Nest project with Herzog and de Meuron, referred to it as a "public relations sham" and the 2008 Olympics as " a pretend smile" (Glancey, 2008a). Shortly before the event in August 2008 he clarified his position toward the stadium. "I don't criticize the stadium. I criticize the government's use of the Olympics for propaganda. I am disappointed that the system is not able to turn this historical event into political reform" (quoted in Watts, 2008).

In sum, the role of architects in contemporary culture is to act as conveyors of meaningful discourses about the buildings and the cultural spaces they produce. The same can be said for the designers and architects of sports facilities and stadia. Through sustaining and perpetuating the global sports mega-event cycle they contribute to and form part of the culture of consumption. Yet, whilst for some consumption has been seen as a means of overcoming many urban problems, investment in the cultural economy "cannot single-handedly save the city" (Miles and Miles, 2004: 2). As Miles and Miles suggest, "*consumption divides as much as it provides*" (p. 2, emphasis in the original). Likewise it remains a central debate among writers on the commodification of

architecture whether it is indeed possible "for designers to resist, escape or offer substantial alternatives to the dominant commercial culture" (Saunders, 2005: viii).

Conclusion

Both critics and boosters of spectacular sports mega-events now conduct research into the organization and networks surrounding them and their impacts, legacies, and outcomes.[8] Research by academics and investigative journalists has also looked at the workings of international sports organizations and international sports federations in examining the background to sports mega-events (e.g., Chappelet and Kubler-Mabbott, 2008; Sugden and Tomlinson, 1998; Jennings, 1996, 2006). In addition to the IOC and FIFA, media corporations, transnational sponsors, politicians, members of bid teams, and national sport organizations have been considered as constituent parts of the networks of power and influence that produce, mediate, and transact sports mega-events. Yet as well as their political, economic, cultural and symbolic impacts – through "showing off" places as global – sports mega-events as spectacles have a spatial impact, in particular upon the built environment, which is generally urban, modernist, and consumerist.

There is nothing new about commercial relations and sports and sport mega-events, nor about relations between sport and politics. What has changed is the way in which sport and sports events are related to both economic and political processes. Sport and sports mega-events, especially the Olympics since the 1980s, have become more commercial and implicated in market relationships. Sports and sports mega-events are experiential commodities and have many attractions for both corporate and governmental agencies seeking a presence in the globalized world. Sports mega-events are also part of the promotional culture of contemporary capitalism. Hence an increased supply of spectacle creates opportunities to attract inward investment and generate consumption spending.

Architecture – especially via airport terminal buildings, tall towers, and domes – has become one of the major means of acquiring an identity for cities and urban spaces in an age of uncertainty and the "institutionalized precariousness" that currently pervades all countries (Horne, 2006: 13). Architecture "has long been a means used by small countries to project their presence on a world stage" (Sudjic, 2005: 154). It is not only small countries that use architecture to signal their existence. As a result of this and the associated growth and spread of the culture ideology of consumerism (Sklair, 2005: 498) architecture and architects increasingly have a higher public profile. Globalization works though agency and it is the agency of the consumerist fraction of the TCC in architecture that has promoted the role of architects.

The basic message of this chapter has been that the relationship between sports mega-events and the urban infrastructure may be "obvious" but it needs examining. Buildings are part of the legacy of sport and sports mega-events, both negative and positive. Architects act as interpreters of the transnational sport spaces they help to design and in so doing they may sustain the work of the TCC and the maintenance of the culture ideology of consumerism, or on some occasions, challenge it. As Hannigan (1998) suggests, seeing the city as a center of consumption is not new but the way we are currently encouraged to consume is. The dreams created through forms of urban development associated with sports mega-events tend not to be those of local, average, or low-waged residents but those of the wealthy, the mobile, and transnational corporations (Rutheiser, 1996). Just as late modern baseball stadia (ballparks) in the United States have become colonized by consumer culture (Ritzer and Stillman, 2001) so too are the other stadia and spaces being built for sports mega-events increasingly seen as places with a "sports theme." It is in these contested spaces that architects play their part and also may face challenges. Whether architects simply impose the will of the marketized world of sport in consumer culture through their designs – and hence for example perpetuate the divisions within sport between the "haves" and "have-nots" – or provide opportunities to challenge such divisions in socially meaningful ways will be the subject of future investigations.

The conflicts, resistances, and negotiations involved in the experience of hosting sports mega-events also resonate among debates about

architecture found elsewhere. This suggests that the main issues worthy of future research in the sociology of sport architecture include the following:

1 Exploration of the ways in which sports architectural styles and architects are dependent and contingent on other social forces in particular contexts, including the relationship of architects to the transnational capitalist class. This would help assist answer "whether and to what extent it is possible for designers to resist, escape, or offer substantial alternatives to the dominant commercial culture" (Saunders, 2005: viii).

2 Examining how global architectural language narrates national (and local) ambitions and hence produces transnational social spaces amidst alternative readings. Whilst architectural work of great technical standard may be produced the urban environment has greater population density, social inequality, and environmental degradation remain (Frampton, 2007).

3 Investigating the power relations involved in local and global forces that collide in the production of sport stadia. These could be conceived as networks as much as a glocal phenomenon. As Short (2004) remarks, winners and losers can be identified. Winners include political regimes seeking to redevelop a city's image, subtle place-specific discourses, and real estate and building companies. The losers are the marginal and weaker social groups, those living in poorer inner city sites who often face relocation with inadequate or no compensation.

Crilley (1993: 249) has argued that the architecture of redevelopment can perform "an effective screening role conducive to geographical and social myopia." Over two decades ago David Harvey (1989: 21) suggested that downtown redevelopments could be likened to a "carnival mask that diverts and entertains, leaving the social problems that lie behind the mask unseen and uncared for." Future research into the social role of sports architects and architecture in producing the spectacle of sports mega-events will enable us to explore what lies behind this mask.

Acknowledgments

This is a revised version of an article published in the *International Review for the Sociology of Sport*, 46 (2), 2011. Earlier sections of this chapter were presented at academic conferences in the United Kingdom and United States. I am extremely grateful to comments made by participants and reviewers since they have improved the focus of the argument considerably.

Notes

1 World Architecture 100 is an annual list compiled on behalf of *Building Design* magazine by research agency Camargue, which combines a sectoral and regional breakdown together with the number of architects employed by participating practices.

2 See http://www.agencetaillibert.com/index_en.html, accessed January 23, 2013.

3 This is the 3rd edition; there is now a 4th edition (John, Sheard, and Vickery, 2006).

4 See http://populous.com, accessed December 17, 2012.

5 See http://populous.com, accessed December 17, 2012.

6 See http://populous.com/expertise/event-design-planning/, accessed January 23, 2012.

7 This can be accessed by searching the archive on www.leodaly.com/search.

8 See for example Cashman (2006) for a critical, yet generally enthusiastic discussion of the IOC-funded Olympic Global Impact project.

References

Ballantyne, A. (2002) *Architecture*, Oxford: Oxford University Press.

Bauman Lyons Architects (2008) *How to Be a Happy Architect*, London: Black Dog.

Bélanger, A. (2009) "The urban sport spectacle: Towards a critical political economy of sports," in Carrington, B. and McDonald, I. (eds.) *Marxism, Cultural Studies and Sport*, London: Routledge, pp. 51–67.

Brecht, B. (1976) *Poems*, ed. J. Willett and R. Mannheim, London: Methuen.

Broudehoux, A.-M. (2004) *The Making and Selling of Post-Mao Beijing*, London: Routledge.

Brownell, S. (1995) "The stadium, the city and the state: Beijing," in Bale, J. and Moen, O. (eds.) *The Stadium and the City*, Keele, UK: Keele University Press, pp. 95–110.

Building Design (2007) "Top 50 most powerful figures in British architecture: Who's got the power?" *Building Design*, January 5, http://www.bdonline.co.uk/comment/top-50-most-powerful-figures-in-british-architecture-31-40/3079432.article, accessed December 29, 2012.

Cashman, R. (2006) *The Bitter-Sweet Awakening*, Sydney: Walla Walla.

CBC News (2006) "Quebec's Big Owe Stadium debt is over," December 19, http://www.cbc.ca/canada/montreal/story/2006/12/19/qc-olympicstadium.html, accessed December 29, 2012.

Chappelet, J.-L. and Kubler-Mabbott, B. (2008) *The International Olympic Committee and the Olympic System: The Governance of World Sport*, London: Routledge.

COHRE (2007) *Fair Play for Housing Rights: Mega-events, Olympic Games and Housing Rights*, Geneva: Centre on Housing Rights and Eviction.

Cornwell, R. (2009) "Yield of dreams." *Independent*, April 17: 48.

Crilley, D. (1993) "Architecture as advertising: Constructing the image of redevelopment," in Kearns, G. and Philo, C. (eds.) *Selling Places: The City as Cultural Capital, Past and Present*, Oxford: Pergamon Press, pp. 231–252.

Culf, A. (2005) "The man who is making a £2bn mark on London." *Guardian*, October 27, Sport section: 8.

Day, M. (2009) "Frank Gehry: 'Don't call me a starchitect." *Independent*, http://www.independent.co.uk/arts-entertainment/architecture/frank-gehry-dont-call-me-a-starchitect-1842870.html, accessed December 29, 2012.

DCMS (2008) *Guide to Safety at Sports Grounds*, London: Department of Media, Culture and Sport.

Delanty, G. and Jones, P. (2002) "European identity and architecture." *European Journal of Social Theory*, 5 (4): 453–466.

Eisinger, P. (2000) "The politics of bread and circuses: Building a city for the visitor class." *Urban Affairs Review*, January: 316–333.

Essex, S. and Chalkley, B. (2003) *Urban Transformation from Hosting the Olympic Games*, Barcelona: Universitat Autònoma de Barcelona, Centre d'Estudis Olimpics, http://olympicstudies.uab.es/lectures/web/pdf/essex.pdf, accessed December 29, 2012.

Ewen, S. (1988) *All Consuming Images*, New York: Basic Books.

Forbes (2011) "Global 500." *CNN Money*, http://money.cnn.com/magazines/fortune/global500/2011/full_list/, accessed December 29, 2012.

Fowler, B. and Wilson, F. (2004) "Women architects and their discontents." *Sociology*, 38 (1): 101–119.

Frampton, K. (2005) "Introduction: The work of architecture in the age of commodification," in Saunders, W. (ed.) *Commodification and Spectacle in Architecture*, Minneapolis: University of Minnesota Press, pp. ix–xviii.

Frampton, K. (2007) *Modern Architecture: A Critical History* (4th edn.), London: Thames & Hudson.

Friedman, M., Andrews, D., and Silk, M. (2004) "Sport and the façade of redevelopment in the postindustrial city." *Sociology of Sport Journal*, 21 (1): 119–139.

Glancey, J. (2008a) "Secrets of the Bird's Nest." *Guardian*, February 11, G2 section: 23–27.

Glancey, J. (2008b) "Architecture." *Guardian*, December 11, G2 section: 22–23.

Glancey, J. (2009) "The wow years." *Guardian*, December 8, G2 section: 17–20.

Glancey, J. (2011) "The flatpack Olympics." *Guardian*, June 13: 24.

Gutman, R. (1988) *Architectural Practice: A Critical View*, Princeton, NJ: Princeton Architectural Press.

Hannigan, J. (1998) *Fantasy City: Pleasure and Profit in the Postmodern Metropolis*, London: Routledge.

Harvey, D. (1989) *The Condition of Postmodernity*, Oxford: Blackwell.

Hayes, G. and Horne, J. (2011) "Sustainable development, shock and awe? London 2012 and civil society." *Sociology*, 45 (5): 749–764.

Hiller, H. (2003) "Toward a science of Olympic outcomes: The urban legacy," in de Moragas, M., Kennett, C., and Puig, N. (eds.) *The Legacy of the Olympic Games 1984–2000*, Lausanne: IOC, pp. 102–109.

Horne, J. (2006) *Sport in Consumer Culture*, Basingstoke, UK: Palgrave Macmillan.

Horne, J. (2007) "The four 'knowns' of sports mega-events." *Leisure Studies*, 26 (1): 81–96.

Horne, J. (2011) "Architects, stadia and sport spectacles: Notes on the role of architects in the building of sport stadia and making of world-class cities." *International Review for the Sociology of Sport*, 46 (2): 205–227.

Horne, J. and Whannel, G. (2012) *Understanding the Olympics*, London: Routledge.

Imrie, R. (2007) "The interrelationships between building regulations and architects' practices." *Environment and Planning B: Planning and Design*, 34: 925–943.

Inglis, S. (1987) *The Football Grounds of Great Britain* (2nd edn.), London: Willow Books.

Inglis, S. (2000) *Sightlines: A Stadium Odyssey*, London: Yellow Jersey.

Inglis, S. (2005) *Engineering Archie: Archibald Leitch – Football Ground Designer*, London: English Heritage/HOK.

Jennings, A. (1996) *The New Lords of the Rings*, New York: Simon & Schuster.

Jennings, A. (2006) *Foul! The Secret World of FIFA*, London: HarperSport.

John, G. and Campbell, K. (1993) *Handbook of Sports and Recreational Building Design*, vol. 1, *Outdoor Sports* (2nd edn.), London: Sports Council, Technical Unit for Sport.

John, G. and Sheard, R. (2000) *Stadia: A Design and Development Guide* (3rd edn.), Oxford: Architectural Press.

John, G., Sheard, R., and Vickery, B. (2006) *Stadia: A Design and Development Guide* (4th edn.), Oxford: Architectural Press.

Jones, P. (2006) "The sociology of architecture and the politics of building." *Sociology*, 40 (3): 549–565.

King, A. (2004) *Spaces of Global Cultures: Architecture, Urbanism, Identity*, London: Routledge.

Larson, M. (1994) "Architectural competitions as discursive events." *Theory and Society*, 23 (4): 469–504.

Liao, H. and Pitts, A. (2006) "A brief historical review of Olympic urbanization." *International Journal of the History of Sport*, 23 (7): 1232–1252.

McNeill, D. (2009) *The Global Architect: Firms, Fame and Urban Form*, London: Routledge.

Marvin, C. (2008) "'All under heaven' – Megaspace in Beijing," in Price, M. and Dayan, D. (eds.) *Owning the Olympics: Narratives of the New China*, Ann Arbor: University of Michigan Press, pp. 229–259.

Merrifield, A. (2002) *Metromarxism: A Marxist Tale of the City*, New York: Routledge.

Miles, S. and Miles, M. (2004) *Consuming Cities*, Basingstoke, UK: Palgrave Macmillan.

Morin, G. (1998) *La Cathédrale inachevée*, Montréal: Éditions XYZ.

Olds, K. (1997) "Globalizing Shanghai: The 'Global Intelligence Corps' and the building of Pudong." *Cities*, 14 (2): 109–123.

Olds, K. (2001) *Globalization and Urban Change: Capital, Culture and Pacific Rim Mega-Projects*, Oxford: Oxford University Press.

Philo, C. and Kearns, G. (1993) "Culture, history, capital: A critical introduction to the selling of places," in Kearns, G. and Philo, C. (eds.) *Selling Places: The City as Cultural Capital, Past and Present*, Oxford: Pergamon Press, pp. 1–32.

Populous (2009a) "About Populous," http://populous. com/about/, accessed January 21, 2013.

Populous (2009b) "Stadia," http://populous.com/ projects/type/stadia/, accessed January 22, 2013.

Preuss, H. (2004) *The Economics of Staging the Olympics*, Cheltenham, UK: Edward Elgar.

Puckett, K. (2009) "Architecture firms look east in 2010." *Building Design*, December 18, www. bdonline.co.uk/architecture-firms-look-east-in-2010/3155179.article, accessed December 29, 2012.

Ren, X. (2008) "Architecture and nation building in the age of globalization: Construction of the national stadium of Beijing for the 2008 Olympics." *Journal of Urban Affairs*, 30 (2): 175–190.

Rimmer, P. (1991) "The global intelligence corps and world cities: Engineering consultancies on the move," in Daniels, P. (ed.) *Services and Metropolitan Development: International Perspectives*, London: Routledge, pp. 66–107.

Ritzer, G. and Stillman, T. (2001) "The postmodern ballpark as a leisure setting: Enchantment and simulated de-McDonaldization." *Leisure Sciences*, 23 (2): 99–113.

RKMA (2006) *The 2007 Architectural/Engineering/ Construction Market Research Handbook*, Loganville, GA: Richard K. Miller and Associates.

Russell, D. (2006) "'We all agree, name the stand after Shankly': Cultures of commemoration in late twentieth-century English football culture." *Sport in History*, 26 (1): 1–25.

Rutheiser, C. (1996) *Imagineering Atlanta: The Politics of Space in the City of Dreams*, New York: Verso.

Sassen, S. (1991) *The Global City*, Princeton, NJ: Princeton University Press.

Saunders, W. (2005) "Preface," in Saunders, W. (ed.) *Commodification and Spectacle in Architecture*, Minneapolis: University of Minnesota Press, pp. vii–viii.

Sheard, R. (2001a) *Sports Architecture*, London: Spon.

Sheard, R. (2001b) "Olympic stadia and the future," in International Union of Architects/IOC, *The Olympic Games and Architecture: The Future for Host Cities*, Lausanne: IOC, pp. 43–47.

Sheard, R. (2005) *The Stadium: Architecture for the New Global Culture*, Singapore: Periplus.

Short, J.R. (2004) *Global Metropolitan: Globalizing Cities in a Capitalist World*, London: Routledge.

Silk, M. and Amis, J. (2005) "Sport tourism, cityscapes and cultural politics." *Sport in Society*, 8 (2): 280–301.

Sinclair, I. (2011) *Ghost Milk: Calling Time on the Grand Project*, London: Hamish Hamilton.

Sklair, L. (2001) *The Transnational Capitalist Class*, Oxford: Blackwell.

Sklair, L. (2002) *Globalization: Capitalism & Its Alternatives*, Oxford: Oxford University Press.

Sklair, L. (2005) "The Transnational Capitalist Class and contemporary architecture in globalizing cities." *International Journal of Urban and Regional Research*, 29 (3): 485–500.

Sklair, L. (2006) "Iconic architecture and capitalist globalization." *City*, 10 (1): 21–47.

Stevens, G. (1998) *The Favored Circle: The Social Foundations of Architectural Distinction*, Cambridge, MA: MIT Press.

Stevens, Q. (2007) *The Ludic City: Exploring the Potential of Public Spaces*, London: Routledge.

Sudjic, D. (2005) *The Edifice Complex: How the Rich and Powerful Shape the World*, London: Penguin Books.

Sugden, J. and Tomlinson, A. (1998) *FIFA and the Contest for World Football*, Cambridge: Polity Press.

Taylor Report (1990) *The Hillsborough Stadium Disaster 15 April 1989. Final Report of the Inquiry by the Rt Hon Lord Justice Taylor*, London: HMSO.

Till, J. (2009) *Architecture Depends*, Cambridge, MA: MIT Press.

Trumpbour, R. (2007) *The New Cathedrals: Politics and Media in the History of Stadium Construction*, Syracuse, NY: Syracuse University Press.

Wainwright, M. (2008) "The happy architect." *Guardian*, November 19, Society Guardian section: 1–2.

Watts, J. (2008) "China using games as 'warfare,' says stadium designer." *Guardian*, August 2: 26.

Whannel, G. (2008) *Culture, Politics and Sport: Blowing the Whistle Revisited*, London: Routledge.

Whitson, D. and Horne, J. (2006) "Underestimated costs and overestimated benefits? Comparing the impact of sports mega-events in Canada and Japan," in Horne, J. and Manzenreiter, W. (eds.) *Sports Mega-events: Social Scientific Analyses of a Global Phenomenon*, Oxford: Blackwell, pp. 73–89.

Whitson, D. and Macintosh, D. (1993) "Becoming a world-class city: Hallmark events and sport franchises in the growth strategies of western Canadian cities." *Sociology of Sport Journal*, 10(3): 221–240.

Zhang, T. and Silk, M. (2006) "Recentering Beijing: Sport, space, subjectivities." *Sociology of Sport Journal*, 23 (4): 438–459.

Zirin, D. (2009) *A People's History of Sports in the United States: 250 Years of Politics, Protest, People and Play*, New York: New Press.

Further Reading

Broudehoux, A.-M. (2004) *The Making and Selling of Post-Mao Beijing*, London: Routledge.

Inglis, S. (2000) *Sightlines: A Stadium Odyssey*, London: Yellow Jersey.

Jones, P. (2006) "The sociology of architecture and the politics of building." *Sociology*, 40 (3): 549–565.

Ren, X. (2008) "Architecture and nation building in the age of globalization: Construction of the national stadium of Beijing for the 2008 Olympics." *Journal of Urban Affairs*, 30 (2): 175–190.

Sklair, L. (2005) "The Transnational Capitalist Class and contemporary architecture in globalizing cities." *International Journal of Urban and Regional Research*, 29 (3): 485–500.

26

Sports, the Beijing Olympics, and Global Media Spectacles

Douglas Kellner and Hui Zhang

Introduction

Professional sports are one of the major spectacles of media culture, hence in contemporary societies sport is an increasingly important part of the culture of the spectacle. In this chapter, we interrogate the sports spectacle from a global perspective, first discussing the sports spectacle in NBA basketball during the Michael Jordan era and then briefly engage the 2006 World Cup as a global media spectacle. The chapter then centers on an in-depth study of the 2008 Beijing Olympics as a spectacle of global sports and of Chinese nationalism, marking the emergence of China as a new global force. We maintain that sport is a largely under-theorized and underrated domain of the society of the spectacle that celebrates its dominant values, products, corporations, state, and socioeconomic system in an unholy alliance between sports celebrity, commercialism, and media spectacle. In the following analysis, we argue that major sports spectacles are complex mixtures of nationalism, localism, and globalism that provide compelling insights into contemporary societies and culture requiring critical reading and contextualizing of sports spectacles like the Beijing Olympics. First, however, we open by conceptually analyzing and historical contextualizing the sports spectacle.

Defining the Sports Spectacle

Sports has always been part of spectacle culture from the beginning of the ancient Greek Olympics in 776 BC through the early modern era. The conjunction of professional sports in the nineteenth century with the rise of a media culture propelled sport into the realm of media spectacle, especially in the era of visual media like film and photography and then broadcasting, in which radio was followed by television. Henceforth, sport became a central part of media culture, amassing large and loyal audiences, and providing high ratings for media corporations and high profits for private corporate media in countries like the United States (see also CHAPTER 3). While sports has always been part of a culture of the spectacle with drama, theatrics, and an aesthetic dimension, in an era of media spectacle the broadcasting media and the sports spectacle have proliferated.

Whereas the activity of participating in sports involves an engagement in creative practice,

A Companion to Sport, First Edition. Edited by David L. Andrews and Ben Carrington.
© 2013 Blackwell Publishing Ltd. Published 2013 by Blackwell Publishing Ltd.

spectator sports enables passive consumption of images of the sports spectacle by mass audiences – although many audiences can be very active in their enthusiasms and appropriation of the sports spectacle. One of the distinguishing features of contemporary post-industrial societies is the extent to which sports have become commercialized and transformed into a spectacle mediated through broadcasting, and now the internet and social networking. During the industrial era, actually playing sports was an adjunct to labor which created strong and skillful bodies for industrial work and which taught individuals how to participate in sports as part of a collective, to fit into a team, to display initiative, and to distinguish themselves, thus training workers for productive labor under industrial capitalism.

During the post-industrial era, by contrast, spectator sport is the correlative to a society that is replacing manual labor with automation and machines, and that requires consumption and passive appropriation of spectacles to reproduce the consumer society. The contemporary era also sees the expansion of a service and high-tech sector and highly differentiated entertainment industry, of which sports are a key part. Thus, significant resources are currently devoted to the expansion and promotion of the sports spectacle and male athletes like Michael Jordan, Kobe Bryant, David Beckham, Yao Ming, Barry Bonds, Zinedine Zidane, and Alex Rodriguez accordingly have the potential to amass high salaries from the profits being generated by the sports/ entertainment colossus.

Modern sports were organized around principles of the division of labor and professionalism, celebrating individualist values of competition and winning. Sports in the modern era replicated the structure of the workplace where both individual initiative and teamwork were necessary and sports celebrated at once both competing values. Sports were part of an autonomous realm with its own professional ethic, carefully regulated rules, and highly organized corporate structure. Post-industrial sport, by contrast, implodes sport into media spectacle, collapses boundaries between professional achievement and commercialization, and between performance and entertainment, attesting to the commodification of all aspects of life in the media and consumer society.

There are many ways in which contemporary sports in the United States and globally are subject to the laws of the spectacle and are becoming totally commercialized, serving to help reproduce the consumer society (see Andrews, 2009). For starters, sport is ever more subject to market logic and commodification with professional athletes making millions of dollars. Further, sports events like basketball games are hypercommodified with such terms as the "Bud player of the game," "Miller Lite genuine moments," the "Reebok half-time report," the "AT&T Time Out," and "Dutch Boy in the Paint," along with ads featuring the star players hucking merchandise. Television networks bid astronomical sums for the rights to broadcast live professional sports events, and super-events like the Superbowl and NBA championship games command some of the highest advertising rates in television. For instance, during the 2010 Superbowl 30-second ads were said to have cost US$2.6 million, while websites have collected the most popular ads, which become popular culture icons.[1]

It appears that North American professional sports, a paradigm of the spectacle, can no longer be played without the accompaniment of cheerleaders, giant mascots who clown with players and spectators, and raffles, promotions, and contests which hawk the products of various sponsors. Instant replays turn the action into high-tech spectacles and stadiums themselves contain electronic reproduction of the action, as well as giant advertisements for various products which rotate for maximum saturation – previewing forthcoming environmental advertising in which entire urban sites will become scenes to promote commodity spectacles. Corporations are now franchising sports arenas to be named after their products, following Great Western Bank's payment to have the Lakers' stadium named the Great Western Forum, the franchising of United Center in Chicago by United Airlines, and the America West Arena in Phoenix by America West. Pacific Telesis paid over US$50 million to name the San Francisco Giants planned new stadium Pacific Bell Park (subsequently to be renamed SBC Park in 2003 as a result of the SBC acquisition of Pacific Bell), and the stadium was ultimately christened AT&T Park on March 3, 2006, after another corporate merger! Philip Morris' Miller Brewing unit paid US$40 million to have its name atop the Milwaukee Brewers' new Brewer Park, a project funded by over US$300 million in public funds and not scheduled for completion until 2014.

The Texas Rangers stadium in Arlington, TX, supplements its sports arena with a shopping mall and commercial area, with office buildings, stores, and a restaurant in which for a hefty price one gets a view of the athletic events, as one consumes food and drink. It probably will not be too long before the uniforms of North American professional sports players are as littered with advertisements as racing cars. In the globally popular sport of soccer, companies such as Canon, Sharp, and Carlsberg sponsor teams and have their names emblazoned on their shirts, making the players epiphenomena of transnational capital. In cycling events like the Tour de France or auto-racing events like the Indianapolis 500, entire teams are sponsored by major corporations whose logos adorn their clothes and cars. And throughout the world, but especially in the United States, the capital of the commodity spectacle, superstars like Michael Jordan commodify themselves from head to foot, selling their various body parts and images to the highest corporate bidders, while swimming champions Mark Spitz and Michael Phelps appeared in every type of imaginable ad, as star athletes commodify their sports images into the spectacles of advertising. In this fashion, the top US athletes augment their salaries, sometimes spectacularly, by endorsing products, thus imploding sports, commerce, and advertising into dazzling spectacles which celebrate the products and values of corporate America.

The 2000s have exhibited a dramatic combining of the sports spectacle, commerce, and entertainment with massive salaries and marketing contracts for superstar players/celebrities. The major media conglomerates are becoming increasingly interested in sports channels and franchises and the most marketable athletes not only earn enormous multi-million dollar salaries but are also able to secure even more lucrative marketing deals to endorse products, star in film or TV programs, and even, in the case of Michael Jordan and other star athletes, to promote their own product lines. While the National Basketball Association (NBA) was once the ne'er-do-well stepchild of the more successful professional

baseball and football franchises, from the late 1980s to the present it has become one of the most popular of the US sports industries on the global scale (Andrews, 1997). While the NBA only fed 35 weekly telecasts to foreign companies in the mid-1980s during the beginning of Jordan's basketball career, by 1996 the roster had swelled to 175 foreign broadcasts in 40 languages to 600 million households. In this process, David Halberstam describes Jordan as "the first great athlete of the wired world" (in Coplon, 1996: 35).

The ongoing evolution of the sports spectacle thus has a global dimension with the major players now becoming international figures, marketed in global advertising campaigns, films, music, and other venue of media culture. As Michael Jordan's superstar agent David Falk puts it, "Michael has transcended sport. He's an international icon" (quoted in Hirschberg, 1996: 46). Indeed, in 1996–1997, Falk put together deals that netted Jordan a record-breaking US$30 million contract for the next season; continuing lucrative deals with Nike and other corporations to promote their products to the estimated tune of US$40 million; the inauguration of his own cologne line, Eau de Michael Jordan; and a high-tech film, *Space Jam*, pairing Jordan with other NBA superstars, Bugs Bunny, and other cartoon characters, together with accompanying product lines and estimates that Jordan could conceivably earn US$20 million from the latter two projects (*USA Today*, October 14, 1996: 6B). During the same era, Los Angeles Lakers star Shaquille O'Neal signed a seven-year, US$120 million deal, leading his agent to comment, "Shaq represents the convergence of sports and entertainment" (*New York Times*, August 23, 1996: C4).

Competing with baseball and football as the American sport of choice of the contemporary era, professional basketball emerged during the Jordan era as the game that best symbolizes the contemporary sports/entertainment colossus. To some extent, the three major US sports encapsulate three periods of socioeconomic development. Baseball represents the challenge of a highly individualist country to merge together individual aspirations and talents with team work and spirit. Emerging in the nineteenth century, baseball disciplined individuals to fit into teams but still rewarded individual accomplishments during a highly entrepreneurial era of capitalist development.

Football is organized on a mass-production industrial model that was appropriate to the era of mass production that reached its highest stage of development in the first half of the twentieth century. Football is a team sport that exemplifies arduous collective physical labor mated with individual achievement. Although the star running-backs, quarter-backs, and touchdown scorers often get the credit and headlines, it is disciplined collective labor that provides the infrastructure for football accomplishments and victory. Without a strong defense and well-coordinated offense even the most spectacular players cannot adequately function and their team cannot win.

NBA basketball, by contrast, has increasingly featured superstar feats of individual brilliance, especially in the era of Michael Jordan, Kobe Bryant, and Yao Ming. Professional basketball is also the perfect television sport, fast-paced, full of action, and resplendent with spectacle. Hard-charging full-court action, balletic shots, and ubiquitous instant replays make basketball the perfect sport for the era of MTV. Perfectly embodying the fragmentary postmodern aesthetics, razzle-dazzle technical effects, and fast pace of today's television, basketball has emerged as the sport of the spectacle, the perfect game for the sports/entertainment society. Once a primarily American game, by the 1990s it had become globally popular (although, as suggested below, soccer is probably the most popular sport globally and the Olympics is still a major global sports spectacle).

Moreover, the sports spectacle is at the center of an almost religious fetishism in which sport becomes surrogate religion and its stars demigods. For many, sport is the "object of ultimate concern" (Paul Tillich's definition of religion in which God is defined as the ultimate concern of a given culture in a specific historical period). Sports provide transcendence from the banality and suffering of everyday life, and its stars constitute its saints and deities, while sports events often have a religious aura of ritual. Sports fans are like a congregation and their cheers and boos are a form of liturgy. In sports events, fans become part of something greater than themselves, the participation provides meaning and significance,

and a higher communal self, fused with the multitudes of believers and the spirit of joy in triumph and suffering in tribulation. Sports are a break from average everyday-ness, providing participation in ritual, mystery, and spiritual aura (although, as our discussion is suggesting, sports also celebrate dominant social values like individuality, winning, teamwork, and, increasingly commercialism). In a global era, as we show in the following sections, the sports spectacle becomes a major feature of globalization that combines sometimes contradictory spectacles of globalism and nationalism.

The Global Sports Spectacle: From the 2006 World Cup to the 2008 Beijing Olympics

Global capitalism and media thrive on sports mega-spectacles and one of the biggest of them all is the men's World Cup football championship. In the 2006 World Cup finals in Germany, billions of dollars were invested in heavy advertising expenditure, special events in the host country of Germany, and unprecedented gambling and media interest. Billions of people watched the games at home, in pubs, in public viewing places, and there was a tremendous outpouring of nationalist sentiment throughout the world. In Germany, for the first time since the end of World War II, German flags were displayed and waved across the nation. The German tricolor was painted on people's faces, and soccer stars' images were seen on billboards and lightshows projecting them on buildings. The financial district of Frankfurt was ablaze with light shows featuring the German team on the eve of the games, while Munich's World Cup arena featured a gigantic red football encompassing the stadium. Global products like McDonald's paid vast sums to have their products advertised and sold in stadiums and there was fierce bidding for the beer franchise, with the Germans deeply disappointed that the US Budweiser brand was chosen. Throughout the World Cup, the competition was as much a celebration of spectacle as a sports event.

The Olympic Games have become an ever-expanding spectacle with fierce bidding wars years in advance to determine the host city, sometimes producing scandal. The Olympic spectacle itself generates discourses about global peace, cooperation, and the collective progress of human race. Yet, the whole idea of organizing athletes into units based on national borders to engage in fierce competitions itself contains the inherent tension between nationalism and cosmopolitanism. While cosmopolitanism was built upon universalist principles which seek to articulate and consolidate an essential human bond and shared humanity, it has long served as an ideological foundation of the modern Olympics. Hence, we should always be wary of cosmopolitanism's underlying complicity with those hegemonic values such as nationalism and racism that it sometimes masks. Yet, on the other hand, as Ben Carrington pointed out (2004: 97), we should not fail to recognize the opportunities for the Olympics' potential, every few years, "to realize a sense of the global, post-national belonging that is grounded in the politics of the local, the city, the regional."

The 2008 summer Olympics held in Beijing was perhaps the most controversial one in recent decades. In many ways, it was similar to the situations of two other previously controversial Olympics, namely the 1936 Berlin Games and the 1980 Moscow Games. The controversies evoked are analogous to these two occasions in that the legitimacy and dominant ideology of the host country's regime in power were conceived as at odds with the cosmopolitanism values which underpinned the Olympic Games (see Guttmann 2006; Edelman, 2006). In China's case, voices of dissent never ceased from the moment the International Olympic Committee made the decision in 2001 to award the status of host city for 2008 to Beijing. As we will discuss, international human rights groups, exiled political dissidents, and a number of national governments disdained the idea of allowing a "totalitarian" regime whose blemished human rights record has constantly been deemed as a disgrace to the global community to hold an event that is the ultimate emblem of cosmopolitanism ideals (Brownell, 2008; Jarvie, Hwang, and Brennan, 2008: 118–119).

China orchestrated, months before the Olympics, a campaign in Beijing to prepare the population for its entry onto the global Olympic stage. In addition to building state-of-the-art Olympic stadia and city, the government tried to teach the population "proper conduct" in interacting with

foreigners, including friendly smiles, no spitting, public urination, or other rude behavior, forming orderly lines, and presenting a positive image of the Chinese people for the global public. Beijing also tried to cut pollution by banning industrial labor in the area, laying off workers for months without wages, and outlawing automotive traffic from various parts of the city in the days before the Olympics.

Yet a negative global spectacle threatened to disrupt Beijing's attempt to mold the Olympic spectacle as a vehicle for Chinese nationalism and its triumphant entry as a superpower on the global stage. From the first lighting of the Olympic torch in Athens through many legs of the symbolic journey of the burning torch through various cities, protests, initially by Tibetans, against repressive Chinese government policies began gaining international media attention. In Athens, a Tibetan protest briefly interrupted the torch's lighting and journey through the streets of that city, in the country that originated the Olympics.

By the time the torch reached London in early April, the protests escalated, as did police protection of the runners bearing the torch, with over 2,000 police in London forming such a phalanx around the torch that the flame and runners were barely visible to the crowds. In Paris, massive demonstrations against the Chinese Olympics reached a high point as over 3,000 police squared off against pro-Tibet protestors and other groups that had a grievance against China, including controversies over China's role in Darfur, Sudan, and the campaigns for a free Tibet. Groups protesting included coalitions involved in the just-mentioned issues with disparate members including Amnesty International, Reporters Without Borders, Taiwanese nationalists, and representatives of the Muslim Uighur minority group in western China. The multiple protests led to at least three incidents where the torch was extinguished, and the need to carry it by bus to its destination, as well as to global publicity (Bennhold and Rosenthal, 2008; see also *Quel Sport*, 2008). In San Francisco, groups of anti- and pro-Chinese demonstrators clashed and blocked traffic, as pro-Chinese demonstrators were bussed in from local colleges around the state into the US city with the largest Chinese population, itself divided into pro- and anti-People's Republic of

China factions, highlighting how media spectacle is a contested terrain among competing groups (on this concept see Kellner, 2003, 2008, 2010). Indeed, the antagonism between a cosmopolitan political principle and nationalist ideology is only one aspect of the Olympics spectacle. The complex relationship between these hegemonic values is much more intricate than a one-dimensional understanding would suggest. As Tomlinson argues (2002: 57), the producers of globalized spectacles are sometimes more than just global consumers, as often the state manufactures spectacles in order to consolidate the legitimacy of its power. In this regard, the 2008 Beijing Olympics was a perfect stage to present the "multifaceted" aspect of the spectacle in which both fierce contestation and alliance of an array of hegemonic values on the national and global scales, as well as the resistance to them, were showcased.

At the same time, there were also domestic critical voices rising to impugn the way the Beijing Olympics was orchestrated. Many opposed the abuse of the administrative advantages of a highly centralized power to mobilize immense material and human resources that were disproportionate to China's status as a still-developing country, with basic infrastructure needs. Further, during the process of destroying neighborhoods to build Olympic facilities for the Games, many citizens' life and rights suffered in detrimental ways.

In general, the voices of critique targeted either the "totalitarian" nature of the regime, or the unethical uses of state power to achieve some self-beneficent goals. Many of these accusations that focused on the "anti-liberal" aspects of the current regime are not groundless. Although the validity of the stereotypical labeling of Chinese government as a "communist" regime by much of Western journalism is highly dubious and contains ideological bias from Cold War legacies, it is true that the current Chinese political system maintains a highly centralized government rule by a party system that lacks flexibility and transparency. It also seems true that the way the current regime operates does indeed include attempts to obstruct many of the commonly accepted precepts of political values in the West such as individual liberty, freedom, and human rights.

This situation produced suspicion that the government was simply using the event as a nationalistic vehicle to consolidate its reign (Zhao, 1998). Yet on the other hand, China's status in recent years as a "rising power" has a lot to do with its avid participation in international market production, and hence the country obtained the role of a pivotal player in advancing the expansion of global capitalism. Such an economic situation and the cultural changes which followed have actually made a type of globalism an imperative element in the prevailing ideology and rhetoric of the Chinese nation. While there has been a distinction between "globalism" as part of the underpinning ideology of globalization driven by capitalist pursuits and the "cosmopolitanism" ideals that emphasize democratic political possibilities that ultimately surpass nation-state sovereignties, such a distinction seems to have become increasingly fuzzy, as specific societies like China that are complicit with global capitalism gradually have adopted the ideology of "cosmopolitanism." Such processes seem to be manifest within the manufacturing and disseminating of Olympics spectacles in recent decades. While the Olympics, as a mega-event, has always in the forefront of the fiercest contestations between the discourses of nationalism and cosmopolitanism, in recent decades, especially since the 1984 Los Angeles Games which marked a watershed in modern Olympics history by its unprecedentedly successful marketing strategies, the unimpeded power of global capitalism has become insinuated into the organization and operation of Olympics media spectacles which have converged and sometimes conflicted with their cosmopolitan ideals. Consequently the power alignment of various political discourses has become increasingly dynamic and complex with conflicting sports, national, cosmopolitan, and commercial discourses at play (Tomlinson, 1996, 2008).

Despite the controversy, seeing the excitement built up in China and through global media coverage in the days preceding the Olympics, the Chinese government fiercely clamped down on protestors. The opening ceremonies of Olympic Games are always occasions for displays of nationalism in which the host country blends its country's iconography and culture with the universalist themes of the Olympics (Tomlinson,

2005: 16–28), and the extravaganza spectacle of the 2008 Beijing Olympic opening ceremony was no exception. The Olympic Games is essentially a competition centering on the "bodies," and the opening ceremony deployed visual strategies focusing on the representation of bodies to construct a spectacle that intertwined both national pride and a sense of earnestness to be recognized in the global community.

The 2008 Opening Ceremony

In the following sections, we engage in an analysis of the opening ceremony of the 29th summer Olympics held on August 8, 2008, which as a global media spectacle employed visual and aural aesthetic strategies to articulate a set of interconnected but nevertheless ambivalent political messages. It is the purpose of this chapter to analyze how the spectacle and discourses regarding the national and the global unfolded and engaged in intricate and intimate contestations with each other. As the global obsessions of the Olympics are essentially fantasies about the spectacle of bodies – bodies that demonstrate strength, beauty, prowess, gender, race, and national characters – our analysis of the opening ceremony will be focused on the performing bodies in this grandiose media spectacle. Through an intermingling of historicized and gendered bodies fused with the symbolism of history, nation, and globalism, the Beijing Olympics spectacle enables a multitude of readings and interpretations. The "encoding" process of the Beijing Olympics involves more than one dimension, with different entities providing different interpretations of the Games, including official Chinese media such as CCTV, popular Western media such as NBC Sports, and grassroots dissidents who articulate their voices through public protesting and the internet. All these voices and perspectives often come from conflicting political views and interests, and constitute a contested terrain over the meanings of spectacles like the Beijing Olympics. Such a situation is further complicated by recognition of how potential readings of the Olympic spectacles' "visual hegemony" contain more than one strand of political thought and practice (Qing, 2010). In the following analysis, through the scrutiny of the Beijing Olympics media spectacle, we attempt to gain a glimpse into the various discourses and imaginaries that shaped the political contestations and complexities of China today, which is also involved in profound polemics of the national and the global as China continues to emerge as a controversial global superpower.

Historicized bodies, invented traditions, and postmodern aesthetic spectacle

Clearly, one of the most important strategies that the Beijing opening ceremony employed is historicizing bodies and spectacle to celebrate China's long and fabled past. Through narration about its glorious history and past cultural legacies, which assembled poignant symbols and myths that contributed to create a strong and prosperous civilization, the opening ceremony tries to present a glamorous spectacle about China to lure the audiences, both domestic and international. For the domestic audience, it combines a sense of nostalgia with national pride, as well as desire for renaissance. For the international audience, the show is clearly targeting audiences in the West, so as to cater to a voyeuristic desire for representations of exotic cultural performances from a mysterious Oriental land.

The result was a dazzling panorama of spectacles dramatizing the "high points" in Chinese history and defining elements of Chinese culture and character. The extravaganza's general director was Zhang Yimou, whose Oscar-winning martial-art epic The Hero (2002) and other epic spectacles of Chinese history were themselves highly mythologized and Hollywoodized. The opening ceremony was controversial precisely because it was ensnared in double accusations, for implicit endorsement of an authoritarian regime in China and for presenting cinematic spectacles to cater to a cultural fetish of the West for icons of the "Chinese." However, it is particularly this representation of Chinese history and of its bodies and culture that reveals a deep rupture within Zhang's attempts at providing a smooth and harmonious display of Chinese history and culture in a totalizing aesthetic spectacle. Rather than presenting a seamless smooth narrative and simple celebration of China, we shall argue that the resulting spectacle produces a picture full of anomalies, ruptures, and contradictions. The glaring inaccuracies in the representation of costumes, historical narratives, and artifacts undermine the authority of this totalizing narrative, and the ideological and idealizing portrait of China lends itself to caricature and critique. While being a highly alluring technical spectacle, its overwhelming and even chaotic assemblage of signifiers also betrayed its banality and problematic status as "Chinese nationalist propaganda." In the following sections, we develop a detailed textual analysis on the representation of this contrived "Chineseness" through the bodies of the performers and the stages and structure of the spectacle.

Although China's official media outlet claimed that the opening ceremony ran on a frugal budget and the cost was considerably less than that of Athens 2004, the international media were almost unanimously suspicious about the statement. Perhaps it is true that the real costs of the ceremony are extremely difficult to calculate, given the scope of infrastructure, technology, and human resources involved, but it is probably fair to say that this is arguably the most extravagant spectacle in the history of Olympics.[2] Further, Zhang's opening ceremony seems to confirm the suspicion that the aesthetic spectacle would showcase a fetish of historicized bodies throughout the performance, just like Zhang's obsessive fetishism of bodies in his cinematic works in recent years, such as *Hero* (2002), *House of Flying Daggers* (2004), and *Curse of the Golden Flower* (2006). Despite the dramatic turn from his early auteur films, which were favorites at international film festival awards, to more commercial productions with stunning visual effects that showcase the aesthetics of violence and spectacle in the past decade, there has been a consistency in Zhang's films that seek to represent "Chinese" culture through the spectacle of bodies. Such attempts evoked criticisms for overt cultural fetishism and self-orientalization by some critics (see Zhang, 1994: 30–41; also Chu, 2008; Harrison, 2006).

In the performative dimension of the opening ceremonies, there is an earnest will to demonstrate and glorify China's ancient civilization. The spectacle presented a complex, but in many aspects trite, assemblage of symbolism of cultural nationalism through showcasing China's past achievements in arts and sciences, as well as the peace-generating, harmonious Confucian tradition. There was a certain awkwardness, however,

in reconciling this nostalgic mode of self-orientalizing of the Chinese body, with the global and idealized universal bodies inherent in the Olympic tradition. Such tensions disrupt the semiotic texture of performances that are mostly built on a presumption about a universal history and essential humanity. Further, the symbols of philosophy, art, and music of ancient China were represented, paradoxically, in the forms of military training and marching. It is in this sense that the historicization of the bodies contain ruptures and present contradictions between a Olympic universalist ideology and the aggressively Chinese figures and symbols.

Other devices also articulate the tension between Olympic universality and Chinese historicity. For instance, the opening rite of welcoming athletes and audiences illustrates how, in this spectacle, the appeal of history aligns itself more with fantasy in spite of a claim of authenticity, and how the visual underpinnings of the spectacle, particularly the body semiotics of the performers, were subversive of the overall narrative of Olympic universality. The opening scene began with a firework display blazing across the darkness of the stadium. This spectacle was followed by a glistening light emerging from one corner of the stadium playground, which gradually expanded to the entire zone. In the flickering lighting, the audience heard the sound of drum beats, which started deep and low, then became amplified and electrifying. The beating sounds ceased all of a sudden, with the playground drowned in total darkness again, but then came close-up shots which made the performers' figures visually accessible, as young and athletic males with short haircuts, uniformly dressed in unconventional silvery robes.

According to the broadcast commentators, this scene featured contemporary performers playing a Chinese instrument from antiquity called *fou*, in a restoration of a traditional rite of welcoming guests from afar (Figure 26.1). A closer shot of the instrument revealed that the exterior of the instrument was cast into the shape of an ancient squared bronze vessel, with intricate ornaments on the sides. Despite this classical design, the surface of the instrument was built with translucent materials, wired to a flashlight installed underneath so that each tap on the plane can trigger a bright beam of light. Under tight orches-

Figure 26.1 Performers playing the "ancient" instrument called *fou*.
Source: *The Opening Ceremony of the Beijing 2008 Olympic Games* DVD, issued by China International Television Corporation, 2008.

trated instructions, different sections of the phalanx hit the instrument with different techniques in prearranged timings, thus forming various aural and visual patterns. Both the sound and the techniques of playing the instrument resembled very much that associated with drums. This percussion instrument, allegedly uncovered and restored through archaeological findings, is utilized to evoke a perennial sense of history peculiar to Chinese civilization.

However, as scholars revealed in the public sphere shortly after the show, this scene is actually filled with inaccurate cultural information. *Fou* was originally a clay-made, pear-shaped vessel used as a wine container. Its function as a musical instrument in the ancient past was an appendage to its utilitarian one, and usually occurred when the amiable atmosphere of the social occasion was heightened by drinking behavior. Hence, when used as a musical instrument *fou* was never associated with any refined form of art, let alone to be played as a welcoming rite on the most reverent occasions. The form of the instrument as displayed in the show actually simulates that of an ancient compound vessel called *jian fou*, which contains two parts as the name indicates. The *fou* component is usually enclosed inside the square shaped *jian*, and again it was used mostly as a container. The authentic design of *jian fou* will actually defy any potential application of it as a musical instrument (for detailed explanations about the origins and uses of *fou*, see Zhang, 2008).

Despite such erroneous historical-cultural iconography, the percussion instrument, with its spurring beats, did successfully stimulate the enthusiastic atmosphere of the audiences. Also "mind-boggling" were the shrill cries uttered by the performers while playing the instrument, charged with passion and a kind of virile strength. The performers' unitary appearance, both visual and aural, as well as the disciplines demonstrated, evoke situations of military training and provide spectacles of well-disciplined and organized Chinese masses. Actually, according to the media reports, there were over 10,000 soldiers and policemen recruited for the performances at the opening ceremony, and all of the performers for this particular scene came from the army (on media coverage of *fou*, see Li and Chen, 2008).

As the *fou* spectacle intensified, the screen inside the stadium displayed subtitles from one of the best-known mottos from Confucius: "How happy we are, to meet friends from afar!" The performers were chanting this line repeatedly, while being accompanied by thundering drum-beatings. However, there existed a deep tension between the amicable hospitality embedded in the words, and the seemingly virulent collective vocal utterances by the performers. The way the sentence was chanted was barely intelligible even for native ears with the aid of subtitles. It seems that in this representation of an ancient rite reproduced without much historical accuracy, the voice features and quality of the performance to some extent destabilized and even overrode the seeming welcoming semantic layer of the chanting.

Similar things occurred in a later scene titled "Chinese characters." Hundreds of performers, all male and costumed uniformly, chanted famous lines from Confucius' *Analects* (Figure 26.2 and Figure 26.3). What was bizarre about the scene was the way the performers constantly shifted the forms of the phalanx in a steady movement, while wielding the bamboo slips they held. This by no means could represent students reciting Confucian classics in the classroom. Rather, it would seem more natural and realistic if the bamboo slips in hand were replaced by some kind of weapon. Such impressions were reinforced when one realized that the meanings of the performers' chanting were completely unintelligible, which inevitably reduced *what*

Figure 26.2 Performers playing Confucius' disciples, in close-up.
Source: *The Opening Ceremony of the Beijing 2008 Olympic Games* DVD, issued by China International Television Corporation, 2008.

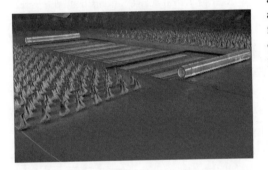

Figure 26.3 Performers playing Confucius' disciples in phalanx.
Source: *The Opening Ceremony of the Beijing 2008 Olympic Games* DVD, issued by China International Television Corporation, 2008.

they were chanting to insignificance compared with *how* they were chanting. Actually, as the spurring drum-beating and the thudding sound emanating from an intentional simulation of the scrapping of ancient bamboo slip amplified and diffused in the stadium, it became so overwhelming that it almost could not help but bring to mind images of leather boots rhythmically stamping the ground. Thus underneath the visual representations that constituted a narrative about the scholarly tradition of ancient China, the sound effect actually imprinted on people's minds and senses contained imaginations and images that were not completely compatible with such narratives.

Chinese civilization, angelic children, and disciplined bodies

After the extravaganza and historically inaccurate welcoming sequence, with multiple occasions for the Chinese president to smile and welcome the guests and express quiet pride in his country's achievements, a long sequence unfolded dramatizing China's contributions to world civilization: paper, printing, the compass, and gunpowder, interspersed with icons of Chinese culture, performed by top musical performers, dancers, classical musicians, and other contemporary culture icons, celebrating both past and contemporary Chinese culture.

In seeming contradiction to the opening masculine, militant, and fictitiously historical imagery and vocal representations of China, there was also an extensive usage of contemporary children's faces and voices as vehicles for the perpetuation of another set of discourses, pertaining to cosmopolitanism rather than nationalism. The imagery of children has become an integral part of the globalization process, and is closely intertwined with powerful discourses related to universal human rights, as well as global poverty and environmental issues (Stephens, 1995: 3–50) . The timeless portrayals of youth represented in this imagery are inscribed with romanticized aspirations for hope, peace and perpetual prosperity in the transmission of generations. Such discourses, while upholding a universal claim, nevertheless stem from the modern construct of Western Europe and America with their fetishization of children and childhood, and thus are potentially in denial of the cultural specificities of China which often held out a harsh life for children of the poor (Fass, 2008).

While serving as vehicles of ideology and pleasant representations of contemporary Chinese people, the imageries of children have also become increasingly complicit with the notion of consumption – consumption of both the visual pleasures derived from the angelic smiles and innocence and of commodities and cultural goods (Fass, 2003). The commodified representations of children are usually dehistoricized particularly through the forgery of angelic features in their physiologies and voices. These imageries of children depict them as vulnerable angels, immaculately innocent, yet constantly at risk of suffering from the harsh realities of the mundane adult world. Widely circulated in the charity groups' advertisements or as media coverage of foreign countries ensnared in a dire war, these images serve to solicit sympathies of the viewers through an imagination of the common identity of global citizens (Fass, 2003).

There was undoubtedly an ostensible attempt at the Beijing Olympics' opening ceremony to appropriate this global discourse of children in order to solicit certain affective responses from the international audiences. The images of children bombarded the audiences almost from the start to the finish of the spectacle. In the scene called "star light" which showcases "modern China," it was arranged for a sweet-looking girl to play piano with Lang Lang – a glamorous international star in the classical music arena, and China's "name card" for its "internationalization" within the high cultural domain (Figure 26.4). Later on in this scene, group performers in uniformed costume emerged and formed yet another exercise of calisthenics in which the pattern of a peace dove unfolding wings came into shape. While the narrators of the live broadcasting on the Chinese CCTV explained that this scene symbolized peace and friendship of the world community, the LED screen at the ground projected images of children's smiling faces simultaneously, providing a universalistic spectacle of global harmony.

Then, toward the climax of the cultural entertainment, as Sarah Brightman and Chinese superstar Liu Huan were singing the theme song, 2,008 pictures featuring beaming faces of children from various races, collected around the world by the Beijing Organizing Committee for the Olympics, appeared at the center of the stadium as well as on the circular screen on top of the stadium (Figure 26.5). These images, together with rising fireworks (also to mimic smiling faces) aimed to immerse the audiences in the glow of an auspicious promise of globalization.

All these appearances of children were presented with attempts to evoke the conviction that China has been fully integrated into the global community and that China has created a harmonious society with a harmonious relation between traditional Chinese civilization and the current state (covering over obvious ruptures in China's turbulent history). The displays of images of children here were always in one way or another conjoined with certain internationally famed icons from China to testify the country's extent of internationalization. Yet, at the same time, there were other elements of discourses that insinuated their way into this spectacle of the children. During the ceremony of the athletes' parade, when the Chinese delegation entered the stadium, the team was led by Yao Ming, who is perhaps the single most internationally renowned athlete from China due to several years' experience serving as a professional sportsman in the NBA until his retirement in

Figure 26.4 Internationally acclaimed musician Lang Lang playing piano with a little girl.
Source: The Opening Ceremony of the Beijing 2008 Olympic Games DVD, issued by China International Television Corporation, 2008.

Figure 26.5 Children's smiling faces collected worldwide.
Source: The Opening Ceremony of the Beijing 2008 Olympic Games DVD, issued by China International Television Corporation, 2008.

2011. Accompanying him was a little boy, tiny in figure, especially in contrast with Yao's giant-like stature. Oftentimes Yao had to slow down his broad strides, and occasionally extend an assisting hand to the boy who was toddling with full strength after him. The boy might have appeared to global audiences as but a cutely clumsy minor, yet he had become a well-known "young hero" hailed by Chinese media just a few months prior to the Games. As a 9-year-old, this boy, whose name is Lin Hao, reportedly saved two of his classmates single-handedly during the tragic earthquake that occurred in Sichuan on May 12, 2008, and since then had been cast into a role model for children and adolescents all across the country through joint efforts by the government and the media.

What is noteworthy here is a merging of two different types of symbolism of children: that of children as innocent, adorably vulnerable, and depoliticized social beings versus children as valiant, dedicated, and strong-willed fellow citizens who will be committed to self-sacrifice at moments of the country's calling. The latter ideal of children is a typical "Chinese" mode of indoctrination that has been constantly articulated in the primary and secondary school moral education curriculum (Reed, 1995; Bulag, 1999).[3] In this scene, the image of Lin Hao condensed two different and to some extent conflicting ideologies, each of which was intended to appeal emotionally to different audiences. On the other hand, it also contained efforts to forge these ideological elements into a hybridity, albeit not without inherent tensions.

Perhaps nowhere else were children's bodily representations displayed with more calculation, and at the same time embodied more intricate tensions, than on the occasion of the rite of national flag-raising. Much of the international media coverage of this scene focused on the lip-singing of the girl who performed the song "Hymn to the Motherland" while 56 other children, dressed in ethnic costumes to represent the 56 ethnic groups in China, were escorting the flag to the pole. Many Western media reports attacked the Chinese government's alleged hypocrisy for replacing the presence of the original singer with a more attractive face while using the voice of the original girl (see Spencer, 2008; Asiaone News, 2008; Riley, 2008).

The international media's obsessions with the issue of the "face," however, diverted attention from the issue of "voice" in this scene, which seemed a much more nuanced and interesting dimension. To many of the Chinese audiences, this scene was perhaps the most emotionally impacting moment during the entire ceremony.[4] Even the general director Zhang Yimou and the music director Chen Qigang later admitted to the media that the scene moved them to tears every time, even during the rehearsals.[5] Although the way it was sung at the opening ceremony did not clearly manifest this, the original version of the song is actually a quite volatile one. Paradoxically, the emotional intensity the song evokes among Chinese audiences was perhaps particularly due to the inherent tensions between the historical memories loaded in the song, and the highly unconventional employment of the little girl's voice as the vehicle for that politically charged memory.

"Hymn to the Motherland," putatively the "second national anthem," was composed by Wang Shen, a fecund songwriter whose work appeared in many important pro-revolution musical productions from the 1930s on. In 1950, inspired by the festive atmosphere of the first national anniversary celebration, Wang Shen caught the spark of the concept of the song while perceiving the mass parade at Tiananmen Square. The song first gained popularity among the schools and factories in Tianjin, and then soon caught the attention of the central government. Thereafter, it won strong support and government promotion from major party leaders such as Mao Zedong and Zhou Enlai, which helped it become a nationwide hit. The lyrics are essentially about mobilizing people's patriotic passions through a retrospection of the country's hardships overcome and a projection of the bright prospect lying ahead. Since its birth in 1950, it has become one of the most popular choices on various social and political occasions where the chorus would be deemed as indispensable to evoke a sense of collective compatriot sentiments. It was chosen, for instance, as the finale for the musical theater *The East is Red*, possibly the most prominent propaganda spectacle created during the 1960s. On October 16, 1964, the day when China detonated its first atomic bomb, after premier Zhou Enlai announced the news to the public, the same song was sung by the performers of the show on stage and cheering (Gu, 1999: 23; 2004: 29–31).

Since the musical form of the song is originally a march, the style of the singing is often highly military in inflection. The conventional mode of singing the song emphasizes a kind of eruptive passion close to rage, a type of valiant determination generated from a sense of collectivity. Yet, when the song appeared at the opening ceremony, the aural aspect contradicted its usual way of presentation. The singing followed closely after the scene where the five Olympic rings were displayed as floating in the air, and a piece of new-age-style music permeated the air with an ambience of smoothness. Almost immediately after a shot of the radiating five rings, the camera cut to a cute girl dressed in red standing on a small stage set up on one side of the stadium ground (Figure 26.6). As the singing started, it appeared that the rhythm of the song was considerably slowed down. The girl's voice was sweet, and the accompanying music eased the strong beats in the original version and was kept low in the background, to allow the girl's voice to appear even more lyrical. Gradually the girl's voice became amplified. It was liltingly ethereal and vulnerably innocent. In this way the atmosphere of the scene interfaced smoothly with the previous scene which was to present Olympic cosmopolitanism as a dream-like ideal.

Parallel to the inherent ambivalence created by the contrast of the girl's immaculately innocent voice with the kind of political assertiveness underlying both the lyrics and the historical memory associated with the song, the visual aspect of the flag-raising rite also embodied a conversion of two contending symbol systems. As the singing went on, the audiences saw 56 other young children, dressed in various ethnic costumes, as representatives of China's 56 ethnic groups, escorting the national flag towards the flagpole (Figure 26.7). As they drew near to the pole, the children handed the flag to eight solemn-looking ceremonial guards, who then goose-stepped to the pole with shiny leather boots thudding the ground resoundingly. This was the instance where the state institution chose to manifest its will of guardianship, strategically yet uncompromisingly, by encapsulating itself with imageries of children's vulnerability and innocence.

The bodily features of the children, themselves being appropriated as a universalist discourse concerning hope, peace, and aspirations for prosperity, when appearing jointly with symbols and signs representing state power, function not only to mitigate the aggressiveness contained within the connotations of the nation-state symbolism but also to lend legitimacy to the agendas behind such representations. Thus the question of guardianship becomes highly intricate here. It seems that in front of the global audiences, the children's faces and voices, with their "irresistible charm" as part of a cosmopolitanism discourse, threw a membrane of affection over the ruthlessness of the state institution, as embodied in the

Figure 26.6 Lin Miaoke lip-singing at the opening ceremony of the Beijing Olympic Games.
Source: *The Opening Ceremony of the Beijing 2008 Olympic Games* DVD, issued by China International Television Corporation, 2008.

Figure 26.7 Fifty-six children in ethnic costumes escorting the Chinese national flag.
Source: *The Opening Ceremony of the Beijing 2008 Olympic Games* DVD, issued by China International Television Corporation, 2008.

lyrics of the song and the symbolism of the nation state. On the other hand, it could also be interpreted as showing that a more humanitarian cosmopolitanism ideal successfully appeased a potentially volatile nationalist discourse. It was through this uncustomary infusion of symbol systems from two ideological parameters that the scene sought both to evoke the compatriot sentiments of the domestic viewers and to satiate the emotional consumption of the global audiences.

Liu Xiang and Lang Ping: Gendered Spectacles of Nationalism and Transnationalism at the Beijing Olympics

In the following section, we discuss two iconic Chinese athletes' stirring spectacles during the Beijing Olympics, focusing on how they were molded by sports institutions and cultures in different periods of China, and engaged in the commodification of bodies and national glories as well as the contestations between nationalism agendas and globalism, in remarkably different ways.

When Liu Xiang won the 110 meters hurdles final at the 2004 Athens Olympics, he became a national hero. His popularity and wide fan base in China largely stems from his breakthrough performance in track and field, in which Chinese athletes, especially male athletes, rarely excelled. Since 2001 when Liu Xiang appeared on the international sport scene, he had consistently ranked as a top competitor and achiever, but his reputation did not reach the level of a highly profitable star until his 2004 Athens gold medal. Public fandom for Liu reached a new peak after the 2006 IAAF Super Grand Prix at Lausanne, Switzerland, where he broke a 13-year-old world record. Later the same year in Stuttgart, Germany, at the IAAF world athletics finals, he became a world champion and thus the first "triple crown" Chinese athlete in track and field.[6]

The rise of Liu's market value was in accordance with his achievements in the sports field. In 2003, his price for branding for a domestic company was merely US$60,000. At the time before the Beijing Olympics, it had risen to US$2 million, an increase by more than 30-fold. While the market displayed its ostensible will of profit

pursuits through overwhelming commercials, another strong player in exploiting Liu Xiang's values, the state, largely exerted its influences either directly through institutional regulations, or more discursively, through various media texts. In this regard, state and market are simultaneously intertwined and contested in constructing Liu Xiang's spectacular imagery. Liu Xiang was hailed as a "national hero" in that he was believed to have subverted the negative stereotype of Chinese males by performing outstandingly in a competitive sport in which Asians were traditionally marginalized. In a media interview right after the Athens Olympic Games, Liu professed that his success retorted the discriminatory belief that Asian men are incapable of entering the finals in certain track and field programs.[7] Thereafter, Liu's numerous commercial presences all seemed to undertake the mission of promoting Chinese masculinity, through a spectacle that forged national pride with his agility, strength, and urban trendy looks.[8] At the same time, the state's track-and-field administration set up an office specifically focusing on cultivating Liu Xiang's commercial values. Hence, the state sport administration also played the role of a broker, while placing both the athlete's acceptance of commercials and his income distributions under close regulations.[9]

Liu Xiang's scandalous withdrawal from the 110 meters hurdle stunned millions of viewers both inside the national stadium and around the TV screen. Especially Chinese audiences suffered tremendous emotional trauma as this seemingly unlikely scene took place right in front of the eyes of the world and was close to becoming a spectacle of national disgrace. The incident soon spawned conspiracy theories which proclaimed that both the sport administration and Liu Xiang knew that his physical strength was not fit enough to compete under such intense pressures, but since Liu as a national icon carried the hopes of the nation, he and his coach staged the entire show to prove to the public that he was still worthy of being a national inspiration (Hook, 2008). This concealment also served to maintain Liu's asset value for the corporations that he represented. While many of the commercial sponsors issued public letters to show support, others quietly edited Liu Xiang out of their TV commercials (PPSJ, 2008). But what is true is perhaps that Liu Xiang's injury did reach an extent where to participate in the games would have been beyond his physical capability at that time. It was indeed the tremendous pressure from the market and the sport administration, plus millions of Chinese audiences' hopes, that helped produce his collapse in the stadium.

If Liu Xiang's dramatic spectacle is one of frustrated national pride, an instance of an individual athlete entrapped in the power relations between a pro-nationalist state and exploitative transnational capital, then another spectacle at the 2008 Olympics told a story from quite a different angle. Jenny Lang (Lang Ping) was a truly legendary figure on world sport stage, for more than 20 years, not just as a famed athlete but also as a successful coach, perhaps the only female coach who has ever achieved that kind of prestige in women's volleyball. (For a brief description of Lang's achievements and popularity in China, see Peterson, 2008).

Lang's reputation was initially built in the early 1980s when serving as a key player of Chinese women's volleyball team (CNWVT), which won five consecutive world championships from 1981 to 1986. It was also during the incipient years of China's post-Cultural Revolution social reform. CNWVT was the only sports team ever to have obtained gold medals in the world among the "three big ball" games (the other two being soccer and basketball).[10] The team's successes in international competitions were timely enough to inspire a country attempting to get rid of its outmoded posture of self-enclosure. The team members acquired "celebrity" status almost overnight and were hailed, honored, and saluted everywhere they showed up. However, at that time, this "celebrity" status was more indebted to the state's deliberate promotion and appropriation than the commercial venues' marketing strategies, though the latter did also play a prominent role in the process (Dong, 2003: 160–163). The term "CNWVT spirit" (*nvpai jingshen*), which emphasized qualities of self-sacrifice and total devotion to the country, was coined and propagated intensely by the government and the media. Thus Lang Ping as an iconic athlete in the 1980s signified a different type of moral exemplar from Liu Xiang. While the former emphasizes perseverance, diligence, and dedication to the country, the latter used TV commercials to promote concepts

of self-confidence, style, and fitness. Both images were tied closely to patriotic sentiments, but Lang as a 1980s team sports icon has always signified the importance of collectivism whereas Liu's imagery, in accordance with a rising China in the context of the global expansion of neoliberalism, is more attuned to individualism.

After retiring from the volleyball team, Lang went abroad to study and in the 1990s, started her coaching career on an international basis. Her career as a head coach was immensely successful. In 1994, she was appointed by the Chinese sports administration to coach the national women's volleyball team. She led the team to win a World Cup bronze medal, an Olympic silver medal, and a World Championship silver medal. After quitting the position in 1998, she coached in Italy's professional league – the world's largest and most successful volleyball league, and again maintained an exceptional record.

One of the most dramatic moments in Lang's career happened in 2005 when she decided to accept the offer to serve as the head coach for the US women's volleyball team. The news provoked tremendous reaction in China, as the US team was widely regarded as among the strongest competitors at the Beijing Olympics. Many Chinese people believed that with her superior coaching skills, and especially her knowledge of the Chinese team's weak spots, Lang's joining the US team would make it an even more formidable rival at the Beijing Olympics. The most difficult part for many people was that the person who helped forge the glory of CNWVT at the 1984 Los Angeles Olympics some 20 years ago would come back to Beijing, but this time she would be commissioned by one of China's strongest rivals to smash the Chinese team's gold medal dream (Qu, 2005). Voices of suspicion and criticism culminated as the Olympic Games approached. Nie Weiping, China's preeminent Go player (also a national icon) attacked Lang and other Chinese coaches serving in foreign teams for betraying their home country. Such news soon stirred heated discussions in the public sphere regarding issues of patriotism and transnationalism in sports.[11] At the Olympics, the Chinese and the US national teams were assigned to the same pool in the preliminary and the US team beat China 3–2. This was an important factor in the Chinese men's volleyball team's failure to reach the final, although the CNWVT eventually won a bronze medal, following the US team's silver medal and Brazil's gold.

Despite many attacks on Lang's prioritizing individual success over China's national glory, the mainstream voices in the media and the internet forum exalted her accomplishments. Most of the media coverage tried to justify this transnational flow of talents in professional sports by citing the many examples of foreign coaches currently working in China. They also contended that the US team's outstanding performance should not be perceived as Lang's personal success but rather as a contribution made by Chinese volleyball professionals to elevate the status of the sport in the world. Lang herself also underscored an understanding of sports that transcends national borders. Yet at the same time, she also credited her success to the training experiences she received as an athlete in China. Hence, Lang strategically maneuvered the rhetoric of national glory and loyalty, and injected new interpretations of the relationship between sport and nation.

Thus the spectacles of Liu Xiang and Lang Ping respectively embodied two sets of attitudes and values regarding sport, national identity, and global community through an interrelated but also contesting manner. Liu's is a heightened sentiment of national glory, constructed and promoted through the collaboration of both the global corporate forces and the strong central state of China. It is a myth that caters to the aspirations of a rising China whose national subjects craved an imagery of a self-confident and agile individual sportsman. Lang's story, however, tried to promote a discourse of "sports without national borders." Her career trajectory delineated the transformation of a national icon into one with claims to defy and transgress nation-state boundaries. Such a transformation, however, also paradoxically contains a tendency of reinforcing the "nationalism agenda," in which Lang's individual success as a transnational sport talent is tied to the triumph of a state-dominated athlete training system.

At the 2008 Beijing Olympics, the Chinese delegation won 51 gold medals and far superseded the US team's 36 medals. For the first time in Olympics history, China won the status of "top

dog." Surely, for many Chinese people, the Beijing Olympics was a landmark event in the new millennium, as in popular discourses there has always been a tendency of associating national glory with the country's performances at the Olympics. The 2008 Olympics was regarded as witnessing China's entry as a major player on the international sports scene. Yet, aside from moments of victory and exhilaration, there were also occasions of loss, regret, and puzzlement. Among them was Liu Xiang's withdrawal from the match right at the starting line. Also dramatic was defeat of the Chinese women's volleyball team by the US team, under the coaching of Lang Ping, one of the legendary, iconic figures from Chinese women's volleyball, in her home country, in front of millions of fellow citizens who bore tremendous hope of China's winning the gold medal.

On the whole, however, triumphant spectacles of nationalism marked China's significant entry on the stage of the global sports spectacle "winner's circle," which was manufactured collaboratively by mass media, transnational corporate forces, and a relentless state politics, in which the Olympics revealed its immense complexity, internal contradictions, and perpetual dialogues between the local, the national, and the global.

Conclusion

We have shown in this chapter how the sports spectacle is co-constructed by global, national, and local cultural forms and in particular how the universalistic Olympics was in 2008 constructed through spectacles and figures of Chinese nationalism. The globally televised spectacle of the 2008 Beijing Olympic opening ceremony illustrates the dynamic cultural process of implementing governmentalizing techniques through "communicative bodies" – bodies that are historicized, mythologized, and aestheticized for the sake of spectatorship (Miller et al., 2001). Condensed onto the site of these performing bodies are the simultaneously contending and complicit ideologies of nationalism and a type of globalism tinged with neoliberal agendas.

Although running on a more frugal fiscal budget of *merely* US$42 million, less than half of the cost of the opening ceremonies at the Beijing Games, the 2012 London Olympics used the opening ceremonies for a media spectacle of British nationalism, one news report commenting on its "replacing Chinese militaristic precision with British fancifulness."[12] Orchestrated by film director Danny Boyle, a cast of thousands illustrated stories from Shakespeare, King Arthur and his Round Table, Mary Poppins, and James Bond, with the Queen of England herself appearing to parachute into the stadium in a Bond narrative. The director managed to get in a promo for Britain's National Health Service, and, as with the Chinese, the British created a media spectacle out of icons of their culture and national history.

We conclude that the spectacle of bodies at the opening ceremony and during the Olympic Games in the 2008 Beijing Olympics was constructed through Chinese nationalist ideological prisms utilizing invented traditions and historical narratives, and at the same time sought to cater to globalized desires for the consumption of utopian cosmopolitanism. These two processes collapsed into each other constantly, and further complicated the power configurations shaped by various imagery discourses presented through the spectacle. Such reciprocal processes seek to mutually reinforce each other, yet at the same time both the substance and the symbolisms of the imaginations of the nation and globalization are undergoing subtle transformations during such processes. Thus, global sports spectacles become the sites of contradictions and tensions as well as the global harmony which the Chinese production of the 2008 Beijing Olympics attempted to generate, and such contradictions and ambiguities will likely be played out for the foreseeable future at Olympic Games to come.

Notes

1   See, for instance, the favorite ads of Superbowl 2011 of one fan at http://www.sb-innovation.de/f53/my-favorite-ads-superbowl-2011-a-24474/, accessed 4 January 2013, and the *USA Today* site in which viewers rank their favorite ads at http://www.usatoday.com/money/advertising/admeter/2011/super-bowl-ad-meter/43271432/1, accessed 4 January 2013.

2   The London Organising Committee of the 2012 Olympics admitted after the Beijing Games that it would be extremely difficult for London to achieve such a level of extravaganza, and that henceforth it might be necessary to reverse the trend and adopt a more budget-wary style of hosting at London. See Grose (2008).

3   Child heroes as a trope of moral education maintained a persistent presence in socialist China's moral education curriculum. It could be traced to the Yan'an period which had a direct lineage to the Soviet Union's moral preaching. In certain aspects, they were also inspired by the Confucian tradition of exemplary children, as argued by both Reed (1995) and Bulag (1999). Famous iconic child heroes include Lei Feng, "The heroic little sisters of the grassland," and Lai Ning, to name just a few.

4   Many netizens left comments on blogs or internet forums and agreed that the "Hymn to the Motherland" was the most moving scene to them. See, for instance, "Ten most memorable moments of the Beijing Olympic opening ceremony" (*Beijing aoyunhui kaimu shi rang ren mingji de shi ge shunjian*), blog of Liuxing Feiyu, August 11, 2008, http://blog.sina.com.cn/s/blog_504ee07a 0100apek.html (in Chinese), accessed January 5, 2013; Hong Tian Pao, "The most moving scene for me at the opening ceremony" (*Kaimushi zui gandong wo de yi huan*), By369.com, August 10, http://www.by369.com/bbs/viewthread.php?tid= 5107, accessed January 5, 2013.

5   See the interview with Zhang Yimou: "Touched by the girl's singing of Hymn to the Motherland every time listening to it" (*Zhang Yimou: Nv hai meici chang "Gechang Zuguo" dou gandong*). *Souhu News*, August 9, http://news.sohu.com/20080809/ n258711258.shtml, accessed January 5, 2013. See also the interview with Chen Qigang: "Qigang Chen and Liu Huan on People Online to talk about Beijing Olympics theme song" (*Chen Qigang, Liu Huan zuoke Renmin Wang, xiangjie Beijing Aoyunhui zhuti ge*). *People Online*, August 13, http://ent.people.com.cn/GB/98772/98778/131721/131722/7661355.html, accessed January 5, 2013.

6   For the introduction of Liu Xiang's achievements, see Liu Xiang's official website: http://liuxiang.sports.cn/meet/highligths/2005-04-12/534962.html, accessed January 5, 2013.

7 See YouTube clip of an interview after Liu Xiang's championship match in Athens (*Liu Xiang yadian guanjun*), http://www.youtube.com/watch?v=Ly_dep10AJM&feature=PlayList&p=F7EB1A2974784F12&playnext=1&playnext_from=PL&index=19 (in Chinese), accessed January 5, 2013.

8 See some of the commercials at "Kia commercial featuring Liu Xiang" (*Liu Xiang daiyan qianlima*), *Sohu Video Blog*, http://v.blog.sohu.com/u/vw/1537831 (in Chinese), accessed January 5, 2013; "Lonoin commercial featuring Liu Xiang" (*Liu Xiang daiyan longxin motuo*), *Sohu Video Blog*, http://v.blog.sohu.com/u/vw/1537398 (in Chinese), accessed January 5, 2013; "Aokang commercial featuring Liu Xiang" (*Liu Xiang daiyan Aokang pixie*), *Boosj.com*, http://www.boosj.com/45607.html (in Chinese), accessed January 5, 2013.

9 See "Five questions concerning Liu Xiang" (*Liu Xiang wu wen*). *Sohu News*, August 23, http://news.sohu.com/20080823/n259149836.shtml, accessed January 5, 2013.

10 This categorization, allegedly based on both the sizes and the popularity of the three games, seems to be uniquely Chinese.

11 For instance, see the thread of the discussions on Lang Ping's being appointed as the US women's volleyball head coach, *tieba.baidu.com*, August 1, 2008, http://tieba.baidu.com/f?kz=455823249, accessed January 5, 2013; thread of the discussions on the US women's volleyball team's defeating the Chinese team at the Beijing Olympics, *zhidao.baidu.com*, August 20, 2008, http://zhidao.baidu.com/question/65089124.html, accessed January 5, 2013.

12 See the report "London 2012 Olympic Games: Billions tune in to watch spectacular opening ceremony." *Belfast Telegraph*, July 28, 2012, http://www.belfasttelegraph.co.uk/sport/olympics/london-2012-olympic-games-billions-tune-in-to-watch-spectacular-opening-ceremony-16191078.html, accessed January 5, 2013.

References

Andrews, D.L. (1997) "The [Trans]National Basketball Association: American commodity-sign culture and global localization," in Cvetovitch, A. and Kellner, D. (eds.), *Politics and Cultural Studies Between the Global and the Local*, Boulder, CO: Westview Press, pp. 72–101.

Andrews, D.L. (2009) "Sport, culture and late capitalism," in Carrington, B. and McDonald, I. (eds.) *Marxism, Cultural Studies and Sport*, London: Routledge, pp. 213–231.

Asiaone News (2008) "Olympic child singing star was a fake." Asiaone News, August 12, http://www.asiaone.com/News/Latest%2BNews/Asia/Story/A1Story20080812-81958.html, accessed January 4, 2013.

Bennhold, K. and Rosenthal, E. (2008) "Olympic torch run in Paris halted as protests spread." *New York Times*, April 8, http://rinf.com/alt-news/activism/olympic-torch-run-in-paris-halted-as-protests-spread/2917/, accessed January 4, 2013.

Brownell, S. (2008) *Beijing's Games: What the Olympics Mean to China*, Lanham, MD: Rowman & Littlefield.

Bulag, U. (1999) "Models and moralities: The parable of the two 'Heroic Little Sisters of the Grassland.'" *China Journal*, 42 (7): 21–41.

Carrington, B. (2004) "Cosmopolitan Olympism, humanism and the spectacle of 'race,'" in Bale, J. and Christensen, M. (eds.) *Post-Olympism? Questioning Sport in the Twenty-First Century*, Oxford: Berg, pp. 81–98.

Chu, Y. (2008) "The importance of being Chinese: Orientalism reconfigured in the age of global modernity." *Boundary 2*, 35 (2): 183–206.

Coplon, J. (1996) "Legends, champions?" *New York Times Magazine*, April 21: 32–35.

Dong, J. (2003) *Women, Sport and Society in Modern China: Holding up More Than Half the Sky*, London: Frank Cass.

Edelman, R. (2006) "Moscow 1980: Stalinism or good, clean fun?" in Tomlinson, A. and Young, C. (eds.) *National Identity and Global Sports Events: Culture, Politics and Spectacle in the Olympics and the Football World Cup*, Albany: State University of New York Press, pp. 149–162.

Fass, P. (2003) "Children and globalization." *Journal of Social History*, 36 (4): 963–977.

Fass, P. (2008) "Childhood and youth as an American/global experience in the context of the past," in Cole, J. and Durham, D. (eds.) *Figuring the Future: Globalization and the Temporalities of Children and Youth*. Santa Fe, NM: School for Advanced Research Press, pp. 25–48.

Grose, T.K. (2008) "London admits it can't top lavish Beijing Olympics when it hosts 2012 Games." *US News and World Report*, August 22, http://www.usnews.com/articles/news/world/2008/08/22/london-admits-it-cant-top-lavish-beijing-olympics-when-it-hosts-2012-games.html, accessed January 4, 2013.

Gu, Y. (1999) "The birth of the Hymn to the Motherland" (*Gechang Zuguo dansheng ji*). *Dang Shi Bo Lan*, 1999 (9): 23.

Gu, Y. (2004) "Zhou Enlai led the choir to sing 'Hymn to the Motherland'" (*Zhou Enlai shuaizhong gao ge "Gechang Zuguo"*). *Xia Yi Dai*, 2004 (10):29–31.

Guttmann, A. (2006) "Berlin 1936: The most controversial Olympics," in Tomlinson, A. and Young, C. (eds.) *National Identity and Global Sports Events: Culture, Politics and Spectacle in the Olympics and the Football World Cup*, Albany: State University of New York Press, pp. 65–82.

Harrison, M. (2006) "Zhang Yimou's hero and the globalisation of propaganda." *Millennium – Journal of International Studies*, 34: 569–572.

Hirschberg, L. (1996) "The big man can deal." *New York Times*, November 17, http://www.nytimes.com/1996/11/17/magazine/the-big-man-can-deal.html?pagewanted=all&src=pm, accessed January 22, 2013.

Hook, L. (2008) "Liu Xiang: The conspiracy theory." *Wall Street Journal Blogs*, August 22, http://blogs.wsj.com/olympics/2008/08/22/liu-xiang-the-conspiracy-theory/, accessed January 5, 2013.

Jarvie, G., Hwang, D., and Brennan, M. (2008) *Sport, Revolution and the Beijing Olympics*, Oxford: Berg.

Kellner, D. (2003) *Media Spectacles*, London: Routledge.

Kellner, D. (2008) *Guys and Guns Amok: Domestic Terrorism and School Shootings from the Oklahoma City Bombing to the Virginia Tech Massacre*, Boulder, CO: Paradigm Publishers.

Kellner, D. (2010) *Cinema Wars: Hollywood Film and Politics in the Bush/Cheney Era*, Oxford: Blackwell.

Li, Y. and Chen, K. (2008) "The soldiers hit on *fou*, and shook the whole world" (*Shibing ji fou, zhenhan shijie*). *Wuhan Evening News*, August 9, http://cjmp.cnhan.com/whwb/html/2008-08/09/content_395481.htm, accessed January 4, 2013.

Miller, T., Lawrence, G., McKay, J., and Rowe, D. (2001) *Globalization and Sport: Playing the World*, London: Sage Publications.

Peterson, A.M. (2008) "US volleyball's Jenny Lang Ping returns to Beijing." *Suelekha.com*, August, http://newshopper.sulekha.com/us-volleyball-s-jenny-lang-ping-returns-to-beijing_news_941514.htm, accessed January 5, 2013.

PPSJ (2008) "Commercials cancelled after Liu Xiang's withdrawal, Aokang decided to keep the contract" (*Liu Xiang tuisai daiyan guanggao fenfen xiapian, Aokang Zuohao xuyue xuanzeti*). *PPSJ.com*, September 4, http://blogs.wsj.com/chinarealtime/2008/08/19/get-well-soon-a-message-from-liu-xiangs-sponsors/ (in Chinese), accessed January 22, 2013.

Qu, B. (2005) "Glad to see open-mindedness matching a rising China – comments on Lang Ping's being appointed as the head coach of the USA women's volleyball team" (*Xijian daguo xintai – Ping Lang Ping churen meiguo nvpai Zhujiaolian*). *People.com. cn*, February 9.

Quel Sport (2008) "Pekin 2008: Boycott des jeux de la honte!" *Quel Sport*, 4/5, May.

Qing, L. (2010) "Encoding the Olympics – visual hegemony? Discussion and interpretation on intercultural communication in the Beijing Olympic games." *International Journal of the History of Sport*, 27 (9/10): 1824–1872.

Reed, G. (1995) "Moral/political education in the People's Republic of China: Learning through role models." *Journal of Moral Education*, 24 (2): 99–111.

Riley, D. (2008) "Not only were the Olympic fireworks fake, so was the 7 year old singer." *The Inquisitr*, August 12, http://www.inquisitr.com/2323/not-only-were-the-olympic-fireworks-fake-so-was-the-7-year-old-singer/, accessed January 4, 2013.

Spencer, R. (2008) "Beijing Olympics: Faking scandal over girl who 'sang' in opening ceremony." *Daily Telegraph*, August 12, http://www.telegraph.co.uk/sport/olympics/2545387/Beijing-Olympics-Faking-scandal-over-girl-who-sang-in-opening-ceremony.html, accessed January 4, 2013.

Stephens, S. (1995) "Children and the politics of culture in 'late capitalism,'" in Stephen, S. (ed.) *Children and the Politics of Culture*, Princeton, NJ: Princeton University Press, pp. 3–50.

Tomlinson, A. (1996) "Olympic spectacle: Opening ceremonies and some paradoxes of globalization." *Media, Culture & Society*, 18 (4): 583–602.

Tomlinson, A. (2002) "Theorizing spectacle: Beyond Debord," in Sugden, J. and Tomlinson, A. (eds.) *Power Games: A Critical Sociology of Sport*, London: Routledge, pp. 44–60.

Tomlinson, A. (2005) *Sport and Leisure Cultures*, Minneapolis: University of Minnesota Press.

Tomlinson, A. (2008) "Olympic values, Beijing's Olympic games and the universal market," in Price, M. and Dayan, D. (eds.) *Owning the Olympics: Narratives of the New China*, Ann Arbor: University of Michigan Press, pp. 67–85.

Zhang, L. (2008) "The fundamental flaw of the '*fou* phalanx,' mistaken *jian fou* for musicial instrument" (*fouzhen yingshang, cuo ba "jianfou" dang yueqi*). *Wuhan Evening News*, August 9, *blogchina.com*, August 11, http://vip.bokee.com/20080811587060.html, accessed January 4, 2013.

Zhang, Y. (1994) "Ideology of the body in *Red Sorghum*: National allegory, national roots and third cinema," in Dissanayake, W. (ed.) *Colonialism and Nationalism in Asian Cinema*, Bloomington: Indiana University Press, pp. 30–41.

Zhao, S. (1998) "A state-led nationalism: The patriotic education campaign in post-Tiananmen China." *Communist and Post-Communist Studies*, 31 (3): 287–302.

Further Reading

Brownell, S. (2008) *Beijing's Games: What the Olympics Mean to China*, Lanham, MD: Rowman & Littlefield.

Jarvie, G., Hwang, D., and Brennan, M. (2008) *Sport, Revolution and the Beijing Olympics*, Oxford: Berg.

Tomlinson, A. and Young, C. (2006) *National Identity and Global Sports Events: Culture, Politics and Spectacle in the Olympics and the Football World Cup*, Albany: State University of New York Press.

Miller, T., Lawrence, G., McKay, J., and Rowe, D. (2001) *Globalization and Sport: Playing the World*, London: Sage.

27

Always Already Excluded
The Gendered Facts of Anti-Blackness and Brazil's Male Seleção

João H. Costa Vargas

Introduction

Not since 1968 has a country hosted an Olympic Games and a World Cup back to back. Inverting the sequence at which these two sports mega-events took place in Mexico, a select group of Brazilian cities will stage the men's 2014 football World Cup finals, while the 2016 summer Olympic Games will take place in Rio de Janeiro. By drawing on a discussion about the gendered inflections of race as they pertain to the Brazilian nation state, common-sense shared understandings, and the places blacks occupy in the nation's symbolic and spatial geographies, this chapter focuses on the black influence on Brazil's football, and indeed the nation, as part of an ongoing political and symbolic struggle. One of the results of this struggle – and here is the point I will argue as I revisit the Brazilian male football team's successful campaign in the 2009 South Africa Confederations Cup – is that it projects an apparent acceptance of blackness. However, this apparent acceptance, when analyzed through an analytical prism that recognizes the mutual imbrications of gender, sexuality, and race, becomes problematic as it also suggests ongoing negative representations of blackness, if only by attempting to mask

them. What do both football and sport mega-events tell us about the projects of nation in the black diaspora? How does an analysis of the gendered inflections of race, as they impact football performance and the organization of mega-events, help us to understand contemporary social conflicts? Inversely, how do social conflicts, and their gendered aspects of race, provide analytical angles through which to comprehend both sport performance and the negotiations and expectations about the men's football World Cup and the summer Olympic Games? This chapter takes up the proposition that "global sport can only be adequately understood if the character of the main political and economic dimension is recognized" (Tomlinson and Young, 2006: 2). It also proposes that the inverse is true: that political and economic processes impacting a context explain specific sport performance as they do strategies employed to organize sport events.

The chapter begins with an analysis and ethnographically informed self-reflective description of a key moment in the 2009 South Africa Confederations Cup final,[1] focusing on the Brazilian male football team – its composition, tactics, management, performance, self-representation, and press coverage. This angle enables us

A Companion to Sport, First Edition. Edited by David L. Andrews and Ben Carrington.
© 2013 Blackwell Publishing Ltd. Published 2013 by Blackwell Publishing Ltd.

to grasp the uneasy gendered and racialized dynamics that define the *seleção*[2] and the hegemonic body politic more generally. Such uneasy dynamics are actualizations of historical and structural facets of the Brazilian modality of racial democracy. At first glance, this modality of racial democracy values particular movements, flair, insights, *ginga* – ephemeral yet critically defining aspects of Brazilian football that distinguish it from approaches common in other nations. This valuing of the immanent Brazilian football qualities requires the recognition that such qualities are indissociable from the African presence in Brazil, modified yet still apparent as a specific diasporic inflection to a sport invented and brought over to Brazil by the British (e.g., Filho, 2003). Here lies a central tension: this black style is valued yet suspect; celebrated yet often taken as reason for Brazil's seemingly perpetual underdevelopment.

Building on this discussion, in the next two sections, which take the 1950 and 1958 World Cups as key moments in football and in the nation's self-understanding, I propose a theoretical perspective that explains the variations in acceptance of the black presence in Brazil. A racial complex informs the ways in which black people in sport and in the national body are *always already excluded*. This exclusion is masked by the authentic celebration of all things black (people and actions) – as during the World Cup victories and other sport and arts achievements. Yet, the work of the racial democracy mythology is such that the celebration not only masks but also unavoidably anticipates the next moment: that of aversion of blacks, and the realization that there is no modern nation that is also a black nation.

Recent social events in Rio de Janeiro, such as police–military pacification operations targeting mostly black neighborhoods, unmistakably connected to the upcoming World Cup and Olympic Games, bring home the point about the aversion of blacks. As much as they are about sport, the intensification in the imposed residential isolation of, and police brutality on, black communities, particularly those in Rio, forcefully illustrate the constitutive contradiction energizing the nationalist project. While former president Lula's statement about the "white, blond and blue-eyed people" as responsible for the world economic crisis reveals an increased sensitivity to race – and

indeed suggests an influence of the Brazilian black movement on the president's statements – it nevertheless reaffirms the ideological pull that racial democracy still exerts (*Veja*, 2009). While this statement surprisingly equates negativity to European and North American Anglos, dialectically it also reinforces default anti-black beliefs. After all, Lula's tirade is precisely this – a surprising, thought-provoking harangue that works only because the default symbology is one that always already devalues blackness. Moreover, the popular Brazilian president's invective does little to address and redress forms of state- and society-sanctioned anti-black discrimination, and thus ends up, quite successfully, reaffirming the white supremacist worldview.

A brief reflection on the alternatives open to the Afro-descended in Brazil concludes the chapter – be they athletes or ordinary citizens, what possibilities are there to oppose their continued dehumanization? The analysis presented in this chapter suggests that Afro-Brazilians will disproportionately experience dislocation, suffering, and death as the preparations begin and the events unfold, even when and as black athletes are celebrated and enshrined.

Brazilian Football Success and the Gendered Facts of Blackness

Luis Fabiano wanted it badly. Fighting a cold, and – considerably more debilitating – the unrealistic yet constant expectations that the press and Brazilians in general attach to the "number 9" yellow jersey, he set himself the objective of scoring at least five times during the 2009 Confederations Cup tournament. He calculated an average of a goal per game would consolidate his starter status for the 2010 South Africa World Cup; it would quell, at least temporarily, the doubts cast over his competence – doubts, of course, that reveal tacit and not so tacit comparisons between Fabiano and legendary former stikers: Vavá (1958 and 1962 World Cups), Tostão (1970), Reinaldo (1978), Careca (1986 and 1990), Romário (1994), and Ronaldo (1998, 2002, 2006), just to cite the most obvious.

"O Fabuloso," as he is known in Brazil, after the moniker Spaniards have given him as a Sevilla player, had not scored in the tough semi-final match against South Africa, and so needed at least one more goal in the Confederations Cup final to fulfill his plan. With Brazil down 0–2 in the final against the United States at the start of the second half, his personal objective became part of an improbable if somewhat desperate and quickly vanishing quest for a comeback.

What the heck, I and certainly other Brazilians thought. It's only the Confederations Cup. The US men's team never wins anything; the title will do good for US football; more importantly, the *seleção* hardly does well in the World Cup after winning the Confederations Cup – the scintillating win in the 2005 final against arch-rivals Argentina, preceding the mediocre 2006 performance in Germany being just the most recent example; plus, Dunga, the hard-headed player turned hard-headed coach, who dares to set up the Brazilian team like any other team – that is, relying on set counter-attacks and thus giving up the traditional, some would say "South American," possession-based tactic – he has been too lucky, let him catch some heat. Many comforting thoughts raced through my mind, finely attuned to the national football/consciousness/hysteria.

But with less than a minute of play into the second half, in the US right intermediary field, Maicon passes the ball to Ramires, who returns it to Maicon, who then finds Luis Fabiano, his back to the US goal, and only one defender guarding him: the sole defender between the Brazilian striker and the US goalkeeper. In that prescient moment, the goal, and indeed the new phase that Brazilian football is entering, are conspicuously configured, rendered inevitable. Unlike Ronaldo, Romário, Careca, and Tostão, who in their good days would have taken a few steps toward their team-mate before receiving the ball so that they could charge toward and beat the defenders facing them, Fabiano's sprint and dribble are not his forte. He is more of the *trombador* striker, like Roberto Dinamite, Vasco da Gama's legendary figure, now the club's president after a relatively successful post-football career as a local elected representative. Or like Serginho, the (only?) unsung member of the still copiously celebrated 1982 World Cup Brazilian team. Roberto, Serginho, and Luis Fabiano, arguably less skilled than the first group I mentioned, and certainly less adept at using or willing to use a flashy arsenal of moves, disproportionately rely on an uncanny

capacity for anticipating the development of key plays and positioning themselves at the right place to do what they do best – to score goals, even if their movements and the goals they produce are not the most aesthetically pleasing. Inventive dancers and painters these strikers are not; they will fight, they will bump, insist, they will use determination above all else; and they score.

So back to Fabiano, in that split second when he has already set the ball in such a way that the defender cannot know what he will do next – will he pass, will he charge, will he run sideways? One detail in the play is crucial: the ball's trajectory is such that there is a movement of all players going from right to left, almost parallel to the offside imaginary line. Remember, Maicon passes the ball to Fabiano from the right to the middle. Fabiano, the defender marking him, and the goalkeeper – indeed like all players closely following the play – are moving in that same direction. Fabiano's right-foot flick backwards, ever so subtly creating a space between him, the ball, and the defender, as unpretentious as it surely seems in real time, generates a pause, an interregnum, a pregnant moment, a shift of pace. In that moment, from which he, and only he, is able to see ahead, he produces a definitive advantage by making time stop, so to speak. Think of it like the trajectory of an object thrown from the ground toward the sky; before it begins falling, it will have a moment of stillness. That is the effect Fabiano created with his flick. While the play's momentum is going left, the ball has found a relative resting coordinate; in that split moment of stillness, Fabiano quickly pivots around his right leg, and kicks the ball, with his left foot, between the defender, the goalie, and the right-hand post. Howard, the US goal keeper, can't fight the inevitable physics: as he lunges to his left, the ball's trajectory and velocity are enough to place it in the net, past his desperately stretching body. Perhaps not as plastically as Reinaldo, Careca, Romário, or even Ronaldo would have done it, just to stick to the automatic number 9 references, but just as effectively. Indeed, in that moment, Fabiano's goal opens up the way, psychologically at least, for what instantaneously becomes an accomplished fact: the Brazilians are irresistible and will beat the United States. By the game's end, the US players experience what the sporting world had come to expect: Brazilian male football global supremacy.

Key to understanding the above description is a vexing aspect of Brazil's triumph in the Confederations Cup – as indeed in the five World Cups won to date, as well as in the many international campaigns (the Brazilian football team is the only one to have participated in all World Cup finals that began in 1930 in Uruguay) – to wit: the facts of anti-blackness – or the ways in which the gendered inflections of race explain, affirm, negate, preserve, and transform such events.[3] To approach the gendered facts of anti-blackness means to revisit a theme rendered classic by Mario Filho's *O Negro no Futebol Brasileiro* (originally published in 1947), and understandably made relevant again as the Brazilian nation-state struggles with its self-definition, both internally and *vis à vis* other nations (e.g., Helal, 2001; Bastidas, 2002; Wisnick, 2008). Immanently racialized, the contours of ideological battles around the national can be captured by a critical cultural and psychological exegesis that forcefully places gender and sexuality at the center of theorizations on race.

The fact that my biographical – and I venture to suggest, national-cultural – memory is organized in no small measure around men's football World Cups and their shared recollections (as they emerge in sociality circles – mostly homosocial but not always – and in news media and specialized literature) indicates that the national male football team, in ways that local male squads, or the female national team, are not able to produce as deeply and comprehensively, is a semantic archive whose conflictive contents point to the continued troubled relationship between the national as a modernist project and as a lived experience, that require and shape bodies according to accepted codes (see Alexander, 2006; Iton, 2008), and the gendered facts of anti-blackness. That Rio's main newspaper, *O Globo* (Jabor, 2009: 1) publicized in its electronic version the all-time black Brazilian male national football team, thus positively gesturing toward the black consciousness day observed on November 20, points to such semantic and political battles.

So when Dunga, the Brazilian men's football team coach, announced on June 29, 2009, after winning the Confederations Cup in South Africa that "to come back from being 2-0 down [at the end of the first half against the United States] is

only possible when you have a team of men, committed to victory until the end" (Jabor, 2009: 1), he was joining such battles. What seems like a redundancy – the emphasis on the fact that the male football team is "a team of men" – is precisely the assertion of the idealized footballer: not only gendered as male but also sexualized as unmistakably heteronormative. That such combination requires emphasis, and becomes celebrated as an explanation for what seemed like an improbable victory, suggests its ambiguous and questioned character. That is, the national squad is not always made up of heteronormative, brave men – the subtext here is most probably a reference to the last World Cup flop in 2006 Germany, when the team's loss in the quarter-finals against France was blamed on the excesses of individualism and less-than-indisputable male warrior ethos, clearly exemplified in the frequent off-day partying in which Ronaldinho, Ronaldo, and Roberto Carlos, among others, were reportedly engaged. As well, Ronaldinho's long hair and alleged post-stardom *ennui*, Ronaldo's excessive weight, and Roberto Carlos' seemingly aesthetic option of fiddling with his socks rather than marking his man, Thierry Henry, who would score France's lone and winning goal – all of these lapses are understood, although rarely explicitly, as evidence of a deficitarian hetoronormative maleness. Due to such deficits, the nation suffers, is not victorious, and a sense of inferiority is quick to reestablish itself, and become dominant.

The gender and sexuality codes are evident in these culturally shared examples – partying, especially when done by famous married men, deviates from and indeed challenges the nuclear monogamous family that Dunga's preferred type of heteronormativity requires, as do too much attention to appearance (Ronaldinho's hair), too little attention to appearance (Ronaldo's waistline), incapacity to defer gratification, or muster resolve. Less apparent in these examples is the role that race plays. How are Dunga's remarks on gender and sexuality loaded with racial cultural knowledge?

Racial inferiority is the semantic matrix informing not only Dunga's diatribe but, more generally, the Brazilian modern national project too. Football, for reasons that I will explain below, is a privileged medium through which to address racial inferiority; more importantly, though, it is one that allows for the social engineering of national viability *in spite of the fact of blackness*. What I am proposing here is that, whereas a historical gendered racial pendulum, apparent in the socially constructed historical football mega-events memory, sways closer to or farther from a positive notion of blackness, it leaves constant the very problem that blackness poses to the national modern project.

Untouched directly (because hardly, if ever, mentioned), yet troubled, white supremacy (the fear of racial mixture, the aversion of blackness, and the reification of patriarchal heteronormativity) reveals its logic as coaches, players, and varied publics (differentiated by and yet intersecting according to race, gender, social class, relative power, sexuality) participate in the performance and idealization of the nation/national team. Not accidentally, Rivaldo, Ronaldinho, Ronaldo, and Roberto Carlos, often against their protests (especially in the case of the latter two), are interpellated, markedly in Europe, as non-white, thus black, Afro-descended Brazilian football stars. Their purported questionable behavior and the consequent national team's loss at the 2006 World Cup become meaningful as, once again, they pose the perennial doubts about blackness and race mixture, and thus the desired race of the nation. Such doubts linger in a historical continuum, and it is only in reference to socially constructed and reconstructed memory – in reference, that is, to dominant, hegemonic discourses – that the muted and blurred acknowledgement of racial inferiority can be heard and made visible. Dunga's exhortation of his men, therefore, is as much an acknowledgement of the 2006 World Cup failure, as it is about the long-standing insecurities about Brazil's human and cultural (that is, racial and gendered) capital.

There would be no national insecurities if it were not for the African presence – a presence that, to make matters seemingly more complicated, provides solutions to the very problems it poses, as when Pelé and Garrincha saved the day in 1958, and as when Rivaldo, Ronaldinho, Ronaldo, and Roberto Carlos, with another black Brazilian, Cafu, as the captain, came back home world champions in 2002 after the defeat to host France in 1998. To delve further into these historical insecurities, let me propose that, whereas

the first World Cup triumph of 1958 quells some of these negative interpretations of blackness, 1950 still stands as the gold standard against which Dunga, and past and future coaches and commentators, elaborate many of their decisions concerning tactics, offer pronouncements about individual players, and even if unintentionally, comment on the modern national viability. As well, arguments about national viability, although obviously not restricted to the realms of sport and football more specifically, nevertheless make the *seleção* a privileged discursive field.

Inasmuch as national insecurities play themselves out in discourse and in action *vis-à-vis* European (and its close derivation, Argentinian) teams and nations, race is a constitutive element, albeit often a submerged one. Further, as significant commentaries about losses and triumphs repeatedly suggest, gender and sexuality become privileged modalities according to which race and nation are rendered palpable. Dunga's victorious manly men, therefore, are presented as not only prime national material but, because of that, evidence against the looming, age-old racial inferiority as well.

Luis Fabiano's current success has to be gauged within this ideological/cultural matrix: he will be accepted and supported as long as he is able to, first, maintain his goal-scoring statistics, and as importantly, keep at bay behaviors that, when associated with male heteronormative blackness, will certainly be interpreted – in ways that are not so determined for unmistakably white players – as reaffirming his unsuitability for the big time, the number 9 yellow jersey. In spite of Luis Fabiano's relatively light complexion, he is certainly not white, and it is his non-whiteness, therefore his blackness, that will make him suspect as a national representative. The gendered facts of anti-blackness here work as a relative field of forces: white players too are under constant scrutiny, and the pressure to prove their national worth is as present as it is for non-white players. Yet, for non-white male players there will always be an additional set of shared understandings that automatically both raises expectations (blacks are more apt at football) and brings them down ruthlessly (blacks are less intelligent, diligent, disciplined, etc.). Below I provide a broader theoretical explanation of these cultural physics.

The Years 1950 and 1958 as the Pendulum's High Points

To speak of the facts of anti-blackness is to make present, unfold, the latent and explicit practices and representations of race attending to the ways the national team plays, is perceived, and talked about, and how these discourses and practices relate to and reveal components of Brazilian social relations and structures of power. Let me propose that, as we engage the facts of anti-blackness as they intersect with the *seleção* – the paradigmatic reference according to which all other sports are evaluated and much of Brazilians' self-understanding is crafted – they oscillate between two landmark football and in fact mega-sport global moments. The first is the 1950 World Cup loss, still evoked as the quintessential national catastrophe, one that goes well beyond the realm of sport. The second is the 1958 triumph in Sweden. Each moment, as reconstituted in the dominant imaginary, cyclically recast in everyday conversation and media events, is a hegemonic argument, one that meshes male football plasticity and efficiency with race, one that invariably conjoins national modern viability and its black diasporic inflections.

The 1950 argument, often tacit but resurfacing in key moments (such as Dunga's affirmation following his team's win at the Confederation's Cup) is that, based on what happened in that tournament's final – meant to symbolize Brazil's concretization of its modern world relevance – certain athletes, those of black and mixed-race backgrounds, are not equipped to express the national consolidated and winning character, and certainly not on the global stage. Substitute people, disposition, cultures, and races for "athletes" above, and the importance of such discourse in the national psyche, self-representation, and the production of social results is evident. To recapitulate briefly: three days before the final against Uruguay, and after a convincing campaign with flashes of brilliance, the team's 6-1 win over Spain in a packed, brand-new, concrete-and-steel mammoth Maracanã stadium, then the largest in the world, inaugurated the title's celebration in advance. It was precisely against that game's collective bliss, when it was reported that the 150,000-plus crowd sang in unison the carnival theme "Touradas de Madri" (Bullfights of Madrid), that the national timeless anticlimax, 72 hours later, made itself palpable in the deafening silence of a stunned crowd. Prominent in the annals of collective memory and historical cultural understanding, on July 16, Brazil lost to Uruguay 2-1, and the arena audience, indeed a considerable part of the nation (if we are to give credence to journalistic, literary, and otherwise social-scientific accounts), plunged into a profound introspection.[4] If leading up to the final the multiracial, celebratory modern national project, suggested forcefully in the monumental stadium and the Brazilian team's racial composition, had emerged victorious against the competing whitening, Eurocentric projects of national purification dominant until the 1930s, then this cultural war witnessed an abrupt turnaround after Uruguay's victory. While this state of ideological suspension lasted – until 1958 to be precise – with obvious gains to the Eurocentric paradigm, the viability of the multiracial national project, which meant black people's accepted integration into both the Brazilian team and society, was seriously put into question. Bigode, the defender accused of being intimidated by the occasion, and principally Barbosa, the goalkeeper, both black, were immediately made responsible for the loss.

Evidence that the catastrophe had long-lasting effects, not the least of which was the pollution, thus bad luck, thus national shame their protagonists embodied, was that Barbosa was barred from visiting the 1994 national team that would win that year's World Cup in the United States (Wisnick, 2008: 349). Despite the four-and-a-half decades removed from the Maracanã catastrophe, the negatively magical power that 1950 exerted on Brazilian football and national psyche was very much present. In barring Barbosa, the often controversial and outspoken Zagalo, well-known former player turned coach, assistant to Parreira in the US campaign, indicated only what was still a consensus, not only among the superstitious. The gendered fact of anti-blackness, transmuted into a metaphysical fear of negative contagion, was in 1994 a significant echo of 1950. Would Zagalo have barred Barbosa had the 1950 goalie been white? That we can't possibly know is less important than the doubt the question itself expresses and generates – a doubt that obviously carries with it the gendered fact of the centrality of anti-blackness. It would be almost six decades before another black goalkeeper, Dida, started a World Cup game, in 2006, for the Brazilian national team.

Yet such negative facts of anti-blackness, as part of Brazil's nuanced, embattled racial and ideological dominant apparatus, require, hail, and depend on their positive modality pre-1950 – precisely the positive modality that would regain ideological momentum in 1958. As much as Zagalo believed in the 1950 curse embodied by Barbosa, he, like most Brazilians, would also vehemently praise the positive contributions that black and mixed-race athletes and citizens bestowed on the national landscape. While the 1994 team disproportionately relied on its defensively minded midfield, where the unmistakably white Dunga commanded the action and imparted to it a decidedly Italian-European approach (a no-nonsense, defend-at-all-costs, then-if-possible-carefully-attack mentality), it was the genial, mercurial mixed-race-interpellated-as-black Romário who differentiated that Brazilian team from its adversaries. Unsurprisingly, he was often described as difficult, undisciplined, lazy, hot-headed, moody, and a plethora of other attributes commonly found in the black diaspora to confirm the always already-known black people's incompatibility with work, rationality, order, and indeed the nation. Resulting from flashes of physical and intellectual brilliance, Romário nevertheless scored at key moments of the tournament, as well as providing several assists to the mixed-race-but-identified-as-white Bebeto, with whom Romário reluctantly shared the attack.

The gendered and racialized controlling images defining Brazilians' expectations about Romário on and off the field, if somewhat blurred by his mixed-race appearance, was readily confirmed when, not infrequently, his origins in and ongoing connections to the embattled Jacarezinho favela, a working-class, predominantly black area in the near-northern part of Rio, were invoked as if to explain both his difficult temperament and his extraordinary skills. Left out of this image, of course, is the fact that Romário's technical prowess and endurance – he played into his 40s, scoring 1,000 career goals – has much to do with his unorthodox but highly effective training regime. The notoriously fit athlete can be seen, to this day, wearing but a diminutive swim-piece at one of Rio's beaches practicing *futvôlei*, a local invention that is a mix of beach volleyball and beach football. Played like beach volleyball, players can use any body part except their arms and hands. It requires an extraordinary amount of ball control; to watch a good game of *futvôlei* is to be reminded of what renders Brazilian football unique.

The 1958 World Cup win, a defining ideological moment as much as an international sport achievement, allows Zagalo and indeed the Brazilian dominant cultural narratives to oscillate between the negative fact of blackness and the necessary, if not reluctant, embracing of blackness. Following the previous World Cup disappointments, of which 1950 was the most hard-felt but by no means the only example, the success in Sweden was unmistakably tied to the ascension of two black athletes, Garrincha and Pelé, whose feats of sheer plasticity and efficiency, and more importantly the setting up and scoring of improbable goals, guaranteed the title. They got their spot in the starting line-up against the Soviet Union, considered one of the tournament's favorites. The enigmatic Soviet team – in spite of the gold they earned in the 1956 Olympics, little was known about its players and strategies up to the tournament's beginning – drew much of its aura from its emphasis on scientific methods applied to football. Combined with their technological supremacy over the United States, made evident as they successfully launched the Sputnik into Earth's orbit on October 1957, and packaged in the carefully developed and conditioned white athlete bodies, in such contrast to the undernourished and mixed-race, already-proven-to-be psychologically weak Brazilians, the Soviets indeed instilled great fear. Brazilian head coach Vicente Feola, as the rest of the world, concerned about the Soviets, was still more preoccupied with Brazil's fragile position in the tournament. After winning the first game against Austria 3-0, and drawing with England scorelessly, he needed the win. Still, as notorious as were Garrincha's first three minutes against the Soviets (his intensive dribbling that astonished adversaries, his first shot, 30 seconds into the game, that smacked Yashin's left post, and the early goals that resulted, are often referred to as the most spectacular ever); and as paradigmatic as the 17-year-old Pelé's goals have become in global football chronicles (which average football connoisseur has not etched in his or her conscience the image of the relatively skinny teenager flicking the ball over European defenders and scoring at least one mythological goal in the final against Sweden?), 1958 is also marked by the coach's resistance against utilizing these two black players in the team.

To grasp Feola's dilemma, and indeed the contradictions of a racial apparatus that up to that historic moment, even though it oscillated between accepting and rejecting blackness, tended most obviously to associate blackness with negativity, we need to take a closer look at the emphasis on the scientific approach that the Brazilian delegation adopted. It was not just the Soviets that brought their specialists and attempted to form a more robust national male football team – one that relied on a plethora of tests, measurements, and dietary and exercise regimes that structured full athletic conditioning. Feola and his assistants – among whom were a nutritionist, a dentist, and a psychologist (at the time innovative if not obviously linked to the damage inflicted in 1950), to strengthen the team and make informed tactical decisions, including line-up – drew from a set of quantitative data extracted from physical and psychological tests. Pelé and Garrincha, according to the team's psychologist, João Carvalhães, were intellectually inept and immature. Carvalhães considered Pelé infantile and incapable of concentrated effort, and thought Garrincha irresponsible.[5] The psychomotor tests gave credence to the expert's analysis; the players' dismal scores confirmed their weakened psyche: out of 10, Pelé got 5.5 and Garrincha 3 (Basthi, 2008).

While the fact of blackness gained alleged scientific correlation with diminished intellectual capacity, it only mirrored the 1950 trauma and its translation into the national team's racial composition. Until Pelé and Garrincha were given starting roles, the legendary Botafogo midfielder Didi was the only unambiguously black player among the starters. Yet, the facts of anti-blackness are malleable to circumstances. To speak of the facts of anti-blackness – to engage with their power – is to acknowledge the underlying symbolic matrix that allows the facts to be plastic. At the core of the nation's self-understanding, white supremacy deflects its centrality by emphasizing its opposite, blackness. Blackness, then, can be made positive

or negative, not because of inherent and varying qualities that black bodies present, but because a white supremacist national project requires shifting discourses that allow for a maximization of desired results. The desired result, in every World Cup, is quite apparent: victory. Victory means not so much the ascension of a harmonious mulatto nation, the de facto racial democracy, as the management of racial differences according to hegemonic Brazilian interests. By such management I mean the degrees of acceptance, proximity, visibility, and significance that racial difference, that is, non-whiteness, acquires. Are there blacks at the helm of any national sports confederation in Brazil? Are there blacks making decisions about the national team? Are there blacks in the national power spheres who are relevant political players? The answers to such question should make it evident that, in spite of the oscillations between degrees of acceptance and exclusion of blacks, the ulterior logic is one that maximizes white Brazilians' interests and therefore their views of the nation. Not that such views are not willingly shared by non-whites; yet such sharing in no manner makes the hegemonic, white-supremacist project any less anti-black.

Although the circumstances leading up to the game against the Soviets were not of the coach's choosing, the reservoir of black talent, as volatile and uncertain as the national psyche rendered it, presented a temptation difficult to resist. Introducing inexperienced yet creative and attack-oriented black players into the line-up could not render much worse the qualifying prospects – a loss or even a draw against the feared Soviets would send the Brazilian team home. The team's defense was not the problem – sufficiently stable, conscious of the moment's importance, the players responsible for the defense and midfield had the technical commission's and, one would surmise, the nation's trust. Didi was capable of producing the brilliant flashes that could decide a game, but so far in the tournament he had not been able to connect with his front line. In other words, the white defenders were reliable, but not creative enough to instantaneously impact a game; the lone black midfielder had no company with whom he could share his recognized legendary insights. So when a group of players, including the captain Bellini, went to talk to Feola about the need for a line-up change, Feola, as was his tendency, acquiesced. It is a telling part of the sports lore about this Cup, in a fascinating parallel with the socially shared knowledge about the 1970 campaign, that the introduction of key players – in the cases of Pelé and Garrincha, all-time greats – was less the coach's decision than the result of players' pressure.

The 1958 argument is thus one that reaffirms the positive black contribution to the national football team, and indeed the national spirit. Although the unmistakably white Bellini held high that year's World Cup trophy – an image that flowed to newspapers, weekly magazines, and postal stamps – etched in the national sports and cultural imagination were the decisive moments in which Pelé and Garrincha were the principal and genial protagonists. Such moments, and indeed the 1958 argument, would gain quite a cultural advantage – a domination – as the male football team repeated the world championship in Chile in 1962 (mostly without Pelé, injured, but with Garrincha carrying the triumphant team on the back of his frightening legend and skills, ending the tournament as the top scorer), and in Mexico, in 1970 (as Pelé, at the pinnacle of his career, was shown to the entire planet, in full televised colors, leading a team which, for the first time, was considerably and undeniably non-white). Carlos Alberto, the right full-back captain, repeated Bellini's gesture, holding high, two-handed, the Jules Rimet trophy, which now, as a prize for the third championship, was to remain in Brazil for good. As a result of the acceptability of the 1958 argument, in 1970 the team captain Carlos Alberto's black body could represent Brazil without the taboo that, up until then, only allowed Bellini, the Brazilian defender of Italian background, to do so.

In 1970 a full-blown right-wing dictatorship, Brazil's military government embraced the considerably black, yellow, and green victorious team as the nation's ultimate symbol. The dictatorship's developmentalist motto "this is a country that moves forward" and its political forcefulness, often based on terror, clearly aimed at the dismantling of leftist dissidents by torture, exile, and death (symbolized in the ubiquitous propaganda "Brazil, love it or leave it"), gained a compelling archive of achievements and imagery in the squad that became known as one of the best ever. Besides Carlos Alberto Torres and Pelé, the team

had Jairzinho, Paulo César Caju, Djalma Santos, Dario, and Zé Maria, that gave it a substantial, and unprecedented – if only because of color television – worldwide black visibility.

The next five winless cups are a study in the imposed black absence in the men's football national team: 1974 in Germany; 1978 in Argentina; 1982 in Spain; 1986 in Mexico; and 1990 in Italy mark a generation of sports aficionados who witness, and thus almost become accustomed to, a mostly white team. Not that black players were completely absent – that indeed would be unthinkable in a polity that is not only numerically at least half black but one which also constantly reaffirms its multiraciality. But like in the United States until recently, when most college and National Football League teams included black players in every position except that of quarter-back, so Brazilian teams' listed black players were hardly significant numerically and, as telling, tactically. Who were the Brazilian stars in these ultimately "failed" campaigns? (And here the reader must take into account that, unlike in most other countries, where a top-three or top-four finish are perfectly honorable achievements, such is not the case in Brazil. Anything less than the title is always a deep disappointment.) Granted, in 1974 Jairzinho, the 1970 hurricane, played his last World Cup, but the team now belonged to Rivelino, also a veteran of the fabled Mexico triumph. Paulo César Caju, now donning a full Afro (as did Jairzinho) was seen as a problematic player whose embattled inclusion in the squad followed an intense debate about his alleged rebellious nature. In 1978, the team acquired a relatively more consolidated white appearance, when Zico, Rivelino, Oscar, Leão, Dirceu, Nelinho, and Polozi, among others, gave it a significantly more marked European appearance and style. In spite of Reinaldo's recognized achievements in his Clube Atlético Mineiro, Belo Horizonte, where, due to his imagination and facility of scoring goals at an impressive frequency, he was greeted as the king (a play on the first syllable of his name, Rei – in Portuguese "king"), he was injured and did not play an entire game in Argentina. Aside from being technically less complex than Reinaldo, Roberto Dinamite, the reserve forward, was neither interpellated as black as Reinaldo was, nor was he as politicized: Reinaldo, after all, often celebrated his goals with a Black Power salute, one hand held high in a closed fist, the other behind his back, head bowed down.

In spite of the 1994 victory, well represented in Dunga's lifting of the Cup, after an excruciating penalty shoot-out against Italy, it is only in 2002 that the pendulum swung back to a greater acceptance of blackness. When Cafu, the team's captain, of mixed race and often interpellated as black, held high the trophy in Japan, after the uncontested 2–0 victory over Germany in the grand final, Juca Kfouri, one of Brazil's most perspicacious sports journalists, celebrated the team's racial hybridity. A featured commentator in one of TV Globo's channels, he exalted the Brazilian mixed-race national make-up and spirit, and used the image of an elated Cafu to reassert the central positive place that non-whites have had in the nation.[6] Implicit in his statement was the idea that Brazilians should feel as proud of the definitely mixed-race 2002 team as they were of the previous successful ones; also, that Brazilians should recognize and embrace the nation's racial multiplicity, and see in it the key to its potential and success. As idealistic as it sounded, Kfouri's statement was a critique directed at what he perceived as a continued resistance against associating blackness with nationality. If Ronaldo, Ronaldinho, Roberto Carlos, Rivaldo, and Kléberson were the main players that led to Brazil's success, then Brazil's success had to be equated with those players' gendered raciality. The victory against Germany, its one black reserve player notwithstanding, made it apparent, once again, that the specter of European whiteness was not insurmountable. Add to this the significant economic and social advancements that Brazilians, especially the underprivileged, were beginning to experience as the twenty-first century began, and the context becomes ripe for optimism and some racial ideology malleability.

"We Are Mutts Again": The Persisting Racial Complex

Despite Kfouri's good intentions, and the seemingly increasing acceptance of race mixture (and therefore of blackness) that began to define Brazil in the early 2000s, the impending questions about national inferiority and superiority are ultimately about global white supremacy (e.g.,Winant, 2002). Kfouri's and analogous claims of Brazilian superiority are fragile and suspect. Fragile because they naïvely exhort the acceptance of blackness without requiring the awareness and critique of the white-supremacist worldview which, until and unless finely understood and challenged, remains the ultimate reference, practical and symbolic. Suspect because, in spite of Kfouri's best intentions, such discourse of racial inclusion is too familiar and thus easily assimilated. What's left untouched is the implicit critique that Kfouri put forward. Because of racial democracy's age-old hold on Brazilians' shared understandings of ourselves, claims of multiraciality are unproblematically accepted, especially in moments of national ecstasy, without the necessary engagement with the otherwise constitutive anti-black ideological and everyday national architectures. Thus, Kfouri's noble argument is suspect precisely because it inadvertently provides additional fodder for, and thus becomes indistinguishable from, the racial democracy thesis, itself based precisely on the well-intentioned logic that requires disengagement with the mechanics of white supremacy. According to this logic, Brazil is a polity characterized by the relative innocuousness of race both as a cognitive-moral category and as a determinant of one's structural social position.

Evidence that the racial democracy symbology is a central organizer of thoughts and actions related to the nation more broadly, and to football in pointed ways, is that in spite of the *seleção*'s long success, the specter of inferiority still emerges frequently. Kfouri's plea for a national pride that embraces race mixture is already quite telling – would there be a need for such plea if the national consensus was not one that associated non-whiteness with shame? More directly, sports commentators often invoke European superiority as a reminder of the Brazilian perpetual struggle against the African presence. In his *O Globo* column, sport writer Fernando Calazans provided an interesting example. On June 12, 2009, as the Brazilian squad arrived in South Africa for the Confederations Cup, Calazans analyzed the team's most recent game in the World Cup qualifying round. It had defeated Uruguay 4–0, in Montevideo. In spite of Uruguay's many weaknesses, Calazans pondered that the Brazilian team was heading in a good direction. It had previously beaten the strong Paraguayan team, in Recife. Although relying heavily on counter-attacks, the team showed consistency and determination. The defense Lúcio commanded was solid – and here Calazans' admiration included the goalkeeper Júlio César, who in his recent appearances with the national squad was repeating brilliant performances. Indeed, in the otherwise lopsided game against Uruguay, Júlio César brought off a few spectacular saves. And here, almost in passing, Calazans invoked the racial complex. The goalkeeper had become a national team starter only after he, like many other Brazilian players, was hired in Italy. Calazans used this fact – that the media and the national team had shunned Júlio César up until he became an Internazionale employee – to argue that Brazilians consider the Europeans "our superiors."

Poet, playwright, and sports writer Nélson Rodrigues often noted that, prior to 1958, we Brazilians thought of ourselves as "mutts" (*vira-latas*), mixed-breed squalid dogs that always looked up to and feared the allegedly pure-bred, fit, and rational Europeans. The complex was manifested in the nation's seemingly intractable multifaceted underdevelopment, and acquired a significant expression in the chronic inability shown by the male national football team to win on the international stage, particularly against European squads. How was it that a country with so many exceptional players faltered against technically limited teams? It all seemingly changed in that prescient World Cup of 1958, when the Brazilian team finally won the tournament. In 1966, in one of his customary *O Globo* columns, Rodrigues (1994: 111) wrote, "In 58, when the game Brazil vs. Sweden was over, every Brazilian felt vindicated, liberated from so much past hunger and biblical humiliations. In the streets, the facial expressions seem to be saying 'I'm not a mutt!'"[7]

The reference to the mutt condenses the comments made by Kfouri and Calazans – indeed, it reveals the central contradiction in the racial democracy worldview. While celebrating racial diversity, the Brazilian dominant set of cultural codes draws on white supremacy's aversion to mixture – and therefore, paradigmatically, to blackness. Instances of undisputed achievement, especially in sport mega-events, momentarily submerge the aversion to mixture and the explicit valuing of whiteness. Yet, this pendular movement is itself prisoner of the same logic: while we Brazilians may not be mutts anymore, the specter is always there. Underdevelopment, which, according to the dominant cultural codes, is indexed appropriately by non-whiteness, or, more directly, race mixture, is over and again unveiled as sporting failures unfold. Indeed, one of Nelson Rodrigues' chronicles is entitled "Voltamos a ser vira-latas" (We are mutts again), written following Brazil's early elimination in the 1966 World Cup in England.

Two points need to be emphasized. First, in spite of the black presence in Brazilian society and successful mixed-race and black male football players more particularly, anti-blackness, expressed commonly in the aversion to the mutt, which exemplarily suggests the valorization of purity and therefore whiteness, is foundational to the nation. Second, insofar as the very logic of racial democracy is not challenged, the negative connotations against citizens and players of African descent will continue, albeit interrupted by the moments of unquestionable success.

Such propositions make it reasonable to trace linkages between this anti-black cultural/ideological matrix, the male national football team, and pressing social problems that the 2014 men's football World Cup and the 2016 summer Olympic Games will inevitably face. To reflect on these events, therefore, is to analyze the challenges that the black presence poses both to sport and to the Brazilian nation. Blacks will always be suspect both as athletes and as citizens. This suspicion, at bottom, is a derivation of the constitutive anti-blackness of the Brazilian state and dominant ideological apparatus. In order to negate the mutt complex, black athletes – more so than their white national counterparts – will have to succeed at the highest level, and in the process negate their own blackness. This impossible existential condition is not lost on many black successful persons. There is a common saying among black successful persons: they will affirm that they, too, know what it is to be black since they were once black. The logic here is the same as the one underlying Rodrigues' and Calazans' inferiority complex: blackness is anathema to success, belonging, and full citizenship.

The 2007 Pan American Games: Foretelling the 2014 World Cup and the 2016 Olympics

The gendered racial inflections that accompany the Brazilian national team are part of a broader semantic and political constellation. The aversion to race mixture is analogous to the fear that the black body always already generates. Arnaldo Jabor (2009: 8), a white Brazilian screenwriter and social commentator, states:

> what bothers the lily-white populations [*população branquinha*] is not just the petty criminal, it is also the ordinary person. Mixed-race people [*pardos*] in flip-flops and shorts fill the Zona Sul [Rio's older, elite area]. They sense the middle-class fear and walk proudly. The white Carioca [as a person from Rio is called] becomes indignant, as if only he were a native. I see that my discomfort about the Carioca chaos is a class feeling. Yes, there's a class horror among the "white" Cariocas; they want Rio to be what it was back in the good old days. It's untrue that we fear only violence; we also fear promiscuity.

"Promiscuity" evokes the forced contact between middle-class whites and the black women and men from the adjoining working-class neighborhoods. Promiscuity is installed as the imagined racial and class purity is challenged. "Brazil did not become Ipanema. Ipanema became Brazil," continues Jabor (2009: 8). The craving of a time when the "dangerous classes" were contained in clearly delimited zones, when the absence of democracy made the work of the military police even more unaccountable – these imaginings, Jabor argues, cannot serve as a blueprint for the future. "The nostalgic ideology only leads to the idea of genocide. To bring back the peaceful [1950s and 1960s] Saturday beers [*chopinhos*], only killing those of the hills . . . Up until now, there have only been 'white' solutions to 'brown' [*pardo*] problems." Jabor evokes the constitutive racial apartheid. It manifests itself, from the privileged perspective, as the expectation of guaranteed barriers, symbolic and actual, that define not only whiteness, but also citizenship and indeed full humanity.

I would like to suggest that, when we reflect on the gendered facts of anti-blackness as they relate to football or indeed as they relate to sport mega events, or taking into account the semantic fields that characterize the Brazilian nation-state, we inevitably confront the constitutive Brazilian apartheid – the same apartheid that makes black athletes always already suspect as it renders the black person less than a citizen and a human being. The non-white players are represented, and find themselves immersed in a symbolic web that, by default, question their full inclusion in the Brazilian modern nation.

In the Brazilian apartheid symbolic and political continuum, the ordinary non-whites of Rio de Janeiro, just like their athlete counterparts, experience the spatial, social, and racial interpellations that define their less-than-full citizenship. Such was the case on June 27, 2007, when the police occupied one of the neighborhoods in the Alemão favela, killing 19 people. The police operation included snipers, helicopters, modified tanks, and an arsenal of precision weapons, scanning devices, and bombs. Among the dead there were at least three teenagers. Photos of the operation, taken by the press and by residents, propose an unmistakable link between race, segregation, and death: the fatal victims were Afro-descended persons while the agents of the state, although at times embodied by black individuals, carried through a policy of social and spatial control whose drive and results were in essence anti-black. The state of Rio de Janeiro's branch of the Ordem dos Advogados do Brasil, the Brazilian equivalent of the US Lawyers Guild, filed a dossier showing evidence of execution in the bodies of at least 13 of the 19 people killed in the operation.

Why is this event significant to our discussion about football and sport mega-events? Simply because this particular massacre occurred a few weeks before the XV Pan American games opening, on July 13, 2007. The Pan American Sports Association had awarded Rio the hosting over San Antonio, TX. During and after the deliberations, urban violence and security for athletes and audience were major concerns. The police operation in the Alemão neighborhood catered to such concerns, and forcefully demonstrated that the military police was in charge. By occupying a well-defined urban area, and isolating it from the rest of the city – the siege lasted through the sporting event, which was considered successful mostly because no violent incidents were reported – it was proposed that crime was curbed, and public order was established.

Following the announcement on October 2, 2009 that Rio was to host the 2016 Olympic Games, the security concerns that were voiced during the long selection process carried over to the preparation phase. Rio state's governor, Sérgio Cabral, signaled his resolve to assure social control by hiring Rudolph Giuliani, New York City's former mayor, as the Games' security advisor. While Giuliani drew much of his municipal and national approval from his zero-tolerance stance on crime, it is also well known that, among the city's black population, few administrators have surpassed his level of disapproval. As if on cue, while the celebrations for the Olympics were still fresh, police operations in Rio became more spectacular. On October 16, 2009 it was reported that, while conducting a "pacifying mission" over a black neighborhood, Morro dos Macacos in Vila Isabel, a near-northern part of the city, during a seven-hour exchange of fire, a police helicopter was shot down by "gang members." Among the 15 dead in the confrontations between alleged drug-dealers and the police were two police casualties – they died as the helicopter they were in caught fire after being shot at, and barely made the landing; the pilot and three other police officers survived. Shortly thereafter, other areas exploded with violence: at least eight vehicles, mostly buses, were set on fire, close to the Jacarezinho favela. To avoid new confrontations, it was reported that over 2,000 police were mobilized to occupy strategic areas around the neighborhoods in Vila Isabel and Jacarezinho.[8]

Besides militarized law enforcement, an intense ideological battle was also at play. The favela and *morro* (hill) residents mostly affected by the gunfire were suspect due to their proximity to – indeed, their alleged entanglement with – the main object of the state's repression: defiant, boastful, and well-armed drug-dealers. In the wake of the helicopter crash, the local media relayed that the police had information on the person responsible for it: Ilan Nogueira, a member of the notorious Fabiano group, and a fugitive of the law, reportedly bragged about his deed during a barbeque celebration in Vila Cruzeiro. The tone of *O Globo*'s article describ-

ing the celebration suggests not only lawlessness and a macho ethos organizing the supposed drug-dealers but also exuberant consumption amid the poverty that otherwise defines such areas. It stated: "the helicopter crash was . . . celebrated on Saturday evening with a *baile funk* (a rap concert), with whisky and cocaine"[9] that Fabiano offered his hosts. The deaths were thus justified as they affected persons rendered suspect by the nature of their appearance and area of residence. That allegations of innocent victims are seldom investigated and given credence only reaffirms the hegemonic understanding about the ultimate suspect nature of those inhabiting black areas. So it was without commotion that on October 21, 2009 the local *O Globo* newspaper revealed that the death toll since the helicopter crash had reached 33. Seven of those deaths occurred earlier that same day. It was evident that the police had cranked up their attempt to re-establish control over embattled favelas. Of the seven people killed, two were at the Morro Santo Amaro, in the central Catete region; three at the Morro do Juramento; one in the Morro dos Prazeres, and one in the Morro da Mangueirinha, in the adjoining Duque de Caxias municipality.[10]

In this pre-World Cup/Olympic context, the US$50 billion the city is expected to receive in the next five years from public and private national sources have at least one well-defined, if not predictable, destination: security. Specifically, Rio state governor Cabral, in an interview to *TV Globo* said that, by 2016, the military police contingent would be doubled.[11] Together with the walls already being built around some of the poorest neighborhoods (justified as ecological measures so that nearby vegetation would not be affected by uncontrolled urban growth), the military police campaigns will recreate, at an unparalleled scale, not only the 2007 forced isolation of the impoverished and therefore black local population but also similar strategies employed in different parts of the planet during similar megaevents. For example, before and during the Atlanta 1996 Olympic Games, about 9,000 homeless residents were arrested and as many as 30,000 impoverished people were displaced. What was missing from the US Olympic experience, namely, indiscriminate police brutality and justified homicide, will certainly be in abundance in Rio, all in preparation for the 2014 men's football World Cup and culminating with the 2016 Games.[12] For Rio's, and indeed Brazil's, poor and black, the countdown is not so much in anticipation of the joys sport mega-events generate (although there is certainly some of this too), as it is about the form of the Brazilian state's anti-black policies and their consequences. Whether the *seleção* or the national athletes will do well is difficult to predict; not so difficult to foresee, however, are the intensified imposed isolation and death the poor and black will experience.

Conclusion: Black Revolt?

In spite of, and because of, the Brazilian state's inexorable and escalating death-prone wishes of black control, in Rio, as in São Paulo, Brazil's largest city, revolt has become more evident. Whereas bus burnings and confrontations with the police used to be largely confined to black and poor urban areas, now a developing scenario suggests a different dynamic. For example, one such act of rebellion took place in the early evening of December 1, 2009 in response to the police occu-

pation of two working-class areas, Pavão-Pavãozinho, in Copacabana and Cantagalo, in Ipanema. Following orders given by armed young men that local commerce should shut down, a bus was burned in one of the main thoroughfares that run parallel to the ocean – this time not in a favela, but smack in the middle of the elite, tourist, and massively policed area, the Avenida Nossa Senhora de Copacabana (Corrêa, 2009).[13]

If revolt against private property and bodies, the state, its agents and buildings, as well as financial institutions, have become more apparent these days, and if these can be reasonably linked to Brazil's enduring social inequalities, which disproportionately negatively impact black communities, what would revolt look like among athletes? Are contemporary global sport spectacles possible and effective arenas in which protest against historical patterns of imposed marginalization can be enacted? Or, are contemporary global sports events, in spite of the ubiquitous black male and female bodies, symptom of racial inequalities even when, and perhaps precisely because of, Afro-descended athletes' success?

Notes

1 The Confederations Cup is an international football tournament organized by FIFA and held every four years in which the winners of the six FIFA confederation championships (UEFA, CONMEBOL, CONCACAF, CAF, AFC, OFC), together with the previous World Cup winner and the host nation compete. The Confederations Cup is held every four years, in the year leading up to the World Cup.

2 The *seleção* is the name given to the men's team that represents Brazil in international football and is run by the Brazilian Football Confederation (CBF). Brazil is widely regarded as one of the world's most exciting and skillful international teams and is currently the most successful team in world football with five World Cup championships (Italy and Germany are the next most successful with four and three World Cup championships respectively). With three titles, Brazil are also the most successful team in the history of the Confederations Cup.

3 This is an obvious reference to Frantz Fanon's *Black Skin, White Masks* (1967), especially the

chapter whose title was translated as "The Fact of Blackness." While my analysis will draw on Fanon's incursions into what it means to be black, which I take to include the colonized, the dispossessed, the displaced, and therefore the diasporic, it will also delve into the place/no-place of gendered blackness in the Brazilian national project. By "national project" I mean a dominant ontological narrative that is at once a project of modernity, and a set of modernizing policies. Spatiality and temporality are intrinsic to and a result of the national project. Inasmuch as the black subject offers no ontological resistance to the white gaze, and insofar as it is forced to inhabit places and times outside of the national project, it is relegated to the condition of imminent negation. In Fanon, this is not a dialectical negation that is a prelude to a transcendental synthesis. Rather, the black subject inhabits spaces and times marked by suspension, suspicion, interruption, rupture, negation; times and spaces of syncope, of death. Here is Fanon, at the beginning of the said chapter: "Ontology – once it is finally admitted as leaving existence by the wayside – does not permit us to understand the being of the black man. For not only must the black man be black; he must be black in relation to the white man. Some critics will take it on themselves to remind us that the proposition has a converse. I say that this is false. The black man has no ontological resistance in the eyes of the white man. Overnight the Negro has been given two frames of reference within which he has had to place himself. His metaphysics, or, less pretentiously, his customs and the sources on which they were based, were wiped out because they were in conflict with a civilization that he did not know and that imposed itself on him" (p. 110).

4   Garrincha, exception to the rule, could not care less about the final. He reportedly went fishing as the nation was glued to the radio and the incipient television sets. But even his off-the-curve take on the catastrophe was only reiteration of the reigning mood – he could not understand why all were so somber.

5   The final proof against Garrincha's suitability for the national team came during a pre-World Cup preparatory friendly game against Fiorentina, in Italy. After dribbling past the entire defense, and faced with an open goal, instead of scoring Garrincha waited for a defender to get back on his feet. Garrincha then proceeded to dribble past the opponent once more and only then score. The next game, against Inter Milan, he was benched in favor of Joel. His ostracism lasted until the World Cup game against the Soviets.

6   That Kfouri's statement was made through one of TV Globo's channels is quite significant. *Globo* holds a historic near-monopoly over Brazilian airwaves and is one of the world's main media conglomerates. Its patriarch, Roberto Marinho, nurtured close ties to the military regime that came to power in 1964, and built the empire by maintaining these ties while managing to forge effective political alliances in the ensuing democracy.

7   My deliberately non-poetic translation of: "Em 58, quando acabou o jogo Brasil X Suécia, cada bra-

sileiro sentiu-se compensado, desagravado de velhas fomes e santas humilhações. Na rua, a cara dos que passavam parecia dizer: – 'eu não sou vira-lata!'"

8   See http://www.guardian.co.uk/world/2009/oct/17/rio-favela-violence-helicopter, accessed January 22, 2013.

9   "Invasão ao Morro dos Macacos teve reforço de dois caminhões-baú e dezenas de motocicletas." *O Globo*, October 20, 2009, http://extra.globo.com/noticias/rio/invasao-ao-morro-dos-macacos-teve-reforco-de-dois-caminhoes-bau-dezenas-de-motocicletas-350807.html, accessed January 24, 2013.

10 "Polícia faz operação em favelas do Rio sob intensa troca de tiros." *O Globo*, October 21, 2009, http://extra.globo.com/noticias/rio/policia-faz-operacoes-em-favelas-do-rio-sob-intensa-troca-de-tiros-351539.html, accessed January 24, 2013.

11 "Cabral diz que Rio receberá US$ 50 bilhões até cinco anos." *O Globo*, October 5, 2009; see http://rio2016evento.blogspot.co.uk/2009/10/us-50-bilhoes.html, accessed January 24, 2013.

12 For a study on police killings in Rio, see Human Rights Watch (2009: 1, 2): "In the state of Rio, alleged resistance killings by the police reached a record high of 1,330 in 2007. While reported killings decreased to 1,137 in 2008, the number remained alarmingly elevated, as it was the third highest on record for Rio. . . . After a comprehensive, two-year investigation into police practices in Rio and in São Paulo, Human Rights Watch has concluded that a substantial portion of the alleged resistance killings reported in both states are in fact extrajudicial executions."

13 In São Paulo in 2006, a group known as the Primeiro Comando da Capital (the First Command of the Capital) carried out more than 100 coordinated attacks against the police, vehicles (mostly buses), banks, and public buildings; 43 police officers were killed in these actions. See Human Rights Watch (2009: 10).

References

Alexander, M.J. (2006) *Pedagogies of Crossing: Meditations on Feminism, Sexual Politics, Memory, and the Sacred*, Durham, NC: Duke University Press.

Basthi, A. (2008) *Pelé: Estrela Negra em Campos Verdes*, Rio de Janeiro: Garamond.

Bastidas, C. (2002) *Driblando a Perversão: Psicanálise, Futebol e Subjetividade Brasileira*, São Paulo: Escuta.

Corrêa, D. (2009) "Ônibus é incendiado em Copacabana e polícia prende suspeitos." *Globo.com*, December 2, 10:45 pm, http://verdesmares.globo.com/v3/canais/noticias.asp?codigo=277258&modulo=967 (in Portuguese), accessed January 22, 2013.

Fanon, F. (1967) *Black Skin, White Masks*, New York: Grove Press.

Filho, M.R. (2003) *O Negro no Futebol Brasileiro*, Rio de Janeiro: Mauad.

Helal, R. (2001) *A Invenção do País do Futebol: Mídia, Raça e Idolatria*, Rio de Janeiro: Mauad.

Human Rights Watch (2009) *Lethal Force: Police Violence and Public Security in Rio de Janeiro and São Paulo*, New York: Human Rights Watch.

Iton, R. (2008) *In Search of the Black Fantastic: Politics and Popular Culture in The Post-Civil Rights Era*, Oxford: Oxford University Press.

Jabor, A. (2009) "Nunca mais voltará Leila Diniz." *O Globo*, June 16: 8.

Rodrigues, N. (1994) *A Pátria em Chuteiras: Novas Crônicas de Futebol*, ed. Ruy Castro, São Paulo: Cia. das Letras.

Tomlinson, A. and Young, C. (2006) *National Identity and Global Sports Events: Culture, Politics and Spectacle in the Olympics and the Football World Cup*, Albany: State University of New York Press.

Veja (2009) "Guilt is blond with blue eyes, says Brazilian president." *Veja*, March 26, http://www.veja. abril.com.br/noticia/brasil/culpa-loiros-olhos-azuis-430909.shtml, accessed March 1, 2013.

Winant, H. (2002) *The World Is a Ghetto: Race and Democracy Since World War II*, New York: Basic Books.

Wisnick, J.M. (2008) *Veneno Remédio: O Fubebol e O Brasil*, São Paulo: Companhia das Letras.

Further Reading

Mason, T. (1995) *Passion of the People? Football in South America*, London: Verso.

Nascimento, A. (1979) *Brazil, Mixture or Massacre?* Dover, MA: Majority Press.

Wisnick, J.M. (2008) *Veneno Remédio: O Fubebol e O Brasil*, São Paulo: Companhia das Letras.

28

To Be Like Everyone Else, Only Better
The US Men's Football Team and the World Cup

Grant Farred

A risk had already been taken when I promised to write something . . . I had already begun to approach . . . with the familiarity of a neophyte, where fascination, admiration, and astonishment were all bound up together, all sorts of troubling questions as well, in particular regarding the form my text might take.

Jacques Derrida, *Athens, Still Remains: The Photographs of Jean-François Bonhomme*, 1996, 1

Introduction

When it comes to the participation and performance of the United States in the 2010 FIFA World Cup finals, hosted, historically, by South Africa, there are indeed "all sorts of troubling questions." After the successful tournament, the first to be hosted on African soil, there remains a deep, and therefore engaging, sense of unease about how the United States fared. One is troubled, perplexed, by something we might, more properly, name *incomprehensibility*. There is something afoot in the relationship between the United States of America and the beautiful game. It is difficult to identify that "something": perhaps it emerges most clearly when one recognizes that the chants of "USA! USA! U-S-A! U-S-A!" – so resonant, so proud, so utterly joyful (especially after beating Algeria 1–0 in the final Group C

game in 2010) – bore within their spontaneous explosion of happiness a certain, might one suggest, innocence? Beating Algeria, a last-gasp goal, 90 seconds into injury time, when all seemed lost and the United States seemed destined to head home, undefeated but eliminated, and drawing, fortunately with England (the result of a goalkeeping blunder by England's Robert Green) and heroically with Slovenia (coming back after trailing 0–2 at half-time), revealed how "fascination, admiration, and astonishment" might "all be bound up together." Despite the fact that the United States was a semi-finalist at the inaugural World Cup in 1930, despite its historic 1–0 Belo Horizonte victory over England in 1950, and despite the fact that it has qualified for six World Cups in a row, there is still something of the "neophyte" about America's participation in the greatest cultural spectacle.

A Companion to Sport, First Edition. Edited by David L. Andrews and Ben Carrington.
© 2013 Blackwell Publishing Ltd. Published 2013 by Blackwell Publishing Ltd.

Football is a game with old roots in the United States, as old as the several waves of European and Latin American immigrants who brought it with them from their "olde countries" (first the English, Irish, Welsh, and Scots, then other European nations; today, of course, Central and Latin American communities bring their own deep love for and history with the game to the United States), but a sport that has never grabbed the nation's imagination (no matter that it is the most widely played sport in the country) in the way that its traditional sports baseball, gridiron (improperly called "football"), ice-hockey, and basketball have (see Wangerin 2006, 2011[1]). And so, like everything that is "new," putatively or not, it is required, every four years, to prove itself. In the process, it is subjected to intense media scrutiny, and not a little derision.

The thing that distinguishes "neophytes," even experienced ones, at the World Cup is simple. It is not so much that they are new to the event (because the United States has a history of participation), it is that no one expects them to win. They are thus, amongst the footballing powers-that-be, willing participants, but they are perpetually new, until they win, that is. That is why they are frequently endowed with other names. They are called "Cinderellas" when they reel off unexpectedly good results, "upstarts" when they beat those who are favored, or "dark horses" when a pundit or three fancies their chances to surprise before the tournament begins. Or, worse, they are, like Spain until they won the Copa Mundial in 2010, "underachievers" – a moniker that now, sadly, belongs almost solely to the Dutch, runners-up to hosts West Germany in 1974 (when they properly introduced the world to their exquisite brand of "total football"), and Argentina in 1978, and again in South Africa when the Spaniards bested them; the Dutch, regrettably, are now in sole possession of the title "perennial underachievers." Spain is only too glad to have rid itself of that stigma.[2] Spain, in fact, has ascended to unprecedented heights in world football: winners of the European championships in 2008 and 2012, and victorious in South Africa in 2010, they are the only nation to have won three successive major tournaments.

No such glories can exist until victory has been achieved. For the "neophytes" the best they can hope for is to be dubbed "willing participants," or "honest triers." We know that these are patronizing names, labels coaches either seek to actively reject or to exploit as a motivational tool, audible in refrains such as "We are not just here to make up the numbers, we are here to compete." This is a song we know too well.

Coaches use the language of low expectation, as we well know, to motivate their charges to achieve the impossible; none of them, of course, believe in the possibility of a neophyte triumph at the Copa Mundial but, in its place, what is there to say? As a result, team officials proffer measurements of success that are relative. "For a team such as ours, qualifying from the Group would be a massive accomplishment." "If we get to the quarterfinals, we will have achieved our goal." "If we can . . . we will have met our expectations." And so on. At the end of the unfinished sentence, is the inevitable expectation of defeat. The "neophytes," their protestations to the contrary notwithstanding, are expected to know their (secondary) place; and, all too often, they do. Of course, the sheer economic and political force of the United States in global affairs is such that it bears few traces of the typical neophyte.

Therein, precisely, lies the tantalizing contradiction that is football in America. In the age of America as a declining imperial power, in the age of China and/or India "Rising" (that is if these nations do not sink under the weight of environmental degradation or are torn asunder by the consumerist greed of their burgeoning middle classes), the United States is respected in international football circles. It is a feared opponent as it showed in the 2009 Confederations Cup tournament, held in South Africa (as a warm-up to the 2010 World Cup finals), when it beat Spain in the semi-finals and lost narrowly, 2–3, to Brazil in the final after leading by two goals at the break (see CHAPTER 27). In the 2009 Confederations Cup final the United States acquitted themselves remarkably well; so much so, in fact, that they won over a fair number of the South African fans.

There is, invariably, a vulnerability attendant to the moment of, shall we say, entrée. Vulnerability is a difficult, even painful lesson, to learn for a nation that considers itself to be not only (all-) powerful but also exceptional. America is, after all, the land founded upon its belief in manifest destiny. And therein lies the rub. If the United States is destined to be singular in its greatness, then how does the superpower enter the world, the World Cup, precisely, as a lesser national entity? Lodged at the core of this question may be exactly what America fears the World Cup represents: the United States entering the world *not* on its own terms. In its participation, it pits itself against other teams, many, though by no means all, of whom are measurably better than its own. It often qualifies at the top of its regional group (CONCACAF, where its toughest opponent is Mexico, a not inconsiderable foe; sometimes the United States finishes behind Mexico in qualifying), but it knows that the sport's tradition in the United States is less grounded. Football is in no way central to America's national sense of self as it is in the case of its southern neighbor. Football in the United States carries none of the weight – the burden, some might say – of national expectation, of national self-hood, that it does in Mexico; or, Brazil, or Argentina, or England, or Italy, for that matter. In the United States, hyperbolic provincialism rules, otherwise there would be no grounds to proclaim the team that wins the Super Bowl "world champs."

The United States participates in the World Cup knowing that there it has no reasonable expectation of victory. In this regard, it is no different from, say, Angola or Slovakia. Such a sense of vulnerability, of historically foreclosed possibility (Cinderella should not bother to come to the dance, should she?), has no place in other American sport. For the world's declining superpower, the expectation always begins with nothing less than the absolute: victory. Prophylactic hope is untenable in American basketball at the Olympics (this is the legacy, of course, of the "Dream Team," the much lauded US basketball representatives at the 1992 Barcelona Olympics) or baseball psyche (though it should, of course, given the massive talent bases that Asian, Caribbean, and Latin American countries boast); American teams do not go to the Olympics expecting not to top the medal count, China's rising Olympic accomplishments notwithstanding. The 2012 London Olympics, as far as the United States is concerned, represents the restoration of the proper order of things: the United States topping China. The fact of foreclosure and *a priori* vulnerability – that is, the inevitability of defeat, of going home losers – is what makes US football such a peculiar beast.

There is always, as Derrida knows, a "risk" that can be identified on the occasion of anticipation of surveying a momentous death that will inaugurate an entire mode of thinking; or, Heidegger might insist, that event that gives birth to the thinking of being. Derrida's "risk" derives from his contemplation of ancient Greece, the city of Athens where Socrates' death will produce nothing less than the birth of philosophy. The logic of foreclosure is, of course, grounded in the expectation of failure, itself a kind of death. The greatest conceptual risk, then, resides in thinking US football against, or, beyond, the prophylactic because such a positing – a new global positioning, as it were – requires nothing less than an argument against foreclosure, against expectation that is girded, guarded, by the limited horizon imposed by the prophylactic – the hope not for victory, but for a defeat that is delayed as long as possible. The desire is not the pleasure of victory, but for a defeat that will not be too painful. Or, at best, a defeat that can be rationalized, that can be made palatable. As every athlete knows, there is no defeat that does not sting, there is no palliative for loss. In refusing the prophylactic, that is where the "troubling questions" about the national US self originate and find their most piercing, irrepressible articulation. Given the complexity of the factors in play, what Derrida names "fascination, admiration and astonishment," it is unsurprising that the contradictions cannot be so easily stilled, so quickly (we might even say "rationally") explained.

For this reason, we must persist in our thinking of the contradictions. We must stay with the contradictions, it is there that thinking finds fecundity.

Football remains, professionally, a minor sport even though more American kids play the game, competitively, recreationally, at university level, than any other sport in the country. During the 2010 World Cup the game found itself dragged into a fight that has nothing to do with it but everything to do with the peculiar provinciality – or perhaps just the pathological small mindedness – of the American Right. Rabid nationalist right-wing media commentator Glenn Beck found it impossible to contain himself when World Cup 2010 rolled around. He ranted, invoking the royal "we" as if in a ritual incantation of national cleansing:

... the soccer thing. I hate it so much – probably because the rest of the world likes it so much, and they riot over it, and they continually try to jam it down our throat. We don't like the World Cup. We don't like soccer. We want nothing to do with it. You can package it any way – you can spend all kinds of money. You can force it on our television sets. We will not enjoy the World Cup. (Beck, quoted in Holden, 2010)

How is it possible to speak, with such authority, in the future imperative tense, to declare "enjoyment" not so much verboten as beyond the pale of what the nation would take pleasure in?

America, to no football fan's surprise, did not take Beck's admonition to heart. Instead, most of the country (or so it seemed if you were following the mainstream media – not only the sports media – or lived in an urban area where bars were filled, at odd hours, with fans of, granted, various affiliations, all equally rambunctious in their support) appeared to enjoy the World Cup. Little wonder then that some "17 million Americans watched the final match alone – and that match didn't even include an *American* team," as Jeremy Holden expressed it in his blog (2010). More tickets were sold in the United States than any country other than the hosts, South Africa. Some of those tickets, it is important to recognize, were bought by fans of other countries, among whom fans of Mexico and other Latin American nations would surely be the most likely buyers. Still, it is a fair bet that most of those tickets were purchased by partisans of "Uncle Sam's Army" – a moniker borrowed, in part, from English and Scottish fans who, respectively, follow the "Barmy Army"[3] and the "Tartan Army"; a moniker that gave a whole new twist to Uncle Sam's age-old call for recruits. Have fans clad in the Stars and Stripes ever looked so silly? Or, endearing? Beck's real target, of course, was not the World Cup but the "socialist" US president Barack Obama. According to Beck, Obama's "socialist" policies resemble that of the World Cup. It is rather difficult to explain this analogy between Obama – part radical opportunist in the Carl Schmitt mold, part proud race man, part unrepentant advocate for neoliberal capital, and part inveterate internationalist intent on resituating the United States as a global presence after the disasters of the Bush regime – and the World Cup except in so far as it

betrays the never-far-from-the-surface American belief in its own providential exceptionalism. US leftists, of course, know better. If only, they muse – or, curse, perhaps – Obama *were* a socialist.

And yet, Adam Smith's famous title achieves a paradoxical interrogative force as regards America's relationship with the World Cup. How does one measure the "wealth of nations," the wealth of a particular nation, in a month-long football tournament? This event, while hardly "nasty, brutish and short" in Smith's sense, and only gently Darwinian, since the tournament is run on the basis that the best are the sole survivors (in making this analogy, of course, one wonders if it might not be better to conceive the survival of the fittest more capaciously, in a non-Schmittian fashion?), raises intriguing questions about how to think of the wealth of the nation – that is, to understand the World Cup as imposing its own conception of "wealth." In the World Cup tournament, the best team (squad, in truth, since injuries or loss of form test the depth of the squad) is that assemblage of players, coaches, and support staff with the most talent, with the best blend of discipline, organization, and creativity. That is the "fittest" team, the squad most likely to win. In some ways, then, the World Cup has everything and nothing to do with the "wealth of (a) nation." It is pure Adam Smith (and Charles Darwin) insofar as it is the most ruthless evaluator of athletic capital; it is the furthest thing from a *Wealth of Nations* logic insofar as it has only a passing regard for economic hegemony. To wit: England's Premier League is the wealthiest in the world, but England seems only capable of mounting an anemic challenge at every World Cup. And then there are cases that defy both economic and cultural logic. For example: New Zealand has no professional league, but at the 2010 World Cup they finished ahead of the ever-cynical Italians who have a proud tradition in the competition.[4] On its own terms, however, the World Cup does let the "market" – even if one makes allowance for the vagaries of fortune (an odd bounce, a lucky break, a freakish save by the goalkeeper), the incompetence of referees – decide who is best.

This chapter on the 2010 World Cup in South Africa, which focuses on the US men's rather than the wonderfully successful women's team, derives its inspiration from an unexpected source. At the core of "To be like everyone else, only better," is two Americans, of different generations, but linked in their thoughtful, culturally nuanced, and politically savvy refusal of nationalist jingoism. Salient about their rejection of flag-waving patriotism, however, is that it does not prohibit their support – by turns thoughtful and wonderfully enthusiastic – for the US team during the 2010 World Cup. The two figures at the core of this chapter are not, of course, presumed to be so much symptomatic of a larger trend (even though they might very well be) as provocative for thinking about the future of football – its affective place, if you will – in the American national psyche. Their fandom is instructive in part because, to me at any rate, it came as such a surprise; a cultural "astonishment," one is almost tempted to suggest. How does one write of surprise? When one is surprised, taken aback, made to think about football in the United States, the United States and football, as if one knew nothing about it?

Because of their capacity to "astonish," these two figures, each in their different way, gave rise to a host of questions about US football. What possibilities for event-specific national affiliation are afoot when the World Cup reveals, as this chapter shows, a new breed of US men's football fan? Moreover, and, more tantalizingly, what prospects for US football are opened up, brought (incipiently) into being, with the inauguration of the anti-jingoistic national subject as a fan of "Uncle Sam's Army?" Can the United States (its players, coaches, administrators and, most importantly, its fans) now, after what happened in 2010 and was certainly afoot before that (though it would be difficult to tell for how long such prospects have existed), dream of winning the World Cup?

Haunting this writing of US men's football is, as it should be, the success of the women's team. For the US women, there is always the expectation of victory. Unlike the men, as Andrew Ross (2007) so mischievously phrases it, "The prodigious achievements of women's soccer . . . are another matter." Indeed, entirely. As their loss in the 2011 women's World Cup to an instrumentalist and defensive-minded Japanese side made clear, not only is there always the expectation of victory, there is also surprise and heartbreak – and, just maybe, vindication for Briana Scurry; how easy it is to dislike the braggadocio of Scur-

ry's loudmouth replacement in the US goal, Hope Solo – when they lose. For the US women not to win, that is failure; how wonderfully fluid and creative they looked in their 2012 triumph in London. What will it take for the US men's team to be released, as it were, from prophylaxis into such an orbit of expectation, into the realm of "prodigious" expectation?

A Song for Alex and Michael

The trouble persists: what form does the question take? Which moves one to ask, what form must the address to the question take? Since any form of address is a risk, and since it is almost impossible to know what is afoot in the relationship between the United States and football without risking a great deal, but by no means everything, it seems useful to turn, in this moment that is so shaped by the "promise to write," to the actual experience of watching the World Cup in the United States. After all, how does one watch in the diaspora when the event itself is taking place in the nation of one's birth? How can one not be troubled by an entire cavalcade of questions? How does one respond to watching in the presence of those native sons who have a relationship to their country, the United States, that is premised on sharp ideological disagreement? How, as a diasporic subject, does one watch in a country where football is a marginal sport when one grew up playing the game every day, thinking, in legendary Liverpool FC manager Bill Shankly's phrase, "Some people believe football is a matter of life and death. I can assure you it is much, much more important than that"? Even, or maybe especially, for those whose enthusiasm is far in excess of their talent?

Without a form for thought that seems especially appropriate or even useful (what is the proper form for writing sport? Only C.L.R. James, Roger Kahn, and Eduardo Galeano can claim to have proposed anything like an answer), it does not appear to be such a bad idea to resort, out of methodological lack as well as philosophical prospect, to the personal and the anecdotal. Because of how I watched the South African event, there is a logic, and a veracity, no doubt, about those daily encounters that marked domestic life in our household for 30 days from June 11 to July 11, 2010, those days that were planned around the World Cup.

There is nothing of the gung-ho American about our older son, Alex. A keen footballer all through his teenage years (how quickly they passed), Alex has no time at all for jingoism of the Glenn Beck variety. As for being a patriot, well, let's just say that this college senior gets his political cues from the world of John Stewart, Stephen Colbert, and *The Onion* rather than Fox News. Not that he'd mind giving offense to Beck, Fox News, and their ilk. Alex's tastes run, almost invariably, to the cutting edge of the cultural spectrum. He is hip to the latest music, from white alternative to rap, leavened by some serious passion for 1970s soul, burnished, always, with an abiding love for Dylan; his reading tastes run from Jack Kerouac to *Rolling Stone* to spending a summer in the company of Ernest Hemingway; he watches, as I said, the "Daily Show" with Jon Stewart and the "Colbert Report" regularly, and shares their acerbic and irreverent take on American politics. Because of excessive exposure to me, he is a fan of England's Liverpool Football Club. Steven Gerrard ranks highly in his football world. (Fernando Torres did too before he left in January 2011 for Chelsea, but we don't talk about that.) Somewhere in his closet is an old Gerrard jersey. We watched most of the 2010 World Cup together. It would be accurate to say that I was moved to second thoughts about what the US men's team means in large measure because of watching the 2010 World Cup with him. The things we learn from our children.

June 12: England versus the USA. After, first, a sex scandal (involving captain John Terry, inexplicably reinstated as skipper, then fired again in February 2012), followed by an injury to the new captain (Rio Ferdinand), Stevie Gerrard became England's World Cup captain. Given this state of affairs, Alex's political inclinations and his general regard for Gerrard and the Liverpool player's elevation to the captaincy, I presumed that our indifferent-to-patriotism son would be supporting the Three Lions – one of the nicknames for the England team, derived from the three lions that constitute the team's crest. After all, why wouldn't he? He did not follow the United States in the qualifying rounds; he hardly, I thought, knew the American players. It only took four minutes for him to disabuse me of any such notion. I am hardly an England fan, but I root for Stevie, and every other Liverpool player at the World Cup, regardless of national affiliation.

Imagine my surprise when Gerrard scored for England in the fourth minute and Alex remained unmoved. I quickly realized that he didn't cheer because his team, his USA, was on the wrong side of the score line. Stevie Gerrard or no Stevie Gerrard. Alex didn't exactly jump up and down when the hard man from Nacogdoches, TX, Clint Dempsey (as tough and combative as they come), scored the softest goal in many a World Cup. There was no venom in Dempsey's shot. The England keeper, Robert Green, more or less guided a tame shot into the net with his hands. Green was immediately dropped for the next game, and he has not played for England since. For his part, Alex accepted the goal with good grace. And, I should add, with nary a glance in my direction. He knows a gift when he sees one, our son, former central midfielder and reluctant (if capable) middle-school goalkeeper. The game ended 1–1 and we both emerged with our honor intact, and my eyes were opened up to this new phenomenon we could call either critical national affiliation or love for US football. (Nation be damned? Okay. Nation tolerated? Okay too.) In any case, we left it at a goal for Liverpool and the United States not losing.

The pattern for the 2010 World Cup was set, at least in our house. I rooted for Liverpool players as Alex became increasingly dedicated to the US team. He couldn't believe that the United States "gifted" tiny Slovenia, in the World Cup match up of biggest versus smallest country in the tournament, a 2–0 lead. I tried to console him by explaining that the Slovenians were no slouches. I assured him that Valter Birsa, scorer of one of the two Slovenian goals, was a valued talent in European circles and that the Slovenians were renowned for playing good football. Such insights provided cold comfort. Only a second-half recovery by the United States could do that. Alex was incensed when the Malian referee, Koman, disallowed Maurice Edu's perfectly legitimate goal. "Robbed," I think I heard him mutter, darkly. On this occasion, it was hard to argue.

Things got worse for Alex in the final Group C game between the United States and Algeria. For at least 91 minutes, that is. Until Landon Donovan scored a goal that was born out of a combination of US striker Jozy Altidore's good work and Donovan's relentless running. Donovan, a bit of a prima donna, worked hard for his goal. He ran at least 60 meters in following up Altidore's shot, parried by the Algerian keeper, so that he was on hand to guide the ball into the Algerian net. No sooner had the ball crossed the line than Alex bounded up, "That's what I'm talking about." And then, the only time I'd ever heard him say it, "U-S-A! U-S-A!" Alex had reason to be ecstatic. It was a historic moment in American football history. Not only had the United States qualified for the knock-out stages of the World Cup, they'd topped their group because of their superior goal difference as well. Gerrard's England was to meet Germany while the United States faced a repeat of their last game in the 2006 World Cup. Once more, Ghana was to be their opponents.

In a small way, a "troubling question" had been answered. Or, at least, a response was offered in outline. For a generation of American kids who have grown up playing football, watching it on TV, and for whom the nation is a frequently alien – or, alienating – concept, the 2010 US team meant something. It drew them in. Landon Donovan, Tim Howard, Clint Dempsey, Jozy Altidore, all offered the opportunity to identify with the team who played a marginal – if culturally and onto-logically definitive, for some – sport, all the while performing colorful but ideologically inoffensive (national) affiliation. After all, how seriously can you take yourself in your Uncle Sam outfit if you do not, really, expect to be the last team standing? Or maybe a dissident national affiliation is simply an alternate way, a non-boorish, un-American way, might one suggest, to take one's place as an American in the world when America is a declin-ing power? All dissidents, as we well know, live with an attendant vulnerability. Dissidents have to, whatever their ideological inclination, open themselves up to the world because there is no real place for them at home.

However, the signal accomplishment of the 2010 men's US football team is that it was adopted by more than one generation. My friend Michael, a casual (sports) fan at best, has for some decades now shuttled between the United States and Italy doing his work as an intellectual. As a result, he (sort of) considers himself a supporter of the Azzurri. This time around, however, he wasn't so sure. Still, he is a loyal guy and he stuck with a

hardly vintage Italian team composed of either aging or already aged stars. Players who, in truth, were so far past their sell-by date as to make their participation in the 2010 World Cup almost a health hazard. The Italians were woeful; no believer in the beautiful game shed a single tear. Released of this onerous burden, Michael said to me that he was, as talked work over the phone, "rooting for this US team."

Even more than Alex, patriotism is not a native sentiment to Michael. Significant, then, that he should have gone on to say "I like this team." Michael and I didn't engage in a great deal of ideological analysis or technical reflection, but there was an awareness of the salient shift in his own position. From alienation to an unexpected warming to this Bob Bradley-coached team. A Princeton man, Bradley (no relation, as far as I can tell, of that other famous son of Princeton, the former New York Knick and senator from New Jersey, Bill Bradley) had fashioned an effi-cient outfit. (Bob Bradley was fired as national coach in December 2010 and now works as in that same capacity for, of all countries, Egypt, "The Pharaohs.") Hard-working, totally dedi-cated to the team, entirely devoid of prima donnas (Donovan excepted), this was not a team designed to win hearts and minds with pretty football. Vulnerable in defense, lacking imagina-tion and creativity in attack, but almost entirely selfless to a man, they were nevertheless extremely good at drawing their countrymen to them. Perhaps it was the lack of selfishness, or the lack of pretense, I know not which, or the overwhelm-ing honesty of their effort, or just that they played for their country without relaying that they were, in any sense, exceptional, that made their nation take them to its heart. It might be their dedication to team and the fact that many of them, including Howard (Everton FC), Dempsey (formerly of Fulham FC, now plying his trade for Tottenham Hotspur in North London), and Donovan (who enjoyed a successful loan spell at Everton), play (or played) in the English Premier League, that ensured that the United States was not cowed by their big-name opponents, as England found out.

Was humility the key? Or, was it their ability to convey how comfortable they were in the world, in this World Cup? They were Americans who represented a mode of national being light years removed from Glenn Beck's verbosity and silliness. Bradley's team seemed to be enjoying themselves. They were possessed of a refreshing capacity for self-reflection, and they gave everything they had. In a word, they seemed almost old-fashioned in their endeavor. In truth, too much so.

How, then, to account for this phenomenon that appealed not only to Alex and Michael but to thousands of Americans in South Africa, across Europe, and in countless bars in American cities and, to a lesser extent, in small heartland towns? Clearly, this team signified across the generations, both to a new generation for whom US football not only matters but has first dibs on their loyalty and to an older generation coming, to this team from some other (trans-)national affiliation, embracing the US football team, belatedly, as their own.

The truth might be simple and run counter to conventional football logic; or, at least, the economic logic of the game. Unlike the rest of the world, football in America does not appear to need to compete with the existing major sports in order to thrive. A modest men's professional league, one that exports its best to Europe and, in return, gets aging European stars who learn to play with moderately talented Americans and other assorted nationalities, Central and Latin Americans not least among them, can sustain a sport that has a genuine grassroots base. US football presents a singular challenge to the game's governing ethos: maybe an enormously healthy football culture in which a few hundred thousand (or more, who knows?) participate, formally and informally, is better than a big-money league.

Maybe there are many truths, each specific to its own set of circumstances. One is that more than 300 million people invariably provide a large enough base from which to select a competitive team. Maybe the American capacity for organization and efficiency, so prized by US business, and robust physicality, so foundational to sports such as gridiron and ice-hockey (without meaning to suggest that basketball and baseball players are any less robust), can compensate for the lack of a professional tradition. Maybe not having a star means that the team, naturally and without the kind of drama that the French team exhibited at the 2010 World Cup (with players refusing to train, team-mates effectively striking in solidarity, a coach who seemed to live in an entirely different dimension from the rest of the universe), always takes priority. After all, there is no more powerful American myth than that of Horatio Alger – up by your bootstraps, work your tail off. There is nothing more foundational to the Puritan ethic than hard work and sacrifice. What's not to like about that, apart from what it has wrought ideologically?

Form

And yet, the matter of form is not restricted to how one writes the "troubling question." It is also crucial, form, to how the game is played. Or, how one imagines the game might be played. Or, how the form in which the game is approached matters, more than anything else, when the game is on the line. It is through and because of form, understood here as an aesthetic approach – commitment – to the game (play like the Spaniards, not like the Italians), that the World Cup can be won.

Form, here, is nothing other than a commitment to, or, better still, a fundamental belief in, creativity. *Joga bonito*, the Brazilians say, the "beautiful game." And with their historic array of talent, and their five World Cups, they know of whence they speak. Or, FC Barcelona, master geometricians, lords of the short pass, innovators of tiki-taka, orchestrated by the magical talents of Lionel Messi, they show us how the game might – the temptation to say "must" is great, and hovers at the edge of the tongue – be played. To play like the Catalans and the Brazilians is to approach the game in the belief that "risk," for beauty, geometric innovation (FC Barcelona creates passing angles which would astonish Archimedes), and individual brilliance must, unfailingly, be taken, not averted – it is only in risk that beauty might be discovered, where genius might flourish, where *joga bonito* might be allowed to show itself to us, in all its glory. The Brazilians have long shown us this; now the Spaniards have been mesmerizing us for almost a decade; and, playing, in truth, with no real forward, just endlessly creative midfielders who can score because of their delicately relentless movement; tiki-taka, move, pass, move, pass, pass, pass, move, score with a tap-in, the opposition's head in a helpless swirl. What's not to like?

To watch those who play for – or with – risk, then, is to encounter a team where players are not so much encouraged as naturally inclined to take on opponents; encouraged to dribble, to beat an opponent with one's skill, encouraged to do so without fear of reprisal from team-mates or coaches if the ball is lost. Differently phrased, for all of the geometrically astounding passing skills of FC Barcelona players such as Xavi, Iniesta, and Busquets (and here one must give kudos to Xabi Alonso, formerly of Liverpool, who seems more a Barça player than a Real Madrid one, because he fits in so effortlessly with his Catalan team-mates when they play together for Spain), sometimes the pass must be superannuated in favor of the dribble. Sometimes there is nothing for Messi to do except be Messi: to mesmerize through his absolute control of the ball, his ability to wrong foot opponents so that they end up sprawled in his wake. Sometimes it is only the team with the player, or, better still, players, who can beat their man, leave their opponents in the dust (preferably on their bottoms after having been turned, again and again, spinning like a top), that will win. Sometimes it is only individual artistry, as possessed by Messi, Pele, Zidane, that can, paradoxically, bring a team – in this instance, a nation – into its own. Players such as Lionel Messi leave a legacy: their exemplarity spawns other individualists who know, at once, their place in the team, and the moment to make it their team. In that signature American phrase, the individualist must know when, the exact moment, to be *the man*. Especially intoxicating if that "man," Messi, is barely 5 feet 5 inches tall.

The United States does not have that player. Yet. The question of record, the troubling question, is: when, how, will it produce that player? (Of course, most nations ask that question, long for that player; Raheem Sterling, are you ready, lad, to be that player for England?) The answer, it might be ventured, turns on a paradox. In order to succeed as a team, the American team must overcome what it lacks by becoming less like itself, its un-American self, we might say, and more like the non-footballing nation. That is because, paradoxically, the American side lacks what is, in the national imagination, conceived of as the characteristic *par excellence*. If a Whitman-esque turn of phrase might be permitted, the American team must submit to the celebration of the individual. "I sing myself, I celebrate my footballing self." American football must think itself in Walt Whitman's poetic terms. Whitman, the great individualist who championed equality and democracy in the young nation, may offer the precise model of how individualism is integral to the life of the collective; Whitman knows when the individual must come into his own. That moment, more than anything, knows itself as the birth of the poetic.

American football can only succeed if it goes in search of a player who is that most American of things: a star. More than that, *the* star, the player everyone wants to see. American football must commit itself to producing a great player so that the world would want to see the great American player. And then, the next one: the greatest player in the world is an American. Like basketball: Bill Russell, Wilt Chamberlain, Magic, Bird, Jordan . . . one after the other. But, for now, one will do. (In Argentina there was Maradona; now, in Spain, there is one greater still, Messi. Who ever imagined that Maradona would be cast in the role of John the Baptist, simply the facilitator for the One who was to come? The Brazilian list is too long, but Pelé, Garrincha, Zico, Socrates, Ronaldo will have to suffice, if only as a starting point.) America the beautiful, America, home of the game where every footballer is expected to be risk-taker. Well, maybe with the exception of defenders under severe pressure in their own penalty box. But, everybody else . . .

Reductively phrased, the American team must not become atomized but seek to transform itself into a collective that has, at its core, a deep desire for the exception, for the exceptional individualist. The American team must become, as it were, more its national itself. Not quite like the nation imagines itself to be, wholly exceptional, but capable of recognizing the importance to itself of the exceptional individual, the individual capable of doing exceptional things. Dribbling, leaving three, four, six opponents sprawling in his mazy wake; scoring spectacular goals, strikes that grab headlines, that grab you by the footballing throat and won't let go until you submit to its particular beauty. The dribbling winger or striker who can, in football parlance, "break down the defense," "leave you a man over." Any time you can beat your man, you create space for your team-mates, you disorganize the opposing defense. You make it easier to score. The player who can do that makes imperative a different chant. Instead of "U-S-A! U-S-A!" one hears, first, "[Messi!] What a player!" Then, "U-S-A! U-S-A!" The triumph of the individual who comes from within, the glorious national Self. And yet . . .

Such an event, such a player, would make America not exceptional but normative, at least in terms of its desire for such a player. The accommodation of the exceptional individual within the concept of the team is what every nation, every coach, whatever the level, every fan, dreams of. Coaches, the media, fans, emphasize the team up to that moment when the game requires something other than the team: a flash of inspiration, genius, visionaries. The United States confronted this dilemma, fatally, in its quarter-final game with Ghana. As it did for all but three minutes of its 2010 World Cup campaign, it found itself behind. Like England, Ghana scored early. Within the first five minutes. Seventeen minutes into the second half, the United States equalized through a Landon Donovan penalty. The game went into extra time and Asamoah Gyan, picking up a hopeful clearance swept by the US captain Carlos Bocanegra, a sturdy but hardly fleet of foot defender, sweetly struck a shot past Tim Howard in goal. Game over, as the pundits say. And yet . . .

Go in Search of Trouble

For the entire game, the United States showed itself capable of winning. The likes of Dempsey and Altidore troubled the inexperienced Ghanaian defense (Ghana fielded the youngest team at the World Cup); Donovan had his moments; the coach's son Michael Bradley had a solid game; but the United States was incapable of breaking down the defense. When a flash of genius, a moment of inspiration was called for, there was not an American player capable of rising to the challenge. To play football like Jon Stewart and Stephen Colbert do comedy, to do comedy like David Chapelle used to, and before them all, of course, there stands Richard Pryor – no comic risked more, caused more trouble, made the expletive funnier, was more willing to offend (although Jim Belushi was no slouch in this department), of that we are

sure. The Richard Pryor way is the only way to do it: risk everything, play for the biggest laugh, or for all the marbles, every time. The risk that is grounded in the commitment to trouble the self into an expectation that will result in nothing, on the football pitch, but trouble for opposing defenders. Trouble (as Pryor taught us) can take many forms, not a few of them self-destructive in the extreme. The risk, of course, is that a dissident form of trouble, if such a redundancy might be indulged, will trouble the team more than the team can sustain.

In order to win at football America must become more itself, after having played unlike its imagined national self now for six consecutive World Cups. It is only when trouble rules that Alex's generation grows in its fidelity to US football, and Michael's develops a new appreciation for its (surprising) loyalty (or, when the loyalty is no longer surprising), will be allowed, will be permitted to dream, beyond the purview of stirring comebacks. At that moment "neophyte" will be cast aside with a rough finality. It is only when trouble is the order of the day that a quarter-final berth will no longer be enough. America must go in search of troublemakers, of jinking wingers, ball-hogging midfielders, and delightfully greedy strikers who think of trouble as the only way in which football should be played. And yet . . .

Isn't the most terrifying part of trying to become yourself in football the fear that you will reveal not your individual exceptionality but, rather, that you will find yourself to be entirely un-exceptional? That is, the American concept of the team with the exceptional individual(s) that is needed to triumph is in no way distinct from that of any other footballing nation. Is that what girds and sustains America's national footballing dissidents? Is that what they dream of? Will that be the team they truly like, the team that they take to their Uncle Sam hearts only to find themselves overwhelmed by love? And what better form for dissident patriotism than to experience the transcendent power of love? What would it mean for America, for football in the United States, when American unexceptionality is thought as a truly exceptional accomplishment? When America has become like everyone else, only better. At least for one World Cup, that World Cup where the dribble is valued above, just for a glorious moment, the organization and efficiency of the team. To be like everyone else, only better: that is the American dream, is it not? That is true to the foundation of American exceptionalism, no matter the tattered state of the empire.

Conclusion

Jürgen Klinsman, the new coach, was already deemed an American before he replaced Bradley. His German compatriots dubbed him "Kalifornia" Klinsman because he'd settled in Los Angeles after his retirement from the game. In his playing days, the gangly Klinsman was a greedy striker. During his time in charge of the German team, he seemed to bring his "Kalifornia kool" to his native land. Youthful, inventive, released from the shackles of Germany's traditional efficiency – dour opportunism is probably the best way to describe it (or, winning on penalties in the more cynical rendering) – Klinsman's team was infinitely easier on the footballing eye. And yet . . .

Klinsman is also a team man in the conventional sense. He has stripped the names off the back of the US jersey and, in a move entirely unheard of in the contemporary game (where players have established the right to decide on their own numbers), returned to the old-fashioned tradition of assigning players numbers based solely on their position – the goalkeeper wears number 1, the right back number 2, and so on up to the wide left player who wears number 11. The substitutes are assigned numbers 12 through 18.

Through his first four games in charge, Klinsman's US team failed to spark the imagination. It might behoove Klinsman to, as it were, return to his American roots. That is, if he could imbue the German national team with West Coast cool, maybe, just maybe, he should make the same gift to his new compatriots: he must give them to themselves. It's all good and well to assign numbers in some long-lost fashion, I have no problem with it since I grew up playing the game that way, as long as you encourage your number 7 to create, show your number 9 video footage of your insatiable hunger for goals, and, yes, Jürgen, glory, and admonish your number 11 if he doesn't dribble at least . . . well, instruct him to dribble a lot. If Klinsman could make the Germans American, his job now is to make the Americans American.

Klinsman could start by handing out copies of *Leaves of Grass* at the next national team practice. If you don't believe me, Jürgen, just ask the Zen meister Phil Jackson how well it worked for him. Jackson tried to find a book, it seems, for every one of his players. One doubts that Shaq read *Poetics*, but surely something happened because all of a sudden he asked to be known as the "Big Aristotle." Begin with the spirit of Whitman who understands the proper place of the American individual in the collective, add a dash of ingenuity, spice it up with verve and panache, and, dare to dream of singing in celebration.

Acknowledgment

This essay is dedicated to Alex and Michael.

Notes

1 This book, *Distant Corners*, is especially useful for charting the history of American football.
2 In the 2010 final, however, unlike their appearances in 1974 and 1978, the Dutch betrayed their cultured heritage. In truth, it was an ugly performance by a country renowned for the "total football" designed by Rinus Michels and executed so sublimely by Johan Cruyff, Johan Neeskens, and the rest of those 1970s stars.
3 The "Barmy Army" is also how England's cricket fans describe themselves on their travels abroad, especially in Australia, the home of the old enemy.
4 Neither New Zealand nor Italy qualified for the knockout stages of the competition, but, in the points standing, the Kiwis topped the Azzurri. Maybe, from time to time, the football gods abhor cynicism and issue small edicts for justice. The purists amongst us bow silently in the direction of Brazil and Spain when the gods heap this kind of humiliation upon the proud anti-footballing inclinations of the Italians.

References

Holden, J. (2010) "Glenn Beck hates the World ... Cup," http://mediamatters.org/blog/2010/06/11/glenn-beck-hates-the-world-cup/166095, accessed January 22, 2013.

Ross, A. (2007) "The ballad of Becks and Posh." *American Quarterly*, 59 (4), 1215.

Wangerin, D. (2006) *Soccer in a Football World: The Story of America's Forgotten Game*, London: WSC Books.

Wangerin, D. (2011) *Distant Corners: America's Soccer History of Missed Opportunities and Lost Causes*, Philadelphia, PA: Temple University Press.

Further Reading

Stark, S. and Harrison S. (2010) *World Cup 2010: The Indispensable Guide to Soccer and Geopolitics*, Indianapolis, IN: Blue River Press.

Trecker, J. (2007) *Love and Blood: At the World Cup with the Footballers, Fans, and Freaks*, Orlando, FL: Harcourt.

Weiland, M. and Wisley, S. (eds.) (2006) *The Thinking Fan's Guide to the World Cup*, New York: Harper Perennial.

29

Sport, Spectacle, and the Political Economy of Mega-events
The Case of the Indian Premier League

Ian McDonald and Abilash Nalapat

Introduction

Since it was launched in 2008, the Indian Premier League (IPL) has transformed the sporting landscape of India, shaken up the international world of cricket and become one of the most lucrative sport leagues in the world. Created by the national governing body, the Board of Control for Cricket in India (BCCI), the IPL is a Twenty20 cricket tournament that runs from April to May each year. Following the model of the franchise system adopted in professional sports in the United States, the IPL consists of ten teams (expanded from eight in its fourth season in 2011). These teams (or franchises) are owned by some of India's top industrialists and Hindi film stars. Following the trend of the football English Premier League, the teams are made up of an array of the finest and best-known players from around the world, thus reversing the dominant trend of East to West, or South to North player migration in sport (Bale and Maguire, 2003). Capitalizing on the twin passions of the Indian masses, cricket and cinema, the IPL was explicitly produced, packaged, and sold as a high-octane media spectacle for a mass audience in India and the vast Indian diaspora. *Forbes Magazine* estimated that

the "brand" value of the IPL exceeded US$4 billion, making it the fourth most valued league in the world. This placed it just below the major American professional sports leagues (National Basketball Association, major league baseball, and the National Football League) but above the English Premier League (Schwartz, 2009).

Described as a "strange hybrid of the English village green, 'Bollywood', and the 'Super Bowl'" (Rowe and Gilmour, 2009: 172), the IPL has captured the imagination of the vast cricket-mad Indian audience. In the very first season, they turned on their televisions, logged onto their computers, switched on their mobiles, and flocked to stadiums in their millions to follow their team and participate in the IPL experience (Gupta, 2009; Mitra, 2010). However, alongside the sporting spectacle have been significant moments of political controversy and intrigue: in its short-lived existence, the IPL has already become embroiled in allegations of match fixing, money laundering, and corruption that has resulted in the downfall and arrest of the IPL's driving force and founding commissioner, Lalit Modi, and the resignation of a senior government minister, Sashi Tharoor (Srinivas and Vivek, 2009). It has soured already tense relations

A Companion to Sport, First Edition. Edited by David L. Andrews and Ben Carrington.
© 2013 Blackwell Publishing Ltd. Published 2013 by Blackwell Publishing Ltd.

between India and Pakistan as a result of the non-selection of Pakistani players in the IPL following the Mumbai attacks of November 2008 by militant Islamic groups. And the increased political clout of the financially flushed BCCI has led to conflicts with the Indian government, the International Cricket Council (ICC), and the England and Wales Cricket Board amongst others.

This chapter provides a context for understanding the significance of the IPL especially in relation to debates about the putative post-Westernization of cricket in the contemporary global sporting landscape. After outlining the ideological gulf between cricket as it has been traditionally understood and its most current incarnation in the Twenty20 format, the chapter situates the IPL in the history of cricket and national identity in India. The chapter then provides an overview of the first four seasons of the IPL from 2008 to 2011 before drawing some conclusions about the success of the IPL as a novel sporting venture and the significance of the IPL as the latest and most stark expression of the post-Westernization of cricket.

Historical Backdrop: The IPL Is Just Not Cricket!

In the discussions of Twenty20 cricket and the IPL, it is easy to forget that at the centre of this frenzy is the erstwhile game of the British imperial elite, emblematic of English rural idyll, and synonymous with a class-bound masculine etiquette (Marqusee, 2005). This is a game that is so drenched in the hierarchical values of the English class system that it can safely proclaim its own disinterested and virtuous morality, summed up in that evocative phrase "It's just not cricket!" A refrain that declares that cricket, uniquely among sports, not only enshrines an ethic of sportsmanship in its rules but also reflects a moral universe that disdains all manner of sharp practices of the pitch. In life as in cricket, one has a duty to play both by the rules and by the spirit of the rules.

Historically, cricket has represented the "gentleman amateur" code of respect for tradition, for hierarchy, for authority, and a "civilizing" code that calls for contained and respectful behavior as opposed to partisan exuberance and a win-at-any-cost mentality. Of course, as the game devel-

oped along professional lines, and as it evolved with the introduction of different formats, this "code" was, over time, observed more rhetorically than practically, but neither can these values be dismissed as mere vestiges from another era. However, the IPL also marks a break with this history and points towards the putative new India. While capitalizing on this history, the IPL marks a new chapter in the development of cricket, and perhaps in the development of sport in general. For the IPL, the point of departure is sport as a form of entertainment for the purpose of profit. The measurement of success is as much to do with the profits generated by the teams, or more accurately the franchises, as with runs accrued or wickets taken. Without any organic connection to the grassroots of the game, Mike Marqusee (2010a) accuses the IPL of being essentially parasitic on the culture of cricket "they (the franchise owners) have neither a mandate for nor an interest in promoting the welfare of the game as a whole.... Since it is a seven-week event, there is little incentive for owners to invest in any wider development."

In professional cricket, there are two main formats: the unlimited-overs game and the limited-overs game. The traditional format is the unlimited-overs game, which is played over a set number of days: three, four, or, at international ("Test") level, five days under the auspices of the ICC. As a counter to the chronic decline in popularity of the five-day format, as registered in falling spectator attendance and television audiences in the post-1945 period, the one-day limited-overs game was first played in England in 1963 and the first international one-day game was played between England and Australia in 1971, followed by the one-day World Cup in 1975 (Gupta, 2009). Similarly, the Twenty20 format was introduced in England in 2003 as a mid-season filler in an attempt to boost poor attendances at domestic league cricket. Each side would bat for 20 overs enabling the game to be completed in three hours. "What followed" notes Gupta (2009: 202) "was an exciting slug-fest of attacking cricket and high scores."

The ICC recognized the potential of this new format to revitalize the game at an international level, and so in 2007 organized the inaugural Twenty20 World Cup in South Africa. India was the surprise winner of this World Cup. This success, which led to exuberant scenes of national(ist) celebrations in India not witnessed since the national team won the one-day World Cup in 1983, confirmed the potential of the Twenty20 format in India. And so it proved to be that in India, where the Twenty20 format was given the blockbuster Bollywood film treatment, that it really took off with the IPL in 2008.

Given the preeminent status of cricket in Indian sports culture (Guha, 2003; Majumdar, 2007) and the increasing dominance of India in world cricket, it is not surprising that the Twenty20 format took off in India (Gupta, 2009). In the relationship between sport and national identity, cricket is invested with far more significance than any other sport in India (McDonald, 1999). Field hockey, for example, is often perceived as India's premier sport, based on the fact that India dominated international hockey for decades (not losing a match in the Olympics from 1928 to 1960). However, a combination of the introduction of artificial pitches in the 1970s, which quite literally created a level playing field to undermine India's superiority that was based on skill rather than pace and strength, and the low international prestige associated with success in hockey, has divested hockey in India of significant political importance. Football (soccer) is another popular sport, especially in certain regions of India such as West Bengal, Goa, and Kerala where it has a significant base of participation (Mills, 2005). However, its utility as a source of national prestige is limited by the woeful position of the national team (India are placed 145th out of 202 in the official FIFA rankings for April 2011; see FIFA, 2011). Traditional forms of physical culture such as wrestling and *kabaddi* are also keenly played and followed, especially in the Punjab (Alter, 1992), but they are without an international profile and so provide little scope for success in the global arena (Guha, 2003). In the relationship between sport and national identity in India, cricket has no parallel.

There are four key phases in the development of Indian cricket and Indian national consciousness. The first phase, stretching from 1870 to 1947, was the era of colonial rule. During this phase, cricket was introduced into India, initially as a "corner of a foreign field" (see Guha, 2003), a means of maintaining a little bit of England in a foreign land. It soon became, alongside other

imperial sports, part of a complex system of control by which the imperialists sought to incorporate a layer of the elite indigenous population into the imperial project. However, rather than becoming a vehicle of cultural imperialism, the game was taken up as an assertion of incipient national identity in the 1930s when India formed a Test side even before independence had been achieved.

The second phase is the era of independent India in the second half of the twentieth century, where cricket underwent a makeover from a colonial to an Indian sport and represented pan-Indian Nehruvian ideals (a form of national unity that cut across religion, caste, and region and was underpinned by progressive social democratic politics). Thus although the cricket of contemporary India emerged out of the British Raj, it has undergone its own process of decolonization, conceptualized by Appadurai as "vernacularization" (1996: 97–105). It is in this period, since gaining independence in 1947, that cricket emerged as the premier game. As India's leading sport, cricket played a key role in contributing to national unity within civil society during the early post-independence years. Although there were divisions and conflicts in cricket from the 1950s to the 1970s, these tended to be based on regional rivalries expressed, for example, in perceptions of selector bias for the national team (Cashman, 1980).

In noting the pivotal role of television in spreading the appeal of the game to all regions and strata of Indian society, Guha asserts (1994/1995: 257), "Cricket is not so much India's national sport as its national obsession. The only opponents of cricket still around are the economists, who call it the opium of the people and do calculations of its negative impact on GNP." However, with the successful rise of the IPL, a commodified spectacle produced and packaged as a form of television entertainment and making enormous profits, now even the economists are on board. The noted Indian sociologist Ashis Nandy neatly captured this complex simultaneous acknowledgement and denial of cricket's colonial heritage in India when he quipped, "Cricket is an Indian game accidentally invented by the English" (1989: 9).

The transition between the second and third phase was marked by the unexpected victory by

Kapil Dev's Indian team against the mighty West Indies in the final of the 1983 one-day World Cup. This triumph can be seen as the culmination of the second phase of Indian cricket in which the sport established itself as truly the national game of the people as opposed to hockey, which even to this date retains the official "national sport" status bestowed by the federal government. The victory in 1983 was instrumental in ensuring that cricket toppled hockey as the most important sport in the north and football as the most followed sport in West Bengal and Kerala. However, the win also was the point of inflection for the aggressive masculine nationalism that gained momentum in the late 1980s, reflected in the growth of the Hindu nationalist Bharatiya Janata Party as a political force to be reckoned with and with the liberalization of the economy (Hansen, 1996).

The third phase has been shaped by the emergence of a new strand of cricket nationalism, the assertion of a narrower national identity through cricket (Marqusee, 1996). In this third phase, from the late 1980s to the early 2000s, cricket came to represent an assertive form of aggressive muscular patriotism. Neoliberal economic reforms went hand in hand with the globalization of Indian society to produce assertive forms of political and cultural nationalism (Hansen, 1996; Bhatt, 2001). An oft-overlooked aspect of the social revolutions that swept aside the command-style economies of the Soviet Union and Eastern Europe in the period from 1989 to 1991 is the impact on India's economic policy. In the post-independence period, high levels of state control and investment dominated India's economy, complete with Soviet-style five-year plans. The adoption of the New Economic Policy (NEP) in 1991 signaled an unequivocal embrace of neoliberalism that was to open up the Indian economy to the global market. Thus, among other measures, the state relinquished its strategic control over domestic operations of the market, taxes were reduced, government welfare programs were pruned back, and a rapid privatization of the public sector implemented. "Globalization" became the mantra of politicians in India, as multinational corporations were welcomed to exploit hitherto protected markets (Kurien, 1994).

In cricket, the impact was soon felt. In 1996, the sixth one-day cricket World Cup tournament was hosted jointly by India, Pakistan, and Sri Lanka. In terms of matches played, spectator attendance, television audience, sponsorship, and media hype, it was, to use the words of one Indian cricket journalist, "Cricket's biggest extravaganza of the century" (Mohan, 1996: 5). The tournament was also the most commercialized event in the history of the sport. Sponsorship deals were signed with multinationals like Coca-Cola (£5.3 million) and the ITC, the Indian tobacco giant (£8 million). Approximately £11.5 million was gained from the sale of television broadcasting rights to Rupert Murdoch's Star network, enabling the organizers to declare that they made a healthy profit of £21 million (Marqusee, 1996). A decade later, the ICC sold the television rights for tournaments between 2007 and 2015 (including the two ICC cricket World Cups in India in 2011 and Australasia in 2015) for US$1.1 billion (Cricinfo, 2006). Although there is a global audience for international cricket events, it is still the burgeoning and increasingly affluent Indian middle class that is the market for this coverage.

The fourth phase can be termed the era of global India: the era when the epicenter of power in the organization and administration of world cricket shifted from the West to Asia. This is what Majumdar (2007: 92) refers to as "The Shift," the transformation of South Asia into the nerve-center of global cricket power – a process that started in earnest in the 1990s. India made the transition from aspiring to achieving global status in the field of cricket. Indeed sport acts as a neat barometer of "India Rising," reflecting the growing economic muscle of India as well as the increasing consciousness on the part of India's sporting administrators of the power of sports in both domestic and international circuits. The staging of the 2010 Commonwealth games in New Delhi and the Indian grand prix in Formula One motor-racing in 2011 are additional indicators of such global aspirations. However, it is in cricket that the shift in the center of geopolitical power from the West towards the vast and passionately committed Indian subcontinent has been interpreted most convincingly as an example of the post-Westernization of the global sports (Rumford, 2007; Rowe and Gilmour, 2008; Gupta, 2009).

The post-Westernization of cricket refers to the shift in the balance of power in world cricket from its traditional centers in the West, most notably England, to the East, most notably India. Thus Gupta (2009: 201) argues that:

> the advent of the IPL indicates two things: one more indicator that India is a factor to be reckoned with in the global economy and is carving out its own niche in that sphere; but also the fact that, increasingly, sporting markets and the control of international sports may be determined by forces in the nonwestern world.

Or in the triumphant tone of Boria Majumdar, "In the modern cricket world, the Indians lead; the others follow" (2007: 88). In Gupta's account, and to a lesser extent in Majumdar also, there is an element of conceiving post-Westernization in binary terms: as the rise of the East at the expense of the West. It is useful then to invoke Rowe and Gilmour's question regarding how India's rise in world cricket might be understood (2008: 192):

> Does the shift in locus of sports governance to the East in the wake of its newfound geopolitical co-operation and media-derived economic domination indicate the decline of the West or the ultimate global success of a cultural form that originated (or was at least fashioned) on the village greens and playing fields of an old imperial power?

Of course, this is actually a rhetorical question that is intended to highlight a false binary. "The Shift," to borrow Majumdar's phrase, is actually a manifestation of both "the decline of the West" and the "ultimate global success" of Western cultural form. To understand how this is the case, it is necessary to outline a more developed conceptualization of post-Westernization than that implicit in the account offered by Gupta (2009). Rumford offers a starting point to develop a more nuanced approached and challenges the tendency to equate post-Westernization with the ending of the Cold War, the bipolar world order, and the decreasing salience of the idea of the West as a reference point for political identification and global leadership. Instead, Rumford (2007) draws on the scholarship of Gerard Delanty (2006) to identify three key dimensions of post-Westernization: namely, the decreasing acceptance and breakdown of a "single Western world view" (p. 205) held between countries in the West; the cor-

responding emergence of different modernities to Western modernity, for example, post-communist and Islamic; and the emergence of "a new East" (p. 206) capable of leading in areas of global affairs previously dominated by the West.

When applied to cricket, post-Westernization signals less "The Shift" and more an intensification of interaction between forms and flows of capital on the one hand and non-Western spheres of institutional and political control on the other. Crudely put, it is a situation in which the new centers of power and control are emerging, such as India in cricket, but within an acceptance of neoliberal economic practices in which the lines of power cut across artificial geographical constructs of West and East. Rumford's approach suggests that the post-Westernization thesis needs to be located within the framework of the global capitalist economy. This then allows further fields of enquiry to be opened up, along the lines articulated by David Andrews (2009). Drawing on Fredric Jameson's (1991) critique of the cultural logic of late capitalism, Andrews argues that originating in the United States and then spreading outwards, the second half of the twentieth century witnessed the systematic capitalization of sport as part of the cultural realm. According to Andrews (2009: 213):

> virtually all aspects of the global sport infrastructure (governing bodies, leagues, tournaments, teams and individual athletes) are now driven and defined by the interrelated processes of: commercialization (the exploitation of an object or practice for capital gain); corporatization (the rational structuring and management of sporting entities according to profit motives); and spectacularization (the production of entertainment-driven experiences).

As a point for analytical departure, these processes of commercialization, corporatization, and spectacularization aptly capture the dynamics of the IPL as a vehicle for capital accumulation. Thus the development of the IPL as a form of post-Westernization cannot be reduced to either a reinscription of cultural imperialism or a manifestation of de-Westernization; it is the latest instantiation of what Andrews calls the "corporatist logics of late sporting capital" (2009: 218). As Andrews elaborates, this "sporting domination" is not "in the sense of an overarching global homo-geneity in prevailing sport forms, events, or athletes, but definitely in the uniform manner through which local sport cultures have been cor-poratized" (p. 221). And it is a logic that is not without an ideological dimension. The accelera-tion in the commodification of sport in India ought not to be perceived naively as a conse-quence of the impersonal global free market. Ideologically, the IPL acts an exemplar of what Andrews (p. 222) describes as "the corporate sport hegemon."

The IPL as Corporate Sport

The IPL was not the first Twenty20 league in India. In 2007, Zee Television, frustrated at losing bids to broadcast cricket by the BCCI, decided to create its own cricket content by setting up an unofficial league, the Indian Cricket League (ICL). Following in the footsteps of other private cricket leagues, most notably Kerry Packer's World Series Cricket in Australia in the late 1970s, the ICL ran for two seasons in 2007 and 2008, organizing a domestic competition (the Indian Championship) and an international competi-tion (the World Series). The ICL ran up against resistance from the BCCI and the associated withdrawal of key players and was eventually sunk by the decision of the BCCI to launch its own official, and ICC-recognized, version of Twenty20: the IPL. In sinking the ICL however, the BCCI not only launched what was soon to become the most lucrative tournament in the history of cricket but also paved the way for the emergence of Lalit Kumar Modi, the charismatic and energetic sporting entrepreneur. The IPL is in effect Modi's brainchild. Modi, BCCI vice president 2005–2010, not only conceived the IPL but was also its first chairman and commissioner between 2008 and 2010. He has been labeled "cricket's answer to Don King of boxing or Bernie Ecclestone of Formula One" (Guha Ray, 2010).

Under the leadership of BCCI vice president Lalit Modi, and involving sports marketing giants the International Management Group (IMG), the blueprint of the billion-dollar league was drawn up and found enough takers in the corporate and the film world. In no other walk of life in the brief history of India after the 1991 economic reforms has "India Incorporated" come together in an exhibition of aggressive entrepreneurial spirit to decisively swing an industry's power pendulum away from the industrialized West and towards India. At a time when corporate India's takeovers of faltering British-based companies – United Breweries Group buying Scottish Distilleries and the Formula One team Spyker (ex-Jordan) and the Tata group taking over Corus and Jaguar – evoked much hype in the Indian media of the mythical "Global Indian Takeover" project (Bist, 2004; Mishra, 2006), Modi, in association with IMG executive Andrew Wildblood, gave the country a real success story to recalibrate its economic prowess, not just against the cricket industries in England and Australia, cricket's rep-resentatives of the industrialized West, but also against the best sporting leagues in Europe and America.

The IPL organizers had their business models well in place: they knew exactly how their fran-chises would be able to generate revenue from the venture. They had elaborately researched the English Premier League and American Pro Sports commercial models to put in place their systems centered on broadcast rights and supported by other revenue streams such as sponsorship, ticket sales, and merchandizing. They also realized they could cash in on the new-found obsessive televi-sion consumption of Twenty20 cricket in India. This consumption had gone through the roof in India when the country, represented by a young team and led by Dhoni, won the inaugural ICC world Twenty20 tournament in South Africa in 2007, beating arch-rival and neighbor Pakistan in the final.

In early 2008, the initial eight franchises, each representing an Indian city (Mumbai, Delhi, Kolkata, Chennai, Bangalore, Hyderabad, Chan-digarh, and Jaipur) were sold for US$723.59 million. The eight franchises were picked up for sums ranging from US$67 million (the Jaipur franchise, which won IPL 1 under the leadership of retired Australian legend Shane Warne) to US$111.9 million (the Mumbai franchise, whose highest placing to date is second in IPL 3) over a ten-year period (*Cricket Today*, 2009: 25). The profile of the eight owners of the franchise teams is significant. Some giant pan-Indian corporate houses, such as Reliance Industries Limited (owners of the Mumbai franchise) and the UB

Group (owners of the Bangalore franchise) wanted to use the IPL predominantly as a platform for a higher profile in the industrialized West. Other franchises aspired for a pan-Indian growth in their traditional business. For example, India Cements, a company that is owned by BCCI secretary N. Srinivasan, is seeking to use the Chennai franchise to expand its existing business strength in south India to other parts of the country. And the Hyderabad franchise, which is owned by the English-language newspaper *Deccan Chronicle*, is seeking to extend its profile beyond south India to Mumbai and Delhi.

However, it is the profiles of the owners of two franchises, Kolkata and Chandigarh, that are the key to understanding the significance of cricket's prime position in Indian culture, and more specifically the IPL's project to reinvent the Twenty20 code of cricket as "Cricketainment," the right mix of "showbiz" glamour and thrill-a-minute experience of reality television that has ensured that the tournament has drawn people from a wider pool of television viewers than just the cricket-lovers (Srinivas and Vivek, 2009). Shah Rukh Khan, one of the biggest stars of the Bollywood film industry during the last decade and a half, won the bid to own the Kolkata franchise team. The franchisees come from several areas that have no previous connection with cricket, testifying to the sport's growing profile as a blue-chip investment in India, prompting the respected cricket web-site, Cricinfo, to declare "Big business and Bollywood grab stakes in IPL" (Cricinfo, 2008).

Marqusee (2010b) noted that of all the IPL's innovations "the most significant, and until recently the least commented on, was the introduction of private ownership of teams." He argues that not since the mid-nineteenth century (with the exception of the Packer interlude) have representative cricket entities been private assets. But what was anathema to an analyst like Marqusee was confirmation of success to advocates of the IPL, such as IMG's Andrew Wildblood. After the franchise bidding in January 2008, Wildblood bombastically declared, "There has never been anything like this in the history of sport. No competition has come from start to where we are today in such a short space of time, or with more financial success" (Srinivas and Vivek, 2009: 42).

It has been through the sale of television and media rights that the vast bulk of income was generated by the IPL. Singapore-based marketing and media company World Sports Group (WSG) paid US$1.026 billion to secure exclusive global broadcast rights to the IPL for 10 years. Sony Entertainment Television, later changed to Multi Screen Media (MSM), would televise the tournament in India as part of the agreement (Viswanath, 2010). The Canadian company Live Current Media bought internet rights for US$50 million over a 10-year period, though this deal came to an end in April 2009 because the company were unable to deliver, and payments were negotiated down to US$20.75 million when it was taken on by Global Cricket Ventures (Pawha, 2009). This contract in turn came to an end in March 2010, and global internet, mobile, and audio rights, along with television and digital rights in specific territories outside India for the next four years, have subsequently been awarded to a consortium led by Times Internet Ltd (*Times of India*, 2011).

Seasons 1 to 4: The Story So Far

For the first time in the history of cricket, in February 2008, Indian and international players were auctioned with each of the eight city franchise teams being allotted a maximum budget of US$5 million to buy up players in the first season. India's captain Mahendra Singh Dhoni, the player with the biggest pulling power in the country's cricket celebrity endorsement bandwagon after batting legend Sachin Tendulkar, was the costliest player. The Chennai franchise bought him for US$1.5 million a season (Monga, 2008). All for a six-week stint of Twenty20 cricket, with no history of traditional rivalries or fan following thought so essential to imbue sport with intensity of the highest level: "Where, in 1977, the best international cricketers had been bought with Australian dollars, now they were bought with Indian rupees" (Mehta, Gemmell, and Malcolm, 2009: 695).

The inaugural Twenty20 match took place at the M. Chinnaswamy Stadium in Bangalore. This poetic-sounding capital city of the southern Indian state of Karnataka, once the center of colonial rule in south India under the British Raj, now celebrated as the "silicon valley of India," was an apt location for the launch of the IPL. With a distinguished imperial legacy and a confident globalized outlook, Bangalore is a distinctively Indian yet modern city, a beacon of neoliberal economic development, youthful innovation, and slick glamour. While 40,000 spectators watched from a stadium bedecked with the corporate logos of Citi, Sony, and Vodafone, 14.4 million television viewers in India and millions more watching on the eight networks that syndicated coverage across the globe witnessed the historic match between the Royal Challengers Bangalore, a franchise owned by the high-profile industrialist Vijay Mallya's United Breweries and the Kolkata Knight Riders, co-owned by Bollywood superstar, Shah Rukh Khan.

It became clear very early on in the tournament that the IPL was going to be big: stadiums were packed, television viewing figures exceeded expectations (Mitra, 2010: 1317–1318); the cricket on display was fast, exciting, and exuded glamour. Before IPL 1, industry experts had predicted that Sony would make a loss of US$4 million in the first season. But the channel turned the prediction on its head as the tournament gained momentum. The 10-second ad slots for the semi-finals and the final of IPL 1 were sold at Rs 100,000 (approximately US$2,100). "We set base prices for ten years, and we were ready to take a hit for the first four years. Instead, we ended with a profit of US$75 million in the first year. We understood cricket and that is why we bet on it," Rohit Gupta, president of Sony Entertainment Television, was quoted as saying (Srinivas and Vivek, 2009). The success of the IPL as a sporting event as well as a media spectacle in its inaugural season was beyond doubt. The unprecedented amounts of money being pumped into the IPL, be it as wages to players or payments for franchises or media rights, were now considered less as a risky investment or a personal indulgence and more as *the* event to invest in, the game to be seen at, and increasingly for players around the world, the teams to play for.

The "Bollywood brigade" in the second season of the IPL was strengthened in early 2009, when Bollywood star and the winner of reality show Celebrity Big Brother on national British TV, Shilpa Shetty, and her British Indian boyfriend Raj Kundra paid US$15 million to buy a 15 percent stake in the Jaipur franchise (*Cricket Today*, 2009: 25). The purchase implied that the value of the Jaipur franchise, just before IPL 2, was US$125 million, or nearly twice the US$67 million paid by Emerging Media, the UK-based consortium that owns the franchise, including London-based entrepreneur Manoj Bedale, Lachlan Murdoch, son of media tycoon Rupert Murdoch, and Suresh Chellaram, brother-in-law of IPL commissioner Lalit Modi (Srinivas and Vivek, 2009).

However, the ineluctable ties between politics and sport were soon to expose the underlying fragility of this newborn sporting phenomenon, a fragility concealed by the media bluster, the marketing hype, and the money generated. On November 26, 2008, Mumbai was subjected to three days of terror when a small group of men representing the Pakistan-based militant organization, Lashkar-e-Taiba, killed 164 people when they laid siege to a number of venues throughout the city, including two showpiece five-star hotels, a Jewish center, the city's main train station, and a local café frequented by Western tourists. Already strained diplomatic relations between India and Pakistan deteriorated further resulting in the Pakistan government denying clearance to all Pakistani cricketers to visit India. Three months later, on March 3, 2009, the worst fears of South Asian cricket-lovers – that there would be an attack on cricketers – turned to reality when the team bus of the visiting Sri Lankan cricket team was ambushed by terrorists in Lahore on the way to the stadium to play a Test match against the home team, Pakistan. Six security personnel were killed in the incident and many Sri Lankan cricketers suffered minor shrapnel injuries (Subramanian, 2009).

In the aftermath of the Mumbai "terror attacks" and the Lahore attack on the Sri Lankan team, it was evident that IPL 2, scheduled from April 10 to May 14, would need a heavy security cover of both Indian central (federal) and state forces just as for the two-Test series against England a month after the Mumbai attacks. However, India's election commission announced that the country's general elections would take place in five stages between mid April and mid May. India's home minister, P. Chidambaram, declared that no central forces would be provided for IPL security owing to the clash with the general elections. Even though the IPL rescheduled the fixtures to ensure that no matches were held on general election day in any city, many of the states were unwilling to give the tournament the all clear due to security concerns. Though the Indian home minister was not averse to the IPL starting after the general elections ended in mid-May, the IPL was adamant that the tournament would have to start in April. A shortened tournament, without the home-and-away model, would have resulted in reduced television coverage and television viewership, which was the bulwark of the commercial success of the IPL. IPL commissioner Lalit Modi started thinking about implementing plan B, staging the tournament abroad, and in a matter of hours he had clinched a deal with Cricket South Africa to hold the tournament in six venues there between April 18 and May 24.

While stadiums were less than full in South Africa, IPL 2 was considered a success in financial and sporting terms. Television audience in India was up on the first season of the IPL, thanks to some spectacular power-hitting, many edge-of-the-seat last-over finishes and some amazing performances from the older generation of cricketers such as Warne and Gilchrist, who led their respective franchises (Jaipur and Hyderabad) to victories. Shifting the tournament to South Africa did not halt the rising profile and appeal of the IPL. In fact, it merely set up the IPL for a triumphant homecoming in 2010. However, IPL 3 proved to be a turning point of a very different kind. While the forward momentum of the IPL was maintained in important respects – for example, the innovation of broadcasting all matches live on YouTube proved to be extremely successful especially in raising awareness of the IPL beyond the borders of India – the expansion of the tournament to include two new franchises designed to confirm the viability and lucrative potential of the IPL actually exposed the lack of financial propriety that had become the norm under the leadership of Modi.

In addition to the developing tensions around the governance of the IPL, the fallout from the deepening diplomatic tensions between India and Pakistan following the Mumbai "terror attacks" resulted in none of the seven Pakistani players, all part of the world Twenty20 championship winning team and including acknowledged world-class players such as Shahid Afridi, Umar Gul, and Umar Akmal, being signed up from the list of 66 players on offer. While the players themselves expressed shock and dismay that none of the franchises had bid for their services, the Pakistan government declared the whole imbroglio an insult and a national humiliation. The franchise owners for their part claimed that they felt unable to bid for the Pakistani players as they could not be confident about their availability as visas still required sorting out. Clearly the players were excluded on political grounds, most likely a combination of fears about potential reprisals that a franchise might face by fielding a Pakistani player in the wake of the Mumbai attacks. Apart from depriving the Indian audience of the talents of some of the best players in the world, this episode undermined the claims made that the IPL was a national league that showcased the best players in the world. Marqusee (2010a) summed it up well:

> On behalf of the IPL, it has been argued that the presence of foreign stars helps internationalise cricket loyalties. "Thanks to the mixture of nationalities in each of the IPL teams," declared no less a person than former Minister of State for External Affairs Shashi Tharoor, "partisanship has suddenly lost its chauvinist flavour. In the IPL, the past poses no impediment to the future." The statement had the hubristic ring of free-market utopianism. A utopianism hopelessly undermined in this case by the exclusion of Pakistani players from the tournament.

In March 2010, a month before the start of IPL 3, marketed in India as the glorious homecoming after the shift to South Africa in 2009, the IPL announced the winners of the auction for the ninth and tenth franchises. The western Indian city of Pune and the southern Indian city of Kochi were declared winners after they bid a staggering US$375 million and US$333.3 million respectively, a combined value that is in excess of the bidding amount of the original eight franchisees. The Sahara Group, the shirt sponsors of the Indian national cricket team, bought the Pune franchise while a consortium of small and middle businesses bought the Kochi franchise. The levels of financial investment in the IPL led Modi to boast, "It only shows that there is no recession for IPL" (Ravindran and Gollapudi, 2010). Modi could not have realized then that within a matter of a few months he would be stripped of his commissioner's office in disgrace after a slew of allegations ranging from corporate malpractice, money laundering, corruption, favoritism in awarding television rights contracts, and manipulation of the franchise auction process.

It all started in April 2010, when Modi, in his Twitter feed, publicly questioned the ownership structure of the new Kochi franchise. Pointing out that Rendezvous Sports World group had been given an additional 25 percent free equity in the franchise, Modi observed in one of his tweets, "Who are the shareholders of Rendezvous? And why have they been given this millions of dollars of bonanza?" (Cricinfo, 2010a). Yet another tweet went thus: "25 per cent of Kochi team is given to Rendezvous Sports for life. The same equity is non-dilutable in perpetuity. What does this mean?" (Cricinfo, 2010a). Modi was implying that Sunanda Pushkar, then girlfriend (now wife) of Shashi Tharoor, the state minister for external affairs in the central Indian government, was a shareholder of Rendezvous Sports and that Tharoor, who had declared himself to be a mentor of the Kochi IPL franchise after the auction, had used his position in the Cabinet to get Pushkar the shares.

Peeved at Modi publicizing ownership details, the Kochi franchise wanted the IPL to declare the ownership structures of the existing franchises. The CEO of Rendezvous Sports World, Satyajit Gaekwad, alleged that a week after Kochi had won the franchise Modi had offered a colleague in Rendezvous US$50 million "to quit the game and get out" (Cricinfo, 2010b). Though Modi denied the allegation, he could not stop the issue attracting media attention and more importantly the attention of the tax authorities, who announced a probe into the Kochi franchise auction. When income-tax officials visited the IPL office and Modi's residence in Mumbai a day later, it became evident that the scope of the probe had been broadened to encompass the entire financial goings-on of IPL. Surprisingly, The IPL had not been under the taxman's scanner during the previous three seasons in spite of the money involved in the tournament. Two days later, Tharoor resigned from his Cabinet post and on the very next day the finance minister in the New Delhi administration, Pranab Mukherjee, declared that "all aspects

regarding the funding of the cash-rich tournament was being probed" (Cricinfo, 2010c).

The BCCI president Shashank Manohar convened the IPL governing council, in which Modi was temporarily suspended from his commissioner's post, and Chirayu Amin, the owner of an Indian pharmaceutical giant and head of the Baroda Cricket Association, was elected as the interim IPL chairman. The charges leveled against Modi involved favoritism in granting the bids for the Rajasthan Royals (the Jaipur franchise) and Kings XI Punjab, favoritism in the award of the broadcast deal, a role in the facilitation fee paid by MSM (the channel with the Indian broadcast rights) to WSG, Mauritius (the sports media organization with the global broadcast rights), the rigging of bids for new franchises in 2010, and the sale of internet rights (Cricinfo, 2010d). The interim IPL chairman, Chirayu Amin, admitted the governing council was "dazzled" by the league's success and overlooked issues, but he promised a clean-up that would assure franchise owners and fans of the IPL's stability and viability. "The success of the IPL was so dazzling that we were all basking in its glory," Amin went on to admit, "I must say as a council member that we did overlook things – certain details were not disclosed to us and we did trust Lalit Modi to run things better. I must admit the governing council could have been more vigilant" (Cricinfo, 2010e).

In September 2010, during the BCCI's annual general meeting in Mumbai, the final nail was driven into Modi's coffin by the BCCI. Lalit Modi, the man most closely identified with the IPL, was formally dropped from all the BCCI operations. Shashank Manohar announced that "Modi is not part of the BCCI any more . . . Now he cannot say that he is the suspended IPL chairman" (Cricinfo, 2010f). The BCCI thereby reduced the strength of the IPL governing council and dramatically curtailed its powers in the name of ensuring transparency. After the controversies and scandals swirling round IPL 3, there was much interest to see how IPL 4 would fare. As a relatively controversy-free tournament, and under the more sedate and measured governance of Amin, IPL 4 emerged as a credible cricket tournament that seems likely to stay for the foreseeable future (Mitra, 2010; Ugra, 2011).

In 2010, the brand value of the IPL was put at US$4.13 billion. Reflecting the turmoil surrounding IPL 3, this dropped by 11 percent to US$3.67 billion by the close of its fourth season (Pande, 2011). Though the percentage decline is steep, the IPL is still the most lucrative tournament in the history of cricket. Sharda Ugra (2011) has aptly described the IPL as "cricket's golden goose" attracting the involvement of some of India's largest corporate houses, "men and women with deep pockets and both a love of the limelight and a nose for profit" (Ugra, 2011). Yet it is difficult to predict the course of the IPL over the next few years. Either it could collapse under the weight of scandal, poor governance, audience fatigue, or as a consequence of global recessionary pressures. Or it could recover from the forward momentum of the first two seasons, but on a more measured pace having now established a more secure, transparent structure of governance. Though the future course of the IPL is uncertain, it is clear that it has accelerated the shift in economic and political power in the governance of cricket away from the West to India. As a result of the increased revenues generated by the IPL, the BCCI is now regarded by the international cricket community as the most influential body in world cricket, more influential even than the international governing body, the ICC.

Conclusion

This chapter has located the IPL within the history of cricket and the politics of national identity in India. The concept of post-Westernization was drawn on and extended in order to explicate the economic and political dimensions of the IPL as a form of corporate sport. This historical and analytical framework then paved the way for a narrative of the first four seasons of the IPL from 2008 to 2011. While it is clear that the IPL represents fertile terrain for analysis and critique of contemporary sporting culture and offers a prism through which to critique the politics of neoliberalizing India, it is still too early to draw firm conclusions about the durability of the IPL as a viable product, and its significance and impact on the global sporting landscape.

The IPL is an ongoing and in many ways an open-ended story. It is nonetheless possible to discern a particular trajectory. That trajectory emerges out of the deeply ambiguous nature of the IPL: it challenges anachronistic (erstwhile imperial) forms of authority in the world of cricket but naturalizes and celebrates an American-based corporatist model of sport, as "cricketainment." As such, the IPL may portend the future development of sport: as a media spectacle designed, produced, and packaged as entertainment for the mass market, based on the convergence of the economy, popular culture, and the mass media (including, crucially, new media). It is difficult to be indifferent to the question of what kind of sporting culture the IPL represents. While for some this "strange hybrid of the English village green, 'Bollywood', and the 'Super Bowl'," to recall Rowe and Gilmour's evocative description quoted earlier, is a refreshing and welcome development to be encouraged, for others it offers a dystopian sporting future to be resisted.

References

Alter, J. (1992) *The Wrestler's Body: Ideology and Identity in North India*, Berkeley: University of California Press.

Andrews, D. (2009) "Sport, culture and late capitalism," in Carrington, B. and McDonald, I. (eds.) *Marxism, Cultural Studies and Sport*, London: Routledge, pp. 213–231.

Appadurai, A. (1996) *Modernity at Large: Cultural Dimensions of Globalization*, Minnesota: University of Minnesota Press.

Bale, J. and Maguire, J. (eds.) (2003) *The Global Sports Arena: Athletic Talent Migration in an Interdependent World*, London: Frank Cass.

Bhatt, C. (2001) *Hindu Nationalism: Origins, Ideologies and Modern Myths*, Oxford: Berg.

Bist, R. (2004) "India's great global takeover game." *Asia Times*, June 22, http://www.atimes.com/atimes/South_Asia/FF22Df04.html, accessed January 8, 2013.

Cashman, R. (1980) *Patrons, Players, and the Crowd: The Phenomenon of Indian Cricket*, New Delhi: Orient Longman.

Cricinfo (2006) "ICC rights go to ESPN-star." ESPN-cricinfo, December 9, http://www.espncricinfo.com/ci/content/story/271994.html, accessed January 8, 2013.

Cricinfo (2008) "Big business and Bollywood grab stakes in IPL." ESPNcricinfo, January 24, http://www.espncricinfo.com/ipl/content/story/333193.html, accessed January 8, 2013.

Cricinfo (2010a) "Concerns over revelation of Kochi ownership details." ESPNcricinfo, April 12, http://www.cricinfo.com/ci/content/story/455821.html, accessed January 8, 2013.

Cricinfo (2010b) "We were offered $50 to quit – Kochi Franchise." ESPNcricinfo, April 14, http://www.espncricinfo.com/ipl2010/content/story/456034.html, accessed January 8, 2013.

Cricinfo (2010c) "Government says all aspects of IPL under scrutiny." ESPNcricinfo, April 19, http://www.cricinfo.com/ipl2010/content/story/456592.html, accessed January 8, 2013.

Cricinfo (2010d) "The charges against Lalit Modi." ESPNcricinfo, April 26, http://www.cricinfo.com/ipl2010/content/story/457373.html, accessed January 8, 2013.

Cricinfo (2010e) "Chirayu Amin promises IPL clean-up." ESPNcricinfo, April 27, http://www.cricinfo.com/ipl2010/content/story/457533.html, accessed January 8, 2013.

Cricinfo (2010f) "BCCI makes major changes to IPL governing council." ESPNcricinfo, September 29, http://www.cricinfo.com/india/content/story/479197.html, accessed January 8, 2013.

Cricket Today (2009) Guide to Indian Premier League Season 2, Delhi: Diamond Pocket Books.

Delanty, G. (2006) "Introduction: The idea of a post-Western Europe," in Delanty, G. (ed.) Europe and Asia beyond East and West, London: Routledge, pp. 1–7.

FIFA (2011) "FIFA/Coca-Cola World Ranking," http://www.fifa.com/worldfootball/ranking/lastranking/gender=m/fullranking.html#confederation=0&rank=204&page=3, accessed January 8, 2011.

Guha, R. (1994/1995) "The empire plays back," in Yearbook of the Institute for Advanced Study Berlin.

Guha, R. (2003) A Corner of a Foreign Field: The Indian History of a British Sport, Basingstoke, UK: Palgrave Macmillan.

Guha Ray, S. (2010) "Lalit Modi: India's maverick impresario." BBC News, http://news.bbc.co.uk/1/hi/8643753.stm, accessed January 8, 2011.

Gupta, A. (2009) "India and the IPL: Cricket's globalized empire." The Round Table, 98 (401): 201–211.

Hansen, T.B. (1996) "Globalization and nationalist imagination: Hindutva's promise of equality through difference." Economic and Political Weekly (Mumbai), March 9: 603–616.

Jameson, F. (1991) Postmodernism, or, The Cultural Logic of Late Capitalism, Durham, NC: Duke University Press.

Kurien, C.T. (1994) Global Capitalism and the Indian Economy, New Delhi: Orient Longman.

Majumdar, B. (2007) "Nationalist romance to postcolonial sport: Cricket in 2006 India." Sport in Society, 10: 88–100.

Marqusee, M. (1996) War Minus the Shooting: A Journey Through South Asia during Cricket's World Cup, London: Heinemann.

Marqusee, M. (2005) Anyone But England: An Outsider Looks at English Cricket (3rd edn.), London: Aurum Press.

Marqusee, M. (2010a) "IPL points to a bleak future for cricket." Guardian, March 12, http://www.guardian.co.uk/commentisfree/2010/mar/12/indian-premier-league-just-not-cricket, accessed January 8, 2011.

Marqusee, M. (2010b) "League of scandals." Frontline, 27 (10), http://www.frontlineonnet.com/fl2710/stories/20100521271000400.htm, accessed January 8, 2013.

McDonald, I. (1999) "Between Saleem and Shiva: The politics of cricket nationalism in 'globalising' India," in Sugden, J. and Bairner, A. (eds.) Sport in Divided Societies, Aachen: Meyer & Meyer.

Mehta, N., Gemmell, J., and Malcolm, D. (2009) "Bombay sport exchange: Cricket, globalization and the future." Sport in Society, 12 (4/5): 694–707.

Mills, J. (ed.) (2005) Subaltern Sports: Politics and Sports in South Asia, London: Anthem Press.

Mishra, P. (2006) "The myth of the new India." New York Times, http://www.nytimes.com/2006/07/06/opinion/06mishra.html, accessed January 8, 2013.

Mitra, S. (2010) "The IPL: India's foray into world sports business." Sport in Society, 13: 1314–1333.

Mohan, R. (1996) "Sri Lanka's Cup: The underdogs win the cricket war." Frontline, 13 (8), April 5: 4–9.

Monga, S. (2008) "The day cricketers sold like stocks." ESPNcricinfo, February 20, http://www.espncricinfo.com/ipl2009/content/story/338107.html, accessed January 8, 2013.

Nandy, A. (1989) The Tao of Cricket: On Games of Destiny and the Destiny of Games, New Delhi: Viking and Penguin.

Pande, B. (2011) "IPL-4: IPL's brand value falls by 11% to $ 3.67 billion." Economic Times, April 7, http://articles.economictimes.indiatimes.com/2011-04-07/news/29392570_1_brand-finance-indian-premier-league-ipl, accessed January 8, 2013.

Pawha, N. (2009) "Live Current Media sells IPL portal rights." Medianama, August 31, http://www.medianama.com/2009/08/223-live-current-media-sells-ipl-portal-rights-cricketcom-exits-cricket-biz/, accessed January 8, 2013.

Ravindran, S. and Gollapudi, N. (2010) "Pune and Kochi unveiled as new IPL franchises." ESPNcricinfo, March 21, http://www.espncricinfo.com/

ipl2010/content/story/452856.html, accessed January 8, 2013.

Rowe, D. and Gilmour, C. (2008) "Contemporary media sport: De- or re-Westernization?" *International Journal of Sport Communication*, 1: 177–194.

Rowe, D. and Gilmour, C. (2009) "Global sport: Where Wembley Way meets Bollywood Boulevard." *Continuum: Journal of Media and Cultural Studies*, 23 (2): 171–182.

Rumford, C. (2007) "More than a game: Globalization and the post-Westernization of world cricket." *Global Networks*, 7 (2): 202–214.

Schwartz, P.J. (2009) "The world's hottest sports league." *Forbes Magazine*, http://www.forbes.com/2009/08/27/cricket-india-ipl-business-sports-ipl_print.html, accessed January 8, 2011.

Srinivas, A. and Vivek, T.R. (2009) *IPL An Inside Story: Cricket and Commerce*, New Delhi: Roli Books.

Subramanian, N. (2009) "Terrorists attack Sri Lankan cricket team in Lahore." *The Hindu*, March 4, http://www.hindu.com/2009/03/04/stories/2009030450060100.htm, accessed January 8, 2011.

Times of India (2011) "TIL-Nimbus bag IPL media rights." *Times of India*, March 22, http://timesofindia.indiatimes.com/sports/cricket/ipl-2011/news/TIL-Nimbus-bag-IPL-media-rights/iplarticleshow/7759083.cms, accessed January 18, 2013.

Ugra, S. (2011) "Moving season for the IPL." ESPNcricinfo, May 30, http://www.espncricinfo.com/magazine/content/story/517189.html, accessed January 8, 2012.

Viswanath, G. (2010) "BCCI cancels IPL media rights contract with WSG." *The Hindu*, June 29, http://www.thehindu.com/news/national/article490724.ece, accessed January 8, 2012.

Further Reading

Chakraborty, R.S., Chakrabarti, S., and Chaterjee, K. (2009) *The Politics of Sport in South Asia*, London: Routledge.

Guha, R. (2003) *A Corner of a Foreign Field: The Indian History of a British Sport*, Basingstoke, UK: Palgrave Macmillan.

Srinivas, A. and Vivek, T.R. (2009) *IPL An Inside Story: Cricket and Commerce*, New Delhi: Roli Books.

Part Six

Sporting Celebrities/ Cultural Icons

Introduction

Having discussed the commercialization and spectacularization of sport in various other sections, it is only appropriate to acknowledge the role played by celebrated sporting bodies within these processes. The transformation of sport in the second half of the twentieth century has occurred in tandem with the flourishing of a celebrity culture in which the individual has seemingly become the primary unit of cultural focus and analysis. Indeed, we are presently ensconced within a context that is culturally, economically, and politically driven and defined by an individualism whose virulence shows little sign of abating. Accordingly, the cultural economy of sport throughout the world has become increasingly structured around, and preoccupied by, the exploits of high-profile athletes both on and off their field of sporting endeavor. Even within team sports, the salacious individualism of the popular media habitually reduces them to contests between notorious individuals (be they heroic or anti-heroic, lionized or demonized). The sporting celebrity, meticulously fabricated as these individuals are as iconic figures able to resonate with prevailing popular preferences and sensibilities, has taken on a more central and influential role within cultural life. As sporting celebrities are metonymic personifications and embodied reaffirmations of their derivative societies, analyzing them provides a way to think about the wider politics of class, race, gender, sexuality, disability, and nation.

In the opening chapter, Barry Smart (CHAPTER 30) provides a genealogy of the contemporary global sport icon, tracing its roots back to Greek antiquity. Therein, the likeness, or *eikon*, of heroic or noteworthy competitors was cast in statue or other representative form. These iconic Greek figures were created because their exceptional performances rendered them worthy of having their image preserved in perpetuity. Smart draws a parallel between the genesis of the sport icon in ancient Greek culture, and an intensified phase of development during the late nineteenth and early twentieth centuries. During this time (a period broaching the 1890s and 1930s at either end), a series of technological innovations in the mass communications industries (most notably the rise of newspaper, magazine, radio, and cinema platforms), combined with the institutionalization and popularization of various sport forms and competitions, precipitated the creation of a new economy of sporting icons. Prompted by the demand of the new media platforms to produce audience engaging content, sport figures such as W.G. Grace in the United Kingdom, Suzanne

A Companion to Sport, First Edition. Edited by David L. Andrews and Ben Carrington.
© 2013 Blackwell Publishing Ltd. Published 2013 by Blackwell Publishing Ltd.

Lenglen in France, and Babe Ruth in the United States, were acclaimed as iconic figures to national and international publics alike. Smart brings the discussion into the television age – and into the age of corporate sport – through recourse to the emergence of Michael Jordan as the quintessential late twentieth-century global sport icon. He posits Jordan as a symbolic expression of global capitalism's ability to transcend national and cultural boundaries, through the global dissemination of sporting imagery, iconography, and ancillary products. It is through this combination of sporting spectacularization, celebritization, and commodification, that figures such as Jordan become globally ubiquitous and familiar. However, Smart also illustrates how shifts in the world economic order, associated with contemporary processes of globalization, have led to the one-time Western domination of the global sporting landscape being challenged by the emergence of non-Western icons such as Sachin Tendulkar (the Indian cricketer), and Yao Ming (the Chinese basketball player).

C.L. Cole and Michael D. Giardina (CHAPTER 31) focus on the iconic figure of the athletic body of the young female white suburbanite which, as they demonstrate, has been a highly valorized and protected part of American nationalist ideology over the past six decades. Whether this iconic figure is celebrated or is referred to in the ubiquitous abstract, Cole and Giardina illustrate how this emotive embodied form has been mobilized to corroborate America's position of exceptionalism, as realized through its combination of moral, cultural, and political superiority. In doing so, these racially and class-coded female athlete bodies are covertly politicized, inasmuch as they have come to represent an American Way of Life, both under threat and in need of protection. The authors' initial example of this process of national differentiation on and through the bodies of female athletes is the anxiety and vitriol which arose following the success of Soviet-bloc athletes in the 1950s and 1960s. Typified by the vilified figure of the highly successful Soviet shot-putter and discus-thrower Tamara Press, the very achievements of these athletes excited American Cold War stereotypes related to the Communist violations of femininity, and the contravening of the *natural* boundaries upon which patriarchal American democracy relied (man/woman,

human/machine, free will/compulsion, American self/Soviet other). Thus, demonized iconic figures such as Press were positioned as threats to idealized forms of white suburban athletic femininity, as metonymic personifications of the American gender formation, and American society more generally. Interestingly, as Cole and Giardina observe, the post-Cold War era has not witnessed a diminution in the influence of this iconic American figure. Rather, the Other threatening white suburban girls, and against whom they need protection, has been explicitly racialized. The Soviet-bloc gender and sex deviant has now been replaced by an enemy from within: the performance-enhancing drug-taking athlete, habitually coded as black, responsible for denying their necessarily virtuous white counterpart of their right to natural, untainted sporting competition. Thus, once celebrated, now demonized, figures such as Marion Jones are affective forces in the re-enchantment of pernicious American ideologies that locate the bodies of white suburban girl athletes – as the progeny of long-coveted heteronormative, racially exclusive, and hierarchical class relations – as the normalized, and normalizing, locus of American life.

While Cole and Giardina point to the process whereby othered sporting bodies contribute to the reinscription of a dominant racial order, Daniel Burdsey (CHAPTER 32) provides an insight into how such nation-based racial formations are disrupted, or at the very least contested. Specifically, Burdsey discusses the iconic figure of Monty Panesar, a British Asian man with Indian parents, who became the first Sikh to play Test Match cricket for England (and indeed the first Sikh to represent any other Test-playing nation apart from India). According to Burdsey, Panesar's background is emblematic of the migrant trajectories of thousands of Indians, Pakistanis, and Bangladeshis, who helped establish the sizeable and vibrant South Asian communities and cultures within the United Kingdom. As such, Panesar can be considered a sporting expression of the "new" Asian Britishness that has emerged (in numerous cultural settings and expressions) in the United Kingdom within the decades either side of the turn of the twenty-first century. Having identified Panesar's broader sociocultural derivation, Burdsey critically examines the popular representations of his highly visible presence within the English cricketing landscape. He illustrates how the popular discourses that enveloped, and helped constitute, the Panesar phenomenon occupy an uncomfortable space between patronizing celebration and demeaning mockery. Hence, the depiction of Panesar as a performatively challenged yet affable figure of amusement is far from innocent, rooted as it is in stereotypical assumptions about South Asian physicality and deference. Significantly, as Burdsey suggests, the popular representation of Panesar (as with that of any minority ethnic sport icon) speaks to the nuances and complexities of the politics of race and multiculturalism within contemporary Britain. In being positioned as the acceptable face of British multiculturalism, with his religiously, politically, and ethnically understated South Asian persona, the popular celebration of Panesar authorizes Britain's self-congratulatory status as a racially tolerant and progressive modern nation, and, by association, the continuance of the prevalent extremist racist stereotypes against which Panesar's atypical affability and acceptability is defined.

Focusing on another purported icon of commercialized multiculturalism, Davis W. Houck (CHAPTER 33) offers an alternative reading of the Tiger Woods phenomenon, focusing on the influence of his father, Earl Woods, who occupied the unusual dual role of father and cultural intermediary. Unlike other accounts, which privilege the role of corporate advertisers, brand managers, and image consultants in the fabrication of the Tiger Woods mythos, Houck points to the central importance of Earl Woods in rhetorically framing the Woods odyssey and persona. The chapter provides a critical interrogation of the racially inflected (as opposed to deflected) rhetorical reinvention of Tiger Woods by his self-preoccupied father; the inference being that Earl Woods overlaid his own racial politics upon a somewhat racially ambivalent Tiger Woods. Houck suggests that Earl Woods single-mindedly engaged in a public form of *post facto* rationalization of his son's very being, and his role in its creation. This cast Tiger Woods as a heavenly ordained and meticulously planned project, groomed as a vehicle for subverting the dominant racial order both in golf and thereby in American society more generally. Earl Woods' mission was advanced through an intertextual media barrage,

wherein various print and television outlets were mobilized in retrofitting Tiger Woods' imaged identity to the pseudo-progressive racial sensibilities of the contemporary American moment. According to Houck, Earl Woods' hand clearly guided the unselfconsciously racial overtones of the notorious (in terms of the public reaction it generated) *Hello World* Nike commercial, which announced Tiger Woods to the broader American populace in 1997. Subsequently, Earl Woods advanced a series of books that carefully cultivated his son's racial and social significance, while simultaneously reinscribing his own indispensable role in the process. Houck draws particular critical attention to the alleged fabrication of an incident of race-based violence against Tiger Woods during his childhood, and to Earl Woods' promulgation of Tiger Woods' long-standing fears of being assassinated while playing golf in the American South. Herein, Earl Woods is presumed to have recognized – and advanced – the cultural, political, and economic value of "fabricating" a figure who had overcome discrimination in the playground, was overcoming it on the golf course, while still being conscious and concerned with the threats posed by his (Earl-proclaimed) sociopolitical significance and potential martyr status.

Finally, Pirkko Markula (CHAPTER 34) extends the understanding of the role of the individual – celebrated or otherwise – in constructing his or her own subjective identities and experiences. Whereas Houck demonstrates how Earl Woods, and to a lesser extent his son, attempted yet ultimately failed to manage his identity project, Markula uses the life experiences of Finnish athlete Tuija Helander to problematize dominant models of identity construction. Of course, Markula's focus is on furthering the understandings of disability, disabled bodies, and disability sport, since Helander is a public figure within Finland, initially renowned for her success as an elite athlete, but later known as a lung-transplant receiver, and successful disabled athlete (despite the exclusion of her category of disability from the frames of Paralympic sport). Markula brings her able-bodied, non-athlete, feminist researcher sensibilities to bear upon the complexities of Helander's life, through a considered engagement with the theorizing of Gilles Deleuze, and problematizes the biomedical, social, and narrative models of disability as an inadequate means by which to understand the complexity of being disabled. Instead, Markula advocates a Deleuzian, rhizomatic approach to reimagining the disabled body. Centered on notions of the individual being involved in the continual process of creating relationships, connections, and affect, this approach offers a corrective to the linear progression implicit within social and narrative models of disabled identity construc-

tion. Through a semi-structured interview with Helander, Markula elicits insights which both confirm and complicate her Deleuzian framework. Helander also reveals the complex power relations underpinning the classification and marginalization of disabled bodies, and highlights the various constituencies with whom she is able to connect, and affect, as a well-known transplant-receiver/athlete. Thus, Markula is able to focus on Helander's body as one in the process of actively becoming.

Further Reading

Coad, D. (2008) *The Metrosexual: Gender, Sexuality, and Sport*, Albany: State University of New York Press.

Heywood, L. and Dworkin, S. (2003) *Built to Win: The Female Athlete as Cultural Icon*, Minneapolis: University of Minnesota Press.

Rojek, C. (2001) *Celebrity*, London: Reaktion.

Smart, B. (2005) *The Sport Star: Modern Sport and the Cultural Economy of Sporting Celebrity*, London: Sage Publications.

Whannel, G. (2001) *Media Sport Stars: Masculinities and Moralities*, London: Routledge.

30

Global Sporting Icons
Consuming Signs of Economic and Cultural Transformation

Barry Smart

Introduction: Fame from Games, Ancient and Modern

From the sacred games of classical antiquity and throughout the history of modern sport, individual competitors have achieved fame and attracted popular interest and acclaim for their performances. Individuals deemed worthy of identification and elevation in status by virtue of their victories, their skills, and the qualities and dedication displayed in competition have been revered as heroes by devoted followers of games and sporting spectacles and their achievements have become matters of public record, recognition, and celebration. From the figurative elevation of successful competitors through the construction of statues in classical antiquity, to the newspaper reports, photographs, and electronic images of modern times, the likenesses of successful competitors have been subject to various forms of public representation and record which have served to evoke memories of performances, confirm heroic qualities, social standing, and cultural significance, and increasingly in late modern societies, signify other attributes such as celebrity status, commercial appeal, and wealth.

As modern sports were becoming established in the late nineteenth and early twentieth centuries in Europe and North America a number of sporting figures achieved heroic status and popular acclaim for their sporting endeavors, not only in their local or national cultural milieu but also, by virtue of the growth of international competition and communication networks, around the world, a development which served to further enhance their standing. For example, in the late nineteenth century the cricketer W.G. Grace transcended "the limits of cricket . . . [and] was soon as well known as anyone in England – by name, by appearance and by that indefinable quality of newsworthiness" (Birley, 2003: 108). Grace did not only help to establish the game of cricket as a national institution in England, his fame spread to the colonies too, and on overseas tours he was "the main attraction, the one everyone wanted to see" (Birley, 2003: 122). A popular hero, Grace enjoyed "the spontaneous, unqualified . . . enthusiasm and goodwill of a whole community" (James, 1969: 182). In his prime he was "the most famous of all English sportsmen and certainly the first national sporting hero" (Holt, 1996: 54).

A Companion to Sport, First Edition. Edited by David L. Andrews and Ben Carrington.
© 2013 Blackwell Publishing Ltd. Published 2013 by Blackwell Publishing Ltd.

In 1919 a 20-year-old Frenchwoman, Suzanne Lenglen, a tennis-player who had never before played on grass, arrived at Wimbledon and proceeded to win the ladies' singles championship at the first attempt and again in each of the following four years. Reports of her tournament successes, powerful style of play, and departure from traditional tennis dress conventions led to her becoming a "household name," one of the first women in sport to be "referred to in the press by her first name" (Walker, 1989: 263). When in 1926 Helen Wills, the United States Lawn Tennis Association's women's singles title holder and number-one-ranked player, traveled to the French Riviera to play in a winter tournament the world's press were in attendance to report on her match with Suzanne Lenglen and described it as "an international grudge match between the United States and France" (Bouchier and Findling, 1983: 239). Suzanne Lenglen became a publicly well-known figure not simply for her remarkable playing successes, which included six Wimbledon and French championships, but also through media representations of the ways in which she was believed to be "actively redefining female sports" and disrupting "conventional images of femininity," which by the time she turned professional in 1926 had led to her becoming "in modern terms, a superstar" (Hargreaves, 1994: 116–117).

Another example is provided by American amateur golfer Bobby Jones who became "famous even to people who knew and cared little" about his sport (Inglis, 1977: 83–85). Jones had an outstanding playing record in the 1920s and his achievement of a Grand Slam in 1930 by winning the British and American Open championships and the British and American Amateur tournaments led to him being described as one of the few amateur sporting heroes, a "casual hero," an outstandingly successful player who acquired the status of a "truly national, even international, golfing celebrity" (Inglis, 1977: 84; Rader, 1983a: 229).

The late nineteenth century and early decades of the twentieth century constituted a period in which professionalism began to have an increasing impact on the development of modern sport as the figure of the amateur began to be displaced by the paid athlete, and in due course increasing growth in media coverage led to the emergence of the sporting celebrity (Rader, 1983a; Smart, 2005). Accounts of games and performances, conveyed in narratives and images in newspapers, radio reports, and later in television coverage and over the internet, have become increasingly influential sources of representations of modern sporting figures, serving to build their reputations, raise their profiles locally and in some instances globally, and over time to transform a minority into virtual legends (Rader, 1983a; McChesney, 1989; Whitson, 1998; Smart, 2005).

Modern electronic media have increasingly eroded differences of "space and time as far as our planet is concerned," transcending the boundaries to communication arising from social and cultural distinctions, and in an "electrically contracted" world the features of very successful sporting figures have become increasingly familiar to the majority of people around the globe (McLuhan, 1973: 11, 12–13). For example, as the twentieth century was drawing to a close US basketball star Michael Jordan, by virtue of satellite television coverage of his outstanding performances for the Chicago Bulls and his prominence in Nike advertising campaigns shown on television screens around the world, was being described as "the first great athlete of the wired world" and as "the global star of a global show" (Halberstam, 1991: 76).

Through the course of the twentieth century several interconnected transformations contributed to the elevation of talented sporting performers to a status on a par with figures from the worlds of entertainment and popular music. Readily available jet air travel made it possible for sport governing bodies and commercial organizations to construct a busy global tournament schedule, safe in the knowledge that leading competitors would be able to participate on a regular basis, which in turn attracted increasing global media coverage and commercial sponsorship (Courier, 2004). Increasing media coverage, especially with the development of television, and satellite television in particular, raised the global profile of sports competitors and sporting events. Growing commercial recognition of sport's cultural capital led to increases in the scale and value of sponsorship of sporting events and endorsement contracts with sporting figures. Such transformations have made it possible for a number of sportsmen and a few sportswomen to acquire international reputations, to become recognized around the world, elevated to a status that is not directly connected with "their teams or even, at times, . . . their sport" and in some instances high-profile sporting competitors have been accorded the status of "global icons" (Klein, 2001: 51).

In the following analysis of the economic and cultural processes that have contributed to the transformation of high-profile sporting figures into global icons, consideration will be given to: (1) icons in sport: ancient and modern; (2) global sporting icons; (3) Sachin Tendulkar and Indian cricket; (4) basketball icons: Michael Jordan and Yao Ming; (5) Athens 2004: Reebok's classical simulation of the Parthenon friezes; (6) iconic global sports brands: Nike and Adidas; (7) consuming icons: Tiger Woods and Thierry Henry.

Icons: Heroes, Stars, and Celebrities

The term "icon" is now used with increasing frequency to describe particular individuals from the world of sport who have become well-known and popular public figures by virtue of a variable combination of closely interconnected factors. These factors include outstanding achievements in a particular sporting field, the scale of financial rewards received from playing professional sport and taking advantage of commercial endorsement opportunities which are now a corollary of sporting success, the wealth subsequently accumulated and lifestyle led, and the media interest attracted which, in turn, serves to create, then to elevate, public profile and reinforces, if it does not increase, the sporting figure's commercial value. By the early years of the twenty-first century the designation of high- and not-so-high-profile sports competitors as "icons" had virtually become the default setting in media narratives on sporting figures.

However, the idea of sporting figures as icons is not peculiar to the modern age. The phenomenon has a long history, one which extends back to the civilizations of classical antiquity. The term "icon" comes from the Greek word *eikon* meaning "likeness" as portrayed in a statue or another form of representation. In classical antiquity effigies were made of heroic competitors, the great majority being men, who by virtue of an exceptional deed or performance were considered to be

"worthy of having their memory perpetuated" (Pollitt, 1990: 30). Historical records reveal that from the sixth century BC when athletes – chariot-racers, discus-throwers, runners, wrestlers – had gained victory in a sacred event, especially at Olympia, a statue would be dedicated to them. Those who had been winners three times would have had a likeness of their features molded, their "effigies" being called "iconicae" or "icons" (Pollitt, 1990: 30). In a few instances women who had bred horses that were successful in chariot races had statues erected in their name.[1] The icons and inscriptions that often accompanied them provided a public representation of heroic competitors and their achievements, a permanent public record of a heroic victory or event.

The icon/statue has continued to be a medium for representing celebrated modern sporting figures from the past whose local and/or national sporting achievements are considered to make them worthy of memory. For example, there is a statue of Babe Ruth, the American major league baseball player, regarded by many as the greatest ever, in Oriole Park at Camden Yards in Baltimore, MD. An icon of Jesse Owens, the African American athlete who won four gold medals at the 1936 Berlin Olympic Games, stands in Jesse Owens Memorial Park, AL. A statue of Bobby Moore, captain of England's 1966 World Cup-winning (association) football team faces down Olympic Way at the new Wembley Stadium in London. Ruth, Owens, and Moore are widely recognized heroic competitors, iconic sporting figures, worthy of remembrance in a manner that bears comparison with the revered figures of classical antiquity whose icons confirmed their place in public memory. There are, of course, other comparable examples, including Jackie Robinson (baseball – Daytona Beach, FL and Jersey City, NJ), Sir Stanley Matthews (football – Britannia Stadium, Stoke, UK), Fred Perry (tennis – Wimbledon), Joe Louis (boxing – Detroit), and exceptionally in an institution that remains male dominated, Suzanne Lenglen (tennis – Roland Garros Stadium, Paris), heroic sporting figures whose achievements warranted and received public recognition in the form of icons/statues.

In America in the period following World War I, and to a lesser extent in Europe, organized sport and sporting figures became an important reporting focus for the developing new media of popular culture (mass-circulation magazines, film, and radio). Disillusioned with war, their lives disturbed by the impact of increasing economic and technological change, people sought solace, distraction, and compensation in the performances of popular cultural figures whose media were film, stage, and entertainment, and in a comparable manner enthusiastically acclaimed the successes of sports figures whose achievements, suitably embellished in media narratives, led them to be designated sporting heroes and stars on a par with those who achieved popularity on stage and screen. In the 1920s, what has been described as the "Golden Age of American Sport," heroes seemed to emerge from virtually every field of sport as journalists and radio reporters constructed compelling images of sporting figures and their achievements and the general public found in the fame and fortune gained by successful competitors compensation "for the passing of the traditional dream of success, the erosion of Victorian values, and feelings of individual powerlessness" (Rader, 1983b: 11).

The continuing development of modern organized sport in the course of the twentieth century, especially the growth of professionalism and the increasing influence of cultural intermediaries in journalism and broadcasting, whose reports have contributed so significantly to the cultural prominence accorded to sporting figures, led concerns to be expressed about the impact such developments were having on the ethos of sport and its potential capacity to nurture "the natural impulses of generosity, elation, heroism, grace [and] decorum" (Inglis, 1977: 35). The influences to which sport and sports competitors have been exposed – increasing professionalism and associated forms of commercialism, as well as a significant growth in media coverage – have led to an increasingly close articulation between the worlds of sport and business, prompting one analyst to designate the emerging cultural and economic form "sportsbiz" (Aris, 1990). Reflecting critically on such developments other analysts have expressed concerns about the loss of sport's "play spirit" and have drawn attention to signs of its degeneration as it has succumbed to "over-seriousness" and a "spectator-orientation" and competitors have been transformed into stars and celebrities who increasingly are "no longer playing . . . for the sake of the game'" but more and more

as a means to improve standing or ranking, raise profile, and enhance brand value and wealth (Inglis, 1977: 155; see also Huizinga, 1949; Hoch, 1972; Rader, 1984; Lasch, 1991; Smart, 2011).

The culture and economy of sport have been dramatically transformed by the growth in media coverage and increase in commercialism. The associated transformation of sporting events and contests into "spectacles" is designed, and is increasingly scheduled, primarily for the entertainment of global television audiences, with stadium spectators serving to complete the cast of "players," albeit off the field, pitch, or court, their presence providing a potential stock of colorful editorialized television images and, more importantly, generating essential qualities of atmosphere and excitement conducive to good live television and buoyant viewing figures. But more significantly, growing media coverage of sports events and the increasing media exposure associated with commercial sponsorship and endorsement opportunities have had a dramatic impact on the public standing and profile of a number of sports competitors.

Contemporary competitive sporting events seem less often to produce moments of genuine heroism. Competitors are now rarely described as heroes and when they are it is questionable whether the description is truly warranted. Late modern professional sportsmen and sportswomen, often armed with exceedingly lucrative playing and commercial endorsement contracts, may from time to time display some of the qualities which have been equated with heroism – "strength, courage, tenacity, endurance . . . sweat and toil" – but only rarely are such qualities deployed, and even then not exclusively, "on behalf of a larger constituency" (Gilchrist, 2005: 122). The late modern professional sportsperson frequently has employed a personal team dedicated to looking after their interest; personal trainers, fitness coaches, agents, and media advisors, for whom the only "constituency" that really counts in the final instance is the player, in particular their playing success, popularity, media profile, and brand value. This creates particular difficulties – tensions and contradictions – in respect of team sports where the all-for-one-and-one-for-all notion of team-spirit is deemed to be so vital for success and frequent reference is made to the importance of loyalty to team or club, signified in some team sports by the staged gesture of kissing the club badge or emblem and the ritualized end-of-game applause given and thanks shown to fans who have paid considerable sums of money to attend the event, often attired in costly team merchandise. Such theatrical simulations of team loyalty and club and community affinity sit uneasily alongside the narcissistic individualism often displayed by players and the increasing frequency with which they are inclined to demand a renegotiation of their contracts or seek to move from one club or team to another to achieve improved terms, an increasingly prominent feature of many modern team sports and Premiership football in particular. Already very well rewarded, players and their agents seem ever ready to initiate contract negotiations for even more lucrative terms, using the threat to join a new club or organization which will meet the desired new terms and to which, should a move occur, the player would in due course rapidly transfer expressions of "loyalty" (Smart, 2011).

Contemporary media references to an athlete or player as an "icon" now generally signify something more than that the individual in question is worthy of memory for the consistently outstanding quality of their sporting performances. Descriptions of a contemporary athlete or player as an icon suggest, in addition to sporting performance and competitive success, other attributes or qualities, including popular cultural profile, commercial appeal, and prominent media presence, as well as, by implication, wealth and a celebrity lifestyle. More often than not the iconic figure will be a sports*man*, an individual whose high media profile has made him well known in a local, national, and/or global context, even to those with little or no interest in sport, for whom the individual in question will be known not so much as a player or competitor, but rather as a celebrity figure, as a recognizable "face" (Klein, 2001).

Global Sporting Icons

A wide range of past and present sporting figures have been designated as "global icons," including Muhammad Ali (boxing), Pelé (association football), Michael Jordan (basketball),Tiger Woods (golf), Michael Phelps (swimming), David Beckham (association football), and Roger Federer (tennis). The media, eager to maintain a supply of "good copy," have continually talked up the prospects of other potential icons, with LeBron James (basketball) and Andy Murray (tennis) being merely the latest in a long line of competitors described as likely candidates for comparable global status, if only they could secure victories in the National Basketball Association (NBA) championship and a Grand Slam tennis tournament, preferably Wimbledon, respectively. LeBron James duly delivered when he led the Miami Heat to victory over the Oklahoma City Thunder in the 2012 NBA finals, as did Andy Murray when he won the gold medal in the men's singles tennis competition at Wimbledon in the London Olympics in the summer of 2012, defeating Roger Federer in three sets, and a month later at Flushing Meadows became US Open Champion.[2]

Tennis is a sport in which women have participated since the game's inception. Female tennis players have campaigned for and gained equality in prize money in the major tournaments, the Grand Slams, and the most successful players have attracted substantial media coverage and considerable commercial endorsement interest. But while some past and present female players, for example Billie-Jean King, Martina Navratilova, and Venus and Serena Williams, have acquired a high media profile, international recognition, and wealth, they have not been accorded comparable iconic status to their male, predominantly American and European, counterparts, even though in respect of playing success, and sporting and wider cultural impact, the designation may appear to be warranted (Smart, 2005). The fact that gender continues to be a differentiating factor in respect of the attribution of global iconic status to high-profile sporting figures serves as confirmation of the enduring patriarchal character of the institution of sport and the processes of media representation that are an integral, and increasingly necessary, part of its operation. Notwithstanding their generally lower global profiles, there are a number of female sporting figures, including King, Navratilova, and the Williams sisters, for whom a good case may be made for iconic status (Overman and Boyer Sagert, 2012).

As two critical observers of the predominantly Western-orientated and American dominated media identification of sporting figures and evaluation and description of sporting prowess and popularity have noted:

> there is a ... tendency to ignore, or at least overlook, a broader range of sporting heroes; individuals who, to all intents and purposes, mean just as much (if not more) to millions of people as national and international celebrities and yet who, for some or other reason, are not considered in quite the same way. (Nalapat and Parker, 2005: 434).[3]

Consideration is given below to two genuinely iconic sporting figures from what has tended to be regarded as the global periphery, two individuals whose relatively marginal status compared to their American and European peers serves in some respects at least to validate the criticism outlined above. Sachin Tendulkar is an Indian cricketer, playing in a sport whose global configuration is changing as it continues to grow in popularity and its political economy and locus of power are significantly transformed by developments on and off the field of play. Yao Ming is a Chinese basketball player from Shanghai whose move to the NBA had a considerable impact on the world of basketball, which has continued its pursuit of global audiences by cultivating potentially lucrative new markets for the sport.

Tendulkar and Indian Cricket

The individuals who have tended to be identified as global sporting icons are invariably American or European and this "geographical and cultural myopia" has led to a relative neglect of sporting figures from (formerly) subaltern cultures and sporting fields, in particular in respect of the Indian subcontinent, the cricketer Sachin Tendulkar, an outstanding and acclaimed competitor and a popular and influential cultural figure within Indian society and diaspora, who has not received the recognition his playing ability, record, and popularity warrant within a "global sport-media complex" oriented primarily towards American and European competitors (Nalapat and Parker, 2005: 434; Maguire, 1999: 146–149).

Tendulkar has been described as a "man of the masses," a symbol of Indian nationhood, and by the late 1990s as "not only famous for his cricketing prowess," or for the celebrity status and instant recognition he received from the public "because of his popular cultural exposure," but as a "fully-fledged sporting icon" (Nalapat and Parker, 2005: 435).

Tendulkar's iconic status is given form through multiple cultural representations of his de-centered identity as "the very face of Indian cricket ... national hero; a 'sporting God' ... [and] the greatest Indian alive" (Nalapat and Parker, 2005: 436) and is bound up with, on the one hand, increasing consumerism, the market economy, and the growth of Indian media and entertainment industries and, on the other hand, a related emergence of a more confident nationalism and expressive patriotism, in respect of which he is deemed to be a "pivotal figure," being described in *Wisden* in 2011 as "the balm of the nation" (Nalapat and Parker, 2005: 436; Guha, 2011: 97). Commercial recognition has followed Tendulkar's multifaceted rise in status, reflecting and significantly reinforcing his popular standing, media profile, and designation as a sporting icon. In 2002 he was reported to hold endorsement contracts with a range of top brands that included "Visa ... Pepsi, Colgate, Boost, Philips ... and Fiat" (Rizvi, 2002) and in 2004 the managing director designate of Adidas India reaffirmed Tendulkar's reputation, popularity, and expanding iconic status, by announcing that they would "use him as a global ambassador" (Razdan, 2004).

Further testimony both to Tendulkar's ascent to something like global iconic status and to the increasingly close articulation between sporting and cultural capital and commercial value and marketing appeal, emerged in June 2009 with Kraken Opus, the British publishing company which publishes limited-edition books on "the biggest names in sport, fashion, music and the arts," announcing a forthcoming *Tendulkar Opus* and the launch of *Tendulkaropus.com*. At a special media event held in the Opus Store in London the assembled photographers and reporters from news organizations around the world witnessed Tendulkar provide a mouth-swab sample, to be used in conjunction with DNA technology to create a two-meter wide multicolored artwork showing "the make-up of a sporting genius," and sign a number of "signature sheets" to be included in the *Tendulkar Opus* publication. As with comparable Opus editions on Arsenal, Celtic, Ferrari, Manchester United, Maradona, and other iconic global sports brands, the *Tendulkar Opus* constitutes a truly monumental publication, "weighing in at over 30 kilos, 800 pages in length, with each page measuring half a metre square" and containing exclusive photographs and special features "among the 1,000 images and 150,000 words" (Opus, 2009).

In the summer of 2010 it was reported that Opus editions were producing a very limited special edition of the *Tendulkar Opus*, just 10 copies of which would be printed, each having Tendulkar's blood mixed in with paper pulp to create the signature page for the book. In response to media interest aroused by the prospect of such a controversial limited edition the CEO of Kraken Media, the publisher of Opus publications, was reported to have remarked that for millions of people Sachin Tendulkar "is a religious icon. And we thought how, in a publishing form, can you get as close to your god as possible?" (Flood, 2010). However, Sachin Tendulkar moved quickly to put an end to the unsavory speculation by telling the *Times of India* (2010) that "There is no truth in my blood being part of the book. The book is basically a photographic publication that celebrates my life and is not an autobiography or a biography."

The selection of Sachin Tendulkar as the subject of an Opus publication, the only cricketer to date to be chosen, did not only reflect his particular status as a record-breaking batsman but also represented recognition of the transformed political economy of late modern cricket. The announcement in 2007 of the Indian Premier League (IPL) Twenty20 competition served as further confirmation of a significant process of transformation already underway in cricket, a shift in the locus of power and influence in the game away from its traditional roots at Lords and the England and Wales Cricket Board, to the Asian subcontinent, more specifically to Mumbai and the Board of Control for Cricket in India (Mitchell, 2006; Suliman, 2008). Cricket has been very popular in India from the colonial era and a late modern combination of a population of a billion or more people with an insatiable appetite for the game, including a "fairly well-off middle-class of some 350 million," who have been the principal beneficiaries of recent rises in economic growth rates and commensurate increases in consumerism, together with increasing television coverage and associated revenue generation, has dramatically redefined the political economy of the sport, the upshot of which is that India now effectively runs cricket (Mitchell, 2006; Suliman, 2008; Smart, 2011).

The development of the IPL in 2008 demonstrated India's increasing economic prowess. Eight city franchise teams were established based in Mumbai, Delhi, Kolkata, Bangalore, Jaipur, Chennai, Chandigarh, and Hyderabad, many of them owned by wealthy entrepreneurs, celebrities, and Bollywood stars, who bid against each other, via an electronically controlled auction, to hire leading cricketers from India and around the world who were attracted to play in the new league by the prospect of earning "as much as £500,000 or more for five weeks work, the sort of money top Premier League footballers get but until now cricketers have only dreamt of" (Bose, 2008; BBC, 2008). India now accounts for "80% of world cricket's income, largely through television rights" (Bose, 2008) and has begun to assume the mantle of the "superpower of cricket," a status powerfully confirmed by the successful introduction by the innovative IPL of 20-over matches played under floodlights (Ganguli, 2008). As a close observer of the game noted, "[f]or the first time in the history of modern sports, a major game is now controlled by a non-European power" (Bose, 2008), but India's ascent to dominance in respect of the political economy of cricket was not mirrored in its playing record in the International Cricket Council Test Match and one-day international rankings, although it did reach the number one Test-ranking position in late 2009 (ICC, 2009).

The IPL and the United States

In his observations on India's increasing influence over cricket Bose (2008) comments that the governance of world sport has tended to be a predominantly European affair, one in which France played a significant part in the late nineteenth and early twentieth centuries by initiating the development in 1894 of the International Olympic Committee and the modern Olympic movement, as well as the foundation in 1904 of the Fédération Internationale de Football Association (FIFA), and that subsequently Europe has "reigned supreme." While the United States is acknowledged to have had a significant influence on economic, cultural, and political life, in Bose's opinion it has had "very little influence" in the world of sport. This is a surprising view, one which fails to recognize a wide range of significant American influences, including the extensive commercialization of sport, and the impact of sponsorship and endorsement initiatives in particular, which became evident first in America; the very significant influence of American sports television coverage innovations, conventions, and styles of reporting, not to mention the effect of rising broadcasting rights revenues on the political economy of all televised sports; the introduction of formats and values from the world of entertainment which have contributed to the "spectacularization of sport," and the related incorporation of sports stars into a culture of celebrity (Goldman and Papson, 1998: 64; Smart, 2005; 2007: 130).

The United States has undoubtedly, to date, had very little impact on cricket, although it is worth recalling the explanation offered by Henry Chadwick for the respectively different appeal of the traditional game of cricket, correctly identified as part of the colonial legacy, and baseball, which was developing rapidly in late 1850s America, and, by virtue of what would ultimately prove to be an unfounded indigenous creation story, was accorded a distinctively American origin (Levine, 1985; Pope, 1997; Smart, 2005). Chadwick is reported to have commented that baseball fitted in better with the American way of life than cricket, because Americans do "[w]hat they want to do in a hurry . . . [and] do not care to dawdle over a sleep-inspiring game" (cited in Pope, 1997: 60–61). Twenty20 certainly fits in better with the hectic pace of late modern life, the demands of television scheduling, and the increasingly competitive commercial imperatives to which broadcasting is subject and to which it has to respond, and the new game format has significantly increased cricket's appeal to the television industry and enhanced its attractiveness to spectators who have not been drawn to the more traditional game.

The success of Twenty20 has led some consideration to be given to areas of potential convergence with baseball, for example it has been noted that there is a similarity in the average time now required to complete the respective games, and that it is possible that baseball's attention to statistical detail may be appropriate and beneficial to the new form of cricket, a view which has been endorsed by New Zealand cricketer Jacob Oram (Cleaver, 2009). But of even greater potential significance is the prospect of the development of US premier league cricket along the lines of the IPL format. The USA Cricket Association announced in July 2009 that it was planning to introduce top-class international cricket in America, already "the second biggest market in the world for cricket television broadcast rights and Internet revenues," where it is reported there are some 15 million fans, "mostly from the South Asian diaspora," and around 200,000 cricketers (Majumdar, 2009). Later that year a strategic partnership was forged with New Zealand cricket to advance the game in the region. In February 2010 the United States participated in the ICC world Twenty20 qualifiers, losing to Afghanistan in their first match in Dubai (UAE); in May the United States played two Twenty20 matches against Jamaica, and in the same month in Florida a historic two-match series between Sri Lanka and New Zealand took place, the first international matches between full ICC members to be held in the United States. It is worth adding that cricket is played in schools in nine states and in over 40 universities across the country, so there is a reasonable grassroots foundation from which to proceed to try to realize the stated USA Cricket Association ambition to be "one of the top 15 cricket playing nations by 2015" (Majumdar, 2009).

Basketball Icons: From Qiao Dan to Yao Ming

In basketball US ambitions have long been realized. Indeed basketball might plausibly claim to be *the* American sport insofar as its origin, unlike baseball and gridiron football, which have their roots in stick-and-ball and folk football games that were brought to the American colonies by

European settlers in the seventeenth century, is vested firmly in the United States, in the persona of James Naismith, a physical education instructor at the Young Men's Christian Association (YMCA) International Training School in Springfield, MA, who is credited with developing the game in the 1890s as an indoor winter sport (Smart, 2005). The game grew in popularity throughout the twentieth century, slowly at first in colleges, then erratically with the establishment of professional leagues, some of which only survived for a few years, finally achieving a degree of stability with the formation of the NBA in 1949. From the late 1960s improved television contracts were secured, viewing audiences increased, and the game's national profile grew. Following the advent of satellite television in the late 1970s and the establishment of Entertainment Sports Programming Network (ESPN), the quantity of television program time available increased significantly and sports events, already taking place, with relatively low production costs, providing potentially dramatic images, and most importantly of all of unrivaled popularity, especially with significant advertising target audiences, were identified as preeminently suitable content. Coverage of college sports, including basketball, a staple of early ESPN television scheduling, served to introduce viewers to up-and-coming college basketball players, many of whom, including Michael Jordan, would subsequently graduate to the professional game and play in the NBA as already relatively well-known faces, effectively icons in the making.

ESPN initiated a major technological revolution in sports broadcasting, which in turn accelerated the process of sport's globalization, providing global audiences for televised sports, global exposure and profiles for clubs, teams, players, sponsors and advertisers, significantly increased scope for marketing sport, club, team, and player merchandise to potential global consumers, as well as generating associated new income streams. Just as America "exported . . . its fast foods, Cokes, and Big Macs; its more relaxed and informal dress codes; its popular music, movies and television shows," so with the advent of satellite television live sports events could be transmitted readily around the globe, and "the ascending new sport," the one that at the time was

growing fastest in popularity was basketball, from whose playing ranks would emerge the first global sporting icon, an individual who would simultaneously become an outstandingly successful athletic competitor and a "signature commercial figure" (Halberstam, 2001: 130). Michael Jordan, by virtue of an outstanding playing record acquired in the course of winning six championships with the Chicago Bulls, extensive television coverage of matches in which he played, the amplificatory benefits of repeated slow-motion replays and analysis of exceptional moves and plays in which he was involved, along with the television advertising exposure and commercial success achieved through his association with Nike in particular, but also other high-profile global corporations cultivating markets for consumer products, became in the 1990s the world's most identifiable athlete, a social and cultural phenomenon, a brand with his own distinctive logo, and the dynamic hub of an expanding sporting and commercial empire which established basketball as "an international phenomenon" and simultaneously extended its global reach and appeal (LaFeber, 2002: 37).

As the twentieth century was drawing to a close, commentators, observers, and analysts were running out of superlatives to describe Jordan's sporting achievements and commercial successes – "the best ever," "a mythic figure," "bigger than basketball," "pop icon," and the century's "greatest endorser" are merely some of the plaudits employed to describe his impact (LaFeber, 2002; Halberstam, 2001; Andrews, 1996). In 1995 *China Sports Daily*, a mass circulation paper, described Jordan in a front-page feature as "the most popular sports star on earth" (Armstrong, 1996: 326). Three years later, following the Chicago Bulls' televised victory in the NBA championship series, a game watched avidly by Chinese people "from all walks of life," chants of "Qiao Dan, Qiao Dan" or "Jordan, Jordan" resounded around the corridors of Beijing University dormitories (LaFeber, 2002: 135). With his image adorning posters and calendars sold on stalls and in shops "alongside those of the late Chairman Mao, father of the Chinese Revolution," Jordan's profile demonstrated China's increasing openness to foreign economic investment and media and its readiness to embrace aspects of Western popular culture and associated consumerist lifestyles (LaFeber, 2002: 102–108).

Jordan, a global sporting icon branded in America, has been a highly significant figure in the promotion in home and export markets around the world of a range of American consumer goods and services, including the NBA and associated merchandise, Nike sportswear and sneakers, Hanes T-shirts and underwear, McDonald's, Coca-Cola, Gatorade, Chevrolet, Wrigley, CBS/Fox Video, and Illinois state lottery, and he undoubtedly contributed enormously to the growth of interest in the game of basketball in China (Andrews, 1998: 203; LaFeber, 2002: 107–108, 135). The game had been part of the cultural cargo carried by YMCA missionaries to China in the 1890s but it was a century later with the formation of the corporate-sport-media complex composed of Nike, the NBA, and Michael Jordan, accompanied by "the hip-hop soundtrack of global youth culture," that basketball really took off in China (Larmer, 2005).

Early in the twenty-first century, in the midst of accumulating signs of global economic and cultural shifts of potentially historic significance, another basketball player, Yao Ming from Shanghai, was drafted into the NBA with Houston Rockets as "overall first pick," an event powerfully symbolizing the changing geopolitical relationship between China and America, the continuing expansion of transnational capitalism, and the increasing globalization of the game (Wang, 2004). Described in media and marketing hype as "the child of globalization," Yao became a "patriotic icon" in his homeland, his 7-foot plus physique and power providing an effective counter to stereotypes and jokes about "short-Asian-males," and in the United States he became the most significant cultural icon of "an ever-globalizing NBA" which in the 2008/2009 season included 77 international players from more than 32 countries (Wang, 2004: 263: NBA, 2009). As one observer of his impact has noted, Yao "alone among Chinese athletes is a global icon, famous both at home and abroad, an instantly recognizable embodiment of China's emergence in the world" (Larmer, 2005).

When he joined the Houston Rockets *Sports Illustrated* said of Yao that he "had the greatest *economic impact* of any NBA rookie since Michael

Jordan" (cited in Wang, 2004: 268, emphasis added). There are undoubted parallels between the two players. In a manner that bears comparison with Jordan and other high-profile NBA players Yao was an important part of a corporate-sport-media complex producing entertaining spectacles for global consumption. Jordan was represented as an "all-American icon" and constituted the catalyst for the globalization of sport and the forms of articulation with the commercial world and communications media which have subsequently become synonymous with the institution as a whole – indeed, increasingly indistinguishable from it in the sense that late modern professional sport is unimaginable without the twin pillars of television coverage bringing lucrative transmission rights revenues, along with global exposure and corporate sponsorship and endorsement contracts. Yao has been described as a transnational sports celebrity "with a marketable ethnicity . . . whose selling power breaks down national boundaries," an individual who embodies "distinct identities . . . Asian, Chinese, and Asian American [which] are collapsed into a vast 'yellow market' to be integrated into the system of global capitalism" (Wang, 2004: 264).

With basketball increasingly operating as a highly commercialized corporate sport the NBA appears to have appreciated that, rather than promoting another all-American idol to accelerate marketing of the game globally, introducing more international players into the American game represented a potentially more effective and profitable way of developing a cosmopolitan world market for the sport as a whole and the NBA in particular. As Wang argues (2004: 271), the NBA corporate commercial sporting strategy to promote diversity within the league has succeeded in "fashioning an assimilating basketball culture that values dominant dispositions and aggressive attitudes, and advocates the American way of life," promoting in particular, its materially acquisitive consumerist culture (Smart, 2010).

All good things are said to come to an end and on July 20, 2011, after a series of ankle and foot injuries that forced him to miss in the region of 250 games in the previous six seasons, Yao Ming announced his retirement from playing the game and added that he intended to join the Shanghai

Sharks possibly as general manager (BBC, 2011). In response to the announcement NBA commissioner David Stern (2011) confirmed Yao Ming's significant status within the game: "Yao has been without question a transformational player for our league . . . [and] I am really very happy that we'll be working with Yao to continue the growth of our game in China. He is iconic in the United States and iconic in China."

Although he has retired, Yao Ming, like Michael Jordan before him, has retained an interest in the sport and continues to hold a number of lucrative endorsement contracts in China. Within the game the expectation of some prominent individuals, including Kobe Bryant of the Los Angeles Lakers, was that the doors that had been opened by Yao Ming's success in the NBA would remain open for other Chinese basketball players and that the youth in China now "believe that it's possible to achieve the dream of being an NBA player' (Lakers, 2011). A more cautious and far less optimistic assessment of future prospects was given by Bob Donewald Jr, American coach of China's national basketball team, who remarked that to date Chinese players who have attempted to follow in Yao Ming's footsteps have not succeeded in the NBA and that there are "structural problems plaguing Chinese basketball," in particular a lack of infrastructure and attention to player development and an absence of "grass roots opportunities for Chinese amateurs to improve" (Levin, 2011).

Athens 2004: Reebok's Classical Simulation

The Reebok advertising campaign in the prelude to the Athens summer Olympic Games in 2004 provides an appropriate illustration of corporate recognition of Yao's lucrative commercial potential, the value of his "marketable ethnicity" and growing global iconic status. It is worth recalling that at the time Reebok was in third place behind Adidas and Nike in branded athletic footwear market share and that Yao signified a potentially lucrative combination of "Chinese ethnicity and American products and sport," a potential which inevitably would be amplified by increased interest in Chinese sporting figures in the build-up to the Beijing Olympics in 2008 (Wang, 2004: 266). Reebok commissioned sculptures of American tennis player, and at the time US Open champion, Andy Roddick, Swedish heptathlete Carolina Kluft, and Yao Ming (Figure 30.1). The sculptures were unveiled as part of Reebok's Outperform advertising campaign, each one designed to look and feel like marble and to mirror the Parthenon friezes at the Acropolis in Athens. The company's vice-president of sports marketing commented, "The Reebok Friezes symbolize everything that is magnificent about Reebok's elite athletes . . . [and] pay homage to the athletes' dedication, perseverance and dream to be the best of the best, a dream to outperform the competition" (Reebok, 2004).

Figure 30.1   Three 3 × 3-meter molded stone-effect bas reliefs of Reebok athletes for the Reebok Center at the 2004 Athens Olympics: a) Andy Roddick, b) Carolina Kluft, c) Yao Ming.
Source: http://www.mccollinbryan.com/index.php/reebok, accessed January 8, 2013.

The life-size sculptures were central to the brand's summer marketing campaign which involved in addition print, billboard, and in-store imagery, and included other Reebok athletes, all designed to be "reminiscent of glorious Greek statues" (Reebok, 2004). The campaign effectively recalled the sacred iconic status accorded to the heroic competitive figures of classical antiquity by utilizing internationally celebrated contemporary sporting figures, quite literally cast "in poses reminiscent of the legendary Parthenon Friezes," to connote and promote the secular iconic status of a commercial brand striving to compete with its two main rival iconic global sporting brands, Nike and Adidas (Reebok, 2004).

Iconic Global Sporting Brands

The consumer commodity sign is inscribed all over late modern sports and sporting figures. The stadiums and courts where sporting events are held, as well as the attire and equipment of competitors taking part, are increasingly adorned with the consumer signs and logos of the corporate world and signify the inextricable articulation of sport and commerce with communications media which deliver the excitement and passion of sporting events and the thrill and intensity of individual and team performances to global audiences beyond the immediate sporting venue. The sports event – match, tournament, competition – is increasingly designed and produced as a commodity made for consumption. It comes wrapped in the signs of consumption. At the venue itself there are pitch perimeters, stadium walls, action-replay jumbo TV screens, and match-day programs displaying and conveying advertisements, as well as club shops selling merchandise, and players and spectators wearing clothing bearing consumer logos. The signs of consumerism are all around the sports event, and television coverage serves to amplify the local images of consumption by relaying them to global audiences, whilst simultaneously adding further layers of consumerist wrapping in the form of commercial program sponsorships and commercial advertising breaks promoting further commodity ranges to audiences of sports fans identified and targeted as potential consumers.

Paralleling the process by which iconic internationally celebrated sports stars have become global brands with their own commercial logos – the most obvious examples, in addition to Michael Jordan, being Tiger Woods and David Beckham – internationally prominent and popular corporate brands, through the calculated articulation of their logos with high-profile sporting events, tournaments, and prominent sports figures, in turn have acquired the status of global sporting icons. Nike and Adidas, which acquired Reebok in 2006, have become global sporting icons in competition with one another, not only in the commercial marketplace but also on the track, court, and field of play, effectively turning sports events into corporate contests (Islam, 2006; Smart, 2007; Branigan, 2008). As one reporter noted of the Beijing summer Olympic Games of 2008:

> Never mind the athletics. The real battle in Beijing is not the struggle to top the medal table, but the multibillion-dollar fight between two giant brands intent on conquering the fastest-growing sportswear market in the world. Adidas and Nike have invested unprecedented sums in wooing Chinese consumers during the Olympics. The German firm is estimated to have spent $190m (£100m) on sponsorship and associated marketing; its US rival has stumped up close to $150m. (Branigan, 2008)

As a member of The Olympic Partner (TOP) program Adidas was one of a select group of official Games sponsors, and all participating officials and volunteers were required to wear the Adidas brand as were all Chinese medal winners when they stood on the podium. But Nike responded in a predictable manner, in its own inimitable fashion. Nike routinely has engaged in "ambush marketing," renting billboard and other advertising sites in close proximity to Olympic and other high-profile sports event stadiums, thereby creating the impression that the brand is officially connected with the event, even though no sponsorship fee will have been paid. At the 1996 Atlanta summer Olympics Nike covered Atlanta advertising hoardings with brand images and slogans and built a "Nike village" close to the athlete's village. A survey conducted after the event revealed that 73 percent of Americans believed Nike was an official sponsor, even though it was not, while "Reebok (which had paid to kit out a third of competing athletes and teams)" did not even register as an official sponsor with most survey respondents (Morgan and Pritchard, 2003: 76–77). In 2008 at the Beijing Olympics Nike responded to its rival Adidas' official Games sponsor status by electing to sponsor Chinese Olympic teams in 22 of 28 sports, thereby ensuring that in the course of events television viewers across China, a market which has been "growing at 30% annually for the past five years," would see their sporting heroes wearing the Nike swoosh in the official setting of an Olympic venue (Branigan, 2008). To coincide with the London Olympic Games in 2012 Nike ran a "Find Your Greatness" advertising campaign featuring everyday athletes which was designed to navigate around the rules on ambush marketing preventing any mention of the London Games or use of Olympic rings imagery by brands that were not official sponsors. Nike used a number of "London" locations in South Africa, Jamaica, and the United States for their television advertisement and ran a high-profile poster campaign taking over billboards in Oxford Circus and Piccadilly Circus (Sweney, 2012).

Although Nike's commercial interest in association football (soccer) only really grew after it had made headway on apparel and footwear competitors in other sporting fields, notably athletics, tennis, and basketball, its global corporate revenue from sale of soccer merchandise rose significantly from an estimated US$20 million in the early 1990s to US$1.5 billion by 2007, aided by individual and team endorsements and increasing television coverage of sport in general and soccer in particular. The logic of the cultural economy of late modern sport dictated that Nike's interest in soccer, the world's most popular sport, would have to increase significantly if it was to continue to increase its share of the global sports goods and equipment market and, simultaneously, raise the global profile and status of its brand (Andrews, 2009). From a low point of no teams, not even the home team, wearing a Nike strip in the 1994 FIFA World Cup held in the United States, the company moved quickly from the mid-1990s to sign up leading international and club sides to wear kit bearing the swoosh, including Brazil, Holland, Portugal, Arsenal, Bar-celona, and Inter Milan, and iconic star players to endorse products, including Ronaldo (Brazil, and a Barcelona player at the time), Eric Cantona (France and Manchester United), and Ian Wright (England and Arsenal) (Howard and Sayce, 2002; Smart, 2005).

Nike was estimated to have a value of US$5.6 billion in 2007, which placed it second in the ranks of global sports business brands just behind ESPN, but by 2010 its value was estimated to have increased to US$10.7 billion making it the most valuable brand amongst sports businesses (Ozanian and Schwartz, 2007; Schwartz, 2010). In 2007 the company had demonstrated its commitment to *the* global game and its willingness to nurture it even at the periphery by cultivating a potential new market in Asia through the establishment of a strategic partnership with the Football Association of Singapore (FAS) which served to reaffirm the company's global status as an iconic sport brand. As the president of the FAS reportedly stated, "The FAS is delighted to welcome Nike as our partner. The strategic alliance will give us the opportunity to leverage the resources, experience and network of global sports icon Nike and the world acclaimed Tiger Beer. . . . We are confident that this partnership will play a key role in the Singapore football roadmap" (Sukaime, 2007).

The commercial agreement announced between the FAS, Tiger Beer, and Nike exemplifies the close articulation of late modern sport with the business world and the way in which, with the development of a global cultural economy, an interest in enhancing sign value or symbolic capital value through sports marketing and branding – that is, the creation of positive lifestyle associations, the ascription of status and prestige, and utilization of attractive and successful images to signify desirability – is shared across the sector. It is shared by global commercial corporations, sports associations, clubs, and teams, as well as by sporting figures whose global iconic status is now constituted not only through outstanding competitive endeavors in sporting events but also through media representations and associated processes of amplification, and, in addition, by virtue of lucrative commercial endorsement contracts and associated forms of marketing exposure.

Consuming Iconic Signs

In an analysis of the myths and structures of consumer society written at the end of the 1960s the French social analyst Jean Baudrillard (1998: 46–47, 79) makes reference to the various ways in which consumption, a "system of signs," is promoted, including through advertising and media representations of the "outrageous expenditure" of celebrated iconic figures drawn from the worlds of film, entertainment, and sport. The athletes of ancient Greece who had achieved success in sacred sporting events were accorded public recognition and status through the creation of statues – icons – presenting a likeness of their features which would promote recall of their heroic sporting endeavors and achievements. In the radically transformed economic and cultural conditions of late modern sport – professional, commercial, and global in scope, and inextricably articulated with the business interests of multinational corporations and communications media – global iconic status is conferred on sports competitors, predominantly sportsmen, not only for an outstanding record of competitive success in their chosen fields but also as a consequence of the significance of their media presence or exposure, international commercial profile and value, and celebrity standing (Smart, 2005; Ozanian and Schwartz, 2007).

At the beginning of 2007 Gillette announced an endorsement deal with US golfer Tiger Woods, Swiss tennis-player Roger Federer, and French footballer Thierry Henry. The campaign to market Gillette's premium shaving products was titled "Gillette Champions" and, estimated at between US$10 million and US$20 million, was reported to be the largest initiative ever conducted by the company in its 108-year history and to be part of a strategy designed to broaden the brand's appeal with consumers. The three high-profile and successful sporting figures chosen to succeed David Beckham, whose three-year £40-million endorsement contract was coming to a close, were reported on two appropriately designated internet web sites – *Athlebrities* and *Celebrity Brands* – to have been described by Gillette's brand manager as having been selected not only because of their "outstanding sporting performances" but also for

their activities, status, and profile outside of their respective sporting fields and "their reputations as icons."

In the space of a few weeks towards the end of 2009 the reputation of two of Gillette's iconic figures lay in ruins, leading some media observers to refer to "the curse of Gillette" (Mesure, 2009). The first of the two global icons to be consumed in a media firestorm was Thierry Henry who was shown over and over again on television replays to have deliberately handled the ball in setting up the decisive goal for his team-mate William Gallas in a crucial FIFA World Cup play-off match against the Republic of Ireland. In the aftermath the Irish prime minister and the justice minister both called for a replay, albeit without success, and the media reported Henry's admission of guilt and commented that he had ruined his sporting reputation. But sports public relations organizations expressed the view that while his personal *sporting* reputation may have been tarnished forever his commercial value would hold firm. In short, the *commercial* judgment was that the iconic Henry *brand* would not be irreversibly damaged, a view which received endorsement from both Gillette and Reebok, who quickly announced that they would stand by their "sponsorship of the star . . . [and] continue to support him" (O'Reilly, 2009).

The second iconic global figure to fall from grace and experience the consequences of critical media exposure was Tiger Woods. The damage inflicted on Woods' reputation was not due to a very *public* departure on his part from the values and codes of conduct associated with his sport, rather it followed from what appeared initially to be nothing more than an unusual early-morning traffic accident. Subsequent investigative journalism and media reporting in the wake of the "accident" led to the uncovering of a series of extramarital affairs, *private* departures from wedding vows and family values, which were reported, in contrast to Henry's sporting lapse, to be of considerable commercial significance and highly detrimental to the Tiger brand. As media interest in Woods' private life grew he announced that he would take an indefinite break from golf. As one reporter commented, in response to statements on the golfer's official web site that the matters preoccupying the media were private and between him and his wife, "When you have been making fortunes upon fortunes – estimated at US$100 million (about £64 million) a year – by selling yourself to the public as a perfect human being . . . the public has a legitimate interest when the lie is exposed" (Barnes, 2010).

Commercial corporations that had offered Tiger Woods lucrative endorsement contracts to promote their goods and services recognized that their marketing slogans were now likely to be interpreted in an altogether different and less commercially appealing manner. After the media meltdown of Woods's iconic status "Go on, be a Tiger" (Accenture); "The best a man can get" (Gillette); "It's in Tiger, is it in you?" (Gatorade); and "What could you and Tiger have in common?" (Lasik Eye Surgery) took on a range of meanings corporate cultural intermediaries could not possibly have anticipated and signified a whole lot more than golfing prowess (Syed, 2010). Although Nike stood by Woods, declaring the indiscretions to be "a minor blip" and the scandal "'part of the game' of sponsorship deals," other corporations took a very different view. Accenture, AT&T, and Gatorade subsequently ended their association with Woods, Tag Heuer pulled most of Woods-related advertising from the United States, and Gillette stated that they would limit his marketing role (Weaver, 2009). Virtually overnight Tiger Woods went from being the most marketable of global sporting figures to at best a flawed icon whose reputation had been tarnished and brand value damaged. However, a decline in marketability, following media disclosure of sensitive personal information or discussion of potentially commercially detrimental matters, need not be permanently damaging, as the previous experiences of other sports stars, including Magic Johnson, David Beckham, and Kobe Bryant demonstrate (Smith, 2009). But if he is to restore his reputation and the value of the Tiger brand Woods needs to start winning major golf tournaments again.

Commercial marketing campaigns, employing globally iconic sporting figures, not only derive promotional benefits for associated consumer brands and products from the aura of authenticity that is a unique quality of exceptional sporting talent, performance, and success, but in turn serve to enhance the popularity and status of the featured individuals, effectively burnishing their global celebrity credentials through circuits of cross-promotion (Klein, 2001; Smart, 2005). Marketing promotional narratives have served to elevate the popular cultural profile achieved by globally iconic sporting figures through their sporting prowess and near-constant media coverage, which is a corollary of participation in the higher reaches of professional sport, leading them to become comparable in many respects, in particular wealth and lifestyle, to globally popular celebrity figures from the worlds of entertainment, film, and music. Sport is now a serious business, a part of the entertainment industry, and the signs – the likenesses, the images, and the logos – of outstanding individual athletes, successful players, and prominent corporate brands have acquired iconic status within the global consumer economy and popular culture.

Acknowledgments

I would like to thank Dr Patricia Mooney Nickel (Assistant Professor, School of Public and International Affairs, Virginia Tech, USA) for helping me to locate the Reebok Parthenon Friezes website; Maureen Bryan of McCollin Bryan for giving permission to use the images; Tim Mathias, one of my students who completed a very fine project on "Indian cricket: cultural supremacy and cricketing swadeshi," for increasing my interest in the Indian Premier League and Sachin Tendulkar in particular; and Sue Viner, artist and gilder, for drawing my attention to the classical antiquity material.

Notes

1 Cynisca, a daughter of the Spartan king Agesilaus II, bred horses that won at the Olympic Games. As owner of the winning team, according to the custom of the ancient Games she was proclaimed victor in the four-horse chariot race in both 396 and 392 BC. At the base of her statue an inscription

proclaimed that she was the first woman to become an Olympic champion in a chariot race: "Kings of Sparta were my forefathers and my brothers. Victorious Cynisca with her chariot drawn by swift-footed horses erected this statue. I assert that I am the only woman in all Greece who has won this crown. Made by Apelleas, son of Kallikles." See M. Lahanas, "Famous ancient Greek athletes," http://www.mlahanas.de/Greeks/Athletes.htm, accessed January 8, 2013.

2   For example, it was said of LeBron James that he needed an NBA championship to realize his ambition to become a global icon: "To achieve greatness on a global scale . . . he needs championships. You look at that triumvirate of what is generally considered global sports icons – Ali, Jordan, Woods – and one thing they all had in common was championships" (*SportsBusiness Daily*, 2008). In the case of

Andy Murray it has been reported that "Wimbledon victory could turn [him] . . . into a global icon . . . [and that he] could become a global brand worth £100 million if he fulfilled his potential" (*MailOnline*, 2009; see also Gillespie and Flatman, 2012). The manner of his comprehensive victory at the London Olympic Games and defeat of Novak Djokovic in the final of the US Open in 2012 to become the first British man to win a Grand Slam title since Fred Perry in 1936 signified that his potential was indeed beginning to be fulfilled at the very highest of levels.

3   One study which shifts the focus of inquiry from European and American contexts and high-profile Western sporting figures is Dennis Frost's (2010) analysis of the emergence and development of sports stardom in modern Japan.

References

Andrews, D.L. (1996) "Deconstructing Michael Jordan: Reconstructing post-industrial America." *Sociology of Sport Journal*, 13: 315–318.

Andrews, D.L. (1998) "Excavating Michael Jordan: Notes on a critical pedagogy of sporting representation," in Rail, G. (ed.) *Sport and Postmodern Times*, Albany: State University of New York Press, pp. 185–219.

Andrews, D.L. (2009) "Sport, culture and late capitalism," in Carrington, B. and McDonald, I. (eds.) *Marxism, Cultural Studies and Sport*, London: Routledge, pp. 213–231.

Armstrong, E.G. (1996) "The commodified 23, or, Michael Jordan as text." *Sociology of Sport Journal*, 13: 325–343.

Aris, S. (1990) *Sportsbiz: Inside the Sports Business*, London: Hutchinson.

Barnes, S. (2010) "The $100m question Tiger will not answer." *The Times*, February 19: 85.

Baudrillard, J. (1998) *The Consumer Society: Myths and Structures* (first pub. 1970), London: Sage Publications.

BBC (2008) "Dhoni tops Indian auction bidding." *BBC Sport News*, February 20, http://news.bbc.co.uk/sport1/hi/cricket/7252238.stm, accessed January 9, 2013.

BBC (2011) "Chinese NBA star Yao Ming retires from basketball." *BBC News Asia-Pacific*, July 20, http://www.bbc.co.uk/news/world-asia-pacific-14214177, accessed January 9, 2013.

Birley, D. (2003) *A Social History of Cricket*, London: Aurum Press.

Bose, M. (2008) "The changing face of cricket." *BBC Sport* blog, March 14, http://www.bbc.co.uk/blogs/thereporters/mihirbose/2008/03/the_changing_face_of_cricket.html, accessed January 9, 2013.

Bouchier, N.B. and Findling, J.E. (1983) "Little miss poker face," in Browne, R.B. and Fishwick, M.W. (eds.) *The Hero in Transition*, Bowling Green, OH: Bowling Green University Press, pp. 229–240.

Branigan, T. (2008) "The real Olympics competition: Nike and Adidas claim China's heroes." *Guardian*, August 18, http://www.guardian.co.uk/sport/2008/aug/18/olympics2008, accessed January 9, 2013.

Cleaver, D. (2009) "Cricket: Baseball the way to go in Twenty20 stats." *New Zealand Herald*, June 14, http://www.nzherald.co.nz/black-caps/news/article.cfm?c_id=128&objectid=10578321, accessed January 9, 2013.

Courier, J. (2004) "Tennis is dependent on jet travel." *CNN.com*, December 6, http://edition.cnn.com/2004/TECH/12/02/explorers.jimcourier, accessed January 9, 2013.

Flood, A. (2010) "Red all over: Fans pay £49,000 for copy of Tendulkar's bloody book." *Guardian*, July 20: 5.

Frost, D.J. (2010) *Seeing Stars: Sports Celebrity, Identity, and Body Culture in Modern Japan*, Boston, MA: Harvard University Asia Center, Harvard University Press.

Ganguli, A. (2008) "India, the new superpower of cricket." *India PRwire* press release, February 23, http://www.indiaenews.com/business/20080223/99556.htm, accessed January 9, 2013.

Gilchrist, P. (2005) "Local heroes and global stars," in Allison, L. (ed.) *The Global Politics of Sport: The Role of Global Institutions in Sport*, London: Routledge, pp. 118–139.

Gillespie, J. and Flatman, B. (2012) "Murray's £100m prize if he wins Wimbledon." *Sunday Times*, July 8: 1.

Goldman, R. and Papson, S. (1998) *Nike Culture*, London: Sage Publications.

Guha, R. (2011) "The leading cricketer in the world: Sachin Tendulkar," in *Wisden Cricketer's Almanack*, Alton, UK: John Wisden & Co., pp. 97–98.

Halberstam, D. (1991) "A hero for the wired world: In the satellite age, Michael Jordan has become the global hero of a global show." *Sports Illustrated*, December 23: 76–81.

Halberstam, D. (2001) *Playing for Keeps: Michael Jordan and the World He Made*, London: Yellow Jersey Press.

Hargreaves, J. (1994) *Sporting Females: Critical Issues in the History and Sociology of Women's Sports*, London: Routledge.

Hoch, P. (1972) *Rip Off the Big Game: The Exploitation of Sports by the Power Elite*, New York: Anchor Doubleday.

Holt, R. (1996) "Cricket and Englishness: The batsman as hero," in Holt, R., Mangan, J.A., and Lanfranchi, P. (eds.) *European Heroes: Myth, Identity, Sport*, London: Frank Cass, pp. 48–70.

Howard, S. and Sayce, R. (2002) *Branding, Sponsorship and Commerce in Football*, Leicester: Sir Norman Chester Centre for Football Research.

Huizinga, J. (1949) *Homo Ludens: A Study of the Play Element in Culture*, London: Routledge & Kegan Paul.

Inglis, F. (1977) *The Name of the Game: Sport and Society*, London: Heinemann.

ICC (2009) "International Cricket Council Rankings," http://www.relianceiccrankings.com/datespecific/test/, accessed January 22, 2013.

Islam, F. (2006) "Stripes versus Swoosh in the marketing World Cup." *Observer*, May 28, http://observer.guardian.co.uk/business/story/0,,1784544,00.html, accessed January 9, 2013.

James, C.L.R. (1969) *Beyond a Boundary*, London: Stanley Paul.

Klein, N. (2001) *NoLogo*, London: Flamingo.

LaFeber, W. (2002) *Michael Jordan and the New Global Capitalism*, New York: W.W. Norton & Co.

Lakers (2011) "Yao Ming's retirement: Kobe Bryant credits his impact on NBA." Lakers blog, *Los Angeles Times*, July, http://lakersblog.latimes.com/lakersblog/2011/07/yao-mings-retirement-kobe-bryant-credits-yaos-impact-on-the-nba.html, accessed January 9, 2012.

Larmer, B. (2005) "The center of the world." *Foreign Policy*, September 15.

Lasch, C. (1991) *The Culture of Narcissism: American Life in an Age of Diminishing Expectations*, New York: W.W. Norton & Co.

Levin, D. (2011) "As towering star retires, China is unprepared to replace him." *New York Times*, July 18, http://www.nytimes.com/2011/07/19/sports/basketball/yaos-retirement-forces-china-to-rethink-basketball-system.html?pagewanted=all, accessed January 9, 2013.

Levine, P. (1985) *A.G. Spalding and the Rise of Baseball: The Promise of American Sport*, Oxford: Oxford University Press.

Maguire, J.A. (1999) *Global Sport: Identities, Societies, Civilizations*, Cambridge: Polity Press.

MailOnline (2009) "Sky's the limit: Wimbledon victory could turn Andy Murray into a 'global icon worth £100m.'" *MailOnline*, June 23, http://www.dailymail.co.uk/news/article-1194986/Skys-limit-Wimbledon-victory-turn-Andy-Murray-global-icon-worth-100m.html, accessed January 8, 2013.

Majumdar, B. (2009) "US plans IPL-style cricket league." *BBC News*, http://news.bbc.co.uk/1/hi/world/americas/8175792.stm, accessed January 9, 2013.

McChesney, R.W. (1989) "Media made sport: A history of sports coverage in the USA," in Wenner, L. (ed.) *Media Sports and Society*, London: Sage, 49–69.

McLuhan, M. (1973) *Understanding Media*, London: Abacus.

Mesure, S. (2009) "Henry, Woods, Federer: The curse of Gillette." *Independent*, November 29, http://www.independent.co.uk/news/media/advertising/henry-woods-federer-the-curse-of-gillette-1830663.html, accessed January 9, 2013.

Mitchell, K. (2006) "Indian chiefs defiant over home rule." *Observer*, January 8, http://www.guardian.co.uk/sport/2006/jan/08/cricket.comment, accessed January 9, 2013.

Morgan, N. and Pritchard, A. (2003) *Advertising in Tourism and Leisure*, Oxford: Butterworth-Heinemann.

Nalapat, A. and Parker, A. (2005) "Sport, celebrity and popular culture: Sachin Tendulkar, cricket and Indian nationalisms." *International Review for the Sociology of Sport*, 40 (4): 433–446.

NBA (2009) "NBA players from around the world: 2008–09 season." *Nba.com*, February 19, http://www.nba.com/players/int_players_0809.html, accessed January 9, 2013.

Opus (2009) "Opus reveals the DNA of a sporting genius," Ferrari Opus, http://www.thisisopus.com/latest/ferrari/opus-reveals-the-dna-of-a-sporting-genius, accessed January 22, 2013.

O'Reilly, G. (2009) "'Thierry Henry brand not irreversibly damaged,' say Sports PR experts." *PRWeek*, November 20, http://www.prweek.com/channel/ConsumerEntertainment/article/968431/thierry-henry-brand-undamaged-say-sports-pr-experts/, accessed January 9, 2013.

Overman, S.J. and Boyer Sagert, K. (2012) *Icons of Women's Sport: From Tomboys to Title XI and Beyond* (2 vols.), Santa Barbara, CA: Greenwood.

Ozanian, M.K. and Schwartz, P.J. (2007) "The world's top sports brands." *Forbes.com*, September 27, http://www.forbes.com/2007/09/26/sports-brands-teams-biz-sports_cz_mo_0927sportsbrands.html, accessed January 9, 2013.

Pollitt, J.J. (1990) *The Art of Ancient Greece* (2nd edn.), Cambridge: Cambridge University Press.

Pope, S.W. (1997) *Patriotic Games: Sporting Traditions in the American Imagination*, Oxford: Oxford University Press.

Rader, B.G. (1983a) *American Sports: From the Age of Folk Games to the Age of Spectators*, Upper Saddle River, NJ: Prentice Hall.

Rader, B.G. (1983b) "Compensatory sport heroes: Ruth, Grange and Dempsey." *Journal of Popular Culture*, 16 (4): 11–22.

Rader, B.G. (1984) *In Its Own Image: How Television Has Transformed Sport*, New York: Free Press.

Razdan, A. (2004) "Tendulkar joins Adidas global endorser line-up." *MediaWeek*, July 30, http://www.mediaweek.co.uk/news/search/448401/, accessed January 9, 2013.

Reebok (2004) "Reebok 'freezes' a moment in athletic history with modern-day versions of Athens' Parthenon Friezes." *PR Newswire*, http://www.prnewswire.com/news-releases/reebok-freezes-a-moment-in-athletic-history-with-modern-day-versions-of-athens-parthenon-friezes-75017727.html, accessed January 22, 2013.

Rizvi, A.A. (2002) "Sachin: Cricket's biggest brand." *Times of India*, August 30, http://timesofindia.indiatimes.com/articleshow/20690291.cms, accessed January 9, 2013.

Schwartz, P.J. (2010) "The world's top sports brands." *Forbes.com*, February 3, http://www.forbes.com/2010/02/03/most-powerful-sports-names-tiger-woods-nike-cmo-network-sports-brands.html, accessed January 9, 2013.

Smart, B. (2005) *The Sport Star – Modern Sport and The Cultural Economy of Sporting Celebrity*, London: Sage Publications.

Smart, B. (2007) "Not playing around: Global capitalism, modern sport and consumer culture." *Global Networks*, 7 (2), special edition on "Globalization and Sport," ed. R. Robertson and R. Giulianotti: 113–134.

Smart, B. (2010) *Consumer Society: Critical Issues & Environmental Consequences*, London, Sage Publications.

Smart, B. (2011) "Global sport and the cultural economy of late capitalism: Play, spectacle and profit," in Cohen, B. (ed.) *Being Cultural*, Auckland, NZ: Pearson, pp. 257–272.

Smith, E. (2009) "Is this the time to buy into the Woods brand?" *The Times*, December 11: 44.

SportsBusiness Daily (2008) "LeBron may need NBA championship to achieve global icon status." *SportsBusiness Daily*, October 22, http://www.sportsbusinessdaily.com/article/12488423/6/09, accessed January 8, 2013.

Stern, D. (2011) "Stern on Yao's retirement." NBA video, http://www.nba.com/video/channels/nba_tv/2011/07/19/stern_yao.nba/, accessed January 9, 2013.

Sukaime, H. (2007) "Just do it Lions, says global sports icon Nike." Soccer Federation blog, January 10, http://soccerextreme.multiply.com/journal/item/3/Just-do-it-Lions-says-global-sports-icon-Nike, accessed January 22, 2013.

Suliman, S. (2008) "'Clearing their way with bat and ball' – cricket, domination and subaltern struggle." *Dialogue e-journal*, 6 (2): 1–20, http://www.polsis.uq.edu.au/dialogue/Vol6/Vol6.2/SamSuliman.pdf, accessed January 22, 2013.

Sweney, M. (2012) "Olympics 2012: Nike plots ambush ad campaign." *Guardian*, July 25, http://www.guardian.co.uk/media/2012/jul/25/olympics-2012-nike-ambush-ad, accessed January 9, 2013.

Syed, M. (2010) "Arch salesman who lost the power to seduce." *The Times*, April 7: 67.

Times of India (2010) "Book won't have my blood: Tendulkar." *Times of India*, July 24, http://articles.timesofindia.indiatimes.com/2010-07-24/top-stories/28300108_1_signature-page-smaller-edition-kraken-media, accessed January 9, 2013.

Walker, H. (1989) "Lawn tennis," in Mason, T. (ed.) *Sport in Britain: A Social History*, Cambridge: Cambridge University Press, pp. 245–275.

Wang, C. (2004) "Capitalizing the big man: Yao Ming, Asian America, and the China Global." *Inter-Asia Cultural Studies*, 5 (2): 263–278.

Weaver, M. (2009) "Nike stands by sponsorship of Tiger Woods despite 'indiscretions.'" *Guardian*, December 14, http://www.guardian.co.uk/sport/2009/dec/14/nike-sponsorship-tiger-woods, accessed January 21, 2013.

Whitson, D. (1998) "Circuits of promotion: Media marketing and the globalization of sport," in Wenner, L.A. (ed.) *MediaSport*, London: Routledge, pp. 57–72.

Further Reading

Andrews, D.L. and Jackson, S.J. (eds.) (2001) *Sport Stars: The Cultural Politics of Sporting Celebrity*, London: Routledge.

Carrington, B. and McDonald, I. (eds.) (2009) *Marxism, Cultural Studies and Sport*, London: Routledge.

Giulianotti, R. and Robertson, R. (eds.) (2007) *Globalization and Sport*, Oxford: Blackwell.

Lasch, C. (1991) "The degradation of sport," in *The Culture of Narcissism: American Life in an Age of Diminishing Expectations*, London: W.W. Norton & Co., ch. 5.

Smart, B. (2005) *The Sport Star: Modern Sport and the Cultural Economy of Sporting Celebrity*, London: Sage.

31

Embodying American Democracy
Performing the Female Sporting Icon

C.L. Cole and Michael D. Giardina

Introduction

In his 2004 State of the Union address, US president George W. Bush offered an interpretation of an America dedicated to what he characterized as "great works of compassion and reform," an America rising to meet what he called "great responsibilities." His optimism wavered momentarily when he took up the theme of America's children, invoking age-old threats to education and health. He simultaneously proclaimed declining drug use among teens while blaming some professional athletes for falling short of their representational role – for the third-party effect of their steroid use. Invoking the imaginary special bond between athletes and children, Bush (2004) declared that "the use of performance-enhancing drugs like steroids . . . is dangerous, and it sends the wrong message: that there are shortcuts to accomplishment, and that performance is more important than character." He then called on "team owners, union representatives, coaches and players to . . . send the right signal. To get tough and to get rid of steroids now."

As if on cue, the following week's *New York Times* sports section featured a front-page article about steroids and sport (Longman, 2004). But the article was not about baseball players Barry Bonds or Mark McGwire, or any of the other key figures in the US scandal that had been unfolding for months. Instead, the article, melodramatically titled "East German Steroids' Toll: 'They Killed Heidi,'" attempted to affectively consolidate the East German sport drug scandal as the most notorious in sporting history, conveniently obscuring the present-day US scandal – one that had left an indelible mark on popular notions of fandom, celebrity, and belief in the purity of athletic performance. In general, the article depicted former East German athletes seeking compensatory justice for damages they experienced under the hand of state sport officials who administered, allegedly without the athletes' consent, performance-enhancing drugs (PEDs). The *New York Times* represented their victimization – coded in terms of *childhood* – as violated trust that led to corrupt athletic performances and a wide range of health problems such as liver tumors, heart disease, infertility, and eating disorders. But most specifically the article concentrated on the "gender death" of Heidi (now Andreas) Krieger, a female-to-male-transsexual, who, for the *New York Times*' US audience, could stand in for the most horrific violence and per-

A Companion to Sport, First Edition. Edited by David L. Andrews and Ben Carrington.
© 2013 Blackwell Publishing Ltd. Published 2013 by Blackwell Publishing Ltd.

verse transformations of an over-rationalized sport system.

The article organized Krieger's experience of the world and self almost exclusively in terms of steroid-induced pain, suffering, and isolation. Krieger's apparent unreadability as female – as well as her shame and humiliation for being seen as gay, a pimp, or a drag queen – serves as the narrative's pivotal atrocity. Isolated from all but the world of sports, where she excelled (she was the 1986 European shot-put champion), Heidi's suffering is resolved not after becoming Andreas (her new male identity), but only after he enters into a heteronormative relationship with another (female) victim of the East German sport system (swimmer Ute Krause) and renounces his former sporting victories as fraudulent. Theirs, as the author put it, "began as a desperate kind of love": two victims, betrayed by adults they trusted, psyches and bodies damaged, both suicidal, who met at the criminal trials of their abusers and are now building a "normal" life together (Longman, 2004).

Against the backdrop of the developing World Anti-Doping Agency (WADA) – an international police force dedicated to "clean [i.e., drug-free] sport" through the constant monitoring of athletes and their urine archive – and an unfolding US-based sport-related drug scandal, one might expect the New York Times to expose the hypocrisy of US accusations against Communist sport. But that is not the case. Instead, "They killed Heidi" reinforces American Cold War stereotypes and a preoccupation with violations of femininity that have long enchanted "America." Indeed, Heidi/Andreas is the literal embodiment of the fantastic figures that have historically propelled America's anti-Communist sport narratives – narratives themselves driven by diagnostic tools like drug- and sex-testing. That is to say, "Heidi" is an expression of a governing narrative about the nation constituted at the crossroads of sport, sex, and American democracy. As systems that, together and in isolation, activate, confirm, and extend a sense of natural bodies, all three bracket the body's technological condition (which, in the Foucauldian sense, can be understood as "an ensemble of knowledges and practices that disciplines, conditions, reshapes, and inscribes the body through the terms and needs of a patriarchal, racist capitalism" – Cole, 1993: 86). In their

press for the natural – and, relatedly, the original – the three systems cultivate, classify, and mark bodies in parallel and divergent ways as deviant, foreign, morally inferior, unproductive, imitations, and hybrids. As Alfred Gell might say, then, these three practices operate as technologies of enchantment in the service of the dominant order, exploiting "innate or derived psychological biases so as to enchant the other person and cause him/her to perceive social reality in a way favorable to the social interests of the enchanter" (1988: 7).[1]

Sport's ethical ground relies on an ontology and epistemology of the human. Thus, while sport draws together and then sorts out bodies, the sorting process is not reducible to athletic performance but, crucially, requires attending to the parameters and performances of the human. Given sport's interpretive ground, remarkable performances – the ostensible goals of high-performance sport – are never simply celebrated as breakthroughs. Instead, they are suspected to be evidence of potential breakdowns – breakdowns that facilitate nightmare fantasies of what and who is responsible for, the origin of, the accomplishment: the hidden hand of drugs? science? an enemy state? And, rather than provoking debates about the boundaries of the supposed natural (e.g., self/other; free will/compulsion; human/machine; man/woman), such performances are domesticated by visualizing strategies (e.g., sex- and drug-testing) that manage and sort the alien and the natural and, by extension, sport's idealized coding.

"Gender verification" is one strategy for making that elusive natural body visible in sport. Between 1966 and 1992, gender verification took the form, first of visual inspection, then a more probing gynecological exam, and now, increasingly, high-tech chromosomal analyses. Not incidentally, the justification for gender verification quickly moved beyond screening for men impersonating women to rationales that rhetorically confused and implicated both non-normative sex and performance-enhancing drug use. In 1990, one international governing body, the International Amateur Athletics Federation (IAAF),[2] revoked its sex-testing requirement, claiming that the test was invasive, humiliating, potentially damaging psychologically, and even resulted in the disqualifications of females who had no physical advantage. But, despite these claims, the organization transformed drug-testing – a space where genitals are seen because urination must been done under observation – into the unofficial official site for sex-testing. Ten years later, the International Olympic Committee (IOC) conditionally suspended sex-testing while maintaining their right to subject "suspect" female athletes to further examination. And, following the IAAF, they, too, gave gender verification refuge in drug-testing. The result? Narratives of international sport, at least in the United States, populated by a wide range of boundary creatures (i.e., drug-crafted athletes, steroid men/women, intersexed, transsexed, hypermasculine, and hypermuscular females) imagined early on as Communist athletes (as we detail below) but also later, and more broadly, as simply "un-natural" by "Western" standards.

With this background in mind, we want to illuminate the cultural history in which "Heidi" is enmeshed. To this end, we begin by tracing the events and anxieties that first fixed America's attention on the Soviet athlete and then more narrowly on Soviet track-and-field athletes, particularly on a "creature" known as "Tamara Press and her sister." We argue that Tamara Press and sex-testing were mutually constitutive: gender verification brought an aura of scientific authority to America's claims about Tamara Press's female masculinity, and Tamara Press (the collectively forged images and history) was the ironic proof of gender verification's necessity. Although Tamara Press and her sister, Irina, never underwent sex-testing, they became America's most fantastic and enduring emblems of the Communist athlete and failed sex (at least until 1976 when America's gaze was directed to East German athletes).

In fact, for America it was the *absence* of the Press sisters from the first sex-testing competition that confirmed their guilt. Additionally, and as we progress forward in our (re)telling of this cultural history, we examine the cultural politics of and backlash to the steroid admission of five-time US Olympic medalist sprinter, Marion Jones, and the gender performativity of South African middle-distance runner Caster Semenya. In so doing, we consider the production of "gender-deviant figures" at the intersection of two cults – the cult of sportsmanship and the cult of "true" suburban womanhood – as they are articulated within two

related contexts: the American Cold War and the post-Civil Rights era. When considered in this historical-cultural context, the biography and bodily habitus of contemporary America's iconic suburban girl athletes (such as Mia Hamm, Brandi Chastain, Lindsay Vonn, and Gabrielle Reece, and Mary Lou Retton, Chris Evert, and Dorothy Hamill before them) can be seen to be born out of an earlier performance of American democracy over and against an imagined gender-deviant Communist athlete. Given this history, Bush's 2004 appeal to end steroid use cannot simply be dismissed, as some have suggested, as a distraction from more pressing political issues. Instead, the deployment of America's sport-drug narrative – a narrative whose meaning is supposedly obvious and non-partisan – is inseparable from the actual making of Bush's political agenda and the production of his image as a quintessential American leader promoting a transparently "American Way of Life."

What the *Other* Superpower Looks Like: Tamara Press and the Communist Athlete

We begin our investigation the year after the Soviets announced that they had an atomic bomb. In 1950, in the midst of a military stalemate, the Soviet Union announced that after a 40-year absence, they would participate in the upcoming Olympic Games. The response was predictable. Prominent US accounts depicted the Soviets as boasting about their athletic prowess; the US media provided semi-detailed reports of the Soviets' supposed systematic violations of fair play; and they documented what they claimed were the Soviets' shameless claims to false victories. The US media self-righteously ridiculed the Soviets for using international sport for propaganda purposes, for advancing *their* political, economic, and moral war in violation of sport's mythic ideals (while at the same time the United States was of course doing the same thing). These violations were framed as symptoms of Soviet character – their excessive competitiveness, deceptiveness, and disregard for rules. Indeed, for America, anxieties about Soviet sport were inseparable both from fears of Soviet imperialism and from anxieties about America's moral superiority, which was marked especially by its so-called truth-telling project. In 1951, Richard B. Walsh (of America's International Information and Education Program) declared America's widespread commitment: "To meet and beat down these [Soviet] lies, the US Government, assisted by private groups, has greatly stepped up its truth-telling programs. . . . Through press, radio, motion pictures, overseas information centers, and the exchange of persons, we are telling the truth on an unprecedented scale. We have done well as far as we have gone." (1951: 1007).

We imagine that Walsh's aim, given his position, was to recruit American athletes for the US state department's "Campaign for Truth." To this end, Walsh flattered the athletes: "We can expect nothing finer than American sportsmanship, for sportsmanship is *democracy at work*" [our emphasis]. Territorializing global sport for the United States, Walsh concluded that, "sportsmanship is deeply rooted in our country's heritage." In this context, America's truth-claims rested on two beliefs: *a belief in the cult of sportsmanship and a belief in the absolute polarity of Soviet and American characters*. Thus, for America, sportsmanship was an instrument for embodying political culture and for linking conduct, performance, and moral superiority to America. In so doing, and in this context, sportsmanship would – and did – yield America's favorite sporting Other: a being recognized as the Communist athlete.

As a product of democracy at work, the Communist athlete, in its negative space, prominently functioned to enchant America's athletic embodiment and America's imagination. In 1952, *Life* magazine depicted the Soviets' appearance at the Olympics in terms of "muscles pop[ping] through the iron curtain," and they did so against a background of the "American cult of sportsmanship" and America's desire to see signs of *visible* transgressions (1952: 15). Comparatively, *US News & World Report* provided a narrative of Soviet sport, under the headline, "Stalin's 'Iron Curtain' for Athletes," built around key codes of corruption: isolation and secrecy, state-sanctioned interactions, violations of the amateur code, political indoctrination, heavy scrutiny and regulation, and their policing of their athletes' susceptibility to the pleasures offered by the Western way of life. Although sex deviance apparently plays no part in the account provided by *US News & World*

Report, the caption of one photograph is symptomatic of the terms that would define America's sporting encounter of the Soviets. The photograph is of Soviet discus-thrower Nina Dumbradze and is simply, without any explanation, captioned "A Russian specialty: Soviet Amazons."

Life seemingly approached the Soviet athlete from a different angle. The article's opening image of US athlete Jim Fuchs gazing in lustful admiration of "the Amazon" herself intimates that even international politics are not powerful enough to overcome the "natural" order of things. While heteronormative sexual difference renders visible a "common humanity," American anxieties about the need to see difference are apparent as *Life*'s visual images repeatedly direct attention to and from sameness. *Life* concretized the image of the Soviet as outsider through a moral geography that measured the Soviets' literal and figurative distance from the Olympic village. In a photograph of several seemingly "ordinary" Soviet athletes, it is this lack of difference that is problematized. This very "ordinariness" is represented as a nefarious impersonation – a state-sanctioned performance of the ideal (American) body. In this case, the American body is represented as the original site of vibrancy and spontaneity, the register of life itself. Yet, *Life* magazine, like *US News & World Report*, offers representations of the sort of mutants that the Soviets would produce if they went uncontrolled.

The photograph is of Soviet athlete Tamara Press, cropped to accentuate her musculature – or, in *Life*'s words, her "tank-shape." As a sign of Soviet militarism and excess, the image calls into question the very integrity of the Soviet body. Certainly the evocation of cyborgs through images of unnatural tank-shaped bodies was not unique to sport – it dominated American depictions of Soviet women in all walks of life. However, the scope of international sport – its competitiveness and regulation of nation and sex and its display of the effects of "democracy at work" – facilitated deep, affective attachments. International sport functioned as a dramatic enactment of the moral and physical chaos associated with the Soviets and its "innocent" American victims. This drama was most vividly played out in what were imagined to be grossly unfair competitions of Communist gender hybrids –

the product of a perverse, over-rationalized, and inhuman sporting system – versus America's "natural" girls.

For at least the next 20 years, albeit alternating in intensity and appearance, Tamara Press and her sister became visual shorthand for threats to American women, the American family, and the American way of life. These dramatic stagings of US sportsmanship were key to mobilizing extraordinary states of indignation and national fervor and negotiating the contradictions of American democracy and, relatedly, America's shame and pride.

Our Girls/*Their* Deviants: Suburban Tranquility Under Fire

In 1964, *Life* prominently featured America's female athletes in a 10-page celebratory photo essay entitled "The Grace of Our Olympic Girls." Arizona diver Barbara Talmage appears on the cover – weightlessly floating backwards in the air from the board, wearing a blue one-piece swimsuit and an angelic smile on her face – next to the issue's caption. The possessive pronoun *our* positions women as part of national culture and points to their bodies as signs of community, nation, gender, and American identity. Throughout the feature article, the bodies of US female athletes are depicted as independent, autonomous, and free of constraints, devoid of mixed signifiers and boundary violations. Quintessential signifiers of masculinity – strength and muscle – are concealed through gesture, clothing, camera angle, distance, and setting. Individualism is asserted in relation to a collective symmetry and proportion established through poses connoting grace, pleasure, and effortlessness. A series of artistic poses, repeated fluid and rhythmic lines and forms, suggest that sameness, unity, and coherence are what matter (not unlike that seen in Leni Riefenstahl's iconic if problematic film, *Olympia*). This was not a singular instance, either. Several months later, another female US Olympian, gold-medal-winning swimmer Donna de Varona, appeared on the cover of the October 9, 1964, issue of *Life*. Though the caption does not similarly infantilize her as one of "our girls," she is presented in a passive, portraiture pose, half-submerged in the water wearing a one-piece

swimsuit with her hair looking professionally styled.[3]

In 1966, and coincidently the same year that the United States would announce that winning was now a national priority, *Life* published an article explaining the need for sex-testing in the Olympics. Asking if girl athletes were *really* girls, *Life* brought tales of suspicion, impersonators, and sex-change surgery to the foreground. On this latter point, *Life* goes so far as to offer a tutorial in what transsexuals might *look like* by presenting before and after photographs of what they claim are transsexual athletes. The accompanying photographs are shot from distorting angles that make the athletes appear unnaturally proportioned: Tamara Press and her sister are two of the featured "monstrosities." Noticeably missing from this account is *America*'s claim to these girls. Yet such a claim defined the very context in which the United States awkwardly and ambivalently reflected and even attempted to legislate the relationship between *its* girls and women and sport.

To wit: on June 27, 1970, CBS aired a celebratory news clip ostensibly devoted to women's liberation's gains in girls' sports. Yet CBS actually takes its cue from an unacknowledged dynamic: a strong yet unstable sense of American masculinity marked by a tension between male privilege and women's liberation, the civil rights movement, and black and Soviet accomplishments in sport. For CBS, its magical resolution comes through America's white suburban girl who successfully negotiates several national burdens, including the gender-deviant Communist athlete. A patronizing tone governs much, but significantly not all, of the narrative.

Indeed, the main shift in tone is *racially* motivated. A slightly out-of-focus still image of a white man with "USA" on his chest going over a hurdle is shown under a voiceover:

> For years the image of track has been of graceful, slender, and, of course, swift men. Whenever women competed they rarely seemed quite feminine. [*Under continuing commentary, there appears an image of Soviet athlete Tamara Press, in an open and aggressive stance.*] But as our society goes through the swirl of women's liberation, so does the world of sport. And the revolution is beginning in the grade schools, as Heywood Halebourne reports from California.

The viewer's perspective is adjusted by Hale-bourne, who appears not at an elementary school but in the private space of a suburban home:

This looks like one of these TV families which speak of dry cereal as if it were pâté de foie. But the subject of conversation is not the crispness of the flakes, but the competitive prospects of the family's nine-year-old candidate for stardom.

Voiceover: Little girls used to set off for school with no thought other than speculation as to which attractive boy would dip one's pigtails in the inkwell. Now, for nine-year-old Jill Boyd there is the bracing prospect of medals and applause for feats of track and field. The girls to whom the recess yard was a place for experimenting with social patterns are now absorbed in physical patterns, as Debbie Kind spins [*image of girls in dresses spinning with petticoats*] through the orbit light-years away from the pantomime tea parties of old. A couple of medium-size Los Angeles suburbs have turned out these well-organized, smartly uniformed Ontario-Montclair Cheetahs. And, even the attendant matrons are pliable to discipline as visions of a medal for the mantel dance in their heads.

Our point of entry, as Halebourne suggests, *is* immediately recognizable, but not simply because of the TV family. Three national myths are summarily invoked: the American way of life defined by the suburbs, Tamara Press, and the American melting-pot. The space that opens our suburban excursion is consistent with that which is fictionalized in 1950s and 1960s family sitcoms like *Leave It to Beaver*, *Ozzie and Harriet*, and *The Donna Reed Show*, and which immediately conjures up ideals about home, family, and a consumer lifestyle.

But although Beaver was never affected by the 1950s Cold War, the 1970s suburban girl is both the stakes and the site of that struggle. In a striking moment of astonishing incoherence, we are told that the monstrous Tamara Press occupies a defining place in America's psyche – a place "fixed" by race, class, sex, and generation: it is, precisely, the young, white, suburban girl who bears the burden of the nightmarish figure. National forces and the complex political conditions that shaped girls' relationship to female masculinity are erased, as the psychic power of "Tamara Press" is invoked to explain the girls'

profound alienation from what is represented as "playing track." We are asked, on the one hand, to applaud the suburban girls' exorcism of the demon that led them to believe that they could not control or would lose control of their muscularity (and that this could be disastrous) and to imagine their track pursuits as a significant accomplishment not just for girls, but, given the gender-deviant Communist athlete, for the *nation*. On the other hand, we are assured that, for these girls, track is simply an expressive vehicle for fun, a temporary, trivial pursuit that will no longer satisfy them upon arriving at adolescence. Suburban girls, unlike Tamara Press – who has, along with the Soviet state, forsaken her biological destiny – will follow their natural (feminine) development and thus their more compelling interests (marriage and motherhood). As track coach Bill Peterson makes clear during the CBS broadcast:

Uh, the critical stage in this is, oh, about 14 … due to the fact that maybe they were a big star in the 12 to 13 division, uh, and then they go into 14 to 17 age group and they're overwhelmed by the competition. Uh, it's very critical at this stage. They either become very interested, or maybe get a little boy crazy and stray off.

The narrative is, in the end, not about women's liberation and a struggle waged on behalf of American girls, but one waged *against* women's liberation and on behalf of America's suburban future – a future in which white, heteronormative masculinity and its related structures, values, and behaviors are projected indefinitely (Rich Benjamin's 2009 *Searching for Whitopia* deftly captures the pockets of the United States where this vision continues to reign supreme).

To a great extent, the narrative's multiracial dimension – a dimension that enacts racialized corporeal norms – is instrumental in securing suburbia's mythic future. Black and white girls might occasionally run alongside one another in CBS's commentary, but America's women's track culture is hardly integrated. Black girls, visibly older, competitive, and apparently unaffected by Tamara Press (a national trauma), are represented in striking contrast to their diminutive, white counterparts. In fact, with the exception of Wilma Rudolph, black women remain outside the scope of the narrative. Even California native Barbara Ferrell's previous performances at the Mount SAC relays – she took first in the 100 meters for three consecutive years – remain unacknowledged. Statements of admiration are instead reserved for Chi Cheng, an Asian immigrant. CBS invites Cheng, its example of racialized productivity and competence and sign of America's women's sporting success, to offer social commentary about America's progress in women's track:

NEWSCASTER: Those who persist think to run in the steps of such idols as Chi Cheng, three times an Olympic competitor, once an Olympic medal winner who runs anything up to 440 yards, flat out or over hurdles. Last year, a coach's poll shows her as the supergirl of track. And as one who has competed through 10 years of geometric growth, she has an historian's viewpoint.

CHI CHENG: I came here in 1963 and, and at that time was, just a few clubs around. But seven years after, now, there are so many clubs around now. It's unbelievable.

VOICEOVER: Vince Reel, Chi Cheng's coach, feels like the erstwhile image of the track girl as a weight-lifting wallflower has completely faded.

VINCE REEL: I think women's track in the United States got off to a bad start when they brought Tamara Press and her sister over here. Most of the girls are now finding out that you have to have a good build to compete in this sport. Well, I think it's becoming a fad, actually. Little girls begin and get their friends interested because they can go on trips and get medals. And, there are hundreds of them, these little characters out there running around, warming up, and putting on track shoes, measuring their steps, and they go clear down to age five. The meet directors are finally waking up in this country to the fact that women's events are more attractive, shall we say, than men's events.

HALEBOURNE: Trampled under all these spikes is the notion that girl athletes come from Frankenstein's laboratory stamped "second" and that a preteen's best friend is her doll. You don't have to look like your brother, or Tamara Press for that matter [close up of Tamara's face], to play his game. Legend has it, Diana the Huntress raced as lightly and swiftly as the moonbeams that lit her path. For a time, her successors seemed to erase their grace with fierce awkwardness. Today's girl runners are a credit to the moonlit body with a bow.

How are we to make sense of such conspicuous erasures? Notably, the CBS report on girls' track aired just two years after black US track athletes Tommie Smith and John Carlos raised a glove-fisted protest on the victory stand at the 1968 Mexico City Olympics (see Hartmann, 2003; Giardina and Newman, 2011). After the United States Olympic Committee (USOC) acquiesced to the IOC both by apologizing for Smith's and Carlos' conduct and then by expelling them from the Olympic village, numerous, primarily black, athletes engaged in various actions to express solidarity. As just one example, the US women's 4 × 100-meter relay team, made up of four black women – Barbara Ferrell, Wyomia Tyus, Midrette Netter, and Margaret Bailes – dedicated their gold medal to the two expelled athletes.

Moreover, during the 1950s and 1960s, and driven by the desire to counter international criticisms of racism in the United States, the US state department had sponsored athletic tours that featured black athletes. Given the role of black athletes in advancing US propaganda and foreign policy, Smith's and Carlos' actions – and those that followed – were seen as a betrayal of America's international image. (In fact, by the time CBS aired its track story, civil rights leaders had fallen under heightened FBI scrutiny and were suspected of being Communists themselves.) Within this context, it seems less remarkable that the only black female athlete named in the story was one who had not competed for 10 years but had taken part in the US state department tours. Importantly, the United States in 1965 abolished the last of its longstanding Asian exclusion laws. One year later, US News & World Report (1966) published an article that defined Chinese Americans as the model minority over and against African Americans, who were depicted as a drag on the nation. Thus, Chi Cheng's elevation to the preeminent figure of social change and, relatedly, to that which redefines women's track as "attractive" entertainment enacted these anti-black civil rights codes. Cheng, who actually married her white coach, Vince Reel, is a remarkable example of the sort of ideological work that the Asian female body is forced to perform in American culture. In this case, submission of a model, minority, female body – through marriage – to the regulation of the American coach serves to contain anxieties about white women's loosening sexuality and about growing Black Power. Indeed, Cheng's national appeal is inextricably bound to the role that the Asian woman's body is forced to play in sustaining the erasure of black women as she negotiates the space where the conflicting meanings between race and sexuality engage the contradictions of democracy.

Our Girls/*Our* Deviants? Marion Jones, Caster Semenya, and National Fantasies

The aforementioned historical legacy remains largely entrenched in the collective consciousness of American (sporting) culture some 40-plus years later. While the late 1970s and early 1980s witnessed slowly growing mainstream success and, importantly, commercial marketability of American female athletes – most notably Chris Evert's exploits on the tennis court, where she won 18 Grand Slam singles titles from 1974 to 1986 and was part of a historic rivalry with Czechoslovakia's Martina Navratilova (see Spencer, 2003), and Mary Lou Retton following her 1984 gold-medal-winning performance over Romania's Ecaterina Szabo in the all-around gymnastics competition that catapulted her into the national imaginary as "America's Sweetheart"[4] – it was not until the 1990s that we witnessed anything resembling a paradigmatic shift toward the widespread, mass-mediated acceptance, celebration, and active promotion of female athletes and women's sports that we see in the present moment. However, as David L. Andrews cautiously reminds us with respect to this time period:

> NBC's representational strategy for the actual coverage of the [1996] Atlanta [Olympic] Games involved manufacturing a stereotypically *feminine* Olympic spectacle. . . . Predictably, NBC's primetime coverage focused on the over-determined hyper-femininity . . . of gymnasts (Shannon Miller, Dominique Dawes, Dominique Moceanu, and Kerri Strug), swimmers (Janet Evans, Amanda Beard, and Amy Van Dyken), and divers (Mary Ellen Clark and Becky Ruchl. (2006: 60–61; emphasis in original)

Andrews further notes that while "there is nothing inherently *feminine* about any of these sporting activities, or any other activity for that matter," all of them "have long been culturally coded as signifying the vulnerable, aesthetic, and hetero-sexualized embodied femininity around which NBC chose to center its Olympic reality" (2006: 61, emphasis in original). Importantly, as before, this celebration was coded in terms of heteronormativity and a focus on the suburban girl-child (and her future well-being). As recently as the 2011 women's soccer World Cup, in fact, this powerful discourse was still in place: ESPN broadcast commentators during the United States–Japan final consistently made remarks reinforcing both the suburban location of the US players (e.g., noting that at least two players on the remarkably *all-white roster* were the daughters of heart surgeons; that players such as goalkeeper Hope Solo and forward Alex Morgan had "modeling careers" ahead of them; that several of the players either had children or were in "serious, long-term" relationships; etc.) and the inspirational role they served for young girls (including direct references to President Obama and his daughters, as the viewer was shown a photo of the First Family watching the game in the White House residence).

Similarly, both Nike and Adidas had, in the last decade, pursued advertising campaigns that articulated women's sporting performance with suburban motherhood. For Nike, it was the "It's only a matter of time" campaign, which featured young girls playing pick-up games of football, addressing the inner machinations of house-league hockey, and jockeying for executive power as they discussed front-office moves *à la* fantasy baseball in a series of ads in which they served as infantilized stand-ins for a "real" (nonexistent) Women's National Football League (WNFL),

Women's National Hockey League (WNHL), or Women's Major League Baseball (WMLB). Likewise Adidas, which produced a series of ads for sports ranging from soccer to jogging in which the key figure in each ad was a pregnant woman or mother (e.g., jogging while pushing a stroller along a peaceful suburban sidewalk; making up a baby's room with soccer paraphernalia; etc.). Moreover, the UN Mine Action Service landmine eradication program featured the visual backdrop of girls' suburban youth soccer as the focal point of its shocking 2004 advertisement (in which the girls were effectively playing on a landmine-laden field). The deployment of youthful innocence and sport as located in girls' youth soccer in the service of terrorism/security narratives should come as no surprise given the previously outlined history (see Giardina, 2009).

The sporting successes born out of the early to mid-1990s, and located squarely within a growing sense of a national conversation on girls and physical activity,[5] contributed in part to the establishment of the Women's National Basketball Association (and its short-lived competitor, the American Basketball League) and Women's United Soccer Association (and its later variant league, Women's Professional Soccer), a slew of magazines such as *Sports Illustrated for Women*, and a noticeable upswing in participation rates across all levels. Jennifer L. Metz, writing about motherhood and suburban girl athletes at this conjunctural moment, reminds us that "the images of WNBA stars as baby-toting, basketball-dribbling, career-oriented superwomen thrust forward the ideal of the 'empowered (heterosexual) female' athlete" while at the same time signaling the limits of widespread acceptance of female athletes: "she is always being reminded to play hard on the field, and look good off the field" (2008: 187).

Correlatively, these rising stars of women's sports were now being read over and against their (black) *male* counterparts who, whether in baseball with a growing specter of steroid use, football with the high-profile arrests of Michael Irvin, Rae Carruth, and Lawrence Phillips, or basketball with so-called anti-heroes Allen Iverson and Latrell Sprewell, were being positioned as dangerous, criminals, and "thugs," and thus as deleterious influences on children, sport, and most importantly, *the nation*. As Martha Brant (1999:

60) wrote for *Newsweek* in her preview of the 1999 Women's World Cup, "Sport marketers, weary of seven-foot egos and Olympic-size scandals, are attracted to women's soccer's wholesome, family-oriented image." Brant went on to make her point in very clear terms:

> For companies used to writing big checks to hire athletes with marquee names, the relative anonymity of the women's team has become an unexpected asset. With the exception of Hamm, a true star, team members haven't spent much time in the spotlight, so they've been gung-ho to promote the event. That's included TV appearances on Rosie O'Donnell and MTV, but it's more likely to mean glamourless soccer clinics and autograph sessions for teen fans. Sometimes you're tired and you don't feel like signing autographs for a half-hour, admits defender Brandi Chastain. The men wouldn't do it. She's no Dennis Rodman. But for that, the sponsors couldn't be happier. (1999: 60)

And, as *Sports Illustrated* columnist, Rick Reilly, exclaimed during the event:

> Well, the revolution is here and it has bright-red toenails. And it shops. And it carries diaper bags. The US women's soccer team is towing the country by the heart in this Women's World Cup and just look at the players. They've got ponytails! They've got kids! They've got (gulp) curves! . . . Whoever they are they are impossible not to watch. (1999: 100)

As the calendar pages turned to 2000, and the impending summer Olympic Games in Sydney, Australia, took center stage in the global sporting arena, all eyes were on another breakout star, African American track and field athlete Marion Jones. Called "America's singular sensation in Sydney" by *Newsweek* in the run-up to that year's Games, Jones and her "dazzling looks, a megawatt smile, obvious smarts, an easy patter, and a down-to-earth style" was positioned as the torch-bearer for America's gold medal hopes (Starr, 2000: 28). A standout sprinter on the national level since she was a 15-year-old high-school sophomore, Jones had skipped the 1992 Olympics[6] and went on to compete at collegiate level for the University of North Carolina in both track and field and basketball (as a freshman, she was the starting point guard on the Tar Heels 1994 national championship team); national media profiles and talk of her competing at the 1996 Olympics soon followed (see Alexander, 1994; Litsky, 1995), though her Olympic hopes for that year were dashed when a severely broken foot suffered while playing basketball kept her off the team. But come the run-up to the 2000 Games, all eyes were on Jones again, as she publicly declared her intent to win an unprecedented five gold medals in the five events in which she was to compete (Coffey, 1998). That she only won three gold (plus two bronze), and went on to become for a time the most dominant and celebrated female athlete in the world, was only part of the story. For just a few short years later, Jones would find herself embroiled in a steroid scandal of her own, caught up in the same tangled web involving Bay Area Laboratory Collective (or BALCO), Barry Bonds, and others.

To review, in 1999 the IAAF not only charged the US Track and Field Association with routine drug use among US athletes but also claimed that US drug officials had been complicit in covering up the positive drug tests. Relatedly, a former USOC official had leaked evidence to the press that confirmed that US officials had routinely covered up US athletes' positive results. In the months before Bush's 2004 State of the Union address, Dick Pound, WADA chairman, specifically took "American sportsmanship" to task as he expressed outrage at Washington's disingenuous stance about performance-enhancing drug use (WADA, 2003). He condemned US professional sports league doping policies, particularly those of major league baseball and the National Football League, as trivializing and dismissive of the war on drugs in sport. More pointedly, Pound claimed that the United States broke its promise to support WADA, first by reducing the amount pledged and then by failing to pay its dues altogether. Pound proposed sanctions that, among other things, would preclude nonpaying members from bidding to host the Olympic Games (a direct threat to New York City's hopes for hosting the 2012 Games, which were eventually awarded to London). And he advocated turning the United States into a sports pariah: "If [IOC president] Jacques Rogge goes around to all the federations and says don't have any events in the United

States, and turns them into a pariah . . . hopefully that will get some attention from Pennsylvania Avenue" (*NBC Sports*, 2005).

By 2004, the US media were making BALCO's new designer steroids – particularly tetrahydrogestrinone (THG), and slang like "the clear" and "the cream" – household names. The hypercharged media coverage of the 18-month federal investigation of BALCO devolved into a circus-like atmosphere as the bodies of African American sport stars were typically used to organize the "leaked" confidential testimony from high-profile athletes. In this context, the United States had to rise – or at least *appear* to rise – to the responsibility of taking drug use in sport seriously. Eight days before Bush's aforementioned State of the Union address, the administration seized that opportunity. In a nationally televised press conference held on February 12, 2004, John Ashcroft, US attorney general, accompanied by the commissioners of the Food and Drug Administration and the Internal Revenue Service, announced the indictment on charges of conspiracy, money laundering, and distribution of steroids, against four individuals (none of whom were athletes). In his statement, Ashcroft said:

> Nothing does more to diminish our potential – both as individuals and as a nation – than illegal drug abuse. The tragedy of so-called performance-enhancing drugs is that they foster the lie that excellence can be bought. . . . Illegal steroid use calls into question not only the integrity of the athletes, but the integrity of the sports they play. (Department of Justice, 2004)

Arizona Senator John McCain, who chaired the Senate Commerce Committee that investigated BALCO (and who coincidentally then sat on the Senate Armed Services Committee that investigated the torture of Iraqi prisoners by the US military), quickly clarified the urgency behind drug-testing in terms of sending a "clean team" to that year's summer Olympics in Athens. In McCain's words, "It [an Olympic doping scandal] will harm our image and will contribute to our image, whether deserved or undeserved, that the United States is a bully and unethical" (quoted in Almond, 2004). Thus, as McCain made clear, the war on drugs in sport is a preemptive strike – in this case, one meant to shore up America's floundering image of exceptionalism and moral superiority rather than address the overwhelming evidence to the contrary.

Predictably, black bodies, popularly invoked since the 1980s to interpret US illegal drug scandals in general, became the metonym for drugs. While the well-established transphobic device that we discussed in the introduction temporarily relieved anxiety about the United States' dubious claims to innocence, the unfolding drama nevertheless played out across the bodies of African American athletes, particularly African American *female* athletes. America's pre-Olympic purification ritual targeted African American athletes Michelle Collins, Chryste Gaines, Regina Jacobs, Kelli White, and the aforementioned Jones. Indeed, in an ironic Catch-22, *their* past athletic accomplishments (Collins was the 2003 world and US titlist in the 200 meters; Gaines held the national title in the 1,500 meters; White was the 100-meters and 200-meters world champion; and Jones was a five-time Olympic medalist) were recast as evidence of their guilt. Thus, the imagined threat those performances posed to American sportsmanship was resolved through a triumphant narrative organized around America's ability to detect their guilt, *even in the absence of positive drug tests.* As a sign of the restoration of the "natural order of things" in its "clean sport" campaign, the United States Anti-Doping Agency (USADA, 2003) unsurprisingly featured America's favorite post-Cold War sporting icon, the suburban white girl.

Jones in particular, the Nike-endorsed "golden girl" and star-of-the-moment in the pantheon of exceptional African American female track athletes ranging from Wilma Rudolph and Barbara Ferrell to Gail Devers, Florence Griffith-Joyner, and Jackie Joyner-Kersee, had fallen from grace; her performance, like that of Bonds – and, importantly, the Communist athletes mentioned previously – was now suspect.[7] Yet while David Leonard and C. Richard King (2011) would say that she had been both "commodified and criminalized," the system got off scot-free; as Dave Zirin (2007) argues:

> Her fall should not be hers alone. It's an indictment of every "employee" of Marion Jones, Inc., every Olympic overseer who basked in her glory,

every corporate sponsor who made her its brand. As steroids entered her orbit and the federal government loomed, they reacted with either benign neglect or malignant intent. They all deserve to shoulder some of this weight.

But the story of Jones and her treatment by the US media, government functionaries, and the court of public opinion does not end there; rather, it is made all the more clear when read in tandem with the curious case of South African middle-distance runner Caster Semenya. Following her gold-medal-winning performance in the women's 800 meters at the 2009 World Championships in Berlin, questions were raised about the 18-year-old's performance and results, which had increased dramatically over the previous two years.[8] Yet rather than simply accuse her of PED use (as one might expect), numerous commentators extraordinarily suggested that the muscular and well-defined Semenya was perhaps not, in fact, "entirely female" (Silkstone, 2009). Such discussion was not simply idle chatter by disgruntled competitors alone;[9] the IAAF confirmed that Semenya would have to undergo a gender verification test "to prove she did not have an unfair biological advantage" (Smith, 2009a).[10]

In the 1940s, as William C. Rhoden (2007) reminds us, an Olympic official named Norman Cox (sarcastically, it is alleged) proposed that in the case of black women the IOC should "create a special category of competition for them – the unfairly advantaged hermaphrodites who regularly defeated 'normal women,' those less skilled 'child bearing' types with 'largish breasts, wide hips and knocked knees'" (p. x). Yet some 60 years later, the notion of Semenya being an unfairly advantaged intersexed competitor out to deceive – if unintentionally – her innocent competitors was given actual credence on the face of her results (and appearance) alone.[11] Interestingly, however, and where before the antiquated Cold War narratives surrounding Tamara Press and her sister celebrated the "modern science" of sextesting, backlash to the IAAF's decision (as well as to her critics) to "test" Semenya rang out not only from South Africa, but also from much of the global media. The *New York Times*, for example, outlined that Semenya had become, like

Sarah Baartman (the so-called Hottentot Venus) before her, "an icon in South Africa of the way colonialism dehumanized black people and pathologized black sexuality" (Gevisser, 2009). The African National Congress "urged the country to rally round 'our golden girl'" (BBC, 2009). And *The Times* (London), the BBC, and the *New Yorker*, to name but a few, all carried significant long-form reporting and pro-Semenya coverage.

Imbedded within the discourse of suspicion was her alleged (visual) unreadability as feminine. That is, as the Young Communist League of South Africa posited, because Semenya did not conform to "the commercial stereotypes of how a woman should look, their facial and physical appearance, as perpetuated by backward Euro-centric definition of beauty," she was always already suspect in the eyes of both her critics and the IAAF (Sawer and Berger, 2009). As if to mollify her detractors, Semenya would, while in the process of undergoing the IAAF's gender verification tests, appear on the cover of *YOU* magazine, a South African publication along the lines of *People* in the United States or *Hello!* in the United Kingdom. Appearing next to the headline "Exclusive: We turn SA's power girl into a glamour girl – and she loves it!" Semenya was featured in a black evening dress, make-up, a new hair style, and dangly gold jewelry. In the interview, which also featured her dressed in leather pants, skirts, and high heels – a "radical departure for the woman who grew up in a rural village wearing trousers and tracksuits, playing football with boys, and eschewing western fashions" (Smith, 2009b) – she is quoted as saying "I'd like to dress up more often and wear dresses but I never get the chance. I'd also like to learn to do my own make-up. I've never bought my own clothes – my mum buys them for me. But now that I know what I can look like, I'd like to dress like this more often." Although there is nothing to suggest that Semenya was insincere in her pronouncement that she liked her made-over self, it is worth remembering, as Anna North (2009) points out, that "magazine 'makeovers' send the message that there's *one* way for women to look good, and the closer you get to it the happier you'll be" (emphasis ours). This becomes all the more problematic when we consider the affective power of her

makeover in tandem with her public celebration within the South African political hierarchy. Writing in *The Times* (London), Owen Slot (2009) critically observed that the public debate surrounding Semenya had indeed morphed "from her very personal medical situation into a national campaign" about "South Africa fighting international oppression" in which "it seems important that the campaign wins," not the athlete's personal issue (which was now, in fact, a public one).[12]

It can thus be argued that the debate surrounding Semenya in South Africa had, in many ways, more to do with her political import *to the nation* and its national fantasies (Berlant, 1991) of itself on the world stage rather than concern for her personal or psychological well-being. That some of the commentary concerning Semenya, both pro and con, referenced her in relation to Baartman, is relevant here. In an op-ed for the *New York Times*, Mark Gevisser (2009), the Alan Paton Award-winning biographer of South Africa's second democratically elected president, Thabo Mbeki, offers that while some of the "adulation of Ms. Semenya is partly rooted in jingoism or wounded pride, perhaps it also celebrates something more salutary – a wish by many South Africans to live up to the values of the Constitution's core statement that 'all persons have the same inherent worth and dignity.'" But while South Africa has legalized same-sex marriage and is ahead of many countries when it comes to transgender rights, Gevisser continues, "one of the difficulties of South Africa is how far ahead of social attitudes its jurisprudence often is. If same-sex marriage (or the right to abortion) were ever put to a plebiscite, they would be voted down by a landslide." And therein lies the balancing act: both government functionaries and the public-at-large claimed Semenya as their own, *but for very different reasons*. That she was later exonerated by the IAAF and cleared to participate in events as a woman is but one part of a more complex national conversation (for more on Semenya, see Vannini and Fornssler, 2011).[13]

All of which brings us back to the case of Marion Jones. Whereas Semenya's innocence, indictment, and eventual exoneration was hailed in South Africa as a symbol of African resistance to colonial legacies of oppression, exploitation, and Eurocentric hegemony, Jones' *guilt*[14] exonerated *the nation* and further enchanted Bush's incoherent War on Drugs (for it was the nation, *not Jones*, that was positioned as vulnerable). That is, the US fantasies of itself and even its place in the global sports community were being undermined as America's sporting order of things became increasingly vulnerable (via threats of drug use, loss of national prestige resulting from Olympic sanctions, etc.). Expurgating those threats – condemning, prosecuting, and indicting Jones (and Bonds, etc.) – thus served to re-enchant and recuperate the national body, discursively performed in the bodies of white suburban girl athletes.

Conclusion: Re-enchanting America

Writing for *Reason* magazine, Matt Welch (2004) once lamented in regards to the steroid-era witch-hunts and the national political ground on which those debates were staged, that "President Bush has indeed 'sent a message' to the kids of America: We can make you look guilty, even when you've never been charged. It's a rough lesson, but they might as well start getting used it." Although George W. Bush's cynical "good sport" pose was, of course, not new to politics, the craven politicization of racialized sporting bodies for, and in the larger context of, epic deception, unprecedented corruption, and American nationalism under Bush should give us pause. As we have witnessed in the cultural history presented throughout this chapter, from "positive" and "negative" representational spaces – the angelic cover images of Barbara Talmage and Hope Solo on the one hand, to the stark and "foreboding" images of Nina Dumbradze and Tamara Press on the other – to modern scientific rationality couched in gender verification and drug-testing technologies, a systematic campaign to guarantee the primacy of the suburban girl athlete and all of the ideological trappings contained and promoted therein has remained a constant organizing principle of modern sport in the United States. For in the last analysis, let us never forget that the true scandal of sport in the United States is the way it is used to enchant already powerful bodies with even more authority by demonizing already vulnerable others.

Acknowledgment

This chapter updates and revisits arguments made in Cole (2007) and Giardina (2009).

Notes

1 As Gell (1988) defines: "In speaking of 'enchantment' I am making use of a cover-term to express the individual premise that human societies depend on the acquiescence of duly socialized individuals in a network of intentionalities whereby, although each individual pursues (what each individual takes to be) his or her own self interests, they all contrive in the final analysis to serve necessities which cannot be comprehended at the level of the individual human being, but only at the level of the collectivities and their dynamics."

2 The name was changed to International Association of Athletics Federations in 2001.

3 Nearly 50 years later, such representational politics are *still* playing out in the pages of the American media; to wit: the cover of *Sports Illustrated* in the week immediately following the 2011 Women's World Cup final featured US goalkeeper Hope Solo on the cover. She was not presented, however, in an action shot, making a diving save, or celebrating a key play. Rather, she was presented in a solitary, serious but attractive pose with nary a hair out of place. That Solo was presented in this manner, not to mention chosen over any member of the *winning* Japanese team or any of her US teammates (such as star player Abby Wambach), speaks volumes about the extent to which "beauty" and "grace" are still privileged with respect to female athletic success.

4 Evert with Converse (and later Nike), Rolex, and Waver; Retton with Wheaties, where she was the first female spokesperson in the brand's history.

5 During the Clinton administration, both the department of health and human services and the President's Council on Physical Fitness and Sports focused attention on the benefits to girls

of participation in sporting endeavors. Said Donna Shalala, secretary of health and human services, "we see physical activity as a cornerstone of our strategy to give 9–14 year old girls the confidence and resilience they need to stay away from the dangers like tobacco, drugs, and teen pregnancy and make the most of their lives . . . Getting involved in sports such as basketball, tennis, and soccer build self-confidence and self-esteem while also keeping young girls physically active. These are vital skills that will help girls throughout their adult lives."

6   At 16, Jones received a bid to be on the 1992 Olympic team, but declined because she did not want to "rush things" (*Washington Post*, 1992).

7   For more on the specific notion of Jones "falling from grace" and seeking public redemption thereafter, see Meân (forthcoming). See also the John Singleton-directed episode of ESPN's *30 for 30*, titled *Marion Jones: Press Pause*, which aired in November 2010, and is available for purchase on DVD or via iTunes.

8   It should be noted that Semenya's winning time of 1:55.45 was not a world record time. In fact, it was almost half a second slower than the previous year's best time (Kenya's Pamela Jelimo ran 1:54.01 in 2008), and on par with Mozambique's Maria de Lurdes Mutola's season's-best times in 1993 and 1994. In other words, questions were raised about Semenya relative to her personal bests, not necessarily to the performances of other sprinters. On her improved times in both the 800-meters and 1500-meters races, David Smith (2009a) notes that they were of 8 seconds and 25 seconds, respectively.

9   Mariya Savinova, a Russian who finished fifth in the race with Semenya, publicly raised doubts over Semenya's gender. Sixth-place finisher, Elisa Piccione of Italy, stated, "For me she is just not a woman" (McDougall, 2009).

10   The notion of an "unfair biological advantage" is, on the face of it, a curious one, and certainly an ephemeral sliding scale when we consider that a 300-lb offensive lineman in football has a biological advantage over a 250-lb defensive lineman, or a 7-foot tall basketball player has a certain biological advantage over a 6-foot small forward. Yet these advantages are considered to be not only part of the game but also a part of what makes an athlete special in his or her field of play.

11   The IAAF, it is noted, stressed that it did not "suspect her of deliberately cheating but question[ed] whether she may have a rare medical condition which [gave] her an unfair advantage" (BBC, 2009).

12   Especially if the speculation that Semenya was unwittingly given some variation of a gender verification test without her knowledge in South Africa prior to competing in Berlin is to be believed.

13   Semenya would go on to win the silver medal in the 800 meters at the 2012 Olympics, finishing second to Russia's Mariya Savinova. Following the race, some reporters, including Tim Layden of *Sports Illustrated*, discussed the notion that Semenya might have "tanked" the race so as to avoid further charges of scandal (see Thomas, 2012).

14   Jones later admitted she had indeed used performance-enhancing drugs, had her Olympic medals stripped, and received a six-month prison sentence for lying to investigators about PEDs and for her involvement in a related check-fraud scam. She is the only major athlete involved in the BALCO scandal to serve prison time (Bonds, Clemens, Palmeiro, etc. have not served time). However, we are not so much concerned with the court case as we are the cultural politics organizing her demonization.

References

Alexander, R. (1994) "Jones sprints to two-sport success." *Washington Post*, July 4: C9.

Almond, E. (2004) "Why John McCain is getting involved" *Mercury News*, May 17, http://www.mercurynews.com/mld/mercury news/sports/8685 231.

Andrews, D.L. (2006) *Sport–Commerce–Culture: Essays on Sport in Late-capitalist America*, New York: Peter Lang.

BBC (2009) "SA fury over athlete gender test." *BBC News*, August 20, http://news.bbc.co.uk/2/hi/8211319.stm, accessed January 9, 2013.

Benjamin, R. (2009) *Searching for Whitopia: An Improbable Journey to the Heart of White America*, New York: Hyperion.

Berlant, L. (1991) *The Anatomy of National Fantasy: Hawthorne, Utopia, and Everyday Life*, Chicago: University of Chicago Press.

Brant, M. (1999) "A cup full of cash." *Newsweek*, June 7: 60.

Bush, G.W. (2004) "State of the Union address." *Washington Post*, http://www.washingtonpost.com/wp-srv/politics/transcripts/bushtext_012004.html, accessed January 22, 2013.

Coffey, W. (1998) "It's tough to keep up with this Jones." *Daily News* (New York), July 19: 90.

Cole, C.L. (1993) "Resisting the canon: Feminist cultural studies, sport, and technologies of the body." *Journal of Sport & Social Issues*, 17 (2): 77–97.

Cole, C.L. (2007) "Bounding American democracy: Sport, sex, and politics," in Denzin, N.K. and Giardina, M.D. (eds.) *Contesting Empire/Globalizing Dissent: Cultural Studies after 9/11*, Boulder, CO: Paradigm, pp. 152–166.

Department of Justice (2004) "Four individuals charged in Bay Area with money laundering and distribution of illegal steroids." US Department of Justice Press release, February 12, http://www.justice.gov/opa/pr/2004/February/04_ag_083.htm, accessed January 24, 2013.

Gell, A. (1988) "The technology of enchantment and the enchantment of technology," in Coote, J. and Sheldon, A. (eds.), *Anthropology, Art, and Aesthetics*, Oxford: Oxford University Press, pp. 40–63.

Gevisser, M. (2009) "South African angst." *New York Times*, September 2, http://www.nytimes.com/2009/09/03/opinion/03iht-edgevisser.html, accessed January 9, 2013.

Giardina, M.D. (2009) "Suburban tranquility, interrupted: Youth sporting culture in the shadows of American vertigo." *Cultural Studies ↔ Critical Methodologies*, 9 (2): 224–247.

Giardina, M.D. and Newman, J.I. (2011) "The Physical and the possible." *Cultural Studies ↔ Critical Methodologies*, 11 (4): 392–402.

Hartmann, D. (2003) *Race, Culture, and the Revolt of the Black Athlete: The 1968 Olympic Protests and Their Aftermath*, Chicago: University of Chicago Press.

Leonard, D.J. and King, C.R. (2011) "Celebrities, commodities, and criminals: African American athletes and the politics of culture," in Leonard, D.J. and King, C.R. (eds.) *Commodified and Criminalized: New Racism and African Americans in Contemporary Sport*, Lanham, MD: Rowman & Littlefield, pp. 1–22.

Life (1952) "Muscles pop through the Iron Curtain." *Life* magazine, July 28: 15–16.

Life (1964) "The grace of our Olympic girls." *Life* magazine, July 31: 38–47.

Life (1966) "Are girl athletes really girls?" *Life* magazine, October 7: 63–66.

Litsky, F. (1995) "Sitting on top of two worlds." *New York Times*, February 17: B11.

Longman, J. (2004) "East German steroids' toll: 'They killed Heidi.'" *New York Times*, January 26, http://www.nytimes.com/2004/01/26/sports/othersports/26STER.html?pagewanted=all, accessed January 22, 2013.

McDougall, D. (2009) "Caster Semenya: Boy, can she run." *The Times* (London), August 23, http://www.timesonline.co.uk/tol/news/world/africa/article6806403.ece, accessed January 21, 2013.

Meân, L.J. (forthcoming) "Off the track and on Oprah: Denials, trials, and redemption-seeking in Marion Jones's fall from grace," in Wenner, L. (ed.) *Fallen Sports Heroes, Media, and Celebrity Culture*, New York: Peter Lang.

Metz, J.L. (2008) "From babies to ballers: Girls' youth basketball and the re-becoming of US motherhood," in Giardina, M.D. and Donnelly, M.K. (eds.), *Youth Culture and Sport: Identity, Power, and Politics*, London: Routledge, pp. 175–192.

NBC Sports (2005) "The most important person in sports? WADA's Pound has forced drug crusade onto U.S. leagues." *NBC Sports*, June 15, http://nbcsports.msnbc.com/id/7916984, accessed January 22, 2013.

North, A. (2009) "How not to solve a gender dispute: Semenya's magazine makeover." *Jezebel*, September 8, http://jezebel.com/5354639/how-not-to-solve-a-gender-dispute-semenyas-magazine-makeover, accessed January 9, 2013.

Reilly, R. (1999) "The goal-goal girls." *Sports Illustrated/CNN*, July 6, http://sportsillustrated.cnn.com/inside_game/magazine/lifeofreilly/1999/0705/, accessed January 22, 2013.

Rhoden, W.C. (2007) "The unpleasant reality for women in sport." *New York Times*, April 9, http://www.nytimes.com/2007/04/09/sports/09rhoden.html?_r=0, accessed January 22, 2103.

Sawer, P. and Berger, S. (2009) "Gender row over Caster Semenya makes athlete South African cause célèbre." *Daily Telegraph* (London), August 23, http://www.telegraph.co.uk/news/worldnews/africaandindianocean/southafrica/6073980/Gender-row-over-Caster-Semenya-makes-athlete-into-a-South-African-cause-celebre.html, accessed January 9, 2013.

Silkstone, D. (2009) "Athlete could be disqualified over gender doubts." *The Age* (Australia), August 19, http://www.theage.com.au/articles/2009/08/18/1250362070807.html, accessed January 9, 2013.

Slot, O. (2009) "World in motion: Caster Semenya photoshoot brings sex back to top of agenda." *The Times* (London), September 8, http://www.timesonline.co.uk/tol/sport/columnists/owen_slot/article6825732.ece, accessed January 23, 2013.

Smith, D. (2009a) "Caster Semenya row: 'Who are white people to question the makeup of an African girl? It is racism.'" *Observer*, August 23, http://www.guardian.co.uk/sport/2009/aug/23/caster-semenya-athletics-gender, accessed January 9, 2013.

Smith, D. (2009b) "Caster is a cover girl: Women's 800m world champion Caster Semenya has been made over by a South African glossy magazine." *Guardian*, September 7, http://www.guardian.co.uk/sport/2009/sep/07/caster-semenya-makeover, accessed January 9, 2013.

Spencer, N. (2003) "'America's Sweetheart' and 'Czech-mate': a discursive analysis of the Evert–Navratilova rivalry." *Journal of Sport & Social Issues*, 27 (1): 18–27.

Starr, M. (2000) "Give me five." *Newsweek*, September 11: 28.

Thomas, J. (2012) Did Caster Semenya lose the women's 800 meters on purpose? *Slate.com*, August 11, http://www.slate.com/blogs/five_ring_circus/2012/08/11/caster_semenya_2012_olympics_did_the_south_african_runner_lose_the_women_s_800_meters_on_purpose_.html, accessed January 9, 2013.

USADA (2003) "US government and WADA's continued cooperation marked by full payment of United States' 2003 dues." Press release, December 22, http://www.letsrun.com/2003/usadapraise.php, accessed January 23, 2013.

US News & World Report (1966) "Success story of one minority in the US." *US News & World Report*, December 26: 73.

Vannini, A. and Fornssler, B. (2011) "Girl, interrupted: Interpreting Semenya's body, gender verification testing, and public discourse." *Cultural Studies ↔ Critical Methodologies*, 11 (3): 243–257.

WADA (2003) "WADA Mulls urging IOC to make US a sports outcast." *Daily Times* (Pakistan), http://www.dailytimes.com.pk/default.asp?page=story_22-11-2003_pg2_19, accessed January 9, 2013.

Walsh, R.B. (1951) "The Soviet athlete in international competition." *State Department Bulletin*, 25 (December 24): 1007–1010.

Washington Post (1992) "Sprinter Jones bypasses Olympics." *Washington Post*, June 6: C2.

Welch, M. (2004) "George W. Bush vs. Barry Bonds: The government's effective smear campaign against baseball's best player." *Reason.com*, December 8, http://reason.com/archives/2004/12/08/george-bush-vs-barry-bonds, accessed January 9, 2013.

Zirin, D. (2007) "The fall of Marion Jones, Inc." *The Nation*, October 29, http://www.thenation.com/article/fall-marion-jones-inc, accessed January 9, 2013.

Further Readings

Cavanagh, S.L. and Sykes, H. (2006) "Transsexual bodies at the Olympics: The International Olympic Committee's policy on transsexual athletes at the 2004 Athens summer Games." *Body and Society*, 12 (3): 75–102.

Cole, C.L. and Hribar, A. (1996) "Celebrity feminism: *Nike Style* post-Fordism, transcendence, and consumer power." *Sociology of Sport Journal*, 12: 347–369.

Heywood, L. and Dworkin, S.L. (2003) *Built to Win: The Female Athlete as Cultural Icon*, Minneapolis: University of Minnesota Press.

Wagg, S. and Andrews, D.L. (eds.) (2006) *East Plays West: Sport and the Cold War*, London: Routledge.

32

Monty Panesar and the New (Sporting) Asian Britishness

Daniel Burdsey

So will the real, the real Great Britain, step forward?
"Real Great Britain," Asian Dub Foundation, 2000

Introduction: Nagpur and the Emergence of the "Sikh of Tweak"

It is early March 2006, and the first match of the cricket Test series between India and England at the Vidarbha Cricket Association ground in Nagpur, Maharashtra, is underway. A tweak of the fingers and one bounce off the dusty ground sends the ball spinning towards the wicket. Striking the batter's pad, a shout goes up from behind the stumps. The umpire's subsequent raised index finger gives the signal that the player is "out." As the batsman trudges back towards the pavilion, the bowler embarks on what will soon become a familiar routine: galloping across the pitch, leaping periodically into the air, and offering "high-fives" to his onrushing team-mates. The wicket-taker is Monty Panesar, who is making his Test debut for the England men's national side.

A young British Asian man, whose Indian parents had migrated to the United Kingdom during the late 1970s, Panesar was the first Sikh to play Test cricket for a nation other than India. Equally symbolically, when he stepped onto the pitch in Nagpur, he also became the first minority ethnic player to represent the England men's Test side after the terrorist attacks on the London transport network on July 7, 2005. This was a time when many young British Asian men were being widely demonized and constructed as the "enemy within" in popular discourses (Lewis, 2007). As such, the appearance of one on a sports field – and a cricket pitch at that – with the Three Lions[1] on his chest held substantial sociopolitical significance (Burdsey, 2008, Carrington, 2008).

The unlucky recipient of the delivery was Sachin Tendulkar. One of the sport's greatest ever talents, Tendulkar is a truly global cricketing icon – a hero not only to his Indian compatriots, but also to South Asian cricket fans the world over, Panesar included (see CHAPTER 30). Through this brief episode the South Asian diaspora had thus conquered fleetingly the homeland and, significantly, sport was the catalyst (see Burdsey, 2006a). At the same time it cemented further the

A Companion to Sport, First Edition. Edited by David L. Andrews and Ben Carrington.
© 2013 Blackwell Publishing Ltd. Published 2013 by Blackwell Publishing Ltd.

popular cultural imbrications of diaspora and homeland(s), demonstrating how their historical relationship has come to impact on the contemporary British sporting landscape. In this regard Panesar opened up an important new chapter in the cultural politics of race and ethnicity in British sport. Indeed, this chapter argues that his achievements and popular reception point towards the (contingent) possibility of a hitherto incongruous concept: a twenty-first-century *sporting* Asian Britishness. In addressing this issue, the chapter is divided into three main sections. First, it provides an account of the emergence of British Asian communities in the United Kingdom and, specifically, articulates the role of sport within them. Second, it provides a critical analysis of the various public responses to, and representations of, Panesar's success. The final section situates – and problematizes – these commentaries further, in the context of dominant discourses around British Asianness and the contemporary politics of multiculturalism.

Preparing the Wicket: The Emergence of British Asian (Sporting) Communities

Mudhsuden Singh Panesar was born in Luton, 30 miles north of London, in 1982. The town is traditionally associated with the manufacture of Vauxhall cars (owned by General Motors of America) and Electrolux vacuum cleaners, together with a professional football team that plummeted from a period of relative success during the 1980s to being relegated from the Football League in 2009. The town is hardly synonymous with celebrities either, with Panesar being described as "the best thing to come out of Luton since Eric Morecambe's wisecracks" (Walters, 2006).[2] However, as British Asian writer Sarfraz Manzoor highlights in his (2007) autobiographical account of growing up in Luton, since the 2005 London terrorist attacks the town has obtained much more pejorative connotations. First, it continues to be perceived as a prominent recruiting ground for Islamist groups, such as Hizb ut-Tahrir and al-Ghurabaa. Most infamously, it was from the town's railway station that the young men who undertook the 2005 terrorist atrocities embarked on the final leg of their

journeys into London. Second, in March 2009, far-right activists and football hooligans in Luton created the English Defence League (EDL) – a racist and violent organization with an overtly Islamophobic agenda. This followed a protest by a handful of Islamic extremists at a homecoming parade in the town for the Royal Anglian Regiment, who were returning from Afghanistan (Lowles, 2011). Luton remains a significant recruiting ground, and venue for marches, for the EDL.

The name Mudhsuden is derived from Madhusudanah, one of the 108 names of the god Krishna who, according to legend, slayed the demon Madhu. The nickname "Monty," by which he is now well known, originated from an affectionate appellation provided by an aunt when he was a child (Panesar, 2007). His father, Paramjit, left the Punjab in 1977, whilst his mother, Gursharan, who was born in Haryana, arrived two years later. The pair met at the *gurdwara* (Sikh temple) they still attend in Coventry. In this regard at least, Monty's background is emblematic of the trajectories undertaken by thousands of Indians, Pakistanis, and Bangladeshis, who left the subcontinent in the mid-to–late twentieth century, to come to live and work in the United Kingdom. Few migrants, however, had aspirations that their sons or daughters would go on to become such iconic members of the British sporting landscape. Indeed, entrenched racial discrimination in sport meant that it would be many years before such an achievement could even become possible.

Although a small South Asian presence in Britain can be traced back to the earliest days of empire and the commercial reign of the East India Company (Visram, 2002), the most rapid and sizable migrations took place during the 1960s and 1970s. Mass population movements were influenced by a wide variety of features. These are often – somewhat simplistically – labeled "push and pull" factors, but they combined a postwar demand for labor within Britain's manual industries and public services, a striving amongst migrants to improve their standard of living, and the desire to escape oppressive regimes or unproductive agricultural environments. The main points of emigration were villages in Gujarat, Punjab, and Kashmir, and later the Sylhet region of Bangladesh; areas that "tended to have particular past histories and present problems which made migration overseas an attractive option for many" (Brown, 2006: 41). Not least of these was the destructive legacy of British imperialism on local economies and the implications of the Partition of India. A significant number of arrivals were also those that have been labeled "twice migrants" (Bhachu, 1985). These were ethnic South Asians resident in East African countries such as Kenya, Tanzania, and Uganda, but who were forced to leave as a result of the Africanization policies implemented by these nations' governments during the 1970s.

For many, migration to Britain was seen as a means of short-term economic advancement and it was originally envisaged that settlement would only be a temporary venture. As a result, the first South Asian migrants were almost exclusively adult males. Their aim was to send earnings home to their families in the subcontinent to contribute towards the purchase and upkeep of housing, land, or machinery (Ballard, 1994). Migratory journeys were characterized by processes of "chain migration" involving specific *biraderi* (kinship networks), whereby those already resident in Britain provided the accommodation and employment contacts for friends and extended-family members leaving the subcontinent. The most popular destinations were London, the industrial urban centers of the Midlands, and mill towns across the northern counties of Lancashire and Yorkshire. Migrants gained employment in a variety of professions and trades: from small retail businesses, and as doctors and nurses in the National Health Service, to less prosperous and secure roles in manufacturing and textile industries. As soon as sufficient income had been earned, the men planned to return to India or Pakistan to reap the benefits of their short, but assiduous, residence in Britain. However, after a number of years, many of these sojourns began to turn into permanent settlements. The establishment of sizable South Asian communities and growing familiarity with their new surroundings, together – somewhat ironically – with increasingly restrictive (and racist) immigration legislation, meant that the late 1960s and early 1970s saw a huge number of family reunifications in the United Kingdom. According to the 2011 census for England and Wales, out of a total population of just over 56 million people, just under 7

percent are South Asian. Around 2.5 percent identified their ethnicity as Indian, 2 percent as Pakistani and 0.8 percent as Bangladeshi.

Judith Brown (2006: 60) argues that migration and the establishment of a particular diaspora "is not a single event, not just a matter of making the journey. It is an ongoing process that continues long after stepping off a boat or plane in a new country." The establishment of settler communities and the subsequent affirmation of group identity are dynamic processes that occur over a number of generations. As increasing numbers of migrants arrived in the United Kingdom, residents of previously majority white, working-class districts soon found themselves living and working alongside South Asian neighbors and colleagues. Religious and cultural institutions, restaurants, grocers, and clothing emporia slowly but surely began to alter the sights, sounds, and smells of local urban landscapes. In some parts of urban Britain, especially England, the *muezzin*'s call to prayer became as noteworthy a quotidian soundtrack as the clamor of heavy industry; *halal* butchers and outlets selling popular Indian movies or beautifully colored fabrics for *saris* and *shalwar kameez* became as common as pubs and pie-'n'-mash shops; and a gaze across city skylines would just as likely take in the crescents, domes, and minarets of *mosques, gurdwaras*, and *mandirs* as tower blocks, church spires, and factory chimneys. Areas such as Brick Lane, Southall and Wembley in London, Melton Road in Leicester, Manningham in Bradford, and Sparkbrook in Birmingham became home to vibrant "Bangla-towns" or "Little Punjabs." Smaller British Asian communities – all with particular histories and futures – also emerged in more provincial towns, including Gravesend, Luton, Oxford, and Southampton.

The new migrants made huge economic, social, and cultural contributions to the nation's fabric. Notwithstanding this, their arrival and settlement "came at a time when British identity was still powerfully moulded by attitudes which had underpinned the British Empire, including ideas of racial superiority and inferiority" (Brown, 2006: 119). It is often pointed out that these discourses signified a shift towards a racism centered primarily on migrants' *cultural* rather than *physical* attributes – their family structures, the languages they spoke, the food they ate, the clothes they wore and the gods they worshipped. Yet, cultural factors were similarly perceived as fixed, static, and immutable traits. Consequently cultural stereotyping represented effectively a homologue for perceptions and assumptions based around phenotype and notions of race.

In the popular imagination, South Asian communities were viewed originally as being inherently incompatible with dominant (white) British values. They were believed consequently to represent a threat to social cohesion – a perception that is still articulated today, although normally targeted more specifically at Muslims. Fears emanated from the belief that migrants were providing competition for already scarce jobs (in fact they took on employment roles and worked shift patterns widely rejected by white workers) and housing (they were actually subjected to racial discrimination in this sphere, as in most other areas of public life). Distinctive South Asian religious and social practices, together with a lack of identification with permissive elements of the host culture, were also regarded as antithetical to a modern, liberal, Western nation. Public concerns about immigration were ignited by far-right parties and right-wing "mainstream" politicians alike. Most infamously, Conservative MP Enoch Powell advocated not only the end of migration from New Commonwealth countries but also the assisted repatriation of minority ethnic populations. Racial discrimination and violence became a habitual experience for South Asian communities living in Britain, culminating tragically in a number of racist murders, including Gurdip Singh Chaggar, Altab Ali, and Akhtar Ali Baig in London in the 1970s.

Despite the rampant racism they faced, South Asian communities fought back. Youth movements emerged in Southall, west London and mobilized across the country to fight discrimination and racist violence (Ramamurthy, 2006); legal precedents were achieved in areas ranging from the provision of *halal* meat in schools with large numbers of Muslim pupils to the rights of Sikh men not to wear hard hats on construction sites or whilst riding motorcycles; and workers attained rights to unionize and protest, as enacted in the strike by South Asian women at the Grunwick photo-processing laboratories in Brent, northwest London in the late 1970s (Wilson, 2006). On a more everyday level, by the second

decade of the twenty-first century, British Asians have made inroads into a plethora of forms of employment and popular culture: politics, the military, art, film, literature, music, comedy, journalism, business and industry, and in shaping the culinary habits of a nation (Ali, Kalra, and Sayyid, 2006; Sardar, 2008). As Sanjay Sharma (2003: 411) states, "in recent times there has been a greater visibility and positivity attached to the sign 'Asian'. Compared to an earlier period of relative obscurity, 'invisibility' and denigration, it has become difficult to ignore the rise of a range of differentiated Asian cultural practices." However, one important institution is absent from the categories mentioned above. What role, therefore, does *sport* play within changing articulations of Asianness in contemporary Britain?

The role of sport in British Asian lifestyles has been habitually ignored, marginalized, or trivialized in both popular and academic accounts (Burdsey, 2007a). Few (otherwise comprehensive) histories of South Asian migration to, and settlement in, the United Kingdom have acknowledged the important role of sport within these communities (e.g., Ramdin, 1999; Visram, 2002). Sporting texts likewise often appear to present British Asian contributions as an afterthought. This oversight is illuminated by the prominence attached to sport in other, more specific, accounts, particularly those based around visual and/or oral histories (e.g., Smith, 2004; Herbert Gallery, 2006).

Sport, primarily cricket, football, hockey, wrestling, and kabaddi, was embedded as a significant pursuit from the very first days of the post-migratory period. It was not only a popular and sociable leisure activity but also a means of articulating ethno-religious identities and attempting to facilitate (contingent) inclusion within majority white communities (Burdsey, 2006b). Much of this was arranged under the auspices of trade unions, such as the Indian Workers' Association, which recognized the potential for using sport as a means of cementing ethnic and class solidarities (Herbert Gallery, 2006). Sanjiev Johal (2001: 162) states that sporting contests, particularly festivals and tournaments, provided "distinct masculinized sites in which men, young and old, indulged themselves in sportive and other hedonistic pursuits, notably the excessive consumption of alcohol." Fifty or so years later, the outcome is an established pattern of sport across British Asian communities. Furthermore, it is one that has finally begun to bridge the gender divide. From being limited to the role of supporters and providers of post-match nourishment during the early days, British Asian women and girls are rapidly developing substantial sporting cultures of their own (see, e.g., Ahmad, 2011; Ratna, 2011).

Sporting participation is no longer confined to recreational spheres. Despite a backdrop of ingrained and pervasive racism, British Asians have begun to forge an important presence and achieve successes in a range of sports. As a result, British Asians finally have sporting heroes that they can really call their own. No longer restricted to subcontinental cricketers like Sachin Tendulkar or Shoaib Akhtar, tennis star Sania Mirza, or iconic kabaddi player Balwinder Singh Fidda, these new sporting idols have grown up in the same communities as their British followers – both men, such as boxer Amir Khan and footballer Zesh Rehman, and women, including golfer Kiran Matharu, cricketer Isa Guha, and tennis player Anne Keothavong. However, there are still few other British Asians who have made the professional grade in these sports and their communities remain heavily underrepresented. Furthermore, at the 2012 London Olympic and Paralympic Games – heralded (rather optimistically) by many commentators as a celebration of multicultural nationhood (Burdsey, 2012) – the absence of British Asians in Team GB was striking.

So where does cricket fit into this state of affairs? An "Indian game accidentally discovered by the English" (Nandy, 2000: 1), it has the most substantial (post-)colonial sporting associations with the Indian subcontinent and is correlated readily with South Asian communities throughout the diaspora. In the United Kingdom, cricket plays a major role within British Asian communities; in recreational (Williams, 2001) and professional playing capacities (Burdsey, 2010b), and in terms of fandom as well (Werbner, 1996; Burdsey, 2006a; Valiotis, 2009). For most of the twentieth century, the only cricketers of South Asian background to play in the English first-class game were "overseas" players (see Williams, 2001). Yet in recent years English cricket has undergone a significant change. The vast majority of first-class

clubs have recruited British Asians to their playing rosters and they are now overrepresented as professional players in comparison to their numbers in the overall population. Indeed, the list of players to be capped by England – for so long a sporting embodiment of hegemonic whiteness and racialized articulations of national identity – now includes a distinct corpus of South Asian names: Afzaal, Ali, Bopara, Habib, Hussain, Khan, Mahmood, Mascarenhas, Panesar, Patel, Rashid, Shah, Shahzad, and Solanki.

Such developments appear far removed from some of the discriminatory commentaries about cricket, race, and nation during the latter twentieth century. In 1990, in the infamous "cricket test," Conservative MP Norman Tebbit suggested that migrants with British passports should jettison their attachments to their homelands and support England in sporting contests. Five years later, journalist Robert Henderson (1995) asserted, equally ridiculously, that minority ethnic players who were born outside the United Kingdom, yet qualified to play for the national team, were not as committed as other players and even gained pleasure from England defeats.

However, a hegemonic discourse of "colorblindness" continues to characterize English cricket and British sport more widely (Burdsey, 2011). Eduardo Bonilla-Silva (2006) uses the framework of color-blind racism to explain how, despite the advances made by the civil rights movement, together with widespread contemporary avowals that racism is no longer an issue, racial inequality remains systemic in twenty-first century US society. While his context is exclusively American, research has shown that similar processes are evident in British sport (Lusted, 2009). The four frames of color-blind racism he identifies are abstract liberalism, naturalization, cultural racism, and minimization of racism. *Abstract liberalism* refers to the manner in which racial inequality is justified on the basis of an individual's right to choose. The second frame describes the way that racial phenomena are explained by the belief that they are *natural* occurrences, whilst the third addresses the shift towards *cultural* attributes, rather than biological ones, within contemporary racist discourses. The fourth frame is *minimization of racism*. This frame posits that prejudicial views and behavior are no longer a major factor affecting the life chances of minorities, it also views discrimination as synonymous with blatant, full-on racist instances, and by doing so "eliminates the bulk of racially motivated actions by individual whites and institutions by fiat" (Bonilla-Silva, 2006: 30). This perception serves to obscure the existence and extent of prejudice and discrimination, and the fact that minority ethnic groups' inclusion in English cricket remains partial and contingent. More specifically, it allows the numerical representation of British Asian players to be often correlated mistakenly with a belief that they are unequivocally included and accepted within the structures and cultures of the game.

Monty Mania: Hero Worship or Modern Day Minstrelsy?

Following the massive impact he made at the start of his international career, arguments have recurred as to whether Monty Panesar has since fulfilled his early cricketing promise (see below). Beyond doubt, however, are his tremendous, enduring popularity and the sizable public profile he generated at the height of his achievements. His fan base transcends supporters of all ethnic backgrounds, and he is highly regarded by teammates in the domestic and international game alike. Specifically, his role within, and on behalf of, the Sikh community, in Britain and beyond, has been widely espoused. Religious leaders in India have labeled him "a true Sikh icon" (Hopps, 2006), whilst Inderjit Singh, editor of the *Sikh Messenger* newspaper in the United Kingdom, argues that "he's had a huge effect on raising the morale and feelings of the Sikh community" (cited in John, 2006). With the exception of television presenter, Hardeep Singh Kohli, and football referee, Jarnail Singh, turban-wearing Sikhs – to be precise Monty and Jarnail wear the smaller bandana-style *patka* – are almost invisible in mainstream British popular culture. Panesar consequently represents an important challenge to this state of affairs.

British Asians have always had their cricketing heroes, but the links between subcontinental stars and the streets of Southall, Sparkbrook, or Stepney have always been tenuous. In addition, former England captain Nasser Hussain's "mixed-race" background (his mother is white), middle-

class manner, and assimilationist tendencies (Brenkley, 2006) have meant that his "Asianness" has been questioned frequently by those who, it is assumed, will regard him as a role model (Burdsey, 2004). However, following Panesar's success, anecdotal evidence suggests that interest in cricket amongst British Asian youths increased considerably. In Luton, for example, the waiting list to join the Luton Town and Indians club, where the player once learned his trade, lengthened quickly. Despite questioning his own applicability for the status and reluctantly adopting the role, it is his heralding as a multicultural icon that is most prominent. As Ranjit Singh Dubb of Luton's Guru Nanak *gurdwara* states, "a lot of people look up to him, not just from our religion, but other religions. Local kids go round to his house and knock on the door for autographs. These are Muslim kids as well as Sikhs" (cited in Beard, 2006).

Panesar's British Asian contemporaries in the first-class game are unequivocal about his popularity and achievements. For example, one player interviewed in 2008 stated:

> Monty is massive. Monty keeps saying in the press that he's not a role model, and he doesn't want to be a role model for British Asians, as they've got other role models and he's just there to play cricket. That's just Monty being Monty. He is a very, you know, average sort of guy, he won't say he's there making a difference to people's lives, that's the way Monty is. But the fact is he *is* making a massive difference to British Asians.

One player claimed that "Monty is like a national hero at the moment. Everybody loves him, doesn't matter if you're English or, what color, whatever"; and another added that "the fans love Monty more than any other cricketer in that [England] dressing room. It's him or [Andrew] Flintoff. Flintoff a true Brit boy, and Monty with a turban and a beard."

The Barmy Army – the boisterous troupe of fans that follow England at home and abroad (see Parry and Malcolm, 2004; Malcolm, 2009) – were also vocal champions of Panesar. Members would sing his name, attach fake beards and wear bandanas during international matches in which he was playing (BBC, 2006). Northamptonshire, his former domestic county club, even organized special "Monty zones" during Twenty20 matches – the shortened, hyper-commercialized form of the game – where his fans could congregate (Panesar, 2007). His personal website once sold a variety of merchandise, while he achieved one of the symbols of postmodern sporting immortality, with the Walkers brand creating a variety of potato crisps named in his honor – the predictably "exotic" chili and tomato chutney-flavored Magic Monty's Spicy Spinners. According to Simon Wilde (2006), "in this age of manicured celebrity, Panesar is refreshingly at home being what he is," spending his spare time doing "normal things and getting away from cricket altogether." This, the public subsequently learnt, extended to relaxing in front of The Simpsons or EastEnders on television, in between playing his Nintendo Wii or listening to hip-hop and garage music. He follows the fortunes both of Luton Town and of Arsenal football clubs, and he likes nothing better than a vegetarian Pizza Hut meal, with cheesy garlic bread and a large Pepsi (Bull, 2008). Put simply, Monty was widely regarded as "one of us," a people's hero, and with "none of [Cristiano] Ronaldo's arrogance, [Kevin] Pietersen's swagger or [David] Beckham's bling" (Sikhnet, 2008). Yet, perhaps tellingly, we knew little beyond superficial accounts of Panesar's leisure and consumption habits. The practicing Sikh and family man were kept very much private, inaccessible – or unappealing – to the celebrity gaze. This calls into question the authenticity of the media-constituted Panesar, yet at the same time demonstrates how – as in many other sporting cases (Andrews and Jackson, 2001) – it often overrides the "real" personality in creating celebrity status in the popular imagination.

The combination of his sporting ability and his unremarkable personal tastes cannot, however, completely account for the manner and speed with which Panesar was taken to the public's hearts. Some have argued that his often comical fielding skills and missed catches helped to bridge the ever-increasing social chasm between professional player and supporter. They may be partly right. Wilde (2006) claims that "fans love nothing more than the sportsman who blends wholehearted effort with a dash of clumsiness. He's Eddie the Eagle, Eric the Eel and court-jester-made-good all rolled into one."[3]

Yet the popularity of players who embody these roles cannot be separated from the racial stereotypes on which they are frequently based. Ben Carrington (2004), for example, highlights the barely veiled racism articulated in media coverage of Eric "the Eel" Moussambani, the swimmer from Equatorial Guinea who struggled to complete a 100-meters freestyle race at the 2004 Olympic Games. Carrington (2004: 90) argues that:

> in addition to the amusing culture clash of the modern West against traditional Africa, and the accounts of untamed wildlife roaming the waters of West Africa, Moussambani, as a signifier, shifted from and between the position of amateur Olympian to archetypal black African. Thus much of the coverage framed him not simply as an individual, or even as an individual from Equatorial Guinea, but as representative, in some fundamental way for Africa itself and black people in general.

Furthermore, the association of African Caribbeans with clowns or entertainers is one of the most ingrained Western racial stereotypes. The capacity of certain black British sport stars to fulfill this function in the public imagination has long been integral to their popularity (Carrington, 2000, 2001). This all points toward the demotic celebration of Panesar being much less innocent than is widely perceived.

With specific regard to South Asian (and other Asian background) sport participants, jokes and mocking discourses have been a prominent way in which they have been historically, and continue to be, effaced and defaced (Burdsey, 2011; King, 2011). Panesar has been subjected to enough "gags" to form his own book. He has been described as "the only Test cricketer in the world who plays and misses when he attempts a high-five to celebrate taking a wicket" (Walters, 2006). His fielding has been labeled "hapless," his batting "incompetent," and his celebrations as "an ecstasy of cartoon-ish disbelief." Monty's decision to live at home with his parents and family – a widespread and highly regarded aspect of South Asian culture – is portrayed through a trivializing and sexist stance: "his mum's an ace cook and he doesn't have to do his own laundry" (John, 2006). By his own admission his nicknames include

Edward Scissorhands (from the eponymous 1990s movie) and Monty Python (coined by Australian legend Shane Warne no less; see Walters, 2006), whilst his "unathletic" style has been compared to Bambi on ice and a giraffe. When he appeared on a 2006 episode of television quiz show *A Question of Sport*, the (usually reverent) introductory footage showed not only his debut dismissal of Tendulkar but also a terrible missed catch off Mahendra Singh Dhoni. Despite the pressures placed on British Asians (and other minority ethnic groups) to downplay discrimination in sport (Burdsey, 2011), it is unsurprising that an intelligent, university graduate started to see through this façade. Monty states in his autobiography that "there were times when I wondered whether [people] were laughing at me rather than with me. I didn't know if they were waiting for the fumbles and taking the mickey as if it was some sort of sideshow, rather than wanting me to succeed" (Panesar, 2007: 121).

As potential nicknames were exhausted and fielding errors were eradicated from his performances, white folk were able to rely on old stereotypes of South Asian culture and physicality. Monty found out that he "could make [his teammates] laugh by getting up to dance to some bhangra music" (Panesar, 2007: 198). As Carrington (2008: 125) argues, "an accomplished, dedicated and thoughtful international cricketer is reduced to a cartoon-like comedic object of ridicule, whose apparent purpose is to entertain ol' massa in the field." There is clearly, therefore, a demeaning strand to the Panesar narrative. Much of this arguably takes on a hypermasculine, heteronormative (and arguably homophobic) theme with the performance of non-hegemonic masculinities and the possession of a gentle, cerebral personality generating ridicule in the contemporary rough-and-tumble of British competitive team sports.

In addition, one needs to consider the influence that Panesar's appearance and corporeal attributes have on public perceptions. As Lee (2007: 24) points out, his visual distinctiveness is immediately apparent and potentially problematic; he "has attached to his head two articles that some interpret as a signal that he does not really belong in the English cricket team." Both his headwear and his beard possess overt religious significance. He might therefore be contrasted

with another British Asian sporting hero, Amir Khan. It has been claimed that Khan – a British Pakistani Muslim boxer who shot to fame at the 2004 Olympic Games – represents the most apposite sporting role model for British Asian youth. This is due to his endorsement of dominant political rhetoric (around Muslim communities and the so-called War on Terror) and his adoption of Westernized, hybrid stylistic sensibilities (Burdsey, 2007b). For example, according to novelist Gautam Malkani (2006), Khan is the most authentic and important contemporary British Asian popular cultural icon, as he "simply oozes desi subculture . . . the right hair, the right swagger, the right speech patterns, the right clothes." Malkani suggests that by embodying a sense of "desiness" – a specific *diasporic* South Asianness – Khan's identity and style "are no less British than [former England cricket captain Nasser] Hussain's cucumber sandwiches" (2006). In other words, "Panesar's outward expression of otherness is in contrast to the short-haired and clean-shaven Sajid Mahmood [Amir Khan's cousin and an England international cricketer], the most likely person after Panesar to be regarded by narrow-minded sports-fans as 'inauthentically' English on account of his Muslim religion" (Lee, 2007: 24).

Panesar retains his popularity despite – or arguably *because of* – his visual otherness. The adorning of clip-on bushy beards by members of the Barmy Army is often perceived as a form of adoration and, misguidedly, heralded as a form of harmless reverence. The popular argument is as follows: "this Asian chap is welcome in the England team and how better for us to demonstrate it than taking his most obvious physical trait and celebrating it?" Wearing Monty beards might, therefore, simply exemplify the polysemic nature of cultural symbols, and the necessarily contextual nature of their reading and interpretation. Yet, as with his representation as a comedic character, the centrality of his beard and *patka* to supporter worship is a much more ambiguous and problematic affair. In the aftermath of the July 2005 London terrorist attacks and the media frenzy surrounding radical Islamists based in the United Kingdom, such as Abu Hamza al-Masri and Omar Bakri Mohammed, the beard has become a key signifier of the "dangerous" Muslim Other in the popular imagination. In sport itself, whilst African Caribbeans' dreadlocks have often been a source of both mirth and criticism within football (Carrington, 1998), Muslim cricketers' beards have likewise been a source of amusement and discrimination amongst some player and supporters (Burdsey, 2010a; see Thangaraj, 2010 for sport in the US context).

This demonstrates that white supporters wearing fake beards can never just be an innocuous act of play; it is always inexorably characterized by a racialized (and often classed and gendered) power dynamic. This patronizing and demeaning appropriation eviscerates immediately the religious significance that the beard holds within Sikhism and the respect it should warrant. Instead it becomes an empty, disposable prop for the merriment of white (male) bodies. As Deborah Root (1996) points out, cultural appropriation is premised upon a belief within white groups that they already possess access to, or even ownership of, desired bodies, images, or artifacts. She adds that "the source of all the fascination can have no say in the terms of the exchange. If we think we already own something, why would we ask anybody's permission to take it?" (Root, 1996: 72). Wearing the beards also represents an all-too-close brush with the neo-minstrelsy of contemporary British television comedian Sacha Baron Cohen, and the shows *Bo' Selecta!*, *Little Britain*, and *Come Fly With Me*. As one British Asian first-class cricket player, interviewed in 2008, argued, "it's a piss-take. It's taking the piss. It is. It's something that looks quite nice, but on the other hand it's taking the piss out of Monty. There's a fine line, isn't there." All of a sudden, white men with false beards on their chin, Three Lions on their chest, and cans of lager in their hand appear as immediately regressive as the sight of Spike Milligan in brown face-paint and a turban in 1970s British comedy sketch shows.[4]

Finally, the issue needs to be understood in the broader context of the complex and contradictory manner in which the exotic, particularly "Asianness," has been appropriated and consumed in Western societies (Hutnyk, 2000). Caroline Nagel and Lynn Staeheli (2008: 83–84) argue that "if certain visible differences are regarded as innocuous, acceptable, and even worthy of protection, others are seen to signify an unwillingness to become part of British society."

Is Monty's beard perceived as an acceptable and available form of cultural appropriation because it is clearly – if not visually, then certainly symbolically – *not Islamic*? For example, David Ligertwood, Panesar's agent, states that "people may have been looking at guys in the street with beards and feeling negative about them. Monty makes them feel good" (cited in Wilde, 2006). Oh well, as long as they feel okay – never mind the Muslim men who are actually forced to endure prejudicial stares.

Monty Panesar and the "Crisis" of Multiculturalism?

It is in this context that the Panesar "story" becomes as much one about the so-called crisis of British multiculturalism as one of personal biography or sport itself. Pitcher (2009: 22) argues that the concept of multiculturalism can be "politically agnostic" and "does not necessarily signify anything beyond a basic recognition of the facticity of social and cultural diversity." Nevertheless, in the United Kingdom – and in much of Western Europe – it has been, to all extents and purposes, jettisoned as a meaningful political concept as neoliberal approaches to race take hold (Goldberg, 2009; Lentin and Titley, 2011). In particular, multiculturalism has been situated in dominant discourses as being at odds with a shared notion of Britishness and the adoption of certain core values. It is widely perceived that local authorities have been reluctant to challenge certain minority religio-cultural practices – primarily those of some British Muslims (Modood, 2005) – because of the culturally relativist policies of municipal governance. Accordingly, multiculturalism is blamed for a perceived absence of "community cohesion" (Cantle, 2008) between these and other groups. The dominant response under the New Labour government to this situation was a decreasing propensity to recognize cultural diversity as a legitimate social benefit in its own right (Burnett, 2004: 8). Minorities' traditions, values, and sense of identity were systematically marginalized within the public sphere. Attempts were made to replace them with state-regulated appropriate "core values," which were believed to be the central tenets of modern British citizenship. Such an approach has been maintained under the subsequent Conservative–Liberal Democrat coalition government.

In such a context, the role of certain racialized celebrity sporting bodies becomes key. Prominent and popular, yet seemingly also transparent and apolitical, such individuals represent an attractive ideological product. As Carrington (2010: 166) notes, sport works as a "racial project," in that it "become(s) productive, and not merely receptive, of racial discourse and this discourse has material effects both within sport and beyond." Mary McDonald and Susan Birrell (1999) have pointed out that focusing on particular sporting celebrities represents an important and insightful way of examining the intricate and fluctuating character of power relations and patterns of social inequality in contemporary society. Furthermore, as Marta Bolognani (2011) argues, celebrity "is produced, consumed and interpreted in specific cultural contexts." As such, the celebrity individual cannot be examined in isolation and "there are certain *qualities* . . . that permit for him/her to emerge in such magnitude at a particular historical moment" (p. 31). Constructions and representations of the minority ethnic sport star at any given time are therefore just as much those of the sociocultural epoch in which they exist. In this regard, an examination of Panesar's position within British sport and society enables an elucidation of much more than ethnic and racial issues in English cricket; rather, it speaks to the nuances and complexities of Asianness, Britishness, race, nation, and multiculturalism in twenty-first-century Britain.

John Hutnyk (2005: 348) argues that dominant representations of British Asians can be described as an "exotica-fanatica" two-step, in that they are "characterized in a double strategy, either as demons or as exotica, and neither stereotype comes close to an appreciation of the diversity of those under anthropological examination. The double strategy makes Asians either, and both, a people of curious culture – bhangra, spicy food, Bollywood – and a people of fanaticism – Islam, Hindutva, religious extremism." Panesar encapsulates notions of exotic culture rather than fanaticism. Perhaps this gets to the crux of the issue. He embodies an Asianness far removed from popular images and discourses of religio-political extremism and segregated communities. Furthermore, his cuddly, effete demeanor and absence of traits usually associated with the excesses of (sporting) masculinity reinforce popular stereotypes about South Asian male physicality (Burdsey, 2007a; Lim, 2008). He is thus a "safe," non-threatening body – physically, politically, and ideologically. Yet, crucially, he still looks *Asian enough* and is appropriately Asian *in the right way* to signify a meaningful and quantifiable engagement with dominant notions of multiculture. Panesar therefore becomes the "legitimate familiar other" (Fortier, 2005: 569), embodying a multiculturalism that the white majority population are comfortable with. According to Anne-Marie Fortier (2008: 64), this is someone "who is expected to display not too much, not too little, but just enough alterity *of the right kind*: moderately religious, successfully heterosexual, not-too-white but White-enough."

In response, one might argue that this line of thinking is contradicted by the case of Amir Khan, who was taken up as a role model *precisely because he was a Muslim*. Yet this was always a contrived construction, based around a specific, dominant, ideological interpretation of what Muslimness should be and look like. It was strongly underpinned by the government's desire for a young, "good" British Muslim man through whom they could project their model of community cohesion, core values, anti-terror legislation, and the repression of radical Islam (Burdsey, 2007b). Panesar has not been cloaked in overt political rhetoric to the same extent as Khan; but then Britain is not currently engaged in acts of state-initiated terror and neo-imperialism against the global Sikh community, nor is it demonizing, carrying out surveillance on, and interning its domestic Sikh population. Khan certainly achieved a significant level of popularity amongst people from all backgrounds (which has arguably diminished somewhat since he embarked on a professional career), but he never received the *affection* that Panesar did. Such a distinction cannot be taken out of the context of the contemporary politics of multiculturalism in the United Kingdom and the trenchant Islamophobia that continues to exist.

In an overly benign interpretation of the relationship between race and nation in contemporary Britain, Wilde (2006) claims that the "rationale is this: the public welcomes [Panesar's] presence because he makes the England cricket team more multicultural. People want their team to look like this." This tendency to draw (tenuous) correlations between particular racialized individuals and national identity can be understood through Fortier's (2008) notion of the "politics of pride." She argues that celebrations of multicultural heroes "separate ethnic 'others' into subjects who must be hailed as figures of the tolerant, multiracial Britain that many commentators 'cherish'. They constitute 'our' diversity, which is what 'we' are proud of" (p. 31). She adds that "in a mimetic relationship between representation and identity, the [misguided] assumption is that if the visual referent changes, 'we' change, consequently satisfying the disenfranchised communities who will feel greater pride in being part of the national community by virtue of seeing 'fellow members' of 'their' communities within the representational field" (Fortier, 2005: 573).

Similarly, Carrington (2008: 125) points out that:

in this moment Panesar becomes the anti-Shazad Tanweer [one of the four perpetrators of the July 2005 terrorist attacks], reassuring 'us' of the redemptive, integrative function that sport – and cricket especially – is supposed to have in making the natives into Englishmen, even if they still refuse to drink the warm beer after the match. And we are also reassured that we really are a fair and welcoming nation. This is the type of multicultural arrangement that we can all settle on.

In reality, as Sharma (2003: 411) argues, "the celebratory constituents of multiculturalism . . . hardly designate that Asian culture has been finally liberated from its orientalized status. On the contrary, the recognition of multiculture cannot be divorced from the concurrent intensification of the fetishization of ethnic otherness in the West." Furthermore, "despite the effervescent cultural industries, the 'hybrid' visibility of Asian cultural forms has not yet translated into any significant socio-economic redress of multi-racial exclusions within Fortress Europe" (Hutnyk, 2000: 4). The birth of "Asian Kool" in music and other aspects of popular culture during the 1990s did not signify an end to the discrimination, social exclusion, unemployment,

and educational under-achievement endured by certain British Asian communities (Sardar, 2008). Likewise, Panesar's cross-cultural take-up as a role model does not signify a universal, unambiguous embracing of multiculture, sporting or otherwise.

The final component of the multicultural sporting jigsaw comes from the fact that Panesar has not spoken publicly about the existence of discrimination, either in relation to any personal experiences or cricket in general. Not discussing, or speaking out against, racism (amongst other forms of discrimination) and the prioritization of a sporting identity over an ethnic one are important facets in the process by which minority ethnic athletes are granted (contingent) inclusion as "one of the lads" in British sport (Carrington, 2000; King, 2004; Burdsey, 2007a). Indeed, allegations of racism are frequently rebuffed by the English cricket establishment, with its members arguing that the game has long shed its colonial baggage and white, middle-class ethos. As Mike Marqusee (1998: 160) argues:

In English cricket, if you mention racism you are seen as an intruder, someone with an ulterior motive, not someone fully and truly dedicated to the game. After all, we're all equal on the cricket field. That is the gentleman's code. Those who decry racism in the game are needlessly introducing conflict into a zone of camaraderie. The truth, of course, is that this conflict is introduced by racists and, more surreptitiously, by racist ideas and assumptions.

Monty does little to challenge dominant perceptions around race in English cricket. As he states in his autobiography and other publications, "I've never encountered prejudice in any dressing room. Quite the opposite. I think players like the idea of being in the same team as somebody from a different culture" (Panesar, 2007: 28). Panesar continues:

I read somewhere that people were happy to see somebody from a different culture being able to integrate so quickly and be so happy in an England side. That was a bit heavy for me. All I ever wanted to do was play cricket for England. I've never felt distinct from any of the other guys in the side, even if I stand out with my beard and my patka. I am a cricketer like [Andrew] Flintoff, [Kevin] Pietersen and all the others. Nothing more, and nothing less. (p. 140)

Similarly, in an article in the alumni magazine of his former university, Panesar is quoted giving the following advice: "Don't believe that you will not be given an opportunity because of your race, if you work hard and prove you're capable then I believe that whatever your race you will be picked for your ability alone" (Loughborough University, 2008: 13). Such sentiments are widely reproduced within the cricket establishment and sections of the media. In contrast, academic research – in which the participants are anonymized – *has* uncovered the existence of racism in the game, and the pressures placed on players to downplay it in order not to mark themselves as "risky" bodies (Carrington and McDonald, 2001; Burdsey, 2011).

In 2006, on England's Ashes tour to Australia, a local spectator was reported to have shouted, "Give us a wave, Monty. You can't speak English you stupid Indian, I'll have to say it in Indian. What are you doing playing in the English side, you're not English?" (Lee, 2007: 23; see also Malcolm, 2009). Panesar responded that, "there was nothing said that I could not cope with and, as at Headingley a few months earlier, my attitude was to laugh it off" (Panesar, 2007: 171). This anecdote simply serves to reinforce his position as a safe individual who does not makes "us" question our credentials as multiculturalists: if Monty says that racism is not present, then who are "we" to argue?

Conclusion: Monty Panesar and the Ephemeral Nature of (Sporting) Celebrity

By the summer of 2010, Panesar had dropped out of the England national team reckoning and had transferred to a new domestic. Struggling for form and to gain a place in the First XI, he was farmed out to play in the Sussex League – a countywide rather than national competition – in the sleepy coastal town of Bexhill-on-Sea. The following year, it came to light that the player had been arrested (although subsequently released

without charge) following a fracas with his wife (*Argus*, 2011).

In the years since the episode with which this chapter began, Panesar has developed a close friendship with Sachin Tendulkar. During the 2011 English cricket season, it was the latter who generated most media attention, with Panesar having all but disappeared from the scene at that time. Tendulkar was part of the Indian touring side playing against a Panesar-less England. He was attempting to score his 100th international century (which he finally achieved in 2012). With the vicissitudes of high-level sport and the "build them up, knock them down" nature of the British tabloid press, Panesar's plight highlights the ephemeral nature of sporting iconography. Arguably more importantly for the present analysis, it also demonstrates the limits of using athletes as national and multicultural icons. Before the 2011 England–India Test Match at Lord's cricket ground in London, it emerged that Panesar had been practicing with Tendulkar in the nets in order to help him prepare for the English spin-bowling attack. The diaspora was now working *in conjunction with* the homeland. For those who tend to operationalize narrow, simplistic (and most likely racialized) concepts of affiliation and loyalty – within the cricket world and beyond – this was simply a step too far (Pringle, 2011). Yet the summer of 2011 saw a return to form for Panesar, as he took the second-highest number of wickets in the national league. In the summer of 2012 he achieved his best-ever innings and match score, taking a total of 13 wickets in a match. In September that year he was rewarded with a recall to the England squad which toured India in 2012–2013 and proved to be an invaluable member as England secured their first Test series win in India for 28 years. Panesar finished the series with an impressive 17 Test wickets (second only to Graeme Swann in the England side) which included twice getting the prized wicket of Tendulkar.

If Stuart Hall (1992: 293) is correct in arguing that national identities are reproduced through popular cultural narratives of the nation, then the role of sport in contributing towards notions of British Asian identities cannot be ignored. In addition, we might also be witnessing the early signs of a new (contingent) formation of *Asian Britishness* – where the national culture comes to be influenced more by the *members* of Britain's South Asian communities than simply by their food and fashion. Any sense of a new Asian Britishness cannot, and will not, be limited to the realm of sport. Yet it is on pitches, courts, and fields, and in gyms and boxing rings that important steps will occur. In an era of both fleeting celebrity and transient sporting stardom, it is unlikely now to be Panesar himself, but the role of sporting heroes – both male and female – in notions of British Asianness and Asian Britishness may well become increasingly important in future years.

Acknowledgements

I would like to express my thanks and appreciation to David Andrews and Ben Carrington for inviting me to contribute to this collection. The interview quotations from British Asian first-class cricketers were generated through a research project that was made possible by a British Academy Small Grant, entitled "The experiences of British Asian players in contemporary county cricket: ethnicity, identity, racism" (SG-46858).

Notes

1 The Three Lions, taken from the royal arms of England, comprise the official emblem for many English national sport sides, including cricket and football.
2 Eric Morecambe (1926–1984) was a British comedian who, with Ernie Wise, formed the award-winning act *Morecambe and Wise*.
3 Eddie Edwards (b. 1963) was a British ski-jumper who achieved cult status after finishing in last place in both jump events at the 1988 winter Olympic Games.
4 Spike Milligan (1918–2002) was an Indian-born, white British comedian and actor (among other roles), who came to fame in the 1950s radio comedy *The Goon Show*.

References

Ahmad, A. (2011) "British Muslim female experiences in football: Islam, identity and the *hijab*," in Burdsey, D. (ed.) *Race, Ethnicity and Football: Persisting Debates and Emergent Issues*, Abingdon: Routledge, pp. 101–114.

Ali, N., Kalra, V., and Sayyid, S. (eds.) (2006) *A Postcolonial People: South Asians in Britain*, London: Hurst.

Andrews, D. and Jackson, S. (eds.) (2001) *Sport Stars: The Cultural Politics of Sporting Celebrity*, London: Routledge.

Argus (2011) "Monty Panesar arrest comes to light." *Argus*, June 12, http://www.theargus.co.uk/news/9079771.Monty_Panesar_arrest_comes_to_light/, accessed January 23, 2013.

Ballard, R. (ed.) (1994) *Desh Pardesh: The South Asian Presence in Britain*, London: Hurst.

BBC (2006) "Monty for England," BBC1 TV, April 12.

Beard, M. (2006) "Monty mania proves to be a potent force for unity as Asian youths rush to emulate cricketing hero." *Independent*, August 5, http://www.independent.co.uk/news/uk/this-britain/monty-mania-proves-to-be-a-potent-force-for-unity-as-asian-youths-rush-to-emulate-cricketing-hero-410606.html, accessed January 23, 2013.

Bhachu, P. (1985) *Twice Migrants: East African Settlers in Britain*, London: Tavistock.

Bolognani, M. (2011) "Star fission: Shoaib Akhtar and fragmentation as transnational celebrity strategy." *Celebrity Studies*, 2 (1): 31–43.

Bonilla-Silva, E. (2006) *Racism Without Racists: Color-blind Racism and the Persistence of Racial Equality in the United States*, Lanham, MD: Rowman & Littlefield.

Brenkley, S. (2006) "The Panesar and Mahmood effect quick to take hold." *Independent on Sunday*, August 13.

Brown, J. (2006) *Global South Asians: Introducing the Modern Diaspora*, Cambridge: Cambridge University Press.

Bull, A. (2008) "Small talk: Monty Panesar." *Guardian*, June 6, http://www.guardian.co.uk/sport/2008/jun/06/englandvnewzealand2008.englandcricketteam4?gusrc=rss&feed=sport, accessed January 10, 2013.

Burdsey, D. (2004) "'One of the lads'? Dual ethnicity and assimilated ethnicities in the careers of British

Asian professional footballers." *Ethnic and Racial Studies*, 27 (5): 757–779.

Burdsey, D. (2006a) "'If I ever play football Dad, can I play for England or India?' British Asians, sport and diasporic national identities." *Sociology*, 40 (1): 11–28.

Burdsey, D. (2006b) "No ball games allowed? A socio-historical examination of the development and social roles of British Asian football clubs." *Journal of Ethnic and Migration Studies*, 32 (3): 477–496.

Burdsey, D. (2007a) *British Asians and Football: Culture, Identity, Exclusion*, Abingdon: Routledge.

Burdsey, D. (2007b) "Role with the punches: The construction and representation of Amir Khan as a role model for multiethnic Britain." *Sociological Review*, 55 (3): 611–631.

Burdsey, D. (2008) "Half of some and half of the Other: The racialised (dis)contents of Englishness," in Perryman, M. (ed.) *Imagined Nation: England after Britain*, London: Lawrence & Wishart, pp. 207–222.

Burdsey, D. (2010a) "British Muslim experiences in English first-class cricket." *International Review for the Sociology of Sport*, 45 (3): 315–334.

Burdsey, D. (2010b) "Midnight's grandchildren at the MCC: British Asians, identity and English first-class cricket," in Rumford, C. and Wagg, S. (eds.) *Cricket and Globalization*, Newcastle upon Tyne: Cambridge Scholars Publishing, pp. 252–269.

Burdsey, D. (2011) "That joke isn't funny anymore: Racial microaggressions, color-blind ideology and the mitigation of racism in Englishmens' first-class cricket." *Sociology of Sport Journal*, 28 (3): 261–283.

Burdsey, D. (2012) "The technicolor Olympics? Race, representation and the 2012 London Games," in Sugden, J. and Tomlinson, A. (eds.) *Watching the Olympics: Politics, Power and Representation*, Abingdon: Routledge, pp. 69–81.

Burnett, J. (2004) "Community, cohesion and the state." *Race and Class*, 45 (3): 1–18.

Cantle, T. (2008) *Community Cohesion: A New Framework for Race and Diversity* (rev. edn.), Basingstoke: Palgrave Macmillan.

Carrington, B. (1998) "'Football's coming home' but whose home? And do we want it? Nation, football and the politics of exclusion," in Brown, A. (ed.) *Fanatics! Power, Identity and Fandom in Football*, London: Routledge, pp. 101–123.

Carrington, B. (2000) "Double consciousness and the black British athlete," in Owusu, K. (ed.) *Black British Culture and Society*, London: Routledge, pp. 133–156.

Carrington, B. (2001) "Postmodern blackness and the celebrity sports star: Ian Wright, 'race' and English identity," in Andrews, D. and Jackson, S. (eds.) *Sport Stars: The Cultural Politics of Sporting Celebrity*, London: Routledge, pp. 102–123.

Carrington, B. (2004) "Cosmopolitan Olympism, humanism and the spectacle of 'race'," in Bale, J. and Christensen, M.K. (eds.) *Post-Olympism? Questioning Sport in the Twenty-first Century*, Oxford: Berg, pp. 81–97.

Carrington, B. (2008) "Where's the white in the Union Jack? Race, identity and the sporting multicultural," in Perryman, M. (ed.) *Imagined Nation: England after Britain*, London: Lawrence & Wishart, pp. 109–133.

Carrington, B. (2010) *Race, Sport and Politics: The Sporting Black Diaspora*, London: Sage Publications.

Carrington, B. and McDonald, I. (2001) "Whose game is it anyway? Racism in local league cricket," in Carrington, B. and McDonald, I. (eds.) *"Race", Sport and British Society*, London: Routledge, pp. 49–69.

Fortier, A.-M. (2005) "Pride politics and multiculturalist citizenship." *Ethnic and Racial Studies*, 28 (3): 559–578.

Fortier, A.-M. (2008) *Multicultural Horizons: Diversity and the Limits of the Civil Nation*, Abingdon: Routledge.

Goldberg, D.T. (2009) *The Threat of Race: Reflections on Racial Neoliberalism*, Oxford: Wiley-Blackwell.

Hall, S. (1992) "The question of cultural identity," in Hall, S., Held, D., and McGrew, T. (eds.) *Modernity and Its Futures*, Cambridge: Polity Press, pp. 273–326.

Henderson, R. (1995) "Is it in the blood?" *Wisden Cricket Monthly*, July.

Herbert Gallery (2006) *Coming To Coventry: Stories From the South Asian Pioneers*, Coventry: Coventry Teaching Primary Care Trust/The Herbert Gallery.

Hopps, D. (2006) "Panesar prepares for McGrath mugging with session on mean streets." *Guardian*, November 11.

Hutnyk, J. (2000) *Critique of Exotica: Music, Politics and the Culture Industry*, London: Pluto Press.

Hutnyk, J. (2005) "The dialectic of here and there: Anthropology 'at home' and British Asian communism." *Social Identities*, 11 (4): 345–361.

Johal, S. (2001) "Playing their own game: A South Asian football experience," in Carrington, B. and McDonald, I. (eds.) *"Race", Sport and British Society*, London: Routledge, pp. 153–169.

John, E. (2006) "Juggling with destiny." *Observer Sport Monthly*, 81, November, http://www.guardian.co.uk/sport/2006/oct/29/cricket.features, accessed January 23, 2013.

King, C. (2004) *Offside Racism: Playing the White Man*, Oxford: Berg.

King, C.R. (2011) *Asian Americans in Sport and Society*, New York: Routledge.

Lee, J. (2007) "Why isn't Panesar a Pommie bastard? Multiculturalism and the implications of Cricket Australia's racial abuse policy." *Anthropology Today*, 24 (2): 23–25.

Lentin, A. and Titley, G. (2011) *The Crises of Multiculturalism: Racism in a Neoliberal Age*, London: Zed Books.

Lewis, P. (2007) *Young, British and Muslim*, London: Continuum.

Lim, J. (2008) "Encountering South Asian masculinity through the event," in Dwyer, C. and Bressey, C. (eds.) *New Geographies of Race and Racism*, Aldershot: Ashgate, pp. 223–238.

Loughborough University (2008) "The Monty effect," *Loughborough University Alumni Magazine*, 18, February.

Lowles, N. (2011) "A town divided?" *Searchlight*, 427, January.

Lusted, J. (2009) "Playing games with 'race': Understanding resistance to 'race' equality initiatives in English local football governance." *Soccer and Society*, 10 (6): 722–739.

McDonald, M. and Birrell, S. (1999) "Reading sport critically: A methodology for interrogating power." *Sociology of Sport Journal*, 16 (4): 283–300.

Malcolm, D. (2009) "Malign or benign? English national identities and cricket." *Sport in Society*, 12 (4/5): 613–628.

Malkani, G. (2006) "Mixing and matching." *Financial Times*, April 22, http://www.ft.com/cms/9f2bb9fc-d03b-11da-b160-0000779e2340.html, accessed January 22, 2013.

Manzoor, S. (2007) *Greetings from Bury Park: Race, Religion and Rock 'n' Roll*, London: Bloomsbury.

Marqusee, M. (1998) *Anyone But England: Cricket, Race and Class* (2nd edn.), London: Two Heads Publishing.

Modood, T. (2005) *Multicultural Politics: Racism, Ethnicity and Muslims in Britain*, Edinburgh: Edinburgh University Press.

Nagel, C. and Staeheli, L. (2008) "Integration and the politics of visibility and invisibility in Britain: The case of British Arab activists," in Dwyer, C. and Bressey, C. (eds.) *New Geographies of Race and Racism*, Aldershot: Ashgate, pp. 83–94.

Nandy, A. (2001) *The Tao of Cricket: On Games of Destiny and the Destiny of Games*, Oxford: Oxford University Press.

Panesar, M., with Hobson, R. (2007) *Monty's Turn: Taking my Chances*, London: Hodder & Stoughton.

Parry, M. and Malcolm, D. (2004) "England's Barmy Army: Commercialization, masculinity and nation-alism." *International Review for the Sociology of Sport*, 39 (1): 73–92.

Pitcher, B. (2009) *The Politics of Multiculturalism: Race and Racism in Contemporary Britain*, Basingstoke: Palgrave Macmillan.

Pringle, D. (2011) "England coach Andy Flower to ban Monty Panesar from giving net practice to Sachin Tendulkar." *Daily Telegraph*, July 26, http://www.telegraph.co.uk/sport/cricket/international/england/8663782/England-coach-Andy-Flower-to-ban-Monty-Panesar-from-giving-net-practice-to-Sachin-Tendulkar.html, accessed January 23, 2013.

Ramamurthy, A. (2006) "The politics of Britain's Asian Youth Movements." *Race and Class*, 48 (2): 38–60.

Ramdin, R. (1999) *Reimagining Britain: 500 Years of Black and Asian History*, London: Pluto Press.

Ratna, A. (2011) "Flying the flag for England? National identities and British Asian female footballers," in Burdsey, D. (ed.) *Race, Ethnicity and Football: Persisting Debates and Emergent Issues*, London: Routledge, pp. 117–130.

Root, D. (1996) *Cannibal Culture: Art, Appropriation and the Commodification of Difference*, Boulder, CO: Westview Press.

Sardar, Z. (2008) *Balti Britain: A Journey Through the British Asian Experience*, London: Granta Books.

Sharma, S. (2003) "The sounds of alterity," in Bull, M. and Back, L. (eds.) *The Auditory Culture Reader*, Oxford: Berg, pp. 409–418.

Sikhnet (2008) "Monty Panesar: The quiet hero." *Sikhnet.com*, August 21 http://www.sikhnet.com/daily-news/monty-panesar-quiet-hero, accessed January 23, 2013.

Smith, T. (2004) *Asians in Britain*, Stockport: Dewi Lewis Publishing.

Thangaraj, S. (2010) "Ballin' Indo-Pak style: Pleasures, desires, and expressive practices of 'South Asian American' masculinity." *International Review for the Sociology of Sport*, 45 (3): 372–389.

Valiotis, C. (2009) "Runs in the outfield: The Pakistani diaspora and cricket in England." *International Journal of the History of Sport*, 26 (12): 1791–1822.

Visram, R. (2002) *Asians in Britain: 400 Years of History*, London: Pluto Press.

Walters, M. (2006) "From joke to cult hero . . . to sports personality of the year?" *Daily Mirror*, August 9, http://www.mirror.co.uk/news/uk-news/from-joke-to-cult-hero-to-sports-personality-637243, accessed January 23, 2013.

Werbner, P. (1996) "'Our blood is green': Cricket, identity and social empowerment among British Pakistanis," in MacClancy, J. (ed.) *Sport, Identity and Ethnicity*, Oxford: Berg, pp. 87–111.

Wilde, S. (2006) "The big interview: Monty Panesar." *Sunday Times*, August 6, also *TimesOnline*, http://www.timesonline.co.uk/tol/sport/article601153.ece, accessed January 22, 2013.

Williams, J. (2001) *Cricket and Race*, Oxford: Berg.

Wilson, A. (2006) *Dreams, Questions, Struggles: South Asian Women in Britain*, London: Pluto Press.

Further Reading

Burdsey, D. (2007) *British Asians and Football: Culture, Identity and Exclusion*, Abingdon: Routledge.

Carrington, B. and McDonald, I. (eds.) (2001) *"Race", Sport and British Society*, London: Routledge.

Gilroy, P. (2002) *There Ain't No Black in the Union Jack: The Cultural Politics of Race and Nation* (2nd edn.), London: Routledge.

Marqusee, M. (2005) *Anyone but England: An Outsider Looks at English Cricket*, London: Aurum Press.

Modood, T. (2005) *Multicultural Politics: Racism, Ethnicity and Muslims in Britain*, Edinburgh: Edinburgh University Press.

33

Earl's Loins – Or, Inventing Tiger Woods

Davis W. Houck

Introduction

The most famous SUV since O.J. Simpson's white Ford Bronco, a black Cadillac Escalade zigzagged violently across Deacon Circle in the exclusive enclave of Isleworth, a suburb of Orlando, in the early hours of November 27, 2009. The vehicle traveled less than the distance of a well-struck lob wedge before plowing into a fire hydrant and coming to an abrupt stop at approximately 2.26 a.m.

The world would find out a few hours later that the vehicle's occupant was also the world's most famous athlete, Eldrick "Tiger" Woods. But what began as a car accident story – initially deemed "serious" by the local media – quickly morphed into an international sensation that seemed equal parts 9/11, O.J.'s freeway "escape," and Princess Diana's death. News helicopters hovered over the sprawling eight-bedroom, nine-bathroom estate; reporters faked serious injury to try and get admitted to Health Central Hospital in Ocoee where Woods had been treated; and boats were launched on Lake Palmer to get a better photographic angle of 6348, Deacon Circle. In just a few hours, Woods had become, in the words of Robert Lusetich (2010: 258), "the Big Story." He still is.

So why all the fuss over a late-night fender bender? On the surface, two reasons: an incognito Woods and wife, Elin, and the exceptionally odd circumstances of the accident. And it didn't hurt that it was Tiger Woods after all, who had been singled out just two months earlier by *Fortune Magazine* as the world's first billion-dollar athlete. Whatever else might be said about Tiger Woods, he made people money. A lot of money. Editors and producers began seeing dollars signs as dawn broke on November 27. I'd be derelict in not mentioning a fourth reason: a not inconsequential cadre of sportswriters had smelled a phony, a horn-dog hypocrite whose peerless image had been erected, so to speak, on the bedrock of family. *Schadenfreude* – in the making for 13 long and lucrative years – was in the Isleworth air. (As but one example of a writer's confession of anti-Tiger motive, see Jones, 2009.)

Unbeknownst to anyone save his small inner circle, upon Woods' release from Health Central that morning he immediately boarded his US$60 million Gulfstream 550 bound for Arizona and emergency plastic surgery on his split lip. Why a split lip needed emergency surgery across the country remains a mystery. The bigger mystery is whether it was Elin's nine-iron that inflicted the

A Companion to Sport, First Edition. Edited by David L. Andrews and Ben Carrington.
© 2013 Blackwell Publishing Ltd. Published 2013 by Blackwell Publishing Ltd.

damage or his Escalade's steering wheel.[1] It didn't take long for American popular culture to vote enthusiastically for the former. Speculation grew even louder as husband and wife refused to speak with the Florida Highway Patrol on three consecutive days. That loudness, in fact, was inversely proportional to televisual absence; updates on his website weren't going to get it done with a public ravenous for details – especially tawdry ones.

And tawdry came quickly. While the Woods crisis management team hunkered down at 6348, Deacon Circle was temporarily successful in getting rumored paramour, Rachel Uchitel, to deny an affair with Woods,[2] the very porous dam broke on December 2. For US$100,000, *US Magazine* bought the rights to Jaimee Grubbs' story – including a voicemail. It quickly became the voicemail heard around the world:

> Hey it's uh, it's Tiger. Can you please, uh, take your name off your phone [message]. My wife went through my phone and, uh, may be calling you. If you can, please take your name off that and, um, what do you call it, just have it as a number on the voice mail; just have it as your telephone number. That's it, okay. You gotta do this for me. Huge. Quickly. All right. Bye. (quoted in Popkin, 2009)

Journalist John Feinstein (2010), whose Tiger BS-meter had initially been activated all the way back in 1996, couldn't resist: "If there was any doubt about his voice, . . . his use of the word 'huge' twice in a few seconds was a dead giveaway. Go back to any Woods interview and listen: everything is huge: making a putt is huge; winning a tournament is huge; being able to help 10 million people is huge."[3] Within hours the voicemail gone viral on the internet, moreover, a soulful (and hilarious) Slow Jam Remix of the message appeared on YouTube that same day. Similarly, and with revelations of multiple dalliances with adult entertainers such as Joslyn James and Holly Sampson, the marketing genius of Eldrick's *nom de plume* was quickly riffed: porn films *Tiger's Wood* and *Tiger's Got Wood* were quickly announced. And filmed.

Stories of Tiger's philandering quickly went "Wilt Chamberlain";[4] after all, there was now money to be made. Back in 2007 Team Tiger –

directed by the International Management Group (IMG) and Woods' agent, Mark Steinberg – had narrowly avoided image and thus economic disaster when Woods decided to sate, if temporarily, his sexual appetite in a church parking lot with Perkins Restaurant and Bakery hostess/waitress Mindy Lawton. Tipped off about Woods' increasingly careless sexual behavior, the *National Enquirer* was present to photograph the pre-dawn and unholy carnal escapade.[5] Though the pictures were hardly clear, the *Enquirer* had other evidence – notably Lawton's sullied tampon. Confronted with the evidence, Steinberg proposed a quid pro quo: kill the *Enquirer* story in exchange for a cover and an exclusive interview with *Men's Fitness* magazine – a sister publication. The deal was consummated sometime that spring; publication followed a few months later in August. Crisis averted. Of course *Men's Fitness* made money. Its editor-in-chief, Neal Boulton, quit in protest. And Tiger saved some, perhaps a lot.

The Chosen One(s)

That article brings us at last to Eldrick[6] Tont Woods' father, Earl Woods. As any Tiger watcher knows well, without Earl there is no "Tiger." And I'm not speaking biologically. There is an Eldrick, but not a "Tiger." But I'm getting ahead of myself. Roy S. Johnson's (2007) 3,000-plus word cover feature in *Men's Fitness* begins thus: "Just about any story on Tiger Woods will involve Earl. He died a little more than a year ago. Yet Earl Woods still lingers about the room like a comfortable, knowing breeze, inspiring stories, laughter and smiles." In an article born directly out of getting caught red-glanded doing the vertical bone dance in the parking lot of Christ the King Lutheran Church, its closing is breathtaking:

> Earl creeps into the room again . . ., "I just hope to be a parent that would raise a child to make the proper decisions," [Tiger] says. "Instill in them the knowledge to make the right choices, the core values, things you don't understand as a kid but when you get to the fork in the road and start reflecting, it gets pretty easy to make those decisions."

Little wonder that the Escalade eventually hit the fire hydrant. Then again, as we'll see, family hypocrisy did not originate with the son.

Prior to December 2009 we'd come to know Earl Dennison Woods as his son's "best friend," a bit of a media-hogging blowhard by dint of his frequently lachrymose declarations of his kid going Gandhi-Mandela-Ashe-Ali; as a frequently cited source when his son wouldn't talk to the press about anything beyond his latest "huge W [win]"; and, an author/parenting consultant who'd quickly churned out three books that capitalized on his relationship with his increasingly famous son. Earl was also something of a rhetorical genius. I'd like to interrogate that genius in this chapter, especially as it relates to race and the rhetorical invention of Tiger Woods. Until his son's Ambien-Vicodin-philandering-induced crash on Deacon Circle, Family Woods had been given a relatively free pass by the nation's media, despite evidence that all wasn't quite what it seemed at the family homestead back in Cypress, California. But to be on the wrong side of Family Woods was to be blackballed from the biggest sports celebrity of the twenty-first century, excommunicated from the Company of the Chosen One where belief in singular golfing genius and God's Will Made Flesh was carefully cultivated and doctrinally enforced. It's no coincidence that the journalists who punctured the myth of Family Woods were not golf writers nor yet sports journalists. The so-called tabloid journalists and independent writers had no financial or ecumenical interest in promulgating the Gospel at the Church of Woods.[7]

It's clear even to the rhetorical novice that Earl Woods loved playing Abraham to his Messianic Son. Or maybe Earl Woods just liked playing God. Not a few quotes were attributed to Him. As we will see, Earl had a rather direct line to the Almighty. That line became a relatively local one after the 1996 Haskins and the 1997 Masters.

The world beyond golf first met Earl Woods in the December 23, 1996, issue of *Sports Illustrated* (Smith, 1996). Many had seen the portly, 60-something black man hovering around his exceptionally talented son, but we hadn't heard much beyond proud fatherly sound bites. This all changed, and rather dramatically, when *Sports Illustrated*'s Gary Smith recorded Earl Woods' introductory remarks at the Fred Haskins Award dinner, honoring the nation's top intercollegiate golfer:

> The world will be a better place to live in . . . by virtue of his existence . . . and his presence . . . I acknowledge only a small part in that [he stated]. I know that I was personally selected by God himself . . . to nurture this young man . . . and bring him to the point where he can make his contribution to humanity . . . This is my treasure. . . . Please accept it . . . and use it wisely. . . . Thank you.

The assembled press, sensing a far bigger story than a 20-year-old golfer getting a trophy, quickly sought clarification from the father. Was he serious when he said that his son would "do more than any other man in history to change the course of humanity"? "Yes," Earl Woods replied, "because he has a larger forum than any of them. . . . He's the bridge between East and West. There is no limit. I don't know yet exactly what form this will take. But he is the Chosen One. The world is just getting a taste of his power" (Smith, 1996).

John Feinstein cried bullshit. So, too, a bit later did Charles Pierce (1998). Perhaps because he didn't want to spoil the "Sportsman of the Year" feature that he was then writing, Smith simply raised a question: was the "maw" of the "machine" set to devour yet another preternaturally talented young athlete whose parents were clearly out of control in touting the virtues of their talented kid? Surely this was Stefano Capriati, Marv Marinovich, and Richard Williams leavened by an unholy exegetical fundamentalism. Read carefully, Earl's Haskins gospel also reveals who, exactly, was the Chosen One.

We should pause here to reflect for a moment on golf, specifically greatness in golf. By the time of Earl's speech, his son had done some remarkable things; in fact, they were completely unprecedented things. For the better part of the last 50 years, Jack Nicklaus has served as the benchmark for golfing greatness. If the golf community spotted a particularly outstanding junior golfer, the "next Nicklaus" label was often quickly applied. Golf writers, television executives, and the golfing public yearned to see the sort of dominating greatness that defined stars in other sports, but which in golf remained very elusive. Tom

Watson drank himself into the "yips" (a dreaded malady in which short putts are missed – often badly – because of jangled nerves; think of the term as something of an onomatopoeia); Bobby Clampett clowned his way into mediocrity;[8] Ian Baker-Finch's head wouldn't allow him to break 90; Scott Verplank won a professional event as an amateur, and then won very little as a professional; Ty Tryon, the *wunderkind* who'd earned his Professional Golfers' Association (PGA) Tour card at age 17, in his mid-twenties can't even find a tour to play; future superstar Jodie Mudd traded golf's pressure for the pastoral landscape of horse-breeding; nobody even remembers Doug Martin,[9] despite being both the top junior and amateur in the nation – and these are just a fraction of the elite golfers who made the PGA Tour. Countless collegiate All-Americans never made it out of the minor leagues of the Hogan Tour, the Nike Tour, and the two most prominent "minor league" professional men's golf tours – the Hooters Tour, and the Nationwide/Web.com Tour. (There are several other more regional tours, but these two are major feeders of the PGA Tour.) In a word, golf is fickle. Perhaps more than any other sport, golf is a game played between the ears. Not coincidentally, it is also a game played completely alone.[10]

And so when Tiger Woods turned professional in August 1996, with the stated intention of being the greatest golfer ever, better even than Jack Nicklaus, the golf community collectively rolled its eyes; they'd heard this all before. That eye-rolling is perhaps best illustrated by ABC's then-expert golf commentator, Curtis Strange, who interviewed Woods during the Greater Milwaukee Open. In response to Tiger Woods' comment that he always played to win, and second place "sucks," and third place "is worse," Strange patronizingly replied, "you'll learn." At Tiger's first professional tournament, after signing record-breaking endorsement deals with Nike and Titleist for nearly US$50 million, his finish in a tie for 60th at a bottom-feeder tournament like the Greater Milwaukee Open only seemed to confirm that collective wisdom. Derision was also directed at Earl Woods, who'd made the outrageous prediction that, given seven chances to play in a PGA tournament that fall, Tiger would be sure to win at least one. Woods' decision to turn pro relatively late in the professional golfing cal-

endar meant that he needed to make enough money to be at least 125th on the official money list. If he cracked the top 125, he would be automatically exempt to compete in nearly all PGA events the following year, 1997. If he didn't make the top 125, he would be subject to the grueling fall event known as "Q school," or qualifying school, which takes place over three separate and very high-pressure tournaments.

How did Earl know Tiger would win? Somewhere outside of Moline, IL, at the Quad Cities Open, God spoke directly to father and son. To John Strege (1997a: 209), Earl later revealed, "I saw it at Quad City. I saw 'the man upstairs' present the young man with the opportunity, let him feel it. Then 'he' said, 'no.' What the 'man' said was, 'you're ready, but patience, my man.'" A few weeks later, at the Las Vegas Invitational, Earl predicted this would be the week. Why? Because it was "only natural that [Tiger] choose an entertainment capital as the stage on which to win his first professional golf tournament" (Strege, 1997a: 209). A funny thing happened in Las Vegas: Tiger won his first professional golf tournament. And then he won a second tournament a few weeks later in his new home town of Orlando.[11] And then he won for a third time in January 1997, dramatically stuffing a 7-iron from 215 yards to 6 inches in a sudden-death playoff against Player of the Year, Tom Lehman. The golf world, and the larger sports world too, was buzzing about the 20-year-old black golfer whose game was actually living up to the Nicklaus hype. Not surprisingly, Earl Woods was frequently mentioned in the same lead paragraph as his famous son; after all, he'd been the creative genius, so he informed anyone who would listen, behind what he openly claimed had been a meticulously crafted, 20-year project.[12] *Newsweek* came calling. So did the US television networks. Earl was ready with the story, and in that narrative of golfing precocity and godly revelation, race – and racism – became central.

Hello World/Hello Earl

Earl Woods had his own story about growing up black in Jim Crow America, and he was eager to tell it – and he now had very willing eyes and ears. His son wasn't nearly so eager, but he was a willing proxy. Initially. At his first press conference as a professional golfer, a nervous Tiger began haltingly, "Well, I guess, hello world." Nobody guessed that this somewhat diffident opening would signal a marketing blitz the likes of which the golf world had never seen. That weekend, ESPN's viewers got a steady dose of Tiger's coming-out commercial – and it was unabashedly loud and confrontational. Set to an ominously percussive score, images of an amateur Tiger danced across the screen. The text propelled and contextualized the visuals:

> Hello World.
> I shot in the 70s when I was eight;
> I shot in the 60s when I was twelve;
> I won the US Junior Amateur when I was fifteen.
> Hello World.
> I played in the Nissan Open when I was sixteen.
> Hello World.
> I won the US Amateur when I was eighteen;
> I played in the Masters when I was nineteen;
> I am the only man to win three consecutive US amateur titles.
> Hello World.[13]

So far the rehearsal of Tiger's remarkable biography stuck to a script of golfing excellence. And then the ad went decidedly off script:

> There are still courses in the US I am not allowed to play because of the color of my skin.
> I've heard I am not ready for you.
> Are you ready for me?

Nike's Hello World advertising campaign generated just as much, if not more, buzz than Tiger's play that week at the Greater Milwaukee Open. Many admired the ad for taking on the aristocratic game's racist past and its unredeemed present. More detested it for crassly commercializing a 20-year-old black kid who hadn't done anything of note in a professional golf tournament – and who could likely play any golf course on the planet, with or without a tee time. Shaun Powell (2008: 14) erroneously claims that "Nike had the good sense to pull the absurd commercial after only a few airings, probably at the request of Tiger." Not only did Nike not prematurely pull the ad, but Woods expressed his support for it.

But Tiger-watchers, those who'd carefully followed him in various professional and amateur tournaments in the United States and abroad, were likely flummoxed by the advertising campaign. After winning his first US amateur title back in the summer of 1994, for example, Woods had this to say about his race (Killion, 1994): "I don't really think about it unless someone [e.g., the press; his father?] brings it up. I just go out and do my part by playing." In the very same article, Earl Woods was quoted to far different effect: "Let's face it, there aren't too many brothers out there on the course. Wherever he's gone, whatever tournament he's in, he's the only one. He has to be a catalyst. And he's accepted that." (For an excellent, though brief, look at some of Woods' race-based contradictions of his own making, see Jones, 2000). The intra-familial tension is palpable: father and "brother" Earl says racial activism is a must; the son thinks about race only when forced to; activism extends only to making statements with his exceptional play. Months later Peter de Jonge (1995) of the *New York Times* noted the same tension after visiting separately with father and son: "One of the few issues on which they diverge is race . . . [Tiger] doesn't see what all the fuss is about." But his father is convinced that by raising a black golfer, Earl "is subverting the racial order." Several years later, Chip Brown (2008), too, noted the tension: "Earl was committing him to an agenda his son seems temperamentally averse to."

And so Tiger-watchers were left to wonder as August turned to September back in 1996: just who was the creative force behind the Hello World advertising campaign? Was it the Wieden and Kennedy advertising agency? Was it Nike, no stranger to controversial ads? Was it Tiger Woods? Or, did Earl Woods, the creative mastermind behind his child's golfing genius, the one chosen by God to expedite racial accord in a balkanized world, provide the inspiration? All the evidence points to the father. Jim Small, the public relations manager at Nike, said as much: "Woods and his family were very much involved in making the ads" (Gross, 1996). But the best evidence for Earl Woods' direct involvement in the Hello World advertisement is in the text itself. As the racial money shot is delivered – "because of the color of my skin" – the camera lingers on Earl Woods hugging his son. Tiger provided the scores; Earl filled in the coloring – and the careful editing.

Earl Woods liked to claim that his time spent as an information officer with the army was all part of the Plan. He didn't know it at the time but doing public relations work for the military functioned to train him for what was coming. No doubt Woods understood that the press which covered a sport as white-dominated, as white-controlled, and with a history of white supremacy that only a Klansman could admire, would be very partial to a talented black golfer. "His dark skin," noted John F. Stacks (1996) of *Time*, makes Tiger . . . all the more appealing in the world of golf, which not only has few nonwhite players but is also played on courses across the country that have systematically excluded minorities. That Tiger could not only crash the party but eventually dominate it is quite delicious." If the "dark-skinned" golfer in question could deliver on the Nicklaus-like comparisons, well, this could only be from a God intent on intervening in the nation's history. Or for the secular hermeneut, and thus profane, Earl's loins.

According to Earl's son, God appeared rather forcefully and emphatically in the second week of April, in the year of our Lord, 1997.

The Master and the Masters, 1997

The Masters golf tournament, played since 1934 at Augusta National golf club, GA, is professional golf's most important and its most prestigious tournament.[14] Its champions form a Who's Who of the history of golf; its signature green jacket has become iconic of golfing excellence. With its 300 members, give or take, Augusta National remains an exclusive sporting bastion. (For two excellent books on the history of Augusta National as well as the Masters, see Owen, 1999; Sampson, 1998). Even Bill Gates had to wait for an invitation to join. But Augusta National is a place not without ugliness. Racial ugliness specifically. Club and tournament founder Bobby Jones, though a major deity in American golf, was a white son of the white-supremacist South. His club manager and tournament chairman, Clifford Roberts, was just a blatant racist. "As long as I'm alive," he infamously declared, "the golfers will be white, and caddies will be black." Only six years after his death – he blew his brains out in his pajamas on the eighth hole at the National

back in 1977 – were professional golfers even allowed to bring white caddies onto the premises. A black golfer didn't receive an invitation to compete in the Masters until Lee Elder broke the color line in 1975, the year Eldrick Woods was born, despite black golfers such as Charlie Sifford winning PGA Tour-sponsored events much earlier.

That Augusta National and the Masters remains a cloistered and conservative haven of privilege is perhaps best reflected in two examples. First, the CBS television announcers are required to use the appellation "patrons" when referring to spectators at the tournament; "fans" would be rhetorically unseemly to its staid tradition of gentlemanly behavior. Second, CBS's popular announcer Gary McCord has been banned from broadcasting since 1994 when he described, on air, that Augusta National's 17th green was so silky smooth, fast, and carefully manicured as to be "bikini waxed." Not only does the membership not like comely metaphor, but it just doesn't much like women, though two women, including former secretary of state Condoleeza Rice, were invited to join in the summer of 2012. Of course in 2001 and 2002, Martha Burke attempted a much-publicized boycott of the tournament and integration of the all-male membership. Despite generating much sympathy, including a rather hyperbolic endorsement from the *New York Times*, her efforts failed rather badly (Khan, 2004).

When Tiger Woods teed it up on Thursday afternoon, April 10, 1997, with reigning champion Nick Faldo, there was much interest in this young black phenomenon attempting to slay the racial ghosts still haunting the National.[15] And slay them, he did. By Sunday evening, Woods had rendered the field and the course largely irrelevant: he'd won by an unprecedented 12 strokes and he'd set the new course record at 18 under par – a record previously held by Jack Nicklaus. He also checked off another first: at 21, he was now the youngest Masters winner in history, again trumping Nicklaus. Conspicuously awaiting him as he came off the 18th hole on Sunday was Earl Woods. A prolonged hug between father and son was broadcast around the world; even today the Hug remains a staple of Masters highlights.[16]

The press was predictably breathless. "This was like Jesse Owens' incredible performance at the

1936 Olympics," exclaimed Ed Sherman (1997), "Joe Louis beating Max Schmeling just before World War II, Jackie Robinson becoming the first black player in the major leagues, Arthur Ashe winning at Wimbledon." Race-inflected conquests all. Tiger aided and abetted that interpretation as he thanked black predecessors Teddy Rhodes, Sifford, and Elder at his victory press conference. Perhaps overcome by the azalea'd splendor and the sheer enormity of what he'd done, Tiger also lapsed metaphysical: "I think I understand why the big guy in the sky has given me some of these talents, and I think the main reason is to help people." Woods continued, "I'm in a very unique position where a lot of kids look up to me just because I'm around their age group. And I think if I can influence their lives in a positive way, then I believe that's what the big guy in the sky had intended for me" (Sherman, 1997). For someone who professed, owing to his mother's Thai influence, to be a practicing Buddhist, it was a most Christian sentiment. Earl Woods couldn't have said it much better himself – with one important exception: Earl would've emphasized his son's race, not his age.

Creating Earl Woods

Along with his nearly deified son, the father became something of a celebrity after the Masters victory. Wherever Tiger went, so too, it seemed did his father. Earl even followed Tiger to Oprah Winfrey's show, the venue for Tiger's much ballyhooed declaration that he fancied himself a "Cablinasian": Ca-caucasian; bl-black; in-Native American; asian-Asian. While many in the multicultural movement swooned over Tiger's neologism, many blacks were miffed that his blackness had been rhetorically diminished (see, e.g., Uchacz, 1998; Ibrahim, 2009; and Rockquemore, 2004). Whenever Tiger was written about – which was daily – so was Earl. When Fuzzy Zoeller's racially charged remarks went public about the "boy" who was winning the Masters and the collard greens and fried chicken he might serve at the champion's dinner the following year, Earl ran interference.[17] He even began appearing in some of his son's golf commercials as Titleist in particular sought to capitalize on the unique father–son relationship.

When Tiger's first self-inflicted media mess occurred with publication of Charles P. Pierce's (1998) GQ article, "The Man. Amen," Tiger sought first to protect his father, who was unflatteringly portrayed. The talented, and very secular Pierce, caught Tiger regaling a limousine driver with all manner of race-inflected jokes, most of which revolved around genitalia size and its corollary: black male hypersexuality. Pierce profaned by publishing them, despite being told by Tiger that he couldn't. Earl attempted to recontextualize, and thus dismiss, the story via age: "Tiger was just a typical 21-year-old. I guess that was shocking to him [Pierce]. . . . Tiger professes to be nothing more, nothing less" (Woods and Mitchell, 1998). "The Chosen" as Pierce (1998) riffed throughout the piece, are never typical.

Further capitalizing on his new-found fame, Earl Woods did what his son steadfastly refused to do: he became an author. In fact, Woods churned out three books in just four years, one of which is central to my arguments about race, the media, and the narrative of Tiger Woods. In his first book, coauthored with black golf journalist Pete McDaniel (Woods and McDaniel, 1997) and titled Training a Tiger: A Father's Guide to Raising a Winner in Both Golf and Life, the emphasis is on the life-teaching aspects of playing golf. Bloated with pictures of Earl instructing his grown son, Woods offers counsel to all would-be parents, not just those with precocious athletic skills. Of course the underlying premise upon which his authorship is grounded is the exceptionalism of his son; in other words, Earl's parenting – and his wife is not terribly visible in the text – has engendered golfing and personal excellence. Earl had always been fond of saying, "Tiger's a better person than he is a golfer," and so why not educate a new generation of parents about how to "raise a Tiger"? In the news cycle of a Masters victory, Earl had become the nation's latest Dr Spock.

There was only one problem with that premise, though: Earl had three other children by his first wife, Barbara Hart Woods Gary, none of whom he was particularly close to.[18] Moreover, since he extolled the virtues of a two-parent household, how did this square with his separation from his second wife, Tiger's mother Kultida Woods? The answers arrived rather quickly in Earl's second book, published the following year in 1998,

Playing Through: Straight Talk on Hard Work, Big Dreams and Adventures with Tiger (Woods and Mitchell, 1998). Part memoir, part self-help, part apologia, always self-serving, and mostly rejoinder, the book is embarrassingly revelatory. Based on the reporting of Sounes (2004) and Callahan (2010), it is chock full of prevarications and half-truths that provide a revealing lens on the Tiger Woods narrative that Earl had peddled from when Tiger was in the womb — literally. It also raises disturbing questions about the role of race in that narrative, so carefully cultivated and so frequently articulated by Earl Woods.

Mabel Lee "Mae" Woods understood her younger brother without having to read the awkward psychological disclosures that constitute *Playing Through*: "He was always searching for something he could do or be that was better than anybody else ... he was so desperate to make his mark" (Callahan, 2010: 14). Perhaps because his own father died before he could see his son become a young man, Earl compensated. And then some. "I love myself. I love who I am. I respect who I am." As if to the mirror, Earl continues to recite, "I need no outside validation of that through either material means or through the opinions of others. I know that I am a good person. I always have been a good person, and I always will be a good person" (Woods and Mitchell, 1998: 9).

The "goodness" of Earl Woods shines through on every page of *Playing Through* because his very unremarkable life had been retroactively redeemed in the visage of his loins; it was up to Earl to limn the rhetorical retrofitting for a beguiled national audience. Not surprisingly God figures prominently in that project — but God needed a fitting partner for the job and He'd found his man in Earl Woods. "I deeply believe that some mystic power up above was preparing me to raise a son who could be articulate, intelligent and learned. . . . I recognize that my own background plays a tremendous and critical role in Tiger's history" (Woods and Mitchell, 1998: 4, 5). Thus could the father read his life in heaven-sent hindsight: joining ROTC at Kansas State was guided by "some external force," since without it "there would be no Tiger"; if he hadn't had the will to survive an early encounter with a racist army officer, "I never would have met my wife Tida, and we would not have had Tiger"; his

death-defying service in Vietnam was guided by a "higher power" eager to redeem communism, lousy generals, and a generation of long-haireds; his 20 years of military service "contributed mightily to Tiger's awesome capacity for mental discipline" (Woods and Mitchell, 1998: 19, 26, 32, 23). As for his crummy first marriage and three children? It was a "test," said, Earl, quoting God again, "'Let's give this guy a boy, and see how he handles it. Give him another one. Well, let's give him a girl and see how he handles that.' Then He put me through the trials and tribulations of an unhappy marriage. He was testing me, always testing me and preparing me" (Woods and Mitchell, 1998: 51). To read Earl's account, he was the most tested man since Job. Most importantly, and because he'd passed all of God's tests — even by failing them — Earl's moment had arrived.

But before Bethlehem, there's the inconvenient detail of how Earl met this story's Mary, Kultida Punswad. As Sounes (2004: 114–118) has argued with no small attention to factual detail, Earl was very much married to his first wife when he first met Kultida in Bangkok, Thailand — and when he asked her out on a date a few minutes later. "I am convinced," claims Earl, "that meeting my current wife, the former Kultida Punswad, was yet another predetermined event. . . . I know without doubt now that it was preordained for us to meet. . . . There was some force that brought us together" (Woods and Mitchell, 1998: 52, 56). The "force" in question more likely originated in Earl's starched Khakis rather than in Elohim playing matchmaker in the Gomorrah of Bangkok. When confronted with the blasphemous question of the date of "the Date," Earl could only reply curtly, "That's my business" (Sounes, 2004: 115).[19] That the union of Earl and Kultida Woods was conceived in the dirty ways of the flesh certainly detracts from the mythic origins narrative.

After marrying in New York in 1969, three years before his divorce was made official, the couple moved west to Cypress, CA. In his early 40s, Earl had found a new passion: golf. He claims to have shot 92 the very first time he played 18 holes, qualifying him as something of a savant. Most golfers find it difficult to break 100 on a regulation golf course, par being in the neighborhood of 70, 71, or 72. Though clearly a fine athlete by virtue of his aptitude in baseball, the likelihood of Earl Woods shooting 92 — even for 17 holes – in his first round of golf is about as likely as his son taking a spin in the Escalade to pick up a pizza on November 27 (see Woods and McDaniel, 1997: xvii). When Kultida became pregnant in the spring of 1975 she would occasionally walk the golf course with her addicted husband. Earl claims that he knew he had a prodigy on his hands before the child was born on December 30: "as soon as we got to the green, he was quiet as a mouse. . . . he seemed to know golf protocol while he was still in the womb" (Woods and Mitchell, 1998: 67). Other signs quickly followed: he would sit in his high-chair and watch his dad hit into a net in the garage for hours; at 11 months he came down from the high-chair and hit his own shot into the net; at age 1 he carried a putter around the house; at 2 he began practicing and even appeared on the Mike Douglas show; at 3 he shot 48 for nine holes on the local Navy Golf Course and he won his first tournament;[20] and, at age 5 he appeared on the national television program, *That's Incredible*. These early markers of golfing precocity form the narrative highlights that Earl Woods peddled to nearly every and any writer. As Polumbaum and Wieting (1999: 93) note, "reporters could hardly invent more felicitous events and details than these facts of the Tiger Woods story." By all accounts, that narrative was quickly accepted; it frames almost every national story ever written about the young Tiger. It also framed local stories of Woods. Early biographies of Tiger Woods are careful to articulate its details (see Strege, 1997a: 7–28). Royster (1998: 63) notes that "Perhaps more than has been done with any other recent athlete, the selling of Tiger Woods has been the selling of Tiger's upbringing." Pope (2006: 326), too, notes the "carefully managed media epic story," one that began in Woods' infancy. Of course it was also the rhetorical frame for Hello World.

Something else supposedly happened to Tiger at age 5.

Kindergarten "Nigger"?

Playing Through details some of the racism Earl Woods had endured as a black man coming of age in the Jim Crow Midwest; in fact the whole of Chapter 9 is dedicated to the subject of race. Earl Woods wanted the world to know that, like

his son, he'd broken new racial ground – in this case, being the first black baseball player in the then-Big Seven Conference while he was at Kansas State. Except he wasn't. Tom Callahan, who clearly had a close and affectionate relationship with Earl, writes, "The rest of Earl's life [beginning in the 1950s] he referred to himself alternately as 'the first black athlete in the entire conference,' or 'the first black baseball player at Kansas State,' neither of which was true. And Earl knew it wasn't true because he was acquainted with both gentlemen." But, "Earl wanted to be first" (Callahan, 2010: 13, 14; see also Sounes, 2004: 30–33). Far more curious is what Earl Woods didn't say about race in *Playing Through*.

Part of the early national narrative of Tiger Woods involved race, specifically an awful and horrifying racist incident that supposedly marked his first day of kindergarten. Writers were not shy about mentioning the incident as part of the narrative of Woods' racial Otherness – and importantly, how he had overcome such racism to become a star golfer in an exceedingly white sport. In other words, the story functioned rhetorically to script Woods in the nation's ongoing racial/racist drama – and to insinuate that racism could be overcome on the way to athletic greatness (for a similar reading of the early Tiger narrative and its rhetorical function, see Perez, 2005).

In examining hundreds of newspaper and magazine articles on father and son, the first mention of the incident I found occurs in a British newspaper in the fall of 1994, just weeks after Woods had enrolled at Stanford. Alan Fraser (1994: 47) wrote, "The middle class boy from Cypress, California, enjoyed opportunity and experienced hurt. As the only black student in his school, he was tied to a tree and called names on his first day." Fraser doesn't reveal his source for the cryptic racial incident that had unmistakable resonances to America's sad history of "rope and faggot." A day later, another British writer, John Hopkins (1994) of *The Times* (London) also wrote of the incident: "The only black student, he was tied to a tree and taunted by fellow pupils on his first day at school." Clearly both Fraser and Hopkins were privy to the same source on the same day. But the second story linked the incident back to golf, and the father, in far less cynical terms: "'My father had a strong mind. He gave it to me. I was not born with it.' [Tiger] has learned how to turn racism to his advantage. 'It makes me want to play even better,' he said." In this context, the harrowing incident gets redeemed in the context of Tiger's unrivaled golfing excellence; it's motivation, nothing else.

Four months later, Earl Woods expressed concern for the safety of his son: "Let's face it. A lot of major black athletes have had threats. It just goes with the territory. I just hope this [possibly earlier death threats] doesn't trigger ideas in other minds around the country." Even as the father was possibly triggering those very thoughts with his disclosure, the writer mentioned, "As the only black kid in the kindergarten class, he was tied to a tree" (DiGiovanna, 1995). With increasing fame, so the article implied, came the bodily threat to a black athlete. On Earl's account, his son was the latest in a line of famous and athletic black bodies imperiled by their own achievements. A month later, and before a much larger national reading audience, *Sports Illustrated*'s Rick Reilly (1995) revealed that, "On his first day of kindergarten Tiger was tied to a tree and taunted by older white kids."

The kindergarten story morphed slightly a week later ahead of Tiger's first appearance at the Masters, and as the nation's press giddily awaited the young black phenomenon's first appearance in a major.[21] John Strege (1995), who had had a relationship with the Woods family since he wrote golf stories for their home-town newspaper, *The Orange County Register*, revealed that "Woods had met racism on his first day of kindergarten in a Cypress school three years before, when older boys tied this son of a black father and Asian mother to a tree and taunted him and pelted him. The boys were later identified and punished." The kindergarten anecdote, though slightly amplified, was part of a much larger narrative that Earl Woods was promulgating that week in Augusta, GA: assassination in the Deep South. For the first time of which I'm aware, and conveniently ahead of the Masters, Earl revealed to Strege that Tiger had suffered nightmares for more than a year when he was eight years old. The cause? "'That he'd be assassinated playing golf in the South,' his father Earl Woods, said." And most likely at Augusta National: "The enemy that disturbed his sleep,

meanwhile, was faceless and posed a greater danger to a boy who dreamed of becoming the greatest golfer who ever lived. Even then," Strege breathlessly disclosed (1995), "Tiger Woods was aware that he could arrive at that destination only via Augusta National Golf Club in Georgia and the Masters, the cornerstone of golf in the South." While the assembled press chose largely to ignore the bloviating father who seemed to harbor a martyr complex for his kid, the race/ assassination angle in the Deep South functioned rhetorically to amplify Tiger Woods to the political importance of Martin Luther King, Jr., and Medgar Evers. Whether Earl had been drinking to excess, dreaming, or both, the story died a quick death.[22] Of course Earl informed Strege that he'd solved his son's nightmare problem: "I've been able to convince him there isn't anything he can do about it. It's been an abiding principle I've taught him, that you don't worry about things over which you have no control" (Strege, 1995). Thus did Earl Woods render childhood nightmares as logical and didactic forms conducive to his rationality and his third grader's will. Tiger lived through the tournament. He even made the cut.[23]

The kindergarten story, though, continued to grow, paralleling Woods' own media prominence and racial importance. After his stunning victory at the Masters in 1997, Tiger disclosed to Barbara Walters in an exclusive interview televised on ABC on May 21, one of the racial incidents he endured while growing up: "One happened when I was 5. I went to kindergarten, my first day of kindergarten, and I was tied up to a tree by the sixth graders and had nigger written on me and rocks thrown at me" (Rogers, 1997).[24] Given that the Woods family had very likely been the progenitor of the story back in 1994, the addition of the grotesque and now-embodied epithet nearly three years later is curious. More curious, and troubling, is what Tiger said to the Associated Press nine months after his televised interview. Re-telling the kindergarten story, he narrated, "Some sixth graders tied me to a tree and threw rocks at me and yelled 'nigger' at me the entire time. The teacher came and let me go but didn't walk me home, and I only lived across the street." After school, he continued, "The sixth graders chased me all the way [just across the street?] home. I had my own friends that were cool; it was just one of those deals" (Woods, 1998). One senses some serious narrative infidelity here. What had become of the corporeal epithet? Presumably this was also the same kindergarten teacher who, according to John Strege (1997b), early in the school year "suggested to [Tiger's] parents that his intelligence and maturity were such that he might want to skip ahead to the first grade." Surely such a vile and misanthropic (racist?) teacher would be expelled from the orbit of the Woods family – and even fired by the Cerritos Elementary School principal or the Orange County school board?

Perhaps most revealing of all in the Tiger Woods kindergarten narrative is that in *Playing Through*, a book that scrupulously documents Earl Woods and his family's encounters with racism, nary a word is mentioned of it. Tom Callahan (2010: 108), sensing a racial con job, broached the subject with Earl: "Do you believe that [the kindergarten racism] really happened?" Earl responded indirectly, "Tiger never lies." Callahan followed up, "Earl, he's the biggest liar on tour." Suffice it to say that Earl never answered the question.

Maureen Decker did, though. In 1981 she was the kindergarten teacher in question. And Howard Sounes somehow managed to find the erstwhile Cerritos Elementary kindergarten teacher. To her shock and horror, she'd watched the Barbara Walters interview. "It's untrue. Absolutely untrue. None of it ever happened" (Sounes, 2004: 127).[25] Her school principal, Donald Hill, who happened to have golfed with Woods in first grade, backed his teacher up: "I have never heard of that story (and) something that was that serious, I would question why didn't the father come to me and complain? . . . It certainly didn't come to my office" (Sounes, 2004: 128). Why did it take a British writer who didn't even write about sports to track down an important and national story – one that should have commenced with a simple phone call to Cerritos Elementary? As Sounes notes, the kindergarten narrative is rhetorically important, "one of the foundation stones in the Tiger Woods story." Furthermore, "Like the stories of Earl's youth, this incident casts Tiger in the sympathetic position of somebody who was unfairly treated at the start of his life, thus making his eventual success more

special" (2004: 127). I would also add, more lucrative. And racially redemptive for a country longing for it. Decker fingered Earl Woods: "Maybe his dad just wanted more publicity" (p. 128).

More than seven years after talking with Sounes, Maureen Decker sought out a larger venue. What looked to be her ostensibly kairotic moment had arrived: the mythic story of Tiger Woods was being punctured on a daily and humiliating basis. And so she did what seemingly every aggrieved woman in the Woods story around 2010 then did: she hired celebrity attorney, Gloria Allred, and called a press conference. Decker told the assembled press much of what she had told Sounes: the golf version of Tawana Brawley wasn't true; the events never happened – and she wanted a public and private apology for her mental and physical suffering. After all, who wants to be the driver of Rosa's bus? The 69-year-old Decker wasn't after a payday nor yet a starring role in a new reality show – rehab, porn, or otherwise. And then a curious thing happened during Decker's 15 minutes: nobody said much, save for what Decker said about what didn't happen. The nation's media couldn't be bothered with an event that went down – or not – nearly 30 years prior. Instead it fixated on the details of Tiger's penchant for anal sex, biting, spanking, choking, lurid texting, and threesomes with Derek Jeter; de-sanctified church tampons; the perennial promise of a sex tape or two; and always the specter of love children and abortions. Of course the Masters and Tiger's return to the game after four long months was less than a week away, too.

The Nation's Dave Zirin was the only national journalist I've found who seemed to care much about what Maureen Decker disclosed. His (2010) blogged story – headlined "A Tiger Woods Story that Actually Matters" – urged Woods to "own" his allegations. "If Tiger was the victim of a hate crime, he needs to bravely own the experience and tell the world that Maureen Decker is the worst kind of liar: a teacher who didn't protect a child and is now using the fog of the sex scandal to seek public redemption." Zirin then chose sides: he couldn't believe the Woods family would "ever lie about being a victim of racist violence." Why couldn't Zirin extend his incredulities to the family? "I don't believe it because the entire marketing strategy behind Tiger, and masterminded by his father, was to make him an avatar of post-racial 'Cablinasian' commercial nirvana" (Zirin, 2010). Zirin gets other important details wrong, including the fact that the story did not originate, as he contends, with the 1997 Barbara Walters interview. (Curiously, the national press, which has a very short memory, traced the origins of the kindergarten saga to Charles Barkley's 2005 book, *Who's Afraid of a Large Black Man*, where the story is recounted.) Zirin also badly confuses Nike, IMG,[26] and the Son for the Father: Earl Woods never embraced a post-racial identity for his son; in fact, as we've seen, quite the contrary. (For an excellent analysis of how corporate America capitalized on these post-racial sentiments, and arguably still does, see Cole and Andrews, 2001; also Andrews, 2006: 68–76.)

Whether or not we believe Maureen Decker, the Woods family could never agree on the details of the alleged racial assault; Earl is silent on the story in *Playing Through* and he deflects it with Callahan; Orange County school officials deny it; and most importantly, in our post-November 27 world, we now know a thing or two about the Woods family and its relationship to the truth. And its relationship to The Brand. Earl Woods knew better than anyone that an otherworldly talented and black golfer who'd overcome racism at the golf course, or on the school playground, would resonate with most Americans – golf fans or not. Such a happy ending appealed to multiple audiences: to blacks it revealed the reality of white racism even in the suburbs; to whites it illustrated that racism could be overcome and ultimately transcended through hard work – even in the lily-white world of golf. In his third and final book, Earl Woods claims only that Tiger got picked on "a lot" as a minority in a predominantly white school (see Woods and Wenk, 2000: 36). Woods returned to parenting in this text but spoke directly to children. Like his two previous efforts, the book is larded with Earl's self-importance. He could say without irony, "Nobody likes a show-off. You know the type: They're always bragging about something they did, how great they are, how much better they are than everyone else. But those people

aren't showing confidence; they're showing the exact opposite" (p. 92).

The Cerritos Elementary narrative played itself out in the months after the 1997 Masters. But as the new millennium began, the race and ethnicity of Tiger Woods dropped out of our public discourse; there was more money to be made pitching Buicks, credit cards, watches, sports drinks, cereal, video games, golf balls, golf clubs, financial planners, clothes, shoes, razors, Japanese beer, Lasik eye surgery, Disney, and communication providers than in race-inflected narratives, however optimistic and nostalgic. Tiger soon fired most of his father's hand-picked employees, including his caddie, lawyer, agent, and financial manager. Tiger didn't want to talk about sexism at the Masters, nor yet racism and the state flag in South Carolina. As many others have written, to say anything too controversial about social and political issues threatened The Brand. As the golf world continued to bank at the Bank of Woods, attention seemed always to return to Jack Nicklaus and Tiger's pursuit of the sport's Holy Grail: 19 major championships.[27]

Resurrecting Earl

Earl Woods watched his son become the world's wealthiest, most famous, and arguably most accomplished, athlete from the family's modest home in Cypress, CA. As his health deteriorated he traveled less frequently. He informed many visiting writers that he stayed in the two-bedroom house to feel Tiger's presence and bask in the memories of their affectionate relationship. He had also carefully executed plans to turn the house into a national monument, a place where visitors could see the high-chair his six-month-old sat in to watch him hit balls out in the garage, the bedroom where Tiger taped a list of Nicklaus' golf accomplishments in order to beat them, and the living room where Tiger hit balls over coffee tables and around furniture and where he dutifully watched golf tournaments with his doting father:

> I have prepared this house so that it can be converted into a national historical monument one day. All the floors in here are granite, they are not

hardwood or any of that other stuff. Granite – the hardest stone. All of the wood you see is walnut. It is built to last – because I am certain that one day the birthplace of Tiger Woods is going to become widely acknowledged. (Donegan, 2002)

Somewhere along the way, though, best friends had become estranged. Callahan (2010) reports that the same team that would do damage control at Deacon Circle was earlier dispatched to Cypress to clean up a "sexual jackpot" of Earl Woods' making (p. 161). What that jackpot was Callahan doesn't say, but he notes, "Any woman who ventured within fifty feet of Earl was a potential plaintiff" (p. 161). Tiger's former high-school girlfriend Dina Gravell-Parr recounted how a distraught Woods would call her from the road because Earl was out philandering (see Sheridan, 2009; also Lusetich, 2010: 264).

Father and son eventually reconciled and not long thereafter Earl Woods died on May 3, 2006, of complications from prostate cancer and heart disease. The press quickly, loudly, and unanimously sung the father's praises: by and large he'd been right about his son. Make that his youngest son.

Earl Woods never publicly doubted the Plan God had for his son, Eldrick. Rarely did he even suggest that his son might not be up to fulfilling it. But at the close of *Playing Through* the father offers this hypothetical "But if he ever loses sight of who he is and stops trying to be a good person and make contributions to others, then I will become very concerned and disappointed." If that ever happened, Earl continued, "believe me, you would see Earl Woods step in and be a very vociferous father. You can believe that" (Woods and Mitchell, 1998: 254). And so with Earl Woods dead and buried for nearly four years, and on the first day of the Masters, April 8, 2010, the tournament that had started the whole thing back in 1997, Nike and Wieden and Kennedy brought Earl Woods back into our living rooms. "Tiger," the black and white ad began, "I am more inclined to be curious, to promote discussion." The voice didn't need a body or a tagline; we just knew. The son eyed us uncomfortably as the camera probed closer. "I want to know what your thinking was. I want to know what your feelings are. And did you learn anything?"[28] Of course Earl Woods would come back to his son in this his greatest hour of need. Nike's, too.

Of course. Huge. Quickly.

Notes

1 Woods has adamantly maintained that there was never any domestic violence between him and his wife. Lusetich (2010: 256) notes that several sources revealed to the *Daily Beast*'s Gerald Posner that Elin chased Woods around their manse with a golf club, mangling all manner of golf trophies in the process. For an excellent parsing of the Florida Highway Patrol's eventual report, see Price (2010).

2 Estimates varied, but most insiders eventually agreed that Uchitel was paid US$10 million for her silence; this after a much-publicized press conference with her attorney, Gloria Allred, was abruptly canceled. That "Team Tiger" was willing to pay such a large sum of hush money, especially in lieu of later text-message revelations of a sexually violent and out-of-control Woods, is indeed suggestive. One can only wonder what exactly was being silenced.

3 Feinstein wrote several columns in 1996 questioning all the hype, especially that espoused by Tiger's father, Earl Woods. Those columns were later synthesized into a small book (Feinstein, 1998).

4 In his 1991 autobiography *A View from Above*, released un-kairotically proximate to Earvin "Magic" Johnson's announcement of HIV infection, Chamberlain bragged of having had sex with 20,000 women. Regardless of whether Wilt kept a daily ledger, or opted for photographic evidence *à la* Kiss frontman Gene Simmons, the math was Hefnerian: 1.37 women per day from the age of 15 till publication day. The revelation did absolutely nothing to kill the recalcitrant myth of the hypersexed and uncontrollable black male.

5 According to Mark Seal (2010a, 2010b), whose investigative reporting for *Vanity Fair* is without peer on the scandal and aftermath, Lawton revealed to him, "He told me to pull my underwear down and pull out my tampon, and we went at it with me pressed against his Escalade. He did it from the back" (2010a).

6 The name Eldrick is reportedly the creation of his mother, Kultida Punswad Woods. The "E" stands

for Earl and the "K" stands for Kultida, thus would their son always be rhetorically surrounded by his parents. Perhaps no story better illustrates the extent of his mother and father's devotion to their only child.

7   Paul Farhi's (2010) rather patronizing treatment of his colleagues in the "mainstream" for following the lead of the "tabloid" media is rife with errors and a lack of understanding about the economic dynamics of the Tiger Woods phenomenon as it played out over many lucrative years. For an account of the media's framing of the post-November Woods story and how fans reacted on social media, see Sanderson (2010).

8   A famed junior golfer growing up in Carmel, CA, Clampett clowned the rather tradition-bound United States Golf Association (USGA) in the 1979 US Open by hitting golf balls off his knees during a competitive round. Today Clampett is a television commentator for CBS.

9   I remember Doug Martin particularly well because I competed against the Van Buren, OH, native on the amateur circuit in the early Reagan years. He went on to be both the top-ranked junior and amateur golfer in the nation, a three time All-American at the University of Oklahoma — and a very forgettable professional career.

10 Of course golf can be played in team formats, but nearly all PGA tournaments are played as individual events over the course of four days and 72 holes. Team formats such as the Ryder Cup (for professionals) and the Walker Cup (for amateurs) use alternate-shot and best-ball formats that pair golfers as a team. That said, team golf is the exception and not the rule.

11 One of Tiger's first professional decisions as a golfer was to move from his boyhood home in Cypress, CA to his new digs in Isleworth, a private golf community in the tiny Orlando suburb of Windermere. Why the precipitous move across country? "I'm trying to get out of California state income taxes," he confessed to family friend and local sportswriter, John Strege (1996). In June 2011, Woods moved into his new US$50 million ocean-front estate on Jupiter Island, FL. That house, designed by ex-wife Elin (née Nordegren) Woods, also boasts a four-hole golf course that abuts the Intracoastal Waterway; its architecture style might best be described as Motel Six-chic.

12 Confessed Earl at the Greater Milwaukee Open: "I've been working on this for 20 years" (Feinstein, 1996). Earl exclaimed to the gathered press in Milwaukee, "I made Tiger privy to all this information to prepare him for his role. I have a vision that all of this is not by accident. I was selected by the man upstairs, I was prepared by the man upstairs" (see Starkman, 1996).

13 See http://www.youtube.com/watch?v=qSRzdXsh Low, accessed January 23, 2013.

14 There are four annually contested "major" championships in professional golf: The Masters, which takes place in April, the United States Open, which is played in June, the British Open, which is contested in late July, and the PGA Championship, which is played in August. For a fine book on "the majors" and how they came to be, see Feinstein (1990).

15 Professional golf tournaments typically begin on Thursday, preceded by practice rounds and "pro-am" (professionals and amateurs play together) events earlier in the week which raise money for local charities. Champions are crowned on Sunday evening following 72 holes of competition. Of course there are exceptions, but most stroke-play tournaments (each score is added to the previous day's scores) proceed in this manner. Less frequently played "match play" tournaments typically feature head-to head competition between players in which each of the 18 holes is either won or lost, with the lowest score always winning a hole. So, for example, if I've won four more holes than my competitor after the 15th hole of our match, I've won 4 and 3 (I'm up by four holes with only three holes left to play, effectively ending the match). Remarkably, Tiger won six straight match-play national championships: three consecutive US junior amateur titles and three consecutive US amateur championships. No one has ever come close to replicating this streak of match-play dominance.

16 The Hug was intertextually riffed to great commercial effect by American Express, one of Woods' former endorsers. In 2002 the company created an advertising campaign featuring a four-armed, tight embrace with eyes closed between a smiling Tiger and his mother, Kultida. It was the first, and to my knowledge, only commercial advertising she's done. It's also one of the only advertisements in which Woods appears without his trademark Nike hat, a cross-marketing trick he no doubt learned from "big brother" and fellow Nike endorser, Michael Jordan. Henry Yu (2002) notes the rhetorical importance of Woods' omission in the now-iconic moment.

17 Frank Urban Zoeller, thus Fuzzy, had a well-earned reputation as a jokester on the PGA Tour. CNN caught the former Masters champion making these remarks and aired them only several days after Woods had won the Masters. The story played out "above the fold" and on broadcast news for several days. Zoeller rather quickly lost his

US$1 million endorsement deal with Kmart and was roundly pilloried in the press. In many respects his career, and persona, have never been the same.

18   Partly to counter some of her ex-husband's self-serving prevarications, Gary published her own memoir in 2000. That she was eager to have her account in press is reflected in the fact that the book was self-published. In a pointed retort to Earl she notes, "I am constantly amazed that they [sons Earl Jr. and Kevin, and daughter Royce] harbor no resentment over the financial invest-ment and paternal pride that has been focused on a single child, since there are actually four children here, who have always been equally entitled to a father's pride, and steadfast love" (Woods Gary, 2000: xiv).

19   No small mystery surrounds Kultida Woods, espe-cially her formative years in Thailand. One scholar, who took the trouble to travel to the country and interview "natives" about her, reports that many think her secretarial work was only her day job; see Weisman (2001). In 2009 Jaime Diaz travelled with Kultida Woods to Thailand. In a story that could've been written by a public relations officer for the erstwhile Mrs Woods, her many mysteries remain unexplored and obvious questions unasked (Diaz, 2009). As a writer for *Golf Digest*, among other elite publications, no doubt Diaz was doing his due diligence to have some access to the planet's most famous athlete via this potentially useful proxy. Earl, after all, had been dead for three years.

20   In one of the only accounts I've located, Tiger corrects his father's narrative of shooting 48 at the age of 3: "Yes, well, I was five. I played from ahead of the teeing grounds and teed up the ball for every shot." A spot-on conclusion follows by Fraser (1994): "He was too familiar with the gimme, if not the cliché."

21   Among the four major championships there is no small debate about which one is the "most" major. European professionals and golf fans would no doubt claim that the British Open – called simply The Open in Europe – is the most venerable tour-nament because of its longer history, its larger field (it is "open" to any golfer, in theory) and its inter-national flavor. While I don't wish to engage in the endless and annual debate, suffice it to say that Helen Mirren is to the British Open what Marilyn Monroe is to the Masters.

22   I could find only two other writers that mentioned this assassination-at-the-Masters story; Cole (1995) and Burch (1995). Strege (1997a: 25) repeats the story with the identical quotes from

Earl in his biography of Woods. The Cole story was reprinted in the *Hamilton Spectator* while the Strege story also appeared in the *Wichita Eagle*, the *St. Louis Post-Dispatch*, and the *Seattle Times*. Interestingly, Michael Madden of the *Boston Globe* wrote two days later that Earl was the one having nightmares about assassination, not his son (Madden, 1995). That Tiger Woods has received, and likely continues to receive, death threats should not be read as evidence against my argu-ment about the rhetorical function of his father publicizing those threats.

23   Most professional golf tournaments have a "cut" after 36 holes in which the field is effectively halved. The bottom half of the field is dismissed from play and make no prize money that week. In a day of guaranteed money and appearance fees, professional golf in the United States remains one of the last bastions of sporting meritocracy.

24   Giacobbi and DeSensi (1999) analyze the Walters interview and a 1997 ESPN *Outside the Lines* episode to generalize about the press coverage of Tiger Woods. The article is rife with problems, perhaps the most obvious (and risible) of which is this claim: "his [Woods'] presence on the [PGA] tour and the threat he represents to the established white upper class males in the golf subculture will remain." Tiger makes lots of money for these EWUCMs; as such, they quite literally worship the ground on which Woods walks. To have him not enter a professional event is an economic cataclysm for that week's tour stop. PGA Tour revenues between 1996 and 2008 increased nearly US$700 million; similarly, prize money at Tour events went from US$70 million to US$277 million (see Lusetich, 2010: 24). Without question, Woods is driving those expo-nential increases.

25   In a delicious bit of irony, Sounes' book was pub-lished by Perennial Currents, an imprint of Harp-erCollins – the same company that published *Playing Through*.

26   IMG, based in Cleveland, OH, was founded by Mark McCormack and represented golfing legend Arnold Palmer, and has represented Tiger Woods from the beginning of his professional career until 2011. Infamously they put Earl Woods on the payroll as a talent scout – they paid his travel expenses to amateur tournaments – when Tiger was 15. Earl Woods hired Hughes Norton as his son's first agent. Norton was fired by Tiger after a year and replaced by his own choice, Mark Steinberg, who continues to repre-sent Woods. IMG reportedly paid Norton to be

silent about his relationship with the Woods family.

27   As of this writing in March 2013, Woods has won 14 major championships. When Woods won his second consecutive US amateur title in 1995, an exultant Earl Woods bragged that his son would one day win 14 major championships (see Rosaforte, 1995).

28   Earl Woods' words were lifted from an interview in *Tiger* (2004).

References

Andrews, D.L. (2006) *Sport–Commerce–Culture: Essays on Sport in Late Capitalist America*, New York: Peter Lang.

Brown, C. (2008) "Just breathing his air, sharing his sun and drinking his water make us more complete." *New York Times Magazine*, June: 50–55, 82–83.

Burch, J. (1995) "Color blind." *Fort Worth Star-Telegram*, April 5: 1.

Callahan, T. (2010) *His Father's Son: Earl and Tiger Woods*, New York: Gotham.

Cole, C. (1995) "Tiger stalks Augusta." *Ottawa Citizen*, April 5: D2.

Cole, C.L. and Andrews, D.L. (2001) "America's new son: Tiger Woods and America's multiculturalism," in Andrews, D.L. and Jackson, S.J. (eds.) *Sports Stars: The Cultural Politics of Sporting Celebrity*, New York: Routledge, pp. 70–86.

de Jonge, P. (1995) "A zone of his own: Tiger Woods." *New York Times Magazine*, February 5: 36–39.

Diaz, J. (2009) "Tida + Thailand." *Golf Digest*, May: 150.

DiGiovanna, M. (1995) "Born golfer." *Fort Worth Star-Telegram*, February 19: 4.

Donegan, L. (2002) "Old father shrine." *Observer*, April 7: 1–8.

Dray, P. (2002) *At the Hands of Persons Unknown: The Lynching of Black America*, New York: Random House.

Farhi, P. (2010) "Lost in the Woods." *American Journalism Review*, 32 (1): 14–19.

Feinstein, J. (1990) *The Majors*, Boston, MA: Little, Brown.

Feinstein, J. (1996) "Tiger by the tail." *Newsweek*, September 9: 58.

Feinstein, J. (1998) *The First Coming: Tiger Woods: Master or Martyr*, New York: Ballantine.

Feinstein, J. (2010) "Secret Tiger." *The Advertiser* (Adelaide, Australia), February 20: W12.

Fraser, A. (1994) "The rare Tiger burning bright." *Daily Mail*, October 10: 47.

Giacobbi, P.R. Jr. and DeSensi, J.T. (1999) "Media portrayals of Tiger Woods: A qualitative deconstructive examination." *Quest*, 51 (4): 408–417.

Gross, L. (1996) "Tiger battles sandtraps of racism." *Tri-State Defender*, October 16: 1A.

Hopkins, J. (1994) "Prodigy now prowling riskier fairways." *The Times* (London), October 11: 46.

Ibrahim, H. (2009) "Toward black and multiracial 'kinship' after 1997, or How a race man became 'Cablinasian.'" *Black Scholar*, 39 (3): 23–31.

Johnson, R.S. (2007) "Tiger!" *Men's Fitness*, August, http://www.mensfitness.com/leisure/entertainment/tiger, accessed January 23, 2013.

Jones, C. (2009) "Where to find the salvation of Tiger Woods." *Esquire*, December 7, http://www.esquire.com/the-side/feature/tiger-woods-mistresses-hit-home-120709, accessed January 10. 2013.

Jones, L. (2000) "Are we Tiger Woods yet?" in Powell, K. (ed.) *Step Into a World: A Global Anthology of the New Black Literature*, New York: John Wiley & Sons, Inc., pp. 49–51.

Khan, A.I. (2004) "Martha, Hootie, and the Masters: Debating gender exclusion at Augusta." Paper presented at the National Communication Association, Chicago.

Killion, A. (1994) "Stanford-bound Woods is more than list of achievements, a college degree is a priority. So is privacy." *Philadelphia Inquirer*, September 4: C03.

Lusetich, R. (2010) *Unplayable: An Inside Account of Tiger's Most Tumultuous Season*, New York: Atria.

Madden, M. (1995) "Woods blazing a trail." *Boston Globe*, April 7, http://www.highbeam.com/doc/1P2-8322753.html, accessed January 10, 2013.

Owen, D. (1999) *The Making of the Masters: Clifford Roberts, Augusta National, and Golf's Most Prestigious Tournament*, New York: Simon & Schuster.

Perez, H. (2005) "How to rehabilitate a mulatto: The iconography of Tiger Woods," in Dave, S., Nishime, L., and Oren, T.G. (eds.) *East Main Street: Asian American Popular Culture*, New York: New York University Press, pp. 224–245.

Pierce, C.P. (1998) "The Man. Amen," in Littlefield, B. (ed.) *The Best American Sports Writing 1998*, Boston, MA: Houghton Mifflin, pp. 165–181.

Polumbaum, J. and Wieting, S.G. (1999) "Stories of sport and the moral order: Unraveling the cultural construction of Tiger Woods." *Journalism & Communication Monographs*, 1 (2): 69–118.

Pope, S.W. (2006) "'Race,' family and nation: The significance of Tiger Woods in American culture," in Wiggins, D.K. (ed.) *Out of the Shadows: A Biographical History of African American Athletes*, Fayetteville: University of Arkansas Press, pp. 325–351.

Popkin, H.A.S. (2009) "Hey, Tiger Woods: Why so dumb about tech? When it comes to digital embarrassment, celebs are apparently just stupid." *Technotica on MSNBC.com*, December 3, http://www.msnbc.msn.com/id/34245443/ns/technology_and_science-tech_and_gadgets/t/hey-tiger-woods-why-so-dumb-about-tech/, accessed January 23, 2013.

Powell, S. (2008) *Souled Out? How Blacks are Winning and Losing in Sports*, Champaign, IL: Human Kinetics.

Price, S.L. (2010) "Truth or consequences." *Sports Illustrated*, April 12: 70–78.

Reilly, R. (1995) "Goodness gracious, he's a great ball of fire." *Sports Illustrated*, March 27: 62–73.

Rockquemore, K.A. (2004) "Deconstructing Tiger Woods: The promise and the pitfalls of multiracial identity," in Dalmage, H.M. (ed.) *The Politics of Multiracialism: Challenging Racial Thinking*, Albany: State University of New York Press, pp. 125–141.

Rogers, P. (1997) "Woods shares childhood racial incident." *Atlanta Journal and Atlanta Constitution*, May 22: D3.

Rosaforte, T. (1995) "Encore! Encore!" *Sports Illustrated*, September 4: 26–28.

Royster, F.T. (1998) "The 'end of race' and the future of early modern cultural studies." *Shakespeare Studies*, 26 (1): 59–64.

Sampson, C. (1998) *The Masters: Golf, Money, and Power in Augusta, Georgia*, New York: Villard.

Sanderson, J. (2010) "Framing Tiger's troubles: Comparing traditional and social media." *International Journal of Sport Communication*, 3 (4): 438–453.

Seal, M. (2010a) "The temptation of Tiger Woods." *Vanity Fair*, May, http://www.vanityfair.com/culture/features/2010/05/tiger-woods-article-full-201005, accessed January 23, 2013.

Seal, M. (2010b) "The temptation of Tiger Woods: Part II: Losing control." *Vanity Fair*, June, http://www.vanityfair.com/culture/features/2010/06/tiger-woods-article-full-201006, accessed January 23, 2013.

Sheridan, P. (2009) "Like father, like son." *Daily Express*, December 18: 24.

Sherman, E. (1997) "Masters marks beginning of the Tiger Woods' era." *Chicago Tribune*, April 15.

Smith, G. (1996) "The Chosen One." *Sports Illustrated*, December 23: 28–43.

Sounes, H. (2004) *The Wicked Game: Arnold Palmer, Jack Nicklaus, Tiger Woods, and the Business of Modern Golf*, New York: Perennial.

Stacks, J.F. (1996) "The Sound of Money." *Time*, September 9: 61.

Starkman, R. (1996) "Portrait of pressure: 'Tiger was sent to do something; he will transcend the game of golf.'" *Toronto Star*, September 7: B1.

Strege, J. (1995) "Erasing the nightmare." *Orange County Register*, April 2: C14.

Strege, J. (1996) "Tiger and the tax man." *Orange County Register*, September 6: B06.

Strege, J. (1997a) *Tiger: A Biography of Tiger Woods*, New York: Broadway.

Strege, J. (1997b) "The 1997 Open – child's play for Tiger – Golf." *Orange County Register*, June 10: D01.

Tiger (2004) *Tiger: The Authorized DVD Collection*, Burbank, CA: Buena Vista Home Entertainment.

Uchacz, C.P. (1998) "Black sports images in transition: The impact of Tiger's roar," in Sailes, G.A. (ed.) *African Americans in Sport*, New Brunswick, NJ: Rutgers University Press, pp. 53–66.

Weisman, J.R. (2001) "The Tiger and his stripes: Thai and American reactions to Tiger Woods's (multi)'racial self,'" in Williams-Leon, T. and Nakashima, C.L. (eds.) *The Sum of Our Parts: Mixed-Heritage Asian Americans*, Philadelphia, PA: Temple University Press, pp. 231–243.

Woods, E. and McDaniel, P. (1997) *Training a Tiger: A Father's Guide to Raising a Winner in Both Golf and Life*, New York: HarperCollins.

Woods, E. and Mitchell, F. (1998) *Playing Through: Straight Talk on Hard Work, Big Dreams and Adventures with Tiger*, New York: HarperCollins.

Woods, E. and Wenk, S.L. (2000) *Start Something: You Can Make a Difference*, New York: Simon & Schuster.

Woods, T. (1998) "Woods praises Sifford, recalls own brushes with racism." *Associated Press Archive*, February 25.

Woods Gary, B. (2000) *"At All Costs": (My Life With the Man Behind the Tiger)*, Salina, KS: BWG Publishing.

Yu, H. (2002) "Tiger Woods at the center of history: Looking back at the twentieth century through the lenses of race, sports, and mass consumption," in Bloom, J. and Willard, M.N. (eds.) *Sports Matters: Race, Recreation, and Culture*, New York: New York University Press, pp. 320–353.

Zirin, D. (2010) "A Tiger Woods story that actually matters." *Nation*, April 5, http://www.thenation.com/blog/tiger-woods-story-actually-matters, accessed January 10, 2013.

Further Reading

Cole, C.L. and Andrews, D.L. (2001) "America's new son: Tiger Woods and America's multiculturalism," in Andrews, D.L. and Jackson, S.J. (eds.) *Sports Stars: The Cultural Politics of Sporting Celebrity*, New York: Routledge, pp. 70–86.

Houck, D.W. (2005) "Crouching Tiger, hidden blackness: Tiger Woods and the disappearance of race," in Raney, A.A. and Bryant, J. (eds.) *Handbook of Sports and Media*, Mahwah, NJ: Erlbaum, pp. 469–484.

Pierce, C.P. (1998) "The Man. Amen," in Littlefield, B. (ed.) *The Best American Sports Writing 1998*, Boston, MA: Houghton Mifflin, pp. 165–181.

Pope, S.W. (2006) "'Race,' family and nation: The significance of Tiger Woods in American culture," in Wiggins, D.K. (ed.) *Out of the Shadows: A Biographical History of African American Athletes*, Fayetteville: University of Arkansas Press, pp. 325–351.

Smith, G. (1996) "The Chosen One," *Sports Illustrated*, December 23: 28–43.

Starn, O. (2011) *The Passion of Tiger Woods: An Anthropologist Reports on Race, Golf, and Celebrity Scandal*, Durham, NC: Duke University Press.

34

Deleuze and the Disabled Sports Star

Pirkko Markula

Like Deleuze and Guattari, cultural studies puts the emphasis on relations and change (becoming and connections).

Lawrence Grossberg, Animations, articulations, and becomings, 5

Introduction

Lawrence Grossberg delineates a close connection between cultural studies and the work of French poststructuralist philosopher Gilles Deleuze and Deleuze's long term collaborator, psychoanalyst Félix Guattari: both aim to make visible "the processes and practices by which identities and identifications, relations and structures, contexts and conjunctures are produced." While drawing from a different theoretical perspective, disability studies has also made visible the processes and practices by which marginalization of the disabled identity is produced. For example, in a special issue on genealogies of disability in *Cultural Studies*, Lisa Diedrich (2005) observes that disability studies and disability activism have strongly embraced identity-based work and through this focus, fought for the civil rights of the disabled as a minority group with single, unified, clearly definable characteristics. Nevertheless, Diedrich detects an emerging shift from identity-based politics toward postmodern or poststructuralist, particularly Foucauldian, analyses of disability, as exemplified by her special issue on genealogies of disability.

This chapter aligns with this distancing from identity politics with a move toward poststructuralism to examine the possibilities of cultural understandings of disability through Deleuzian rhizomatics. It is particularly inspired by the potential of Deleuzian experimentation to animate the cultural studies of disability sport with imaginative theoretical thinking. I will, thus, discuss Deleuze's concept of rhizome more closely later in this chapter. Through Deleuzian rhizomatics and empiricism I aim to draw lines between the current constructions of disability, the body, and sport performance. In this process I, an "able-bodied," non-athlete feminist researcher, follow Grossberg's "rule" of conducting Deleuzian analyses: "construct multiplicities, be imaginative in forging connections, and don't let anything stop you" (2003: 2). Consequently, I define the purpose of this chapter as an exploration of further theoretical resources to examine performance(s) of the athletic body.

To forge connections with the current field of disability sport studies, I first provide a brief discussion of Deleuze's rhizomatics and empiricism to argue for its usefulness in deterritorializing

A Companion to Sport, First Edition. Edited by David L. Andrews and Ben Carrington.
© 2013 Blackwell Publishing Ltd. Published 2013 by Blackwell Publishing Ltd.

the current structures of disability studies of sport. I then re-describe this context through a Deleuzian lens and finally, in an attempt for Deleuzian pragmatics, I animate the philosophical concepts with the life experience of the Finnish athlete Tuija Helander who, as a former sport star and current lung-transplant receiver, is officially classified as disabled, yet excluded from the disability sport movement associated with the Paralympics. Her performance, thus, potentially problematizes the meaning(s) of disabled sports star.

Deleuzian Deterritorializations: The Arborescent Model of Thought

While Deleuze is a relative newcomer into disability studies,[1] there are some researchers who have engaged with rhizomatics to begin to deterritorialize the currently dominant theorizing of disability as a socially constructed identity. For example, Dan Goodley (2007) credits Deleuze and Guattari with providing heuristic devices, modes of experimentation, and methodologies for addressing the current construction of the human subject in disability studies. By creating lines of flight between Goodley's research and my own feminist Deleuzian examinations of the physically active body (Markula, 2004, 2006a, 2006b, 2008), I will address how Deleuzian concepts can animate disability studies through the materiality of the life of a woman athlete with a lung transplant.

In his work with Félix Guattari, Deleuze embarks on a critique of "modern" philosophy, which he describes as the arborescent model of thought (Deleuze and Guattari, 1987). This model of thought, for Deleuze and Guattari, "is the most classical and well reflected, oldest, and weariest kind of thought" (p. 5). Deleuze uses the image of a tree as supported by one principal root to illustrate this model. Even if the root divides, each new "shoot" or thought stems always from the main root (the "truth" or the deeply rooted belief of what is true). In addition, the arborescent model is typically divided, hierarchically, into clear-cut segments. Deleuze and Guattari identify three segments or "strata" that organize the logic of modern Western philosophical thought. *Organism* refers to the organization of

the natural life, including the human body, based on the logic of science. *Signifiance* refers to the necessity of interpreting human experiences and actions through language (an interplay of a signified and a signifier). *Subjectification* refers to the logic according to which an individual is turned into a singular subject or is assigned a unified identity. While disability studies cannot be directly compared to modern Western philosophy, it can be seen as a stem, similar to feminism, from the same tree. It might not be possible to name the strata of disability studies imitating Deleuze and Guattari, but a certain hierarchy of thought, akin to the arborescent model, can be identified.

The Arborescent Thought of Sport Disability Studies: The Medical Model, the Social Model, and the Narrative Model

When reading contemporary disability studies research, it is evident that much of the current debate occurs in the intersections of four inter-related "models": the biomedical, the social, the narrative, and the poststructuralist/postmodern models.[2] The biomedical models view disability as a biological, physical impairment that should be fixed through the means of medical science to make disabled people as normal as possible (see, e.g., Diedrich, 2005; Galvin, 2003; Hughes, 2005; Siebers, 2005; Tremain, 2005, 2006). Thomas (2004), for example, notes that this type of understanding of disability is associated with medical sociology which posits that "disability is caused by illness and impairment and entails suffering and some social disadvantage" (p. 570). This view of disability studies can be seen to resemble the stratum Deleuze and Guattari (1987) identified as "organism." While such an approach to disability has undoubtedly provided much needed ability, access, and help for numerous people, disability scholars argue that this model tends to "perceive and classify disability in terms of a meta-narrative of deviance, lack, and tragedy, and assume it to be logically separate from and inferior to 'normalcy'" (Corker and Shakespeare, 2002: 2, cited in Diedrich, 2005: 649). It situates disability exclusively in individual bodies and "strives to cure them with particular treatment, isolating the patient as diseased or defective" (Siebers, 2005: 173).

The social model of disability sport studies

The social model of disability grew out of these critiques and also coincided with disability rights activism in the United Kingdom (see, e.g., Hughes, 2005; Thomas, 2004) and with the disability rights movement in the United States where it resulted in the groundbreaking Americans with Disabilities Act in 1990 (Tremain, 2005).[3] Vic Finkelstein, who, with Paul Hunt, established the Union of the Physically Impaired Against Segregation (UPIAS) and Mike Oliver, a sociologist, are often considered the "founders" of the social model of disability (Gabel and Peters, 2004; Thomas, 2004). Therefore, the social model has strong roots in disability activism in the United Kingdom and some scholars refer to this "original" British model as the "strong social model" of understanding disability. Many also agree that this model comprises the dominant model – "disability studies" proper (Gabel and Peters, 2004; Thomas, 2004) – in the current field.[4] In brief, this model understands disability as socially constructed in a sense that the physical impairment leads to social exclusion which then, comprises a form of oppression. Disability is "imposed" upon an impairment and thus, disabled people turn into an oppressed group.

Embedded in the historical materialism of critical theory, the social model of disability moved the focus from the "impaired" (biological) body to disability as a marginalized social identity with defendable human rights. The aim of this social critique is to discard the oppressive image of disability (as deviant, abnormal, and dependent) to seek to define an alternative, empowering disabled identity through which the rights of this marginalized group can be actualized. The social model, thus, "offers people with impairment an alternative frame of reference in which to build their own identities" (Huang and Brittain, 2006: 354). Following Deleuze, this type of thought regarding disability appears embedded in the strata of significance and subjectification where the individual's experiences are interpreted against a clearly defined identity. This model is also the dominant model within sport disability studies.

From the perspective of the social model, sport participation both reflects the ideological construction of disability and provides an avenue to resist this construction. Because sport embodies desirable and accepted Western values such as physical prowess, independence, and individualism, it offers a place where disabled people can also overcome the perceptions of dependency and physical frailty often connected to disability (Hardin and Hardin, 2003). Through sport, a disabled athlete is able to resist the "ableist" constructions through which people with disabilities are defined as a deviation from the norm: different and abnormal (DePauw, 1997; Duncan, 2001; Hargreaves, 2000). Consequently, following other disability scholars, sport researchers argue that the "real problem is not physical but social: it is the way people with able bodies view persons with disabilities and the institutionalization of these views that is the genuine handicap . . . Thus do people with disabilities become 'nonpersons'" (Duncan, 2001: 1). It is possible, for example, through participation in disability sports, to demonstrate that it is the society, not the individual, that is the problem. Disability sport studies research, from this perspective, focuses on the meaning of sport as constructing a disabled identity through inclusion/exclusion from disabled sport. For example, while the disability sport movement and Paralympics offer opportunities for sport involvement for people with disabilities, it is debated whether the inclusion of disability sport and mainstream sport or clear separation of the two would best aid the creation of positive disability identity.

Nixon (2007), for example, sees inclusion as potentially creating a positive identity as "people with disabilities are able to compete in integrated settings without stigma" (p. 419).[5] In their study, however, Promis, Erevelles, and Matthews (2001) find that their mobility-impaired respondents did not see a total inclusion of disabled to the able-bodied program as providing more positive physical activity experiences. Amid the promotion of sport as a positive practice, several scholars have also observed the domination of physical excellence, performance ethics, and masculine ideologies in disability sport to question whether compliance to such values promotes a positive disability identity (e.g., Howe and Jones, 2006; Promis et al., 2001). The media representation of disabled athletes certainly tends to support traditional sporting values. This leads to the second theme within the social studies of disability sport: the identity of a disabled athlete as a celebrated "supercrip."

Supercrip athletes have, with hard work and dedication, achieved high-performance standards despite the disadvantage of their disabled bodies. They are viewed as closest to "normal" athletes and provide the most common image of a disabled athlete: the male wheelchair athlete (Hardin and Hardin, 2003). There is, however, a vigorous debate among disability scholars as to whether such an image should represent the "authentic" or real voice for disability sport. From the point of view of the social model, this image is antithetical to the goals of a progressive understanding of disability in society and hampers the social change required for the more positive treatment of people with disabilities (Berger, 2008; Hardin and Hardin, 2003; Nixon, 2007). While the social model of disability sport condemns the supercrip image, some researchers have examined how disabled athletes themselves perceive this representation. This research finds the athletes living in a contradiction: they simultaneously comply with and resist the image.

In their examination of Hope Lewellen, a highly successful wheelchair athlete, Schell and Rodriguez (2001) discover that while the media portrayed her as a supercrip, she herself preferred a more "progressive model" where she would have been talked about as a sportswoman with remarkable performance ability rather than a disabled athlete overcoming great obstacles to succeed. Hardin and Hardin (2003), Berger (2008), and Huang and Brittain (2006) further examine athletes' attitudes toward the supercrip image to find that the image of "a dedicated athlete" offers both disempowering and empowering experiences. The supercrip narrative reproduced oppressive, ideologically constructed gender ideals: the male athletes confirmed with and celebrated the hegemonic masculine sport image and the female athletes expressed a need to look feminine and thus reinforced the current able-bodied feminine identity ideologically connected with the ideal, perfect body. However, the athletes also longed to change the societal perceptions of disability by emphasizing participation in high-performance sport. In this sense, the

identity as an elite athlete can "challenge the dominant perceptions of the medical model of disability" (Huang and Brittain, 2006: 372). Guthrie and Castelnuovo (2001) also argue that disabled women who participated in competitive sport, but not necessarily at an elite level, resisted the ideologically constructed femininity and some also engaged in political activism to promote sport participation as liberation for women with disabilities.[6] Sport liberated disabled women from the perfect body ideal and thus, for these researchers, sport served as a resistant activity through which to construct a more positive collective and self identity.

In sum, the social model of disability effectively demonstrates the social construction of disability as a marginalized identity. Disability sport has acted as one way of creating a more positive identity, because in sport, disabled athletes can demonstrate their independence and celebrate their physical ability. As Berger notes: "adopting the discourse of identity politics and multiculturalism, they [the advocates of the social model] challenged societal notions of normality and promoted disability as an acceptable, even celebrated form of social difference" (2008: 648). Despite such positives, the social model has also been critiqued for prioritizing the social construction of a disabled identity at the expense of individual experiences of disability. According to these critics, disabled sport is not only about changing the social construction of disability as "abnormal" but also about corporeal beings with feelings, understandings, and bodily experiences (e.g., Best, 2007; Sparkes and Smith, 2008). Consequently, there has been an increasing interest in the lived experiences of disability and the use of narrative inquiry to tap into these experiences.

Narratives of coherent construction of disabled (sporting) identity

There is a substantial literature on disability and particularly illness as "narratives." A majority of this research could be located within the interpretive paradigm as identified by Gabel and Peters (2004). In Deleuzian terms this type of narrative inquiry, similar to the social model of disability studies, draws from the strata of significance and subjectification because the experiences embedded in the stories are used to assign a coherent identity to the disabled subjects. An interpretive (sport) disability researcher recognizes how the participants' reflections essentially engage in coherent ways of understanding a self. For example, while disabled participants' stories might involve several stages of identity development – and not necessarily in chronological, clear order – the researchers actively analyze how "storytellers do coherence" (Smith and Sparkes, 2002: 144). One of the seminal representations of this type of approach is Arthur Frank's (1995) book *The Wounded Storyteller* where he identified three narrative types – restitution, chaos, and quest – in the gradual development of a new identity in the process of illness/recovery.[7] In sport studies, Smith and Sparkes (e.g., 2004, 2005, 2007, 2008; Sparkes and Smith, 2008) have produced a series of articles on male athletes with spinal-cord injury using Frank's narrative approach. They identify how spinal-cord-injured male athletes went through restitution, chaos, and quest stages to construct new coherent identities after their athletic identity. While some athletes remained at the first restitution stage and others had difficulty leaving the chaos state, some reached the final, quest stage where they could again have a meaningfully constructed, coherent identity as a disabled former athlete. Smith and Sparkes do not locate the spinal-cord-injured athletes' experiences into an ideological construction of sport, masculinity, or disability but rather advocate that narratives can help other athletes in similar situations resonate with the stories through which they can join the current collective of disability movement. They assert, therefore, that narrative inquiry is particularly useful for disability studies as it offers insights into how impairment is negotiated and constructed.

In sum, this model of narrative inquiry and narrative analysis advocates a linear search for a coherent identity as a "healthy" self. Therefore, it is important to provide stories others can relate to and learn from to then make "sense" of themselves as individuals in the otherwise "chaotic" world (e.g., Crossley, 2000; Frank, 1995; Sparkes and Smith, 2008). While the individual stories are to be understood in their social context, there is less emphasis on understanding the ideological construction of disability experiences than tracing how the narrative practice can help detect the construction of a coherent self. Consequently,

while locating itself as a resistant mode to the social model, both of these models rest on the conceptualization of a unified, coherent, disabled identity. From a Deleuzian perspective, the social model and interpretive-narrative inquiry, thus, draw from the modernist foundations of social science research that looks for the formation of a coherent self through the logic of the arborescent model. Scholars of disability sport have already evoked some limitations of the unified identity model.

The umbrella term "disability" covers a huge variety of impairments ranging from mental to physical, from visible to invisible, from acquired to congenial. While this diversity, no doubt, provides richness within the disability sport movement, it also creates difficulties in terms of defining collective goals based on a unified identity (e.g., Berger, 2008). For example, it is difficult to assign the supercrip image as representative of the entire disability movement, yet this image has gained the most visibility and most support for disability sport as a collective. In addition, as the social model has demonstrated, this image creates contradictory experiences between disempowerment and empowerment for disabled athletes. Nevertheless, within this model, the disability movement as a political movement will have to rest on a collective identity while not representative of the multiplicity within it. Both the social model and the interpretive-narrative inquiry fundamentally differ from a poststructuralist conceptualization of identity as continually formed and negotiated – in a process of becoming – within power relations. Deleuzian rhizomatics, along with other poststructuralist/postmodern models of understanding disability, aims to challenge the need for a singular, unified identity to renegotiate how we can understand disability in more inclusive terms.

Renegotiating Identity: The Poststructuralist/Postmodern Model of Disability

A Deleuzian approach to disability is part of the emerging poststructuralist disability studies. These perspectives aim to smooth the hierarchical striation of theorizing in disability studies. Poststructuralist critics do not locate themselves in opposition to the biomedical, social, or narrative model of disability, but rather are interested in challenging the underlying binary structure that necessitates dichotomous politics. Poststructuralists aim to reveal the limitations of this logic on two main fronts. First, with its focus on the social construction of disability, the social model creates a strict separation between the medical model (which is based on definitions of "impairment") and the social model (which focuses on the social construction of disability by entirely ignoring the meaning of "impairment" in the construction of disability). Second, the social and narrative models construct a stifling, unified identity that essentializes difference and retains the dichotomies it is supposed to erase.

Several scholars observe a conceptual separation between "impairment" and disability stemming from the social model of disability. Similar to Deleuzian scholars, Thomas (2004), Tremain (2005, 2006), and Hughes (2005) – while drawing from different theoretical perspectives – critique the binary between the biological body (impairment) and disability (the socially constructed oppression) inherent in the social model of disability. From a Foucauldian perspective,[8] for example, Tremain argues that an "impairment," rather than a biological, non-historical entity, is socially constructed similar to the identity of disability. For Tremain, impairment is "an historical artifact of the regime of 'bio-power'" (2006: 185). The disabled body is, through scientific (also social scientific) definitions of impairment and identity, linked with webs of power relations and knowledge production. In this system, Tremain argues, subjects become objectivized into such categories as healthy/sick, non-impaired/impaired, unrestricted/restricted, or abled/disabled through which we come to understand what constitutes normal and how we should try to discipline our bodies towards normalcy (healthy, able-bodied). Tremain adds that the idea of normalcy makes subjects governable. In a society of biopower, a unified identity for the disabled produces governable subjects that are easily controlled through governmental disability policies. From a Foucauldian perspective, then, the social model that aims to use a politicized identity of disability as a tool for emancipation will not be successful as it reproduces bodies disciplined by biopower: "politicized identity both produces

and potentially accelerates that aspect of disciplinary society that incessantly characterizes, classifies, and specializes through on-going surveillance, unremitting registration, and perpetual assessment" (Tremain, 2006: 193). The subversive potential of such an identity will, thus, be limited.

Foucauldian scholars, however, remain committed to overcoming the current limitations of the unified identity promoted by both the social model and the narrative model. Galvin, for example, draws from Foucault's work to seek ways to escape the uniform disability identity. While she acknowledges that the social model has undoubtedly acted as a liberating factor for many people with disabilities who previously have been "trapped in the net of individualism that masked their oppression under the guise of personal troubles" (Galvin, 2003: 677), she also questions why so many people with "impairments" choose not to identify as disabled. In addition, as the disability sport movement demonstrates, instead of unity, there is an internal political struggle as to who is to represent the "authentic voice" for all the disabled. Instead of reversing the dichotomies which define who is privileged (the able-bodied) and who is excluded (the disabled) in society, Gavin aims to challenge this binary logic. She calls for fluid forms of local resistance that can be strategically employed to take "into account the specificity of each claim to a more positive identity" (p. 685). Such politics, according to her, enable, rather than fix, the disabled identity.

This Foucauldian work has alerted scholars of disability to the connection between knowledge production and power relations: research tends to reproduce the polarities of the political field when it is embedded within the same binary juridico-discursive understanding of power (see Tremain, 2006). Without a challenge to the structure, any attempt at resistance only reverses the binary and social change becomes impossible. Foucault's later but unfinished work on the technologies of the self could provide a means to rethink the idea of social change with a focus on the ethics of the care of the self. Deleuze was, of course, an admirer of Foucault's thinking and also provided his own reading of Foucault's large body of work, developing, particularly, the technologies of the self as a way toward social change through his concepts of "fold" and the "body without organs" (Deleuze, 1986; Deleuze and

Guattari, 1987). In the second half of this chapter, I am interested in moving beyond identity politics with a particular emphasis on the body's ability to facilitate positive change. While Foucault and Deleuze both emphasized the role of the body in power relations, I turn to Deleuze to examine what disability research might gain from moving beyond the theoretical limitations of an identity-based politics to refocus on the body's ability to act and affect.

Becoming Minority: The Body without Organs

In his work, Deleuze understands theoretical concepts as solutions to problems (Buchanan, 1997). The poststructuralist critique of the social model demonstrates that an identity-based politics of the social model or the narrative model has limitations. From a Deleuzian perspective, also much of the current research on disability sport is built on an assumption of unified identity. This type of thinking, Deleuze and Guattari (1987) argue, stems from the philosophical root model which is characterized by a binary logic. In this logic, each representation or identity is reflected against the originary unity (the root) and has, thus, resulted in such clear-cut, yet unified, binary categories as masculine versus feminine, white versus black, upper-class versus working-class, the self versus the other, or able-bodied versus disabled. Deleuze and Guattari (1987) title these binaries *molar categories*. Individuals come to know an identity "from the outside and recognize from experience, through science, or by habit" (Deleuze and Guattari, 1987: 275). The "outside" includes disability sport studies that promotes a coherent, unified identity. For example, following Deleuze and Guattari, a molar identity of a disabled athlete is characterized by a person with an impaired "organism," whose "form" is further defined through disability classification and who, then, has been assigned a subjectivity as Paralympian. In addition to being defined as a binary opposition to "ability," *dis*ability as an identity, according to the root-tree model, turns into a unity that exists in the totality of the social world, an identity that is realized or found in a negative reflection to its binary opposition. By definition, then, the identity of an disabled athlete is always

constructed as a binary and thus, it necessarily results in further binaries (inclusion/exclusion, supercrip narrative/performance narrative, wheelchair sports/other sports, masculinity/femininity, empowerment/disempowerment, coherence/chaos) that, according to Deleuze and Guattari (1987: 5), will never help us reach "an understanding of multiplicities." From a Deleuzian perspective, new theoretical concepts are needed to rethink the molar identity (and the strata of significance and subjectification). To do this, Deleuze and Guattari (1987) draw from the body's ability to act. However, to understand their philosophy more fully, it is necessary to briefly detail the principles of their rhizomatic philosophy.

Rejecting the deep-root model of philosophical thought, Deleuze and Guattari (1987) compare their work on a type of root that grows horizontally as a rhizome where the roots take off from any point of the root to multiple directions. The rhizomatic model of thinking is based on the ideas of heterogeneous (not unified) thought, multiplicities (not singularities), and asignifying ruptures (not signification of meaning according to a unifying logic). Within this rhizomatic model, Deleuze and Guattari have developed concepts such as *the body without organs* and *assemblage* to further explore the multiplicity of thought.

The body without organs (BwO) is a concept developed by Deleuze and Guattari (1987) to move away from the molar identity to thinking of multiplicities or minorities. Instead of thinking what a body is (an identity), the BwO draws from what the body can do. The BwO does not refer to the functions of the body (with organs) *per se*, neither does it stem from the strata of organism (e.g., medicine) which aims to understand the body by hierarchically organizing it into a functional unit. At the same time, the BwO is not in opposition with the material body, the organs, but rather aims to direct us to think outside of the strata that currently define the logic for the body. In this sense, the BwO is a tool for change.

A BwO works by gradually unhinging the strata and thus, the purpose of constructing a BwO is not to oppose or to step out of the strata, but rather to create new territories that gradually allow the strata to smooth out. This can be done by looking for advantageous places within the current strata and then gradually, alleviate, sediment, coagulate, fold, and recoil the composition of the current organism, signification, and subject (Deleuze and Guattari, 1987). They add that "we are a social formation; first see how it is stratified for us and in us and at the place where we are; then descend from the strata to the deeper assemblage which we are held, gently tip the assemblage, making it pass over to the side of the plane of consistency" (p. 161). For example, I have aimed to identify how the current strata construct sport disability research, and then rethink how to create new territories through an advantageous place, the body, that is already of a current interest in the field. This way I have constructed my "own little machine, ready when needed to be plugged into other collective machines" (Deleuze and Guattari, 1987: 161). However, to further illustrate how a BwO "reveals itself for what it is: connection of desires, conjunction of flows, continuum of intensities" in disability sport, my researcher's body needs to create relationships with sporting bodies.

According to Deleuze and Guattari, the body is able to create relationships and thus, affects (Buchanan, 1997). Through its capacity to connect, the body can affect its surroundings. In this sense, the body's "doing" should be talked about in terms of qualities and quantities of forces (Buchanan, 1997). The BwO is a way of creating a (virtual) "body" with force, a body that has a capacity to create multiple relationships and thus, affects. The BwO is not something to be discovered (for example, under ideological construction), but it has to be actively created. If an identity is something given, assigned from "outside," something that the body is (disabled, woman, black, lesbian), a BwO is defined by what the body does when continually in the process of creating relationships and affect, continually becoming. This allows the Deleuzian researchers to rethink bodies positively: what relationships can a body, currently identified negatively as "disabled," create? Thus, what affects does this particular body have? What can the body do? Through its affects, the body incessantly creates linkages and connections with its surroundings and other bodies. It rearranges its surroundings but is also continually rearranged. Deleuze and Guattari title these "force-relations" as "assem-blages." Through assemblages the body is continually a part of large compounds and can, thus, create lines of flight through which affects carry further, to become "machines" that harness forces purposefully (Buchanan, 1997).

My interest in this chapter is primarily to investigate how to problematize the molar understanding of identity and then, to reimagine the role of the body in the life of a disabled athlete. To understand how Deleuzian concepts can be meaningful for expanding the boundaries of disability studies beyond identity-based politics, I paraphrase Diane Currier's (2003) conceptualization of Deleuzian feminism in which each instance of creating force-relations, or assembling, produces a particular instantiation of ability, in concert with the other elements of that assemblage (such as sport). Disability studies would then attend to the specificities of constituent elements – the forms of bodies, populations, technologies, and practices – that are actualized through the flow of energy, intensities, speeds, and slowness that traverse the assemblage. In this process the object of disability studies "becomes much more fragmented and local" (Currier, 2003: 335).

It is important to remember, however, that because Deleuze and Guattari are primarily interested in relations, and while their analysis relocates the focus to the local, they are concerned with how relations of power permeate different abilities, operations, practices, events, and fields. Nevertheless, an individual's attempt to create a BwO is a crucial aspect of their philosophy. Accentuating the local, however, enables a Deleuzian disability studies scholar to think otherwise: to imagine radical transformation within which ability is not bound to a category of disabled as subordinate to the able-bodied. To identify a BwO that has the "right Place, Power (puissance), and Collectivity" (Deleuze and Guattari, 1987: 152), I need to further seek connections to disability sport.

Further Connection: Collection of Empirical Material

When I was asked to write this chapter, I sensed a chance to be plugged into another collective machine that can use poststructuralist tools to analyze physically active bodies. As a Deleuzian, I intentionally wanted to challenge the boundaries of disability as an identity category. As a feminist researcher I was also interested in women's experiences of molarity and thus, preferred to involve women in my research. With no apparent connections with the disability sport community, I became interested in involving my cousin, Tuija Helander, a Finnish former Olympian who has undergone a lung transplant operation and currently continues her athletic career as a transplant athlete and a masters (veteran) athlete. Therefore, she is a former elite athlete, and while officially categorized as "disabled," she is, as a transplant athlete, excluded from Paralympic sport. I felt, therefore, that her body might send interesting lines of flight to deterritorialize the molarity dominating disability sport research.

I reconnected with her story through collecting textual material and through semi-structured interviewing. To prepare for the interview, I tracked her achievements as an elite athlete through the official website of her sport club, Euran Raiku. In addition, Helander appears in a Wikipedia page that primarily accounts her career as a 400-meter hurdler. I was able to follow her current career as a masters athlete through the Finnish Masters Athletes Association (Suomen Veteraaniurheiluliitto, SVU).[9] Consequently, these numerical records helped to trace what her body was capable of doing as an athlete. Moreover, her life after the lung-transplant operation was described in some newspaper articles, for example, in *Helsingin Sanomat*, the biggest daily newspaper in Finland and in the local newspaper, *Alasatakunta*. Through the newspaper accounts I discovered that Helander was active in several organizations such as the Finnish Heart and Lung Transplant Association (SYKE) where she was the vice-president, The Finnish Transplant Sport Association (ELLI), and Pulmonary Association (HELI). She also wrote a monthly blog during HELI's physical activity "Keuhkot Pihalle" (Blow Your Lungs Out) campaign.[10] While these blogs no longer appear on the HELI website, they provided interesting insights about the importance of physical activity for Helander. Although she is not educated as a physical activity professional (she obtained a Masters degree in economics), Helander began to offer physical activity advice also in the Finnish

Sport Federation's online magazine, *Liikunnan ja Urheilun Maailma* (the World of Sport and Physical Activity) in 2002 shortly after her operation, and later in the SYKE website article "Ten Reasons to Get out of the House."[11] Helander promotes moderate physical activity performed every day in small doses. In addition, she is an advocate of everyday physical activity – taking stairs, cycling instead of driving, gardening, and picking berries or mushrooms in the forest – as an effective and time-efficient way to keep active. This information shed some light into the elements of the assemblages with which Helander created linkages and provided me with more understanding of the collectivities she connected. From textual material, it is, nevertheless, difficult to detect the ways she thought about her body or the energy and intensity that might flow from her body's actions. Therefore, I contacted Helander for a possible interview.

As I have always followed Helander's career and had already obtained very detailed accounts of her athletic achievements, in the interview I wanted to focus on her potential to affect, her possible ability to think otherwise about disability sport, disability identity, or the disabled body. Therefore, I opted for a semi-structured interview (e.g., Kvale, 1996; Patton, 2002) rather than a life-history interview. I created the interview guide based on my reading of the previous literature on disability sport and Helander's career as an athlete to talk about her experiences as a transplant and masters athlete, the differences between disability sport and transplant sport, her understandings of disability as an identity, her role as a "transplant activist," and the relationships she has created as a transplant athlete. I obtained ethical approval for this project through the appropriate University of Alberta Research Ethics Board. During this process, the question of how to secure Helander's anonymity was raised. She is a well-known figure in Finland and thus, even with a pseudonym, she would most likely be recognizable. Therefore, as part of the informed consent, Helander opted to allow me to use her real name. Helander invited me to interview her at her home in Eura in western Finland and the interview took about two hours. It was conducted entirely in Finnish and I have translated the direct quotations presented in this paper. Helander has,

DELEUZE AND THE DISABLED SPORTS STAR 591

however, read the manuscript to check that I have done so in a manner that is acceptable to her. In the following section I map how a woman athlete's body creates force-relations in different instantiations of ability: as an elite, 400-meters hurdler and Olympian, as a person with a rare lung disease, and as a transplant and masters athlete.

Connecting: Particular Instantiations of Ability

Based on Deleuze and Guattari's (1987) recommendation to find an advantageous place in the current strata, I included interview questions that, based on the previous research, connect with the current dominant strata of disability sport (organism/medical understandings of disability; social and narrative model/disability as a molar identity). Through these strata I also hoped to gain an understanding of what Helander's body is able to do to possibly transgress the boundaries of the current strata. Before I had time to begin with my preplanned question, Helander explained how she classifies her life into three phases: during the first phase "running and breathing were natural and easy"; during the second, illness phase, breathing was no longer natural, but laborious, even painful; and during the third phase, there was "new life" when breathing was again possible. While it is not entirely surprising that Helander should think of her life through her ability to "breathe," it certainly offers a different starting point – based on her body's ability – from identity-based understanding of "disability." As a researcher, I could not quite let go of the molar lines that supported the research knowledge on disability sport when I asked how Helander now, as a transplant receiver, identifies herself. Helander found this "a really difficult question" as she did not identify as a disabled (athlete), but rather described herself as "I am just me." It was obvious that I had to be sensitive to the lines of flight through which Helander's body deterritorialized my research strata. As a result, my discussion here follows the three phases described by Helander to observe the relationships with which her body allowed her to connect to several different assemblages.

Running as natural as breathing

Helander's athletic career began when, as a 6-year-old, she made her debut in a local cross-country running meet in Eura, Finland. Running was always her "thing," her sport: as natural as breathing. Through running she describes finding "self-actualization": she loved to "push" herself, to "take everything out of herself." Already as a little girl she remembers dreaming of participating in the Olympic Games. Early on she started competing at regional (county) level in 100-meters sprints and hurdles, but happened to try 400-meters hurdles as a warm up for one of her 100-meters events. She loved the event in which she could push herself further than was possible during a sprint. She won her warm-up event and at the age of 16 became the Finnish women's champion in 400-meters hurdles in 1977. Through this achievement, she was selected to train with the Finnish Olympic team. Helander describes her own career:

> It lasted 15 years, the last five years as the captain of the women's team. I participated twice in the European and World Championships and once in the Olympics. The Olympics were in Los Angeles 1984, where I surprisingly reached the final, placing seventh. My best achievement was three years later in the world championships in Rome 1987, where I came fifth in the 400-meters hurdles with a Finnish record 54.62 seconds, which still stands. (Helander, 2006: 18)

Alongside her athletic career, Helander finished a Masters degree at the Helsinki School of Economics. Already during her active career Helander experienced the collapse of both of her lungs:

> Problems with my lungs appeared during my athletic career. In 1986 I had a collapsed lung, and the other lung collapsed in 1988, when I was preparing for the Olympics in Seoul. After the second operation my results began to decline no matter how hard I trained, and I never got back to the shape I was in 1987. I had big problems especially with endurance training, which afterwards could be explained by the worsening of my lungs. (Helander, 2006: 18)

Despite these problems Helander continued her career until 1990 when she won the 400-meters hurdles in the Finnish national championships and also participated in the European Championships in 400-meters hurdles as well as the 400-meters relay which meant running several heats in addition to the final, which the Finnish women's team reached that year. She now remembers that these European championships were her "hardest competitions," yet her best as she now understands under what strain her high-performance body was. Therefore, with a slow-advancing illness like LAM (lymphangioleiomyomatosis), the two first phases of Helander's life overlap quite extensively and differ thus, from the life stories of the spinal-cord-injured athletes in Smith and Sparkes' research (2004, 2005, 2007, 2008; Sparkes and Smith, 2008). In addition, she can now, in retrospect, consider the quite hidden impact of LAM on her elite career whereas a spinal-cord-injury ends one's athletic career. During the interview, we discussed how her endurance mysteriously declined and how her training program had to be changed to emphasize anaerobic power and muscle strength. We openly drew from the biomedical discourse of "organism" to make sense of Helander's feelings about her body's ability at the time, but at the same time, we connected with the field of high-performance sport to locate her experience within the localized context of her everyday bodily practice. Evidently, Helander embodied an advantageous psychological make-up for an elite athlete: she was determined to have goals and constantly improve her results. Therefore, as an elite athlete she had purposefully harnessed forces – often supported by science and psychology of correct high-performance training – to become a high-performance body.

The breathless body

After the 1990 European championships, Helander's physical "condition collapsed" quite drastically and she also remembers a "psychological" change from when she was an athlete who was like a "Formula One driver" in her starting block itching to go, and became more concerned and careful competitor. This attitude change made her realize that she had to give up her career as an elite athlete. Her increased breathlessness – she could not even walk uphill "like normal people" – led to further medical tests and in 1992 she was diagnosed with LAM with a devastating prognosis that she would have 5–15 years to live. She left the doctor's office "hysterical and disoriented" and hardly registered the doctor mentioning a possibility for a lung transplant. Drawing further from a medical understanding of "organism" we detailed the possible causes for LAM such as disruptions in oestrogen production, cancerous cell formation, gene mutation, and difficulties of diagnosing such a rare illness. Although her body's ability to move was severely restricted, Helander certainly did not adopt an identity as a terminally ill patient. On the contrary, she experimented with drawing different lines of flight from the athlete's life.

A couple of years after her diagnosis, Helander became pregnant with her first and only child. To ensure enough oxygen for the baby she had to continually wear oxygen tubes during the nine months of her pregnancy. The birth of her son almost killed Helander and she ended up in an intensive care unit in a hospital for several months. After the pregnancy, her lungs did not recover and she was forced to always use extra oxygen. For the next five years, she wore oxygen tubes connected to an oxygen container that she carried with her.

Although her body's ability to move was severely restricted – she was unable to exercise at all and could only ascend two steps of the stairs at the time – Helander remembered these five years as "quiet time," but also "very happy time" during which she lived "fully." At this point, Helander was a single parent and moved back to her home town, Eura. While leaving her athletic career was by no means painless, she began to realize that there was more to life than running and took on, for example, a new hobby, photography. She reflected, "when you are at the point where you talk about life or death, you are satisfied with less, with being able to live with your child and wake to a new day in the morning . . . a human being is quite adaptable in those ways . . . and I did not miss sport. . . . It was better to enjoy different things."

In 1996 Helander officially began to receive governmental disability compensation as she was deemed unable to work due to the disease. As Helander's condition deteriorated, her physician advised her to consider joining the queue of people waiting for a lung transplant. This was a big hurdle for Helander who felt that she was doing quite well with new lighter oxygen-support equipment and by doing things slowly. Her body could still do many things. At this point she felt strong and full of life; it was "just those lungs that don't work." After hospitalization due to a respiratory illness, Helander realized, however, that she had to act, to do something, about her continually deteriorating physical condition. After making that decision, Helander was again "behind her starting blocks," ready for the gun to go. Sport, she explained, helped her mentally: once behind the starting line, an athlete is determined to go and do her best without worrying about every detail in advance.

While Helander could no longer perform as an elite athlete, she drew from her athletic career to perform on a different stage. Therefore, her positive use of past sporting experiences differs from Frank's (1995) illness stories or Smith and Sparkes' research where the researchers classified such references to a past that is no longer possible after illness/disability as locking the individual into impossible and unproductive body–self relationship. Helander's transplant operation, which took place 18 months later, went well. Helander describes the recovery process as surprisingly fast in terms of being able to breathe again without fear of oxygen running out. After five days, she was able to ride a stationary bike and only had to stop because her legs were too tired to continue.

The new life: breathing again

With her body's ability to move returned, Helander described her life after the operation as a continually positive experience. To keep her lungs functional she continues to exercise every day until out of breath. I asked if Helander, as a former athlete, immediately began competing in transplant sport. Her first thought was that she "had had enough of sport and I don't need to show off in sport anymore," but when her close friends within ELLI asked her to try competing, six months after her operation, Helander decided, after all, to take part in the Finnish national heart-and-lung transplant championships in the 3-km walk. She gained silver (there were only two participants) after taking more than 30 minutes

to complete the distance. For a former elite athlete this was a dismal result, but Helander considers it as the most valued of her "transplant medals" because simply being able to complete such a distance felt, at the time, remarkable.

Since her first 3-km competition she has enjoyed a very successful international career as a transplant athlete. In the 2002 World Transplant Games, in France, she was the best female athlete, winning the 100-meters sprint, the long jump, the 100-meters hurdles, and the badminton competition, and gaining silver in the ball throw. In the European championships in 2008,[12] Helander obtained the most medals in the Finnish team. She currently participates in a much broader range of sports than from her elite career and obtained seven gold medals in 100 meters, 4 × 100-meters relay, long jump, high jump, shot put, badminton, and volleyball. In addition, she competes at the national indoor Masters Games ("healthy people's games" as she calls them) in 60-meters hurdles, 60 meters, 200 meters, and long jump in which she holds the Finnish records for the W45 category. She participated in the 2009 World Masters Games 100 meters and obtained silver in the 4 × 100-meters relay in the W45 category. In addition to being a successful athlete, Helander is a freelance journalist, vice-chair of the Finnish Transplant Sport Association,[13] an athlete, and a coach.

In summary, telling what her body can do, Helander has, as an athlete, as a severely ill person and a lung-transplant receiver, constructed a type of BwO. Her understanding of life based on her ability to breathe has also forced me to divert my attention from the molar identities of elite athlete or disability. Although this Deleuzian analysis draws from the specificities of the local (Currier, 2003), similar to the narrative model, it also aims to deterritorialize the arborescence of this model.

Instead of "narrative practice in action" (Smith and Sparkes, 2002) to produce coherent identities through different stages of illness/disability, Deleuzian analysis is sensitized for lines of flight that deterritorialize the modernist assumptions behind the construction of chronological, linear progress narratives of a coherent self. For example, I could have labeled Helander's three life phases – breathing as natural, breathing as difficult, breathing again – as stages toward a final quest narrative (Frank, 1995) where Helander has reconciled her previous identities to assume a new meaningful, coherent "disabled" identity. Unlike the spinal-cord-injured athletes in Smith and Sparkes' research, transplant provided a "new" body and a new life for Helander where she was able "to do things again" and thus, her story is quite different from permanently disabled athletes. Nevertheless, even with a transplant she, in her own words, "is not quite healthy" and could, thus, be assumed to need a new narrative for a coherent self. Helander did not articulate a need for a new self: it is "just her" who is doing things through her life, albeit with differing levels of intensity or purpose. Neither does she leave her elite athlete "identity" behind her but continues to draw force from it: the determination and organization of an athlete has helped her through the lung operation and continues to enable her to exercise every day for the health of her lungs. Her story, thus, highlights her continual becoming that, rather than a linear and progressive construction of a particular self (assigned from the outside), demonstrates how a focus on the doing body can help researchers transgress the strata defining current disability identity politics. When she refused my attempt to clarify her identity, she demonstrated how I, through my research, tried to assign her a molar identity from "outside," instead of allowing her to present what her body can do. Therefore, rather than being forced into the unifying logic of signification of a coherent self, her body, like a rhizome, can create asignifying ruptures to the ways we currently understand the meanings of disability.

While Helander's doing body forced me to problematize the molarity of disability, she did not challenge the exercise science according to which she continues to train her athlete's body or the medical science that provided the diagnosis of her illness and the "new" transplant body. Perhaps I didn't ask her to elaborate on these issues. Both of these sciences, nevertheless, can be located within the stratum of organism. It is important to remember, however, that Deleuze and Guattari (1987) did not advocate a violent collapse of the strata but a process of deterritorialization through rhizomatic tactics of finding an advantageous place within the strata. Therefore, the idea is not to condemn medicine or exercise science as entirely oppressive, akin to the social model of disability research, but to think

how one can use these sciences without being dominated by their unifying, singular thought structure. In Helander's case, both seem to have also produced positive bodily force, particularly in relation to sport. In the next section, I aim to highlight further how Helander's body has enabled her to assemble with other bodies and communities and thus, provide potential affects (Buchanan, 1997).

Conjugations: Multiplicity and Continual Becoming

Although Helander does not talk in Deleuzian terms, I find her body creating several flow conjunctions. As an elite athlete, she appeared to connect mostly with the high-performance world of elite running. Her "disabled" body, nevertheless, has enabled her to connect with multiple different communities: the lung- and heart-transplant community, the national and international world of transplant athletics, the disability sport community, the masters athletic community, and the media. While several of these are sport-related communities, she has also assumed a visible position as an advocate for understanding and prevention of lung diseases.

As discussed previously, Helander has been a phenomenally successful transplant athlete with multiple international medals. When I note how remarkable such an achievement is, Helander explains that the majority of participants in the transplant games have never been able to participate in sport (e.g., many have been born with debilitating heart conditions) and she is one of the few previous athletes in these games. According to her, while some participants might feel that the medals are important, this is not her motivation to participate in the transplant games: "While some might think that I am there for the medals, I participate for the satisfaction that I can do this . . . however, I cannot move without goals. . . . Competitive sport, for me, is exercising with definite goals . . . competitions, then, keep me practicing."

Helander clearly distinguished her current sport participation from her elite athlete career, but continued to reflect the affect of her elite training:

I turned 45, I felt that I can no longer have targets where I improve so and so much from the previous results, but more like: I hope I only become this much worse. This has been bitter for me. . . . It's that elite athlete in me who always wants to improve . . . it is not so bad, but I must occasionally say to myself: you are not an elite athlete any more, you are not even entirely healthy.

I wondered if her second sport competition assemblage with the Masters games allows that "elite athlete" body to connect with other former elite athletes. She found the men in these events particularly serious about competition, but women spend time to chat and socialize together. While the Masters athletics obviously has a more competitive oeuvre than the transplant games, Helander found the Paralympic athletes and their Finnish association the most serious of all of these sports. The transplant athletes, it turns out, are actually not part of the disability sport movement connected with the Paralympics. Although they are "officially" classified as "disabled" (e.g., Helander receives governmental disability compensation), they do not fall within Nixon's (2007) definition of sport participants who have a disability of physical mobility, sight, hearing, or mental functioning. Helander counted three further reasons for this separation: first, transplant athletes tend to be "too old" ("young people don't need transplants"), second, transplant athletes do not have same ability to train ("we often have some infection"), and third, the reasons for sport participation are very different ("winning is not so important, but it is great to be able to it [sport]").

Such exclusion within the disability sport movement is almost invisible within the previous research on disability sport studies that locate the inclusion/exclusion debate primarily within the further binary of ability/disability. Helander's transplant athlete's body reveals more complex power relations regarding the marginalization and definition of the disabled body. Her comments on the concept of "elite athlete" leads to a further discussion of what this can mean in terms of disability sport and connects with the supercrip/elite athlete division analyzed by the social model of disability sport (e.g., Hardin and Hardin, 2003; Huang and Brittain, 2006; Schell and Rodriques, 2001). Helander approaches this

debate from quite a different angle from the social model: she is neither an elite athlete nor a supercrip. Helander obviously does not currently consider herself as an "elite athlete" despite her international success in transplant games. Although her results are good even when compared to the "Para" results, they are still results produced by someone with transplant lungs. This is a leveling factor and for her, elite sport does not consider such bodily "equalizers." She was, nevertheless, voted as the Finnish Disabled Athlete of the Year in 2005 and received her award in a gala where the Finnish Athlete of the Year title also was awarded. The other contenders for the title of Disabled Athlete of the Year were both male Paralympic athletes. Such a title came as quite a surprise for Helander, as she does not necessarily identify as a disabled athlete. Rather than disability sport, she prefers the terms *special sport* or *special elite sport* (Antola, 2005). During our interview, Helander reinforces her distinction between elite sport and "special sport." For example, as the vice-president of SYKE she insisted that the term "elite" needs to be replaced with another term in their constitutional terms of reference. The World Transplant Games website (www.wtgf.org/default.asp) reinforces participation rather than winning as the main point, but also establishes its reputation as an elite sport event.

For Helander, nevertheless, participation in transplant sports is an advantageous place to conjugate sport, to find potential movements to experiment with thinking differently. She considers elite sport as quite a different field from transplant sport where she wishes to operate based on a different premise, capacity, and ability. Our discussion demonstrates the competing and contradictory views of "special" sport participation and the difficulty of reconciling a broad physical activity movement under a unified umbrella of disability sport. The current organization is obviously stratified based on several factors and our discussion on transplant sport touched the surface of complex power politics within this movement. While not possible within the limits of this chapter, these aspects obviously require further examination.

In addition to her current career as a lung-transplant athlete, Helander is an active member of the Finnish Pulmonary Association (HELI) and the Finnish Health and Lung Transplant Association (SYKE). HELI is an umbrella organization that provides information regarding all lung diseases from asthma to rare diseases like Helander's LAM. SYKE represents a smaller clientele of actual transplant receivers. Through these organizations, Helander hopes to emphasize the importance of physical activity for well-being. Helander promotes active living and moderate physical activity, not sport, as a means for better physical fitness. She does not, therefore, problematize the stratum of organism that informs medical science and allows for the signification of physical activity as a type of medicine. Connecting with the governmental health promotion strategies, she justifies the importance of physical activity through its ability to prevent illness. Her physical activity advocacy has not been entirely successful: "When I have given talks, I have realized that humans are lazy and comfortable . . . it is a worldwide problem that people do not move enough . . . but I am a bit tired of this now, as there does not seem to be much change. . . . I have lost some of the idealism, I can't live and do sport for everyone." As a former elite athlete for whom moving was as natural a breathing she does not readily empathize with inactive people who might find physical activity cumbersome, tiresome, and unpleasant. While Helander does not problematize the stratum of organism that defines her physical activity promotion, she is, nevertheless, in a continuous process of becoming "herself": a minority creating relations through different physical activity contexts.

In addition to sport participation and lung-transplant activism, Helander continues to work as a freelance journalist for *Juoksija* magazine.[14] She also is a celebrated athlete and continues to be of interest to the Finnish media. Already at an early stage when her illness was visibly marked by the oxygen tank she had to carry with her, Helander made a conscious decision to assemble with the media: she wanted to use her celebrity status to act as a positive role model by providing information about lung transplants. As a journalist herself, she is well aware of the representational economy of the media that assumes a certain type of signification will sell and therefore, in her own words, she "came out of the

'closet'" before a journalist could attempt to sensationalize her illness. Currently, she observes that the media is interested in her story at steady intervals, but she is more selective of the type of media she is willing to engage with. She particularly dislikes stories that color her life with many features similar to the supercrip narrative. These types of stories are sedimented on the stratum of signifiance: Helander's identity as a former elite athlete is used to dramatize her current identity into an illness sufferer signified by her transplant body. Such representation, for Helander, accentuates her life as a great emotional and physical tragedy that, like the medical model, assumes suffering and social disadvantage as necessary aspects of disability instead of depicting a "good life." As an example, Helander described a recent story by *Iltasanomat*, one of the Finnish tabloids, that portrayed her almost dying after giving birth and then living confined to an oxygen tank before becoming an active transplant athlete. Under the headline "From the Shadows of Death," the article cited her telling the story of her illness and transplant operation with a highly emotional, shaking voice. The picture accompanying the story depicted her as a "sufferer" of a rare lung disease with drawn face and dark eyes. Like the disabled athletes, Helander detests such narratives because they are based on a negative, "false" dramatization of overcoming a debilitating illness. However, unlike the disabled athletes, she does not long to be represented as an elite, transplant athlete, but rather as an active, content person with a functioning transplant body.

In her current life, Helander has many possibilities to create lines of flight that produce flow conjunctions. Consequently, she has entered a small new plot in the intersecting fields of transplant activism and sport. As a transplant receiver she connects to elite sport by coaching young athletes as well as creating relationships with disability sport, transplant sport, masters sport, physical activity, and transplant "activism" to instigate affect. Paraphrasing Deleuze and Guatteri (1987), Helander has a place (sport), power (as a former elite athlete), and collectivity (the Finnish Transplant Sport Association and the transplant community) through which she can affect the ways transplant receivers are perceived.

Conclusion: Finding Localized Connections

In this chapter, I set out to investigate whether it is possible to deterritorialize the current dominant strata – the medical model, the social model, the narrative model – of disability sport studies through a Deleuzian reading. I first problematized the arborescent premise of these strata to offer Deleuzian concepts of the Body without Organs and assemblage to attempt a rhizomatic analysis of disability sport. I chose to localize these concepts through the experiences of former Finnish Olympian and current transplant athlete and activist Tuija Helander who is located outside of the Paralympic disability sport movement.

Helander's athletic body certainly tests the boundaries of physical "disability": as a multiple medal winner in international transplant sport, a national champion in masters sports and an avid exerciser, her body's physical ability exceeds, for example, my body's ability. In addition, while her body has enabled her to do multiple sports, it has also allowed her to create relationships with multiple communities. Through this assembling her body has affect on transplant sport, transplant recipients' attitudes, and, through the media, public attitudes about the transplant recipients. As a transplant athlete, Helander follows the developments within disability sport and directs me to the decision to unite all the Finnish associations representing different disability sport groups, including the Finnish Transplant Sport Association, under one umbrella association. In this sense, her BwO links with the constituent elements of assemblage of disability sports in Finland and to the larger machine of the disability sport movement. Helander's body can also affect the research on disability sport through her assemblage with me.

In Deleuzian terms, Helander and I have identified stratification in our respective, yet connected strata: I identified several models in the current disability studies (medical, social, narrative, poststructuralist) and Helander identified multiple sport assemblages (the elite, the special, the masters sports). We have both descended to a new assemblage: I have connected with disability sport studies and Helander with the world of transplant sports. Did this Deleuzian analysis, nevertheless, tip the assemblage of research away from stratification, towards smoothness, towards a plane of consistency? Will my chapter change disability sport studies? Will I be able to create poststructuralist based disability sport activism?

It is clear that Deleuzian rhizomatics offers quite a different approach from the current strata of disability sport studies. Its emphasis on the body allows a researcher to move beyond the mere organism of the medical model. A Deleuzian analysis prioritizes the body's affect that is absent in the social model. While the narrative model concerns both with the individual's bodily experiences and with their social context, it remains anchored in the arborescent model of seeking the true, unified, coherent, linear construction of an identity/self. Deleuzian analysis is sensitive to lines of flight that deterritorialize such assumptions. For example, Helander's refusal to accept an identity defined to her from outside, while first puzzling to me, allowed an understanding of her life through breathing. Breathing was always there, but allowed different aspects of the moving body to emerge in different times. Consequently, Helander did not create linear stages of a narrative of the self, but rather continually became something different based on her body's ability and its affect in different contexts. Through this affect she also continually created relationships with different communities. Her story gave a glimpse of the complex molar lines defining the disability sport movement and one individual's desire to create positive change through her advantageous spaces. The Deleuzian concepts sensitized me to the affects of Helander's body: instead of locking myself into examining what her body is (identity), I desired to connect with what her body does (affect). This examination, I hope, has exposed some of the molar lines connected to the dominant disability studies strata and through an example of Helander's sporting body – and also my researcher's writing body – highlights some possibilities of constructing small machines ready to be "plugged into other collective machines" (Deleuze and Guattari, 1987: 161). That is a start – one attempt, as called for by Grossberg (2003), to put the emphasis on relations and change (becoming and connections).

Acknowledgments

I would like to thank Danielle Peers for pointing me to the poststructuralist literature in disability studies and listening to my struggles with the strata; Donna Goodwin for her expertise, encouragement, and providing me with the details on disability studies as a field and the Americans with Disabilities Act; Jim Denison for his assistance with my writing process; and finally, Tuija Helander for generously providing her time and sharing her life story with me.

Notes

1 Disability studies is an interdisciplinary field of studies that emerged through the 1980s and 1990s to challenge the medical and rehabilitative interventionist view of disability as an individual deficit or defect. Disability studies refers to the examination of disability as a social, cultural, economic, and political phenomenon and the model that can provide individual and collective responses to perceived inequality by diverse groups of people (Barnes, Oliver, and Barton, 2002).

2 Gabel and Peters (2004) identify four paradigmatic approaches to studying disability: functionalism, historical-materialism, interpretivism, and postmodernism. In their classification they also introduce dimensions of macro–micro, objectivism–subjectivism, and structuralism–poststructuralism. According to these parameters, medical research on disability characterizes the functionalist disability research that focuses on macro-level, objective, and structuralist research. The "social model" tends be characterized by historical-materialism with a focus on objective analysis of structuralist constraints, yet at micro-level. The interpretivist research focuses on individual concerns of disability, yet assume a macro-level social context, within a poststructuralist stance. Postmodern disability research is subjective, micro-level, poststructuralist analysis. While Gabel and Peters' classification has some similarities with Deleuze's three strata (e.g., organism characterizes the functionalist medical research), his critique of modern philosophy would criticize the founding dualism, such as subjectivism–objectivism, micro–macro, on which Gabel and Peters base their model. In addition, their use of poststructuralism differs from the way poststructuralism is discussed in this chapter. While Gabel and Peters do not define their term *poststructuralism*, structuralism, according to them, focuses on "material conditions of existence and emphasizes processes or relations of production within class structure or identity categories" (2004: 587). If poststructuralism is defined as the opposite to this type of structuralism it denotes an unconcern of the sociopolitical system of structures of power in favor of a more subjective, micro-understanding of disability. Deleuze's and Foucault's poststructuralism grew out of a critique of Saussure's structuralism that was concerned with how meanings become fixed through certain structures of language, not as a call for more focus on micro-level analysis as opposed to macro-level structure. Consequently, both Foucault and Deleuze devoted considerable time to defining how structures of power (power relations) can be theorized. Therefore, my later discussion of poststructuralist disability research does not correspond with Gabel and Peters' characterization of postmodern disability research.

3 The Americans with Disabilities Act is a law that was enacted by the US Congress in 1990 to establish comprehensive and clear prohibition of discrimination on the basis of disability, defined as physical or mental impairment that subsequently limits major life activities in the domains of employment, public entities, public accommodations and commercial facilities, and telecommunications. The Act was the culmination of joint efforts by groups dedicated to disability rights, civil rights, and social justice. (For more information on the Act go to http://finduslaw.com/, accessed January 11, 2013, and search Americans with Disabilities Act 1990.)

4 Some argue that the social model was never meant to provide a theory to explain what a disability is, but rather to provide a political agenda for action. Gabel and Peters note that there are now several modifications of the social model (e.g., the biosocial model in Thomas, 2001, expanded in Thomas, 2004). They do, nevertheless, locate the "strong social model" within historical-materialism in their discussion of disability research paradigms.

5 For an ideal type model for a structure of disability sports, see Nixon (2007) who suggests a continuum of seven categories of sports. Nixon

draws from Brasile's (1990) concept of reverse integration: inclusion of the able-bodied into disability sport.

6   While some scholars have used Foucault's theory to read disability sport (Guthrie and Castelnuovo, 2001; Huang and Brittain, 2006), their framework can be located within the social model of disability: they focus on the empowerment/disempowerment dichotomy of disability sport rather than challenging underlying theoretical binaries of the social model.

7   "Restitution narrative" refers to a construction of a restored self after illness/disability. As Frank (1995) describes, "yesterday I was healthy, today I'm sick, but tomorrow I'll be healthy again" (p. 77). This type of narrative of the self, nevertheless, locks individuals in their past body–self relationship that is no longer possible after illness/disability. In turn, the chaos narratives, where the protagonist imagines never getting better, lack narrative order and are told without coherent sequence. Frank advocates that individuals at this stage need to tell stories to regain coherent self and develop new relations within a community. In quest narratives, the individual has overcome the chaos stage and accepts the illness/disability and aims to use it toward a more or less clearly defined goal.

8   Other scholars approach disability studies through a Foucauldian perspective (e.g., Allen, 2005; Diedrich, 2005; Corker and Shakespeare, 2002). Hughes (2005) offers a critique of Foucault's work, claiming that his notion of the body does not allow for the (disabled) body to act as an agent of transformation. Hughes, while briefly acknowledging Foucault's work on the technologies of the self, insists that phenomenology offers a corrective to Foucault's theory (see also Guthrie and Castelnuovo, 2001).

9   For Euran Raiku see www.euranraiku.fi, accessed January 11, 2013; Helander's Wikipedia entry can be found at fi.wikipedia.org/wiki/Tuija_Helander, accessed January 11, 2013; the Finnish Masters Athletes Association can be found at www.svu.fi, accessed January 11, 2013.

10 See "Blow you lungs out" at www.keuhkotpihalle.fi, accessed January 11, 2013.

11 Finnish Sport Federation, www2.slu.fi/lehti/arkisto/verkkolehti200210/pienuutinen.2586, accessed July, 2009 but no longer available; and

http://www.syke-elinsiirrot.fi (SYKE), accessed January 27, 2013.

12 The European Lung and Heart Transplant Games are organized biennially by the European Lung and Heart Transplant Federation (EHLTF). According to their website, the federation was formally established in Helsinki, Finland 1994, when representatives from 15 European national heart or heart–lung transplant associations signed the protocol accepting the statues of the federation. The games, which they call "a celebration of life," are organized in one of the member countries and comprise of 20 track and field athletic events as well as tennis, table tennis, volleyball, badminton, cycling, golf, and swimming. From a modest start in 1989, the Games have become increasingly popular and have, in recent years attracted almost 600 participants and supporters from the member Associations (http://www.ehltf.info/main.php?page=games, accessed January 11, 2013). During the last 20 years the World Transplant Games Federation has organized the World Transplant Games. Currently, the World Transplant Games Federation is officially recognized by the International Olympic Committee. The main purpose of the Federation is to demonstrate the physical success of transplant surgery and to raise awareness of the need to increase organ donation. There are over 50 events including athletics, ten-pin bowling, swimming, racquet sports, golf, volleyball, lawn bowls, and cycling (http://www.wtgf.org/default.asp, accessed January 11, 2013).

13 At the time of the interview, Helander was the vice-chair of the Finnish Transplant Sport Association (ELLI). In 2010 four Finnish associations – Finnish Transplant Sport Association, Finnish Invalid Sport Association, Finnish Sport and Physical Activity Association for the Mentally Disabled, and Finnish Association for the Visually Impaired – formed a new central sport organization: Finnish Disability Sport Association (VAU). With the disappearance of ELLI, Helander is now a board member of VAU and a "physical activity coordinator" for the Finnish Lung and Heart Plant Association (SYKE).

14 Juoksija-lehti (The Runner magazine) is a monthly magazine that covers endurance sports with an emphasis on elite and serious competitive running (www.juoksija-lehti.fi, accessed January 11, 2013).

References

Allen, B. (2005) "Foucault's nominalism," in Tremain, S. (ed.) Foucault and the Government of Disability, Ann Arbor: University of Michigan Press, pp. 93–107.

Antola, P. (2005) "Valinta vuoden vammaisurheilijaksi yllätti täysin" (Selection to the Disabled Athlete of the Year was a Total Surprise). *Alasatakunta*, December 29, n.p.

Barnes, C., Oliver, M., and Barton, L. (2002) *Disability Studies Today*, Cambridge: Polity Press.

Berger, R.J. (2008) "Disability and the dedicated wheelchair athlete: Beyond the 'supercrip' critique." *Journal of Contemporary Ethnography*, 37: 647–678.

Best, S. (2007) "The social construction of pain: An evaluation." *Disability & Society*, 22: 161–171.

Brasile, F.M. (1990) "Wheelchair sports: A new perspective on integration." *Adapted Physical Activity Quarterly*, 7 (1): 3–11.

Buchanan, I. (1997) "The problem of the body in Deleuze and Guattari, or, What can a body do?" *Body & Society*, 3: 73–91.

Corker, M., and Shakespeare, T. (2002) "Mapping the terrain," in Corker, M. and Shakespeare, T. (eds.) *Disability/Postmodernity*, London: Continuum, pp. 1–17.

Currier, D. (2003) "Feminist technological futures: Deleuze and the body/technology assemblages." *Feminist Theory*, 4: 321–338.

Crossley, M. (2000) *Introducing Narrative Psychology: Self, Trauma and the Construction of Meaning*, Buckingham: Open University Press.

Deleuze, G. (1986) *Foucault*, London: Athlone Press.

Deleuze, G. and Guattari, F. (1987) *A Thousand Plateaus: Capitalism and Schizophrenia*, London: Athlone Press.

DePauw, K.P. (1997) "The (in)visibility of disability: Cultural contexts and 'sporting bodies.'" *Quest*, 49: 416–430.

Diedrich, L. (2005) "Introduction: Genealogies of disability." *Cultural Studies*, 19: 649–666.

Duncan, M.C. (2001) "The sociology of ability and disability in physical activity." *Sociology of Sport Journal*, 18: 1–4.

Frank, A. (1995) *The Wounded Storyteller*, Chicago: University of Chicago Press.

Gabel, S. and Peters, S. (2004) "Presage of a paradigm shift? Beyond the social model of disability toward resistance theories of disability." *Disability & Society*, 19: 585–600.

Galvin, R. (2003) "The paradox of disability culture: the need to combine versus the imperative to let go." *Disability & Society*, 18: 675–690.

Goodley, D. (2007) "Becoming rhizomatic parents: Deleuze, Guattari and disabled babies." *Disability & Society*, 22: 145–160.

Grossberg, L. (2003) "Animations, articulations, and becomings: An introduction," in Slack, J.D. (ed.) *Animations (of Deleuze and Guattari)*, New York: Peter Lang, pp. 1–8.

Guthrie, S.R. and Castelnuovo, S. (2001) "Disability management among women with physical impairments: The contribution of physical activity." *Sociology of Sport Journal*, 18: 5–20.

Hardin, B. and Hardin, M. (2003) "Conformity and conflict: Wheelchair athletes discuss sport media." *Adapted Physical Activity Quarterly*, 20: 246–259.

Hargreaves, J.A. (2000) *Heroines of Sport: The Politics of Difference and Identity*, London: Routledge.

Helander, T. (2006) "From top athlete to transplant patient." *Transworld*, 1: 18.

Howe, P.D. and Jones, C. (2006) "Classification of disabled athletes: (Dis)empowering the Paralympic practice community." *Sociology of Sport Journal*, 23: 29–46.

Huang, C.-J. and Brittain, I. (2006) "Negotiating identities through disability sport." *Sociology of Sport Journal*, 23: 352–375.

Hughes, B. (2005) "What can a Foucauldian analysis contribute to disability theory?" in Tremain, S. (ed.) *Foucault and the Government of Disability*, Ann Arbor: University of Michigan Press, pp. 78–92.

Kvale, S. (1996) *InterViews: An Introduction to Qualitative Research Interviewing*, London: Sage Publications.

Markula, P. (2004) "'Cute with vague feminist gender shift': Posh and Becks United," in Andrews, D.L. (ed.) *Manchester United: An Interdisciplinary Study*, London: Routledge, pp. 160–172.

Markula, P. (2006a) "The dancing body without organs: Deleuze, femininity and performing research." *Qualitative Inquiry*, 12: 3–27.

Markula, P. (2006b) "Deleuze and the body without organs: Disreading the fit feminine identity." *Journal of Sport & Social Issues*, 30: 29–44.

Markula, P. (2008) "'Affecting' bodies: Political pedagogy of Pilates." *International Review of Qualitative Research*, 1: 381–408.

Nixon, H.L. (2007) "Constructing diverse sports opportunities for people with disabilities." *Journal of Sport & Social Issues*, 31: 417–433.

Patton, M.Q. (2002) *Qualitative Research & Evaluative Methods* (3rd edn.), Thousand Oaks, CA: Sage.

Promis, D., Erevelles, N., and Matthews, J. (2001) "Reconceptualizing inclusion: The politics of university sports and recreation programs for students with mobility impairments." *Sociology of Sport Journal*, 18: 37–50.

Schell, L.A.B. and Rodriguez, S. (2001) "Subverting bodies/ambivalent representations: Media analysis of Paralympian Hope Lewellen." *Sociology of Sport Journal*, 18: 127–135.

Siebers, T. (2005) "Disability in theory: From social constructionism to the new realism of the body," in Davis, L.J. (ed.) *The Disability Studies Reader* (2nd edn.), New York: Routledge, pp. 173–183.

Smith, B. and Sparkes, A.C. (2002) "Men, sport, spinal cord injury and the construction of coherence: Narrative practice in action." *Qualitative Research*, 2: 143–171.

Smith, B. and Sparkes, A.C. (2004) "Men, sport, and spinal cord injury: An analysis of metaphors and narratives types." *Disability & Society*, 19: 613–626.

Smith, B. and Sparkes, A.C. (2005) "Men, sport, spinal cord injury, and narratives of hope." *Social Science and Medicine*, 61: 1095–1105.

Smith, B. and Sparkes, A.C. (2007) "Changing bodies, changing narratives and the consequences of tellability: A case study of becoming disabled through sport." *Sociology of Health & Illness*, 30: 217–236.

Smith, B. and Sparkes, A.C. (2008) "Narrative and its potential contribution to disability studies." *Disability & Society*, 23: 17–28.

Sparkes, A.C. (1999) "Exploring body narratives." *Sport, Education and Society*, 4: 17–30.

Sparkes, A.C. and Smith, B. (2008) "Men, spinal cord injury, memories and the narrative performance of pain." *Disability & Society*, 23: 679–690.

Thomas, C. (2001) "Feminism and disability: The theoretical and political significance of the personal and the experiential," in Barton, L. (ed.) *Disability, Politics and the Struggle for Change*, London: David Fulton.

Thomas, C. (2004) "How is disability understood? An examination of sociological approaches." *Disability & Society*, 19: 569–583.

Tremain, S. (2005) "Foucault, governmentality, and critical disability theory: An introduction," in Tremain, S. (ed.) *Foucault and the Government of Disability*, Ann Arbor: University of Michigan Press, pp. 1–26.

Tremain, S. (2006) "On the government of disability: Foucault, power, and the subject of impairment," in Davis, L.J. (ed.) *The Disability Studies Reader* (2nd edn.), New York: Routledge, pp. 185–196.

Further Reading

Corker, M. and Shakespeare, T. (2002) *Disability/Postmodernity*, London: Continuum.

Deleuze, G. and Guattari, F. (1987) *A Thousand Plateaus: Capitalism and Schizophrenia*, London: Athlone Press.

Diedrich, L. (ed.) (2005) "Genealogies of disability." *Cultural Studies*, 19 (6), special issue.

Duncan, M. (ed.) (2001) "The sociology of ability and disability in physical activity." *Sociology of Sport Journal*, 18 (1), special issue.

Tremain, S. (2005) *Foucault and the Government of Disability*, Ann Arbor: University of Michigan Press.

Index

A Companion to Sport, First Edition. Edited by David L. Andrews and Ben Carrington.
© 2013 Blackwell Publishing Ltd. Published 2013 by Blackwell Publishing Ltd.

Printed and bound by CPI Group (UK) Ltd, Croydon, CR0 4YY